A CONCORDANCE
to the
English Poetry of

GERARD MANLEY HOPKINS

A CONCORDANCE
to the
English Poetry of

GERARD MANLEY HOPKINS

Compiled by
ROBERT J. DILLIGAN
and
TODD K. BENDER

THE UNIVERSITY OF WISCONSIN PRESS
Madison, Milwaukee, and London
1970

Published by the University of Wisconsin Press
Box 1379, Madison, Wisconsin 53701
The University of Wisconsin Press, Ltd.
27—29 Whitfield Street, London, W.1

Printed in the United States of America by
NAPCO, INC., Milwaukee, Wisconsin
LC 70—101504
SBN 299—05330—X

The text used for this concordance is the edition published by Oxford
University Press in 1967, *The Poems of Gerard Manley Hopkins*,
edited by W. H. Gardner and N. H. MacKenzie.

CONTENTS

v

FOREWORD

For many years one of the most serious needs for scholarly work
in Nineteenth-Century English poetry has been for a concordance to
Gerard Manley Hopkins. This dense and contorted vocabulary, full of
verbal resonances on multiple levels, demands the careful and syste-
matic study for which a reliable concordance can be an indispensable
help. We are pleased to be able to offer at this time, therefore, a
concordance to the English poems of Hopkins which conforms to the
best technical standard for such publications, which has primary reference to the best existing text of his work (*The Poems of Gerard
Manley Hopkins*, fourth edition, published by Oxford University Press
in 1967), and which carries the kind approval of Oxford University
Press and of Professor Norman H. MacKenzie, the surviving editor of
the fourth edition. Although this edition is the most accurate and
complete existing text, because of certain complex editorial problems
it cannot be said to be final. In all likelihood, the only text of Hopkins which will satisfy all scholars would be a facsimile, reproducing
all of his unique notations and metrical markings as well as full variants. As a general rule, it would be desirable from a technical consideration if the standard critical edition of an author's work and the
concordance to that edition could be produced simultaneously as two
different output statements of the same input data. Such a project is
not practical, however, for Hopkins. This concordance can be used,
however, with all current editions of Hopkins's work.

Grants from the American Council of Learned Societies and the
American Philosophical Society, although given to support other as-
pects of my work, have substantially assisted in the preparation of
this volume and the project generally of which this book is a part. I
wish to thank also the Centre Universitaire International and the
Bibliothèque Nationale of France for much gracious assistance.

We also wish to thank Oxford University Press and Professor
Norman H. MacKenzie for their cooperation and in compliance with
Professor MacKenzie's request we include the following statement:
"Although Professor MacKenzie was reluctant to see the Fourth Edition used for this Concordance (because he was still in the process
of re-editing the poems for inclusion in the Oxford English Texts
series), he has agreed to its use, on the clear understanding that in
certain finer details the Fourth Edition must be regarded as only an
interim edition."

T. K. B.

Paris, 1969

TECHNICAL PREFACE

A concordance produced by programmed computer is different in kind from a hand-made concordance. The printed text of the hand-made concordance is the sole repository of the information and it has only that particular printed form; but the printed text of a computer concordance is merely one expression among many possible expressions of the information recorded on the electronic tape which directs the machine. The "real" depository of information for our concordance of Hopkins is an electronic tape, not a printed page. We can make that tape print a number of different forms. This printed concordance sorts words on the basis of their initial letters and frequency of occurrence; but, if we wished, we could have the output in any number of different statements. We might sort out all words involving certain combinations such as SCAPE, for example, if we were interested in finding out how Hopkins formed combinations on analogy to his enigmatic *inscape*. Or we could search out trisyllabic words which have primary stress on the first syllable to see if these are common in the antepenultimate foot in Hopkins' lines as they are in Virgil. Or we might make other analytic statements. In making this concordance as we have done, we have chosen to sort the information on our tapes a certain way. Our choice resulted in a form closely resembling that of a traditional concordance which, we hope, is useful in all the ways a hand-made concordance might be. But there is no particular sanctity about the appearance of a traditional concordance. In the future, thought should be given to the conception of the form itself of a published concordance. It is possible to conceive of radically different kinds of cross reference between vocabulary and text.

Our aim is not only to use computers to produce concordances; but to conduct an investigation into the nature of poetic language based on a very large body of data. This publication conforms to the standard of the best work in the Cornell series whose pioneer publications in the field have been an immense help and model to all who follow. We hope that this printed version of a small part of our data will be useful to all serious students of literature. If it proves welcome we would be happy to prepare comparable works on other poets, especially those in the circle of Robert Bridges. But we must insist that these printed concordances are just one form (a useful, but arbitrary form) of information which "really" resides in electronic tape and which we hope to find even more meaningful when organized in a radically different manner. We feel that this concordance is a step forward in the techniques of production because of its cost efficiency which results from the circumstances surrounding its production.

This volume is not produced as an end in itself, but as a by-product of a larger investigation in the course of which the data involved pass through a stage very similar in form to that of the traditional concordance. For the past several years Professor Bender has been supervising a group of investigators who hope to develop programmed techniques for approaching literary problems. In general, the kinds of applications we hope to find are of two sorts: First, we hope to make positively verified descriptive statements about large samples of language so as to be able to answer with precision questions such as, "Can Chatman's theory of meter serve as the basis for a computational approach to prosody?" A second aim of our work has been to develop a system for collating and editing complex texts. In the preparation of our input tapes for our larger investigation, the material passes through a phase very near the form of a standard concordance and, as we began to receive requests from scholars to use our material in both electronic tape and printout form, we decided to divert some of our research effort to the preparation of interim material, such as this concordance, likely to be of use to the scholarly public.

But a printed concordance is of little use by itself. It must be used generally in conjunction with a printed text. In everyday speech, one sometimes says that a concordance is *based on* a particular text. *Based on* is a metaphor which only serves to obscure the real relationship of a computer tape to a previously published text. We see one aim of our computer work to generate scholarly editions, not to depend on previously published texts. It is more accurate to say that a computer concordance *refers to* a text. The concordance organizes the vocabulary of a writer one way; a critical edition organizes the words another. Some uses of the concordance illuminate the writer's art when one organization is made to refer to the other. In this way, this concordance refers equally to all texts of Hopkins' work.

This concordance has been produced with funds supplied by the Graduate Research Council of the University of Wisconsin as part of a project whose general aim is the development of computer techniques which will facilitate the study of diction and prosody in large bodies of English verse. The present state of computer technology and recent developments in linguistically oriented theories of prosody by such scholars as Halle and Keyser, Levin, and Chatman suggest that techniques can be developed which will remove much of the routine drudgery from such studies and place at the disposal of scholars the widest possible body of information upon which to base generalizations. Computers seem particularly suited to such work as prosody which involves basically the recognition and tabulation of phonemic

patterns. By employing the computer to deal with the presemantic
levels of language for which it is suited, the prosodist is freed to
consider broad questions of comparison and interpretation.

The poetry of Gerard Manley Hopkins, Coventry Patmore, and
Robert Bridges has been selected as the focus of this project because
it represents a unique confluence of the three traditional approaches
to English prosody; very briefly, Hopkins's verse evolves from a consideration of stress, Patmore's from a consideration of time, and
Bridges' from a consideration of syllable count. Both Patmore and
Bridges produced rather elaborate statements of their prosodic theories, while Hopkins, though his remarks on prosody are somewhat
cryptic compared to those of Patmore and Bridges, has produced a
body of verse of the greatest interest to the study of prosody. Cer-
tainly techniques which aid in the description and interpretation of
his practice will be of wide application.

As a first step in developing such techniques, concordances of
the English-language verse of these three poets are being produced.
These concordances, besides being indispensable in any study of
diction, provide word lists which facilitate the transcription of verse
into machine-readable phonemic text. After encoding the word list
provided by the concordance in the received pronunciation of late 19th-
Century British English, the computer, by means of a look-up table,
substitutes phonemic for orthographic symbols in the text. The broad
phonemic transcription which results can then be scanned by the computer for such things as metrical pattern, assonance, alliteration,
vowel chime, enjambment, caesura, and rhyme. The computer also
organizes the results of the scansion of each line so that the distri-
bution of a given prosodic feature in the entire corpus of a poet's
work is immediately evident.

These concordances are being produced on a CDC 3600 computer
using the University of Wisconsin Bibcon system, a modification of
the CDC KWIC indexing system developed by Richard Venezky. It
took slightly over one half-hour to compile the Hopkins concordance.
Since the CDC 3600 does not include full punctuation on its print
chain, a number of mathematical signs were substituted for standard
punctuation in encoding the text. Camera copy was therefore produced
on a Univac 1108 whose print chain does include standard punctuation.
To produce this copy, I wrote an editing program for the 1108 which
restored standard punctuation, removed various sorting marks, marked
entries continued over more than one page, added pagination, and
sorted the word frequency list. The Univac 1108 provided the quick-
est, least expensive, and most readily available method of producing
camera copy. One guiding principle for this publication has been that
a computer concordance must cost less to produce than a hand-made
concordance. From such considerations of cost efficiency we ruled
that upper and lower case discrimination should not appear in this

printout. The total project proved so economical, however, that future publications can safely include upper and lower case with no unjustifiable cost. Such discrimination is, of course, feasible by means of any of several output devices currently available and would have been undertaken had the project been interested in producing by computer what has traditionally been done at great expense by hand. But besides the desire not to be sidetracked by considerations not relevant to our immediate objectives, we were also swayed in our decision by our awareness that the fourth edition of *The Poems of Gerard Manley Hopkins*, which the reader will be using, would eventually be superseded by an edition which might possibly reveal the need for a revision of this material. This is not to express any doubt about the soundness of the fourth edition which adopts "the latest variants or author's corrections, as far as these are discernible, ... as the best available text, except in some of the more fragmentary early verses where the writing, still fluid, had apparently not approached the final stage...."[1] This concordance is being published in order to make available to scholars who do not have access to computers a version of data assembled for our own purposes but which we feel is of general interest and immediate use. We have not included either Hopkins's Latin, Greek, and Welsh verse, or such variants as the notes to the fourth edition provide. We have recorded, however, all variants listed in the text itself of that edition.

We are now planning the publication of a concordance to the poems of Robert Bridges which will utilize a new technique so as to represent upper and lower case discrimination as well as all other features of the text in the visible printout.[2] For scholars interested either in the Hopkins circle or computer studies of nineteenth-century verse in general, we should also mention that Professor Bender's current research project includes editorial work on a concordance to Patmore, a concordance and critical edition of R. W. Dixon, and a complete concordance of Keats with all variants in machine-readable form. Related projects under other supervision are also in progress here. Present plans for the Dixon project are to collate the text by computer and to produce simultaneously an edition and concordance. We invite inquiries from scholars who would be interested in any of this work. We have on file a listing of those entries not included in the published version of this concordance.

---

1. *The Poems of Gerard Manley Hopkins*, 4th edition, ed. W. H. Gardner and N. H. MacKenzie (London: Oxford University Press, 1967) p. 236.
2. See Richard L. Venezky, "Computer-Aided Humanities Research at the University of Wisconsin," *Computers and the Humanities* (January, 1969), 129–38.

I would like to take this opportunity to express my gratitude to all those who have assisted in this project. Special thanks are due to the Graduate Research Council of the University of Wisconsin, the University of Wisconsin Computer Center, to Karl Kroeber who first suggested to me the possibility of undertaking computer-assisted literary research, and to Richard Venezky who has most generously made available both his own technical knowledge and that of his staff.

R. J. D.

Madison, 1969

NOTE
TO THE USER

This concordance refers primarily to *The Poems of Gerard Manley Hopkins*, 4th edition, edited by W. H. Gardner and N. H. MacKenzie, London: Oxford University Press, 1967. The line identifiers to the right of each entry correspond, in general, to the poem, stanza, and line numbers of this edition; e.g., 028 03 004 corresponds to poem 28, stanza 3, line 4. The second column in this sequence of three is used also for fragment identification or sonnet, act, or epigram number as given in this edition. For example the three parts of the dramatic fragment, "St. Winifred's Well," are identified as 01, 02, and C in this column. Where fragmentary stanzas are printed without being numbered, as in poem 80, consecutive numbering has been supplied. The two parts of poem 59, "The Leaden Echo and the Golden Echo," are identified as L and G. Entries are arranged alphabetically according to the CDC 3600 computer's standard collating sequence in which hyphen (-) comes between the letters I and J and apostrophe (') comes between R and S. Possessive forms marked only by apostrophe are listed as if they ended with s. The Bibcon system which generated this concordance alphabetizes words of more than 16 letters in length by their first 16 letters and enters them in the concordance as if they were only 16 letters long. Thus "before-time-taken" is entered as "BEFORE-TIME-TAKE."

Two marks not found in the fourth edition, C and V, have been added at the end of certain lines. A line marked in this manner by a V is a line printed in the text as a variant. A line marked by a C is not a full line but part of a line divided because it was too long to fit on a single hollerith card. Square brackets have been added at the beginning of lines in emended passages of lengths greater than two lines. In all other respects the text of the fourth edition has been followed as far as the print chain on the Univac 1108 computer allowed. Metrical marks, though encoded, were edited out by the computer for this reason. To facilitate cross reference and to aid users who do not have the fourth edition at hand, the table of contents to that edition is printed below. We have silently amended a few obvious typographical errors.

EARLY POEMS (1860–75?)

POEMS (1876—89)

UNFINISHED POEMS, FRAGMENTS, LIGHT VERSE, &c. (1862—89)

WORDS OMITTED FROM CONCORDANCE

AGAIN	HAD	ME	SOMETHING	WERE
ALTHOUGH	HADST	MIGHT*	THAT	WERT
AM	HAS	MINE	THAT'S	WHAT
AN	HAST	MUST	THE	WHATE'ER
AND	HATH	MY	THEE	WHAT'S
ANOTHER	HAVE	MYSELF	THEIR	WHEN
ARE	HE	NEITHER	THEM	WHERE
ART*	HE'S	NOR	THEMSELVES	WHERE'ER
AT	HER	NOT	THEN	WHEREVER
BE	HERE	NOW	THERE	WHICH
BECAUSE	HERS	OF	THERE'S	WHO
BEING*	HERSELF	ON	THESE	WHO'LL
BEEN	HIM	ONE	THEY	WHOM
BUT	HIMSELF	OR	THEY'RE	WHOSE
BY	HIS	OTHER	THIS	WHY
CAN	HOW	OTHER'S	THO	WILL*
CAN'T	IF	OTHERS	THOROUGH	WILT
CANNOT	IN	OUGHT	THOSE	WITH
CANST	IN'T	OUR	THOU	WOULD
COULD	INTO	OURS	THOUGH	WOULDST
DID	IS	OUT	THRO'	YE
DIDST	IT	SHALL	THROUGH	YOU
DO	ITS	SHALT	THUS	YOU'LL
DOES	ITSELF	SHE	THY	YOU'VE
DONE	IT'S	SHE'LL	TO	YOUR
DON'T	I'D	SHE'S	TOO	YOURS
DOST	I'LL	SHOULD	UPON	YOURSELF
DOWN*	I'M	SO	US	'TIS
EACH	I'VE	SOME	WAS	'TS
FOR	MAY*	SOMEONE	WE	'TWAS
FROM				

---

*These words are partially stopped, so that only noun forms appear in the concordance.

A CONCORDANCE

to the
English Poetry of

GERARD MANLEY HOPKINS

ABAKE
    THE DOG-STAR WITH THE FIELDS ABAKE · · · · · · · · · ∫ · 166 00 031
ABANDONED
    ABANDONED BY HER SAINTS, TURN'D BLACK AND BLASTED, · · · · · 102 02 011
ABEL
    ABEL IS CAIN'S BROTHER AND BREASTS THEY HAVE SUCKED THE SAME.) · · 028 20 008
ABELES
    WIND-BEAT WHITEBEAM! AIRY ABELES SET ON A FLARE! · · · · · 032 00 006
ABIDE
    TOO NEAR THEE, AND THOU MUST ABIDE · · · · · · · · 106 00 003
ABIDES
    DEATH WITH A SOVEREIGNTY THAT HEEDS BUT HIDES, BODES BUT ABIDES; · · 028 32 008
ABJECT
    I CEASE THE MOURNING AND THE ABJECT FAST, · · · · · · 014 01 008
ABODE
    HOUSES THAT MAKE ABODE BESIDE THE LAKE, · · · · · · 080 06 006
ABOLISHED
    HE HATH ABOLISHED THE OLD DROUTH, · · · · · · · 008 00 001
ABOUND
    FOR THESE, MAKE ALL THE VIRTUES TO ABOUND, -- · · · · 013 00 013
ABOUT
    SO GLASSY WHITE ABOUT THE SKY, · · · · · · · 003 00 016
    AND RISE AND GO ABOUT MY WORKS AGAIN · · · · · · 014 01 009
    CONTENDS ABOUT ITS MANY CREEDS · · · · · · · 023 00 032
    ABOUT MAN'S BEATING HEART, · · · · · · · · 060 00 050
    WHEN WHOLESOME SPIRITS RUSTLE ABOUT, · · · · · · 077 00 027
    WERE LIMN'D ABOUT WITH RADIANCE RARE · · · · · · 077 00 060
    AND SOME OF THOSE WHO STAND ABOUT, -- · · · · · · 080 09 004
    ABOUT HERSELF SHE IS MOST SENSITIVE, · · · · · · 094 00 021
    IN SKEINS ABOUT THE BRAKES, · · · · · · · · 098 10 003
    ---- ---- -- SILVER PLIGHTED TUFT ABOUT V · · · · 102 01 070
    THE RIVER WOUND ABOUT IT AS A WAIST. · · · · · · 107 04 002
    WHICH WORDSWORTH WOULD HAVE DWELT ON, ABOUT THE PLACE · · 107 04 016
    WHEN EYES THAT CAST ABOUT IN HEIGHTS OF HEAVEN · · · 113 00 001
    BESIDE THEM, ABOUT THE HEDGES, HEARING HIM: · · · · 113 00 008
    AS WISHING ALL ABOUT US SWEET, · · · · · · · 139 00 001
    HAD SWARTHED ABOUT WITH LION-BROWN · · · · · · 144 00 003
    DAYS AND DAYS CAME ROUND ABOUT · · · · · · · 145 00 023
    IT WILL NOT WELL, SO SHE WOULD BRING ABOUT · · · · 151 00 003
    THAT RIDES THE AIR SO RICH ABOUT THEE, C · · · · · 152 01 017
    FROM THY HAND OUT, SWAYED ABOUT · · · · · · · 155 00 003
    ALL BY TURN AND TURN ABOUT. C · · · · · · · 159 00 018
    WHILE HE LOOKS ABOUT HIM, LAUGHS, SWIMS. C · · · · 159 00 042
ABOVE
    THERE IS A MASSY PILE ABOVE THE WASTE · · · · · · 001 01 001
    IN BOWS ABOVE MY HEAD, AS FALSIFIED · · · · · · 012 02 004
    ECLIPSING PARAPET; YET ABOVE THE WALL · · · · · · 012 02 007
    I CANNOT BUOY MY HEART ABOVE; · · · · · · · 018 00 005
    ABOVE IT CANNOT ENTRANCE WIN. · · · · · · · 018 00 006
    LOVE, IT GROWS DARKER HERE AND THOU ART ABOVE! · · · 020 00 005
    IF I SHALL OVERTAKE THEE AT LAST ABOVE. · · · · · 020 00 016
    IN ACRES ALL ABOVE THE WOOD. · · · · · · · 021 00 035
    O BREATH OF IT BATHES GREAT HEAVEN ABOVE, · · · · · 027 00 045
    GNASHED: BUT THOU ART ABOVE, THOU ORION OF LIGHT! · · 028 21 005
    FURRED SNOWS, CHARGED TUFT ABOVE TUFT, TOWER · · · · 030 00 031
    AROUND! UP ABOVE, WHAT WIND-WALKS! WHAT LOVELY BEHAVIOUR · · 038 00 002
    THROSTLE ABOVE HER NESTED · · · · · · · · 042 00 020
    ABOVE ME, ROUND ME LIE · · · · · · · · 060 00 118
    LIFTS THEM A LITTLE WAY ABOVE. · · · · · · · 081 00 038
    THE ANGEL LIFTED US ABOVE. · · · · · · · · 081 00 119
    ABOVE THEM, DOWN THE DRAUGHT OF AIR, · · · · · · 083 00 012
    ABOVE · · · · · · · · · · · 098 21 001
    THE PROPER SWEET RE-ATTRIBUTING ABOVE. V · · · · · 113 00 011
    THAT SWEETNESS RE-ATTRIBUTING ABOVE. -- V · · · · · 113 00 012
    NOR FRUIT ABOVE, -- · · · · · · · · 127 00 008
    I AM, THAT HERE ABOVE US IS! · · · · · · · APPEN D 26
    FOR THY LOVE ABOVE OTHER, · · · · · · · APPEN D 44
ABREAST
    MARCH, KIND COMRADE, ABREAST HIM! · · · · · · 048 00 019
ABROAD
    AND LOOK ABROAD ON SUNNY CLUSTERS · · · · · · 077 00 134
    LOWLY ALICE LOOK'D ABROAD · · · · · · · · 109 17 001
ABRUPT
    OF OWN, OF ABRUPT SELF THERE SO THRUSTS ON, SO THRONGS THE EAR. · · 045 00 008
ABUNDANT
    NEXT TO MEADOWS ABUNDANT, PIERCED WITH FLOWERS, · · · 098 12 002
ABUTMENTS
    WITH OUR ABUTMENTS: THERE WE SEE · · · · · · 166 00 034
ABYSMAL
    THE ABYSMAL OCEAN HOARDS OF STRANGE AND RARE. · · · · 002 00 055
ABYSSES
    AND STILL TH' ABYSSES INFINITE · · · · · · · 023 00 025

ACANTHUS-CROWN'D
  BROAD-FLUTED, NOR WITH SHAFTS ACANTHUS-CROWN'D, ... 001 07 003
ACCENTS
  FIRM ACCENTS STRIKE HER FINE AND SCROLLED EAR, ... 136 00 021
ACCEPT
  THOU WHO CANST BEST ACCEPT THE CERTAINTY 013 00 005
ACCEPTANCE
  ACCEPTANCE ROUND HIS MISTRESS' MOUTH: 083 00 008
ACCEPTED
  THOSE CHARMS ACCEPTED OF MY INMOST THOUGHT, ... 012 01 009
ACCESSORIES
  WITH FICKLE SPOTS OF SADNESS: ACCESSORIES 125 00 041
ACCIDENTS
  AND, SAVE BY DARTING ACCIDENTS, FORGET. 014 01 010
ACCUMULATED
  DIMM'D IN THE LONG ACCUMULATED DUST: 001 12 006
ACHES
  HOLDS TILL HAND ACHES AND WONDERS WHAT IS THERE: 151 00 008
ACHIEVE
  STIRRED FOR A BIRD, -- THE ACHIEVE OF, THE MASTERY OF THE THING! . . 036 00 008
ACHING
  BUT COME, THOU BALM TO ACHING SOUL, ... 077 00 011
ACKNOWLEDGING
  AS ACKNOWLEDGING THY STRESS 155 00 006
ACORN
  SUCKS CLOSE THE ACORN: AS THE HAND AND GLOVE: 101 00 003
ACORN-CUP
  THE HAND DRAWS OFF THE GLOVE: THE ACORN-CUP 101 00 009
ACQUAINTANCE
  AND BRED ACQUAINTANCE OF UNUSED TOWNS? 107 02 002
ACRE
  IN THE ACRE OF GETHSEMANE: 006 00 016
  MEET IN ONE ACRE OF ONE LAND, ... 008 00 011
ACRES
  IN ACRES ALL ABOVE THE WOOD, ... 021 00 035
ACROSS
  ANON, ACROSS THEIR SWIMMING SPLENDOUR STROOK, ... 002 00 015
  IS THIS MADE PLAIN? WHAT HAVE I COME ACROSS 014 03 010
  MEAL-DRIFT MOULDED EVER AND MELTED ACROSS SKIES? 038 00 004
  ACROSS MY FOUNDERING DECK SHONE 072 00 018
  LET INCENSE HANG ACROSS THE ROOM 077 00 019
  ROLLS ACROSS THE LABOURING WILLOWS: 078 00 004
  PLY FOLD ON FOLD ACROSS HIS DANGEROUS EYES, ... 102 01 019
  THUS HE TIES SPIDER'S WEB ACROSS HIS SIGHT 102 03 028
  SUCH SPIDER'S WEB HE TIES ACROSS HIS SIGHT, V 102 03 034
  (I KNOW IT, KNOWING NOT) ACROSS FROM THOSE 119 00 007
  THE WORDS CAME FROM A COURT ACROSS THE WAY. 136 00 023
  FLINTY KINDCOLD ELEMENT LET BREAK ACROSS HIS LIMBS 159 00 041
ACT
  BRUTE BEAUTY AND VALOUR AND ACT, OH, AIR, PRIDE, PLUME, HERE . . 036 00 009
  SWEETLY THEN AND OF FREE ACT 077 00 089
  SEES THE RIGHT THING TO DO, AND DOES NOT ACT: 094 00 020
ACTS
  TWO TEDIOUS ACTS WERE PAST: 054 00 029
  ACTS IN GOD'S EYE WHAT IN GOD'S EYE HE IS -- 057 00 011
ADAMANTINE
  WOULD BRANDLE ADAMANTINE HEAVEN WITH RIDE AND JAR, DID . . . 048 00 046
ADAZZLE
  WITH SWIFT, SLOW: SWEET, SOUR: ADAZZLE, DIM: 037 00 009
ADD
  WILL ADD A FOOTREST THERE TO STAND, ... 080 13 002
ADELA
  SELVAGGIA, ORINDA, AND ADELA, AND THE REST. 125 00 038
ADMIRE
  I ADMIRE THEE, MASTER OF THE TIDES, ... 028 32 001
  FOR ALL TO SEE AND TO ADMIRE, ... 131 00 004
  O I ADMIRE AND SORROW! THE HEART'S EYE GRIEVES 157 00 001
ADMIRED
  SHE WAS ADMIRED, THE SPIRIT OF HELL 145 00 017
ADORE
  GODHEAD HERE IN HIDING, WHOM I DO ADORE 168 00 001
ADORED
  BE ADORED AMONG MEN, ... 028 09 001
  MASTERY, BUT BE ADORED, BUT BE ADORED KING. 028 10 008
  MASTERY, BUT BE ADORED, BUT BE ADORED KING. 028 10 008
ADOWN
  ADOWN THE CLATTERING GULLIES SWEPT THE RAIN: 001 13 002
  THEIR FILMY TAILS ADOWN WHOSE LENGTH THERE SHOW'D 002 00 104
ADVANCE
  EIGHT THOUSAND FURLONGS IN ADVANCE. 083 00 016
ADVERSITY
  SHE'S FRAMED TO TRIUMPH IN ADVERSITY: 094 00 023
ADVISE
  SOUL, SELF: COME, POOR JACKSELF, I DO ADVISE 069 00 009
AEOLIS
  OF GLASSY-CLEAR AEOLIS, METAL-LUSTRED 002 00 069
AEONS
  WHILE AGES AND WHILE AEONS RUN, ... 023 00 020

2

AERIAL
   SPLENDID WITH PHANTASIES AERIAL, ... 001 08 002
   AND FLOCKBELLS OFF THE AERIAL 041 00 007
AETHER
   MELTING INTO AETHER RARE 077 00 074
AFAR
   AFAR IN CORRIDORS WITH PAINED STRAIN 001 13 007
AFFECTION
   IS VERY CAPABLE OF STRONG AFFECTION 094 00 013
AFFINED
   AFFINED WELL TO THAT SWEET SOLITUDE, ... 107 01 015
AFFLICTED
   I HEARD HER SAY, POOR POOR AFFLICTED SOUL, -- 111 00 011
AFFLICTIVE
   THE SUN WHOSE VAST AFFLICTIVE HEAT 080 02 002
AFFLICTS
   AFFLICTS NO LESS, WHAT YET I HOPE MAY BLOW, ... 017 00 006
AFLASH
   AND CRUSH-SILK POPPIES AFLASH, ... 138 00 021
AFOOT
   ARE AFOOT! HEAVEN-VAULT FAST PURPLING PORTENDS, C 152 02 031
AFRAID
   BRING SLEEP ROUND THEN? -- SLEEP NOT AFRAID 166 00 021
AFRESH
   THY DOING! AND DOST THOU TOUCH ME AFRESH? 028 01 007
AFTER
   AFTER THE SANDFIELD AND THE UNVEINED GLARE! 005 00 029
   AFTER THE SUNSET I WOULD LIE, ... 015 00 042
   AND AFTER IT ALMOST UNMADE, WHAT WITH DREAD, ... 028 01 006
   O UNTEACHABLY AFTER EVIL, BUT UTTERING TRUTH, ... 028 18 005
   WHAT MOST I MAY EYE AFTER, BE IN AT THE END 040 00 010
   HIM, AFTER AN HOUR OF WINTRY WAVES, ... 041 00 069
   THIS VERY VERY DAY CAME DOWN TO US AFTER A BOON HE ON . . 048 00 005
   DAYS AFTER, SO I IN A SORT DESERVE TO 048 00 026
   AND NONE RECK OF WORLD AFTER, THIS BIDS WEAR 058 00 013
   IT FANCIES, FEIGNS, DEEMS, DEARS THE ARTIST AFTER HIS ART! . 063 00 006
   WHO COULD FORGIVE WITHOUT GRUDGE AFTER 077 00 057
   LIKE SHUTTLES FLEET THE CLOUDS, AND AFTER 098 03 001
   AND AFTER THAT SAD SORROW. 110 00 004
   WHAT WOULD BE A BIRTHDAY LETTER THAT AFTER THE BIRTHDAY CAME? . 128 00 004
   TIME WAS, NEXT WHITEST AFTER MARY'S OWN. 136 00 004
   WELL, AFTER ALL! AH BUT HARK -- 138 00 010
   AND AFTER THAT OFF THE BOUGH 138 00 039
   AFTER THAT IN PERFECT HUSH 145 00 058
   NEXT AFTER SWEET SUCCESS. I AM NOT LEFT EVEN THIS! . . . 152 02 059
   AFTER DAYLIGHT, DRAUGHTS OF DAYLIGHT, C . . . . . . 152 C 014
   MAKES GLADNESS AFTER HE IS GONE! 167 00 002
   THOU, THOU, MY JESUS, AFTER ME 170 00 005
AFTERCAST
   IN ONE FAIR FALL! BUT, FOR TIME'S AFTERCAST, ... 157 00 007
AFTERDRAUGHT
   NOW HER AFTERDRAUGHT GULLIES HIM TOO DOWN! 041 00 061
AFTER-COMERS
   AFTER-COMERS CANNOT GUESS THE BEAUTY BEEN. 043 00 019
AFTER-WORDS
   IT'S THE DAY THAT MAKES THE CHARM! NO AFTER-WORDS COULD SUCCEED . 128 00 007
AFTERNOON
   THEN THROUGH THE AFTERNOON THE SUMMER BEAM 001 12 001
AGAINST
   TRENCH -- RIGHT, THE TIDE THAT RAMPS AGAINST THE SHORE! . . 035 00 002
   THEY RAIN AGAINST OUR MUCH-THICK AND MARSH AIR 040 00 007
   THOUGHTS AGAINST THOUGHTS IN GROANS GRIND. C 061 00 014
   THY WRING-WORLD RIGHT FOOT ROCK? LAY A LIONLIMB AGAINST ME? SCAN . 064 00 006
   SIR! CHRIST! AGAINST THIS MULTITUDE I STRAIN. -- . . . 080 08 005
   THE FRUIT AGAINST THE WALL 105 00 012
   MY THOUGHT WAS, THERE TO REST AGAINST THE TREES 125 00 008
   ARE SHUT AGAINST THE CANVASSING OF ART. 126 00 006
   ON ONE THAT WENT AGAINST ME WHEREAS I HAD WARNED HER -- . . 152 02 006
   AGAINST THE WILD AND WANTON WORK OF MEN. 157 00 036
   AGAINST THY POWER PUT UNDER FEET 169 00 009
AGE
   OR SUNDER'D FROM MY SIGHT IN THE AGE THAT IS 013 00 003
   COULD COUNT ON PREDILUVIAN AGE. 015 00 010
   THIS IN DRUDGERY, DAY-LABOURING-OUT LIFE'S AGE. 039 00 004
   AN AGE IS NOW SINCE PASSED, SINCE PARTED! WITH THE REVERSAL . 045 00 003
   AGE AND AGE'S EVILS, HOAR HAIR, ... 059 0L 011
   MANWOLF, WORSE! AND THEIR PACKS INFEST THE AGE. 070 0G 020
   AGE GASP! WHOSE BREATH IS OUR MEMENTO MORI -- 075 00 007
   TO THAT FIRST GOLDEN AGE OF GOSPEL TIMES 136 00 005
AGE-OLD
   WOE, WORLD-SORROW! ON AN AGE-OLD ANVIL WINCE AND SING -- . . 065 00 006
AGE'S
   AND SILVER DAMASQU'D PLATES OBSCUR'D IN AGE'S CRUST. . . . 001 12 009
   AGE AND AGE'S EVILS, HOAR HAIR, ... 059 0L 011
AGES
   THIS TO REMOTEST AGES WAS TO BE 001 08 008
   WHILE AGES AND WHILE AEONS RUN, ... 023 00 020

AGGRANDISE
    THERE / GOD TO AGGRANDISE, GOD TO GLORIFY. --   •   •   •   •   •   •   •   046 00 008
AGO
    THE MONKS LEFT LONG AGO: SINCE WHICH NO MORE   •   •   •   •   •   001 15 004
    WHAT WAS ITS SEASON THEN? HOW LONG AGO?   •   •   •   •   •   •   027 00 013
    JEWS KILLED JESUS LONG AGO   •   •   •   •   •   •   •   •   145 00 052
AH
    BUT AH! IF YOU COULD UNDERSTAND HOW THEN   •   •   •   •   •   014 01 011
    AH DIP IN BLOOD THE PALMTREE PEN   •   •   •   •   •   •   •   025 00 037
    AH, TOUCHED IN YOUR BOWER OF BONE,   •   •   •   •   •   •   028 18 001
    AH! THERE WAS A HEART RIGHT!   •   •   •   •   •   •   •   028 29 001
    WORLD BROODS WITH WARM BREAST AND WITH AH! BRIGHT WINGS.   •   •   031 00 014
    AH WELL! IT IS ALL A PURCHASE, ALL IS A PRIZE.   •   •   •   032 00 008
    SHINE, AND BLUE-BLEAK EMBERS, AH MY DEAR,   •   •   •   •   036 00 013
    YET AH! THIS AIR I GATHER AND I RELEASE   •   •   •   •   •   044 00 009
    THERE! AND YOUR SWEETEST SENDINGS, AH DIVINE,   •   •   •   048 00 013
    TENDERED TO HIM. AH WELL, GOD REST HIM ALL ROAD EVER HE OFFENDED!   •   053 00 008
    AH NATURE, FRAMED IN FAULT,   •   •   •   •   •   •   •   054 00 038
    AH! AS THE HEART GROWS OLDER   •   •   •   •   •   •   •   055 00 005
    ELSE, BUT IN DEAR AND DOGGED MAN? -- AH, THE HEIR   •   •   •   058 00 010
    SOMEWHERE ELSEWHERE THERE IS AH WELL WHERE! ONE,   •   •   •   059 0G 006
    THE FLOWER OF BEAUTY, FLEECE OF BEAUTY, TOO TOO APT TO, AH! TO FLEET,   059 0G 011
    LET LIFE, WANED, AH LET LIFE WIND C   •   •   •   •   •   061 00 010
    BUT AH, BUT O THOU TERRIBLE, WHY WOULDST THOU RUDE ON ME   •   •   064 00 005
    I PLEAD: AND AH! HOW MUCH IN VAIN!   •   •   •   •   •   081 00 029
    AH FLORIS, FLORIS, LET ME SPEAK THIS LITTLE   •   •   •   •   102 01 050
    AH! SURELY ALL WHO HAVE WRITTEN WILL PROFESS   •   •   •   117 00 008
    AH NO! AND SHE WHO SITS BESIDE   •   •   •   •   •   •   120 00 014
    WELL, AFTER ALL! AH BUT HARK --   •   •   •   •   •   •   138 00 010
    AH YES! WHY, GET THEE GONE THEN: TELL THY MOTHER I WANT HER,   •   152 01 010
    ONE SPELL AND WELL THAT ONE. THERE, AH THEREBY   •   •   •   153 00 007
    BUT AH, BRIGHT FORELOCK, CLUSTER THAT YOU ARE   •   •   •   157 00 017
    AH WELL A DAY! --   •   •   •   •   •   •   •   •   160 00 019
    AH CHILD, NO PERSIAN-PERFECT ART!   •   •   •   •   •   165 00 001
    THEO. AH MYRTLE-BEND NEVER SIT,   •   •   •   •   •   APPEN A 37
AID
    SHE LENDS, IN AID OF WORK AND WILL,   •   •   •   •   •   139 00 003
AIDENN
    AND, WHERE THOU DWELLEST IN DEEP-GROVED AIDENN,   •   •   •   026 00 023
AIM
    THE WIDOW OF AN INSIGHT LOST SHE LIVES, WITH AIM   •   •   •   076 00 007
AIR
    THE ZENITH MELTED TO A ROSE OF AIR: •   •   •   •   •   002 00 023
    OF SOMETHING DRIFTING THRO' DELIGHTED AIR,   •   •   •   002 00 028
    SWIRLING OUT BLOOM TILL ALL THE AIR IS BLIND   •   •   •   002 00 089
    -- A LITTLE SICKNESS IN THE AIR   •   •   •   •   •   •   004 00 003
    YOUR PARCHED NOSTRILS SNUFF EGYPTIAN AIR,   •   •   •   005 00 027
    BELOW ME IN THE BEARING AIR: •   •   •   •   •   •   015 00 030
    AND SILENCE AND A GULF OF AIR.   •   •   •   •   •   •   015 00 040
    ' I THOUGHT THE AIR MUST CUT AND STRAIN   •   •   •   •   021 00 036
    YOU WENT INTO THE PARTLESS AIR.   •   •   •   •   •   025 00 030
    FOR THE INFINITE AIR IS UNKIND,   •   •   •   •   •   028 13 004
    WITH THE BURL OF THE FOUNTAINS OF AIR, BUCK AND THE FLOOD OF THE WAVE?   028 16 008
    SHE TO THE BLACK-ABOUT AIR, TO THE BREAKER, THE THICKLY   •   •   028 24 005
    O LOOK AT ALL THE FIRE-FOLK SITTING IN THE AIR!   •   •   •   032 00 002
    THAT CORDIAL AIR MADE THOSE KIND PEOPLE A HOOD   •   •   •   034 00 005
    ALL THE AIR THINGS WEAR THAT BUILD THIS WORLD OF WALES: •   •   034 00 010
    OF THE ROLLING LEVEL UNDERNEATH HIM STEADY AIR, AND STRIDING   •   036 00 003
    BRUTE BEAUTY AND VALOUR AND ACT, OH, AIR, PRIDE, PLUME, HERE   •   036 00 009
    THEY RAIN AGAINST OUR MUCH-THICK AND MARSH AIR   •   •   •   040 00 007
    NOW HE SHOOTS SHORT UP TO THE ROUND AIR;   •   •   •   •   041 00 065
    YET AH! THIS AIR I GATHER AND I RELEASE   •   •   •   •   044 00 009
    LET HIM OH! WITH HIS AIR OF ANGELS THEN LIFT ME, LAY ME! ONLY I'LL   045 00 009
    WITH THE SWEETEST AIR THAT SAID, STILL PLIED AND PRESSED,   •   •   047 00 003
    PILLOWY AIR HE TREADS A TIME AND HANGS   •   •   •   •   050 00 010
    TALL SUN'S TINGEING, OR TREACHEROUS THE TAINTING OF THE EARTH'S AIR,   059 0G 005
    WILD AIR, WORLD-MOTHERING AIR,   •   •   •   •   •   •   060 00 001
    WILD AIR, WORLD-MOTHERING AIR,   •   •   •   •   •   •   060 00 001
    THIS AIR, WHICH, BY LIFE'S LAW,   •   •   •   •   •   •   060 00 013
    AS IF WITH AIR: THE SAME   •   •   •   •   •   •   •   060 00 036
    HER LIFE AS LIFE DOES AIR.   •   •   •   •   •   •   060 00 045
    HOW AIR IS AZURED: •   •   •   •   •   •   •   •   060 00 074
    WHEREAS DID AIR NOT MAKE   •   •   •   •   •   •   •   060 00 094
    OF GOD'S LOVE, O LIVE AIR,   •   •   •   •   •   •   060 00 122
    WORLD-MOTHERING AIR, AIR WILD,   •   •   •   •   •   060 00 124
    WORLD-MOTHERING AIR, AIR WILD,   •   •   •   •   •   060 00 124
    TO WHOM THE COMMON EARTH AND AIR   •   •   •   •   •   077 00 059
    TO DRIFT IN AIR, THE CIRCLED EARTH   •   •   •   •   •   077 00 069
    IN BREEZY BELTS OF UPPER AIR   •   •   •   •   •   •   077 00 073
    AND ALL IN LONE AIR STOOD THE SUN,   •   •   •   •   •   077 00 076
    BREATHES IN THE MYSTERIOUS AIR: •   •   •   •   •   077 00 128
    HIGH UP THE BALANCED STONY AIR --   •   •   •   •   •   080 04 002
    ABOVE THEM, DOWN THE DRAUGHT OF AIR,   •   •   •   •   083 00 012
    BREAKING THE . . . AIR OF SPRING.   •   •   •   •   •   098 03 007
    THE LIBERTIES OF AIR.   •   •   •   •   •   •   •   098 29 004
    THE SPARKY AIR   •   •   •   •   •   •   •   •   098 33 001
    HE SHOOK WITH RACING NOTES THE STANDING AIR.   •   •   •   098 38 001

```
AIR        (CONTINUED)
      ONE STAR BY DAYLIGHT FROM THE STRONG BLUE AIR,    .   .   .   .   .  102 03 010
      SPRINGS IN THE FLOATING AIR AND THE SKIES SWIM, --  .   .   .   .  113 00 006
      FALLING ALONG THE BREAKLESS POOL OF AIR,    .   .   .   .   .   .  122 00 009
      WHICH DRIVES THE STONY AIR TO UTTERANCE? --  .   .   .   .   .   .  122 00 018
      AND DAYLIGHT AND SWEET AIR,     .   .   .   .   .   .   .   .   .  133 00 014
      THE LIBERTIES OF AIR.    .   .   .   .   .   .   .   .   .   .   .  135 00 022
      THE AIR SMELLS STRONG OF SWEETBRIAR IN THE PARK,   .   .   .   .  135 00 024
      TO THE POINT OF SILENCE IN THE AIR    .   .   .   .   .   .   .   .  135 00 032
      SPENT PEGASUS DOWN THE STARK-PRECIPITOUS AIR   .   .   .   .   .  136 00 008
      WHEN THE AIR WAS SWEET-AND-SOUR OF THE FLOWN FINEFLOUR OF  .   .  142 00 004
      LIKE AIR HE CHANGED IN CHOICE,    .   .   .   .   .   .   .   .   .  148 00 018
      THAT RIDES THE AIR SO RICH ABOUT THEE, C    .   .   .   .   .   .  152 01 017
      THEIR CRUTCHES SHALL CAST FROM THEM, ON HEELS OF AIR DEPARTING,  .  152  C 023
      OUT ON THE GIANT AIR; TELL SUMMER NO,    .   .   .   .   .   .   .  154 00 003
      DEALT SO, PAINTED ON THE AIR, C   .   .   .   .   .   .   .   .   .  159 00 025
      DIVINITY OF AIR, FLEET-FEATHER'D GALES,    .   .   .   .   .   .   .  160 00 001
      OR BIRD WITH PIPE, VIOL WITH AIR   .   .   .   .   .   .   .   .   .  166 00 020
      THEO.   YOU FELL INTO THE PARTLESS AIR.    .   .   .   .   .   .  APPEN A 30
AIRBUILT
      TOSSED PILLOWS FLAUNT FORTH, THEN CHEVY ON AN AIR- C   .   .   .  072 00 001
      BUILT THOROUGHFARE: HEAVEN-ROYSTERERS, C   .   .   .   .   .   .  072 00 002
AIR-BLENDED
      OF THE AIR-BLENDED DIADEM,     .   .   .   .   .   .   .   .   .  077 00 115
AIR-CRISPING
      OR BAT WITH TENDER AND AIR-CRISPING WINGS   .   .   .   .   .   .  019 00 002
AIR'S
      LAYING, LIKE AIR'S FINE FLOOD,    .   .   .   .   .   .   .   .   .  060 00 051
AIRS
      -- THEY SHOOK IN THE HURLING AND HORRIBLE AIRS, C   .   .   .   .  028 15 008
      COME THEN, YOUR WAYS AND AIRS AND LOOKS, LOCKS, C   .   .   .   .  059 06 014
      WINNING WAYS, AIRS INNOCENT, MAIDEN MANNERS, C   .   .   .   .   .  059 06 015
AIRWARDS
      AIRWARDS, DISTURB'D: AND THE SCARCE TROUBLED SEA   .   .   .   .  002 00 110
AIRWORLD
      ARE EARTHWORLD, AIRWORLD, WATERWORLD THOROUGH HURLED, C   .   .  159 00 018
AIRY
      TRIUMPH OF AIRY GRACE AND PERFECT HARMONY,    .   .   .   .   .  001 07 009
      WIND-BEAT WHITEBEAM! AIRY ABELES SET ON A FLARE!    .   .   .   .  032 00 006
      MY ASPENS DEAR, WHOSE AIRY CAGES QUELLED,    .   .   .   .   .   .  043 00 001
      THE AIRY EMPIRE AT HIS WILL:    .   .   .   .   .   .   .   .   .  077 00 078
      THERE THEY DID APPEAL. THEREFORE AIRY VENGEANCES   .   .   .   .  152 02 030
AIRY-GREY
      THE GOLD-WISP, THE AIRY-GREY    .   .   .   .   .   .   .   .   .  049 00 003
A-WANTING
      I PLOD WONDERING, A-WANTING, JUST FOR LACK    .   .   .   .   .  046 00 006
      OF ANSWER THE EAGERER A-WANTING JESSY OR JACK   .   .   .   .   .  046 00 007
AKIN
      AND TO THOSE STONES BECOME AKIN   .   .   .   .   .   .   .   .   .  080 03 002
ALARMS
      ALARMS OF WARS, THE DAUNTING WARS, THE DEATH OF IT?   .   .   .  051 00 006
ALAS
      AND THEY ARE PURER, BUT ALAS! NOT SOLELY    .   .   .   .   .   .  016 00 005
      THREE HUNDRED SOULS, O ALAS! ON BOARD,    .   .   .   .   .   .   .  041 00 002
      TO DEAREST HIM THAT LIVES ALAS! AWAY,    .   .   .   .   .   .   .  067 00 008
      ALAS! I RAVE, WHERE CALM IS DUE!   .   .   .   .   .   .   .   .   .  081 00 070
      THAT I WAS SO NEAR LAUGHTER? ALAS NOW    .   .   .   .   .   .   .  102 01 030
      ALAS! BUT I AM ALL AT FAULT,    .   .   .   .   .   .   .   .   .  120 00 024
ALBEIT
      WHEN THE FIERCE SKIES ARE BLUE TO BLACK, ALBEIT   .   .   .   .  080 02 005
      BUT IF THOU HATE ME WHO LOVE THEE, ALBEIT   .   .   .   .   .   .  161 00 002
ALE
      NOT HONOUR IT? ) ALE LIKE GOLDY FOAM    .   .   .   .   .   .   .  030 00 035
ALERT
      DENIS, WHOSE MOTIONABLE, ALERT, MOST VAULTING WIT   .   .   .   .  143 00 001
ALFONSO
      THAT IN MAJORCA ALFONSO WATCHED THE DOOR.    .   .   .   .   .   .  073 00 014
ALICE
      LOWLY ALICE SAT IN HER BOWER    .   .   .   .   .   .   .   .   .  109 16 001
      LOWLY ALICE LOOK'D ABROAD    .   .   .   .   .   .   .   .   .   .  109 17 001
      ' AND ALICE THEY CALL ME. '    .   .   .   .   .   .   .   .   .  109 19 002
ALIEN
      ALIEN FROM YOURS AS HEAVEN FROM NADIR-FIRES:    .   .   .   .   .  077 00 004
      NOW COMING FROM THE ALIEN EAVES, --   .   .   .   .   .   .   .   .  081 00 003
      TO ALIEN EAVES YOU FLED AND WENT, --   .   .   .   .   .   .   .  081 00 005
ALIGHT
      MOUNTS: THEN TO ALIGHT DISARMING, NO ONE DREAMS,   .   .   .   .  050 00 013
ALIGHTED
      ALL AS THE MOTH CALL'D UNDERWING ALIGHTED,    .   .   .   .   .  108 00 001
ALIKE
      ALL ALIKE IS GRIEF TO ME:    .   .   .   .   .   .   .   .   .   .  160 00 016
ALIVE
      'TIS MARVEL SHE IS YET ALIVE.    .   .   .   .   .   .   .   .   .  081 00 010
      ALIVE OR DEAD MY GIRL IS CARRIED IN IT, ENDLESSLY   .   .   .   .  152 01 021
ALL
      BY CONQU'RORS RUDE OF HONOR: AND NOT ALL    .   .   .   .   .   .  001 08 004
      INTO THE COOLING GLOOM: TILL SLOWLY ALL    .   .   .   .   .   .  001 12 005
```

5

```
NOW ALL THINGS ROSY TURN'D: THE WEST HAD GROWN     .   .   .   .   .   .   .   002 00 019
WITH SPIKED QUILLS ALL OF INTENSEST HUE:  .   .   .   .   .   .   .   .   002 00 044
SWIRLING OUT BLOOM TILL ALL THE AIR IS BLIND   .   .   .   .   .   .   002 00 089
A GLORIOUS WANTON! -- ALL THE WRECKS IN SHOWERS    .   .   .   .   .   002 00 093
IS ALL THE WINTER BIRD DARE TRY.   .   .   .   .   .   .   .   .   003 00 014
DROPS OUT AND ALL OUR DAY IS DONE.    .   .   .   .   .   .   .   003 00 032
ARE ALL THE MANNA-BUSHES IN THE LAND     .   .   .   .   .   .   005 00 021
UNBAKES MY PORES, AND STREAMS, AND MAKES ALL FRESH.    .   .   .   005 00 032
BLAZE FOR HIM ALL THIS WHILE.    .   .   .   .   .   .   .   .   005 00 036
CHRIST AT ALL HAZARDS FRUIT HATH SHEWED.   .   .   .   .   .   .   007 00 010
AND RIVERS RUN WHERE ALL WAS DRY.   .   .   .   .   .   .   .   008 00 002
GOD COMES ALL SWEETNESS TO YOUR LENTEN LIPS.   .   .   .   .   .   011 00 002
LO, GOD SHALL STRENGTHEN ALL THE FEEBLE KNEES.    .   .   .   .   011 00 014
ALL MINE, YET COMMON TO MY EVERY PEER.   .   .   .   .   .   .   012 01 008
THE WINDOW-CIRCLES, THESE MAY ALL BE SOUGHT    .   .   .   .   .   012 01 011
AND ALL LIKE ME MAY BOAST, IMPEACHED NOT,  .   .   .   .   .   012 01 013
SO THAT THE MASON'S LEVELS, COURSES, ALL   .   .   .   .   .   .   012 02 002
FOR THESE, MAKE ALL THE VIRTUES TO ABOUND, --  .   .   .   .   013 00 013
INTO ALL SEASONS, THOUGH NO WINTER CAST    .   .   .   .   .   014 01 005
AND SO, THOUGH EACH HAVE ONE WHILE I HAVE ALL,    .   .   .   016 00 012
AND FAIL OR SCATTER ALL AWAY.    .   .   .   .   .   .   .   .   018 00 002
AND OTHER SCIENCE ALL GONE OUT OF DATE   .   .   .   .   .   .   019 00 011
HEAR YET MY PARADOX: LOVE, WHEN ALL IS GIVEN,  .   .   .   .   020 00 013
IN ALL OUR WESTERN SHIRES WAS RARE.  .   .   .   .   .   .   .   021 00 023
IN ACRES ALL ABOVE THE WOOD.   .   .   .   .   .   .   .   .   021 00 035
ALL DOWN THE STAIR-WAY OF THE COPSE  .   .   .   .   .   .   .   021 00 045
FROM THERE WHERE ALL SURRENDERS COME    .   .   .   .   .   .   022 00 007
BUT NOT THE HAND THAT WROUGHT THEM ALL:    .   .   .   .   .   023 00 008
UPON CHRIST THROW ALL AWAY:  .   .   .   .   .   .   .   .   .   024 00 005
WHERE WINTER-WHILE IS ALL FORGOT, --    .   .   .   .   .   .   025 00 014
FROM ALL THE PAIN OF THE PAST'S UNREST!    .   .   .   .   .   026 00 012
TO THEE WE TENDER THE BEAUTIES ALL   .   .   .   .   .   .   .   026 00 021
WE, ALL WE, THRO' THE LENGTH OF OUR DAYS,  .   .   .   .   .   026 00 034
BUT ROPED WITH, ALWAYS, ALL THE WAY DOWN FROM THE TALL    .   028 04 006
MAKE MERCY IN ALL OF US, OUT OF US ALL   .   .   .   .   .   .   028 10 007
MAKE MERCY IN ALL OF US, OUT OF US ALL   .   .   .   .   .   .   028 10 007
FOR ALL HIS DREADNOUGHT BREAST AND BRAIDS OF THEW:   .   .   028 16 005
HAVE YOU! MAKE WORDS BREAK FROM ME HERE ALL ALONE, .   .   028 18 003
GROUND OF BEING, AND GRANITE OF IT: PAST ALL   .   .   .   .   028 32 006
THE ALL OF WATER, AN ARK   .   .   .   .   .   .   .   .   .   028 33 002
AND ALL THE LANDSCAPE UNDER SURVEY,  .   .   .   .   .   .   .   030 00 013
FOR ALL THEY SHINE SO, HIGH IN HEAVEN,   .   .   .   .   .   .   030 00 019
AND MAZY SANDS ALL WATER-WATTLED   .   .   .   .   .   .   .   030 00 023
AND ALL IS SEARED WITH TRADE; BLEARED, SMEARED WITH TOIL:  .   031 00 006
AND FOR ALL THIS, NATURE IS NEVER SPENT;   .   .   .   .   .   031 00 009
O LOOK AT ALL THE FIRE-FOLK SITTING IN THE AIR!    .   .   .   032 00 002
AH WELL! IT IS ALL A PURCHASE, ALL IS A PRIZE.    .   .   .   032 00 008
AH WELL! IT IS ALL A PURCHASE, ALL IS A PRIZE.    .   .   .   032 00 008
CHRIST HOME, CHRIST AND HIS MOTHER AND ALL HIS HALLOWS.    .   032 00 014
THE DESCENDING BLUE: THAT BLUE IS ALL IN A RUSH    .   .   .   033 00 007
WHAT IS ALL THIS JUICE AND ALL THIS JOY?   .   .   .   .   .   033 00 009
WHAT IS ALL THIS JUICE AND ALL THIS JOY?   .   .   .   .   .   033 00 009
I REMEMBER A HOUSE WHERE ALL WERE GOOD   .   .   .   .   .   034 00 001
ALL OVER, AS A BEVY OF EGGS THE MOTHERING WING .   .   .   034 00 006
ALL THE AIR THINGS WEAR THAT BUILD THIS WORLD OF WALES!    .   034 00 010
WITH A FLOOD OR A FALL, LOW LULL-OFF OR ALL ROAR,  .   .   035 00 003
FOR ROSE-MOLES ALL IN STIPPLE UPON TROUT THAT SWIM;    .   037 00 003
AND ALL TRADES, THEIR GEAR AND TACKLE AND TRIM.    .   .   037 00 006
ALL THINGS COUNTER, ORIGINAL, SPARE, STRANGE:  .   .   .   037 00 007
DOWN ALL THAT GLORY IN THE HEAVENS TO GLEAN OUR SAVIOUR:   .   038 00 006
WITH, ALL DOWN DARKNESS WIDE, HIS WADING LIGHT?    .   .   040 00 004
SOME ASLEEP UNAWAKENED, ALL UN-  .   .   .   .   .   .   .   041 00 003
ROYAL, AND ALL HER ROYALS WORE.   .   .   .   .   .   .   .   041 00 034
' ALL HANDS FOR THEMSELVES ' THE CRY RAN THEN; .   .   .   041 00 042
ALL UNDER CHANNEL TO BURY IN A BEACH HER   .   .   .   .   041 00 049
DOFFS ALL, DRIVES FULL FOR RIGHTEOUSNESS.  .   .   .   .   .   041 00 056
HE WAS ALL OF LOVELY MANLY MOULD,    .   .   .   .   .   .   041 00 074
LOOK, FOOT TO FORELOCK, HOW ALL THINGS SUIT! HE    .   .   041 00 077
UNCHRIST, ALL ROLLED IN RUIN --  .   .   .   .   .   .   .   041 00 096
FRESH, TILL DOOMFIRE BURN ALL,   .   .   .   .   .   .   .   041 00 119
GRASS AND GREENWORLD ALL TOGETHER;   .   .   .   .   .   .   042 00 018
ALL THINGS RISING, ALL THINGS SIZING .   .   .   .   .   .   042 00 025
ALL THINGS RISING, ALL THINGS SIZING .   .   .   .   .   .   042 00 025
CAPS, CLEARS, AND CLINCHES ALL -- .   .   .   .   .   .   .   042 00 044
THIS ECSTASY ALL THROUGH MOTHERING EARTH   .   .   .   .   042 00 045
ALL FELLED, FELLED, ARE ALL FELLED;  .   .   .   .   .   .   043 00 003
ALL FELLED, FELLED, ARE ALL FELLED;  .   .   .   .   .   .   043 00 003
BUT A PRICK WILL MAKE NO EYE AT ALL, .   .   .   .   .   .   043 00 015
HE HAUNTED WHO OF ALL MEN MOST SWAYS MY SPIRITS TO PEACE;  .   044 00 011
OR LOVE OR PITY OR ALL THAT SWEET NOTES NOT HIS MIGHT NURSLES;  .   045 00 006
ALL, IN THIS CASE, BATHED IN HIGH HALLOWING GRACE. .   .   047 00 011
RUN ALL YOUR RACE, O BRACE STERNER THAT STRAIN!    .   .   047 00 014
WHEN LIMBER LIQUID YOUTH, THAT TO ALL I TEACH  .   .   .   048 00 022
NOTHING ELSE IS LIKE IT, NO, NOT ALL SO STRAINS    .   .   048 00 029
US! FRESH YOUTH FRETTED IN A BLOOMFALL ALL PORTENDING  .   048 00 030
EYE, ALL IN FELLOWSHIP -- .   .   .   .   .   .   .   .   .   049 00 004
```

```
THIS, ALL THIS BEAUTY BLOOMING,        .  .  .  .  .  .  .  .  .  049 00 005
THIS, ALL THIS FRESHNESS FUMING,       .  .  .  .  .  .  .  .  .  049 00 006
A WILDER BEAST FROM WEST THAN ALL WERE, MORE     .  .  .  .  .  .  050 00 007
ALL WHILE HER PATIENCE, MORSELLED INTO PANGS,    .  .  .  .  .  .  050 00 012
FELIX RANDAL THE FARRIER, O IS HE DEAD THEN? MY DUTY ALL ENDED,   .  053 00 001
FATAL FOUR DISORDERS, FLESHED THERE, ALL CONTENDED?    .  .  .  .  053 00 004
BEING ANOINTED AND ALL! THOUGH A HEAVENLIER HEART BEGAN SOME    .  053 00 006
TENDERED TO HIM. AH WELL, GOD REST HIM ALL ROAD EVER HE OFFENDED!  053 00 008
HOW FAR FROM THEN FORETHOUGHT OF, ALL THY MORE BOISTEROUS YEARS,.  053 00 012
LIFE ALL LACED IN THE OTHER'S,         .  .  .  .  .  .  .  .  .  054 00 002
NOW THE NIGHT COME! ALL  .  .  .  .  .  .  .  .  .  .  .  .  .  .  054 00 010
FOR, WRUNG ALL ON LOVE'S RACK,         .  .  .  .  .  .  .  .  .  054 00 017
KEEPS GRACE! THAT KEEPS ALL HIS GOINGS GRACES!   .  .  .  .  .  .  057 00 010
THY RIVER, AND O'ER GIVES ALL TO RACK OR WRONG.  .  .  .  .  .  .  058 00 008
IT IS AN EVERLASTINGNESS OF, O IT IS AN ALL YOUTH! C   .  .  .  .  059 06 013
BIRTH, MILK, AND ALL THE REST          .  .  .  .  .  .  .  .  .  060 00 021
LET ALL GOD'S GLORY THROUGH,           .  .  .  .  .  .  .  .  .  060 00 030
TOWARDS ALL OUR GHOSTLY GOOD           .  .  .  .  .  .  .  .  .  060 00 048
MORE MAKES, WHEN ALL IS DONE,          .  .  .  .  .  .  .  .  .  060 00 071
WITH BLACKNESS BOUND, AND ALL          .  .  .  .  .  .  .  .  .  060 00 098
TRAY OR ASWARM, ALL THROUGHTHER, IN THRONGS! C   .  .  .  .  .  .  061 00 006
DISREMEMBERING, DISMEMBERING ALL NOW. HEART, YOU ROUND ME RIGHT .  061 00 007
UPON, ALL ON TWO SPOOLS! PART, PEN, PACK C       .  .  .  .  .  .  061 00 011
NOW HER ALL IN TWO FLOCKS, TWO FOLDS C .  .  .  .  .  .  .  .  .  061 00 012
OUR LAW SAYS! LOVE WHAT ARE LOVE'S WORTHIEST, WERE ALL KNOWN!   .  062 00 010
YEA, WISH THAT THOUGH, WISH ALL, GOD'S BETTER BEAUTY, GRACE.    .  062 00 014
YES, WHY DO WE ALL, SEEING OF A SOLDIER, BLESS HIM? BLESS   .  .  063 00 001
AND FAIN WILL FIND AS STERLING ALL AS ALL IS SMART,    .  .  .  .  063 00 007
AND FAIN WILL FIND AS STERLING ALL AS ALL IS SMART,    .  .  .  .  063 00 007
HE OF ALL CAN REEVE A ROPE BEST. THERE HE BIDES IN BLISS    .  .  063 00 010
NOW, AND SEEING SOMEWHERE SOME MAN DO ALL THAT MAN CAN DO,  .  .  063 00 011
NAY IN ALL THAT TOIL, THAT COIL, SINCE ( SEEMS ) I KISSED THE ROD, 064 00 010
WRETCH, UNDER A COMFORT SERVES IN A WHIRLWIND! ALL     .  .  .  .  065 00 013
ENGLAND, WHOSE HONOUR O ALL MY HEART WOOS, WIFE   .  .  .  .  .  .  066 00 005
REMOVE. NOT BUT IN ALL REMOVES I CAN   .  .  .  .  .  .  .  .  .  066 00 010
PURPLE EYES AND SEAS OF LIQUID LEAVES ALL DAY.   .  .  .  .  .  .  068 00 008
THIRST'S ALL-IN-ALL IN ALL A WORLD OF WET.       .  .  .  .  .  .  069 00 008
TOM HEART-AT-EASE, TOM NAVVY: HE IS ALL FOR HIS MEAL   .  .  .  .  070 00 004
LITTLE I RECK HO! LACKLEVEL IN, IF ALL HAD BREAD!  .  .  .  .  .  070 00 009
WHAT! COUNTRY IS HONOUR ENOUGH IN ALL US -- LORDLY HEAD,    .  .  070 00 010
OF EARTH'S GLORY, EARTH'S EASE, ALL! NO ONE, NOWHERE,  .  .  .  .  070 00 016
IN HIM, ALL QUAIL TO THE WALLOWING O' THE PLOUGH. C    .  .  .  .  071 00 010
BOTH ARE IN AN UNFATHOMABLE, ALL IS IN AN ENORMOUS DARK     .  .  072 00 012
IS ANY OF HIM AT ALL SO STARK          .  .  .  .  .  .  .  .  .  072 00 015
I AM ALL AT ONCE WHAT CHRIST IS, SINCE HE WAS WHAT I AM, AND    .  072 00 022
EARTH, ALL, OUT! WHO, WITH TRICKLING INCREMENT,  .  .  .  .  .  .  073 00 010
DISAPPOINTMENT ALL I ENDEAVOUR END?    .  .  .  .  .  .  .  .  .  074 00 004
WHEN STRANGELY LOOM ALL SHAPES THAT BE,.  .  .  .  .  .  .  .  .  077 00 031
AND THE WAKED STARS ARE ALL ALONE,     .  .  .  .  .  .  .  .  .  077 00 034
WHO KNOWING ALL THE SINS AND SORES     .  .  .  .  .  .  .  .  .  077 00 053
AND ALL IN LONE AIR STOOD THE SUN,     .  .  .  .  .  .  .  .  .  077 00 076
ALL THE WELKIN OVERHEAD,               .  .  .  .  .  .  .  .  .  077 00 096
ALL A SEVENFOLD-SINGLE GEM,            .  .  .  .  .  .  .  .  .  077 00 116
THERE IS A DAY OF ALL THE YEAR         .  .  .  .  .  .  .  .  .  080 08 001
THEY ALL COME HERE AND STAND BEFORE ME CLEAR     .  .  .  .  .  .  080 08 003
AND ALL IN ONE SAY ' CRUCIFY! '        .  .  .  .  .  .  .  .  .  080 08 007
C AND ALL J INTO THE DUOMO RAN!        .  .  .  .  .  .  .  .  .  081 00 088
'TWAS SAID OF NONE BUT ALL MEN KNEW!   .  .  .  .  .  .  .  .  .  081 00 091
BUT ALL THE WHILE IT SEEM'D TO ME .    .  .  .  .  .  .  .  .  .  081 00 112
MY LOVE! AND ALL WAS SWEET AND WELL.   .  .  .  .  .  .  .  .  .  081 00 121
FOR MORE WITH HIM WHO GIVES THEE ALL,  .  .  .  .  .  .  .  .  .  081 00 150
FOR ALL THE MILES THAT THEY WERE SPED! .  .  .  .  .  .  .  .  .  081 00 158
HAS DANCED WITH HER! AND ALL THE WHILE .  .  .  .  .  .  .  .  .  083 00 023
SEE ONE BOW EACH, YET NOT THE SAME TO ALL,       .  .  .  .  .  .  091 00 006
WHAT WERE WORTH NOTHING IF ALL COMPLIMENT!       .  .  .  .  .  .  094 00 006
AND CANNOT SEE AT ALL WITH OTHERS' EYES!         .  .  .  .  .  .  094 00 026
THEY'RE OUT OF DATE -- LENT SERMONS ALL THE YEAR.  .  .  .  .  .  096 05 002
OF FALLING WATER. THIS AND ALL OF THESE.  .  .  .  .  .  .  .  .  098 02 003
OF ALL THE GOLDEN PRESS.               .  .  .  .  .  .  .  .  .  098 27 002
TO ALL THE STARRY PRESS. --            .  .  .  .  .  .  .  .  .  098 28 006
WELL, I KNOW NOT, BUT ALL THINGS SEEM TO-NIGHT   .  .  .  .  .  .  102 01 010
THOU JACINTH! NOR HAVE SKILL OF ALL THY VIRTUES,  .  .  .  .  .  102 01 059
LIKE KNOCKING THUNDER ALL ROUND BRITAIN'S WELKIN,  .  .  .  .  .  102 02 003
WHERE ALL THE VIRTUES WERE ILLUSTRATED .  .  .  .  .  .  .  .  .  102 02 009
AND GIVES FOR TROPES HIS JUDGMENT ALL AWAY,      .  .  .  .  .  .  102 03 029
AND GIVES FOR TROPES HIS JUDGMENT ALL AWAY, V    .  .  .  .  .  .  102 03 035
ALL QUESTS SAVE THE RECITAL OF THEIR GREATNESS!  .  .  .  .  .  .  104 00 003
THEIR CLARIONS FROM ALL CORNERS OF THE FIELD     .  .  .  .  .  .  104 00 004
THEY DRAW ALL COVERTS, CUT THE FIELDS, AND SUCK  .  .  .  .  .  .  104 00 012
THE TREASURE FROM ALL CITIES.          .  .  .  .  .  .  .  .  .  104 00 013
OR NEVER BEEN AT ALL!                  .  .  .  .  .  .  .  .  .  105 00 015
THEIR CHANGING FEET IN FLICKER ALL THE TIME      .  .  .  .  .  .  107 01 013
BEYOND THE RIVER, ALL THE MEADOW'S ROUND,.  .  .  .  .  .  .  .  107 04 010
I HOPE THAT ALL THE PLACES ON OUR TRIP .  .  .  .  .  .  .  .  .  107 04 027
ALL AS THE MOTH CALL'D UNDERWING ALIGHTED,       .  .  .  .  .  .  108 00 001
LORD WILLIAM IS KING OF ALL THIS LAND  .  .  .  .  .  .  .  .  .  109 27 003
```

8

ALLOWS
    THAT PIECEMEAL PEACE IS POOR PEACE. WHAT PURE PEACE ALLOWS • • • 051 00 005
    ALLOWS THE SOUND OF BELLS IN HAMLETS ROUND • • • • • 080 04 006
    THEO. WHAT THE COLD MONTH ALLOWS -- • • • • • APPEN A 40
ALL'S
    THE BALD AND BOLD BLINKING GOLD WHEN ALL'S DONE • • • 143 00 004
    HOW ALL'S TO ONE THING WROUGHT! • • • • • 148 00 001
ALLSEEING
    THOU SUN, ALLSEEING EYEBALL OF THE DAY, • • • 160 00 004
ALMONER
    NAY, MORE THAN ALMONER, • • • • • 060 00 042
ALMOST
    AND AFTER IT ALMOST UNMADE, WHAT WITH DREAD, • • • 028 01 006
    THERE WAS A MEADOW LEVEL ALMOST: YOU TRACED • • • 107 04 001
    AND SAID ' I LIKE THIS: IT IS ALMOST ISLED, • • • 107 04 025
    YOU HAVE MADE ME QUOTE ALMOST THE DISMALEST PROVERB I KNOW: • • 128 00 018
ALMS
    BUY THEN! BID THEN! -- WHAT? -- PRAYER, PATIENCE, ALMS, VOWS, • • 032 00 009
    THE SWEET ALMS' SELF IS HER • • • • 060 00 043
ALOFT
    THOUGH ALOFT ON TURF OR PERCH OR POOR LOW STAGE, • • • 039 00 005
    ON THINGS ALOOF, ALOFT, • • • • • 060 00 091
ALONE
    HAVE YOU! MAKE WORDS BREAK FROM ME HERE ALL ALONE, • • 028 18 003
    HOME AT HEART, HEAVEN'S SWEET GIFT: THEN LEAVE, LET THAT ALONE. • • 062 00 013
    AND THE WAKED STARS ARE ALL ALONE. • • • • 077 00 034
    WHICH TO PURE SOULS ALONE MAY BE. • • • • 077 00 142
    NOW LIKE THE BIRD THAT SHAPES ALONE • • • • 081 00 006
    THIS HEART IS WARM TO YOU ALONE: • • • • 081 00 129
    OF HIM THAT LOOKS, YET NOT IN THAT ALONE, • • • 091 00 003
    BUT I'M ALONE, FOR MY LOVE'S GONE . • • • 095 00 007
    ALONE UPON THE HILL-TOP, HEAVEN O'ER HIM, • • • 107 01 008
    YET I'D NOT SAY IT IS HER FACE ALONE • • • 125 00 055
    IN A WIDE WORLD OF DEFIANCE CARADOC LIVES ALONE, • • 152 02 039
    WORLD WITHOUT END ALONE IN THEE. • • • • 167 00 028
ALONG
    POURTRAY'D ALONG THE FRIEZE WITH TITAN'S BROOD • • • 001 07 004
    LAY ALONG THE GRASSES GREEN • • • • • 004 00 022
    ALONG THE SANCTUARY SIDE! • • • • • 022 00 020
    I MOVE ALONG LIFE'S TOMB-DECKED WAY • • • • 023 00 039
    SOMETIMES A LANTERN MOVES ALONG THE NIGHT, • • • 040 00 001
    WITH, ALONG THEM, CRAGIRON UNDER AND COLD FURLS -- C • • 071 00 014
    GLIMMER'D ALONG THE SQUARE-CUT STEEP. • • • 092 00 001
    TOLD OFF THEIR LEAVES ALONG THE PIERCING GALE, • • 098 05 002
    ONE AND THEN ONE, ALONG THEIR WALKS, AND KEPT • • 107 01 012
    FALLING ALONG THE BREAKLESS POOL OF AIR, • • • 122 00 009
    CREPT ALL ALONG A HILL UPON OUR LEFT, • • • 125 00 003
    GALLOP ALONG THE MEADOW GRASS, -- . • • • 130 00 026
    THOSE GOLDNAILS AND THEIR GAYLINKS THAT HANG ALONG A LIME! • • 142 00 005
    THAT LEANS ALONG THE LOINS OF HILLS, WHERE A CANDYCOLOURED, C • • 159 00 005
ALOOF
    ON THINGS ALOOF, ALOFT, • • • • • 060 00 091
    OR, LIKE A LARK TO GLIDE ALOOF • • • • 077 00 065
    FOLDS OFF ALOOF, THAT SIGNAL IS AND PROOF • • • 080 06 003
ALP
    YOU'LL DARE THE ALP? YOU'LL DART THE SKIFF? • • • 030 00 005
ALSO
    A RAINBOW ALSO SHAPES ITSELF BEYOND • • • 107 03 006
    HEAVED DRUM ON DRUM: BUT HANDS ALSO • • • 145 00 006
ALTAR
    UPON HIS ALTAR, AND WITH RAREST STORE • • • 001 02 008
    THOU KNOWEST THE WALLS, ALTAR AND HOUR AND NIGHT: • • 028 02 005
ALTAR-TAPERS
    THE ALTAR-TAPERS FLAR'D IN GUSTS! IN VAIN • • • 001 13 005
ALTAR-VESSELS
    NOW IN OUR ALTAR-VESSELS STORED • • • • 006 00 019
ALTARS
    AND, ON A THOUSAND ALTARS LAID, • • • • 006 00 009
ALTER
    PERFECT, NOT ALTER IT. • • • • • 060 00 089
ALTER'D
    LEAVES SPENT, NEW SEASONS, ALTER'D SKY, • • • 015 00 002
    FROM PARTS UNLOOK'D FOR, ALTER'D, SPENT, • • • 081 00 024
    YOU HEAR AND, ALTER'D, DO NOT HEAR • • • 081 00 041
ALTHO
    ALTHO' UNCHALLENGED, WHERE SHE SITS, • • • 083 00 009
ALTOGETHER
    THEY WERE ELSE-MINDED THEN, ALTOGETHER, THE MEN • • 028 25 005
ALWAY
    HENCEFORTH LET YOUR SOULS ALWAY • • • • 024 00 029
    NOW BEGINNING, AND ALWAY! • • • • • 129 00 008
ALWAYS
    AS I MARK'D, NOT ALWAYS DIED • • • • 004 00 028
    BUT ROPED WITH, ALWAYS, ALL THE WAY DOWN FROM THE TALL • • 028 04 006
    ALWAYS THE TIME REMEMBERETH • • • • 081 00 061
    AND, HEADED ALWAYS DOWNWARDS, WITH LESS SOUNDING • • 112 00 002
    HAD ALWAYS DOOMED HER DOWN TO THIS -- • • • 145 00 003

9

ALWAYS   (CONTINUED)
    SECOND THIS FIERY STRAIN? NOT ALWAYS: O NO NO! 152 02 046
AMAIN
    UPON THE MOULD'RING TERRACES AMAIN: 001 13 004
    WHILE THE SUN STREAMS FORTH AMAIN 077 00 103
AMANSSTRENGTH
    CHURLSGRACE, TOO, CHILD OF AMANSSTRENGTH, HOW IT HANGS OR HURLS   .   . 071 00 012
AMAZE
    IT DOES AMAZE ME, WHEN THE CLICKING HOUR 102 01 001
AMAZED
    MEN ARE AMAZED TO WATCH ME PASS 025 00 003
AMBER
    WHOSE KEN THROUGH AMBER OF DARK EYES 077 00 051
    DOES INTO AMBER SPLENDOURS FAIL, ... 077 00 100
AMEN
    TO THE GLORY OF THE FATHER. AMEN. 169 00 011
    FOR BEING MY KING AND GOD. AMEN. 170 00 021
    TILL HE US TO HIM TAKE.   AMEN.   .   .   .   . APPEN D 50
AMEND
    CHRIST MINDS: CHRIST'S INTEREST, WHAT TO AVOW OR AMEND 040 00 012
AMENDS
    AND I MUST TAKE YOUR AMENDS, CRY PARDON, AND THEN BE DUMB.   .   .   . 128 00 020
AMERICAN-OUTWARD
    AMERICAN-OUTWARD-BOUND, ... 028 12 002
AMETHYST
    BROIDERS THE NETS WITH FANS OF AMETHYST 002 00 066
AMIDST
    THEY TELL ITS STORY THUS: AMIDST THE HEAT 001 02 001
    AND MELTS AMIDST ANOTHER: CIEL'D ON HIGH 001 06 008
    PLASHES AMIDST THE BILLOWY APPLE-TREES 002 00 087
    WHEN THOU AT THE RANDOM GRIM FORGE, POWERFUL AMIDST PEERS,   .   .   . 053 00 013
    AMIDST THE SISTERING PLANETS, TILL SHE COMES 103 00 014
AMISS
    CONCEIVING WHOM I MUST CONCEIVE AMISS? 013 00 002
AMONG
    OTHERS WITH FINGERS WHITE WOULD COMB AMONG 002 00 112
    A MOANING VOICE AMONG THE REEDS. 023 00 036
    BE ADORED AMONG MEN. 028 09 001
    DROWNED, AND AMONG OUR SHOALS, ... 028 35 002
    AMONG STRANGERS. FATHER AND MOTHER DEAR, ... 066 00 002
    AMONG HIS BROTHERS THREE, ... 109 23 002
    AMONG THE LILIES AND THY GOOD DOMAIN. 123 00 006
AMONGST
    AMONGST CASTILIAN BARRENS MOUNTAIN-BOUND: 001 01 002
    AMONGST COME-BACK-AGAIN THINGS, C .   .   .   . 152 C 029
ANCIENT
    OR ANCIENT MOUNDS THAT COVER BONES, ... 015 00 037
ANCLES
    EARTHLESS DEWS ON ANCLES SLEEK: 077 00 016
ANDROMEDA
    NOW TIME'S ANDROMEDA ON THIS ROCK RUDE, ... 050 00 001
ANEW
    THIS SWEET DESERTER LISTS HERSELF ANEW 102 01 062
ANGEL
    AN ANGEL CAME: ' THE JUDGMENT DONE, ... 081 00 104
    THE ANGEL LIFTED US ABOVE. 081 00 119
    NOR ANGEL INSIGHT CAN 148 00 005
    THE ANGEL SAID: ' O DREAD THEE NOUGHT. .   .   .   . APPEN D 15
    THE ANGEL SHE ANSWERED: .   .   .   . APPEN D 24
    THE ANGEL WENT AWAY THEREON .   .   .   . APPEN D 31
ANGEL-WARDER
    FROWNING AND FOREFENDING ANGEL-WARDER 048 00 017
ANGEL'S
    FAR FROM ITS HEAD AN ANGEL'S HOVERINGS. 089 00 008
    AND THE ANGEL'S WORDS HAD HEARD, ... APPEN D 22
ANGELS
    LET HIM OH! WITH HIS AIR OF ANGELS THEN LIFT ME, LAY ME! ONLY I'LL   . 045 00 009
    OF IT. ANGELS FALL, THEY ARE TOWERS, FROM HEAVEN -- A STORY   .   .   . 075 00 003
    TO WHAT THE CHORDS OF ANGELS ARE: 077 00 046
    CAUGHT FROM ANGELS' WINGS IN HEAVEN, ... 077 00 110
    WHO SAY THAT ANGELS, IN YOUR EAR 081 00 122
    AS THE STARS OR AS THE ANGELS THERE, C 159 00 026
ANIGH
    WHAT WAS THAT ECHO CAUGHT ANIGH ME, ... 160 00 020
ANOINTED
    BEING ANOINTED AND ALL: THOUGH A HEAVENLIER HEART BEGAN SOME   .   . 053 00 006
ANON
    ANON, ACROSS THEIR SWIMMING SPLENDOUR STROOK, ... 002 00 015
    LIES IN HER LAP, WHICH SHE ANON SWEEPS OFF, ... 111 00 009
    ' WOULD IT WERE SUMMER-TIME. ' ANON SHE SANG 111 00 012
    IN HER WAS CHRIST CONTAINED ANON, ... APPEN D 35
ANSWER
    OF ANSWER THE EAGERER A-WANTING JESSY OR JACK 046 00 007
    THE HEAVEN-ENFORCED ANSWER COMES, ... 081 00 144
    YEA, TO MYSELF I ANSWER MAKE: 081 00 145
    TWO MADE ANSWER IN ONE BREATH 109 26 001
    GENTLY TO HIM GAVE ANSWER .   .   .   . APPEN D 11

10

ANSWERED
    THE ANGEL SHE ANSWERED: • • • • • • • • • • • • APPEN D 24
ANSWERING
    NO ANSWERING VOICE COMES FROM THE SKIES: • • • • • • 023 00 002
ANTINOUS
    BUT, HAPLESS YOUTH, ANTINOUS THE WHILE • • • • • • 001 11 005
ANTIPODES
    THEY ARE ANTIPODES APART. • • • • • • • • • • 083 00 024
ANTIQUE
    AN ANTIQUE CHAUNT AND IN AN UNKNOWN TONGUE. • • • • • 002 00 131
ANVIL
    WOE, WORLD-SORROW: ON AN AGE-OLD ANVIL WINCE AND SING -- • • 065 00 006
ANVIL-DING
    WITH AN ANVIL-DING • • • • • • • • • • • 028 10 001
ANY
    I MUST FEED FANCY. SHOW ME ANY ONE • • • • • • 014 02 001
    COULD MOULD, IF ANY TEARS THERE WERE. • • • • • • 018 00 014
    IS SET IN ANY ORCHARD: NO, • • • • • • • • 025 00 010
    HOW TO KEEP -- IS THERE ANY ANY, IS THERE NONE SUCH, C • • 059 0L 001
    HOW TO KEEP -- IS THERE ANY ANY, IS THERE NONE SUCH, C • • 059 0L 001
    IS ANY OF HIM AT ALL SO STARK • • • • • • • 072 00 015
    WHEN SKIES ARE HARD AS ANY STONE. • • • • • • 081 00 008
    THE SPELL OF WOE IF ANY COULD. • • • • • • • 081 00 079
    IS FOND OF FLATTERY, AS ANY SHE, • • • • • • 094 00 015
    FROM ANY HEDGEROW, ANY COPSE, • • • • • • • 098 18 001
    FROM ANY HEDGEROW, ANY COPSE, • • • • • • • 098 18 001
    -- CAN I DO ANY HARM? • • • • • • • • • 125 00 017
    BY ANY LAUDED STATUE, NOR AGAIN • • • • • • • 125 00 026
    C ANYWHERE ANY MORE JOY TO BE IN. • • • • • • 138 00 033
    SUCK ANY SENSE FROM THAT WHO CAN: • • • • • • 147 00 003
    ANY INSTANT FALLS MEANS ME. AND I DO NOT REPENT: • • • 152 02 032
    NOT FOR ANY GAINS I SEE: • • • • • • • : • 170 00 017
    ANG. IS SET IN ANY ORCHARD, NO: • • • • • • APPEN A 10
ANYTHING
    IS IT ANYTHING TRUE? DOES IT GROW UPON GROUND? • • • 027 00 002
    IS ANYTHING A MILK TO THE MIND SO, SO SIGHS DEEP • • • 149 A 002
ANYWHERE
    ANYWHERE IN THE SUNLIGHT. • • • • • • • • 138 00 009
    C ANYWHERE ANY MORE JOY TO BE IN. • • • • • • 138 00 033
APART
    APART, BETWIXT TEN THOUSAND PETALL'D LIPS • • • • • 002 00 021
    THE APPEALING OF THE PASSION IS TENDERER IN PRAYER APART: • • 028 27 006
    YOUR SIGNAL, WHEN APART WE STOOD, • • • • • • 081 00 017
    THEY ARE ANTIPODES APART. • • • • • • • • 083 00 024
    THE STRANDED KEEL AND KELSON WARP APART: • • • • • 101 00 011
    HE HAS HIS PORTION. GOD, WHO STRETCH'D APART • • • • 126 00 002
    APART WIDE AND NEW-NESTLE AT HEAVEN MOST HIGH. • • • 149 A 006
APOLLO
    APOLLO VIEWS THE SMITTEN PYTHON WRITHE AND DIE. • • • 001 11 009
APPAL
    VACANT CREATION'S LAMPS APPAL. • • • • • • • 023 00 012
APPAREL'D
    BEING A STOLED APPAREL'D STAR. • • • • • • • 081 00 042
APPEAL
    AND LOUCHED LOW GRASS, HEAVEN THAT DOST APPEAL • • • 058 00 002
    THERE THEY DID APPEAL. THEREFORE AIRY VENGEANCES • • • 152 02 030
APPEALING
    THE APPEALING OF THE PASSION IS TENDERER IN PRAYER APART: • • 028 27 006
APPEAR
    AND MORE, ON EACH HAND, THICKEN, AND APPEAR • • • • 002 00 030
    AND SCARCELY DOES APPEAR • • • • • • •• • • 105 00 004
    AS VOID AS THOSE THE GENTLE DOWNS APPEAR • • • • 107 01 003
    AND PRESSED VIOLETS IN THE FOLDS APPEAR, • • • • 119 00 004
    I WILL APPEAR, LOOKING SUCH CHARITY • • • • • 140 00 003
APPEARING
    HOVERS OFF, THE JAY-BLUE HEAVENS APPEARING • • • • 028 26 003
APPEAR'D
    APPEAR'D NOT FOR THE PRESENT, TILL • • • • • • 092 00 008
APPLEDURCOMBE
    NOW IT OVERVAULTS APPLEDURCOMBE: • • • • • • 041 00 030
APPLE-TREES
    PLASHES AMIDST THE BILLOWY APPLE-TREES • • • • • 002 00 087
APPLES
    WITH GREEN-WHITE APPLES ON THE BOUGH. • • • • • 124 00 020
APPLY
    AND TO MY PALM THE POINT APPLY, • • • • • • 080 14 002
APPREHEND
    WITH TWICE AS FINE A SENSE TO APPREHEND THEM, • • • 102 01 012
APPROVE
    WHICH ENDS THOSE ONLY STRAINS THAT I APPROVE, • • • 019 00 010
APPROVED
    WHO SAY THAT HAD I KNOWN I HAD APPROVED THEE, -- • • • 013 00 012
    A HOPE OF AN APPROVED DEVICE: • • • • • • 080 12 002
APRIL
    LATE IN THE GREEN WEEKS OF APRIL • • • • • • 081 00 021
    OUR SEX SHOULD BE BORN IN APRIL PERHAPS OR THE LILY-TIME: • • 128 00 013
    AND WHERE COLD DAFFODILS IN APRIL ARE • • • • • 135 00 029

11

APRIL-WEATHER
    GOLD GALLANT, FLOWERS MUCH LOOKED AT IN APRIL-WEATHER • • • • 098 16 002
APT
    THE FLOWER OF BEAUTY, FLEECE OF BEAUTY, TOO TOO APT TO, AH! TO FLEET, 059 06 011
    THO' APT TO THROW IT IN A STRANGE DIRECTION; • • • • • 094 00 014
ARC
    THEN WHILE THE RAIN-BORN ARC GLOWS HIGHER • • • • 077 00 123
    THESE RATHER ARE THE ARC WHERE BEAUTY SHINES, • • • • 102 03 003
ARCADIA
    THAT NOT ARCADIA KNEW NOR HAEMONY. • • • • • 107 01 017
ARCADIAN
    HE WAS A SHEPHERD OF THE ARCADIAN MOOD • • • • 107 01 016
ARCH
    BREATHE, ARCH AND ORIGINAL BREATH, • • • • • 028 25 002
ARCHED
    DEEPLY IN THE ARCHED LUSTRES, • • • • • 077 00 133
ARCHES
    DOWN ROUGHCAST, DOWN DAZZLING WHITEWASH, WHEREVER AN ELM ARCHES, • 072 00 003
ARCHING
    WHEN THE RAINBOW ARCHING HIGH • • • • • 077 00 107
ARCH-ESPECIAL
    TO ME, SO ARCH-ESPECIAL A SPIRIT AS HEAVES IN HENRY PURCELL, • • 045 00 002
ARCS
    PLUNGE ORB'D IN RAINBOW ARCS, AND TRAMPLE AND TREAD • • • 002 00 078
ARCTURUS-SET
    AT HAEDUS-RISE, ARCTURUS-SET, • • • • • 166 00 028
ARGENT
    WITH ARM AND FIN; THE ARGENT BUBBLES STREAM'D • • • • 002 00 109
    SWOLL'N IS THE WIND THAT IN ARGENT BILLOWS • • • • 078 00 003
ARGUED
    I ARGUED ILL? • • • • • • • • 127 00 012
ARIGHT
    ' HAIL BE THOU, FULL OF GRACE ARIGHT! • • • • APPEN D 05
ARISE
    SAVE BY TWO STARS, MORE CROWDING LIGHTS ARISE, • • • 002 00 032
    COME UP, ARISE AND SLAY. • • • • • • • 005 00 018
    IT MELTS, NEW LIGHTS ARISE AS FAIR, • • • • • 077 00 118
ARK
    THE ALL OF WATER, AN ARK • • • • • • 028 33 002
ARM
    WITH ARM AND FIN; THE ARGENT BUBBLES STREAM'D • • • • 002 00 109
    WHAT STROKE HAS CARADOC'S RIGHT ARM DEALT? WHAT DONE? HEAD OF A REBEL 152 02 002
ARMS
    AND DAMASQU'D ARMS AND FOLIAG'D CARVING PILED. -- • • • • 001 10 002
    O FOR NOW CHARMS, ARMS, WHAT BANS OFF BAD • • • • 048 00 034
    HARD AS HURDLE ARMS, WITH A BROTH OF GOLDISH FLUE • • 071 00 001
    IT IS HARDLY A PROPER TREAT FOR A BIRTHDAY TO REST IN HER ARMS, • 128 00 012
    DIDST REACH THINE ARMS OUT DYING, • • • • • 170 00 006
AROSE
    AROSE IN GLOOM, A SOLEMN MOCKERY • • • • • 001 08 006
    TILL A LIONESS AROSE BREASTING THE BABBLE, • • • 028 17 007
AROUND
    AROUND THE WATER-NYMPHS IN FRETTED FALLS, • • • • 002 00 050
    HOW SOLDIERS PLATTING THORNS AROUND CHRIST'S HEAD • • 007 00 004
    AROUND; UP ABOVE, WHAT WIND-WALKS! WHAT LOVELY BEHAVIOUR • 038 00 002
    WAS AROUND THEM, BOUND THEM OR WOUND THEM WITH HER, • • 041 00 044
    QUESTIONING WINDS AROUND THE HILLS; • • • • • 077 00 044
    AROUND IT BALANCES THE LEVEL SEA, • • • • • 098 04 002
    ROUND A RING, AROUND A RING • • • • • • 138 00 014
AROUSED
    THE BLAME BEAR WHO AROUSED ME. WHAT I HAVE DONE VIOLENT • • 152 02 034
ARRAY
    RETURNING THANKS, MIGHT OFFER SUCH ARRAY. • • • • 089 00 004
ARTHUR
    YET ARTHUR IS A BOWMAN: HIS THREE-HEELED TIMBER'LL HIT • • 143 00 003
ARTHUR'S
    BUT DROPP'D ITS COIL OF WOES: ARTHUR'S BRITAIN, • • • 102 02 007
ARTIST
    IT FANCIES, FEIGNS, DEEMS, DEARS THE ARTIST AFTER HIS ART; • • 063 00 006
ART
    OF ART BEST FOLLOW NATURE) IN A MAZE • • • • • 001 06 005
    AND ART AND BEAUTY: TITLE NOW TOO FULL -- • • • • 001 15 006
    IT FANCIES, FEIGNS, DEEMS, DEARS THE ARTIST AFTER HIS ART; • • 063 00 006
    TAKE COURAGE; THIS SHALL NEED NO FURTHER ART. • • • • 080 11 005
    ARE SHUT AGAINST THE CANVASSING OF ART. • • • • • 126 00 006
    THE RUINS OF, RIFLED, ONCE A WORLD OF ART? • • • • 153 00 004
    AH CHILD, NO PERSIAN-PERFECT ART! • • • • • 165 00 001
ARTS
    WHAT TAUGHT THE HUMANITIES AND THE ROUND OF ARTS? • • • 107 02 006
AS
    HE RAIS'D THE CONVENT AS A MONSTROUS GRATE; • • • 001 04 001
    THE STRETCHING PALACE LAY AS HANDLE FIX'D, • • • 001 04 006
    IN SHOALS OF BLOOM: AS IN UNPEOPLED SKIES, • • • 002 00 031
    AND WAS AS THO' SOME SAPPHIRE MOLTEN-BLUE • • • 002 00 045
    TO MANTLE-O'ER THE TAIL, SUCH AS IS SHED • • • 002 00 049
    SOON -- AS WHEN SUMMER OF HIS SISTER SPRING • • • 002 00 084
    OF DRIVING VERMEIL-RAIN; AND, AS HE LISTS, • • • 002 00 091

AS POETS SING! OR THAT IT IS A PAIN	002	00	121
AS I WALK'D A STILLY WOOD,	004	00	005
SUMMER WAS AS FULL OF FLAME;	004	00	025
AS I MARK'D, NOT ALWAYS DIED	004	00	028
GIVE US THE TALE OF BRICKS AS HERETOFORE!	005	00	049
AND FAINT AS THOUGH TO DIE.	005	00	060
SHALL SHAKE HER FRUIT AS LIBANUS,	006	00	028
THAT MEN MUST WONDER AS I PASS	010	00	003
AS PUBLIC IS MY GREATER PRIVACY,	012	01	007
IN BOWS ABOVE MY HEAD, AS FALSIFIED	012	02	004
OF GOD'S DEAR PLEADINGS HAVE AS YET NOT MOVED THEE, --	013	00	010
WITH SUCH MALIGN CONJUCTIONS AS BEFORE	014	02	006
AT HOPES SO EVIL-HEAVEN'D AS MINE ARE.	014	02	014
LET ME BE TO THEE AS THE CIRCLING BIRD,	019	00	001
AS SILKEN GARDEN-POPPIES DO.	021	00	007
THE BATS' WINGS LISPING AS THEY FLEW	021	00	019
' YET AS HE CHANGED HIS MIGHTY STOPS	021	00	043
AS ERST UPON CHAOTIC FLOODS	023	00	021
ONE WORD -- AS WHEN A MOTHER SPEAKS	023	00	050
THEN, TO BEHOLD THEE AS THOU ART,	023	00	053
YET MADE ITS MARKET HERE AS WELL!	025	00	032
MAID YET MOTHER AS MAY HATH BEEN --	026	00	020
FOR THOU, AS SHE, WERT THE ONE FAIR DAUGHTER	026	00	025
THAT WAS UNTO JUDAH AS MAY, AND BROUGHT HER	026	00	031
WHO TO US ARE AS DEW UNTO GRASS AND TREE,	026	00	038
I STEADY AS A WATER IN A WELL, TO A POISE, TO A PANE,	028	04	005
OR RATHER, RATHER THEN, STEALING AS SPRING	028	10	003
WHETHER AT ONCE, AS ONCE AT A CRASH PAUL,	028	10	005
OR AS AUSTIN, A LINGERING-OUT SWEET SKILL,	028	10	006
O FATHER, NOT UNDER THY FEATHERS NOR EVER AS GUESSING	028	12	005
IS IT LOVE IN HER OF THE BEING AS HER LOVER HAD BEEN?	028	25	003
NOT A DOOMS-DAY DAZZLE IN HIS COMING NOR DARK AS HE CAME!	028	34	006
MORE BRIGHTENING HER, RARE-DEAR BRITAIN, AS HIS REIGN ROLLS,	028	35	006
NOTHING IS SO BEAUTIFUL AS SPRING --	033	00	001
FETCHED FRESH, AS I SUPPOSE, OFF SOME SWEET WOOD.	034	00	004
ALL OVER, AS A BEVY OF EGGS THE MOTHERING WING	034	00	006
AS A SKATE'S HEEL SWEEPS SMOOTH ON A BOW-BEND: THE HURL AND GLIDING	036	00	006
FOR SKIES OF COUPLE-COLOUR AS A BRINDED COW!	037	00	002
MAJESTIC -- AS A STALLION STALWART, VERY-VIOLET-SWEET! --	038	00	010
AS A DARE-GALE SKYLARK SCANTED IN A DULL CAGE	039	00	001
AS HALF SHE HAD RIGHTED AND HOPED TO RISE --	041	00	038
AS SHEER DOWN THE SHIP GOES.	041	00	060
TO ME, SO ARCH-ESPECIAL A SPIRIT AS HEAVES IN HENRY PURCELL,	045	00	002
FALLS LIGHT AS TEN YEARS LONG TAUGHT HOW TO AND WHY.	047	00	008
BY IT, HEAVENS, BEFALL HIM! AS A HEART CHRIST'S DARLING, DAUNTLESS!	048	00	014
YIELDS TENDER AS A PUSHED PEACH,	048	00	023
TAKE AS FOR TOOL, NOT TOY MEANT	049	00	013
AH! AS THE HEART GROWS OLDER	055	00	005
AS KINGFISHERS CATCH FIRE, DRAGONFLIES DRAW FLAME!	057	00	001
AS TUMBLED OVER RIM IN ROUNDY WELLS	057	00	002
YONDER. -- WHAT HIGH AS THAT! WE FOLLOW, C	059	06	031
GREAT AS NO GODDESS'S	060	00	027
AS IF WITH AIR! THE SAME	060	00	036
HER LIFE AS LIFE DOES AIR.	060	00	045
AND FAIN WILL FIND AS STERLING ALL AS ALL IS SMART,	063	00	007
AND FAIN WILL FIND AS STERLING ALL AS ALL IS SMART,	063	00	007
AS I AM MINE, THEIR SWEATING SELVES; BUT WORSE.	067	00	014
'S NOT WRUNG, SEE YOU! UNFORESEEN TIMES RATHER -- AS SKIES	069	00	013
HARD AS HURDLE ARMS, WITH A BROTH OF GOLDISH FLUE	071	00	001
THOUGH AS A BEECHBOLE FIRM, FINDS HIS, AS AT A ROLLCALL, RANK	071	00	007
THOUGH AS A BEECHBOLE FIRM, FINDS HIS, AS AT A ROLLCALL, RANK	071	00	007
ALIEN FROM YOURS AS HEAVEN FROM NADIR-FIRES!	077	00	004
AND DEATH FALLS GENTLY AS THE SNOW;	077	00	026
MELT AS FROM A HEAVENLY CHRISM!	077	00	062
IT MELTS, NEW LIGHTS ARISE AS FAIR,	077	00	118
FAIR, BUT OF FAIRNESS AS A VISION DREAM'D;	079	00	001
WHITE-FACED, AS ONE IN SAD ASSAY TO FLY	079	00	008
AS THOUGH THEY WERE NOT FROM WITHIN	080	03	004
AND NUMBS AND STARVES, AS BETWEEN ICY WHARVES	080	03	006
THUS CRUCIFIED AS I DID CRUCIFY.	080	14	005
WHEN SKIES ARE HARD AS ANY STONE,	081	00	008
YOUR COMFORT IS AS SHARP AS SWORDS!	081	00	032
YOUR COMFORT IS AS SHARP AS SWORDS!	081	00	032
YOU SHOULD HAVE BEEN WITH ME AS NEAR	081	00	043
AS HALVES OF SWEET-PEA-BLOSSOM ARE!	081	00	044
AS THE LAST PLEIAD, YEA BEHIND	081	00	046
'TIS FALSELY GIVEN -- AS LOVE IN MEN!	081	00	049
AS A SELF-EMBRACED SWEET THOUGHTS!V	085	00	003
HE PLAY'D HIS WINGS AS THOUGH FOR FLIGHT!	087	00	001
AS WRECKS OF MINED EMBERS WILL.	092	00	013
HER FACE WAS SUCH, AS BEING DIAPERED	093	B	003
IS FOND OF FLATTERY, AS ANY SHE,	094	00	015
-- YES FOR A TIME THEY HELD AS WELL	101	00	001
TOGETHER, AS THE CRISS-CROSS'D SHELLY CUP	101	00	002
SUCKS CLOSE THE ACORN; AS THE HAND AND GLOVE;	101	00	003
AS WATER MOULDED TO THE DUCT IT RUNS IN;	101	00	004

```
AS KEEL LOCKS CLOSE TO KELSON --  .  .  .  .  .  .  .  .  .  .  .  .  .  101 00 005
DOUBLE AS SHARP, MEANING AND FORCIBLE,  .  .  .  .  .  .  .  .  .  .  .  102 01 011
WITH TWICE AS FINE A SENSE TO APPREHEND THEM,  .  .  .  .  .  .  .  .  .  102 01 012
AS EVER I REMEMBER IN MY LIFE.  .  .  .  .  .  .  .  .  .  .  .  .  .  .  102 01 013
LODGE HIS EYES FAST; BUT YET AS EASY AND LIGHT  .  .  .  .  .  .  .  .  .  102 01 020
AS THE LAID GOSSAMERS OF MICHAELMAS  .  .  .  .  .  .  .  .  .  .  .  .  102 01 021
I FIND I AM AS READY WITH MY TEARS  .  .  .  .  .  .  .  .  .  .  .  .  102 01 031
AS THE FINE MORSELS OF A DWINDLING CLOUD  .  .  .  .  .  .  .  .  .  .  .  102 01 032
MY COUSIN WILL NOT LOVE YOU AS I LOVE,  .  .  .  .  .  .  .  .  .  .  .  102 01 057
AND SUCKS THE LIGHT AS FULL AS GIDEON'S FLEECE;  .  .  .  .  .  .  .  .  .  103 00 011
AND SUCKS THE LIGHT AS FULL AS GIDEON'S FLEECE;  .  .  .  .  .  .  .  .  .  103 00 011
AND AS SHE DWINDLES SHREDS HER SMOCK OF GOLD  .  .  .  .  .  .  .  .  .  103 00 013
AS VOID AS CLOUDS THAT HOUSE AND HARBOUR NONE,  .  .  .  .  .  .  .  .  .  107 01 001
AS VOID AS CLOUDS THAT HOUSE AND HARBOUR NONE,  .  .  .  .  .  .  .  .  .  107 01 001
AS VOID AS THOSE THE GENTLE DOWNS APPEAR  .  .  .  .  .  .  .  .  .  .  .  107 01 003
AS VOID AS THOSE THE GENTLE DOWNS APPEAR  .  .  .  .  .  .  .  .  .  .  .  107 01 003
HIS SHEEP SEEM'D TO COME FROM IT AS THEY STEPT,  .  .  .  .  .  .  .  .  .  107 01 011
THEN SOUGHT SUCH LEAFY SHELTER AS IT YIELDS,  .  .  .  .  .  .  .  .  .  107 03 016
THE RIVER WOUND ABOUT IT AS A WAIST.  .  .  .  .  .  .  .  .  .  .  .  .  107 04 002
WITH PARALLEL SHAFTS, -- AS UPWARD-PARTED ASHES, --  .  .  .  .  .  .  .  107 04 005
THEIR HIGHEST SPRAYS WERE DRAWN AS FINE AS LASHES,  .  .  .  .  .  .  .  .  107 04 006
THEIR HIGHEST SPRAYS WERE DRAWN AS FINE AS LASHES,  .  .  .  .  .  .  .  .  107 04 006
ALL AS THE MOTH CALL'D UNDERWING ALIGHTED,  .  .  .  .  .  .  .  .  .  .  108 00 001
TO COLOUR AS SMOOTH AND FRESH AS CHEEKS OF ROSES,  .  .  .  .  .  .  .  .  108 00 004
TO COLOUR AS SMOOTH AND FRESH AS CHEEKS OF ROSES,  .  .  .  .  .  .  .  .  108 00 004
AS WEDDED YOU MUST BE?  .  .  .  .  .  .  .  .  .  .  .  .  .  .  .  .  .  109 08 004
HIS THREE BROTHERS ARE EACH AS TALL  .  .  .  .  .  .  .  .  .  .  .  .  109 21 003
AND EACH AS FAIR AS HE.  .  .  .  .  .  .  .  .  .  .  .  .  .  .  .  .  109 21 004
AND EACH AS FAIR AS HE.  .  .  .  .  .  .  .  .  .  .  .  .  .  .  .  .  109 21 004
AS SHE LAY WEEPING AT THE NIGHT  .  .  .  .  .  .  .  .  .  .  .  .  .  .  109 29 001
' IT IS AS COLD AS DEATH WITHOUT:  .  .  .  .  .  .  .  .  .  .  .  .  .  109 29 003
' IT IS AS COLD AS DEATH WITHOUT:  .  .  .  .  .  .  .  .  .  .  .  .  .  109 29 003
HE GAVE HER KISSES COLD AS ICE:  .  .  .  .  .  .  .  .  .  .  .  .  .  .  109 39 001
NOW COMES AS LOW BENEATH.  .  .  .  .  .  .  .  .  .  .  .  .  .  .  .  .  115 00 004
AS DEVONSHIRE LETTERS, EARLIER IN THE YEAR  .  .  .  .  .  .  .  .  .  .  119 00 001
' AS WHEN A SOUL LAMENTS, WHICH HATH BEEN BLEST ' --  .  .  .  .  .  .  .  119 00 009
AS STRUCK WITH RINGS OF SOUND THE CLOSE-SHUT PALMS  .  .  .  .  .  .  .  .  122 00 010
[ AS MIGHT HAVE STRUCK AND SHOOK THE CLOSE-SHUT PALMS ]  .  .  .  .  .  .  122 00 013
AS THE WOOD-SORREL AND ALL THINGS SENSITIVE  .  .  .  .  .  .  .  .  .  .  122 00 014
BUT SING CONTENTED AS THE DOVE  .  .  .  .  .  .  .  .  .  .  .  .  .  .  124 00 003
GUILTY OF SILENCE? QUITE, AS LADIES GO.  .  .  .  .  .  .  .  .  .  .  .  125 00 023
BUT THE LILY IS PAST, AS I SAY, AND THE ROSE IS NOT IN ITS PRIME:  .  .  128 00 014
AS IT FELL UPON A DAY  .  .  .  .  .  .  .  .  .  .  .  .  .  .  .  .  .  131 00 001
AS SURE AS HEAVEN IT IS  .  .  .  .  .  .  .  .  .  .  .  .  .  .  .  .  133 00 006
AS SURE AS HEAVEN IT IS  .  .  .  .  .  .  .  .  .  .  .  .  .  .  .  .  133 00 006
AND ALL WITHIN THE HOUSE WERE SOUND AS POSTS,  .  .  .  .  .  .  .  .  .  135 00 017
THINK YOU WANT DAFFODILS AND FOLLOW AS FAR  .  .  .  .  .  .  .  .  .  .  135 00 030
AS WHERE THE LITTLE HURLING SOUND  .  .  .  .  .  .  .  .  .  .  .  .  .  135 00 031
SHE, HIGH AT THE HOUSETOP SITTING, AS THEY SAY,  .  .  .  .  .  .  .  .  .  136 00 013
ALL OVER, SOME SUCH WORDS AS THESE, THOUGH DARK,  .  .  .  .  .  .  .  .  136 00 029
AS WISHING ALL ABOUT US SWEET,  .  .  .  .  .  .  .  .  .  .  .  .  .  .  139 00 001
POETRY TO IT, AS A TREE WHOSE BOUGHS BREAK IN THE SKY,  .  .  .  .  .  .  149  A 003
THEY WASTE, THEY WITHER WORSE: THEY AS THEY RUN  .  .  .  .  .  .  .  .  150 00 003
WORK WHICH TO SEE SCARCE SO MUCH AS BEGUN  .  .  .  .  .  .  .  .  .  .  150 00 007
HER GLASS IS BLEST BUT SHE AS GOOD AS BLIND  .  .  .  .  .  .  .  .  .  .  151 00 007
HER GLASS IS BLEST BUT SHE AS GOOD AS BLIND  .  .  .  .  .  .  .  .  .  .  151 00 007
WITH DREADFUL DISTILLATION OF THOUGHTS SOUR AS BLOOD,  .  .  .  .  .  .  .  152 02 064
BRAVE ALL, AND TAKE WHAT COMES -- AS HERE THIS RABBLE IS COME.  .  .  .  152 02 068
AS LONG AS MEN ARE MORTAL AND GOD MERCIFUL,  .  .  .  .  .  .  .  .  .  .  152  C 010
AS LONG AS MEN ARE MORTAL AND GOD MERCIFUL,  .  .  .  .  .  .  .  .  .  .  152  C 010
OR THEY GO RICH AS ROSELEAVES HENCE THAT LOATHSOME CAME HITHER!  .  .  .  152  C 024
AS SURE AS WHAT IS MOST SURE, SURE AS THAT SPRING PRIMROSES  .  .  .  .  152  C 027
AS SURE AS WHAT IS MOST SURE, SURE AS THAT SPRING PRIMROSES  .  .  .  .  152  C 027
AS SURE AS WHAT IS MOST SURE, SURE AS THAT SPRING PRIMROSES  .  .  .  .  152  C 027
SHALL NEW-DAPPLE NEXT YEAR, SURE AS TO-MORROW MORNING,  .  .  .  .  .  .  152  C 028
AS ACKNOWLEDGING THY STRESS  .  .  .  .  .  .  .  .  .  .  .  .  .  .  155 00 006
OF MY BEING AND AS SEEING  .  .  .  .  .  .  .  .  .  .  .  .  .  .  .  155 00 007
AS WELL THE SISTER SITS, WOULD WELL THE WIFE:  .  .  .  .  .  .  .  .  .  157 00 014
AS THE STARS OR AS THE ANGELS THERE, C  .  .  .  .  .  .  .  .  .  .  .  159 00 026
HANG AS STILL AS HAWK OR HAWKMOTH, C  .  .  .  .  .  .  .  .  .  .  .  .  159 00 026
HANG AS STILL AS HAWK OR HAWKMOTH, C  .  .  .  .  .  .  .  .  .  .  .  .  159 00 026
LOVE ME AS I LOVE THEE, O DOUBLE SWEET!  .  .  .  .  .  .  .  .  .  .  .  161 00 001
THOU CANST NOT HATE SO MUCH AS I DO LOVE THEE.  .  .  .  .  .  .  .  .  .  161 00 004
FOR WEALTH AS WIDE AS WEARINESS?  .  .  .  .  .  .  .  .  .  .  .  .  .  166 00 048
FOR WEALTH AS WIDE AS WEARINESS?  .  .  .  .  .  .  .  .  .  .  .  .  .  166 00 048
AS JESUS GOD THE FATHER'S SON  .  .  .  .  .  .  .  .  .  .  .  .  .  .  167 00 008
AS BY AND BY OUR PRIZE ART THOU,  .  .  .  .  .  .  .  .  .  .  .  .  .  167 00 026
BUT CAN PLAINLY CALL THEE LORD AND GOD AS HE:  .  .  .  .  .  .  .  .  .  168 00 014
BE IN THY SERVANTS' HEARTS AS WELL,  .  .  .  .  .  .  .  .  .  .  .  .  169 00 002
THEO.  YET MADE YOUR MARKET HERE AS WELL:  .  .  .  .  .  .  .  .  .  .  APPEN A 32
AS TOUCHING ME FULFILLED BE THY SAW:  .  .  .  .  .  .  .  .  .  .  .  .  APPEN D 27
```

ASCEND

```
LEFT HAND, OFF LAND, I HEAR THE LARK ASCEND,  .  .  .  .  .  .  .  .  035 00 005
```

ASCENDANCY

```
IN THE ASCENDANCY OF RAINBOW'S HORNS,  .  .  .  .  .  .  .  .  .  .  .  084 00 002
```

ASCRIBED

```
ALL GLORY BE ASCRIBED TO  .  .  .  .  .  .  .  .  .  .  .  .  .  .  .  133 00 003
```

ASH
    AND THE BEADBONNY ASH THAT SITS OVER THE BURN. • • • • • • • 056 00 012
    FALL TO THE RESIDUARY WORM! WORLD'S WILDFIRE, LEAVE BUT ASH! • • • 072 00 020
    FAIRYLAND! SILK-BEECH, SCROLLED ASH, PACKED SYCAMORE, C • • • 159 00 024
ASHBOUGHS
    SAY IT IS ASHBOUGHS! WHETHER ON A DECEMBER DAY AND FURLED • • • 149 A 004
ASHES
    BEAUTY NOW FOR ASHES WEAR, • • • • • • • • • 024 00 019
    WITH PARALLEL SHAFTS, -- AS UPWARD-PARTED ASHES, -- • • • • 107 04 005
ASHINESS
    AND TANTALEAN SLATY ASHINESS • • • • -• • • • 117 00 005
ASH-TOPS
    WHICH BETWEEN ASH-TOPS SUFFERS LOSS • • • • • • 121 00 005
ASIDE
    AND TO PUT GRAVER SINS ASIDE • • • • • • • • 096 01 003
ASK
    NEVER ASK IF MEANING IT, WANTING IT, WARNED OF IT -- MEN GO. • • 028 08 008
    ASK OF HER, THE MIGHTY MOTHER! • • • • • • • 042 00 013
    MISS STORY'S CHARACTER! TOO MUCH YOU ASK, • • • • 094 00 001
    YOU ASK WHY CAN'T CLARISSA HOLD HER TONGUE. • • • 096 04 001
    WHAT I DID ASK THEN WAS A CIRCLE OF ROSE-RED SEALING-WAX • • 128 00 015
    ASK WHOM HE SERVES OR NOT • • • • • • • • 148 00 023
    SO KIND TO THOSE WHO ASK THE WAY, • • • • • • 167 00 010
ASKED
    AND I HAVE ASKED TO BE • • • • • • • • 009 00 005
ASKING
    TIME'S TASKING, IT IS FATHERS THAT ASKING FOR EASE • • • 028 27 003
    WHO STOPS HIS ASKING MOOD AT PAR • • • • • 166 00 025
ASK'D
    THE MORE SHE ASK'D, THE MORE HE SPOKE, • • • • 109 36 001
    BUT WHAT INDEED IS ASK'D OF ME? • • • • • 118 00 001
    THIS WAS NOT ASK'D, BUT WHAT INSTEAD? • • • • 118 00 007
ASKS
    BUT BID FOR, PATIENCE IS! PATIENCE WHO ASKS • • • 068 00 002
    WHO ASKS NOT LIFE BUT ONLY PLACE TO DIE. • • • 079 00 009
ASLANT
    GAZES ASLANT HIS SHOULDER, VIEWING NIGH • • • 001 11 006
ASLEEP
    FEASTS, WHEN WE SHALL FALL ASLEEP, • • • • 029 00 009
    SOME ASLEEP UNAWAKENED, ALL UN- • • • • • 041 00 003
ASPECT
    BAD SATURN WITH A SWART ASPECT • • • • • 083 00 018
ASPEN'S
    AND BARED IS THE ASPEN'S SILKY SKIRTING! • • • 078 00 006
ASPENS
    MY ASPENS DEAR, WHOSE AIRY CAGES QUELLED, • • • 043 00 001
ASSAULT
    BE AT EVERY ASSAULT FRESH FOILED, WORSE FLUNG, DEEPER DISAPPOINTED, • 152 02 056
ASSAULTING
    A JAUNTING VAUNTING VAULTING ASSAULTING TRUMPET TELLING. V • • 141 00 007
ASSAY
    WHITE-FACED, AS ONE IN SAD ASSAY TO FLY • • • 079 00 008
ASSIGN'D
    NO, LOVE PRESCRIPTIVE, LOVE WITH PLACE ASSIGN'D, • • • 102 03 013
ASSURED
    ELSE I AM WELL ASSURED I SHOULD OFFEND • • • 014 03 005
ASSYRIAN
    LIKE AN ASSYRIAN PRINCE, WITH BUDS UNSHEATH'D • • 002 00 062
ASTERN
    A MILE ASTERN LAY THE BLUE SHORES AWAY! • • • 002 00 005
ASTRAIN
    AND THE MIDRIFF ASTRAIN WITH LEANING OF, LACED WITH FIRE OF STRESS. • 028 02 008
ASTRAL
    CIRCLET OF ASTRAL FLOWERETS -- DIADEM'D • • • 002 00 061
ASTRAY
    HER DAPPLE IS AT AN END, AS- C • • • • 061 00 005
    TRAY OR ASWARM, ALL THROUGHTHER, IN THRONGS! C • • 061 00 006
    SOMEWHERE WE SLIPT ASTRAY, YOU CANNOT DOUBT. • • 125 00 014
    JESU, THEIR HOPE WHO GO ASTRAY, • • • • 167 00 009
ASTREW
    LILY SHOWERS -- SWEET HEAVEN WAS ASTREW IN THEM. C • • 028 21 008
ASTROLOGIC
    THAT READS OR HOLDS THE ASTROLOGIC LORE, • • • 014 02 002
ASWARM
    TRAY OR ASWARM, ALL THROUGHTHER, IN THRONGS! C • • 061 00 006
ATLANTIC
    NO ATLANTIC SQUALL OVERWROUGHT HER • • • 041 00 017
ATMOSPHERE
    MOTHER, MY ATMOSPHERE! • • • • • • • 060 00 115
ATONE
    AND DIED FOR US T'ATONE. • • • • • • APPEN D 40
ATTAIN
    MIGHT SO ATTAIN THEIR HERITAGE, • • • • 015 00 012
    ATTAIN THE WINDY LEVELS OF THE SKY • • • 121 00 004
ATTEMPTED
    TIME PAST SHE HAS BEEN ATTEMPTED AND PURSUED • • 050 00 005
ATTIRE
    SHE WAS DRESSED IN SILK ATTIRE • • • • • 131 00 003

```
ATTRIBUTES
    WITH ATTRIBUTES WE DEEM ARE MEET:  .   .   .   .   .   .   .   .   .   .   .   .   023 00 014
ATTUNEABLE
    EARNEST, EARTHLESS, EQUAL, ATTUNEABLE, C   .   .   .   .   .   .   .   .   .   061 00 001
ATTUNING
    MILKY AND DARK, WITH AN ATTUNING STRESS   .   .   .   .   .   .   .   .   107 04 013
AUREOLES
    UPWARDS AT ONCE AND WIN THEIR AUREOLES.   .   .   .   .   .   .   .   .   126 00 008
AUSTIN
    OR AS AUSTIN, A LINGERING-OUT SWEET SKILL,   .   .   .   .   .   .   .   028 10 006
AUTHENTIC
    THE AUTHENTIC CADENCE WAS DISCOVERED LATE   .   .   .   .   .   .   .   019 00 009
AUTUMN
    BUT FROM THE MOUNTAIN GLENS IN AUTUMN LATE   .   .   .   .   .   .   001 13 001
    THE AUTUMN YELLOW FEATHER IN THE BOUGHS   .   .   .   .   .   .   .   105 00 005
    ONLY THE DAHLIAS BLOW, AND ALL IS AUTUMN HERE.   .   .   .   .   .   128 00 010
AUTUMN-TIME
    WHICH I MAY TELL AT AUTUMN-TIME, '   .   .   .   .   .   .   .   .   .   004 00 015
    AUTUMN-TIME NO EARLIER CAME.   .   .   .   .   .   .   .   .   .   .   004 00 026
AVENGE
    HIS INJURY SHE'LL AVENGE WITH RAGING SHAME.   .   .   .   .   .   .   082 00 006
AVOID
    ME FRANTIC TO AVOID THEE AND FLEES? C   .   .   .   .   .   .   .   .   064 00 008
AVOW
    CHRIST MINDS: CHRIST'S INTEREST, WHAT TO AVOW OR AMEND   .   .   .   040 00 012
AWAY
    A MILE ASTERN LAY THE BLUE SHORES AWAY:   .   .   .   .   .   .   .   002 00 005
    THE ROSY ISLES: SO THAT I STOLE AWAY   .   .   .   .   .   .   .   .   002 00 140
    AND FAIL OR SCATTER ALL AWAY.   .   .   .   .   .   .   .   .   .   .   018 00 002
    WHICH PRAYING FAILS TO DO AWAY.   .   .   .   .   .   .   .   .   .   018 00 012
    LOVE, IT IS EVENING NOW AND THOU AWAY:   .   .   .   .   .   .   .   020 00 004
    AND PUT AWAY MY SUN,   .   .   .   .   .   .   .   .   .   .   .   .   021 00 011
    UPON CHRIST THROW ALL AWAY:   .   .   .   .   .   .   .   .   .   .   024 00 005
    EARTH THROWS WINTER'S ROBES AWAY,   .   .   .   .   .   .   .   .   .   024 00 017
    AND LIVES AT LAST WERE WASHING AWAY:   .   .   .   .   .   .   .   .   028 15 007
    AWAY IN THE LOVEABLE WEST,   .   .   .   .   .   .   .   .   .   .   028 24 001
    AWAY FROM COUNTER, COURT, OR SCHOOL   .   .   .   .   .   .   .   .   030 00 002
    AWAY FROM COUNTER, COURT, OR SCHOOL,   .   .   .   .   .   .   .   030 00 038
    DONE AWAY WITH, UNDONE, C   .   .   .   .   .   .   .   .   .   .   .   059 06 008
    SEEMS TO US SWEET OF US AND SWIFTLY AWAY WITH, C   .   .   .   .   059 06 008
    . . . FROM VANISHING AWAY? C   .   .   .   .   .   .   .   .   .   059 0L 002
    TO DEAREST HIM THAT LIVES ALAS! AWAY.   .   .   .   .   .   .   .   067 00 008
    RARE PATIENCE ROOTS IN THESE, AND, THESE AWAY,   .   .   .   .   .   068 00 005
    A HEART'S-CLARION! AWAY GRIEF'S GASPING, JOYLESS DAYS, DEJECTION,  .   .   072 00 017
    WINKS AWAY ITS RING OF GREEN,   .   .   .   .   .   .   .   .   .   086 00 002
    HEAVEN COMFORT SENDS, BUT HARRY IT AWAY,   .   .   .   .   .   .   089 00 005
    AND GIVES FOR TROPES HIS JUDGMENT ALL AWAY,   .   .   .   .   .   .   102 03 029
    AND GIVES FOR TROPES HIS JUDGMENT ALL AWAY, V   .   .   .   .   .   102 03 035
    HERE AT THE VERY FURTHEST REACH AWAY   .   .   .   .   .   .   .   .   107 04 019
    I HEAR A NOISE OF WATERS DRAWN AWAY,   .   .   .   .   .   .   .   .   112 00 001
    FLUNG RIDER AND WINGS AWAY: THOUGH THESE WERE NONE,   .   .   .   136 00 009
    IS ALL, ALL SHEARED AWAY, THUS! ' THEN I SWEAT FOR FEAR.   .   .   .   152 01 018
    IT STOOPED AND FLASHED AND FELL AND RAN LIKE WATER AWAY.   .   .   .   152 02 021
    NOT SLEEK AWAY: FALERNIAN-GROWN   .   .   .   .   .   .   .   .   .   166 00 043
    THE ANGEL WENT AWAY THEREON   .   .   .   .   .   .   .   .   .   .   APPEN D 31
    AWAY OUR SIN AND GUILT SHOULD TAKE,   .   .   .   .   .   .   .   .   APPEN D 45
AWFUL
    HAVE, AT THE AWFUL OVERTAKING,   .   .   .   .   .   .   .   .   .   .   041 00 114
AWHILE
    YOU, JADED, LET BE: CALL OFF THOUGHTS AWHILE   .   .   .   .   .   .   069 00 010
AWOKE
    I AWOKE IN THE MIDSUMMER NOT-TO-CALL NIGHT, C   .   .   .   .   .   137 00 001
AY
    THESE DAREDEATHS, AY THIS CREW, IN   .   .   .   .   .   .   .   .   .   041 00 095
    AY, SWEET TO TASTE BESIDE THIS WOE.   .   .   .   .   .   .   .   .   080 07 007
    NOT HOPE, NOT PRAY: DESPAIR! AY, THAT: BRAZEN DESPAIR OUT,   .   .   152 02 067
AYE
    THAN CHANGEFUL POMP OF COURTS IS AYE MORE WONDERFUL.   .   .   .   001 15 009
AZURE
    AN AZURE RIDGE: OR CLOUDS OF VIOLET GLOW'D   .   .   .   .   .   .   002 00 105
    PAVES THE CLOUDS ON THE SWEPT AZURE.   .   .   .   .   .   .   .   .   078 00 010
    BARTER'D FOR AN AZURE DYE,   .   .   .   .   .   .   .   .   .   .   086 00 003
    WITH THE READY AZURE AND HIGH CARMINE: -- THINK   .   .   .   .   093 8 002
    SHALL SEE THE AZURE TURN EXPRESSIONLESS   .   .   .   .   .   .   .   117 00 004
AZURED
    HOW AIR IS AZURED:   .   .   .   .   .   .   .   .   .   .   .   .   .   060 00 074
AZURING-OVER
    AND AZURING-OVER GREYBELL MAKES   .   .   .   .   .   .   .   .   .   042 00 041
AZUROUS
    AND THE AZUROUS HUNG HILLS ARE HIS WORLD-WIELDING SHOULDER   .   .   038 00 009


BABBLE
    TILL A LIONESS AROSE BREASTING THE BABBLE,   .   .   .   .   .   .   .   028 17 007
```
16

BABBLE   (CONTINUED)
    WHY, HEAR HIM, HEAR HIM BABBLE AND DROP DOWN TO HIS NEST, •   •   •   • 039 00 010
BABES
    MOTHERS ARE DOUBTLESS HAPPIER FOR THEIR BABES   •   •   •   •   • 123 00 001
BABYHOOD
    WHO BREATHE, FROM GROUNDLONG BABYHOOD TO HOARY   •   •   •   • 075 00 006
BACK
    WHAT TIME THE BAFFLED FRANK SWEPT BACK PURSU'D   •   •   •   • 001 14 008
    EBB'D BACK BENEATH ITS SNOWY LIDS, UNSEEN,   •   •   •   •   • 002 00 018
    AND WHEN HE TURNED IT BACK AGAIN   •   •   •   •   •   •   • 021 00 038
    AND THEN LAY BACK TO SLEEP,   •   •   •   •   •   •   •   • 021 00 053
    STARTLE·THE POOR SHEEP BACK! IS THE SHIPWRACK THEN A HARVEST, C   • 028 31 008
    OUR KING BACK, OH, UPON ENGLISH SOULS!   •   •   •   •   • 028 35 004
    I MUSE AT HOW ITS BEING PUTS BLISSFUL BACK   •   •   •   • 046 00 002
    BACK TO GOD, BEAUTY'S SELF AND BEAUTY'S GIVER, C   •   •   • 059 06 019
    GIVE BEAUTY BACK, BEAUTY, BEAUTY, BEAUTY, C   •   •   •   • 059 06 019
    BACK BEAUTY, KEEP IT, BEAUTY, BEAUTY, BEAUTY, C   •   •   • 059 0L 002
    HE LEANS TO IT, HARRY BENDS, LOOK, BACK, ELBOW, AND LIQUID WAIST   • 071 00 009
    FORWARD SHE LEANS, WITH HOLLOWING BACK, STOCK-STILL,   •   •   • 099 00 001
    AT ONCE THE SENSES GIVE THE MUSIC BACK,   •   •   •   •   • 113 00 010
    TO KEEP THE LOADED BOLT FROM PLUNGING BACK.   •   •   •   • 135 00 006
    STEPPED FROM THE STOOL, DREW BACK FROM C   •   •   •   •   • 137 00 004
    BID JOY BACK, HAVE AT THE HARVEST, KEEP HOPE PALE.   •   •   • 154 00 004
    TREAD BACK -- AND BACK, THE LEWD AND LAY! --   •   •   •   • 166 00 001
    TREAD BACK -- AND BACK, THE LEWD AND LAY! --   •   •   •   • 166 00 001
    AND BACK FROM SORROW BROUGHT. '   •   •   •   •   •   •   • APPEN D 20
BACKED
    ONE BETTER BACKED COMES CROWDING BY: --   •   •   •   •   • 166 00 013
BACKWARD
    BACKWARD ARE LAID HER PRETTY BLACK-FLEECED EARS!   •   •   • 099 00 013
BACKWHEELS
    IN BACKWHEELS THOUGH BOUND HOME? --   •   •   •   •   •   • 048 00 043
BAD
    O FOR NOW CHARMS, ARMS, WHAT BANS OFF BAD   •   •   •   • 048 00 034
    NATURE, BAD, BASE, AND BLIND,   •   •   •   •   •   •   •   • 054 00 040
    BAD SATURN WITH A SWART ASPECT   •   •   •   •   •   •   • 083 00 018
    BAD I AM, BUT YET THY CHILD.   •   •   •   •   •   •   •   • 155 00 013
BAFFLE
    MORE CHRIST AND BAFFLE DEATH!   •   •   •   •   •   •   • 060 00 067
BAFFLED
    WHAT TIME THE BAFFLED FRANK SWEPT BACK PURSU'D   •   •   •   • 001 14 008
BAFFLING
    WISEST MY HEART BREEDS DARK HEAVEN'S BAFFLING BAN   •   •   • 066 00 012
BALANCE
    TO THE NEST'S NOOK I BALANCE AND BUOY   •   •   •   •   • 138 00 043
BALANCED
    HIGH UP THE BALANCED STONY AIR --   •   •   •   •   •   • 080 04 002
    SHAKE THE BALANCED DAFFODILS.   •   •   •   •   •   •   • 098 07 002
    JARR'D DOWN THE BALANCED STORM! THE BLEEDING HEAVENS   •   • 102 02 004
BALANCES
    AROUND IT BALANCES THE LEVEL SEA.   •   •   •   •   •   • 098 04 002
BALD
    THE BALD AND BOLD BLINKING GOLD WHEN ALL'S DONE   •   •   • 143 00 004
BALDBRIGHT
    A BEETLING BALDBRIGHT CLOUD THOROUGH ENGLAND   •   •   •   • 041 00 025
BALES
    BOUNDEN BALES OR A HOARD OF BULLION? --   •   •   •   •   • 041 00 010
BALL
    THAT, LIKE THIS SLEEK AND SEEING BALL   •   •   •   •   • 043 00 014
    A BLEAR AND BLINDING BALL   •   •   •   •   •   •   •   • 060 00 097
    OF NERVE! THE CLAMMY BALL WAS DRY.   •   •   •   •   •   • 081 00 098
BALLAD
    WITH A BALLAD, WITH A BALLAD, A REBOUND   •   •   •   •   • 146 00 003
    WITH A BALLAD, WITH A BALLAD, A REBOUND   •   •   •   •   • 146 00 003
BALLS
    AND DANCED THE BALLS OF DEW THAT STOOD   •   •   •   •   • 021 00 034
    DANCES THE BALLS FOR LOW OR HIGH!   •   •   •   •   •   • 166 00 015
BALM
    BUT COME, THOU BALM TO ACHING SOUL,   •   •   •   •   •   • 077 00 011
BAN
    WISEST MY HEART BREEDS DARK HEAVEN'S BAFFLING BAN   •   •   • 066 00 012
BAND
    WE SHALL BE SHEAVED WITH ONE BAND   •   •   •   •   •   • 008 00 014
    LOCK WITH MY RIGHT! THEN KNOT A BARKEN BAND   •   •   •   • 080 13 005
BANDS
    SHEAVED IN CRUEL BANDS, BRUISED SORE,   •   •   •   •   • 006 00 005
    WHY SHOULD THEIR FOOLISH BANDS, THEIR HOPELESS HEARSES   •   • 089 00 001
    AND IN GREY BANDS THE SUN SHOULD LIE STILL BORN!   •   •   • 090 00 003
    THOUGH SELF-MADE BANDS AT LAST MAY TRUE LOVE BIND,   •   •   • 102 03 019
    THEY HAVE HELD HIS EYES WITH BLINDFOLD BANDS   •   •   •   • 109 13 001
BANES
    BY MANY BLOWS AND BANES! BUT NOW HEARS ROAR   •   •   •   • 050 00 006
    MAY BUT CALL ON YOUR BANES TO MORE CAROUSE.   •   •   •   • 157 00 030
BANK
    AND SHE BEAT THE BANK DOWN WITH HER BOWS AND THE RIDE OF HER KEEL!   • 028 14 005
    ON MEADOW AND RIVER AND WIND-WANDERING WEED-WINDING BANK.   •   • 043 00 008
BANKRUPT
    MY BANKRUPT HEART HAS NO MORE TEARS TO SPEND.   •   •   •   • 014 03 004

17

BANK'S
    AND LAPPED IN SHINING HAIR, ROLL TO THE BANK'S EDGE; THEN 152 02 019
BANKS
    WOOD BANKS AND BRAKES WASH WET LIKE LAKES 042 00 042
    SIR, LIFE UPON THY CAUSE. SEE, BANKS AND BRAKES 074 00 009
    ON CHEBAR'S BANKS, AND WHY THEY WENT 077 00 049
    LIKE SCALDED BANKS TOPP'D ONCE WITH PRINCIPAL FLOWERS; 102 02 012
    BEYOND, THE BANKS WERE STEEP; A BRUSH OF TREES 107 04 003
    NEVER, NEVER, NEVER IN THEIR BLUE BANKS AGAIN. 152 02 016
    DOWN THE BEETLING BANKS, LIKE WATER IN WATERFALLS, ... 152 02 020
    ENTRIES OR BANKS ALL OVER SHADE 166 00 023
BANNED
    BANNED BY THE LAND OF THEIR BIRTH, ... 028 21 002
BANNER
    BE UNDER HER BANNER AND LIVE FOR HER HONOUR; 156 00 003
    UNDER HER BANNER I'LL LIVE FOR HER HONOUR. 156 00 004
    UNDER HER BANNER WE LIVE FOR HER HONOUR. 156 00 005
    TO FOLLOW A BANNER AND FIGHT FOR HONOUR. 156 00 009
    WE FOLLOW HER BANNER, WE FIGHT FOR HER HONOUR. 156 00 010
    BUT UNDER HER BANNER I LIVE FOR HER HONOUR. 156 00 014
    UNDER HER BANNER WE MARCH FOR HER HONOUR. 156 00 015
    IF UNDER HER BANNER I FALL FOR HER HONOUR. 156 00 019
    UNDER HER BANNER WE FALL FOR HER HONOUR. 156 00 020
BANN'D
    AND COUNT THE ROSY CROSS WITH BANN'D DISASTROUS THINGS. . . . 089 00 009
BANQUET
    WE SCARCELY CALL THAT BANQUET FOOD, ... 006 00 031
BANQUET-HALL
    THAT WONT TO THRONG ZEUS' BANQUET-HALL; 160 00 029
BANS
    O FOR NOW CHARMS, ARMS, WHAT BANS OFF BAD 048 00 034
BAR
    ON TANGLED SHOALS THAT BAR THE BROOK -- A CROWD 002 00 096
BARBAROUS
    SUMMER ENDS NOW; NOW, BARBAROUS IN BEAUTY, THE STOOKS RISE . . 038 00 001
BARE
    THE BOUGHS, THE BOUGHS ARE BARE ENOUGH 003 00 001
    IS BARE NOW, NOR CAN FOOT FEEL, BEING SHOD. 031 00 008
    TO THRIFTLESS REAVE BOTH OUR RICH ROUND WORLD BARE 058 00 012
    WHOSE GLORY BARE WOULD BLIND 060 00 108
    IN WIDE THE WORLD'S WEAL; RARE GOLD, BOLD STEEL, BARE . . . 070 00 017
    ROPES, WRESTLES, BEATS EARTH BARE C 072 00 005
    THE HANGING SNOWS RUSH DOWN AND BARE 080 04 004
    BREATHE O'ER MY BARE NERVE RATHER. I DESIRE 080 05 005
    BARE THE CONDITION OF A REALM AT RIOT 082 00 004
    THERE IS NO PARTING OR BARE INTERSTICE 098 22 004
    RIGHT ROOTING IN THE BARE BUTT'S WINCING NAVEL C 143 00 005
    TILL WALK THE WORLD HE CAN WITH BARE HIS FEET 159 00 035
    MASKED BY THESE BARE SHADOWS, SHAPE AND NOTHING MORE, . . . 168 00 002
BAREBILL
    WITH GORGON'S GEAR AND BAREBILL / THONGS AND FANGS, . . . 050 00 014
BARED
    AND BARED IS THE ASPEN'S SILKY SKIRTING! 078 00 006
BARELY
    BARELY A SIGH TO THOUGHT OF HOPES FORGONE. 014 03 009
    AND BARELY TO ESCAPE THE CURSE, ... 081 00 170
BARGAIN
    TO THE BARGAIN OF ITS HATE TO THROW 145 00 020
BARGE
    ON BRAZED BARGE AND HARD BEHIND 166 00 039
BARKEN
    LOCK WITH MY RIGHT; THEN KNOT A BARKEN BAND 080 13 005
BARLEY
    AND BARLEY TURN TO WEED AND WILD; 114 00 005
BARN
    THESE ARE INDEED THE BARN; WITHINDOORS HOUSE 032 00 012
BARRACK
    A BUGLER BOY FROM BARRACK (IT IS OVER THE HILL . . . 048 00 001
BARRED
    HER BARRED FINGERS CLASP'D UPON HER EYES, ... 111 00 006
BARREL
    UNDERNEATH, THEIR GLASSY BARREL, OF A FAIRY GREEN. . . . 141 00 006
BARRELLED
    ROPE-OVER THIGH; KNEE-NAVE; AND BARRELLED SHANK -- C . . . 071 00 003
BARREN
    WITH BARREN RIGOUR AND A FRIGID GLOOM -- 001 01 008
    IT SEEMS; FOR GRANDEUR BARREN LEFT AND DULL 001 15 008
    TO MAN, THAT NEEDS WOULD WORSHIP BLOCK OR BARREN STONE; . . 062 00 009
BARRENS
    AMONGST CASTILIAN BARRENS MOUNTAIN-BOUND; 001 01 002
BARRIERS
    OR WRING THEIR BARRIERS IN BURSTS OF FEAR OR RAGE. . . . 039 00 008
BARROW
    THE BARROW OF DARK MAENEFA THE MOUNTAIN; C 137 00 004
    OR RINGLET-RACE ON BURLING BARROW BROWN. 157 00 012
BARROWY
    STAND AT STRESS. EACH LIMB'S BARROWY BRAWN, HIS THEW . . . 071 00 005

BARR'D
    AND WITH COFFIN-BLACK HE BARR'D THE GREEN.　.　.　.　.　.　.　.　.　004 00 011
BARS
    FORMED BARS OF STONE: BEYOND IN STIFFEN'D STATE　.　.　.　.　.　001 04 003
    BARS OR HELL'S SPELL THWARTS. THIS TO HOARD UNHEARD,　.　.　.　066 00 013
    THROUGH OTHER BARS IT USED TO THRILL.　.　.　.　.　.　.　.　081 00 015
    O'ER PASSES BLEAK, O'ER PERILOUS BARS　.　.　.　.　.　.　.　083 00 003
BARTER
    WHO CAN BUT BARTER SLENDER SUMS　.　.　.　.　.　.　.　.　.　081 00 146
BARTER'D
    BARTER'D FOR AN AZURE DYE,　.　.　.　.　.　.　.　.　.　.　086 00 003
BASE
    THOU HAST A BASE AND BRICKISH SKIRT THERE, SOURS　.　.　.　044 00 005
    NATURE, BAD, BASE, AND BLIND,　.　.　.　.　.　.　.　.　.　054 00 040
BASKET
    I BEAR A BASKET LINED WITH GRASS:　.　.　.　.　.　.　.　.　010 00 001
    AND AT THE BASKET THAT I BEAR,　.　.　.　.　.　.　.　.　.　010 00 004
    I BEAR A BASKET LINED WITH GRASS:　.　.　.　.　.　.　.　.　025 00 001
    WITH THE BASKET I BEAR,　.　.　.　.　.　.　.　.　.　.　025 00 004
    A BASKET BROAD OF WOVEN WHITE RODS　.　.　.　.　.　.　.　098 19 001
    ANG.　I BEAR A BASKET LINED WITH GRASS.　.　.　.　.　.　.　APPEN A 01
    ANG.　AND THE BASKET I BEAR,　.　.　.　.　.　.　.　.　.　APPEN A 04
BASKS
    OUR RUINS OF WRECKED PAST PURPOSE. THERE SHE BASKS　.　.　.　068 00 007
BASON
    AND IN A BASON BRINGS THE BLOCKS.　.　.　.　.　.　.　.　.　080 09 007
BASS
    WHAT BASS IS OUR VIOL FOR TRAGIC TONES?　.　.　.　.　.　.　075 00 008
BAST
    CROWNS COMPOSITE AND BRAIDED BAST　.　.　.　.　.　.　.　.　165 00 002
BAT
    OR BAT WITH TENDER AND AIR-CRISPING WINGS　.　.　.　.　.　019 00 002
BATH
    THIS BATH OF BLUE AND SLAKE　.　.　.　.　.　.　.　.　.　060 00 095
    SHE BRIMS HER BATH IN COLD OR HEAT:　.　.　.　.　.　.　.　139 00 002
BATHE
    TO BATHE IN HIS FALL-GOLD MERCIES, TO BREATHE IN HIS ALL-FIRE GLANCES.　028 23 008
    BATHE ME, JESU LORD, IN WHAT THY BOSOM RAN --　.　.　.　.　168 00 022
BATHED
    ALL, IN THIS CASE, BATHED IN HIGH HALLOWING GRACE.　.　.　.　047 00 011
BATHES
    O BREATH OF IT BATHES GREAT HEAVEN ABOVE.　.　.　.　.　.　027 00 045
BATHING
    BATHING: IT IS SUMMER'S SOVEREIGN GOOD.　.　.　.　.　.　.　159 00 013
BATS
    THE BATS' WINGS LISPING AS THEY FLEW　.　.　.　.　.　.　.　021 00 019
BATTERING
    HIS BRIGHT AND BATTERING SANDAL! C　.　.　.　.　.　.　.　053 00 014
BATTLE
    OF BATTLE ONCE UPON ST. LAWRENCE' DAY　.　.　.　.　.　.　.　001 02 002
BATTLED
    THAT BATTLED GODS FOR HEAVEN: BRILLIANT-HUED,　.　.　.　.　001 07 005
BATTLING
    BATTLING WITH GOD, IS NOW MY PRAYER.　.　.　.　.　.　.　.　018 00 016
BAY
    AND GAIN'D THRO' GROWING DUSK THE STIRLESS BAY:　.　.　.　.　002 00 141
    WHAT NONE WOULD HAVE KNOWN OF IT, ONLY THE HEART, BEING HARD AT BAY,　028 07 008
    YET DID THE DARK SIDE OF THE BAY OF THY BLESSING　.　.　.　028 12 007
    BRIGHT SUN LANCED FIRE IN THE HEAVENLY BAY:　.　.　.　.　041 00 022
    TO KEEP AT BAY　.　.　.　.　.　.　.　.　.　.　.　.　.　059 0L 010
    (THE FURTHEST REACH THIS SIDE, ON THAT THE BAY　.　.　.　107 04 020
BAYS
    OR ELSE THEIR COOINGS CAME FROM BAYS OF TREES,　.　.　.　.　098 02 001
BEACH
    ALL UNDER CHANNEL TO BURY IN A BEACH HER　.　.　.　.　.　041 00 049
BEACON
    TARPEIAN-FAST, BUT A BLOWN BEACON OF LIGHT.　.　.　.　.　028 29 008
    A BEACON, AN ETERNAL BEAM. FLESH FADE, AND MORTAL TRASH　.　.　072 00 019
BEAD
    THAT BROW AND BEAD OF BEING,　.　.　.　.　.　.　.　.　.　048 00 039
    THAT BEAD THE PLAIN! DID EVER HAVERING CHURCH-TOWER　.　.　100 00 006
BEADBONNY
    AND THE BEADBONNY ASH THAT SITS OVER THE BURN.　.　.　.　056 00 012
BEAKLEAVED
    ONLY THE BEAKLEAVED BOUGHS DRAGONISH C　.　.　.　.　.　.　061 00 009
BEAM
    THEN THROUGH THE AFTERNOON THE SUMMER BEAM　.　.　.　.　.　001 12 001
    THE BREAKERS ROLLED ON HER BEAM WITH RUINOUS SHOCK!　.　.　028 14 006
    A BEACON, AN ETERNAL BEAM. FLESH FADE, AND MORTAL TRASH　.　.　072 00 019
BEAMING
    FOAMFALLING IS NOT FRESH TO IT, RAINBOW BY IT NOT BEAMING,　.　.　152 02 024
BEAM-BLIND
    WHAT HINDERS? ARE YOU BEAM-BLIND, YET TO A FAULT　.　.　.　046 00 012
BEAMS
    RICH BEAMS, TILL DEATH OR DISTANCE BUYS THEM QUITE.　.　.　040 00 008
    THEIR HARNESS BEAMS LIKE SCYTHES IN MORNING GRASS:　.　.　104 00 006
    AND ARE THEY THUS? THE FINE, THE FINGERING BEAMS　.　.　.　157 00 009

BEAN
```
    AND THE PIECE THAT'S LIKE A BEAN,  .   .   .   .   .   .   .   .   .   .   086 00 004
```
BEAR
```
    WHEN HE HAS MADE US BEAR HIS LEAF. --  .   .   .   .   .   .   .   .   006 00 030
    BEAR HIM TO HEAVEN ON EASEFUL WINGS.  .   .   .   .   .   .   .   .   007 00 015
    I BEAR A BASKET LINED WITH GRASS:  .   .   .   .   .   .   .   .   .   010 00 001
    AND AT THE BASKET THAT I BEAR,  .   .   .   .   .   .   .   .   .   .   010 00 004
    I BEAR A BASKET LINED WITH GRASS.  .   .   .   .   .   .   .   .   .   025 00 001
    WITH THE BASKET I BEAR,  .   .   .   .   .   .   .   .   .   .   .   .   025 00 004
    CONFIRMED BEAUTY WILL NOT BEAR A STRESS: --   .   .   .   .   .   .   117 00 001
    THEY BROUGHT THEIR HUNDREDWEIGHTS TO BEAR.  .   .   .   .   .   .   145 00 051
    THE BLAME BEAR WHO AROUSED ME, WHAT I HAVE DONE VIOLENT  .   .   152 02 034
    O BUT I BEAR MY BURNING WITNESS THOUGH  .   .   .   .   .   .   .   157 00 035
    ANG.  I BEAR A BASKET LINED WITH GRASS.  .   .   .   .   .   .   .   APPEN A 01
    ANG.  AND THE BASKET I BEAR,  .   .   .   .   .   .   .   .   .   .   APPEN A 04
    ' AND IN WHAT WISE SHOULD I BEAR  .   .   .   .   .   .   .   .   .   APPEN D 13
```
BEARER
```
    STOOD CAPITAL, EMINENT, . . . GONFALON BEARER   .   .   .   .   .   098 28 005
```
BEARING
```
    BELOW ME IN THE BEARING AIR:  .   .   .   .   .   .   .   .   .   .   015 00 030
    BEAUTY'S BEARING OR MUSE OF MOUNTING VEIN,  .   .   .   .   .   .   047 00 010
    MORTAL MY MATE, BEARING MY ROCK-A-HEART   .   .   .   .   .   .   .   153 00 001
```
BEARS
```
    WITHIN HER WEARS, BEARS, CARES AND COMBS THE SAME:  .   .   .   .   076 00 006
```
BEAST
```
    CHRIST'S LILY AND BEAST OF THE WASTE WOOD:  .   .   .   .   .   .   028 20 006
    A WILDER BEAST FROM WEST THAN ALL WERE, MORE   .   .   .   .   .   050 00 007
    SITS TO THE BEAST THAT SEATS HIM -- CARE.  .   .   .   .   .   .   .   166 00 040
```
BEAT
```
    HUNG LIKE A WRECK THAT FLAMES NOT BILLOWS BEAT --  .   .   .   .   001 03 004
    THE DRIVING STORM AT HOUR OF VESPERS BEAT  .   .   .   .   .   .   001 13 003
    AND BEAT UPON MY WHORLED EAR,  .   .   .   .   .   .   .   .   .   .   022 00 002
    AND SHE BEAT THE BANK DOWN WITH HER BOWS AND THE RIDE OF HER KEEL:   028 14 005
    BURDEN, IN WIND'S BURLY AND BEAT OF ENDRAGONED SEAS.  .   .   .   028 27 008
    DOWNS' FOREFALLS BEAT TO THE BURIAL.  .   .   .   .   .   .   .   .   041 00 008
    THAT BEAT AND BREATHE IN POWER --  .   .   .   .   .   .   .   .   .   049 00 011
    BEAT, HEAVE AND THE STRONG MOUNTAIN TIRE  .   .   .   .   .   .   080 05 002
    O HEART, HAVE DONE, YOU BEAT YOU BEAT SO HIGH,  .   .   .   .   .   135 00 035
    O HEART, HAVE DONE, YOU BEAT YOU BEAT SO HIGH,  .   .   .   .   .   135 00 035
    WHAT BEAUTY BEAT BEHIND. ]  .   .   .   .   .   .   .   .   .   .   .   148 00 012
    WARM BEAT WITH COLD BEAT COMPANY, SHALL I  .   .   .   .   .   .   153 00 002
    WARM BEAT WITH COLD BEAT COMPANY, SHALL I  .   .   .   .   .   .   153 00 002
    BEAT FROM OUR BRAINS THE THICKY NIGHT  .   .   .   .   .   .   .   167 00 023
```
BEATING
```
    ABOUT MAN'S BEATING HEART.  .   .   .   .   .   .   .   .   .   .   .   060 00 050
```
BEATS
```
    ROPES, WRESTLES, BEATS EARTH BARE C  .   .   .   .   .   .   .   .   072 00 005
    BUT VASTNESS BLURS AND TIME BEATS LEVEL. ENOUGH! THE RESURRECTION,   072 00 016
```
BEAUTIES
```
    TO THEE WE TENDER THE BEAUTIES ALL   .   .   .   .   .   .   .   .   026 00 021
```
BEAUTIFUL
```
    NOTHING IS SO BEAUTIFUL AS SPRING --  .   .   .   .   .   .   .   .   033 00 001
    MARBLED RIVER, BOISTEROUSLY BEAUTIFUL, BETWEEN  .   .   .   .   .   159 00 006
```
BEAUTY
```
    AND SCARCELY TRACES WHERE ONE BEAUTY STRAYS  .   .   .   .   .   001 06 007
    AND ART AND BEAUTY: TITLE NOW TOO FULL --  .   .   .   .   .   .   001 15 006
    NONE BESIDES ME THIS BYE-WAYS BEAUTY TRY.  .   .   .   .   .   .   012 02 009
    BEAUTY NOW FOR ASHES WEAR.  .   .   .   .   .   .   .   .   .   .   .   024 00 019
    BRUTE BEAUTY AND VALOUR AND ACT, OH, AIR, PRIDE, PLUME, HERE   .   036 00 009
    HE FATHERS-FORTH WHOSE BEAUTY IS PAST CHANGE:  .   .   .   .   .   037 00 010
    SUMMER ENDS NOW! NOW, BARBAROUS IN BEAUTY, THE STOOKS RISE  .   038 00 001
    MEN GO BY ME WHOM EITHER BEAUTY BRIGHT  .   .   .   .   .   .   .   040 00 005
    IS STRUNG BY DUTY, IS STRAINED TO BEAUTY,  .   .   .   .   .   .   041 00 078
    AFTER-COMERS CANNOT GUESS THE BEAUTY BEEN,  .   .   .   .   .   043 00 019
    THAT NEIGHBOUR-NATURE THY GREY BEAUTY IS GROUNDED   .   .   .   044 00 006
    THIS, ALL THIS BEAUTY BLOOMING,   .   .   .   .   .   .   .   .   .   049 00 005
    THE FLOWER OF BEAUTY, FLEECE OF BEAUTY, TOO TOO APT TO, AH! TO FLEET,   059 0G 011
    THE FLOWER OF BEAUTY, FLEECE OF BEAUTY, TOO TOO APT TO, AH! TO FLEET,   059 0G 011
    GIVE BEAUTY BACK, BEAUTY, BEAUTY, BEAUTY, C  .   .   .   .   .   059 0G 019
    GIVE BEAUTY BACK, BEAUTY, BEAUTY, BEAUTY, C  .   .   .   .   .   059 0G 019
    GIVE BEAUTY BACK, BEAUTY, BEAUTY, BEAUTY, C  .   .   .   .   .   059 0G 019
    GIVE BEAUTY BACK, BEAUTY, BEAUTY, BEAUTY, C  .   .   .   .   .   059 0G 019
    BACK BEAUTY, KEEP IT, BEAUTY, BEAUTY, BEAUTY, C  .   .   .   .   059 0L 002
    BACK BEAUTY, KEEP IT, BEAUTY, BEAUTY, BEAUTY, C  .   .   .   .   059 0L 002
    BACK BEAUTY, KEEP IT, BEAUTY, BEAUTY, BEAUTY, C  .   .   .   .   059 0L 002
    BACK BEAUTY, KEEP IT, BEAUTY, BEAUTY, BEAUTY, C  .   .   .   .   059 0L 002
    TO WHAT SERVES MORTAL BEAUTY -- DANGEROUS! DOES SET DANC-  .   062 00 001
    WHAT DO THEN? HOW MEET BEAUTY? MERELY MEET IT: OWN,  .   .   062 00 012
    YEA, WISH THAT THOUGH, WISH ALL, GOD'S BETTER BEAUTY, GRACE.  .   062 00 014
    BEAUTY IT MAY BE IS THE MEET OF LINES.  .   .   .   .   .   .   .   102 03 001
    THESE RATHER ARE THE ARC WHERE BEAUTY SHINES,  .   .   .   .   102 03 003
    SAY BEAUTY LIES BUT IN THE MEET OF LINES, V  .   .   .   .   .   102 03 021
    CONFIRMED BEAUTY WILL NOT BEAR A STRESS: --  .   .   .   .   .   117 00 001
    WHY. THERE'S AN INTEREST AND SWEET SOUL IN BEAUTY  .   .   .   125 00 035
    THE CHRIST-ED BEAUTY OF HER MIND  .   .   .   .   .   .   .   .   .   145 00 015
    WHAT BEAUTY BEAT BEHIND. ]  .   .   .   .   .   .   .   .   .   .   .   148 00 012
    IN ALL HER BEAUTY, AND SUNLIGHT TO IT IS A PIT, DEN, DARKNESS,   .   152 02 023
```

BEAUTY   (CONTINUED)
    MAY'S BEAUTY MASSACRE AND WISPED WILD CLOUDS GROW 154 00 002
    IMMORTAL BEAUTY IS DEATH WITH DUTY, ... 156 00 018
BEAUTY-BOW
    FOR A BEAUTY-BOW TO HIS HAT, ... 144 00 016
BEAUTY-IN-THE-GH
    THEM: BEAUTY-IN-THE-GHOST, DELIVER IT, EARLY NOW, LONG BEFORE DEATH . 059 06 018
BEAUTY'S
    BEAUTY'S BEARING OR MUSE OF MOUNTING VEIN, ... 047 00 010
    WITH NOT HER EITHER BEAUTY'S EQUAL OR 050 00 002
    BACK TO GOD, BEAUTY'S SELF AND BEAUTY'S GIVER, C 059 06 019
    BACK TO GOD, BEAUTY'S SELF AND BEAUTY'S GIVER, C 059 06 019
    AND BEAUTY'S DEAREST VERIEST VEIN IS TEARS. 157 00 004
BECKONED
    BECKONED ME BESIDE HIM: 054 00 013
    BY THERE COMES A LISTLESS STRANGER: BECKONED BY THE NOISE . . . 159 00 014
BECOME
    AND TO THOSE STONES BECOME AKIN 080 03 002
BED
    (LOW LIE HIS MATES NOW ON WATERY BED) 041 00 058
    GROOM, AND GRACE YOU, BRIDE, YOUR BED 052 00 002
    SURE, 'S BED NOW, LOW BE IT; LUSTILY HE HIS LOW LOT (FEEL . 070 00 005
    SO WASTE IN TEARS OVER THIS BED OF SWEETNESS, ... 102 01 035
    CREPT TREMBLING OUT OF BED. 135 00 004
    THE CART ROAD WITH A SHALLOW BED 135 00 026
    AND BRIDEGROOM WAITS AND READY ARE BOWER AND BED. . . . 136 00 018
BEDDED
    AND THEY WERE BEDDED TILL DAYLIGHT 109 01 003
BEDS
    FAIR BEDS THEY SEEM'D OF WATER-LILY FLAKES 002 00 013
    IN BEDS, IN GARDENS, IN THICK PLOTS I STAND, ... 005 00 037
BEE
    THAT'S BUILT FOR BY THE BEE. 148 00 036
BEECHBOLE
    THOUGH AS A BEECHBOLE FIRM, FINDS HIS, AS AT A ROLLCALL, RANK . 071 00 007
BEES
    STARS LIKE GOLDEN BEES. 098 25 003
BEETLE-BROWED
    A BUSH-BROWED, BEETLE-BROWED BILLOW IS IT? 141 00 003
BEETLING
    A BEETLING BALDBRIGHT CLOUD THOROUGH ENGLAND 041 00 025
    DOWN THE BEETLING BANKS, LIKE WATER IN WATERFALLS, . . . 152 02 020
BEFAL
    WHAT WOULD BEFAL THE GODLESS FLOCK 092 00 007
BEFALL
    BY IT, HEAVENS, BEFALL HIM! AS A HEART CHRIST'S DARLING, DAUNTLESS; . 048 00 014
BEFORE
    -- BEFORE THE SEPULCHRE THERE STOOD A GATE: 001 04 006
    MORE WONDROUS TO HAVE BORNE SUCH HOPE BEFORE 001 15 007
    SUDDEN, DEATH BEFORE ME STOOD: 004 00 006
    WITH SUCH MALIGN CONJUNCTIONS AS BEFORE 014 02 006
    BUT NOW BEFORE THE POT CAN GLOW 015 00 013
    BEFORE ME, THE HURTLE OF HELL 028 03 002
    THOUGH FELT BEFORE, THOUGH IN HIGH FLOOD YET -- . . . 028 07 007
    IN EDEN GARDEN. -- HAVE, GET, BEFORE IT CLOY, ... 033 00 011
    BEFORE IT CLOUD, CHRIST, LORD, AND SOUR WITH SINNING, . . . 033 00 012
    THEM: BEAUTY-IN-THE-GHOST, DELIVER IT, EARLY NOW, LONG BEFORE DEATH . 059 06 018
    SHE STOOD BEFORE A LIGHT NOT HERS, AND SEEM'D 079 00 003
    THEY ALL COME HERE AND STAND BEFORE ME CLEAR 080 08 003
    BEFORE THAT ROCK, MY SEAT, HE STANDS; 080 09 001
    TO WASH BEFORE THE MULTITUDE 080 10 002
    BEFORE THE MOUNTAIN? -- NO, NOT ONE, ... 081 00 143
    AND SAW THE MEN BEFORE THE FLOOD . . . . . . 093 A 002
    LEAPS UP BEFORE MY VISION, -- THOU ART GONE. 098 33 002
    YET THERE CAME ONE WHO SENT HIS FLOCK BEFORE HIM, . . . 107 01 007
    BEFORE HE WENT TO SEA. 109 01 004
    SHE STOOD BEFORE THEM IN THE GLEN. 109 25 001
    I THOUGHT: BEFORE I GATHER STRENGTH 118 00 013
    FOR A LETTER COMES AT LAST: (SHALL I SAY BEFORE CHRISTMAS IS COME?) 128 00 019
    BEFORE OR BEHIND OR FAR OR AT HAND 138 00 007
    BEFORE THE SPRING WAS DONE. 144 00 004
    A GROWING BURNISH BRIGHTER THAN BEFORE 151 00 004
BEFORE-TIME-TAKE
    BEFORE-TIME-TAKEN, DEAREST PRIZED AND PRICED -- 028 22 006
BEGAN
    ' FOR HE BEGAN AT ONCE AND SHOOK 021 00 029
    BEING ANOINTED AND ALL; THOUGH A HEAVENLIER HEART BEGAN SOME . 053 00 006
    HEARD UNHEEDED, LEAVES ME A LONELY BEGAN. 066 00 014
    THAT NIGHT THE JUDGMENT DAY BEGAN: 081 00 090
BEGGED
    MY LATE BEING THERE BEGGED OF ME, OVERFLOWING 048 00 006
BEGIN
    WHITE TO BEGIN WITH, IMMACULATE WHITE. 027 00 032
    LET CHARITY THUS BEGIN AT HOME, -- 081 00 124
    NOW BEGIN, ON CHRISTMAS DAY. 129 00 009
BEGINNING
    A STRAIN OF THE EARTH'S SWEET BEING IN THE BEGINNING . . . 033 00 010

21

BELL-SWARMED
CUCKOO-ECHOING, BELL-SWARMED, LARK-CHARMED, C • • • • • • • 044 00 002
BELLOWS
AT LENGTH THE BELLOWS SHALL NOT BLOW, • • • • • • • 015 00 015
BELL'S
STONES RING; LIKE EACH TUCKED STRING TELLS, EACH HUNG BELL'S • 057 00 003
BELLS
THOUGH NO HIGH-HUNG BELLS OR DIN • • • • • • • 029 00 001
ALLOWS THE SOUND OF BELLS IN HAMLETS ROUND • • • • • 080 00 006
FROM OXFORD COMES THE THRONG AND HUM OF BELLS • • • • 098 03 006
AND TO THEIR FEET THE NARROW BELLS GAVE RHYME. • • • • 107 01 014
GAVE THE MUCH MUSIC OF OUR OXFORD BELLS? • • • • • 107 02 008
BELONG
FOR LIPS AND HEARTS THEY BELONG TO THEE • • • • • 026 00 037
BELOW
IS SET UPON YOUR BOUGHS BELOW; • • • • • • • 010 00 010
BELOW ME IN THE BEARING AIR; • • • • • • • 015 00 030
THE WILD WOMAN-KIND BELOW, • • • • • • • 028 16 002
THE DAPPLE-EARED LILY BELOW THEE; THAT COUNTRY AND TOWN DID • • 044 00 003
OF MILE-LONG REACHES OF OUR ROAD BELOW US. • • • • 125 00 007
HEAVEN TURNED ITS STARLIGHT EYES BELOW • • • • • • 145 00 046
JESU WHOM I LOOK AT SHROUDED HERE BELOW, • • • • • 168 00 025
BELTS
IN BREEZY BELTS OF UPPER AIR • • • • • • • 077 00 073
BELVEDERE
I WALK MY BREEZY BELVEDERE • • • • • • • 015 00 025
BEND
OF US WE DO BID GOD BEND TO HIM EVEN SO. • • • • • 068 00 011
BENDS
HE LEANS TO IT, HARRY BENDS, LOOK. BACK, ELBOW, AND LIQUID WAIST • 071 00 009
BENEATH
WHEREIN BENEATH THE CORNICE, HORSEMEN RODE • • • • • 001 07 007
EBB'D BACK BENEATH ITS SNOWY LIDS, UNSEEN. • • • • • 002 00 018
AND SILVER FILMS, BENEATH WITH PEARLY MIST, • • • • • 002 00 067
YOU WOULD NOT HOUSE BENEATH MY OWN; • • • • • • 081 00 004
NOW COMES AS LOW BENEATH. • • • • • • • 115 00 004
BENEATH THE TACKLED VINE. • • • • • • • 165 00 008
BENEDICTION
THEN CAME THE BENEDICTION. • • • • • • • 081 00 099
BENEFITS
BUT SINCE I HAVE NO SCOPE FOR BENEFITS • • • • • 102 01 052
BENT
YOUR SCARCE-SHEATHED BONES ARE WEARY OF BEING BENT; • • • 011 00 013
BECAUSE THE HOLY GHOST OVER THE BENT • • • • • 031 00 013
HER WILL WAS BENT AT GOD. FOR THAT • • • • • 145 00 037
THOUGH DOWN HIS BEING'S BENT • • • • • • 148 00 017
BEREFT
OF MAZY SHAPE AND HUE, BUT NOW BEREFT • • • • • 001 08 003
WHAT WOULD THE WORLD BE, ONCE BEREFT • • • • • 056 00 013
BERG
SO LIKE A BERG OF HYALINE, • • • • • • 003 00 017
BERYL
CLUSTERING ENTRANCINGLY IN BERYL LAKES; • • • • • 002 00 014
BERYL-COVERED
IN BERYL-COVERED FENS SO DIM, • • • • • • 003 00 026
BESEECH
I BESEECH THEE SEND ME WHAT I THIRST FOR SO, • • • • 168 00 026
BESIDE
BECKONED ME BESIDE HIM; • • • • • • • 054 00 013
AND IN THE DEWS BESIDE HIS NEST • • • • • • 077 00 091
HOUSES THAT MAKE ABODE BESIDE THE LAKE. • • • • • 080 06 006
AY, SWEET TO TASTE BESIDE THIS WOE. • • • • • 080 07 007
THE RINGED BLINDWORM HARD BESIDE. • • • • • • 106 00 004
THAT WAS BESIDE THE SEA. • • • • • • • 109 15 002
BESIDE HIS BROTHERS THREE? ' • • • • • • 109 20 002
BESIDE HIS BROTHERS THREE? • • • • • • 109 21 002
BESIDE HIS BROTHERS THREE: • • • • • • 109 22 004
BESIDE THEM, ABOUT THE HEDGES, HEARING HIM; • • • • 113 00 008
AH NO! AND SHE WHO SITS BESIDE • • • • • • 120 00 014
BESIDES
NONE BESIDES ME THIS BYE-WAYS BEAUTY TRY. • • • • • 012 02 009
BESPOKEN
BUT HE SCORES IT IN SCARLET HIMSELF ON HIS OWN BESPOKEN, • • 028 22 005
BEST
OF ART BEST FOLLOW NATURE) IN A MAZE • • • • • 001 06 005
THOU WHO CANST BEST ACCEPT THE CERTAINTY • • • • • 013 00 005
NO BETTER SERVES ME NOW, SAVE BEST; NO OTHER • • • • 016 00 013
WE LASH WITH THE BEST OR WORST • • • • • • 028 08 002
CHRISTENS HER WILD-WORST BEST. C • • • • • • 028 24 008
MAN'S SPIRIT WILL BE FLESH-BOUND WHEN FOUND AT BEST, • • • 039 00 012
OF THE BEST WE BOAST OUR SAILORS ARE. • • • • • 041 00 076
BEST IN: GRACELESS GROWTH, THOU HAST CONFOUNDED • • • 044 00 007
YOU? ' -- ' FATHER, WHAT YOU BUY ME I LIKE BEST. ' • • • 047 00 002
SHARES THEIR BEST GIFTS SURELY, FALL HOW THINGS WILL) , • • 048 00 004
TO ITS OWN BEST BEING AND ITS LOVELINESS OF YOUTH C • • 059 06 013
HE OF ALL CAN REEVE A ROPE BEST. THERE HE BIDES IN BLISS • • 063 00 010
I NEVER SAW THOSE FIELDS WHEREON THEIR BEST • • • • 119 00 011

23

BEST (CONTINUED)
```
ILL MEANT, YET TRUE, I BEST SHOULD FLATTER THEN,   .   .   .   .   .   . 125 00 019
IN COPYING WELL WHAT YOU HAVE BEST BEGUN. .   .   .   .   .   .   .   . 125 00 020
THE BEST IDEAL IS THE TRUE   .   .   .   .   .   .   .   .   .   .   . 133 00 001
WORST WILL THE BEST.   WHAT WORM WAS HERE, WE CRY,   .   .   .   . 157 00 031
THAT HE HIES TO A POOL NEIGHBOURING; SEES IT IS THE BEST   .   .   . 159 00 022
```
BESTOWING
```
BOON IN MY BESTOWING,   .   .   .   .   .   .   .   .   .   .   .   . 048 00 007
```
BETHLEHEM
```
BUT THE BETHLEHEM STAR MAY LEAD ME   .   .   .   .   .   .   .   . 129 00 003
```
BETHLEM
```
BETHLEM OR NAZARETH,   .   .   .   .   .   .   .   .   .   .   .   . 060 00 065
```
BETHLEMS
```
NEW BETHLEMS, AND HE BORN .   .   .   .   .   .   .   .   .   .   . 060 00 063
```
BETIMES
```
THE LOCK OF CLOUDS BETIMES AND HANGS THE DAY,   .   .   .   .   . 098 31 003
```
BETRAY
```
AND WHAT IF SHE MY CONFIDENCE BETRAY!   .   .   .   .   .   .   . 094 00 004
```
BETRAY'D
```
A THREAD OF LIGHT BETRAY'D THE HILL   .   .   .   .   .   .   .   . 092 00 009
```
BETTER
```
NO BETTER SERVES ME NOW, SAVE BEST; NO OTHER   .   .   .   .   . 016 00 013
YEA, WISH THAT THOUGH, WISH ALL, GOD'S BETTER BEAUTY, GRACE. .   . 062 00 014
AND YET I KNOW IT WOULD BE BETTER SO, .   .   .   .   .   .   .   . 080 07 006
DIAMONDS ARE BETTER CUT; WHO PARE, REPAIR;   .   .   .   .   .   . 096 07 005
BUT LATE IS BETTER THAN NEVER: YOU SEE YOU HAVE MANAGED SO,   .   . 128 00 017
REASON, SELFDISPOSAL, CHOICE OF BETTER OR WORSE WAY,   .   .   . 152 02 061
EVEN THUS I HAVE THE BETTER OF THEE;   .   .   .   .   .   .   .   . 161 00 003
ONE BETTER BACKED COMES CROWDING BY; --   .   .   .   .   .   . 166 00 013
```
BETTER'D
```
I BETTER'D ALL OUR PATH WITH SANGUINE EYES. .   .   .   .   .   . 125 00 016
```
BETWEEN
```
HIS CHARNELHOUSE-GRATE RIBS BETWEEN,   .   .   .   .   .   .   . 004 00 010
BETWEEN THE TOWER-TOP AND THE GROUND   .   .   .   .   .   .   . 015 00 029
TOWERY CITY AND BRANCHY BETWEEN TOWERS;   .   .   .   .   .   . 044 00 001
AND NUMBS AND STARVES, AS BETWEEN ICY WHARVES   .   .   .   . 080 03 006
TINGLING BETWEEN DUSK AND SILVER. .   .   .   .   .   .   .   .   . 098 01 004
' NO TRUTH BETWEEN YOU THREE. .   .   .   .   .   .   .   .   . 109 28 002
WHICH BETWEEN ASH-TOPS SUFFERS LOSS   .   .   .   .   .   .   . 121 00 005
MOONLESS DARKNESS STANDS BETWEEN. .   .   .   .   .   .   .   . 129 00 001
MARBLED RIVER, BOISTEROUSLY BEAUTIFUL, BETWEEN   .   .   .   . 159 00 006
HIS HEART AT FARMING, WHAT BETWEEN   .   .   .   .   .   .   . 166 00 030
```
BETWEENPIE
```
BETWEENPIE MOUNTAINS -- LIGHTS A LOVELY MILE.   .   .   .   .   . 069 00 014
```
BETWEENS
```
BETWEENS I HEARD THE WATER STILL   .   .   .   .   .   .   .   . 021 00 044
```
BETWEENWHILES
```
BETWEENWHILES, BUT SHE SEES HERSELF NOT HIM. .   .   .   .   . 151 00 012
```
BETWIXT
```
THE CLOISTERS CROSS'D WITH EQUAL COURTS BETWIXT   .   .   .   . 001 04 002
APART, BETWIXT TEN THOUSAND PETALL'D LIPS .   .   .   .   .   . 002 00 021
GIRDLES; GOES HOME BETWIXT   .   .   .   .   .   .   .   .   .   . 060 00 004
```
BEUNO
```
LORD BEUNO COMES TONIGHT. TONIGHT, SIR! SOON, NOW; THEREFORE   . 152 01 005
BEUNO. O NOW WHILE SKIES ARE BLUE, NOW WHILE SEAS ARE SALT,   .   . 152 C 001
```
BEVY
```
ALL OVER, AS A BEVY OF EGGS THE MOTHERING WING   .   .   .   . 034 00 006
SEES THE BEVY OF THEM, HOW THE BOYS   .   .   .   .   .   .   . 159 00 016
```
BEYOND
```
FORMED BARS OF STONE; BEYOND IN STIFFEN'D STATE   .   .   .   . 001 04 003
BEYOND THE HURST WITH SUCH A HUE   .   .   .   .   .   .   .   . 021 00 006
OH! TILL THOU GIVEST THAT SENSE BEYOND,   .   .   .   .   .   . 023 00 043
BEYOND SAYING SWEET, PAST TELLING OF TONGUE,   .   .   .   .   . 028 09 005
THAT BIRD BEYOND THE REMEMBERING HIS FREE FELLS;   .   .   .   . 039 00 003
UNDENIZENED, BEYOND BOUND   .   .   .   .   .   .   .   .   .   . 070 00 015
BUT WITH HIS OTHER FOOT THREE MILES BEYOND   .   .   .   .   . 100 00 004
BEYOND, AND ONE WITHIN THE LOOKER'S EYE;   .   .   .   .   .   . 102 03 006
A RAINBOW ALSO SHAPES ITSELF BEYOND   .   .   .   .   .   .   . 107 03 006
BEYOND, THE BANKS WERE STEEP; A BRUSH OF TREES   .   .   .   . 107 04 003
BEYOND THE RIVER, ALL THE MEADOW'S ROUND,   .   .   .   .   . 107 04 010
BEYOND THE WORLD; THE STREAMS ARE FULL   .   .   .   .   .   . 130 00 024
BEYOND MAGDALEN AND BY THE BRIDGE, ON A PLACE CALLED THERE THE PLAIN, 142 00 001
BUT FROM BEYOND SEAS, ERIN, FRANCE AND FLANDERS, EVERYWHERE,   .   . 152 C 020
HIS LOOKS, THE SOUL'S OWN LETTERS, SEE BEYOND,   .   .   .   . 157 00 015
WHAT NEED I STRAIN MY HEART BEYOND MY KEN?   .   .   .   .   . 157 00 034
```
BID
```
AND BID TO CATCH HIM ERE THE DROP OF DAY.   .   .   .   .   . 020 00 002
BUY THEN! BID THEN! -- WHAT? -- PRAYER, PATIENCE, ALMS, VOWS, .   . 032 00 009
BUT BID FOR, PATIENCE IS! PATIENCE WHO ASKS   .   .   .   .   . 068 00 002
OF US WE DO BID GOD BEND TO HIM EVEN SO. .   .   .   .   .   . 068 00 011
TO RISE YOU BID ME WITH THE LARK;   .   .   .   .   .   .   . 096 06 001
BID YOUR PAPA GOODNIGHT. SWEET EXHIBITION! .   .   .   .   .   . 097 00 007
BID JOY BACK, HAVE AT THE HARVEST, KEEP HOPE PALE.   .   .   . 154 00 004
I BID THE BOYS AND MAIDENS HEAR. .   .   .   .   .   .   .   . 166 00 004
```
BIDDER'S
```
OF COUNTRY BIDDER'S CALLS OR LOW   .   .   .   .   .   .   .   . 166 00 022
```
BIDES
```
HE OF ALL CAN REEVE A ROPE BEST. THERE HE BIDES IN BLISS   .   .   . 063 00 010
```

BIDS
  ' A CRIMSON EAST, THAT BIDS FOR RAIN. 021 00 008
  THY LOVELY DALE DOWN THUS AND THUS BIDS REEL 058 00 007
  AND NONE RECK OF WORLD AFTER, THIS BIDS WEAR 058 00 013
  BIDS HIM THIS WAY HIS GAZES FIX. 120 00 015
BIDST
  BUT THOU BIDST, AND JUST THOU ART, ... 155 00 021
BIG
  REBUFFED THE BIG WIND. MY HEART IN HIDING 036 00 007
BIG-BONED
  WHO HAVE WATCHED HIS MOULD OF MAN, BIG-BONED AND HARDY-HANDSOME . . 053 00 002
BILL
  TO PAUSE -- THEN FROM HIS GURGLING BILL 077 00 083
  (BECAUSE THE MUSIC FROM HIS BILL FORTH-DRIVEN 113 00 003
BILLION
  BUCKLE! AND THE FIRE THAT BREAKS FROM THEE THEN, A BILLION . . 036 00 010
BILLOW
  OR REARING BILLOW OF THE BISCAY WATER: 041 00 018
  A BUSH-BROWED, BEETLE-BROWED BILLOW IS IT? 141 00 003
BILLOWS
  HUNG LIKE A WRECK THAT FLAMES NOT BILLOWS BEAT -- 001 03 004
  SWOLL'N IS THE WIND THAT IN ARGENT BILLOWS 078 00 003
BILLOWY
  PLASHES AMIDST THE BILLOWY APPLE-TREES 002 00 087
  YE RIVER-HEADS, THOU BILLOWY DEEP THAT LAUGH'ST 160 00 002
BILLS
  WITH BILLS OF RIME THE BRAMBLES SHEW. 003 00 004
BIND
  FAST YOU EVER, FAST BIND. 052 00 008
  THOUGH SELF-MADE BANDS AT LAST MAY TRUE LOVE BIND, ... 102 03 019
BIND'ST
  AND STILL THOU BIND'ST ME TO FRESH FEALTY 012 01 003
BINES
  TAMPERING WITH THOSE SWEET BINES, DRAWS THEM OUT, C . . . 152 01 015
BIRD
  IS ALL THE WINTER BIRD DARE TRY. 003 00 014
  LET ME BE TO THEE AS THE CIRCLING BIRD. 019 00 001
  A SINGING BIRD IN MORNING CLEAR 021 00 041
  FOR WARBLING OF THE WARBLING BIRD. ' 021 00 049
  STIRRED FOR A BIRD, -- THE ACHIEVE OF, THE MASTERY OF THE THING! . 036 00 008
  THAT BIRD BEYOND THE REMEMBERING HIS FREE FELLS! 039 00 003
  AND BIRD AND BLOSSOM SWELL 042 00 023
  NOW LIKE THE BIRD THAT SHAPES ALONE 081 00 006
  AT LAST THE BIRD IS FOUND A FLICKERING SHAPE AND SLIM. . . . 113 00 009
  CUCKOO, BIRD, AND OPEN EAR WELLS, HEART-SPRINGS, DELIGHTFULLY SWEET, 146 00 002
  OR BIRD WITH PIPE, VIOL WITH AIR 166 00 020
BIRDS
  THEM! BIRDS BUILD -- BUT NOT I BUILD! NO, BUT STRAIN, . . . 074 00 012
  ' BOUGHS BEING PRUNED, BIRDS PREENED, SHOW MORE FAIR! . . . 096 07 001
BIRTH
  NIGHT TO A MYRIAD WORLDS GIVES BIRTH, ... 023 00 009
  TILL A MAID IN DAVID'S HOUSE HAD BIRTH, ... 026 00 030
  SINCE ITS BIRTH, AND ITS BLOOM, AND ITS BREATHING ITS LAST. . . 027 00 016
  BANNED BY THE LAND OF THEIR BIRTH, ... 028 21 002
  BUT HERE WAS HEART-THROE, BIRTH OF A BRAIN, ... 028 30 007
  TELLS MARY HER MIRTH TILL CHRIST'S BIRTH 042 00 046
  BIRTH, MILK, AND ALL THE REST 060 00 021
  MY SPIRIT HATH A BIRTH 077 00 003
BIRTHDAY
  I THOUGHT THAT YOU WOULD HAVE WRITTEN! MY BIRTHDAY CAME AND WENT, . 128 00 001
  WHAT WOULD BE A BIRTHDAY LETTER THAT AFTER THE BIRTHDAY CAME? . 128 00 004
  WHAT WOULD BE A BIRTHDAY LETTER THAT AFTER THE BIRTHDAY CAME? . 128 00 004
  THINK THIS, MY BIRTHDAY FALLS IN SADDENING TIME OF YEAR! . . . 128 00 009
  IT IS HARDLY A PROPER TREAT FOR A BIRTHDAY TO REST IN HER ARMS. . 128 00 012
BISCAY
  OR REARING BILLOW OF THE BISCAY WATER: 041 00 018
BIT
  SMILED, BLUSHED, AND BIT HIS LIP! 054 00 019
BITE
  I BITE MY HANDS, MY LOOKS I SHROUD; 081 00 065
BITTEN
  I KNOW OF THE BORED AND BITTEN ROCKS 120 00 020
BITTER
  SWEET FLOWERS I CARRY, -- SWEETS FOR BITTER. 010 00 006
  THEREFORE HOW BITTER, AND LEARNT HOW LATE, THE TRUTH! . . . 017 00 014
  CARRIES TREATS OF SWEET FOR BITTER. 025 00 006
  BITTER WOULD HAVE ME TASTE: MY TASTE WAS ME! 067 00 010
  ANG. CARRIES TREATS OF SWEET FOR BITTER. . . . . . APPEN A 06
BITTERER
  HEART, GO AND BLEED AT A BITTERER VEIN FOR THE 028 31 003
BITTERNESS
  THE BITTERNESS OF DEATH WAS PAST, ... 081 00 120
  INTO THE BITTERNESS OF SIN. 092 00 006
BLACK
  BUT THROUGH BLACK BRANCHES, RARELY DREST 003 00 020
  WITH A SUBTLE WEB OF BLACK. 004 00 020
  AND THOUGH THE LAST LIGHTS OFF THE BLACK WEST WENT 031 00 011

25

BLACK   (CONTINUED)
    BUT WHAT BLACK BOREAS WRECKED HER? HE 041 00 023
    WITH YELLOW MOISTURE MILD NIGHT'S BLEAR-ALL BLACK, ... 046 00 003
    DAMASK THE TOOLSMOOTH BLEAK LIGHT; BLACK, C 061 00 009
    EVER SO BLACK ON IT, OUR TALE, O OUR ORACLE! C 061 00 012
    -- BLACK, WHITE; RIGHT, WRONG; RECKON BUT, RECK BUT, MIND C . 061 00 012
    WHAT HOURS, O WHAT BLACK HOURS WE HAVE SPENT 067 00 002
    SHEER OFF, DISSEVERAL, A STAR, DEATH BLOTS BLACK OUT; NOR MARK . 072 00 014
    WHEN THE FIERCE SKIES ARE BLUE TO BLACK, ALBEIT 080 02 005
    HER NOSTRIL GLISTENS; AND HER WET BLACK EYE 099 00 005
    HER FINGER-LONG NEW HORNS ARE CAPP'D WITH BLACK; 099 00 007
    ABANDONED BY HER SAINTS, TURN'D BLACK AND BLASTED, ... 102 02 011
    GILDS WITH SOME SPARKY FANCIES HIS BLACK NIGHT 102 03 030
BLACKEST
    DEEP CALLS TO DEEP, AND BLACKEST NIGHT 023 00 027
BLACK-ABOUT
    SHE TO THE BLACK-ABOUT AIR, TO THE BREAKER, THE THICKLY . . 028 24 005
BLACK-BACKED
    AND THE SEA FLINT-FLAKE, BLACK-BACKED IN THE REGULAR BLOW, . . 028 13 005
BLACK-FLEECED
    BACKWARD ARE LAID HER PRETTY BLACK-FLEECED EARS; 099 00 013
BLACKNESS
    WITH BLACKNESS BOUND, AND ALL 060 00 098
BLACKS
    AND A FEW LEAVES NOT LILY-WHITE BUT CHARACTERED OVER WITH BLACKS. . 128 00 016
BLADE
    STILL THE SCARLET SWINGS AND DANCES ON THE BLADE. . . . 152 02 013
    SINNER WHO SAW THE BLADE THAT HUNG 166 00 017
BLADE-GASH
    THE BLOOD-GUSH BLADE-GASH 138 00 022
BLADE'S
    DOES LAY MEN LOW WITH ONE BLADE'S SUDDEN BLOW 080 02 003
BLADES
    BLADES OF MILAN IN CIRCLES RANG'D, GREW RUST 001 12 008
    AND LEAVES THE BLADES, WHERE'ER HE WILL VEER, ... 098 01 003
BLADY
    I'LL TAKE IN HAND THE BLADY STONE 080 14 001
BLAME
    THE BLAME BEAR WHO AROUSED ME. WHAT I HAVE DONE VIOLENT . . 152 02 034
BLAST
    THE SIMON PETER OF A SOUL! TO THE BLAST 028 29 007
    BLAST BOLE AND BLOOM TOGETHER? 041 00 016
    AND FEEL NO BLAST. -- THE FRETFUL FIRE 080 05 004
    AND LIKE A SELF-OUTWITTED BLAST 081 00 074
    INTO HIS HOLLOW'D PALM SHOULD MOAN THE BLAST; 090 00 002
BLASTED
    ABANDONED BY HER SAINTS, TURN'D BLACK AND BLASTED, . . . 102 02 011
BLASTS
    DOORS SLAMM'D TO THE BLASTS CONTINUALLY; MORE LOW, . . . 001 13 008
BLAZE
    BLAZE FOR HIM ALL THIS WHILE. 005 00 036
    THE SHEARING RAYS CONTRACT ME WITH THEIR BLAZE 080 02 006
BLAZON
    IN BLAZON, GILT   AND IMAGES OF BRONZE, V 102 02 010
    -- GILT AND BLAZON -- BRONZE STATUARY, V 102 02 010
    OR BRING MORE OR MORE BLAZON MAN'S DISTRESS. 150 00 004
BLAZONED
    WITH BLAZONED GROINS, AND CROWNED WITH HUES OF MAJESTY. . . 001 06 009
    AND, BLAZONED IN HOWEVER BOLD THE NAME, ... 075 00 010
BLAZONRY
    WITH GOLDEN FILLETS AND RICH BLAZONRY, ... 001 07 006
BLEACHED
    HIS BLEACHED BOTH AND WOOLWOVEN WEAR; 159 00 029
BLEAK
    HOW IT DOES MY HEART GOOD, VISITING AT THAT BLEAK HILL, . . 048 00 021
    DAMASK THE TOOLSMOOTH BLEAK LIGHT; BLACK, C 061 00 009
    O'ER PASSES BLEAK, O'ER PERILOUS BARS 083 00 003
BLEAR
    THE SOUR SCYTHE CRINGE, AND THE BLEAR SHARE COME. . . . 028 11 008
    A BLEAR AND BLINDING BALL 060 00 097
BLEARED
    AND ALL IS SEARED WITH TRADE; BLEARED, SMEARED WITH TOIL; . . 031 00 006
BLEAR-ALL
    WITH YELLOW MOISTURE MILD NIGHT'S BLEAR-ALL BLACK, . . . 046 00 003
BLEAT
    MY CRY IS LIKE A BLEAT; A FEW 081 00 066
    THERE WAS NO BLEAT OF EWE, NO CHIME OF WETHER, . . . 107 01 005
BLEATS
    EPISTLES, WHILE THE RUNNING PASTORAL BLEATS 107 04 022
BLEED
    HEART, GO AND BLEED AT A BITTERER VEIN FOR THE . . . 028 31 003
    INTOLERABLE TEARS I BLEED. 081 00 067
BLEEDING
    AND BLEEDING SAW. -- THUS HUNG FROM ROOM TO ROOM . . . 001 10 008
    LAY BLEEDING, TO MADRID THE LAST THEY BORE, ... 001 15 002
    JARR'D DOWN THE BALANCED STORM; THE BLEEDING HEAVENS . . . 102 02 004
BLEEDS
    AND ZEAL IS FLUSHED AND PITY BLEEDS 023 00 034

26

BLESS
FOR I GREET HIM THE DAYS I MEET HIM, AND BLESS WHEN I UNDERSTAND. . . . 028 05 008
YES. WHY DO WE ALL, SEEING OF A SOLDIER, BLESS HIM? BLESS 063 00 001
YES. WHY DO WE ALL, SEEING OF A SOLDIER, BLESS HIM? BLESS 063 00 001
OF VIRTUES I MOST WARMLY BLESS, ... 096 01 001
WHAT I KNOW OF THEE I BLESS, ... 155 00 005
BLESSED
HOW TO NAME IT, BLESSED IT! 025 00 025
FOR SOULS THAT MIGHT HAVE BLESSED THE TIME 133 00 009
BLESSED BE EVERYTHING. 135 00 016
THEO. HOW TO NAME IT, BLESSED IT, ... APPEN A 25
BLESSING
YET DID THE DARK SIDE OF THE BAY OF THY BLESSING 028 12 007
BLESS'D
THE YOUNG CHIEF OF THE BLESS'D OF HEAVEN 160 00 011
BLEST
THAT WAS BLEST IN IT ONCE, THOUGH NOW IT IS NOT? -- 027 00 008
' AS WHEN A SOUL LAMENTS, WHICH HATH BEEN BLEST ' -- . . . 119 00 009
HER GLASS IS BLEST BUT SHE AS GOOD AS BLIND 151 00 007
NOT THAT, BUT THUS FAR, ALL WITH FRAILTY, BLEST 157 00 006
AND BE BLEST FOR EVER WITH THY GLORY'S SIGHT. 168 00 028
BLIGHT
IT IS THE BLIGHT MAN WAS BORN FOR. 055 00 014
BLIND
SWIRLING OUT BLOOM TILL ALL THE AIR IS BLIND 002 00 089
MORE POWERLESS THAN THE BLIND OR LAME. 015 00 020
NATURE, BAD, BASE, AND BLIND, ... 054 00 040
WHOSE GLORY BARE WOULD BLIND 060 00 108
BY GROPING ROUND MY COMFORTLESS, THAN BLIND 069 00 006
HER GLASS IS BLEST BUT SHE AS GOOD AS BLIND 151 00 007
WHILE BLIND MEN'S EYES SHALL THIRST C . . . . . . 152 C 004
BLINDFOLD
THEY HAVE HELD HIS EYES WITH BLINDFOLD BANDS 109 13 001
BLINDING
GIDDIES THE SOUL WITH BLINDING DAZE 023 00 028
A BLEAR AND BLINDING BALL 060 00 097
GILDS WITH SOME SPARKY FANCIES BLINDING NIGHT, V 102 03 036
BLINDNESS
BLINDNESS! A LEARNED FOOL AND WELL-BRED CHURL 102 03 032
BLINDS
BLINDS HER! BUT SHE THAT WEATHER SEES ONE THING, ONE! . . . 028 19 005
BLINDWORM
THE RINGED BLINDWORM HARD BESIDE. 106 00 004
BLINKING
THE BALD AND BOLD BLINKING GOLD WHEN ALL'S DONE 143 00 004
BLISS
THAT THOU HADST BORNE PROPORTION IN MY BLISS, ... 013 00 006
NOT OUT OF HIS BLISS 028 06 001
SPRING'S UNIVERSAL BLISS 042 00 034
HE OF ALL CAN REEVE A ROPE BEST. THERE HE BIDES IN BLISS . . 063 00 010
MY WINTER WORLD, THAT SCARCELY BREATHES THAT BLISS . . . 076 00 013
BUT CHAPTERED IN THE CHIEF OF BLISS 145 00 002
A MAID WITH MOTHER'S BLISS. ' . . . . APPEN D 30
AND HEAVEN'S BLISS, WHEN OUR TIME IS TO DIE, ... APPEN D 47
BLISSFUL
I MUSE AT HOW ITS BEING PUTS BLISSFUL BACK 046 00 002
BROUGHT TO HER BLISSFUL TIDING . . . . APPEN D 03
BLOCK
TO MAN, THAT NEEDS WOULD WORSHIP BLOCK OR BARREN STONE, . . 062 00 009
THE OUTGOINGS OF THE VALE DOES BLOCK. 092 00 011
HELP'D BY THE DARKNESS OF A BLOCK OF COPSE 107 03 014
BLOCKS
AND IN A BASON BRINGS THE BLOCKS. 080 09 007
AND COME WHERE LIES A COFFER, BURLY ALL OF BLOCKS 159 00 036
BLOOD
BUT EVEN OUR SAVIOUR'S AND OUR BLOOD, ... 006 00 032
AH DIP IN BLOOD THE PALMTREE PEN 025 00 037
THE DEATHDANCE IN HIS BLOOD; 060 00 052
ING BLOOD -- THE O-SEAL-THAT-SO FEATURE, FLUNG PROUDER FORM . . 062 00 002
BONES BUILT IN ME, FLESH FILLED, BLOOD BRIMMED THE CURSE. . . 067 00 011
FROM HANDS NOW CLAMMY WITH STRANGE BLOOD. 080 10 004
NOW STARS OF BLOOD. 098 26 002
SO LATE THERE IS NO FORCE IN SAP OR BLOOD; 105 00 011
WITH DREADFUL DISTILLATION OF THOUGHTS SOUR AS BLOOD, . . 152 02 064
OF BLOOD TO OUR GREEN HUSTINGS GOES; 166 00 011
BLOOD THAT BUT ONE DROP OF HAS THE WORTH TO WIN 168 00 023
THEO. DIP IN BLOOD THE PALMTREE-PEN . . . . . APPEN A 43
BLOOD-GUSH
THE BLOOD-GUSH BLADE-GASH 138 00 022
BLOOD-LIGHT
AN INTENSE LINE OF THROBBING BLOOD-LIGHT SHOOK 002 00 016
BLOOD-VIVID
THRO' SILVER, GLOOM'D TO A BLOOD-VIVID CLOT. 002 00 107
BLOODS
WHOSE BLOODS I RECK NO MORE OF, NO MORE RANK WITH HERS . . 152 02 069
BLOODY
OR TENDER PINKS WITH BLOODY TYRIAN DYE. 002 00 047

27

BLOODY   (CONTINUED)
         AND EVERY SAINT OF BLOODY HOUR 145 00 044
         IN BLOODY LETTERS, LESSONS OF EARNEST, OF REVENGE: 152 02 004
BLOOM
         AND HELD A CROSS OF FLOWERS, IN PURPLE BLOOM: 001 10 006
         IN SHOALS OF BLOOM: AS IN UNPEOPLED SKIES, ...   002 00 031
         SWIRLING OUT BLOOM TILL ALL THE AIR IS BLIND 002 00 089
         AND THICKEN'D, LIKE THAT DRIFTED BLOOM, THE FLOCK 002 00 099
         AND BROKE INTO BLOOM UPON NAZARETH HILL. 027 00 010
         SINCE ITS BIRTH, AND ITS BLOOM, AND ITS BREATHING ITS LAST. . . 027 00 016
         BLAST BOLE AND BLOOM TOGETHER? 041 00 016
         BLOOM LIGHTS THE ORCHARD-APPLE 042 00 038
         BREATHING BLOOM OF A CHASTITY IN MANSEX FINE. 048 00 016
         BLOOM BREATHE, THAT ONE BREATH MORE 060 00 092
         HOW WHEN THIS BLOOM, THIS HONEYSUCKLE, C 152 01 017
         BY HER BLOOM, FAST BY HER FRESH, HER FLEECED BLOOM, . . . 152 02 051
         BY HER BLOOM, FAST BY HER FRESH, HER FLEECED BLOOM, . . . 152 02 051
BLOOMFALL
         US: FRESH YOUTH FRETTED IN A BLOOMFALL ALL PORTENDING . . . 048 00 030
BLOOMING
         THIS, ALL THIS BEAUTY BLOOMING, ... 049 00 005
BLOOMS
         WITH GARNET WREATHS AND BLOOMS OF ROSY-BUDDED FIRE. . . . 002 00 026
         THE FLOATING BLOOMS AND WITH TIDE FLOWING QUENCH'D . . . 002 00 139
         THE GLASSY PEARTREE LEAVES AND BLOOMS; THEY BRUSH . . . 033 00 006
         C HIS BRIGHTEST BLOOMS LIE THERE UNBLOWN, ... 148 00 041
BLOSSOM
         WITH ROSY FOAM AND PELTING BLOSSOM AND MISTS 002 00 090
         BUT THE BLOSSOM, THE BLOSSOM THERE, WHO CAN IT BE? -- . . 027 00 026
         BUT THE BLOSSOM, THE BLOSSOM THERE, WHO CAN IT BE? -- . . 027 00 026
         WHAT WAS THE COLOUR OF THAT BLOSSOM BRIGHT? -- . . . 027 00 031
         AND BIRD AND BLOSSOM SWELL 042 00 023
BLOSSOM-HITTING
         OF STANDING TO THE BLOSSOM-HITTING SHOWER 107 03 004
BLOT
         BLOT THE PERPETUAL FESTIVAL OF DAY? 089 00 002
         THEIR HEADS TOGETHER IN A STORMY BLOT. 090 00 006
BLOTLESS
         THE UNQUESTION'D READINGS OF A BLOTLESS BOOK.   . . . 016 00 006
BLOTS
         SHEER OFF, DISSEVERAL, A STAR, DEATH BLOTS BLACK OUT: NOR MARK . . 072 00 014
         AND BREATHES THE BLOTS OFF ALL WITH SIGHS ON SIGHS, . . . 151 00 006
BLOW
         A STEALTHY WIND CREPT ROUND SEEKING TO BLOW,   . . . 002 00 137
         AND A FEW LILIES BLOW. 009 00 006
         NONE IN CAESAR'S GARDENS BLOW, -- 010 00 008
         AT LENGTH THE BELLOWS SHALL NOT BLOW, ... 015 00 015
         AFFLICTS NO LESS, WHAT YET I HOPE MAY BLOW, ... 017 00 006
         NONE IN CAESAR'S GARDEN BLOW. 025 00 008
         WHEN WAS THE SUMMER THAT SAW THE BUD BLOW? -- 027 00 014
         AND THE SEA FLINT-FLAKE, BLACK-BACKED IN THE REGULAR BLOW, . . 028 13 005
         HE WAS PITCHED TO HIS DEATH AT A BLOW, ... 028 16 004
         AND THE BLOW BORE FROM LAND. 041 00 020
         DOES LAY MEN LOW WITH ONE BLADE'S SUDDEN BLOW   . . . 080 02 003
         ONLY THE DAHLIAS BLOW, AND ALL IS AUTUMN HERE.   . . . 128 00 010
         PERHAPS WE STRUCK NO BLOW, GWENVREWI LIVES PERHAPS: . . . 152 02 009
         OR TEMPE WITH THE WEST TO BLOW. 166 00 024
         ANG. NONE IN CAESAR'S GARDENS BLOW -- . . . . . APPEN A 08
BLOWING
         OF THE COLD WIND BLOWING. 132 00 003
BLOWN
         TO AN ORB'D ROSE, WHICH, BY HOT PANTINGS BLOWN   . . . 002 00 020
         TARPEIAN-FAST, BUT A BLOWN BEACON OF LIGHT. 028 29 008
         LIFE, THIS WILDWORTH BLOWN SO SWEET, ... 041 00 094
         NOR NIGHT IS BLOWN WITH FLAME-RINGS EVERYWHERE. 099 00 018
BLOWPIPE
         SPUR, LIVE AND LANCING LIKE THE BLOWPIPE FLAME,   . . . 076 00 002
BLOWS
         BY MANY BLOWS AND BANES: BUT NOW HEARS ROAR 050 00 006
         NEWS FROM BELLEISLE, EVEN SUCH A SWEETNESS BLOWS 119 00 006
BLUE
         A MILE ASTERN LAY THE BLUE SHORES AWAY: 002 00 005
         AND PENCILLED BLUE SO DAINTILY. 003 00 018
         INTO THE FLAT BLUE MIST THE SUN 003 00 031
         THE DESCENDING BLUE: THAT BLUE IS ALL IN A RUSH   . . . 033 00 007
         THE DESCENDING BLUE: THAT BLUE IS ALL IN A RUSH   . . . 033 00 007
         AND YOU WERE A LIAR, O BLUE MARCH DAY. 041 00 021
         CLUSTER OF BUGLE BLUE EGGS THIN 042 00 021
         BLUE BE IT: THIS BLUE HEAVEN 060 00 086
         BLUE BE IT: THIS BLUE HEAVEN 060 00 086
         THIS BATH OF BLUE AND SLAKE 060 00 095
         OF A MASTERING HEAVEN UTTERLY BLUE: 078 00 002
         WHEN THE FIERCE SKIES ARE BLUE TO BLACK, ALBEIT   . . . 080 02 005
         AT LAST UP THE BLUE ELEMENT. 087 00 006
         ONE STAR BY DAYLIGHT FROM THE STRONG BLUE AIR, ... 102 03 010
         THE BLUE WITH BRIGHTER PLACES NOT REMOTE. 107 03 020
         DRY UP THE BLUE AND BE NOT SLAKED THEREBY. 117 00 007

BONE   (CONTINUED)
    PENANCE SHALL CLOTHE ME TO THE BONE.   • • • • • • • • • 081 00 135
    TRUE GOD, TRUE MAN, IN FLESH AND BONE! • • • • • • • APPEN D 36
BONE-HOUSE
    MAN'S MOUNTING SPIRIT IN HIS BONE-HOUSE, MEAN HOUSE, DWELLS -- • • 039 00 002
BONES
    FOR, WHERE THE MARTYR'S BONES WERE THICKEST TROD, • • • • 001 05 008
    YOUR SCARCE-SHEATHED BONES ARE WEARY OF BEING BENT! • • • • 011 00 013
    OR ANCIENT MOUNDS THAT COVER BONES, • • • • • • 015 00 037
    THOU HAST BOUND BONES AND VEINS IN ME, FASTENED ME FLESH, • • 028 01 005
    FOR A RAINBOW FOOTING IT NOR HE FOR HIS BONES RISEN. • • • 039 00 014
    BONES, THIS SINEW, AND WILL NOT WAKEN. • • • • • • 041 00 084
    WITH DARKSOME DEVOURING EYES MY BRUISED BONES? AND FAN, • • 064 00 007
    BONES BUILT IN ME, FLESH FILLED, BLOOD BRIMMED THE CURSE. • • 067 00 011
    BUT MAN -- WE, SCAFFOLD OF SCORE BRITTLE BONES! • • • 075 00 005
    THEIR CHEEKS MOVED AND THE BONES THEREIN. • • • • 092 00 003
    DEATH'S BONES FELL IN WITH SUDDEN CLANK • • • • • 092 00 012
BONFIRE
    FOOTFRETTED IN IT. MILLION-FUELED, NATURE'S BONFIRE BURNS ON. • 072 00 009
BONIFACE
    IT HURLS, HURLS OFF BONIFACE DOWN. • • • • • • • 041 00 032
BONNIEST
    BUT QUENCH HER BONNIEST, DEAREST TO HER, HER CLEAREST-SELVED SPARK • 072 00 010
BOOK
    IN THE MOST MURDEROUS PASSAGE OF HIS BOOK! • • • • • 014 02 011
    THE UNQUESTION'D READINGS OF A BLOTLESS BOOK. • • • • 016 00 006
BOOKISH
    THEO. SIT NO MORE THESE BOOKISH BROWS! • • • • • APPEN A 38
BOON
    OF HEAVEN WHAT BOON TO BUY YOU, BOY, OR GAIN • • • • 047 00 012
    THIS VERY VERY DAY CAME DOWN TO US AFTER A BOON HE ON • • 048 00 005
    BOON IN MY BESTOWING, • • • • • • • • • 048 00 007
BOONS
    THOSE DEARER, MORE DIVINE BOONS WHOSE HAVEN THE HEART IS. • • 152 C 026
BOOTS
    OVER FINGER-TEASING TASK, HIS TWINY BOOTS • • • • • 159 00 033
BORDERS
    STARS FLOAT FROM THE BORDERS OF THE MAIN. • • • • • 098 20 001
BORE
    THE RICHEST GIFT ST. LAWRENCE EVER BORE, • • • • • 001 02 006
    LAY BLEEDING, TO MADRID THE LAST THEY BORE, • • • • • 001 15 002
    ARE SPATTER'D. WE DESIRE THE YOKE WE BORE, • • • • 005 00 053
    AND THE BLOW BORE FROM LAND. • • • • • • • 041 00 020
    TOO PROUD, TOO PROUD, WHAT A PRESS SHE BORE! • • • 041 00 033
    WONDERING WHY MY MASTER BORE IT, • • • • • • 041 00 098
BOREAS
    BUT WHAT BLACK BOREAS WRECKED HER? HE • • • • • 041 00 023
BORED
    I KNOW OF THE BORED AND BITTEN ROCKS • • • • • 120 00 020
BORES
    ITS DEAREST CHANGED TO BORES. • • • • • • • 114 00 016
BORN
    WHEN A SISTER, BORN FOR EACH STRONG MONTH-BROTHER, • • 026 00 001
    NOW BURN, NEW BORN TO THE WORLD, • • • • • • 028 34 001
    MY PEOPLE AND BORN OWN NATION, • • • • • • 041 00 087
    THERE) -- BOY BUGLER, BORN, HE TELLS ME, OF IRISH • 048 00 002
    IT IS THE BLIGHT MAN WAS BORN FOR, • • • • • 055 00 014
    NEW BETHLEMS, AND HE BORN • • • • • • • 060 00 063
    WHO, BORN SO, COMES TO BE • • • • • • • 060 00 068
    BUT SLEEP AGAIN ERE DAY BE BORN! • • • • • 077 00 024
    AND IN GREY BANDS THE SUN SHOULD LIE STILL BORN! • • 090 00 003
    SO THOSE WHO [BORN IN] THEE • • • • • • 123 00 004
    OUR SEX SHOULD BE BORN IN APRIL PERHAPS OR THE LILY-TIME! • 128 00 013
    BORN OF HER TOO WHEN TIME WAS DUE! WHO THEN • • • APPEN D 37
BORNE
    MORE WONDROUS TO HAVE BORNE SUCH HOPE BEFORE • • • 001 15 007
    YOUR HANDS HAVE BORNE THE TENT-POLES: ON YOU PLOD! • • 005 00 007
    THAT THOU HADST BORNE PROPORTION IN MY BLISS, • • • 013 00 006
BOROUGHS
    THE BRIGHT BOROUGHS, THE CIRCLE-CITADELS THERE! • • 032 00 003
BORROW
    AND FAIN IN THE SPRINGTIME SURCEASE WOULD BORROW • • 026 00 011
BOSOM
    BATHE ME, JESU LORD, IN WHAT THY BOSOM RAN -- • • • 168 00 022
BOSS'D
    TUGG'D THE BOSS'D, SMOOTH-LIPP'D, GIANT STROMBUS-SHELL. • • 002 00 057
BOTH
    FROM BOTH OF WHOM A CHANGELESS NOTE IS HEARD. • • • 019 00 004
    BOTH SING SOMETIMES THE SWEETEST, SWEETEST SPELLS, • • 039 00 006
    YET BOTH DROOP DEADLY SOMETIMES IN THEIR CELLS • • • 039 00 007
    REALM BOTH CHRIST IS HEIR TO AND THERE REIGNS. • • • 048 00 032
    BOTH THOUGHT AND THEW NOW BOLDER • • • • • • 049 00 008
    HER INJURY'S, LOOKS OFF BY BOTH HORNS OF SHORE, • • 050 00 003
    TO THRIFTLESS REAVE BOTH OUR RICH ROUND WORLD BARE • • 058 00 012
    BOTH GOD'S AND MARY'S SON. • • • • • • • 060 00 072
    OUR REDCOATS, OUR TARS? BOTH THESE BEING, THE GREATER PART, • 063 00 002
    KIND LOVE BOTH GIVE AND GET. ONLY WHAT WORD • • • 066 00 011

31

BRACE   (CONTINUED)
    NOWHERE KNOWN SOME, BOW OR BROOCH OR BRAID OR BRACE, C • • • • • 059 OL 001
    LOW-COVERED PASS, AND BRACE THE WOODLAND CLODS • • • • • 112 00 006
BRAES
    ARE THE GROINS OF THE BRAES THAT THE BROOK TREADS THROUGH, • • 056 00 010
BRAGGART
    OF BRAGGART BUGLES CRY IT IN -- • • • • • • • 029 00 002
    WHOSE BRAGGART 'SCUTCHEON, WHOSE COMPLAISANT CREST • • • 098 32 001
BRAGS
    THE THUNDER BRAGS, IN JOINTS AND SPARKLING JAGS • • • • 080 07 003
BRAID
    NOWHERE KNOWN SOME, BOW OR BROOCH OR BRAID OR BRACE, C • • • 059 OL 001
BRAIDED
    CROWNS COMPOSITE AND BRAIDED BAST • • • • • • 165 00 002
BRAIDS
    THE GLAUCUS CLEPED; OTHERS SMALL BRAIDS ENCLUSTER'D • • • 002 00 068
    FOR ALL HIS DREADNOUGHT BREAST AND BRAIDS OF THEW; • • • 028 16 005
BRAIN
    BUT HERE WAS HEART-THROE, BIRTH OF A BRAIN, • • • • 028 30 007
    CLEAVES NOT MY BRAIN, BURNS NOT MY FEET, • • • • • 080 02 004
    PHRENZY, BUT EDGED AND CLEAR OF BRAIN • • • • • 081 00 052
BRAINS
    AND DID THE CHILDREN OF HIS BRAINS ENJOY • • • • • 097 00 003
    BEAT FROM OUR BRAINS THE THICKY NIGHT • • • • • 167 00 023
BRAKES
    WOOD BANKS AND BRAKES WASH WET LIKE LAKES • • • • 042 00 042
    SIR, LIFE UPON THY CAUSE. SEE, BANKS AND BRAKES • • • 074 00 009
    IN SKEINS ABOUT THE BRAKES, • • • • • • • 098 10 003
    OF THE BRAKES OF LILIES. • • • • • • • 098 19 004
BRAMBLES
    WITH BILLS OF RIME THE BRAMBLES SHEW. • • • • • 003 00 004
BRANCH
    A BRANCH OF WALNUT LEAVES, AND THAT • • • • • 120 00 006
BRANCHES
    BUT THROUGH BLACK BRANCHES, RARELY DREST • • • • 003 00 020
    FIVE WAYS THE PRECIOUS BRANCHES TORN; • • • • • 006 00 014
BRANCHY
    TOWERY CITY AND BRANCHY BETWEEN TOWERS; • • • • 044 00 001
    OF SOME BRANCHY BUNCHY BUSHYBOWERED WOOD, • • • 159 00 003
BRAND
    BUT BE THE WAR WITHIN, THE BRAND WE WIELD • • • • 073 00 006
BRANDLE
    WOULD BRANDLE ADAMANTINE HEAVEN WITH RIDE AND JAR, DID • 048 00 046
BRANDS
    THEY HAVE TAKEN OUT THEIR LONG BRANDS, • • • • 109 14 001
BRASS
    MY HEAVEN IS BRASS AND IRON MY EARTH; • • • • • 018 00 009
BRASS-BOLD
    NOW THE OTHER WAS BRASS-BOLD: • • • • • • 054 00 025
BRAVE
    WITH A ROPE'S END ROUND THE MAN, HANDY AND BRAVE -- • 028 16 003
    BRAVE ALL, AND TAKE WHAT COMES -- AS HERE THIS RABBLE IS COME, • 152 02 068
BRAVEST
    ' HOLIEST, LOVELIEST, BRAVEST, • • • • • • 041 00 111
BRAWLING
    TO THE MEN IN THE TOPS AND THE TACKLE RODE OVER THE STORM'S BRAWLING. 028 19 008
BRAWN
    STAND AT STRESS. EACH LIMB'S BARROWY BRAWN, HIS THEW • • • 071 00 005
BRAZED
    ON BRAZED BARGE AND HARD BEHIND • • • • • • 166 00 039
BRAZEN
    MY PRAYERS MUST MEET A BRAZEN HEAVEN • • • • • 018 00 001
    NOT HOPE, NOT PRAY; DESPAIR; AY, THAT: BRAZEN DESPAIR OUT. • • 152 02 067
BREAD
    AT MORN WE FOUND THE HEAVENLY BREAD, • • • • • 006 00 008
    HE IS WITH YOU IN THE BREAKING OF THE BREAD. • • • 020 00 018
    GOD! GIVER OF BREATH AND BREAD; • • • • • • 028 01 002
    LITTLE I RECK HO! LACKLEVEL IN, IF ALL HAD BREAD; • • 070 00 009
    TO GENTLE MANNA AND SIMPLE BREAD? • • • • • 081 00 175
    LIVING BREAD THE LIFE OF US FOR WHOM HE DIED, • • • 168 00 018
BREADTH
    BUT EACH A HAND'S BREADTH FURTHER THAN THE NEXT. • • • 091 00 007
BREAK
    THEN SAW I SUDDEN FROM THE WATERS BREAK • • • • 002 00 074
    BREAK THE BOX AND SHED THE NARD; • • • • • 024 00 001
    HAVE YOU! MAKE WORDS BREAK FROM ME HERE ALL ALONE, • • 028 18 003
    OUR MAKE AND MAKING BREAK, ARE BREAKING, DOWN • • • 035 00 013
    AND THEN MY HEART GOES NEAR TO BREAK. • • • • • 080 06 007
    I WILL BREAK FREE FROM THE JEWS' COMPANY, • • • 080 12 003
    I NEED NOT, LOVE, I NEED NOT BREAK • • • • • 081 00 138
    AND HEDGES BREAK, AND LOSE THE KINE, • • • • • 114 00 002
    POETRY TO IT, AS A TREE WHOSE BOUGHS BREAK IN THE SKY. • 149 A 003
    FLINTY KINDCOLD ELEMENT LET BREAK ACROSS HIS LIMBS • • 159 00 041
    FOR HAIL UPON THE VINE NOR BREAK • • • • • 166 00 029
BREAKER
    SHE TO THE BLACK-ABOUT AIR, TO THE BREAKER, THE THICKLY • • 028 24 005
BREAKERS
    THE BREAKERS ROLLED ON HER BEAM WITH RUINOUS SHOCK; • • 028 14 006

32

BREAKING
HE IS WITH YOU IN THE BREAKING OF THE BREAD.	. . . . . .	020 00 018
OUR MAKE AND MAKING BREAK, ARE BREAKING, DOWN	. . . . .	035 00 013
THE WIND COMES BREAKING HERE AND THERE WITH LAUGHTER:	. . .	098 03 003
BREAKING THE . . . AIR OF SPRING.	. . . . . .	098 03 007
THE BREAKING LEAVES OF GOLD ARE CURL'D UPON HER LIPS.	. . .	098 14 003

BREAKLESS
FALLING ALONG THE BREAKLESS POOL OF AIR.	. . . . . .	122 00 009

BREAKS
I'LL WAIT TILL MORN ETERNAL BREAKS.	. . . . . .	023 00 054
BUCKLE! AND THE FIRE THAT BREAKS FROM THEE THEN, A BILLION	. .	036 00 010
POINTED WITH PIERCED LIGHTS, AND BREAKS OF RAYS	. . .	098 24 002
LIKE A CUPP'D CHESTNUT DAMASK'D WITH DARK BREAKS,	. . .	099 00 012
DROPS THE FRUIT OUT! THE DUCT RUNS DRY OR BREAKS:	. . .	101 00 010
SO LATE THE HOAR GREEN CHESTNUT BREAKS A BUD,	. . . .	105 00 009

BREAST
LIES IN THE BREAST OF THE YOUNG YEAR—MOTHER	. . . .	026 00 003
AND THE PROMISE OF SUMMER WITHIN HER BREAST!	. . . .	026 00 016
TO THY BREAST, TO THY REST, TO THY GLORY DIVINE	. . . .	027 00 047
FOR ALL HIS DREADNOUGHT BREAST AND BRAIDS OF THEW:	. . .	028 16 005
FINGER OF A TENDER OF, O OF A FEATHERY DELICACY, THE BREAST OF THE		028 31 006
WORLD BROODS WITH WARM BREAST AND WITH AH! BRIGHT WINGS.	. . .	031 00 014
WELCOME IN WOMB AND BREAST.	. . . . . .	060 00 020
UNSEEN, THE HEROIC BREAST NOT OUTWARD—STEELED,	. . . .	073 00 007
TO COOL HIS PLUMY THROBBING BREAST.	. . . . . .	077 00 092
ARE MEASURED OUTWARDS FROM MY BREAST.	. . . . .	130 00 002
THIS GARLAND OF THEIR GAMBOL FLASHES IN HIS BREAST	. . .	159 00 019

BREASTING
TILL A LIONESS AROSE BREASTING THE BABBLE.	. . . . .	028 17 007

BREAST'S
THE BREAST'S DESPONDING SOB I QUELL:	. . . . .	023 00 038

BREASTS
ABEL IS CAIN'S BROTHER AND BREASTS THEY HAVE SUCKED THE SAME.)	. .	028 20 008

BREATH
ONLY WITH UTTERANCE OF SWEET BREATH THEY SUNG	. . . .	002 00 130
THE WINDPIPE WHEN HE SUCKED HIS BREATH	. . . .	021 00 037
NOSTRILS, YOUR CARELESS BREATH THAT SPEND	. . . . .	022 00 017
AT THE TOUCH OF HER WANDERING WONDERING BREATH	. . .	026 00 006
O BREATH OF IT BATHES GREAT HEAVEN ABOVE,	. . . . .	027 00 045
GOD! GIVER OF BREATH AND BREAD:	. . . . . .	028 01 002
BREATHE, ARCH AND ORIGINAL BREATH.	. . . . .	028 25 002
NOW HE WRINGS FOR BREATH WITH THE DEATHGUSH BROWN:	. . .	041 00 062
RESIGN THEM, SIGN THEM, SEAL THEM, SEND THEM, MOTION THEM WITH BREATH,		059 06 016
MEN HERE MAY DRAW LIKE BREATH	. . . . . .	060 00 066
BLOOM BREATHE, THAT ONE BREATH MORE	. . . . .	060 00 092
AGE GASP! WHOSE BREATH IS OUR MEMENTO MORI --	. . .	075 00 007
SILENCE HOLDS BREATH UPON HER THRONE,	. . . . .	077 00 033
AT ONCE I STRUGGLE WITH MY BREATH.	. . . . .	081 00 058
TWO MADE ANSWER IN ONE BREATH	. . . . . .	109 26 001
AND BREATH UPON IT. THAT IS, HER FACE IS THIS.	. . .	125 00 052
AND BREATHED DELIGHTFUL BREATH	. . . . . .	133 00 010
WHAT BEING IN RANK—OLD NATURE SHOULD EARLIER HAVE THAT BREATH BEEN		141 00 001
AND BREATH IMMORTAL THRONGED THAT SHOW!	. . . . .	145 00 045

BREATHE
BREATHE EASTER NOW! YOU SERGED FELLOWSHIPS,	. . . .	011 00 007
PLUCK THE HARP AND BREATHE THE HORN!	. . . . .	024 00 011
TO BATHE IN HIS FALL—GOLD MERCIES, TO BREATHE IN HIS ALL—FIRE GLANCES.		028 23 008
BREATHE, ARCH AND ORIGINAL BREATH.	. . . . .	028 25 002
BREATHE, BODY OF LOVELY DEATH.	. . . . .	028 25 004
THAT BEAT AND BREATHE IN POWER --.	. . . . .	049 00 011
NOW BUT TO BREATHE ITS PRAISE.	. . . . .	060 00 015
BLOOM BREATHE, THAT ONE BREATH MORE	. . . . .	060 00 092
WHO BREATHE, FROM GROUNDLONG BABYHOOD TO HOARY	. . .	075 00 006
BREATHE O'ER MY BARE NERVE RATHER. I DESIRE	. . . .	080 05 005
THEY BREATHE NOT WHO ARE LATE TO RUN. --	. . . .	081 00 148
BREATHE IN SUCH ETHER? OR THE QUICKLY ELMS	. . . .	100 00 007

BREATHED
COMFORTING SMELL BREATHED AT VERY ENTERING,	. . . .	034 00 003
BREATHED ROUND: THE RACK OF RIBS! THE SCOOPED FLANK: LANK	. .	071 00 002
AND BREATHED DELIGHTFUL BREATH	. . . . . .	133 00 010

BREATHES
BREATHES ONCE AND, QUENCHED FASTER THAN IT CAME,	. . .	076 00 003
MY WINTER WORLD, THAT SCARCELY BREATHES THAT BLISS	. . .	076 00 013
BREATHES IN THE MYSTERIOUS AIR:	. . . . .	077 00 128
AND BREATHES THE BLOTS OFF ALL WITH SIGHS ON SIGHS.	. . .	151 00 006

BREATHING
SINCE ITS BIRTH, AND ITS BLOOM, AND ITS BREATHING ITS LAST.	. .	027 00 016
ONLY THE BREATHING TEMPLE AND FLEET	. . . . .	041 00 093
BREATHING BLOOM OF A CHASTITY IN MANSEX FINE.	. . . .	048 00 016
THEIR CLOUDS WITH BREATHING EDGES WHITE	. . . .	130 00 023
THAT SCENT FROM BREEZES BREATHING BY ME,	. . . .	160 00 021

BREATH—TAKING
YOU STRIPED IN SECRET WITH BREATH—TAKING WHIPS,	. . .	011 00 003

BRED
OUT OF HALLOWED BODIES BRED.	. . . . . .	052 00 004
THIS, BY DESPAIR, BRED HANGDOG DULL: BY RAGE,	. . . .	070 00 019
AND BRED ACQUAINTANCE OF UNUSED TOWNS?	. . . .	107 02 002

33

BRED   (CONTINUED)
      WHAT SHALL I DO FOR THE LAND THAT BRED ME, ... 156 00 001
BREED
      TIME'S EUNUCH, AND NOT BREED ONE WORK THAT WAKES, ... 074 00 013
BREEDS
      WISEST MY HEART BREEDS DARK HEAVEN'S BAFFLING BAN 066 00 012
BREEZE
      WHILE THE BREEZE BY RANK AND MEASURE 078 00 009
      AND KEEPS THE BREEZE AND CLEARS THE SEAS 083 00 013
      PLAYS TO THE BREEZE: WHERE NOW ARE FLED HER FEARS, ... 099 00 015
      TO THESE CASTARA IS RAIN OR BREEZE OR SPRING, ... 125 00 048
BREEZES
      THAT SCENT FROM BREEZES BREATHING BY ME, ... 160 00 021
BREEZY
      I WALK MY BREEZY BELVEDERE 015 00 025
      IN BREEZY BELTS OF UPPER AIR 077 00 073
BREMEN
      ON SATURDAY SAILED FROM BREMEN, ... 028 12 001
BRICKISH
      THOU HAST A BASE AND BRICKISH SKIRT THERE, SOURS 044 00 005
BRICKS
      GIVE US THE TALE OF BRICKS AS HERETOFORE! 005 00 049
BRIDE
      AND, POVERTY, BE THOU THE BRIDE 022 00 025
      GROOM, AND GRACE YOU, BRIDE, YOUR BED 052 00 002
      THEN SHE SEEMS SWEET WHO SEEMS HIS BRIDE, ... 120 00 016
      C THEN SWEETEST SEEMS THE SEEMING BRIDE 120 00 018
BRIDEGROOM
      AND BRIDEGROOM WAITS AND READY ARE BOWER AND BED. 136 00 018
BRIDGE
      BEYOND MAGDALEN AND BY THE BRIDGE, ON A PLACE CALLED THERE THE PLAIN, 142 00 001
BRIDGING
      BRIDGING THE SLENDER DIFFERENCE OF TWO STARS, ... 103 00 003
BRIEF
      ERING! LET ME BE FELL! FORCE I MUST BE BRIEF ' 065 00 008
      RUPTURE, RUNNING SORES, WHAT MORE? IN BRIEF, IN BURDEN, ... 152 C 009
BRIER
      FOR BRIER, BOUGH, FURROW, OR GREEN GROUND 138 00 006
BRIGHT
      MY EYES HOLD YET THE RINDS AND BRIGHT 025 00 033
      WHAT WAS THE COLOUR OF THAT BLOSSOM BRIGHT? -- 027 00 031
      WORLD BROODS WITH WARM BREAST AND WITH AH! BRIGHT WINGS. .   .   . 031 00 014
      THE BRIGHT BOROUGHS, THE CIRCLE-CITADELS THERE! 032 00 003
      MEN GO BY ME WHOM EITHER BEAUTY BRIGHT 040 00 005
      BRIGHT SUN LANCED FIRE IN THE HEAVENLY BAY! 041 00 022
      HIS BRIGHT AND BATTERING SANDAL! C 053 00 014
      DELIGHTFULLY THE BRIGHT WIND BOISTEROUS C 072 00 005
      AND GATHER IN LIKE HURDLES BRIGHT 098 29 003
      HE DROPS HIS BRIGHT ROOTS IN THE WATER'D SWARD, ... 100 00 002
      WARN'D BY THE BRIGHT PROCESSION OF THE STARS, ... 102 01 056
      BRIGHT HUES LONG LOOK'D AT THIN, DISSOLVE AND FLY! 117 00 002
      HAMPSTEAD WAS NEVER BRIGHT! AND WHATEVER MISS CULLY'S CHARMS   .   . 128 00 011
      AND GATHER IN LIKE HURDLES BRIGHT 135 00 021
      AND BRIGHT ICONIUM EASTWARDS REACH MY RHYMES. 136 00 006
      BUT AH, BRIGHT FORELOCK, CLUSTER THAT YOU ARE 157 00 017
      THEO. MY EYES HOLD YET THE RINDS AND BRIGHT   .   .   .   .   .   . APPEN A 33
      FLESH OF THEE, MAIDEN BRIGHT, ... APPEN D 08
BRIGHTEN
      FAIRER THAN THIS ONE TO BRIGHTEN OUR DAY? 026 00 008
BRIGHTENING
      MORE BRIGHTENING HER, RARE-DEAR BRITAIN, AS HIS REIGN ROLLS, .   . 028 35 006
BRIGHTER
      SHEW BRIGHTER SHAKEN IN PENMAEN POOL. 030 00 020
      IS IT ONLY ITS BEING BRIGHTER 042 00 009
      THE BLUE WITH BRIGHTER PLACES NOT REMOTE. 107 03 020
      A GROWING BURNISH BRIGHTER THAN BEFORE 151 00 004
BRIGHTEST
      C HIS BRIGHTEST BLOOMS LIE THERE UNBLOWN, ... 148 00 041
BRIGHT-COUNTER
      EYE-GREETING DOVES BRIGHT-COUNTER TO THE ROOK, ... 016 00 003
BRIGHT-LIFTING
      BRIGHT-LIFTING WITH A LITTLE-LASTING SMILE 125 00 051
BRIGHT-MASK'D
      SLIGHT WITH SUCH VIOLET THEIR BRIGHT-MASK'D GREEN? V 100 00 009
BRIGHTNESS
      BUT, BEING LIFTED, IMMORTAL, OF IMMORTAL BRIGHTNESS. 152 02 027
BRILLIANCE
      FLARES HIS WET BRILLIANCE IN THE DINTLESS HEAVEN. 098 34 002
BRILLIANT
      THE VAST OF HEAVEN STUNG WITH BRILLIANT STARS. 098 21 002
      GEM-FLEECED AT MORN, SO BRILLIANT IS THE WEATHER. 099 00 004
BRILLIANT-HUED
      THAT BATTLED GODS FOR HEAVEN; BRILLIANT-HUED, ... 001 07 005
BRIM
      ITS BRINDLED WHARVES AND YELLOW BRIM, ... 003 00 028
      BRIM, IN A FLASH, FULL! -- HITHER THEN, LAST OR FIRST,   .   .   . 028 08 006
BRIMMED
      BONES BUILT IN ME, FLESH FILLED, BLOOD BRIMMED THE CURSE. .   .   . 067 00 011

34

BRIMS
   SHE BRIMS HER BATH IN COLD OR HEAT; 139 00 002
   AND WITH HEAVENFALLEN FRESHNESS DOWN FROM MOORLAND STILL BRIMS, . . 159 00 039
BRINDED
   FOR SKIES OF COUPLE-COLOUR AS A BRINDED COW; 037 00 002
BRINDLED
   ITS BRINDLED WHARVES AND YELLOW BRIM, ... 003 00 028
BRINE
   THE RASH SMART SLOGGERING BRINE 028 19 004
   WITH BRINE AND SHINE AND WHIRLING WIND. 041 00 080
BRING
   AND BRING YOUR OFFERINGS TO A GRATEFUL GOD, ... 005 00 011
   BRING IN THE GLISTERY STRAW, ... 005 00 046
   YET KNOW NOT HOW OUR GIFTS TO BRING, ... 023 00 017
   HITHER BRING PEARL, OPAL, SARD; 024 00 003
   THE PRAISE OF THE LIPS AND THE HEARTS OF US BRING TO THEE, . 026 00 035
   BRING ME PALM WITH PEARLED KNOPS, ... 098 18 002
   AND PRIMROSE BRING, AND MAKE A SHEAF 098 18 003
   AND BRING A CROWN FOR THEE. ' 109 23 004
   OR BRING MORE OR MORE BLAZON MAN'S DISTRESS. 150 00 004
   IT WILL NOT WELL, SO SHE WOULD BRING ABOUT 151 00 003
   BRING NATURAL MYRTLE, AND HAVE DONE; 165 00 005
   BRING SLEEP ROUND THEN? -- SLEEP NOT AFRAID . . . 166 00 021
   BRING THE TENDER TALE TRUE OF THE PELICAN; 168 00 021
   SHALL BE THIS THING WHEREOF TIDING I BRING; . . . . APPEN D 17
BRINGING
   O THIS IS BRINGING! TEARS MAY SWARM 025 00 035
   BRINGING HEADS OF DAFFODILLIES, ... 098 16 001
   THEO. O THIS IS BRINGING! TEARS MAY SWARM . . . . APPEN A 35
BRINGS
   FROM WASTES OF ROCK HE BRINGS 007 00 011
   AND IN A BASON BRINGS THE BLOCKS. 080 09 007
   FIELD-FLOWN, THE DEPARTED DAY NO MORNING BRINGS . . . 153 00 009
BRINK
   OH, MORNING, AT THE BROWN BRINK EASTWARD, SPRINGS -- . . . 031 00 012
BRISTOL-BRED
   SYDNEY FLETCHER, BRISTOL-BRED, ... 041 00 057
BRITAIN
   MORE BRIGHTENING HER, RARE-DEAR BRITAIN, AS HIS REIGN ROLLS, . 028 35 006
   BUT DROPP'D ITS COIL OF WOES; ARTHUR'S BRITAIN, ... 102 02 007
BRITAIN'S
   LIKE KNOCKING THUNDER ALL ROUND BRITAIN'S WELKIN, . . . 102 02 003
BRITTLE
   BUT MAN -- WE, SCAFFOLD OF SCORE BRITTLE BONES; 075 00 005
   A BRITTLE SHEEN, RUNS UPWARD LIKE A CLIFF, ... 098 06 002
   -- AND ON THEIR BRITTLE GREEN QUILS 098 07 001
   WITH SULPHUR-COLOUR'D LILIES, BRITTLE IN STALK, . . . 098 12 003
BROAD
   IN SOME BROAD PALMY MEAD, AND SAINTLY SMILED, . . . 001 10 005
   BOW SWUNG FINDS TONGUE TO FLING OUT BROAD ITS NAME; . . 057 00 004
   THEM -- BROAD IN BLUFF HIDE HIS FROWNING FEET LASHED! RACED . 071 00 013
   IN WANDERING UNTIL BROAD LIGHT OF DAY; 079 00 006
   A BASKET BROAD OF WOVEN WHITE RODS 098 19 001
BROAD-FLUTED
   BROAD-FLUTED, NOR WITH SHAFTS ACANTHUS-CROWN'D. . . . 001 07 003
BROAD-SHED
   BUD SWELLING OR BROAD-SHED 138 00 024
BROIDERS
   BROIDERS THE NETS WITH FANS OF AMETHYST 002 00 066
BROKE
   AND BROKE INTO BLOOM UPON NAZARETH HILL. 027 00 010
   SICKNESS BROKE HIM, IMPATIENT, HE CURSED AT FIRST, BUT MENDED . 053 00 005
BROKEN
   BY SPEECH SO SWEETLY BROKEN UP AND GONE. 125 00 027
BRONZE
   IN BLAZON, GILT AND IMAGES OF BRONZE, V . . . 102 02 010
   -- GILT AND BLAZON -- BRONZE STATUARY, V . . . 102 02 010
   -- -- -- ---- -- MAIL'D SHAPES OF BRONZE, V . . . 102 02 010
BRONZEN
   THEIR PANSY-DARK OR BRONZEN LOCKS WERE STRUNG . . . 002 00 053
BROOCH
   NOWHERE KNOWN SOME, BOW OR BROOCH OR BRAID OR BRACE, C . . 059 0L 001
BROOD
   POURTRAY'D ALONG THE FRIEZE WITH TITAN'S BROOD . . . 001 07 004
   HE COMES TO BROOD AND SIT. 051 00 011
BROODS
   AND STILL TH' UNBROKEN SILENCE BROODS 023 00 019
   WORLD BROODS WITH WARM BREAST AND WITH AH! BRIGHT WINGS. . . 031 00 014
   THESE SHOULD HAVE STARV'D WITH THE GREEN BROODS OF SPRING, . 105 00 014
BROOK
   ON TANGLED SHOALS THAT BAR THE BROOK -- A CROWD . . . 002 00 096
   THE CLOGGED BROOK RUNS WITH CHOKING SOUND 003 00 009
   A ROW OF RIPPLES IN THE BROOK, ... 021 00 031
   ARE THE GROINS OF THE BRAES THAT THE BROOK TREADS THROUGH, . 056 00 010
   THEY SAID WE COULD NOT MISS. A PUSHING BROOK . . . 125 00 005
   I KNEW THE BROOK THAT PARTS IN TWO 135 00 025
BROOKS
   FRESH BROOKS TO SALT SAND-TEASING WATERS SHOALY; -- . . . 016 00 004

BROOKS   (CONTINUED)
    WHILE RUSHY RAINS SHALL FALL OR BROOKS SHALL FLEET FROM FOUNTAINS,   .   152   C 002
BROTH
    TURNS AND TWINDLES OVER THE BROTH 056 00 006
    HARD AS HURDLE ARMS, WITH A BROTH OF GOLDISH FLUE 071 00 001
BROTHER
    HE HAS A SIN OF MINE, HE ITS NEAR BROTHER! 016 00 009
    ABEL IS CAIN'S BROTHER AND BREASTS THEY HAVE SUCKED THE SAME.)   .   .   028 20 008
    THEN UP AND SPAKE THE THIRD BROTHER, ...   109 27 001
    TOWARDS MY BROTHER, EVERY OTHER 155 00 023
BROTHER'S
    HOW LOVELY THE ELDER BROTHER'S 054 00 001
BROTHERS
    BROTHERS AND SISTERS ARE IN CHRIST NOT NEAR 066 00 003
    HE SAW HIS BROTHERS THREE. 109 07 002
    BESIDE HIS BROTHERS THREE? ' 109 20 002
    BESIDE HIS BROTHERS THREE? 109 21 002
    HIS THREE BROTHERS ARE EACH AS TALL 109 21 003
    BESIDE HIS BROTHERS THREE! 109 22 004
    AMONG HIS BROTHERS THREE, ...   109 23 002
    BUT SAW HIS BROTHERS THREE. 109 24 004
    FATHER, MOTHER, BROTHERS, SISTERS, FRIENDS 159 00 049
BROUGHT
    THE DAY THAT BROUGHT MY LASTING PAIN 021 00 010
    THAT WAS UNTO JUDAH AS MAY, AND BROUGHT HER 026 00 031
    OUR BOYS' PLAYS BROUGHT ON 054 00 006
    AND BROUGHT THE SENSE OF GENTLE FELLOWSHIP, ...   107 02 004
    THEY BROUGHT THEIR HUNDREDWEIGHTS TO BEAR. 145 00 051
    BROUGHT TO HER BLISSFUL TIDING   .   .   .   .   APPEN D 03
    AND BACK FROM SORROW BROUGHT. '   .   .   .   .   APPEN D 20
BROW
    WARM ON HIS BROW; LO! WHERE IS ANOTHER 026 00 007
    THAT BROW AND BEAD OF BEING, ...   048 00 039
    THE SHEPHERD'S BROW, FRONTING FORKED LIGHTNING, OWNS   .   .   .   075 00 001
    AND WHERE THE BROW IN FIRST DESCENDING BOW'D 107 01 009
    WITH YELLOW FLAGS WILL SUIT HIS BROW, ...   124 00 018
    [HOVER-FLOAT TO THE HEDGE BROW.] 138 00 040
BROWN
    OH, MORNING, AT THE BROWN BRINK EASTWARD, SPRINGS --   .   .   .   031 00 012
    NOW HE WRINGS FOR BREATH WITH THE DEATHGUSH BROWN;   .   .   041 00 062
    THIS DARKSOME BURN, HORSEBACK BROWN, ...   056 00 001
    HER HUE'S A VARIOUS BROWN WITH CREAMY LAKES, ...   099 00 011
    OR RINGLET-RACE ON BURLING BARROW BROWN. 157 00 012
BROWN-AS-DAWNING
    AND BROWN-AS-DAWNING-SKINNED 041 00 079
BROWS
    DROOP'D O'ER THE BROWS LIKE HECTOR'S CASQUE, AND SWAY'D   .   .   002 00 042
    EARTH BROWS OF SUCH CARE, CARE AND DEAR CONCERN.   .   .   .   058 00 014
    THE SERAPH BROWS OF GALAHAD. 077 00 042
    THEO.   SIT NO MORE THESE BOOKISH BROWS!   .   .   .   .   .   APPEN A 38
BROWZED
    WHOSE GAPS AND HOLLOWS ARE NOT BROWZED UPON, ...   107 01 002
BRUISE
    TO BRUISE THEM DEARER, YET THE REBELLIOUS WILLS 068 00 010
BRUISED
    SHEAVED IN CRUEL BANDS, BRUISED SORE, ...   006 00 005
    WITH DARKSOME DEVOURING EYES MY BRUISED BONES? AND FAN,   .   .   064 00 007
BRUSH
    THE GLASSY PEARTREE LEAVES AND BLOOMS, THEY BRUSH 033 00 006
    THEY WATCHED THE BRUSH OF THE SWIFT STRINGY DROPS,   .   .   .   107 03 013
    BEYOND, THE BANKS WERE STEEP; A BRUSH OF TREES 107 04 003
    AT HIGHEST WHEN HE SEEMS TO BRUSH THE CLOUDS, ...   122 00 004
BRUTE
    BRUTE BEAUTY AND VALOUR AND ACT, OH, AIR, PRIDE, PLUME, HERE   .   036 00 009
BUBBLES
    WITH BUBBLES BUGLE-EYED, STRUGGLE AND STICK 002 00 095
    WITH ARM AND FIN; THE ARGENT BUBBLES STREAM'D 002 00 109
BUCK
    WITH THE BURL OF THE FOUNTAINS OF AIR, BUCK AND THE FLOOD OF THE WAVE?   028 16 008
BUCKLE
    BUCKLE! AND THE FIRE THAT BREAKS FROM THEE THEN, A BILLION   .   .   036 00 010
BUD
    AND PLANETS BUD WHERE'ER WE TURN OUR MAZED EYES, ...   002 00 033
    WHEN WAS THE SUMMER THAT SAW THE BUD BLOW? -- 027 00 014
    SO LATE THE HOAR GREEN CHESTNUT BREAKS A BUD, ...   105 00 009
    BUD SHELLING OR BROAD-SHED 138 00 024
BUDS
    LIKE AN ASSYRIAN PRINCE, WITH BUDS UNSHEATH'D 002 00 062
    NOT SET, BECAUSE THEIR BUDS NOT SPRING! 010 00 011
    IS IT A WONDER IF THE BUDS ARE SLOW? 017 00 003
    NOT SET BECAUSE THEIR BUDS NOT SPRING! 025 00 011
    THE ENDS OF THE CRISP BUDS SHE CHIPS 098 14 001
    WITH THE WARM'D AND THE WATER'D BUDS 098 19 007
    THAN WE IN THE EAST DARE LOOK FOR BUDS, DISCLOSE   .   .   .   119 00 002
    ANG.   NOT SET BECAUSE THEIR BUDS NOT SPRING!   .   .   .   .   APPEN A 11
BUGLE
    THE BUGLE MOON BY DAYLIGHT FLOATS 003 00 015

BUGLE   (CONTINUED)
    AND STORMS BUGLE HIS FAME. 028 11 004
    CLUSTER OF BUGLE BLUE EGGS THIN 042 00 021
BUGLE-EYED
    WITH BUBBLES BUGLE-EYED, STRUGGLE AND STICK 002 00 095
BUGLER
    A BUGLER BOY FROM BARRACK (IT IS OVER THE HILL 048 00 001
    THERE) -- BOY BUGLER, BORN, HE TELLS ME, OF IRISH .   .   .   048 00 002
BUGLES
    OF BRAGGART BUGLES CRY IT IN -- 029 00 002
BUILD
    BUT MEN AND MASTERS PLAN AND BUILD! 015 00 006
    BUILD HIS CHURCH AND DECK HIS SHRINE, ...   024 00 007
    ALL THE AIR THINGS WEAR THAT BUILD THIS WORLD OF WALES! .   .   034 00 010
    THEM! BIRDS BUILD -- BUT NOT I BUILD! NO, BUT STRAIN, .   .   074 00 012
    THEM! BIRDS BUILD -- BUT NOT I BUILD! NO, BUT STRAIN, .   .   074 00 012
BUILT
    BONES BUILT IN ME, FLESH FILLED, BLOOD BRIMMED THE CURSE. .   .   067 00 011
    THAT'S BUILT FOR BY THE BEE. 148 00 036
    C WHO BUILT THESE WALLS MADE KNOWN 148 00 037
    BUILT OF CHANCEQUARRIED, SELFQUAINED, HOAR-HUSKED ROCKS .   .   159 00 037
BULK
    MUST SEE THE EAGLE'S BULK, RENDER'D IN MISTS, ...   088 00 003
BULKY
    CIRCLED THE SAFE FLANKS OF THE BULKY HILLS. 125 00 010
BULLION
    BOUNDEN BALES OR A HOARD OF BULLION? -- 041 00 010
BUNCHY
    OF SOME BRANCHY BUNCHY BUSHYBOWERED WOOD, ...   159 00 003
BUOY
    I CANNOT BUOY MY HEART ABOVE! 018 00 005
    TO THE NEST'S NOOK I BALANCE AND BUOY 138 00 043
BURDEN
    THE EASY BURDEN OF YORE. 005 00 054
    BURDEN, IN WIND'S BURLY AND BEAT OF ENDRAGONED SEAS. .   .   028 27 008
    OF BURDEN CAME AND BOW'D MY HEAD. 118 00 011
    RUPTURE, RUNNING SORES, WHAT MORE? IN BRIEF, IN BURDEN, .   .   152 C 009
BURIAL
    DOWNS' FOREFALLS BEAT TO THE BURIAL. 041 00 008
BURL
    WITH THE BURL OF THE FOUNTAINS OF AIR, BUCK AND THE FLOOD OF THE WAVE? 028 16 008
BURLING
    OR RINGLET-RACE ON BURLING BARROW BROWN. 157 00 012
BURLY
    BURDEN, IN WIND'S BURLY AND BEAT OF ENDRAGONED SEAS. .   .   028 27 008
    UPON MY FOREHEAD HIT THE BURLY WIND. 135 00 012
    AND COME WHERE LIES A COFFER, BURLY ALL OF BLOCKS .   .   .   159 00 036
    THE BURLY SEA MAY QUITE FORGET 166 00 026
BURN
    NOW BURN, NEW BORN TO THE WORLD, ...   028 34 001
    FRESH, TILL DOOMFIRE BURN ALL, ...   041 00 119
    THIS DARKSOME BURN, HORSEBACK BROWN, ...   056 00 001
    AND THE BEADBONNY ASH THAT SITS OVER THE BURN. 056 00 012
BURNING
    AND SLENDERING TO HIS BURNING RIM 003 00 030
    O BUT I BEAR MY BURNING WITNESS THOUGH 157 00 035
    IN THE EVERLASTING BURNING. 170 00 004
BURNISH
    A GROWING BURNISH BRIGHTER THAN BEFORE 151 00 004
    I CAN SCOUR THEE, FRESH BURNISH THEE, C 152 02 015
BURNISH'D
    AND FRETTED CLOUDS WITH BURNISH'D RIM, ...   077 00 101
BURNS
    SOME CANDLE CLEAR BURNS SOMEWHERE I COME BY. 046 00 001
    FOOTFRETTED IN IT, MILLION-FUELED, NATURE'S BONFIRE BURNS ON, .   072 00 009
    CLEAVES NOT MY BRAIN, BURNS NOT MY FEET, ...   080 02 004
BURST
    IN SUMMER, IN A BURST OF SUMMERTIME 142 00 002
BURSTS
    OR WRING THEIR BARRIERS IN BURSTS OF FEAR OR RAGE. .   .   .   039 00 008
BURTHEN
    THE DREAR DULL BURTHEN OF UNENDING PAINS. 160 00 018
BURY
    ALL UNDER CHANNEL TO BURY IN A BEACH HER 041 00 049
BUSHES
    QUT-FLEECED BUSHES LIKE A SPANIEL'S EAR V 098 11 001
    THICK-FLEECED BUSHES LIKE A HEIFER'S EAR V 098 11 001
BUSH-BROWED
    A BUSH-BROWED, BEETLE-BROWED BILLOW IS IT? 141 00 003
BUSHYBOWERED
    OF SOME BRANCHY BUNCHY BUSHYBOWERED WOOD, ...   159 00 003
BUSINESS
    WHO, LIKE ME, KNOWING HIS NATURE TO THE HEART HOME, NATURE'S BUSINESS, 152 02 044
BUSY
    ROBBERY'S HAND IS BUSY TO 041 00 091
BUTCHER
    SO BE IT. THOU STEEL, THOU BUTCHER, ...   152 02 014

                                37

BUTTERFLIES
    TWO TONGUES LIKE BUTTERFLIES. 098 12 007
BUTTER-BURR
    GREAT BUTTER-BURR LEAVES FLOOR'D THE SLOPE CORPSE GROUND . . . 107 04 009
BUTT'S
    RIGHT ROOTING IN THE BARE BUTT'S WINCING NAVEL C 143 00 005
BUY
    BUY THEN! BID THEN! -- WHAT? -- PRAYER, PATIENCE, ALMS, VOWS, . . 032 00 009
    ' BUT TELL ME, CHILD, YOUR CHOICE! WHAT SHALL I BUY . . . 047 00 001
    YOU? ' -- ' FATHER, WHAT YOU BUY ME I LIKE BEST. ' . . . 047 00 002
    OF HEAVEN WHAT BOON TO BUY YOU, BOY, OR GAIN 047 00 012
BUYS
    RICH BEAMS, TILL DEATH OR DISTANCE BUYS THEM QUITE. 040 00 008
BYE-WAYS
    NONE BESIDES ME THIS BYE-WAYS BEAUTY TRY. 012 02 009
BYGONES
    I MIGHT LET BYGONES BE -- OUR CURSE 041 00 089
BYPLAY
    TURN MOST ON TENDER BYPLAY. 054 00 016

CADAIR
    COME, PLANT THE STAFF BY CADAIR CLIFF! 030 00 007
CADENCE
    THE AUTHENTIC CADENCE WAS DISCOVERED LATE 019 00 009
CAERWYS
    YOU CAME BY CAERWYS, SIR? I CAME BY CAERWYS. THERE . . 152 01 002
    YOU CAME BY CAERWYS, SIR? I CAME BY CAERWYS. THERE . . 152 01 002
CAESAR'S
    NONE IN CAESAR'S GARDENS BLOW, -- 010 00 008
    NONE IN CAESAR'S GARDEN BLOW. 025 00 008
    ANG. NONE IN CAESAR'S GARDENS BLOW -- . . . . . . APPEN A 08
CAGE
    AS A DARE-GALE SKYLARK SCANTED IN A DULL CAGE 039 00 001
CAGES
    MY ASPENS DEAR, WHOSE AIRY CAGES QUELLED, ... 043 00 001
CAIN'S
    ABEL IS CAIN'S BROTHER AND BREASTS THEY HAVE SUCKED THE SAME,) . 028 20 008
CAKED
    'MID FEVER'D FUMES AND SLIME AND CAKED CLOT! 077 00 008
CALENDAR
    NOR FEAR THE VIOLENT CALENDAR 166 00 027
CALL
    THE GROSS FLOCK CALL THEM QUAILS, ... 005 00 016
    MOST WIDE YE ARE WHO CALL THIS GUST SIMOOM. 005 00 026
    WE SCARCELY CALL THAT BANQUET FOOD, ... 006 00 031
    SAVE CHRIST! TO CHRIST I LOOK, ON CHRIST I CALL. . . . 016 00 014
    MY PRAYERS I SCARCELY CALL TO PRAY. 018 00 004
    LOVE, O MY GOD, TO CALL THEE LOVE AND LOVE. 019 00 014
    EARS, AND THE CALL OF THE TALL NUN 028 19 007
    JACK'S CALL AND CUE AT LAST! 054 00 030
    YOU, JADED, LET BE! CALL OFF THOUGHTS AWHILE 069 00 010
    WITH POTENT LIPS CALL DOWN CEMENTED TOWERS! 104 00 005
    HOW SHALL I CALL MY LOVE, ' SHE SAID, ... 109 04 003
    ' LORD WILLIAM THEY CALL ME. 109 05 002
    ' AND ALICE THEY CALL ME. ' 109 19 002
    CALL NO SUCH MAIDEN ' MINE ' . THE DEEPER GROWS HER DEARNESS . 152 01 012
    CALL ME ENGLAND'S FAME'S FOND LOVER, ... 156 00 011
    MAY BUT CALL ON YOUR BANES TO MORE CAROUSE. 157 00 030
    BUT CAN PLAINLY CALL THEE LORD AND GOD AS HE! . . . 168 00 014
    THEO. PROCONSUL, -- CALL HIM NEAR -- . . . . . APPEN A 47
CALLED
    HAD CALLED THE SEASONS' CHANGEFUL MOODS 023 00 023
    OF THE MONTH BY MEN CALLED VIRGINAL. 026 00 022
    I CAME WHERE CALLED, AND EYED HIM 054 00 014
    NOR CAN YOU LONG BE, WHAT YOU NOW ARE, CALLED FAIR. . . 059 0L 006
    AND CALLED TO COME AT MEALTIME SHE WOULD NOT! . . . 136 00 033
    BEYOND MAGDALEN AND BY THE BRIDGE, ON A PLACE CALLED THERE THE PLAIN, 142 00 001
CALLING
    SISTER, A SISTER CALLING 028 19 001
    WAS CALLING ' O CHRIST, CHRIST, COME QUICKLY ' : . . . 028 24 007
    SINCE, PROUD, IT CALLS THE CALLING MANLY, GIVES A GUESS . . 063 00 004
CALL'D
    I CALL'D THEM AND I THOUGHT THEM THEN -- 081 00 164
    ALL AS THE MOTH CALL'D UNDERWING ALIGHTED, ... 108 00 001
CALLS
    DEEP CALLS TO DEEP, AND BLACKEST NIGHT 023 00 027
    THE CROSS TO HER SHE CALLS CHRIST TO HER, C 028 24 008
    WITH DELIGHT CALLS TO MIND 042 00 030
    SINCE, PROUD, IT CALLS THE CALLING MANLY, GIVES A GUESS . . 063 00 004
    CUCKOO CALLS CUCKOO UP THE WOOD, ... 081 00 022
    WHEN CUCKOO CALLS AND I MAY HEAR, ... 098 37 001
    BUT THEN HER TETHER CALLS HER! SHE FALLS OFF, . . . 103 00 012

CALLS (CONTINUED)
    OF COUNTRY BIDDER'S CALLS OR LOW 166 00 022
CALM
    ALAS! I RAVE, WHERE CALM IS DUE! 081 00 070
    I CANNOT CALM, I CANNOT HEED. 081 00 072
CALVARY
    TO HERO OF CALVARY, CHRIST,'S FEET -- 028 08 007
CALVARY'S
    FOR US BY CALVARY'S DISTRESS 006 00 017
CAME
    WHEN CHIEFS AND MONARCHS CAME THEIR GIFTS TO LAY 001 02 007
    CAME MIDST THE DRIZZLE TELLING HOW LAST NIGHT 001 14 002
    AND THRO' THEIR PARTING LIDS THERE CAME AND WENT 002 00 011
    AUTUMN-TIME NO EARLIER CAME. 004 00 026
    BUT THEY CAME FROM THE SOUTH. 025 00 013
    THAT CAME WHEN A LINE OF KINGS DID CEASE. 026 00 026
    SHE WAS FIRST OF A FIVE AND CAME 028 20 001
    NOT A DOOMS-DAY DAZZLE IN HIS COMING NOR DARK AS HE CAME! . 028 34 006
    CAME EQUIPPED, DEADLY-ELECTRIC, ... 041 00 024
    HE HAS LOST COUNT WHAT CAME NEXT, POOR BOY, -- 041 00 072
    THIS VERY VERY DAY CAME DOWN TO US AFTER A BOON HE ON . . 048 00 005
    CAME, I SAY, THIS DAY TO IT -- TO A FIRST COMMUNION . . 048 00 008
    I CAME WHERE CALLED, AND EYED HIM 054 00 014
    CRYING WHAT I DO IS ME! FOR THAT I CAME. 057 00 008
    A MOTHER CAME TO MOULD 060 00 104
    BREATHES ONCE AND, QUENCHED FASTER THAN IT CAME, . . . 076 00 003
    THEN CAME THE BENEDICTION. 081 00 099
    AN ANGEL CAME! ' THE JUDGMENT DONE, ... 081 00 104
    OR ELSE THEIR COOINGS CAME FROM BAYS OF TREES, ... 098 02 001
    THEY CAME 098 12 001
    YET THERE CAME ONE WHO SENT HIS FLOCK BEFORE HIM, . . . 107 01 007
    SYLVESTER CAME! THEY WENT BY CUNNOR HILL. 107 03 009
    SOUNDS REACH'D HIM. RICHARD CAME. SYLVESTER SMILED . . . 107 04 024
    CAME RUNNING OVER THE LEA. 109 17 004
    AND SHE CAME OUT TO SEE. 109 24 002
    WHEN YOU CAME FORTH FOR ME? ' 109 33 004
    WHEN I CAME FORTH FOR THEE, ... 109 34 002
    WHO CAME FROM FURTHER THAN THE STARS 115 00 003
    OF BURDEN CAME AND BOW'D MY HEAD. 118 00 011
    I THOUGHT THAT YOU WOULD HAVE WRITTEN: MY BIRTHDAY CAME AND WENT, . 128 00 001
    WHAT WOULD BE A BIRTHDAY LETTER THAT AFTER THE BIRTHDAY CAME? . 128 00 004
    THE WORDS CAME FROM A COURT ACROSS THE WAY. 136 00 023
    DAYS AND DAYS CAME ROUND ABOUT 145 00 023
    YOU CAME BY CAERWYS, SIR? I CAME BY CAERWYS, THERE . . . 152 01 002
    YOU CAME BY CAERWYS, SIR? I CAME BY CAERWYS, THERE . . . 152 01 002
    ROUND AND ROUND THEY CAME AND FLASHED TOWARDS HEAVEN! O THERE, . 152 02 029
    OR THEY GO RICH AS ROSELEAVES HENCE THAT LOATHSOME CAME HITHER! . 152 C 024
    THEO. BUT THEY CAME FROM THE SOUTH. . . . . . . APPEN A 13
CAMPION
    ROUGH-ROBIN OR FIVE-LIPPED CAMPION CLEAR 144 00 015
CANAAN
    TAKE CANAAN WITH YOUR SWORD AND WITH YOUR BOW. 005 00 056
CANCER
    STONE, PALSY, CANCER, COUGH, LUNG-WASTING, WOMB-NOT-BEARING, . 152 C 008
CANDLE
    SOME CANDLE CLEAR BURNS SOMEWHERE I COME BY. 046 00 001
    MEND FIRST AND VITAL CANDLE IN CLOSE HEART'S VAULT! . . . 046 00 010
    OF A FINGERNAIL HELD TO THE CANDLE, C 137 00 002
    WITH TEARS TO PUT HER CANDLE OUT! 145 00 024
CANDLEMAS
    CANDLEMAS, LADY DAY! 042 00 005
CANDLES
    BY SHINE OF CANDLES THREE, ... 109 01 002
CANDOUR
    BUT CANDOUR NEVER HURT THE DEAREST FRIEND. 094 00 008
CANDYCOLOURED
    THAT LEANS ALONG THE LOINS OF HILLS, WHERE A CANDYCOLOURED, C . 159 00 005
CANNON
    O WELCOME THERE THEIR STEEL OR CANNON. 156 00 017
CANVAS
    AND CANVAS AND COMPASS, THE WHORL AND THE WHEEL . . . 028 14 007
CANVASS
    TO CANVASS THE RETIREMENT OF THE LARK 113 00 002
CANVASSING
    ARE SHUT AGAINST THE CANVASSING OF ART. 126 00 006
CAP
    HIS CAP SHALL BE SHINING FUR, ... 124 00 013
CAPABLE
    IS VERY CAPABLE OF STRONG AFFECTION 094 00 013
CAPES
    THEY SEEM TO FOLD THE HILLS WITH GOLDEN CAPES! . . . 104 00 011
CAPITAL
    STOOD CAPITAL, EMINENT, . . . GONFALON BEARER . . . 098 28 005
CAPP'D
    HER FINGER-LONG NEW HORNS ARE CAPP'D WITH BLACK! . . . 099 00 007
CAPS
    CAPS, CLEARS, AND CLINCHES ALL -- 042 00 044

CASQUE
    DROOP'D O'ER THE BROWS LIKE HECTOR'S CASQUE, AND SWAY'D   •   •   •   002 00 042
CAST
    INTO ALL SEASONS, THOUGH NO WINTER CAST   • • • • • • 014 01 005
    THAT DARES TO CAST ITS SEARCHING SIGHT   • • • • • • 023 00 029
    HE WAS TO CURE THE EXTREMITY WHERE HE HAD CAST HER;   • • • 028 28 006
    AND, CAST BY CONSCIENCE OUT, SPENDSAVOUR SALT?   • • • • 046 00 014
    I CAST FOR COMFORT I CAN NO MORE GET   • • • • • 069 00 005
    AND, SWARTER STILL, THE ROLLING PINES SHOULD CAST   • • • 090 00 005
    WHEN EYES THAT CAST ABOUT IN HEIGHTS OF HEAVEN   • • • • 113 00 001
    NO PIECE MATCHED THOSE EYES KEPT MOST PART MUCH CAST DOWN   • • 152 02 026
    WHILE SICK MEN SHALL CAST SIGHS, OF SWEET HEALTH ALL DESPAIRING,   • 152 C 003
    THEIR CRUTCHES SHALL CAST FROM THEM, ON HEELS OF AIR DEPARTING,   • 152 C 023
    JESUS TO CAST ONE THOUGHT UPON   • • • / • • • 167 00 001
CASTARA
    WHY SHOULD I GO BECAUSE CASTARA GOES?   • • • • • • 125 00 032
    BUT WHY THEN SHOULD CASTARA WEIGH WITH ME?   • • • • 125 00 034
    TO THESE CASTARA IS RAIN OR BREEZE OR SPRING,   • • • 125 00 048
    TO SAY I GO BECAUSE CASTARA GOES;   • • • • • 125 00 054
    MUCH CAUSE TO GO BECAUSE CASTARA GOES.   • • • • • 125 00 059
CASTARA'S
    THAT THIS IS TRUE OF: 'TIS CASTARA'S SELF;   • • • • 125 00 056
CASTILIAN
    AMONGST CASTILIAN BARRENS MOUNTAIN-BOUND;   • • • • 001 01 002
CATARACT
    TO QUENCH THE FINE-DRAWN CATARACT;   • • • • • 077 00 090
CATCH
    AND BID TO CATCH HIM ERE THE DROP OF DAY.   • • • • 020 00 002
    AS KINGFISHERS CATCH FIRE, DRAGONFLIES DRAW FLAME!   • • 057 00 001
    LACE, LATCH OR CATCH OR KEY TO KEEP C   • • • • • 059 0L 001
    CATCH SUNLIGHT AND ONE STRAIN OF STUPID PRAISE.   • • 098 32 002
CATCHES
    FALLING FLAKES, TO THE THRONG THAT CATCHES AND QUAILS   • • 028 24 006
CAUGHT
    I CAUGHT THIS MORNING MORNING'S MINION, KING-   • • • 036 00 001
    CAUGHT ON THE DANK-YTRESSED TREES,   • • • • • 077 00 106
    CAUGHT FROM ANGELS' WINGS IN HEAVEN,   • • • • • 077 00 110
    SHE CAUGHT THE CRYING OF THOSE THREE,   • • • • 145 00 029
    WHAT WAS THAT ECHO CAUGHT ANIGH ME,   • • • • • 160 00 020
CAUSE
    I KNOW THE SADNESS BUT THE CAUSE KNOW NOT.   • • • • 002 00 125
    GROWS LESS AND LESS SWEET TO HIM, AND KNOWS NO CAUSE,   • • 014 03 014
    SIR, LIFE UPON THY CAUSE. SEE, BANKS AND BRAKES   • • 074 00 009
    I KNOW I MAR MY CAUSE WITH WORDS: • • • • • 081 00 030
    AND IF IT IS WHY THERE IS CAUSE ENOUGH   • • • • 125 00 053
    MUCH CAUSE TO GO BECAUSE CASTARA GOES.   • • • • 125 00 059
CAVERNOUS
    AND THEN GOES OUT INTO THE CAVERNOUS DARK.   • • • 103 00 016
CEASE
    I CEASE THE MOURNING AND THE ABJECT FAST,   • • • • 014 01 008
    THAT CAME WHEN A LINE OF KINGS DID CEASE,   • • • • 026 00 026
CEASELESS
    THE MOTES IN CEASELESS EDDY SHINE AND FALL   • • • • 001 12 004
CELL
    BUT BOTH WILL SHARE ONE CELL. -- THIS WAS GOOD NEWS, GWENVREWI.   • 152 01 009
CELLS
    YET BOTH DROOP DEADLY SOMETIMES IN THEIR CELLS   • • • 039 00 007
CEMENTED
    WITH POTENT LIPS CALL DOWN CEMENTED TOWERS;   • • • 104 00 005
CENSERS
    WHAT RELISH SHALL THE CENSERS SEND   • • • • • 022 00 019
CENTRAL
    A FORTRESS OF TRUE FAITH, AND CENTRAL STAND   • • • 001 05 003
    WERE EYES OF CENTRAL PRIMROSE; BLUEBELLS RAN   • • • 098 10 002
    AND SPINS HER SKIRTS OUT, WHILE HER CENTRAL STAR   • • 103 00 007
CENTRE
    WOULD NOT PUT OUT SOME TINY GOLDEN CENTRE.   • • • 098 22 006
    THE MOUTHED CENTRE OF A VIOLET.   • • • • • 102 01 071
    AND I MUST HAVE THE CENTRE IN MY HEART   • • • • 102 03 007
CENTREINGS
    ROUNDS ITS STILL-PURPLING CENTREINGS OF CLOUD.   • • 098 30 003
CENTRE-DARKS
    ROUNDS ITS STILL-PURPLING CENTRE-DARKS OF CLOUD.   • • 098 30 006
CENTRES
    THAT MANY CENTRES FOUND IN MANY HEARTS?   • • • • 107 02 005
    WITH CENTRES DULY TOUCH'D AND NESTLIKE SPOTS, --   • • 107 04 007
CENTURION
    VESPILLO MY CENTURION HACKS OUT   • • • • • 080 09 005
CERES
    TO GOLDEN-GIRDLED CYPRIS, -- CERES THERE   • • • • 001 11 003
CERTAINTY
    THOU WHO CANST BEST ACCEPT THE CERTAINTY   • • • • 013 00 005
CHAFF
    WHY? THAT MY CHAFF MIGHT FLY: MY GRAIN LIE, SHEER AND CLEAR.   • 064 00 009
CHAINED
    CHRIST'S ONLY CHARITY CHARMED AND CHAINED THESE TWO.   • • 136 00 012
CHAINS
    THIS INDIGNITY OF CHAINS.   • • • • • • • 160 00 014

CHAIR
THREE RIVALS THRONG HER GARDEN CHAIR, ... 083 00 010
CHALKY
OF WRINGING TREE-TOPS, CHALKY LANES, ... 077 00 135
CHAMFER'D
ENRICHED POSTS ARE CHAMFER'D: EVERYWHERE 096 07 003
CHAMP-WHITE
HIS CHARGE THROUGH THE CHAMP-WHITE WATER-IN-A-WALLOW, ... 041 00 048
CHANCE
ED ROME? BUT GOD TO A NATION DEALT THAT DAY'S DEAR CHANCE. . . . 062 00 008
CHANCEQUARRIED
BUILT OF CHANCEQUARRIED, SELFQUAINED, HOAR-HUSKED ROCKS 159 00 037
CHANGE
HE FATHERS-FORTH WHOSE BEAUTY IS PAST CHANGE: 037 00 010
AND WATCHES CHANGE UPON THE SEA: 077 00 032
BUT THIS DISTEMPER'D COURT WILL CHANGE IT ALL: -- 125 00 057
THE UNCHANGING REGISTER OF CHANGE 130 00 005
O LOVELY EASE IN CHANGE OF PLACE! 130 00 027
IS CORPSE NOW, CANNOT CHANGE! MY OTHER SELF, THIS SOUL, . . . 152 02 062
WHY SHOULD I CHANGE A SABINE DALE 166 00 047
CHANGED
' YET AS HE CHANGED HIS MIGHTY STOPS 021 00 043
ITS DEAREST CHANGED TO BORES. 114 00 016
LIKE AIR HE CHANGED IN CHOICE, ... 148 00 018
CHANGEFUL
FAIR RELICS TOO THE CHANGEFUL MOOR HAD LEFT 001 08 001
THAN CHANGEFUL POMP OF COURTS IS AYE MORE WONDERFUL. . . . 001 15 009
HAD CALLED THE SEASONS' CHANGEFUL MOODS 023 00 023
CHANGELESS
FROM BOTH OF WHOM A CHANGELESS NOTE IS HEARD. 019 00 004
CHANGING
THEIR CHANGING FEET IN FLICKER ALL THE TIME 107 01 013
HIS PLEASURE TO THE CHANGING CLIME, ... 124 00 006
C HIS PLEASURE TO THE CHANGING CLIME, ... 124 00 010
CHANG'D
CHANG'D TO A FLOWER: AND THERE, WITH PLACID EYE 001 11 008
CHANNEL
HIS CHANNEL UNDER CLAMMY COATS 003 00 011
ALL UNDER CHANNEL TO BURY IN A BEACH HER 041 00 049
CHANNELLED
SEEMS BY A DIVINE DOOM CHANNELLED, NOR DO I CRY 048 00 041
CHAOTIC
AS ERST UPON CHAOTIC FLOODS 023 00 021
CHAPEL-SIDE
THUS, I COME UNDERNEATH THIS CHAPEL-SIDE, ... 012 02 001
CHAPLETED
WITH LACE OF ROSY WEED WERE CHAPLETED: 002 00 059
CHAPLETS
CHAPLETS FOR DISHEVELLED HAIR, ... 024 00 021
CHAPTERED
BUT CHAPTERED IN THE CHIEF OF BLISS 145 00 002
CHARACTER
MISS STORY'S CHARACTER! TOO MUCH YOU ASK, ... 094 00 001
HER CHARACTER SHE DOES NOT REALIZE. 094 00 025
CHARACTERED
AND A FEW LEAVES NOT LILY-WHITE BUT CHARACTERED OVER WITH BLACKS. . 128 00 016
CHARGE
HIS CHARGE THROUGH THE CHAMP-WHITE WATER-IN-A-WALLOW, ... 041 00 048
WE WILL CHARGE OUR FLOCKS THAT THEY NOT FEED. 098 15 002
CHARGED
FURRED SNOWS, CHARGED TUFT ABOVE TUFT, TOWER 030 00 031
THE WORLD IS CHARGED WITH THE GRANDEUR OF GOD. 031 00 001
CHARGED, STEEPED SKY WILL NOT 060 00 080
CHARITABLE
CHARITABLE! NOT LIVE THIS TORMENTED MIND 069 00 003
CHARITY
IN GRACE THAT IS CHARITY, GRACE THAT IS LOVE. 027 00 046
DRAW ME BY CHARITY, MOTHER OF MINE. 027 00 048
DIVINE CHARITY, DEAR CHARITY, ... 052 00 007
DIVINE CHARITY, DEAR CHARITY, ... 052 00 007
LET CHARITY THUS BEGIN AT HOME, -- 081 00 124
CHRIST'S ONLY CHARITY CHARMED AND CHAINED THESE TWO. . . . 136 00 012
I WILL APPEAR, LOOKING SUCH CHARITY 140 00 003
FILLED FULL OF CHARITY, ... APPEN D 41
CHARITY'S
OUR HEARTS' CHARITY'S HEARTH'S FIRE, C 028 35 008
CHARLES'S
AND CHARLES'S WAIN, THE WONDROUS SEVEN, ... 030 00 017
CHARM
HAVE LOST THAT CHEER AND CHARM OF EARTH'S PAST PRIME! . . . 035 00 012
THERE WAS A CHARM WOULD COUNTERVAIL 081 00 078
IT'S THE DAY THAT MAKES THE CHARM: NO AFTER-WORDS COULD SUCCEED . 128 00 007
CHARMED
CHRIST'S ONLY CHARITY CHARMED AND CHAINED THESE TWO. . . . 136 00 012
CHARMS
THOSE CHARMS ACCEPTED OF MY INMOST THOUGHT, ... 012 01 009
C FOR NOW CHARMS, ARMS, WHAT BANS OFF BAD 048 00 034

CHARMS   (CONTINUED)
    HAMPSTEAD WAS NEVER BRIGHT; AND WHATEVER MISS CULLY'S CHARMS   • • 128 00 011
CHARNELHOUSE-GRA
    HIS CHARNELHOUSE-GRATE RIBS BETWEEN.   • • • • • • • 004 00 010
CHART
    DOOMSDAY AND DEATH -- WHOSE DATELESS THOUGHT MUST CHART   • • • 126 00 003
CHARTED
    BECAUSE ITS PLACE IS KNOWN AND CHARTED THERE.   • • • • • 102 03 012
CHARTER
    HAS NOT A CHARTER THAT ITS SAP SHALL LAST • • • • • • 014 01 004
CHASE
    BUT I MUST YIELD THE CHASE, OR REST AND EAT. -- • • • • 020 00 011
CHASMS
    OF SEAMEN WHELM'D IN CHASMS OF THE MID-MAIN.   • • • • 002 00 120
CHASTENING
    LET PATIENCE WITH HER CHASTENING WAND   • • • • • 023 00 045
CHASTITY
    BREATHING BLOOM OF A CHASTITY IN MANSEX FINE.   • • • 048 00 016
CHAUNT
    AN ANTIQUE CHAUNT AND IN AN UNKNOWN TONGUE.   • • • • 002 00 131
CHEAP
    FRIGHTFUL, SHEER, NO-MAN-FATHOMED. HOLD THEM CHEAP   • • • 065 00 010
CHEBAR'S
    ON CHEBAR'S BANKS, AND WHY THEY WENT   • • • • • 077 00 049
CHECK
    THE WOMAN'S WAILING, THE CRYING OF CHILD WITHOUT CHECK -- • • • 028 17 006
CHEE
    TEEVO CHEEVO CHEEVIO CHEE: • • • • • • • 138 00 001
CHEEK
    CHEEK AND THE WIMPLED LIP.   • • • • • • • 049 00 002
    'S CHEEK CRIMSON; CURLS C   • • • • • • • 071 00 010
    CRISP LIPS, STRAIGHT NOSE, AND TENDER-SLANTED CHEEK.   • • • 136 00 016
CHEEKS
    TILL DIMPLED JOY STEALS O'ER ITS CHEEKS. • • • • • 023 00 052
    CHEEKS; RIGHT, RUDE OF FEATURE,   • • • • • • 041 00 050
    HIS TEAR-TRICKED CHEEKS OF FLAME   • • • • • • 054 00 036
    THEIR CHEEKS MOVED AND THE BONES THEREIN. • • • • • 092 00 003
    TO COLOUR AS SMOOTH AND FRESH AS CHEEKS OF ROSES. • • • • 108 00 004
    HIS CHEEKS THE FORTH-AND-FLAUNTING SUN   • • • • • 144 00 002
CHEER
    HAVE LOST THAT CHEER AND CHARM OF EARTH'S PAST PRIME;   • • 035 00 012
    STOLE JOY, WOULD LAUGH, CHEER. C   • • • • • • 064 00 011
    CHEER WHOM THOUGH? THE HERO WHOSE HEAVEN-HANDLING FLUNG ME, FOOT TROD 064 00 012
    THAT STRUGGLING SHOULD NOT SEAR HIM, A GIFT SHOULD CHEER HIM   • • 142 00 008
       BUT MORE CHEER IS WHEN I MAY V • • • • • • 149 B 010
CHEERED
    PEACE AND FOOD CHEERED ME WHERE FOUR ROUGH WAYS MEET.   • • • 020 00 012
CHEERING
    FOR HOW TO THE HEART'S CHEERING • • • • • • • 028 26 001
CHEERLESS
    STRIKE, CHURL; HURL, CHEERLESS WIND, THEN; HELTERING HAIL • • • 154 00 001
CHEER'S
    CHEER'S DEATH, WOULD FOLLOW • • • • • • • 041 00 047
CHEEVIO
    TEEVO CHEEVO CHEEVIO CHEE: • • • • • • • 138 00 001
    CHEEVIO: I WHEN THE CRY WITHIN • • • • • • 138 00 034
CHEEVO
    TEEVO CHEEVO CHEEVIO CHEE: • • • • • • • 138 00 001
CHEQUERS
    THOSE CROOKED ROUGH-SCORED CHEQUERS MAY BE PIECED • • • • 011 00 004
CHERRY
    WITH SILVER-SURFED CHERRY • • • • • • • • 042 00 040
CHERVIL
    WITH FRETTY CHERVIL, LOOK, AND FRESH WIND SHAKES • • • • 074 00 011
CHESTNUT
    LIKE A CUPP'D CHESTNUT DAMASK'D WITH DARK BREAKS. • • • • 099 00 012
    SO LATE THE HOAR GREEN CHESTNUT BREAKS A BUD.   • • • • 105 00 009
CHESTNUT-FALLS
    FRESH-FIRECOAL CHESTNUT-FALLS; FINCHES' WINGS: • • • • 037 00 004
CHESTNUT-FANS
    THE CHESTNUT-FANS ARE LOOSELY FLIRTING.   • • • • • 078 00 005
CHEVALIER
    TIMES TOLD LOVELIER, MORE DANGEROUS, O MY CHEVALIER!   • • • 036 00 011
CHEVY
    TOSSED PILLOWS FLAUNT FORTH, THEN CHEVY ON AN AIR- C   • • • 072 00 001
CHEW'D
    THEY CHEW'D THE CUD IN HOLLOWS DEEP. • • • • • • 092 00 002
CHIEF
    BUT CHAPTERED IN THE CHIEF OF BLISS • • • • • • 145 00 002
    THE YOUNG CHIEF OF THE BLESS'D OF HEAVEN • • • • • • 160 00 011
CHIEFS
    WHEN CHIEFS AND MONARCHS CAME THEIR GIFTS TO LAY • • • • 001 02 007
CHIEFTAIN
    AND CHOOSE FOR CHIEFTAIN ONE.   • • • • • • 148 00 028
CHIEFWOE
    MY CRIES HEAVE, HERDS-LONG; HUDDLE IN A MAIN, A CHIEF-   • • • 065 00 005
    WOE, WORLD-SORROW; ON AN AGE-OLD ANVIL WINCE AND SING --   • • • 065 00 006

CHILD
    HERE PLAY'D THE VIRGIN MOTHER WITH HER CHILD   •   •   •   •   •   •   001 10 004
    SPRING'S ONE DAUGHTER, THE SWEET CHILD MAY. •   •   •   .026 00 002
    THE WOMAN'S WAILING, THE CRYING OF CHILD WITHOUT CHECK -- •   •   028 17 006
    MOST, O MAID'S CHILD, THY CHOICE AND WORTHY THE WINNING. •   •   •   033 00 014
    ' BUT TELL ME, CHILD, YOUR CHOICE! WHAT SHALL I BUY •   •   •   047 00 001
    THY TEARS THAT TOUCHED MY HEART, CHILD, FELIX, POOR FELIX RANDAL! •   053 00 011
    NOW NO MATTER, CHILD, THE NAME! •   •   •   •   •   •   •   055 00 010
    FOLD HOME, FAST FOLD THY CHILD. •   •   •   •   •   •   060 00 126
    CHURLSGRACE, TOO, CHILD OF AMANSSTRENGTH, HOW IT HANGS OR HURLS •   071 00 012
    WITH A TWO YEARS CHILD AT HER KNEE. •   •   •   •   •   109 16 002
    AND MOTHER HAVE NO MILK FOR CHILD, •   •   •   •   •   114 00 007
    WITHIN HER WOMB THE CHILD WAS QUICK. •   •   •   •   •   145 00 039
    ' THE CHILD IS FATHER TO THE MAN. ' •   •   •   •   •   147 00 001
    ' THE CHILD IS FATHER TO THE MAN. ' •   •   •   •   •   147 00 004
    ' THE MAN IS FATHER TO THE CHILD. ' •   •   •   •   •   147 00 006
    ' THE CHILD IS FATHER TO THE MAN! ' •   •   •   •   •   147 00 007
    BAD I AM, BUT YET THY CHILD. •   •   •   •   •   •   155 00 013
    AND SHE SHALL CHILD THEM ON THE NEW-WORLD STRAND. ' •   •   158 00 004
    AH CHILD, NO PERSIAN-PERFECT ART! •   •   •   •   •   •   165 00 001
    CHILD, THAT KNOW NOT MAN? ' •   •   •   •   •   •   APPEN D 14
CHILDBEARING
    BY THY SWEET CHILDBEARING, •   •   •   •   •   •   APPEN D 19
CHILD-LIKE
    AND LEAD ME CHILD-LIKE BY THE HAND •   •   •   •   •   023 00 047
CHILDLESS
    AND RISEN SONS: YET ARE THE CHILDLESS FREE •   •   •   123 00 002
CHILDREN
    AND DID THE CHILDREN OF HIS BRAINS ENJOY •   •   •   •   097 00 003
CHILDREN'S
    FROM TEARS SHED OVER CHILDREN'S GRAVES. •   •   •   •   123 00 003
CHILD'S
    AN OUR DAY'S GOD'S OWN GALAHAD. THOUGH THIS CHILD'S DRIFT •   •   048 00 040
CHILDS
    HEAVEN WHOM SHE CHILDS US BY. •   •   •   •   •   •   149 A 011
    HEAVEN WITH IT WHOM SHE CHILDS THINGS BY. V •   •   •   149 B 013
CHILL
    I HAD SLEPT A LITTLE AND WAS CHILL. •   •   •   •   •   021 00 016
    WHEN CHILL WOODS WAKE AND THINK OF MORN, •   •   •   •   077 00 023
CHILLING
    CHILLING REMEMBRANCE OF MY DAYS OF OLD •   •   •   •   017 00 005
CHIME
    LET THE CHIME OF A RHYME •   •   •   •   •   •   029 00 019
    THERE WAS NO BLEAT OF EWE, NO CHIME OF WETHER, •   •   107 01 005
CHIPS
    THE ENDS OF THE CRISP BUDS SHE CHIPS •   •   •   •   098 14 001
CHIVALRY
    WITH FORM DIVINE, A FIERY CHIVALRY -- •   •   •   •   001 07 008
CHIVALRY'S
    OUR THOUGHTS' CHIVALRY'S THRONG'S LORD. C •   •   •   028 35 008
CHOICE
    MOST, O MAID'S CHILD, THY CHOICE AND WORTHY THE WINNING. •   •   033 00 014
    ' BUT TELL ME, CHILD, YOUR CHOICE! WHAT SHALL I BUY •   •   047 00 001
    HER CHOICE IN ROSES KNOWS BY HEART! •   •   •   •   083 00 022
    LIKE AIR HE CHANGED IN CHOICE, •   •   •   •   •   148 00 018
    REASON, SELFDISPOSAL, CHOICE OF BETTER OR WORSE WAY, •   152 02 061
CHOICEST
    THE CHOICEST REMNANTS THENCE: -- SUCH HOME FORLORN •   •   001 15 003
    YE HAVE KEPT YOUR CHOICEST WINE -- •   •   •   •   024 00 009
CHOIR
    WITH HEAVENLY CITHERN FROM HIGH CHOIR, •   •   •   •   077 00 013
CHOKE
    AND THEN -- I CHOKE TO TELL THIS OUT -- •   •   •   •   080 09 002
    SHOULD CHOKE SWEET VIRTUE'S GLORY IS TIME'S GREAT GUILT. •   136 00 002
    SHE WAS WITH THE CHOKE OF WOE. -- •   •   •   •   145 00 060
    AND SPITING SNOWS TO CHOKE THE GREEN. •   •   •   •   166 00 032
CHOKING
    THE CLOGGED BROOK RUNS WITH CHOKING SOUND •   •   •   003 00 009
CHOOSE
    CAN SOMETHING, HOPE, WISH DAY COME, NOT CHOOSE NOT TO BE. •   •   064 00 004
    I CHOOSE ONE! BUT WHEN I DESIRE •   •   •   •   •   080 10 001
    CHOOSE, ONE FOR HELL AND ONE FOR HEAVEN! ' •   •   •   081 00 106
    AND CHOOSE FOR CHIEFTAIN ONE. •   •   •   •   •   148 00 028
CHORDS
    OR STRETCH'D CHORDS TUNEABLE ON TURTLE'S SHELL! •   •   002 00 129
    TO WHAT THE CHORDS OF ANGELS ARE! •   •   •   •   •   077 00 046
CHOSE
    ' AND IF I CHOSE A LOVE TO WED •   •   •   •   •   109 10 001
    PERHAPS IT WAS FOR THIS SHE CHOSE THE PLACE. •   •   111 00 015
CHRISM
    MELT AS FROM A HEAVENLY CHRISM! •   •   •   •   •   077 00 062
CHRIST
    CHRIST OUR SACRIFICE IS MADE! •   •   •   •   •   006 00 010
    CHRIST AT ALL HAZARDS FRUIT HATH SHEWED. •   •   •   007 00 010
    NO, BUT FOR CHRIST WHO HATH FOREKNOWN AND LOVED THEE. •   013 00 014
    SAVE CHRIST: TO CHRIST I LOOK, ON CHRIST I CALL. •   •   016 00 014
    SAVE CHRIST: TO CHRIST I LOOK, ON CHRIST I CALL. •   •   016 00 014

CHRIST   (CONTINUED)
     SAVE CHRIST; TO CHRIST I LOOK, ON CHRIST I CALL. 016 00 014
     UPON CHRIST THROW ALL AWAY; 024 00 005
     CHRIST JESUS, OUR LORD, HER GOD AND HER SON. 027 00 028
     THY TERROR, O CHRIST, O GOD; 028 02 004
     AND CIPHER OF SUFFERING CHRIST. 028 22 002
     WAS CALLING ' O CHRIST, CHRIST, COME QUICKLY ' ; 028 24 007
     WAS CALLING ' O CHRIST, CHRIST, COME QUICKLY ' ; 028 24 007
     THE CROSS TO HER SHE CALLS CHRIST TO HER, C 028 24 008
     IPSE, THE ONLY ONE, CHRIST, KING, HEAD; 028 28 005
     THE CHRIST OF THE FATHER COMPASSIONATE, C 028 33 008
     CHRIST HOME, CHRIST AND HIS MOTHER AND ALL HIS HALLOWS. 032 00 014
     CHRIST HOME, CHRIST AND HIS MOTHER AND ALL HIS HALLOWS. 032 00 014
     BEFORE IT CLOUD, CHRIST, LORD, AND SOUR WITH SINNING, ...   033 00 012
     CHRIST MINDS: CHRIST'S INTEREST, WHAT TO AVOW OR AMEND 040 00 012
     BUT TO CHRIST LORD OF THUNDER 041 00 109
     FORTH CHRIST FROM CUPBOARD FETCHED, HOW FAIN I OF FEET 048 00 010
     REALM BOTH CHRIST IS HEIR TO AND THERE REIGNS, ...   048 00 032
     CHRIST, FOR CHRIST PLAYS IN TEN THOUSAND PLACES, ...   057 00 012
     CHRIST, FOR CHRIST PLAYS IN TEN THOUSAND PLACES, ...   057 00 012
     BE CHRIST OUR SAVIOUR STILL. 060 00 054
     MORE CHRIST AND BAFFLE DEATH; 060 00 067
     MARK CHRIST OUR KING. HE KNOWS WAR, SERVED THIS SOLDIERING THROUGH;   063 00 009
     WERE I COME O'ER AGAIN ' CRIES CHRIST ' IT SHOULD BE THIS ' .   .   .   063 00 014
     BROTHERS AND SISTERS ARE IN CHRIST NOT NEAR 066 00 003
     I AM ALL AT ONCE WHAT CHRIST IS, SINCE HE WAS WHAT I AM, AND   .   .   072 00 022
     ON CHRIST THEY DO AND ON THE MARTYR MAY; 073 00 005
     IS THIS, FROM CHRIST TO BE SHUT OUT. 080 01 002
     BUT YET THEY SAY CHRIST COMES AT THE LAST DAY. 080 01 006
     SIR! CHRIST! AGAINST THIS MULTITUDE I STRAIN. --   .   .   .   .   .   o   080 08 005
     FOR LOVE AND GREATER GLORY OF CHRIST. 118 00 004
     CHRIST LIVED IN MARGARET CLITHEROE. 145 00 028
     HOPE HOLDS TO CHRIST THE MIND'S OWN MIRROR OUT 151 00 001
     THERE'S NONE BUT TRUTH CAN STEAD YOU. CHRIST IS TRUTH. 157 00 020
     O THOU OUR REMINDER OF CHRIST CRUCIFIED, ...   168 00 017
     IN HER WAS CHRIST CONTAINED ANON, ...   APPEN D 35
CHRISTENS
     CHRISTENS HER WILD-WORST BEST. C 028 24 008
CHRISTIAN
     I FIND ANOTHER CHRISTIAN HERE. 025 00 042
     THEO. I FIND ANOTHER CHRISTIAN HERE. .   .   .   .   APPEN A 48
CHRISTIANS
     THE PANG OF TARTARUS, CHRISTIANS HOLD. 080 01 001
CHRIST-DONE
     AND CRY ' O CHRIST-DONE DEED! SO GOD-MADE-FLESH DOES TOO; .   .   .   063 00 013
CHRIST-ED
     THE CHRIST-ED BEAUTY OF HER MIND 145 00 015
CHRISTMAS
     FOR A LETTER COMES AT LAST! (SHALL I SAY BEFORE CHRISTMAS IS COME?)   128 00 019
     NOW BEGIN, ON CHRISTMAS DAY. 129 00 009
CHRIST'S
     HOW SOLDIERS PLATTING THORNS AROUND CHRIST'S HEAD 007 00 004
     OF THE GOSPEL PROFFER, A PRESSURE, A PRINCIPLE, CHRIST'S GIFT. .   .   028 04 008
     CHRIST'S LILY AND BEAST OF THE WASTE WOOD; 028 20 006
     CHRIST MINDS: CHRIST'S INTEREST, WHAT TO AVOW OR AMEND   .   .   .   040 00 012
     TELLS MARY HER MIRTH TILL CHRIST'S BIRTH 042 00 046
     BY IT, HEAVENS, BEFALL HIM! AS A HEART CHRIST'S DARLING, DAUNTLESS;   048 00 014
     JUST SUCH SLIPS OF SOLDIERY CHRIST'S ROYAL RATION. 048 00 028
     AND HOLD AT CHRIST'S EMPLOYMENT. 049 00 014
     CHRIST'S ONLY CHARITY CHARMED AND CHAINED THESE TWO. 136 00 012
CHRISTUS
     I TRY THE CHRISTUS O'ER AGAIN. 080 08 004
CHRIST,'S
     TO HERO OF CALVARY, CHRIST,'S FEET -- 028 08 007
CHRYSOLITE
     SAPPHIRE, JACINTH, CHRYSOLITE, ...   077 00 119
CHURCH
     BUILD HIS CHURCH AND DECK HIS SHRINE, ...   024 00 007
CHURCH-TOWER
     THAT BEAD THE PLAIN; DID EVER HAVERING CHURCH-TOWER 100 00 006
CHURL
     BLINDNESS! A LEARNED FOOL AND WELL-BRED CHURL 102 03 032
     A LEARNED FOOL INDEED AND WELL-BRED CHURL V 102 03 038
     STRIKE, CHURL; HURL, CHEERLESS WIND, THEN; HELTERING HAIL .   .   .   154 00 001
CHURLSGRACE
     CHURLSGRACE, TOO, CHILD OF AMANSSTRENGTH, HOW IT HANGS OR HURLS .   071 00 012
CHURNING
     AND CHURNING IN THE MILL. 021 00 046
CIEL'D
     AND MELTS AMIDST ANOTHER; CIEL'D ON HIGH 001 06 008
CINQUEFOIL
     STIGMA, SIGNAL, CINQUEFOIL TOKEN 028 22 007
CIPHER
     AND CIPHER OF SUFFERING CHRIST. 028 22 002
CIRCLE
     AND EACH A DINTED CIRCLE. THE GRASS WAS RED 107 04 011
     WHAT I DID ASK THEN WAS A CIRCLE OF ROSE-RED SEALING-WAX .   .   .   128 00 015

CIRCLED
TO DRIFT IN AIR, THE CIRCLED EARTH 077 00 069
CIRCLED THE SAFE FLANKS OF THE BULKY HILLS. 125 00 010
CIRCLE-CITADELS
THE BRIGHT BOROUGHS, THE CIRCLE-CITADELS THERE! 032 00 003
CIRCLES
BLADES OF MILAN IN CIRCLES RANG'D, GREW RUST 001 12 008
CIRCLET
CIRCLET OF ASTRAL FLOWERETS -- DIADEM'D 002 00 061
CIRCLING
LET ME BE TO THEE AS THE CIRCLING BIRD, ... 019 00 001
CITE
I'LL CITE NO FURTHER WHAT THE INITIATE KNOW. 119 00 010
CITHERN
WITH HEAVENLY CITHERN FROM HIGH CHOIR, ... 077 00 013
CITIES
THE TREASURE FROM ALL CITIES. 104 00 013
CITY
NO, I SHOULD LOVE THE CITY LESS 015 00 021
I SEE THE CITY PIGEONS VEER, ... 015 00 027
TOWERY CITY AND BRANCHY BETWEEN TOWERS! 044 00 001
THE CITY TIRES TO DEATH, ... 133 00 012
CLAD
GRANT THAT CLOSE-FOLDED PEACE THAT CLAD 077 00 041
I AM WARMLY CLAD. 132 00 004
CLAIM
WIDER, MORE WHOLESALE; ONE WITH CLAIM 166 00 010
CLAMMY
HIS CHANNEL UNDER CLAMMY COATS 003 00 011
FROM HANDS NOW CLAMMY WITH STRANGE BLOOD. 080 10 004
OF NERVE; THE CLAMMY BALL WAS DRY. 081 00 098
THE MORE SOME MONSTROUS HAND GROPES WITH CLAMMY FINGERS THERE, . 152 01 014
CLAMMYISH
FAST OR THEY IN CLAMMYISH LASHTENDER COMBS CREEP . . . . 149 A 005
CLANK
DEATH'S BONES FELL IN WITH SUDDEN CLANK 092 00 012
CLARION-CLEAR
NOW RINGING CLARION-CLEAR TO WHENCE IT ROSE 002 00 134
CLARIONS
THEIR CLARIONS FROM ALL CORNERS OF THE FIELD 104 00 004
CLARISSA
YOU ASK WHY CAN'T CLARISSA HOLD HER TONGUE. 096 04 001
CLASPED
CLUTCHED HANDS THROUGH CLASPED KNEES! 054 00 021
A CUSP STILL CLASPED HIM, C 137 00 005
CLASP'D
HER BARRED FINGERS CLASP'D UPON HER EYES, ... 111 00 006
CLASSIC
THIS WAS NO CLASSIC TEMPLE ORDER'D ROUND 001 07 001
CLATTERING
ADOWN THE CLATTERING GULLIES SWEPT THE RAIN! . . . 001 13 002
CLAUDE
THE SKILL OF DREAMY CLAUDE, AND TITIAN'S MELLOW GLOOM. . . 001 10 009
CLAY
TO PLASH WITH COOL FEET THE CLAY JUICY SOIL. . . . 005 00 050
YEA IRON IS MINGLED WITH MY CLAY, ... 018 00 010
NOR TEARS, NOR TEARS THIS CLAY UNCOUTH 018 00 013
BUT FRAIL CLAY, NAY BUT FOUL CLAY, HERE IT IS; THE HEART, . . 063 00 003
BUT FRAIL CLAY, NAY BUT FOUL CLAY, HERE IT IS; THE HEART, . . 063 00 003
CLAYFIELD'S
NOR CLOSE THE CLAYFIELD'S SHARDED SORES, ... 114 00 014
CLEAN
AND CLEAN OF EVERY STAIN US MAKE . . . . . APPEN D 46
CLEANER
ONE WITH MORE CONSCIENCE, CLEANER FAME! 166 00 012
CLEAR
A SINGING BIRD IN MORNING CLEAR 021 00 041
SOME CANDLE CLEAR BURNS SOMEWHERE I COME BY. . . . 046 00 001
WHY? THAT MY CHAFF MIGHT FLY; MY GRAIN LIE, SHEER AND CLEAR. . 064 00 009
NOT OF CLEAR SKIES, BUT STORM TO BE. 080 06 004
THEY ALL COME HERE AND STAND BEFORE ME CLEAR . . . 080 08 003
PHRENZY, BUT EDGED AND CLEAR OF BRAIN 081 00 052
ROUGH-ROBIN OR FIVE-LIPPED CAMPION CLEAR 144 00 015
CLEAREST-SELVED
BUT QUENCH HER BONNIEST, DEAREST TO HER, HER CLEAREST-SELVED SPARK . 072 00 010
CLEARS
CAPS, CLEARS, AND CLINCHES ALL -- 042 00 044
AND KEEPS THE BREEZE AND CLEARS THE SEAS 083 00 013
CLEAVE
SOUTHERN DEAN OR LANCASHIRE CLOUGH OR DEVON CLEAVE, . . . 159 00 004
CLEAVES
CLEAVES NOT MY BRAIN, BURNS NOT MY FEET, ... 080 02 004
AND CLEAVES, I STRUGGLE AND AM DUMB. 080 10 007
CLEPED
THE GLAUCUS CLEPED; OTHERS SMALL BRAIDS ENCLUSTER'D . . . 002 00 068
CLICKING
IT DOES AMAZE ME, WHEN THE CLICKING HOUR 102 01 001

CLIFF
    COME, PLANT THE STAFF BY CADAIR CLIFF; 030 00 007
    BUT HIS EYE NO CLIFF, NO COAST OR 041 00 067
    A BRITTLE SHEEN, RUNS UPWARD LIKE A CLIFF, ... 098 06 002
CLIFFS
    SHOWER'D THE CLIFFS AND EVERY FRET AND SPIRE 002 00 025
    O THE MIND, MIND HAS MOUNTAINS; CLIFFS OF FALL . . . 065 00 009
    LIKE FLAME THEY GATHER ON OUR CLIFFS AT EVENING, . . 104 00 007
CLIMB
    CLIMB QUITS; ONE BOARDS THE MASTER THERE 166 00 038
CLIME
    WHERE WINTER IS THE CLIME FORGOT. -- 010 00 014
    HIS PLEASURE TO THE CHANGING CLIME, ... 124 00 006
    C HIS PLEASURE TO THE CHANGING CLIME, ... 124 00 010
CLINCHES
    CAPS, CLEARS, AND CLINCHES ALL -- 042 00 044
CLINCHING-BLIND
    BEING TO HER VIRTUE CLINCHING-BLIND 145 00 018
CLING
    WILL ON THE MOULDING STRIKE AND CLING, ... 130 00 010
CLINGS
    COME WHEN NIGHT CLINGS TO WHAT IS HERS 077 00 021
    IN HOLLOWS OF HER FORM THE SHADOW CLINGS; 099 00 008
    CLINGS ON THE STROKE OF DEATH, THAT I CAN SMILE. . . 102 01 002
CLITHEROE
    MUST DEAL WITH MARGARET CLITHEROE. 145 00 007
    IS A SHROUD FOR MARGARET CLITHEROE. 145 00 014
    THE BODY OF MARGARET CLITHEROE. 145 00 021
    CHRIST LIVED IN MARGARET CLITHEROE. 145 00 028
    TO THE DEATH WITH MARGARET CLITHEROE! 145 00 035
    TO THE MURDER OF MARGARET CLITHEROE. 145 00 047
    GOD'S DAUGHTER MARGARET CLITHEROE. 145 00 054
    IT IS OVER, MARGARET CLITHEROE. 145 00 061
CLODS
    LOW-COVERED PASS, AND BRACE THE WOODLAND CLODS . . . 112 00 006
CLOGGED
    THE CLOGGED BROOK RUNS WITH CHOKING SOUND 003 00 009
CLOISTER-LIGHT
    UNDER THE CLOISTER-LIGHT OF GREENHOUSE VINES, . . . 084 00 006
CLOISTER'D
    A CLOISTER'D CONVENT FIRST, THE PROUDEST HOME . . . 001 01 006
CLOISTERS
    THE CLOISTERS CROSS'D WITH EQUAL COURTS BETWIXT . . . 001 04 002
CLOSE
    SLUMBER'D AT LAST IN ONE SWEET, DEEP, HEART-BROKEN CLOSE. . . 002 00 135
    THE DARKNESS DID NOT CLOSE THAT NIGHT 021 00 003
    MEND FIRST AND VITAL CANDLE IN CLOSE HEART'S VAULT; . 046 00 010
    THE STARS WERE PACKED SO CLOSE THAT NIGHT 098 29 001
    SUCKS CLOSE THE ACORN; AS THE HAND AND GLOVE; . . . 101 00 003
    AS KEEL LOCKS CLOSE TO KELSON -- 101 00 005
    THAT TEARS AND LAUGHTER ARE HUNG CLOSE TOGETHER. . . 102 01 016
    NOR CLOSE THE CLAYFIELD'S SHARDED SORES, ... 114 00 014
CLOSE-BARRED
    THAT NEST WITHIN CLOSE-BARRED DOORS, ... 077 00 054
CLOSE-FOLDED
    GRANT THAT CLOSE-FOLDED PEACE THAT CLAD 077 00 041
CLOSE-PLY
    ARE STILL; HER NECK IS CREASED IN CLOSE-PLY RINGS; . 099 00 010
CLOSE-ROOTED
    CLOSE-ROOTED IN THE DOWNWARD-HOLLOWING FIELDS; . . . 107 03 015
CLOSE-SHUT
    AS STRUCK WITH RINGS OF SOUND THE CLOSE-SHUT PALMS . 122 00 010
    C AS MIGHT HAVE STRUCK AND SHOOK THE CLOSE-SHUT PALMS] . 122 00 013
CLOSER
    CLOSER BECAUSE FAINT MORNING STIRS; 077 00 022
CLOSES
    OF FLOWERS THAT COUNTING CLOSES, ... 098 19 006
CLOT
    THRO' SILVER, GLOOM'D TO A BLOOD-VIVID CLOT. 002 00 107
    'MID FEVER'D FUMES AND SLIME AND CAKED CLOT; 077 00 008
CLOTHE
    WE GUESS; WE CLOTHE THEE, UNSEEN KING, ... 023 00 013
    PENANCE SHALL CLOTHE ME TO THE BONE. 081 00 135
CLOTHES
    AND LILY-COLOURED CLOTHES PROVIDE 022 00 027
CLOUD
    OF FILMY GLOBES AND ROSY FLOATING CLOUD; -- 002 00 097
    BEFORE IT CLOUD, CHRIST, LORD, AND SOUR WITH SINNING, . 033 00 012
    A BEETLING BALDBRIGHT CLOUD THOROUGH ENGLAND . . . 041 00 025
    ON TO LEDGES OF GREY CLOUD; 077 00 080
    AND WITH WEEPING CLOUD IS SPREAD 077 00 095
    MY TEARS ARE BUT A CLOUD OF RAIN; 081 00 036
    ROUNDS ITS STILL-PURPLING CENTREINGS OF CLOUD. . . . 098 30 003
    ROUNDS ITS STILL-PURPLING CENTRE-DARKS OF CLOUD. . . 098 30 006
    AS THE FINE MORSELS OF A DWINDLING CLOUD 102 01 032
    HE SAT AND WROUGHT HIS OUTLINE ON A CLOUD. 107 01 010
CLOUD-FESTOONED
    UNDER THE CLOUD-FESTOONED ROOF, ... 077 00 066

CLOUD-PUFFBALL
    CLOUD-PUFFBALL, TORN TUFTS, C   •   •   •   •   •   •   •   •   •   072 00 001
CLOUDS
    AN AZURE RIDGE: OR CLOUDS OF VIOLET GLOW'D   •   •   •   •   •   •   002 00 105
    MY WINDOW SHOWS THE TRAVELLING CLOUDS,   •   •   •   •   •   •   015 00 001
    AND SHEEP-FLOCK CLOUDS LIKE WORLDS OF WOOL,   •   •   •   •   •   030 00 018
    OF SILK-SACK CLOUDS! HAS WILDER, WILFUL-WAVIER   •   •   •   •   038 00 003
    TILL THE LIFTED CLOUDS WERE NIGH, •   •   •   •   •   •   •   077 00 072
    AND FRETTED CLOUDS WITH BURNISH'D RIM,   •   •   •   •   •   •   077 00 101
    PAVES THE CLOUDS ON THE SWEPT AZURE,   •   •   •   •   •   •   078 00 010
    THEN CLOUDS COME, LIKE ILL-BALANCED CRAGS,   •   •   •   •   •   080 07 001
    LIKE SHUTTLES FLEET THE CLOUDS, AND AFTER •   •   •   •   •   098 03 001
    THE LOCK OF CLOUDS BETIMES AND HANGS THE DAY,   •   •   •   •   098 31 003
    COVERS WITH SHALLOW SILVER, THE LOCK OF CLOUDS   •   •   •   •   098 31 005
    THERE WAS NO CREASE OR GATHER IN THE CLOUDS   •   •   •   •   102 02 006
    AS VOID AS CLOUDS THAT HOUSE AND HARBOUR NONE,   •   •   •   107 01 001
    OF STREAMS: AND CLOUDS LIKE MESH'D AND PARTED MOSS V   •   •   121 00 002
    OF WATER. CLOUDS LIKE PARTED MOSS V   •   •   •   •   •   •   121 00 003
    AT HIGHEST WHEN HE SEEMS TO BRUSH THE CLOUDS,   •   •   •   122 00 004
    THEIR CLOUDS WITH BREATHING EDGES WHITE   •   •   •   •   •   130 00 023
    MAY'S BEAUTY MASSACRE AND WISPED WILD CLOUDS GROW •   •   •   154 00 002
CLOUGH
    SOUTHERN DEAN OR LANCASHIRE CLOUGH OR DEVON CLEAVE,   •   •   159 00 004
CLOY
    IN EDEN GARDEN. -- HAVE, GET, BEFORE IT CLOY,   •   •   •   •   033 00 011
CLUSTER
    CLUSTER OF BUGLE BLUE EGGS THIN •   •   •   •   •   •   •   •   042 00 021
    BUT AH, BRIGHT FORELOCK, CLUSTER THAT YOU ARE   •   •   •   •   157 00 017
CLUSTERING
    CLUSTERING ENTRANCINGLY IN BERYL LAKES: •   •   •   •   •   002 00 014
CLUSTER'D
    CLUSTER'D IN TROOPS AND HALO'D BY THE LIGHT,   •   •   •   •   002 00 036
CLUSTERS
    AND LOOK ABROAD ON SUNNY CLUSTERS •   •   •   •   •   •   •   077 00 134
CLUTCHED
    CLUTCHED HANDS THROUGH CLASPED KNEES!   •   •   •   •   •   •   054 00 021
COAL
    FLASHING LIKE FLECKS OF COAL,   •   •   •   •   •   •   •   •   060 00 100
COAST
    BUT HIS EYE NO CLIFF, NO COAST OR •   •   •   •   •   •   •   041 00 067
COAT
    HER SILKY COAT IS SHEENY, LIKE A HILL,   •   •   •   •   •   •   099 00 003
COATS
    HIS CHANNEL UNDER CLAMMY COATS   •   •   •   •   •   •   •   003 00 011
COBBLED
    THROUGH THE COBBLED FOAM-FLEECE. WHAT COULD HE DO •   •   •   028 16 007
COCOONING
    SHAKES ITS COCOONING MISTS: AND SO SHE COMES   •   •   •   •   103 00 008
COFFER
    AND COME WHERE LIES A COFFER, BURLY ALL OF BLOCKS •   •   •   159 00 036
COFFIN-BLACK
    AND WITH COFFIN-BLACK HE BARR'D THE GREEN.   •   •   •   •   004 00 011
COGGED
    SO FAGGED, SO FASHED, SO COGGED, SO CUMBERED, C   •   •   •   059 0G 026
COIFED
    OF A COIFED SISTERHOOD.   •   •   •   •   •   •   •   •   •   028 20 002
COIL
    NAY IN ALL THAT TOIL, THAT COIL, SINCE (SEEMS) I KISSED THE ROD,   •   064 00 010
    BUT DROPP'D ITS COIL OF WOES: ARTHUR'S BRITAIN,   •   •   •   102 02 007
COILS
    COILS, KEEPS, AND TEASES SIMPLE SIGHT.   •   •   •   •   •   022 00 012
COINAGE
    THUS WE SHALL PROFIT, WHILE GOLD COINAGE STILL   •   •   •   096 07 007
COLD
    WITH LOATH'D COLD FISHES, FAR FROM MAN -- OR WHAT: --   •   •   002 00 124
    WITH DRAUGHT OF THIN AND PURSUANT COLD SO NIPS   •   •   •   011 00 006
    THE FURNACE SHALL AT LAST BE COLD.   •   •   •   •   •   •   015 00 016
    SEE HOW SPRING OPENS WITH DISABLING COLD,   •   •   •   •   017 00 001
    THEY FOUGHT WITH GOD'S COLD --   •   •   •   •   •   •   •   028 17 001
    THE GREY LAWNS COLD WHERE GOLD, WHERE QUICKGOLD LIES!   •   •   032 00 005
    THEY SAY WHO SAW ONE SEA-CORPSE COLD   •   •   •   •   •   041 00 073
    WITH, ALONG THEM, CRAGIRON UNDER AND COLD FURLS -- C   •   •   071 00 014
    THIS OUTER COLD, MY EXILE FROM OF OLD   •   •   •   •   •   080 01 003
    THE COLD WHIP-ADDER UNESPIED   •   •   •   •   •   •   •   106 00 001
    ' IT IS AS COLD AS DEATH WITHOUT!   •   •   •   •   •   •   109 29 003
    HE GAVE HER KISSES COLD AS ICE!   •   •   •   •   •   •   •   109 39 001
    OF THE COLD WIND BLOWING. •   •   •   •   •   •   •   •   132 00 003
    AND WHERE COLD DAFFODILS IN APRIL ARE   •   •   •   •   •   135 00 029
    SHE BRIMS HER BATH IN COLD OR HEAT!   •   •   •   •   •   •   139 00 002
    WARM BEAT WITH COLD BEAT COMPANY, SHALL I •   •   •   •   •   153 00 002
    THEO.   WHAT THE COLD MONTH ALLOWS --   •   •   •   •   •   APPEN A 40
COLDER
    IT WILL COME TO SUCH SIGHTS COLDER   •   •   •   •   •   •   055 00 006
COLDLY
    AND COLDLY DO BELIE THE THOUGHT OF THEE?   •   •   •   •   117 00 012
COLDNESS
    THE STABBING COLDNESS OF REBUFF. •   •   •   •   •   •   •   083 00 028

COLLAPSING
    THEN FAIL'D THE TONGUE; THE POOR COLLAPSING FRAME, ... 001 03 003
COLOMB
    THAT HAS IT; AND SHE IS FAIRER THAN COLOMB, ... 125 00 037
COLOSSAL
    IF A WUTHERING OF HIS PALMY SNOW-PINIONS SCATTER A COLOSSAL SMILE . 045 00 013
COLOUR
    OF COLOUR IN HIGH CASEMENTS FACE TO FACE; 001 06 003
    BUT WATCHING WHILE THE COLOUR GREW 021 00 012
    WHAT WAS THE COLOUR OF THAT BLOSSOM BRIGHT? -- 027 00 031
    WHEN EVERY COLOUR GLOWS, ... 060 00 084
    NO COLOUR IN THE OVERHEAD, ... 081 00 160
    TO COLOUR AS SMOOTH AND FRESH AS CHEEKS OF ROSES, ... 108 00 004
COLOURED
    CARELESS THESE IN COLOURED WISP 159 00 030
COLOURING
    WE FOUND WERE DABBLED WITH A COLOURING GROWTH, ... 098 09 002
COLOUR'D
    AND LONG, THE TREES WERE COLOUR'D, BUT THE O'ER-HEAD, . . . 107 04 012
COLOURS
    THE WAXEN COLOURS WEEP AND RUN, ... 003 00 029
    AND MARCHING TO FALSE COLOURS! THOSE FEW STROKES 102 01 065
COLUMNAR-SEVERE
    GOD'S COUNSEL COLUMNAR-SEVERE 145 00 001
COLUMNS
    FLUSH THRO' THEIR HEAVING COLUMNS; WHEN THEY HALT 104 00 010
COMB
    OTHERS WITH FINGERS WHITE WOULD COMB AMONG 002 00 112
    IN COOP AND IN COMB THE FLEECE OF HIS FOAM 056 00 003
COMBATING
    THE KEENER TO COME AT THE COMFORT FOR FEELING THE COMBATING KEEN? . 028 25 008
COMBES
    LOVELY THE WOODS, WATERS, MEADOWS, COMBES, VALES, ... 034 00 009
COMBS
    AND IT CROWDS AND IT COMBS TO THE FALL; 028 04 004
    BUT THE COMBS OF A SMOTHER OF SAND; NIGHT DREW HER . . . 028 14 003
    HIS CRISP COMBS, AND THAT COMES THOSE WAYS WE KNOW, . . . 068 00 014
    WITHIN HER WEARS, BEARS, CARES AND COMBS THE SAME; . . . 076 00 006
    FAST OR THEY IN CLAMMYISH LASHTENDER COMBS CREEP . . . 149 A 006
COME
    COME BY THE FLESH-POTS! YOU SHALL SIT UNSHOD . . . 005 00 009
    COME UP, ARISE AND SLAY. 005 00 018
    YE WEARY, COME INTO THE SHADE. 006 00 026
    WHERE NO STORMS COME. 009 00 006
    THUS, I COME UNDERNEATH THIS CHAPEL-SIDE, . . . 012 02 001
    YOU SEE THAT I HAVE COME TO PASSION'S END; . . . 014 03 001
    IS THIS MADE PLAIN? WHAT HAVE I COME ACROSS . . . 014 03 010
    LOVE, COME DOWN TO ME IF THY NAME BE LOVE. . . . 020 00 006
    FROM THERE WHERE ALL SURRENDERS COME . . . 022 00 007
    SO FRESH THAT COME IN FASTS DIVINE! . . . 022 00 016
    AND MAY HAS COME, HAIR-BOUND IN FLOWERS, . . 026 00 013
    I SHALL COME HOME TO THEE, MOTHER OF MINE. . . 027 00 024
    THE SOUR SCYTHE CRINGE, AND THE BLEAR SHARE COME. . . 028 11 008
    WAS CALLING ' O CHRIST, CHRIST, COME QUICKLY ' : . . 028 24 007
    THE KEENER TO COME AT THE COMFORT FOR FEELING THE COMBATING KEEN? . 028 25 008
    REACH ME A . . . FANCY, COME FASTER -- . . 028 28 002
    COME, PLANT THE STAFF BY CADAIR CLIFF; . . . 030 00 007
    COME, SWING THE SCULLS ON PENMAEN POOL. . . 030 00 008
    THEN COME WHO PINE FOR PEACE OR PLEASURE . . 030 00 037
    SHE HAD COME FROM A CRUISE, TRAINING SEAMEN -- . . 041 00 013
    SOME CANDLE CLEAR BURNS SOMEWHERE I COME BY. . . 046 00 001
    COME YOU INDOORS, COME HOME; YOUR FADING FIRE . . 046 00 009
    COME YOU INDOORS, COME HOME; YOUR FADING FIRE . . 046 00 009
    TO OWN MY HEART; I YIELD YOU DO COME SOMETIMES; BUT . 051 00 004
    HE COMES WITH WORK TO DO, HE DOES NOT COME TO COO, . 051 00 010
    NOW THE NIGHT COME; ALL 054 00 010
    IT WILL COME TO SUCH SIGHTS COLDER . . 055 00 006
    COME THEN, YOUR WAYS AND AIRS AND LOOKS, LOCKS, C . . 059 06 014
    WERE I COME O'ER AGAIN ' CRIES CHRIST ' IT SHOULD BE THIS ' . 063 00 014
    CAN SOMETHING, HOPE, WISH DAY COME, NOT CHOOSE NOT TO BE. . 064 00 004
    SOUL, SELF! COME, POOR JACKSELF, I DO ADVISE . . 069 00 009
    BUT COME, THOU BALM TO ACHING SOUL, . . 077 00 011
    COME WHEN NIGHT CLINGS TO WHAT IS HERS . . 077 00 021
    COME BECAUSE THEN MOST THINLY LIES . . 077 00 035
    MY SEVERAL MOANS COME DISTANT IN THEIR TONES . . 080 03 003
    TO COME TO ME FROM THE UNDERGROUND. . . 080 04 007
    THEN CLOUDS COME, LIKE ILL-BALANCED CRAGS, . . 080 07 001
    THEY ALL COME HERE AND STAND BEFORE ME CLEAR . . 080 08 003
    AND I COME LADEN FROM SUCH FLOODS . . 098 19 005
    COME OUT OF SPACE, OR SUDDENLY ENGENDER'D . . 103 00 004
    NO, THEY ARE COME; THEIR HORN IS LIFTED UP; . . 104 00 001
    AT MORN THEY COME UPON OUR LANDS LIKE RAINS; . . 104 00 008
    HIS SHEEP SEEM'D TO COME FROM IT AS THEY STEPT, . . 107 01 011
    ' SYLVESTER, COME, SYLVESTER! YOU MAY TRUST . . 107 03 001
    THE SHINING SLATES AND HOUSES. COME AND SEE. . . 107 03 007
    WHEN I COME HOME FROM SEA. ' . . 109 05 004
    COME WITH YOU FROM OVER THE SEA? ' . . 109 07 004

COME (CONTINUED)

COME WITH ME FROM OVER THE SEA. 109 08 002
THE CROWN HAS COME TO THEE. ' 109 09 004
THAT THIS HAS COME TO THEE. ' 109 14 004
AND HE WILL COME TO THEE. 109 19 004
HE WOULD HAVE COME FOR ME. 109 28 004
AND ART THOU COME FROM ENGLISH LAND, ... 109 31 003
OR COME FROM OVER THE SEA? 109 31 004
' I AM NOT COME FROM ENGLISH LAND, ... 109 32 001
IF I WERE COME FROM PARADISE, ... 109 32 003
O DEATH, DEATH, HE IS COME. 115 00 001
THE KING OF GLORY WILL COME IN. 115 00 010
WHO IS IT? HOW COME TO THIS FORGOTTEN LAND? 122 00 019
WE HAVE COME FOUR, DO YOU THINK? 125 00 013
COME, DAPHNIS. GOOD VALERIAN, I WILL COME. 125 00 031
COME, DAPHNIS. GOOD VALERIAN, I WILL COME. 125 00 031
FOR A LETTER COMES AT LAST: (SHALL I SAY BEFORE CHRISTMAS IS COME?) 128 00 019
AND CALLED TO COME AT MEALTIME SHE WOULD NOT: 136 00 033
BRAVE ALL, AND TAKE WHAT COMES -- AS HERE THIS RABBLE IS COME, . 152 02 068
THAN SEWERS WITH SACRED OILS. MANKIND, THAT MOB, COMES. COME! . 152 02 070
THEE, GOD, I COME FROM, TO THEE GO, ... 155 00 001
AND COME WHERE LIES A COFFER, BURLY ALL OF BLOCKS 159 00 036
IS TO COME NEAR AND TAKE HIM HOME. 167 00 004

COME-BACK-AGAIN

AMONGST COME-BACK-AGAIN THINGS, C . . . . 152 C 029

COMES

A PRESS OF WINGED THINGS COMES DOWN THIS WAY: 005 00 015
GOD COMES ALL SWEETNESS TO YOUR LENTEN LIPS. 011 00 002
NO ANSWERING VOICE COMES FROM THE SKIES: 023 00 002
HE COMES WITH WORK TO DO, HE DOES NOT COME TO COO, ... 051 00 010
HE COMES TO BROOD AND SIT. 051 00 011
WHO, BORN SO, COMES TO BE 060 00 068
HIS CRISP COMBS, AND THAT COMES THOSE WAYS WE KNOW. 068 00 014
BUT YET THEY SAY CHRIST COMES AT THE LAST DAY. 080 01 006
THE HEAVEN-ENFORCED ANSWER COMES, ... 081 00 144
THE WIND COMES BREAKING HERE AND THERE WITH LAUGHTER: . . . 098 03 003
FROM OXFORD COMES THE THRONG AND HUM OF BELLS 098 03 006
SHAKES ITS COCOONING MISTS: AND SO SHE COMES 103 00 008
AMIDST THE SISTERING PLANETS, TILL SHE COMES 103 00 014
' LORD WILLIAM COMES HUNTING TOMORROW MORNING, ... 109 19 003
NOW COMES AS LOW BENEATH. 115 00 004
THAT COMES AGAIN TO THE WOODLAND TREE. 124 00 004
THE HATRED COMES WITH A GOOD GRACE FROM YOU: 125 00 029
FOR A LETTER COMES AT LAST: (SHALL I SAY BEFORE CHRISTMAS IS COME?) 128 00 019
LORD BEUNO COMES TONIGHT, TONIGHT, SIR! SOON, NOW: THEREFORE . 152 01 005
BRAVE ALL, AND TAKE WHAT COMES -- AS HERE THIS RABBLE IS COME, . 152 02 068
THAN SEWERS WITH SACRED OILS. MANKIND, THAT MOB, COMES. COME! . 152 02 070
BY THERE COMES A LISTLESS STRANGER: BECKONED BY THE NOISE . . 159 00 014
COMES ONE TO GAZE UPON MY ILL: 160 00 025
AND ALL THAT COMES IS FRAUGHT TO ME WITH FEAR. 160 00 036
ONE BETTER BACKED COMES CROWDING BY: -- 166 00 013

COMET

-- I AM LIKE A SLIP OF COMET, ... 103 00 001

COMFORT

THE KEENER TO COME AT THE COMFORT FOR FEELING THE COMBATING KEEN? . 028 25 008
EACH BE OTHER'S COMFORT KIND: 052 00 005
MY TONGUE HAD TAUGHT THEE COMFORT, TOUCH HAD QUENCHED THY TEARS, . 053 00 010
THERE'S COMFORT THEN, THERE'S SALT: 054 00 039
NOT, I'LL NOT, CARRION COMFORT, DESPAIR, NOT FEAST ON THEE: . . 064 00 001
WRETCH, UNDER A COMFORT SERVES IN A WHIRLWIND: ALL 065 00 013
I CAST FOR COMFORT I CAN NO MORE GET 069 00 005
ELSEWHERE: LEAVE COMFORT ROOT-ROOM: LET JOY SIZE 069 00 011
YOUR COMFORT IS AS SHARP AS SWORDS: 081 00 032
HEAVEN COMFORT SENDS, BUT HARRY IT AWAY, ... 089 00 005
AND IN THIS DARKSOME WORLD WHAT COMFORT CAN I FIND? 152 02 048
DOWN THIS DARKSOME WORLD COMFORT WHERE CAN I FIND 152 02 049
AND OILS OF SHUSHAN COMFORT NOT, ... 166 00 044

COMFORTABLE

THE COMFORTABLE GLOOM 005 00 028

COMFORTER

COMFORTER, WHERE, WHERE IS YOUR COMFORTING? 065 00 003

COMFORTING

COMFORTING SMELL BREATHED AT VERY ENTERING, ... 034 00 003
COMFORTER, WHERE, WHERE IS YOUR COMFORTING? 065 00 003

COMFORTLESS

COMFORTLESS UNCONFESSED OF THEM -- 028 31 004
BY GROPING ROUND MY COMFORTLESS, THAN BLIND 069 00 006

COMFORT'S

IS COMFORT'S CAROL OF ALL OR WOE'S WORST SMART. 153 00 008

COMING

NOT A DOOMS-DAY DAZZLE IN HIS COMING NOR DARK AS HE CAME: . . 028 34 006
NOW COMING FROM THE ALIEN EAVES, -- 081 00 003

COMMANDER

' HER COMMANDER! AND THOU TOO, AND THOU THIS WAY. ' 041 00 052

COMMANDS

I GIVE COMMANDS FOR WATER FOR MY HANDS: 080 09 003

COMMON

ALL MINE, YET COMMON TO MY EVERY PEER. 012 01 008

COMMON   (CONTINUED)
    I HAVE FOUND MY MUSIC IN A COMMON WORD, ... 019 00 005
    TO WHOM THE COMMON EARTH AND AIR 077 00 059
COMMONWEAL
    THOUSANDS OF THORNS, THOUGHTS) SWINGS THOUGH, COMMONWEAL . . . 070 00 008
    YOUR WILL IS LAW IN THAT SMALL COMMONWEAL. 150 00 011
COMMUNION
    CAME, I SAY, THIS DAY TO IT -- TO A FIRST COMMUNION. . . . 048 00 008
COMPANION
    LET WHAT THERE NEEDS BE DONE. STAY! WITH HIM ONE COMPANION, . . 152 01 007
COMPANY
    FAR OFF A NEREID COMPANY, AND SHAKE 002 00 075
    OUR COMPANY THRONGED THE HALL; 054 00 011
    I WILL BREAK FREE FROM THE JEWS' COMPANY, ... 080 12 003
    WITH A GOLDEN COMPANY. 109 06 004
    WARM BEAT WITH COLD BEAT COMPANY, SHALL I 153 00 002
COMPARISON
    THAT HERE WILL SERVE ME FOR COMPARISON? 014 03 011
COMPASS
    AT CORNERS FLANK THE STRETCHING COMPASS ROUND; 001 01 004
    AND CANVAS AND COMPASS, THE WHORL AND THE WHEEL 028 14 007
    WENT FORTH TO COMPASS MYSTERIES; 077 00 052
    AND COULD NOT COMPASS IT. 095 00 004
    WHERE THE STINT COMPASS OF A SKYLARK'S WINGS 098 22 005
    TO SPREAD THE COMPASS ON THE ALL-STARR'D SKY; 102 03 008
    TO TURN THE COMPASS ON THE ALL-STARR'D SKY V 102 03 023
COMPASSION
    AND KIND COMPASSION, AT HIS LIFE'S LAST NEED 140 00 004
COMPASSIONATE
    THE CHRIST OF THE FATHER COMPASSIONATE, C 028 33 008
COMPLAISANT
    WHOSE BRAGGART 'SCUTCHEON, WHOSE COMPLAISANT CREST . . . 098 32 001
COMPLETE
    COMPLETE THY CREATURE DEAR O WHERE IT FAILS; 034 00 013
COMPLIMENT
    WHAT WERE WORTH NOTHING IF ALL COMPLIMENT! 094 00 006
COMPOSITE
    CROWNS COMPOSITE AND BRAIDED BAST 165 00 002
COMPULSION
    BY VISUAL COMPULSION, TILL I HIDE 012 02 005
COMRADE
    MARCH, KIND COMRADE, ABREAST HIM; 048 00 019
CONCAVITY
    OF ITS CONCAVITY. 121 00 006
CONCEIVE
    CONCEIVING WHOM I MUST CONCEIVE AMISS? 013 00 002
    FOR SO CONCEIVED, SO TO CONCEIVE THEE IS DONE; 028 30 006
    WHERE SHE SHALL YET CONCEIVE 060 00 061
CONCEIVED
    FOR SO CONCEIVED, SO TO CONCEIVE THEE IS DONE; 028 30 006
    'TIS SO CONCEIVED IN HIS LINEAMENT. 102 01 046
    ['TIS SO CONCEIVED IN HIS TRUE LINEAMENT.] 102 01 047
    AND STRAIGHTWAY SHE CONCEIVED A SON . . . . APPEN D 33
CONCEIVING
    CONCEIVING WHOM I MUST CONCEIVE AMISS? 013 00 002
CONCERN
    EARTH BROWS OF SUCH CARE, CARE AND DEAR CONCERN. 058 00 014
CONCERNED
    THE EURYDICE -- IT CONCERNED THEE, O LORD! 041 00 001
CONCH
    WITHOUTEN INSTRUMENT, OR CONCH, OR BELL, ... 002 00 128
CONCORDING
    OR TAKE IT THUS -- THAT THE CONCORDING STARS 122 00 007
CONDITION
    IN ITS CONDITION. NO, THE TROPIC TREE 014 01 003
    BARE THE CONDITION OF A REALM AT RIOT. 082 00 004
CONFESS
    THOU HEARDST ME TRUER THAN TONGUE CONFESS 028 02 003
CONFESSION
    BOTH ARE MY CONFESSION, BOTH ARE MY BELIEF, ... 168 00 011
CONFIDANTE
    WHEN 'TIS THE CONFIDANTE THAT SETS THE TASK. 094 00 002
CONFIDENCE
    AND WHAT IF SHE MY CONFIDENCE BETRAY! 094 00 004
CONFINED
    LOVE BY PRENATAL SERFDOM STILL CONFINED 102 03 015
CONFIRMED
    CONFIRMED BEAUTY WILL NOT BEAR A STRESS; -- 117 00 001
CONFOUND
    OF THOSE WHO STROVE GOD'S GOSPEL TO CONFOUND 001 01 007
CONFOUNDED
    BEST IN: GRACELESS GROWTH, THOU HAST CONFOUNDED 044 00 007
CONFRONT
    AND HOSTS CONFRONT WITH FLAGS UNFURLED 023 00 033
CONFUSED
    AND SO MY TRUST, CONFUSED, STRUCK, AND SHOOK 016 00 007
CONJECTURE
    WHO MADE CONJECTURE NEAREST FAR 077 00 045

CONJUNCTIONS
    WITH SUCH MALIGN CONJUNCTIONS AS BEFORE 014 02 006
CONQUEST
    COULD CROWD CAREER WITH CONQUEST WHILE THERE WENT 073 00 012
CONQU'RORS
    BY CONQU'RORS RUDE OF HONOR; AND NOT ALL 001 08 004
CONSCIENCE
    AND, CAST BY CONSCIENCE OUT, SPENDSAVOUR SALT? 046 00 014
    ONE WITH MORE CONSCIENCE, CLEANER FAME; 166 00 012
CONSIDERATE
    GOD, LOVER OF SOULS, SWAYING CONSIDERATE SCALES, ... 034 00 012
CONSIDERED
    SHE NOT CONSIDERED WHETHER OR NO 145 00 033
CONSOLATION
    THEN THOUGH I SHOULD TREAD TUFTS OF CONSOLATION 048 00 025
    SITS WITHOUT CONSOLATION, MARKING NOT 111 00 004
CONSTANCY
    UPRAIS'D AN EMBLEM OF THAT FIERY CONSTANCY. 001 03 008
CONSUMES
    DEATH OR DISTANCE SOON CONSUMES THEM; WIND 040 00 009
CONSUMING
    GIVE GOD WHILE WORTH CONSUMING. 049 00 007
CONTAGIOUS
    I HAVE DRAWN HEAT FROM THIS CONTAGIOUS SUN; 103 00 018
CONTAINED
    IN HER WAS CHRIST CONTAINED ANON, ... APPEN D 35
CONTEND
    THOU ART INDEED JUST, LORD, IF I CONTEND 074 00 001
CONTENDED
    FATAL FOUR DISORDERS, FLESHED THERE, ALL CONTENDED? 053 00 004
CONTENDS
    CONTENDS ABOUT ITS MANY CREEDS 023 00 032
CONTENTED
    GO THEN; I AM CONTENTED HERE TO LIE. 005 00 055
    LIKE A CONTENTED WIND, OR GENTLE SHOCKS 098 02 002
    BUT SING CONTENTED AS THE DOVE 124 00 003
CONTENTMENT
    SHE LEANS ON HIM WITH SUCH CONTENTMENT FOND 157 00 013
CONTINENCE
    HE PRAISED THE LOVELY LOT OF CONTINENCE; 136 00 028
CONTINENT
    YET GOD (THAT HEWS MOUNTAIN AND CONTINENT, ... 073 00 009
CONTINUALLY
    DOORS SLAMM'D TO THE BLASTS CONTINUALLY; MORE LOW, ... 001 13 008
CONTRACT
    THE SHEARING RAYS CONTRACT ME WITH THEIR BLAZE 080 02 006
CONTROLL'D
    CONTROLL'D THEM TO A (EY-GREEN TEMPERATENESS, ... 107 04 014
CONVENT
    A CLOISTER'D CONVENT FIRST, THE PROUDEST HOME 001 01 006
    HE RAIS'D THE CONVENT AS A MONSTROUS GRATE; 001 04 001
    FLING TO THE CONVENT WICKET FAST. 081 00 075
COO
    THE WOOD; BUT NOT A DOVE WOULD COO. 021 00 021
    HE COMES WITH WORK TO DO, HE DOES NOT COME TO COO, ... 051 00 010
COOINGS
    OR ELSE THEIR COOINGS CAME FROM BAYS OF TREES, ... 098 02 001
COOL
    TO PLASH WITH COOL FEET THE CLAY JUICY SOIL. 005 00 050
    WHEN GREY SHOWERS GATHER AND GUSTS ARE COOL? -- 030 00 026
    TO COOL HIS PLUMY THROBBING BREAST. 077 00 092
COOLING
    INTO THE COOLING GLOOM; TILL SLOWLY ALL 001 12 005
    IN SILK-ASH KEPT FROM COOLING. 049 00 017
COOP
    IN COOP AND IN COMB THE FLEECE OF HIS FOAM 056 00 003
COPED
    ONCE ENCOUNTER IN, HERE COPED AND POISED POWERS; 044 00 004
COPSE
    OF FOLIAGE FALLEN IN THE COPSE. 003 00 012
    THE COPSE WAS NEVER MORE THAN GREY. 021 00 002
    ALL DOWN THE STAIR-WAY OF THE COPSE 021 00 045
    THE PEACOCK'D COPSE WERE KNOWN TO FILL; 081 00 014
    THAT LICK THE SHELLY LEAVES WHICH FLOOR THE COPSE, ... 084 00 004
    FROM ANY HEDGEROW, ANY COPSE, ... 098 18 001
    HELP'D BY THE DARKNESS OF A BLOCK OF COPSE 107 03 014
    WORK THROUGH A COVER'D COPSE WHOSE HOLLOW ROUNDING 112 00 003
COPSES
    THE VIOLET MOVES AND COPSES ROCK. 098 03 004
COPYING
    IN COPYING WELL WHAT YOU HAVE BEST BEGUN. 125 00 020
    IN COPYING? HOW? MUST I GIVE TONGUE AGAIN? 125 00 021
    IN COPYING YOUR SWEET SILENCE. AM I SO 125 00 022
CORAL
    WITH CORAL, SHELLS, THICK-PEARLED CORDS, WHATE'ER 002 00 054
CORDED
    AND THE CORN IS CORDED AND SHOULDERS ITS SHEAF, ... 138 00 019

CORDIAL
    THAT CORDIAL AIR MADE THOSE KIND PEOPLE A HOOD • • • • • • 034 00 005
CORDS
    WITH CORAL, SHELLS, THICK-PEARLED CORDS, WHATE'ER • • • • • 002 00 054
CORN
    AND NEVER TURNED TO CORN. • • • • • • • • • 007 00 008
    WITH CORN THAT THEY SHALL LAUGH AND SING. • • • • • • 008 00 017
    AND SEVEN EARS CROWN THE LODGED CORN, • • • • • • 114 00 006
    AND THE CORN IS CORDED AND SHOULDERS ITS SHEAF, • • • • 138 00 019
CORNER
    TO GRACE THEM SPIRES ARE SHAPED WITH CORNER SQUINCHES: • • • 096 07 002
    SCARCE WORTH DISCOVERY, IN SOME CORNER SEEN • • • • • 103 00 002
CORNERS
    AT CORNERS FLANK THE STRETCHING COMPASS ROUND: • • • • 001 01 004
    THEIR CLARIONS FROM ALL CORNERS OF THE FIELD • • • • • 104 00 004
CORNICE
    WHEREIN BENEATH THE CORNICE, HORSEMEN RODE • • • • • 001 07 007
    PENDANT IN FORMAL LINE FROM CORNICE TALL • • • • • • 001 12 007
CORNIC'D
    HE RANG'D LONG CORRIDORS AND CORNIC'D HALLS, • • • • • 001 10 001
CORONET
    I HAVE WRONG'D IT OF ITS CORONET, AND NOW • • • • • 102 01 048
CORPSE
    GREAT BUTTER-BURR LEAVES FLOOR'D THE SLOPE CORPSE GROUND • • 107 04 009
    IS CORPSE NOW, CANNOT CHANGE: MY OTHER SELF, THIS SOUL, • • 152 02 062
CORPSES
    HE HIDES OUR CORPSES DROPPING BY THE WAY • • • • • • 005 00 005
CORRESPOND
    ONLY THE INMATE DOES NOT CORRESPOND: • • • • • • 034 00 011
CORRIDORS
    HE RANG'D LONG CORRIDORS AND CORNIC'D HALLS, • • • • • 001 10 001
    AFAR IN CORRIDORS WITH PAINED STRAIN • • • • • • 001 13 007
CORRUPTION
    ENOUGH: CORRUPTION WAS THE WORLD'S FIRST WOE. • • • • 157 00 033
CORSE
    TO NEWBORN PRINCE, AND ROYAL CORSE INANIMATE, • • • • 001 04 009
    AND THE POOR CORSE IMPALE WITH IT AND FRAY • • • • • 089 00 007
COST
    STOP NOT NOW TO COUNT THE COST: • • • • • • • • 024 00 002
COT
    NO TUMBLER WOKE AND SHOOK THE COT, • • • • • • • 135 00 013
COTTAGES
    DOWN-SPLINTER'D ROCKS CRUSH'D COTTAGES. -- DREAR SIGHT, • • 001 14 005
COUGH
    STONE, PALSY, CANCER, COUGH, LUNG-WASTING, WOMB-NOT-BEARING, • 152 C 008
COULDST
    AND THOU COULDST SEE ME SINNING: • • • • • • • 170 00 012
COUNCIL
    SHE PLEASED THE QUEEN AND COUNCIL. SO • • • • • • 145 00 034
COUNSEL
    GOD'S COUNSEL COLUMNAR-SEVERE • • • • • • • • 145 00 001
COUNT
    COULD COUNT ON PREDILUVIAN AGE, • • • • • • • 015 00 010
    STOP NOT NOW TO COUNT THE COST: • • • • • • • 024 00 002
    HE HAS LOST COUNT WHAT CAME NEXT, POOR BOY, -- • • • 041 00 072
    AND COUNT THE ROSY CROSS WITH BANN'D DISASTROUS THINGS. • • 089 00 009
COUNTENANCE
    MASTER MORE MAY THAN GAZE, GAZE OUT OF COUNTENANCE. • • • 062 00 005
    MOCKED AND MARRED COUNTENANCE, • • • • • • • 170 00 008
COUNTER
    AWAY FROM COUNTER, COURT, OR SCHOOL • • • • • • 030 00 002
    AWAY FROM COUNTER, COURT, OR SCHOOL, • • • • • • 030 00 038
    ALL THINGS COUNTER, ORIGINAL, SPARE, STRANGE: • • • • 037 00 007
COUNTERFEIT
    THIS DOWNY COUNTERFEIT UPON MY LIP, • • • • • • 102 01 005
COUNTERFOILING
    HER SHOWY LEAVES STAID WATCHET COUNTERFOILING V • • • 108 00 005
COUNTER-ROUNDELS
    THAT STILL MAKES COUNTER-ROUNDELS IN THE POND. • • • • 107 03 005
COUNTERPART
    I [DREAM'D] MY COUNTERPART. IT SEEM'D • • • • • 081 00 086
    MAN MY MATE AND COUNTERPART. • • • • • • • • 155 00 024
COUNTERVAIL
    THERE WAS A CHARM WOULD COUNTERVAIL • • • • • • 081 00 078
COUNTING
    OF FLOWERS THAT COUNTING CLOSES, • • • • • • • 098 19 006
COUNTLESS
    IS CRIES COUNTLESS, CRIES LIKE DEAD LETTERS SENT • • • 067 00 007
    A COUNTLESS LAUGHTER, EARTH MOTHER OF ALL, • • • • 160 00 003
COUNTRY
    SINCE COUNTRY IS SO TENDER • • • • • • • • 043 00 012
    THE DAPPLE-EARED LILY BELOW THEE: THAT COUNTRY AND TOWN DID • 044 00 003
    WHAT! COUNTRY IS HONOUR ENOUGH IN ALL US -- LORDLY HEAD, • • 070 00 010
    WHILE THE UPGAZING COUNTRY SEEMS • • • • • • • 077 00 125
    WHAT PUT TAUGHT GRACES ON HIS COUNTRY LIP, • • • • 107 02 003
    THE COUNTRY SONG OF WILLOW. ' THE POOR SOUL -- • • • 111 00 013

COUNTRY   (CONTINUED)
    A WONDER IN THE COUNTRY, AND A LANDMARK 125 00 004
    BUT COUNTRY AND FLAG, THE FLAG I AM UNDER -- 156 00 007
    OF COUNTRY BIDDER'S CALLS OR LOW 166 00 022
COUNTY
    IN THE RUDDIED COUNTY OF THE DAY'S UPBRINGING 098 28 004
COUPLE-COLOUR
    FOR SKIES OF COUPLE-COLOUR AS A BRINDED COW: 037 00 002
COURAGE
    TAKE COURAGE: THIS SHALL NEED NO FURTHER ART. 080 11 005
COURSE
    WHY, IT SEEMED OF COURSE: SEEMED OF RIGHT IT SHOULD. 034 00 008
COURSES
    SO THAT THE MASON'S LEVELS, COURSES, ALL 012 02 002
COURT
    AWAY FROM COUNTER, COURT, OR SCHOOL 030 00 002
    AWAY FROM COUNTER, COURT, OR SCHOOL, ... 030 00 038
    BUT THIS DISTEMPER'D COURT WILL CHANGE IT ALL: -- 125 00 057
    THE WORDS CAME FROM A COURT ACROSS THE WAY. 136 00 023
COURTESIES
    THE MINT OF CURRENT COURTESIES, THE FORGE 102 02 008
COURTS
    THE CLOISTERS CROSS'D WITH EQUAL COURTS BETWIXT 001 04 002
    THAN CHANGEFUL POMP OF COURTS IS AYE MORE WONDERFUL. . . . 001 15 009
COUSIN
    MY COUSIN WILL NOT LOVE YOU AS I LOVE, ... 102 01 057
    THE SKYLARK IS MY COUSIN AND HE 138 00 012
COVER
    WHICH THE TIDES COVER IN THEIR OVERFLOW, ... 002 00 002
    OR ANCIENT MOUNDS THAT COVER BONES, ... 015 00 037
    MIGHT COVER THE NEIGHBOUR DOWNS WITH A SPAN OF SINGING, . . 098 28 002
    DO COVER FROM THE STARRY SPREAD, ... 135 00 002
    THAT THE HANGING HONEYSUCK, THE DOGEARED HAZELS IN THE COVER . 159 00 009
COVERLID
    HER SOBER SIMPLE COVERLID UNDERPLIGHTED 108 00 003
COVER'D
    WORK THROUGH A COVER'D COPSE WHOSE HOLLOW ROUNDING 112 00 003
COVERS
    THE VEIL THAT COVERS MYSTERIES: 077 00 036
    COVERS WITH SHALLOW SILVER, THAT UNSETS 098 31 002
    COVERS WITH SHALLOW SILVER, THE LOCK OF CLOUDS 098 31 005
COVERTS
    THEY DRAW ALL COVERTS, CUT THE FIELDS, AND SUCK 104 00 012
COW
    FOR SKIES OF COUPLE-COLOUR AS A BRINDED COW: 037 00 002
CRACK'D
    WHILE HIS CRACK'D FLESH LAY HISSING ON THE GRATE: 001 03 002
CRADOCK
    THE WOEFUL, CRADOCK, O THE WOEFUL WORD! THEN WHAT, ... 152 02 017
CRAGIRON
    WITH, ALONG THEM, CRAGIRON UNDER AND COLD FURLS -- C . . . 071 00 014
CRAGS
    THEN CLOUDS COME, LIKE ILL-BALANCED CRAGS, ... 080 07 001
CRAMPS
    CRAMPS ALL DOING. WHAT DO? NOT YIELD, C 152 02 066
CRASH
    WHETHER AT ONCE, AS ONCE AT A CRASH PAUL, ... 028 10 005
    IN A FLASH, AT A TRUMPET CRASH, ... 072 00 021
CRAWL
    THE HOARSE LEAVES CRAWL ON HISSING GROUND 003 00 005
CREAMY
    HER HUE'S A VARIOUS BROWN WITH CREAMY LAKES, ... 099 00 011
CREASE
    THERE WAS NO CREASE OR GATHER IN THE CLOUDS 102 02 006
CREASED
    WHICH WITH ITS LINED AND CREASED FLANK 092 00 010
    ARE STILL: HER NECK IS CREASED IN CLOSE-PLY RINGS: 099 00 010
CREASES
    OF YESTERTEMPEST'S CREASES: IN POOL AND RUTPEEL PARCHES . . 072 00 006
CREATING
    TO MY CREATING THOUGHT, WOULD NEITHER HEAR 066 00 006
CREATION
    THE ROLL, THE RISE, THE CAROL, THE CREATION, ... 076 00 012
CREATION'S
    VACANT CREATION'S LAMPS APPAL. 023 00 012
CREATURE
    COMPLETE THY CREATURE DEAR O WHERE IT FAILS, ... 034 00 013
CREATURES
    CREATURES ALL HEFT, HOPE, HAZARD, INTEREST. 157 00 008
CREDIT
    AND I'LL PRETEND THE CREDIT GIVEN OF YORE: 014 02 003
CREEDS
    CONTENDS ABOUT ITS MANY CREEDS 023 00 032
CREEP
    SEE, LOVE, I CREEP AND THOU ON WINGS DOST RIDE: 020 00 003
    DURANCE DEAL WITH THAT STEEP OR DEEP, HERE! CREEP, ... 065 00 012
    FAST OR THEY IN CLAMMYISH LASHTENDER COMBS CREEP . . . . . 149 A 005

CREPT
   A STEALTHY WIND CREPT ROUND SEEKING TO BLOW, • • • • • • 002 00 137
   CREPT ALL ALONG A HILL UPON OUR LEFT, • • • • • • • 125 00 003
   CREPT TREMBLING OUT OF BED. • • • • • • • • • 135 00 004
CREST
   THIS WAS THEIR MANNER: ONE TRANSLUCENT CREST • • • • 002 00 038
   WHOSE BRAGGART 'SCUTCHEON, WHOSE COMPLAISANT CREST • • 098 32 001
CREW
   BOUND FOR THE HARBOUR AND YOUR CREW. • • • • • • 021 00 014
   THESE DAREDEATHS, AY THIS CREW, IN • • • • • • 041 00 095
   BY A GREY EYE'S HEED STEERED WELL, ONE CREW, FALL TO: • • 071 00 004
CRIED
   OR IS IT THAT SHE CRIED FOR THE CROWN THEN, • • • • 028 25 007
   YOU CRIED ' BUT I HAVE SERVED THEE WELL, • • • • • 081 00 107
   I YIELD ' I WOULD HAVE CRIED. AT LAST • • • • • 081 00 117
   I CRIED WITH MY DESIRE. • • • • • • • • 135 00 010
CRIES
   THIS MEANS YOU NEED NOT FEAR THE STORMS, THE CRIES, • • 014 03 002
   WERE I COME O'ER AGAIN ' CRIES CHRIST ' IT SHOULD BE THIS ' • 063 00 014
   MY CRIES HEAVE, HERDS-LONG: HUDDLE IN A MAIN, A CHIEF- • • 065 00 005
   IS CRIES COUNTLESS, CRIES LIKE DEAD LETTERS SENT • • • 067 00 007
   IS CRIES COUNTLESS, CRIES LIKE DEAD LETTERS SENT • • • 067 00 007
   MEANTIME SOME TONGUE CRIES C • • • • • • • 152 01 016
CRIME
   IN SORDIDNESS OF CARE AND CRIME • • • • • • 133 00 011
CRIMSON
   THE WAVES WERE ROSY-LIPP'D: THE CRIMSON GLARE • • • 002 00 024
   TO SHEW THE CRIMSON STREAMS THAT INWARD SHINE, • • • 002 00 071
   WHERE YONDER CRIMSON FIREBALL SITS • • • • • 003 00 023
   ' A CRIMSON EAST, THAT BIDS FOR RAIN. • • • • • 021 00 008
   'S CHEEK CRIMSON: CURLS C • • • • • • • 071 00 010
   MANTLING PASSION IN A GRANDEUR, CRIMSON GRANDEUR. • • 152 02 037
   AND CRIMSON WEAR OF STARRY SHOT • • • • • 166 00 042
CRIMSONINGS
   WHEN THE ROSE RAN IN CRIMSONINGS DOWN THE CROSS-WOOD! • 027 00 034
CRIMSON-CRESSETE
   BE A CRIMSON-CRESSETED EAST, C • • • • • • 028 35 005
CRIMSON-GOLDEN
   THRO' CRIMSON-GOLDEN FLOODS PASS SWALLOW'D INTO FIRE. • • 002 00 083
CRIMSON-WHITE
   SPEAR'D OPEN LUSTROUS GASHES, CRIMSON-WHITE: • • • 002 00 008
CRINGE
   THE SOUR SCYTHE CRINGE, AND THE BLEAR SHARE COME. • • • • 028 11 008
CRIPPLES
   WHILE CRIPPLES ARE, WHILE LEPERS, DANCERS IN DISMAL LIMBDANCE, • 152 C 006
CRISP
   HIS CRISP COMBS, AND THAT COMES THOSE WAYS WE KNOW. • • 068 00 014
   THE ENDS OF THE CRISP BUDS SHE CHIPS • • • • 098 14 001
   CRISP LIPS, STRAIGHT NOSE, AND TENDER-SLANTED CHEEK. • • 136 00 016
   WILL CRISP ITSELF OR SETTLE AND SPIN • • • • 145 00 010
   FORWARD FALLING, FOREHEAD FROWNING, LIPS CRISP • • • 159 00 032
CRISP'D
   CRISP'D UP AND STARCHY FROM A SHORT HALF-HOUR • • • 107 03 003
CRISPS
   IN CRISPS OF CURL OFF WILD WINCH WHIRL, AND POUR • • 035 00 007
CRISS-CROSS'D
   TOGETHER, AS THE CRISS-CROSS'D SHELLY CUP • • • • • 101 00 002
CROCODILES
   FAWNING FAWNING CROCODILES • • • • • • • 145 00 022
CROOKED
   THOSE CROOKED ROUGH-SCORED CHEQUERS MAY BE PIECED • • • 011 00 004
CROSS
   AND HELD A CROSS OF FLOWERS, IN PURPLE BLOOM: • • • 001 10 006
   THE CROSS TO HER SHE CALLS CHRIST TO HER, C • • • 028 24 008
   THUS I SHALL MAKE A CROSS, AND IN'T • • • • 080 13 001
   AND COUNT THE ROSY CROSS WITH BANN'D DISASTROUS THINGS. • 089 00 009
   ON THE CROSS THY GODHEAD MADE NO SIGN TO MEN: • • • 168 00 009
CROSSBRIDLE
   WAG OR CROSSBRIDLE, IN A WIND LIFTED, WINDLACED -- C • • 071 00 011
CROSSES
   TO CROSSES MEANT FOR JESU'S: YOU WHOM THE EAST • • • 011 00 005
CROSS-BARRED
   I TOOK OF VINE A CROSS-BARRED ROD OR ROOD. • • • • 020 00 008
CROSS-COLOUR
   THAT MAKE MY EYES SORE AND CROSS-COLOUR THINGS • • • 125 00 040
CROSS-WOOD
   WHEN THE ROSE RAN IN CRIMSONINGS DOWN THE CROSS-WOOD! • 027 00 034
CROSS'D
   THE CLOISTERS CROSS'D WITH EQUAL COURTS BETWIXT • • • 001 04 002
CROUCH
   CROUCH: LAY KNEE BY EARTH LOW UNDER: • • • • 041 00 110
CROWD
   CROWD DOWN UPON A STREAM, AND, JOSTLING THICK • • • 002 00 094
   ON TANGLED SHOALS THAT BAR THE BROOK -- A CROWD • • • 002 00 096
   COULD CROWD CAREER WITH CONQUEST WHILE THERE WENT • • 073 00 012
CROWDED
   SO THOSE MERMAIDENS CROWDED TO MY ROCK, • • • • 002 00 098

CROWDED   (CONTINUED)
    CROWDED LET HIS TABLE BE: 024 00 026
CROWDING
    SAVE BY TWO STARS, MORE CROWDING LIGHTS ARISE, ... 002 00 032
    ONE BETTER BACKED COMES CROWDING BY: -- 166 00 013
CROWDS
    THE MAKING AND THE MELTING CROWDS: 015 00 003
    AND IT CROWDS AND IT COMBS TO THE FALL: 028 04 004
CROWN
    FROM CROWN TO TAIL-FIN FLOATING, FRINGED THE SPINE, ... 002 00 041
    OR IS IT THAT SHE CRIED FOR THE CROWN THEN, ... 028 25 007
    BEING PURE: WE, LIFE'S PRIDE AND CARED-FOR CROWN, ... 035 00 011
    THE CROWN HAS COME TO THEE. ' 109 09 004
    THE CROWN SHOULD BE UNTO HER HEAD 109 10 003
    THE CROWN SHALL BE FOR ME. 109 15 004
    IF HE WEAR THE CROWN UPON HIS HEAD 109 23 001
    IF HE WEAR A CROWN UPON HIS HEAD 109 23 003
    AND BRING A CROWN FOR THEE. ' 109 23 004
    ' IS THAT THE KING'S CROWN ON YOUR HEAD, ... 109 35 001
    AND HAVE YOU A CROWN FOR ME? ' 109 35 002
    ' IF IT WERE A CROWN OF PARADISE, ... 109 35 003
    I HAVE A CROWN FOR THEE. ' 109 37 004
    AND SEVEN EARS CROWN THE LODGED CORN, ... 114 00 006
CROWNALS
    AND FOLIAG'D CROWNALS (POINTING HOW THE WAYS 001 06 004
    HE, WHERE THE CROWNALS DROOP'D, HIMSELF REVILED 001 10 007
CROWNED
    WITH BLAZONED GROINS, AND CROWNED WITH HUES OF MAJESTY. . . . 001 06 009
CROWNING
    I SEE THE CROWNING OF THEIR TOWERS, ... 015 00 007
    THERE SHALL HER CROWNING BE. 109 39 004
CROWN'D
    A PIOUS WORK WITH THREEFOLD PURPOSE CROWN'D -- 001 01 005
CROWNS
    THAN ALL THE CROWNS TO ME. ' 109 38 004
    CROWNS COMPOSITE AND BRAIDED BAST 165 00 002
CRUCIFIED
    LOVESCAPE CRUCIFIED 028 23 004
    THUS CRUCIFIED AS I DID CRUCIFY, ... 080 14 005
    (JUST LIKE JESUS CRUCIFIED) : 145 00 050
    O THOU OUR REMINDER OF CHRIST CRUCIFIED, ... 168 00 017
CRUCIFY
    AND ALL IN ONE SAY ' CRUCIFY! ' 080 08 007
    FOR HE WHOM I SEND FORTH TO CRUCIFY, ... 080 11 003
    THUS CRUCIFIED AS I DID CRUCIFY, ... 080 14 005
CRUEL
    SHEAVED IN CRUEL BANDS, BRUISED SORE, ... 006 00 005
CRUISE
    SHE HAD COME FROM A CRUISE, TRAINING SEAMEN -- 041 00 013
CRUMBLED
    FROM ONE FRAIL HORN THAT CRUMBLED TO THE PLAIN 107 03 011
CRUMBLING
    OF CRUMBLING, FORE-FOUNDERING, THUNDERING ALL-SURFY SEAS IN: SEEN . 141 00 005
CRUSH
    AND THEY WHO CRUSH THE OIL 005 00 052
    WHEN SHE FELT THE KILL-WEIGHTS CRUSH 145 00 055
CRUSHED
    (CRUSHED THEM) OR WATER (AND DROWNED THEM) OR ROLLED . . . 028 17 003
    CRUSHED. WHY DO MEN THEN NOW NOT RECK HIS ROD? 031 00 004
    WORD WENT SHE SHOULD BE CRUSHED OUT FLAT 145 00 038
CRUSHES
    CRUSHES AND TEARS THE RARE ENJEWELLING, ... 002 00 085
CRUSH-SILK
    AND CRUSH-SILK POPPIES AFLASH, ... 138 00 021
CRUSH'D
    DOWN-SPLINTER'D ROCKS CRUSH'D COTTAGES. -- DREAR SIGHT, . . . 001 14 005
    YEA, CRUSH'D MY HEART, AND MADE ME DUMB, ... 118 00 012
CRUST
    AND SILVER DAMASQU'D PLATES OBSCUR'D IN AGE'S CRUST. 001 12 009
    THE CAN MUST BE SO SWEET, THE CRUST 022 00 015
    SQUANDERING OOZE TO SQUEEZED DOUGH, CRUST, DUST: STANCHES, STARCHES . 072 00 007
    THAT SHALL UNGLUE THE CRUST OF SIN. 081 00 133
CRUTCHES
    WHAT SIGHTS SHALL BE WHEN SOME THAT SWUNG, WRETCHES, ON CRUTCHES . 152 C 022
    THEIR CRUTCHES SHALL CAST FROM THEM, ON HEELS OF AIR DEPARTING, . 152 C 023
CRY
    THEY SHRIVE THEMSELVES AND CRY, ' GOOD SERVICE TO OUR GOD, ' . . 001 05 009
    OF BRAGGART BUGLES CRY IT IN -- 029 00 002
    ' ALL HANDS FOR THEMSELVES ' THE CRY RAN THEN: 041 00 042
    SEEMS BY A DIVINE DOOM CHANNELLED, NOR DO I CRY 048 00 041
    AND CRY ' O CHRIST-DONE DEED! SO GOD-MADE-FLESH DOES TOO: . . 063 00 013
    IN ME OR, MOST WEARY, CRY I CAN NO MORE. I CAN: 064 00 003
    I CRY ' O ROCKS AND MOUNTAIN MAKE ME ROOM ' 080 07 005
    LORD, BUT THEY CRY SO LOUD, AND WHAT AM I? 080 08 006
    AND I CRY OUT FOR WOUNDED LOVE, ... 081 00 033
    MY CRY IS LIKE A BLEAT: A FEW 081 00 066
    ARE HEARD, THAT CRY ' SHE DOES REPENT ', ... 081 00 123

56

CRY   (CONTINUED)
    I CAN SEND UP AN ESAU'S CRY: 081 00 126
    AND I MUST TAKE YOUR AMENDS, CRY PARDON, AND THEN BE DUMB.   .   .   .   128 00 020
        CHEEVIO:] WHEN THE CRY WITHIN 138 00 034
    WORST WILL THE BEST.   WHAT WORM WAS HERE, WE CRY, ...   157 00 031
CRYING
    THE WOMAN'S WAILING, THE CRYING OF CHILD WITHOUT CHECK --   .   .   .   028 17 006
    CRYING WHAT I DO IS ME: FOR THAT I CAME. 057 00 008
    SHE CAUGHT THE CRYING OF THOSE THREE. 145 00 029
CRYSTAL-ENDING
    THE BLUEBELLS UP WHOSE CRYSTAL-ENDING RODS 112 00 008
CRYSTALLINE
    WITH GROWTHS OF MYRIAD FEELERS, CRYSTALLINE 002 00 070
CUCKOO
    CUCKOO CALLS CUCKOO UP THE WOOD, ...   081 00 022
    CUCKOO CALLS CUCKOO UP THE WOOD, ...   081 00 022
    WHEN CUCKOO CALLS AND I MAY HEAR, ...   098 37 001
    CUCKOO, BIRD, AND OPEN EAR WELLS, HEART-SPRINGS, DELIGHTFULLY SWEET,   146 00 002
CUCKOOCALL
    AND MAGIC CUCKOOCALL 042 00 043
CUCKOO-ECHOING
    CUCKOO-ECHOING, BELL-SWARMED, LARK-CHARMED, C 044 00 002
CUD
    THEY CHEW'D THE CUD IN HOLLOWS DEEP. 092 00 002
CUE
    JACK'S CALL AND CUE AT LAST: 054 00 030
CULLY'S
    HAMPSTEAD WAS NEVER BRIGHT: AND WHATEVER MISS CULLY'S CHARMS   .   128 00 011
CUMBER
    BUT FOUL AND CUMBER NOT 077 00 009
    SWEAT AND CARE AND CUMBER, ...   170 00 010
CUMBERED
    SO FAGGED, SO FASHED, SO COGGED, SO CUMBERED, C 059 06 026
CUMBROUS
    THE INCAPABLE AND CUMBROUS SHAME 015 00 018
CUMNOR
    SYLVESTER CAME: THEY WENT BY CUMNOR HILL. 107 03 009
CUP
    TOGETHER, AS THE CRISS-CROSS'D SHELLY CUP 101 00 002
CUPBOARD
    FORTH CHRIST FROM CUPBOARD FETCHED, HOW FAIN I OF FEET   .   .   .   048 00 010
CUPP'D
    LIKE A CUPP'D CHESTNUT DAMASK'D WITH DARK BREAKS. 099 00 012
CURB
    LORD NOW CURB HIM FOR EVER. O DARING! O DEEP INSIGHT!   .   .   .   152 02 041
CURDED
    THAT ONEWHERE CURDED, ONEWHERE SUCKED OR SANK -- SOARED OR SANK --   071 00 006
CURE
    HE WAS TO CURE THE EXTREMITY WHERE HE HAD CAST HER: .   .   .   028 28 006
CURFEW
    IT IS THE SHUT, THE CURFEW SENT 022 00 006
CURL
    IN CRISPS OF CURL OFF WILD WINCH WHIRL, AND POUR 035 00 007
CURL'D
    THE BREAKING LEAVES OF GOLD ARE CURL'D UPON HER LIPS.   .   .   .   098 14 003
CURLS
    'S CHEEK CRIMSON: CURLS C 071 00 010
CURRENT
    IS WORTH AND CURRENT WITH A LESSEN'D MILL.' 096 07 008
    THE MINT OF CURRENT COURTESIES, THE FORGE 102 02 008
CURSE
    I MIGHT LET BYGONES BE -- OUR CURSE 041 00 089
    BONES BUILT IN ME, FLESH FILLED, BLOOD BRIMMED THE CURSE.   .   .   067 00 011
    AND BARELY TO ESCAPE THE CURSE, ...   081 00 170
    WEEPING, -- EVEN NOW I CURSE MYSELF REMEMBERING: --   .   .   .   102 01 041
CURSED
    SITTING EASTNORTHEAST, IN CURSED QUARTER, THE WIND: .   .   .   028 13 006
    SICKNESS BROKE HIM, IMPATIENT, HE CURSED AT FIRST, BUT MENDED   .   053 00 005
CURSES
    RAVENS, FOR PROSPEROUSLY-BODED CURSES 089 00 003
    LEFT NOT A ROOD WITH CURSES UNIMPREGNATE: 102 02 005
CURSING
    AND HATE THE ILL-VISAGED CURSING TARS, ...   114 00 010
CURVES
    WITH SHINING-HILTED CURVES, THAT THEY MAY STAY 112 00 007
CUSP
    A CUSP STILL CLASPED HIM, C 137 00 005
CUSTOMARY
    THESE NAMES, THESE FACES? THEY ARE CUSTOMARY 125 00 045
CUT
    ' I THOUGHT THE AIR MUST CUT AND STRAIN 021 00 036
    DIAMONDS ARE BETTER CUT: WHO PARE, REPAIR: 096 07 005
    THEY DRAW ALL COVERTS, CUT THE FIELDS, AND SUCK 104 00 012
CYCLADS
    THOSE CYCLADS MADE THAT THICKEN'D ON MY SIGHT. 002 00 037
CYPRIS
    TO GOLDEN-GIRDLED CYPRIS, -- CERES THERE 001 11 003

57

DABBLED
    WE FOUND WERE DABBLED WITH A COLOURING GROWTH, ... 098 09 002
DAFFODIL
    FOR ORIENCE OF THE DAFFODIL: 081 00 012
DAFFODILLIES
    BRINGING HEADS OF DAFFODILLIES, ... 098 16 001
DAFFODILS
    SHAKE THE BALANCED DAFFODILS. 098 07 002
    AND WHERE COLD DAFFODILS IN APRIL ARE 135 00 029
    THINK YOU WANT DAFFODILS AND FOLLOW AS FAR 135 00 030
DAHLIAS
    ONLY THE DAHLIAS BLOW, AND ALL IS AUTUMN HERE. 128 00 010
DAILY
    DAILY MAKE ME HARDER HOPE AND DEARER LOVE. 168 00 016
DAINTILY
    AND PENCILLED BLUE SO DAINTILY, ... 003 00 018
DAINTY
    THE DAINTY ONYX-CORONALS DEFLOWERS, ... 002 00 092
    DANDY-HUNG DAINTY HEAD. 138 00 026
DAINTY-DELICATE
    WITH THE DAINTY-DELICATE FRETTED FRINGE OF FINGERS 002 00 064
DAISIES
    I SPY THE NEAREST DAISIES THROUGH THE DARK, ... 135 00 023
DALE
    THAT MORE HE SHUNS OUR SPECIAL DALE 021 00 024
    THY LOVELY DALE DOWN THUS AND THUS BIDS REEL 058 00 007
    WHY SHOULD I CHANGE A SABINE DALE 166 00 047
DALLIES
    HE DALLIES YET AND YET WITH ME 110 00 006
DAMASK
    DAMASK THE TOOLSMOOTH BLEAK LIGHT: BLACK, C 061 00 009
DAMASK'D
    LIKE A CUPP'D CHESTNUT DAMASK'D WITH DARK BREAKS. 099 00 012
DAMASQU'D
    AND DAMASQU'D ARMS AND FOLIAG'D CARVING PILED, -- 001 10 002
    AND SILVER DAMASQU'D PLATES OBSCUR'D IN AGE'S CRUST. . . . 001 12 009
DAME
    DAME, AT OUR DOOR 028 35 001
DAMP
    IN A HOLLOW LUSH AND DAMP, ... 004 00 007
DANCE
    LIKE SHIVER'D RUBIES DANCE OR SHEEN OF SAPPHIRE HAIL. . . . 002 00 073
DANCED
    AND DANCED THE BALLS OF DEW THAT STOOD 021 00 034
    HAS DANCED WITH HER: AND ALL THE WHILE 083 00 023
    ROOTS AND ROCKS IS DANCED AND DANDLED, C 159 00 007
DANCERS
    WHILE CRIPPLES ARE, WHILE LEPERS, DANCERS IN DISMAL LIMBDANCE, . . 152 C 006
DANCES
    DANCES FOR SAD FOOTSTEPS SLOW: 024 00 022
    STILL THE SCARLET SWINGS AND DANCES ON THE BLADE. 152 02 013
    DANCES THE BALLS FOR LOW OR HIGH: 166 00 015
DANCING
    TO WHAT SERVES MORTAL BEAUTY -- DANGEROUS: DOES SET DANC- . . 062 00 001
    ING BLOOD -- THE O-SEAL-THAT-SO FEATURE, FLUNG PROUDER FORM . . 062 00 002
DANDLED
    THEY COULD TELL HIM FOR HOURS, DANDLED THE TO AND FRO . . . 028 16 006
    THAT DANDLED A SANDALLED 043 00 006
    AND THE SUNLIGHT SIDLED, LIKE DEWDROPS, LIKE DANDLED DIAMONDS . . 144 00 017
    ROOTS AND ROCKS IS DANCED AND DANDLED, C 159 00 007
DANDY-HUNG
    DANDY-HUNG DAINTY HEAD. 138 00 026
DANGER
    NOT DANGER, ELECTRICAL HORROR: THEN FURTHER IT FINDS . . . 028 27 005
DANGEROUS
    TIMES TOLD LOVELIER, MORE DANGEROUS, O MY CHEVALIER! . . . 036 00 011
    TO WHAT SERVES MORTAL BEAUTY -- DANGEROUS: DOES SET DANC- . . 062 00 001
    PLY FOLD ON FOLD ACROSS HIS DANGEROUS EYES. 102 01 019
DANGEROUSLY
    AND YET DEARLY AND DANGEROUSLY SWEET C 059 06 009
DANK
    DOWN THAT DANK ROCK O'ER WHICH THEIR LUSH LONG TRESSES WEEP. . 002 00 115
    AND FROM DANK FEATHERS WRING THE DROPS 003 00 008
DANK-YTRESSED
    CAUGHT ON THE DANK-YTRESSED TREES, ... 077 00 106
DANTE'S
    HOW SHAKESPEARE'S ENGLAND WEDS WITH DANTE'S ITALY. 098 35 002
DAPHNIS
    COME, DAPHNIS, GOOD VALERIAN, I WILL COME. 125 00 031
DAPPLE
    HER DAPPLE IS AT AN END, AS- C 061 00 005

DAPPLED
    GLORY BE TO GOD FOR DAPPLED THINGS -- 037 00 001
    THE DAPPLED DIE-AWAY 049 00 001
    DEGGED WITH DEW, DAPPLED WITH DEW 056 00 009
    DAPPLED WITH DIMINISH'D TREES 098 08 002
DAPPLED-WITH-DAM
    KISS MY HAND TO THE DAPPLED-WITH-DAMSON WEST: . . . 028 05 005
DAPPLE-DAWN-DRAW
    DOM OF DAYLIGHT'S DAUPHIN, DAPPLE-DAWN-DRAWN FALCON, IN HIS RIDING . 036 00 002
DAPPLE-EARED
    THE DAPPLE-EARED LILY BELOW THEE: THAT COUNTRY AND TOWN DID . . 044 00 003
DARE
    IS ALL THE WINTER BIRD DARE TRY. 003 00 014
    YOU'LL DARE THE ALP? YOU'LL DART THE SKIFF? 030 00 005
    HOW DARE I PAINT MISS STORY TO MISS MAY? 094 00 003
    THAN WE IN THE EAST DARE LOOK FOR BUDS, DISCLOSE . . . 119 00 002
    I DARE NOT TASTE THE THICKENING SALT, ... 120 00 026
    WITH DARE AND WITH DOWNDOLPHINRY AND BELLBRIGHT BODIES HUDDLING OUT, 159 00 017
DARED
    DROPPED EYES AND DARED NOT LOOK. 054 00 032
    TO DREAM I DARED SO MUCH FOR THEE. 118 00 006
DAREDEATHS
    THESE DAREDEATHS, AY THIS CREW, IN 041 00 095
DARE-GALE
    AS A DARE-GALE SKYLARK SCANTED IN A DULL CAGE . . . 039 00 001
DARES
    THAT DARES TO CAST ITS SEARCHING SIGHT 023 00 029
DARING
    MIGHT WE NOT THINK THE SWEET (?) AND DARING RISES . . 122 00 002
    LORD NOW CURB HIM FOR EVER. O DARING! O DEEP INSIGHT! . . 152 02 041
DARK
    BE SHELLED, EYES, WITH DOUBLE DARK 022 00 009
    HAST THY DARK DESCENDING AND MOST ART MERCIFUL THEN. . . 028 09 008
    YET DID THE DARK SIDE OF THE BAY OF THY BLESSING . . . 028 12 007
    SHE DROVE IN THE DARK TO LEEWARD. 028 14 001
    LOWER THAN DEATH AND THE DARK: 028 33 004
    NOT A DOOMS-DAY DAZZLE IN HIS COMING NOR DARK AS HE CAME: . 028 34 006
    WISEST MY HEART BREEDS DARK HEAVEN'S BAFFLING BAN . . 066 00 012
    I WAKE AND FEEL THE FELL OF DARK, NOT DAY. 067 00 001
    EYES IN THEIR DARK CAN DAY OR THIRST CAN FIND . . . 069 00 007
    BOTH ARE IN AN UNFATHOMABLE, ALL IS IN AN ENORMOUS DARK . 072 00 012
    WHOSE KEN THROUGH AMBER OF DARK EYES 077 00 051
    WITH ME 'TIS RISING IN THE DARK. 096 06 002
    WHILE PHOSPHOR, RISEN UPON THE SHALLOWING DARK, . . 098 28 003
    IN MORE PRECISION NOW OF LIGHT AND DARK 098 30 001
    LIKE A CUPP'D CHESTNUT DAMASK'D WITH DARK BREAKS, . . 099 00 012
    AND THEN GOES OUT INTO THE CAVERNOUS DARK. 103 00 016
    MILKY AND DARK, WITH AN ATTUNING STRESS 107 04 013
    I SPY THE NEAREST DAISIES THROUGH THE DARK, . . . 135 00 023
    ALL OVER, SOME SUCH WORDS AS THESE, THOUGH DARK, . . 136 00 029
    THE BARROW OF DARK MAENEFA THE MOUNTAIN: C 137 00 004
    GOD LIGHTEN YOUR DARK HEART -- BUT NO, ... 145 00 027
    SHEATHE THEE IN THY DARK LAIR: THESE DROPS C . . . 152 02 015
    DISCOVERING YOU, DARK TRAMPLERS, TYRANT YEARS, . . . 157 00 002
    DARK OR DAYLIGHT ON AND ON. HERE HE WILL THEN, HERE HE WILL THE FLEET 159 00 040
DARKENED
    THEE, MAY-HOPE OF OUR DARKENED WAYS! 026 00 040
DARKEN'D
    HERE IN SOME DARKEN'D LANDSCAPE PARIS FAIR 001 11 001
DARKER
    LOVE, IT GROWS DARKER HERE AND THOU ART ABOVE: . . . 020 00 005
    TO DEATH'S MORE SILENT, DARKER SPELL. 023 00 042
DARKLES
    HER GLASS DRINKS LIGHT, SHE DARKLES DOWN BEHIND, . . . 151 00 009
DARKNESS
    A FAITHFUL GUARD OF INNER DARKNESS FIX'D -- 001 04 007
    THE DARKNESS DID NOT CLOSE THAT NIGHT 021 00 003
    IF STILL IN DARKNESS NOT IN FEAR. 023 00 048
    WITH, ALL DOWN DARKNESS WIDE, HIS WADING LIGHT? . . . 040 00 004
    DOFF DARKNESS, HOMING NATURE KNOWS THE REST -- . . . 047 00 006
    OF NOW DONE DARKNESS I WRETCH LAY WRESTLING WITH (MY GOD!) MY GOD. 064 00 014
    LIGHT AND DARKNESS FROM HIM FLINGS: 077 00 068
    HELP'D BY THE DARKNESS OF A BLOCK OF COPSE 107 03 014
    MOONLESS DARKNESS STANDS BETWEEN. 129 00 001
    IN THE STARING DARKNESS 132 00 001
    IN ALL HER BEAUTY, AND SUNLIGHT TO IT IS A PIT, DEN, DARKNESS, . 152 02 023
DARKSOME
    FROM DARKSOME DARKSOME PENMAEN POOL. 030 00 032
    FROM DARKSOME DARKSOME PENMAEN POOL. 030 00 032
    THIS DARKSOME BURN, HORSEBACK BROWN, ... 056 00 001
    WITH DARKSOME DEVOURING EYES MY BRUISED BONES? AND FAN, . . 064 00 007
    AND IN THIS DARKSOME WORLD WHAT COMFORT CAN I FIND? . . 152 02 048
    DOWN THIS DARKSOME WORLD COMFORT WHERE CAN I FIND . . 152 02 049
DARLING
    BY IT, HEAVENS, BEFALL HIM! AS A HEART CHRIST'S DARLING, DAUNTLESS: 048 00 014
DART
    YOU'LL DARE THE ALP? YOU'LL DART THE SKIFF? 030 00 005

DARTING
    AND, SAVE BY DARTING ACCIDENTS, FORGET.   •   •   •   •   •   •   •   •   •   014 01 010
DASHED
    HIDEOUS DASHED DOWN, LEAVING EARTH A WINTER WITHERING   •   •   •   •   152 02 052
DATE
    AND OTHER SCIENCE ALL GONE OUT OF DATE   •   •   •   •   •   •   •   019 00 011
    THEY'RE OUT OF DATE -- LENT SERMONS ALL THE YEAR.   •   •   •   •   •   096 05 002
DATED
    DATED DUE TO SEASON --   •   •   •   •   •   •   •   •   •   •   042 00 004
DATELESS
    DOOMSDAY AND DEATH -- WHOSE DATELESS THOUGHT MUST CHART   •   •   •   126 00 003
DATES
    IT DATES FROM DAY   •   •   •   •   •   •   •   •   •   •   •   028 07 001
DAUGHTER
    SPRING'S ONE DAUGHTER, THE SWEET CHILD MAY.   •   •   •   •   •   •   026 00 002
    FOR THOU, AS SHE, WERT THE ONE FAIR DAUGHTER   •   •   •   •   •   026 00 025
    GOD'S DAUGHTER MARGARET CLITHEROE.   •   •   •   •   •   •   •   145 00 054
    NO MAN HAS SUCH A DAUGHTER. THE FATHERS OF THE WORLD   •   •   •   152 01 011
DAUGHTERS
    AND SEAL OF HIS SERAPH-ARRIVAL! AND THESE THY DAUGHTERS   •   •   028 23 005
    ' I HAVE TALL DAUGHTERS DEAR THAT HEED MY HAND: •   •   •   •   158 00 002
DAUNTING
    ALARMS OF WARS, THE DAUNTING WARS, THE DEATH OF IT?   •   •   •   051 00 006
DAUNTLESS
    BY IT, HEAVENS, BEFALL HIM! AS A HEART CHRIST'S DARLING, DAUNTLESS;   •   048 00 014
DAUPHIN
    DOM OF DAYLIGHT'S DAUPHIN, DAPPLE-DAWN-DRAWN FALCON, IN HIS RIDING   •   036 00 002
DAVID'S
    TILL A MAID IN DAVID'S HOUSE HAD BIRTH,   •   •   •   •   •   •   026 00 030
DAWN
    SO FROM THE DAWN WAS ILL BEGUN   •   •   •   •   •   •   •   •   021 00 009
    FROM LIFE'S DAWN IT IS DRAWN DOWN,   •   •   •   •   •   •   •   028 20 007
    THE HEIGHTENING DAWN WITH MILKY ORIENCE   •   •   •   •   •   •   098 30 002
    DAWN THAT THE PEBBLY LOW-DOWN EAST   •   •   •   •   •   •   •   098 31 001
    DAWN THAT THE LOW-DOWN PEBBLY EAST   •   •   •   •   •   •   •   098 31 004
    -- ---- ------ -- DEW, IS DAWN, IS DAY,   •   •   •   •   •   •   125 00 049
DAY
    OF BATTLE ONCE UPON ST. LAWRENCE' DAY   •   •   •   •   •   •   001 02 002
    AND IT WAS AT THE SETTING OF THE DAY.   •   •   •   •   •   •   002 00 006
    DROPS OUT AND ALL OUR DAY IS DONE.   •   •   •   •   •   •   •   003 00 032
    HE FEEDS ME WITH HIS MANNA EVERY DAY: •   •   •   •   •   •   005 00 013
    AND BID TO CATCH HIM ERE THE DROP OF DAY.   •   •   •   •   •   020 00 002
    BUT DAY PASSED INTO DAY.   •   •   •   •   •   •   •   •   •   021 00 004
    BUT DAY PASSED INTO DAY.   •   •   •   •   •   •   •   •   •   021 00 004
    THE DAY THAT BROUGHT MY LASTING PAIN   •   •   •   •   •   •   021 00 010
    SUMMONING MEN FROM SPEECHLESS DAY   •   •   •   •   •   •   •   023 00 041
    KNOW YE, THIS IS EASTER DAY.   •   •   •   •   •   •   •   •   024 00 006
    DECKS HERSELF FOR EASTER DAY.   •   •   •   •   •   •   •   •   024 00 018
    LET IN JOY THIS EASTER DAY.   •   •   •   •   •   •   •   •   024 00 024
    MAKE EACH MORN AN EASTER DAY.   •   •   •   •   •   •   •   •   024 00 030
    FAIRER THAN THIS ONE TO BRIGHTEN OUR DAY?   •   •   •   •   •   026 00 008
    IT DATES FROM DAY   •   •   •   •   •   •   •   •   •   •   •   028 07 001
    AND FRIGHTFUL A NIGHTFALL FOLDED RUEFUL A DAY   •   •   •   •   028 15 005
    AND YOU WERE A LIAR, O BLUE MARCH DAY.   •   •   •   •   •   •   041 00 021
    DAY AND NIGHT I DEPLORE   •   •   •   •   •   •   •   •   •   041 00 086
    GRACE THAT DAY GRACE WAS WANTED, '   •   •   •   •   •   •   •   041 00 116
    CANDLEMAS, LADY DAY;   •   •   •   •   •   •   •   •   •   •   042 00 005
    THIS VERY VERY DAY CAME DOWN TO US AFTER A BOON HE ON   •   •   •   048 00 005
    CAME, I SAY, THIS DAY TO IT -- TO A FIRST COMMUNION.   •   •   •   048 00 008
    IN SCARLET OR SOMEWHERE OF SOME DAY SEEING   •   •   •   •   048 00 038
    CAN SOMETHING, HOPE, WISH DAY COME, NOT CHOOSE NOT TO BE.   •   •   064 00 004
    LIFE DEATH DOES END AND EACH DAY DIES WITH SLEEP.   •   •   •   •   065 00 014
    I WAKE AND FEEL THE FELL OF DARK, NOT DAY.   •   •   •   •   •   067 00 001
    PURPLE EYES AND SEAS OF LIQUID LEAVES ALL DAY.   •   •   •   •   068 00 008
    EYES IN THEIR DARK CAN DAY OR THIRST CAN FIND   •   •   •   •   069 00 007
    AND, ON THE FIGHTER, FORGE HIS GLORIOUS DAY.   •   •   •   •   073 00 008
    BUT SLEEP AGAIN ERE DAY BE BORN: •   •   •   •   •   •   •   077 00 024
    IN WANDERING UNTIL BROAD LIGHT OF DAY: •   •   •   •   •   •   079 00 006
    BUT YET THEY SAY CHRIST COMES AT THE LAST DAY.   •   •   •   •   080 01 006
    THE LIGHTNINGS LEAP, THE DAY OF DOOM!   •   •   •   •   •   •   080 07 004
    THERE IS A DAY OF ALL THE YEAR   •   •   •   •   •   •   •   •   080 08 001
    THAT NIGHT THE JUDGMENT DAY BEGAN: •   •   •   •   •   •   081 00 090
    HE MEETS UPON MIDSUMMER DAY   •   •   •   •   •   •   •   •   083 00 027
    BLOT THE PERPETUAL FESTIVAL OF DAY?   •   •   •   •   •   •   •   089 00 002
    IF THAT WERE TRUE, IT COULD NOT LIVE A DAY.   •   •   •   •   •   097 00 002
    THE LOCK OF CLOUDS BETIMES AND HANGS THE DAY.   •   •   •   •   098 31 003
    THAT EARLY 'SPERSES, AND HIGH HANGS THE DAY.   •   •   •   •   098 31 006
    AND STUMBLING SWEARS HE WALKS BY LIGHT OF DAY.   •   •   •   •   102 03 031
    AND STUMBLING SWEARS HE WALKS BY LIGHT OF DAY. V   •   •   •   102 03 037
    ON SUCH A SEASON OF THE DAY AND YEAR.   •   •   •   •   •   •   107 01 004
    -- ---- ------ -- DEW, IS DAWN, IS DAY,   •   •   •   •   •   •   125 00 049
    IT'S THE DAY THAT MAKES THE CHARM: NO AFTER-WORDS COULD SUCCEED   •   128 00 007
    NOW BEGIN, ON CHRISTMAS DAY.   •   •   •   •   •   •   •   •   129 00 009
    AS IT FELL UPON A DAY   •   •   •   •   •   •   •   •   •   •   131 00 007
    YOUNG THECLA, SCANNED THE DAZZLING STREETS ONE DAY: •   •   •   136 00 014
    SHE LOOKED, SHE LISTENED: PAUL TAUGHT LONG THAT DAY.   •   •   •   136 00 024
    A DAY OFF SHEARING DAY.   •   •   •   •   •   •   •   •   •   144 00 012

DAY   (CONTINUED)
    A DAY OFF SHEARING DAY. 144 00 012
    SAY IT IS ASHBOUGHS; WHETHER ON A DECEMBER DAY AND FURLED .   .   .   .   149 A 004
    MUST ALL DAY LONG TASTE MURDER. WHAT DO NOW THEN? DO? NAY, ...   152 02 065
    WITH THE UPROLL AND THE DOWNCAROL OF DAY AND NIGHT DELIVERING   .   .   .   152 C 013
    FIELD-FLOWN, THE DEPARTED DAY NO MORNING BRINGS 153 00 009
    ALL DAY LONG I LIKE FOUNTAIN FLOW 155 00 002
    THOU SUN, ALLSEEING EYEBALL OF THE DAY, ...   160 00 004
    AH WELL A DAY! -- 160 00 019
    THIS FAITH EACH DAY DEEPER BE MY HOLDING OF, ...   168 00 015
    SOME DAY TO GAZE ON THEE FACE TO FACE IN LIGHT 168 00 027
DAY-BREAK
    AND LIGHT US, LORD, WITH THY DAY-BREAK. 167 00 022
DAY-DISSOLVED
    THAT FLEETED ELSE LIKE DAY-DISSOLVED DREAMS 157 00 011
DAY-LABOURING-OU
    THIS IN DRUDGERY, DAY-LABOURING-OUT LIFE'S AGE. 039 00 004
DAYLIGHT
    THE BUGLE MOON BY DAYLIGHT FLOATS 003 00 015
    IN THE GARDENS OF GOD, IN THE DAYLIGHT DIVINE 027 00 005
    IN THE GARDENS OF GOD, IN THE DAYLIGHT DIVINE 027 00 011
    IN THE GARDENS OF GOD, IN THE DAYLIGHT DIVINE 027 00 017
    IN THE GARDENS OF GOD, IN THE DAYLIGHT DIVINE 027 00 023
    IN THE GARDENS OF GOD, IN THE DAYLIGHT DIVINE 027 00 029
    IN THE GARDENS OF GOD, IN THE DAYLIGHT DIVINE 027 00 035
    IN THE GARDENS OF GOD, IN THE DAYLIGHT DIVINE 027 00 041
    ONE STAR BY DAYLIGHT FROM THE STRONG BLUE AIR, ...   102 03 010
    AND THEY WERE BEDDED TILL DAYLIGHT 109 01 003
    AND DAYLIGHT AND SWEET AIR, ...   133 00 014
    AFTER DAYLIGHT, DRAUGHTS OF DAYLIGHT, C   .   .   .   .   152 C 004
    AFTER DAYLIGHT, DRAUGHTS OF DAYLIGHT, C   .   .   .   .   152 C 004
    DARK OR DAYLIGHT ON AND ON. HERE HE WILL THEN, HERE HE WILL THE FLEET   159 00 040
    DAYLIGHT TO HEAD AND TREAT TO HEART, ...   167 00 018
DAYLIGHT'S
    DOM OF DAYLIGHT'S DAUPHIN, DAPPLE-DAWN-DRAWN FALCON, IN HIS RIDING   .   036 00 002
DAY'S
    AN OUR DAY'S GOD'S OWN GALAHAD. THOUGH THIS CHILD'S DRIFT   .   .   .   048 00 040
    ED ROME? BUT GOD TO A NATION DEALT THAT DAY'S DEAR CHANCE.   .   .   .   062 00 008
    IN THE RUDDIED COUNTY OF THE DAY'S UPBRINGING 098 28 004
    BUT HERE, HERE IS A WORKMAN FROM HIS DAY'S TASK SWEATS. 152 02 011
DAYS
    IN FORTY DAYS REACH'D HEAVEN FROM EARTH! 006 00 024
    CHILLING REMEMBRANCE OF MY DAYS OF OLD 017 00 005
    WE, ALL WE, THRO' THE LENGTH OF OUR DAYS, ...   026 00 034
    FOR I GREET HIM THE DAYS I MEET HIM, AND BLESS WHEN I UNDERSTAND. .   028 05 008
    DRESS HIS DAYS TO A DEXTEROUS AND STARLIGHT ORDER. 048 00 020
    DAYS AFTER, SO I IN A SORT DESERVE TO 048 00 026
    THE GLASS-BLUE DAYS ARE THOSE 060 00 083
    A HEART'S-CLARION! AWAY GRIEF'S GASPING, JOYLESS DAYS, DEJECTION. .   072 00 017
    MOST DEAD-ALIVE UPON THOSE DAYS. 080 02 007
    ? I THINK IT IS SEVEN DAYS, ' SHE SAID, ...   109 16 003
    AND KINDRED TO MY LAMENTABLE DAYS, ...   125 00 046
    DAYS AND DAYS CAME ROUND ABOUT 145 00 023
    DAYS AND DAYS CAME ROUND ABOUT 145 00 023
DAYSPRING
    LET HIM EASTER IN US, BE A DAYSPRING TO THE DIMNESS OF US, C   .   .   028 35 005
DAYSTAR
    WHAT MUST MAKE OUR DAYSTAR 060 00 106
DAZE
    GIDDIES THE SOUL WITH BLINDING DAZE 023 00 028
DAZZLE
    NOT A DOOMS-DAY DAZZLE IN HIS COMING NOR DARK AS HE CAME!   .   .   .   028 34 006
DAZZLING
    DOWN ROUGHCAST, DOWN DAZZLING WHITEWASH, WHEREVER AN ELM ARCHES,   072 00 003
    YOUNG THECLA, SCANNED THE DAZZLING STREETS ONE DAY! 136 00 014
DEACON
    HIS DEACON, DIRVAN. WARM TWICE OVER MUST THE WELCOME BE, .   .   .   152 01 008
DEAD
    LORD OF LIVING AND DEAD! 028 01 004
    DEAD TO THE KENTISH KNOCK! 028 14 004
    DO, DEAL, LORD IT WITH LIVING AND DEAD! 028 28 007
    FELIX RANDAL THE FARRIER, O IS HE DEAD THEN? MY DUTY ALL ENDED,   053 00 001
    IS CRIES COUNTLESS, CRIES LIKE DEAD LETTERS SENT 067 00 007
    IN WHOSE DEAD LAKE EVEN A VOICE MAY MAKE 080 04 003
    THEY ARE NOT DEAD WHO DIE, THEY ARE BUT LOST WHO LIVE.   .   .   .   098 40 001
    HER JAILOR WITH HIS VIGIL-ORGAN DEAD? 099 00 016
    ERE YOU SET SAIL THE KING WAS DEAD. 109 09 003
    AND JOHN SHALL LIE, WHERE WINDS ARE DEAD, ...   114 00 009
    I PROVE IT. WHAT THEN WHEN THESE LINES ARE DEAD 117 00 011
    ALIVE OR DEAD MY GIRL IS CARRIED IN IT. ENDLESSLY 152 01 021
DEAD-ALIVE
    MOST DEAD-ALIVE UPON THOSE DAYS. 080 02 007
DEADLY
    YET BOTH DROOP DEADLY SOMETIMES IN THEIR CELLS 039 00 007
DEADLY-ELECTRIC
    CAME EQUIPPED, DEADLY-ELECTRIC, ...   041 00 024
DEAD'NING
    AN ENDLESS ROUND OF DEAD'NING SOLITUDE! 001 14 006

DEAF

OR DEAF EARS SHALL DESIRE THAT LIPMUSIC THAT'S LOST UPON THEM.   •   • 152 C 005

DEAL

WHICH MAKES ME WHEN WITH MEN I DEAL   •   •   •   •   •   •   • 015 00 019
DO, DEAL, LORD IT WITH LIVING AND DEAD!   •   •   •   •   •   •   • 028 28 007
THY PLEA WITH HIM WHO DEALT, NAY DOES NOW DEAL,   •   •   •   •   • 058 00 006
DURANCE DEAL WITH THAT STEEP OR DEEP. HERE! CREEP,   •   •   •   • 065 00 012
MUST DEAL WITH MARGARET CLITHEROE.   •   •   •   •   •   •   • 145 00 007
HER URN TAKES ALL, HER DEAL IS JUST.   •   •   •   •   •   •   • 166 00 016

DEALS

DEALS TRIUMPH AND IMMORTAL YEARS!   •   •   •   •   •   •   • 052 00 012
DEALS OUT THAT BEING INDOORS EACH ONE DWELLS;   •   •   •   • 057 00 006

DEALT

SWINGS THE STROKE DEALT --   •   •   •   •   •   •   •   • 028 06 004
THY PLEA WITH HIM WHO DEALT, NAY DOES NOW DEAL,   •   •   •   • 058 00 006
ED ROME? BUT GOD TO A NATION DEALT THAT DAY'S DEAR CHANCE.   •   • 062 00 008
WHAT STROKE HAS CARADOC'S RIGHT ARM DEALT? WHAT DONE? HEAD OF A REBEL 152 02 002
DEALT SO, PAINTED ON THE AIR, C   •   •   •   •   •   •   • 159 00 025

DEAN

THIS DRY DEAN, NOW NO LONGER DRY NOR DUMB, BUT MOIST AND MUSICAL   • 152 C 012
SOUTHERN DEAN OR LANCASHIRE CLOUGH OR DEVON CLEAVE,   •   •   • 159 00 004
WHAT IS • • • • • • • THE DELIGHTFUL DEAN?   •   •   •   • 159 00 046

DEAR

OF GOD'S DEAR PLEADINGS HAVE AS YET NOT MOVED THEE, --   •   • 013 00 010
COMPLETE THY CREATURE DEAR O WHERE IT FAILS,   •   •   •   • 034 00 013
SHINE, AND BLUE-BLEAK EMBERS, AH MY DEAR,   •   •   •   •   • 036 00 013
MY ASPENS DEAR, WHOSE AIRY CAGES QUELLED,   •   •   •   •   • 043 00 001
HAVE FAIR FALLEN, O FAIR, FAIR HAVE FALLEN, SO DEAR   •   •   • 045 00 001
DIVINE CHARITY, DEAR CHARITY,   •   •   •   •   •   •   • 052 00 007
ELSE, BUT IN DEAR AND DOGGED MAN? -- AH, THE HEIR   •   •   • 058 00 010
EARTH BROWS OF SUCH CARE, CARE AND DEAR CONCERN.   •   •   • 058 00 014
BE THOU THEN, O THOU DEAR   •   •   •   •   •   •   •   • 060 00 114
ED ROME? BUT GOD TO A NATION DEALT THAT DAY'S DEAR CHANCE.   •   • 062 00 008
AMONG STRANGERS, FATHER AND MOTHER DEAR,   •   •   •   •   • 066 00 002
DULY, DEAR LORD, MY PRIZE IS WON.   •   •   •   •   •   • 081 00 109
THIS FLOWER, THIS FLORIS, THIS DEAR MAJESTY,   •   •   •   • 102 01 036
MEADOWS TO THEM INEXPLICABLY DEAR.   •   •   •   •   •   • 119 00 008
DEAR GRACE AND GIRDER OF MINE AND ME.   •   •   •   •   • 134 00 002
MAKES WELCOME DEATH, DOES DEAR FORGETFULNESS.   •   •   •   • 150 00 008
' I HAVE TALL DAUGHTERS DEAR THAT HEED MY HAND;   •   •   • 158 00 002

DEARER

MUCH DEARER TO MANKIND!   •   •   •   •   •   •   •   • 060 00 107
TO BRUISE THEM DEARER. YET THE REBELLIOUS WILLS   •   •   • 068 00 010
THOSE DEARER, MORE DIVINE BOONS WHOSE HAVEN THE HEART IS.   •   • 152 C 026
DAILY MAKE ME HARDER HOPE AND DEARER LOVE.   •   •   •   • 168 00 016

DEAREST

BEFORE-TIME-TAKEN, DEAREST PRIZED AND PRICED --   •   •   • 028 22 006
THERE LIVES THE DEAREST FRESHNESS DEEP DOWN THINGS!   •   •   • 031 00 010
TO DEAREST HIM THAT LIVES ALAS! AWAY.   •   •   •   •   • 067 00 008
BUT QUENCH HER BONNIEST, DEAREST TO HER, HER CLEAREST-SELVED SPARK 072 00 010
BUT CANDOUR NEVER HURT THE DEAREST FRIEND.   •   •   •   • 094 00 008
ITS DEAREST CHANGED TO BORES.   •   •   •   •   •   •   • 114 00 016
AND BEAUTY'S DEAREST VERIEST VEIN IS TEARS.   •   •   •   • 157 00 004

DEARLY

DEARLY THOU CANST BE KIND!   •   •   •   •   •   •   •   • 054 00 041
THERE DEARLY THEN, DEARLY,   •   •   •   •   •   •   •   • 054 00 042
THERE DEARLY THEN, DEARLY,   •   •   •   •   •   •   •   • 054 00 042
DEARLY THOU CANST BE KIND.   •   •   •   •   •   •   •   • 054 00 043
AND YET DEARLY AND DANGEROUSLY SWEET C   •   •   •   •   • 059 06 009

DEARNESS

CALL NO SUCH MAIDEN ' MINE ' . THE DEEPER GROWS HER DEARNESS   • 152 01 012

DEARS

IT FANCIES, FEIGNS, DEEMS, DEARS THE ARTIST AFTER HIS ART;   •   • 063 00 006

DEARTH

AND NEVER THIRST OR DEARTH.   •   •   •   •   •   •   •   • 005 00 048
SO HARDEN'D IS IT IN THIS DEARTH   •   •   •   •   •   •   • 018 00 011

DEATH

BUT OPEN'D TWICE, IN LIFE AND DEATH, TO STATE,   •   •   •   • 001 04 008
SUDDEN, DEATH BEFORE ME STOOD!   •   •   •   •   •   •   • 004 00 006
' DEATH, ' SAID I, ' WHAT DO YOU HERE   •   •   •   •   • 004 00 012
DEATH WAS VANISH'D FROM THE GLADE.   •   •   •   •   •   • 004 00 017
DEATH, TO MARK THEM IN THE SPRING.   •   •   •   •   •   • 004 00 032
THE MUSIC MUST BE DEATH.   •   •   •   •   •   •   •   • 021 00 039
AND LIFE'S FIRST GERMS FROM DEATH HAD WON.   •   •   •   • 023 00 024
FANG, OR FLOOD ' GOES DEATH ON DRUM,   •   •   •   •   • 028 11 003
HE WAS PITCHED TO HIS DEATH AT A BLOW,   •   •   •   •   • 028 16 004
BREATHE, BODY OF LOVELY DEATH.   •   •   •   •   •   •   • 028 25 004
DEATH WITH A SOVEREIGNTY THAT HEEDS BUT HIDES, BODES BUT ABIDES;   • 028 32 008
LOWER THAN DEATH AND THE DARK;   •   •   •   •   •   •   • 028 33 004
RICH BEAMS, TILL DEATH OR DISTANCE BUYS THEM QUITE.   •   •   • 040 00 008
DEATH OR DISTANCE SOON CONSUMES THEM! WIND   •   •   •   • 040 00 009
DEATH TEEMING IN BY HER PORTHOLES   •   •   •   •   •   • 041 00 039
CHEER'S DEATH, WOULD FOLLOW   •   •   •   •   •   •   • 041 00 047
WHAT DEATH HALF LIFTS THE LATCH OF,   •   •   •   •   •   • 049 00 019
ALARMS OF WARS, THE DAUNTING WARS, THE DEATH OF IT?   •   •   • 051 00 006
THEM! BEAUTY-IN-THE-GHOST, DELIVER IT, EARLY NOW, LONG BEFORE DEATH   • 059 06 018
MORE CHRIST AND BAFFLE DEATH;   •   •   •   •   •   •   • 060 00 067

DEATH   (CONTINUED)
    LIFE DEATH DOES END AND EACH DAY DIES WITH SLEEP. 065 00 014
    SHEER OFF, DISSEVERAL, A STAR, DEATH BLOTS BLACK OUT; NOR MARK   .   .   072 00 014
    AND DEATH FALLS GENTLY AS THE SNOW; 077 00 026
    RUINOUS HEART-BEAT, WANDERING, DEATH. 081 00 053
    THE BITTERNESS OF DEATH WAS PAST. 081 00 120
    CLINGS ON THE STROKE OF DEATH, THAT I CAN SMILE. 102 01 002
    TO NOT UNGENTLE DEATH NOW FORTH I RUN. 103 00 019
    ' IT IS AS COLD AS DEATH WITHOUT; 109 29 003
    O DEATH, DEATH, HE IS COME. 115 00 001
    O DEATH, DEATH, HE IS COME. 115 00 001
    THY RIBBED PORTS, O DEATH 115 00 005
    DOOMSDAY AND DEATH -- WHOSE DATELESS THOUGHT MUST CHART   .   .   .   126 00 003
    THE CITY TIRES TO DEATH. 133 00 012
    PRESSED TO DEATH. HE PLANTS THE YEAR; 145 00 004
    TO THE DEATH WITH MARGARET CLITHEROE! 145 00 035
    MAKES WELCOME DEATH, DOES DEAR FORGETFULNESS. 150 00 008
    IMMORTAL BEAUTY IS DEATH WITH DUTY, ...   156 00 018
    YEA AND DEATH, AND THIS FOR ME, ...   170 00 011
DEATHDANCE
    THE DEATHDANCE IN HIS BLOOD; 060 00 052
DEATHGUSH
    NOW HE WRINGS FOR BREATH WITH THE DEATHGUSH BROWN; 041 00 062
DEATH'S
    TO DEATH'S MORE SILENT, DARKER SPELL. 023 00 042
    RUCK AND WRINKLE, DROOPING, DYING, DEATH'S WORST, C 059 0L 012
    GATHER THE SOOTY PLUMAGE FROM DEATH'S WINGS 089 00 006
    DEATH'S BONES FELL IN WITH SUDDEN CLANK 092 00 012
DEATHS
    AND I THAT DIE THESE DEATHS, THAT FEED THIS FLAME, ...   075 00 012
DEBT
    FREELY FORGIVES THE MONSTROUS DEBT! 081 00 151
    YEA A DEBT TO PAY THEE YET; 155 00 019
DECAY
    WINDING SHEETS, TOMBS AND WORMS AND TUMBLING TO DECAY; C .   .   059 0L 012
DECAYING
    AND YIELD A SONG TO THE DECAYING YEAR; 105 00 002
DECEIVED
    SEEING, TOUCHING, TASTING ARE IN THEE DECEIVED; 168 00 005
DECEMBER
    SAY IT IS ASHBOUGHS; WHETHER ON A DECEMBER DAY AND FURLED .   .   149 A 004
DECK
    TO DECK AND MAKE MOST LORDLY EVERMORE. ' 001 02 009
    WHILE HE WAS WASHING FROM ON DECK 021 00 054
    BUILD HIS CHURCH AND DECK HIS SHRINE, ...   024 00 007
    AND THEY COULD NOT AND FELL TO THE DECK 028 17 002
    ACROSS MY FOUNDERING DECK SHONE 072 00 018
DECKS
    DECKS HERSELF FOR EASTER DAY. 024 00 018
    RACED DOWN DECKS, ROUND MESSES OF MORTALS. 041 00 040
DECREASED
    YOU VIGIL-KEEPERS WITH LOW FLAMES DECREASED, ...   011 00 008
DECREE
    I AM GALL, I AM HEARTBURN. GOD'S MOST DEEP DECREE 067 00 009
DEED
    AND CRY ' O CHRIST-DONE DEED! SO GOD-MADE-FLESH DOES TOO; .   .   063 00 013
    AND FEATURES, IN FLESH, WHAT DEED HE C 071 00 008
    OR EVER DID FOR MY SAKE SOME GOOD DEED 140 00 002
    DEED-BOUND I AM; ONE DEED TREADS ALL DOWN HERE C 152 02 066
DEED-BOUND
    DEED-BOUND I AM; ONE DEED TREADS ALL DOWN HERE C 152 02 066
DEEM
    WITH ATTRIBUTES WE DEEM ARE MEET; 023 00 014
DEEMED
    WAS DEEMED, DREAMED; WHO 060 00 028
DEEMS
    IT FANCIES, FEIGNS, DEEMS, DEARS THE ARTIST AFTER HIS ART; .   .   063 00 006
DEEP
    SWIMMING, AND LANGUISH'D GREEN UPON THE DEEP 002 00 114
    SLUMBER'D AT LAST IN ONE SWEET, DEEP, HEART-BROKEN CLOSE. .   .   002 00 135
    MADE HEADWAY IN THE FROTHY DEEP, ...   021 00 051
    DEEP CALLS TO DEEP, AND BLACKEST NIGHT 023 00 027
    DEEP CALLS TO DEEP, AND BLACKEST NIGHT 023 00 027
    THERE LIVES THE DEAREST FRESHNESS DEEP DOWN THINGS; .   .   .   031 00 010
    DEEP, DEEPER THAN DIVINED, ...   052 00 006
    O IS THERE NO FROWNING OF THESE WRINKLES, RANKED WRINKLES DEEP, .   059 0L 003
    DURANCE DEAL WITH THAT STEEP OR DEEP. HERE! CREEP, .   .   .   065 00 012
    I AM GALL, I AM HEARTBURN. GOD'S MOST DEEP DECREE 067 00 009
    THEY CHEW'D THE CUD IN HOLLOWS DEEP. 092 00 002
    DEEP SHAME IT WERE TO BE DISCOVER'D SO. 102 01 039
    THE RIVER SPANS IT WITH SO DEEP A HIP. 107 04 026
    IS ANYTHING A MILK TO THE MIND SO, SO SIGHS DEEP .   .   .   .   149 A 002
    LORD NOW CURB HIM FOR EVER. O DARING! O DEEP INSIGHT! .   .   .   152 02 041
    YE RIVER-HEADS, THOU BILLOWY DEEP THAT LAUGH'ST 160 00 002
DEEPENING
    THE DEEPENING INTENSITY 077 00 114
DEEPER
    DEEP, DEEPER THAN DIVINED, ...   052 00 006

63

DEEPER   (CONTINUED)
    CALL NO SUCH MAIDEN ' MINE ' . THE DEEPER GROWS HER DEARNESS   •   •   152 01 012
    BE AT EVERY ASSAULT FRESH FOILED, WORSE FLUNG, DEEPER DISAPPOINTED,   •   152 02 056
    THIS FAITH EACH DAY DEEPER BE MY HOLDING OF,   •   •   •   •   •   •   168 00 015
DEEP-GROVED
    AND, WHERE THOU DWELLEST IN DEEP-GROVED AIDENN,   •   •   •   •   •   026 00 023
DEEPLY
    DEEPLY SURELY I NEED TO DEPLORE IT,   •   •   •   •   •   •   •   •   041 00 097
    DEEPLY IN THE ARCHED LUSTRES,   •   •   •   •   •   •   •   •   •   077 00 133
DEEPS
    RIS'N FROM THE DEEPS TO GAZE ON SUN AND HEAVEN,   •   •   •   •   002 00 035
    SPINS TO THE WIDOW-MAKING UNCHILDING UNFATHERING DEEPS.   •   •   •   028 13 008
DEFEAT
    PHILIP TOOK OATH, WHILE GLORY OR DEFEAT   •   •   •   •   •   •   001 02 003
    DEFEAT, THWART ME? OH, THE SOTS AND THRALLS OF LUST   •   •   •   074 00 007
DEFIANCE
    IN A WIDE WORLD OF DEFIANCE CARADOC LIVES ALONE,   •   •   •   •   152 02 039
DEFLOWERS
    THE DAINTY ONYX-CORONALS DEFLOWERS,   •   •   •   •   •   •   •   002 00 092
DEFT-HANDED
    IN A NEIGHBOUR DEFT-HANDED? ARE YOU THAT LIAR   •   •   •   •   •   046 00 013
DEGGED
    DEGGED WITH DEW, DAPPLED WITH DEW •   •   •   •   •   •   •   •   056 00 009
DEGREE
    ' YOUR NAME AND YOUR DEGREE?   •   •   •   •   •   •   •   •   •   109 04 002
    THAT WAS OF LOW DEGREE?   •   •   •   •   •   •   •   •   •   •   109 10 002
    WITH ONE OF LOW DEGREE.   •   •   •   •   •   •   •   •   •   •   109 12 004
    THAT IS OF LOW DEGREE? '   •   •   •   •   •   •   •   •   •   •   109 18 004
    AND THOU OF LOW DEGREE. '   •   •   •   •   •   •   •   •   •   •   109 27 004
    IS TASTELESS NOTHING; AND IN MY DEGREE   •   •   •   •   •   •   •   117 00 010
    WITH WEALTH THAT MOCKS HIS HIGH DEGREE,   •   •   •   •   •   •   124 00 022
DEGREES
    ROUNDED IT, THINNING SKYWARDS BY DEGREES,   •   •   •   •   •   •   107 04 004
DEJECTION
    A HEART'S-CLARION! AWAY GRIEF'S GASPING, JOYLESS DAYS, DEJECTION.   •   •   072 00 017
DELAY
    AND MORE MUST, IN YET LONGER LIGHT'S DELAY.   •   •   •   •   •   067 00 004
DELICACY
    FINGER OF A TENDER OF, O OF A FEATHERY DELICACY, THE BREAST OF THE   •   028 31 006
DELICIOUS
    DELICIOUS KINDNESS? -- HE IS PATIENT. PATIENCE FILLS   •   •   •   068 00 013
DELIGHT
    THAN THE MOST ARE MUST DELIGHT HER?   •   •   •   •   •   •   •   042 00 010
    WITH DELIGHT CALLS TO MIND   •   •   •   •   •   •   •   •   •   042 00 030
    THE FINE DELIGHT THAT FATHERS THOUGHT! THE STRONG   •   •   •   •   076 00 001
    AND FILL THE WORLD UP WITH DELIGHT.   •   •   •   •   •   •   •   167 00 024
    BE OUR DELIGHT, O JESU, NOW   •   •   •   •   •   •   •   •   •   167 00 025
DELIGHTED
    OF SOMETHING DRIFTING THRO' DELIGHTED AIR,   •   •   •   •   •   002 00 028
DELIGHTFUL
    AND BREATHED DELIGHTFUL BREATH   •   •   •   •   •   •   •   •   133 00 010
    THEIR YOUNG DELIGHTFUL HOUR DO FEATURE DOWN   •   •   •   •   •   157 00 010
    WHAT IS •   •   •   •   •   •   •   •   THE DELIGHTFUL DEAN?   •   •   •   159 00 046
DELIGHTFULLY
    DELIGHTFULLY THE BRIGHT WIND BOISTEROUS C   •   •   •   •   •   •   072 00 005
    CUCKOO, BIRD, AND OPEN EAR WELLS, HEART-SPRINGS, DELIGHTFULLY SWEET,   146 00 002
DELIVER
    STROKE AND A STRESS THAT STARS AND STORMS DELIVER,   •   •   •   •   028 06 005
    AND WITH SIGHS SOARING, SOARING SIGHS, DELIVER   •   •   •   •   059 06 017
    THEM! BEAUTY-IN-THE-GHOST, DELIVER IT, EARLY NOW, LONG BEFORE DEATH   •   059 06 018
DELIVERING
    WITH THE UPROLL AND THE DOWNCAROL OF DAY AND NIGHT DELIVERING   •   152 C 013
DELL
    AND PLEDGED PURPLY IN A HALF-LIT DELL.   •   •   •   •   •   •   112 00 012
DELVE
    WHEN WE DELVE OR HEW --   •   •   •   •   •   •   •   •   •   043 00 010
    WHEN WE HEW OR DELVE!   •   •   •   •   •   •   •   •   •   •   043 00 018
DELVES
    DOWN IN DIM WOODS THE DIAMOND DELVES! THE ELVES'-EYES!   •   •   •   032 00 004
DEN
    WRING THY REBEL, DOGGED IN DEN,   •   •   •   •   •   •   •   •   028 09 003
    IN ALL HER BEAUTY, AND SUNLIGHT TO IT IS A PIT, DEN, DARKNESS,   •   152 02 023
DENIAL
    AND WILL NOT TAKE DENIAL.   •   •   •   •   •   •   •   •   •   110 00 007
DENIS
    DENIS, WHOSE MOTIONABLE, ALERT, MOST VAULTING WIT   •   •   •   •   143 00 001
DENSE
    THE DENSE AND THE DRIVEN PASSION, AND FRIGHTFUL SWEAT!   •   •   •   028 07 005
DENTED
    MOST DENTED) LAY SYLVESTER, READING KEATS'   •   •   •   •   •   107 04 021
DEPARTED
    FIELD-FLOWN, THE DEPARTED DAY NO MORNING BRINGS   •   •   •   •   153 00 009
DEPARTING
    THAT SHAPES IN HALF-LIGHT HIS DEPARTING RINGS,   c   •   •   •   •   019 00 003
    THEIR CRUTCHES SHALL CAST FROM THEM, ON HEELS OF AIR DEPARTING,   •   152 C 023
DEPEND
    YOU MAY DEPEND THAT ERE A WEEK WAS FLED,   •   •   •   •   •   •   097 00 005

DEPLORE
    DAY AND NIGHT I DEPLORE • • • • • • • • • • • • • • 041 00 086
    DEEPLY SURELY I NEED TO DEPLORE IT, • • • • • • • • • • • 041 00 097
DEPTHS
    TO KNOW THE DUSK DEPTHS OF THE PONDEROUS SEA, • • • • • 002 00 122
DESCEND
    TO HEAR HIS STRAIN DESCEND LESS LOUD • • • • • • • 077 00 079
    THE TIME SAVE WHEN HER TEARS WHICH STILL [DESCEND] • • • 111 00 005
DESCENDING
    HAST THY DARK DESCENDING AND MOST ART MERCIFUL THEN, • • 028 09 008
    THE DESCENDING BLUE! THAT BLUE IS ALL IN A RUSH • • • • 033 00 007
    AND WHERE THE BROW IN FIRST DESCENDING BOW'D • • • • 107 01 009
DESCRIED
    AND FIND IT WILL NOT THEREFORE BE DESCRIED • • • • • 102 03 011
DESERT
    OUR PRAYER SEEMS LOST IN DESERT WAYS, • • • • • • 023 00 005
DESERTER
    THIS SWEET DESERTER LISTS HERSELF ANEW • • • • • • 102 01 062
DESERVE
    DAYS AFTER, SO I IN A SORT DESERVE TO • • • • • • 048 00 026
DESERVING
    TO ME, GOD KNOWS, DESERVING NO SUCH THING! • • • • 034 00 002
DESIRABLE
    THIS WAS THE PRIZED, THE DESIRABLE SIGHT, C • • • • 137 00 006
DESIRE
    ARE SPATTER'D, WE DESIRE THE YOKE WE BORE, • • • • 005 00 053
    BUT I DESIRE THE WILDERNESS • • • • • • • • 015 00 023
    DESIRE NOT TO BE RINSED WITH WINE! • • • • • • 022 00 014
    WHAT BY YOUR MEASURE IS THE HEAVEN OF DESIRE, • • • 028 26 007
    YOU THERE ARE MASTER, DO YOUR OWN DESIRE! • • • • 046 00 011
    BREATHE O'ER MY BARE NERVE RATHER. I DESIRE • • • 080 05 005
    I CHOOSE ONE! BUT WHEN I DESIRE • • • • • • 080 10 001
    I CRIED WITH MY DESIRE, • • • • • • • • 135 00 010
    OR DEAF EARS SHALL DESIRE THAT LIPMUSIC THAT'S LOST UPON THEM, • 152 C 005
DESIRED
    I HAVE DESIRED TO GO • • • • • • • • • • 009 00 001
    I HAVE DESIRED, DESIRED TO PASS • • • • • • • • • 130 00 028
    I HAVE DESIRED, DESIRED TO PASS • • • • • • • • • 130 00 028
DESIRES
    HENCE SENSUAL GROSS DESIRES, • • • • • • • • 077 00 001
DESIROUS
    TO THE OFTEN TAKINGS OF DESIROUS WINDS, • • • • • 111 00 003
DESPAIR
    IT ROUNDS AND ROUNDS DESPAIR TO DROWNING. • • • • 056 00 008
    AND WISDOM IS EARLY TO DESPAIR! • • • • • • 059 OL 008
    SO BE BEGINNING, BE BEGINNING TO DESPAIR. • • • • 059 OL 013
    BE BEGINNING TO DESPAIR, TO DESPAIR, • • • • • 059 OL 015
    BE BEGINNING TO DESPAIR, TO DESPAIR, • • • • • 059 OL 015
    DESPAIR, DESPAIR, DESPAIR, DESPAIR, • • • • • 059 OL 016
    DESPAIR, DESPAIR, DESPAIR, DESPAIR, • • • • • 059 OL 016
    DESPAIR, DESPAIR, DESPAIR, DESPAIR, • • • • • 059 OL 016
    DESPAIR, DESPAIR, DESPAIR, DESPAIR, • • • • • 059 OL 016
    NOT, I'LL NOT, CARRION COMFORT, DESPAIR, NOT FEAST ON THEE! • 064 00 001
    THIS, BY DESPAIR, BRED HANGDOG DULL! BY RAGE, • • 070 00 019
    NOT HOPE, NOT PRAY! DESPAIR! AY, THAT! BRAZEN DESPAIR OUT, • 152 02 067
    NOT HOPE, NOT PRAY! DESPAIR! AY, THAT! BRAZEN DESPAIR OUT, • 152 02 067
DESPAIRING
    WHILE SICK MEN SHALL CAST SIGHS, OF SWEET HEALTH ALL DESPAIRING, • 152 C 003
DESPATCH
    DESPATCH AND HAVE DONE WITH HIS DOOM THERE. C • • • 028 28 008
    YOUR OFFERING, WITH DESPATCH, OF! • • • • • • 049 00 021
DESPATCHES
    DESPATCHES WITH NO FLINCHING. BUT WILL FLESH, O CAN FLESH • • 152 02 045
DESPERATE
    WITH FIERCER WEEPINGS OF THESE DESPERATE EYES • • • 014 03 006
    (O DEUTSCHLAND, DOUBLE A DESPERATE NAME! • • • • 028 20 003
DESPISE
    THAT GAVE YOU VANTAGE WHEN YOU WOULD DESPISE! • • • 014 03 003
    THINGS THAT SHE LIKES SEEMS OFTEN TO DESPISE, • • • 094 00 017
DESPONDING
    THE BREAST'S DESPONDING SOB I QUELL! • • • • • 023 00 038
DESTINED
    THE DESTINED LOVER, WHOM HIS STARS • • • • • • 083 00 001
DESTINY
    A GOD ENCHAIN'D OF DESTINY, • • • • • • • • 160 00 027
DEUTSCHLAND
    THE DEUTSCHLAND, ON SUNDAY! AND SO THE SKY KEEPS, • • 028 13 003
    (O DEUTSCHLAND, DOUBLE A DESPERATE NAME! • • • • 028 20 003
DEVICE
    A HOPE OF AN APPROVED DEVICE! • • • • • • • 080 12 002
DEVILISH
    THAT NO RECORDED DEVILISH THING WAS DONE • • • • 014 02 008
DEVIL'S
    OF SIN AND DEVIL'S MIGHT.' • • • • • • • • APPEN D 10
DEVIS'D
    HATH DEVIS'D NEW PAINS FOR ME • • • • • • • 160 00 012
DEVON
    SOUTHERN DEAN OR LANCASHIRE CLOUGH OR DEVON CLEAVE, • • • • 159 00 004

DEVONSHIRE
    AS DEVONSHIRE LETTERS, EARLIER IN THE YEAR   • • • • • • • • 119 00 001
DEVOURING
    WITH DARKSOME DEVOURING EYES MY BRUISED BONES? AND FAN, • • • • 064 00 007
DEW
    THE FIELD IS SOPP'D WITH MERCIFUL DEW. • • • • • • • • 008 00 003
    THESE DROPS: WHICH BE THEY? STARS OR DEW? • • • • • • • 010 00 018
    UP TILL THAT MORNING'S FALL OF DEW, • • • • • • • • 021 00 027
    AND DANCED THE BALLS OF DEW THAT STOOD • • • • • • • 021 00 034
    WHICH IS IT, STAR OR DEW? • • • • • • • • • • 025 00 010
    WHO TO US ARE AS DEW UNTO GRASS AND TREE, • • • • • 026 00 038
    DEGGED WITH DEW, DAPPLED WITH DEW • • • • • • • • 056 00 009
    DEGGED WITH DEW, DAPPLED WITH DEW • • • • • • • • 056 00 009
    —— ———— ————— —— DEW, IS DAWN, IS DAY, • • • • • • 125 00 049
    ANG. WHICH ARE THEY? STARS OR DEW? • • • • • • APPEN A 18
DEWBELL
    THE DEWBELL IN THE MALLOW'S MOUTH • • • • • • • • 025 00 015
DEWDROP
    THE DEWDROP ON THE LARKSPUR'S MOUTH • • • • • • • 010 00 015
DEWDROPS
    AND THE SUNLIGHT SIDLED, LIKE DEWDROPS, LIKE DANDLED DIAMONDS • • 144 00 017
DEW-LAP
    HER MILK-WHITE THROAT AND FOLDED DEW-LAP SLACK • • • • 099 00 009
DEWS
    EARTHLESS DEWS ON ANKLES SLEEK! • • • • • • • • 077 00 016
    AND IN THE DEWS BESIDE HIS NEST • • • • • • • • 077 00 091
DEWY
    OF DEWY GORSE BLURR'D WITH THE GOSSAMER FINE, • • • • 002 00 040
    DEWY FIELDS IN THE MORNING UNDER THE SUN • • • • • 098 13 001
DEXTEROUS
    DRESS HIS DAYS TO A DEXTEROUS AND STARLIGHT ORDER. • • • 048 00 020
DIADEM
    OF THE AIR-BLENDED DIADEM, • • • • • • • • • 077 00 115
DIADEM'D
    CIRCLET OF ASTRAL FLOWERETS —— DIADEM'D • • • • • 002 00 061
DIAMOND
    DOWN IN DIM WOODS THE DIAMOND DELVES! THE ELVES'-EYES! • • • 032 00 004
    THIS JACK, JOKE, POOR POTSHERD, PATCH, MATCHWOOD, IMMORTAL DIAMOND, • 072 00 023
    IS IMMORTAL DIAMOND. • • • • • • • • • • 072 00 024
DIAMONDS
    DIAMONDS ARE BETTER CUT: WHO PARE, REPAIR! • • • • 096 07 005
    AND THE SUNLIGHT SIDLED, LIKE DEWDROPS, LIKE DANDLED DIAMONDS • 144 00 017
DIAPERED
    HER FACE WAS SUCH, AS BEING DIAPERED • • • • • • 093 B 003
DIAPERS
    OF FINISH'D DIAPERS, THAT FILLS THE EYE • • • • • 001 06 006
DICK
    BY HIM AND RIPS OUT ROCKFIRE HOMEFORTH —— STURDY DICK! • • • 070 00 003
DIE
    APOLLO VIEWS THE SMITTEN PYTHON WRITHE AND DIE. • • • 001 11 009
    AND FAINT AS THOUGH TO DIE. • • • • • • • • 005 00 060
    THAT I SHALL LIVE, I SHALL NOT DIE, • • • • • • 008 00 007
    WITH FREE LONG LOOKING, ERE I DIE. • • • • • • 015 00 044
    AND I THAT DIE THESE DEATHS, THAT FEED THIS FLAME, • • • 075 00 012
    TO HEAR THE SHEEP-BELLS DIMLY DIE • • • • • • • 077 00 071
    WHO ASKS NOT LIFE BUT ONLY PLACE TO DIE. • • • • 079 00 009
    I DIE, I DIE, I DO NOT LIVE. —— • • • • • • ° 081 00 069
    I DIE, I DIE, I DO NOT LIVE. —— • • • • • • • 081 00 069
    THEY ARE NOT DEAD WHO DIE, THEY ARE BUT LOST WHO LIVE. • • 098 40 001
    NOT ALL, BUT WE WERE FRAMED TO FAIL AND DIE —— • • • 153 00 006
    AND HEAVEN'S BLISS, WHEN OUR TIME IS TO DIE, • • • • APPEN D 47
DIED
    AS I MARK'D, NOT ALWAYS DIED • • • • • • • 004 00 028
    DRAWN TO THE LIFE THAT DIED: • • • • • • • 028 23 002
    LIVING BREAD THE LIFE OF US FOR WHOM HE DIED, • • • 168 00 018
    AND DIED FOR US T'ATONE. • • • • • • • • APPEN D 40
DIE-AWAY
    THE DAPPLED DIE-AWAY • • • • • • • • • 049 00 001
DIES
    OUR HYMN IN THE VAST SILENCE DIES. • • • • • • 023 00 006
    LIFE DEATH DOES END AND EACH DAY DIES WITH SLEEP. • • • 065 00 014
    DIES OFF IN HYACINTHED GROUND, • • • • • • • 135 00 033
DIET
    SHE KEPT HER LOVE-THOUGHTS ON MOST LENTEN DIET, • • • 082 00 007
DIFFERENCE
    BRIDGING THE SLENDER DIFFERENCE OF TWO STARS, • • • 103 00 003
DIGHT
    THE RIM WITH RUBY FRINGES DIGHT, • • • • • • • 077 00 120
DIM
    IN BERYL-COVERED FENS SO DIM, • • • • • • • 003 00 026
    WHAT'S YONDER? GRIZZLED DYPHWYS DIM: • • • • • 030 00 009
    DOWN IN DIM WOODS THE DIAMOND DELVES! THE ELVES'-EYES! • • 032 00 004
    WITH SWIFT, SLOW; SWEET, SOUR; ADAZZLE, DIM! • • • 037 00 009
    MADE SWEETER, NOT MADE DIM, • • • • • • • 060 00 111
    I TOLD YOU THAT SHE TURNED HER MIRROR DIM • • • • 151 00 011
DIMINISHES
    HE HEIGHTENS WORTH WHO GUARDEDLY DIMINISHES! • • • • 096 07 004

DIMINISH'D
    DAPPLED WITH DIMINISH'D TREES 098 08 002
DIMLY
    TO HEAR THE SHEEP-BELLS DIMLY DIE 077 00 071
DIMM'D
    DIMM'D IN THE LONG ACCUMULATED DUST! 001 12 006
DIMNESS
    LET HIM EASTER IN US, BE A DAYSPRING TO THE DIMNESS OF US, C   .   .   028 35 005
DIMPLED
    TILL DIMPLED JOY STEALS O'ER ITS CHEEKS. 023 00 052
DIMPLING
    THE LANGUENT SMOOTH WITH DIMPLING DROPS, AND FLASH 002 00 103
DIN
    THOUGH NO HIGH-HUNG BELLS OR DIN 029 00 001
DINGLE-A-DANGLED
    TATTER-TANGLED AND DINGLE-A-DANGLED 138 00 025
DINGS
    NO MORE! OFF WITH -- DOWN HE DINGS C 159 00 028
DINT
    AND WITH SHARP FLINT WILL PART MY FEET AND DINT 080 13 003
DINTED
    AND EACH A DINTED CIRCLE. THE GRASS WAS RED 107 04 011
DINTLESS
    FLARES HIS WET BRILLIANCE IN THE DINTLESS HEAVEN. 098 34 002
DIP
    AH DIP IN BLOOD THE PALMTREE PEN 025 00 037
    OR DROVE, WITH A DIVER'S DIP, ...   054 00 020
    SWEETNESS FROM THE HOUR, AND DIP 077 00 132
    THEO. DIP IN BLOOD THE PALMTREE-PEN   .   .   .   .   APPEN A 43
DIPP'D
    TRESSES DIPP'D IN RAINBOW FIRE, ...   077 00 014
DIRECTION
    THO' APT TO THROW IT IN A STRANGE DIRECTION! 094 00 014
DIRECTLY
    GAZE ON, AND FALL DIRECTLY FORTH ON LIFE. 157 00 016
DIRVAN
    HIS DEACON, DIRVAN. WARM TWICE OVER MUST THE WELCOME BE,   .   .   .   152 01 008
DISMAY
    THE LORN MOON, PALE WITH PITEOUS DISMAY. 079 00 004
DISABLING
    SEE HOW SPRING OPENS WITH DISABLING COLD, ...   017 00 001
DISALLOW
    MASK'D WITH SUCH VIOLET DISALLOW THEIR GREEN? V 100 00 010
DISAPPOINTED
    BE AT EVERY ASSAULT FRESH FOILED, WORSE FLUNG, DEEPER DISAPPOINTED,   .   152 02 056
DISAPPOINTMENT
    THE SCEPTIC DISAPPOINTMENT AND THE LOSS 014 03 012
    LET ME THOUGH SEE NO MORE OF HIM, AND NOT DISAPPOINTMENT   .   .   .   048 00 036
    DISAPPOINTMENT ALL I ENDEAVOUR END? 074 00 004
DISARMING
    MOUNTS! THEN TO ALIGHT DISARMING, NO ONE DREAMS, ...   050 00 013
DISARRAY
    SWUNG DOWN AT A DISARRAY. 144 00 008
DISASTER
    DISASTER THERE! BUT MAY HE NOT RANKLE AND ROAM 048 00 042
DISASTROUS
    AND COUNT THE ROSY CROSS WITH BANN'D DISASTROUS THINGS.   .   .   .   089 00 009
DISCHARGE
    THENCE THE DISCHARGE OF IT, THERE ITS SWELLING TO BE,   .   .   .   028 07 006
DISCHARGED
    THE LADES DISCHARGED AND LADED NEW, ...   166 00 035
DISCHARGING
    GROSS MIND DISCHARGING FOULED LAUGHTER! 077 00 058
DISCLOSE
    THAN WE IN THE EAST DARE LOOK FOR BUDS, DISCLOSE 119 00 002
DISCLOSES
    TURNING AND PACING, SO BY SLIPS DISCLOSES 108 00 002
DISCONTENT
    THESE ARE MY VERY TEXT OF DISCONTENT! 125 00 044
DISCORD
    SINCE TRAMPLED SPAIN BY ROYAL DISCORD TORN 001 15 001
DISCOVERED
    THE AUTHENTIC CADENCE WAS DISCOVERED LATE 019 00 009
DISCOVERING
    DISCOVERING YOU, DARK TRAMPLERS, TYRANT YEARS. 157 00 002
DISCOVER'D
    WITH NOT TO BE DISCOVER'D GOLD, ...   015 00 014
    BE DISCOVER'D TO MY SIGHT 077 00 017
    THEN WAS DISCOVER'D IN THE PATHLESS SKY, ...   079 00 007
    DISCOVER'D EVERYWHERE. 098 24 003
    DEEP SHAME IT WERE TO BE DISCOVER'D SO. 102 01 039
DISCOVERY
    SCARCE WORTH DISCOVERY, IN SOME CORNER SEEN 103 00 002
DISHEVELLED
    CHAPLETS FOR DISHEVELLED HAIR, ...   024 00 021
DISMAL
    HE SEEM'D A DISMAL MIRKY STAMP 004 00 008

67

DISMAL   (CONTINUED)
     IT SEEM'D SO HARD AND DISMAL THING, ...   004 00 031
     WHY IF IT BE SO, FOR THE DISMAL MORN 090 00 001
     WHILE CRIPPLES ARE, WHILE LEPERS, DANCERS IN DISMAL LIMBDANCE,   .   .   152 C 006
DISMALEST
     YOU HAVE MADE ME QUOTE ALMOST THE DISMALEST PROVERB I KNOW;   .   .   128 00 018
DISMEMBERING
     DISREMEMBERING, DISMEMBERING ALL NOW, HEART, YOU ROUND ME RIGHT   .   061 00 007
DISOBEDIENT
     WHICH ONCE WERE DISOBEDIENT   .   .   .   .   093 A 003
DISORDERS
     FATAL FOUR DISORDERS, FLESHED THERE, ALL CONTENDED? 053 00 004
DISPARADISED
     HAVE WILL'D TO BE DISPARADISED 118 00 003
DISPEL
     DISPEL THE DOUBT AND DRY THE TEAR; 023 00 046
DISPENSE
     SINCE GOD HAS LET DISPENSE 060 00 040
DISPENSES
     AND ROSING PART, ON PART DISPENSES GREEN; 100 00 003
DISPOSES
     EVEN SO MY THOUGHT THE ROSE AND GREY DISPOSES 108 00 007
DISQUIET
     WITH LEVELL'D LASHES STILLING THEIR DISQUIET; 082 00 002
DISREGARDED
     PRAYER GO DISREGARDED; 048 00 047
DISREMEMBERING
     DISREMEMBERING, DISMEMBERING ALL NOW, HEART, YOU ROUND ME RIGHT   .   061 00 007
DISSEVERAL
     SHEER OFF, DISSEVERAL, A STAR, DEATH BLOTS BLACK OUT; NOR MARK   .   072 00 014
DISSOLVE
     BRIGHT HUES LONG LOOK'D AT THIN, DISSOLVE AND FLY; 117 00 002
DISTANCE
     RICH BEAMS, TILL DEATH OR DISTANCE BUYS THEM QUITE. 040 00 008
     DEATH OR DISTANCE SOON CONSUMES THEM: WIND 040 00 009
     DISTANCE 098 08 001
DISTANCED
     WITH SUCH A VIOLET SLIGHT THEIR DISTANCED GREEN? V 100 00 008
DISTANT
     MY SEVERAL MOANS COME DISTANT IN THEIR TONES 080 03 003
     ALL TIME AT ONCE AND SPAN THE DISTANT GOALS, ...   126 00 004
DISTEMPER'D
     BUT THIS DISTEMPER'D COURT WILL CHANGE IT ALL: -- 125 00 057
DISTILLATION
     WITH DREADFUL DISTILLATION OF THOUGHTS SOUR AS BLOOD,   .   .   .   152 02 064
DISTILLS
     AND WHERE IS HE WHO MORE AND MORE DISTILLS 068 00 012
DISTINCTION
     AND I'LL LOVE MY DISTINCTION: NEAR OR FAR 014 02 012
DISTRESS
     FOR US BY CALVARY'S DISTRESS 006 00 017
     OR BRING MORE OR MORE BLAZON MAN'S DISTRESS. 150 00 004
DISTRESSED
     BUT UNCUMBERED: MEADOW-DOWN IS NOT DISTRESSED 039 00 013
DISTURB'D
     AIRWARDS, DISTURB'D; AND THE SCARCE TROUBLED SEA 002 00 110
DITHER
     MAKES DITHER, MAKES HOVER 159 00 010
DIVE
     ALL ELSE MAY WHIRL OR DIVE OR FLY. 130 00 008
DIVER'S
     OR DROVE, WITH A DIVER'S DIP, ...   054 00 020
DIVIDE
     FOR ONLY TRY BY GAZING TO DIVIDE 102 03 009
DIVIDED
     PARTED ME LEAF AND LEAF, DIVIDED ME, EYELID AND EYELID OF SLUMBER.   .   137 00 007
DIVINE
     WITH FORM DIVINE, A FIERY CHIVALRY -- 001 07 008
     I NEVER SAW HER SO DIVINE. 003 00 019
     SO FRESH THAT COME IN FASTS DIVINE! 022 00 016
     IN THE GARDENS OF GOD, IN THE DAYLIGHT DIVINE 027 00 005
     IN THE GARDENS OF GOD, IN THE DAYLIGHT DIVINE 027 00 011
     IN THE GARDENS OF GOD, IN THE DAYLIGHT DIVINE 027 00 017
     IN THE GARDENS OF GOD, IN THE DAYLIGHT DIVINE 027 00 023
     IN THE GARDENS OF GOD, IN THE DAYLIGHT DIVINE 027 00 029
     IN THE GARDENS OF GOD, IN THE DAYLIGHT DIVINE 027 00 035
     IN THE GARDENS OF GOD, IN THE DAYLIGHT DIVINE 027 00 041
     TO THY BREAST, TO THY REST, TO THY GLORY DIVINE 027 00 047
     HAS ONE FETCH IN HER: SHE REARS HERSELF TO DIVINE 028 19 006
     THERE! AND YOUR SWEETEST SENDINGS, AH DIVINE, ...   048 00 013
     SEEMS BY A DIVINE DOOM CHANNELLED, NOR DO I CRY 048 00 041
     DIVINE CHARITY, DEAR CHARITY, ...   052 00 007
     AND, HIDE IT THOUGH SHE DOES, ONE MAY DIVINE 094 00 011
     THOSE DEARER, MORE DIVINE BOONS WHOSE HAVEN THE HEART IS.   .   .   152 C 026
DIVINED
     DEEP, DEEPER THAN DIVINED, ...   052 00 006
DIVINELY
     LIES DIVINELY STILL, AT REST, ...   077 00 098

68

DIVING
    SOME, DIVING MERRILY, DOWNWARD DROVE, AND GLEAM'D 002 00 108
DIVINITY
    DIVINITY OF AIR, FLEET-FEATHER'D GALES, ... 160 00 001
DIZZY
    MELTED IN THE DIZZY BOW 077 00 140
DOFF
    DOFF DARKNESS, HOMING NATURE KNOWS THE REST -- 047 00 006
DOFFS
    DOFFS ALL, DRIVES FULL FOR RIGHTEOUSNESS. 041 00 056
DOG
    DOG, HE DID GIVE TONGUE! 054 00 034
DOGEARED
    THAT THE HANGING HONEYSUCK, THE DOGEARED HAZELS IN THE COVER . 159 00 009
DOGGED
    WRING THY REBEL, DOGGED IN DEN, ... 028 09 003
    ELSE, BUT IN DEAR AND DOGGED MAN? -- AH, THE HEIR 058 00 010
DOGG'D
    SUCH HEATHENISH MISADVENTURE DOGG'D ONE SIN. V 102 02 013
DOG-STAR
    THE DOG-STAR WITH THE FIELDS ABAKE 166 00 031
DOGROSE
    THE FURL OF FRESH-LEAVED DOGROSE DOWN 144 00 001
DOGS
    SUCH HEATHENISH MISADVENTURE DOGS ONE SIN. V 102 02 013
DOING
    THY DOING! AND DOST THOU TOUCH ME AFRESH? 028 01 007
    HAVE ALL THINGS READY IN HIS ROOM. THERE NEEDS BUT LITTLE DOING. . 152 01 006
    CRAMPS ALL DOING. WHAT DO? NOT YIELD, C 152 02 066
DOMAIN
    AMONG THE LILIES AND THY GOOD DOMAIN. 123 00 006
DOMINANT
    I HAVE FOUND THE DOMINANT OF MY RANGE AND STATE -- . . . 019 00 013
DOOM
    THE GOAL WAS A SHOAL, OF A FOURTH THE DOOM TO BE DROWNED! . . 028 12 006
    DESPATCH AND HAVE DONE WITH HIS DOOM THERE. C . . . 028 28 008
    SEEMS BY A DIVINE DOOM CHANNELLED, NOR DO I CRY . . . 048 00 041
    THE LIGHTNINGS LEAP, THE DAY OF DOOM! 080 07 004
    THE SEA TOOK PITY: IT INTERPOSED WITH DOOM! . . . 158 00 001
DOOMED
    HER FLOWER, HER PIECE OF BEING, DOOMED DRAGON FOOD. . . 050 00 004
    HAD ALWAYS DOOMED HER DOWN TO THIS -- 145 00 003
DOOMFIRE
    FRESH, TILL DOOMFIRE BURN ALL, ... 041 00 119
DOOMSDAY
    DOOMSDAY AND DEATH -- WHOSE DATELESS THOUGHT MUST CHART . . 126 00 003
DOOMS-DAY
    NOT A DOOMS-DAY DAZZLE IN HIS COMING NOR DARK AS HE CAME! . . 028 34 006
DOOR
    WHERE STANDS NO HOST AT DOOR OR HEARTH 023 00 011
    DAME, AT OUR DOOR 028 35 001
    THAT IN MAJORCA ALFONSO WATCHED THE DOOR. 073 00 014
    OPEN THE DOOR TO ME. ' 109 29 004
    WHEN SHE HAD MADE THE DOOR WIDE 109 30 003
    THEN AT THE DOOR WHAT WORK THERE WAS, GOOD LACK, . . 135 00 005
    I PUT THE DOOR TO WITH THE BOLTS UNPINNED, . . . 135 00 011
DOORS
    DOORS SLAMM'D TO THE BLASTS CONTINUALLY: MORE LOW, . . 001 13 008
    THAT NEST WITHIN CLOSE-BARRED DOORS, ... 077 00 054
    BE YE LIFT UP, YE EVERLASTING DOORS 115 00 009
DORIC
    WITH MASSY PILLARS OF THE DORIC MOOD 001 07 002
DOROTHEA
    DOROTHEA -- OR WAS YOUR WRIT 025 00 027
    THEO. DOROTHEA -- OR WAS YOUR WRIT . . . . APPEN A 27
DOROTHY
    NOR FRUIT, NOR FLOWERS, NOR DOROTHY. . . . 010 00 024
    FRUIT NOR FLOWER NOR DOROTHY. 025 00 024
    CAT. NOR FRUIT NOR FLOWERS NOR DOROTHY. . . APPEN A 24
DOUBLE
    BE SHELLED, EYES, WITH DOUBLE DARK . . . 022 00 009
    (O DEUTSCHLAND, DOUBLE A DESPERATE NAME! . . 028 20 003
    DOUBLE, AND HIGHER THAN HIS WONT, . . . 077 00 111
    DOUBLE AS SHARP, MEANING AND FORCIBLE. . . 102 01 011
    LOVE ME AS I LOVE THEE. O DOUBLE SWEET! . . 161 00 001
DOUBLE-MUSICAL
    MAKING THEM DOUBLE-MUSICAL. AND THEY . . 112 00 005
DOUBLE-NATURED
    DOUBLE-NATURED NAME, ... 028 34 002
DOUBLET
    ROUND THIS UNSEXING DOUBLET, -- WHILE I SET . . 102 01 004
DOUBT
    DISPEL THE DOUBT AND DRY THE TEAR: . . 023 00 046
    FROM GOD AND MAN, IS HELL NO DOUBT. . . 080 01 004
    SOMEWHERE WE SLIPT ASTRAY, YOU CANNOT DOUBT. . 125 00 014
DOUBTLESS
    DOUBTLESS THE VOICE! NOW FALL'N NOW SPENT, . . 081 00 002

DOUBTLESS   (CONTINUED)
    MOTHERS ARE DOUBTLESS HAPPIER FOR THEIR BABES 123 00 001
DOUGH
    SELFYEAST OF SPIRIT A DULL DOUGH SOURS. I SEE 067 00 012
    SQUANDERING OOZE TO SQUEEZED DOUGH, CRUST, DUST; STANCHES, STARCHES   . 072 00 007
DOVE
    THE WOOD: BUT NOT A DOVE WOULD COO. 021 00 021
    BUT SING CONTENTED AS THE DOVE 124 00 003
DOVES
    EYE-GREETING DOVES BRIGHT-COUNTER TO THE ROOK, ... 016 00 003
DOVEWINGED
    MY HEART, BUT YOU WERE DOVEWINGED, I CAN TELL, ... 028 03 006
DOWNCAROL
    WITH THE UPROLL AND THE DOWNCAROL OF DAY AND NIGHT DELIVERING   . . 152 C 013
DOWNDOLPHINRY
    WITH DARE AND WITH DOWNDOLPHINRY AND BELLBRIGHT BODIES HUDDLING OUT, 159 00 017
DOWN-DUGGED
    THE DOWN-DUGGED GROUND-HUGGED GREY 028 26 002
DOWN-SPLINTER'D
    DOWN-SPLINTER'D ROCKS CRUSH'D COTTAGES. -- DREAR SIGHT,   . . . 001 14 005
DOWNRIGHT
    AT DOWNRIGHT ' NO OR YES? ' 041 00 055
DOWN
    NO WONDER OF IT: SHEER PLOD MAKES PLOUGH DOWN SILLION   . . . 036 00 012
    WITH, ALL DOWN DARKNESS WIDE, HIS WADING LIGHT? 040 00 004
    IT HURLS, HURLS OFF BONIFACE DOWN. 041 00 032
    THY LOVELY DALE DOWN THUS AND THUS BIDS REEL 058 00 007
    DOWN ROUGHCAST, DOWN DAZZLING WHITEWASH, WHEREVER AN ELM ARCHES, . 072 00 003
    DOWN ROUGHCAST, DOWN DAZZLING WHITEWASH, WHEREVER AN ELM ARCHES, . 072 00 003
    AND TANGLES ON A DOWN OF FRANCE, ... 083 00 014
    AND DOWN . . . THE FURROW DRY 138 00 027
DOWNS
    DOWNS' FOREFALLS BEAT TO THE BURIAL. 041 00 008
    MIGHT COVER THE NEIGHBOUR DOWNS WITH A SPAN OF SINGING,   . . . 098 28 002
    AS VOID AS THOSE THE GENTLE DOWNS APPEAR 107 01 003
    BUT WHAT DREW SHEPHERD RICHARD FROM HIS DOWNS, ... 107 02 001
DOWNWARD
    SOME, DIVING MERRILY, DOWNWARD DROVE, AND GLEAM'D   . . . 002 00 108
DOWNWARD-HOLLOWI
    CLOSE-ROOTED IN THE DOWNWARD-HOLLOWING FIELDS: 107 03 015
DOWNWARDS
    AND, HEADED ALWAYS DOWNWARDS, WITH LESS SOUNDING 112 00 002
DOWNY
    THIS DOWNY COUNTERFEIT UPON MY LIP, ... 102 01 005
DRAGON
    HER FLOWER, HER PIECE OF BEING, DOOMED DRAGON FOOD. 050 00 004
DRAGONFLIES
    AS KINGFISHERS CATCH FIRE, DRAGONFLIES DRAW FLAME; 057 00 001
DRAGONISH
    ONLY THE BEAKLEAVED BOUGHS DRAGONISH C 061 00 009
DRAGONS
    THERE RID THE DRAGONS, ROOT OUT THERE THE SIN. 150 00 010
DRAIN
    TO MAN'S LAST DUST, DRAIN FAST TOWARDS MAN'S FIRST SLIME. . . . 035 00 014
DRAINING
    AND WATER DRAINING THROUGH AND THROUGH 021 00 020
DRAUGHT
    WITH DRAUGHT OF THIN AND PURSUANT COLD SO NIPS 011 00 006
    ABOVE THEM, DOWN THE DRAUGHT OF AIR, ... 083 00 012
DRAUGHTS
    AFTER DAYLIGHT, DRAUGHTS OF DAYLIGHT, C   . . . . . . 152 C 004
DRAW
    PURE FASTED FACES DRAW UNTO THIS FEAST: 011 00 001
    DRAW ME BY CHARITY, MOTHER OF MINE. 027 00 048
    AS KINGFISHERS CATCH FIRE, DRAGONFLIES DRAW FLAME; 057 00 001
    MY LUNG MUST DRAW AND DRAW 060 00 014
    MY LUNG MUST DRAW AND DRAW 060 00 014
    MEN HERE MAY DRAW LIKE BREATH 060 00 066
    THEY DRAW ALL COVERTS, CUT THE FIELDS, AND SUCK 104 00 012
DRAWER
    ONCE IN A DRAWER OF INDIAN WOOD 081 00 080
DRAWING
    FISH FEEL THEIR WATERS DRAWING TO 166 00 033
DRAWN
    WHICH IN NEWLY DRAWN GREEN LITTER 025 00 005
    FROM LIFE'S DAWN IT IS DRAWN DOWN, ... 028 20 007
    DRAWN TO THE LIFE THAT DIED; 028 23 002
    I HAVE DRAWN HEAT FROM THIS CONTAGIOUS SUN; 103 00 018
    THEIR HIGHEST SPRAYS WERE DRAWN AS FINE AS LASHES,   . . . 107 04 006
    I HEAR A NOISE OF WATERS DRAWN AWAY, ... 112 00 001
DRAWS
    THE HAND DRAWS OFF THE GLOVE: THE ACORN-CUP 101 00 009
    TAMPERING WITH THOSE SWEET BINES, DRAWS THEM OUT, C   . . . 152 01 015
DRAYHORSE
    DIDST FETTLE FOR THE GREAT GREY DRAYHORSE C 053 00 014
DREAD
    ON BEING'S DREAD AND VACANT MAZE. 023 00 030

DREAD   (CONTINUED)
    AND AFTER IT ALMOST UNMADE, WHAT WITH DREAD, ... 028 01 006
    THE ANGEL SAID: ' O DREAD THEE NOUGHT.   .   .   .   . APPEN D 15
DREADFUL
    BUT MINE IS DREADFUL LEAPING PAIN, ... 081 00 051
    WITH DREADFUL DISTILLATION OF THOUGHTS SOUR AS BLOOD,   .   .   . 152 02 064
    FALLERS IN DREADFUL FROTHPITS, WATERFEARERS WILD, ... 152 C 007
DREADNOUGHT
    FOR ALL HIS DREADNOUGHT BREAST AND BRAIDS OF THEW; 028 16 006
DREAM
    I HAD A DREAM, A WONDROUS THING: 004 00 001
    BUT WE DREAM WE ARE ROOTED IN EARTH -- DUST! 028 11 005
    TO DREAM I DARED SO MUCH FOR THEE. 118 00 006
DREAMED
    WAS DEEMED, DREAMED; WHO 060 00 028
    .   .   .   UPON YOU DREAMED; 081 00 085
DREAM'D
    FAIR, BUT OF FAIRNESS AS A VISION DREAM'D; 079 00 001
    I [DREAM'D] MY COUNTERPART. IT SEEM'D 081 00 086
DREAMS
    MOUNTS; THEN TO ALIGHT DISARMING, NO ONE DREAMS, ... 050 00 013
    TOUCH'D FROM HEAVEN IN SWEET DREAMS; 077 00 126
    THAT FLEETED ELSE LIKE DAY-DISSOLVED DREAMS 157 00 011
DREAMY
    THE SKILL OF DREAMY CLAUDE, AND TITIAN'S MELLOW GLOOM.   .   .   . 001 10 009
DREAR
    DOWN-SPLINTER'D ROCKS CRUSH'D COTTAGES. -- DREAR SIGHT,   .   .   . 001 14 005
    THE DREAR DULL BURTHEN OF UNENDING PAINS. 160 00 018
DRENCHED
    THE DRENCHED HAIR OF SLABBY WEEDS THAT SWUNG 002 00 113
DRENCH'D
    LINGER'D, THEN RAISED THE WASHING WAVES AND DRENCH'D   .   .   . 002 00 138
    HAS DRENCH'D THE MOLTEN SUNSET HOUR, ... 077 00 094
DRESS
    DRESS, HOAR-HALLOWED SHRINES UNVISITED! 041 00 092
    DRESS HIS DAYS TO A DEXTEROUS AND STARLIGHT ORDER,   .   .   . 048 00 020
    YOU FOLDED (DID YOU NOT?) YOUR DRESS, ... 081 00 081
    HE SHALL HAVE SUMMER SWEETS AND DRESS 124 00 005
DRESSED
    SHE WAS DRESSED IN SILK ATTIRE 131 00 003
DREST
    BUT THROUGH BLACK BRANCHES, RARELY DREST 003 00 020
DREW
    IN STARRY WATER-MEADS THEY DREW 010 00 017
    BUT THE COMBS OF A SMOTHER OF SAND; NIGHT DREW HER   .   .   . 028 14 003
    BUT WHAT DREW SHEPHERD RICHARD FROM HIS DOWNS, ... 107 02 001
    AND EACH DREW BLUEBELLS UP, AND FOR RELIEF 107 03 017
    STEPPED FROM THE STOOL, DREW BACK FROM C 137 00 004
    ANG. THESE DROPS IN STARRY SHIRE THEY DREW;   .   .   .   . APPEN A 17
DRIFT
    FAST, BUT MINED WITH A MOTION, A DRIFT, ... 028 04 003
    AN OUR DAY'S GOD'S OWN GALAHAD, THOUGH THIS CHILD'S DRIFT   .   . 048 00 040
    TO DRIFT IN AIR, THE CIRCLED EARTH 077 00 069
DRIFTED
    AND THICKEN'D, LIKE THAT DRIFTED BLOOM, THE FLOCK   .   .   . 002 00 099
DRIFTING
    OF SOMETHING DRIFTING THRO' DELIGHTED AIR, ... 002 00 028
DRILLED
    THE SHAPEN FLAGS AND DRILLED HOLES OF SKY, ... 012 02 011
DRINK
    WHO WOULD DRINK WATER FROM A STONY ROCK? 005 00 020
    STRIKE TIMBRELS, SING, EAT, DRINK, BE FULL OF MIRTH,   .   .   . 005 00 043
    MY MORE THAN MEAT AND DRINK, ... 060 00 011
    THAT I MAY DRINK THAT ECSTACY 077 00 141
DRINKS
    HER GLASS DRINKS LIGHT, SHE DARKLES DOWN BEHIND,   .   .   . 151 00 009
DRIPPING
    ONE BOUND O'ER DRIPPING GOLD A TURQUOISE-GEMM'D 002 00 060
DRIVEN
    THE DENSE AND THE DRIVEN PASSION, AND FRIGHTFUL SWEAT;   .   . 028 07 005
DRIVES
    DOFFS ALL, DRIVES FULL FOR RIGHTEOUSNESS. 041 00 056
    WHICH DRIVES THE STONY AIR TO UTTERANCE? -- 122 00 018
DRIVING
    THE DRIVING STORM AT HOUR OF VESPERS BEAT 001 13 003
    OF DRIVING VERMEIL-RAIN; AND, AS HE LISTS, ... 002 00 091
DRIZZLE
    CAME MIDST THE DRIZZLE TELLING HOW LAST NIGHT 001 14 002
DRON'D
    LOUDER THE MONKS DRON'D OUT GREGORIANS SLOW; 001 13 006
DROOP
    SLIM-POINTED SEA-GULL PLUMES, AND DROOP BEHIND 002 00 080
    YET BOTH DROOP DEADLY SOMETIMES IN THEIR CELLS 039 00 007
    THEY SEEM TO PRESS AND DROOP AND STARE, ... 135 00 020
DROOPING
    GRAINS FROM HIS DROOPING HEAD; 007 00 013
    RUCK AND WRINKLE, DROOPING, DYING, DEATH'S WORST, C   .   .   . 059 OL 012

71

DROOP'D

HE, WHERE THE CROWNALS DROOP'D, HIMSELF REVILED 001 10 007
DROOP'D O'ER THE BROWS LIKE HECTOR'S CASQUE, AND SWAY'D 002 00 042

DROP

AND BID TO CATCH HIM ERE THE DROP OF DAY. 020 00 002
WHY, HEAR HIM, HEAR HIM BABBLE AND DROP DOWN TO HIS NEST, ... 039 00 010
A DROP OF SHADE ROLLS OVER FIELD AND FLOCK. 098 03 002
SHAPE ON THE UNDER SIDE AND SIZE AND DROP. 111 00 007
BUT DOWN DROP, IF IT SAYS STOP, ... 138 00 037
BLOOD THAT BUT ONE DROP OF HAS THE WORTH TO WIN 168 00 023

DROP-OF-BLOOD-AN

WHEN DROP-OF-BLOOD-AND-FOAM-DAPPLE 042 00 037

DROPPED

DROPPED EYES AND DARED NOT LOOK. 054 00 032

DROPPING

HE HIDES OUR CORPSES DROPPING BY THE WAY 005 00 005

DROPP'D

BUT DROPP'D ITS COIL OF WOES: ARTHUR'S BRITAIN, ... 102 02 007

DROPS

THE LANGUENT SMOOTH WITH DIMPLING DROPS, AND FLASH 002 00 103
AND FROM DANK FEATHERS WRING THE DROPS 003 00 008
DROPS OUT AND ALL OUR DAY IS DONE. 003 00 032
GRAPES GREW AND DROPS OF WINE WERE SHED. 007 00 005
THESE DROPS: WHICH BE THEY? STARS OR DEW? 010 00 018
IN THE FIRST SIGNALS OF THE SEVERAL DROPS 084 00 003
WHEN THE WIND DROPS YOU HEAR THE SKYLARKS SING: 098 03 005
HE DROPS HIS BRIGHT ROOTS IN THE WATER'D SWARD, ... 100 00 002
DROPS THE FRUIT OUT: THE DUCT RUNS DRY OR BREAKS: 101 00 010
THAT PIECE THEMSELVES INTO A RACE OF DROPS 102 01 033
THEY WATCHED THE BRUSH OF THE SWIFT STRINGY DROPS, ... 107 03 013
HE DROPS UPON THE WIND AGAIN: 130 00 013
SHEATHE THEE IN THY DARK LAIR: THESE DROPS C 152 02 015
HE DROPS TOWARDS THE RIVER: UNSEEN 159 00 015
ANG. THESE DROPS IN STARRY SHIRE THEY DREW: . . . . APPEN A 17

DROUTH

HE HATH ABOLISHED THE OLD DROUTH, ... 008 00 001

DROVE

SOME, DIVING MERRILY, DOWNWARD DROVE, AND GLEAM'D 002 00 108
SHE DROVE IN THE DARK TO LEEWARD, ... 028 14 001
OR DROVE, WITH A DIVER'S DIP, ... 054 00 020

DROVES

KINGS HERD IT ON THEIR SUBJECT DROVES 166 00 005

DROWNED

THE GOAL WAS A SHOAL, OF A FOURTH THE DOOM TO BE DROWNED: . . . 028 12 006
(CRUSHED THEM) OR WATER (AND DROWNED THEM) OR ROLLED . . . 028 17 003
DROWNED, AND AMONG OUR SHOALS, ... 028 35 002
DROWNED. O PITY AND INDIGNATION: MANSHAPE, THAT SHONE 072 00 013

DROWNING

IT ROUNDS AND ROUNDS DESPAIR TO DROWNING. 056 00 008

DROWSY

GLAZED WATER VAULTED O'ER A DROWSY STONE. 098 39 001

DRUDGERY

THIS IN DRUDGERY, DAY-LABOURING-OUT LIFE'S AGE. 039 00 004

DRUM

FANG, OR FLOOD ' GOES DEATH ON DRUM, ... 028 11 003
HEAVED DRUM ON DRUM: BUT HANDS ALSO 145 00 006
HEAVED DRUM ON DRUM: BUT HANDS ALSO 145 00 006

DRY

THOSE WHOSE DRY PLOT FOR MOISTURE GAPES, ... 006 00 011
THE RIV'N VINE, LEAFLESS, LIFELESS, DRY: 006 00 022
AND RIVERS RUN WHERE ALL WAS DRY, ... 008 00 002
DISPEL THE DOUBT AND DRY THE TEAR: 023 00 046
DRY WERE HER SAD EYES THAT WOULD FAIN HAVE STREAM'D 079 00 002
OF NERVE: THE CLAMMY BALL WAS DRY. 081 00 098
DROPS THE FRUIT OUT: THE DUCT RUNS DRY OR BREAKS: 101 00 010
LIKE PHAROH'S EARS OF WINDY HARVEST DRY 117 00 006
DRY UP THE BLUE AND BE NOT SLAKED THEREBY. 117 00 007
MY ROOT IS DRY. 127 00 004
AND DOWN . . . . THE FURROW DRY 138 00 027
THIS DRY DEAN, NOW NO LONGER DRY NOR DUMB, BUT MOIST AND MUSICAL . 152 C 012
THIS DRY DEAN, NOW NO LONGER DRY NOR DUMB, BUT MOIST AND MUSICAL . 152 C 012

DUCT

AS WATER MOULDED TO THE DUCT IT RUNS IN: 101 00 004
DROPS THE FRUIT OUT: THE DUCT RUNS DRY OR BREAKS: 101 00 010

DUE

DATED DUE TO SEASON -- 042 00 004
ALAS: I RAVE, WHERE CALM IS DUE: 081 00 070
BORN OF HER TOO WHEN TIME WAS DUE: WHO THEN . . . . APPEN D 37

DULL

IT SEEMS: FOR GRANDEUR BARREN LEFT AND DULL 001 15 008
AS A DARE-GALE SKYLARK SCANTED IN A DULL CAGE 039 00 001
SELFYEAST OF SPIRIT A DULL DOUGH SOURS. I SEE 067 00 012
THIS, BY DESPAIR, BRED HANGDOG DULL: BY RAGE, ... 070 00 019
THE DREAR DULL BURTHEN OF UNENDING PAINS. 160 00 018

DULY

DULY, DEAR LORD, MY PRIZE IS WON. 081 00 109
WITH CENTRES DULY TOUCH'D AND NESTLIKE SPOTS, -- 107 04 007

DUMB
    WHERE THE GREEN SWELL IS IN THE HAVENS DUMB, ...   009 00 007
    AND CLEAVES, I STRUGGLE AND AM DUMB, ...   080 10 007
    YEA, CRUSH'D MY HEART, AND MADE ME DUMB, ...   118 00 012
    AND I MUST TAKE YOUR AMENDS, CRY PARDON, AND THEN BE DUMB,   .   .   .   128 00 020
    THIS DRY DEAN, NOW NO LONGER DRY NOR DUMB, BUT MOIST AND MUSICAL   .   .   152 C 012
DUOMO
    C AND ALL J INTO THE DUOMO RAN; 081 00 088
DURANCE
    DURANCE DEAL WITH THAT STEEP OR DEEP, HERE! CREEP, ...   065 00 012
DURING
    DURING THE EASTERING OF UNTAINTED MORNS, ...   084 00 001
DUSK
    TO KNOW THE DUSK DEPTHS OF THE PONDEROUS SEA, ...   002 00 122
    AND GAIN'D THRO' GROWING DUSK THE STIRLESS BAY; 002 00 141
    TINGLING BETWEEN DUSK AND SILVER. 098 01 004
DUSK=DEEP
    WERE VEIN'D AND STREAK'D WITH DUSK-DEEP LAZULI, ...   002 00 046
DUST
    DIMM'D IN THE LONG ACCUMULATED DUST; 001 12 006
    BUT WE DREAM WE ARE ROOTED IN EARTH -- DUST! 028 11 005
    TO MAN'S LAST DUST, DRAIN FAST TOWARDS MAN'S FIRST SLIME.   .   .   .   035 00 014
    SQUANDERING OOZE TO SQUEEZED DOUGH, CRUST, DUST; STANCHES, STARCHES   .   072 00 007
    YOUR FOOTING NOW TO THE MUCH-DREADED DUST, ...   107 03 002
DUTY
    IS STRUNG BY DUTY, IS STRAINED TO BEAUTY, ...   041 00 078
    FELIX RANDAL THE FARRIER, O IS HE DEAD THEN? MY DUTY ALL ENDED,   .   053 00 001
    IMMORTAL BEAUTY IS DEATH WITH DUTY, ...   156 00 018
DUTY=SWERVER
    IN MANKIND'S MEDLEY A DUTY-SWERVER, ...   041 00 054
DWARF
    THERE WAS A WOOD OF DWARF AND SOURED OAKS 125 00 002
DWARFS
    A FREEZING RUNNEL SOBS AND DWARFS. 080 03 007
DWELL
    JESU THAT DOST IN MARY DWELL, ...   169 00 001
DWELLEST
    AND, WHERE THOU DWELLEST IN DEEP#GROVED AIDENN, ...   026 00 023
DWELLS
    I KNEW NOT WHY, -- BUT KNOW THAT SADNESS DWELLS 002 00 118
    MAN'S MOUNTING SPIRIT IN HIS BONE-HOUSE, MEAN HOUSE, DWELLS --   .   039 00 002
    DEALS OUT THAT BEING INDOORS EACH ONE DWELLS; 057 00 006
DWELT
    AND A SWEET SADNESS DWELT ON EVERYONE; 002 00 117
    WHICH WORDSWORTH WOULD HAVE DWELT ON, ABOUT THE PLACE   .   .   .   107 04 016
DWINDLED
    DWINDLED TO INFANCY 060 00 019
    THE MOON, DWINDLED AND THINNED TO THE FRINGE C 137 00 002
DWINDLES
    AND AS SHE DWINDLES SHREDS HER SMOCK OF GOLD 103 00 013
DWINDLING
    AS THE FINE MORSELS OF A DWINDLING CLOUD 102 01 032
DYE
    OR TENDER PINKS WITH BLOODY TYRIAN DYE. 002 00 047
    BARTER'D FOR AN AZURE DYE, ...   086 00 003
DYING
    RUCK AND WRINKLE, DROOPING, DYING, DEATH'S WORST, C 059 0L 012
    AND I PRAY THE PRAYER OF THE DYING THIEF. 168 00 012
    DIDST REACH THINE ARMS OUT DYING, ...   170 00 006
DYPHWYS
    WHAT'S YONDER? GRIZZLED DYPHWYS DIM; 030 00 009

EAGER
    BUT THEN I MAKE AN EAGER SHIFT TO SEE 080 06 005
EAGERER
    OF ANSWER THE EAGERER A-WANTING JESSY OR JACK 046 00 007
EAGLE'S
    MUST SEE THE EAGLE'S BULK, RENDER'D IN MISTS, ...   088 00 003
EAR
    AND BEAT UPON MY WHORLED EAR, ...   022 00 002
    THE EAR, IT STRIKES LIKE LIGHTNINGS TO HEAR HIM SING;   .   .   .   033 00 005
    ON EAR AND EAR TWO NOISES TOO OLD TO END 035 00 001
    ON EAR AND EAR TWO NOISES TOO OLD TO END 035 00 001
    OF OWN, OF ABRUPT SELF THERE SO THRUSTS ON, SO THRONGS THE EAR.   .   045 00 008
    WHO SAY THAT ANGELS, IN YOUR EAR 081 00 122
    OUT-FLEECED BUSHES LIKE A SPANIEL'S EAR V 098 11 001
    THICK-FLEECED BUSHES LIKE A HEIFER'S EAR V 098 11 001
    RATHER TO EAR THAN EYE SHEWS WHERE THEY STRAY, ...   112 00 004
    FIRM ACCENTS STRIKE HER FINE AND SCROLLED EAR, ...   136 00 021
    THE EAR IN MILK, LUSH THE SASH. 138 00 020
    CUCKOO, BIRD, AND OPEN EAR WELLS, HEART-SPRINGS, DELIGHTFULLY SWEET,   146 00 002
    GRACE LOVE YOUR LIPS! -- WHAT NEVER EAR 166 00 002

73

EAR   (CONTINUED)
     SONG NEVER WAS SO SWEET IN EAR, ... 167 00 005
EAR-CARESSING
     WITH EAR-CARESSING SPEECH? WHERE IS THE TONGUE 122 00 017
EARLIER
     AUTUMN-TIME NO EARLIER CAME. 004 00 026
     MONTHS EARLIER, SINCE I HAD OUR SWEET REPRIEVE AND RANSOM . . . 053 00 007
     AS DEVONSHIRE LETTERS, EARLIER IN THE YEAR 119 00 001
     WHAT BEING IN RANK-OLD NATURE SHOULD EARLIER HAVE THAT BREATH BEEN . 141 00 001
     EARLIER OR YOU FAIL AT OUR FORCE, AND LIE 153 00 003
EARLIEST
     WASTE! HER EARLIEST STARS, EARLSTARS, STARS PRINCIPAL, OVERBEND US, . 061 00 004
     THE PLACE IN THE EAST WITH EARLIEST MILKY MORN 098 30 005
EARLSTARS
     WASTE! HER EARLIEST STARS, EARLSTARS, STARS PRINCIPAL, OVERBEND US, . 061 00 004
EARLY
     THEM: BEAUTY-IN-THE-GHOST, DELIVER IT, EARLY NOW, LONG BEFORE DEATH . 059 0G 018
     AND WISDOM IS EARLY TO DESPAIR; 059 0L 008
     OR EVER THE EARLY STIRRINGS OF SKYLARK 098 28 001
     THAT EARLY 'SPERSES, AND HIGH HANGS THE DAY. 098 31 006
EARNEST
     EARNEST, EARTHLESS, EQUAL, ATTUNEABLE, C 061 00 001
     AND GRAVE PAST GIRLHOOD EARNEST IN HER EYES. 136 00 020
     IN BLOODY LETTERS, LESSONS OF EARNEST, OF REVENGE; 152 02 004
     MONUMENTS OF MY EARNEST, RECORDS OF MY REVENGE, ... 152 02 005
     YOUR FEAST OF: THAT MOST IN YOU EARNEST EYE 157 00 029
EARNEST-HEARTED
     THE EARNEST-HEARTED MAIDEN SAT AND HEARD, ... 136 00 032
EARS
     EARS, AND THE CALL OF THE TALL NUN 028 19 007
     THEN LET THE MARCH TREAD OUR EARS; 052 00 009
     STIR IN MY EARS, SPEAK THERE 060 00 121
     BACKWARD ARE LAID HER PRETTY BLACK-FLEECED EARS; 099 00 013
     THEN OFTEN THE EARS IN A NEW FASHION HARK, ... 113 00 007
     AND SEVEN EARS CROWN THE LODGED CORN. 114 00 006
     LIKE PHAROH'S EARS OF WINDY HARVEST DRY 117 00 006
     OR DEAF EARS SHALL DESIRE THAT LIPMUSIC THAT'S LOST UPON THEM, . 152 C 005
EARTH
     EIGHTH WONDER OF THE EARTH, IN SIZE, IN STORE 001 15 005
     BUT EARTH HAS NEVER FELT THE SNOW. 003 00 002
     SPREAD O'ER THE SWART FACE OF THIS PRODIGAL EARTH. 005 00 045
     IN FORTY DAYS REACH'D HEAVEN FROM EARTH: 006 00 024
     MY HEAVEN IS BRASS AND IRON MY EARTH: 018 00 009
     WE SEE THE GLORIES OF THE EARTH 023 00 007
     EMPTY THOUGH IT BE ON EARTH: 024 00 008
     EARTH THROWS WINTER'S ROBES AWAY, ... 024 00 017
     AND LIKE THE STORM-MONTHS SMOTE THE EARTH 026 00 029
     BUT WE DREAM WE ARE ROOTED IN EARTH -- DUST! 028 11 005
     SURF, SNOW, RIVER AND EARTH 028 21 004
     HEAVEN AND EARTH ARE WORD OF, WORDED BY? -- 028 29 006
     AND HURLS FOR HIM, O HALF HURLS EARTH FOR HIM OFF UNDER HIS FEET. . 038 00 014
     CROUCH! LAY KNEE BY EARTH LOW UNDER; 041 00 110
     THIS ECSTASY ALL THROUGH MOTHERING EARTH 042 00 045
     EARTH, SWEET EARTH, SWEET LANDSCAPE, WITH LEAVES THRONG . . . 058 00 001
     EARTH, SWEET EARTH, SWEET LANDSCAPE, WITH LEAVES THRONG . . . 058 00 001
     EARTH BROWS OF SUCH CARE, CARE AND DEAR CONCERN. 058 00 014
     EARTH IS THE FAIRER FOR. 060 00 093
     ROPES, WRESTLES, BEATS EARTH BARE C 072 00 005
     EARTH HEARS NO HURTLE THEN FROM FIERCEST FRAY. 073 00 008
     EARTH, ALL, OUT: WHO, WITH TRICKLING INCREMENT, ... 073 00 010
     RIGHT OFFSPRING OF YOUR GRIMY MOTHER EARTH! 077 00 002
     AND THAT GRIEF MASTERS JOY ON EARTH, ... 077 00 055
     TO WHOM THE COMMON EARTH AND AIR 077 00 059
     TO DRIFT IN AIR, THE CIRCLED EARTH 077 00 069
     MIX O'ER THE NOT UNMOVED EARTH, -- 077 00 130
     AND A GREY HEAVEN DOES THE HUSH'D EARTH HOUSE, ... 105 00 007
     THE EARTH AND HEAVEN, SO LITTLE KNOWN, ... 130 00 001
     OF GREENERY AND OLD EARTH GROPES FOR, GRASPS AT STEEP V . . . 149 8 012
     HIDEOUS DASHED DOWN, LEAVING EARTH A WINTER WITHERING . . . 152 02 052
     LIKE THE THING THAT NEVER KNEW THE EARTH, NEVER OFF ROOTS . . 159 00 027
     A COUNTLESS LAUGHTER, EARTH MOTHER OF ALL, ... 160 00 003
EARTHLESS
     EARNEST, EARTHLESS, EQUAL, ATTUNEABLE, C 061 00 001
     EARTHLESS DEWS ON ANCLES SLEEK: 077 00 016
EARTH'S
     IT WAS MADE OF EARTH'S MOULD BUT IT WENT FROM MEN'S EYES . . 027 00 003
     A STRAIN OF THE EARTH'S SWEET BEING IN THE BEGINNING . . . 033 00 010
     HAVE LOST THAT CHEER AND CHARM OF EARTH'S PAST PRIME: . . . 035 00 012
     AND WHAT IS EARTH'S EYE, TONGUE, OR HEART ELSE, WHERE . . . 058 00 009
     TALL SUN'S TINGEING, OR TREACHEROUS THE TAINTING OF THE EARTH'S AIR, . 059 0G 005
     OF EARTH'S GLORY, EARTH'S EASE, ALL: NO ONE, NOWHERE, . . . 070 00 016
     OF EARTH'S GLORY, EARTH'S EASE, ALL: NO ONE, NOWHERE, . . . 070 00 016
     OF GREENERY: IT IS OLD EARTH'S GROPING TOWARDS THE STEEP . . 149 A 010
EARTHWORLD
     ARE EARTHWORLD, AIRWORLD, WATERWORLD THOROUGH HURLED, C . . . 159 00 018
EASE
     GIVE MYRRHY-THREADED GOLDEN FOLDS OF EASE. 011 00 012

74

EASE (CONTINUED)
TIME'S TASKING, IT IS FATHERS THAT ASKING FOR EASE • • • • • 028 27 003
OF EARTH'S GLORY, EARTH'S EASE, ALL! NO ONE, NOWHERE, • • • • 070 00 016
YET LEAVES HIM IN UNGIRDLED EASE • • • • • • • • • 083 00 015
O LOVELY EASE IN CHANGE OF PLACE! • • • • • • • • • 130 00 027
EASEFUL
BEAR HIM TO HEAVEN ON EASEFUL WINGS. • • • • • • • 007 00 015
EASILY
THE HEART GUESSES EASILY: IS IT THE SAME? -- • • • • • 027 00 020
UNSOUGHT, PRESENTED SO EASILY, C • • • • • • • • 137 00 006
EAST
BUT THESE WERE FOUND IN THE EAST AND SOUTH • • • • • 010 00 013
TO CROSSES MEANT FOR JESU'S: YOU WHOM THE EAST • • • • 011 00 005
' A CRIMSON EAST, THAT BIDS FOR RAIN, • • • • • • 021 00 008
BE A CRIMSON-CRESSETED EAST, C • • • • • • • • 028 35 005
THE PLACE IN THE EAST WITH EARLIEST MILKY MORN • • • • 098 30 005
DAWN THAT THE PEBBLY LOW-DOWN EAST • • • • • • • 098 31 001
DAWN THAT THE LOW-DOWN PEBBLY EAST • • • • • • • 098 31 004
THAN WE IN THE EAST DARE LOOK FOR BUDS, DISCLOSE • • • 119 00 002
AND JUSTIFY THE EAST AND WEST: • • • • • • • • 130 00 004
EASTER
ON EASTER MORN THE TREE WAS FORTH, • • • • • • • 006 00 023
BREATHE EASTER NOW! YOU SERGED FELLOWSHIPS, • • • • 011 00 007
KNOW YE, THIS IS EASTER DAY. • • • • • • • • 024 00 006
KNOW YE NOT 'TIS EASTER MORN? • • • • • • • • 024 00 012
DECKS HERSELF FOR EASTER DAY, • • • • • • • • 024 00 018
LET IN JOY THIS EASTER DAY. • • • • • • • • 024 00 024
MAKE EACH MORN AN EASTER DAY. • • • • • • • • 024 00 030
LET HIM EASTER IN US, BE A DAYSPRING TO THE DIMNESS OF US, C • 028 35 005
EASTERING
DURING THE EASTERING OF UNTAINTED MORNS, • • • • • 084 00 001
EASTERN
TWICE LOVELY, TINTED EASTERN, TURNED GREEK -- • • • • 136 00 015
EASTNORTHEAST
SITTING EASTNORTHEAST, IN CURSED QUARTER, THE WIND: • • • 028 13 006
EASTWARD
OH, MORNING, AT THE BROWN BRINK EASTWARD, SPRINGS -- • • • 031 00 012
EASTWARDS
AND BRIGHT ICONIUM EASTWARDS REACH MY RHYMES. • • • • 136 00 006
EASY
FROM EASY RUNNELS THE RICH-PIECED LAND • • • • • 005 00 039
THE EASY BURDEN OF YORE. • • • • • • • • • 005 00 054
LODGE HIS EYES FAST: BUT YET AS EASY AND LIGHT • • • • 102 01 020
EAT
STRIKE TIMBRELS, SING, EAT, DRINK, BE FULL OF MIRTH. • • • 005 00 043
BUT I MUST YIELD THE CHASE, OR REST AND EAT. -- • • • 020 00 011
UNPALATEABLE FRUITS TO EAT. • • • • • • • • 081 00 167
EATEN
THE LAWLESS HONEY EATEN OF OLD • • • • • • • 092 00 004
EAVES
NOW COMING FROM THE ALIEN EAVES, -- • • • • • • 081 00 003
TO ALIEN EAVES YOU FLED AND WENT, -- • • • • • • 081 00 005
EBB
WAYLAY HER AT EBB, PAST PENMAEN POOL. • • • • • 030 00 024
EBB'D
EBB'D BACK BENEATH ITS SNOWY LIDS, UNSEEN. • • • • 002 00 018
ECHO
WHAT WAS THAT ECHO CAUGHT ANIGH ME, • • • • • • 160 00 020
ECHOING
THROUGH THE ECHOING TIMBER DOES SO RINSE AND WRING • • • 033 00 004
HAVE HERE A TRUE ONE, ECHOING THE SOUND: • • • • • 116 00 002
ECHOING-OF-EARTH
UPON THIS ONLY GAMBOLLING AND ECHOING-OF-EARTH NOTE -- • • 159 00 045
ECLIPSE
BY INTERCHANGE GASP'D SPLENDOUR AND ECLIPSE. • • • • 002 00 022
ECLIPSING
ECLIPSING PARAPET: YET ABOVE THE WALL • • • • • 012 02 007
ECSTACY
THAT I MAY DRINK THAT ECSTACY • • • • • • • 077 00 141
LATE I FELL IN THE ECSTACY • • • • • • • • 093 A 001
ECSTASY
IN HIS ECSTASY! THEN OFF, OFF FORTH ON SWING, • • • • 036 00 005
THIS ECSTASY ALL THROUGH MOTHERING EARTH • • • • • 042 00 045
KEEPS A KIND OF JOY IN IT, A ZEST, AN EDGE, AN ECSTASY, • • 152 02 058
EDDIES
IN EDDIES OF THE WIND HE WENT • • • • • • • 087 00 005
EDDY
THE MOTES IN CEASELESS EDDY SHINE AND FALL • • • • • 001 12 004
EDEN
IN EDEN GARDEN. -- HAVE, GET, BEFORE IT CLOY, • • • • 033 00 011
EDGE
AND LAPPED IN SHINING HAIR, ROLL TO THE BANK'S EDGE: THEN • • 152 02 019
KEEPS A KIND OF JOY IN IT, A ZEST, AN EDGE, AN ECSTASY, • • 152 02 058
EDGED
PHRENZY, BUT EDGED AND CLEAR OF BRAIN • • • • • 081 00 052
EDGES
THEIR CLOUDS WITH BREATHING EDGES WHITE • • • • • 130 00 023

EFFECTUAL
    [HAD BEEN EFFECTUAL TO HAVE SOWN WITH NOTES] • • • • • • 122 00 012
EGGS
    THRUSH'S EGGS LOOK LITTLE LOW HEAVENS, AND THRUSH • • • • • 033 00 003
    ALL OVER, AS A BEVY OF EGGS THE MOTHERING WING • • • • • 034 00 006
    CLUSTER OF BUGLE BLUE EGGS THIN • • • • • • • • 042 00 021
EGYPT
    EGYPT, THE VALLEY OF OUR PLEASANCE, THERE! • • • • • 005 00 025
EGYPTIAN
    HE SLEW THE EGYPTIAN YESTERDAY, TO-DAY • • • • • 005 00 003
    YOUR PARCHED NOSTRILS SNUFF. EGYPTIAN AIR, • • • • • 005 00 027
    MY NATIONAL OLD EGYPTIAN REED GAVE WAY! • • • • • 020 00 007
EIGHT
    EIGHT THOUSAND FURLONGS IN ADVANCE. • • • • • • 083 00 016
EIGHTH
    EIGHTH WONDER OF THE EARTH, IN SIZE, IN STORE • • • • 001 15 005
EITHER
    A TINTED FIN ON EITHER SHOULDER HUNG! • • • • • 002 00 052
    THAT LIKEST IN ME EITHER THAT OR THIS, -- • • • • • 013 00 007
    MEN GO BY ME WHOM EITHER BEAUTY BRIGHT • • • • • 040 00 005
    WITH NOT HER EITHER BEAUTY'S EQUAL OR • • • • • 050 00 002
    AND PRESS IT DOWN, ON EITHER SIDE A BONE, • • • • 080 14 003
    LAUGHING OR TEARS, I THINK I COULD DO EITHER -- • • • 102 01 014
    EITHER LEFT EITHER RIGHT • • • • • • • • • 138 00 008
    EITHER LEFT EITHER RIGHT • • • • • • • • • 138 00 008
ELBOW
    HE LEANS TO IT, HARRY BENDS, LOOK. BACK, ELBOW, AND LIQUID WAIST • 071 00 009
ELDER
    HOW LOVELY THE ELDER BROTHER'S • • • • • • • 054 00 001
    RAN REVEL IN THE ELDER BOY. • • • • • • • • 054 00 009
ELECTED
    ELECTED SILENCE, SING TO ME • • • • • • • 022 00 001
ELECTRICAL
    NOT DANGER, ELECTRICAL HORROR! THEN FURTHER IT FINDS • • 028 27 005
ELEMENT
    AND NURSING ELEMENT! • • • • • • • • • 060 00 010
    I CAN STAND PENT IN THE MONSTROUS ELEMENT • • • • 080 05 003
    THE PENETRATIVE ELEMENT • • • • • • • • 081 00 132
    AT LAST UP THE BLUE ELEMENT. • • • • • • • 087 00 006
    AND SLENDER ELEMENT TO PIECE AND PLOT. V • • • • 102 03 025
    FLINTY KINDCOLD ELEMENT LET BREAK ACROSS HIS LIMBS • • 159 00 041
ELEMENTED
    SO STRANGELY ELEMENTED IS MY MIND'S WEATHER, • • • 102 01 015
ELEMENTS
    PIECING THE ELEMENTS OUT BY PLAN AND PLOT. • • • • 102 03 018
    THE ---- ELEMENTS -- ---- -- ---- V • • • • 102 03 026
    BY HEADY ELEMENTS, FOR NO MAN KNOWS! • • • • 103 00 005
ELEVEN
    WARNED, ELEVEN FATHOMS FALLEN • • • • • • 041 00 004
ELIM
    BEHOLD AT ELIM WELLS ON EVERY HAND • • • • • 005 00 023
ELKHOR
    EXILED MOST REMOTE ELKHOR. • • • • • • • 081 000 47
ELM
    DOWN ROUGHCAST, DOWN DAZZLING WHITEWASH, WHEREVER AN ELM ARCHES, 072 00 003
ELM-HEADS
    THE VEX'D ELM-HEADS ARE PALE WITH THE VIEW • • • • 078 00 001
ELMS
    BREATHE IN SUCH ETHER? OR THE QUICKLY ELMS • • • • 100 00 007
ELMY
    AND NOT FROM PURPLE WALES ONLY NOR FROM ELMY ENGLAND, • • 152 C 019
ELOQUENT
    WHICH ONLY MAKES YOU ELOQUENT. • • • • • • 022 00 008
ELSE
    ELSE I AM WELL ASSURED I SHOULD OFFEND • • • • 014 03 005
    IN MOULD OR MIND OR WHAT NOT ELSE MAKES RARE! • • • 040 00 006
    NOTHING ELSE IS LIKE IT, NO, NOT ALL SO STRAINS • • • 048 00 029
    AND WHAT IS EARTH'S EYE, TONGUE, OR HEART ELSE, WHERE • • 058 00 009
    ELSE, BUT IN DEAR AND DOGGED MAN? -- AH, THE HEIR • • • 058 00 010
    HOW THEN SHOULD GREGORY, A FATHER, HAVE GLEANED ELSE FROM SWARM- 062 00 007
    OR THIS, OR ELSE I DO NOT LOVE, • • • • • • 081 00 114
    OR ELSE THEIR COOINGS CAME FROM BAYS OF TREES, • • • 098 02 001
    TOO LATE OR ELSE MUCH, MUCH TOO SOON, • • • • 105 00 016
    WHILE ALL THINGS ELSE MAY STIR AND RANGE • • • • 130 00 007
    ALL ELSE MAY WHIRL OR DIVE OR FLY. • • • • • 130 00 008
    OR WHAT IS ELSE? THERE IS YOUR WORLD WITHIN. • • • 150 00 009
    OR ELSE A FUNERAL, AND YET 'TIS NOT A FUNERAL, • • • 152 01 019
    THAT FLEETED ELSE LIKE DAY-DISSOLVED DREAMS • • • • 157 00 011
ELSE-MINDED
    THEY WERE ELSE-MINDED THEN, ALTOGETHER, THE MEN • • • 028 25 005
ELSEWHERE
    NOR ELSEWHERE CAN THY SWEETNESS UNENDEAR. • • • • 012 01 005
    SOMEWHERE ELSEWHERE THERE IS AH WELL WHERE! ONE, • • 059 06 006
    ELSEWHERE! LEAVE COMFORT ROOT-ROOM! LET JOY SIZE • • 069 00 011
ELVES'-EYES
    DOWN IN DIM WOODS THE DIAMOND DELVES! THE ELVES'-EYES! • • 032 00 004
EMBERS
    SHINE, AND BLUE-BLEAK EMBERS, AH MY DEAR, • • • • 036 00 013

EMBERS   (CONTINUED)
    AS WRECKS OF MINED EMBERS WILL. 092 00 013
EMBLEM
    UPRAIS'D AN EMBLEM OF THAT FIERY CONSTANCY. 001 03 008
EMINENT
    STOOD CAPITAL, EMINENT, . . . GONFALON BEARER 098 28 005
EMPIRE
    THE AIRY EMPIRE AT HIS WILL; 077 00 078
EMPLOYMENT
    AND HOLD AT CHRIST'S EMPLOYMENT. 049 00 014
EMPTY
    YET LIKE A LIGHTED EMPTY HALL 023 00 010
    EMPTY THOUGH IT BE ON EARTH; 024 00 008
ENCHAIN'D
    A GOD ENCHAIN'D OF DESTINY, ... 160 00 027
ENCLUSTER'D
    THE GLAUCUS CLEPED; OTHERS SMALL BRAIDS ENCLUSTER'D 002 00 068
ENCOUNTER
    ONCE ENCOUNTER IN, HERE COPED AND POISED POWERS; 044 00 004
ENCRIMSONING
    (WHERE THE EYE FIX'D, FLED THE ENCRIMSONING SPOT, ... 002 00 009
END
    YOU SEE THAT I HAVE COME TO PASSION'S END; 014 03 001
    WITH A ROPE'S END ROUND THE MAN, HANDY AND BRAVE -- 028 16 003
    ON EAR AND EAR TWO NOISES TOO OLD TO END 035 00 001
    WHAT MOST I MAY EYE AFTER, BE IN AT THE END 040 00 010
    TO MEND HER WE END HER. 043 00 017
    YOUR ROUND ME ROAMING END, AND UNDER BE MY BOUGHS? 051 00 002
    HER DAPPLE IS AT AN END, AS— C 061 00 005
    OUR NIGHT WHELMS, WHELMS, AND WILL END US. C 061 00 008
    LIFE DEATH DOES END AND EACH DAY DIES WITH SLEEP. 065 00 014
    DISAPPOINTMENT ALL I ENDEAVOUR END? 074 00 004
    SPEND ME OR END ME WHAT GOD SHALL SEND ME, ... 156 00 013
    TO THE WORLD'S END, TO THE LAST HILL 160 00 024
    WORLD WITHOUT END ALONE IN THEE.   c 167 00 028
ENDEARS
    THIS SEEING THE SICK ENDEARS THEM TO US, US TOO IT ENDEARS,   .   .   . 053 00 009
    THIS SEEING THE SICK ENDEARS THEM TO US, US TOO IT ENDEARS,   .   .   . 053 00 009
    I PLEAD; FAMILIARNESS ENDEARS 081 00 026
ENDEAVOUR
    DISAPPOINTMENT ALL I ENDEAVOUR END? 074 00 004
ENDED
    FELIX RANDAL THE FARRIER, O ;S HE DEAD THEN? MY DUTY ALL ENDED,   .   . 053 00 001
    AND THESE ARE SPENT AND ENDED QUITE; 130 00 021
ENDING
    THAT SWEET'S SWEETER ENDING; 048 00 031
    ENDING IN SWEET UNCERTAINTY 077 00 121
ENDLESS
    AN ENDLESS ROUND OF DEAD'NING SOLITUDE; 001 14 006
ENDLESSLY
    ALIVE OR DEAD MY GIRL IS CARRIED IN IT, ENDLESSLY 152 01 021
ENDRAGONED
    BURDEN. IN WIND'S BURLY AND BEAT OF ENDRAGONED SEAS. 028 27 008
ENDS
    WHICH ENDS THOSE ONLY STRAINS THAT I APPROVE, ... 019 00 010
    SUMMER ENDS NOW; NOW, BARBAROUS IN BEAUTY, THE STOOKS RISE   .   .   . 038 00 001
    THE ENDS OF THE CRISP BUDS SHE CHIPS 098 14 001
ENDURED
    IDLE FOR EVER TO WAFT HER OR WIND HER WITH, THESE SHE ENDURED.   .   . 028 14 008
ENDURING
    A THING THAT WEEPS, ENDURING LONG; 081 00 050
ENEMY
    WERT THOU MY ENEMY, O THOU MY FRIEND, ... 074 00 005
ENGEMMING
    WITH FLOWING TRACERY ENGEMMING RAYS 001 06 002
ENGENDER'D
    COME OUT OF SPACE, OR SUDDENLY ENGENDER'D 103 00 004
ENGLAND
    A BEETLING BALDBRIGHT CLOUD THOROUGH ENGLAND 041 00 025
    ENGLAND, WHOSE HONOUR O ALL MY HEART WOOS, WIFE 066 00 005
    HOW SHAKESPEARE'S ENGLAND WEDS WITH DANTE'S ITALY. 098 35 002
    AND NOT FROM PURPLE WALES ONLY NOR FROM ELMY ENGLAND, ... 152 C 019
ENGLAND'S
    CALL ME ENGLAND'S FAME'S FOND LOVER, ... 156 00 011
ENGLISH
    OUR KING BACK, OH, UPON ENGLISH SOULS! 028 35 004
    MOTHER TO AN ENGLISH SIRE (HE 048 00 003
    ' THEN WILL YOU WED WITH AN ENGLISH LADY, ... 109 08 003
    AND ART THOU COME FROM ENGLISH LAND, ... 109 31 003
    ' I AM NOT COME FROM ENGLISH LAND, ... 109 32 001
ENJEWELLING
    CRUSHES AND TEARS THE RARE ENJEWELLING, ... 002 00 085
ENJOY
    AND DID THE CHILDREN OF HIS BRAINS ENJOY 097 00 003
ENJOYMENT
    THIS PRIDE OF PRIME'S ENJOYMENT 049 00 012
ENORMOUS
    BOTH ARE IN AN UNFATHOMABLE, ALL IS IN AN ENORMOUS DARK 072 00 012

ENORMOUS   (CONTINUED)
```
    THE SMOULDERING ENORMOUS WINTER WELKIN! MAY    .  .   .   .   .   .   .   .   149   A  008
    THE SMOULDERING ENORMOUS WINTER WELKIN. [ EYE, V  .  .  .   .   .   .   .   149   B  009
```
ENOUGH
```
    THE BOUGHS, THE BOUGHS ARE BARE ENOUGH   .   .   .   .   .   .   .   003  00  001
    WHAT! COUNTRY IS HONOUR ENOUGH IN ALL US -- LORDLY HEAD,  .  .  .   .   070  00  010
    BUT VASTNESS BLURS AND TIME BEATS LEVEL. ENOUGH! THE RESURRECTION,  .   072  00  016
    MERCY IS LEFT ENOUGH FOR ONE:   .   .   .   .   .   .   .   .   .   081  00  105
    NOT WIN, IF THIS BE NOT ENOUGH.  .   .   .   .   .   .   .   .   .   083  00  026
    HAS WIT ENOUGH, BUT LESS THAN FEMALE TACT,   .   .   .   .   .   094  00  019
    ' SOME ARE PRETTY ENOUGH, AND SOME ARE POOR INDEED. '   .   .   .   098  15  004
    AND IF IT IS WHY THERE IS CAUSE ENOUGH   .   .   .   .   .   .   125  00  053
    ENOUGH! CORRUPTION WAS THE WORLD'S FIRST WOE.   .   .   .   .   .   157  00  033
    ENOUGH NOW! SINCE THE SACRED MATTER THAT I MEAN   .   .   .   .   159  00  043
```
ENRICHED
```
    ENRICHED POSTS ARE CHAMFER'D: EVERYWHERE  .   .   .   .   .   .   096  07  003
```
ENROLL'D
```
    ENROLL'D AND SEXING WITH -- ---- ---- V   .   .   .   .   .   .   102  01  064
    ENROLL'D AND SEXED WITH -- ---- ---- V    .   .   .   .   .   .   102  01  064
```
ENTANGLED
```
    A FLUKE YET FANGED HIM, ENTANGLED HIM. NOT QUIT UTTERLY. C   .   .   137  00  005
```
ENTER
```
    YOU HAVE YOUR WISH! ENTER THESE WALLS, ONE SAID:   .   .   .   .   020  00  017
```
ENTERING
```
    COMFORTING SMELL BREATHED AT VERY ENTERING,   .   .   .   .   .   034  00  003
```
ENTRANCE
```
    ABOVE IT CANNOT ENTRANCE WIN.   .   .   .   .   .   .   .   .   018  00  006
```
ENTRANCINGLY
```
    CLUSTERING ENTRANCINGLY IN BERYL LAKES:   .   .   .   .   .   .   002  00  014
```
ENTRIES
```
    ENTRIES OR BANKS ALL OVER SHADE   .   .   .   .   .   .   .   .   166  00  023
```
ENVIED
```
    STRETCHES THE ENVIED FRUIT WITH FATAL SMILE   .   .   .   .   .   001  11  002
```
EPISTLES
```
    EPISTLES, WHILE THE RUNNING PASTORAL BLEATS   .   .   .   .   .   107  04  022
```
EQUAL
```
    THE CLOISTERS CROSS'D WITH EQUAL COURTS BETWIXT   .   .   .   .   001  04  002
    WITH NOT HER EITHER BEAUTY'S EQUAL OR   .   .   .   .   .   .   050  00  002
    EARNEST, EARTHLESS, EQUAL, ATTUNEABLE, C  .   .   .   .   .   .   061  00  001
```
EQUIPPED
```
    CAME EQUIPPED, DEADLY-ELECTRIC,   .   .   .   .   .   .   .   .   041  00  024
```
ERE
```
    ' I MARK THE FLOWERS ERE THE PRIME   .   .   .   .   .   .   .   004  00  014
    ERE I HAD FURTHER QUESTION MADE   .   .   .   .   .   .   .   .   004  00  016
    WITH FREE LONG LOOKING, ERE I DIE.   .   .   .   .   .   .   .   015  00  044
    WHICH SHOULD ERE NOW HAVE LED MY FEET TO THE FIELD,   .   .   .   017  00  009
    AND BID TO CATCH HIM ERE THE DROP OF DAY.   .   .   .   .   .   020  00  002
    THE SPIRIT HOVERED ERE THE SUN   .   .   .   .   .   .   .   .   023  00  022
    BUT SLEEP AGAIN ERE DAY BE BORN:   .   .   .   .   .   .   .   077  00  024
    YOU MAY DEPEND THAT ERE A WEEK WAS FLED,   .   .   .   .   .   097  00  005
    ERE YOU SET SAIL THE KING WAS DEAD.   .   .   .   .   .   .   .   109  09  003
```
ERIN
```
    BUT FROM BEYOND SEAS, ERIN, FRANCE AND FLANDERS, EVERYWHERE,   .   152  C  020
```
ERST
```
    AS ERST UPON CHAOTIC FLOODS   .   .   .   .   .   .   .   .   .   023  00  021
```
ESAU'S
```
    I CAN SEND UP AN ESAU'S CRY:   .   .   .   .   .   .   .   .   .   081  00  126
```
ESCAPE
```
    AND BARELY TO ESCAPE THE CURSE,   .   .   .   .   .   .   .   .   081  00  170
```
ESCORIAL
```
    UNMINDFUL OF THEIR GRACE, THE ESCORIAL   .   .   .   .   .   .   001  08  005
```
ESPECIAL
```
    THE SWEET ESPECIAL SCENE.   .   .   .   .   .   .   .   .   .   043  00  022
    SWEET ESPECIAL RURAL SCENE.   .   .   .   .   .   .   .   .   .   043  00  024
```
ESPIAL
```
    FEAR HINDRANCE AND ESPIAL   .   .   .   .   .   .   .   .   .   110  00  003
```
ESSENCE
```
    THE ESSENCE NE'ER FORGOT THE FOLD:   .   .   .   .   .   .   .   081  00  082
```
ESTATES
```
    LAY OPEN THINE ESTATES.   .   .   .   .   .   .   .   .   .   .   115  00  007
```
ESTEEM'D
```
    AND I ESTEEM'D THE SANDAL GOOD   .   .   .   .   .   .   .   .   081  00  083
```
ETC
```
    AND YOUR TWO ETC.   .   .   .   .   .   .   .   .   .   .   .   101  00  012
```
ETERNAL
```
    I'LL WAIT TILL MORN ETERNAL BREAKS.   .   .   .   .   .   .   .   023  00  054
    PRAYER SHALL FETCH PITY ETERNAL.   .   .   .   .   .   .   .   .   041  00  120
    A BEACON, AN ETERNAL BEAM, FLESH FADE, AND MORTAL TRASH   .   .   072  00  019
    THE IMMORTALS OF THE ETERNAL RING,   .   .   .   .   .   .   .   145  00  030
```
ETHER
```
    BREATHE IN SUCH ETHER? OR THE QUICKLY ELMS   .   .   .   .   .   100  00  007
```
EUCHARIST
```
    THAT LEFT TO THE LORD OF THE EUCHARIST, I HERE LIE BY:   .   .   048  00  044
```
EUNUCH
```
    TIME'S EUNUCH, AND NOT BREED ONE WORK THAT WAKES.   .   .   .   074  00  013
```
EURYDICE
```
    THE EURYDICE -- IT CONCERNED THEE, O LORD:   .   .   .   .   .   041  00  001
```

EVE
HIM, MORNING, NOON, AND EVE; 060 00 062
I WALK TOWARDS EVE OUR WALKS AGAIN; 081 00 054
EVEN
BUT EVEN OUR SAVIOUR'S AND OUR BLOOD, ... 006 00 032
OH! EVEN FOR THE WEAKNESS OF THE PLEA 013 00 008
THAT LESS IS HEAVENS HIGHER EVEN YET 014 01 012
EVEN YOUR UNPASSION'D EYELIDS MIGHT BE WET. 014 01 014
EVEN THAN THIS MY THANKLESS LORE; 015 00 022
OF THY MERCY NOT REEVE EVEN THEM IN? C 028 12 008
THEN EVEN IN WEARIEST WINTRY HOUR 030 00 029
IT IS EVEN SEEN, TIME'S SOMETHING SERVER, ... 041 00 053
WHERE WE, EVEN WHERE WE MEAN 043 00 016
OF US WE DO BID GOD BEND TO HIM EVEN SO. 068 00 011
IN WHOSE DEAD LAKE EVEN A VOICE MAY MAKE 080 04 003
WITH LOOPS OF VEINS; NOT OF AN EVEN PINK, ... 093 B 004
WEEPING, -- EVEN NOW I CURSE MYSELF REMEMBERING; -- . . 102 01 041
EVEN TO THE TILLAGE OF THE SWEETEST SPOT, -- . . . 102 03 016
EVEN SO MY THOUGHT THE ROSE AND GREY DISPOSES . . . 108 00 007
NEWS FROM BELLEISLE, EVEN SUCH A SWEETNESS BLOWS . . 119 00 006
NEXT AFTER SWEET SUCCESS. I AM NOT LEFT EVEN THIS; . 152 02 059
NOT NOW TO NAME EVEN . . . . 152 C 025
EVEN THUS I HAVE THE BETTER OF THEE; 161 00 003
EVENING
IT SEEM'D AN EVENING IN THE SPRING; 004 00 002
LOVE, IT IS EVENING NOW AND THOU AWAY; 020 00 004
IN TUFTS OF EVENING SKY. -- SO SOON? 025 00 022
THERE, EVENING, NOON, AND MORN -- 060 00 064
EVENING STRAINS TO BE TIME'S VAST, C 061 00 002
WITH; OUR EVENING IS OVER US; C 061 00 008
LIKE FLAME THEY GATHER ON OUR CLIFFS AT EVENING, . . 104 00 007
CAT. IN FLOATS OF EVENING SKY. -- SO SOON? . . . APPEN A 22
EVENT
THOSE YEARS AND YEARS BY OF WORLD WITHOUT EVENT . . . 073 00 013
EVER
THE RICHEST GIFT ST. LAWRENCE EVER BORE, ... 001 02 006
MUST YOU BE GORGED WITH PROOF? DID EVER SAND . . . 005 00 041
NO INFLUENTIAL HEAVEN EVER WORE; 014 02 007
O FATHER, NOT UNDER THY FEATHERS NOR EVER AS GUESSING 028 12 005
IDLE FOR EVER TO WAFT HER OR WIND HER WITH, THESE SHE ENDURED. 028 14 008
NOR WAS EVER GUESSED WHAT FOR THE HEARINGS? C . . . 028 26 008
AND EVER, IF BOUND HERE HARDEST HOME, ... 030 00 033
MEAL-DRIFT MOULDED EVER AND MELTED ACROSS SKIES? . . 038 00 004
AND LOCKS LOVE EVER IN A LAD! 048 00 035
WHEN WILL YOU EVER, PEACE, WILD WOODDOVE, SHY WINGS SHUT, 051 00 001
FAST YOU EVER, FAST BIND. 052 00 008
TENDERED TO HIM. AH WELL, GOD REST HIM ALL ROAD EVER HE OFFENDED! 053 00 008
EVER SO BLACK ON IT. OUR TALE, O OUR ORACLE! C . . 061 00 010
AND THERE FOR EVER GROVEL 077 00 007
OR EVER THE EARLY STIRRINGS OF SKYLARK 098 28 001
THAT BEAD THE PLAIN; DID EVER HAVERING CHURCH-TOWER . 100 00 006
AS EVER I REMEMBER IN MY LIFE. 102 01 013
OR EVER HE SET HIS FOOT TO THE LAND 109 07 001
TO HIM WHO EVER THOUGHT WITH LOVE OF ME 140 00 001
OR EVER DID FOR MY SAKE SOME GOOD DEED 140 00 002
LORD NOW CURB HIM FOR EVER. O DARING! O DEEP INSIGHT! 152 02 041
AND BE BLEST FOR EVER WITH THY GLORY'S SIGHT. . . . 168 00 028
EVER-FRETTING
AND THE EVER-FRETTING SHIRT OF PUNISHMENT 011 00 011
EVERLASTING
BE YE LIFT UP, YE EVERLASTING DOORS 115 00 009
IN THE EVERLASTING BURNING. 170 00 004
EVERLASTINGNESS
IT IS AN EVERLASTINGNESS OF, O IT IS AN ALL YOUTH! C 059 06 013
EVERMORE
TO DECK AND MAKE MOST LORDLY EVERMORE. ' 001 02 009
EVERY
SHOWER'D THE CLIFFS AND EVERY FRET AND SPIRE . . . 002 00 025
HE FEEDS ME WITH HIS MANNA EVERY DAY; 005 00 013
BEHOLD AT ELIM WELLS ON EVERY HAND 005 00 023
ALL MINE, YET COMMON TO MY EVERY PEER. 012 01 008
AND EVERY PRAISED SEQUENCE OF SWEET STRINGS, . . . 019 00 007
EVERY INCH A TAR, ... 041 00 075
NOT THE LEAST LASH LOST; EVERY HAIR C 059 06 020
IN EVERY LEAST THING'S LIFE; 060 00 008
WHEN EVERY COLOUR GLOWS, ... 060 00 084
HEAVEN AND EVERY FIELD, ARE STILL 085 00 002
SPANN'D WITH SHADOW EVERY ONE. 098 08 003
AND EVERY HEART THINK LOATHINGLY 114 00 015
I AM THE MIDST OF EVERY ZONE 130 00 003
AND EVERY SAINT OF BLOODY HOUR 145 00 044
BE AT EVERY ASSAULT FRESH FOILED, WORSE FLUNG, DEEPER DISAPPOINTED, 152 02 056
TOWARDS MY BROTHER, EVERY OTHER 155 00 023
AND EVERY POWER IN US THAT IS 169 00 008
AND CLEAN OF EVERY STAIN US MAKE . . . . APPEN D 46
EVERYONE
AND A SWEET SADNESS DWELT ON EVERYONE; 002 00 117

79

EVERYONE   (CONTINUED)
   IN HIS HEART SAID EVERYONE 109 15 003
EVERYTHING
   GROWTH IN EVERYTHING -- 042 00 016
   EVERYTHING THAT'S FRESH AND FAST FLYING OF US, C 059 06 008
   BLESSED BE EVERYTHING! 135 00 016
EVERYWHERE
   FROM TOO MUCH FRAGRANCE EVERYWHERE: -- 004 00 004
   NOW HE GASPS, NOW HE GAZES EVERYWHERE: 041 00 066
   NESTLING ME EVERYWHERE, ... 060 00 002
   ENRICHED POSTS ARE CHAMFER'D: EVERYWHERE 096 07 003
   DISCOVER'D EVERYWHERE, ... 098 24 003
   NOR NIGHT IS BLOWN WITH FLAME-RINGS EVERYWHERE. 099 00 018
   BUT FROM BEYOND SEAS, ERIN, FRANCE AND FLANDERS, EVERYWHERE, . 152 C 020
EVIL
   O UNTEACHABLY AFTER EVIL, BUT UTTERING TRUTH, ... 028 18 005
   MY EVIL WORDS THORNY WITH PAIN: 081 00 027
EVIL-HEAVEN'D
   AT HOPES SO EVIL-HEAVEN'D AS MINE ARE. 014 02 014
EVILS
   AGE AND AGE'S EVILS, HOAR HAIR, ... 059 0L 011
EWE
   THERE WAS NO BLEAT OF EWE, NO CHIME OF WETHER, ... 107 01 005
EXCEPT
   (EXCEPT FOR SIN), ... 127 00 007
EXCESS
   AT ONCE PERCEIVED, WITH EXCESS 118 00 010
EXHIBITION
   BID YOUR PAPA GOODNIGHT, SWEET EXHIBITION! 097 00 007
EXILE
   THIS OUTER COLD, MY EXILE FROM OF OLD 080 01 003
EXILED
   EXILED MOST REMOTE ELKHOR. 081 00U 47
EXPLANATION
   NOW, YIELDS YOU, WITH SOME SIGHS, OUR EXPLANATION. . . . 076 00 014
EXPLOIT
   HONOUR IS FLASHED OFF EXPLOIT, SO WE SAY: 073 00 001
EXPRESS
   AND SCARLET WEAR THE SPIRIT OF WAR THERE EXPRESS. . . . 063 00 008
EXPRESSED
   NOR MOUTH HAD, NO NOR MIND, EXPRESSED 055 00 012
EXPRESSIONLESS
   SHALL SEE THE AZURE TURN EXPRESSIONLESS 117 00 004
EXQUISITE
   ARE YOU! TURNED FOR AN EXQUISITE SMART, ... 028 18 002
   SOME GOOD! AND SO HE DOES LEAVE PATIENCE EXQUISITE, . . . 051 00 008
   LIT WITH EXQUISITE TINTS SEVEN 077 00 109
EXTREMES
   HER PERSEUS LINGER AND LEAVE HER TO HER EXTREMES? -- . . 050 00 009
EXTREMITY
   HE WAS TO CURE THE EXTREMITY WHERE HE HAD CAST HER: . . . 028 28 006
EXULTATION
   TO REMEMBER AND EXULTATION 042 00 047
EYE
   OF FINISH'D DIAPERS, THAT FILLS THE EYE 001 06 006
   CHANG'D TO A FLOWER: AND THERE, WITH PLACID EYE 001 11 008
   (WHERE THE EYE FIX'D, FLED THE ENCRIMSONING SPOT, . . . 002 00 009
   A QUIVERING PENNON: THEN, FOR EYE TOO KEEN, ... 002 00 017
   THE ONE PECULIAR OF THEIR PLEASURED EYE, ... 012 02 013
   THERE WAS SINGLE EYE! 028 29 002
   WHAT MOST I MAY EYE AFTER, BE IN AT THE END 040 00 010
   BUT HIS EYE NO CLIFF, NO COAST OR 041 00 067
   BUT A PRICK WILL MAKE NO EYE AT ALL, ... 043 00 015
   HAVE AN EYE TO THE SAKES OF HIM, C 045 00 010
   OR TO-FRO TENDER TRAMBEAMS TRUCKLE AT THE EYE. 046 00 004
   EYE, ALL IN FELLOWSHIP -- 049 00 004
   ACTS IN GOD'S EYE WHAT IN GOD'S EYE HE IS -- 057 0U 011
   ACTS IN GOD'S EYE WHAT IN GOD'S EYE HE IS -- 057 00 011
   AND WHAT IS EARTH'S EYE, TONGUE, OR HEART ELSE, WHERE . . 058 00 009
   FRONTING MY FROWARD EYE 060 00 119
   MARK YOU HOW THE PEACOCK'S EYE 086 00 001
   WHICH YET IS IN THE EYE OR IN THE THOUGHT. 091 00 009
   HER NOSTRIL GLISTENS; AND HER WET BLACK EYE 099 0U 005
   BEYOND, AND ONE WITHIN THE LOOKER'S EYE: 102 03 006
   RATHER TO EAR THAN EYE SHEWS WHERE THEY STRAY, ... 112 0U 004
   WHICH MAKES US EYE-ATTENTIVE TO THE EYE 125 0U 036
   MY ALL-ACCEPTING FIXED EYE, ... 130 0U 006
   THE SMOULDERING ENORMOUS WINTER WELKIN. C EYE, V . . . 149 B 009
   O I ADMIRE AND SORROW! THE HEART'S EYE GRIEVES 157 0U 001
   YOUR FEAST OF: THAT MOST IN YOU EARNEST EYE 157 0U 029
EYEBALL
   THOU SUN, ALLSEEING EYEBALL OF THE DAY, ... 160 0U 004
EYEBROW
   MERE EYEBROW ROCKS THIS ROUND OF THINGS. 166 0U 008
EYED
   I CAME WHERE CALLED, AND EYED HIM 054 0U 014
EYE-ATTENTIVE
   WHICH MAKES US EYE-ATTENTIVE TO THE EYE 125 0U 036

FACE   (CONTINUED)

```
    I MUST NOT TURN THE LANTERN ON HIS FACE, --  .   .   .   .   .   .   . 102 01 024
    SINCE ON THE FACE IT IS UNSAFE TO LOOK;  .   .   .   .   .   .   . 102 01 044
    SHE LOVES HIS FACE, SHE KNOWS THE SPOT;  .   .   .   .   .   .   . 120 00 002
    A SOMETHING IN HER FACE OF GUILE, .   .   .   .   .   .   .   . 120 00 010
    AND BREATH UPON IT. THAT IS, HER FACE IS THIS.  .   .   .   .   . 125 00 052
    YET I'D NOT SAY IT IS HER FACE ALONE  .   .   .   .   .   .   . 125 00 055
    SOME DAY TO GAZE ON THEE FACE TO FACE IN LIGHT  .   .   .   .   . 168 00 027
    SOME DAY TO GAZE ON THEE FACE TO FACE IN LIGHT  .   .   .   .   . 168 00 027
```

FACES

```
    PURE FASTED FACES DRAW UNTO THIS FEAST;  .   .   .   .   .   .   . 011 00 001
    TO THE FATHER THROUGH THE FEATURES OF MEN'S FACES.  .   .   .   . 057 00 014
    THESE NAMES, THESE FACES? THEY ARE CUSTOMARY  .   .   .   .   . 125 00 045
    AND FACES FIT FOR LEISURE GAZE  .   .   .   .   .   .   .   . 133 00 013
```

FADE

```
    A BEACON, AN ETERNAL BEAM. FLESH FADE, AND MORTAL TRASH  .   .   . 072 00 019
```

FADED

```
    RICH TITIANS FADED; IN THE STRAYING GLEAM  .   .   .   .   .   . 001 12 003
    AND JAMES SHALL HATE HIS FADED RED.  .   .   .   .   .   .   . 114 00 011
```

FADING

```
    COME YOU INDOORS, COME HOME; YOUR FADING FIRE  .   .   .   .   . 046 00 009
```

FAGGED

```
    SO FAGGED, SO FASHED, SO COGGED, SO CUMBERED, C  .   .   .   .   . 059 06 026
```

FAIL

```
    WHERE SPRINGS NOT FAIL,  .   .   .   .   .   .   .   .   .   . 009 00 002
    AND FAIL OR SCATTER ALL AWAY.  .   .   .   .   .   .   .   . 018 00 002
    DOES INTO AMBER SPLENDOURS FAIL,  .   .   .   .   .   .   . 077 00 100
    I STORM AND SHOCK YOU, SO I FAIL.  .   .   .   .   .   .   . 081 00 073
    THAT SHALL NOT FAIL IN WINTER-TIME.  .   .   .   .   .   .   . 124 00 008
    EARLIER OR YOU FAIL AT OUR FORCE, AND LIE  .   .   .   .   .   . 153 00 003
    NOT ALL, BUT WE WERE FRAMED TO FAIL AND DIE --  .   .   .   .   . 153 00 006
```

FAILING

```
    WAS A ROSE, OR, FAILING THAT,  .   .   .   .   .   .   .   . 144 00 014
```

FAIL'D

```
    THEN FAIL'D THE TONGUE; THE POOR COLLAPSING FRAME,  .   .   .   . 001 03 003
```

FAILS

```
    MY SOUL DOES LOATHE IT AND MY SPIRIT FAILS.  .   .   .   .   . 005 00 014
    WHICH PRAYING FAILS TO DO AWAY.  .   .   .   .   .   .   .   . 018 00 012
    COMPLETE THY CREATURE DEAR O WHERE IT FAILS,  .   .   .   .   . 034 00 013
```

FAILURE

```
    FOR POOR LOVE'S FAILURE THAN HIS HOPELESS RISE.  .   .   .   .   . 014 03 007
```

FAIN

```
    AND FAIN IN THE SPRINGTIME SURCEASE WOULD BORROW  .   .   .   . 026 00 011
    FORTH CHRIST FROM CUPBOARD FETCHED, HOW FAIN I OF FEET  .   .   . 048 00 010
    AND FAIN WILL FIND AS STERLING ALL AS ALL IS SMART,  .   .   .   . 063 00 007
    DRY WERE HER SAD EYES THAT WOULD FAIN HAVE STREAM'D  .   .   .   . 079 00 002
    AND FAIN WOULD FOLLOW I WHO LED.  .   .   .   .   .   .   . 081 00 172
```

FAINT

```
    AND FAINT AS THOUGH TO DIE.  .   .   .   .   .   .   .   .   . 005 00 060
    CLOSER BECAUSE FAINT MORNING STIRS;  .   .   .   .   .   .   . 077 00 022
```

FAINTER

```
    AND FAINTER, FINER, TRICKLE FAR  .   .   .   .   .   .   .   . 077 00 081
```

FAIR

```
    FAIR RELICS TOO THE CHANGEFUL MOOR HAD LEFT  .   .   .   .   . 001 08 001
    HERE IN SOME DARKEN'D LANDSCAPE PARIS FAIR  .   .   .   .   . 001 11 001
    FAIR BEDS THEY SEEM'D OF WATER-LILY FLAKES  .   .   .   .   . 002 00 013
    GOSHEN IS GREEN AND FAIR.  .   .   .   .   .   .   .   .   . 005 00 030
    I AM SO LIGHT, I AM SO FAIR,  .   .   .   .   .   .   .   . 010 00 002
    I AM SO LIGHT AND FAIR  .   .   .   .   .   .   .   .   . 025 00 002
    FOR THOU, AS SHE, WERT THE ONE FAIR DAUGHTER  .   .   .   .   . 026 00 025
    WITH RICHNESS; THE RACING LAMBS TOO HAVE FAIR THEIR FLING.  .   . 033 00 008
    HAVE FAIR FALLEN, O FAIR, FAIR HAVE FALLEN, SO DEAR  .   .   .   . 045 00 001
    HAVE FAIR FALLEN, O FAIR, FAIR HAVE FALLEN, SO DEAR  .   .   .   . 045 00 001
    HAVE FAIR FALLEN, O FAIR, FAIR HAVE FALLEN, SO DEAR  .   .   .   . 045 00 001
    NOR CAN YOU LONG BE, WHAT YOU NOW ARE, CALLED FAIR,  .   .   .   . 059 0L 006
    IT MELTS, NEW LIGHTS ARISE AS FAIR,  .   .   .   .   .   .   . 077 00 118
    FAIR, BUT OF FAIRNESS AS A VISION DREAM'D;  .   .   .   .   . 079 00 001
    ' BOUGHS BEING PRUNED, BIRDS PREENED, SHOW MORE FAIR;  .   .   . 096 07 001
    ' AND IS SO FAIR TO SEE. '  .   .   .   .   .   .   .   .   . 109 20 004
    AND EACH AS FAIR AS HE.  .   .   .   .   .   .   .   .   . 109 21 004
    HAVE TOLD ME I AM FAIR TO SEE.  .   .   .   .   .   .   .   . 124 00 024
    ARE NEVER KNOWN FOR FAIR,  .   .   .   .   .   .   .   .   . 133 00 016
    IN ONE FAIR FALL; BUT, FOR TIME'S AFTERCAST,  .   .   .   .   . 157 00 007
    ANG.  I AM SO LIGHT AND FAIR  .   .   .   .   .   .   .   . APPEN A 02
    AND FAIR 'GAN HER TO GREET.  .   .   .   .   .   .   .   . APPEN D 04
```

FAIRER

```
    AND BOASTING ' I HAVE FAIRER THINGS THAN THESE '  .   .   .   . 002 00 086
    FAIRER THAN THIS ONE TO BRIGHTEN OUR DAY?  .   .   .   .   . 026 00 008
    EARTH IS THE FAIRER FOR.  .   .   .   .   .   .   .   .   . 060 00 093
    THE FAIRER WAXED HE.  .   .   .   .   .   .   .   .   .   . 109 36 002
    THAT HAS IT; AND SHE IS FAIRER THAN COLOMB.  .   .   .   .   . 125 00 037
    FAIRER? THESE ARE THE FLARING SHOWS UNLOVELY  .   .   .   .   . 125 00 039
```

FAIRLY

```
    SNOWFLAKE; THAT'S FAIRLY MIXED  .   .   .   .   .   .   .   . 060 00 006
```

FAIRNESS

```
    FAIR, BUT OF FAIRNESS AS A VISION DREAM'D;  .   .   .   .   . 079 00 001
```

FAIRY

```
    IN FRANK, IN FAIRY PENMAEN POOL.  .   .   .   .   .   .   . 030 00 016
```

FALSE
    AND MARCHING TO FALSE COLOURS! THOSE FEW STROKES 102 01 065
FALSELY
    'TIS FALSELY GIVEN -- AS LOVE IN MEN! 081 00 049
FALSIFIED
    IN BOWS ABOVE MY HEAD, AS FALSIFIED 012 02 004
FALTER
    HIS SICK STARS FALTER. MORE HE MAY 083 00 025
FAME
    AND STORMS BUGLE HIS FAME. 028 11 004
    THEY STAND, THEY SHINE IN THE SUN: FAME HAS FOREGONE . . . 104 00 002
    HER FAME TO KEEP, HER FAME TO RECOVER. 156 00 012
    HER FAME TO KEEP, HER FAME TO RECOVER. 156 00 012
    ONE WITH MORE CONSCIENCE, CLEANER FAME! 166 00 012
FAME'S
    CALL ME ENGLAND'S FAME'S FOND LOVER. 156 00 011
FAMILIAR
    FAMILIAR AND SO HATED BY THE SICK; V 125 00 042
    HATED AND TOO FAMILIAR TO -- ----; V 125 00 043
FAMILIARNESS
    I PLEAD: FAMILIARNESS ENDEARS 081 00 026
FAN
    WITH DARKSOME DEVOURING EYES MY BRUISED BONES? AND FAN, . . 064 00 007
    THAN FAN OR HOOD OR STRAWY PLAIT. 120 00 008
FANCIED
    MUST BE THAT FANCIED IT. 148 00 004
FANCIES
    IT FANCIES, FEIGNS, DEEMS, DEARS THE ARTIST AFTER HIS ART! . 063 00 006
    GILDS WITH SOME SPARKY FANCIES HIS BLACK NIGHT . . . 102 03 030
    GILDS WITH SOME SPARKY FANCIES BLINDING NIGHT, V . . . 102 03 036
FANCIFUL
    THIS IS TOO MUCH THE FATHER: NAY THE MOTHER. FANCIFUL! . . 152 01 023
FANCY
    I MUST FEED FANCY. SHOW ME ANY ONE 014 02 001
    REACH ME A . . . FANCY, COME FASTER -- 028 28 002
FANG
    FANG, OR FLOOD ? GOES DEATH ON DRUM. 028 11 003
    AND FIND A FLINT, A FANG OF ICE, ... 080 12 004
FANGED
    A FLUKE YET FANGED HIM, ENTANGLED HIM, NOT QUIT UTTERLY. C . 137 00 005
FANGS
    WITH GORGON'S GEAR AND BAREBILL / THONGS AND FANGS. . . 050 00 014
FANS
    BROIDERS THE NETS WITH FANS OF AMETHYST 002 00 066
    OFF HIM, BUT MEANING MOTION FANS FRESH OUR WITS WITH WONDER. . 045 00 014
FANTASTIC
    SO, GROWN FANTASTIC IN HIS PIETY, ... 001 03 005
FAR
    FAR OFF A NEREID COMPANY, AND SHAKE 002 00 075
    WITH LOATH'D COLD FISHES, FAR FROM MAN -- OR WHAT; -- . . 002 00 124
    AND I'LL LOVE MY DISTINCTION: NEAR OR FAR 014 02 012
    HOW FAR FROM THEN FORETHOUGHT OF, ALL THY MORE BOISTEROUS YEARS, . 053 00 012
    FAR WITH FONDER A CARE C 059 06 029
    WHO MADE CONJECTURE NEAREST FAR 077 00 045
    AND FAINTER, FINER, TRICKLE FAR 077 00 081
    THO' FAR OR SICK OR HEAVY OR STILL 081 00 018
    AND YOU ARE GONE SO HEAVENLY FAR 081 00 034
    SO FAR BUT I HAVE YET WITHIN 081 00 131
    NOT FURTHER'D FAR MY TRAVELL'D FEET 081 00 157
    NOT SO FAR FROM THE POLE. 088 00 008
    NOT SO FAR FROM THE POLE. V 088 00 012
    FAR FROM ITS HEAD AN ANGEL'S HOVERINGS. 089 00 008
    NOT SO FAR OUTWARD IN THE SEA: 120 00 021
    THINK YOU WANT DAFFODILS AND FOLLOW AS FAR 135 00 030
    BEFORE OR BEHIND OR FAR OR AT HAND 138 00 007
    NOT THAT, BUT THUS FAR, ALL WITH FRAILTY, BLEST . . . 157 00 006
FARE
    VERTICAL HOME, COULD SICILY FARE 166 00 018
FAR-OFF
    OR FAR-OFF PROMISE OF A TIME TO BE! 013 00 004
FARMING
    HIS HEART AT FARMING, WHAT BETWEEN 166 00 030
FARMYARD
    FLAKE-DOVES SENT FLOATING FORTH AT A FARMYARD SCARE! -- . . 032 00 007
FARRIER
    FELIX RANDAL THE FARRIER, O IS HE DEAD THEN? MY DUTY ALL ENDED, . 053 00 001
FASHED
    SO FAGGED, SO FASHED, SO COGGED, SO CUMBERED, C . . . 059 06 026
FASHION
    THEN OFTEN THE EARS IN A NEW FASHION HARK, ... 113 00 007
FAST
    SPHERED SO FAST, SWEET SOUL? -- WE SEE 010 00 023
    I CEASE THE MOURNING AND THE ABJECT FAST, ... 014 01 008
    SPHERED SO FAST, SWEET SOUL? -- WE SEE 025 00 023
    FAST, BUT MINED WITH A MOTION, A DRIFT, ... 028 04 003
    TO MAN'S LAST DUST, DRAIN FAST TOWARDS MAN'S FIRST SLIME. . . 035 00 014
    THEIR RANSOM, THEIR RESCUE, AND FIRST, FAST, LAST FRIEND. . . 040 00 014

FAST   (CONTINUED)
    FAST FOUNDERING OWN GENERATION. 041 00 088
    FAST YOU EVER, FAST BIND. 052 00 008
    FAST YOU EVER, FAST BIND. 052 00 008
    EVERYTHING THAT'S FRESH AND FAST FLYING OF US, C 059 06 008
    FOLD HOME, FAST FOLD THY CHILD. 060 00 126
    MAN, HOW FAST HIS FIREDINT, HIS MARK ON MIND, IS GONE!   .   .   072 00 011
    THE POINT FAST IN, AND MY LEFT HAND 080 13 004
    FLING TO THE CONVENT WICKET FAST. 081 00 075
    HIS LIPS MOVED FAST IN SENSE TOO THICK! 081 00 100
    AND STRAIGHT SHOWERS PARALLEL SHOULD FOLLOW FAST;   .   .   090 00 004
    LODGE HIS EYES FAST; BUT YET AS EASY AND LIGHT   .   .   .   102 01 020
    FAST OR THEY IN CLAMMYISH LASHTENDER COMBS CREEP   .   .   149 A 005
    ARE AFOOT; HEAVEN-VAULT FAST PURPLING PORTENDS, C   .   .   152 02 031
    BY HER BLOOM, FAST BY HER FRESH, HER FLEECED BLOOM,   .   .   152 02 051
    HAPPY THE FATHER, MOTHER OF THESE! TOO FAST; 157 00 005
    FAST FURLED AND ALL FOREDRAWN TO NO OR YES. 157 00 028
    FAST HE OPENS, LAST HE OFF WRINGS 159 00 034
    CAT. SPHERED SO FAST, SWEET SOUL? -- WE SEE   .   .   .   .   APPEN A 23
FASTED
    PURE FASTED FACES DRAW UNTO THIS FEAST; 011 00 001
FASTEN
    WHY FASTEN THAT UPON HER, ...   042 00 007
FASTENED
    THOU HAST BOUND BONES AND VEINS IN ME, FASTENED ME FLESH,   .   028 01 005
    NEVER FLEETS MORE, FASTENED WITH THE TENDEREST TRUTH   .   .   059 06 012
FASTER
    REACH ME A . . . FANCY, COME FASTER -- 028 28 002
    BREATHES ONCE AND, QUENCHED FASTER THAN IT CAME,   .   .   .   076 00 003
FAST-FLOWING
    THAT HIS FAST-FLOWING HOURS WITH SANDY SILT 136 00 001
FAST-LODGED
    MY FAST-LODGED TONGUE, ' [TO HER THE GIFT] 081 00 116
FASTS
    SO FRESH THAT COME IN FASTS DIVINE! 022 00 016
FATAL
    STRETCHES THE ENVIED FRUIT WITH FATAL SMILE 001 11 002
    FATAL FOUR DISORDERS, FLESHED THERE, ALL CONTENDED?   .   .   053 00 004
    AND LOVES -- A FATAL FAULT -- TO PATRONIZE; 094 00 018
FATHER
    SUN-FLUSH'D, UNTIL IT SEEM'D THEIR FATHER SEA 002 00 100
    FATHER AND FONDLER OF HEART THOU HAST WRUNG; 028 09 007
    O FATHER, NOT UNDER THY FEATHERS NOR EVER AS GUESSING   .   028 12 005
    JOY FALL TO THEE, FATHER FRANCIS. 028 23 001
    THE CHRIST OF THE FATHER COMPASSIONATE, C 028 33 008
    BEING MIGHTY A MASTER, BEING A FATHER AND FOND.   .   .   .   034 00 014
    YOU? ' -- ' FATHER, WHAT YOU BUY ME I LIKE BEST. '   .   .   .   047 00 002
    TO THE FATHER THROUGH THE FEATURES OF MEN'S FACES.   .   .   057 00 014
    HOW THEN SHOULD GREGORY, A FATHER, HAVE GLEANED ELSE FROM SWARM-   062 00 007
    AMONG STRANGERS. FATHER AND MOTHER DEAR, ...   066 00 002
    ' THY FATHER THOU SHALT SEE. ' 109 16 004
    AND FATHER BE OVERWORN. 114 00 008
    HE SPOKE OF GOD THE FATHER AND HIS SON, ...   136 00 025
    ' THE CHILD IS FATHER TO THE MAN. ' 147 00 001
    ' THE CHILD IS FATHER TO THE MAN. ' 147 00 004
    ' THE MAN IS FATHER TO THE CHILD. ' 147 00 006
    ' THE CHILD IS FATHER TO THE MAN! ' 147 00 007
    ' WHAT, TERYTH! WHAT, THOU POOR FOND FATHER! C   .   .   .   152 01 016
    THIS IS TOO MUCH THE FATHER; NAY THE MOTHER. FANCIFUL!   .   152 01 023
    FATHER, BE THOU RECONCILED. 155 00 014
    HAPPY THE FATHER, MOTHER OF THESE! TOO FAST; 157 00 005
    FATHER, MOTHER, BROTHERS, SISTERS, FRIENDS 159 00 049
    TO THE GLORY OF THE FATHER. AMEN. 169 00 011
FATHER'D
    OR FATHER'D BY THE SUNDER'D SOUTH, ...   083 00 006
FATHER'S
    AS JESUS GOD THE FATHER'S SON. 167 00 008
FATHERS
    TIME'S TASKING, IT IS FATHERS THAT ASKING FOR EASE   .   .   .   028 27 003
    THE FINE DELIGHT THAT FATHERS THOUGHT; THE STRONG   .   .   .   076 00 001
    NO MAN HAS SUCH A DAUGHTER. THE FATHERS OF THE WORLD   .   .   152 01 011
FATHERS-FORTH
    HE FATHERS-FORTH WHOSE BEAUTY IS PAST CHANGE; 037 00 010
FATHOMS
    WARNED, ELEVEN FATHOMS FALLEN 041 00 004
FAULT
    THIS FAULT IN ONE I FOUND, THAT IN ANOTHER; 016 00 011
    WHAT HINDERS? ARE YOU BEAM-BLIND, YET TO A FAULT   .   .   .   046 00 012
    AH NATURE, FRAMED IN FAULT, ...   054 00 038
    AND LOVES -- A FATAL FAULT -- TO PATRONIZE; 094 00 018
    ALAS! BUT I AM ALL AT FAULT, ...   120 00 024
FAULT-NOT-FOUND-
    THIS FAULT-NOT-FOUND-WITH GOOD 148 00 031
FAVOUR
    AND FIVE-LIVED AND LEAVED FAVOUR AND PRIDE, ...   028 23 006
FAVOURABLE
    FORWARD-LIKE, BUT HOWEVER, AND LIKE FAVOURABLE HEAVEN HEARD THESE.   .   048 00 048

FAVOURED
OF FAVOURED MAKE AND MIND AND HEALTH AND YOUTH, ... 157 00 018
FAVOURING
AND FAVOURING VIRGIN FRESHNESS YET. 139 00 006
FAVOURITE
THE SWALLOW, FAVOURITE OF THE GALE, ... 130 00 009
FAWNING
FAWNING FAWNING CROCODILES 145 00 022
FAWNING FAWNING CROCODILES 145 00 022
FAWN=FROTH
A WINDPUFF=BONNET OF FAWN=FROTH 056 00 005
FEALTY
AND STILL THOU BIND'ST ME TO FRESH FEALTY 012 01 003
FEAR
AND FEAR NO IRON ROD. 005 00 012
THIS MEANS YOU NEED NOT FEAR THE STORMS, THE CRIES, ... 014 03 002
WITH NOT A THING TO MAKE ME FEAR, ... 021 00 040
IF STILL IN DARKNESS NOT IN FEAR. 023 00 048
OR WRING THEIR BARRIERS IN BURSTS OF FEAR OR RAGE. 039 00 008
NOT MOOD IN HIM NOR MEANING, PROUD FIRE OR SACRED FEAR, ... 045 00 005
YOUNG JOHN! THEN FEAR, THEN JOY 054 00 008
FEAR HINDRANCE AND ESPIAL 110 00 003
IS ALL, ALL SHEARED AWAY, THUS! ' THEN I SWEAT FOR FEAR. 152 01 018
AND ALL THAT COMES IS FRAUGHT TO ME WITH FEAR. 160 00 036
NOR FEAR THE VIOLENT CALENDAR 166 00 027
FEARED
I ONLY FEARED THE WET FOR YOU 021 00 013
FEARFUL
AND FOR THAT FEARFUL HOUR LIFE IS MORE THIN 080 03 005
FEARING
TILL, (FEARING RAVAGE WORSE THAN IN HIS FLIGHT, ... 001 14 007
NOR FEARING NOT TO LOVE AND BE 170 00 003
FEAR'D
-- LATELY I FEAR'D 102 01 006
FEARS
BECAUSE SHE FEARS HER FINGERS WILL BE STUNG. 096 04 002
PLAYS TO THE BREEZE! WHERE NOW ARE FLED HER FEARS, ... 099 00 015
I HERE FORBID MY THOUGHTS TO FOOL THEMSELVES WITH FEARS. 152 01 024
BUT FEARS, FORE=MOTIONS OF THE MIND, ... 166 00 037
FEAST
PURE FASTED FACES DRAW UNTO THIS FEAST! 011 00 001
AND NOW THE MARRIAGE FEAST BEGUN, ... 022 00 026
WHAT WAS THE FEAST FOLLOWED THE NIGHT 028 30 003
FEAST OF THE ONE WOMAN WITHOUT STAIN, ... 028 30 005
NOT, I'LL NOT, CARRION COMFORT, DESPAIR, NOT FEAST ON THEE! 064 00 001
YOUR FEAST OF! THAT MOST IN YOU EARNEST EYE 157 00 029
LEND THIS LIFE TO ME THEN! FEED AND FEAST MY MIND, ... 168 00 019
FEASTING
LOOKS LAID FOR FEASTING AND FOR REST. 003 00 024
WITH A FEASTING IN HER HONOUR? 042 00 008
FEASTS
FEASTS, WHEN WE SHALL FALL ASLEEP, ... 029 00 009
HER FEASTS FOLLOW REASON, ... 042 00 003
ROSE. HERE HE FEASTS: LOVELY ALL IS! C 159 00 028
FEATHER
ONE SCARLET FEATHER TRAILING TO THE WIND! 002 00 081
FLESH AND FLEECE, FUR AND FEATHER, ... 042 00 017
THE AUTUMN YELLOW FEATHER IN THE BOUGHS 105 00 005
FEATHERS
AND FROM DANK FEATHERS WRING THE DROPS 003 00 008
O FATHER, NOT UNDER THY FEATHERS NOR EVER AS GUESSING 028 12 005
FEATHERY
FINGER OF A TENDER OF, O OF A FEATHERY DELICACY, THE BREAST OF THE . 028 31 006
THE KNOT OF FEATHERY LOCKS UPON HER HEAD 099 00 014
FEATURE
CHEEKS! RIGHT, RUDE OF FEATURE, ... 041 00 050
IT IS THE FORGED FEATURE FINDS ME! IT IS THE REHEARSAL 045 00 007
ING BLOOD -- THE O=SEAL=THAT=SO FEATURE, FLUNG PROUDER FORM . . . 062 00 002
THEIR YOUNG DELIGHTFUL HOUR DO FEATURE DOWN 157 00 010
FEATURES
TO THE FATHER THROUGH THE FEATURES OF MEN'S FACES. 057 00 014
AND FEATURES, IN FLESH, WHAT DEED HE C 071 00 008
HER MOULD OF FEATURES MATED WELL. 145 00 016
FED
HER HOMES AND FIELDS THAT FOLDED AND FED ME? 156 00 002
FEE
THAT HAS BOTH GOLD AND FEE. 109 09 002
SHEWN HIM BOTH GOLD AND FEE: 109 11 002
BECAUSE OF GOLD AND FEE. 109 12 002
FEEBLE
LO, GOD SHALL STRENGTHEN ALL THE FEEBLE KNEES. 011 00 014
FEED
I MUST FEED FANCY. SHOW ME ANY ONE 014 02 001
AND I THAT DIE THESE DEATHS, THAT FEED THIS FLAME, ... 075 00 012
WE WILL CHARGE OUR FLOCKS THAT THEY NOT FEED. 098 15 002
LEND THIS LIFE TO ME THEN! FEED AND FEAST MY MIND, ... 168 00 019
FEEDS
HE FEEDS ME WITH HIS MANNA EVERY DAY: 005 00 013

86

```
FEEDS        (CONTINUED)
      AND FEEDS NEW LEAVES UPON THE WINDS OF FALL;    .    .    .    .    .    .  105 00 010
FEEL
      BUT FEEL THE LONG SUCCESS OF SIN.  .    .    .    .    .    .    .    .    .  018 00 008
      OVER AGAIN I FEEL THY FINGER AND FIND THEE.    .    .    .    .    .    .  028 01 008
      IS BARE NOW, NOR CAN FOOT FEEL, BEING SHOD.    .    .    .    .    .    .  031 00 008
      TO, WITH NO TONGUE TO PLEAD, NO HEART TO FEEL;    .    .    .    .    .  058 00 003
      I WAKE AND FEEL THE FELL OF DARK, NOT DAY.    .    .    .    .    .    .  067 00 001
      SURE, 'S BED NOW, LOW BE IT; LUSTILY HE HIS LOW LOT ( FEEL    .    .  070 00 005
      AND HARD MEN FEEL A SOFTENING TOUCH;    .    .    .    .    .    .    .  077 00 030
      AND FEEL NO BLAST. -- THE FRETFUL FIRE    .    .    .    .    .    .    .  080 05 004
      SOME KNELT, SOME STOOD; I SEEM'D TO FEEL    .    .    .    .    .    .  081 00 093
      FISH FEEL THEIR WATERS DRAWING TO .    .    .    .    .    .    .    .    .  166 00 033
FEELERS
      WITH GROWTHS OF MYRIAD FEELERS, CRYSTALLINE    .    .    .    .    .  002 00 070
FEELING
      THE KEENER TO COME AT THE COMFORT FOR FEELING THE COMBATING KEEN?    .  028 25 008
      SOME PAGEANT WHICH TAKES TEARS AND I MUST FOOT WITH FEELING THAT    .  152 01 020
FEEL-OF-PRIMROSE
      O FEEL-OF-PRIMROSE HANDS, O FEET    .    .    .    .    .    .    .    .    .  022 00 021
FEELS
      A BOY FEELS WHEN THE POET HE PORES UPON    .    .    .    .    .    .  014 03 013
FEET
      THE TRUMPET WAXES LOUD; TIRED ARE YOUR FEET.    .    .    .    .    .  005 00 008
      TO PLASH WITH COOL FEET THE CLAY JUICY SOIL.    .    .    .    .    .    .  005 00 050
      WHICH SHOULD ERE NOW HAVE LED MY FEET TO THE FIELD.    .    .    .    .  017 00 009
      O FEEL-OF-PRIMROSE HANDS, O FEET    .    .    .    .    .    .    .    .    .  022 00 021
      WHERE SEEK THEE WITH UNSANDALLED FEET.    .    .    .    .    .    .    .  023 00 018
      TO HERO OF CALVARY, CHRIST, 'S FEET --    .    .    .    .    .    .    .  028 08 007
      AND HURLS FOR HIM, O HALF HURLS EARTH FOR HIM OFF UNDER HIS FEET.    .  038 00 014
      FORTH CHRIST FROM CUPBOARD FETCHED, HOW FAIN I OF FEET    .    .    .  048 00 010
      THEM -- BROAD IN BLUFF HIDE HIS FROWNING FEET LASHED! RACED    .    .  071 00 013
      CLEAVES NOT MY BRAIN, BURNS NOT MY FEET.    .    .    .    .    .    .    .  080 02 004
      AND WITH SHARP FLINT WILL PART MY FEET AND DINT    .    .    .    .    .  080 13 003
      NOT FURTHER'D FAR MY TRAVELL'D FEET    .    .    .    .    .    .    .    .  081 00 157
      THEIR CHANGING FEET IN FLICKER ALL THE TIME    .    .    .    .    .    .  107 01 013
      AND TO THEIR FEET THE NARROW BELLS GAVE RHYME.    .    .    .    .    .  107 01 014
      THEY HAVE BOUND HIS FEET, THEY HAVE BOUND HIS HANDS;    .    .    .  109 13 003
      TILL WALK THE WORLD HE CAN WITH BARE HIS FEET    .    .    .    .    .  159 00 035
      AGAINST THY POWER PUT UNDER FEET .    .    .    .    .    .    .    .    .  169 00 009
FEIGNS
      IT FANCIES, FEIGNS, DEEMS, DEARS THE ARTIST AFTER HIS ART;    .    .  063 00 006
FELIX
      FELIX RANDAL THE FARRIER, O IS HE DEAD THEN? MY DUTY ALL ENDED,    .  053 00 001
      THY TEARS THAT TOUCHED MY HEART, CHILD, FELIX, POOR FELIX RANDAL;    .  053 00 011
      THY TEARS THAT TOUCHED MY HEART, CHILD, FELIX, POOR FELIX RANDAL!    .  053 00 011
FELL
      FELL ON THE PALACE, AND THE LUST OF RABBLE RUDE, )    .    .    .    .  001 14 009
      THE WINGED FOWLS TOOK PART; PART FELL IN THORN    .    .    .    .    .  007 00 007
      AND THEY COULD NOT AND FELL TO THE DECK    .    .    .    .    .    .    .  028 17 002
      THIS WAS THAT FELL CAPSIZE.    .    .    .    .    .    .    .    .    .    .  041 00 037
      WITNESSED; SO FORTUNE FELL.    .    .    .    .    .    .    .    .    .    .  054 00 004
      ERING! LET ME BE FELL; FORCE I MUST BE BRIEF '    .    .    .    .    .  065 00 008
      I WAKE AND FEEL THE FELL OF DARK, NOT DAY.    .    .    .    .    .    .  067 00 001
      SOMETHING I SAID: I SWOONED AND FELL,    .    .    .    .    .    .    .  081 00 118
      DEATH'S BONES FELL IN WITH SUDDEN CLANK    .    .    .    .    .    .    .  092 00 012
      LATE I FELL IN THE ECSTACY    .    .    .    .    .    .    .    .    .    .  093  A 001
      DOWN UPON GROUND FELL SHE.    .    .    .    .    .    .    .    .    .    .  109 39 002
      A STANDING FELL    .    .    .    .    .    .    .    .    .    .    .    .  112 00 010
      AS IT FELL UPON A DAY    .    .    .    .    .    .    .    .    .    .    .  131 00 001
      IT STOOPED AND FLASHED AND FELL AND RAN LIKE WATER AWAY.    .    .    .  152 02 021
      THE RACE OF MAN; AND HENCE I FELL.    .    .    .    .    .    .    .    .  160 00 031
      THEO.   YOU FELL INTO THE PARTLESS AIR.    .    .    .    .    .    .  APPEN A 30
FELLED
      FELLED AND FURLED THEM, THE HEARTS OF OAK!    .    .    .    .    .    .  041 00 006
      ALL FELLED, FELLED, ARE ALL FELLED;    .    .    .    .    .    .    .    .  043 00 003
      ALL FELLED, FELLED, ARE ALL FELLED;    .    .    .    .    .    .    .    .  043 00 003
      ALL FELLED, FELLED, ARE ALL FELLED;    .    .    .    .    .    .    .    .  043 00 003
FELL-FROWNING
      OF A POOL SO PITCHBLACK, FELL-FROWNING,    .    .    .    .    .    .    .  056 00 007
FELLOWSHIP
      EYE, ALL IN FELLOWSHIP -- .    .    .    .    .    .    .    .    .    .    .  049 00 004
      AND BROUGHT THE SENSE OF GENTLE FELLOWSHIP,    .    .    .    .    .    .  107 02 004
FELLOWSHIPS
      BREATHE EASTER NOW! YOU SERGED FELLOWSHIPS,    .    .    .    .    .    .  011 00 007
FELLS
      FELLS OR FLANKS OF THE VOEL, A VEIN    .    .    .    .    .    .    .    .  028 04 007
      THAT BIRD BEYOND THE REMEMBERING HIS FREE FELLS;    .    .    .    .    .  039 00 003
FELT
      BUT EARTH HAS NEVER FELT THE SNOW.    .    .    .    .    .    .    .    .  003 00 002
      SPRINGS THE STRESS FELT .    .    .    .    .    .    .    .    .    .    .  028 06 002
      THOUGH FELT BEFORE, THOUGH IN HIGH FLOOD YET --    .    .    .    .    .  028 07 007
      WHEN SHE FELT THE KILL-WEIGHTS CRUSH    .    .    .    .    .    .    .  145 00 055
FEMALE
      HAS WIT ENOUGH, BUT LESS THAN FEMALE TACT,    .    .    .    .    .    .  094 00 019
FENCED
      FOR US THE VINE WAS FENCED WITH THORN,    .    .    .    .    .    .    .  006 00 013
```

87

FENS
IN BERYL-COVERED FENS SO DIM, ... 003 00 026
FERN
WIRY HEATHPACKS, FLITCHES OF FERN, ... 056 00 011
FERTILE
HAD BEEN MORE FERTILE AND HAD SOWN WITH NOTES 122 00 005
FESTIVAL
BLOT THE PERPETUAL FESTIVAL OF DAY? 089 00 002
FETCH
HAS ONE FETCH IN HER: SHE REARS HERSELF TO DIVINE .   .   . 028 19 006
PRAYER SHALL FETCH PITY ETERNAL. 041 00 120
FETCHED
FETCHED IN THE STORM OF HIS STRIDES. C 028 33 008
FETCHED FRESH, AS I SUPPOSE, OFF SOME SWEET WOOD,   .   . 034 00 004
FORTH CHRIST FROM CUPBOARD FETCHED, HOW FAIN I OF FEET .   . 048 00 010
FETTLE
DIDST FETTLE FOR THE GREAT GREY DRAYHORSE C 053 00 014
FEVER
MY TEMPESTS THERE, MY FIRE AND FEVER FUSSY. 075 00 014
FEVER'D
'MID FEVER'D FUMES AND SLIME AND CAKED CLOT: 077 00 008
FEW
AND A FEW LILIES BLOW. 009 00 004
NOR FIRST FROM HEAVEN (AND FEW KNOW THIS) 028 06 003
FIVE NOTES OR SEVEN, LATE AND FEW: 081 00 023
MY CRY IS LIKE A BLEAT: A FEW 081 00 066
AND MARCHING TO FALSE COLOURS: THOSE FEW STROKES   .   .   . 102 01 065
AND A FEW LEAVES NOT LILY-WHITE BUT CHARACTERED OVER WITH BLACKS.   .   . 128 00 016
FICKLE
WHATEVER IS FICKLE, FRECKLED (WHO KNOWS HOW?)   .   .   . 037 00 008
WITH FICKLE SPOTS OF SADNESS: ACCESSORIES 125 00 041
FIE
' FIE, YOU ARE NOT LORD WILLIAM, ' SHE SAID: 109 26 003
' O FIE THAT THIS SHOULD BE. ' 109 26 004
' FIE, ' SHE SAID UNTO THEM ALL, ... 109 28 001
FIELD
THE FIELD WHERE HE HAS PLANTED US 006 00 027
THE FIELD IS SOPP'D WITH MERCIFUL DEW. 008 00 003
WHICH SHOULD ERE NOW HAVE LED MY FEET TO THE FIELD,   .   . 017 00 009
SHOULD TONGUE THAT TIME NOW, TRUMPET NOW THAT FIELD,   .   . 073 00 003
HEAVEN AND EVERY FIELD, ARE STILL 085 00 002
A DROP OF SHADE ROLLS OVER FIELD AND FLOCK: 098 03 002
WHOSE SILVER SKINS LIE LEVEL AND THICK IN FIELD.   .   .   . 102 01 022
THEIR CLARIONS FROM ALL CORNERS OF THE FIELD 104 00 004
OVER FIELD AND TREE, ... 109 17 002
WHERE IS THE FIELD I MUST PLAY THE MAN ON? 156 00 016
FIELD-FLOWERS
AND FIELD-FLOWERS MAKE THE FIELDS FORLORN, ... 114 00 003
FIELD-FLOWN
FIELD-FLOWN, THE DEPARTED DAY NO MORNING BRINGS   .   .   . 153 00 009
FIELDS
TO FIELDS WHERE FLIES NO SHARP AND SIDED HAIL 009 00 003
DEWY FIELDS IN THE MORNING UNDER THE SUN 098 13 001
TO SPILL O'ER FIELDS OF LILIES. SO COULD I 102 01 034
TO FIELDS OF LIGHT: MILLIONS OF TRAVELLING RAYS   .   .   . 103 00 009
THEY DRAW ALL COVERTS, CUT THE FIELDS, AND SUCK   .   .   . 104 00 012
CLOSE-ROOTED IN THE DOWNWARD-HOLLOWING FIELDS: .   .   . 107 03 015
OF SHEEP FROM THE HIGH FIELDS AND OTHER WILD 107 04 023
AND FIELD-FLOWERS MAKE THE FIELDS FORLORN, ... 114 00 003
I NEVER SAW THOSE FIELDS WHEREON THEIR BEST 119 00 011
HER HOMES AND FIELDS THAT FOLDED AND FED ME?   .   .   . 156 00 002
THE DOG-STAR WITH THE FIELDS ABAKE 166 00 031
FIERCE
HUNG IN THE SWAYING OF THE FIERCE MELEE, ... 001 02 004
WHEN THE FIERCE SKIES ARE BLUE TO BLACK, ALBEIT   .   .   . 080 02 005
FIERCER
WITH FIERCER WEEPINGS OF THESE DESPERATE EYES 014 03 006
FIERCEST
EARTH HEARS NO HURTLE THEN FROM FIERCEST FRAY.   .   .   . 073 00 008
FIERY
UPRAIS'D AN EMBLEM OF THAT FIERY CONSTANCY. 001 03 008
LEGATES MIGHT RUSH, ZEAL-RAMPANT, FIERY, ... 001 05 005
WITH FORM DIVINE, A FIERY CHIVALRY -- 001 07 008
SECOND THIS FIERY STRAIN? NOT ALWAYS: O NO NO!   .   .   . 152 02 046
FIG
HANDLE THE FIG, SUCK THE FULL-SAPP'D VINE-SHOOT.   .   .   . 005 00 038
FIGHT
TO FOLLOW A BANNER AND FIGHT FOR HONOUR. 156 00 009
WE FOLLOW HER BANNER, WE FIGHT FOR HER HONOUR.   .   .   . 156 00 010
FIGHTER
AND, ON THE FIGHTER, FORGE HIS GLORIOUS DAY. 073 00 004
FILES
SEXING AND RANKING WITH OUR RUDER FILES V 102 01 063
FILIAL
THEY KISS THE ROD WITH FILIAL SUBMISSION. 097 00 008
FILL
AND HAVE YOUR FILL OF MEAT: 005 00 010

88

FILL   (CONTINUED)
    TO SING SCARCE HEARD, AND SINGING FILL 077 00 077
    THE PEACOCK'D COPSE WERE KNOWN TO FILL; 081 00 014
    I HAVE FILL'D, THAT HARD TO FILL IS, ...   098 19 002
    MET A NEW SHOWER, AND SAW THE RAINBOW FILL 107 03 010
    AND FILL THE WORLD UP WITH DELIGHT. 167 00 024
FILLED
    BONES BUILT IN ME, FLESH FILLED, BLOOD BRIMMED THE CURSE.   .   .   .   067 00 011
    FILLED FULL OF CHARITY, ...   APPEN D 41
FILLETED
    FILLETED WITH GLASSY GRASSY QUICKSILVERY SHIVES AND SHOOTS C   .   .   159 00 038
FILLETS
    WITH GOLDEN FILLETS AND RICH BLAZONRY, ...   001 07 006
FILL'D
    I HAVE FILL'D, THAT HARD TO FILL IS, ...   098 19 002
FILLS
    OF FINISH'D DIAPERS, THAT FILLS THE EYE 001 06 006
    DELICIOUS KINDNESS? -- HE IS PATIENT, PATIENCE FILLS 068 00 013
    WHO KNEW THE INNER SPIRIT THAT FILLS 077 00 043
FILM
    OF TREMULOUS FILM, MORE SUBTLE THAN THE VEST 002 00 039
FILMS
    AND SILVER FILMS, BENEATH WITH PEARLY MIST, ...   002 00 067
FILMY
    OF FILMY GLOBES AND ROSY FLOATING CLOUD; -- 002 00 097
    THEIR FILMY TAILS ADOWN WHOSE LENGTH THERE SHOW'D 002 00 104
FILTH
    SCOOP YOU FROM TEEMING FILTH SOME SICKLY HOVEL, ...   077 00 006
FIN
    A TINTED FIN ON EITHER SHOULDER HUNG; 002 00 052
    WITH ARM AND FIN; THE ARGENT BUBBLES STREAM'D 002 00 109
FINCHES
    FRESH-FIRECOAL CHESTNUT-FALLS; FINCHES' WINGS; 037 00 004
FIND
    THEN FIND IN THE HORIZON-ROUND 015 00 031
    AND FIND THE UNCREATED LIGHT; 022 00 010
    I FIND ANOTHER CHRISTIAN HERE. 025 00 042
    FIND ME A PLACE BY THEE, MOTHER OF MINE. 027 00 006
    OVER AGAIN I FEEL THY FINGER AND FIND THEE. 028 01 008
    ' SOME FIND ME A SWORD; SOME 028 11 001
    AND FAIN WILL FIND AS STERLING ALL AS ALL IS SMART, ...   063 00 007
    EYES IN THEIR DARK CAN DAY OR THIRST CAN FIND 069 00 007
    AND FIND A FLINT, A FANG OF ICE, ...   080 12 004
    BUT NOW ARE FLED, AND HARD TO FIND 081 00 045
    NO FLOWERS TO FIND, NO PLACE TO HALT, ...   081 00 159
    SHALL, WHEN HIS STAR IS ZENITH'D, FIND 083 00 007
    I FIND I AM AS READY WITH MY TEARS 102 01 031
    AND FIND IT WILL NOT THEREFORE BE DESCRIED 102 03 011
    SO TAKES THE SISTER SENSE I CAN FIND NO MARK, ...   113 00 004
    WOULD HE NOT FIND 127 00 018
    YOU LOOK AGAIN AND CANNOT FIND, ...   130 00 019
    AND I SHOULD FIND HIM THERE. 135 00 034
    YOU SPOIL THE PLOT I FIND MY TRUE LOVE BY. 135 00 036
    AND IN THIS DARKSOME WORLD WHAT COMFORT CAN I FIND?   .   .   .   152 02 048
    DOWN THIS DARKSOME WORLD COMFORT WHERE CAN I FIND 152 02 049
    TO THOSE WHO FIND WHAT MUST THOU BE? 167 00 012
    THERE BE THOU THE SWEETNESS MAN WAS MEANT TO FIND.   .   .   .   168 00 020
    THEO. I FIND ANOTHER CHRISTIAN HERE.   .   .   .   .   APPEN A 48
FINDING
    FIVE; THE FINDING AND SAKE 028 22 001
FINDS
    NOT DANGER, ELECTRICAL HORROR; THEN FURTHER IT FINDS   .   .   .   028 27 005
    AND FLOWERS FINDS SOONEST? 042 00 012
    IT IS THE FORGED FEATURE FINDS ME; IT IS THE REHEARSAL   .   .   .   045 00 007
    BOW SWUNG FINDS TONGUE TO FLING OUT BROAD ITS NAME;   .   .   .   057 00 004
    THOUGH AS A BEECHBOLE FIRM, FINDS HIS, AS AT A ROLLCALL, RANK   .   071 00 007
    THERE IS THE SHILLING THAT FINDS ME WILLING 156 00 008
FINE
    OF DEWY GORSE BLURR'D WITH THE GOSSAMER FINE, ...   002 00 040
    TO ITS OWN FINE FUNCTION, WILD AND SELF-INSTRESSED,   .   .   .   047 00 007
    BREATHING BLOOM OF A CHASTITY IN MANSEX FINE. 048 00 016
    LAYING, LIKE AIR'S FINE FLOOD, ...   060 00 051
    THE FINE DELIGHT THAT FATHERS THOUGHT; THE STRONG   .   .   .   076 00 001
    WITH TWICE AS FINE A SENSE TO APPREHEND THEM, ...   102 01 012
    AS THE FINE MORSELS OF A DWINDLING CLOUD 102 01 032
    THEIR HIGHEST SPRAYS WERE DRAWN AS FINE AS LASHES,   .   .   .   107 04 006
    FIRM ACCENTS STRIKE HER FINE AND SCROLLED EAR, ...   136 00 021
    THE MOTION OF THAT MAN'S HEART IS FINE 142 00 006
    AND ARE THEY THUS? THE FINE, THE FINGERING BEAMS 157 00 009
FINEFLOUR
    WHEN THE AIR WAS SWEET-AND-SOUR OF THE FLOWN FINEFLOUR OF   .   .   142 00 004
FINE-DRAWN
    TO QUENCH THE FINE-DRAWN CATARACT; 077 00 090
FINER
    (AND WE, WE SHOULD HAVE LOST IT) FINER, FONDER C 059 06 029
    AND FAINTER, FINER, TRICKLE FAR 077 00 081
FINGER
    OVER AGAIN I FEEL THY FINGER AND FIND THEE. 028 01 008

FINGER   (CONTINUED)
       FINGER OF A TENDER OF, O OF A FEATHERY DELICACY, THE BREAST OF THE   .   028 31 006
       O HIS NIMBLE FINGER, HIS GNARLED GRIP! 041 00 081
FINGERGAPS
       ROUND THE FOUR FINGERGAPS. 060 00 078
FINGERING
       AND ARE THEY THUS? THE FINE, THE FINGERING BEAMS 157 00 009
FINGER-LONG
       HER FINGER-LONG NEW HORNS ARE CAPP'D WITH BLACK! 099 00 007
FINGER-TEASING
       OVER FINGER-TEASING TASK, HIS TWINY BOOTS 159 00 033
FINGERNAIL
       OF A FINGERNAIL HELD TO THE CANDLE, C 137 00 002
FINGERS
       WITH THE DAINTY-DELICATE FRETTED FRINGE OF FINGERS 002 00 064
       OTHERS WITH FINGERS WHITE WOULD COMB AMONG 002 00 112
       BY THAT WINDOW WHAT TASK WHAT FINGERS PLY, ...   046 00 005
       BECAUSE SHE FEARS HER FINGERS WILL BE STUNG. 096 04 002
       RUNS HIS FINGERS THROUGH THE WHEAT, ...   098 01 002
       HER BARRED FINGERS CLASP'D UPON HER EYES, ...   111 00 006
       I SEE HER RIVING FINGERS TEAR 120 00 005
       THE LAST THING MARGARET'S FINGERS SEW 145 00 013
       THE MORE SOME MONSTROUS HAND GROPES WITH CLAMMY FINGERS THERE,   .   152 01 014
FINISH'D
       NO FINISH'D PROOF WAS THIS OF GOTHIC GRACE 001 06 001
       OF FINISH'D DIAPERS, THAT FILLS THE EYE 001 06 006
FIRE
       WITH GARNET WREATHS AND BLOOMS OF ROSY-BUDDED FIRE. 002 00 026
       THRO' CRIMSON-GOLDEN FLOODS PASS SWALLOW'D INTO FIRE.   .   .   .   002 00 083
       AND THE MIDRIFF ASTRAIN WITH LEANING OF, LACED WITH FIRE OF STRESS.   028 02 008
       AND WITH FIRE IN HIM FORGE THY WILL 028 10 002
       WITH BELLED FIRE AND THE MOTH-SOFT MILKY WAY, ...   028 26 006
       NOT A LIGHTNING OF FIRE HARD-HURLED. C 028 34 008
       OUR HEARTS' CHARITY'S HEARTH'S FIRE, C 028 35 008
       BUCKLE! AND THE FIRE THAT BREAKS FROM THEE THEN, A BILLION   .   .   036 00 010
       BRIGHT SUN LANCED FIRE IN THE HEAVENLY BAY! 041 00 022
       NOT MOOD IN HIM NOR MEANING, PROUD FIRE OR SACRED FEAR,   .   .   .   045 00 005
       COME YOU INDOORS, COME HOME! YOUR FADING FIRE 046 00 009
       AS KINGFISHERS CATCH FIRE, DRAGONFLIES DRAW FLAME! 057 00 001
       HIS FIRE, THE SUN WOULD SHAKE, ...   060 00 096
       MY TEMPESTS THERE, MY FIRE AND FEVER FUSSY. 075 00 014
       SWEET FIRE THE SIRE OF MUSE, MY SOUL NEEDS THIS! 076 00 009
       TRESSES DIPP'D IN RAINBOW FIRE, ...   077 00 014
       AND FEEL NO BLAST, -- THE FRETFUL FIRE 080 05 004
       THE VITAL FIRE DOES SUDDENLY RETIRE 080 10 003
       I SAW THE STARS LIKE FLASH OF FIRE. 135 00 008
FIREBALL
       WHERE YONDER CRIMSON FIREBALL SITS 003 00 023
FIRED
       WHO FIRED FRANCE FOR MARY WITHOUT SPOT. 044 00 014
FIREDINT
       MAN, HOW FAST HIS FIREDINT, HIS MARK ON MIND, IS GONE!   .   .   .   072 00 011
FIRE-FOLK
       O LOOK AT ALL THE FIRE-FOLK SITTING IN THE AIR! 032 00 002
FIRM
       THOUGH AS A BEECHBOLE FIRM, FINDS HIS, AS AT A ROLLCALL, RANK   .   071 00 007
       FIRM ACCENTS STRIKE HER FINE AND SCROLLED EAR, ...   136 00 021
FIRMAMENT
       KEEN GLIMPSES OF THE INNER FIRMAMENT! 002 00 012
       UNSWERVING THROUGH THE FIRMAMENT! 077 00 050
FIRST
       A CLOISTER'D CONVENT FIRST, THE PROUDEST HOME 001 01 006
       AND LIFE'S FIRST GERMS FROM DEATH HAD WON, ...   023 00 024
       NOR FIRST FROM HEAVEN (AND FEW KNOW THIS) 028 06 003
       BRIM, IN A FLASH, FULL! -- HITHER THEN, LAST OR FIRST,   .   .   .   028 08 006
       SHE WAS FIRST OF A FIVE AND CAME 028 20 001
       TO MAN'S LAST DUST, DRAIN FAST TOWARDS MAN'S FIRST SLIME.   .   .   035 00 014
       THEIR RANSOM, THEIR RESCUE, AND FIRST, FAST, LAST FRIEND.   .   .   040 00 014
       MEND FIRST AND VITAL CANDLE IN CLOSE HEART'S VAULT! 046 00 010
       HE SWUNG TO HIS FIRST POISED PURPORT OF REPLY. 047 00 004
       CAME, I SAY, THIS DAY TO IT -- TO A FIRST COMMUNION.   .   .   .   048 00 008
       SICKNESS BROKE HIM. IMPATIENT, HE CURSED AT FIRST, BUT MENDED   .   053 00 005
       IN THE FIRST SIGNALS OF THE SEVERAL DROPS 084 00 003
       WHO FIRST KNEW MOONLIGHT BY THE HUNTERS' MOON. 105 00 017
       AND WHERE THE BROW IN FIRST DESCENDING BOW'D 107 01 009
       TO THAT FIRST GOLDEN AGE OF GOSPEL TIMES 136 00 005
       AND WHAT FIRST LIGHTNING C 152 02 031
       ENOUGH! CORRUPTION WAS THE WORLD'S FIRST WOE. 157 00 033
FIRST-FRUITS
       FOR US WAS GATHER'D THE FIRST-FRUITS, ...   006 00 003
FISH
       FISH FEEL THEIR WATERS DRAWING TO 166 00 033
FISHES
       WITH LOATH'D COLD FISHES, FAR FROM MAN -- OR WHAT! --   .   .   .   002 00 124
FIT
       FIT FOR FLOWERS, WATER-PIERCED AND RILLY. 098 15 006
       AND FACES FIT FOR LEISURE GAZE 133 00 013

FIT   (CONTINUED)
    CAPS OCCASION WITH AN INTELLECTUAL FIT. 143 00 002
    THEO. I WANT, I WANT, IF I WERE FIT, ...   APPEN A 39
FITS
    IN FITS OF MUSIC TILL SUNSET 077 00 087
FIVE
    FIVE WAYS THE PRECIOUS BRANCHES TORN; 006 00 014
    FOOD FOR FIVE THOUSAND; ON THE THORNS HE SHED 007 00 012
    HOW MANY LEAVES HAD IT? FIVE THEY WERE THEN, ...   027 00 037
    FIVE LIKE THE SENSES AND MEMBERS OF MEN; 027 00 038
    FIVE IS THEIR NUMBER BY NATURE, BUT NOW 027 00 039
    SHE WAS FIRST OF A FIVE AND CAME 028 20 001
    FIVE! THE FINDING AND SAKE 028 22 001
    FIVE AND TWENTY YEARS HAVE RUN 029 00 005
    A TURN OF SEVEN NOTES OR FIVE, ...   081 00 007
    FIVE NOTES OR SEVEN, LATE AND FEW; 081 00 023
    THE SWEETEST SONNET FIVE OR SIX TIMES READ 117 00 009
FIVE-LIPPED
    ROUGH-ROBIN OR FIVE-LIPPED CAMPION CLEAR 144 00 015
FIVE-LIVED
    AND FIVE-LIVED AND LEAVED FAVOUR AND PRIDE, ...   028 23 006
FIX
    BIDS HIM THIS WAY HIS GAZES FIX. 120 00 015
FIXED
    MY ALL-ACCEPTING FIXED EYE. 130 00 006
FIXEDLY
    WITH HOPE, WITH SHUT EYES, FIXEDLY; 080 14 004
FIX'D
    THE STRETCHING PALACE LAY AS HANDLE FIX'D. 001 04 004
    A FAITHFUL GUARD OF INNER DARKNESS FIX'D -- 001 04 007
    (WHERE THE EYE FIX'D, FLED THE ENCRIMSONING SPOT,   .   .   .   002 00 009
    TO HOLD ME QUITE FIX'D IN THE SELFSAME PLIGHT; 080 13 006
FLAG
    BUT COUNTRY AND FLAG, THE FLAG I AM UNDER -- 156 00 007
    BUT COUNTRY AND FLAG, THE FLAG I AM UNDER -- 156 00 007
FLAGS
    THE SHAPEN FLAGS AND DRILLED HOLES OF SKY, ...   012 02 011
    AND HOSTS CONFRONT WITH FLAGS UNFURLED 023 00 033
    WITH YELLOW FLAGS WILL SUIT HIS BROW, ...   124 00 018
FLAKE
    BY, RAFTS AND RAFTS OF FLAKE LEAVES LIGHT, C 159 00 025
FLAKE-DOVES
    FLAKE-DOVES SENT FLOATING FORTH AT A FARMYARD SCARE! --   .   .   032 00 007
FLAKES
    FAIR BEDS THEY SEEM'D OF WATER-LILY FLAKES 002 00 013
    BUT WHAT A WILD FLUSH ON THE FLAKES OF IT STOOD   .   .   .   027 00 033
    STORM FLAKES WERE SCROLL-LEAVED FLOWERS, C 028 21 008
    FALLING FLAKES, TO THE THRONG THAT CATCHES AND QUAILS   .   .   028 24 006
FLAME
    SUMMER WAS AS FULL OF FLAME; 004 00 025
    TO FLASH FROM THE FLAME TO THE FLAME THEN, C   .   .   .   028 03 008
    TO FLASH FROM THE FLAME TO THE FLAME THEN, C   .   .   .   028 03 008
    THE FLANGE AND THE RAIL; FLAME, ...   028 11 002
    IT WILL FLAME OUT, LIKE SHINING FROM SHOOK FOIL;   .   .   .   031 00 002
    HIS TEAR-TRICKED CHEEKS OF FLAME 054 00 036
    AS KINGFISHERS CATCH FIRE, DRAGONFLIES DRAW FLAME;   .   .   057 00 001
    AND I THAT DIE THESE DEATHS, THAT FEED THIS FLAME,   .   .   075 00 012
    SPUR, LIVE AND LANCING LIKE THE BLOWPIPE FLAME,   .   .   .   076 00 002
    LIKE FLAME THEY GATHER ON OUR CLIFFS AT EVENING,   .   .   .   104 00 007
FLAME-CASED
    PIERCE HER; SHE HANGS UPON THE FLAME-CASED SUN,   .   .   .   103 00 010
FLAME-RASH
    FLAME-RASH RUDRED 138 00 023
FLAME-RINGS
    NOR NIGHT IS BLOWN WITH FLAME-RINGS EVERYWHERE.   .   .   .   099 00 018
FLAMES
    HUNG LIKE A WRECK THAT FLAMES NOT BILLOWS BEAT --   .   .   .   001 03 004
    YOU VIGIL-KEEPERS WITH LOW FLAMES DECREASED, ...   011 00 008
    SKY PEAK'D WITH TINY FLAMES. 098 25 005
FLANDERS
    BUT FROM BEYOND SEAS, ERIN, FRANCE AND FLANDERS, EVERYWHERE,   .   .   152 C 020
FLANGE
    THE FLANGE AND THE RAIL; FLAME, ...   028 11 002
FLANK
    AT CORNERS FLANK THE STRETCHING COMPASS ROUND;   .   .   .   001 01 004
    BREATHED ROUND; THE RACK OF RIBS; THE SCOOPED FLANK; LANK .   .   071 00 002
    WHICH WITH ITS LINED AND CREASED FLANK 092 00 010
FLANKS
    FELLS OR FLANKS OF THE VOEL, A VEIN 028 04 007
    CIRCLED THE SAFE FLANKS OF THE BULKY HILLS. 125 00 010
FLARE
    WIND-BEAT WHITEBEAM! AIRY ABELES SET ON A FLARE!   .   .   .   032 00 006
    THEY PLOUGH OUR VALES; YOU SEE THE UNSTEADY FLARE   .   .   .   104 00 009
FLARES
    FLAKES HIS WET BRILLIANCE IN THE DINTLESS HEAVEN.   .   .   .   098 34 002
FLARING
    FAIRER? THESE ARE THE FLARING SHOWS UNLOVELY 125 00 039

91

FLAR'D
    THE ALTAR-TAPERS FLAR'D IN GUSTS: IN VAIN 001 13 005
FLASH
    THE LANGUENT SMOOTH WITH DIMPLING DROPS, AND FLASH 002 0U 103
    TO FLASH FROM THE FLAME TO THE FLAME THEN, C 028 03 008
    BRIM, IN A FLASH, FULL! -- HITHER THEN, LAST OR FIRST, . . . 028 0B 006
    A RELEASED SHOWER, LET FLASH TO THE SHIRE, C 028 34 008
    IN A FLASH, AT A TRUMPET CRASH, ... 072 0U 021
    I SAW THE STARS LIKE FLASH OF FIRE. 135 0U 008
FLASHED
    HONOUR IS FLASHED OFF EXPLOIT, SO WE SAY: 073 0U 001
    IT STOOPED AND FLASHED AND FELL AND RAN LIKE WATER AWAY. . . 152 02 021
    ROUND AND ROUND THEY CAME AND FLASHED TOWARDS HEAVEN: O THERE, . 152 02 029
FLASHES
    WORLD'S LOVELIEST -- MEN'S SELVES. SELF FLASHES OFF FRAME AND FACE. 062 0U 011
    THIS GARLAND OF THEIR GAMBOL FLASHES IN HIS BREAST 159 0U 019
FLASHING
    FLASHING LIKE FLECKS OF COAL, ... 060 0U 100
FLAT
    INTO THE FLAT BLUE MIST THE SUN 003 0U 031
    WORD WENT SHE SHOULD BE CRUSHED OUT FLAT 145 0U 038
FLATS
    NO RAINS SHALL FRESH THE FLATS OF SEA, ... 114 0U 013
FLATTER
    ILL MEANT, YET TRUE. I BEST SHOULD FLATTER THEN, ... 125 0U 019
FLATTERY
    IS FOND OF FLATTERY, AS ANY SHE, ... 094 0U 015
    WHAT IF I HATED FLATTERY? SAY YOU DO: 125 0U 028
FLATTERY'S
    FLATTERY'S ALL OUT OF PLACE WHERE PRAISE IS TRUE. 125 0U 030
FLAUNT
    TOSSED PILLOWS FLAUNT FORTH, THEN CHEVY ON AN AIR- C . . . 072 0U 001
FLAWED
    AND WORDY WARRANTS ARE FLAWED THROUGH. 025 0U 038
    THEO. AND WORDY WARRANTS ARE FLAWED THROUGH: . . . . APPEN A 44
FLECKS
    FLASHING LIKE FLECKS OF COAL, ... 060 0U 100
FLED
    (WHERE THE EYE FIX'D, FLED THE ENCRIMSONING SPOT, . . . 002 0U 009
    AND FLED WITH A FLING OF THE HEART TO THE HEART OF THE HOST. . 028 03 005
    TO ALIEN EAVES YOU FLED AND WENT, -- 081 0U 005
    BUT NOW ARE FLED, AND HARD TO FIND 081 0U 045
    YOU MAY DEPEND THAT ERE A WEEK WAS FLED, ... 097 0U 005
    PLAYS TO THE BREEZE: WHERE NOW ARE FLED HER FEARS, . . . 099 0U 015
FLEDGED
    FLEDGED THINGS DO RUSTLE NEAR: 160 0U 033
FLEECE
    FOR LETTERING OF THE LAMB'S FLEECE, RUDDYING OF THE ROSE-FLAKE. . 028 22 008
    FLESH AND FLEECE, FUR AND FEATHER, ... 042 0U 017
    IN COOP AND IN COMB THE FLEECE OF HIS FOAM 056 0U 003
    THE FLOWER OF BEAUTY, FLEECE OF BEAUTY, TOO TOO APT TO, AH! TO FLEET, 059 0G 011
    AND SUCKS THE LIGHT AS FULL AS GIDEON'S FLEECE: 103 0U 011
FLEECED
    SKY FLEECED WITH THE MILKY WAY. 098 23 002
    BY HER BLOOM, FAST BY HER FRESH, HER FLEECED BLOOM, . . . 152 02 051
FLEECES
    OR WIND-LONG FLEECES ON THE FLOCK 144 0U 011
FLEECIEST
    THE FLEECIEST, FRAILEST-FLIXED 060 0U 005
FLEES
    ME FRANTIC TO AVOID THEE AND FLEES? C 064 0U 008
FLEET
    ONLY THE BREATHING TEMPLE AND FLEET 041 0U 093
    THE FLOWER OF BEAUTY, FLEECE OF BEAUTY, TOO TOO APT TO, AH! TO FLEET, 059 0G 011
    THE WIND, THAT PASSES BY SO FLEET, ... 098 01 001
    LIKE SHUTTLES FLEET THE CLOUDS, AND AFTER 098 03 001
    WHILE RUSHY RAINS SHALL FALL OR BROOKS SHALL FLEET FROM FOUNTAINS, 152 C 002
    DARK OR DAYLIGHT ON AND ON, HERE HE WILL THEN, HERE HE WILL THE FLEET 159 0U 040
FLEETED
    THAT FLEETED ELSE LIKE DAY-DISSOLVED DREAMS 157 0U 011
FLEET-FEATHER'D
    DIVINITY OF AIR, FLEET-FEATHER'D GALES, ... 160 0U 001
FLEETS
    NEVER FLEETS MORE, FASTENED WITH THE TENDEREST TRUTH . . . 059 0G 012
FLEMING
    UPON THE STUBBORN FLEMING: AND THE ROD 001 05 006
FLESH
    WHILE HIS CRACK'D FLESH LAY HISSING ON THE GRATE: . . . 001 03 002
    OF LEAVES OF GREENEST FLESH. 005 0U 034
    THOU HAST BOUND BONES AND VEINS IN ME, FASTENED ME FLESH, . . 028 01 005
    FLESH FALLS WITHIN SIGHT OF US, WE, THOUGH OUR FLOWER THE SAME, . 028 11 006
    FLESH AND FLEECE, FUR AND FEATHER, ... 042 0U 017
    OF HER FLESH HE TOOK FLESH: 060 0U 055
    OF HER FLESH HE TOOK FLESH: 060 0U 055
    NOT FLESH BUT SPIRIT NOW 060 0U 058
    BONES BUILT IN ME, FLESH FILLED, BLOOD BRIMMED THE CURSE. . . 067 0U 011
    AND FEATURES, IN FLESH, WHAT DEED HE C 071 0U 008

FLESH   (CONTINUED)
    A BEACON, AN ETERNAL BEAM. FLESH FADE, AND MORTAL TRASH •   •   •   • 072 00 019
    AND THOSE STROKES ONCE THAT GASHED FLESH OR GALLED SHIELD •   •   • 073 00 002
    AND SOUL IS SUBTLE AND FLESH WEAK •   •   •   •   •   •   •   • 077 00 037
    DESPATCHES WITH NO FLINCHING. BUT WILL FLESH, O CAN FLESH •   •   • 152 02 045
    DESPATCHES WITH NO FLINCHING. BUT WILL FLESH, O CAN FLESH •   •   • 152 02 045
    FLESH OF THEE, MAIDEN BRIGHT, •   •   •   •   •   •   • APPEN D 08
    TRUE GOD, TRUE MAN, IN FLESH AND BONE: •   •   •   •   • APPEN D 36
FLESHED
    FATAL FOUR DISORDERS, FLESHED THERE, ALL CONTENDED? •   •   • 053 00 004
FLESH-BOUND
    MAN'S SPIRIT WILL BE FLESH-BOUND WHEN FOUND AT BEST, •   •   • 039 00 012
FLESH-BURST
    WILL, MOUTHED TO FLESH-BURST, •   •   •   •   •   •   • 028 08 004
FLESH-FLOWERS
    FROM FLESH-FLOWERS OF THE ROCK: BUT MORE WERE WREATH'D •   • 002 00 063
FLESH-POTS
    COME BY THE FLESH-POTS: YOU SHALL SIT UNSHOD •   •   •   • 005 00 009
FLETCHER
    SYDNEY FLETCHER, BRISTOL-BRED, •   •   •   •   •   •   • 041 00 057
FLEW
    THE BATS' WINGS LISPING AS THEY FLEW •   •   •   •   • 021 00 019
FLICKER
    THEIR CHANGING FEET IN FLICKER ALL THE TIME •   •   •   • 107 01 013
FLICKERING
    FLICKERING WITH SUNNY SPOKES, AND LEFT AND RIGHT •   •   • 002 00 077
    AT LAST THE BIRD IS FOUND A FLICKERING SHAPE AND SLIM. •   • 113 00 009
FLIES
    TO FIELDS WHERE FLIES NO SHARP AND SIDED HAIL •   •   •   • 009 00 003
    AND ITALY FLIES FROM ITALY. •   •   •   •   •   •   •   • 166 00 036
FLIGHT
    TILL, (FEARING RAVAGE WORSE THAN IN HIS FLIGHT, •   •   • 001 14 007
    HE PLAY'D HIS WINGS AS THOUGH FOR FLIGHT: •   •   •   • 087 00 001
    OF THE FLOWN SKYLARK, AND HIS TRAVERSE FLIGHT •   •   •   • 122 00 003
FLIGHTY
    SHE SCHOOLS THE FLIGHTY PUPILS OF HER EYES, •   •   •   • 082 00 001
FLINCHING
    DESPATCHES WITH NO FLINCHING. BUT WILL FLESH, O CAN FLESH •   • 152 02 045
FLING
    AND FLED WITH A FLING OF THE HEART TO THE HEART OF THE HOST. • 028 03 005
    WITH RICHNESS: THE RACING LAMBS TOO HAVE FAIR THEIR FLING. •   • 033 00 008
    BOW SWUNG FINDS TONGUE TO FLING OUT BROAD ITS NAME: •   • 057 00 004
    THEN WOULD I FLING ME UP TO SIP •   •   •   •   •   •   • 077 00 131
    FLING TO THE CONVENT WICKET FAST. •   •   •   •   •   • 081 00 075
FLINGS
    LIGHT AND DARKNESS FROM HIM FLINGS: •   •   •   •   •   • 077 00 068
FLINT
    AND FIND A FLINT, A FANG OF ICE, •   •   •   •   •   • 080 12 004
    AND WITH SHARP FLINT WILL PART MY FEET AND DINT •   •   • 080 13 003
FLINT-FLAKE
    AND THE SEA FLINT-FLAKE, BLACK-BACKED IN THE REGULAR BLOW, •   • 028 13 005
FLINTS
    OF SMALL AND SUGAR FLINTS, I KNEW •   •   •   •   •   • 135 00 027
FLINTY
    PART FOUND NO ROOT UPON THE FLINTY ROAD, -- •   •   •   • 007 00 009
    FLINTY KINDCOLD ELEMENT LET BREAK ACROSS HIS LIMBS •   •   • 159 00 041
FLIRTING
    THE CHESTNUT-FANS ARE LOOSELY FLIRTING, •   •   •   •   • 078 00 005
FLITCHES
    WIRY HEATHPACKS, FLITCHES OF FERN, •   •   •   •   •   • 056 00 011
FLITS
    AND THO' THE SILVER SEED THAT FLITS •   •   •   •   •   • 083 00 011
FLOAT
    STARS FLOAT FROM THE BORDERS OF THE MAIN. •   •   •   • 098 20 001
    I SHOULD BE WRONGING LONGER LEAVING IT TO FLOAT •   •   • 159 00 044
FLOATED
    AND GATHERING, FLOATED WHERE THE GAZE WAS NOT:) •   •   • 002 00 010
FLOATING
    WITH A THIN FLOATING VEIL OF WATER HOAR. •   •   •   • 002 00 004
    FROM CROWN TO TAIL-FIN FLOATING, FRINGED THE SPINE, •   •   • 002 00 041
    OF FILMY GLOBES AND ROSY FLOATING CLOUD: -- •   •   •   • 002 00 097
    THE FLOATING BLOOMS AND WITH TIDE FLOWING QUENCH'D •   •   • 002 00 139
    FLAKE-DOVES SENT FLOATING FORTH AT A FARMYARD SCARE! -- •   • 032 00 007
    SPRINGS IN THE FLOATING AIR AND THE SKIES SWIM, -- •   •   • 113 00 006
FLOATS
    THE BUGLE MOON BY DAYLIGHT FLOATS •   •   •   •   •   • 003 00 015
    CAT. IN FLOATS OF EVENING SKY, -- SO SOON? •   •   •   • APPEN A 22
FLOCK
    THEN, LIKE A FLOCK OF SEA-FOWL MOUNTING HIGHER, •   •   • 002 00 082
    AND THICKEN'D, LIKE THAT DRIFTED BLOOM, THE FLOCK •   •   • 002 00 099
    THE GROSS FLOCK CALL THEM QUAILS. •   •   •   •   •   • 005 00 016
    A SHELTER FOR THIS FLOCK? •   •   •   •   •   •   •   • 005 00 022
    WHAT WOULD BEFAL THE GODLESS FLOCK •   •   •   •   •   • 092 00 007
    A DROP OF SHADE ROLLS OVER FIELD AND FLOCK: •   •   •   • 098 03 002
    YET THERE CAME ONE WHO SENT HIS FLOCK BEFORE HIM, •   •   • 107 01 007
    OR WIND-LONG FLEECES ON THE FLOCK •   •   •   •   •   • 144 00 011
FLOCKBELLS
    AND FLOCKBELLS OFF THE AERIAL •   •   •   •   •   •   • 041 00 007

93

FLOCKS
```
RURAL RURAL KEEPING -- FOLK, FLOCKS, AND FLOWERS.  .   .   .   .   .   . 044 00 008
NOW HER ALL IN TWO FLOCKS, TWO FOLDS C  .   .   .   .   .   .   . 061 00 012
WE WILL CHARGE OUR FLOCKS THAT THEY NOT FEED.  .   .   .   .   .   . 098 15 002
HE RISES FROM THE FLOCKS OF VILLAGES  .   .   .   .   .   . 100 00 005
AND BLUER GREY THE FLOCKS OF TREES LOOK IN THE PLAIN.  .   .   .   . 105 00 008
```
FLOOD
```
THOUGH FELT BEFORE, THOUGH IN HIGH FLOOD YET --  .   .   .   .   . 028 07 007
FANG, OR FLOOD ' GOES DEATH ON DRUM,  .   .   .   .   .   . 028 11 003
WITH THE BURL OF THE FOUNTAINS OF AIR, BUCK AND THE FLOOD OF THE WAVE? 028 16 008
WITH A FLOOD OR A FALL, LOW LULL-OFF OR ALL ROAR,  .   .   .   .   . 035 00 003
LAYING, LIKE AIR'S FINE FLOOD,  .   .   .   .   .   .   . 060 00 051
AND SAW THE MEN BEFORE THE FLOOD  .   .   .   .   .   .   . 093 A 002
```
FLOODS
```
THRO' CRIMSON-GOLDEN FLOODS PASS SWALLOW'D INTO FIRE.  .   .   . 002 00 083
AS ERST UPON CHAOTIC FLOODS  .   .   .   .   .   .   . 023 00 021
AND I COME LADEN FROM SUCH FLOODS  .   .   .   .   .   . 098 19 005
```
FLOODTIDE
```
IF FLOODTIDE TEEMING THRILLS HER FULL,  .   .   .   .   .   . 030 00 022
```
FLOOR
```
THAT LICK THE SHELLY LEAVES WHICH FLOOR THE COPSE,  .   .   . 084 00 004
```
FLOOR'D
```
GREAT BUTTER-BURR LEAVES FLOOR'D THE SLOPE CORPSE GROUND  .   .   . 107 04 009
```
FLORIS
```
MY SIGNALLING TEARS MIGHT RING UP FLORIS! NOW  .   .   .   .   . 102 01 007
SLEEP FLORIS WHILE I ROB YOU, TIGHTEN, O SLEEP,  .   .   .   . 102 01 017
THIS FLOWER, THIS FLORIS, THIS DEAR MAJESTY,  .   .   .   .   . 102 01 036
WORSE THAN WHEN FLORIS FOUND ME IN THE GARDEN  .   .   .   . 102 01 040
AH FLORIS, FLORIS, LET ME SPEAK THIS LITTLE  .   .   .   .   . 102 01 050
AH FLORIS, FLORIS, LET ME SPEAK THIS LITTLE  .   .   .   .   . 102 01 050
THOUGH ILL-CONTENTED, PRECIOUS PRECIOUS FLORIS,  .   .   .   . 102 01 053
FLORIS! SHE WILL NOT HIT THY SUM OF WORTH,  .   .   .   .   . 102 01 058
FLORIS, THOU LATE-FOUND ALL-HEAL!  .   .   .   .   .   . 102 01 060
```
FLOW
```
LET IT FLOW FOR HEAVENLY MIRTH!  .   .   .   .   .   .   . 024 00 010
THROUGH HER AND FROM HER FLOW  .   .   .   .   .   .   . 060 00 032
ALL DAY LONG I LIKE FOUNTAIN FLOW  .   .   .   .   .   . 155 00 002
```
FLOWER
```
CHANG'D TO A FLOWER! AND THERE, WITH PLACID EYE  .   .   .   . 001 11 008
FRUIT NOR FLOWER NOR DOROTHY.  .   .   .   .   .   .   . 025 00 024
FLESH FALLS WITHIN SIGHT OF US, WE, THOUGH OUR FLOWER THE SAME, 028 11 006
HER FLOWER, HER PIECE OF BEING, DOOMED DRAGON FOOD,  .   .   . 050 00 004
THE FLOWER OF BEAUTY, FLEECE OF BEAUTY, TOO TOO APT TO, AH! TO FLEET, 059 0G 011
AND THE FLOWER STRIPS,  .   .   .   .   .   .   .   . 098 14 002
THIS FLOWER, THIS FLORIS, THIS DEAR MAJESTY,  .   .   .   .   . 102 01 036
THE TEMPER'D SOIL WHERE ONLY HER FLOWER IS FOUND.  .   .   .   . 102 03 004
IF IT WERE A FLOWER OF PARADISE,  .   .   .   .   .   . 109 34 003
```
FLOWERETS
```
CIRCLET OF ASTRAL FLOWERETS -- DIADEM'D  .   .   .   .   .   . 002 00 061
```
FLOWERS
```
AND HELD A CROSS OF FLOWERS, IN PURPLE BLOOM!  .   .   .   . 001 1U 006
ON THE FLOWERS THAT WERE SEEN  .   .   .   .   .   .   . 004 0U 009
' I MARK THE FLOWERS ERE THE PRIME  .   .   .   .   .   . 004 00 014
MANY TREES AND FLOWERS ROUND  .   .   .   .   .   .   . 004 0U 019
AND THE FLOWERS THAT HE HAD TIED,  .   .   .   .   .   . 004 0U 027
SWEET FLOWERS I CARRY, -- SWEETS FOR BITTER.  .   .   .   . 010 0U 006
NOR FRUIT, NOR FLOWERS, NOR DOROTHY.  .   .   .   .   .   . 010 00 024
FLOWERS DO OPE THEIR HEAVENWARD EYES  .   .   .   .   .   . 024 0U 015
AND MAY HAS COME, HAIR-BOUND IN FLOWERS,  .   .   .   . 026 00 013
STORM FLAKES WERE SCROLL-LEAVED FLOWERS, C  .   .   .   . 028 21 008
AND FLOWERS FINDS SOONEST?  .   .   .   .   .   .   . 042 00 012
RURAL RURAL KEEPING -- FOLK, FLOCKS, AND FLOWERS.  .   .   . 044 0U 008
NO FLOWERS TO FIND, NO PLACE TO HALT,  .   .   .   .   . 081 0U 159
NEXT TO MEADOWS ABUNDANT, PIERCED WITH FLOWERS,  .   .   . 098 12 002
FIT FOR FLOWERS, WATER-PIERCED AND RILLY.  .   .   .   . 098 15 006
GOLD GALLANT, FLOWERS MUCH LOOKED AT IN APRIL-WEATHER  .   . 098 16 002
OF FLOWERS THAT COUNTING CLOSES,  .   .   .   .   .   . 098 19 006
LIKE SCALDED BANKS TOPP'D ONCE WITH PRINCIPAL FLOWERS;  .   . 102 02 012
CAT.  NOR FRUIT NOR FLOWERS NOR DOROTHY.  .   .   .   . APPEN A 24
```
FLOWING
```
WITH FLOWING TRACERY ENGEMMING RAYS  .   .   .   .   .   . 001 06 002
THE FLOATING BLOOMS AND WITH TIDE FLOWING QUENCH'D  .   .   . 002 00 139
```
FLOWN
```
OF THE FLOWN SKYLARK, AND HIS TRAVERSE FLIGHT  .   .   .   . 122 00 003
WHEN THE AIR WAS SWEET-AND-SOUR OF THE FLOWN FINEFLOUR OF  .   . 142 0U 004
```
FLUE
```
HARD AS HURDLE ARMS, WITH A BROTH OF GOLDISH FLUE  .   .   . 071 00 001
```
FLUKE
```
A FLUKE YET FANGED HIM, ENTANGLED HIM, NOT QUIT UTTERLY. C  .   . 137 00 005
```
FLUNG
```
BUT HARRY -- IN HIS HANDS HE HAS FLUNG  .   .   .   .   . 054 00 035
ING BLOOD -- THE O-SEAL-THAT-SO FEATURE, FLUNG PROUDER FORM  . 062 00 002
CHEER WHOM THOUGH? THE HERO WHOSE HEAVEN-HANDLING FLUNG ME, FOOT TROD 064 00 012
FLUNG RIDER AND WINGS AWAY! THOUGH THESE WERE NONE,  .   .   . 136 00 009
BE AT EVERY ASSAULT FRESH FOILED, WORSE FLUNG, DEEPER DISAPPOINTED, 152 02 056
```
FLUSH
```
BUT WHAT A WILD FLUSH ON THE FLAKES OF IT STOOD  .   .   .   . 027 0U 033
```

FLUSH   (CONTINUED)
    GUSH! -- FLUSH THE MAN, THE BEING WITH IT, SOUR OR SWEET,   .   .   .   028 08 005
    FLUSH THRO' THEIR HEAVING COLUMNS! WHEN THEY HALT 104 00 010
FLUSHED
    AND ZEAL IS FLUSHED AND PITY BLEEDS 023 00 034
    THAT GUILT IS HUSHED BY, HEARTS ARE FLUSHED BY AND MELT --   .   .   .   028 06 006
FLUSHES
    THE WHOLE LANDSCAPE FLUSHES ON A SUDDEN AT A SOUND. 146 00 005
FLUTES
    FLUTES AND LOW TO THE LAKE FALLS HOME. 056 00 004
FLY
    WHAT THE HEART IS! WHICH, LIKE CARRIERS LET FLY -- 047 00 005
    WHY? THAT MY CHAFF MIGHT FLY! MY GRAIN LIE, SHEER AND CLEAR.   .   .   064 00 009
    WHITE-FACED, AS ONE IN SAD ASSAY TO FLY 079 00 008
    BRIGHT HUES LONG LOOK'D AT THIN, DISSOLVE AND FLY; 117 00 002
    ALL ELSE MAY WHIRL OR DIVE OR FLY. 130 00 008
FLYING
    EVERYTHING THAT'S FRESH AND FAST FLYING OF US, C 059 06 008
    FLYING A BOW. 098 06 003
FOAM
    THE SATIN-PURFLED SMOOTH TO FOAM, AND SPREAD 002 00 079
    WITH ROSY FOAM AND PELTING BLOSSOM AND MISTS 002 00 090
    NOT HONOUR IT?) ALE LIKE GOLDY FOAM 030 00 035
    IN COOP AND IN COMB THE FLEECE OF HIS FOAM 056 00 003
FOAMFALLING
    FOAMFALLING IS NOT FRESH TO IT, RAINBOW BY IT NOT BEAMING,   .   .   152 02 024
FOAM-FALLOW
    FALLOW, FOAM-FALLOW, HANKS -- FALL'N OFF THEIR RANKS,   .   .   .   144 00 007
FOAM-FLEECE
    THROUGH THE COBBLED FOAM-FLEECE. WHAT COULD HE DO 028 16 007
FOAM-TUFT
    FOAM-TUFT FUMITORY. 138 00 030
FOE
    FOE OF ZEUS AND HATE OF ALL 160 00 028
FOIL
    IT WILL FLAME OUT, LIKE SHINING FROM SHOOK FOIL! 031 00 002
FOILED
    BE AT EVERY ASSAULT FRESH FOILED, WORSE FLUNG, DEEPER DISAPPOINTED,   .   152 02 056
FOILING
    HER SHOWY LEAVES WITH GENTLE WATCHET FOILING V 108 00 006
FOLD
    LANDSCAPE PLOTTED AND PIECED -- FOLD, FALLOW, AND PLOUGH! .   .   .   037 00 005
    FOLD HOME, FAST FOLD THY CHILD. 060 00 126
    FOLD HOME, FAST FOLD THY CHILD. 060 00 126
    THE ESSENCE NE'ER FORGOT THE FOLD! 081 00 082
    PLY FOLD ON FOLD ACROSS HIS DANGEROUS EYES, ...   102 01 019
    PLY FOLD ON FOLD ACROSS HIS DANGEROUS EYES, ...   102 01 019
    THEY SEEM TO FOLD THE HILLS WITH GOLDEN CAPES! 104 00 011
FOLDED
    AND FRIGHTFUL A NIGHTFALL FOLDED RUEFUL A DAY 028 15 005
    OF A FRESH AND FOLLOWING FOLDED RANK 043 00 004
    YOU FOLDED (DID YOU NOT?) YOUR DRESS. 081 00 081
    HER MILK-WHITE THROAT AND FOLDED DEW-LAP SLACK 099 00 009
    HER HOMES AND FIELDS THAT FOLDED AND FED ME? 156 00 002
FOLDS
    GIVE MYRRHY-THREADED GOLDEN FOLDS OF EASE. 011 00 012
    NOW HER ALL IN TWO FLOCKS, TWO FOLDS C 061 00 012
    FOLDS OFF ALOOF, THAT SIGNAL IS AND PROOF 080 06 003
    -- THE SHALLOW FOLDS OF THE WOOD 098 09 001
    AND PRESSED VIOLETS IN THE FOLDS APPEAR. 119 00 004
FOLIAGE
    OF FOLIAGE FALLEN IN THE COPSE. 003 00 012
FOLIAG'D
    AND FOLIAG'D CROWNALS (POINTING HOW THE WAYS 001 06 004
    AND DAMASQU'D ARMS AND FOLIAG'D CARVING PILED. -- 001 10 002
FOLK
    RURAL RURAL KEEPING -- FOLK, FLOCKS, AND FLOWERS. 044 00 008
FOLLOW
    OF ART BEST FOLLOW NATURE) IN A MAZE 001 06 005
    CHEER'S DEATH, WOULD FOLLOW 041 00 047
    HER FEASTS FOLLOW REASON, ...   042 00 003
    NOW WE FOLLOW. -- .YONDER, YES YONDER, YONDER, C 059 06 031
    YONDER. -- WHAT HIGH AS THAT! WE FOLLOW, C 059 06 031
    AND FAIN WOULD FOLLOW I WHO LED. 081 00 172
    AND STRAIGHT SHOWERS PARALLEL SHOULD FOLLOW FAST;   .   .   .   090 00 004
    LEAD SHEPHERD, NOW WE FOLLOW, SHEPHERD LEAD. 098 15 007
    ' WILT THOU FOLLOW ME, MY TRUE LOVE, ...   109 37 001
    WILT THOU FOLLOW ME, MY TRUE LOVE? 109 37 003
    ' O I WILL FOLLOW THEE, MY TRUE LOVE. 109 38 001
    THINK YOU WANT DAFFODILS AND FOLLOW AS FAR 135 00 030
    TO FOLLOW A BANNER AND FIGHT FOR HONOUR. 156 00 009
    WE FOLLOW HER BANNER, WE FIGHT FOR HER HONOUR. 156 00 010
FOLLOWED
    WHAT WAS THE FEAST FOLLOWED THE NIGHT 028 30 003
FOLLOWING
    OF A FRESH AND FOLLOWING FOLDED RANK 043 00 004
    RAN THROUGH IT, FOLLOWING WHICH WE SHOULD HAVE SIGHT   .   .   .   125 00 006

FOLLOWING   (CONTINUED)
    FOLLOWING FALLS AND FALLS OF RAIN, ...   142 00 003
FOLLOWS
    THERE, EYES THEM, HEART WANTS, CARE HAUNTS, FOOT FOLLOWS KIND,   . .   040 00 013
FOND
    BEING MIGHTY A MASTER, BEING A FATHER AND FOND. 034 00 014
    FOR FOND LOVE AND FOR SHAME. 054 00 037
    HER FOND YELLOW HORNLIGHT WOUND TO THE WEST, C 061 00 003
    IS FOND OF FLATTERY, AS ANY SHE, ...   094 00 015
    ' WHAT, TERYTH! WHAT, THOU POOR FOND FATHER! C 152 01 016
    CALL ME ENGLAND'S FAME'S FOND LOVER, ...   156 00 011
    SHE LEANS ON HIM WITH SUCH CONTENTMENT FOND 157 00 013
FONDER
    WHEN THE THING WE FREELY FORFEIT IS KEPT WITH FONDER A CARE,   . .   059 06 027
    FONDER A CARE KEPT THAN WE COULD HAVE KEPT IT, KEPT 059 06 028
    FAR WITH FONDER A CARE C 059 06 029
    (AND WE, WE SHOULD HAVE LOST IT) FINER, FONDER C 059 06 029
FONDLER
    FATHER AND FONDLER OF HEART THOU HAST WRUNG: 028 09 007
FONT
    THE WROUGHT RIM OF HEAVEN'S FONT, -- 077 00 112
FOOD
    WE SCARCELY CALL THAT BANQUET FOOD, ...   006 00 031
    FOOD FOR FIVE THOUSAND: ON THE THORNS HE SHED 007 00 012
    OR ONCE OR NEVER TOOK LOVE'S PROPER FOOD: 020 00 010
    PEACE AND FOOD CHEERED ME WHERE FOUR ROUGH WAYS MEET,   . . .   020 00 012
    HER FLOWER, HER PIECE OF BEING, DOOMED DRAGON FOOD. 050 00 004
FOODS
    ARE WASTE, AND HAD NO WHOLESOME FOODS, ...   081 00 166
FOOL
    BLINDNESS! A LEARNED FOOL AND WELL-BRED CHURL 102 03 032
    A LEARNED FOOL INDEED AND WELL-BRED CHURL V 102 03 038
    I HERE FORBID MY THOUGHTS TO FOOL THEMSELVES WITH FEARS.   . . .   152 01 024
FOOLISH
    MY PASSION LIKE A FOOLISH WIND 081 00 037
    WHY SHOULD THEIR FOOLISH BANDS, THEIR HOPELESS HEARSES   . . .   089 00 001
FOOT
    I WATER WITH MY FOOT. 005 00 040
    IS BARE NOW, NOR CAN FOOT FEEL, BEING SHOD, ...   031 00 008
    THERE, EYES THEM, HEART WANTS, CARE HAUNTS, FOOT FOLLOWS KIND,   . .   040 00 013
    LOOK, FOOT TO FORELOCK, HOW ALL THINGS SUIT! HE 041 00 077
    THY WRING-WORLD RIGHT FOOT ROCK? LAY A LIONLIMB AGAINST ME? SCAN   .   064 00 006
    CHEER WHOM THOUGH? THE HERO WHOSE HEAVEN-HANDLING FLUNG ME, FOOT TROD   064 00 012
    THAT MAMMOCKS, MIGHTY FOOT. BUT NO WAY SPED, ...   070 00 012
    HEAD AND FOOT, SHOULDER AND SHANK -- C 071 00 003
    BUT WITH HIS OTHER FOOT THREE MILES BEYOND 100 00 004
    OR EVER HE SET HIS FOOT TO THE LAND 109 07 001
    SOME PAGEANT WHICH TAKES TEARS AND I MUST FOOT WITH FEELING THAT   .   152 01 020
FOOTFRETTED
    FOOTFRETTED IN IT. MILLION-FUELED, NATURE'S BONFIRE BURNS ON.   . .   072 00 009
FOOTING
    FOR A RAINBOW FOOTING IT NOR HE FOR HIS BONES RISEN.   . . .   039 00 014
    YOUR FOOTING NOW TO THE MUCH-DREADED DUST, ...   107 03 002
FOOTREST
    WILL ADD A FOOTREST THERE TO STAND, ...   080 13 002
FOOTSTEPS
    DANCES FOR SAD FOOTSTEPS SLOW: 024 00 022
FOOTWAY
    THE FOOTWAY, STEPHEN SAID, ...   135 00 028
FORBID
    I HERE FORBID MY THOUGHTS TO FOOL THEMSELVES WITH FEARS.   . . .   152 01 024
    BOUND ON WHAT THOU HADST FORBID: 155 00 010
FORCE
    ERING! LET ME BE FELL: FORCE I MUST BE BRIEF ' 065 00 008
    SO LATE THERE IS NO FORCE IN SAP OR BLOOD: 105 00 011
    EARLIER OR YOU FAIL AT OUR FORCE, AND LIE 153 00 003
    IN THE FULLNESS OF THY FORCE AND STRESS, ...   169 00 004
FORCED
    THEY ROSE AT LAST AND FORCED HER FROM THE SPOT. 136 00 034
FORCIBLE
    DOUBLE AS SHARP, MEANING AND FORCIBLE, ...   102 01 011
FORCIBLY
    SO FORCIBLY HE SUNG, ...   021 00 032
FORC'D
    OF FORC'D PERSUASION ISSUE O'ER THE FREE. -- 001 05 007
FORECAST
    NOT KIND! TO FREEZE ME WITH FORECAST, ...   134 00 001
    NO WISDOM CAN FORECAST BY GAUGE OR GUESS, ...   157 00 026
FOREDRAWN
    FAST FURLED AND ALL FOREDRAWN TO NO OR YES. 157 00 028
FOREFALLS
    DOWNS' FOREFALLS BEAT TO THE BURIAL. 041 00 008
FOREFENDING
    FROWNING AND FOREFENDING ANGEL-WARDER 048 00 017
FOREGONE
    THEY STAND, THEY SHINE IN THE SUN: FAME HAS FOREGONE   . . .   104 00 002
FOREHEAD
    ON A PASTORAL FOREHEAD OF WALES, ...   028 24 002

96

FORTH   (CONTINUED)
      WENT FORTH TO COMPASS MYSTERIES: 077 00 052
      WHILE THE SUN STREAMS FORTH AMAIN 077 00 103
      FOR HE WHOM I SEND FORTH TO CRUCIFY, ...   080 11 003
      TO NOT UNGENTLE DEATH NOW FORTH I RUN. 103 00 019
      WHEN YOU CAME FORTH FOR ME? ' 109 33 004
      WHEN I CAME FORTH FOR THEE. 109 34 002
      GAZE ON, AND FALL DIRECTLY FORTH ON LIFE. 157 00 016
FORTH-AND-FLAUNT
      HIS CHEEKS THE FORTH-AND-FLAUNTING SUN 144 00 002
FORTH-DRIVEN
      (BECAUSE THE MUSIC FROM HIS BILL FORTH-DRIVEN 113 00 003
FORTRESS
      A FORTRESS OF TRUE FAITH, AND CENTRAL STAND 001 05 003
FORTUNE
      WITNESSED: SO FORTUNE FELL. 054 00 004
FORTY
      IN FORTY DAYS REACH'D HEAVEN FROM EARTH: 006 00 024
FORWARD
      THEN A LURCH FORWARD, FRIGATE AND MEN: 041 00 041
      FORWARD SHE LEANS, WITH HOLLOWING BACK, STOCK-STILL, ...   099 00 001
      FORWARD FALLING, FOREHEAD FROWNING, LIPS CRISP 159 00 032
FORWARD-LIKE
      FORWARD-LIKE, BUT HOWEVER, AND LIKE FAVOURABLE HEAVEN HEARD THESE.   .   048 00 048
FOUGHT
      THEY FOUGHT WITH GOD'S COLD -- 028 17 001
      ME? OR ME THAT FOUGHT HIM? O WHICH ONE? C 064 00 013
FOUL
      BUT FRAIL CLAY, NAY BUT FOUL CLAY. HERE IT IS: THE HEART, ...   063 00 003
      BUT FOUL AND CUMBER NOT 077 00 009
FOULED
      GROSS MIND DISCHARGING FOULED LAUGHTER: 077 00 058
FOUND
      AT MORN WE FOUND THE HEAVENLY BREAD, ...   006 00 008
      PART FOUND NO ROOT UPON THE FLINTY ROAD, -- 007 00 009
      BUT THESE WERE FOUND IN THE EAST AND SOUTH 010 00 013
      AND FOR THOSE VIRTUES I IN THEE HAVE FOUND, ...   013 00 011
      THIS FAULT IN ONE I FOUND, THAT IN ANOTHER: 016 00 011
      I HAVE FOUND MY MUSIC IN A COMMON WORD, ...   019 00 005
      I HAVE FOUND THE DOMINANT OF MY RANGE AND STATE -- 019 00 013
      ' I DID NOT MEAN TO SLEEP, BUT FOUND 021 00 015
      AND A SPRING-TIME JOY HAVE FOUND: 024 00 016
      THE ROSE IN A MYSTERY -- WHERE IS IT FOUND? 027 00 001
      THOU ART LIGHTNING AND LOVE, I FOUND IT, A WINTER AND WARM: .   .   028 09 004
      MAN'S SPIRIT WILL BE FLESH-BOUND WHEN FOUND AT BEST, ...   039 00 012
      YET FOUND UNSTINTED PLACE FOR MIRTH: 077 00 056
      I FOUND THE WAYS WERE SOWN WITH SALT 081 00 155
      WE FOUND WERE DABBLED WITH A COLOURING GROWTH, ...   098 09 002
      WORSE THAN WHEN FLORIS FOUND ME IN THE GARDEN 102 01 040
      THE TEMPER'D SOIL WHERE ONLY HER FLOWER IS FOUND. 102 03 004
      THAT MANY CENTRES FOUND IN MANY HEARTS? 107 02 005
      AT LAST THE BIRD IS FOUND A FLICKERING SHAPE AND SLIM. 113 00 009
      AND ALL ROUND NOT TO BE FOUND 138 00 005
      ONE ONCE THAT WAS FOUND WANTING WHEN GOOD WEIGHED. 157 00 024
FOUNDERED
      WHERE SHE FOUNDERED! ONE STROKE 041 00 005
FOUNDERING
      FAST FOUNDERING OWN GENERATION. 041 00 088
      ACROSS MY FOUNDERING DECK SHONE 072 00 018
FOUNTAIN
      ALL DAY LONG I LIKE FOUNTAIN FLOW 155 00 002
FOUNTAINS
      WITH THE BURL OF THE FOUNTAINS OF AIR, BUCK AND THE FLOOD OF THE WAVE?   028 16 008
      SINCE SACRED FOUNTAINS TO THE SUN 029 00 006
      WHILE RUSHY RAINS SHALL FALL OR BROOKS SHALL FLEET FROM FOUNTAINS,   .   152 C 002
FOUNTS
      THEN LAVER'D FOUNTS AND POSTUR'D STONE HE MIX'D. 001 04 005
FOUR
      A SOMBRE LENGTH OF GREY: FOUR TOWERS PLACED 001 01 003
      PEACE AND FOOD CHEERED ME WHERE FOUR ROUGH WAYS MEET, ...   020 00 012
      FATAL FOUR DISORDERS, FLESHED THERE, ALL CONTENDED? 053 00 004
      ROUND THE FOUR FINGERGAPS. 060 00 008
      AND THRICE AND FOUR TIMES AND AGAIN. 098 37 002
      WE HAVE COME FOUR, DO YOU THINK? 125 00 013
      SEVERAL TIMES I SAW THEM, THRICE OR FOUR TIMES TURNING: .   .   .   152 02 028
FOURTH
      THE GOAL WAS A SHOAL, OF A FOURTH THE DOOM TO BE DROWNED: .   .   .   028 12 006
FOWLS
      THE WINGED FOWLS TOOK PART, PART FELL IN THORN 007 00 007
FOXGLOVES
      ONLY THE BELLED FOXGLOVES LISP'D TOGETHER. 107 01 006
FRAGRANCE
      FROM TOO MUCH FRAGRANCE EVERYWHERE: -- 004 00 004
      IN THE QUICK FRAGRANCE OF TALL ROLLING PINES, ...   084 00 005
FRAIL
      HOW THESE TWO SHAME THIS SHALLOW AND FRAIL TOWN! 035 00 009
      BUT FRAIL CLAY, NAY BUT FOUL CLAY. HERE IT IS: THE HEART,   .   .   .   063 00 003

FRAIL   (CONTINUED)
    FROM ONE FRAIL HORN THAT CRUMBLED TO THE PLAIN   •   •   •   •   •   •   107 03 011
    BUT IN PALE WATER, FRAIL WATER, WILD RASH AND REELING WATER,   •   •   152 C 015
FRAILEST-FLIXED
    THE FLEECIEST, FRAILEST-FLIXED   •   •   •   •   •   •   •   •   •   060 00 005
FRAILTY
    NOT THAT, BUT THUS FAR, ALL WITH FRAILTY, BLEST   •   •   •   •   •   157 00 006
FRAME
    THEN FAIL'D THE TONGUE: THE POOR COLLAPSING FRAME,   •   •   •   •   001 03 003
    WORLD'S LOVELIEST -- MEN'S SELVES. SELF FLASHES OFF FRAME AND FACE.   •   062 00 011
FRAMED
    AH NATURE, FRAMED IN FAULT,   •   •   •   •   •   •   •   •   •   054 00 038
    SHE'S FRAMED TO TRIUMPH IN ADVERSITY: •   •   •   •   •   •   094 00 023
    NOT ALL, BUT WE WERE FRAMED TO FAIL AND DIE --   •   •   •   •   •   153 00 006
FRANCE
    WHO FIRED FRANCE FOR MARY WITHOUT SPOT.   •   •   •   •   •   •   044 00 014
    AND TANGLES ON A DOWN OF FRANCE,   •   •   •   •   •   •   •   •   083 00 014
    BUT FROM BEYOND SEAS, ERIN, FRANCE AND FLANDERS, EVERYWHERE,   •   •   152 C 020
FRANCES
    THUS FRANCES SIGHED AT HOME, WHILE LUKE   •   •   •   •   •   •   021 00 050
FRANCIS
    JOY FALL TO THEE, FATHER FRANCIS,   •   •   •   •   •   •   •   •   028 23 001
FRANK
    WHAT TIME THE BAFFLED FRANK SWEPT BACK PURSU'D   •   •   •   •   •   001 14 008
    IN FRANK, IN FAIRY PENMAEN POOL.   •   •   •   •   •   •   •   •   030 00 016
FRANTIC
    ME FRANTIC TO AVOID THEE AND FLEES? C   •   •   •   •   •   •   064 00 008
FRAUGHT
    AND ALL THAT COMES IS FRAUGHT TO ME WITH FEAR.   •   •   •   •   •   160 00 036
FRAY
    EARTH HEARS NO HURTLE THEN FROM FIERCEST FRAY.   •   •   •   •   •   073 00 008
    OR FRAY A GRANITE FROM THE PRECIPICE: •   •   •   •   •   •   080 12 005
    AND THE POOR CORSE IMPALE WITH IT AND FRAY   •   •   •   •   •   •   089 00 007
    MELLS BLUE AND SNOWWHITE THROUGH THEM, A FRINGE AND FRAY   •   •   149 A 009
    MELLS BLUE WITH SNOWWHITE THROUGH THEIR FRINGE AND FRAY V   •   •   149 B 011
FRECKLED
    WHATEVER IS FICKLE, FRECKLED (WHO KNOWS HOW?)   •   •   •   •   037 00 008
FREE
    OF FORC'D PERSUASION ISSUE O'ER THE FREE. --   •   •   •   •   •   001 05 007
    THEN FREE AND KIND THE WILDERNESS.   •   •   •   •   •   •   •   015 00 036
    WITH FREE LONG LOOKING, ERE I DIE.   •   •   •   •   •   •   •   015 00 044
    THAT BIRD BEYOND THE REMEMBERING HIS FREE FELLS: •   •   •   •   039 00 003
    AND DOWN THE WELKIN, GUSHING FREE,   •   •   •   •   •   •   •   077 00 085
    SWEETLY THEN AND OF FREE ACT   •   •   •   •   •   •   •   •   •   077 00 089
    I WILL BREAK FREE FROM THE JEWS' COMPANY,   •   •   •   •   •   080 12 003
    NEW LOVE IS FREE LOVE, OR TRUE LOVE 'TIS NOT.   •   •   •   •   102 03 020
    NEW LOVE IS FREE LOVE, OR TRUE LOVE 'TIS NOT. V   •   •   •   102 03 027
    AND RISEN SONS: YET ARE THE CHILDLESS FREE   •   •   •   •   •   123 00 002
    NEAR BY IS PAUL'S FREE TARSUS, FABLED WHERE   •   •   •   •   •   136 00 007
    NOT FREE IN THIS BECAUSE   •   •   •   •   •   •   •   •   •   148 00 013
    HIS POWERS SEEMED FREE TO PLAY: •   •   •   •   •   •   •   •   148 00 014
    MANKIND FREE FOR TO MAKE   •   •   •   •   •   •   •   •   •   APPEN D 09
FREED
    TO THE SIGHT OF HIM WHO FREED ME   •   •   •   •   •   •   •   129 00 004
    REPENT HE SINNED AND ALL HIS SINS BE FREED.   •   •   •   •   •   140 00 006
FREELY
    WHEN THE THING WE FREELY FORFEIT IS KEPT WITH FONDER A CARE,   •   •   059 0G 027
    FREELY FORGIVES THE MONSTROUS DEBT!   •   •   •   •   •   •   •   081 00 151
FREEZE
    NOT KIND! TO FREEZE ME WITH FORECAST,   •   •   •   •   •   •   134 00 001
FREEZING
    A FREEZING RUNNEL SOBS AND DWARFS.   •   •   •   •   •   •   •   080 03 007
FREIGHTED
    FOR DID SHE PRIDE HER, FREIGHTED FULLY, ON   •   •   •   •   •   041 00 009
FRENZIED
    MY FRENZIED WORKING IS NOT UNDERSTOOD.   •   •   •   •   •   •   080 10 005
FREQUENTING
    FREQUENTING THERE WHILE MOON SHALL WEAR AND WEND.   •   •   •   035 00 004
FRESH
    UNBAKES MY PORES, AND STREAMS, AND MAKES ALL FRESH.   •   •   •   005 00 032
    AND STILL THOU BIND'ST ME TO FRESH FEALTY   •   •   •   •   •   012 01 003
    FRESH BROOKS TO SALT SAND-TEASING WATERS SHOALY: --   •   •   •   016 00 004
    SO FRESH THAT COME IN FASTS DIVINE!   •   •   •   •   •   •   •   022 00 016
    FETCHED FRESH, AS I SUPPOSE, OFF SOME SWEET WOOD.   •   •   •   034 00 004
    FRESH, TILL DOOMFIRE BURN ALL,   •   •   •   •   •   •   •   •   041 00 119
    OF A FRESH AND FOLLOWING FOLDED RANK   •   •   •   •   •   •   043 00 004
    OFF HIM, BUT MEANING MOTION FANS FRESH OUR WITS WITH WONDER,   •   045 00 014
    US: FRESH YOUTH FRETTED IN A BLOOMFALL ALL PORTENDING   •   •   048 00 030
    WITH YOUR FRESH THOUGHTS CARE FOR, CAN YOU?   •   •   •   •   055 00 004
    EVERYTHING THAT'S FRESH AND FAST FLYING OF US, C   •   •   •   059 0G 008
    HE DOES TAKE FRESH AND FRESH,   •   •   •   •   •   •   •   •   060 00 056
    HE DOES TAKE FRESH AND FRESH,   •   •   •   •   •   •   •   •   060 00 056
    WITH FRETTY CHERVIL, LOOK, AND FRESH WIND SHAKES   •   •   •   074 00 011
    TO COLOUR AS SMOOTH AND FRESH AS CHEEKS OF ROSES,   •   •   •   108 00 004
    NO RAINS SHALL FRESH THE FLATS OF SEA,   •   •   •   •   •   •   114 00 013
    WHICH SAYS AT LEAST THEN GO WHILE ALL IS FRESH, --   •   •   •   125 00 058
    I CAN SCOUR THEE, FRESH BURNISH THEE, C   •   •   •   •   •   •   152 02 015

FRESH   (CONTINUED)
    FOAMFALLING IS NOT FRESH TO IT, RAINBOW BY IT NOT BEAMING,   .   .   .   152 02 024
    BY HER BLOOM, FAST BY HER FRESH, HER FLEECED BLOOM, ...   152 02 051
    BE AT EVERY ASSAULT FRESH FOILED, WORSE FLUNG, DEEPER DISAPPOINTED,   .   152 02 056
FRESHEST
    THERE! SWEETEST, FRESHEST, SHADOWIEST! 159 00 023
FRESH-FIRECOAL
    FRESH-FIRECOAL CHESTNUT-FALLS! FINCHES' WINGS! 037 00 004
FRESH-LEAVED
    THE FURL OF FRESH-LEAVED DOGROSE DOWN 144 00 001
FRESHLY
    I'LL LAY THEM BY, AND FRESHLY TURN INSTEAD 117 00 013
FRESHNESS
    THERE LIVES THE DEAREST FRESHNESS DEEP DOWN THINGS! 031 00 010
    THIS, ALL THIS FRESHNESS FUMING, ...   049 00 006
    AND FAVOURING VIRGIN FRESHNESS YET, ...   139 00 006
    AND WITH HEAVENFALLEN FRESHNESS DOWN FROM MOORLAND STILL BRIMS,   .   159 00 039
FRET
    SHOWER'D THE CLIFFS AND EVERY FRET AND SPIRE 002 00 025
    TOWARDS WASTES WHERE ROUND THE ICE-BLOCKS TILT AND FRET   .   .   .   088 00 007
    TOWARDS THOSE WASTES WHERE THE ICE-BLOCKS TILT AND FRET, V   .   .   088 00 011
FRETFUL
    AND FEEL NO BLAST. -- THE FRETFUL FIRE 080 05 004
FRETS
    A GOLD-WATER PACTOLUS FRETS 003 00 027
FRETTED
    AROUND THE WATER-NYMPHS IN FRETTED FALLS, ...   002 00 050
    WITH THE DAINTY-DELICATE FRETTED FRINGE OF FINGERS   .   .   .   002 00 064
    US! FRESH YOUTH FRETTED IN A BLOOMFALL ALL PORTENDING   .   .   .   048 00 030
    AND FRETTED CLOUDS WITH BURNISH'D RIM, ...   077 00 101
FRETTY
    WITH FRETTY CHERVIL, LOOK, AND FRESH WIND SHAKES 074 00 011
    WILD WYCHELM, HORNBEAM FRETTY OVERSTOOD C 159 00 024
FRIEND
    WHERE ART THOU FRIEND, WHOM I SHALL NEVER SEE, ...   013 00 001
    THEIR RANSOM, THEIR RESCUE, AND FIRST, FAST, LAST FRIEND.   .   .   040 00 014
    WERT THOU MY ENEMY, O THOU MY FRIEND, ...   074 00 005
    BUT CANDOUR NEVER HURT THE DEAREST FRIEND. 094 00 008
    THE KING'S FRIEND TOLD THE THING THAT WAS HID 109 12 001
FRIENDS
    TO THE SWEET LIVING OF MY FRIENDS I LOOK -- 016 00 002
    SO IS IT WITH MY FRIENDS, I NOTE, TO HEAR 119 00 005
    FATHER, MOTHER, BROTHERS, SISTERS, FRIENDS 159 00 049
FRIEZE
    POURTRAY'D ALONG THE FRIEZE WITH TITAN'S BROOD 001 07 004
    WITH OIL OF GLADNESS! FOR SACKCLOTH AND FRIEZE 011 00 010
FRIGATE
    THEN A LURCH FORWARD, FRIGATE AND MEN! 041 00 041
FRIGHTFUL
    THE DENSE AND THE DRIVEN PASSION, AND FRIGHTFUL SWEAT!   .   .   .   028 07 005
    AND FRIGHTFUL A NIGHTFALL FOLDED RUEFUL A DAY 028 15 005
    FRIGHTFUL, SHEER, NO-MAN-FATHOMED. HOLD THEM CHEAP   .   .   .   065 00 010
FRIGID
    WITH BARREN RIGOUR AND A FRIGID GLOOM -- 001 01 008
FRINGE
    WITH THE DAINTY-DELICATE FRETTED FRINGE OF FINGERS   .   .   .   002 00 064
    THE MOON, DWINDLED AND THINNED TO THE FRINGE C 137 00 002
    MELLS BLUE AND SNOWWHITE THROUGH THEM, A FRINGE AND FRAY   .   .   149 A 009
    MELLS BLUE WITH SNOWWHITE THROUGH THEIR FRINGE AND FRAY V   .   .   149 B 011
FRINGED
    FROM CROWN TO TAIL-FIN FLOATING, FRINGED THE SPINE,   .   .   .   002 00 041
FRINGES
    THE RIM WITH RUBY FRINGES DIGHT, ...   077 00 120
FRO
    THEY COULD TELL HIM FOR HOURS, DANDLED THE TO AND FRO   .   .   .   028 16 006
FROCKS
    THAT FROCKS AN OAR IN PENMAEN POOL, ...   030 00 036
FROLICLAVISH
    LONG, WHERE WE LEAVE HIM, FROLICLAVISH, C 159 00 042
FRONTING
    FRONTING MY FROWARD EYE 060 00 119
    THE SHEPHERD'S BROW, FRONTING FORKED LIGHTNING, OWNS   .   .   .   075 00 001
FRONTS
    FRONTS VENUS. -- HIS ILL-LAUNCHED HOPE 083 00 019
FROST-FURRED
    FROST-FURRED OUR IVIES ARE AND ROUGH 003 00 003
FROTH
    ALL IN FROTH AND WATERBLOWBALLS, DOWN. C 159 00 007
FROTHPITS
    FALLERS IN DREADFUL FROTHPITS, WATERFEARERS WILD, ...   152 C 007
FROTHY
    MADE HEADWAY IN THE FROTHY DEEP, ...   021 00 051
FROWARD
    FRONTING MY FROWARD EYE 060 00 119
FROWN
    THE FROWN OF HIS FACE 028 03 001
FROWNING
    FROWNING AND FOREFENDING ANGEL-WARDER 048 00 017

FROWNING   (CONTINUED)
O IS THERE NO FROWNING OF THESE WRINKLES, RANKED WRINKLES DEEP, . . . 059 OL 003
THEM -- BROAD IN BLUFF HIDE HIS FROWNING FEET LASHED! RACED . . . 071 00 013
FORWARD FALLING, FOREHEAD FROWNING, LIPS CRISP 159 00 032
FRUIT
STRETCHES THE ENVIED FRUIT WITH FATAL SMILE 001 11 002
TERRIBLE FRUIT WAS ON THE TREE 006 00 015
SHALL SHAKE HER FRUIT AS LIBANUS, ... 006 00 028
CHRIST AT ALL HAZARDS FRUIT HATH SHEWED. 007 00 010
NOR FRUIT, NOR FLOWERS, NOR DOROTHY. 010 00 024
FRUIT NOR FLOWER NOR DOROTHY. 025 00 024
DROPS THE FRUIT OUT! THE DUCT RUNS DRY OR BREAKS! . . . 101 00 010
THE FRUIT AGAINST THE WALL 105 00 012
NOR FRUIT ABOVE, -- 127 00 008
OR PARING OF PARADISAICAL FRUIT, LOVELY IN WANING BUT LUSTRELESS, . 137 00 003
CAT. NOR FRUIT NOR FLOWERS NOR DOROTHY. . . . . . APPEN A 24
FRUIT-CLOISTERIN
FRUIT-CLOISTERING HYACINTH-WARDING WOODS, ... 081 00 163
FRUITS
UNPALATEABLE FRUITS TO EAT. 081 00 167
FULFIL
AND THY PURPOSE TO FULFIL! 155 00 018
FULFILLED
AS TOUCHING ME FULFILLED BE THY SAW! . . . . . . APPEN D 27
FULFILL'D
AND HAPPY PROMISES FULFILL'D. 015 00 008
FULL
AND ART AND BEAUTY! TITLE NOW TOO FULL -- 001 15 006
THEN THEY, THUS RANGED, 'GAN MAKE FULL PLAINTIVELY . . . 002 00 126
SUMMER WAS AS FULL OF FLAME! 004 00 025
STRIKE TIMBRELS, SING, EAT, DRINK, BE FULL OF MIRTH. . . . 005 00 043
BRIM, IN A FLASH, FULL! -- HITHER THEN, LAST OR FIRST, . . 028 08 006
IF FLOODTIDE TEEMING THRILLS HER FULL. 030 00 022
DOFFS ALL, DRIVES FULL FOR RIGHTEOUSNESS. 041 00 056
THEN IS MY MISERY FULL INDEED! 081 00 068
AND SUCKS THE LIGHT AS FULL AS GIDEON'S FLEECE! . . . 103 00 011
HIS STEADY WHEEL QUITE TO THE FULL AGAIN. 107 03 012
BEYOND THE WORLD! THE STREAMS ARE FULL 130 00 024
' HAIL BE THOU, FULL OF GRACE ARIGHT! . . . . . APPEN D 05
FILLED FULL OF CHARITY. . . . . APPEN D 41
FULLER
THEIR FALL WAS FULLER OF REGRET! 004 00 030
FULL-LEAVED
NOW WHILE THE FULL-LEAVED HURSTS UNALTER'D STAND, . . . 105 00 003
FULL-SAPP'D
HANDLE THE FIG, SUCK THE FULL-SAPP'D VINE-SHOOT. . . . 005 00 038
FULLNESS
IN THE FULLNESS OF THY FORCE AND STRESS, ... 169 00 004
FULLY
FOR DID SHE PRIDE HER, FREIGHTED FULLY, ON 041 00 009
FUMES
'MID FEVER'D FUMES AND SLIME AND CAKED CLOT! 077 00 008
FUMING
THIS, ALL THIS FRESHNESS FUMING, ... 049 00 006
FUMITORY
FOAM-TUFT FUMITORY. 138 00 030
FUNCTION
TO ITS OWN FINE FUNCTION, WILD AND SELF-INSTRESSED, . . . 047 00 007
FUNERAL
OR ELSE A FUNERAL, AND YET 'TIS NOT A FUNERAL, . . . 152 01 019
OR ELSE A FUNERAL, AND YET 'TIS NOT A FUNERAL, . . . 152 01 019
FUR
FLESH AND FLEECE, FUR AND FEATHER, ... 042 00 017
HIS CAP SHALL BE SHINING FUR, ... 124 00 013
FURL
THE FURL OF FRESH-LEAVED DOGROSE DOWN 144 00 001
FURLED
FELLED AND FURLED THEM, THE HEARTS OF OAK! 041 00 006
SAY IT IS ASHBOUGHS! WHETHER ON A DECEMBER DAY AND FURLED . 149 A 004
FAST FURLED AND ALL FOREDRAWN TO NO OR YES. . . . 157 00 028
FURLONGS
EIGHT THOUSAND FURLONGS IN ADVANCE. 083 00 016
FURLS
WITH-A-FOUNTAIN'S SHINING-SHOT FURLS. C 071 00 014
WITH, ALONG THEM, CRAGIRON UNDER AND COLD FURLS -- C . . 071 00 014
FURNACE
THE FURNACE SHALL AT LAST BE COLD. 015 00 016
FURRED
FURRED SNOWS, CHARGED TUFT ABOVE TUFT, TOWER . . . 030 00 031
FURROW
YAWN'D LIKE LONG FURROW IN THE HEART! 077 00 064
FOR BRIER, BOUGH, FURROW, OR GREEN GROUND 138 00 006
AND DOWN . . . . THE FURROW DRY 138 00 027
FURROWS
FROM FURROWS OF THE POOR AND STINTING WEALD. . . . 017 00 013
FURTHER
BUT FURTHER DOWN THE VALLEY, LEFT AND RIGHT, . . . 001 14 004

FURTHER   (CONTINUED)
         ERE I HAD FURTHER QUESTION MADE 004 00 016
         NOT DANGER, ELECTRICAL HORROR! THEN FURTHER IT FINDS 028 27 005
         TAKE COURAGE! THIS SHALL NEED NO FURTHER ART. 080 11 005
         BUT EACH A HAND'S BREADTH FURTHER THAN THE NEXT. 091 00 007
         WHO CAME FROM FURTHER THAN THE STARS 115 00 003
         I'LL CITE NO FURTHER WHAT THE INITIATE KNOW. 119 00 010
FURTHER'D
         NOT FURTHER'D FAR MY TRAVELL'D FEET 081 00 157
FURTHEST
         HERE AT THE VERY FURTHEST REACH AWAY 107 04 019
         (THE FURTHEST REACH THIS SIDE, ON THAT THE BAY 107 04 020
FURY
         THEN LULL, THEN LEAVE OFF, FURY HAD SHRIEKED ' NO LING- . . . 065 00 007
FUSSY
         MY TEMPESTS THERE, MY FIRE AND FEVER FUSSY. 075 00 014
FUTILITY
         I REASON'D THE FUTILITY. 081 00 113

GABRIEL
         GABRIEL, FROM HEAVEN'S KING . . . . APPEN D 01
GAIETY
         MAIDENGEAR, GALLANTRY AND GAIETY AND GRACE, C 059 0G 014
GAIN
         OF HEAVEN WHAT BOON TO BUY YOU, BOY, OR GAIN 047 00 012
GAININGS
         ALL OF HER GLORIOUS GAININGS UNAWARE. 151 00 010
GAIN'D
         AND GAIN'D THRO' GROWING DUSK THE STIRLESS BAY! 002 00 141
GAINS
         NOT FOR ANY GAINS I SEE! 170 00 017
GALAHAD
         AN OUR DAY'S GOD'S OWN GALAHAD. THOUGH THIS CHILD'S DRIFT . . 048 00 040
         THE SERAPH BROWS OF GALAHAD. 077 00 042
GALAXY
         NOW QUICKEN, SHEATHED IN THE YELLOW GALAXY. 098 22 003
GALE
         TOO LATE! LOST! GONE WITH THE GALE. 041 00 036
         TOLD OFF THEIR LEAVES ALONG THE PIERCING GALE, ... 098 05 002
         THE SWALLOW, FAVOURITE OF THE GALE, ... 130 00 009
GALES
         AND THEY THE PREY OF THE GALES! 028 24 004
         DIVINITY OF AIR, FLEET-FEATHER'D GALES; 160 00 001
GALILEE
         OF HIS GOING IN GALILEE! 028 07 002
GALILEE'S
         IT IS GALILEE'S GROWTH: IT GREW AT GOD'S WILL 027 00 009
GALL
         FALL, GALL THEMSELVES, AND GASH GOLD-VERMILION. . . . 036 00 014
         I AM GALL, I AM HEARTBURN. GOD'S MOST DEEP DECREE . . . 067 00 009
GALLANT
         GAYGEAR, GOING GALLANT, GIRLGRACE -- C 059 0G 015
         GOLD GALLANT, FLOWERS MUCH LOOKED AT IN APRIL-WEATHER . . 098 16 002
GALLANTRY
         MAIDENGEAR, GALLANTRY AND GAIETY AND GRACE, C 059 0G 014
GALLED
         AND THOSE STROKES ONCE THAT GASHED FLESH OR GALLED SHIELD . . 073 00 002
GALLERIES
         SLOP'D ON THE GALLERIES: UPON THE WALL 001 12 002
GALLOP
         GALLOP ALONG THE MEADOW GRASS. -- 130 00 026
GAMBOL
         THIS GARLAND OF THEIR GAMBOL FLASHES IN HIS BREAST . . . 159 00 019
GAMBOLLING
         UPON THIS ONLY GAMBOLLING AND ECHOING-OF-EARTH NOTE -- . . 159 00 045
GAPES
         THOSE WHOSE DRY PLOT FOR MOISTURE GAPES, ... 006 00 011
GAPS
         WHOSE GAPS AND HOLLOWS ARE NOT BROWZED UPON, ... 107 01 002
GARB
         PERFUMES FOR THE GARB OF WOE. 024 00 020
GARDEN
         IN JOSEPH'S GARDEN THEY THREW BY 006 00 021
         NONE IN CAESAR'S GARDEN BLOW. 025 00 008
         IN EDEN GARDEN. -- HAVE, GET, BEFORE IT CLOY, ... 033 00 011
         THREE RIVALS THRONG HER GARDEN CHAIR, ... 083 00 010
         WORSE THAN WHEN FLORIS FOUND ME IN THE GARDEN 102 01 040
         DID YOU PULL IT IN THE KING'S GARDEN 109 33 003
         ' I DID NOT PULL IT IN KING'S GARDEN 109 34 001
GARDEN-POPPIES
         AS SILKEN GARDEN-POPPIES DO. 021 00 007
GARDENS
         IN BEDS, IN GARDENS, IN THICK PLOTS I STAND, ... 005 00 037

GARDENS   (CONTINUED)
       NONE IN CAESAR'S GARDENS BLOW. -- 010 00 008
       IN THE GARDENS OF GOD, IN THE DAYLIGHT DIVINE 027 00 005
       IN THE GARDENS OF GOD, IN THE DAYLIGHT DIVINE 027 00 011
       IN THE GARDENS OF GOD, IN THE DAYLIGHT DIVINE 027 00 017
       IN THE GARDENS OF GOD, IN THE DAYLIGHT DIVINE 027 00 023
       IN THE GARDENS OF GOD, IN THE DAYLIGHT DIVINE 027 00 029
       IN THE GARDENS OF GOD, IN THE DAYLIGHT DIVINE 027 00 035
       IN THE GARDENS OF GOD, IN THE DAYLIGHT DIVINE 027 00 041
       ANG.   NONE IN CAESAR'S GARDENS BLOW -- . . . . APPEN A 08
GARLAND
       THIS GARLAND OF THEIR GAMBOL FLASHES IN HIS BREAST 159 00 019
GARLANDED
       TOM -- GARLANDED WITH SQUAT AND SURLY STEEL 070 00 001
       NOR MIND NOR MAINSTRENGTH: GOLD GO GARLANDED 070 00 013
GARNERED
       FOR LEARNING STORED AND GARNERED? 081 00 169
GARNERING
       IN HARVEST AND IN GARNERING, ... 008 00 015
GARNET
       WITH GARNET WREATHS AND BLOOMS OF ROSY-BUDDED FIRE.   . . . 002 00 026
GASH
       FALL, GALL THEMSELVES, AND GASH GOLD-VERMILION. 036 00 014
GASHED
       AND THOSE STROKES ONCE THAT GASHED FLESH OR GALLED SHIELD . . 073 00 002
GASHES
       SPEAR'D OPEN LUSTROUS GASHES, CRIMSON-WHITE; 002 00 008
GASP
       AGE GASP: WHOSE BREATH IS OUR MEMENTO MORI -- 075 00 007
GASPING
       A HEART'S-CLARION! AWAY GRIEF'S GASPING, JOYLESS DAYS, DEJECTION. . 072 00 017
GASP'D
       BY INTERCHANGE GASP'D SPLENDOUR AND ECLIPSE. 002 00 022
GASPS
       NOW HE GASPS, NOW HE GAZES EVERYWHERE; 041 00 066
GATE
       -- BEFORE THE SEPULCHRE THERE STOOD A GATE, ... 001 04 006
GATES
       LIFT UP YOUR HEADS, O GATES; 115 00 008
GATHER
       I GATHER POINTS OF LOTE-FLOWER FROM AN ISLE 005 00 033
       ON THISTLES THAT MEN LOOK NOT GRAPES TO GATHER, ... 007 00 002
       GATHER GLADNESS FROM THE SKIES; 024 00 013
       OTHER, I GATHER, IN MEASURE HER MIND'S 028 27 007
       WHEN GREY SHOWERS GATHER AND GUSTS ARE COOL? -- 030 00 026
       YET AH! THIS AIR I GATHER AND I RELEASE 044 00 009
       GATHER THE SOOTY PLUMAGE FROM DEATH'S WINGS 089 00 006
       AND GATHER IN LIKE HURDLES BRIGHT 098 29 003
       THERE WAS NO CREASE OR GATHER IN THE CLOUDS 102 02 006
       LIKE FLAME THEY GATHER ON OUR CLIFFS AT EVENING, ... 104 00 007
       I THOUGHT; BEFORE I GATHER STRENGTH 118 00 013
       AND GATHER IN LIKE HURDLES BRIGHT 135 00 021
GATHERING
       AND GATHERING, FLOATED WHERE THE GAZE WAS NOT;) 002 00 010
GATHER'D
       FOR US WAS GATHER'D THE FIRST-FRUITS, ... 006 00 003
GATHERS
       IT GATHERS TO A GREATNESS, LIKE THE OOZE OF OIL 031 00 003
GAUGE
       NO WISDOM CAN FORECAST BY GAUGE OR GUESS, ... 157 00 026
GAVE
       THAT GAVE YOU VANTAGE WHEN YOU WOULD DESPISE; 014 03 003
       MY NATIONAL OLD EGYPTIAN REED GAVE WAY; 020 00 007
       AND, EYES, HEART, WHAT LOOKS, WHAT LIPS YET GAVE YOU A   . . 038 00 007
       GAVE GOD'S INFINITY 060 00 018
       AND TO THEIR FEET THE NARROW BELLS GAVE RHYME. 107 01 014
       GAVE THE MUCH MUSIC OF OUR OXFORD BELLS? 107 02 008
       HE GAVE HER KISSES COLD AS ICE; 109 39 001
       GENTLY TO HIM GAVE ANSWER . . . . APPEN D 11
GAY
       THERE WAS A LADY VERY GAY, ... 131 00 002
GAYGEAR
       GAYGEAR, GOING GALLANT, GIRLGRACE -- C 059 06 015
GAY-GANGS
       IN GAY-GANGS THEY THRONG; THEY GLITTER IN MARCHES. C   . . . 072 00 002
GAYLINKS
       THOSE GOLDNAILS AND THEIR GAYLINKS THAT HANG ALONG A LIME;   . 142 00 005
GAZE
       AND GATHERING, FLOATED WHERE THE GAZE WAS NOT;) 002 00 010
       RIS'N FROM THE DEEPS TO GAZE ON SUN AND HEAVEN, ... 002 00 035
       HAD SHE A QUINCE IN HAND? YET GAZE; 010 00 019
       SURROUND THE PEAK FROM WHICH WE GAZE. 023 00 026
       MASTER MORE MAY THAN GAZE, GAZE OUT OF COUNTENANCE.   . . . 062 00 005
       MASTER MORE MAY THAN GAZE, GAZE OUT OF COUNTENANCE.   . . . 062 00 005
       THEN MAY I UPWARDS GAZE AND SEE 077 00 113
       AND FACES FIT FOR LEISURE GAZE 133 00 013
       GAZE ON, AND FALL DIRECTLY FORTH ON LIFE. 157 00 016

103

GAZE (CONTINUED)
    COMES ONE TO GAZE UPON MY ILL! 160 00 025
    SOME DAY TO GAZE ON THEE FACE TO FACE IN LIGHT 168 00 027
GAZED
    I GAZED UNHINDER'D: MERMAIDS SIX OR SEVEN, ... 002 00 034
GAZES
    GAZES ASLANT HIS SHOULDER, VIEWING NIGH 001 11 006
    NOW HE GASPS, NOW HE GAZES EVERYWHERE: 041 00 066
    BIDS HIM THIS WAY HIS GAZES FIX. 120 00 015
GAZING
    FOR ONLY TRY BY GAZING TO DIVIDE 102 03 009
GEAR
    AND ALL TRADES, THEIR GEAR AND TACKLE AND TRIM. . . 037 00 006
    WITH GORGON'S GEAR AND BAREBILL / THONGS AND FANGS. . . 050 00 014
GEM
    ALL A SEVENFOLD-SINGLE GEM, ... 077 00 116
GEM-FLEECED
    GEM-FLEECED AT MORN, SO BRILLIANT IS THE WEATHER. . . 099 00 004
GENERATION
    FAST FOUNDERING OWN GENERATION. 041 00 088
GENERATIONS
    GENERATIONS HAVE TROD, HAVE TROD, HAVE TROD; . . . 031 00 005
GENNESARETH
    WOKE THEE WITH A WE ARE PERISHING IN THE WEATHER OF GENNESARETH. . 028 25 006
GENTLE
    TO GENTLE MANNA AND SIMPLE BREAD? 081 00 175
    LIKE A CONTENTED WIND, OR GENTLE SHOCKS 098 02 002
    AS VOID AS THOSE THE GENTLE DOWNS APPEAR 107 01 003
    AND BROUGHT THE SENSE OF GENTLE FELLOWSHIP, . . . 107 02 004
    HER SHOWY LEAVES WITH GENTLE WATCHET FOILING V . . 108 00 006
    THE GENTLE MAIDEN THEN: . . . . APPEN D 12
GENTLY
    AND DEATH FALLS GENTLY AS THE SNOW: 077 00 026
    GENTLY TO HIM GAVE ANSWER . . . . . . APPEN D 11
GERMS
    AND LIFE'S FIRST GERMS FROM DEATH HAD WON. . . . 023 00 024
GERTRUDE
    BUT GERTRUDE, LILY, AND LUTHER, ARE TWO OF A TOWN, . 028 20 005
GET
    IN EDEN GARDEN. -- HAVE, GET, BEFORE IT CLOY, . . . 033 00 011
    KIND LOVE BOTH GIVE AND GET, ONLY WHAT WORD . . . 066 00 011
    I CAST FOR COMFORT I CAN NO MORE GET 069 00 005
    AND NOW I GET SOME PRECIOUS SLIPS. 081 00 084
    SAYS ' GET YOU, GET YOU A LADY TO WED 109 09 001
    SAYS ' GET YOU, GET YOU A LADY TO WED 109 09 001
    AH YES! WHY, GET THEE GONE THEN! TELL THY MOTHER I WANT HER. . 152 01 010
GETHSEMANE
    IN THE ACRE OF GETHSEMANE: 006 00 016
GHOST
    BECAUSE THE HOLY GHOST OVER THE BENT 031 00 013
    WHAT HEART HEARD OF, GHOST GUESSED: 055 00 013
    IN THE HOLY GHOST THE PARACLETE 169 00 010
    'TIS THROUGH THE HOLY GHOST THAT WROUGHT . . . APPEN D 16
    THROUGH TH' HOLY GHOST HIS MIGHT. . . . . APPEN D 34
GHOSTLY
    TOWARDS ALL OUR GHOSTLY GOOD 060 00 048
GHOSTS
    OR LISTENING THOUGHT OF LINEN-WINDED GHOSTS. . . . 135 00 018
GIANT
    TUGG'D THE BOSS'D, SMOOTH-LIPP'D, GIANT STROMBUS-SHELL. . 002 00 057
    OUR PASSION-PLUNGED GIANT RISEN. 028 33 007
    OF JUST, MAJESTICAL, AND GIANT GROANS. 075 00 004
    OUT ON THE GIANT AIR! TELL SUMMER NO, ... 154 00 003
GIANT'S
    THE TRIPLE-HUMMOCKED GIANT'S STOOL, ... 030 00 010
GIANTS
    JOVE OF THE GIANTS: SIMPLE JOVE'S 166 00 007
GIDDIES
    GIDDIES THE SOUL WITH BLINDING DAZE 023 00 028
GIDEON'S
    AND SUCKS THE LIGHT AS FULL AS GIDEON'S FLEECE: . . 103 00 011
GIFT
    THE RICHEST GIFT ST. LAWRENCE EVER BORE, . . . 001 02 006
    PHILIP, SUPPOSING THAT THE GIFT MOST MEET, . . . 001 03 006
    OF THE GOSPEL PROFFER, A PRESSURE, A PRINCIPLE, CHRIST'S GIFT. . 028 04 008
    HOME AT HEART, HEAVEN'S SWEET GIFT: THEN LEAVE, LET THAT ALONE. . 062 00 013
    GIVE HIM THE GIFT. ' I CANNOT TELL 081 00 111
    MY FAST-LODGED TONGUE. ' [TO HER THE GIFT] . . . 081 00 116
    THAT STRUGGLING SHOULD NOT SEAR HIM, A GIFT SHOULD CHEER HIM . 142 00 008
GIFTS
    WHEN CHIEFS AND MONARCHS CAME THEIR GIFTS TO LAY . . 001 02 007
    YET KNOW NOT HOW OUR GIFTS TO BRING, ... 023 00 017
    SHARES THEIR BEST GIFTS SURELY, FALL HOW THINGS WILL) . . 048 00 004
GILDED
    HIS GILDED ROWELS 098 26 001
GILDS
    GILDS WITH SOME SPARKY FANCIES HIS BLACK NIGHT . . . 102 03 030

GILDS   (CONTINUED)
        GILDS WITH SOME SPARKY FANCIES BLINDING NIGHT, V 102 03 036
GILT
        OF THOSE GILT WEBS THAT LANGUISH'D IN A FALL. 001 08 007
        IN BLAZON, GILT   AND IMAGES OF BRONZE, V 102 02 010
        -- GILT AND BLAZON -- BRONZE STATUARY, V 102 02 010
GIRDER
        DEAR GRACE AND GIRDER OF MINE AND ME. 134 00 002
GIRDLES
        GIRDLES: GOES HOME BETWIXT 060 00 004
GIRL
        INNOCENT MIND AND MAYDAY IN GIRL AND BOY, ...   033 00 013
        WHAT IS IT, GWEN, MY GIRL? WHY DO YOU HOVER AND HAUNT ME? .   .   .   152 01 001
        ALIVE OR DEAD MY GIRL IS CARRIED IN IT, ENDLESSLY 152 01 021
GIRLGRACE
        GAYGEAR, GOING GALLANT, GIRLGRACE -- C 059 06 015
GIRLHOOD
        AND GRAVE PAST GIRLHOOD EARNEST IN HER EYES. 136 00 020
GIRTH
        THE GIRTH OF IT AND THE WHARF OF IT AND THE WALL: 028 32 004
        SPREADING STILL ITS SUNNED GIRTH: 077 00 070
GIVE
        GIVE US THE TALE OF BRICKS AS HERETOFORE: 005 00 049
        GIVE MYRRHY-THREADED GOLDEN FOLDS OF EASE. 011 00 012
        GIVE GOD WHILE WORTH CONSUMING. 049 00 007
        DOG, HE DID GIVE TONGUE! 054 00 034
        GIVE BEAUTY BACK, BEAUTY, BEAUTY, BEAUTY, C 059 06 019
        KIND LOVE BOTH GIVE AND GET, ONLY WHAT WORD 066 00 011
        I GIVE COMMANDS FOR WATER FOR MY HANDS: 080 09 003
        I PLEAD: AND YOU WILL GIVE YOUR TEARS: 081 00 028
        GIVE HIM THE GIFT. ' I CANNOT TELL 081 00 111
        GIVE US OUR GREEN LOTS IN ANOTHER MEAD 098 15 005
        IS TO GIVE REGIMEN TO THE IMPERFECT WIND, V 102 03 024
        I GIVE YOU MY LOVE AND I GIVE YOU MY LAND, ...   109 05 003
        I GIVE YOU MY LOVE AND I GIVE YOU MY LAND, ...   109 05 003
        IF I GIVE THEE KISSES THREE? 109 37 002
        GIVE ME THY KISSES THREE. 109 38 002
        AT ONCE THE SENSES GIVE THE MUSIC BACK, ...   113 00 010
        IN COPYING? HOW? MUST I GIVE TONGUE AGAIN? 125 00 021
        WOULD GIVE US FOR THY SAKE: .   .   .   .   APPEN D 48
GIVEN
        AND I'LL PRETEND THE CREDIT GIVEN OF YORE: 014 02 003
        HEAR YET MY PARADOX: LOVE, WHEN ALL IS GIVEN,   .   .   .   020 00 013
        'TIS FALSELY GIVEN -- AS LOVE IN MEN: 081 00 049
        HIS TALE AND TELLING HAS BEEN GIVEN TO ME. 107 01 018
        AND HATH GIVEN 160 00 013
GIVER
        GOD! GIVER OF BREATH AND BREAD: 028 01 002
        BACK TO GOD, BEAUTY'S SELF AND BEAUTY'S GIVER, C .   .   .   059 06 019
GIVES
        INTO MY HAND HE GIVES A HOST FOR PREY, ...   005 00 017
        NIGHT TO A MYRIAD WORLDS GIVES BIRTH, ...   023 00 009
        THY RIVER, AND O'ER GIVES ALL TO RACK OR WRONG, .   .   .   058 00 008
        SINCE, PROUD, IT CALLS THE CALLING MANLY, GIVES A GUESS   .   063 00 004
        FOR MORE WITH HIM WHO GIVES THEE ALL, ...   081 00 150
        AND GIVES FOR TROPES HIS JUDGMENT ALL AWAY,   .   .   .   102 03 029
        AND GIVES FOR TROPES HIS JUDGMENT ALL AWAY, V .   .   .   102 03 035
GIVEST
        OH! TILL THOU GIVEST THAT SENSE BEYOND, ...   023 00 043
GLACIER
        SOME ICE THAT LOCKS THE GLACIER TO THE ROCKS   .   .   .   080 09 006
GLAD
        AND I'M VERY GLAD 132 00 005
        I AM SO VERY, O SO VERY GLAD 138 00 031
        AND MATCHED WITH THEE THERE 'S NOTHING GLAD   .   .   .   167 00 019
GLADDEST
        THE GLADDEST THING THAT OUR EYES HAVE SEEN,   .   .   .   026 00 018
GLADE
        DEATH WAS VANISH'D FROM THE GLADE. 004 00 017
GLADNESS
        WITH OIL OF GLADNESS: FOR SACKCLOTH AND FRIEZE   .   .   .   011 00 010
        GATHER GLADNESS FROM THE SKIES: 024 00 013
        MAKES GLADNESS AFTER HE IS GONE: 167 00 002
GLANCE
        MEN'S WITS TO THE THINGS THAT ARE: WHAT GOOD MEANS -- WHERE A GLANCE   062 00 004
GLANCES
        TO BATHE IN HIS FALL-GOLD MERCIES, TO BREATHE IN HIS ALL-FIRE GLANCES.   028 23 008
GLARE
        THE WAVES WERE ROSY-LIPP'D: THE CRIMSON GLARE   .   .   .   002 00 024
        SICKEN'D AND THICKEN'D BY THE GLARE AND SAND   .   .   .   005 00 019
        AFTER THE SANDFIELD AND THE UNVEINED GLARE!   .   .   .   005 00 029
GLASS
        HER GLASS IS BLEST BUT SHE AS GOOD AS BLIND   .   .   .   151 00 007
        HER GLASS DRINKS LIGHT, SHE DARKLES DOWN BEHIND, .   .   .   151 00 009
GLASSES
        AND SET THE GLASSES FROM THE SUN 165 00 007
GLASS-BLUE
        THE GLASS-BLUE DAYS ARE THOSE 060 00 083

GLASSY
    SO GLASSY WHITE ABOUT THE SKY, ... 003 00 016
    THE GLASSY PEARTREE LEAVES AND BLOOMS, THEY BRUSH 033 00 006
    THEY WEBB'D THE SKY WITH GLASSY LIGHT. 087 00 002
    UNDERNEATH, THEIR GLASSY BARREL, OF A FAIRY GREEN. 141 00 006
    FILLETED WITH GLASSY GRASSY QUICKSILVERY SHIVES AND SHOOTS C . . 159 00 038
GLASSY-CLEAR
    OF GLASSY-CLEAR AEOLIS, METAL-LUSTRED 002 00 069
GLAUCUS
    THE GLAUCUS CLEPED: OTHERS SMALL BRAIDS ENCLUSTER'D 002 00 068
GLAZED
    GLAZED WATER VAULTED O'ER A DROWSY STONE. 098 39 001
GLEAM
    RICH TITIANS FADED: IN THE STRAYING GLEAM 001 12 003
GLEAM'D
    WITH PAINTING GLEAM'D THE RICH PILASTER'D WALLS -- 001 10 003
    SOME, DIVING MERRILY, DOWNWARD DROVE, AND GLEAM'D 002 00 108
GLEAN
    DOWN ALL THAT GLORY IN THE HEAVENS TO GLEAN OUR SAVIOUR: . . . 038 00 006
GLEANED
    HOW THEN SHOULD GREGORY, A FATHER, HAVE GLEANED ELSE FROM SWARM- . 062 00 007
GLEE
    WHAT CAN IT BE, THIS GLEE? THE GOOD YOU HAVE THERE OF YOUR OWN? . 028 18 008
GLEN
    SHE STOOD BEFORE THEM IN THE GLEN, ... 109 25 001
GLENS
    BUT FROM THE MOUNTAIN GLENS IN AUTUMN LATE 001 13 001
GLIDE
    OR, LIKE A LARK TO GLIDE ALOOF 077 00 065
    WITH WAVED PASSES THERE SHALL GLIDE 106 00 002
GLIDES
    FOR THE LISTENER: FOR THE LINGERER WITH A LOVE GLIDES . . . 028 33 003
GLIDING
    AS A SKATE'S HEEL SWEEPS SMOOTH ON A BOW-BEND: THE HURL AND GLIDING . 036 00 006
GLIMMER'D
    GLIMMER'D ALONG THE SQUARE-CUT STEEP. 092 00 001
GLIMPSES
    KEEN GLIMPSES OF THE INNER FIRMAMENT: 002 00 012
GLISTENS
    HER NOSTRIL GLISTENS: AND HER WET BLACK EYE 099 00 005
GLISTERY
    BRING IN THE GLISTERY STRAW. 005 00 046
GLITTER
    IN GAY-GANGS THEY THRONG: THEY GLITTER IN MARCHES. C . . . 072 00 002
GLOBES
    OF FILMY GLOBES AND ROSY FLOATING CLOUD: -- 002 00 097
GLOOM
    WITH BARREN RIGOUR AND A FRIGID GLOOM -- 001 01 008
    AROSE IN GLOOM, A SOLEMN MOCKERY 001 08 006
    THE SKILL OF DREAMY CLAUDE, AND TITIAN'S MELLOW GLOOM. . . . 001 10 009
    INTO THE COOLING GLOOM: TILL SLOWLY ALL 001 12 005
    THE COMFORTABLE GLOOM 005 00 028
    NOW CARISBROOK KEEP GOES UNDER IN GLOOM: 041 00 029
    AND SOBER LUSTRES TAKE THE GLOOM: 077 00 020
    SHOULDERING, DOWN VALLEYS SMOKES THE GLOOM. 080 07 002
    NOW MORE PRECISELY TOUCHED IN LIGHT AND GLOOM, ... 098 30 004
GLOOM'D
    THRO' SILVER, GLOOM'D TO A BLOOD-VIVID CLOT. 002 00 107
GLORIES
    WE SEE THE GLORIES OF THE EARTH 023 00 007
GLORIFY
    THERE / GOD TO AGGRANDISE, GOD TO GLORIFY. -- 046 00 008
GLORIOUS
    A GLORIOUS WANTON: -- ALL THE WRECKS IN SHOWERS 002 00 093
    AND, ON THE FIGHTER, FORGE HIS GLORIOUS DAY. 073 00 004
    ALL OF HER GLORIOUS GAININGS UNAWARE. 151 00 010
GLORY
    PHILIP TOOK OATH, WHILE GLORY OR DEFEAT 001 02 003
    TO THY BREAST, TO THY REST, TO THY GLORY DIVINE 027 00 047
    GLOW, GLORY IN THUNDER: 028 05 004
    THOU HADST GLORY OF THIS NUN? -- 028 30 004
    GLORY BE TO GOD FOR DAPPLED THINGS -- 037 00 001
    DOWN ALL THAT GLORY IN THE HEAVENS TO GLEAN OUR SAVIOUR: . . 038 00 006
    LET ALL GOD'S GLORY THROUGH, ... 060 00 030
    GOD'S GLORY WHICH WOULD GO 060 00 031
    WHOSE GLORY BARE WOULD BLIND 060 00 108
    OF EARTH'S GLORY, EARTH'S EASE, ALL: NO ONE, NOWHERE, . . . 070 00 016
    THE HORROR AND THE HAVOC AND THE GLORY 075 00 002
    THE KING OF GLORY WILL COME IN. 115 00 010
    FOR LOVE AND GREATER GLORY OF CHRIST. 118 00 004
    ALL GLORY BE ASCRIBED TO 133 00 003
    SHOULD CHOKE SWEET VIRTUE'S GLORY IS TIME'S GREAT GUILT. . . 136 00 002
    TO THE GLORY OF THE FATHER. AMEN. 169 00 011
GLORYING
    AND GRANT OUR GLORYING MAY BE 167 00 027
GLORY'S
    AND BE BLEST FOR EVER WITH THY GLORY'S SIGHT. 168 00 028

GLOSS
    A SILVER SCARCE=CALL=SILVER GLOSS 098 17 001
GLOVE
    MANTLES THE GUILTY GLOVE. 060 00 039
    SUCKS CLOSE THE ACORN! AS THE HAND AND GLOVE! 101 00 003
    THE HAND DRAWS OFF THE GLOVE! THE ACORN=CUP 101 00 009
GLOW
    BUT NOW BEFORE THE POT CAN GLOW 015 00 013
    GLOW, GLORY IN THUNDER! 028 05 004
    MOTE=LIKE IN THY MIGHTY GLOW. 155 00 004
GLOWLESS
    THE MOONLIGHT=MATED GLOWLESS GLOWWORMS SHINE. 098 36 001
GLOW'D
    AN AZURE RIDGE! OR CLOUDS OF VIOLET GLOW'D 002 00 105
GLOWS
    WHEN EVERY COLOUR GLOWS, ... 060 00 084
    THEN WHILE THE RAIN=BORN ARC GLOWS HIGHER 077 00 123
GLOWWORMS
    THE MOONLIGHT=MATED GLOWLESS GLOWWORMS SHINE. 098 36 001
GLUE
    OR SWEET THE GOLDEN GLUE 148 00 035
GLUEGOLD=BROWN
    WHERE A GLUEGOLD=BROWN C 159 00 005
GNARLED
    O HIS NIMBLE FINGER, HIS GNARLED GRIP! 041 00 081
GNARLS
    WITH THE GNARLS OF THE NAILS IN THEE, NICHE OF THE LANCE, HIS . . 028 23 003
GNASHED
    GNASHED! BUT THOU ART ABOVE, THOU ORION OF LIGHT! 028 21 005
GO
    GO THEN! I AM CONTENTED HERE TO LIE. 005 00 055
    AT KIRJATH=ARBA! GO. -- 005 00 058
    I HAVE DESIRED TO GO 009 00 001
    AND RISE AND GO ABOUT MY WORKS AGAIN 014 01 009
    NEVER ASK IF MEANING IT, WANTING IT, WARNED OF IT -- MEN GO. . . 028 08 008
    HEART, GO AND BLEED AT A BITTERER VEIN FOR THE 028 31 003
    MEN GO BY ME WHOM EITHER BEAUTY BRIGHT 040 00 005
    PRAYER GO DISREGARDED! 048 00 047
    GOD'S GLORY WHICH WOULD GO 060 00 031
    NOR MIND NOR MAINSTRENGTH! GOLD GO GARLANDED 070 00 013
    NO, LET THAT GO! I HAVE SAID GOODNIGHT TO SHAME. 102 01 042
    SO I GO OUT! MY LITTLE SWEET IS DONE! 103 00 017
    OR IF I GO, SHE STAYS MEANWHILE. 120 00 028
    GUILTY OF SILENCE? QUITE, AS LADIES GO. 125 00 023
    WHY SHOULD I GO BECAUSE CASTARA GOES? 125 00 032
    TO SAY I GO BECAUSE CASTARA GOES. 125 00 054
    WHICH SAYS AT LEAST THEN GO WHILE ALL IS FRESH, -- . . . 125 00 058
    MUCH CAUSE TO GO BECAUSE CASTARA GOES. 125 00 059
    SAYS GO ON THEN I GO ON 138 00 035
    SAYS GO ON THEN I GO ON 138 00 035
    SHE MENDS THE WAY SHE MEANS TO GO. 145 00 012
    TO TAKE HER! WHILE THEIR TONGUES WOULD GO -- 145 00 026
    OR THEY GO RICH AS ROSELEAVES HENCE THAT LOATHSOME CAME HITHER! . 152 C 024
    THEE, GOD, I COME FROM, TO THEE GO, ... 155 00 001
    JESU, THEIR HOPE WHO GO ASTRAY, ... 167 00 009
GOAL
    THE GOAL WAS A SHOAL, OF A FOURTH THE DOOM TO BE DROWNED! . . 028 12 006
GOALS
    ALL TIME AT ONCE AND SPAN THE DISTANT GOALS, ... 126 00 004
GOATS
    THEY ARE THE GOATS WHO STAND, SAID I. 081 00 095
GOD
    THEY SHRIVE THEMSELVES AND CRY, ' GOOD SERVICE TO OUR GOD. ' . . 001 05 009
    AND BRING YOUR OFFERINGS TO A GRATEFUL GOD. 005 00 011
    GOD COMES ALL SWEETNESS TO YOUR LENTEN LIPS. 011 00 002
    GOD SHALL O'ER=BRIM THE MEASURES YOU HAVE SPENT 011 00 009
    LO, GOD SHALL STRENGTHEN ALL THE FEEBLE KNEES. 011 00 014
    BATTLING WITH GOD, IS NOW MY PRAYER. 018 00 016
    LOVE, O MY GOD, TO CALL THEE LOVE AND LOVE. 019 00 014
    GOD, THOUGH TO THEE OUR PSALM WE RAISE 023 00 001
    IN THE GARDENS OF GOD, IN THE DAYLIGHT DIVINE 027 00 005
    IN THE GARDENS OF GOD, IN THE DAYLIGHT DIVINE 027 00 011
    IN THE GARDENS OF GOD, IN THE DAYLIGHT DIVINE 027 00 017
    IN THE GARDENS OF GOD, IN THE DAYLIGHT DIVINE 027 00 023
    CHRIST JESUS, OUR LORD, HER GOD AND HER SON. 027 00 028
    IN THE GARDENS OF GOD, IN THE DAYLIGHT DIVINE 027 00 029
    IN THE GARDENS OF GOD, IN THE DAYLIGHT DIVINE 027 00 035
    IN THE GARDENS OF GOD, IN THE DAYLIGHT DIVINE 027 00 041
    SWEET UNTO GOD, AND THE SWEETNESS IS GRACE! 027 00 044
    GOD! GIVER OF BREATH AND BREAD! 028 01 002
    THY TERROR, O CHRIST, O GOD! 028 02 004
    GOD, THREE=NUMBERED FORM! 028 09 002
    GRASP GOD, THRONED BEHIND 028 32 007
    THE WORLD IS CHARGED WITH THE GRANDEUR OF GOD. 031 00 001
    TO ME, GOD KNOWS, DESERVING NO SUCH THING! 034 00 002
    GOD, LOVER OF SOULS, SWAYING CONSIDERATE SCALES, . . . 034 00 012
    GLORY BE TO GOD FOR DAPPLED THINGS -- 037 00 001

107

GOD (CONTINUED)

```
IN᷑ GOD WHO WAS HER SALVATION.  . . . . ./ .  . . . . . 042 00 048
THERE / GOD TO AGGRANDISE, GOD TO GLORIFY. --  . . . . . 046 00 008
THERE / GOD TO AGGRANDISE, GOD TO GLORIFY. --  . . . . . 046 00 008
AND DO SERVE GOD TO SERVE TO  . . . . . . . . 048 00 027
GIVE GOD WHILE WORTH CONSUMING.  . . . . . . . 049 00 007
GOD WITH HONOUR HANG YOUR HEAD.  . . . . . . . 052 00 001
TENDERED TO HIM. AH WELL, GOD REST HIM ALL ROAD EVER HE OFFENDED! . 053 00 008
BACK TO GOD, BEAUTY'S SELF AND BEAUTY'S GIVER. C  . . . . 059 0G 019
SINCE GOD HAS LET DISPENSE  . . . . . . . . . 060 00 040
SO GOD WAS GOD OF OLD:  . . . . . . . . . . 060 00 103
SO GOD WAS GOD OF OLD:  . . . . . . . . . . 060 00 103
ED ROME? BUT GOD TO A NATION DEALT THAT DAY'S DEAR CHANCE,  . 062 00 008
OF NOW DONE DARKNESS I WRETCH LAY WRESTLING WITH ( MY GOD! ) MY GOD. 064 00 014
OF NOW DONE DARKNESS I WRETCH LAY WRESTLING WITH ( MY GOD! ) MY GOD. 064 00 014
OF US WE DO BID GOD BEND TO HIM EVEN SO.  . . . . . 068 00 011
AT GOD KNOWS WHEN TO GOD KNOWS WHAT: WHOSE SMILE  . . . 069 00 012
AT GOD KNOWS WHEN TO GOD KNOWS WHAT: WHOSE SMILE  . . . 069 00 012
YET GOD ( THAT HEWS MOUNTAIN AND CONTINENT,  . . . . . 073 00 009
FROM GOD AND MAN, IS HELL NO DOUBT.  . . . . . . 080 01 004
MAKE IT TO GOD. I AM NOT SPENT  . . . . . . . 081 00 130
HE HAS HIS PORTION. GOD, WHO STRETCH'D APART  . . . . 126 00 002
MAN IS MOST LOW. GOD IS MOST HIGH.  . . . . . . 133 00 005
HE SPOKE OF GOD THE FATHER AND HIS SON.  . . . . . 136 00 025
GOD LIGHTEN YOUR DARK HEART -- BUT NO,  . . . . . . 145 00 027
HER WILL WAS BENT AT GOD.   FOR THAT  . . . . . 145 00 037
AS LONG AS MEN ARE MORTAL AND GOD MERCIFUL,  . . . . 152 C 010
THEE, GOD, I COME FROM, TO THEE GO.  . . . . . . 155 00 001
SPEND ME OR END ME WHAT GOD SHALL SEND ME,  . . . . 156 00 013
NONE GOOD BUT GOD -- A WARNING WAVED TO  . . . . . 157 00 023
WITNESS TO ME! LOOK YOU, I AM A GOD,  . . . . . . 160 00 005
A GOD ENCHAIN'D OF DESTINY,  . . . . . . . . 160 00 027
AS JESUS GOD THE FATHER'S SON.  . . . . . . . 167 00 008
LOST, ALL LOST IN WONDER AT THE GOD THOU ART.  . . . 168 00 004
BUT CAN PLAINLY CALL THEE LORD AND GOD AS HE:  . . . 168 00 014
O GOD, I LOVE THEE: I LOVE THEE --  . . . . . . 170 00 001
FOR BEING MY KING AND GOD. AMEN.  . . . . . . 170 00 021
TRUE GOD, TRUE MAN, IN FLESH AND BONE:  . . . . . APPEN D 36
```

GODDESS'S

```
GREAT AS NO GODDESS'S  . . . . . . . . . . 060 00 027
```

GODHEAD

```
LOW-LATCHED IN LEAF-LIGHT HOUSEL HIS TOO HUGE GODHEAD.  . . 048 00 012
GODHEAD HERE IN HIDING, WHOM I DO ADORE  . . . . . 168 00 001
ON THE CROSS THY GODHEAD MADE NO SIGN TO MEN:  . . . 168 00 009
```

GOD-MADE-FLESH

```
AND CRY ' O CHRIST-DONE DEED! SO GOD-MADE-FLESH DOES TOO:  . 063 00 013
```

GODLESS

```
WHAT WOULD BEFAL THE GODLESS FLOCK  . . . . . . 092 00 007
```

GOD'S

```
OF THOSE WHO STROVE GOD'S GOSPEL TO CONFOUND  . . . . 001 01 007
OF GOD'S DEAR PLEADINGS HAVE AS YET NOT MOVED THEE, --  . 013 00 010
SEEK GOD'S HOUSE IN HAPPY THRONG;  . . . . . . . 024 00 025
IT IS GALILEE'S GROWTH: IT GREW AT GOD'S WILL  . . . 027 00 009
THEY FOUGHT WITH GOD'S COLD --  . . . . . . . 028 17 001
TILL A LIFEBELT AND GOD'S WILL  . . . . . . . 041 00 063
AN OUR DAY'S GOD'S OWN GALAHAD, THOUGH THIS CHILD'S DRIFT  . 048 00 040
ACTS IN GOD'S EYE WHAT IN GOD'S EYE HE IS --  . . . 057 00 011
ACTS IN GOD'S EYE WHAT IN GOD'S EYE HE IS --  . . . 057 00 011
GAVE GOD'S INFINITY  . . . . . . . . . . 060 00 018
LET ALL GOD'S GLORY THROUGH,  . . . . . . . . 060 00 030
GOD'S GLORY WHICH WOULD GO  . . . . . . . . 060 00 031
BOTH GOD'S AND MARY'S SON.  . . . . . . . . 060 00 072
OF GOD'S LOVE, O LIVE AIR,  . . . . . . . . 060 00 122
YEA, WISH THAT THOUGH, WISH ALL, GOD'S BETTER BEAUTY, GRACE.  . 062 00 014
I AM GALL, I AM HEARTBURN. GOD'S MOST DEEP DECREE  . . 067 00 009
GOD'S COUNSEL COLUMNAR-SEVERE  . . . . . . . 145 00 001
GOD'S SON: THESE ( THEY DID NOT KNOW )  . . . . . 145 00 053
GOD'S DAUGHTER MARGARET CLITHEROE  . . . . . . 145 00 054
WHAT GOD'S SON HAS TOLD ME, TAKE FOR TRUTH I DO:  . . 168 00 007
FOR SO GOD'S SON, THE HEAVEN'S LIGHT,  . . . . . APPEN D 06
```

GODS

```
THAT BATTLED GODS FOR HEAVEN: BRILLIANT-HUED,  . . . . 001 07 005
AND THESE FROM THE GODS MY PENALTIES.  . . . . . 160 00 006
SPED OF GODS, OR MORTAL SIGN.  . . . . . . . 160 00 022
```

GOES

```
FANG, OR FLOOD ' GOES DEATH ON DRUM,  . . . . . 028 11 003
THAT INTERESTS OUR EYES. AND WHO GOES THERE?  . . . 040 00 002
NOW CARISBROOK KEEP GOES UNDER IN GLOOM;  . . . . 041 00 029
AS SHEER DOWN THE SHIP GOES.  . . . . . . . 041 00 060
SELVES -- GOES ITSELF; MYSELF IT SPEAKS AND SPELLS,  . . 057 00 007
GIRDLES; GOES HOME BETWIXT  . . . . . . . . 060 00 004
AND THEN MY HEART GOES NEAR TO BREAK.  . . . . . 080 06 007
AND THEN GOES OUT INTO THE CAVERNOUS DARK.  . . . . 103 00 016
WHY SHOULD I GO BECAUSE CASTARA GOES?  . . . . . 125 00 032
TO SAY I GO BECAUSE CASTARA GOES.  . . . . . . 125 00 054
MUCH CAUSE TO GO BECAUSE CASTARA GOES.  . . . . . 125 00 059
GOES MARCHING THRO' MY MIND. WHAT SENSE IS THIS? IT HAS NONE,  . 152 01 022
```

GOES   (CONTINUED)
     OF BLOOD TO OUR GREEN HUSTINGS GOES! 166 00 011
     IN THE VERY WAYS THAT THY LIFE GOES 169 00 005
GOING
     OF HIS GOING IN GALILEE! 028 07 002
     GAYGEAR, GOING GALLANT, GIRLGRACE -- C 059 0G 015
GOINGS
     KEEPS GRACE; THAT KEEPS ALL HIS GOINGS GRACES! 057 00 010
GOLD
     ONE BOUND O'ER DRIPPING GOLD A TURQUOISE-GEMM'D 002 00 060
     WITH NOT TO BE DISCOVER'D GOLD, ...   015 00 014
     THE GREY LAWNS COLD WHERE GOLD, WHERE QUICKGOLD LIES!   .   .   .   032 00 005
     NOR MIND NOR MAINSTRENGTH; GOLD GO GARLANDED 070 00 013
     IN WIDE THE WORLD'S WEAL; RARE GOLD, BOLD STEEL, BARE   .   .   .   070 00 017
     THUS WE SHALL PROFIT, WHILE GOLD COINAGE STILL 096 07 007
     THE BREAKING LEAVES OF GOLD ARE CURL'D UPON HER LIPS,   .   .   .   098 14 003
     A PURE GOLD LILY, BUT BY THE PURE GOLD LILY 098 15 001
     A PURE GOLD LILY, BUT BY THE PURE GOLD LILY 098 15 001
     GOLD GALLANT, FLOWERS MUCH LOOKED AT IN APRIL-WEATHER   .   .   .   098 16 002
     STARS LIKE GOLD TUFTS. 098 25 002
     AND AS SHE DWINDLES SHREDS HER SMOCK OF GOLD 103 00 013
     THAT HAS BOTH GOLD AND FEE. 109 09 002
     SHEWN HIM BOTH GOLD AND FEE; 109 11 002
     BECAUSE OF GOLD AND FEE. 109 12 002
     THE BALD AND BOLD BLINKING GOLD WHEN ALL'S DONE 143 00 004
GOLDEN
     WITH GOLDEN FILLETS AND RICH BLAZONRY, ...   001 07 006
     GIVE MYRRHY-THREADED GOLDEN FOLDS OF EASE. 011 00 012
     BUT YOU SHALL WALK THE GOLDEN STREET 022 00 023
     MORE GOLDEN THAN THE WORLD OF LIGHTS. 083 00 002
     WOULD NOT PUT OUT SOME TINY GOLDEN CENTRE. 098 22 006
     THE SKY MINTED INTO GOLDEN SEQUINS. 098 25 001
     STARS LIKE GOLDEN BEES. 098 25 003
     STARS LIKE GOLDEN ROWELS. 098 25 004
     OF ALL THE GOLDEN PRESS. 098 27 002
     THEY SEEM TO FOLD THE HILLS WITH GOLDEN CAPES! 104 00 011
     THEN HE SET SAIL IN A GOLDEN SHIP 109 06 003
     WITH A GOLDEN COMPANY. 109 06 004
     AND STAINED, AND KNOTS OF GOLDEN THREAD. 124 00 014
     TO THAT FIRST GOLDEN AGE OF GOSPEL TIMES 136 00 005
     OR SWEET THE GOLDEN GLUE 148 00 035
GOLDENGROVE
     OVER GOLDENGROVE UNLEAVING? 055 00 002
GOLDEN-GIRDLED
     TO GOLDEN-GIRDLED CYPRIS, -- CERES THERE 001 11 003
GOLDISH
     HARD AS HURDLE ARMS, WITH A BROTH OF GOLDISH FLUE 071 00 001
GOLD-VERMILION
     FALL, GALL THEMSELVES, AND GASH GOLD-VERMILION. 036 00 014
GOLD-WATER
     A GOLD-WATER PACTOLUS FRETS 003 00 027
GOLD-WISP
     THE GOLD-WISP, THE AIRY-GREY 049 00 003
GOLDNAILS
     THOSE GOLDNAILS AND THEIR GAYLINKS THAT HANG ALONG A LIME!   .   .   142 00 005
GOLDY
     NOT HONOUR IT?) ALE LIKE GOLDY FOAM 030 00 035
GONE
     AND OTHER SCIENCE ALL GONE OUT OF DATE 019 00 011
     NOW HER MALLOW-ROW IS GONE 025 00 021
     HOPE WAS TWELVE HOURS GONE! 028 15 004
     TOO LATE! LOST! GONE WITH THE GALE. 041 00 036
     WHEN SHROVETIDE, TWO YEARS GONE, ...   054 00 005
     MAN, HOW FAST HIS FIREDINT, HIS MARK ON MIND, IS GONE!   .   .   .   072 00 011
     AND YOU ARE GONE SO HEAVENLY FAR 081 00 034
     BUT I'M ALONE, FOR MY LOVE'S GONE 095 00 007
     LEAPS UP BEFORE MY VISION, -- THOU ART GONE. 098 33 002
     NOW ONE WORD MORE AND THEN I AM GONE INDEED, ...   102 01 055
     ONE HAS GONE TO THE KING'S STEWARD, ...   109 11 001
     SHE HAS GONE WITH HIM TO PARADISE. 109 39 003
     BY SPEECH SO SWEETLY BROKEN UP AND GONE. 125 00 027
     YOU TO BE GONE AND I LAG LAST -- 134 00 003
     TILL THE LONGING IS LESS AND THE GOOD GONE, ...   138 00 036
     AH YES! WHY, GET THEE GONE THEN! TELL THY MOTHER I WANT HER.   .   152 01 010
     MAKES GLADNESS AFTER HE IS GONE! 167 00 002
     CAT.   NOW HER MALLOW-ROW IS GONE   .   .   .   .   APPEN A 21
GONFALON
     STOOD CAPITAL, EMINENT, . . . GONFALON BEARER 098 28 005
GOOD
     THEY SHRIVE THEMSELVES AND CRY, ' GOOD SERVICE TO OUR GOD. '   .   .   001 05 009
     THAT SEED WHICH THE GOOD SOWER ONCE DID SOW, ...   017 00 007
     WHAT CAN IT BE, THIS GLEE? THE GOOD YOU HAVE THERE OF YOUR OWN?   .   028 18 008
     O WORLD WIDE OF ITS GOOD! 028 20 004
     I REMEMBER A HOUSE WHERE ALL WERE GOOD 034 00 001
     THOUGH GRIEF YIELD THEM NO GOOD 041 00 107
     WITH THAT WORLD OF GOOD. 042 00 027
     HOW IT DOES MY HEART GOOD, VISITING AT THAT BLEAK HILL,   .   .   .   048 00 021

GOOD   (CONTINUED)
       SOME GOOD! AND SO HE DOES LEAVE PATIENCE EXQUISITE, ... 051 00 008
       TOWARDS ALL OUR GHOSTLY GOOD 060 00 048
       MEN'S WITS TO THE THINGS THAT ARE: WHAT GOOD MEANS -- WHERE A GLANCE 062 00 004
       AND I ESTEEM'D THE SANDAL GOOD 081 00 083
       TUNE IT TO WORDS OF GOOD INTENT. 081 00 127
       ' O WHAT WILL YOU NOW, GOOD SERVINGMAN, ... 109 18 001
       AMONG THE LILIES AND THY GOOD DOMAIN. 123 00 006
       THE HATRED COMES WITH A GOOD GRACE FROM YOU: 125 00 029
       COME, DAPHNIS, GOOD VALERIAN, I WILL COME. 125 00 031
       THEN AT THE DOOR WHAT WORK THERE WAS, GOOD LACK, ... 135 00 005
       TILL THE LONGING IS LESS AND THE GOOD GONE, ... 138 00 036
       OR EVER DID FOR MY SAKE SOME GOOD DEED 140 00 002
       FOR GOOD GROWS WILD AND WIDE, ... 148 00 025
       THIS FAULT-NOT-FOUND-WITH GOOD 148 00 031
       HER GLASS IS BLEST BUT SHE AS GOOD AS BLIND 151 00 007
       BUT BOTH WILL SHARE ONE CELL. -- THIS WAS GOOD NEWS, GWENVREWI: 152 01 009
       THERE'S NONE BUT GOOD CAN BE GOOD, BOTH FOR YOU 157 00 021
       THERE'S NONE BUT GOOD CAN BE GOOD, BOTH FOR YOU 157 00 021
       NONE GOOD BUT GOD -- A WARNING WAVED TO 157 00 023
       ONE ONCE THAT WAS FOUND WANTING WHEN GOOD WEIGHED. 157 00 024
       BATHING: IT IS SUMMER'S SOVEREIGN GOOD. 159 00 013
       SO GOOD TO THOSE WHO LOOK FOR THEE, ... 167 00 011
       WISH US GOOD MORNING WHEN WE WAKE 167 00 021
GOODNIGHT
       BID YOUR PAPA GOODNIGHT. SWEET EXHIBITION! 097 00 007
       NO, LET THAT GO! I HAVE SAID GOODNIGHT TO SHAME. 102 01 042
GOODS
       (HE SHALL HAVE SUMMER GOODS AND TRIM 124 00 009
GORE
       WHO TREAD THE GRAPES ARE SPLAY'D WITH STRIPES OF GORE,   .   .   . 005 00 051
GORGED
       MUST YOU BE GORGED WITH PROOF? DID EVER SAND 005 00 041
GORGON'S
       WITH GORGON'S GEAR AND BAREBILL / THONGS AND FANGS.   .   .   . 050 00 014
GORSE
       OF DEWY GORSE BLURR'D WITH THE GOSSAMER FINE, ... 002 00 040
GOSHEN
       GOSHEN IS GREEN AND FAIR. 005 00 030
       NOT GOSHEN. WASTEFUL WIDE HUGE-GIRTHED NILE 005 00 031
GOSPEL
       OF THOSE WHO STROVE GOD'S GOSPEL TO CONFOUND 001 01 007
       OF THE GOSPEL PROFFER, A PRESSURE, A PRINCIPLE, CHRIST'S GIFT.   . 028 04 008
       TO THAT FIRST GOLDEN AGE OF GOSPEL TIMES 136 00 005
GOSSAMER
       OF DEWY GORSE BLURR'D WITH THE GOSSAMER FINE, ... 002 00 040
GOSSAMERS
       AS THE LAID GOSSAMERS OF MICHAELMAS 102 01 021
GOT
       THE TREASURE NEVER EYESIGHT GOT, (. 028 26 008
       THAT I'VE GOT A HOME. 132 00 006
GOTHIC
       NO FINISH'D PROOF WAS THIS OF GOTHIC GRACE 001 06 001
GOTTEN
       HAD GOTTEN HIM A WREATH OF SWEET SPRING-BROIDERY. 002 00 101
GRACE
       NO FINISH'D PROOF WAS THIS OF GOTHIC GRACE 001 06 001
       TRIUMPH OF AIRY GRACE AND PERFECT HARMONY. 001 07 009
       UNMINDFUL OF THEIR GRACE, THE ESCORIAL 001 08 005
       SUITING ITS GRACE WITH HIM OR HER? 025 00 026
       SWEET UNTO GOD, AND THE SWEETNESS IS GRACE: 027 00 044
       IN GRACE THAT IS CHARITY, GRACE THAT IS LOVE. 027 00 046
       IN GRACE THAT IS CHARITY, GRACE THAT IS LOVE. 027 00 046
       TOWER FROM THE GRACE TO THE GRACE, (. 028 03 008
       TOWER FROM THE GRACE TO THE GRACE, (. 028 03 008
       SO AT HOME, TIME WAS, TO HIS TRUTH AND GRACE 041 00 100
       GRACE THAT DAY GRACE WAS WANTED. 041 00 116
       GRACE THAT DAY GRACE WAS WANTED. ' 041 00 116
       ALL, IN THIS CASE, BATHED IN HIGH HALLOWING GRACE.   .   .   . 047 00 011
       GROOM, AND GRACE YOU, BRIDE, YOUR BED 052 00 002
       KEEPS GRACE: THAT KEEPS ALL HIS GOINGS GRACES! 057 00 010
       MAIDENGEAR, GALLANTRY AND GAIETY AND GRACE, (.   .   .   . 059 06 014
       BUT MOTHERS EACH NEW GRACE 060 00 022
       AND PLAYS IN GRACE HER PART 060 00 049
       YEA, WISH THAT THOUGH, WISH ALL, GOD'S BETTER BEAUTY, GRACE.   . 062 00 014
       TO GRACE THEM SPIRES ARE SHAPED WITH CORNER SQUINCHES: .   . 096 07 002
       WITH WHAT BOLD GRACE 102 01 061
       MAKING THE SHADOW SWEETER, A SPIRITUAL GRACE 107 04 015
       THE HATRED COMES WITH A GOOD GRACE FROM YOU: 125 00 029
       DEAR GRACE AND GIRDER OF MINE AND ME. 134 00 002
       GRACE LOVE YOUR LIPS! -- WHAT NEVER EAR 166 00 002
       THEO. SUITING ITS GRACE BY HIM AND HER?   .   .   .   .   . APPEN A 26
       ' HAIL BE THOU, FULL OF GRACE ARIGHT!   .   .   .   .   .   . APPEN D 05
       WITH GRACE TO SERVE HIM BY   .   .   .   . APPEN D 49
GRACEFULLY
       BUT HAS NOT LEARNT TO TAKE IT GRACEFULLY: 094 00 016
GRACELESS
       BEST IN: GRACELESS GROWTH, THOU HAST CONFOUNDED   .   .   . 044 00 007

110

GRACES
    KEEPS GRACE; THAT KEEPS ALL HIS GOINGS GRACES; • • • • • • 057 00 010
    WHAT PUT TAUGHT GRACES ON HIS COUNTRY LIP, • • • • • • 107 02 003
GRAFTED
    WE ARE SO GRAFTED ON HIS WOOD. • • • • • • • • 006 00 033
GRAIN
    DOES TEMPEST CARRY THE GRAIN FOR THEE? C • • • • • 028 31 008
    WHY? THAT MY CHAFF MIGHT FLY; MY GRAIN LIE, SHEER AND CLEAR. • • 064 00 009
GRAINS
    GRAINS FROM HIS DROOPING HEAD; • • • • • • • 007 00 013
GRANDEUR
    IT SEEMS; FOR GRANDEUR BARREN LEFT AND DULL • • • • 001 15 008
    THE WORLD IS CHARGED WITH THE GRANDEUR OF GOD. • • • • 031 00 001
    MANTLING PASSION IN A GRANDEUR, CRIMSON GRANDEUR. • • • • 152 02 037
    MANTLING PASSION IN A GRANDEUR, CRIMSON GRANDEUR. • • • • 152 02 037
GRANITE
    GROUND OF BEING, AND GRANITE OF IT; PAST ALL • • • • 028 32 006
    OR FRAY A GRANITE FROM THE PRECIPICE; • • • • • 080 12 005
GRANT
    GRANT THAT CLOSE-FOLDED PEACE THAT CLAD • • • • • 077 00 041
    BUT GRANT MY PENITENCE BEGUN; • • • • • • • 081 00 137
    AND GRANT OUR GLORYING MAY BE • • • • • • • 167 00 027
GRANTED
    HEARD! HAVE HEARD AND GRANTED • • • • • • • 041 00 115
    NOT GRANTED! -- ONLY . . . O ON THAT PATH YOU PACE • • • 047 00 013
GRAPES
    WHO TREAD THE GRAPES ARE SPLAY'D WITH STRIPES OF GORE, • • • 006 00 051
    WE SHOUT WITH THEM THAT TREAD THE GRAPES; • • • • • 006 00 012
    ON THISTLES THAT MEN LOOK NOT GRAPES TO GATHER, • • • • 007 00 002
    GRAPES GREW AND DROPS OF WINE WERE SHED. • • • • • 007 00 005
GRASP
    GRASP GOD, THRONED BEHIND • • • • • • • • 028 32 007
GRASPS
    OF GREENERY AND OLD EARTH GROPES FOR, GRASPS AT STEEP V • • • 149 8 012
GRASS
    I BEAR A BASKET LINED WITH GRASS; • • • • • • 010 00 001
    I BEAR A BASKET LINED WITH GRASS. • • • • • • 025 00 001
    WHO TO US ARE AS DEW UNTO GRASS AND TREE, • • • • • 026 00 038
    GRASS AND GREENWORLD ALL TOGETHER; • • • • • • 042 00 018
    AND LOUCHED LOW GRASS, HEAVEN THAT DOST APPEAL • • • • 058 00 002
    THEIR HARNESS BEAMS LIKE SCYTHES IN MORNING GRASS; • • • 104 00 006
    AND EACH A DINTED CIRCLE. THE GRASS WAS RED • • • • 107 04 011
    WHO LIES ON GRASS AND PORES UPON THE SKY • • • • • 117 00 003
    GALLOP ALONG THE MEADOW GRASS. -- • • • • • • 130 00 026
    ANG. I BEAR A BASKET LINED WITH GRASS. • • • • • APPEN A 01
GRASSES
    LAY ALONG THE GRASSES GREEN • • • • • • • 004 00 022
GRASSY
    FILLETED WITH GLASSY GRASSY QUICKSILVERY SHIVES AND SHOOTS C • • 159 00 038
GRATE
    WHILE HIS CRACK'D FLESH LAY HISSING ON THE GRATE; • • • 001 03 002
    HE RAIS'D THE CONVENT AS A MONSTROUS GRATE; • • • • 001 04 001
    WE HEAR OUR HEARTS GRATE ON THEMSELVES; IT KILLS • • • 068 00 009
GRATEFUL
    AND BRING YOUR OFFERINGS TO A GRATEFUL GOD, • • • • 005 00 011
GRAVE
    WARM-LAID GRAVE OF A WOMB-LIFE GREY; • • • • • 028 07 003
    AND GRAVE PAST GIRLHOOD EARNEST IN HER EYES. • • • • 136 00 020
GRAVER
    AND TO PUT GRAVER SINS ASIDE • • • • • • • 096 01 003
GRAVES
    FROM TEARS SHED OVER CHILDREN'S GRAVES. • • • • • 123 00 003
GREAT
    O BREATH OF IT BATHES GREAT HEAVEN ABOVE. • • • • • 027 00 045
    WINGS; SO SOME GREAT STORMFOWL, WHENEVER HE HAS WALKED HIS WHILE • 045 00 011
    DIDST FETTLE FOR THE GREAT GREY DRAYHORSE C • • • • 053 00 014
    GREAT AS NO GODDESS'S • • • • • • • • 060 00 027
    HAVING THE INFINITELY GREAT • • • • • • • 081 00 152
    GREAT BUTTER-BURR LEAVES FLOOR'D THE SLOPE CORPSE GROUND • • 107 04 009
    SHOULD CHOKE SWEET VIRTUE'S GLORY IS TIME'S GREAT GUILT. • • 136 00 002
    GREAT THECLA, THE PLUMED PASSIONFLOWER, • • • • • 145 00 042
GREATER
    AS PUBLIC IS MY GREATER PRIVACY, • • • • • • 012 01 007
    OUR REDCOATS, OUR TARS? BOTH THESE BEING, THE GREATER PART, • • 063 00 002
    BUT, HAVING THAT, BELIEVES IT GREATER STILL; • • • • 094 00 010
    FOR LOVE AND GREATER GLORY OF CHRIST. • • • • • 118 00 004
GREATNESS
    IT GATHERS TO A GREATNESS, LIKE THE OOZE OF OIL • • • 031 00 003
    ALL QUESTS SAVE, THE RECITAL OF THEIR GREATNESS; • • • 104 00 003
GREECE
    RIVALLED INSIGHT, BE RIVAL ITALY OR GREECE; • • • • 044 00 013
GREEK
    TWICE LOVELY, TINTED EASTERN, TURNED GREEK -- • • • • 136 00 015
GREEN
    SWIMMING, AND LANGUISH'D GREEN UPON THE DEEP • • • • 002 00 114
    THE MILES PROFOUND OF SOLID GREEN, AND BE • • • • • 002 00 123
    AND WITH COFFIN-BLACK HE BARR'D THE GREEN. • • • • 004 00 011

GREEN   (CONTINUED)
   LAY ALONG THE GRASSES GREEN 004 00 022
   GOSHEN IS GREEN AND FAIR. 005 00 030
   WHERE THE GREEN SWELL IS IN THE HAVENS DUMB, ... 009 00 007
   WHERE IN A NEWLY-DRAWN GREEN LITTER 010 00 005
   WHICH IN NEWLY DRAWN GREEN LITTER 025 00 005
   HACK AND RACK THE GROWING GREEN! 043 00 011
   LATE IN THE GREEN WEEKS OF APRIL 081 00 021
   WINKS AWAY ITS RING OF GREEN, ... 086 00 002
   MUST SEE THE GREEN SEAS ROLL V 088 00 009
   -- AND ON THEIR BRITTLE GREEN QUILS 098 07 001
   IN THE GREEN SPOTS OF THAT WOOD 098 10 001
   GIVE US OUR GREEN LOTS IN ANOTHER MEAD 098 15 005
   AND ROSING PART, ON PART DISPENSES GREEN; 100 00 003
   WITH SUCH A VIOLET SLIGHT THEIR DISTANCED GREEN? V . . . 100 00 008
   SLIGHT WITH SUCH VIOLET THEIR BRIGHT-MASK'D GREEN? V . . 100 00 009
   MASK'D WITH SUCH VIOLET DISALLOW THEIR GREEN? V 100 00 010
   SO LATE THE HOAR GREEN CHESTNUT BREAKS A BUD, ... 105 00 009
   THESE SHOULD HAVE STARV'D WITH THE GREEN BROODS OF SPRING, . 105 00 014
   BUT THE BOATMAN ON THE GREEN 131 00 005
   FOR BRIER, BOUGH, FURROW, OR GREEN GROUND 138 00 006
   UNDERNEATH, THEIR GLASSY BARREL, OF A FAIRY GREEN. . . . 141 00 006
   OF BLOOD TO OUR GREEN HUSTINGS GOES; 166 00 011
   AND SPITING SNOWS TO CHOKE THE GREEN. 166 00 032
   ANG. WHICH IN NEWLY-DRAWN GREEN LITTER . . . . APPEN A 05
   THEO. NOTHING GREEN OR GROWING BUT . . . . APPEN A 41
GREENERY
   OF GREENERY; IT IS OLD EARTH'S GROPING TOWARDS THE STEEP . 149 A 010
   OF GREENERY AND OLD EARTH GROPES FOR, GRASPS AT STEEP V . . 149 B 012
GREENEST
   OF LEAVES OF GREENEST FLESH. 005 00 034
GREENHOUSE
   UNDER THE CLOISTER-LIGHT OF GREENHOUSE VINES, ... 084 00 006
GREEN-WHITE
   WITH GREEN-WHITE APPLES ON THE BOUGH. 124 00 020
GREENNESS
   THAT THRIVE IN THE LOAMY GREENNESS OF THIS PLACE? . . . 122 00 015
GREENWORLD
   GRASS AND GREENWORLD ALL TOGETHER; 042 00 018
GREET
   FOR I GREET HIM THE DAYS I MEET HIM, AND BLESS WHEN I UNDERSTAND. . 028 05 008
   AND FAIR 'GAN HER TO GREET. . . . . APPEN D 04
GREETING
   RAPTUROUS LOVE'S GREETING OF REALER, OF ROUNDER REPLIES? . . 038 00 008
GREGORIANS
   LOUDER THE MONKS DRON'D OUT GREGORIANS SLOW; 001 13 006
GREGORY
   HOW THEN SHOULD GREGORY, A FATHER, HAVE GLEANED ELSE FROM SWARM- . 062 00 007
GREW
   BLADES OF MILAN IN CIRCLES RANG'D, GREW RUST 001 12 008
   GRAPES GREW AND DROPS OF WINE WERE SHED. 007 00 005
   BUT WATCHING WHILE THE COLOUR GREW 021 00 012
   IN STARRY, STARRY SHIRE IT GREW; 025 00 017
   IT IS GALILEE'S GROWTH; IT GREW AT GOD'S WILL 027 00 009
GREY
   A SOMBRE LENGTH OF GREY; FOUR TOWERS PLACED 001 01 003
   THE COPSE WAS NEVER MORE THAN GREY. 021 00 002
   WARM-LAID GRAVE OF A WOMB-LIFE GREY; 028 07 003
   HOPE HAD GROWN GREY HAIRS. 028 15 001
   THE DOWN-DUGGED GROUND-HUGGED GREY 028 26 002
   WHEN GREY SHOWERS GATHER AND GUSTS ARE COOL? -- 030 00 026
   THE GREY LAWNS COLD WHERE GOLD, WHERE QUICKGOLD LIES! . . 032 00 005
   THAT NEIGHBOUR-NATURE THY GREY BEAUTY IS GROUNDED . . . 044 00 006
   DIDST FETTLE FOR THE GREAT GREY DRAYHORSE C 053 00 014
   STILL MESSENGERS, SAD AND STEALING MESSENGERS OF GREY? -- C . 059 OL 004
   BY A GREY EYE'S HEED STEERED WELL, ONE CREW, FALL TO; . . 071 00 004
   ON TO LEDGES OF GREY CLOUD! 077 00 080
   AND IN GREY BANDS THE SUN SHOULD LIE STILL BORN; 090 00 003
   AND A GREY HEAVEN DOES THE HUSH'D EARTH HOUSE, ... 105 00 007
   AND BLUER GREY THE FLOCKS OF TREES LOOK IN THE PLAIN. . . 105 00 008
   EVEN SO MY THOUGHT THE ROSE AND GREY DISPOSES 108 00 007
GREYBELL
   AND AZURING-OVER GREYBELL MAKES 042 00 041
GREY-GREEN
   CONTROLL'D THEM TO A GREY-GREEN TEMPERATENESS, ... 107 04 014
GRIEF
   THOUGH GRIEF YIELD THEM NO GOOD 041 00 107
   NO WORST, THERE IS NONE. PITCHED PAST PITCH OF GRIEF, . . 065 00 001
   AND THAT GRIEF MASTERS JOY ON EARTH, ... 077 00 055
   ALL ALIKE IS GRIEF TO ME! 160 00 016
GRIEF'S
   A HEART'S-CLARION! AWAY GRIEF'S GASPING, JOYLESS DAYS, DEJECTION. . 072 00 017
GRIEVANCE
   BUT IS NOT THAT MY GRIEVANCE -- YOU PROMISED AND YOU FORGOT? . 128 00 006
GRIEVES
   O I ADMIRE AND SORROW! THE HEART'S EYE GRIEVES 157 00 001
GRIEVING
   MARGARET, ARE YOU GRIEVING 055 00 001

112

GRIM
WHEN THOU AT THE RANDOM GRIM FORGE, POWERFUL AMIDST PEERS, • • • 053 00 013
GRIMY
IN GRIMY VASTY VAULT. • • • • • • • • • • • • 060 00 102
RIGHT OFFSPRING OF YOUR GRIMY MOTHER EARTH! • • • • • • • 077 00 002
GRIND
HAILROPES HUSTLE AND GRIND THEIR • • • • • • • • • 041 00 027
THOUGHTS AGAINST THOUGHTS IN GROANS GRIND. C • • • • • • 061 00 014
GRIP
O HIS NIMBLE FINGER, HIS GNARLED GRIP! • • • • • • • 041 00 081
GRIZZLED
WHAT'S YONDER? GRIZZLED DYPHWYS DIM! • • • • • • 030 00 009
GROANS
THOUGHTS AGAINST THOUGHTS IN GROANS GRIND. C • • • • • • 061 00 014
OF JUST, MAJESTICAL, AND GIANT GROANS. • • • • • • • 075 00 004
GROINS
WITH BLAZONED GROINS, AND CROWNED WITH HUES OF MAJESTY. • • • 001 06 009
ARE THE GROINS OF THE BRAES THAT THE BROOK TREADS THROUGH, • • 056 00 010
GROOM
GROOM, AND GRACE YOU, BRIDE, YOUR BED • • • • • • • 052 00 002
GROPES
OF GREENERY AND OLD EARTH GROPES FOR, GRASPS AT STEEP V • • • 149 B 012
THE MORE SOME MONSTROUS HAND GROPES WITH CLAMMY FINGERS THERE, • • 152 01 014
GROPING
BY GROPING ROUND MY COMFORTLESS, THAN BLIND • • • • • 069 00 006
OF GREENERY: IT IS OLD EARTH'S GROPING TOWARDS THE STEEP • • • 149 A 010
GROSS
THE GROSS FLOCK CALL THEM QUAILS. • • • • • • • 005 00 016
HENCE SENSUAL GROSS DESIRES. • • • • • • • • 077 00 001
GROSS MIND DISCHARGING FOULED LAUGHTER! • • • • • • • 077 00 058
GROUND
THE HOARSE LEAVES CRAWL ON HISSING GROUND • • • • • • 003 00 005
BETWEEN THE TOWER-TOP AND THE GROUND • • • • • • • 015 00 029
TAKE A LESSON FROM THE GROUND! • • • • • • • • 024 00 014
IS IT ANYTHING TRUE? DOES IT GROW UPON GROUND? • • • • • 027 00 002
GROUND OF BEING, AND GRANITE OF IT: PAST ALL • • • • • 028 32 006
GREAT BUTTER-BURR LEAVES FLOOR'D THE SLOPE CORPSE GROUND • • • 107 04 009
DOWN UPON GROUND FELL SHE. • • • • • • • • 109 39 002
AND ONE TO EACH OF US IS HOLY GROUND! • • • • • • 116 00 003
DIES OFF IN HYACINTHED GROUND, • • • • • • • • 135 00 033
FOR BRIER, BOUGH, FURROW, OR GREEN GROUND • • • • • • 138 00 006
HOLLOW HOLLOW HOLLOW GROUND! C • • • • • • • 146 00 004
OFF TRUNDLED TIMBER AND SCOOPS OF THE HILLSIDE GROUND, C • • 146 00 004
GROUNDED
THAT NEIGHBOUR-NATURE THY GREY BEAUTY IS GROUNDED • • • • 044 00 006
GROUND-HUGGED
THE DOWN-DUGGED GROUND-HUGGED GREY • • • • • • 028 26 002
GROUNDLONG
WHO BREATHE, FROM GROUNDLONG BABYHOOD TO HOARY • • • • 075 00 006
GROUNDS
O GROUNDS OF HELL MAKE ROOM. • • • • • • • • 115 00 002
GROVE
THE TOWERS MUSICAL, QUIET-WALLED GROVE. • • • • • • 012 01 010
LEAVE IT WITH ITS GROVE HARD BY • • • • • • • 098 15 003
GROVEL
AND THERE FOR EVER GROVEL • • • • • • • • • 077 00 007
GROW
IS IT ANYTHING TRUE? DOES IT GROW UPON GROUND? • • • • • 027 00 002
NOW I GROW NUMB. MY TONGUE STRIKES ON THE GUM • • • • 080 10 006
THE WEIGHTY WEEKS WITHOUT HANDS GROW, • • • • • • 145 00 005
MAY'S BEAUTY MASSACRE AND WISPED WILD CLOUDS GROW • • • • 154 00 002
GROWING
AND GAIN'D THRO' GROWING DUSK THE STIRLESS BAY! • • • • 002 00 141
HACK AND RACK THE GROWING GREEN! • • • • • • • 043 00 011
A GROWING BURNISH BRIGHTER THAN BEFORE • • • • • • 151 00 004
THEO. NOTHING GREEN OR GROWING BUT • • • • • • APPEN A 41
GROWN
SO, GROWN FANTASTIC IN HIS PIETY, • • • • • • • 001 03 005
NOW ALL THINGS ROSY TURN'D; THE WEST HAD GROWN • • • • 002 00 019
HOPE HAD GROWN GREY HAIRS; • • • • • • • • 028 15 001
GROWN WICKED IN THE WICKED WARS. • • • • • • • 114 00 012
GROWS
MORE SWEET-FAMILIAR GROWS MY LOVE TO THEE. • • • • • 012 01 002
GROWS LESS AND LESS SWEET TO HIM, AND KNOWS NO CAUSE. • • • 014 03 014
LOVE, IT GROWS DARKER HERE AND THOU ART ABOVE! • • • • 020 00 005
AH! AS THE HEART GROWS OLDER • • • • • • • • 055 00 005
BUT WHEN SHE SIGHTS THE SUN SHE GROWS AND SIZES • • • • 103 00 006
FOR GOOD GROWS WILD AND WIDE, • • • • • • • 148 00 025
THE TIMES ARE NIGHTFALL, LOOK, THEIR LIGHT GROWS LESS! • • • 150 00 001
CALL NO SUCH MAIDEN ' MINE ' . THE DEEPER GROWS HER DEARNESS • 152 01 012
GROWTH
IT IS GALILEE'S GROWTH: IT GREW AT GOD'S WILL • • • • 027 00 009
GROWTH IN EVERYTHING -- • • • • • • • • 042 00 016
BEST IN! GRACELESS GROWTH, THOU HAST CONFOUNDED • • • • 044 00 007
WE FOUND WERE DABBLED WITH A COLOURING GROWTH, • • • • 098 09 002
GROWTHS
WITH GROWTHS OF MYRIAD FEELERS, CRYSTALLINE • • • • • 002 00 070

113

GRUDGE
    WHO COULD FORGIVE WITHOUT GRUDGE AFTER 077 00 057
GUARD
    A FAITHFUL GUARD OF INNER DARKNESS FIX'D -- 001 04 007
GUARDEDLY
    HE HEIGHTENS WORTH WHO GUARDEDLY DIMINISHES: 096 07 004
GUESS
    WE GUESS: WE CLOTHE THEE, UNSEEN KING, ... 023 00 013
    AFTER-COMERS CANNOT GUESS THE BEAUTY BEEN. 043 00 019
    SINCE, PROUD, IT CALLS THE CALLING MANLY, GIVES A GUESS . . 063 00 004
    SOMETHING WE GUESS OR KNOW: SOME SPIRITS START 126 00 007
    NO WISDOM CAN FORECAST BY GAUGE OR GUESS, ... 157 00 026
    BUT THEY CAN GUESS WHO HAVE TASTED OF 167 00 015
GUESSED
    NOR WAS EVER GUESSED WHAT FOR THE HEARINGS? C 028 26 008
    WHAT HEART HEARD OF, GHOST GUESSED: 055 00 013
GUESSES
    THE HEART GUESSES EASILY: IS IT THE SAME? -- 027 00 020
GUESSING
    O FATHER, NOT UNDER THY FEATHERS NOR EVER AS GUESSING . . 028 12 005
GUILE
    WHERE PHOEBUS WEEPS FOR HIM WHOM ZEPHYR'S GUILE . . . 001 11 007
    A SOMETHING IN HER FACE OF GUILE, ... 120 00 010
    AND SPEEDS UNCHECK'D HER MURDEROUS GUILE 120 00 030
GUILT
    THAT GUILT IS HUSHED BY, HEARTS ARE FLUSHED BY AND MELT -- . . 028 06 006
    SHOULD CHOKE SWEET VIRTUE'S GLORY IS TIME'S GREAT GUILT. . . 136 00 002
    AWAY OUR SIN AND GUILT SHOULD TAKE, ... APPEN D 45
GUILTY
    MANTLES THE GUILTY GLOVE, ... 060 00 039
    GUILTY OF SILENCE? QUITE, AS LADIES GO. 125 00 023
GUINEVERE
    -- O GUINEVERE 102 02 001
GULF
    AND SILENCE AND A GULF OF AIR. 015 00 040
GULF'S
    THE RECURB AND THE RECOVERY OF THE GULF'S SIDES, ... 028 32 003
GULLIES
    ADOWN THE CLATTERING GULLIES SWEPT THE RAIN: 001 13 002
    NOW HER AFTERDRAUGHT GULLIES HIM TOO DOWN: 041 00 061
GUM
    NOW I GROW NUMB. MY TONGUE STRIKES ON THE GUM 080 10 006
GURGLED
    MARKING THE SPOT, WHEN THEY HAVE GURGLED O'ER, ... 002 00 003
    GURGLED, WHERE THEY HAD SUNK, MELODIOUSLY, ... 002 00 111
GURGLING
    WHITE LOOM'D MY ROCK, THE WATER GURGLING O'ER, ... 002 00 142
    TO PAUSE -- THEN FROM HIS GURGLING BILL 077 00 083
GUSH
    GUSH! -- FLUSH THE MAN, THE BEING WITH IT, SOUR OR SWEET, . . 028 08 005
GUSHING
    AND DOWN THE WELKIN, GUSHING FREE, ... 077 00 085
GUST
    MOST WIDE YE ARE WHO CALL THIS GUST SIMOOM. 005 00 026
GUSTS
    THE ALTAR-TAPERS FLAR'D IN GUSTS: IN VAIN 001 13 005
    HIS LUSTY HANDS, IN GUSTS OF SCENTED WIND 002 00 088
    WHEN GREY SHOWERS GATHER AND GUSTS ARE COOL? -- . . . 030 00 026
GUSTY
    AND SILVER-SHOT WITH GUSTY LIGHT: 078 00 008
GWEN
    WHAT IS IT, GWEN, MY GIRL? WHY DO YOU HOVER AND HAUNT ME? . . 152 01 001
GWENVREWI
    BUT BOTH WILL SHARE ONE CELL. -- THIS WAS GOOD NEWS, GWENVREWI. . . 152 01 009
    PERHAPS WE STRUCK NO BLOW, GWENVREWI LIVES PERHAPS: . . 152 02 009
    WITH NO NOW, NO GWENVREWI. I MUST MISS HER MOST 152 02 053

HACK
    HACK AND RACK THE GROWING GREEN! 043 00 011
HACKED
    I ALL MY BEING HAVE HACKED IN HALF WITH HER NECK: ONE PART, , . 152 02 060
HACKS
    VESPILLO MY CENTURION HACKS OUT 080 09 005
HAEDUS-RISE
    AT HAEDUS-RISE, ARCTURUS-SET, ... 166 00 028
HAEMONY
    THAT NOT ARCADIA KNEW NOR HAEMONY. 107 01 017
HAGGARD
    O WHY ARE WE SO HAGGARD AT THE HEART, SO CARE-COILED, CARE-KILLED, C 059 0G 026
HAGGLE
    O HIDEOUS VICE TO HAGGLE YET 081 00 149
HAIL
    LIKE SHIVER'D RUBIES DANCE OR SHEEN OF SAPPHIRE HAIL. . . . 002 00 073

114

HAIL   (CONTINUED)
    TO FIELDS WHERE FLIES NO SHARP AND SIDED HAIL   • • • • • •   009 00 003
    WHO WOULD NOT SHELTER FROM THE HAIL?   • • • • •   081 00 076
    STRIKE, CHURL; HURL, CHEERLESS WIND, THEN; HELTERING HAIL • • •   154 00 001
    FOR HAIL UPON THE VINE NOR BREAK • • • • • •   166 00 029
    ' HAIL BE THOU, FULL OF GRACE ARIGHT! • • • • •   APPEN D 05
HAILROPES
    HAILROPES HUSTLE AND GRIND THEIR • • • • • •   041 00 027
HAIR
    THE DRENCHED HAIR OF SLABBY WEEDS THAT SWUNG • • • •   002 00 113
    CHAPLETS FOR DISHEVELLED HAIR, • • • • • •   024 00 021
    NOT THE LEAST LASH LOST; EVERY HAIR C • • • • •   059 06 020
    SEE; NOT A HAIR IS, NOT AN EYELASH, C • • • • •   059 06 020
    IS, HAIR OF THE HEAD, NUMBERED. • • • • • •   059 06 021
    AGE AND AGE'S EVILS, HOAR HAIR. • • • • • •   059 0L 011
    THAT EACH EYELASH OR HAIR • • • • • • •   060 00 003
    MORE SWEETLY SHADES HER STOLEN HAIR • • • • •   120 00 007
    AND LAPPED IN SHINING HAIR, ROLL TO THE BANK'S EDGE; THEN • •   152 02 019
HAIR-BOUND
    AND MAY HAS COME, HAIR-BOUND IN FLOWERS, • • • • •   026 00 013
HAIRS
    HOPE HAD GROWN GREY HAIRS, • • • • • • •   028 15 001
HALF
    AND HURLS FOR HIM, O HALF HURLS EARTH FOR HIM OFF UNDER HIS FEET. •   038 00 014
    AS HALF SHE HAD RIGHTED AND HOPED TO RISE • • • •   041 00 038
    WHAT DEATH HALF LIFTS THE LATCH OF, • • • • •   049 00 019
    BUT HALF THE PAINS HE SPENDS UPON HIS BOY, • • • •   097 00 004
    C AND HALF MISLIKE HER LOVELESS KISS.] • • • • •   120 00 013
    I ALL MY BEING HAVE HACKED IN HALF WITH HER NECK; ONE PART, • •   152 02 060
    THOUGHT HALF SO SWEET THERE IS NOT ONE • • • • •   167 00 007
HALF-CIRCLE
    BUT MOST IN A HALF-CIRCLE WATCH'D THE SUN; • • • •   002 00 116
HALF-DIVINE
    OR HALF-HUMAN, HALF-DIVINE? • • • • • • •   160 00 023
HALF-HOUR
    CRISP'D UP AND STARCHY FROM A SHORT HALF-HOUR • • •   107 03 003
HALF-HUMAN
    OR HALF-HUMAN, HALF-DIVINE? • • • • • • •   160 00 023
HALF-LIGHT
    THAT SHAPES IN HALF-LIGHT HIS DEPARTING RINGS, • • •   019 00 003
HALF-LIT
    AND PLEDGED PURPLY IN A HALF-LIT DELL. • • • • •   112 00 012
HALF-MESHING
    HER LIDS HALF-MESHING SHELTER FROM THE SKY. • • • •   099 00 006
HALL
    YET LIKE A LIGHTED EMPTY HALL • • • • • • •   023 00 010
    OUR COMPANY THRONGED THE HALL; • • • • • •   054 00 011
    THERE! THE HALL RUNG! • • • • • • • •   054 00 033
HALLOWED
    OUT OF HALLOWED BODIES BRED. • • • • • •   052 00 004
HALLOWING
    ALL, IN THIS CASE, BATHED IN HIGH HALLOWING GRACE. • •   047 00 011
HALLOWS
    CHRIST HOME, CHRIST AND HIS MOTHER AND ALL HIS HALLOWS. • •   032 00 014
HALLS
    HE RANG'D LONG CORRIDORS AND CORNIC'D HALLS, • • •   001 10 001
HALO'D
    CLUSTER'D IN TROOPS AND HALO'D BY THE LIGHT, • • •   002 00 036
HALT
    NO FLOWERS TO FIND, NO PLACE TO HALT, • • • •   081 00 159
    FLUSH THRO' THEIR HEAVING COLUMNS; WHEN THEY HALT • • •   104 00 010
HALVE
    TO HALVE THE BOWL OF PENMAEN POOL. • • • • •   030 00 012
HALVES
    AS HALVES OF SWEET-PEA-BLOSSOM ARE; • • • • •   081 00 044
HAMLETS
    ALLOWS THE SOUND OF BELLS IN HAMLETS ROUND • • •   080 04 006
HAMPSTEAD
    HAMPSTEAD WAS NEVER BRIGHT; AND WHATEVER MISS CULLY'S CHARMS •   128 00 011
HAND
    AND MORE, ON EACH HAND, THICKEN, AND APPEAR • • •   002 00 030
    INTO MY HAND HE GIVES A HOST FOR PREY, • • • •   005 00 017
    BEHOLD AT ELIM WELLS ON EVERY HAND • • • • •   005 00 023
    SO TRICKLE FROM YOUR HAND? • • • • • • •   005 00 042
    AND A QUINCE IN HAND, -- NOT ONE • • • • •   010 00 009
    HAD SHE A QUINCE IN HAND? YET GAZE; • • • • •   010 00 019
    BUT NOT THE HAND THAT WROUGHT THEM ALL; • • • •   023 00 008
    MY HAND UPON MY LIPS I LAY; • • • • • •   023 00 037
    AND LEAD ME CHILD-LIKE BY THE HAND • • • • •   023 00 047
    I KISS MY HAND • • • • • • • • •   028 05 001
    KISS MY HAND TO THE DAPPLED-WITH-DAMSON WEST; • •   028 05 005
    LEFT HAND, OFF LAND, I HEAR THE LARK ASCEND, • •   035 00 005
    HOME WAS HARD AT HAND • • • • • • •   041 00 019
    OF RUINOUS SHRINE NO HAND OR, WORSE, • • • •   041 00 090
    ROBBERY'S HAND IS BUSY TO • • • • • •   041 00 091
    HEAD, HEART, HAND, HEEL, AND SHOULDER • • •   049 00 010
    WHERE YOU CAN LIFT YOUR HAND • • • • • •   060 00 076

HAND   (CONTINUED)
        AND HER HAND LEAVES HIS LIGHT 060 00 112
        HAND RATHER, MY HEART LO! LAPPED STRENGTH, C 064 00 011
        HE! HAND TO MOUTH HE LIVES, AND VOIDS WITH SHAME; 075 00 009
        NOW KNOWN AND HAND AT WORK NOW NEVER WRONG. 076 00 008
        THE POINT FAST IN, AND MY LEFT HAND 080 13 004
        I'LL TAKE IN HAND THE BLADY STONE 080 14 001
        WHO KNELT WERE FOR THE LORD'S RIGHT HAND; 081 00 094
        SEE ON ONE HAND 100 00 001
        SUCKS CLOSE THE ACORN; AS THE HAND AND GLOVE; 101 00 003
        THE HAND DRAWS OFF THE GLOVE; THE ACORN-CUP 101 00 009
        NO I'LL NOT HAZARD IT. ONLY HIS HAND. 102 01 025
        NOW LET ME SEE YOU, YOU LARGE PRINCELY HAND, ...   102 01 043
        YET THIS COULD BE NO OTHER'S HAND THAN HIS, ...   102 01 045
        NOW I AM MINDED TO TAKE PIPE IN HAND 105 00 001
        IF IT BE A WHITE ROSE IN HIS HAND, ...   109 22 001
        ' IS IT A LILY IN YOUR HAND, ...   109 33 001
        BEFORE OR BEHIND OR FAR OR AT HAND 138 00 007
        HER HAND FROM HEAVEN TO TURN A MILL -- 139 00 004
        THAT HE WILL OUT OF HAND AND HEARTILY 140 00 005
        HOLDS TILL HAND ACHES AND WONDERS WHAT IS THERE; 151 00 008
        THE MORE SOME MONSTROUS HAND GROPES WITH CLAMMY FINGERS THERE, ...   152 01 014
        WHEN 'TS LIGHT I QUENCHED! ITS ROSE, TIME'S ONE RICH ROSE, MY HAND,   .   .   .   152 02 050
        FROM THY HAND OUT, SWAYED ABOUT 155 00 003
        ' I HAVE TALL DAUGHTERS DEAR THAT HEED MY HAND; 158 00 002
HANDLE
        THE STRETCHING PALACE LAY AS HANDLE FIX'D. 001 04 004
        HANDLE THE FIG, SUCK THE FULL-SAPP'D VINE-SHOOT. 005 00 038
        UNCHILL'D I HANDLE STINGING SNOW; 080 02 001
HANDMAIDEN
        ' OUR LORD HIS HANDMAIDEN, I WIS.   .   .   .   .   APPEN D 25
HAND'S
        BUT EACH A HAND'S BREADTH FURTHER THAN THE NEXT. 091 00 007
HANDS
        HIS LUSTY HANDS, IN GUSTS OF SCENTED WIND 002 00 088
        YOUR HANDS HAVE BORNE THE TENT-POLES! ON YOU PLOD; 005 00 007
        O FEEL-OF-PRIMROSE HANDS, O FEET 022 00 021
        ' ALL HANDS FOR THEMSELVES ' THE CRY RAN THEN; 041 00 042
        CLUTCHED HANDS THROUGH CLASPED KNEES! 054 00 021
        BUT HARRY -- IN HIS HANDS HE HAS FLUNG 054 00 035
        I GIVE COMMANDS FOR WATER FOR MY HANDS; 080 09 003
        FROM HANDS NOW CLAMMY WITH STRANGE BLOOD. 080 10 004
        I BITE MY HANDS, MY LOOKS I SHROUD; 081 00 065
        THEY HAVE BOUND HIS FEET, THEY HAVE BOUND HIS HANDS; 109 13 003
        THE WEIGHTY WEEKS WITHOUT HANDS GROW, ...   145 00 005
        HEAVED DRUM ON DRUM; BUT HANDS ALSO 145 00 006
        SHE HELD HER HANDS TO, LIKE IN PRAYER; 145 00 048
HANDSOME
        MANNERLY-HEARTED! MORE THAN HANDSOME FACE -- 047 00 009
HANDY
        WITH A ROPE'S END ROUND THE MAN, HANDY AND BRAVE -- 028 16 003
HANG
        GOD WITH HONOUR HANG YOUR HEAD, ...   052 00 001
        LET INCENSE HANG ACROSS THE ROOM 077 00 019
        HANG OF A TREBLE SIZE. 088 00 004
        THOSE GOLDNAILS AND THEIR GAYLINKS THAT HANG ALONG A LIME; 142 00 005
        HANG AS STILL AS HAWK OR HAWKMOTH, C 159 00 026
HANGDOG
        THIS, BY DESPAIR, BRED HANGDOG DULL! BY RAGE, ...   070 00 019
HANGING
        THE HANGING SNOWS RUSH DOWN AND BARE 080 04 004
        THAT THE HANGING HONEYSUCK, THE DOGEARED HAZELS IN THE COVER   .   .   .   159 00 009
HANGS
        PILLOWY AIR HE TREADS A TIME AND HANGS 050 00 010
        CHURLSGRACE, TOO, CHILD OF AMANSSTRENGTH, HOW IT HANGS OR HURLS   .   .   .   071 00 012
        SAY, O'ER IT HANGS A WATER-CLOUD 081 00 056
        THE LOCK OF CLOUDS BETIMES AND HANGS THE DAY, ...   098 31 003
        THAT EARLY 'SPERSES, AND HIGH HANGS THE DAY, ...   098 31 006
        PIERCE HER; SHE HANGS UPON THE FLAME-CASED SUN, ...   103 00 010
HANKER
        THEREWITH TO HANKER FOR THE SMALL! 081 00 153
HANKS
        FALLOW, FOAM-FALLOW, HANKS -- FALL'N OFF THEIR RANKS, ...   144 00 007
HAPLESS
        BUT, HAPLESS YOUTH, ANTINOUS THE WHILE 001 11 005
HAPPIER
        OR IF THEY TRY IT, I AM HAPPIER THEN; 012 02 010
        MY HAPPIER WORLD, WHEREIN 060 00 116
        MOTHERS ARE DOUBTLESS HAPPIER FOR THEIR BABES 123 00 001
HAPPINESS
        AND I CAN TEACH HIM HAPPINESS 124 00 007
HAPP'D
        THEY HAVE HAPP'D HIM WITH THE SAND AND STONE 109 15 001
HAPPY
        THE HAPPY LEAFING. IT IS SO WITH ME; 014 01 006
        AND HAPPY PROMISES FULFILL'D. 015 00 008
        SEEK GOD'S HOUSE IN HAPPY THRONG; 024 00 025

                                        116

HAPPY   (CONTINUED)
     HAPPY THE FATHER, MOTHER OF THESE! TOO FAST: •   •   •   •   •   •   157 00 005
HARBOUR
     BOUND FOR THE HARBOUR AND YOUR CREW.   •   •   •   •   •   •   •   021 00 014
     AS VOID AS CLOUDS THAT HOUSE AND HARBOUR NONE,   •   •   •   •   •   107 01 001
HARD
     HARD BY A ROYAL PALACE AND A ROYAL TOMB.   •   •   •   •   •   •   001 01 009
     IT SEEM'D SO HARD AND DISMAL THING.   •   •   •   •   •   •   •   004 00 031
     HARD DOWN WITH A HORROR OF HEIGHT: •   •   •   •   •   •   •   028 02 007
     WHAT NONE WOULD HAVE KNOWN OF IT, ONLY THE HEART, BEING HARD AT BAY,   028 07 008
     HOME WAS HARD AT HAND   •   •   •   •   •   •   •   •   •   041 00 019
     PATIENCE, HARD THING! THE HARD THING BUT TO PRAY,   •   •   •   •   068 00 001
     PATIENCE, HARD THING! THE HARD THING BUT TO PRAY,   •   •   •   •   068 00 001
     HARD AS HURDLE ARMS, WITH A BROTH OF GOLDISH FLUE   •   •   •   071 00 001
     AND HARD MEN FEEL A SOFTENING TOUCH: •   •   •   •   •   •   077 00 030
     WHEN SKIES ARE HARD AS ANY STONE,   •   •   •   •   •   •   •   081 00 008
     BUT NOW ARE FLED, AND HARD TO FIND   •   •   •   •   •   •   081 00 045
     IT WAS A HARD THING TO UNDO THIS KNOT.   •   •   •   •   •   091 00 001
     IT WAS A HARD THING TO UNDO THIS KNOT.   •   •   •   •   •   091 00 010
     LEAVE IT WITH ITS GROVE HARD BY   •   •   •   •   •   •   •   098 15 003
     I HAVE FILL'D, THAT HARD TO FILL IS,   •   •   •   •   •   •   098 19 007
     THE RINGED BLINDWORM HARD BESIDE.   •   •   •   •   •   •   •   106 00 004
     ON BRAZED BARGE AND HARD BEHIND   •   •   •   •   •   •   •   166 00 039
HARDEN'D
     SO HARDEN'D IS IT IN THIS DEARTH   •   •   •   •   •   •   •   018 00 011
HARDER
     DAILY MAKE ME HARDER HOPE AND DEARER LOVE.   •   •   •   •   •   168 00 016
HARDEST
     AND EVER, IF BOUND HERE HARDEST HOME,   •   •   •   •   •   •   030 00 033
HARD-HURLED
     NOT A LIGHTNING OF FIRE HARD-HURLED. C   •   •   •   •   •   •   028 34 008
HARDLY
     IT IS HARDLY A PROPER TREAT FOR A BIRTHDAY TO REST IN HER ARMS.   •   128 00 012
HARDY-HANDSOME
     WHO HAVE WATCHED HIS MOULD OF MAN, BIG-BONED AND HARDY-HANDSOME   •   053 00 002
HARE
     MARCUS HARE, HIGH HER CAPTAIN,   •   •   •   •   •   •   •   041 00 045
HARK
     HARK THE MOLTEN MELODY: •   •   •   •   •   •   •   •   077 00 086
     THEN OFTEN THE EARS IN A NEW FASHION HARK,   •   •   •   •   •   113 00 007
     WELL, AFTER ALL! AH BUT HARK --   •   •   •   •   •   •   •   138 00 010
     HARK, HEARER, HEAR WHAT I DO; LEND A THOUGHT NOW, MAKE BELIEVE   •   159 00 001
HARM
     -- CAN I DO ANY HARM?   •   •   •   •   •   •   •   •   •   125 00 017
     WHAT WORK? WHAT HARM'S DONE? THERE IS NO HARM DONE, NONE YET;   •   152 02 008
HARMONIES
     WHENCE SPRING THE JEWELL'D HARMONIES   •   •   •   •   •   •   077 00 138
     WE TUNED TO ONE KEY AND MADE THEIR HARMONIES.   •   •   •   •   098 02 004
HARMONY
     TRIUMPH OF AIRY GRACE AND PERFECT HARMONY.   •   •   •   •   •   001 07 009
HARM'S
     WHAT WORK? WHAT HARM'S DONE? THERE IS NO HARM DONE, NONE YET;   •   152 02 008
HARNESS
     THEIR HARNESS BEAMS LIKE SCYTHES IN MORNING GRASS;   •   •   •   104 00 006
HARP
     PLUCK THE HARP AND BREATHE THE HORN: •   •   •   •   •   •   024 00 011
HARRY
     BUT HARRY -- IN HIS HANDS HE HAS FLUNG   •   •   •   •   •   054 00 035
     HE LEANS TO IT, HARRY BENDS, LOOK, BACK, ELBOW, AND LIQUID WAIST   •   071 00 009
     HEAVEN COMFORT SENDS, BUT HARRY IT AWAY,   •   •   •   •   •   089 00 005
HARSHNESS
     I CAN HEAR THE HARSHNESS   •   •   •   •   •   •   •   •   132 00 002
HARVEST
     BEHOLD WE HAVE THE JOY IN HARVEST: •   •   •   •   •   •   006 00 002
     IN HARVEST AND IN GARNERING,   •   •   •   •   •   •   •   008 00 015
     STARTLE THE POOR SHEEP BACK! IS THE SHIPWRACK THEN A HARVEST, C   •   028 31 008
     LIKE PHAROH'S EARS OF WINDY HARVEST DRY   •   •   •   •   •   117 00 006
     BID JOY BACK, HAVE AT THE HARVEST, KEEP HOPE PALE.   •   •   •   •   154 00 004
HASTEN'D
     YOU MET ME, I HAD HASTEN'D DOWN;   •   •   •   •   •   •   081 00 089
HAT
     FOR A BEAUTY-BOW TO HIS HAT,   •   •   •   •   •   •   •   144 00 016
HATE
     AND THEN I HATE THE MOST THAT LORE   •   •   •   •   •   •   015 00 033
     AND HATE THE ILL-VISAGED CURSING TARS,   •   •   •   •   •   114 00 010
     AND JAMES SHALL HATE HIS FADED RED,   •   •   •   •   •   •   114 00 011
     TO THE BARGAIN OF ITS HATE TO THROW   •   •   •   •   •   •   145 00 020
     FOE OF ZEUS AND HATE OF ALL   •   •   •   •   •   •   •   160 00 028
     BUT IF THOU HATE ME WHO LOVE THEE, ALBEIT   •   •   •   •   •   161 00 002
     THOU CANST NOT HATE SO MUCH AS I DO LOVE THEE.   •   •   •   •   161 00 004
HATED
     WHAT IF I HATED FLATTERY? SAY YOU DO: •   •   •   •   •   125 00 028
     FAMILIAR AND SO HATED BY THE SICK: V   •   •   •   •   •   •   125 00 042
     HATED AND TOO FAMILIAR TO -- ----; V   •   •   •   •   •   •   125 00 043
HATRED
     THE HATRED COMES WITH A GOOD GRACE FROM YOU: •   •   •   •   125 00 029
HAUNT
     WHAT IS IT, GWEN, MY GIRL? WHY DO YOU HOVER AND HAUNT ME?   •   •   •   152 01 001

117

HEAR   (CONTINUED)
   LEFT HAND, OFF LAND, I HEAR THE LARK ASCEND, ... 035 00 005
   WHY, HEAR HIM, HEAR HIM BABBLE AND DROP DOWN TO HIS NEST, . . . 039 00 010
   WHY, HEAR HIM, HEAR HIM BABBLE AND DROP DOWN TO HIS NEST, . . . 039 00 010
   TO MY CREATING THOUGHT, WOULD NEITHER HEAR 066 00 006
   WE HEAR OUR HEARTS GRATE ON THEMSELVES: IT KILLS 068 00 009
   TO HEAR THE SHEEP-BELLS DIMLY DIE 077 00 071
   TO HEAR HIS STRAIN DESCEND LESS LOUD 077 00 079
   WOULD I COULD HEAR THE OTHER PILATES SHOUT. 080 01 005
   I HEAR THE MULTITUDE TRAMP BY. 080 11 001
   AT LAST I HEAR THE VOICE WELL KNOWN: 081 00 001
   AT LAST I HEAR THE VOICE I KNEW. 081 00 025
   YOU HEAR NOR CARE OF LOVE AND PAIN. 081 00 035
   YOU HEAR AND, ALTER'D, DO NOT HEAR 081 00 041
   YOU HEAR AND, ALTER'D, DO NOT HEAR 081 00 041
   THE OTHERS HEARD: I COULD NOT HEAR 081 00 101
   HERCLOT'S PREACHINGS I'LL NO LONGER HEAR: 096 05 001
   WHEN THE WIND DROPS YOU HEAR THE SKYLARKS SING: 098 03 005
   WHEN CUCKOO CALLS AND I MAY HEAR, ... 098 37 001
   I HEAR A NOISE OF WATERS DRAWN AWAY. 112 00 001
   SO IS IT WITH MY FRIENDS, I NOTE, TO HEAR 119 00 005
   I CAN HEAR THE HARSHNESS 132 00 002
   HARK, HEARER, HEAR WHAT I DO: LEND A THOUGHT NOW, MAKE BELIEVE . 159 00 001
   WE ARE THERE, WHEN WE HEAR A SHOUT 159 00 008
   WOE IS ME, WHAT DO I HEAR? 160 00 032
   I BID THE BOYS AND MAIDENS HEAR. 166 00 004
   WORD NEVER WAS SUCH NEWS TO HEAR, ... 167 00 006
HEARD
   FROM BOTH OF WHOM A CHANGELESS NOTE IS HEARD. 019 00 004
   BETWEENS I HEARD THE WATER STILL 021 00 044
   YOUR PASSING STEPS, I NEVER HEARD 021 00 048
   AND TRUTH IS HEARD, WITH TEARS IMPEARLED, ... 023 00 035
   WORD, THAT HEARD AND KEPT THEE AND UTTERED THEE OUTRIGHT. . . 028 30 008
   HE THOUGHT HE HEARD SAY 041 00 051
   HEARD: HAVE HEARD AND GRANTED 041 00 115
   HEARD: HAVE HEARD AND GRANTED 041 00 115
   FORWARD-LIKE, BUT HOWEVER, AND LIKE FAVOURABLE HEAVEN HEARD THESE. 048 00 048
   WHAT HEART HEARD OF, GHOST GUESSED: 055 00 013
   HEARD UNHEEDED, LEAVES ME A LONELY BEGAN. 066 00 014
   TO SING SCARCE HEARD, AND SINGING FILL 077 00 077
   THE OTHERS HEARD: I COULD NOT HEAR 081 00 101
   ARE HEARD, THAT CRY ' SHE DOES REPENT ', ... 081 00 123
   SHE HEARD THE HUNT THE MORROW MORNING 109 24 001
   SHE HEARD BUT KNOCKINGS THREE. 109 29 002
   I HEARD HER SAY, POOR POOR AFFLICTED SOUL, -- 111 00 011
   THE EARNEST-HEARTED MAIDEN SAT AND HEARD. 136 00 032
   HEARD YET, THE MUSES' MAN, TODAY, ... 166 00 003
   AND THE ANGEL'S WORDS HAD HEARD, ... APPEN D 22
HEARDST
   THOU HEARDST ME TRUER THAN TONGUE CONFESS 028 02 003
HEARER
   HARK, HEARER, HEAR WHAT I DO: LEND A THOUGHT NOW, MAKE BELIEVE . 159 00 001
HEARERS
   THEMSELVES LIVE SINGING AND THEIR HEARERS KILL. 096 02 002
HEARING
   NIGHT ROARED, WITH THE HEART-BREAK HEARING A HEART-BROKE RABBLE, . 028 17 005
   BESIDE THEM, ABOUT THE HEDGES, HEARING HIM: 113 00 008
   HOW SAYS TRUSTY HEARING? THAT SHALL BE BELIEVED: 168 00 006
HEARINGS
   NOR WAS EVER GUESSED WHAT FOR THE HEARINGS? C 028 26 008
HEARS
   BY MANY BLOWS AND BANES: BUT NOW HEARS ROAR 050 00 006
   EARTH HEARS NO HURTLE THEN FROM FIERCEST FRAY. 073 00 008
HEARSE-OF-ALL
   WOMB-OF-ALL, HOME-OF-ALL, HEARSE-OF-ALL NIGHT. C 061 00 002
HEARSES
   WHY SHOULD THEIR FOOLISH BANDS, THEIR HOPELESS HEARSES . . . 089 00 001
HEARST
   AND THE PRAYER THOU HEARST ME MAKING 041 00 113
HEART
   MY BANKRUPT HEART HAS NO MORE TEARS TO SPEND. 014 03 004
   I CANNOT BUOY MY HEART ABOVE: 018 00 005
   SPEAK! WHISPER TO MY WATCHING HEART 023 00 049
   THE HEART GUESSES EASILY: IS IT THE SAME? -- 027 00 020
   MARY THE VIRGIN, WELL THE HEART KNOWS, ... 027 00 021
   THE SWOON OF A HEART THAT THE SWEEP AND THE HURL OF THEE TROD . 028 02 006
   AND FLED WITH A FLING OF THE HEART TO THE HEART OF THE HOST. . 028 03 005
   AND FLED WITH A FLING OF THE HEART TO THE HEART OF THE HOST. . 028 03 005
   MY HEART, BUT YOU WERE DOVEWINGED, I CAN TELL. 028 03 006
   WHAT NONE WOULD HAVE KNOWN OF IT, ONLY THE HEART, BEING HARD AT BAY, 028 07 008
   FATHER AND FONDLER OF HEART THOU HAST WRUNG: 028 09 007
   DO YOU! -- MOTHER OF BEING IN ME, HEART, ... 028 18 004
   OF THE SODDEN-WITH-ITS-SORROWING HEART, ... 028 27 004
   AH! THERE WAS A HEART RIGHT! 028 29 001
   HEART, GO AND BLEED AT A BITTERER VEIN FOR THE 028 31 003
   REBUFFED THE BIG WIND. MY HEART IN HIDING 036 00 007
   I WALK, I LIFT UP, I LIFT UP HEART, EYES, ... 038 00 005

~ AND, EYES, HEART, WHAT LOOKS, WHAT LIPS, YET GAVE YOU A • • • • 038 00 007
THE HEART REARS WINGS BOLD AND BOLDER • • • • • • • 038 00 013
THERE, EYES THEM, HEART WANTS, CARE HAUNTS, FOOT FOLLOWS KIND, • • 040 00 013
WHAT THE HEART IS! WHICH, LIKE CARRIERS LET FLY -- • • • • 047 00 005
BY IT, HEAVENS, BEFALL HIM! AS A HEART CHRIST'S DARLING, DAUNTLESS; • 048 00 014
HOW IT DOES MY HEART GOOD, VISITING AT THAT BLEAK HILL, • • • 048 00 021
HEAD, HEART, HAND, HEEL, AND SHOULDER • • • • • • • 049 00 010
TO OWN MY HEART: I YIELD YOU DO COME SOMETIMES; BUT • • • 051 00 004
BEING ANOINTED AND ALL; THOUGH A HEAVENLIER HEART BEGAN SOME • • 053 00 006
THY TEARS THAT TOUCHED MY HEART, CHILD, FELIX, POOR FELIX RANDAL; • 053 00 011
HIS HEART UP AT THE STRAIN; • • • • • • • • 054 00 027
AH! AS THE HEART GROWS OLDER • • • • • • • • 055 00 005
WHAT HEART HEARD OF, GHOST GUESSED: • • • • • • • 055 00 013
TO, WITH NO TONGUE TO PLEAD, NO HEART TO FEEL; • • • • 058 00 003
AND WHAT IS EARTH'S EYE, TONGUE, OR HEART ELSE, WHERE • • • 058 00 009
O WHY ARE WE SO HAGGARD AT THE HEART, SO CARE-COILED, CARE-KILLED, C 059 0G 026
ABOUT MAN'S BEATING HEART. • • • • • • • • 060 00 050
DISREMEMBERING, DISMEMBERING ALL NOW. HEART, YOU ROUND ME RIGHT • 061 00 007
HOME AT HEART, HEAVEN'S SWEET GIFT; THEN LEAVE, LET THAT ALONE. • 062 00 013
BUT FRAIL CLAY, NAY BUT FOUL CLAY, HERE IT IS: THE HEART, • • 063 00 003
HAND RATHER, MY HEART LO! LAPPED STRENGTH, C • • • • 064 00 011
ENGLAND, WHOSE HONOUR O ALL MY HEART WOOS, WIFE • • • • 066 00 005
WISEST MY HEART BREEDS DARK HEAVEN'S BAFFLING BAN • • • • 066 00 012
THIS NIGHT! WHAT SIGHTS YOU, HEART, SAW; WAYS YOU WENT! • • 067 00 003
MY OWN HEART LET ME MORE HAVE PITY ON; LET • • • • 069 00 001
YAWN'D LIKE LONG FURROW IN THE HEART; • • • • • • 077 00 064
AND THEN MY HEART GOES NEAR TO BREAK, • • • • • • 080 06 007
WHISPERS ' IF THOU HAVE WARMTH AT HEART • • • • • • 080 11 004
THIS HEART IS WARM TO YOU ALONE; • • • • • • • 081 00 129
HER CHOICE IN ROSES KNOWS BY HEART! • • • • • • 083 00 022
WHERE MY HEART LISTS. • • • • • • • • • 088 00 002
AND WEAR IT THUS, A PECTORAL, BY MY HEART. • • • • • 102 01 028
AND I MUST HAVE THE CENTRE IN MY HEART • • • • • • 102 03 007
IN HIS HEART SAID EVERYONE • • • • • • • • 109 15 003
AND EVERY HEART THINK LOATHINGLY • • • • • • • 114 00 015
YEA, CRUSH'D MY HEART, AND MADE ME DUMB, • • • • • 118 00 012
MY HEART IRREGULARLY SHOOK, • • • • • • • • 135 00 009
O HEART, HAVE DONE, YOU BEAT YOU BEAT SO HIGH, • • • • 135 00 035
THE MOTION OF THAT MAN'S HEART IS FINE • • • • • • 142 00 006
GOD LIGHTEN YOUR DARK HEART -- BUT NO, • • • • • • 145 00 027
LEARN HOW THE HEART IS HENCE; • • • • • • • 148 00 006
AND MORE AND MORE TIMES LACES ROUND AND ROUND MY HEART, • • • 152 01 013
MY HEART, WHERE HAVE WE BEEN? WHAT HAVE WE SEEN, MY MIND? • • 152 02 001
WHAT IS VIRTUE? VALOUR: ONLY THE HEART VALIANT. • • • • 152 02 042
WHO, LIKE ME, KNOWING HIS NATURE TO THE HEART HOME, NATURE'S BUSINESS, 152 02 044
THOSE DEARER, MORE DIVINE BOONS WHOSE HAVEN THE HEART IS. • • 152 C 026
ME SHEW MERCY FROM MY HEART • • • • • • • • 155 00 022
WHAT NEED I STRAIN MY HEART BEYOND MY KEN? • • • • • 157 00 034
HIS HEART AT FARMING, WHAT BETWEEN • • • • • • • 166 00 030
DAYLIGHT TO HEAD AND TREAT TO HEART, • • • • • • 167 00 018
SEE, LORD, AT THY SERVICE LOW LIES HERE A HEART • • • • 168 00 003

HEARTBURN
I AM GALL, I AM HEARTBURN. GOD'S MOST DEEP DECREE • • • • 067 00 009

HEARTH
WHERE STANDS NO HOST AT DOOR OR HEARTH • • • • • • 023 00 011

HEARTH'S
OUR HEARTS' CHARITY'S HEARTH'S FIRE, C • • • • • • 028 35 008

HEARTILY
THAT HE WILL OUT OF HAND AND HEARTILY • • • • • • 140 00 005

HEART-AT-EASE
TOM HEART-AT-EASE, TOM NAVVY: HE IS ALL FOR HIS MEAL • • • 070 00 004

HEART-BEAT
RUINOUS HEART-BEAT, WANDERING, DEATH. • • • • • • 081 00 053

HEART-BREAK
NIGHT ROARED, WITH THE HEART-BREAK HEARING A HEART-BROKE RABBLE, • 028 17 005

HEART-BROKE
NIGHT ROARED, WITH THE HEART-BREAK HEARING A HEART-BROKE RABBLE, • 028 17 005

HEART-BROKEN
SLUMBER'D AT LAST IN ONE SWEET, DEEP, HEART-BROKEN CLOSE. • • • 002 00 135

HEART-FLESHED
THE HEAVEN-FLUNG, HEART-FLESHED, MAIDEN-FURLED • • • • 028 34 003

HEART-FORSOOK
WHEN HENRY, HEART-FORSOOK, • • • • • • • • 054 00 031

HEART-SONG
THAT HERE PERSONAL TELLS OFF THESE HEART-SONG POWERFUL PEALS? -- • 141 00 002

HEART-SPRINGS
CUCKOO, BIRD, AND OPEN EAR WELLS, HEART-SPRINGS, DELIGHTFULLY SWEET, 146 00 002

HEART-THROE
BUT HERE WAS HEART-THROE, BIRTH OF A BRAIN, • • • • • 028 30 007

HEART'S
FOR HOW TO THE HEART'S CHEERING • • • • • • • 028 26 001
JESU, HEART'S LIGHT, • • • • • • • • • 028 30 001
MEND FIRST AND VITAL CANDLE IN CLOSE HEART'S VAULT: • • • • 046 00 010
TOLD TALES WITH WHAT HEART'S STRESS • • • • • • 054 00 023
NOWHERE. NATURAL HEART'S IVY, PATIENCE MASKS • • • • • 068 00 006
O I ADMIRE AND SORROW! THE HEART'S EYE GRIEVES • • • • 157 00 001

HEART'S-CLARION
    A HEART'S-CLARION! AWAY GRIEF'S GASPING, JOYLESS DAYS, DEJECTION. •   •   072 00 017
HEARTS
    OPEN WIDE YOUR HEARTS THAT THEY • • • • • • • • •   •   •   024 00 023
    THE PRAISE OF THE LIPS AND THE HEARTS OF US BRING TO THEE,   •   •   026 00 035
    FOR LIPS AND HEARTS THEY BELONG TO THEE • • • • •   •   •   026 00 037
    THAT GUILT IS HUSHED BY, HEARTS ARE FLUSHED BY AND MELT --   •   •   028 06 006
    OUR HEARTS' CHARITY'S HEARTH'S FIRE, C • • • • • •   •   •   028 35 008
    FELLED AND FURLED THEM, THE HEARTS OF OAK! • • • •   •   •   041 00 006
    WE HEAR OUR HEARTS GRATE ON THEMSELVES! IT KILLS • •   •   •   068 00 009
    WHEN WAKING HEARTS CAN PARDON MUCH • • • • • •   •   •   077 00 029
    AND PRIDE IS NERVELESS AND HEARTS MEEK. • • • • •   •   •   077 00 038
    THAT MANY CENTRES FOUND IN MANY HEARTS? • • • •   •   •   107 02 005
    BE IN THY SERVANTS' HEARTS AS WELL, • • • • • •   •   •   169 00 002
HEARTSORE
    SELDOMER HEARTSORE! THAT TREADS THROUGH, PRICKPROOF, THICK   •   •   070 00 007
HEAT
    THEY TELL ITS STORY THUS! AMIDST THE HEAT • • • • •   •   •   001 02 001
    THE SUN WHOSE VAST AFFLICTIVE HEAT • • • • • •   •   •   080 02 002
    I HAVE DRAWN HEAT FROM THIS CONTAGIOUS SUN! • • •   •   •   103 00 018
    SHE BRIMS HER BATH IN COLD OR HEAT! • • • • •   •   •   139 00 002
HEATHENISH
    SUCH HEATHENISH MISADVENTURE DOGS ONE SIN. V • •   •   •   102 02 013
    SUCH HEATHENISH MISADVENTURE DOGG'D ONE SIN. V • •   •   •   102 02 013
HEATHPACKS
    WIRY HEATHPACKS, FLITCHES OF FERN, • • • • • •   •   •   056 00 011
HEAVE
    MY CRIES HEAVE, HERDS-LONG! HUDDLE IN A MAIN, A CHIEF-   •   •   065 00 005
    BEAT, HEAVE AND THE STRONG MOUNTAIN TIRE • • • •   •   •   080 05 002
HEAVED
    HEAVED DRUM ON DRUM! BUT HANDS ALSO • • • • •   •   •   145 00 006
HEAVEN
    THAT BATTLED GODS FOR HEAVEN! BRILLIANT-HUED, • •   •   •   001 07 005
    RIS'N FROM THE DEEPS TO GAZE ON SUN AND HEAVEN, • •   •   •   002 00 035
    IN FORTY DAYS REACH'D HEAVEN FROM EARTH! • • •   •   •   006 00 024
    BEAR HIM TO HEAVEN ON EASEFUL WINGS. • • • •   •   •   007 00 015
    NO INFLUENTIAL HEAVEN EVER WORE! • • • • • •   •   •   014 02 007
    MY PRAYERS MUST MEET A BRAZEN HEAVEN • • • • •   •   •   018 00 001
    MY HEAVEN IS BRASS AND IRON MY EARTH: • • • •   •   •   018 00 009
    I MUST O'ERTAKE THEE AT ONCE AND UNDER HEAVEN • •   •   •   020 00 015
    O BREATH OF IT BATHES GREAT HEAVEN ABOVE, • • • •   •   •   027 00 045
    NOR FIRST FROM HEAVEN (AND FEW KNOW THIS) • •   •   •   028 06 003
    LILY SHOWERS -- SWEET HEAVEN WAS ASTREW IN THEM. C   •   •   028 21 008
    WHAT BY YOUR MEASURE IS THE HEAVEN OF DESIRE, • •   •   •   028 26 007
    HEAVEN AND EARTH ARE WORD OF, WORDED BY? -- • • •   •   •   028 29 006
    FOR ALL THEY SHINE SO, HIGH IN HEAVEN, • • • • •   •   •   030 00 019
    OF HEAVEN WHAT BOON TO BUY YOU, BOY, OR GAIN • •   •   •   047 00 012
    WOULD BRANDLE ADAMANTINE HEAVEN WITH RIDE AND JAR, DID   •   •   048 00 046
    FORWARD-LIKE, BUT HOWEVER, AND LIKE FAVOURABLE HEAVEN HEARD THESE.   048 00 048
    AND LOUCHED LOW GRASS, HEAVEN THAT DOST APPEAL • •   •   •   058 00 002
    BLUE BE IT! THIS BLUE HEAVEN • • • • • • •   •   •   060 00 086
    OF IT. ANGELS FALL, THEY ARE TOWERS, FROM HEAVEN -- A STORY   •   •   075 00 003
    ALIEN FROM YOURS AS HEAVEN FROM NADIR-FIRES! • •   •   •   077 00 004
    WHERE LIQUID HEAVEN SAPPHIRE-PALE • • • • • •   •   •   077 00 099
    CAUGHT FROM ANGELS' WINGS IN HEAVEN, • • • • •   •   •   077 00 110
    TOUCH'D FROM HEAVEN IN SWEET DREAMS! • • • • •   •   •   077 00 126
    OF A MASTERING HEAVEN UTTERLY BLUE! • • • • •   •   •   078 00 002
    CHOOSE, ONE FOR HELL AND ONE FOR HEAVEN! ' • • •   •   •   081 00 106
    HEAVEN AND EVERY FIELD, ARE STILL • • • • • •   •   •   085 00 002
    HEAVEN COMFORT SENDS, BUT HARRY IT AWAY, • • • •   •   •   089 00 005
    THE VAST OF HEAVEN STUNG WITH BRILLIANT STARS. • •   •   •   098 21 000
    FLARES HIS WET BRILLIANCE IN THE DINTLESS HEAVEN. • •   •   •   098 34 002
    AND A GREY HEAVEN DOES THE HUSH'D EARTH HOUSE, • •   •   •   105 00 007
    ALONE UPON THE HILL-TOP, HEAVEN O'ER HIM, • • • •   •   •   107 01 008
    ' HEAVEN MAKE THE TIME BE SHORT, ' SHE SAID, • • •   •   •   109 03 001
    HEAVEN MAKE IT SWEET TO YOU, ' SHE SAID, • • • •   •   •   109 03 003
    WHEN EYES THAT CAST ABOUT IN HEIGHTS OF HEAVEN • •   •   •   113 00 001
    THE UNENDURING FALLOWS OF THE HEAVEN? • • • • •   •   •   122 00 006
    THE EARTH AND HEAVEN, SO LITTLE KNOWN, • • • • •   •   •   130 00 001
    AS SURE AS HEAVEN IT IS • • • • • • • •   •   •   133 00 006
    NOR I NOR HEAVEN WOULD HAVE IT BE. • • • • •   •   •   134 00 004
    HER HAND FROM HEAVEN TO TURN A MILL -- • • • •   •   •   139 00 004
    HEAVEN TURNED ITS STARLIGHT EYES BELOW • • • • •   •   •   145 00 046
    APART WIDE AND NEW-NESTLE AT HEAVEN MOST HIGH. • •   •   •   149   A 006
    THEY TOUCH HEAVEN, TABOUR ON IT! HOW THEIR TALONS SWEEP   •   •   149   A 007
    HEAVEN WHOM SHE CHILDS US BY. • • • • • • •   •   •   149   A 011
    HEAVEN WITH IT WHOM SHE CHILDS THINGS BY. V • • •   •   •   149   B 013
    ROUND AND ROUND THEY CAME AND FLASHED TOWARDS HEAVEN: O THERE,   •   •   152 02 029
    THE YOUNG CHIEF OF THE BLESS'D OF HEAVEN • • • •   •   •   160 00 011
    NOT OUT OF HOPE OF HEAVEN FOR ME • • • • •   •   •   170 00 002
HEAVENFALLEN
    AND WITH HEAVENFALLEN FRESHNESS DOWN FROM MOORLAND STILL BRIMS,   159 00 039
HEAVENGRAVEL
    HEAVENGRAVEL? WOLFSNOW, WORLDS OF IT, WIND THERE? • •   •   •   041 00 028
HEAVEN-ENFORCED
    THE HEAVEN-ENFORCED ANSWER COMES, • • • • • •   •   •   081 00 144
HEAVEN-FLUNG
    THE HEAVEN-FLUNG, HEART-FLESHED, MAIDEN-FURLED • • •   •   •   028 34 003

HEAVEN-HANDLING
  CHEER WHOM THOUGH? THE HERO WHOSE HEAVEN-HANDLING FLUNG ME, FOOT TROD   064 00 012
HEAVEN-HAVEN
  REMEMBER US IN THE ROADS, THE HEAVEN-HAVEN OF THE REWARD; 028 35 003
HEAVEN-ROYSTERER
  BUILT THOROUGHFARE: HEAVEN-ROYSTERERS, C 072 00 002
HEAVEN-VAULT
  ARE AFOOT: HEAVEN-VAULT FAST PURPLING PORTENDS, C 152 02 031
HEAVENLIER
  BEING ANOINTED AND ALL: THOUGH A HEAVENLIER HEART BEGAN SOME   . .   053 00 006
HEAVENLY
  AT MORN WE FOUND THE HEAVENLY BREAD, ...   006 00 008
  WHEN HEAVENLY VALES SO THICK SHALL STAND 008 00 016
  LET IT FLOW FOR HEAVENLY MIRTH; 024 00 010
  BRIGHT SUN LANCED FIRE IN THE HEAVENLY BAY; 041 00 022
  WITH HEAVENLY CITHERN FROM HIGH CHOIR, ...   077 00 013
  MELT AS FROM A HEAVENLY CHRISM; 077 00 062
  AND YOU ARE GONE SO HEAVENLY FAR 081 00 034
HEAVEN'S
  HOME AT HEART, HEAVEN'S SWEET GIFT: THEN LEAVE, LET THAT ALONE. . .   062 00 013
  WISEST MY HEART BREEDS DARK HEAVEN'S BAFFLING BAN 066 00 012
  WITH HEAVEN'S LIGHTS HIGH HUNG ROUND, OR, MOTHER-GROUND   . .   070 00 011
  THE WROUGHT RIM OF HEAVEN'S FONT, -- 077 00 112
  NOT FOR HEAVEN'S SAKE! NOT TO BE 170 00 015
  GABRIEL, FROM HEAVEN'S KING   . . . .   APPEN D 01
  FOR SO GOD'S SON, THE HEAVEN'S LIGHT, ...   APPEN D 06
  AND HEAVEN'S BLISS, WHEN OUR TIME IS TO DIE, ...   APPEN D 47
HEAVENS
  LO, LINKED HEAVENS WITH MILKY WAYS! 010 00 021
  THAT LESS IS HEAVENS HIGHER EVEN YET 014 01 012
  HOVERS OFF, THE JAY-BLUE HEAVENS APPEARING 028 26 003
  THRUSH'S EGGS LOOK LITTLE LOW HEAVENS, AND THRUSH 033 00 003
  DOWN ALL THAT GLORY IN THE HEAVENS TO GLEAN OUR SAVIOUR; . .   038 00 006
  BY IT, HEAVENS, BEFALL HIM! AS A HEART CHRIST'S DARLING, DAUNTLESS!   048 00 014
  JARR'D DOWN THE BALANCED STORM: THE BLEEDING HEAVENS . . .   102 02 004
HEAVENWARD
  FLOWERS DO OPE THEIR HEAVENWARD EYES 024 00 015
HEAVES
  TO ME, SO ARCH-ESPECIAL A SPIRIT AS HEAVES IN HENRY PURCELL, .   045 00 002
HEAVING
  FLUSH THRO' THEIR HEAVING COLUMNS: WHEN THEY HALT 104 00 010
HEAVY
  THO' FAR OR SICK OR HEAVY OR STILL 081 00 018
HEAVYHEADED
  THIS SIDE, THAT SIDE HURLING A HEAVYHEADED HUNDREDFOLD   . .   059 06 024
HECTOR'S
  DROOP'D O'ER THE BROWS LIKE HECTOR'S CASQUE, AND SWAY'D   . .   002 00 042
HEDGE
  [HOVER-FLOAT TO THE HEDGE BROW.] 138 00 040
HEDGEROW
  FROM ANY HEDGEROW, ANY COPSE, ...   098 18 001
HEDGES
  BESIDE THEM, ABOUT THE HEDGES, HEARING HIM; 113 00 008
  AND HEDGES BREAK, AND LOSE THE KINE, ...   114 00 002
HEED
  BY A GREY EYE'S HEED STEERED WELL, ONE CREW, FALL TO;   . .   071 00 004
  I CANNOT CALM, I CANNOT HEED. 081 00 072
  ' I HAVE TALL DAUGHTERS DEAR THAT HEED MY HAND: . . .   158 00 002
HEEDS
  DEATH WITH A SOVEREIGNTY THAT HEEDS BUT HIDES, BODES BUT ABIDES; .   028 32 008
HEEL
  AS A SKATE'S HEEL SWEEPS SMOOTH ON A BOW-BEND: THE HURL AND GLIDING .   036 00 006
  HEAD, HEART, HAND, HEEL, AND SHOULDER 049 00 010
HEELS
  THEIR CRUTCHES SHALL CAST FROM THEM, ON HEELS OF AIR DEPARTING, .   152 C 023
HEFT
  CREATURES ALL HEFT, HOPE, HAZARD, INTEREST. 157 00 008
HEIFER'S
  THICK-FLEECED BUSHES LIKE A HEIFER'S EAR V 098 11 001
HEIGHT
  THERE ON A LONG AND SQUARED HEIGHT 015 00 041
  HARD DOWN WITH A HORROR OF HEIGHT; 028 02 007
  BLUE-BEATING AND HOARY-GLOW HEIGHT; OR NIGHT, STILL HIGHER, . .   028 26 005
  HER WILD HOLLOW HOARLIGHT HUNG TO THE HEIGHT C   . . .   061 00 004
  AND WHEN THE SILENT HEIGHT WERE WON, ...   077 00 075
HEIGHTENING
  THE HEIGHTENING DAWN WITH MILKY ORIENCE 098 30 002
HEIGHTENS
  HE HEIGHTENS WORTH WHO GUARDEDLY DIMINISHES;   . . .   096 07 004
HEIGHTS
  WHEN EYES THAT CAST ABOUT IN HEIGHTS OF HEAVEN 113 00 001
HEIR
  REALM BOTH CHRIST IS HEIR TO AND THERE REIGNS. 048 00 032
  ELSE, BUT IN DEAR AND DOGGED MAN? -- AH, THE HEIR . . .   058 00 010
HELD
  AND HELD A CROSS OF FLOWERS, IN PURPLE BLOOM;   . . .   001 10 006
  -- YES FOR A TIME THEY HELD AS WELL 101 00 001

HELD   (CONTINUED)
    THEY HAVE HELD HIS EYES WITH BLINDFOLD BANDS 109 13 001
    OF A FINGERNAIL HELD TO THE CANDLE, C 137 00 002
    SHE HELD HER HANDS TO, LIKE IN PRAYER; 145 00 048
HELEN
    DID HELEN STEAL MY LOVE FROM ME? 095 00 001
    IT MIGHT BE HELEN, JANE, OR KATE, ... 095 00 005
HELL
    BEFORE ME, THE HURTLE OF HELL 028 03 002
    NOT THAT HELL KNOWS REDEEMING, ... 041 00 117
    WHAT HELL HOPES SOON THE SNATCH OF, ... 049 00 020
    FROM GOD AND MAN, IS HELL NO DOUBT. 080 01 004
    CHOOSE, ONE FOR HELL AND ONE FOR HEAVEN! ' 081 00 106
    O GROUNDS OF HELL MAKE ROOM. 115 00 002
    SHE WAS ADMIRED, THE SPIRIT OF HELL 145 00 017
    OUT OF HELL BY LOVING THEE! 170 00 016
HELL-ROOK
    SQUANDER THE HELL-ROOK RANKS SALLY TO MOLEST HIM;   .   .   . 048 00 018
HELL'S
    BARS OR HELL'S SPELL THWARTS, THIS TO HOARD UNHEARD,   .   . 066 00 013
HELP
    AND I NOT HELP, NOR WORD NOW OF SUCCESS: 150 00 005
    HELP ME, SIR, AND SO I WILL. 155 00 020
HELP'D
    HELP'D BY THE DARKNESS OF A BLOCK OF COPSE 107 03 014
HELPS
    HE SAYS HIS SCIENCE HELPS HIM NOT TO LOOK 014 02 013
HELTERING
    STRIKE, CHURL! HURL, CHEERLESS WIND, THEN; HELTERING HAIL   .   . 154 00 001
HEMPEN
    WITH HEMPEN STRANDS IN SPRAY -- 144 00 006
HENCE
    HENCE SENSUAL GROSS DESIRES, ... 077 00 001
    LEARN HOW THE HEART IS HENCE; 148 00 006
    OR THEY GO RICH AS ROSELEAVES HENCE THAT LOATHSOME CAME HITHER!   . 152 C 024
    THE RACE OF MAN; AND HENCE I FELL. 160 00 031
HENCEFORTH
    HENCEFORTH LET YOUR SOULS ALWAY 024 00 029
    NOW BE MY PRIDE THEN PERFECT, ALL ONE PIECE. HENCEFORTH   .   . 152 02 038
HENRY
    TO ME, SO ARCH-ESPECIAL A SPIRIT AS HEAVES IN HENRY PURCELL,   .   . 045 00 002
    HENRY, BY THE WALL, ... 054 00 012
    WHEN HENRY, HEART-FORSOOK, ... 054 00 031
HERCLOT'S
    HERCLOT'S PREACHINGS I'LL NO LONGER HEAR! 096 05 001
HERD
    KINGS HERD IT ON THEIR SUBJECT DROVES 166 00 005
    BUT JOVE'S THE HERD THAT KEEPS THE KINGS -- 166 00 006
HERDS-LONG
    MY CRIES HEAVE, HERDS-LONG; HUDDLE IN A MAIN, A CHIEF-   .   . 065 00 005
HEREAFTER
    ME LIVE TO MY SAD SELF HEREAFTER KIND, ... 069 00 002
HERESY
    OF THE OUTWARD SENTENCE LOW LAYS HIM, LISTED TO A HERESY, HERE.   . 045 00 004
HERETIC
    WHILE FROM THE PULPIT IN A HERETIC LAND 001 05 001
HERETOFORE
    GIVE US THE TALE OF BRICKS AS HERETOFORE! 005 00 049
HERITAGE
    MIGHT SO ATTAIN THEIR HERITAGE, ... 015 00 012
    LOVE BY MONITION, HERITAGE, OR LOT, ... 102 03 014
HERO
    TO HERO OF CALVARY, CHRIST,'S FEET -- 028 08 007
    PRIDE, ROSE, PRINCE, HERO OF US, HIGH-PRIEST, ... 028 35 007
    SAVE MY HERO, O HERO SAVEST. 041 00 112
    SAVE MY HERO, O HERO SAVEST. 041 00 112
    CHEER WHOM THOUGH? THE HERO WHOSE HEAVEN-HANDLING FLUNG ME, FOOT TROD   064 00 012
HEROIC
    UNSEEN, THE HEROIC BREAST NOT OUTWARD-STEELED, ... 073 00 007
HEW
    WHEN WE DELVE OR HEW -- 043 00 010
    WHEN WE HEW OR DELVE; 043 00 018
HEWS
    YET GOD (THAT HEWS MOUNTAIN AND CONTINENT, ... 073 00 009
HID
    THE KING'S FRIEND TOLD THE THING THAT WAS HID 109 12 001
    BE HID BEHIND 127 00 020
    ONCE I TURNED FROM THEE AND HID, ... 155 00 009
HIDE
    BY VISUAL COMPULSION, TILL I HIDE 012 02 005
    THEM -- BROAD IN BLUFF HIDE HIS FROWNING FEET LASHED! RACED   .   . 071 00 013
    AND, HIDE IT THOUGH SHE DOES, ONE MAY DIVINE 094 00 011
HIDEOUS
    O HIDEOUS VICE TO HAGGLE YET 081 00 149
    HIDEOUS DASHED DOWN, LEAVING EARTH A WINTER WITHERING   .   .   . 152 02 052

HO
    LITTLE I RECK HO! LACKLEVEL IN, IF ALL HAD BREAD! 070 00 009
HOAR
    WITH A THIN FLOATING VEIL OF WATER HOAR. 002 00 004
    HOAR MESSMATE, HOBS AND NOBS WITH HIM 030 00 011
    AGE AND AGE'S EVILS, HOAR HAIR, ...   059 OL 011
    SO LATE THE HOAR GREEN CHESTNUT BREAKS A BUD, ...   105 00 009
HOARD
    BOUNDEN BALES OR A HOARD OF BULLION? -- 041 00 010
    BARS OR HELL'S SPELL THWARTS, THIS TO HOARD UNHEARD, .   .   066 00 013
HOARDS
    THE ABYSMAL OCEAN HOARDS OF STRANGE AND RARE. 002 00 055
HOAR-HALLOWED
    DRESS, HOAR-HALLOWED SHRINES UNVISITED! 041 00 092
HOAR-HUSKED
    BUILT OF CHANCEQUARRIED, SELFQUAINED, HOAR-HUSKED ROCKS .   .   159 00 037
HOARLIGHT
    HER WILD HOLLOW HOARLIGHT HUNG TO THE HEIGHT C .   .   .   061 00 003
HOARSE
    THE HOARSE LEAVES CRAWL ON HISSING GROUND 003 00 005
HOARY
    WHO BREATHE, FROM GROUNDLONG BABYHOOD TO HOARY .   .   .   075 00 006
HOARY-GLOW
    BLUE-BEATING AND HOARY-GLOW HEIGHT! OR NIGHT, STILL HIGHER, .   .   028 26 005
HOBS
    HOAR MESSMATE, HOBS AND NOBS WITH HIM 030 00 011
HOLD
    MY EYES HOLD YET THE RINDS AND BRIGHT 025 00 033
    AND HOLD AT CHRIST'S EMPLOYMENT. 049 00 014
    HE HAD NO WORK TO HOLD 054 00 026
    FRIGHTFUL, SHEER, NO-MAN-FATHOMED. HOLD THEM CHEAP .   .   065 00 010
    THE PANG OF TARTARUS, CHRISTIANS HOLD, ...   080 01 001
    TO HOLD ME QUITE FIX'D IN THE SELFSAME PLIGHT! 080 13 000
    YOU ASK WHY CAN'T CLARISSA HOLD HER TONGUE. .   .   .   096 04 001
    HOLD HIM. -- 102 01 023
    THEO. MY EYES HOLD YET THE RINDS AND BRIGHT .   .   .   APPEN A 33
HOLDING
    THIS FAITH EACH DAY DEEPER BE MY HOLDING OF, ...   168 00 015
HOLDS
    THAT READS OR HOLDS THE ASTROLOGIC LORE, ...   014 02 002
    THAT HOLDS NO PROMISE OF SUCCESS! 015 00 034
    SHE HOLDS HIGH MOTHERHOOD 060 00 047
    SILENCE HOLDS BREATH UPON HER THRONE, ...   077 00 033
    HOPE HOLDS TO CHRIST THE MIND'S OWN MIRROR OUT .   .   .   151 00 001
    HOLDS TILL HAND ACHES AND WONDERS WHAT IS THERE! .   .   151 00 008
HOLES
    THE SHAPEN FLAGS AND DRILLED HOLES OF SKY, ...   012 02 011
HOLIER
    YOU SEE BUT WITH A HOLIER MIND -- 081 00 040
HOLIEST
    ' HOLIEST, LOVELIEST, BRAVEST, ...   041 00 111
HOLINESS
    SOMETHING OF THY HOLINESS. 155 00 008
    IN THE SPIRIT OF THY HOLINESS, ...   169 00 003
HOLLOW
    IN A HOLLOW LUSH AND DAMP, ...   004 00 007
    HER WILD HOLLOW HOARLIGHT HUNG TO THE HEIGHT C .   .   .   061 00 003
    WORK THROUGH A COVER'D COPSE WHOSE HOLLOW ROUNDING .   .   112 00 003
    HOLLOW HOLLOW HOLLOW GROUND! C 146 00 004
    HOLLOW HOLLOW HOLLOW GROUND; C 146 00 004
    HOLLOW HOLLOW HOLLOW GROUND; C 146 00 004
HOLLOWING
    FORWARD SHE LEANS, WITH HOLLOWING BACK, STOCK-STILL, .   .   099 00 001
HOLLOW'D
    INTO HIS HOLLOW'D PALM SHOULD MOAN THE BLAST! 090 00 002
HOLLOWS
    THEY CHEW'D THE CUD IN HOLLOWS DEEP. 092 00 002
    IN HOLLOWS OF HER FORM THE SHADOW CLINGS! 099 00 006
    WHOSE GAPS AND HOLLOWS ARE NOT BROWZED UPON, .   .   .   107 01 002
HOLY
    DOES IT SMELL SWEET TOO IN THAT HOLY PLACE? -- .   .   .   027 00 043
    BECAUSE THE HOLY GHOST OVER THE BENT 031 00 013
    AND ONE TO EACH OF US IS HOLY GROUND! 116 00 003
    MAKE ME PURE, LORD! THOU ART HOLY! 129 00 006
    THE HOLY THREE IN ONE. 133 00 004
    HERE TO THIS HOLY WELL SHALL PILGRIMAGES BE, .   .   .   152 C 018
    IN THE HOLY GHOST THE PARACLETE 169 00 010
    'TIS THROUGH THE HOLY GHOST THAT WROUGHT .   .   .   .   APPEN D 16
    THROUGH TH' HOLY GHOST HIS MIGHT. .   .   .   .   .   APPEN D 34
HOME
    A CLOISTER'D CONVENT FIRST, THE PROUDEST HOME .   .   .   001 01 006
    THE PRIDE OF FAITH, AND HOME OF STERNEST PIETY. .   .   001 08 009
    THE CHOICEST REMNANTS THENCE! -- SUCH HOME FORLORN .   001 15 003
    THUS FRANCES SIGHED AT HOME, WHILE LUKE 021 00 050
    I SHALL COME HOME TO THEE, MOTHER OF MINE. .   .   .   027 00 024
    AND EVER, IF BOUND HERE HARDEST HOME, ...   030 00 033
    CHRIST HOME, CHRIST AND HIS MOTHER AND ALL HIS HALLOWS. .   .   032 00 014

126

HOPES
    AT HOPES SO EVIL-HEAVEN'D AS MINE ARE.   • • • • • • • •   014 02 014
    BARELY A SIGH TO THOUGHT OF HOPES FORGONE.   • • • • • • 014 03 009
    THOSE SWEET HOPES QUELL WHOSE LEAST ME QUICKENINGS LIFT,   • • • 048 00 037
    WHAT HELL HOPES SOON THE SNATCH OF.   • • • • • • • 049 00 020
    THAT, HOPES THAT, MAKESBELIEVE, THE MEN MUST BE NO LESS;   • • 063 00 005
    MY HOPES AND MY UNWORTHINESS,   • • • • • • • • 118 00 009
HORIZON-ROUND
    THEN FIND IN THE HORIZON-ROUND   • • • • • • • 015 00 031
HORIZONTALS
    THE VIGOROUS HORIZONTALS, EACH WAY FALL   • • • • 012 02 003
HORN
    PLUCK THE HARP AND BREATHE THE HORN;   • • • • • • 024 00 011
    NO, THEY ARE COME; THEIR HORN IS LIFTED UP;   • • • • 104 00 001
    FROM ONE FRAIL HORN THAT CRUMBLED TO THE PLAIN   • • • 107 03 011
HORNBEAM
    WILD WYCHELM, HORNBEAM FRETTY OVERSTOOD C   • • • 159 00 024
HORNLIGHT
    HER FOND YELLOW HORNLIGHT WOUND TO THE WEST, C   • • 061 00 003
HORNS
    HER INJURY'S, LOOKS OFF BY BOTH HORNS OF SHORE,   • • 050 00 003
    IN THE ASCENDANCY OF RAINBOW'S HORNS,   • • • • 084 00 002
    HER FINGER-LONG NEW HORNS ARE CAPP'D WITH BLACK;   • • 099 00 007
HOROSCOPE
    BUT IN THE OTHER'S HOROSCOPE   • • • • • • • 083 00 017
HORRIBLE
    -- THEY SHOOK IN THE HURLING AND HORRIBLE AIRS. C   • • 028 15 008
HORROR
    HARD DOWN WITH A HORROR OF HEIGHT;   • • • • • • 028 02 007
    NOT DANGER, ELECTRICAL HORROR; THEN FURTHER IT FINDS   • • 028 27 005
    THE HORROR AND THE HAVOC AND THE GLORY   • • • • 075 00 002
HORSEBACK
    THIS DARKSOME BURN, HORSEBACK BROWN,   • • • • 056 00 001
HORSEMEN
    WHEREIN BENEATH THE CORNICE, HORSEMEN RODE   • • • 001 07 007
HORSES
    AND WATCH UNTIL OUR HORSES AND THE MEN   • • • • 125 00 009
HOST
    INTO MY HAND HE GIVES A HOST FOR PREY,   • • • • • 005 00 017
    WHERE STANDS NO HOST AT DOOR OR HEARTH   • • • • 023 00 011
    AND FLED WITH A FLING OF THE HEART TO THE HEART OF THE HOST.   • 028 03 005
HOSTS
    AND HOSTS CONFRONT WITH FLAGS UNFURLED   • • • • 023 00 033
HOT
    TO AN ORB'D ROSE, WHICH, BY HOT PANTINGS BLOWN   • • 002 00 020
    IN HOT SANDS PERILOUS   • • • • • • • • • 005 00 004
HOUR
    THE DRIVING STORM AT HOUR OF VESPERS BEAT   • • • 001 13 003
    IN THE WORST HOUR THAT'S MEASURED BY THE SUN,   • • 014 02 005
    THOU KNOWEST THE WALLS, ALTAR AND HOUR AND NIGHT;   • • 028 02 005
    THEN EVEN IN WEARIEST WINTRY HOUR   • • • • • 030 00 029
    HIM, AFTER AN HOUR OF WINTRY WAVES,   • • • • 041 00 069
    HAS DRENCH'D THE MOLTEN SUNSET HOUR.   • • • • 077 00 094
    SWEETNESS FROM THE HOUR, AND DIP   • • • • • 077 00 132
    AND FOR THAT FEARFUL HOUR LIFE IS MORE THIN   • • 080 03 005
    IT DOES AMAZE ME, WHEN THE CLICKING HOUR   • • • 102 01 001
    AND EVERY SAINT OF BLOODY HOUR   • • • • • • 145 00 044
    FOR A QUARTER OF AN HOUR OR SO   • • • • • • 145 00 059
    THEIR YOUNG DELIGHTFUL HOUR DO FEATURE DOWN   • • 157 00 010
HOURGLASS
    IN AN HOURGLASS -- AT THE WALL   • • • • • • 028 04 002
HOURS
    THEY DO NOT WASTE THEIR METED HOURS,   • • • • 015 00 005
    WITH EYES THAT SMILE THRO' THE TEARS OF THE HOURS,   • • 026 00 014
    HOPE WAS TWELVE HOURS GONE;   • • • • • • • 028 15 004
    THEY COULD TELL HIM FOR HOURS, DANDLED THE TO AND FRO   • 028 16 006
    WHAT HOURS, O WHAT BLACK HOURS WE HAVE SPENT   • • 067 00 002
    WHAT HOURS, O WHAT BLACK HOURS WE HAVE SPENT   • • 067 00 002
    HOURS I MEAN YEARS, MEAN LIFE. AND MY LAMENT   • • 067 00 006
    DO IN SPARE HOURS MORE THRIVE THAN I THAT SPEND,   • • 074 00 008
    THAT HIS FAST-FLOWING HOURS WITH SANDY SILT   • • 136 00 001
HOUSE
    AND YOU UNHOUSE AND HOUSE THE LORD.   • • • • 022 00 024
    SEEK GOD'S HOUSE IN HAPPY THRONG;   • • • • • 024 00 025
    TILL A MAID IN DAVID'S HOUSE HAD BIRTH,   • • • 026 00 030
    THESE ARE INDEED THE BARN; WITHINDOORS HOUSE   • • 032 00 012
    I REMEMBER A HOUSE WHERE ALL WERE GOOD   • • • 034 00 001
    MAN'S MOUNTING SPIRIT IN HIS BONE-HOUSE, MEAN HOUSE, DWELLS --   • 039 00 002
    THAT PLUMES TO PEACE THEREAFTER. AND WHEN PEACE HERE DOES HOUSE   • 051 00 009
    YOU WOULD NOT HOUSE BENEATH MY OWN;   • • • • 081 00 004
    NO HOUSE OF RIMMON MAY I TAKE,   • • • • • • 081 00 140
    AND A GREY HEAVEN DOES THE HUSH'D EARTH HOUSE,   • • 105 00 007
    AS VOID AS CLOUDS THAT HOUSE AND HARBOUR NONE,   • • 107 01 001
    AND ALL WITHIN THE HOUSE WERE SOUND AS POSTS,   • • 135 00 017
HOUSED
    BUT SHE WHO HAD HOUSED THEM THITHER   • • • • 041 00 043
HOUSEL
    LOW-LATCHED IN LEAF-LIGHT HOUSEL HIS TOO HUGE GODHEAD.   • • 048 00 012

HOUSELESS
  THEN SWEETEST SEEMS THE HOUSELESS SHORE, ... 015 00 035
HOUSES
  HOUSES THAT MAKE ABODE BESIDE THE LAKE, ... 080 06 006
  THE SHINING SLATES AND HOUSES, COME AND SEE. 107 03 007
HOUSETOP
  SHE, HIGH AT THE HOUSETOP SITTING, AS THEY SAY, ... 136 00 013
HOVEL
  SCOOP YOU FROM TEEMING FILTH SOME SICKLY HOVEL, ... 077 00 006
HOVER
  THEY TOUCH, THEY TABOUR ON IT, HOVER ON IT [: HERE, THERE HURLED] ,V 149 B 007
  WHAT IS IT, GWEN, MY GIRL? WHY DO YOU HOVER AND HAUNT ME? . . . 152 01 001
  MAKES DITHER, MAKES HOVER 159 00 010
HOVERED
  THE SPIRIT HOVERED ERE THE SUN 023 00 022
HOVERINGS
  FAR FROM ITS HEAD AN ANGEL'S HOVERINGS, ... 089 00 008
HOVER-FLOAT
  [HOVER-FLOAT TO THE HEDGE BROW.] 138 00 040
HOVERS
  HOVERS OFF, THE JAY-BLUE HEAVENS APPEARING 028 26 003
HOWEVER
  FORWARD-LIKE, BUT HOWEVER, AND LIKE FAVOURABLE HEAVEN HEARD THESE. . 048 00 048
  AND, BLAZONED IN HOWEVER BOLD THE NAME, ... 075 00 010
HUDDLE
  MY CRIES HEAVE, HERDS-LONG: HUDDLE IN A MAIN, A CHIEF- . . . 065 00 005
HUDDLING
  WITH DARE AND WITH DOWNDOLPHINRY AND BELLBRIGHT BODIES HUDDLING OUT, 159 00 017
HUE
  OF MAZY SHAPE AND HUE, BUT NOW BEREFT 001 08 003
  WITH SPIKED QUILLS ALL OF INTENSEST HUE: 002 00 044
  BEYOND THE HURST WITH SUCH A HUE 021 00 006
  EACH HUE SO RARELY WROUGHT THAT WHERE 077 00 117
  'TWIXT REAL HUE AND PHANTASY, ... 077 00 122
HUED
  HUED SUNBEAM WILL TRANSMIT 060 00 088
HUE'S
  HER HUE'S A VARIOUS BROWN WITH CREAMY LAKES, ... 099 00 011
HUES
  WITH BLAZONED GROINS, AND CROWNED WITH HUES OF MAJESTY. . . . 001 06 009
  MOST LIKE THOSE HUES THAT IN THE PRISM 077 00 061
  BRIGHT HUES LONG LOOK'D AT THIN, DISSOLVE AND FLY: 117 00 002
HUGE
  LOW-LATCHED IN LEAF-LIGHT HOUSEL HIS TOO HUGE GODHEAD. . . . 048 00 012
HUGE-GIRTHED
  NOT GOSHEN, WASTEFUL WIDE HUGE-GIRTHED NILE 005 00 031
HUM
  FROM OXFORD COMES THE THRONG AND HUM OF BELLS 098 03 006
HUMAN
  HERE THY VERY MANHOOD STEALS FROM HUMAN KEN: 168 00 010
HUMANITIES
  WHAT TAUGHT THE HUMANITIES AND THE ROUND OF ARTS? 107 02 006
HUNDRED
  TWO HUNDRED SOULS IN THE ROUND -- 028 12 004
  THREE HUNDRED SOULS, O ALAS! ON BOARD, ... 041 00 002
HUNDREDFOLD
  THIS SIDE, THAT SIDE HURLING A HEAVYHEADED HUNDREDFOLD . . . 059 06 024
HUNDREDWEIGHTS
  THEY BROUGHT THEIR HUNDREDWEIGHTS TO BEAR. 145 00 051
HUNG
  HUNG IN THE SWAYING OF THE FIERCE MELEE. 001 02 004
  HUNG LIKE A WRECK THAT FLAMES NOT BILLOWS BEAT -- 001 03 004
  AND BLEEDING SAW. -- THUS HUNG FROM ROOM TO ROOM 001 10 008
  A TINTED FIN ON EITHER SHOULDER HUNG: 002 00 052
  AND THE AZUROUS HUNG HILLS ARE HIS WORLD-WIELDING SHOULDER . . . 038 00 009
  HE HUNG ON THE IMP'S SUCCESS. 054 00 024
  STONES RING: LIKE EACH TUCKED STRING TELLS, EACH HUNG BELL'S . . 057 00 003
  HER WILD HOLLOW HOARLIGHT HUNG TO THE HEIGHT [. . . . 061 00 003
  MAY WHO NE'ER HUNG THERE. NOR DOES LONG OUR SMALL 065 00 011
  WITH HEAVEN'S LIGHTS HIGH HUNG ROUND, OR, MOTHER-GROUND . . . 070 00 011
  YET WHEN MY UNSET TRESSES HUNG LOOSE-TRACED 102 01 003
  THAT TEARS AND LAUGHTER ARE HUNG CLOSE TOGETHER. 102 01 016
  SINNER WHO SAW THE BLADE THAT HUNG 166 00 017
HUNGER
  ONE SPOT AND HUNGER TO BE THERE. 015 00 032
  THAT NE'ER NEED HUNGER, TOM: TOM SELDOM SICK, ... 070 00 006
  TO HUNGER AND NOT HAVE, YET HOPE ON FOR, TO STORM AND STRIVE AND . 152 02 055
HUNGERED
  THEN NEXT I HUNGERED: LOVE WHEN HERE, THEY SAY, ... 020 00 009
HUNG-HEAVENWARD
  TO HAVE HAVOC-POCKED SO, SEE, THE HUNG-HEAVENWARD BOUGHS? . . 157 00 032
HUNT
  I MUST HUNT DOWN THE PRIZE 088 00 001
  SHE HEARD THE HUNT THE MORROW MORNING 109 24 001
HUNTERS
  WHO FIRST KNEW MOONLIGHT BY THE HUNTERS' MOON. 105 00 017
HUNTING
  AND HUNTING WINDS AND THE LONG-LYING SNOW. 017 00 002

HUNTING   (CONTINUED)
    ' LORD WILLIAM COMES HUNTING TOMORROW MORNING;   •   •   •   •   •   •   . 109 19 003
HURDLE
    HARD AS HURDLE ARMS, WITH A BROTH OF GOLDISH FLUE •   •   •   •   •   •   . 071 00 001
HURDLES
    AND GATHER IN LIKE HURDLES BRIGHT •   •   •   •   •   •   •   •   •   . 098 29 003
    AND GATHER IN LIKE HURDLES BRIGHT •   •   •   •   •   •   •   •   •   . 135 00 021
HURL
    THE SWOON OF A HEART THAT THE SWEEP AND THE HURL OF THEE TROD   •   . 028 02 006
    AS A SKATE'S HEEL SWEEPS SMOOTH ON A BOW-BEND; THE HURL AND GLIDING • 036 00 006
    STRIKE, CHURL; HURL, CHEERLESS WIND, THEN; HELTERING HAIL •   •   . 154 00 001
HURLED
    THEY TOUCH, THEY TABOUR ON IT, HOVER ON IT [; HERE, THERE HURLED] V 149 8 007
    ARE EARTHWORLD, AIRWORLD, WATERWORLD THOROUGH HURLED, C •   •   . 159 00 018
HURLING
    HURLING THE HAVEN BEHIND, •   •   •   •   •   •   •   •   •   •   . 028 13 002
    -- THEY SHOOK IN THE HURLING AND HORRIBLE AIRS. C •   •   •   •   . 028 15 008
    THIS SIDE, THAT SIDE HURLING A HEAVYHEADED HUNDREDFOLD •   •   . 059 06 024
    AS WHERE THE LITTLE HURLING SOUND •   •   •   •   •   •   •   . 135 00 031
HURLS
    AND HURLS FOR HIM, O HALF HURLS EARTH FOR HIM OFF UNDER HIS FEET. • 038 00 014
    AND HURLS FOR HIM, O HALF HURLS EARTH FOR HIM OFF UNDER HIS FEET. • 038 00 014
    IT HURLS, HURLS OFF BONIFACE DOWN. •   •   •   •   •   •   •   . 041 00 032
    IT HURLS, HURLS OFF BONIFACE DOWN. •   •   •   •   •   •   •   . 041 00 032
    CHURLSGRACE, TOO, CHILD OF AMANSSTRENGTH, HOW IT HANGS OR HURLS • 071 00 012
HURRIED
    NOCTURNS I THOUGHT WERE HURRIED THROUGH. •   •   •   •   •   . 081 00 092
HURST
    BEYOND THE HURST WITH SUCH A HUE •   •   •   •   •   •   •   . 021 00 006
HURSTS
    NOW WHILE THE FULL-LEAVED HURSTS UNALTER'D STAND, •   •   •   . 105 00 003
HURT
    BUT CANDOUR NEVER HURT THE DEAREST FRIEND. •   •   •   •   •   . 094 00 008
HURTLE
    BEFORE ME, THE HURTLE OF HELL •   •   •   •   •   •   •   •   . 028 03 002
    EARTH HEARS NO HURTLE THEN FROM FIERCEST FRAY. •   •   •   •   . 073 00 008
HUSH
    THERE IS ONE, YES I HAVE ONE (HUSH THERE!) , •   •   •   •   . 059 06 002
    AFTER THAT IN PERFECT HUSH •   •   •   •   •   •   •   •   . 145 00 058
HUSHED
    THAT GUILT IS HUSHED BY, HEARTS ARE FLUSHED BY AND MELT -- •   •   . 028 06 006
HUSH'D
    AND A GREY HEAVEN DOES THE HUSH'D EARTH HOUSE, •   •   •   •   . 105 00 007
HUSSY
    MAN JACK THE MAN IS, JUST; HIS MATE A HUSSY. •   •   •   •   •   . 075 00 011
HUSTINGS
    OF BLOOD TO OUR GREEN HUSTINGS GOES; •   •   •   •   •   •   . 166 00 011
HUSTLE
    HAILROPES HUSTLE AND GRIND THEIR •   •   •   •   •   •   •   . 041 00 027
HUTCH
    PALATE, THE HUTCH OF TASTY LUST, •   •   •   •   •   •   •   . 022 00 013
HYACINTHED
    DIES OFF IN HYACINTHED GROUND, •   •   •   •   •   •   •   . 135 00 033
HYACINTH-WARDING
    FRUIT-CLOISTERING HYACINTH-WARDING WOODS. •   •   •   •   •   . 081 00 163
HYACINTHS
    OF HYACINTHS •   •   •   •   •   •   •   •   •   •   •   . 112 00 011
HYALINE
    SO LIKE A BERG OF HYALINE, •   •   •   •   •   •   •   •   . 003 00 017
HYMN
    OUR HYMN IN THE VAST SILENCE DIES. •   •   •   •   •   •   . 023 00 006
HYPOCRITE
    WHEN, WHEN, PEACE, WILL YOU, PEACE? I'LL NOT PLAY HYPOCRITE •   •   . 051 00 003

ICE
    SOME ICE THAT LOCKS THE GLACIER TO THE ROCKS •   •   •   •   •   . 080 09 006
    AND FIND A FLINT, A FANG OF ICE, •   •   •   •   •   •   •   . 080 12 004
    THIS ICE, THIS LEAD, THIS STEEL, THIS STONE, •   •   •   •   •   . 081 00 128
    HE GAVE HER KISSES COLD AS ICE; •   •   •   •   •   •   •   . 109 39 001
ICE-BLOCKS   ,
    TOWARDS WASTES WHERE ROUND THE ICE-BLOCKS TILT AND FRET •   •   . 088 00 007
    TOWARDS THOSE WASTES WHERE THE ICE-BLOCKS TILT AND FRET, V •   •   . 088 00 011
ICONIUM
    AND BRIGHT ICONIUM EASTWARDS REACH MY RHYMES. •   •   •   •   . 136 00 006
ICY
    AND NUMBS AND STARVES, AS BETWEEN ICY WHARVES •   •   •   •   . 080 03 006
IDEAL
    THE BEST IDEAL IS THE TRUE •   •   •   •   •   •   •   •   . 133 00 001
IDLE
    IDLE FOR EVER TO WAFT HER OR WIND HER WITH, THESE SHE ENDURED. •   . 028 14 008
    Y OF IDLE A BEING BUT BY WHERE WARS ARE RIFE. •   •   •   •   •   . 066 00 008
IGNORANTLY
    BUT I WAS IGNORANTLY BOLD •   •   •   •   •   •   •   •   •   . 118 00 005

ILL
    SO FROM THE DAWN WAS ILL BEGUN 021 00 009
    AND THE TIDE OF ILL IS OUT: 077 00 028
    ILL MEANT, YET TRUE, I BEST SHOULD FLATTER THEN, ... 125 00 019
    I ARGUED ILL? 127 00 012
    COMES ONE TO GAZE UPON MY ILL: 160 00 025
ILL-BALANCED
    THEN CLOUDS COME, LIKE ILL-BALANCED CRAGS, ... 080 07 001
ILL-CONTENT
    MOST ILL-CONTENT, THIS LEAST LEAST THING I DO. 102 01 054
ILL-CONTENTED
    THOUGH ILL-CONTENTED, PRECIOUS PRECIOUS FLORIS, ... 102 01 053
ILL-LAUNCHED
    FRONTS VENUS. -- HIS ILL-LAUNCHED HOPE 083 00 019
ILL-VISAGED
    AND HATE THE ILL-VISAGED CURSING TARS, ... 114 00 010
ILLUMINED
    THINK OF AN OPENING PAGE ILLUMINED 093 8 001
ILLUSTRATED
    WHERE ALL THE VIRTUES WERE ILLUSTRATED 102 02 009
IMAGE
    THE SCULPTUR'D IMAGE OF SUCH FAITH WOULD BE, ... 001 03 007
IMAGES
    IN BLAZON, GILT AND IMAGES OF BRONZE, V 102 02 010
IMAGINING
    EACH IN HIS OWN IMAGINING 023 00 015
IMMACULATE
    WHITE TO BEGIN WITH, IMMACULATE WHITE. 027 00 032
    MARY IMMACULATE, ... 060 00 024
IMMORTAL
    DEALS TRIUMPH AND IMMORTAL YEARS. 052 00 012
    THIS JACK, JOKE, POOR POTSHERD, PATCH, MATCHWOOD, IMMORTAL DIAMOND, . 072 00 023
    IS IMMORTAL DIAMOND. 072 00 024
    LEAVES YET THE MIND A MOTHER OF IMMORTAL SONG. . . . 076 00 004
    AND BREATH IMMORTAL THRONGED THAT SHOW: 145 00 045
    BUT, BEING LIFTED, IMMORTAL, OF IMMORTAL BRIGHTNESS. . . 152 02 027
    BUT, BEING LIFTED, IMMORTAL, OF IMMORTAL BRIGHTNESS. . . 152 02 027
    IMMORTAL BEAUTY IS DEATH WITH DUTY. 156 00 018
IMMORTALS
    THE IMMORTALS OF THE ETERNAL RING, ... 145 00 030
IMPALE
    AND THE POOR CORSE IMPALE WITH IT AND FRAY 089 00 007
IMPALED
    OR THORN-ENGAGED, IMPALED AND PENT 081 00 019
IMPALPABLE
    THY IMPALPABLE OPPRESSION. PIN HIM DOWN, ... 102 01 018
IMPATIENT
    SICKNESS BROKE HIM. IMPATIENT, HE CURSED AT FIRST, BUT MENDED . 053 00 005
IMPEACHED
    AND ALL LIKE ME MAY BOAST, IMPEACHED NOT, ... 012 01 013
IMPEARLED
    AND TRUTH IS HEARD, WITH TEARS IMPEARLED, ... 023 00 035
IMPEDIMENT
    HAD LET SUCH MUSIC DOWN, WITHOUT IMPEDIMENT 122 00 008
IMPENITENT
    OFTEN WHEN WINDS IMPENITENT 080 05 001
IMPERFECT
    IT IS A REGIMEN ON THE IMPERFECT WIND. 102 03 017
    IS TO GIVE REGIMEN TO THE IMPERFECT WIND, V 102 03 024
IMP'S
    HE HUNG ON THE IMP'S SUCCESS. 054 00 024
INANIMATE
    TO NEWBORN PRINCE, AND ROYAL CORSE INANIMATE. . . . 001 04 009
INBOARD
    AND THE INBOARD SEAS RUN SWIRLING AND HAWLING: . . . 028 19 003
INCAPABLE
    THE INCAPABLE AND CUMBROUS SHAME 015 00 018
INCENSE
    LET INCENSE HANG ACROSS THE ROOM 077 00 019
INCH
    EVERY INCH A TAR, ... 041 00 075
INCHES
    IS STATUARY RATED BY ITS INCHES? 096 07 006
INCREASE
    THAT, WARRING, WASTED THE LAND'S INCREASE, ... 026 00 028
INCREMENT
    EARTH, ALL, OUT: WHO, WITH TRICKLING INCREMENT, . . . 073 00 010
INDEED
    INDEED WHILE SUCH A WONDER'S WARM. 025 00 036
    THESE ARE INDEED THE BARN: WITHINDOORS HOUSE . . . 032 00 012
    THOU ART INDEED JUST, LORD, IF I CONTEND 074 00 001
    THEN IS MY MISERY FULL INDEED: 081 00 068
    ' SOME ARE PRETTY ENOUGH, AND SOME ARE POOR INDEED. ' . . 098 15 004
    NOW ONE WORD MORE AND THEN I AM GONE INDEED, . . . 102 01 055
    A LEARNED FOOL INDEED AND WELL-BRED CHURL V . . . 102 03 038
    BUT WHAT INDEED IS ASK'D OF ME? 118 00 001
    THREE MILES INDEED. 125 00 012

JAMES
    AND JAMES SHALL HATE HIS FADED RED. 114 00 011
JANE
    OR WAS IT JANE? SHE IS TOO PLAIN, ... 095 00 003
    IT MIGHT BE HELEN, JANE, OR KATE, ... 095 00 005
JAR
    THE JADING AND JAR OF THE CART, ... 028 27 002
    WOULD BRANDLE ADAMANTINE HEAVEN WITH RIDE AND JAR, DID . . . 048 00 046
JARR'D
    JARR'D DOWN THE BALANCED STORM; THE BLEEDING HEAVENS 102 02 004
JAUNTING
    A JAUNTING VAUNTING VAULTING ASSAULTING TRUMPET TELLING. V . . 141 00 007
JAY-BLUE
    HOVERS OFF, THE JAY-BLUE HEAVENS APPEARING 028 26 003
JESSY
    OF ANSWER THE EAGERER A-WANTING JESSY OR JACK 046 00 007
JESU
    JESU, HEART'S LIGHT, ... 028 30 001
    JESU, MAID'S SON, ... 028 30 002
    JESU, THEIR HOPE WHO GO ASTRAY, ... 167 00 009
    JESU, A SPRINGING WELL THOU ART, ... 167 00 017
    BE OUR DELIGHT, O JESU, NOW 167 00 025
    BATHE ME, JESU LORD, IN WHAT THY BOSOM RAN -- 168 00 022
    JESU WHOM I LOOK AT SHROUDED HERE BELOW, ... 168 00 025
    JESU THAT DOST IN MARY DWELL, ... 169 00 001
    JESU SO MUCH IN LOVE WITH ME? 170 00 014
JESU'S
    TO CROSSES MEANT FOR JESU'S; YOU WHOM THE EAST 011 00 005
JESUS
    CHRIST JESUS, OUR LORD, HER GOD AND HER SON. 027 00 028
    (JUST LIKE JESUS CRUCIFIED) 145 00 050
    JEWS KILLED JESUS LONG AGO 145 00 052
    JESUS TO CAST ONE THOUGHT UPON 167 00 001
    AS JESUS GOD THE FATHER'S SON. 167 00 008
    WHAT JESUS IS AND WHAT IS LOVE. 167 00 016
    THOU, THOU, MY JESUS, AFTER ME 170 00 005
JET
    THE PUPIL, PLAYS ITS LIQUID JET 086 00 005
JEWELL'D
    WHENCE SPRING THE JEWELL'D HARMONIES 077 00 138
JEWS
    I WILL BREAK FREE FROM THE JEWS' COMPANY, ... 080 12 003
    JEWS KILLED JESUS LONG AGO 145 00 052
JOHN
    PART WAS PICKED FOR JOHN, ... 054 00 007
    YOUNG JOHN; THEN FEAR, THEN JOY 054 00 008
    AND JOHN SHALL LIE, WHERE WINDS ARE DEAD, ... 114 00 009
JOINTS
    THE THUNDER BRAGS, IN JOINTS AND SPARKLING JAGS 080 07 003
JOKE
    THIS JACK, JOKE, POOR POTSHERD, PATCH, MATCHWOOD, IMMORTAL DIAMOND, . 072 00 023
JOLT
    JOLT V 101 00 007
JOSEPH'S
    IN JOSEPH'S GARDEN THEY THREW BY 006 00 021
JOSTLING
    CROWD DOWN UPON A STREAM, AND, JOSTLING THICK 002 00 094
    ONCE, JOSTLING THICK, THE BLUEBELL SHEAVES 081 00 013
    OR LIKE A JUICY AND JOSTLING SHOCK 144 00 009
JOVE
    JOVE OF THE GIANTS; SIMPLE JOVE'S 166 00 007
JOVE'S
    BUT JOVE'S THE HERD THAT KEEPS THE KINGS -- 166 00 006
    JOVE OF THE GIANTS; SIMPLE JOVE'S 166 00 007
JOY
    BEHOLD WE HAVE THE JOY IN HARVEST; 006 00 002
    TILL DIMPLED JOY STEALS O'ER ITS CHEEKS. 023 00 052
    AND A SPRING-TIME JOY HAVE FOUND; 024 00 016
    LET IN JOY THIS EASTER DAY. 024 00 024
    WITH JOY FOR TO-DAY AND HOPE FOR TO-MORROW 026 00 015
    AND WE THAT JOY IN THIS-MONTH JOY-LADEN, ... 026 00 017
    JOY FALL TO THEE, FATHER FRANCIS, ... 028 23 001
    WHAT IS ALL THIS JUICE AND ALL THIS JOY? 033 00 009
    AND HE BOARDS HER IN OH! SUCH JOY 041 00 071
    YOUNG JOHN; THEN FEAR, THEN JOY 054 00 008
    STOLE JOY, WOULD LAUGH, CHEER. C 064 00 011
    ELSEWHERE; LEAVE COMFORT ROOT-ROOM; LET JOY SIZE 069 00 011
    AND THAT GRIEF MASTERS JOY ON EARTH, ... 077 00 055
    OF WHICH I SAY THERE IS NO JOY IN THEM. 125 00 047
    C ANYWHERE ANY MORE JOY TO BE IN. 138 00 033
    WITH A SWEET JOY OF A SWEET JOY, ... 138 00 044
    WITH A SWEET JOY OF A SWEET JOY, ... 138 00 044
    SWEET, OF A SWEET, OF A SWEET JOY 138 00 045
    OF A SWEET -- A SWEET -- SWEET -- JOY. ' 138 00 046
    KEEPS A KIND OF JOY IN IT, A ZEST, AN EDGE, AN ECSTASY, . . . 152 02 058
    BID JOY BACK, HAVE AT THE HARVEST, KEEP HOPE PALE. . . . 154 00 004
JOY-LADEN
    AND WE THAT JOY IN THIS MONTH JOY-LADEN, ... 026 00 017

KEEPS   (CONTINUED)
    KEEPS GRACE: THAT KEEPS ALL HIS GOINGS GRACES;   •   •   •   •   •   •   057 00 010
    KEEPS GRACE: THAT KEEPS ALL HIS GOINGS GRACES;   •   •   •   •   •   •   057 00 010
    THAN PURCELL TUNE LETS TREAD TO? SEE: IT DOES THIS: KEEPS WARM   •   •   062 00 003
    AND KEEPS THE BREEZE AND CLEARS THE SEAS   •   •   •   •   •   •   083 00 013
    KEEPS A KIND OF JOY IN IT, A ZEST, AN EDGE, AN ECSTASY,   •   •   •   152 02 058
    WATER, WHICH KEEPS THY NAME, (FOR NOT IN ROCK WRITTEN,   •   •   •   152 C 014
    BUT JOVE'S THE HERD THAT KEEPS THE KINGS --   •   •   •   •   •   •   166 00 006
KELSON
    AS KEEL LOCKS CLOSE TO KELSON --   •   •   •   •   •   •   •   101 00 005
    THE STRANDED KEEL AND KELSON WARP APART;   •   •   •   •   •   101 00 011
KEN
    WHOSE KEN THROUGH AMBER OF DARK EYES   •   •   •   •   •   •   077 00 051
    WHAT NEED I STRAIN MY HEART BEYOND MY KEN?   •   •   •   •   •   157 00 034
    HERE THY VERY MANHOOD STEALS FROM HUMAN KEN: •   •   •   •   168 00 010
KENTISH
    DEAD TO THE KENTISH KNOCK;   •   •   •   •   •   •   •   028 14 004
KEPT
    YE HAVE KEPT YOUR CHOICEST WINE --   •   •   •   •   •   •   024 00 009
    WORD, THAT HEARD AND KEPT THEE AND UTTERED THEE OUTRIGHT.   •   •   028 30 008
    KEPT TO HER -- CARE-DROWNED AND WRAPPED IN   •   •   •   •   041 00 046
    IN SILK-ASH KEPT FROM COOLING,   •   •   •   •   •   •   049 00 017
    WHEN THE THING WE FREELY FORFEIT IS KEPT WITH FONDER A CARE,   •   059 06 027
    FONDER A CARE KEPT THAN WE COULD HAVE KEPT IT, KEPT   •   •   •   059 06 028
    FONDER A CARE KEPT THAN WE COULD HAVE KEPT IT, KEPT   •   •   •   059 06 028
    FONDER A CARE KEPT THAN WE COULD HAVE KEPT IT, KEPT   •   •   •   059 06 028
    A CARE KEPT. -- WHERE KEPT? DO BUT TELL US WHERE KEPT, WHERE. --   059 06 030
    A CARE KEPT. -- WHERE KEPT? DO BUT TELL US WHERE KEPT, WHERE. --   059 06 030
    A CARE KEPT. -- WHERE KEPT? DO BUT TELL US WHERE KEPT, WHERE. --   059 06 030
    SHE KEPT HER LOVE-THOUGHTS ON MOST LENTEN DIET,   •   •   •   082 00 007
    ONE AND THEN ONE, ALONG THEIR WALKS, AND KEPT   •   •   •   •   107 01 012
    NO PIECE MATCHED THOSE EYES KEPT MOST PART MUCH CAST DOWN   •   •   152 02 026
KEY
    ONE. YES I CAN TELL SUCH A KEY, I DO KNOW SUCH A PLACE,   •   •   059 06 007
    LACE, LATCH OR CATCH OR KEY TO KEEP C   •   •   •   •   •   059 0L 001
    WE TUNED TO ONE KEY AND MADE THEIR HARMONIES.   •   •   •   •   098 02 004
KILL
    THEMSELVES LIVE SINGING AND THEIR HEARERS KILL.   •   •   •   •   096 02 002
    WHO MEANS TO WED OR MEANS TO KILL,   •   •   •   •   •   •   120 00 029
KILLED
    JEWS KILLED JESUS LONG AGO   •   •   •   •   •   •   •   145 00 052
KILL-WEIGHTS
    WHEN SHE FELT THE KILL-WEIGHTS CRUSH   •   •   •   •   •   145 00 055
KILLS
    WE HEAR OUR HEARTS GRATE ON THEMSELVES: IT KILLS   •   •   •   068 00 009
KIND
    THEN FREE AND KIND THE WILDERNESS.   •   •   •   •   •   •   015 00 036
    KIND, BUT ROYALLY RECLAIMING HIS OWN: •   •   •   •   •   028 34 007
    THAT CORDIAL AIR MADE THOSE KIND PEOPLE A HOOD   •   •   •   034 00 005
    THERE, EYES THEM, HEART WANTS, CARE HAUNTS, FOOT FOLLOWS KIND,   •   040 00 013
    THEIR MAGNIFYING OF EACH ITS KIND   •   •   •   •   •   •   042 00 029
    MARCH, KIND COMRADE, ABREAST HIM!   •   •   •   •   •   •   048 00 019
    EACH BE OTHER'S COMFORT KIND: •   •   •   •   •   •   052 00 005
    DEARLY THOU CANST BE KIND!   •   •   •   •   •   •   •   054 00 041
    DEARLY THOU CANST BE KIND.   •   •   •   •   •   •   •   054 00 043
    KIND LOVE BOTH GIVE AND GET. ONLY WHAT WORD   •   •   •   •   066 00 011
    ME LIVE TO MY SAD SELF HEREAFTER KIND,   •   •   •   •   •   069 00 002
    NOT KIND! TO FREEZE ME WITH FORECAST,   •   •   •   •   •   134 00 001
    AND KIND COMPASSION, AT HIS LIFE'S LAST NEED   •   •   •   •   140 00 004
    KEEPS A KIND OF JOY IN IT, A ZEST, AN EDGE, AN ECSTASY,   •   •   152 02 058
    LIFE'S QUICK, THIS KIND, THIS KEEN SELF-FEELING,   •   •   •   152 02 063
    SO KIND TO THOSE WHO ASK THE WAY,   •   •   •   •   •   •   167 00 010
KINDCOLD
    FLINTY KINDCOLD ELEMENT LET BREAK ACROSS HIS LIMBS   •   •   •   159 00 041
KINDNESS
    DELICIOUS KINDNESS? -- HE IS PATIENT. PATIENCE FILLS   •   •   •   068 00 013
KINDRED
    AND KINDRED TO MY LAMENTABLE DAYS,   •   •   •   •   •   •   125 00 046
KINE
    AND HEDGES BREAK, AND LOSE THE KINE,   •   •   •   •   •   114 00 002
KING
    WE GUESS; WE CLOTHE THEE, UNSEEN KING,   •   •   •   •   •   023 00 013
    A SON FOR KING, WHOSE NAME WAS PEACE.   •   •   •   •   •   026 00 032
    MASTERY, BUT BE ADORED, BUT BE ADORED KING.   •   •   •   •   028 10 008
    IPSE, THE ONLY ONE, CHRIST, KING, HEAD: •   •   •   •   •   028 28 005
    OUR KING BACK, OH, UPON ENGLISH SOULS!   •   •   •   •   •   028 35 004
    MARK CHRIST OUR KING. HE KNOWS WAR, SERVED THIS SOLDIERING THROUGH: 063 00 009
    ERE YOU SET SAIL THE KING WAS DEAD.   •   •   •   •   •   •   109 09 003
    SAID, IT WAS NOT MEET THE KING SHOULD WED   •   •   •   •   109 12 003
    AND THERE SHE NEVER SAW THE KING,   •   •   •   •   •   •   109 24 003
    LORD WILLIAM IS KING OF ALL THIS LAND   •   •   •   •   •   109 27 003
    IF HE WERE KING OF ALL THIS LAND   •   •   •   •   •   •   109 28 003
    THE KING OF GLORY WILL COME IN.   •   •   •   •   •   •   115 00 010
    FOR BEING MY KING AND GOD. AMEN.   •   •   •   •   •   •   170 00 021
    GABRIEL, FROM HEAVEN'S KING   •   •   •   •   •   •   •   APPEN D 01
KINGDOM
    I CAUGHT THIS MORNING MORNING'S MINION, KING-   •   •   •   •   036 00 001

135

KINGDOM   (CONTINUED)
    DOM OF DAYLIGHT'S DAUPHIN, DAPPLE-DAWN-DRAWN FALCON, IN HIS RIDING   . 036 00 002
KINGFISHERS
    AS KINGFISHERS CATCH FIRE, DRAGONFLIES DRAW FLAME; 057 00 001
KING'S
    ' O I AM THE KING'S SON, ' HE SAID, ... 109 05 001
    ONE HAS GONE TO THE KING'S STEWARD, ... 109 11 001
    THE KING'S FRIEND TOLD THE THING THAT WAS HID 109 12 001
    DID YOU PULL IT IN THE KING'S GARDEN 109 33 003
    ' I DID NOT PULL IT IN KING'S GARDEN 109 34 001
    ' IS THAT THE KING'S CROWN ON YOUR HEAD, ... 109 35 001
KINGS
    THAT CAME WHEN A LINE OF KINGS 'DID CEASE, ... 026 00 026
    KINGS HERD IT ON THEIR SUBJECT DROVES 166 00 005
    BUT JOVE'S THE HERD THAT KEEPS THE KINGS -- 166 00 006
KIRJATH-ARBA
    AT KIRJATH-ARBA: GO. -- 005 00 058
KISS
    I KISS MY HAND 028 05 001
    KISS MY HAND TO THE DAPPLED-WITH-DAMSON WEST; 028 05 005
    FOR LOVE HE LEANS FORTH, NEEDS HIS NECK MUST FALL ON, KISS,   .   .   . 063 00 012
    THEY KISS THE ROD WITH FILIAL SUBMISSION. 097 00 008
    AND RELISH NOT HER LOVELESS KISS 120 00 011
    [AND HALF MISLIKE HER LOVELESS KISS.] 120 00 013
KISSED
    NAY IN ALL THAT TOIL, THAT COIL, SINCE (SEEMS) I KISSED THE ROD,   . 064 00 010
KISSES
    IF I GIVE THEE KISSES THREE? 109 37 002
    GIVE ME THY KISSES THREE. 109 38 002
    SWEETER THY KISSES, MY OWN LOVE, ... 109 38 003
    HE GAVE HER KISSES COLD AS ICE; 109 39 001
KISSING
    I OUTRAGE IT WITH TREASONABLE KISSING. 102 01 049
KNEADING
    KNEADING THE MOUNDED MIRE THAT STOPS 003 00 010
KNEE
    MANGER, MAIDEN'S KNEE; 028 07 004
    CROUCH! LAY KNEE BY EARTH LOW UNDER; 041 00 110
    THEY MADE HIM KNEEL ON KNEE. 109 14 002
    WITH A TWO YEARS CHILD AT HER KNEE. 109 16 002
    SHE KNEELED UPON HER KNEE. 109 25 002
KNEE-NAVE
    ROPE-OVER THIGH; KNEE-NAVE; AND BARRELLED SHANK -- C 071 00 003
KNEEL
    I STOOD; BUT DOES SHE STAND OR KNEEL? 081 00 096
    THEY MADE HIM KNEEL ON KNEE. 109 14 002
KNEELED
    SHE KNEELED UPON HER KNEE. 109 25 002
KNEES
    LO, GOD SHALL STRENGTHEN ALL THE FEEBLE KNEES. 011 00 014
    CLUTCHED HANDS THROUGH CLASPED KNEES; 054 00 021
    HER WHITE WEED-BATHED KNEES ARE SHUT TOGETHER, ... 099 00 002
KNELLS
    ON MERMAIDS -- WHETHER THAT THEY RING THE KNELLS 002 00 119
KNELT
    HERE HE KNELT THEN IN REGIMENTAL RED, ... 048 00 009
    SOME KNELT, SOME STOOD; I SEEM'D TO FEEL 081 00 093
    WHO KNELT WERE FOR THE LORD'S RIGHT HAND; 081 00 094
KNEW
    I KNEW NOT WHY, -- BUT KNOW THAT SADNESS DWELLS 002 00 118
    LOATHED FOR A LOVE MEN KNEW IN THEM, ... 028 21 001
    AND KNEW THE WHO AND THE WHY; 028 29 004
    O IF WE BUT KNEW WHAT WE DO 043 00 009
    WHO KNEW THE INNER SPIRIT THAT FILLS 077 00 043
    AT LAST I HEAR THE VOICE I KNEW. 081 00 025
    'TWAS SAID OF NONE BUT ALL MEN KNEW; 081 00 091
    WHO FIRST KNEW MOONLIGHT BY THE HUNTERS' MOON. 105 00 017
    THAT NOT ARCADIA KNEW NOR HAEMONY. 107 01 017
    AND WITH THE LAST POST OVER I KNEW NO LETTER WAS SENT. 128 00 002
    I KNEW THE BROOK THAT PARTS IN TWO 135 00 025
    OF SMALL AND SUGAR FLINTS, I KNEW 135 00 027
    WARNED HER! WELL SHE KNEW I WARNED HER OF THIS WORK, ... 152 02 007
    LIKE THE THING THAT NEVER KNEW THE EARTH, NEVER OFF ROOTS   .   .   . 159 00 027
KNOCK
    DEAD TO THE KENTISH KNOCK; 028 14 004
KNOCKING
    LIKE KNOCKING THUNDER ALL ROUND BRITAIN'S WELKIN, ... 102 02 003
KNOCKINGS
    SHE HEARD BUT KNOCKINGS THREE. 109 29 002
KNOPS
    BRING ME PALM WITH PEARLED KNOPS, ... 098 18 002
KNOPT
    IN SUMMER ARE OUR ORCHARDS KNOPT 124 00 019
KNOT
    LOCK WITH MY RIGHT! THEN KNOT A BARKEN BAND 080 13 005
    IT WAS A HARD THING TO UNDO THIS KNOT. 091 00 001
    IT WAS A HARD THING TO UNDO THIS KNOT. 091 00 010

KNOT   (CONTINUED)
    THE KNOT OF FEATHERY LOCKS UPON HER HEAD • •   •   •   •   •   •   •   •   099 00 014
    NO TIME TO THINK, I'LL KNOT IT ON THIS RIBBON, •   •   •   •   •   •   •   102 01 027
KNOTS
    AND OAKS, -- BUT THESE WERE LEAVED IN SHARPER KNOTS.   •   •   •   •   •   107 04 008
    AND STAINED, AND KNOTS OF GOLDEN THREAD, •   •   •   •   •   •   •   •   124 00 014
KNOW
    I KNEW NOT WHY, -- BUT KNOW THAT SADNESS DWELLS   •   •   •   •   •   •   002 00 118
    TO KNOW THE DUSK DEPTHS OF THE PONDEROUS SEA,   •   •   •   •   •   •   002 00 122
    I KNOW THE SADNESS BUT THE CAUSE KNOW NOT.   •   •   •   •   •   •   •   002 00 125
    I KNOW THE SADNESS BUT THE CAUSE KNOW NOT.   •   •   •   •   •   •   •   002 00 125
    SURE, THIS IS NILE: I SICKEN, I KNOW NOT WHY,   •   •   •   •   •   •   005 00 059
    AND KNOW INFALLIBLY WHICH I PREFERRED.   •   •   •   •   •   •   •   •   019 00 008
    ' YOU KNOW YOU SAID THE NIGHTINGALE   •   •   •   •   •   •   •   •   •   021 00 022
    YET KNOW NOT HOW OUR GIFTS TO BRING,   •   •   •   •   •   •   •   •   •   023 00 017
    KNOW YE, THIS IS EASTER DAY.   •   •   •   •   •   •   •   •   •   •   •   024 00 006
    KNOW YE NOT 'TIS EASTER MORN?   •   •   •   •   •   •   •   •   •   •   024 00 012
    NOR FIRST FROM HEAVEN (AND FEW KNOW THIS)   •   •   •   •   •   •   •   028 06 003
    AND YET YOU WILL WEEP AND KNOW WHY.   •   •   •   •   •   •   •   •   •   055 00 009
    ONE. YES I CAN TELL SUCH A KEY, I DO KNOW SUCH A PLACE,   •   •   •   •   059 06 007
    HIS CRISP COMBS, AND THAT COMES THOSE WAYS WE KNOW.   •   •   •   •   068 00 014
    SOME OF THE SECRETS I WOULD KNOW.   •   •   •   •   •   •   •   •   •   077 00 040
    AND YET I KNOW IT WOULD BE BETTER SO,   •   •   •   •   •   •   •   •   080 07 006
    I KNOW I MAR MY CAUSE WITH WORDS: •   •   •   •   •   •   •   •   •   081 00 030
    WELL, I KNOW NOT, BUT ALL THINGS SEEM TO-NIGHT   •   •   •   •   •   •   102 01 010
    BUT HOW WILL YOU LORD WILLIAM KNOW   •   •   •   •   •   •   •   •   •   109 20 001
    ' YET HOW WILL YOU LORD WILLIAM KNOW.   •   •   •   •   •   •   •   •   109 21 001
    IN THIS WISE YOU MAY KNOW YOUR LORD   •   •   •   •   •   •   •   •   •   109 22 003
    (I KNOW IT, KNOWING NOT) ACROSS FROM THOSE   •   •   •   •   •   •   119 00 007
    I'LL CITE NO FURTHER WHAT THE INITIATE KNOW.   •   •   •   •   •   •   119 00 010
    I KNOW OF THE BORED AND BITTEN ROCKS   •   •   •   •   •   •   •   •   120 00 020
    C AND I SHALL KNOW OF SWEETS FOR HIM   •   •   •   •   •   •   •   •   124 00 011
    IF YOU ARE SILENT, THAT I KNOW OF, NONE.   •   •   •   •   •   •   •   125 00 018
    SOMETHING WE GUESS OR KNOW: SOME SPIRITS START   •   •   •   •   •   126 00 007
    I KNOW WHAT YOU WILL TELL ME -- NEGLECTFUL THAT YOU WERE NOT.   •   128 00 005
    YOU HAVE MADE ME QUOTE ALMOST THE DISMALEST PROVERB I KNOW: •   128 00 018
    GOD'S SON: THESE (THEY DID NOT KNOW)   •   •   •   •   •   •   •   •   145 00 053
    WHAT I KNOW OF THEE I BLESS,   •   •   •   •   •   •   •   •   •   •   155 00 005
    THEY TEASE ME. NEVER KNOW THE PART   •   •   •   •   •   •   •   •   165 00 003
    CHILD, THAT KNOW NOT MAN? '   •   •   •   •   •   •   •   •   •   •   APPEN D 14
KNOWEST
    THOU KNOWEST THE WALLS, ALTAR AND HOUR AND NIGHT: •   •   •   •   •   028 02 005
KNOWING
    KNOWING THEM WELL I CAN BUT SEE THE FALL.   •   •   •   •   •   •   •   016 00 010
    WHO KNOWING ALL THE SINS AND SORES   •   •   •   •   •   •   •   •   •   077 00 053
    (I KNOW IT, KNOWING NOT) ACROSS FROM THOSE   •   •   •   •   •   •   119 00 007
    WHO, LIKE ME, KNOWING HIS NATURE TO THE HEART HOME, NATURE'S BUSINESS,   152 02 044
KNOWLEDGE
    KNOWLEDGE IS STRONG BUT LOVE IS SWEET. --   •   •   •   •   •   •   •   081 00 154
KNOWN
    WHO SAY THAT HAD I KNOWN I HAD APPROVED THEE, --   •   •   •   •   •   013 00 012
    WHAT NONE WOULD HAVE KNOWN OF IT, ONLY THE HEART, BEING HARD AT BAY,   028 07 008
    NOWHERE KNOWN SOME, BOW OR BROOCH OR BRAID OR BRACE, C   •   •   •   059 0L 001
    OUR LAW SAYS: LOVE WHAT ARE LOVE'S WORTHIEST, WERE ALL KNOWN: •   062 00 010
    NOW KNOWN AND HAND AT WORK NOW NEVER WRONG,   •   •   •   •   •   076 00 008
    AT LAST I HEAR THE VOICE WELL KNOWN: •   •   •   •   •   •   •   •   081 00 001
    THE PEACOCK'D COPSE WERE KNOWN TO FILL: •   •   •   •   •   •   •   081 00 014
    BECAUSE ITS PLACE IS KNOWN AND CHARTED THERE.   •   •   •   •   •   102 03 012
    BUT LET ME SING THAT WHICH IS KNOWN TO ME.   •   •   •   •   •   •   116 00 004
    ARE KNOWN: BUT I --   •   •   •   •   •   •   •   •   •   •   •   •   127 00 002
    THE EARTH AND HEAVEN, SO LITTLE KNOWN,   •   •   •   •   •   •   •   •   130 00 001
    ARE NEVER KNOWN FOR FAIR.   •   •   •   •   •   •   •   •   •   •   •   133 00 016
    WHO THINKS OF THECLA? YET HER NAME WAS KNOWN,   •   •   •   •   •   136 00 003
    IS KNOWN TO MEN MORE THAN ME.   •   •   •   •   •   •   •   •   •   138 00 013
    C MADE KNOWN, THOUGH THICK THROUGH STONE,   •   •   •   •   •   •   148 00 011
    C WHO BUILT THESE WALLS MADE KNOWN   •   •   •   •   •   •   •   •   148 00 037
KNOWS
    GROWS LESS AND LESS SWEET TO HIM, AND KNOWS NO CAUSE.   •   •   •   014 03 014
    MARY THE VIRGIN, WELL THE HEART KNOWS.   •   •   •   •   •   •   •   027 00 021
    TO ME, GOD KNOWS, DESERVING NO SUCH THING: •   •   •   •   •   •   034 00 002
    WHATEVER IS FICKLE, FRECKLED (WHO KNOWS HOW?)   •   •   •   •   •   037 00 008
    NOT THAT HELL KNOWS REDEEMING,   •   •   •   •   •   •   •   •   •   041 00 117
    DOFF DARKNESS, HOMING NATURE KNOWS THE REST --   •   •   •   •   •   047 00 006
    MARK CHRIST OUR KING. HE KNOWS WAR, SERVED THIS SOLDIERING THROUGH: 063 00 009
    AT GOD KNOWS WHEN TO GOD KNOWS WHAT: WHOSE SMILE   •   •   •   •   069 00 012
    AT GOD KNOWS WHEN TO GOD KNOWS WHAT: WHOSE SMILE   •   •   •   •   069 00 012
    HER CHOICE IN ROSES KNOWS BY HEART: •   •   •   •   •   •   •   •   083 00 022
    BY HEADY ELEMENTS, FOR NO MAN KNOWS: •   •   •   •   •   •   •   103 00 005
    SHE LOVES HIS FACE, SHE KNOWS THE SPOT: •   •   •   •   •   •   •   120 00 002

LABOURED-AT
    YOUR SPOUSE NOT LABOURED-AT NOR SPUN.   •   •   •   •   •   •   •   •   022 00 028

LABOURING
~ ROLLS ACROSS THE LABOURING WILLOWS: 078 00 004
LABOURS
THE LABOURS I SHOULD THEN HAVE SPENT 015 00 011
LACE
WITH LACE OF ROSY WEED WERE CHAPLETED: 002 00 059
THAT LACE THE FACE OF PENMAEN POOL. 030 00 028
LACE, LATCH OR CATCH OR KEY TO KEEP C 059 0L 001
SHIVELIGHTS AND SHADOWTACKLE IN LONG LASHES LACE, LANCE, AND PAIR. . 072 00 004
THEY SWATHE AND LACE THE SHROUD-PLAITS O'ER MY FACE, . . . 080 05 006
LACED
AND THE MIDRIFF ASTRAIN WITH LEANING OF, LACED WITH FIRE OF STRESS. . 028 02 008
LIFE ALL LACED IN THE OTHER'S, ... 054 00 002
NOW, LEAVED HOW THICK! LACED THEY ARE AGAIN 074 00 010
LACE-LEAVED
AND LACE-LEAVED LOVELY 138 00 029
LACES
AND MORE AND MORE TIMES LACES ROUND AND ROUND MY HEART, . . 152 01 013
LACK
I PLOD WONDERING, A-WANTING, JUST FOR LACK 046 00 006
THEN AT THE DOOR WHAT WORK THERE WAS, GOOD LACK, . . . 135 00 005
LACKLEVEL
LITTLE I RECK HO! LACKLEVEL IN, IF ALL HAD BREAD: . . . 070 00 009
LAD
AND LOCKS LOVE EVER IN A LAD! 048 00 035
MY LAD, AND LOST IN JACK, ... 054 00 018
LADE
LADS AND MEN HER LADE AND TREASURE. 041 00 012
LADED
THE LADES DISCHARGED AND LADED NEW, ... 166 00 035
LADEN
AND I COME LADEN FROM SUCH FLOODS 098 19 005
LADES
THE LADES DISCHARGED AND LADED NEW, ... 166 00 035
LADIES
GUILTY OF SILENCE? QUITE, AS LADIES GO. 125 00 023
LADS
LADS AND MEN HER LADE AND TREASURE. 041 00 012
THOSE LOVELY LADS ONCE, WET-FRESH WINDFALLS OF WAR'S STORM, . . 062 00 006
LADY
CANDLEMAS, LADY DAY! 042 00 005
BUT THE LADY MONTH, MAY, ... 042 00 006
' O HAVE YOU HERE A FOREIGN LADY 109 07 003
' O I HAVE HERE NO FOREIGN LADY 109 08 001
' THEN WILL YOU WED WITH AN ENGLISH LADY, ... 109 08 003
SAYS ' GET YOU, GET YOU A LADY TO WED 109 09 001
THERE WAS A LADY VERY GAY, ... 131 00 002
LADY-STAR
SUCH OPPOSITION TO THE LADY-STAR 014 02 010
LAG
YOU TO BE GONE AND I LAG LAST -- 134 00 003
LAGGING
O THEN IF IN MY LAGGING LINES YOU MISS 076 00 011
LAID
LOOKS LAID FOR FEASTING AND FOR REST. 003 00 024
AND, ON A THOUSAND ALTARS LAID, ... 006 00 009
BACKWARD ARE LAID HER PRETTY BLACK-FLEECED EARS: . . . 099 00 013
AS THE LAID GOSSAMERS OF MICHAELMAS 102 01 021
THEY HAD THEM OUT AND LAID THEM WIDE 145 00 049
LAIR
SHEATHE THEE IN THY DARK LAIR! THESE DROPS C . . . 152 02 015
LAKE
FLUTES AND LOW TO THE LAKE FALLS HOME. 056 00 004
IN WHOSE DEAD LAKE EVEN A VOICE MAY MAKE 080 04 003
HOUSES THAT MAKE ABODE BESIDE THE LAKE, ... 080 06 006
LAKES
CLUSTERING ENTRANCINGLY IN BERYL LAKES: 002 00 014
WOOD BANKS AND BRAKES WASH WET LIKE LAKES . . . 042 00 042
IN LAKES OF BLUEBELLS, PIECED WITH PRIMROSES. . . . 098 09 003
HER HUE'S A VARIOUS BROWN WITH CREAMY LAKES, . . . 099 00 011
LAMB'S
FOR LETTERING OF THE LAMB'S FLEECE, RUDDYING OF THE ROSE-FLAKE. . 028 22 008
LAMBS
WITH RICHNESS! THE RACING LAMBS TOO HAVE FAIR THEIR FLING. . . 033 00 008
LAME
MORE POWERLESS THAN THE BLIND OR LAME. 015 00 020
LAMENT
NOT TODAY WE NEED LAMENT 029 00 013
HOURS I MEAN YEARS, MEAN LIFE. AND MY LAMENT . . . 067 00 006
LAMENTABLE
AND KINDRED TO MY LAMENTABLE DAYS, ... 125 00 046
LAMENTS
' AS WHEN A SOUL LAMENTS, WHICH HATH BEEN BLEST ' -- . . 119 00 009
LAMPS
VACANT CREATION'S LAMPS APPAL. 023 00 012
LANCASHIRE
SOUTHERN DEAN OR LANCASHIRE CLOUGH OR DEVON CLEAVE, . . 159 00 004

138

LANCE
    WITH THE GNARLS OF THE NAILS IN THEE, NICHE OF THE LANCE, HIS • • 028 23 003
    SHIVELIGHTS AND SHADOWTACKLE IN LONG LASHES LACE, LANCE, AND PAIR. • 072 00 004
    FOR MY SAKE SUFFEREDST NAILS AND LANCE, • • • • • • 170 00 007
LANCED
    BRIGHT SUN LANCED FIRE IN THE HEAVENLY BAY; • • • • • 041 00 022
LANCING
    SPUR, LIVE AND LANCING LIKE THE BLOWPIPE FLAME, • • • • 076 00 002
LAND
    WHILE FROM THE PULPIT IN A HERETIC LAND • • • • • 001 05 001
    ARE ALL THE MANNA-BUSHES IN THE LAND • • • • • 005 00 021
    FROM EASY RUNNELS THE RICH-PIECED LAND • • • • • 005 00 039
    MEET IN ONE ACRE OF ONE LAND, • • • • • 008 00 011
    BANNED BY THE LAND OF THEIR BIRTH, • • • • • 028 21 002
    LEFT HAND, OFF LAND, I HEAR THE LARK ASCEND, • • • • 035 00 005
    AND THE BLOW BORE FROM LAND. • • • • • 041 00 020
    I GIVE YOU MY LOVE AND I GIVE YOU MY LAND, • • • • 109 05 003
    OR EVER HE SET HIS FOOT TO THE LAND • • • • • 109 07 001
    LORD WILLIAM IS KING OF ALL THIS LAND • • • • • 109 27 003
    IF HE WERE KING OF ALL THIS LAND • • • • • 109 28 003
    AND ART THOU COME FROM ENGLISH LAND, • • • • 109 31 003
    ‘ I AM NOT COME FROM ENGLISH LAND, • • • • 109 32 001
    WHO IS IT? HOW COME TO THIS FORGOTTEN LAND? • • • 122 00 019
    WHAT SHALL I DO FOR THE LAND THAT BRED ME? • • • 156 00 001
LANDMARK
    A WONDER IN THE COUNTRY, AND A LANDMARK • • • • 125 00 004
    WHERE LIES YOUR LANDMARK, SEAMARK, OR SOUL'S STAR? • • • 157 00 019
LAND'S
    THAT, WARRING, WASTED THE LAND'S INCREASE, • • • • 026 00 028
LANDS
    AT MORN THEY COME UPON OUR LANDS LIKE RAINS; • • • 104 00 008
LANDSCAPE
    HERE IN SOME DARKEN'D LANDSCAPE PARIS FAIR • • • 001 11 001
    AND ALL THE LANDSCAPE UNDER SURVEY, • • • • 030 00 013
    LANDSCAPE PLOTTED AND PIECED -- FOLD, FALLOW, AND PLOUGH; • 037 00 005
    EARTH, SWEET EARTH, SWEET LANDSCAPE, WITH LEAVES THRONG • 058 00 001
    THE WHOLE LANDSCAPE FLUSHES ON A SUDDEN AT A SOUND. • • 146 00 005
LANDSLIPS
    OR WEEDED LANDSLIPS OF THE SHORE. • • • • 015 00 024
LANES
    OF WRINGING TREE-TOPS, CHALKY LANES, • • • • 077 00 135
LANGUENT
    THE LANGUENT SMOOTH WITH DIMPLING DROPS, AND FLASH • • • 002 00 103
LANGUISH'D
    OF THOSE GILT WEBS THAT LANGUISH'D IN A FALL. • • • 001 06 007
    SWIMMING, AND LANGUISH'D GREEN UPON THE DEEP • • • 002 00 114
LANK
    BREATHED ROUND; THE RACK OF RIBS; THE SCOOPED FLANK; LANK • 071 00 002
LANTERN
    SOMETIMES A LANTERN MOVES ALONG THE NIGHT, • • • 040 00 001
    NIGHT'S LANTERN • • • • • • • • 098 24 001
    I MUST NOT TURN THE LANTERN ON HIS FACE. -- • • • 102 01 024
LAP
    LIES IN HER LAP, WHICH SHE ANON SWEEPS OFF. • • • 111 00 009
LAPPED
    HAND RATHER, MY HEART LO! LAPPED STRENGTH, C • • • 064 00 011
    AND LAPPED IN SHINING HAIR, ROLL TO THE BANK'S EDGE; THEN • • 152 02 019
LAPS
    SKYWARDS: RICH, RICH IT LAPS • • • • • 060 00 077
LAPSED
    BUT WHEN THE SUN HAD LAPSED TO OCEAN, LO • • • • 002 00 136
LARGE
    IT IS TOO LARGE FOR ME. WHAT DOES THAT MEAN? • • • 102 01 026
    NOW LET ME SEE YOU, YOU LARGE PRINCELY HAND, • • • 102 01 043
LARK
    LEFT HAND, OFF LAND, I HEAR THE LARK ASCEND, • • • 035 00 005
    OR, LIKE A LARK TO GLIDE ALOOF • • • • • 077 00 065
    TO RISE YOU BID ME WITH THE LARK; • • • • • 096 06 001
    TO CANVASS THE RETIREMENT OF THE LARK • • • • 113 00 002
LARK-CHARMED
    CUCKOO-ECHOING, BELL-SWARMED, LARK-CHARMED, C • • • 044 00 002
LARKSPUR
    THAT WAS HER LARKSPUR ROW. -- SO SOON? • • • • 010 00 022
LARKSPUR'S
    THE DEWDROP ON THE LARKSPUR'S MOUTH • • • • 010 00 015
LASH
    WE LASH WITH THE BEST OR WORST • • • • • 028 08 002
    NOT THE LEAST LASH LOST; EVERY HAIR C • • • • 059 06 020
LASHED
    O AT LIGHTNING AND LASHED ROD; • • • • • 028 02 002
    THEM -- BROAD IN BLUFF HIDE HIS FROWNING FEET LASHED! RACED • • 071 00 013
LASHES
    SHIVELIGHTS AND SHADOWTACKLE IN LONG LASHES LACE, LANCE, AND PAIR. • 072 00 004
    WITH LEVELL'D LASHES STILLING THEIR DISQUIET; • • • 082 00 002
    THEIR HIGHEST SPRAYS WERE DRAWN AS FINE AS LASHES, • • 107 04 006
LASHTENDER
    FAST OR THEY IN CLAMMYISH LASHTENDER COMBS CREEP • • • 149 A 005

LAST
    CAME MIDST THE DRIZZLE TELLING HOW LAST NIGHT · · · · · · · 001 14 002
    LAY BLEEDING, TO MADRID THE LAST THEY BORE, · · · · · · · 001 15 002
    SLUMBER'D AT LAST IN ONE SWEET, DEEP, HEART-BROKEN CLOSE. · · 002 00 135
    THE STEEP-UP ROOF AT LAST BEHIND THE SMALL · · · · · · 012 02 006
    HAS NOT A CHARTER THAT ITS SAP SHALL LAST · · · · · · 014 01 004
    THE FURNACE SHALL AT LAST BE COLD. · · · · · · · 015 00 016
    IF I SHALL OVERTAKE THEE AT LAST ABOVE, · · · · · · 020 00 016
    SINCE ITS BIRTH, AND ITS BLOOM, AND ITS BREATHING ITS LAST. · · 027 00 016
    WORD LAST! HOW A LUSH-KEPT PLUSH-CAPPED SLOE · · · · 028 08 003
    BRIM, IN A FLASH, FULL! -- HITHER THEN, LAST OR FIRST, · · 028 08 006
    AND LIVES AT LAST WERE WASHING AWAY; · · · · · · 028 15 007
    AND THOUGH THE LAST LIGHTS OFF THE BLACK WEST WENT · · · 031 00 011
    TO MAN'S LAST DUST, DRAIN FAST TOWARDS MAN'S FIRST SLIME. · · 035 00 014
    THEIR RANSOM, THEIR RESCUE, AND FIRST, FAST, LAST FRIEND. · · 040 00 014
    JACK'S CALL AND CUE AT LAST; · · · · · · · · 054 00 030
    NOT UNTWIST -- SLACK THEY MAY BE -- THESE LAST STRANDS OF MAN · 064 00 002
    BUT YET THEY SAY CHRIST COMES AT THE LAST DAY. · · · · 080 01 006
    AT LAST I HEAR THE VOICE WELL KNOWN; · · · · · · 081 00 001
    AT LAST I HEAR THE VOICE I KNEW. · · · · · · · 081 00 025
    AS THE LAST PLEIAD, YEA BEHIND · · · · · · · 081 00 046
    I YIELD ' I WOULD HAVE CRIED. AT LAST · · · · · 081 00 117
    AT LAST UP THE BLUE ELEMENT. · · · · · · · · 087 00 006
    THOUGH SELF-MADE BANDS AT LAST MAY TRUE LOVE BIND, · · · 102 03 019
    TO SINGLE SATURN, LAST AND SOLITARY; · · · · · · 103 00 015
    AT LAST THE BIRD IS FOUND A FLICKERING SHAPE AND SLIM. · · 113 00 009
    AND WITH THE LAST POST OVER I KNEW NO LETTER WAS SENT. · · 128 00 002
    AND IF YOU WRITE AT LAST, IT NEVER CAN BE THE SAME; · · · 128 00 003
    FOR A LETTER COMES AT LAST; (SHALL I SAY BEFORE CHRISTMAS IS COME?) 128 00 019
    YOU TO BE GONE AND I LAG LAST -- · · · · · · · 134 00 003
    THEY ROSE AT LAST AND FORCED HER FROM THE SPOT. · · · 136 00 034
    AND KIND COMPASSION, AT HIS LIFE'S LAST NEED · · · · 140 00 004
    THE LAST THING MARGARET'S FINGERS SEW · · · · · · 145 00 013
    AND THEN THAT LAST AND SHORTEST · · · · · · · 153 00 011
    FAST HE OPENS, LAST HE OFF WRINGS · · · · · · · 159 00 034
    TO THE WORLD'S END, TO THE LAST HILL · · · · · · 160 00 024
    WHERE ROSES LINGER LAST. · · · · · · · · · 165 00 004
LASTING
    THE DAY THAT BROUGHT MY LASTING PAIN · · · · · · 021 00 010
LATCH
    WHAT DEATH HALF LIFTS THE LATCH OF, · · · · · · 049 00 019
    LACE, LATCH OR CATCH OR KEEP C · · · · · · · 059 0L 001
LATE
    BUT FROM THE MOUNTAIN GLENS IN AUTUMN LATE · · · · · 001 13 001
    YET IT IS NOW TOO LATE TO HEAL · · · · · · · 015 00 017
    THEREFORE HOW BITTER, AND LEARNT HOW LATE, THE TRUTH! · · 017 00 014
    THE AUTHENTIC CADENCE WAS DISCOVERED LATE · · · · 019 00 009
    TOO LATE; LOST; GONE WITH THE GALE. · · · · · · 041 00 036
    MY LATE BEING THERE BEGGED OF ME, OVERFLOWING · · · 048 00 006
    WHO RISING LATE HAD MISS'D HER PAINFUL WAY · · · · 079 00 005
    LATE IN THE GREEN WEEKS OF APRIL · · · · · · 081 00 021
    FIVE NOTES OR SEVEN, LATE AND FEW; · · · · · · 081 00 023
    THEY BREATHE NOT WHO ARE LATE TO RUN, -- · · · · 081 00 148
    LATE I FELL IN THE ECSTACY · · · · · · · · 093 A 001
    THE TIME WAS LATE AND THE WET YELLOW WOODS · · · · 098 05 001
    SO LATE THE HOAR GREEN CHESTNUT BREAKS A BUD, · · · 105 00 009
    SO LATE THERE IS NO FORCE IN SAP OR BLOOD; · · · · 105 00 011
    TOO LATE OR ELSE MUCH, MUCH TOO SOON, · · · · · 105 00 016
    BUT LATE IS BETTER THAN NEVER: YOU SEE YOU HAVE MANAGED SO, · 128 00 017
LATE-FOUND
    FLORIS, THOU LATE-FOUND ALL-HEAL! · · · · · · 102 01 060
LATE-LEARNT
    THAT I MAY WIN WITH LATE-LEARNT SKILL UNCOUTH · · · 017 00 012
LATELY
    -- LATELY I FEAR'D · · · · · · · · · · 102 01 006
    DID I SAY BUT LATELY · · · · · · · · · 102 01 029
LAUDED
    BY ANY LAUDED STATUE, NOR AGAIN · · · · · · · 125 00 026
LAUGH
    WITH CORN THAT THEY SHALL LAUGH AND SING. · · · · 008 00 017
    STOLE JOY, WOULD LAUGH, CHEER, C · · · · · · 064 00 011
LAUGHING
    LAUGHING OR TEARS. I THINK I COULD DO EITHER -- · · · 102 01 014
LAUGH'ST
    YE RIVER-HEADS, THOU BILLOWY DEEP THAT LAUGH'ST · · · 160 00 002
LAUGHS
    WHILE HE LOOKS ABOUT HIM, LAUGHS, SWIMS. C · · · · 159 00 042
LAUGHTER
    GROSS MIND DISCHARGING FOULED LAUGHTER; · · · · · 077 00 058
    THE WIND COMES BREAKING HERE AND THERE WITH LAUGHTER; · · 098 03 003
    METHINKS MY LAUGHTER IS MORE PERILOUS V · · · · 102 01 008
    ------ THERE IS MORE PERIL FROM MY LAUGHTER. V · · · 102 01 009
    THAT TEARS AND LAUGHTER ARE HUNG CLOSE TOGETHER. · · · 102 01 016
    THAT I WAS SO NEAR LAUGHTER? ALAS NOW · · · · · 102 01 030
    A COUNTLESS LAUGHTER, EARTH MOTHER OF ALL, · · · · 160 00 003
LAVER'D
    THEN LAVER'D FOUNTS AND POSTUR'D STONE HE MIX'D. · · · 001 04 005

LAW
  FORGET THE WAKING TRUMPET, THE LONG LAW. • • • • • • • • • 005 00 044
  THIS AIR, WHICH, BY LIFE'S LAW, • • • • • • • • • • 060 00 013
  OUR LAW SAYS: LOVE WHAT ARE LOVE'S WORTHIEST, WERE ALL KNOWN! • • 062 00 010
  YOUR WILL IS LAW IN THAT SMALL COMMONWEAL• • • • • • • 150 00 011
  LOYAL TO HIS OWN SOUL, LAYING HIS OWN LAW DOWN, NO LAW NOR • • • 152 02 040
  LOYAL TO HIS OWN SOUL, LAYING HIS OWN LAW DOWN, NO LAW NOR • • • 152 02 040
  BE, OUT OF NATURE'S LAW • • • • • • • • • • • APPEN D 29
LAWLESS
  RIFE IN HER WRONGS, MORE LAWLESS, AND MORE LEWD. • • • • • 050 00 008
  THE LAWLESS HONEY EATEN OF OLD • • • • • • • • • 092 00 004
LAWNS
  THE GREY LAWNS COLD WHERE GOLD, WHERE QUICKGOLD LIES! • • • 032 00 005
LAWRENCE
  OF BATTLE ONCE UPON ST. LAWRENCE' DAY • • • • • • • 001 02 002
  THE RICHEST GIFT ST. LAWRENCE EVER BORE, • • • • • • • 001 02 006
LAW'S
  IS LAW'S INDIFFERENCE. • • • • • • • • • • • 148 00 008
LAY
  WHEN CHIEFS AND MONARCHS CAME THEIR GIFTS TO LAY • • • • • 001 02 007
  WHILE HIS CRACK'D FLESH LAY HISSING ON THE GRATE; • • • • • 001 03 002
  THE STRETCHING PALACE LAY AS HANDLE FIX'D. • • • • • • 001 04 004
  LAY BLEEDING, TO MADRID THE LAST THEY BORE, • • • • • • 001 15 002
  A MILE ASTERN LAY THE BLUE SHORES AWAY! • • • • • • • 002 00 005
  LAY ALONG THE GRASSES GREEN • • • • • • • • • 004 00 022
  AND THEN LAY BACK TO SLEEP. • • • • • • • • • 021 00 053
  MY HAND UPON MY LIPS I LAY! • • • • • • • • • 023 00 037
  CROUCH! LAY KNEE BY EARTH LOW UNDER: • • • • • • • 041 00 110
  LET HIM OH! WITH HIS AIR OF ANGELS THEN LIFT ME, LAY ME! ONLY I'LL • 045 00 009
  THY WRING-WORLD RIGHT FOOT ROCK? LAY A LIONLIMB AGAINST ME? SCAN • 064 00 006
  OF NOW DONE DARKNESS I WRETCH LAY WRESTLING WITH (MY GOD!) MY GOD. • 064 00 014
  DOES LAY MEN LOW WITH ONE BLADE'S SUDDEN BLOW • • • • • 080 02 003
  MOST DENTED) LAY SYLVESTER, READING KEATS' • • • • • 107 04 021
  AS SHE LAY WEEPING AT THE NIGHT • • • • • • • • 109 29 001
  LAY OPEN THINE ESTATES. • • • • • • • • • • 115 00 007
  I'LL LAY THEM BY, AND FRESHLY TURN INSTEAD • • • • • • 117 00 013
  TREAD BACK -- AND BACK, THE LEWD AND LAY! -- • • • • • 166 00 001
LAYING
  LAYING, LIKE AIR'S FINE FLOOD, • • • • • • • • 060 00 051
  LOYAL TO HIS OWN SOUL, LAYING HIS OWN LAW DOWN, NO LAW NOR • • 152 02 040
LAYS
  OF THE OUTWARD SENTENCE LOW LAYS HIM, LISTED TO A HERESY, HERE. • • 045 00 004
LAZULI
  WERE VEIN'D AND STREAK'D WITH DUSK-DEEP LAZULI, • • • • • 002 00 046
LEA
  CAME RUNNING OVER THE LEA. • • • • • • • • • 109 17 004
LEAD
  AND LEAD ME CHILD-LIKE BY THE HAND • • • • • • • 023 00 047
  THIS ICE, THIS LEAD, THIS STEEL, THIS STONE, • • • • • • 081 00 128
  OF RIVERS, LEAD, THRO' STORMS AND NIGHTS, • • • • • • 083 00 004
  BUT SINGLE, LEAD A MISDIRECTED LIFE. • • • • • • • 094 00 032
  LEAD SHEPHERD, NOW WE FOLLOW, SHEPHERD LEAD. • • • • • 098 15 007
  LEAD SHEPHERD, NOW WE FOLLOW, SHEPHERD LEAD. • • • • • 098 15 007
  BUT THE BETHLEHEM STAR MAY LEAD ME • • • • • • • 129 00 003
LEAF
  WHEN HE HAS MADE US BEAR HIS LOAD. -- • • • • • • 006 00 030
  OR WHERE IS STRENGTH TO MAKE THE LEAF UNFOLD? • • • • • 017 00 004
  MAKE ME A LEAF IN THEE, MOTHER OF MINE. • • • • • • 027 00 042
  WITH HIS PULL'D AND PLOTTED LEAF. • • • • • • • 098 18 004
  TOOK PRIMROSES, THEIR PULL'D AND PLOTTED LEAF • • • • • 107 03 018
  PARTED ME LEAF AND LEAF, DIVIDED ME, EYELID AND EYELID OF SLUMBER. • 137 00 007
  PARTED ME LEAF AND LEAF, DIVIDED ME, EYELID AND EYELID OF SLUMBER. • 137 00 007
LEAFING
  THE HAPPY LEAFING. IT IS SO WITH ME: • • • • • • 014 01 006
LEAF-LIGHT
  LOW-LATCHED IN LEAF-LIGHT HOUSEL HIS TOO HUGE GODHEAD. • • • 048 00 012
LEAFLESS
  THE RIV'N VINE, LEAFLESS, LIFELESS, DRY: • • • • • • 006 00 022
LEAFMEAL
  THOUGH WORLDS OF WANWOOD LEAFMEAL LIE: • • • • • • 055 00 008
LEAFWHELMED
  WE ARE LEAFWHELMED SOMEWHERE WITH THE HOOD • • • • • 159 00 002
LEAFY
  THEN SOUGHT SUCH LEAFY SHELTER AS IT YIELDS, • • • • • 107 03 016
  SO LONG TO THIS SWEET SPOT, THIS LEAFY LEAN-OVER, • • • • 152 C 011
LEAGUES
  LEAGUES, LEAGUES OF SEAMANSHIP • • • • • • • 041 00 082
  LEAGUES, LEAGUES OF SEAMANSHIP • • • • • • • 041 00 082
LEANING
  AND THE MIDRIFF ASTRAIN WITH LEANING OF, LACED WITH FIRE OF STRESS, • 028 02 008
  MAN LIVES THAT LIST, THAT LEANING IN THE WILL • • • • • 157 00 025
LEAN-OVER
  SO LONG TO THIS SWEET SPOT, THIS LEAFY LEAN-OVER, • • • • 152 C 011
LEANS
  FOR LOVE HE LEANS FORTH, NEEDS HIS NECK MUST FALL ON, KISS, • • 063 00 012
  HE LEANS TO IT, HARRY BENDS, LOOK. BACK, ELBOW, AND LIQUID WAIST • 071 00 009
  FORWARD SHE LEANS, WITH HOLLOWING BACK, STOCK-STILL, • • • 099 00 001

LEANS   (CONTINUED)
        SHE LEANS ON HIM WITH SUCH CONTENTMENT FOND 157 00 013
        THAT LEANS ALONG THE LOINS OF HILLS, WHERE A CANDYCOLOURED, C . . 159 00 005
LEAP
        THE LIGHTNINGS LEAP, THE DAY OF DOOM! 080 07 004
LEAPING
        QUELLED OR QUENCHED IN LEAVES THE LEAPING SUN, ... 043 00 002
        BUT MINE IS DREADFUL LEAPING PAIN, ... 081 00 051
LEAPS
        LEAPS UP BEFORE MY VISION, -- THOU ART GONE. 098 33 002
LEARN
        LEARN HOW THE HEART IS HENCE: 148 00 006
LEARNED
        BLINDNESS! A LEARNED FOOL AND WELL-BRED CHURL 102 03 032
        A LEARNED FOOL INDEED AND WELL-BRED CHURL V 102 03 038
LEARNER
        WHEN YOU WERE LEARNER AND I READ, ... 081 00 165
LEARNING
        FOR LEARNING STORED AND GARNERED? 081 00 169
LEARNT
        THEREFORE HOW BITTER, AND LEARNT HOW LATE, THE TRUTH! . . 017 00 014
        AND LEARNT HER NOT TO STARTLE AT HIS NAME. 082 00 008
        BUT HAS NOT LEARNT TO TAKE IT GRACEFULLY: 094 00 016
LEAS
        STREAKS OF SHADOW, THISTLED LEAS, ... 077 00 137
LEASE
        O WHERE LIVE WELL YOUR LEASE OF LEISURE 030 00 003
LEASH
        SHE PUTS IN LEASH HER PAIR'D LIPS LEST SURPRISE 082 00 003
LEAST
        THOSE SWEET HOPES QUELL WHOSE LEAST ME QUICKENINGS LIFT, . . 048 00 037
        NOT THE LEAST LASH LOST: EVERY HAIR C 059 06 020
        IN EVERY LEAST THING'S LIFE: 060 00 008
        WHAT I DO NOW IS BUT THE LEAST LEAST THING. 102 01 051
        WHAT I DO NOW IS BUT THE LEAST LEAST THING. 102 01 051
        MOST ILL-CONTENT, THIS LEAST LEAST THING I DO. 102 01 054
        MOST ILL-CONTENT, THIS LEAST LEAST THING I DO. 102 01 054
        ALLOW AT LEAST IT HAS ONE TERM AND PART 102 03 005
        WHICH SAYS AT LEAST THEN GO WHILE ALL IS FRESH, -- . . . 125 00 058
LEAVE
        THE SUMPTUOUS RIDGE-CREST LEAVE TO POISE AND RIDE, . . . 012 02 008
        HER PERSEUS LINGER AND LEAVE HER TO HER EXTREMES? -- . . 050 00 009
        O SURELY, REAVING PEACE, MY LORD SHOULD LEAVE IN LIEU . . 051 00 007
        SOME GOOD! AND SO HE DOES LEAVE PATIENCE EXQUISITE, . . . 051 00 008
        HOME AT HEART, HEAVEN'S SWEET GIFT: THEN LEAVE, LET THAT ALONE. 062 00 013
        THEN LULL, THEN LEAVE OFF. FURY HAD SHRIEKED ' NO LING- . . 065 00 007
        ELSEWHERE! LEAVE COMFORT ROOT-ROOM: LET JOY SIZE . . . 069 00 011
        FALL TO THE RESIDUARY WORM: WORLD'S WILDFIRE, LEAVE BUT ASH: 072 00 020
        OR IF HE LEAVE THE WEST BEHIND, ... 083 00 005
        LEAVE IT WITH ITS GROVE HARD BY 098 15 003
        LONG. WHERE WE LEAVE HIM, FROLICLAVISH, C 159 00 042
LEAVED
        AND FIVE-LIVED AND LEAVED FAVOUR AND PRIDE, ... 028 23 006
        NOW, LEAVED HOW THICK! LACED THEY ARE AGAIN 074 00 010
        AND OAKS, -- BUT THESE WERE LEAVED IN SHARPER KNOTS. . . 107 04 008
LEAVES
        THE HOARSE LEAVES CRAWL ON HISSING GROUND 003 00 005
        OF LEAVES OF GREENEST FLESH. 005 00 034
        LEAVES SPENT, NEW SEASONS, ALTER'D SKY, ... 015 00 002
        THE MIST UPON THE LEAVES HAVE STREWED, ... 021 00 033
        HOW MANY LEAVES HAD IT? FIVE THEY WERE THEN, ... 027 00 037
        THE GLASSY PEARTREE LEAVES AND BLOOMS, THEY BRUSH . . . 033 00 006
        QUELLED OR QUENCHED IN LEAVES THE LEAPING SUN, ... 043 00 002
        LEAVES, LIKE THE THINGS OF MAN, YOU 055 00 003
        EARTH, SWEET EARTH, SWEET LANDSCAPE, WITH LEAVES THRONG . . 058 00 001
        AND HER HAND LEAVES HIS LIGHT 060 00 112
        HEARD UNHEEDED, LEAVES ME A LONELY BEGAN. 066 00 014
        PURPLE EYES AND SEAS OF LIQUID LEAVES ALL DAY. 068 00 008
        LEAVES YET THE MIND A MOTHER OF IMMORTAL SONG. 076 00 004
        THE FALL IS O'ER, TOLD OFF THE LEAVES, ... 081 00 009
        YET LEAVES HIM IN UNGIRDLED EASE 083 00 015
        THAT LICK THE SHELLY LEAVES WHICH FLOOR THE COPSE, . . . 084 00 004
        AND LEAVES THE BLADES, WHERE'ER HE WILL VEER, ... 098 01 003
        TOLD OFF THEIR LEAVES ALONG THE PIERCING GALE, ... 098 05 002
        THE BREAKING LEAVES OF GOLD ARE CURL'D UPON HER LIPS. . . 098 14 003
        LIGHTED THE WATERY-PLATED LEAVES. V 098 17 002
        AND FEEDS NEW LEAVES UPON THE WINDS OF FALL: 105 00 010
        GREAT BUTTER-BURR LEAVES FLOOR'D THE SLOPE CORPSE GROUND . . 107 04 009
        HER SHOWY LEAVES STAID WATCHET COUNTERFOILING V 108 00 005
        HER SHOWY LEAVES WITH GENTLE WATCHET FOILING V 108 00 006
        WHOSE ALL-BELATED LEAVES YIELD UP THEMSELVES 111 00 002
        MEANWHILE A LITTER OF THE JAGGED LEAVES 111 00 008
        A BRANCH OF WALNUT LEAVES, AND THAT 120 00 006
        AND A FEW LEAVES NOT LILY-WHITE BUT CHARACTERED OVER WITH BLACKS. . 128 00 016
        A JUICE RIDES RICH THROUGH BLUEBELLS, IN VINE-LEAVES, . . 157 00 003
        BY, RAFTS AND RAFTS OF FLAKE LEAVES LIGHT, C 159 00 025
LEAVING
        HIDEOUS DASHED DOWN, LEAVING EARTH A WINTER WITHERING . . . 152 02 052

142

LEAVING   (CONTINUED)
    I SHOULD BE WRONGING LONGER LEAVING IT TO FLOAT 159 00 044
LED
    WHICH SHOULD ERE NOW HAVE LED MY FEET TO THE FIELD. 017 00 009
    AND FAIN WOULD FOLLOW I WHO LED. 081 00 172
    LED RICHARD WITH A SWEET UNDOING PAIN 107 04 017
LEDGES
    ON TO LEDGES OF GREY CLOUD: 077 00 080
LEEWARD
    SHE DROVE IN THE DARK TO LEEWARD, ... 028 14 001
LEFT
    FAIR RELICS TOO THE CHANGEFUL MOOR HAD LEFT 001 08 001
    BUT FURTHER DOWN THE VALLEY, LEFT AND RIGHT, ... 001 14 004
    THE MONKS LEFT LONG AGO: SINCE WHICH NO MORE 001 15 004
    IT SEEMS: FOR GRANDEUR BARREN LEFT AND DULL 001 15 008
    FLICKERING WITH SUNNY SPOKES, AND LEFT AND RIGHT 002 00 077
    YOU'VE PARLOUR-PASTIME LEFT AND { WHO'LL 030 00 034
    LEFT HAND, OFF LAND, I HEAR THE LARK ASCEND, ... 035 00 005
    THAT LEFT TO THE LORD OF THE EUCHARIST, I HERE LIE BY: . . 048 00 044
    OF WET AND OF WILDNESS? LET THEM BE LEFT, ... 056 00 014
    O LET THEM BE LEFT, WILDNESS AND WET: 056 00 015
    NAY, WHAT WE HAD LIGHTHANDED LEFT IN SURLY THE MERE MOULD . 059 04 022
    THE POINT FAST IN, AND MY LEFT HAND 080 13 004
    MERCY IS LEFT ENOUGH FOR ONE: 081 00 105
    LEFT NOT A ROOD WITH CURSES UNIMPREGNATE: 102 02 005
    CREPT ALL ALONG A HILL UPON OUR LEFT, ... 125 00 003
    EITHER LEFT EITHER RIGHT 138 00 008
    NEXT AFTER SWEET SUCCESS, I AM NOT LEFT EVEN THIS: . . . 152 02 059
    I HAVE LIFE LEFT WITH ME STILL 155 00 017
LEGATES
    LEGATES MIGHT RUSH, ZEAL-RAMPANT, FIERY, ... 001 05 005
LEGER
    AND SHEATHE AT ONCE HIS LEGER WING. 130 00 012
LEGION
    AND WOULD NOT HAVE THAT LEGION OF WINGED THINGS 007 00 014
LEISURE
    O WHERE LIVE WELL YOUR LEASE OF LEISURE 030 00 003
    AND FACES FIT FOR LEISURE GAZE 133 00 013
LEND
    LEND HIM A LIFT FROM THE SEA-SWILL. 041 00 064
    HARK, HEARER, HEAR WHAT I DO; LEND A THOUGHT NOW, MAKE BELIEVE . 159 00 001
    LEND THIS LIFE TO ME THEN: FEED AND FEAST MY MIND, . . . 168 00 019
LENDS
    SHE LENDS, IN AID OF WORK AND WILL, ... 139 00 003
LENGTH
    A SOMBRE LENGTH OF GREY: FOUR TOWERS PLACED 001 01 003
    THEIR FILMY TAILS ADOWN WHOSE LENGTH THERE SHOW'D . . . 002 00 104
    AT LENGTH THE BELLOWS SHALL NOT BLOW, ... 015 00 015
    WE, ALL WE, THRO' THE LENGTH OF OUR DAYS, ... 026 00 034
LENT
    ONCE IT WAS SCARCE PERCEIVED LENT 081 00 011
    THEY'RE OUT OF DATE -- LENT SERMONS ALL THE YEAR. . . . 096 05 002
LENTEN
    GOD COMES ALL SWEETNESS TO YOUR LENTEN LIPS. 011 00 002
    SHE KEPT HER LOVE-THOUGHTS ON MOST LENTEN DIET, ... 082 00 007
LEPERS
    WHILE CRIPPLES ARE, WHILE LEPERS, DANCERS IN DISMAL LIMBDANCE, . 152 C 006
LESS
    MY LOVE IS LESS, MY LOVE IS LESS FOR THEE. 014 01 007
    MY LOVE IS LESS, MY LOVE IS LESS FOR THEE. 014 01 007
    THAT LESS IS HEAVENS HIGHER EVEN YET 014 01 012
    GROWS LESS AND LESS SWEET TO HIM, AND KNOWS NO CAUSE. . . 014 03 014
    GROWS LESS AND LESS SWEET TO HIM, AND KNOWS NO CAUSE. . . 014 03 014
    NO, I SHOULD LOVE THE CITY LESS 015 00 021
    AFFLICTS NO LESS, WHAT YET I HOPE MAY BLOW, ... 017 00 006
    OR LESS WOULD WIN MAN'S MIND. 060 00 109
    THAT, HOPES THAT, MAKESBELIEVE, THE MEN MUST BE NO LESS: . 063 00 005
    TO HEAR HIS STRAIN DESCEND LESS LOUD 077 00 079
    HAS WIT ENOUGH, BUT LESS THAN FEMALE TACT. 094 00 019
    THE MORE HE TOLD, THE LESS SHE SPOKE. 109 36 003
    AND, HEADED ALWAYS DOWNWARDS, WITH LESS SOUNDING 112 00 002
    THAT ARE NOT LESS IN WINTER-TIME. J 124 00 012
    TILL THE LONGING IS LESS AND THE GOOD GONE, ... 138 00 036
    THE TIMES ARE NIGHTFALL, LOOK, THEIR LIGHT GROWS LESS: . . 150 00 001
LESSENED
    MY LOVE IS LESSENED AND MUST SOON BE PAST. 014 01 001
LESSEN'D
    ---- -- LESSEN'D STARS RAY --. V 085 00 006
    IS WORTH AND CURRENT WITH A LESSEN'D MILL. ' 096 07 008
LESSON
    TAKE A LESSON FROM THE GROUND: 024 00 014
LESSONS
    IN BLOODY LETTERS, LESSONS OF EARNEST, OF REVENGE: . . . 152 02 004
LEST
    SHE PUTS IN LEASH HER PAIR'D LIPS LEST SURPRISE 082 00 003
LET
    AND LET HIM PROVE MY PASSION WAS BEGUN 014 02 004

LET   (CONTINUED)
                    LET ME BE TO THEE AS THE CIRCLING BIRD, ... 019 00 001
                    LET PATIENCE WITH HER CHASTENING WAND 023 00 045
                    LET IT FLOW FOR HEAVENLY MIRTH; 024 00 010
                    LET IN JOY THIS EASTER DAY. 024 00 024
                    CROWDED LET HIS TABLE BE; 024 00 026
                    HENCEFORTH LET YOUR SOULS ALWAY 024 00 029
                    LET HIM RIDE, HER PRIDE, IN HIS TRIUMPH, C 028 28 008
                    A RELEASED SHOWER, LET FLASH TO THE SHIRE, C 028 34 008
                    LET HIM EASTER IN US, BE A DAYSPRING TO THE DIMNESS OF US, C 028 35 005
                    LET THE CHIME OF A RHYME 029 00 019
                    I MIGHT LET BYGONES BE -- OUR CURSE 041 00 089
                    AND ONE -- BUT LET BE, LET BE; 041 00 103
                    AND ONE -- BUT LET BE, LET BE; 041 00 103
                    LET HIM OH! WITH HIS AIR OF ANGELS THEN LIFT ME, LAY ME! ONLY I'LL . . 045 00 009
                    WHAT THE HEART IS! WHICH, LIKE CARRIERS LET FLY -- 047 00 005
                    LET ME THOUGH SEE NO MORE OF HIM, AND NOT DISAPPOINTMENT 048 00 036
                    THEN LET THE MARCH TREAD OUR EARS: 052 00 009
                    OF WET AND OF WILDNESS? LET THEM BE LEFT, ... 056 00 014
                    O LET THEM BE LEFT, WILDNESS AND WET; 056 00 015
                    LET ALL GOD'S GLORY THROUGH, ... 060 00 030
                    SINCE GOD HAS LET DISPENSE 060 00 040
                    LET LIFE, WANED, AH LET LIFE WIND C 061 00 010
                    LET LIFE, WANED, AH LET LIFE WIND C 061 00 010
                    HOME AT HEART, HEAVEN'S SWEET GIFT; THEN LEAVE, LET THAT ALONE. . . . 062 00 013
                    ERING! LET ME BE FELL: FORCE I MUST BE BRIEF ' 065 00 008
                    MY OWN HEART LET ME MORE HAVE PITY ON; LET 069 00 001
                    MY OWN HEART LET ME MORE HAVE PITY ON; LET 069 00 001
                    YOU, JADED, LET BE; CALL OFF THOUGHTS AWHILE 069 00 010
                    ELSEWHERE; LEAVE COMFORT ROOT-ROOM; LET JOY SIZE 069 00 011
                    LET INCENSE HANG ACROSS THE ROOM 077 00 019
                    LET THE WARBLED SWEETNESS RILL, ... 077 00 084
                    LET CHARITY THUS BEGIN AT HOME, -- 081 00 124
                    LET ME NOW 101 00 006
                    NO, LET THAT GO! I HAVE SAID GOODNIGHT TO SHAME. 102 01 042
                    NOW LET ME SEE YOU, YOU LARGE PRINCELY HAND, ... 102 01 043
                    AH FLORIS, FLORIS, LET ME SPEAK THIS LITTLE 102 01 050
                    BUT LET ME SING THAT WHICH IS KNOWN TO ME. 116 00 004
                    HAD LET SUCH MUSIC DOWN, WITHOUT IMPEDIMENT 122 00 008
                    SMALL MATTER OF THAT THEN! LET HIM SMOTHER 145 00 040
                    LET WHAT THERE NEEDS BE DONE. STAY! WITH HIM ONE COMPANION, ... 152 01 007
                    LET WINTER WED ONE, SOW THEM IN HER WOMB, ... 158 00 003
                    FLINTY KINDCOLD ELEMENT LET BREAK ACROSS HIS LIMBS 159 00 041
LETS
                    THAN PURCELL TUNE LETS TREAD TO? SEE: IT DOES THIS; KEEPS WARM . . 062 00 003
LETTER
                    ALTHOUGH THE LETTER SAID 007 00 001
                    AND WITH THE LAST POST OVER I KNEW NO LETTER WAS SENT. 128 00 002
                    WHAT WOULD BE A BIRTHDAY LETTER THAT AFTER THE BIRTHDAY CAME? . . 128 00 004
                    FOR A LETTER COMES AT LAST: (SHALL I SAY BEFORE CHRISTMAS IS COME?) 128 00 019
LETTERING
                    FOR LETTERING OF THE LAMB'S FLEECE, RUDDYING OF THE ROSE-FLAKE. . . 028 22 008
LETTERS
                    IS CRIES COUNTLESS, CRIES LIKE DEAD LETTERS SENT 067 00 007
                    AS DEVONSHIRE LETTERS, EARLIER IN THE YEAR 119 00 001
                    IN BLOODY LETTERS, LESSONS OF EARNEST, OF REVENGE; 152 02 004
                    HIS LOOKS, THE SOUL'S OWN LETTERS, SEE BEYOND, ... 157 00 015
                    NOR LETTERS SUIT TO SPELL IT TRUE: 167 00 014
LEVANT
                    TO WATCH THE LOW OR LEVANT SUN, ... 015 00 026
LEVEL
                    OF THE ROLLING LEVEL UNDERNEATH HIM STEADY AIR, AND STRIDING . . 036 00 003
                    BUT VASTNESS BLURS AND TIME BEATS LEVEL. ENOUGH! THE RESURRECTION, . 072 00 016
                    AROUND IT BALANCES THE LEVEL SEA. 098 04 002
                    WHOSE SILVER SKINS LIE LEVEL AND THICK IN FIELD. 102 01 022
                    THERE WAS A MEADOW LEVEL ALMOST: YOU TRACED 107 04 001
                    THAT LEVEL POWER WHOSE WORD IS MUST 166 00 014
LEVELL'D
                    WITH LEVELL'D LASHES STILLING THEIR DISQUIET; 082 00 002
LEVELS
                    SO THAT THE MASON'S LEVELS, COURSES, ALL 012 02 002
                    ATTAIN THE WINDY LEVELS OF THE SKY 121 00 004
LEWD
                    RIFE IN HER WRONGS, MORE LAWLESS, AND MORE LEWD. 050 00 008
                    TREAD BACK -- AND BACK, THE LEWD AND LAY! -- 166 00 001
LIAR
                    AND YOU WERE A LIAR, O BLUE MARCH DAY. 041 00 021
                    IN A NEIGHBOUR DEFT-HANDED? ARE YOU THAT LIAR 046 00 013
LIBANUS
                    SHALL SHAKE HER FRUIT AS LIBANUS, ... 006 00 028
LIBERTIES
                    THE LIBERTIES OF AIR. 098 29 004
                    THE LIBERTIES OF AIR. 135 00 022
LICK
                    THAT LICK THE SHELLY LEAVES WHICH FLOOR THE COPSE, ... 084 00 004
LID
                    SHOT LIGHTNING TO THE STIFLING LID OF NIGHT 125 00 050

144

LIDS
AND THRO' THEIR PARTING LIDS THERE CAME AND WENT 002 00 011
EBB'D BACK BENEATH ITS SNOWY LIDS, UNSEEN. 002 00 018
HER LIDS HALF-MESHING SHELTER FROM THE SKY. 099 00 006
LIE
GO THEN: I AM CONTENTED HERE TO LIE. 005 00 055
AFTER THE SUNSET I WOULD LIE, ... 015 00 042
(LOW LIE HIS MATES NOW ON WATERY BED) 041 00 058
THAT LEFT TO THE LORD OF THE EUCHARIST, I HERE LIE BY: 048 00 044
THOUGH WORLDS OF WANWOOD LEAFMEAL LIE: 055 00 008
ABOVE ME, ROUND ME LIE 060 00 118
WHY? THAT MY CHAFF MIGHT FLY: MY GRAIN LIE, SHEER AND CLEAR. . . 064 00 009
AND IN GREY BANDS THE SUN SHOULD LIE STILL BORN: 090 00 003
WHOSE SILVER SKINS LIE LEVEL AND THICK IN FIELD, ... 102 01 022
AND JOHN SHALL LIE, WHERE WINDS ARE DEAD, ... 114 00 009
C HIS BRIGHTEST BLOOMS LIE THERE UNBLOWN, ... 148 00 041
EARLIER OR YOU FAIL AT OUR FORCE, AND LIE 153 00 003
ALL LIE TUMBLED-TO: THEN WITH LOOP-LOCKS 159 00 031
LIES
LIES IN THE BREAST OF THE YOUNG YEAR-MOTHER 026 00 003
THE GREY LAWNS COLD WHERE GOLD, WHERE QUICKGOLD LIES! 032 00 005
TO SEEM THE STRANGER LIES MY LOT, MY LIFE 066 00 001
COME BECAUSE THEN MOST THINLY LIES 077 00 035
LIES DIVINELY STILL, AT REST, ... 077 00 098
SAY BEAUTY LIES BUT IN THE MEET OF LINES, V 102 03 021
LIES IN HER LAP, WHICH SHE ANON SWEEPS OFF. 111 00 009
WHO LIES ON GRASS AND PORES UPON THE SKY 117 00 003
WHERE LIES YOUR LANDMARK, SEAMARK, OR SOUL'S STAR? 157 00 019
AND COME WHERE LIES A COFFER, BURLY ALL OF BLOCKS 159 00 036
SEE, LORD, AT THY SERVICE LOW LIES HERE A HEART 168 00 003
LIEU
O SURELY, REAVING PEACE, MY LORD SHOULD LEAVE IN LIEU 051 00 007
LIFE
BUT OPEN'D TWICE, IN LIFE AND DEATH, TO STATE, ... 001 04 008
DRAWN TO THE LIFE THAT DIED: 028 23 002
YOUR WEALTH OF LIFE IS SOME WAY SPENT: 029 00 014
LIFE, THIS WILDWORTH BLOWN SO SWEET, ... 041 00 094
FORMS AND WARMS THE LIFE WITHIN: 042 00 022
LIFE ALL LACED IN THE OTHER'S, ... 054 00 002
IN EVERY LEAST THING'S LIFE: 060 00 008
HER LIFE AS LIFE DOES AIR. 060 00 045
HER LIFE AS LIFE DOES AIR. 060 00 045
LET LIFE, WANED, AH LET LIFE WIND C 061 00 010
LET LIFE, WANED, AH LET LIFE WIND C 061 00 010
LIFE DEATH DOES END AND EACH DAY DIES WITH SLEEP. 065 00 014
TO SEEM THE STRANGER LIES MY LOT, MY LIFE 066 00 001
HOURS I MEAN YEARS, MEAN LIFE. AND MY LAMENT 067 00 006
SIR, LIFE UPON THY CAUSE. SEE, BANKS AND BRAKES 074 00 009
MINE, O THOU LORD OF LIFE, SEND MY ROOTS RAIN, ... 074 00 014
WHO ASKS NOT LIFE BUT ONLY PLACE TO DIE. 079 00 009
AND FOR THAT FEARFUL HOUR LIFE IS MORE THIN 080 03 005
WHEN LIFE REVISITS ME, NERVE AND VEIN. 080 00 002
BUT SINGLE, LEAD A MISDIRECTED LIFE. 094 00 032
AS EVER I REMEMBER IN MY LIFE. 102 01 013
IF LIFE WITHIN 127 00 005
WE CANNOT LIVE THIS LIFE OUT: SOMETIMES WE MUST WEARY . . . 152 02 047
I HAVE LIFE LEFT WITH ME STILL 155 00 017
GAZE ON, AND FALL DIRECTLY FORTH ON LIFE. 157 00 016
LIVING BREAD THE LIFE OF US FOR WHOM HE DIED, ... 168 00 018
LEND THIS LIFE TO ME THEN: FEED AND FEAST MY MIND, ... 168 00 019
IN THE VERY WAYS THAT THY LIFE GOES 169 00 005
LIFEBELT
TILL A LIFEBELT AND GOD'S WILL 041 00 063
LIFELESS
THE RIV'N VINE, LEAFLESS, LIFELESS, DRY: 006 00 022
LIFE'S
AND LIFE'S FIRST GERMS FROM DEATH HAD WON. 023 00 024
I MOVE ALONG LIFE'S TOMB-DECKED WAY 023 00 039
FROM LIFE'S DAWN IT IS DRAWN DOWN, ... 028 20 007
BEING PURE! WE, LIFE'S PRIDE AND CARED-FOR CROWN, ... 035 00 011
THIS IN DRUDGERY, DAY-LABOURING-OUT LIFE'S AGE. 039 00 004
THIS AIR, WHICH, BY LIFE'S LAW, ... 060 00 013
THAT . . . IN SMOOTH SPOONS SPY LIFE'S MASQUE MIRRORED: TAME . . 075 00 013
AND KIND COMPASSION, AT HIS LIFE'S LAST NEED 140 00 004
LIFE'S QUICK, THIS KIND, THIS KEEN SELF-FEELING, ... 152 02 063
LIFT
I WALK, I LIFT UP, I LIFT UP HEART, EYES, ... 038 00 005
I WALK, I LIFT UP, I LIFT UP HEART, EYES, ... 038 00 005
LEND HIM A LIFT FROM THE SEA-SWILL. 041 00 064
LET HIM OH! WITH HIS AIR OF ANGELS THEN LIFT ME, LAY ME! ONLY I'LL . 045 00 009
THOSE SWEET HOPES QUELL WHOSE LEAST ME QUICKENINGS LIFT, . . . 048 00 037
WHERE YOU CAN LIFT YOUR HAND 060 00 076
LIFT UP YOUR HEADS, O GATES! 115 00 008
BE YE LIFT UP, YE EVERLASTING DOORS 115 00 009
LIFTED
FOR US WAS LIFTED FROM THE ROOTS, ... 006 00 004
WAG OR CROSSBRIDLE, IN A WIND LIFTED, WINDLACED -- C . . . 071 00 011

145

LIFTED   (CONTINUED)
       TILL THE LIFTED CLOUDS WERE NIGH, ... 077 00 072
       THE ANGEL LIFTED US ABOVE. 081 00 119
       NO, THEY ARE COME! THEIR HORN IS LIFTED UP; 104 00 001
       BUT, BEING LIFTED, IMMORTAL, OF IMMORTAL BRIGHTNESS. . . . 152 02 027
LIFTS
       WHAT DEATH HALF LIFTS THE LATCH OF, ... 049 00 019
       LIFTS THEM A LITTLE WAY ABOVE. 081 00 038
LIGHT
       PLUM-PURPLE WAS THE WEST! BUT SPIKES OF LIGHT 002 00 007
       CLUSTER'D IN TROOPS AND HALO'D BY THE LIGHT, ... 002 00 036
       FROM WINGS SWAN-FLEDGED A WHEEL OF WATERY LIGHT 002 00 076
       I AM SO LIGHT, I AM SO FAIR 010 00 002
       AND PIERCE THE YELLOW WAXEN LIGHT 015 00 043
       ' FROM NINE O'CLOCK TILL MORNING LIGHT 021 00 001
       AND FIND THE UNCREATED LIGHT: 022 00 001
       I AM SO LIGHT AND FAIR 025 00 002
       IT WANED INTO THE WORLD OF LIGHT, ... 025 00 031
       WITH LIGHT ON HER FACE LIKE THE WAVES AT PLAY, ... 026 00 004
       GNASHED: BUT THOU ART ABOVE, THOU ORION OF LIGHT; . . . 028 21 005
       TARPEIAN-FAST, BUT A BLOWN BEACON OF LIGHT. 028 29 008
       JESU, HEART'S LIGHT, ... 028 30 001
       WITH, ALL DOWN DARKNESS WIDE, HIS WADING LIGHT? . . . 040 00 004
       FALLS LIGHT AS TEN YEARS LONG TAUGHT HOW TO AND WHY. . . 047 00 008
       STAIN LIGHT. YEA, MARK YOU THIS: 060 00 081
       AND HER HAND LEAVES HIS LIGHT 060 00 112
       DAMASK THE TOOLSMOOTH BLEAK LIGHT; BLACK, C 061 00 009
       FROM A HAZE OF SAPPHIRE LIGHT, ... 077 00 018
       LIGHT AND DARKNESS FROM HIM FLINGS: 077 00 068
       AND SILVER-SHOT WITH GUSTY LIGHT; 078 00 008
       SHE STOOD BEFORE A LIGHT NOT HERS, AND SEEM'D 079 00 003
       IN WANDERING UNTIL BROAD LIGHT OF DAY; 079 00 006
       ' THE LIGHT WAS SO, THE WIND SO LOUD 081 00 059
       THEY WEBB'D THE SKY WITH GLASSY LIGHT. 087 00 002
       A THREAD OF LIGHT BETRAY'D THE HILL 092 00 009
       IN MORE PRECISION NOW OF LIGHT AND DARK 098 30 001
       NOW MORE PRECISELY TOUCHED IN LIGHT AND GLOOM, ... 098 30 004
       LODGE HIS EYES FAST; BUT YET AS EASY AND LIGHT 102 01 020
       AND STUMBLING SWEARS HE WALKS BY LIGHT OF DAY. 102 03 031
       AND STUMBLING SWEARS HE WALKS BY LIGHT OF DAY. V . . . 102 03 037
       TO FIELDS OF LIGHT: MILLIONS OF TRAVELLING RAYS 103 00 009
       AND SUCKS THE LIGHT AS FULL AS GIDEON'S FLEECE: 103 00 011
       THE TIMES ARE NIGHTFALL, LOOK, THEIR LIGHT GROWS LESS! . . 150 00 001
       HER GLASS DRINKS LIGHT, SHE DARKLES DOWN BEHIND, . . . 151 00 009
       WHEN 'TS LIGHT I QUENCHED: ITS ROSE, TIME'S ONE RICH ROSE, MY HAND, 152 02 050
       BY. RAFTS AND RAFTS OF FLAKE LEAVES LIGHT, C 159 00 025
       WITH LIGHT PULSE OF PINIONS SKIRRING, ... 160 00 035
       AND LIGHT US, LORD, WITH THY DAY-BREAK. 167 00 022
       SOME DAY TO GAZE ON THEE FACE TO FACE IN LIGHT 168 00 027
       ANG. I AM SO LIGHT AND FAIR . . . . APPEN A 02
       THEO. YOU WANED INTO THE WORLD OF LIGHT, ... APPEN A 31
       FOR SO GOD'S SON, THE HEAVEN'S LIGHT. . . . . . . APPEN D 06
LIGHTED
       YET LIKE A LIGHTED EMPTY HALL 023 00 010
       LIGHTED THE WATERY-PLATED LEAVES. V 098 17 002
LIGHTEN
       GOD LIGHTEN YOUR DARK HEART -- BUT NO, ... 145 00 027
LIGHTENING
       WHICH, LIGHTENING O'ER THE BODY ROSY-PALE, ... 002 00 072
LIGHTHANDED
       NAY, WHAT WE HAD LIGHTHANDED LEFT IN SURLY THE MERE MOULD . . 059 06 022
LIGHTNING
       O AT LIGHTNING AND LASHED ROD! 028 02 002
       THOU ART LIGHTNING AND LOVE, I FOUND IT, A WINTER AND WARM; . 028 09 006
       NOT A LIGHTNING OF FIRE HARD-HURLED. C 028 34 008
       THE SHEPHERD'S BROW, FRONTING FORKED LIGHTNING, OWNS . . 075 00 001
       SHOT LIGHTNING TO THE STIFLING LID OF NIGHT 125 00 050
       AND WHAT FIRST LIGHTNING C 152 02 031
LIGHTNINGS
       THE EAR, IT STRIKES LIKE LIGHTNINGS TO HEAR HIM SING; . . . 033 00 005
       THE LIGHTNINGS LEAP. THE DAY OF DOOM! 080 07 004
LIGHT'S
       AND MORE MUST, IN YET LONGER LIGHT'S DELAY. 067 00 004
LIGHTS
       SAVE BY TWO STARS, MORE CROWDING LIGHTS ARISE, ... 002 00 032
       AND THOUGH THE LAST LIGHTS OFF THE BLACK WEST WENT . . . 031 00 011
       BLOOM LIGHTS THE ORCHARD-APPLE 042 00 038
       BETWEENPIE MOUNTAINS -- LIGHTS A LOVELY MILE. 069 00 014
       WITH HEAVEN'S LIGHTS HIGH HUNG ROUND, OR, MOTHER-GROUND . . 070 00 011
       WHEN SICK MEN TURN, AND LIGHTS ARE LOW, ... 077 00 025
       IT MELTS, NEW LIGHTS ARISE AS FAIR, ... 077 00 118
       MORE GOLDEN THAN THE WORLD OF LIGHTS, ... 083 00 002
       POINTED WITH PIERCED LIGHTS, AND BREAKS OF RAYS 098 24 002
LIGHTSHIP
       NOR RESCUE, ONLY ROCKET AND LIGHTSHIP, SHONE, ... 028 15 006
LIKE
       HUNG LIKE A WRECK THAT FLAMES NOT BILLOWS BEAT -- 001 03 004

146

```
DROOP'D O'ER THE BROWS LIKE HECTOR'S CASQUE, AND SWAY'D    .   .   .   .   002 00 042
LIKE AN ASSYRIAN PRINCE, WITH BUDS UNSHEATH'D    .   .   .   .   .   .   002 00 062
LIKE SHIVER'D RUBIES DANCE OR SHEEN OF SAPPHIRE HAIL.   .   .   .   .   002 00 073
THEN, LIKE A FLOCK OF SEA-FOWL MOUNTING HIGHER,    .   .   .   .   .   002 00 082
AND THICKEN'D, LIKE THAT DRIFTED BLOOM, THE FLOCK    .   .   .   .   002 00 099
SO LIKE A BERG OF HYALINE,   .   .   .   .   .   .   .   .   .   .   003 00 017
AND ALL LIKE ME MAY BOAST, IMPEACHED NOT, .   .   .   .   .   .   .   012 01 013
YET LIKE A LIGHTED EMPTY HALL    .   .   .   .   .   .   .   .   .   023 00 010
WITH LIGHT ON HER FACE LIKE THE WAVES AT PLAY,    .   .   .   .   .   026 00 004
AND LIKE THE STORM-MONTHS SMOTE THE EARTH .   .   .   .   .   .   .   026 00 029
FIVE LIKE THE SENSES AND MEMBERS OF MEN;    .   .   .   .   .   .   027 00 038
BUT IT RIDES TIME LIKE RIDING A RIVER    .   .   .   .   .   .   .   028 06 007
AND SHEEP-FLOCK CLOUDS LIKE WORLDS OF WOOL,    .   .   .   .   .   030 00 018
NOT HONOUR IT? ) ALE LIKE GOLDY FOAM    .   .   .   .   .   .   .   030 00 035
IT WILL FLAME OUT, LIKE SHINING FROM SHOOK FOIL;    .   .   .   .   031 00 002
IT GATHERS TO A GREATNESS, LIKE THE OOZE OF OIL    .   .   .   .   031 00 003
LOOK, LOOK: A MAY-MESS, LIKE ON ORCHARD BOUGHS!    .   .   .   .   032 00 010
LOOK! MARCH-BLOOM, LIKE ON MEALED-WITH-YELLOW SALLOWS!    .   .   .   032 00 011
THE EAR, IT STRIKES LIKE LIGHTNINGS TO HEAR HIM SING;    .   .   .   033 00 005
HE WAS BUT ONE LIKE THOUSANDS MORE.    .   .   .   .   .   .   .   041 00 085
WOOD BANKS AND BRAKES WASH WET LIKE LAKES .   .   .   .   .   .   042 00 042
THAT, LIKE THIS SLEEK AND SEEING BALL    .   .   .   .   .   .   .   043 00 014
YOU? ' -- ' FATHER, WHAT YOU BUY ME I LIKE BEST. '    .   .   .   047 00 002
WHAT THE HEART IS! WHICH, LIKE CARRIERS LET FLY --    .   .   .   047 00 005
NOTHING ELSE IS LIKE IT, NO, NOT ALL SO STRAINS    .   .   .   .   048 00 029
FORWARD-LIKE, BUT HOWEVER, AND LIKE FAVOURABLE HEAVEN HEARD THESE.    .   048 00 048
AND MANY A MARK LIKE THESE,   .   .   .   .   .   .   .   .   .   054 00 022
LEAVES, LIKE THE THINGS OF MAN, YOU    .   .   .   .   .   .   .   055 00 003
STONES RING! LIKE EACH TUCKED STRING TELLS, EACH HUNG BELL'S    .   057 00 003
LAYING, LIKE AIR'S FINE FLOOD,    .   .   .   .   .   .   .   .   060 00 051
MEN HERE MAY DRAW LIKE BREATH    .   .   .   .   .   .   .   .   060 00 066
FLASHING LIKE FLECKS OF COAL,    .   .   .   .   .   .   .   .   060 00 100
THOSE LIMBS LIKE OURS WHICH ARE    .   .   .   .   .   .   .   .   060 00 105
IS CRIES COUNTLESS, CRIES LIKE DEAD LETTERS SENT    .   .   .   .   067 00 007
THE LOST ARE LIKE THIS, AND THEIR SCOURGE TO BE    .   .   .   .   067 00 013
SPUR, LIVE AND LANCING LIKE THE BLOWPIPE FLAME,    .   .   .   .   076 00 002
MOST LIKE THOSE HUES THAT IN THE PRISM    .   .   .   .   .   .   077 00 061
YAWN'D LIKE LONG FURROW IN THE HEART;    .   .   .   .   .   .   077 00 064
OR, LIKE A LARK TO GLIDE ALOOF    .   .   .   .   .   .   .   .   077 00 065
THEN CLOUDS COME, LIKE ILL-BALANCED CRAGS,    .   .   .   .   .   080 07 001
NOW LIKE THE BIRD THAT SHAPES ALONE    .   .   .   .   .   .   .   081 00 006
MY PASSION LIKE A FOOLISH WIND    .   .   .   .   .   .   .   .   081 00 037
MY CRY IS LIKE A BLEAT; A FEW    .   .   .   .   .   .   .   .   081 00 066
AND LIKE A SELF-OUTWITTED BLAST    .   .   .   .   .   .   .   .   081 00 074
AND THE PIECE THAT'S LIKE A BEAN,    .   .   .   .   .   .   .   086 00 004
LIKE A WIND-PERPLEXED ROSE!    .   .   .   .   .   .   .   .   .   087 00 004
LIKE A CONTENTED WIND, OR GENTLE SHOCKS    .   .   .   .   .   .   098 02 002
LIKE SHUTTLES FLEET THE CLOUDS, AND AFTER    .   .   .   .   .   .   098 03 001
A BRITTLE SHEEN, RUNS UPWARD LIKE A CLIFF,    .   .   .   .   .   098 06 002
OUT-FLEECED BUSHES LIKE A SPANIEL'S EAR V    .   .   .   .   .   .   098 11 001
THICK-FLEECED BUSHES LIKE A HEIFER'S EAR V    .   .   .   .   .   .   098 11 001
TWO TONGUES LIKE BUTTERFLIES.    .   .   .   .   .   .   .   .   098 12 007
STARS LIKE GOLD TUFTS.    .   .   .   .   .   .   .   .   .   .   098 25 002
STARS LIKE GOLDEN BEES.    .   .   .   .   .   .   .   .   .   .   098 25 003
STARS LIKE GOLDEN ROWELS.    .   .   .   .   .   .   .   .   .   098 25 004
AND GATHER IN LIKE HURDLES BRIGHT    .   .   .   .   .   .   .   098 29 003
HER SILKY COAT IS SHEENY, LIKE A HILL,    .   .   .   .   .   .   099 00 003
LIKE A CUPP'D CHESTNUT DAMASK'D WITH DARK BREAKS.    .   .   .   099 00 012
MOST LIKE THE TUFT OF PLIGHTED SILVER ROUND V    .   .   .   .   102 01 068
LIKE KNOCKING THUNDER ALL ROUND BRITAIN'S WELKIN,    .   .   .   102 02 003
LIKE SCALDED BANKS TOPP'D ONCE WITH PRINCIPAL FLOWERS;    .   .   102 02 012
-- I AM LIKE A SLIP OF COMET,    .   .   .   .   .   .   .   .   103 00 001
THEIR HARNESS BEAMS LIKE SCYTHES IN MORNING GRASS;    .   .   .   104 00 006
LIKE FLAME THEY GATHER ON OUR CLIFFS AT EVENING,    .   .   .   104 00 007
AT MORN THEY COME UPON OUR LANDS LIKE RAINS!    .   .   .   .   104 00 008
YOU MAY QUOTE WORDSWORTH, IF YOU LIKE, TO ME. '    .   .   .   107 03 008
AND SAID ' I LIKE THIS: IT IS ALMOST ISLED,    .   .   .   .   .   107 04 025
IT WERE MORE LIKE TO BE.    .   .   .   .   .   .   .   .   .   109 32 004
IT WERE MORE LIKE TO BE. '    .   .   .   .   .   .   .   .   .   109 34 004
IT WERE MORE LIKE TO BE. '    .   .   .   .   .   .   .   .   .   109 35 004
( LIKE ME ) -- SAT SIGHING BY A SYCAMORE-TREE. '    .   .   .   111 00 014
LIKE PHAROH'S EARS OF WINDY HARVEST DRY    .   .   .   .   .   .   117 00 006
OF STREAMS! AND CLOUDS LIKE MESH'D AND PARTED MOSS V    .   .   121 00 002
OF WATER, CLOUDS LIKE PARTED MOSS V    .   .   .   .   .   .   121 00 003
I SAW THE STARS LIKE FLASH OF FIRE.    .   .   .   .   .   .   .   135 00 008
AND GATHER IN LIKE HURDLES BRIGHT    .   .   .   .   .   .   .   135 00 021
LIKE THAT POOR POCKET OF PENCE, POOR PENCE OF MINE.    .   .   142 00 009
HIS LOCKS LIKE ALL A RAVEL-ROPE'S-END,    .   .   .   .   .   .   144 00 005
OR LIKE A JUICY AND JOSTLING SHOCK    .   .   .   .   .   .   .   144 00 009
AND THE SUNLIGHT SIDLED, LIKE DEWDROPS, LIKE DANDLED DIAMONDS    .   144 00 017
AND THE SUNLIGHT SIDLED, LIKE DEWDROPS, LIKE DANDLED DIAMONDS    .   144 00 017
LIKE WATER SOON TO BE SUCKED IN    .   .   .   .   .   .   .   145 00 009
SHE HELD HER HANDS TO, LIKE IN PRAYER;    .   .   .   .   .   .   145 00 048
( JUST LIKE JESUS CRUCIFIED ) ;    .   .   .   .   .   .   .   .   145 00 050
LIKE AIR HE CHANGED IN CHOICE,    .   .   .   .   .   .   .   .   148 00 018
DOWN THE BEETLING BANKS, LIKE WATER IN WATERFALLS,    .   .   .   152 02 020
```

147

LIKE   (CONTINUED)
IT STOOPED AND FLASHED AND FELL AND RAN LIKE WATER AWAY. 152 02 021
IN ALL HER BODY, I SAY, NO PLACE WAS LIKE HER EYES, ... 152 02 025
I HAVE LIKE A LION DONE, LIONLIKE DONE, ... 152 02 035
WHO, LIKE ME, KNOWING HIS NATURE TO THE HEART HOME, NATURE'S BUSINESS, 152 02 044
ALL DAY LONG I LIKE FOUNTAIN FLOW 155 00 002
THAT FLEETED ELSE LIKE DAY-DISSOLVED DREAMS 157 00 011
LIKE THE THING THAT NEVER KNEW THE EARTH, NEVER OFF ROOTS . . . 159 00 027
I AM NOT LIKE THOMAS, WOUNDS I CANNOT SEE. 168 00 013
LIKENESS
TO TAKE HIS LOVELY LIKENESS MORE AND MORE. 151 00 002
LIKES
THINGS THAT SHE LIKES SEEMS OFTEN TO DESPISE, ... 094 00 017
LIKEST
THAT LIKEST IN ME EITHER THAT OR THIS, -- 013 00 007
LILIES
AND A FEW LILIES BLOW. 009 00 004
LILIES I SHEW YOU, LILIES NONE, ... 010 00 007
LILIES I SHEW YOU, LILIES NONE, ... 010 00 007
SEE MY LILIES: LILIES NONE, ... 025 00 007
SEE MY LILIES: LILIES NONE, ... 025 00 007
WITH SULPHUR-COLOUR'D LILIES, BRITTLE IN STALK, ... 098 12 003
OF THE BRAKES OF LILIES. 098 19 004
TO SPILL O'ER FIELDS OF LILIES. SO COULD I 102 01 034
AMONG THE LILIES AND THY GOOD DOMAIN. 123 00 006
ANG. SEE MY LILIES: LILIES NONE, ... APPEN A 07
ANG. SEE MY LILIES: LILIES NONE, ... APPEN A 07
LILY
SHE PILLOWING LOW HER LILY NECK 021 00 055
BUT GERTRUDE, LILY, AND LUTHER, ARE TWO OF A TOWN, . . . 028 20 005
CHRIST'S LILY AND BEAST OF THE WASTE WOOD: 028 20 006
LILY SHOWERS -- SWEET HEAVEN WAS ASTREW IN THEM. C . . . 028 21 008
THE DAPPLE-EARED LILY BELOW THEE! THAT COUNTRY AND TOWN DID . . 044 00 003
A PURE GOLD LILY, BUT BY THE PURE GOLD LILY 098 15 001
A PURE GOLD LILY, BUT BY THE PURE GOLD LILY 098 15 001
A LILY IF IT SHOULD BE, ... 109 22 002
' IS IT A LILY IN YOUR HAND, ... 109 33 001
BUT THE LILY IS PAST, AS I SAY, AND THE ROSE IS NOT IN ITS PRIME: . 128 00 014
LILY-BUDS
WITH THE MULTITUDE OF THE LILY-BUDS 098 19 003
LILY-COLOURED
AND LILY-COLOURED CLOTHES PROVIDE 022 00 027
LILY-TIME
OUR SEX SHOULD BE BORN IN APRIL PERHAPS OR THE LILY-TIME! . . 128 00 013
LILY-WHITE
AND A FEW LEAVES NOT LILY-WHITE BUT CHARACTERED OVER WITH BLACKS. . 128 00 016
LILY-YELLOW
WHEN LILY-YELLOW IS THE WEST. 081 00 055
LILYLOCKS
SEE HIS WIND- LILYLOCKS -LACED: C 071 00 011
LIMBDANCE
WHILE CRIPPLES ARE, WHILE LEPERS, DANCERS IN DISMAL LIMBDANCE, . 152 C 006
LIMBER
WHEN LIMBER LIQUID YOUTH, THAT TO ALL I TEACH 048 00 022
LIMB'S
STAND AT STRESS. EACH LIMB'S BARROWY BRAWN, HIS THEW . . . 071 00 005
LIMBS
LOVELY IN LIMBS, AND LOVELY IN EYES NOT HIS 057 00 013
THOSE LIMBS LIKE OURS WHICH ARE 060 00 105
STRUCK OFF IT HAS: WRITTEN UPON LOVELY LIMBS, ... 152 02 003
FLINTY KINDCOLD ELEMENT LET BREAK ACROSS HIS LIMBS . . . 159 00 041
LIME
THOSE GOLDNAILS AND THEIR GAYLINKS THAT HANG ALONG A LIME: . . 142 00 005
LIMN'D
WERE LIMN'D ABOUT WITH RADIANCE RARE 077 00 060
LINE
PENDANT IN FORMAL LINE FROM CORNICE TALL 001 12 007
AN INTENSE LINE OF THROBBING BLOOD-LIGHT SHOOK 002 00 016
THAT CAME WHEN A LINE OF KINGS DID CEASE, ... 026 00 026
LINEAMENT
'TIS SO CONCEIVED IN HIS LINEAMENT. 102 01 046
C 'TIS SO CONCEIVED IN HIS TRUE LINEAMENT.] 102 01 047
LINED
I BEAR A BASKET LINED WITH GRASS! 010 00 001
I BEAR A BASKET LINED WITH GRASS! 025 00 001
WHICH WITH ITS LINED AND CREASED FLANK 092 00 010
LINED ALL WITH SILK OF JUICY RED. 124 00 013
ANG. I BEAR A BASKET LINED WITH GRASS. . . . . . . APPEN A 01
LINEN-WINDED
OR LISTENING THOUGHT OF LINEN-WINDED GHOSTS. 135 00 018
LINES
O THEN IF IN MY LAGGING LINES YOU MISS 076 00 011
BEAUTY IT MAY BE IS THE MEET OF LINES, ... 102 03 001
SAY BEAUTY LIES BUT IN THE MEET OF LINES, V 102 03 021
I PROVE IT. WHAT THEN WHEN THESE LINES ARE DEAD 117 00 011
LINGER
HER PERSEUS LINGER AND LEAVE HER TO HER EXTREMES? -- . . . 050 00 009

LINGER   (CONTINUED)
     WHERE ROSES LINGER LAST. 165 00 004
LINGERER
     FOR THE LISTENER; FOR THE LINGERER WITH A LOVE GLIDES   .   .   .   028 33 003
LINGERING
     THEN LULL, THEN LEAVE OFF. FURY HAD SHRIEKED ' NO LING- 065 00 007
     ERING! LET ME BE FELL: FORCE I MUST BE BRIEF ' 065 00 008
LINGERING-OUT
     OR AS AUSTIN, A LINGERING-OUT SWEET SKILL, ...   028 10 006
LINGER'D
     LINGER'D, THEN RAISED THE WASHING WAVES AND DRENCH'D   .   .   .   002 00 138
LINGERS
     OF THAT JACINTHINE THING, THAT, WHERE IT LINGERS, ...   002 00 065
LINKED
     LO, LINKED HEAVENS WITH MILKY WAYS! 010 00 021
LION
     I HAVE LIKE A LION DONE, LIONLIKE DONE, ...   152 02 035
LIONESS
     TILL A LIONESS AROSE BREASTING THE BABBLE, ...   028 17 007
LION-BROWN
     HAD SWARTHED ABOUT WITH LION-BROWN 144 00 003
LIONLIKE
     I HAVE LIKE A LION DONE, LIONLIKE DONE, ...   152 02 035
LIONLIMB
     THY WRING-WORLD RIGHT FOOT ROCK? LAY A LIONLIMB AGAINST ME? SCAN .   064 00 006
LIP
     CHEEK AND THE WIMPLED LIP, ...   049 00 002
     SMILED, BLUSHED, AND BIT HIS LIP; 054 00 019
     THIS DOWNY COUNTERFEIT UPON MY LIP, ...   102 01 005
     TO MANHOOD, ON THE UPPER LIP, -- THEY LOOK'D 102 01 067
     WHAT PUT TAUGHT GRACES ON HIS COUNTRY LIP, ...   107 02 003
LIPMUSIC
     OR DEAF EARS SHALL DESIRE THAT LIPMUSIC THAT'S LOST UPON THEM,   .   152 C 005
LIPS
     APART, BETWIXT TEN THOUSAND PETALL'D LIPS 002 00 021
     AND TAUGHT MY LIPS TO QUOTE THIS WORD 008 00 006
     GOD COMES ALL SWEETNESS TO YOUR LENTEN LIPS, ...   011 00 002
     A WARFARE OF MY LIPS IN TRUTH, ...   018 00 015
     SHAPE NOTHING, LIPS! BE LOVELY-DUMB! 022 00 005
     MY HAND UPON MY LIPS I LAY; 023 00 037
     MAN FROM THE LIPS OF HIM SPEAKETH AND SAITH, ...   026 00 005
     THE PRAISE OF THE LIPS AND THE HEARTS OF US BRING TO THEE,   .   .   026 00 035
     FOR LIPS AND HEARTS THEY BELONG TO THEE 026 00 037
     AND, EYES, HEART, WHAT LOOKS, WHAT LIPS YET GAVE YOU A   .   .   .   038 00 007
     RECORDED ONLY, I HAVE PUT MY LIPS ON PLEAS 048 00 045
     HIS LIPS MOVED FAST IN SENSE TOO THICK! 081 00 100
     SHE PUTS IN LEASH HER PAIR'D LIPS LEST SURPRISE 082 00 003
     THE BREAKING LEAVES OF GOLD ARE CURL'D UPON HER LIPS,   .   .   .   098 14 003
     WITH POTENT LIPS CALL DOWN CEMENTED TOWERS! 104 00 005
     CRISP LIPS, STRAIGHT NOSE, AND TENDER-SLANTED CHEEK, ...   136 00 016
     FORWARD FALLING, FOREHEAD FROWNING, LIPS CRISP 159 00 032
     GRACE LOVE YOUR LIPS! -- WHAT NEVER EAR 166 00 002
LIQUID
     WHEN LIMBER LIQUID YOUTH, THAT TO ALL I TEACH 048 00 022
     PURPLE EYES AND SEAS OF LIQUID LEAVES ALL DAY, ...   068 00 008
     HE LEANS TO IT, HARRY BENDS, LOOK, BACK, ELBOW, AND LIQUID WAIST .   071 00 009
     WHERE LIQUID HEAVEN SAPPHIRE-PALE 077 00 099
     THE PUPIL, PLAYS ITS LIQUID JET 086 00 005
LISPING
     THE BATS' WINGS LISPING AS THEY FLEW 021 00 019
LISP'D
     ONLY THE BELLED FOXGLOVES LISP'D TOGETHER. 107 01 006
LISSOME
     WITH LISSOME SCIONS, SWEET SCIONS, ...   052 00 003
LIST
     MAN LIVES THAT LIST, THAT LEANING IN THE WILL 157 00 025
LISTED
     OF THE OUTWARD SENTENCE LOW LAYS HIM, LISTED TO A HERESY, HERE. .   045 00 004
LISTEN
     AND LISTEN TO THE PASSING BELL 023 00 040
     SAID ' LISTEN NOW TO ME. 109 27 002
     AND WHILE I SAIL (MUST LISTEN) I SING. 138 00 015
LISTENED
     SHE LISTENED HOW THE SEA-GUST SHOOK 021 00 052
     SHE LOOKED, SHE LISTENED: PAUL TAUGHT LONG THAT DAY. 136 00 024
LISTENER
     FOR THE LISTENER; FOR THE LINGERER WITH A LOVE GLIDES   .   .   .   028 33 003
LISTENING
     TO WHERE THE LISTENING UPLANDS ARE; 077 00 082
     OR LISTENING THOUGHT OF LINEN-WINDED GHOSTS. 135 00 018
LISTLESS
     BY THERE COMES A LISTLESS STRANGER: BECKONED BY THE NOISE   .   .   159 00 014
LISTS
     OF DRIVING VERMEIL-RAIN; AND, AS HE LISTS, ...   002 00 091
     WHERE MY HEART LISTS. 088 00 002
     THIS SWEET DESERTER LISTS HERSELF ANEW 102 01 062
LIT
     LIT WITH EXQUISITE TINTS SEVEN 077 00 109

149

```
          THE  WATERY-PLATED  PLANE-LEAVES  LIT.  V    .    .    .    .    .    .    .    .    098  17  003
LITTER
          WHERE  IN  A  NEWLY-DRAWN  GREEN  LITTER    .    .    .    .    .    .    .    .    010  00  005
          WHICH  IN  NEWLY  DRAWN  GREEN  LITTER   .    .    ✓    .    .    .    .    .    025  00  005
          MEANWHILE  A  LITTER  OF  THE  JAGGED  LEAVES    .    .    .    .    .    .    111  00  008
          ANG.  WHICH  IN  NEWLY-DRAWN  GREEN  LITTER    .    .    .    .    .    .    .    APPEN  A  05
LITTLE
          --  A  LITTLE  SICKNESS  IN  THE  AIR    .    .    .    .    .    .    .    .    004  00  003
          I  HAD  SLEPT  A  LITTLE  AND  WAS  CHILL.    .    .    .    .    .    .    .    021  00  016
          THRUSH'S  EGGS  LOOK  LITTLE  LOW  HEAVENS,  AND  THRUSH    .    .    .    .    033  00  003
          LITTLE  I  RECK  HO!  LACKLEVEL  IN,  IF  ALL  HAD  BREAD:    .    .    .    .    070  00  009
          LIFTS  THEM  A  LITTLE  WAY  ABOVE.    .    .    .    .    .    .    .    .    081  00  038
          TO  BOW  BUT  LITTLE,  AND  WORSHIP  NOT?    .    .    .    .    .    .    .    081  00  141
          IS  NOT  SOME  LITTLE  BELA  SET    .    .    .    .    .    .    .    .    081  00  142
          AH  FLORIS,  FLORIS,  LET  ME  SPEAK  THIS  LITTLE    .    .    .    .    .    102  01  050
          SO  I  GO  OUT:  MY  LITTLE  SWEET  IS  DONE:    .    .    .    .    .    .    103  00  017
          THE  EARTH  AND  HEAVEN,  SO  LITTLE  KNOWN,    .    .    .    .    .    .    130  00  001
          HIS  LITTLE  PENNON  IS  UNFURLED.    .    .    .    .    .    .    .    .    130  00  014
          AS  WHERE  THE  LITTLE  HURLING  SOUND    .    .    .    .    .    .    .    135  00  031
           '  I  AM  THE  LITTLE  WOODLARK.    .    .    .    .    .    .    .    .    138  00  011
          HAVE  ALL  THINGS  READY  IN  HIS  ROOM.  THERE  NEEDS  BUT  LITTLE  DOING.    .    .    152  01  006
LITTLE-LASTING
          BRIGHT-LIFTING  WITH  A  LITTLE-LASTING  SMILE    .    .    .    .    .    .    125  00  051
LIVE
          THAT  I  SHALL  LIVE,  I  SHALL  NOT  DIE,    .    .    .    .    .    .    .    008  00  007
          O  WHERE  LIVE  WELL  YOUR  LEASE  OF  LEISURE    .    .    .    .    .    .    030  00  003
          LONG  LIVE  THE  WEEDS  AND  THE  WILDERNESS  YET.    .    .    .    .    .    056  00  016
          OF  GOD'S  LOVE,  O  LIVE  AIR,    .    .    .    .    .    .    .    .    060  00  122
          ME  LIVE  TO  MY  SAD  SELF  HEREAFTER  KIND,    .    .    .    .    .    .    069  00  002
          CHARITABLE:  NOT  LIVE  THIS  TORMENTED  MIND    .    .    .    .    .    .    069  00  003
          SPUR,  LIVE  AND  LANCING  LIKE  THE  BLOWPIPE  FLAME,    .    .    .    .    076  00  002
          I  DIE,  I  DIE,  I  DO  NOT  LIVE,  --    .    .    .    .    .    .    .    081  00  069
          THEMSELVES  LIVE  SINGING  AND  THEIR  HEARERS  KILL.    .    .    .    .    096  02  002
          IF  THAT  WERE  TRUE,  IT  COULD  NOT  LIVE  A  DAY.    .    .    .    .    .    097  00  002
          --  ----  --  LIVE  ------  ----  --  ----  V    .    .    .    .    .    .    098  12  005
          WE  LIVE  TO  SEE    .    .    .    .    .    .    .    .    .    .    .    098  35  001
          THEY  ARE  NOT  DEAD  WHO  DIE,  THEY  ARE  BUT  LOST  WHO  LIVE.    .    .    .    098  40  001
          WE  CANNOT  LIVE  THIS  LIFE  OUT:  SOMETIMES  WE  MUST  WEARY    .    .    .    152  02  047
          BE  UNDER  HER  BANNER  AND  LIVE  FOR  HER  HONOUR:    .    .    .    .    156  00  003
          UNDER  HER  BANNER  I'LL  LIVE  FOR  HER  HONOUR.    .    .    .    .    .    156  00  004
          UNDER  HER  BANNER  WE  LIVE  FOR  HER  HONOUR.    .    .    .    .    .    156  00  005
          BUT  UNDER  HER  BANNER  I  LIVE  FOR  HER  HONOUR.    .    .    .    .    156  00  014
LIVED
          HE  LIVED  ON:  THESE  WEEDS  AND  WATERS,  THESE  WALLS  ARE  WHAT    .    .    .    044  00  010
          CHRIST  LIVED  IN  MARGARET  CLITHEROE.    .    .    .    .    .    .    .    145  00  028
LIVES
          AND  LIVES  AT  LAST  WERE  WASHING  AWAY:    .    .    .    .    .    .    028  15  007
          THERE  LIVES  THE  DEAREST  FRESHNESS  DEEP  DOWN  THINGS;    .    .    .    .    031  00  010
          TO  DEAREST  HIM  THAT  LIVES  ALAS!  AWAY.    .    .    .    .    .    .    067  00  008
          HE!  HAND  TO  MOUTH  HE  LIVES,  AND  VOIDS  WITH  SHAME!    .    .    .    .    075  00  009
          THE  WIDOW  OF  AN  INSIGHT  LOST  SHE  LIVES,  WITH  AIM    .    .    .    076  00  007
          THERE  LIVES  THE  WITCH  SHALL  WIN  MY  LOCKS    .    .    .    .    .    120  00  022
          PERHAPS  WE  STRUCK  NO  BLOW,  GWENVREWI  LIVES  PERHAPS:    .    .    .    152  02  009
          IN  A  WIDE  WORLD  OF  DEFIANCE  CARADOC  LIVES  ALONE,    .    .    .    152  02  039
          MAN  LIVES  THAT  LIST,  THAT  LEANING  IN  THE  WILL    .    .    .    .    157  00  025
LIVING
          TO  THE  SWEET  LIVING  OF  MY  FRIENDS  I  LOOK  --    .    .    .    .    016  00  002
          LORD  OF  LIVING  AND  DEAD:    .    .    .    .    .    .    .    .    028  01  004
          DO,  DEAL,  LORD  IT  WITH  LIVING  AND  DEAD:    .    .    .    .    .    028  28  007
          LIVING  BREAD  THE  LIFE  OF  US  FOR  WHOM  HE  DIED,    .    .    .    .    168  00  018
LO
          BUT  WHEN  THE  SUN  HAD  LAPSED  TO  OCEAN,  LO    .    .    .    .    .    002  00  136
          LO,  LINKED  HEAVENS  WITH  MILKY  WAYS!    .    .    .    .    .    .    .    010  00  021
          LO,  GOD  SHALL  STRENGTHEN  ALL  THE  FEEBLE  KNEES.    .    .    .    .    011  00  014
          WARM  ON  HIS  BROW:  LO!  WHERE  IS  ANOTHER    .    .    .    .    .    026  00  007
          HAND  RATHER,  MY  HEART  LO!  LAPPED  STRENGTH,  C    .    .    .    .    064  00  011
LOADED
          TO  KEEP  THE  LOADED  BOLT  FROM  PLUNGING  BACK.    .    .    .    .    .    135  00  006
LOADING
          SO  LOADING  WITH  OBSTRUCTION  THAT  THRESHOLD    .    .    .    .    .    017  00  008
LOAMY
          THAT  THRIVE  IN  THE  LOAMY  GREENNESS  OF  THIS  PLACE?    .    .    .    .    122  00  015
LOATHE
          MY  SOUL  DOES  LOATHE  IT  AND  MY  SPIRIT  FAILS.    .    .    .    .    .    005  00  014
LOATHED
          LOATHED  FOR  A  LOVE  MEN  KNEW  IN  THEM,    .    .    .    .    .    .    028  21  001
LOATHINGLY
          AND  EVERY  HEART  THINK  LOATHINGLY    .    .    .    .    .    .    .    114  00  015
LOATH'D
          WITH  LOATH'D  COLD  FISHES,  FAR  FROM  MAN  --  OR  WHAT:  --    .    .    .    002  00  124
LOATHSOME
          OR  THEY  GO  RICH  AS  ROSELEAVES  HENCE  THAT  LOATHSOME  CAME  HITHER!    .    .    152  C  024
LOCK
          LOCK  WITH  MY  RIGHT:  THEN  KNOT  A  BARKEN  BAND    .    .    .    .    .    080  13  005
          THE  LOCK  OF  CLOUDS  BETIMES  AND  HANGS  THE  DAY.    .    .    .    .    098  31  003
          COVERS  WITH  SHALLOW  SILVER,  THE  LOCK  OF  CLOUDS    .    .    .    .    098  31  005
```

LOCKS
    THEIR PANSY-DARK OR BRONZEN LOCKS WERE STRUNG 002 00 053
    AND LOCKS LOVE EVER IN A LAD! 048 00 035
    COME THEN, YOUR WAYS AND AIRS AND LOOKS, LOCKS, C 059 06 014
    SWEET LOOKS, LOOSE LOCKS, LONG LOCKS, LOVELOCKS, C 059 06 015
    SWEET LOOKS, LOOSE LOCKS, LONG LOCKS, LOVELOCKS, C 059 06 015
    SOME ICE THAT LOCKS THE GLACIER TO THE ROCKS 080 09 006
    THE KNOT OF FEATHERY LOCKS UPON HER HEAD 099 00 014
    AS KEEL LOCKS CLOSE TO KELSON -- 101 00 005
    AND THERE SHE WAITS WITH LOCKS UNWET 120 00 005
    THERE LIVES THE WITCH SHALL WIN MY LOCKS 120 00 022
    NOR LOCKS NOR EYES SHALL WIN AGAIN. 120 00 025
    HIS LOCKS LIKE ALL A RAVEL-ROPE'S-END, ... 144 00 005
LODGE
    LODGE HIS EYES FAST: BUT YET AS EASY AND LIGHT 102 01 020
LODGED
    AND SEVEN EARS CROWN THE LODGED CORN, ... 114 00 006
LODGES
    OR NEVER LODGES THERE: 021 00 025
    THEIR ROCKY LODGES, THEN THE WEATHER RARE 080 04 005
    IN THE LODGES OF THE PERISHABLE SOULS 126 00 001
LOINS
    THAT LEANS ALONG THE LOINS OF HILLS, WHERE A CANDYCOLOURED, C   .   . 159 00 005
LONE
    AND ALL IN LONE AIR STOOD THE SUN, ... 077 00 076
LONELY
    HEARD UNHEEDED, LEAVES ME A LONELY BEGAN. 066 00 014
LONG
    HE RANG'D LONG CORRIDORS AND CORNIC'D HALLS, ... 001 10 001
    DIMM'D IN THE LONG ACCUMULATED DUST: 001 12 006
    THE MONKS LEFT LONG AGO: SINCE WHICH NO MORE 001 15 004
    DOWN THAT DANK ROCK O'ER WHICH THEIR LUSH LONG TRESSES WEEP.   .   . 002 00 115
    I SEE LONG REEFS OF VIOLETS 003 00 025
    FORGET THE WAKING TRUMPET, THE LONG LAW. 005 00 044
    THERE ON A LONG AND SQUARED HEIGHT 015 00 041
    WITH FREE LONG LOOKING, ERE I DIE. 015 00 044
    BUT FEEL THE LONG SUCCESS OF SIN. 018 00 008
    WHAT WAS ITS SEASON THEN? HOW LONG AGO? 027 00 013
    WHO LONG FOR REST, WHO LOOK FOR PLEASURE 030 00 001
    WHEN WEEDS, IN WHEELS, SHOOT LONG AND LOVELY AND LUSH: .   .   . 033 00 002
    FALLS LIGHT AS TEN YEARS LONG TAUGHT HOW TO AND WHY.   .   .   . 047 00 008
    LONG LIVE THE WEEDS AND THE WILDERNESS YET. 056 00 016
    THAT CANST BUT ONLY BE, BUT DOST THAT LONG -- 058 00 004
    SWEET LOOKS, LOOSE LOCKS, LONG LOCKS, LOVELOCKS, C 059 06 015
    THEM: BEAUTY-IN-THE-GHOST, DELIVER IT, EARLY NOW, LONG BEFORE DEATH . 059 06 018
    NOR CAN YOU LONG BE, WHAT YOU NOW ARE, CALLED FAIR.   .   .   . 059 0L 006
    MAY WHO NE'ER HUNG THERE. NOR DOES LONG OUR SMALL 065 00 011
    SHIVELIGHTS AND SHADOWTACKLE IN LONG LASHES LACE, LANCE, AND PAIR.   . 072 00 004
    NINE MONTHS SHE THEN, NAY YEARS, NINE YEARS SHE LONG   .   .   . 076 00 005
    YAWN'D LIKE LONG FURROW IN THE HEART: 077 00 064
    A THING THAT WEEPS, ENDURING LONG: 081 00 050
    AND LONG, THE TREES WERE COLOUR'D, BUT THE O'ER-HEAD,   .   .   . 107 04 012
    THEY HAVE TAKEN OUT THEIR LONG BRANDS. 109 14 001
    BRIGHT HUES LONG LOOK'D AT THIN, DISSOLVE AND FLY: .   .   . 117 00 002
    AND HOW LONG WAS THE WAY? THIS SHORTER WAY? 125 00 011
    SHE LOOKED, SHE LISTENED: PAUL TAUGHT LONG THAT DAY.   .   .   . 136 00 024
    JEWS KILLED JESUS LONG AGO 145 00 052
    MUST ALL DAY LONG TASTE MURDER. WHAT DO NOW THEN? DO? NAY,   .   . 152 02 065
    AS LONG AS MEN ARE MORTAL AND GOD MERCIFUL, ... 152 C 010
    SO LONG TO THIS SWEET SPOT, THIS LEAFY LEAN-OVER, ... 152 C 011
    ALL DAY LONG I LIKE FOUNTAIN FLOW. 155 00 002
    LONG, WHERE WE LEAVE HIM, FROLICLAVISH, C 159 00 042
LONGER
    AND MORE MUST, IN YET LONGER LIGHT'S DELAY. 067 00 004
    HERCLOT'S PREACHINGS I'LL NO LONGER HEAR: 096 05 001
    THIS DRY DEAN, NOW NO LONGER DRY NOR DUMB, BUT MOIST AND MUSICAL   . 152 C 012
    I SHOULD BE WRONGING LONGER LEAVING IT TO FLOAT 159 00 044
LONGING
    TILL THE LONGING IS LESS AND THE GOOD GONE. 138 00 036
LONG-LYING
    AND HUNTING WINDS AND THE LONG-LYING SNOW. 017 00 002
LONG-SUPERFLUOUS
    WITH LONG-SUPERFLUOUS TIES, FOR NOTHING HERE 012 01 004
LOOK
    ON THISTLES THAT MEN LOOK NOT GRAPES TO GATHER, ... 007 00 002
    HE SAYS HIS SCIENCE HELPS HIM NOT TO LOOK 014 02 013
    TO THE SWEET LIVING OF MY FRIENDS I LOOK -- 016 00 002
    SAVE CHRIST: TO CHRIST I LOOK, ON CHRIST I CALL. 016 00 014
    QUINCES, LOOK, WHEN NOT ONE 025 00 009
    I SHALL LOOK ON THY LOVELINESS, MOTHER OF MINE. 027 00 012
    STRIKE YOU THE SIGHT OF IT? LOOK AT IT LOOM THERE.   .   .   . 028 28 003
    WHO LONG FOR REST, WHO LOOK FOR PLEASURE 030 00 001
    LOOK AT THE STARS! LOOK, LOOK UP AT THE SKIES! 032 00 001
    LOOK AT THE STARS! LOOK, LOOK UP AT THE SKIES! 032 00 001
    LOOK AT THE STARS! LOOK, LOOK UP AT THE SKIES! 032 00 001
    O LOOK AT ALL THE FIRE-FOLK SITTING IN THE AIR! 032 00 002
    LOOK, LOOK: A MAY-MESS, LIKE ON ORCHARD BOUGHS! 032 00 010

LORD   (CONTINUED)
   THOU ART INDEED JUST, LORD, IF I CONTEND 074 00 001
   MINE, O THOU LORD OF LIFE, SEND MY ROOTS RAIN. 074 00 014
   LORD, BUT THEY CRY SO LOUD, AND WHAT AM I? 080 08 006
   O LORD! BUT I HAVE WROUGHT AND STRIVEN! 081 00 108
   DULY, DEAR LORD, MY PRIZE IS WON. 081 00 109
   ' LORD WILLIAM THEY CALL ME. 109 05 002
   SAYS ' ARE YOU NOT LORD WILLIAM'S LOVE 109 18 003
   ' I AM LORD WILLIAM'S LOVE, ' SHE SAID, ... 109 19 001
   ' LORD WILLIAM COMES HUNTING TOMORROW MORNING, ... 109 19 003
   BUT HOW WILL YOU LORD WILLIAM KNOW 109 20 001
   ' YET HOW WILL YOU LORD WILLIAM KNOW 109 21 001
   IN THIS WISE YOU MAY KNOW YOUR LORD 109 22 003
   ' O WHERE IS LORD WILLIAM, MY LORDS, ' SHE SAID, ... 109 25 003
   ' FIE, YOU ARE NOT LORD WILLIAM, ' SHE SAID; 109 26 003
   LORD WILLIAM IS KING OF ALL THIS LAND 109 27 003
   MAKE WIDE; -- THOU, O LORD OF SIN, ... 115 00 006
   MAKE ME PURE, LORD: THOU ART HOLY! 129 00 006
   MAKE ME MEEK, LORD: THOU WERT LOWLY! 129 00 007
   LORD BEUNO COMES TONIGHT. TONIGHT, SIR! SOON, NOW; THEREFORE . 152 01 005
   LORD NOW CURB HIM FOR EVER. O DARING! O DEEP INSIGHT! . . 152 02 041
   AND LIGHT US, LORD, WITH THY DAY-BREAK. 167 00 022
   SEE, LORD, AT THY SERVICE LOW LIES HERE A HEART 168 00 003
   BUT CAN PLAINLY CALL THEE LORD AND GOD AS HE! 168 00 014
   BATHE ME, JESU LORD, IN WHAT THY BOSOM RAN -- 168 00 022
   WHAT MUST I LOVE THEE, LORD, FOR THEN? -- 170 00 020
   ' OUR LORD HIS HANDMAIDEN, I WIS, ... APPEN D 25
LORDLY
   TO DECK AND MAKE MOST LORDLY EVERMORE. ' 001 02 009
   WHAT! COUNTRY IS HONOUR ENOUGH IN ALL US -- LORDLY HEAD, . . . 070 00 010
LORD'S
   WHO KNELT WERE FOR THE LORD'S RIGHT HAND; 081 00 094
LORDS
   ' O WHERE IS LORD WILLIAM, MY LORDS, ' SHE SAID, ... 109 25 003
LORE
   THAT READS OR HOLDS THE ASTROLOGIC LORE. 014 02 002
   EVEN THAN THIS MY THANKLESS LORE! 015 00 022
   AND THEN I HATE THE MOST THAT LORE 015 00 033
LORN
   THE LORN MOON, PALE WITH PITEOUS DISMAY, ... 079 00 004
LOSE
   AND HEDGES BREAK, AND LOSE THE KINE, ... 114 00 002
LOSS
   THE SCEPTIC DISAPPOINTMENT AND THE LOSS 014 03 012
   TO TRACE SOME TRACELESS LOSS OF THOUGHT AGAIN. 107 04 018
   WHICH BETWEEN ASH-TOPS SUFFERS LOSS 121 00 005
LOSSES
   BY SLENDER LOSSES ARE UNDONE; 081 00 147
LOST
   OUR PRAYER SEEMS LOST IN DESERT WAYS, ... 023 00 005
   RECK NOT WHAT THE POOR HAVE LOST! 024 00 004
   HAVE LOST THAT CHEER AND CHARM OF EARTH'S PAST PRIME! . . . 035 00 012
   TOO LATE! LOST! GONE WITH THE GALE. 041 00 036
   HE HAS LOST COUNT WHAT CAME NEXT, POOR BOY. -- 041 00 072
   O WELL WEPT, MOTHER HAVE LOST SON; 041 00 105
   MY LAD, AND LOST IN JACK, ... 054 00 018
   NOT THE LEAST LASH LOST; EVERY HAIR C 059 06 020
   (AND WE, WE SHOULD HAVE LOST IT) FINER, FONDER C 059 06 029
   THE LOST ARE LIKE THIS, AND THEIR SCOURGE TO BE 067 00 013
   THE WIDOW OF AN INSIGHT LOST SHE LIVES, WITH AIM 076 00 007
   I STROVE TO LOOK! I LOST THE TRICK 081 00 097
   HAS LOST ITS SAVOUR AND IS ROLL'D D 092 00 005
   THEY ARE NOT DEAD WHO DIE, THEY ARE BUT LOST WHO LIVE. . . . 098 40 001
   OF WORLD MADE, MARRED, AND MENDED, LOST AND WON! 136 00 026
   OR DEAF EARS SHALL DESIRE THAT LIPMUSIC THAT'S LOST UPON THEM, . 152 C 005
   LOST, ALL LOST IN WONDER AT THE GOD THOU ART. 168 00 004
   LOST, ALL LOST IN WONDER AT THE GOD THOU ART. 168 00 004
   LOST MANKIND SHALL BE BOUGHT . . . . APPEN D 18
LOT
   TO SEEM THE STRANGER LIES MY LOT, MY LIFE 066 00 001
   SURE, 'S BED NOW, LOW BE IT! LUSTILY HE HIS LOW LOT (FEEL . . 070 00 005
   LOVE BY MONITION, HERITAGE, OR LOT, ... 102 03 014
   HE PRAISED THE LOVELY LOT OF CONTINENCE: 136 00 028
LOTE-FLOWER
   I GATHER POINTS OF LOTE-FLOWER FROM AN ISLE 005 00 033
LOTS
   GIVE US OUR GREEN LOTS IN ANOTHER MEAD 098 15 005
LOUCHED
   AND LOUCHED LOW GRASS, HEAVEN THAT DOST APPEAL 058 00 002
LOUD
   THE TRUMPET WAXES LOUD: TIRED ARE YOUR FEET. 005 00 008
   TO HEAR HIS STRAIN DESCEND LESS LOUD 077 00 079
   LORD, BUT THEY CRY SO LOUD, AND WHAT AM I? 080 08 006
   ' THE LIGHT WAS SO, THE WIND SO LOUD 081 00 059
LOUDER
   LOUDER THE MONKS DRON'D OUT GREGORIANS SLOW; 001 13 006
   NO LOUDER, WHEN I WAS WITH YOU. 081 00 060

LOVE

```
MORE SWEET-FAMILIAR GROWS MY LOVE TO THEE,    .   .   .   .   .   .   .   . 012 01 002
THEIR SPECIAL-GENERAL TITLE TO THY LOVE. .    .   .   .   .   .   .   .   . 012 01 014
MY LOVE IS LESSENED AND MUST SOON BE PAST.    .   .   .   .   .   .   .   . 014 01 001
MY LOVE IS LESS, MY LOVE IS LESS FOR THEE,    .   .   .   .   .   .   .   . 014 01 007
MY LOVE IS LESS, MY LOVE IS LESS FOR THEE.    .   .   .   .   .   .   .   . 014 01 007
AND I'LL LOVE MY DISTINCTION: NEAR OR FAR .   .   .   .   .   .   .   .   . 014 02 012
NO, I SHOULD LOVE THE CITY LESS   .   .   .   .   .   .   .   .   .   .   . 015 00 021
I RECKON PRECEDENTS OF LOVE,   .   .   .   .   .   .   .   .   .   .   .   . 018 00 007
LOVE, O MY GOD, TO CALL THEE LOVE AND LOVE.   .   .   .   .   .   .   .   . 019 00 014
LOVE, O MY GOD, TO CALL THEE LOVE AND LOVE.   .   .   .   .   .   .   .   . 019 00 014
LOVE, O MY GOD, TO CALL THEE LOVE AND LOVE.   .   .   .   .   .   .   .   . 019 00 014
LOVE I WAS SHEWN UPON THE MOUNTAIN-SIDE   .   .   .   .   .   .   .   .   . 020 00 001
SEE, LOVE, I CREEP AND THOU ON WINGS DOST RIDE:   .   .   .   .   .   .   . 020 00 003
LOVE, IT IS EVENING NOW AND THOU AWAY:    .   .   .   .   .   .   .   .   . 020 00 004
LOVE, IT GROWS DARKER HERE AND THOU ART ABOVE:    .   .   .   .   .   .   . 020 00 005
LOVE, COME DOWN TO ME IF THY NAME BE LOVE,    .   .   .   .   .   .   .   . 020 00 006
LOVE, COME DOWN TO ME IF THY NAME BE LOVE.    .   .   .   .   .   .   .   . 020 00 006
THEN NEXT I HUNGERED: LOVE WHEN HERE, THEY SAY,   .   .   .   .   .   .   . 020 00 009
HEAR YET MY PARADOX: LOVE, WHEN ALL IS GIVEN,     .   .   .   .   .   .   . 020 00 013
TO SEE THEE I MUST SEE THEE, TO LOVE, LOVE:   .   .   .   .   .   .   .   . 020 00 014
TO SEE THEE I MUST SEE THEE, TO LOVE, LOVE:   .   .   .   .   .   .   .   . 020 00 014
WHEREFORE WE LOVE THEE, WHEREFORE WE SING TO THEE,    .   .   .   .   .   . 026 00 033
IN GRACE THAT IS CHARITY, GRACE THAT IS LOVE.     .   .   .   .   .   .   . 027 00 046
THOU ART LIGHTNING AND LOVE, I FOUND IT, A WINTER AND WARM:   .   .   .   . 028 09 006
LOATHED FOR A LOVE MEN KNEW IN THEM,  .   .   .   .   .   .   .   .   .   . 028 21 001
IS IT LOVE IN HER OF THE BEING AS HER LOVER HAD BEEN?     .   .   .   .   . 028 25 003
FOR THE LISTENER: FOR THE LINGERER WITH A LOVE GLIDES    .   .   .   .   . 028 33 003
OR LOVE OR PITY OR ALL THAT SWEET NOTES NOT HIS MIGHT NURSLES;    .   .   . 045 00 006
AND LOCKS LOVE EVER IN A LAD!     .   .   .   .   .   .   .   .   .   .   . 048 00 035
FOR FOND LOVE AND FOR SHAME,   .   .   .   .   .   .   .   .   .   .   .   . 054 00 037
OF GOD'S LOVE, O LIVE AIR,     .   .   .   .   .   .   .   .   .   .   .   . 060 00 122
OUR LAW SAYS: LOVE WHAT ARE LOVE'S WORTHIEST, WERE ALL KNOWN;     .   .   . 062 00 010
FOR LOVE HE LEANS FORTH, NEEDS HIS NECK MUST FALL ON, KISS,   .   .   .   . 063 00 012
KIND LOVE BOTH GIVE AND GET. ONLY WHAT WORD   .   .   .   .   .   .   .   . 066 00 011
AND I CRY OUT FOR WOUNDED LOVE.   .   .   .   .   .   .   .   .   .   .   . 081 00 033
YOU HEAR NOR CARE OF LOVE AND PAIN.   .   .   .   .   .   .   .   .   .   . 081 00 035
THE LOVE OF WOMEN IS NOT SO STRONG, --    .   .   .   .   .   .   .   .   . 081 00 048
'TIS FALSELY GIVEN -- AS LOVE IN MEN:     .   .   .   .   .   .   .   .   . 081 00 049
I WOULD REMEMBER, LOVE, FORGIVE,  .   .   .   .   .   .   .   .   .   .   . 081 00 071
OR THIS, OR ELSE I DO NOT LOVE,   .   .   .   .   .   .   .   .   .   .   . 081 00 114
MY LOVE: AND ALL WAS SWEET AND WELL.  .   .   .   .   .   .   .   .   .   . 081 00 121
I NEED NOT, LOVE, I NEED NOT BREAK    .   .   .   .   .   .   .   .   .   . 081 00 138
KNOWLEDGE IS STRONG BUT LOVE IS SWEET. --     .   .   .   .   .   .   .   . 081 00 154
DID HELEN STEAL MY LOVE FROM ME?  .   .   .   .   .   .   .   .   .   .   . 095 00 001
MY COUSIN WILL NOT LOVE YOU AS I LOVE,    .   .   .   .   .   .   .   .   . 102 01 057
MY COUSIN WILL NOT LOVE YOU AS I LOVE,    .   .   .   .   .   .   .   .   . 102 01 057
NO, LOVE PRESCRIPTIVE, LOVE WITH PLACE ASSIGN'D,  .   .   .   .   .   .   . 102 03 013
NO, LOVE PRESCRIPTIVE, LOVE WITH PLACE ASSIGN'D,  .   .   .   .   .   .   . 102 03 013
LOVE BY MONITION, HERITAGE, OR LOT,   .   .   .   .   .   .   .   .   .   . 102 03 014
LOVE BY PRENATAL SERFDOM STILL CONFINED   .   .   .   .   .   .   .   .   . 102 03 015
THOUGH SELF-MADE BANDS AT LAST MAY TRUE LOVE BIND,    .   .   .   .   .   . 102 03 019
NEW LOVE IS FREE LOVE, OR TRUE LOVE 'TIS NOT.     .   .   .   .   .   .   . 102 03 020
NEW LOVE IS FREE LOVE, OR TRUE LOVE 'TIS NOT.     .   .   .   .   .   .   . 102 03 020
NEW LOVE IS FREE LOVE, OR TRUE LOVE 'TIS NOT.     .   .   .   .   .   .   . 102 03 020
NEW LOVE IS FREE LOVE, OR TRUE LOVE 'TIS NOT. V   .   .   .   .   .   .   . 102 03 027
NEW LOVE IS FREE LOVE, OR TRUE LOVE 'TIS NOT. V   .   .   .   .   .   .   . 102 03 027
NEW LOVE IS FREE LOVE, OR TRUE LOVE 'TIS NOT. V   .   .   .   .   .   .   . 102 03 027
' WHEN ARE YOU HOME, MY LOVE, ' SHE SAID,     .   .   .   .   .   .   .   . 109 02 001
' YOU MAY LOOK FOR ME HOME, MY LOVE, ' HE SAID,   .   .   .   .   .   .   . 109 02 002
HOW SHALL I CALL MY LOVE, ' SHE SAID,     .   .   .   .   .   .   .   .   . 109 04 003
I GIVE YOU MY LOVE AND I GIVE YOU MY LAND,    .   .   .   .   .   .   .   . 109 05 003
HE YEARN'D, HE YEARN'D TO HAVE HIS LOVE,  .   .   .   .   .   .   .   .   . 109 06 001
' AND IF I CHOSE A LOVE TO WED    .   .   .   .   .   .   .   .   .   .   . 109 10 001
SAYS ' ARE YOU NOT LORD WILLIAM'S LOVE    .   .   .   .   .   .   .   .   . 109 18 003
' I AM LORD WILLIAM'S LOVE, ' SHE SAID,   .   .   .   .   .   .   .   .   . 109 19 001
' BECAUSE HE IS MY LOVE, ' SHE SAID,  .   .   .   .   .   .   .   .   .   . 109 20 001
HER TRUE LOVE SHE MIGHT SEE.   .   .   .   .   .   .   .   .   .   .   .   . 109 30 004
' WILT THOU FOLLOW ME, MY TRUE LOVE,  .   .   .   .   .   .   .   .   .   . 109 37 001
WILT THOU FOLLOW ME, MY TRUE LOVE?    .   .   .   .   .   .   .   .   .   . 109 37 003
' O I WILL FOLLOW THEE, MY TRUE LOVE. .   .   .   .   .   .   .   .   .   . 109 38 001
SWEETER THY KISSES, MY OWN LOVE,  .   .   .   .   .   .   .   .   .   .   . 109 38 003
FOR LOVE AND GREATER GLORY OF CHRIST. .   .   .   .   .   .   .   .   .   . 118 00 004
AND UNDIVULGED LOVE DOES OVERFLOW.    .   .   .   .   .   .   .   .   .   . 119 00 012
WHO LOVES ME HERE AND HAS MY LOVE,    .   .   .   .   .   .   .   .   .   . 124 00 001
I DO NOT LOVE.    .   .   .   .   .   .   .   .   .   .   .   .   .   .   . 127 00 010
YOU SPOIL THE PLOT I FIND MY TRUE LOVE BY.    .   .   .   .   .   .   .   . 135 00 036
TO HIM WHO EVER THOUGHT WITH LOVE OF ME   .   .   .   .   .   .   .   .   . 140 00 001
WEDLOCK. WHAT THE WATER? SPOUSAL LOVE.    .   .   .   .   .   .   .   .   . 159 00 047
LOVE ME AS I LOVE THEE. O DOUBLE SWEET!   .   .   .   .   .   .   .   .   . 161 01 001
LOVE ME AS I LOVE THEE. O DOUBLE SWEET!   .   .   .   .   .   .   .   .   . 161 01 001
BUT IF THOU HATE ME WHO LOVE THEE, ALBEIT     .   .   .   .   .   .   .   . 161 00 002
THOU CANST NOT HATE SO MUCH AS I DO LOVE THEE.    .   .   .   .   .   .   . 161 00 004
GRACE LOVE YOUR LIPS! -- WHAT NEVER EAR   .   .   .   .   .   .   .   .   . 166 00 002
WHAT JESUS IS AND WHAT IS LOVE.   .   .   .   .   .   .   .   .   .   .   . 167 00 016
DAILY MAKE ME HARDER HOPE AND DEARER LOVE.    .   .   .   .   .   .   .   . 168 00 016
O GOD, I LOVE THEE, I LOVE THEE --    .   .   .   .   .   .   .   .   .   . 170 00 001
```

LOVE
    O GOD, I LOVE THEE, I LOVE THEE --   • • • • • • • • • 170 00 001
    NOR FEARING NOT TO LOVE AND BE   • • • • • • • • 170 00 003
    THEN I, WHY SHOULD NOT I LOVE THEE; • • • • • • • 170 00 013
    JESU SO MUCH IN LOVE WITH ME?   • • • • • • • • 170 00 014
    I DO LOVE AND I WILL LOVE THEE: • • • • • • • • 170 00 019
    I DO LOVE AND I WILL LOVE THEE: • • • • • • • • 170 00 019
    WHAT MUST I LOVE THEE, LORD, FOR THEN? -- • • • • • 170 00 020
    FOR THY LOVE ABOVE OTHER, • • • • • • • • • APPEN D 44
LOVEABLE
    AWAY IN THE LOVEABLE WEST, • • • • • • • • • 028 24 001
LOVED
    NO, BUT FOR CHRIST WHO HATH FOREKNOWN AND LOVED THEE. • • • 013 00 014
LOVE-LACED
    LOVE-LACED! -- WHAT ONCE I WELL • • • • • • • • 054 00 003
LOVE-THOUGHTS
    SHE KEPT HER LOVE-THOUGHTS ON MOST LENTEN DIET, • • • • 082 00 007
LOVELESS
    AND RELISH NOT HER LOVELESS KISS • • • • • • • • 120 00 011
    [AND HALF MISLIKE HER LOVELESS KISS.] • • • • • • 120 00 013
LOVELIER
    TIMES TOLD LOVELIER, MORE DANGEROUS, O MY CHEVALIER! • • 036 00 011
LOVELIEST
    ' HOLIEST, LOVELIEST, BRAVEST, • • • • • • • • • 041 00 111
    WORLD'S LOVELIEST -- MEN'S SELVES. SELF FLASHES OFF FRAME AND FACE. • 062 00 011
LOVELINESS
    I SHALL LOOK ON THY LOVELINESS, MOTHER OF MINE. • • • • 027 00 012
    TO ITS OWN BEST BEING AND ITS LOVELINESS OF YOUTH [• • • 059 0G 013
LOVELOCKS
    SWEET LOOKS, LOOSE LOCKS, LONG LOCKS, LOVELOCKS, [• • 059 0G 015
LOVELY
    BREATHE, BODY OF LOVELY DEATH. • • • • • • • • 028 25 004
    WHEN WEEDS, IN WHEELS, SHOOT LONG AND LOVELY AND LUSH: • • 033 00 002
    LOVELY THE WOODS, WATERS, MEADOWS, COMBES, VALES, • • • 034 00 009
    AROUND! UP ABOVE, WHAT WIND-WALKS! WHAT LOVELY BEHAVIOUR • • 038 00 002
    HE WAS ALL OF LOVELY MANLY MOULD. • • • • • • • 041 00 074
    HOW LOVELY THE ELDER BROTHER'S • • • • • • • • 054 00 001
    LOVELY IN LIMBS, AND LOVELY IN EYES NOT HIS • • • • 057 00 013
    LOVELY IN LIMBS, AND LOVELY IN EYES NOT HIS • • • • 057 00 013
    THY LOVELY DALE DOWN THUS AND THUS BIDS REEL • • • 058 00 007
    THOSE LOVELY LADS ONCE, WET-FRESH WINDFALLS OF WAR'S STORM, • 062 00 006
    BETWEENPIE MOUNTAINS -- LIGHTS A LOVELY MILE. • • • 069 00 014
    O LOVELY EASE IN CHANGE OF PLACE? • • • • • • • 130 00 027
    TWICE LOVELY, TINTED EASTERN, TURNED GREEK -- • • • 136 00 015
    HE PRAISED THE LOVELY LOT OF CONTINENCE: • • • • 136 00 028
    OR PARING OF PARADISAICAL FRUIT, LOVELY IN WANING BUT LUSTRELESS, • 137 00 003
    AND LACE-LEAVED LOVELY • • • • • • • • • • 138 00 029
    TO TAKE HIS LOVELY LIKENESS MORE AND MORE. • • • 151 00 002
    STRUCK OFF IT HAS: WRITTEN UPON LOVELY LIMBS, • • • 152 02 003
    ROSE. HERE HE FEASTS: LOVELY ALL IS! [• • • • • 159 00 028
LOVELY-ASUNDER
    TO THE STARS, LOVELY-ASUNDER • • • • • • • 028 05 002
LOVELY-DUMB
    SHAPE NOTHING, LIPS! BE LOVELY-DUMB: • • • • • 022 00 005
LOVELY-FELICITOU
    NO NOT UNCOMFORTED: LOVELY-FELICITOUS PROVIDENCE • • 028 31 005
LOVER
    IS IT LOVE IN HER OF THE BEING AS HER LOVER HAD BEEN? • • 028 25 003
    GOD, LOVER OF SOULS, SWAYING CONSIDERATE SCALES, • • 034 00 012
    THE DESTINED LOVER, WHOM HIS STARS • • • • • • 083 00 001
    CALL ME ENGLAND'S FAME'S FOND LOVER, • • • • • 156 00 011
LOVE'S
    FOR POOR LOVE'S FAILURE THAN HIS HOPELESS RISE. • • • 014 03 007
    OR ONCE OR NEVER TOOK LOVE'S PROPER FOOD: • • • 020 00 010
    RAPTUROUS LOVE'S GREETING OF REALER, OF ROUNDER REPLIES? • 038 00 008
    FOR, WRUNG ALL ON LOVE'S RACK, • • • • • • • 054 00 017
    OUR LAW SAYS: LOVE WHAT ARE LOVE'S WORTHIEST, WERE ALL KNOWN: • 062 00 010
    BUT I'M ALONE, FOR MY LOVE'S GONE • • • • • • 095 00 007
LOVES
    AND LOVES -- A FATAL FAULT -- TO PATRONIZE: • • • 094 00 018
    SHE LOVES HIS FACE, SHE KNOWS THE SPOT: • • • • 120 00 002
    WHO LOVES ME HERE AND HAS MY LOVE, • • • • • 124 00 001
    LOVES MAN, THAT HE A MAN WILL BE AND TAKE • • • APPEN D 07
LOVESCAPE
    LOVESCAPE CRUCIFIED • • • • • • • • • • 028 23 004
LOVING
    OUT OF HELL BY LOVING THEE: • • • • • • • • 170 00 016
LOV'D
    SITH I LOV'D AND LOV'D TOO WELL • • • • • • 160 00 030
    SITH I LOV'D AND LOV'D TOO WELL • • • • • • 160 00 030
LOW
    DOORS SLAMM'D TO THE BLASTS CONTINUALLY: MORE LOW, • • 001 13 008
    ROWING, I REACH'D A ROCK -- THE SEA WAS LOW -- • • • 002 00 001
    BECAUSE THE SIGHING WIND IS LOW. • • • • • • 003 00 006
    YOU VIGIL-KEEPERS WITH LOW FLAMES DECREASED, • • • 011 00 008
    TO WATCH THE LOW OR LEVANT SUN, • • • • • • 015 00 026
    SHE PILLOWING LOW HER LILY NECK • • • • • • 021 00 055

LOW   (CONTINUED)
     THRUSH'S EGGS LOOK LITTLE LOW-HEAVENS, AND THRUSH 033 00 003
     WITH A FLOOD OR A FALL, LOW LULL-OFF OR ALL ROAR, ... 035 00 003
     THOUGH ALOFT ON TURF OR PERCH OR POOR LOW STAGE, ... 039 00 005
     (LOW LIE HIS MATES NOW ON WATERY BED) 041 00 058
     CROUCH; LAY KNEE BY EARTH LOW UNDER: 041 00 110
     OF THE OUTWARD SENTENCE LOW LAYS HIM, LISTED TO A HERESY, HERE, . . 045 00 004
     FLUTES AND LOW TO THE LAKE FALLS HOME. 056 00 004
     AND LOUCHED LOW GRASS, HEAVEN THAT DOST APPEAL 058 00 002
     SURE, 'S BED NOW, LOW BE IT: LUSTILY HE HIS LOW LOT (FEEL . . 070 00 005
     SURE, 'S BED NOW, LOW BE IT: LUSTILY HE HIS LOW LOT (FEEL . . 070 00 005
     WHEN SICK MEN TURN, AND LIGHTS ARE LOW, ... 077 00 025
     DOES LAY MEN LOW WITH ONE BLADE'S SUDDEN BLOW 080 02 003
     THAT WAS OF LOW DEGREE? 109 10 002
     WITH ONE OF LOW DEGREE. 109 12 004
     THAT IS OF LOW DEGREE? , ... 109 18 004
     AND THOU OF LOW DEGREE, ' 109 27 004
     NOW COMES AS LOW BENEATH. 115 00 004
     MAN IS MOST LOW, GOD IS MOST HIGH, ... 133 00 005
     DANCES THE BALLS FOR LOW OR HIGH; 166 00 015
     OF COUNTRY BIDDER'S CALLS OR LOW 166 00 022
     SEE, LORD, AT THY SERVICE LOW LIES HERE A HEART 168 00 003
LOWER
     LOWER THAN DEATH AND THE DARK; 028 33 004
LOW-COVERED
     LOW-COVERED PASS, AND BRACE THE WOODLAND CLODS 112 00 006
LOW-DOWN
     DAWN THAT THE PEBBLY LOW-DOWN EAST 098 31 001
     DAWN THAT THE LOW-DOWN PEBBLY EAST 098 31 004
LOW-LATCHED
     LOW-LATCHED IN LEAF-LIGHT HOUSEL HIS TOO HUGE GODHEAD. . . . 048 00 012
LOWLY
     SAID ' WHO THEN IS THIS LOWLY WOMAN, ... 109 11 003
     ' IT IS FOR THE SHAME OF THE LOWLY WOMAN 109 14 003
     LOWLY ALICE SAT IN HER BOWER 109 16 001
     LOWLY ALICE LOOK'D ABROAD 109 17 001
     MAKE ME MEEK, LORD: THOU WERT LOWLY; 129 00 007
LOYAL
     LOYAL TO HIS OWN SOUL, LAYING HIS OWN LAW DOWN, NO LAW NOR . . 152 02 040
LUKE
     THUS FRANCES SIGHED AT HOME, WHILE LUKE 021 00 050
LULL
     THEN LULL, THEN LEAVE OFF, FURY HAD SHRIEKED ' NO LING- . . . 065 00 007
LULL-OFF
     WITH A FLOOD OR A FALL, LOW LULL-OFF OR ALL ROAR, ... 035 00 003
LUNG
     MY LUNG MUST DRAW AND DRAW 060 00 014
LUNG-WASTING
     STONE, PALSY, CANCER, COUGH, LUNG-WASTING, WOMB-NOT-BEARING, . . 152 C 008
LURCH
     THEN A LURCH FORWARD, FRIGATE AND MEN; 041 00 041
LUSH
     DOWN THAT DANK ROCK O'ER WHICH THEIR LUSH LONG TRESSES WEEP. . 002 00 115
     IN A HOLLOW LUSH AND DAMP, ... 004 00 007
     WHEN WEEDS, IN WHEELS, SHOOT LONG AND LOVELY AND LUSH; . . 033 00 002
     THE EAR IN MILK, LUSH THE SASH, ... 138 00 020
LUSH-KEPT
     WORD LAST! HOW A LUSH-KEPT PLUSH-CAPPED SLOE 028 08 003
LUST
     FELL ON THE PALACE, AND THE LUST OF RABBLE RUDE,) . . . 001 14 009
     PALATE, THE HUTCH OF TASTY LUST, ... 022 00 013
     DEFEAT, THWART ME? OH, THE SOTS AND THRALLS OF LUST . . . 074 00 007
LUSTILY
     SURE, 'S BED NOW, LOW BE IT: LUSTILY HE HIS LOW LOT (FEEL . 070 00 005
LUSTRELESS
     OR PARING OF PARADISAICAL FRUIT, LOVELY IN WANING BUT LUSTRELESS, . 137 00 003
LUSTRES
     AND SOBER LUSTRES TAKE THE GLOOM; 077 00 020
     DEEPLY IN THE ARCHED LUSTRES, ... 077 00 133
LUSTROUS
     SPEAR'D OPEN LUSTROUS GASHES, CRIMSON-WHITE; 002 00 008
LUSTY
     HIS LUSTY HANDS, IN GUSTS OF SCENTED WIND 002 00 088
LUTHER
     BUT GERTRUDE, LILY, AND LUTHER, ARE TWO OF A TOWN, . . . 028 20 005

MADAM
     TRUE, MADAM. I AM SORRY NOW TO SEE 125 00 015
MADDEST
     WHEN MADDEST LOOKS THE SLIGHTED NIX.] 120 00 019
MADE
     THOSE CYCLADS MADE THAT THICKEN'D ON MY SIGHT. 002 00 037

156

MADE   (CONTINUED)
    ERE I HAD FURTHER QUESTION MADE 004 00 016
    WHO IS THIS MOSES? WHO MADE HIM, WE SAY, ...   005 00 001
    CHRIST OUR SACRIFICE IS MADE! 006 00 010
    WHEN HE HAS MADE US BEAR HIS LEAF. -- 006 00 030
    IS THIS MADE PLAIN? WHAT HAVE I COME ACROSS 014 03 010
    AND MINOR SWEETNESS SCARCE MADE MENTION OF: 019 00 012
    MADE HEADWAY IN THE FROTHY DEEP. 021 00 051
    YET MADE ITS MARKET HERE AS WELL: 025 00 032
    IT WAS MADE OF EARTH'S MOULD BUT IT WENT FROM MEN'S EYES   .   .   .   027 00 003
    THAT CORDIAL AIR MADE THOSE KIND PEOPLE A HOOD 034 00 005
    MADE SWEETER, NOT MADE DIM, ...   060 00 111
    MADE SWEETER, NOT MADE DIM, ...   060 00 111
    WHO MADE CONJECTURE NEAREST FAR 077 00 045
    WE TUNED TO ONE KEY AND MADE THEIR HARMONIES. 098 02 004
    THEY MADE HIM KNEEL ON KNEE. 109 14 002
    TWO MADE ANSWER IN ONE BREATH 109 26 001
    WHEN SHE HAD MADE THE DOOR WIDE 109 30 003
    YEA, CRUSH'D MY HEART, AND MADE ME DUMB, ...   118 00 012
    YOU HAVE MADE ME QUOTE ALMOST THE DISMALEST PROVERB I KNOW: .   .   128 00 018
    OF WORLD MADE, MARRED, AND MENDED, LOST AND WON: 136 00 026
    THE WORLD WAS SAVED BY VIRGINS, MADE THE MARK. 136 00 030
    C MADE KNOWN, THOUGH THICK THROUGH STONE. 148 00 011
    C WHO BUILT THESE WALLS MADE KNOWN 148 00 037
    ON THE CROSS THY GODHEAD MADE NO SIGN TO MEN: 168 00 009
    THEO. YET MADE YOUR MARKET HERE AS WELL: .   .   .   .   APPEN A 32
MADRID
    LAY BLEEDING, TO MADRID THE LAST THEY BORE, ...   001 15 002
MADRIGAL
    WHY, TEARS! IS IT? TEARS: SUCH A MELTING, A MADRIGAL START!   .   .   028 18 006
MAENEFA
    THE BARROW OF DARK MAENEFA THE MOUNTAIN: C 137 00 004
MAGDALEN
    BEYOND MAGDALEN AND BY THE BRIDGE, ON A PLACE CALLED THERE THE PLAIN,   142 00 001
MAGIC
    AND MAGIC CUCKOOCALL 042 00 043
MAGNIFY
    MAGNIFY THE LORD. 042 00 032
MAGNIFYING
    THEIR MAGNIFYING OF EACH ITS KIND 042 00 029
MAID
    MAID YET MOTHER AS MAY HATH BEEN -- 026 00 020
    TILL A MAID IN DAVID'S HOUSE HAD BIRTH, ...   026 00 030
    NEXT MARY MOTHER OF MAID AND NUN, ...   145 00 043
    AND WHAT SWAYS WITH YOU, MAYBE THIS SWEET MAID: 157 00 022
    A MAID WITH MOTHER'S BLISS. '   .   .   .   .   APPEN D 30
MAIDEN
    OH THOU, PROUD MOTHER AND MUCH PROUD MAIDEN -- 026 00 019
    THEE, OH MAIDEN, MOST WORTHY OF PRAISE! 026 00 036
    MAIDEN COULD OBEY SO, BE A BELL TO, RING OF IT, AND 028 31 007
    WINNING WAYS, AIRS INNOCENT, MAIDEN MANNERS, C 059 06 015
    HER WEEDS ALL MARK HER MAIDEN, THOUGH TO WED, ...   136 00 017
    THE EARNEST-HEARTED MAIDEN SAT AND HEARD, ...   136 00 032
    CALL NO SUCH MAIDEN ' MINE ' . THE DEEPER GROWS HER DEARNESS   .   152 01 012
    SENT TO THE MAIDEN SWEET, ...   APPEN D 02
    FLESH OF THEE, MAIDEN BRIGHT, ...   APPEN D 08
    THE GENTLE MAIDEN THEN: .   .   .   .   APPEN D 12
    WHEN THE MAIDEN UNDERSTOOD   .   .   .   .   APPEN D 21
MAIDENGEAR
    MAIDENGEAR, GALLANTRY AND GAIETY AND GRACE, C 059 06 014
MAIDEN-FURLED
    THE HEAVEN-FLUNG, HEART-FLESHED, MAIDEN-FURLED 028 34 003
MAIDEN-MOTHER
    THOU MATCHLESS MAIDEN-MOTHER, ...   APPEN D 42
MAIDEN'S
    MANGER, MAIDEN'S KNEE: 028 07 004
MAIDENS
    MAIDENS SHALL WEEP AT MERRY MORN, ...   114 00 001
    I BID THE BOYS AND MAIDENS HEAR. 166 00 004
MAID-MONTH'S
    SALUTE THEE, MOTHER, THE MAID-MONTH'S QUEEN! 026 00 024
MAID'S
    JESU, MAID'S SON, ...   028 30 002
    MOST, O MAID'S CHILD, THY CHOICE AND WORTHY THE WINNING.   .   .   .   033 00 014
MAIL'D
    -- -- -- ---- -- MAIL'D SHAPES OF BRONZE, V 102 02 010
MAIM
    SO BE IT: I MUST MAIM AND MAR. 081 00 031
MAIN
    MY CRIES HEAVE, HERDS-LONG: HUDDLE IN A MAIN, A CHIEF-   .   .   .   065 00 005
    THERE IS AN ISLAND, WESTER'D IN THE MAIN, ...   098 04 001
    STARS FLOAT FROM THE BORDERS OF THE MAIN. 098 20 001
    I CANNOT MEET THE SWALLOWING MAIN. 120 00 027
MAINSTRENGTH
    NOR MIND NOR MAINSTRENGTH: GOLD GO GARLANDED 070 00 013
MAJESTIC
    MAJESTIC -- AS A STALLION STALWART, VERY-VIOLET-SWEET! --   .   .   .   038 00 010

157

MAJESTICAL
    OF JUST, MAJESTICAL, AND GIANT GROANS. • • • • • • • • • • • 075 0U 004
MAJESTY
    WITH BLAZONED GROINS, AND CROWNED WITH HUES OF MAJESTY. • • • 001 06 009
    THE MAJESTY! WHAT DID SHE MEAN? • • • • • • • • • 028 25 001
    THIS FLOWER, THIS FLORIS, THIS DEAR MAJESTY, • • • • • 102 01 036
MAJORCA
    THAT IN MAJORCA ALFONSO WATCHED THE DOOR. • • • • • • 073 0U 014
MAKE
    TO DECK AND MAKE MOST LORDLY EVERMORE. • • • • • • 001 02 009
    THEN THEY, THUS RANGED, 'GAN MAKE FULL PLAINTIVELY • • 002 0U 126
    FOR THESE, MAKE ALL THE VIRTUES TO ABOUND, -- • • • 013 0U 013
    OR WHERE IS STRENGTH TO MAKE THE LEAF UNFOLD? • • • 017 0U 004
    WITH NOT A THING TO MAKE ME FEAR, • • • • • • 021 0U 040
    MAKE EACH MORN AN EASTER DAY. • • • • • • • 024 0U 030
    MAKE ME A LEAF IN THEE, MOTHER OF MINE. • • • • 027 0U 042
    MAKE MERCY IN ALL OF US, OUT OF US ALL • • • • 028 10 007
    HAVE YOU! MAKE WORDS BREAK FROM ME HERE ALL ALONE, • • 028 18 003
    MARK, THE MARK IS OF MAN'S MAKE • • • • • • 028 22 003
    BUT HOW SHALL I • • • MAKE ME ROOM THERE! • • • 028 28 001
    OUR MAKE AND MAKING BREAK, ARE BREAKING, DOWN • • 035 0U 013
    BUT A PRICK WILL MAKE NO EYE AT ALL, • • • • • 043 0U 015
    WHEREAS DID AIR NOT MAKE • • • • • • • • 060 0U 094
    WHAT MUST MAKE OUR DAYSTAR • • • • • • • 060 0U 106
    IN WHOSE DEAD LAKE EVEN A VOICE MAY MAKE • • • 080 04 003
    BUT THEN I MAKE AN EAGER SHIFT TO SEE • • • • 080 06 005
    HOUSES THAT MAKE ABODE BESIDE THE LAKE. • • • • 080 06 006
    I CRY ' O ROCKS AND MOUNTAIN MAKE ME ROOM ' • • 080 07 005
    THUS I SHALL MAKE A CROSS, AND IN'T • • • • 080 13 001
    MAKE IT TO GOD. I AM NOT SPENT • • • • • 081 0U 130
    YEA, TO MYSELF I ANSWER MAKE: • • • • • • 081 0U 145
    MARRIED, WILL MAKE A SWEET AND MATCHLESS WIFE, • • 094 0U 031
    AND PRIMROSE BRING, AND MAKE A SHEAF • • • 098 18 003
    ' HEAVEN MAKE THE TIME BE SHORT, ' SHE SAID, • • 109 03 001
    HEAVEN MAKE IT SWEET TO YOU, ' SHE SAID, • • • 109 03 003
    ' AND MAKE IT SHORT TO ME. • • • • • • • 109 03 004
    I WOULD NOT MAKE THE TRIAL. • • • • • • • 110 0U 002
    AND FIELD-FLOWERS MAKE THE FIELDS FORLORN, • • • 114 0U 003
    O GROUNDS OF HELL MAKE ROOM. • • • • • • 115 0U 002
    MAKE WIDE; -- THOU, O LORD OF SIN, • • • • 115 0U 006
    THAT MAKE MY EYES SORE AND CROSS-COLOUR THINGS • 125 0U 040
    MAKE ME PURE, LORD: THOU ART HOLY: • • • • 129 0U 006
    MAKE ME MEEK, LORD: THOU WERT LOWLY; • • • 129 0U 007
    WHOM WANT COULD NOT MAKE PINE, PINE • • • • 142 0U 007
    SINCE ALL THE MAKE OF MAN • • • • • • 148 0U 007
    TO MAKE BELIEVE MY MOOD WAS -- MOCK. O I MIGHT THINK SO 152 0Z 010
    OF FAVOURED MAKE AND MIND AND HEALTH AND YOUTH, • 157 0U 018
    HARK, HEARER, HEAR WHAT I DO; LEND A THOUGHT NOW, MAKE BELIEVE 159 0U 001
    DAILY MAKE ME HARDER HOPE AND DEARER LOVE. • • • 168 0U 016
    MANKIND FREE FOR TO MAKE • • • • • • • APPEN D 09
    AND CLEAN OF EVERY STAIN US MAKE • • • • • • APPEN D 46
MAKES
    WHEREIN HE MAKES US STRAY. • • • • • • • 005 0U 006
    UNBAKES MY PORES, AND STREAMS, AND MAKES ALL FRESH. • 005 0U 032
    WHICH MAKES ME WHEN WITH MEN I DEAL • • • • 015 0U 019
    WHICH MAKES SO SMALL THE PROMISE OF THAT YIELD • • 017 0U 011
    WHICH ONLY MAKES YOU ELOQUENT. • • • • • 022 0U 008
    MAKES THE SILVER JUBILEE. • • • • • • • 029 0U 004
    NO WONDER OF IT: SHEER PLOD MAKES PLOUGH DOWN SILLION 036 0U 012
    IN MOULD OR MIND OR WHAT NOT ELSE MAKES RARE; • • 040 0U 006
    MARK MAKES IN THE RIVELLING SNOWSTORM. • • • 041 0U 068
    AND AZURING-OVER GREYBELL MAKES • • • • • 042 0U 041
    AND MAKES, O MARVELLOUS! • • • • • • • 060 0U 059
    MORE MAKES, WHEN ALL IS DONE, • • • • • • 060 0U 071
    VEINS VIOLETS AND TALL TREES MAKES MORE AND MORE) • 073 0U 011
    FOR WHO MAKES RAINBOWS BY INVENTION? • • • • 091 0U 004
    THAT STILL MAKES COUNTER-ROUNDELS IN THE POND. • • 107 03 005
    WHAT SPIRIT IS THAT MAKES STILLNESS OBSOLETE • • 122 0U 016
    WHICH MAKES US EYE-ATTENTIVE TO THE EYE • • • 125 0U 036
    IT'S THE DAY THAT MAKES THE CHARM; NO AFTER-WORDS COULD SUCCEED 128 0U 007
    WHAT MAKES THE MAN AND WHAT • • • • • • 148 0U 021
    THE MAN WITHIN THAT MAKES: • • • • • • • 148 0U 022
    MAKES WELCOME DEATH, DOES DEAR FORGETFULNESS. • • 150 0U 008
    MAKES DITHER, MAKES HOVER • • • • • • • 159 0U 010
    MAKES DITHER, MAKES HOVER • • • • • • • 159 0U 010
    MAKES GLADNESS AFTER HE IS GONE; • • • • • 167 0U 002
MAKESBELIEVE
    THAT, HOPES THAT, MAKESBELIEVE, THE MEN MUST BE NO LESS; • 063 0U 005
MAKING
    THE MAKING AND THE MELTING CROWDS: • • • • 015 0U 003
    OUR MAKE AND MAKING BREAK, ARE BREAKING, DOWN • • 035 0U 013
    AND THE PRAYER THOU HEARST ME MAKING • • • 041 0U 113
    BY MEANWHILES: MAKING MY PLAY • • • • • • 054 0U 015
    MAKING THE SHADOW SWEETER, A SPIRITUAL GRACE • • 107 04 015
    MAKING THEM DOUBLE-MUSICAL, AND THEY • • • 112 0U 005
MALICE
    MAN'S MALICE, WITH WRECKING AND STORM. • • • • 028 0Y 004

MALIGN
  WITH SUCH MALIGN CONJUNCTIONS AS BEFORE   •   •   •   •   •   •   014 02 006
MALLOW-ROW
  NOW HER MALLOW-ROW IS GONE   • • • • • • • • • 025 00 021
  CAT. NOW HER MALLOW-ROW IS GONE   • • • • • • • APPEN A 21
MALLOW'S
  THE DEWBELL IN THE MALLOW'S MOUTH   • • • • • • 025 00 015
  ANG. THE BELL-DROPS IN MY MALLOW'S MOUTH   • • • • • APPEN A 15
MAMMOCKS
  THAT MAMMOCKS, MIGHTY FOOT. BUT NO WAY SPED,   • • • 070 00 012
MAN
  WITH LOATH'D COLD FISHES, FAR FROM MAN -- OR WHAT: --   • • 002 00 124
  MAN FROM THE LIPS OF HIM SPEAKETH AND SAITH,   • • • 026 00 005
  GUSH! -- FLUSH THE MAN, THE BEING WITH IT, SOUR OR SWEET,   • 028 08 005
  WITH A ROPE'S END ROUND THE MAN, HANDY AND BRAVE -- • • • 028 16 003
  WHO HAVE WATCHED HIS MOULD OF MAN, BIG-BONED AND HARDY-HANDSOME   053 00 002
  LEAVES, LIKE THE THINGS OF MAN, YOU   • • • • • 055 00 003
  IT IS THE BLIGHT MAN WAS BORN FOR.   • • • • • 055 00 014
  I SAY MORE: THE JUST MAN JUSTICES;   • • • • • 057 00 009
  ELSE, BUT IN DEAR AND DOGGED MAN? -- AH, THE HEIR • • • 058 00 010
  TO MAN, THAT NEEDS WOULD WORSHIP BLOCK OR BARREN STONE, • • 062 00 009
  NOW, AND SEEING SOMEWHERE SOME MAN DO ALL THAT MAN CAN DO, • 063 00 011
  NOW, AND SEEING SOMEWHERE SOME MAN DO ALL THAT MAN CAN DO, • 063 00 011
  NOT UNTWIST -- SLACK THEY MAY BE -- THESE LAST STRANDS OF MAN   064 00 002
  MAN, HOW FAST HIS FIREDINT, HIS MARK ON MIND, IS GONE! • • 072 00 011
  BUT MAN -- WE, SCAFFOLD OF SCORE BRITTLE BONES; • • • 075 00 005
  MAN JACK THE MAN IS, JUST; HIS MATE A HUSSY. • • • • 075 00 011
  MAN JACK THE MAN IS, JUST; HIS MATE A HUSSY. • • • • 075 00 011
  FROM GOD AND MAN, IS HELL NO DOUBT.   • • • • • 080 01 004
  BY HEADY ELEMENTS, FOR NO MAN KNOWS;   • • • • • 103 00 005
  MAN IS MOST LOW, GOD IS MOST HIGH.   • • • • • 133 00 005
  ' THE CHILD IS FATHER TO THE MAN.   • • • • • 147 00 001
  ' THE CHILD IS FATHER TO THE MAN.   • • • • • 147 00 004
  ' THE MAN IS FATHER TO THE CHILD.   • • • • • 147 00 006
  ' THE CHILD IS FATHER TO THE MAN! '   • • • • • 147 00 007
  SINCE ALL THE MAKE OF MAN   • • • • • • • 148 00 007
  WHAT MAKES THE MAN AND WHAT   • • • • • • 148 00 021
  THE MAN WITHIN THAT MAKES: • • • • • • • 148 00 022
  NO MAN HAS SUCH A DAUGHTER, THE FATHERS OF THE WORLD • • 152 01 011
  MAN MY MATE AND COUNTERPART.   • • • • • • 155 00 024
  WHERE IS THE FIELD I MUST PLAY THE MAN ON? • • • • 156 00 016
  MAN LIVES THAT LIST, THAT LEANING IN THE WILL • • • 157 00 025
  THE RACE OF MAN; AND HENCE I FELL.   • • • • • 160 00 031
  HEARD YET, THE MUSES' MAN, TODAY   • • • • • 166 00 003
  SAY MAN THAN MAN MAY RANK HIS ROWS   • • • • 166 00 009
  SAY MAN THAN MAN MAY RANK HIS ROWS   • • • • 166 00 009
  THERE BE THOU THE SWEETNESS MAN WAS MEANT TO FIND. • • 168 00 020
  LOVES MAN, THAT HE A MAN WILL BE AND TAKE • • • APPEN D 07
  LOVES MAN, THAT HE A MAN WILL BE AND TAKE • • • APPEN D 07
  CHILD, THAT KNOW NOT MAN? '   • • • • • • APPEN D 14
  TRUE GOD, TRUE MAN, IN FLESH AND BONE; • • • • APPEN D 36
MANMARKS
  SQUADRONED MASKS AND MANMARKS TREADMIRE TOIL THERE • • 072 00 008
MANAGED
  BUT LATE IS BETTER THAN NEVER: YOU SEE YOU HAVE MANAGED SO, • 128 00 017
  BE MANAGED TASTY TO THAT TONGUE? • • • • • • 166 00 019
MANGER
  MANGER, MAIDEN'S KNEE: • • • • • • • • 028 07 004
MANHOOD
  THIS ROYAL MANHOOD. -- 'TIS IN ME REBELLION • • • 102 01 037
  TO MANHOOD, ON THE UPPER LIP -- THEY LOOK'D • • • 102 01 067
  HERE THY VERY MANHOOD STEALS FROM HUMAN KEN; • • • 168 00 010
MANKIND
  MUCH DEARER TO MANKIND;   • • • • • • • • 060 00 107
  THAN SEWERS WITH SACRED OILS. MANKIND, THAT MOB, COMES. COME! • 152 02 070
  MANKIND FREE FOR TO MAKE   • • • • • • • APPEN D 09
  LOST MANKIND SHALL BE BOUGHT   • • • • • • APPEN D 18
MANKIND'S
  IN MANKIND'S MEDLEY A DUTY-SWERVER.   • • • • • 041 00 054
MANLY
  HE WAS ALL OF LOVELY MANLY MOULD,   • • • • • 041 00 074
  SINCE, PROUD, IT CALLS THE CALLING MANLY, GIVES A GUESS • 063 00 004
MANNA
  HE FEEDS ME WITH HIS MANNA EVERY DAY; • • • • 005 00 013
  TO GENTLE MANNA AND SIMPLE BREAD?   • • • • • 081 00 175
MANNA-BUSHES
  ARE ALL THE MANNA-BUSHES IN THE LAND • • • • • 005 00 021
MANNER
  THIS WAS THEIR MANNER: ONE TRANSLUCENT CREST • • • 002 00 038
MANNERLY-HEARTED
  MANNERLY-HEARTED! MORE THAN HANDSOME FACE -- • • 047 00 009
MANNERS
  WINNING WAYS, AIRS INNOCENT, MAIDEN MANNERS, C • • 059 06 015
MAN'S
  MAN'S MALICE, WITH WRECKING AND STORM. • • • • 028 09 004
  MARK, THE MARK IS OF MAN'S MAKE   • • • • • 028 22 003
  AND WEARS MAN'S SMUDGE AND SHARES MAN'S SMELL: THE SOIL • 031 00 007

MAN'S   (CONTINUED)
      AND WEARS MAN'S SMUDGE AND SHARES MAN'S SMELL: THE SOIL • •   •   • 031 00 007
      TO MAN'S LAST DUST, DRAIN FAST TOWARDS MAN'S FIRST SLIME. • •   •   • 035 00 014
      TO MAN'S LAST DUST, DRAIN FAST TOWARDS MAN'S FIRST SLIME. • •   •   • 035 00 014
      MAN'S MOUNTING SPIRIT IN HIS BONE-HOUSE, MEAN HOUSE, DWELLS --   •   • 039 00 002
      MAN'S SPIRIT WILL BE FLESH-BOUND WHEN FOUND AT BEST, •   •   •   • 039 00 012
      ABOUT MAN'S BEATING HEART, •   •   •   •   •   •   •   •   • 060 00 050
      OR LESS WOULD WIN MAN'S MIND. •   •   •   •   •   •   •   • 060 00 109
      A MAN'S VOICE AND A NEW VOICE SPEAKING NEAR. •   •   •   •   • 136 00 022
      THE MOTION OF THAT MAN'S HEART IS FINE •   •   •   •   •   • 142 00 006
      OR BRING MORE OR MORE BLAZON MAN'S DISTRESS. •   •   •   •   • 150 00 004
MANSEX
      BREATHING BLOOM OF A CHASTITY IN MANSEX FINE. •   •   •   •   • 048 00 016
MANSHAPE
      DROWNED. O PITY AND INDIGNATION! MANSHAPE, THAT SHONE •   •   • 072 00 013
MANTLE-O'ER
      TO MANTLE-O'ER THE TAIL, SUCH AS IS SHED •   •   •   •   •   • 002 00 049
MANTLES
      MANTLES THE GUILTY GLOVE. •   •   •   •   •   •   •   •   • 060 00 039
MANTLING
      MANTLING PASSION IN A GRANDEUR, CRIMSON GRANDEUR. •   •   •   • 152 02 037
MANWOLF
      MANWOLF, WORSE! AND THEIR PACKS INFEST THE AGE. •   •   •   •   • 070 00 020
MANY
      RAVES THROUGH SICILIAN PASTURES MANY A MILE! •   •   •   •   • 001 11 004
      MANY TREES AND FLOWERS ROUND •   •   •   •   •   •   •   • 004 00 019
      ARE YOU SANDBLIND? SLABS OF WATER MANY A MILE •   •   •   •   • 005 00 035
      JUST SEEN, MAY BE TO MANY UNKNOWN MEN •   •   •   •   •   •   • 012 02 012
      CONTENDS ABOUT ITS MANY CREEDS •   •   •   •   •   •   •   • 023 00 032
      HOW MANY LEAVES HAD IT? FIVE THEY WERE THEN, •   •   •   •   • 027 00 037
      BY MANY BLOWS AND BANES: BUT NOW HEARS ROAR •   •   •   •   • 050 00 006
      AND MANY A MARK LIKE THESE, •   •   •   •   •   •   •   •   • 054 00 022
      MINDS ME IN MANY WAYS •   •   •   •   •   •   •   •   •   • 060 00 016
      AND MANY STANDING ROUND A WATERFALL •   •   •   •   •   •   • 091 00 005
      THAT MANY CENTRES FOUND IN MANY HEARTS? •   •   •   •   •   • 107 02 005
      THAT MANY CENTRES FOUND IN MANY HEARTS? •   •   •   •   •   • 107 02 005
      BUT MANY A SILVER VISIONARY SPARK •   •   •   •   •   •   • 113 00 005
MAR
      I KNOW I MAR MY CAUSE WITH WORDS! •   •   •   •   •   •   •   • 081 00 030
      SO BE IT! I MUST MAIM AND MAR. •   •   •   •   •   •   •   • 081 00 031
MARBLED
      MARBLED RIVER, BOISTEROUSLY BEAUTIFUL, BETWEEN •   •   •   •   • 159 00 006
MARCH
      AND YOU WERE A LIAR, O BLUE MARCH DAY. •   •   •   •   •   •   • 041 00 021
      MARCH, KIND COMRADE, ABREAST HIM! •   •   •   •   •   •   •   • 048 00 019
      THEN LET THE MARCH TREAD OUR EARS! •   •   •   •   •   •   •   • 052 00 009
      UNDER HER BANNER WE MARCH FOR HER HONOUR. •   •   •   •   •   • 156 00 015
MARCHES
      IN GAY-GANGS THEY THRONG! THEY GLITTER IN MARCHES. C •   •   • 072 00 002
MARCHING
      AND MARCHING TO FALSE COLOURS! THOSE FEW STROKES •   •   •   • 102 01 065
      GOES MARCHING THRO' MY MIND. WHAT SENSE IS THIS? IT HAS NONE. • 152 01 022
MARCH-BLOOM
      LOOK! MARCH-BLOOM, LIKE ON MEALED-WITH-YELLOW SALLOWS! •   •   • 032 00 011
MARCUS
      MARCUS HARE, HIGH HER CAPTAIN, •   •   •   •   •   •   •   • 041 00 045
MARGARET
      MARGARET, ARE YOU GRIEVING •   •   •   •   •   •   •   •   • 055 00 001
      IT IS MARGARET YOU MOURN FOR. •   •   •   •   •   •   •   • 055 00 015
      MUST DEAL WITH MARGARET CLITHEROE. •   •   •   •   •   •   • 145 00 007
      IS A SHROUD FOR MARGARET CLITHEROE. •   •   •   •   •   •   • 145 00 014
      THE BODY OF MARGARET CLITHEROE. •   •   •   •   •   •   •   • 145 00 021
      CHRIST LIVED IN MARGARET CLITHEROE. •   •   •   •   •   •   • 145 00 028
      TO THE DEATH WITH MARGARET CLITHEROE! •   •   •   •   •   •   • 145 00 035
      TO THE MURDER OF MARGARET CLITHEROE. •   •   •   •   •   •   • 145 00 047
      GOD'S DAUGHTER MARGARET CLITHEROE. •   •   •   •   •   •   • 145 00 054
      IT IS OVER, MARGARET CLITHEROE. •   •   •   •   •   •   •   • 145 00 061
MARGARET'S
      THE LAST THING MARGARET'S FINGERS SEW •   •   •   •   •   •   • 145 00 013
MARK
      ' I MARK THE FLOWERS ERE THE PRIME •   •   •   •   •   •   • 004 00 014
      DEATH, TO MARK THEM IN THE SPRING. •   •   •   •   •   •   • 004 00 032
      I MARK THE TOWER SWALLOWS RUN •   •   •   •   •   •   •   • 015 00 028
      MARK, THE MARK IS OF MAN'S MAKE •   •   •   •   •   •   •   • 028 22 003
      MARK, THE MARK IS OF MAN'S MAKE •   •   •   •   •   •   •   • 028 22 003
      THE-LAST-BREATH PENITENT SPIRITS -- THE UTTERMOST MARK •   •   • 028 33 006
      MARK MAKES IN THE RIVELLING SNOWSTORM. •   •   •   •   •   • 041 00 068
      AND MANY A MARK LIKE THESE, •   •   •   •   •   •   •   •   • 054 00 022
      STAIN LIGHT. YEA, MARK YOU THIS: •   •   •   •   •   •   •   • 060 00 081
      MARK CHRIST OUR KING. HE KNOWS WAR, SERVED THIS SOLDIERING THROUGH! 063 00 009
      MAN, HOW FAST HIS FIREDINT, HIS MARK ON MIND, IS GONE! •   •   • 072 00 011
      SHEER OFF, DISSEVERAL, A STAR, DEATH BLOTS BLACK OUT: NOR·MARK • 072 00 014
      MARK YOU HOW THE PEACOCK'S EYE •   •   •   •   •   •   •   • 086 00 001
      SO TAKES THE SISTER SENSE) CAN FIND NO MARK, •   •   •   •   • 113 00 004
      HER WEEDS ALL MARK HER MAIDEN, THOUGH TO WED, •   •   •   •   • 136 00 017
      THE WORLD WAS SAVED BY VIRGINS, MADE THE MARK. •   •   •   •   • 136 00 030
MARKET
      YET MADE ITS MARKET HERE AS WELL: •   •   •   •   •   •   •   • 025 00 032

160

MARKET   (CONTINUED)
   THEO. YET MADE YOUR MARKET HERE AS WELL: . .   .   . APPEN A 32
MARKING
   MARKING THE SPOT, WHEN THEY HAVE GURGLED O'ER, ... 002 00 003
   SITS WITHOUT CONSOLATION, MARKING NOT 111 00 004
MARK'D
   AS I MARK'D, NOT ALWAYS DIED 004 00 028
   SHE MARK'D WHERE I AND FABIAN MET: 120 00 001
MARRED
   OF WORLD MADE, MARRED, AND MENDED, LOST AND WON: 136 00 026
   MOCKED AND MARRED COUNTENANCE, ... 170 00 008
MARRIAGE
   AND NOW THE MARRIAGE FEAST BEGUN, , ... 022 00 026
MARRIED
   MARRIED, WILL MAKE A SWEET AND MATCHLESS WIFE, ... 094 00 031
MARSH
   THEY RAIN AGAINST OUR MUCH-THICK AND MARSH AIR 040 00 007
MARTINMAS
   ' THIS WEARY MARTINMAS, WOULD IT WERE SUMMER ' 111 00 010
MARTYR
   ON CHRIST THEY DO AND ON THE MARTYR MAY: 073 00 005
MARTYR-MASTER
   THOU MARTYR-MASTER: IN THY SIGHT 028 21 007
MARTYR'S
   FOR, WHERE THE MARTYR'S BONES WERE THICKEST TROD, ... 001 05 008
MARVEL
   'TIS MARVEL SHE IS YET ALIVE. 081 00 010
MARVELLOUS
   THE MARVELLOUS MILK WAS WALSINGHAM WAY 041 00 102
   AND MAKES, O MARVELLOUS! 060 00 059
MARY
   MARY THE VIRGIN, WELL THE HEART KNOWS, ... 027 00 021
   IS MARY THE ROSE, THEN? MARY THE TREE? 027 00 025
   IS MARY THE ROSE, THEN? MARY THE TREE? 027 00 025
   MARY SEES, SYMPATHISING 042 00 026
   TO OFFERING MARY MAY. 042 00 036
   TELLS MARY HER MIRTH TILL CHRIST'S BIRTH 042 00 046
   WHO FIRED FRANCE FOR MARY WITHOUT SPOT. 044 00 014
   MARY IMMACULATE, ... 060 00 024
   IS MARY, MORE BY NAME. 060 00 037
   MARY, MOTHER OF US, WHERE IS YOUR RELIEF? 065 00 004
   NEXT MARY MOTHER OF MAID AND NUN, ... 145 00 043
   JESU THAT DOST IN MARY DWELL, ... 169 00 001
MARY'S
   MAY IS MARY'S MONTH, AND I 042 00 001
   BOTH GOD'S AND MARY'S SON, ... 060 00 072
   TIME WAS, NEXT WHITEST AFTER MARY'S OWN. 136 00 004
MASKED
   MASKED BY THESE BARE SHADOWS, SHAPE AND NOTHING MORE,   .   .   . 168 00 002
MASK'D
   MASK'D WITH SUCH VIOLET DISALLOW THEIR GREEN? V 100 00 010
MASKS
   NOWHERE. NATURAL HEART'S IVY, PATIENCE MASKS 068 00 006
   SQUADRONED MASKS AND MANMARKS TREADMIRE TOIL THERE   .   .   . 072 00 008
MASON'S
   SO THAT THE MASON'S LEVELS, COURSES, ALL 012 02 002
MASQUE
   THAT . . . IN SMOOTH SPOONS SPY LIFE'S MASQUE MIRRORED: TAME   . 075 00 013
MASSACRE
   MAY'S BEAUTY MASSACRE AND WISPED WILD CLOUDS GROW 154 00 002
MASSY
   THERE IS A MASSY PILE ABOVE THE WASTE 001 01 001
   WITH MASSY PILLARS OF THE DORIC MOOD 001 07 002
MASTER
   THROUGH HIM, MELT HIM BUT MASTER HIM STILL: 028 10 004
   A MASTER, HER MASTER AND MINE! -- 028 19 002
   A MASTER, HER MASTER AND MINE! -- 028 19 002
   THING THAT SHE...THERE THEN! THE MASTER, ... 028 28 004
   I ADMIRE THEE, MASTER OF THE TIDES, ... 028 32 001
   BEING MIGHTY A MASTER, BEING A FATHER AND FOND. 034 00 014
   WONDERING WHY MY MASTER BORE IT. 041 00 098
   YOU THERE ARE MASTER, DO YOUR OWN DESIRE: 046 00 011
   MASTER MORE MAY THAN GAZE, GAZE OUT OF COUNTENANCE.   .   .   . 062 00 005
   CLIMB QUITS: ONE BOARDS THE MASTER THERE 166 00 038
MASTERHOOD
   THEREFORE THIS MASTERHOOD, ... 148 00 029
MASTERING
   THOU MASTERING ME 028 01 001
   OF A MASTERING HEAVEN UTTERLY BLUE! 078 00 002
MASTER'S
   FOR THAT STAUNCH SAINT STILL PRAIS'D HIS MASTER'S NAME   .   .   . 001 03 001
MASTERS
   BUT MEN AND MASTERS PLAN AND BUILD: 015 00 006
   AND THAT GRIEF MASTERS JOY ON EARTH, ... 077 00 055
MASTERY
   MASTERY, BUT BE ADORED, BUT BE ADORED KING. 028 10 008
   STIRRED FOR A BIRD, -- THE ACHIEVE OF, THE MASTERY OF THE THING!   .   . 036 00 008

161

MASTERY   (CONTINUED)
    AND MASTERY IN THE MIND, ... 049 00 016
MATCH
    RISE: MATCH YOUR STRENGTH WITH MONSTROUS TALMAI 005 00 057
MATCHED
    NO PIECE MATCHED THOSE EYES KEPT MOST PART MUCH CAST DOWN . . . 152 02 026
    AND MATCHED WITH THEE THERE 'S NOTHING GLAD 167 00 019
MATCHLESS
    MARRIED, WILL MAKE A SWEET AND MATCHLESS WIFE, ... 094 00 031
    THOU MATCHLESS MAIDEN-MOTHER, ... APPEN D 42
MATCHWOOD
    THIS JACK, JOKE, POOR POTSHERD, PATCH, MATCHWOOD, IMMORTAL DIAMOND, . 072 00 023
MATE
    MAN JACK THE MAN IS, JUST; HIS MATE A HUSSY. 075 00 011
    MORTAL MY MATE, BEARING MY ROCK-A-HEART 153 00 001
    MAN MY MATE AND COUNTERPART. 155 00 024
MATED.
    HER MOULD OF FEATURES MATED WELL. 145 00 016
MATES
    SOONER THAN THEIR MATES; AND YET 004 00 029
    (LOW LIE HIS MATES NOW ON WATERY BED) 041 00 058
MATTER
    NOW NO MATTER, CHILD, THE NAME; 055 00 010
    SMALL MATTER OF THAT THEN! LET HIM SMOTHER 145 00 040
    ENOUGH NOW; SINCE THE SACRED MATTER THAT I MEAN . . . 159 00 043
MAWDDACH
    THE MAWDDACH, HOW SHE TRIPS! THOUGH THROTTLED . . . 030 00 021
MAYBE
    AND WHAT SWAYS WITH YOU, MAYBE THIS SWEET MAID; . . . 157 00 022
MAYDAY
    INNOCENT MIND AND MAYDAY IN GIRL AND BOY, ... 033 00 013
MAY-HOPE
    THEE, MAY-HOPE OF OUR DARKENED WAYS! 026 00 040
MAY-MESS
    LOOK, LOOK: A MAY-MESS, LIKE ON ORCHARD BOUGHS! . . . 032 00 010
MAY'S
    MAY'S BEAUTY MASSACRE AND WISPED WILD CLOUDS GROW . . . 154 00 002
MAY
    SPRING'S ONE DAUGHTER, THE SWEET CHILD MAY. 026 00 002
    AND MAY HAS COME, HAIR-BOUND IN FLOWERS, ... 026 00 013
    MAID YET MOTHER AS MAY HATH BEEN -- 026 00 020
    THAT WAS UNTO JUDAH AS MAY, AND BROUGHT HER . . . 026 00 031
    OF PIED AND PEELED MAY! 028 26 004
    MAY IS MARY'S MONTH, AND I 042 00 001
    BUT THE LADY MONTH, MAY, ... 042 00 006
    TO OFFERING MARY MAY. 042 00 036
    HOW DARE I PAINT MISS STORY TO MISS MAY? 094 00 003
    OF BLUEBELLS SHEAVED IN MAY 144 00 010
    THE SMOULDERING ENORMOUS WINTER WELKIN! MAY . . . 149 A 008
    BUT MORE CHEER IS WHEN J MAY V . . . . . . 149 B 010
MAZE
    OF ART BEST FOLLOW NATURE) IN A MAZE 001 06 005
    ON BEING'S DREAD AND VACANT MAZE. 023 00 030
MAZED
    TWO MAZED SHEPHERDS PERISH'D IN THE TIDE; 001 14 003
    AND PLANETS BUD WHERE'ER WE TURN OUR MAZED EYES. . . 002 00 033
MAZY
    OF MAZY SHAPE AND HUE, BUT NOW BEREFT 001 08 003
    AND MAZY SANDS ALL WATER-WATTLED 030 00 023
MEAD
    IN SOME BROAD PALMY MEAD, AND SAINTLY SMILED, . . . 001 10 005
    GIVE US OUR GREEN LOTS IN ANOTHER MEAD 098 15 005
MEADOW
    WAVE WITH THE MEADOW, FORGET THAT THERE MUST . . . 028 11 007
    ON MEADOW AND RIVER AND WIND-WANDERING WEED-WINDING BANK. . 043 00 008
    THERE WAS A MEADOW LEVEL ALMOST: YOU TRACED . . . 107 04 001
    GALLOP ALONG THE MEADOW GRASS. -- 130 00 026
MEADOW-DOWN
    BUT UNCUMBERED: MEADOW-DOWN IS NOT DISTRESSED . . . 039 00 013
MEADOW'S
    BEYOND THE RIVER, ALL THE MEADOW'S ROUND, ... 107 04 010
MEADOWS
    LOVELY THE WOODS, WATERS, MEADOWS, COMBES, VALES, . . 034 00 009
    NEXT TO MEADOWS ABUNDANT, PIERCED WITH FLOWERS, . . 098 12 002
    MEADOWS TO THEM INEXPLICABLY DEAR. 119 00 008
MEAL
    TOM HEART-AT-EASE, TOM NAVVY; HE IS ALL FOR HIS MEAL . . 070 00 004
MEALED-WITH-YELL
    LOOK! MARCH-BLOOM, LIKE ON MEALED-WITH-YELLOW SALLOWS! . . 032 00 011
MEAL-DRIFT
    MEAL-DRIFT MOULDED EVER AND MELTED ACROSS SKIES? . . . 038 00 004
MEALTIME
    AND CALLED TO COME AT MEALTIME SHE WOULD NOT; . . . 136 00 033
MEAN
    ' I DID NOT MEAN TO SLEEP, BUT FOUND 021 00 015
    THE MAJESTY! WHAT DID SHE MEAN? 028 25 001
    MAN'S MOUNTING SPIRIT IN HIS BONE-HOUSE, MEAN HOUSE, DWELLS -- . 039 00 002

MEAN   (CONTINUED)
WHERE WE, EVEN WHERE WE MEAN 043 00 016
HOURS I MEAN YEARS, MEAN LIFE, AND MY LAMENT 067 00 006
HOURS I MEAN YEARS, MEAN LIFE, AND MY LAMENT 067 00 006
IT IS TOO LARGE FOR ME. WHAT DOES THAT MEAN? 102 01 026
ENOUGH NOW! SINCE THE SACRED MATTER THAT I MEAN 159 00 043
MEANING
NEVER ASK IF MEANING IT, WANTING IT, WARNED OF IT -- MEN GO. . 028 08 008
NOT MOOD IN HIM NOR MEANING, PROUD FIRE OR SACRED FEAR, . . 045 00 005
OFF HIM, BUT MEANING MOTION FANS FRESH OUR WITS WITH WONDER. . 045 00 014
DOUBLE AS SHARP, MEANING AND FORCIBLE, ... 102 01 011
MEANS
THIS MEANS YOU NEED NOT FEAR THE STORMS, THE CRIES, . . . 014 03 002
MEN'S WITS TO THE THINGS THAT ARE! WHAT GOOD MEANS -- WHERE A GLANCE 062 00 004
WHO MEANS TO WED OR MEANS TO KILL, ... 120 00 029
WHO MEANS TO WED OR MEANS TO KILL, ... 120 00 029
SHE MENDS THE WAY SHE MEANS TO GO, ... 145 00 012
ANY INSTANT FALLS MEANS ME, AND I DO NOT REPENT! 152 02 032
MEANT
TO CROSSES MEANT FOR JESU'S! YOU WHOM THE EAST 011 00 005
TAKE AS FOR TOOL, NOT TOY MEANT 049 00 013
AND MEN ARE MEANT TO SHARE 060 00 044
ILL MEANT, YET TRUE. I BEST SHOULD FLATTER THEN, ... 125 00 019
THERE BE THOU THE SWEETNESS MAN WAS MEANT TO FIND. . . . 168 00 020
MEANTIME
MEANTIME SOME TONGUE CRIES C 152 01 016
MEANWHILE
MEANWHILE A LITTER OF THE JAGGED LEAVES 111 00 008
OR IF I GO, SHE STAYS MEANWHILE, ... 120 00 028
MEANWHILES
BY MEANWHILES! MAKING MY PLAY 054 00 015
MEASURE
WHAT BY YOUR MEASURE IS THE HEAVEN OF DESIRE, ... 028 26 007
OTHER, I GATHER, IN MEASURE HER MIND'S 028 27 007
SPEND HERE YOUR MEASURE OF TIME AND TREASURE 030 00 039
PRECIOUS PASSING MEASURE, ... 041 00 011
WHILE THE BREEZE BY RANK AND MEASURE 078 00 009
MEASURED
IN THE WORST HOUR THAT'S MEASURED BY THE SUN, ... 014 02 005
ARE MEASURED OUTWARDS FROM MY BREAST, ... 130 00 002
MEASURES
GOD SHALL O'ER-BRIM THE MEASURES YOU HAVE SPENT 011 00 009
MEAT
AND HAVE YOUR FILL OF MEAT! 005 00 010
MY MORE THAN MEAT AND DRINK, ... 060 00 011
MEDALLION'D
AT RED POMPEII ON MEDALLION'D WALLS. 002 00 051
MEDLEY
IN MANKIND'S MEDLEY A DUTY-SWERVER, ... 041 00 054
MEEK
AND PRIDE IS NERVELESS AND HEARTS MEEK. 077 00 038
MAKE ME MEEK, LORD! THOU WERT LOWLY! 129 00 007
MEET
PHILIP, SUPPOSING THAT THE GIFT MOST MEET, ... 001 03 006
WE MEET TOGETHER, YOU AND I. 008 00 010
MEET IN ONE ACRE OF ONE LAND, ... 008 00 011
AND YOU SHALL MEET ME WITH REPLY, ... 008 00 013
MY PRAYERS MUST MEET A BRAZEN HEAVEN 018 00 001
PEACE AND FOOD CHEERED ME WHERE FOUR ROUGH WAYS MEET. . . 020 00 012
WITH ATTRIBUTES WE DEEM ARE MEET! 023 00 014
FOR I GREET HIM THE DAYS I MEET HIM, AND BLESS WHEN I UNDERSTAND. . 028 05 008
WANTING! WHICH TWO WHEN THEY ONCE MEET, ... 038 00 012
TO WEND AND MEET NO SIN! 060 00 117
WHAT DO THEN? HOW MEET BEAUTY? MERELY MEET IT! OWN, . . 062 00 012
WHAT DO THEN? HOW MEET BEAUTY? MERELY MEET IT! OWN, . . 062 00 012
THAT MEET IN MID-AIR! AND BE SO 077 00 139
AND PASSAGES WHERE WE USED TO MEET, -- 081 00 162
BEAUTY IT MAY BE IS THE MEET OF LINES, ... 102 03 001
SAY BEAUTY LIES BUT IN THE MEET OF LINES, V 102 03 021
SAID, IT WAS NOT MEET THE KING SHOULD WED 109 12 003
TOMORROW MEET YOU? O NOT TOMORROW. 110 00 001
I CANNOT MEET THE SWALLOWING MAIN. 120 00 027
MEETS
HE MEETS HER, STINTLESS OF HER SMILE! 083 00 021
HE MEETS UPON MIDSUMMER DAY 083 00 027
MELANCHOLY
YIELDS TO THE SULTRY SIEGE OF MELANCHOLY. 016 00 008
MELEE
HUNG IN THE SWAYING OF THE FIERCE MELEE, ... 001 02 004
MELLOW
THE SKILL OF DREAMY CLAUDE, AND TITIAN'S MELLOW GLOOM. . . 001 10 009
WHEN HIS MELLOW SMILE HE SEES 077 00 105
MELLS
MELLS BLUE AND SNOWWHITE THROUGH THEM, A FRINGE AND FRAY . . 149 A 009
MELLS BLUE WITH SNOWWHITE THROUGH THEIR FRINGE AND FRAY V . . 149 B 011
MELODIOUS
SWELL'D THE SWEET STRAIN TO A MELODIOUS WAIL! 002 00 133

163

MELODIOUSLY
    GURGLED, WHERE THEY HAD SUNK, MELODIOUSLY. 002 00 111
MELODY
    HARK THE MOLTEN MELODY; 077 00 086
MELT
    THAT GUILT IS HUSHED BY, HEARTS ARE FLUSHED BY AND MELT -- . . 028 06 006
    THROUGH HIM, MELT HIM BUT MASTER HIM STILL; 028 10 004
    MELT AS FROM A HEAVENLY CHRISM; 077 00 062
MELTED
    THE ZENITH MELTED TO A ROSE OF AIR; 002 00 023
    MEAL-DRIFT MOULDED EVER AND MELTED ACROSS SKIES? 038 00 004
    MELTED IN THE DIZZY BOW 077 00 140
    STEEL MAY BE MELTED AND ROCK RENT. 081 00 134
MELTING
    NOW MELTING UPWARD THRO' THE SLOPING SCALE 002 00 132
    THE MAKING AND THE MELTING CROWDS; 015 00 003
    WHY, TEARS! IS IT? TEARS! SUCH A MELTING, A MADRIGAL START! . . 028 18 004
    MELTING INTO AETHER RARE 077 00 074
MELTS
    AND MELTS AMIDST ANOTHER; CIEL'D ON HIGH 001 06 008
    IT MELTS, NEW LIGHTS ARISE AS FAIR. 077 00 118
MEMBERS
    FIVE LIKE THE SENSES AND MEMBERS OF MEN; 027 00 038
    THE MEMBERS, HOW THEY SIT! 148 00 002
MEMENTO
    AGE GASP! WHOSE BREATH IS OUR MEMENTO MORI -- 075 00 007
MEMORY
    TO THY NOT-STALED UNCHARTED MEMORY. 117 00 014
MEN
    ON THISTLES THAT MEN LOOK NOT GRAPES TO GATHER, ... 007 00 002
    THAT MEN MUST WONDER AS I PASS 010 00 003
    JUST SEEN, MAY BE TO MANY UNKNOWN MEN 012 02 012
    THAN TREBLE-FERVENT MORE OF OTHER MEN, ... 014 01 013
    BUT MEN AND MASTERS PLAN AND BUILD; 015 00 006
    WHICH MAKES ME WHEN WITH MEN I DEAL 015 00 019
    SUMMONING MEN FROM SPEECHLESS DAY 023 00 041
    MEN ARE AMAZED TO WATCH ME PASS 025 00 003
    OF THE MONTH BY MEN CALLED VIRGINAL. 026 00 022
    FIVE LIKE THE SENSES AND MEMBERS OF MEN; 027 00 038
    NEVER ASK IF MEANING IT, WANTING IT, WARNED OF IT -- MEN GO. . 028 08 008
    BE ADORED AMONG MEN, ... 028 09 001
    TAKE SETTLER AND SEAMEN, TELL MEN WITH WOMEN, ... 028 12 003
    TO THE MEN IN THE TOPS AND THE TACKLE RODE OVER THE STORM'S BRAWLING. 028 19 008
    LOATHED FOR A LOVE MEN KNEW IN THEM, ... 028 21 001
    THEY WERE ELSE-MINDED THEN, ALTOGETHER, THE MEN . . . 028 25 005
    CRUSHED. WHY DO MEN THEN NOW NOT RECK HIS ROD? . . . 031 00 004
    MEN GO BY ME WHOM EITHER BEAUTY BRIGHT 040 00 005
    LADS AND MEN HER LADE AND TREASURE. 041 00 012
    MEN, BOLDBOYS SOON TO BE MEN; 041 00 014
    MEN, BOLDBOYS SOON TO BE MEN; 041 00 014
    THEN A LURCH FORWARD, FRIGATE AND MEN; 041 00 041
    HE HAUNTED WHO OF ALL MEN MOST SWAYS MY SPIRITS TO PEACE; . 044 00 011
    AND MEN ARE MEANT TO SHARE 060 00 044
    MEN HERE MAY DRAW LIKE BREATH 060 00 066
    THAT, HOPES THAT, MAKESBELIEVE, THE MEN MUST BE NO LESS; . 063 00 005
    WHEN SICK MEN TURN, AND LIGHTS ARE LOW, ... 077 00 025
    AND HARD MEN FEEL A SOFTENING TOUCH; 077 00 030
    DOES LAY MEN LOW WITH ONE BLADE'S SUDDEN BLOW 080 02 003
    'TIS FALSELY GIVEN -- AS LOVE IN MEN; 081 00 049
    'TWAS SAID OF NONE BUT ALL MEN KNEW; 081 00 091
    WHAT HAVE I MORE THAN OTHER MEN, ... 081 00 168
    AND SAW THE MEN BEFORE THE FLOOD . . . . 093 A 002
    AND WATCH UNTIL OUR HORSES AND THE MEN 125 00 009
    IS KNOWN TO MEN MORE THAN ME. 138 00 013
    WHILE SICK MEN SHALL CAST SIGHS, OF SWEET HEALTH ALL DESPAIRING, . 152 C 003
    AS LONG AS MEN ARE MORTAL AND GOD MERCIFUL, ... 152 C 010
    AGAINST THE WILD AND WANTON WORK OF MEN. 157 00 036
    THAT MEN HAVE WISHED FOR OR HAVE HAD, ... 167 00 020
    ON THE CROSS THY GODHEAD MADE NO SIGN TO MEN; 168 00 009
    ANG. MEN MUST START TO SEE ME PASS . . . . . . APPEN A 03
MEND
    TO MEND HER WE END HER, ... 043 00 017
    MEND FIRST AND VITAL CANDLE IN CLOSE HEART'S VAULT; . . . 046 00 010
MENDED
    SICKNESS BROKE HIM. IMPATIENT, HE CURSED AT FIRST, BUT MENDED . 053 00 005
    OF WORLD MADE, MARRED, AND MENDED, LOST AND WON; . . . 136 00 026
MENDS
    SHE MENDS THE WAY SHE MEANS TO GO. 145 00 012
MEN'S
    IT WAS MADE OF EARTH'S MOULD BUT IT WENT FROM MEN'S EYES . . 027 00 003
    TO THE FATHER THROUGH THE FEATURES OF MEN'S FACES. . . . 057 00 014
    MEN'S WITS TO THE THINGS THAT ARE; WHAT GOOD MEANS -- WHERE A GLANCE 062 00 004
    WORLD'S LOVELIEST -- MEN'S SELVES, SELF FLASHES OFF FRAME AND FACE. 062 00 011
    WHILE BLIND MEN'S EYES SHALL THIRST_C . . . . . . 152 C 004
MENTION
    AND MINOR SWEETNESS SCARCE MADE MENTION OF; 019 00 012
MERCIES
    TO BATHE IN HIS FALL-GOLD MERCIES, TO BREATHE IN HIS ALL-FIRE GLANCES. 028 23 008

MIGHT   (CONTINUED)
   OF SIN AND DEVIL'S MIGHT.'   . . . . APPEN D 10
   THROUGH TH' HOLY GHOST HIS MIGHT. . . . . APPEN D 34
MIGHTY
   ' YET AS HE CHANGED HIS MIGHTY STOPS 021 00 043
   BEING MIGHTY A MASTER, BEING A FATHER AND FOND. . . 034 00 014
   ASK OF HER, THE MIGHTY MOTHER; 042 00 013
   THAT MAMMOCKS, MIGHTY FOOT, BUT NO WAY SPED,   . . . 070 00 012
   MOTE-LIKE IN THY MIGHTY GLOW. 155 00 004
MILAN
   BLADES OF MILAN IN CIRCLES RANG'D, GREW RUST   . . . 001 12 008
MILD
   WILL, OR MILD NIGHTS THE NEW MORSELS OF SPRING;   . . 034 00 007
   WITH YELLOWY MOISTURE MILD NIGHT'S BLEAR-ALL BLACK, . 046 00 003
   WITH THY MIGHT THAT THOU ART MILD. 155 00 016
   MILDLY, OF HER OWN MILD MOOD. . . . . APPEN D 23
MILDLY
   MILDLY, OF HER OWN MILD MOOD, ... APPEN D 23
MILE
   RAVES THROUGH SICILIAN PASTURES MANY A MILE;   . . . 001 11 004
   A MILE ASTERN LAY THE BLUE SHORES AWAY; 002 00 005
   ARE YOU SANDBLIND? SLABS OF WATER MANY A MILE   . . . 005 00 035
   BETWEENPIE MOUNTAINS -- LIGHTS A LOVELY MILE. . . . 069 00 014
MILE-LONG
   OF MILE-LONG REACHES OF OUR ROAD BELOW US. 125 00 007
MILES
   THE MILES PROFOUND OF SOLID GREEN, AND BE 002 00 123
   FOR ALL THE MILES THAT THEY WERE SPED; 081 00 158
   BUT WITH HIS OTHER FOOT THREE MILES BEYOND 100 00 004
   THREE MILES INDEED. 125 00 012
MILK
   THE MARVELLOUS MILK WAS WALSINGHAM WAY 041 00 102
   BIRTH, MILK, AND ALL THE REST 060 00 021
   AND MOTHER HAVE NO MILK FOR CHILD, ... 114 00 007
   THE EAR IN MILK, LUSH THE SASH, ... 138 00 020
   IS ANYTHING A MILK TO THE MIND SO, SO SIGHS DEEP . . 149 A 002
MILK-WHITE
   HER MILK-WHITE THROAT AND FOLDED DEW-LAP SLACK   . . 099 00 009
MILKY
   LO, LINKED HEAVENS WITH MILKY WAYS! 010 00 021
   WITH BELLED FIRE AND THE MOTH-SOFT MILKY WAY,   . . . 028 26 006
   SKY FLEECED WITH THE MILKY WAY. 098 23 002
   THE HEIGHTENING DAWN WITH MILKY ORIENCE 098 30 002
   THE PLACE IN THE EAST WITH EARLIEST MILKY MORN   . . 098 30 005
   MILKY AND DARK, WITH AN ATTUNING STRESS 107 04 013
MILL
   AND CHURNING IN THE MILL. 021 00 046
   IS WORTH AND CURRENT WITH A LESSEN'D MILL.' 096 07 008
   HER HAND FROM HEAVEN TO TURN A MILL -- 139 00 004
MILLBROOK-SLIPS
   AND MILLBROOK-SLIPS WITH PRETTY PACE 130 00 025
MILLION
   NOT VAULT THEM, THE MILLION OF ROUNDS C 028 12 008
   THE MILLION SORTS OF UNACCOUNTED MOTES 098 22 002
MILLION-FUELED
   FOOTFRETTED IN IT. MILLION-FUELED, NATURE'S BONFIRE BURNS ON,   . 072 00 009
MILLIONS
   TO FIELDS OF LIGHT; MILLIONS OF TRAVELLING RAYS . . 103 00 009
MILL-STONE
   WHERE THE UPPER MILL-STONE ROOF'D HIS HEAD, ... 006 00 007
MIND
   STANCHING QUENCHING OCEAN OF A MOTIONABLE MIND;   . . 028 32 005
   INNOCENT MIND AND MAYDAY IN GIRL AND BOY, ... 033 00 013
   IN MOULD OR MIND OR WHAT NOT ELSE MAKES RARE;   . . . 040 00 006
   I CANNOT, AND OUT OF SIGHT IS OUT OF MIND. 040 00 011
   WITH DELIGHT CALLS TO MIND 042 00 030
   AND MASTERY IN THE MIND, ... 049 00 016
   NOR MOUTH HAD, NO NOR MIND, EXPRESSED 055 00 012
   OR LESS WOULD WIN MAN'S MIND. 060 00 109
   -- BLACK, WHITE; RIGHT, WRONG; RECKON BUT, RECK BUT, MIND C . . 061 00 012
   O THE MIND, MIND HAS MOUNTAINS; CLIFFS OF FALL . . . 065 00 009
   O THE MIND, MIND HAS MOUNTAINS; CLIFFS OF FALL . . . 065 00 009
   CHARITABLE; NOT LIVE THIS TORMENTED MIND 069 00 003
   WITH THIS TORMENTED MIND TORMENTING YET. 069 00 004
   NOR MIND NOR MAINSTRENGTH; GOLD GO GARLANDED   . . . 070 00 013
   MAN, HOW FAST HIS FIREDINT, HIS MARK ON MIND, IS GONE!   . 072 00 011
   LEAVES YET THE MIND A MOTHER OF IMMORTAL SONG. . . . 076 00 004
   GROSS MIND DISCHARGING FOULED LAUGHTER; 077 00 058
   YOU SEE BUT WITH A HOLIER MIND -- 081 00 040
   THE CHRIST-ED BEAUTY OF HER MIND 145 00 015
   C THE MUSIC OF HIS MIND, ... 148 00 010
   C THE MUSIC OF HIS MIND, ... 148 00 038
   IS ANYTHING A MILK TO THE MIND SO, SO SIGHS DEEP . . 149 A 002
   GOES MARCHING THRO' MY MIND. WHAT SENSE IS THIS? IT HAS NONE,   . 152 01 022
   MY HEART, WHERE HAVE WE BEEN? WHAT HAVE WE SEEN, MY MIND? . . 152 02 001
   OF FAVOURED MAKE AND MIND AND HEALTH AND YOUTH,   . . 157 00 018
   BUT FEARS, FORE-MOTIONS OF THE MIND, ... 166 00 037

MIND   (CONTINUED)
    LEND THIS LIFE TO ME THEN: FEED AND FEAST MY MIND, ... 168 00 019
MINDED
    NOW I AM MINDED TO TAKE PIPE IN HAND 105 00 001
MIND'S
    OTHER, I GATHER, IN MEASURE HER MIND'S 028 27 007
    SO STRANGELY ELEMENTED IS MY MIND'S WEATHER, ... 102 01 015
    HOPE HOLDS TO CHRIST THE MIND'S OWN MIRROR OUT 151 00 001
MINDS
    CHRIST MINDS: CHRIST'S INTEREST, WHAT TO AVOW OR AMEND   .   . 040 00 012
    MINDS ME IN MANY WAYS 060 00 016
MINED
    FAST, BUT MINED WITH A MOTION, A DRIFT, ... 028 04 003
    AS WRECKS OF MINED EMBERS WILL. 092 00 013
MINGLE
    MINGLE PRAISES, PRAYER AND SONG, ... 024 00 027
    RIDING: THERE DID STORMS NOT MINGLE? AND 041 00 026
MINGLED
    YEA IRON IS MINGLED WITH MY CLAY, ... 018 00 010
MINION
    I CAUGHT THIS MORNING MORNING'S MINION, KING- 036 00 001
MINIVER
    HE SHALL BE WARM WITH MINIVER 124 00 015
MINOR
    AND MINOR SWEETNESS SCARCE MADE MENTION OF: 019 00 012
MINT
    THE MINT OF CURRENT COURTESIES, THE FORGE 102 02 008
MINTED
    THE SKY MINTED INTO GOLDEN SEQUINS. 098 25 001
MIRACLE
    REMAINDER OF A MIRACLE. 025 00 034
    THEO. REMAINDER OF A MIRACLE.   .   .   .   .   .   . APPEN A 34
MIRACLE-IN-MARY-
    MIRACLE-IN-MARY-OF-FLAME, ... 028 34 004
MIRE
    KNEADING THE MOUNDED MIRE THAT STOPS 003 00 010
MIRKY
    HE SEEM'D A DISMAL MIRKY STAMP 004 00 008
MIRROR
    HOPE HOLDS TO CHRIST THE MIND'S OWN MIRROR OUT 151 00 001
    I TOLD YOU THAT SHE TURNED HER MIRROR DIM 151 00 011
MIRRORED
    THAT . . . IN SMOOTH SPOONS SPY LIFE'S MASQUE MIRRORED: TAME   . 075 00 013
MIRTH
    STRIKE TIMBRELS, SING, EAT, DRINK, BE FULL OF MIRTH.   .   .   . 005 00 043
    LET IT FLOW FOR HEAVENLY MIRTH: 024 00 010
    TELLS MARY HER MIRTH TILL CHRIST'S BIRTH 042 00 046
    YET FOUND UNSTINTED PLACE FOR MIRTH: 077 00 056
    WHILE SHEENY TEARS AND SUNLIT MIRTH 077 00 129
MISADVENTURE
    SUCH HEATHENISH MISADVENTURE DOGS ONE SIN. V   .   .   . 102 02 013
    SUCH HEATHENISH MISADVENTURE DOGG'D ONE SIN. V   .   .   . 102 02 013
MISDIRECTED
    BUT SINGLE, LEAD A MISDIRECTED LIFE. 094 00 032
MISERY
    THEN IS MY MISERY FULL INDEED: 081 00 068
MISLIKE
    [AND HALF MISLIKE HER LOVELESS KISS.] 120 00 013
MISS
    (AND HERE THE FAITHFUL WAVER, THE FAITHLESS FABLE AND MISS) .   . 028 06 008
    O THEN IF IN MY LAGGING LINES YOU MISS 076 00 011
    MISS STORY'S CHARACTER! TOO MUCH YOU ASK, ... 094 00 001
    HOW DARE I PAINT MISS STORY TO MISS MAY? 094 00 003
    HOW DARE I PAINT MISS STORY TO MISS MAY? 094 00 003
    MISS STORY HAS A MODERATE POWER OF WILL, ... 094 00 009
    MISS M.'S A NIGHTINGALE. 'TIS WELL 096 03 001
    HOW LOOKS THE NIGHT? THERE DOES NOT MISS A STAR.   .   .   . 098 22 001
    HE SEES HER, O BUT HE MUST MISS 120 00 009
    THEY SAID WE COULD NOT MISS. A PUSHING BROOK 125 00 005
    HAMPSTEAD WAS NEVER BRIGHT: AND WHATEVER MISS CULLY'S CHARMS   . 128 00 011
    WITH NO NOW, NO GWENVREWI. I MUST MISS HER MOST   .   .   . 152 02 053
MISSING
    MISSING PROSPERITY AND PRAISE, ... 133 00 015
MISS'D
    WHO RISING LATE HAD MISS'D HER PAINFUL WAY 079 00 005
MIST
    AND SILVER FILMS, BENEATH WITH PEARLY MIST, ... 002 00 067
    INTO THE FLAT BLUE MIST THE SUN 003 00 031
    THE MIST UPON THE LEAVES HAVE STREWED, ... 021 00 033
MISTRESS
    ACCEPTANCE ROUND HIS MISTRESS' MOUTH: 083 00 008
MISTS
    WITH ROSY FOAM AND PELTING BLOSSOM AND MISTS 002 00 090
    MUST SEE THE EAGLE'S BULK, RENDER'D IN MISTS, ... 088 00 003
    SHAKES ITS COCOONING MISTS: AND SO SHE COMES   .   .   . 103 00 008
MIX
    MIX O'ER THE NOT UNMOVED EARTH, -- 077 00 130

                                        167

MIXED
    SNOWFLAKE! THAT'S FAIRLY MIXED   •   •   •   •   •   •   •   •   060 00 006
MIX'D
    THEN LAVER'D FOUNTS AND POSTUR'D STONE HE MIX'D.   •   •   •   001 04 005
M.'S
    MISS M.'S A NIGHTINGALE. 'TIS WELL   •   •   •   •   •   •   096 03 001
MOAN
    INTO HIS HOLLOW'D PALM SHOULD MOAN THE BLAST;   •   •   •   090 00 002
MOANING
    A MOANING VOICE AMONG THE REEDS.   •   •   •   •   •   023 00 036
MOANS
    MY SEVERAL MOANS COME DISTANT IN THEIR TONES   •   •   •   080 03 003
MOB
    THAN SEWERS WITH SACRED OILS. MANKIND, THAT MOB, COMES. COME!   •   152 02 070
MOCK
    TO MAKE BELIEVE MY MOOD WAS -- MOCK. O I MIGHT THINK SO   •   152 02 010
MOCKED
    MOCKED AND MARRED COUNTENANCE,   •   •   •   •   •   •   170 00 008
MOCKERY
    AROSE IN GLOOM, A SOLEMN MOCKERY   •   •   •   •   •   001 08 006
MOCKS
    WITH WEALTH THAT MOCKS HIS HIGH DEGREE,   •   •   •   •   124 00 022
MODERATE
    MISS STORY HAS A MODERATE POWER OF WILL,   •   •   •   094 00 009
MODEST
    WITHAL HER MIEN IS MODEST, WAYS ARE WISE,   •   •   •   136 00 019
MOIST
    THIS DRY DEAN, NOW NO LONGER DRY NOR DUMB, BUT MOIST AND MUSICAL   •   152 C 012
MOISTURE
    THOSE WHOSE DRY PLOT FOR MOISTURE GAPES,   •   •   •   006 00 011
    WITH YELLOWY MOISTURE MILD NIGHT'S BLEAR-ALL BLACK,   •   •   046 00 003
MOLEST
    SQUANDER THE HELL-ROOK RANKS SALLY TO MOLEST HIM;   •   •   048 00 018
MOLTEN
    HARK THE MOLTEN MELODY;   •   •   •   •   •   •   077 00 086
    HAS DRENCH'D THE MOLTEN SUNSET HOUR,   •   •   •   •   077 00 094
MOLTEN-BLUE
    AND WAS AS THO' SOME SAPPHIRE MOLTEN-BLUE   •   •   •   002 00 045
MONARCHS
    WHEN CHIEFS AND MONARCHS CAME THEIR GIFTS TO LAY   •   •   001 02 007
MONITION
    LOVE BY MONITION, HERITAGE, OR LOT,   •   •   •   •   102 03 014
MONKS
    LOUDER THE MONKS DRON'D OUT GREGORIANS SLOW;   •   •   001 13 006
    THE MONKS LEFT LONG AGO; SINCE WHICH NO MORE   •   •   001 15 004
MONSTROUS
    HE RAIS'D THE CONVENT AS A MONSTROUS GRATE;   •   •   001 04 001
    RISE: MATCH YOUR STRENGTH WITH MONSTROUS TALMAI   •   •   005 00 057
    I CAN STAND PENT IN THE MONSTROUS ELEMENT   •   •   •   080 05 003
    FREELY FORGIVES THE MONSTROUS DEBT!   •   •   •   •   081 00 151
    THE MORE SOME MONSTROUS HAND GROPES WITH CLAMMY FINGERS THERE,   •   152 01 014
MONTH
    AND WE THAT JOY IN THIS MONTH JOY-LADEN,   •   •   •   026 00 017
    OF THE MONTH BY MEN CALLED VIRGINAL.   •   •   •   •   026 00 022
    OF NEW YEAR'S MONTH OR SURLY YULE   •   •   •   •   030 00 030
    MAY IS MARY'S MONTH, AND I   •   •   •   •   •   042 00 001
    BUT THE LADY MONTH, MAY,   •   •   •   •   •   042 00 006
    THEO. WHAT THE COLD MONTH ALLOWS --   •   •   •   APPEN A 40
MONTH-BROTHER
    WHEN A SISTER, BORN FOR EACH STRONG MONTH-BROTHER,   •   •   026 00 001
MONTHS
    MONTHS EARLIER, SINCE I HAD OUR SWEET REPRIEVE AND RANSOM   •   053 00 007
    NINE MONTHS SHE THEN, NAY YEARS, NINE YEARS SHE LONG   •   •   076 00 005
MONUMENTS
    MONUMENTS OF MY EARNEST, RECORDS OF MY REVENGE,   •   •   152 02 005
MOOD
    WITH MASSY PILLARS OF THE DORIC MOOD   •   •   •   •   001 07 002
    NOT MOOD IN HIM NOR MEANING, PROUD FIRE OR SACRED FEAR,   •   045 00 005
    HE WAS A SHEPHERD OF THE ARCADIAN MOOD   •   •   •   107 01 016
    TO MAKE BELIEVE MY MOOD WAS -- MOCK. O I MIGHT THINK SO   •   152 02 010
    WHO STOPS HIS ASKING MOOD AT PAR   •   •   •   •   166 00 025
    MILDLY, OF HER OWN MILD MOOD,   •   •   •   •   APPEN D 23
MOODS
    HAD CALLED THE SEASONS' CHANGEFUL MOODS   •   •   •   023 00 023
MOON
    THE BUGLE MOON BY DAYLIGHT FLOATS   •   •   •   •   003 00 015
    RATHER IT IS THE SIZING MOON.   •   •   •   •   •   010 00 020
    O NO IT IS THE SIZING MOON.   •   •   •   •   •   025 00 020
    FREQUENTING THERE WHILE MOON SHALL WEAR AND WEND.   •   •   035 00 004
    THE LORN MOON, PALE WITH PITEOUS DISMAY,   •   •   •   079 00 004
    WHO FIRST KNEW MOONLIGHT BY THE HUNTERS' MOON.   •   •   105 00 017
    THE MOON, DWINDLED AND THINNED TO THE FRINGE C   •   •   137 00 002
    CAT. O NO, IT IS THE SIZING MOON.   •   •   •   APPEN A 20
MOONLESS
    MOONLESS DARKNESS STANDS BETWEEN.   •   •   •   •   129 00 001
MOONLIGHT
    WHO FIRST KNEW MOONLIGHT BY THE HUNTERS' MOON.   •   •   105 00 017

MOONLIGHT-MATED
    THE MOONLIGHT-MATED GLOWLESS GLOWWORMS SHINE. 098 36 001
MOONMARKS
    QUAINT MOONMARKS, TO HIS PELTED PLUMAGE UNDER C 045 00 010
MOOR
    FAIR RELICS TOO THE CHANGEFUL MOOR HAD LEFT 001 08 001
MOORLAND
    AND WITH HEAVENFALLEN FRESHNESS DOWN FROM MOORLAND STILL BRIMS, .   . 159 00 039
MORE
    DOORS SLAMM'D TO THE BLASTS CONTINUALLY! MORE LOW, ... 001 13 008
    THE MONKS LEFT LONG AGO; SINCE WHICH NO MORE 001 15 004
    MORE WONDROUS TO HAVE BORNE SUCH HOPE BEFORE 001 15 007
    THAN CHANGEFUL POMP OF COURTS IS AYE MORE WONDERFUL. .   .   . 001 15 009
    AND MORE, ON EACH HAND, THICKEN, AND APPEAR 002 00 030
    SAVE BY TWO STARS, MORE CROWDING LIGHTS ARISE, ... 002 00 032
    OF TREMULOUS FILM, MORE SUBTLE THAN THE VEST 002 00 039
    FROM FLESH-FLOWERS OF THE ROCK; BUT MORE WERE WREATH'D .   . 002 00 063
    WHENCE OFT I WATCH BUT SEE THOSE MERMAIDS NOW NO MORE. .   . 002 00 143
    MORE SWEET-FAMILIAR GROWS MY LOVE TO THEE, ... 012 01 002
    THAN TREBLE-FERVENT MORE OF OTHER MEN, ... 014 01 013
    MY BANKRUPT HEART HAS NO MORE TEARS TO SPEND. 014 03 004
    MORE POWERLESS THAN THE BLIND OR LAME. 015 00 020
    THE COPSE WAS NEVER MORE THAN GREY. 021 00 002
    THAT MORE HE SHUNS OUR SPECIAL DALE 021 00 024
    TO DEATH'S MORE SILENT, DARKER SPELL. 023 00 042
    MORE WILL WEAR THIS WAND AND THEN 025 00 039
    MORE BRIGHTENING HER, RARE-DEAR BRITAIN, AS HIS REIGN ROLLS, .   . 028 35 006
    TIMES TOLD LOVELIER, MORE DANGEROUS, O MY CHEVALIER! .   .   . 036 00 011
    HE WAS BUT ONE LIKE THOUSANDS MORE. 041 00 085
    MORE, MORE THAN WAS WILL YET BE. -- 041 00 104
    MORE, MORE THAN WAS WILL YET BE. -- 041 00 104
    WELL BUT THERE WAS MORE THAN THIS: 042 00 033
    MANNERLY-HEARTED! MORE THAN HANDSOME FACE -- 047 00 009
    LET ME THOUGH SEE NO MORE OF HIM, AND NOT DISAPPOINTMENT .   . 048 00 036
    A WILDER BEAST FROM WEST THAN ALL WERE, MORE 050 00 007
    RIFE IN HER WRONGS, MORE LAWLESS, AND MORE LEWD. .   .   . 050 00 008
    RIFE IN HER WRONGS, MORE LAWLESS, AND MORE LEWD. .   .   . 050 00 008
    HOW FAR FROM THEN FORETHOUGHT OF, ALL THY MORE BOISTEROUS YEARS, . 053 00 012
    I SAY MORE: THE JUST MAN JUSTICES! 057 00 009
    NEVER FLEETS MORE, FASTENED WITH THE TENDEREST TRUTH .   .   . 059 06 012
    MY MORE THAN MEAT AND DRINK, ... 060 00 011
    IS MARY, MORE BY NAME. 060 00 037
    NAY, MORE THAN ALMONER, ... 060 00 042
    MORE CHRIST AND BAFFLE DEATH; 060 00 067
    MORE MAKES, WHEN ALL IS DONE, ... 060 00 071
    BLOOM BREATHE, THAT ONE BREATH MORE 060 00 092
    MASTER MORE MAY THAN GAZE, GAZE OUT OF COUNTENANCE. .   .   . 062 00 005
    IN ME OR, MOST WEARY, CRY I CAN NO MORE. I CAN; .   .   . 064 00 003
    MORE PANGS WILL, SCHOOLED AT FOREPANGS, WILDER WRING, .   . 065 00 002
    AND MORE MUST, IN YET LONGER LIGHT'S DELAY. 067 00 004
    AND WHERE IS HE WHO MORE AND MORE DISTILLS 068 00 012
    AND WHERE IS HE WHO MORE AND MORE DISTILLS 068 00 012
    MY OWN HEART LET ME MORE HAVE PITY ON: LET 069 00 001
    I CAST FOR COMFORT I CAN NO MORE GET 069 00 005
    VEINS VIOLETS AND TALL TREES MAKES MORE AND MORE) .   .   . 073 00 011
    VEINS VIOLETS AND TALL TREES MAKES MORE AND MORE) .   .   . 073 00 011
    DO IN SPARE HOURS MORE THRIVE THAN I THAT SPEND, .   .   . 074 00 008
    AND FOR THAT FEARFUL HOUR LIFE IS MORE THIN 080 03 005
    BUT YOU, SO SPHERED, SEE NO MORE -- 081 00 039
    FOR MORE WITH HIM WHO GIVES THEE ALL, ... 081 00 150
    WHAT HAVE I MORE THAN OTHER MEN, ... 081 00 168
    MORE GOLDEN THAN THE WORLD OF LIGHTS, ... 083 00 002
    HIS SICK STARS FALTER. MORE HE MAY 083 00 025
    ' BOUGHS BEING PRUNED, BIRDS PREENED, SHOW MORE FAIR! .   .   . 096 07 001
    IN MORE PRECISION NOW OF LIGHT AND DARK 098 30 001
    NOW MORE PRECISELY TOUCHED IN LIGHT AND GLOOM, ... 098 30 004
    METHINKS MY LAUGHTER IS MORE PERILOUS V 102 01 008
    ------ THERE IS MORE PERIL FROM MY LAUGHTER. V 102 01 009
    NOW ONE WORD MORE AND THEN I AM GONE INDEED, ... 102 01 055
    IT WERE MORE LIKE TO BE. ' 109 32 004
    IT WERE MORE LIKE TO BE. ' 109 34 004
    IT WERE MORE LIKE TO BE. ' 109 35 004
    THE MORE SHE ASK'D, THE MORE HE SPOKE, ... 109 36 001
    THE MORE SHE ASK'D, THE MORE HE SPOKE, ... 109 36 001
    THE MORE HE TOLD, THE LESS SHE SPOKE, ... 109 36 003
    MORE SWEETLY SHADES HER STOLEN HAIR 120 00 007
    HAD BEEN MORE FERTILE AND HAD SOWN WITH NOTES 122 00 005
    PAST, THE PAST, NO MORE BE SEEN! 129 00 002
    IS KNOWN TO MEN MORE THAN ME. 138 00 013
    C ANYWHERE ANY MORE JOY TO BE IN. 138 00 033
    NO MORE THAN RED AND BLUE, ... 148 00 033
    NO MORE THAN RE AND MI, ... 148 00 034
        BUT MORE CHEER IS WHEN J MAY V 149 8 010
    OR BRING MORE OR MORE BLAZON MAN'S DISTRESS. 150 00 004
    OR BRING MORE OR MORE BLAZON MAN'S DISTRESS. 150 00 004
    TO TAKE HIS LOVELY LIKENESS MORE AND MORE. 151 00 002
    TO TAKE HIS LOVELY LIKENESS MORE AND MORE. 151 00 002

MOST   (CONTINUED)
      HAST THY DARK DESCENDING AND MOST ART MERCIFUL THEN. 028 09 008
      MOST, O MAID'S CHILD, THY CHOICE AND WORTHY THE WINNING. 033 00 014
      WHAT MOST I MAY EYE AFTER, BE IN AT THE END 040 00 010
      THAN THE MOST ARE MUST DELIGHT HER? 042 00 010
      HE HAUNTED WHO OF ALL MEN MOST SWAYS MY SPIRITS TO PEACE: .   .   . 044 00 011
      TURN MOST ON TENDER BYPLAY. 054 00 016
      DOWN? NO WAVING OFF OF THESE MOST MOURNFUL MESSENGERS, C   .   . 059 0L 004
      IN ME OR, MOST WEARY, CRY I CAN NO MORE. I CAN; 064 00 003
      I AM GALL, I AM HEARTBURN. GOD'S MOST DEEP DECREE 067 00 009
      COME BECAUSE THEN MOST THINLY LIES 077 00 035
      MOST LIKE THOSE HUES THAT IN THE PRISM 077 00 061
      MOST DEAD-ALIVE UPON THOSE DAYS. 080 02 007
      O HERE IS THE MOST PITEOUS PART, ... 080 11 002
      EXILED MOST REMOTE ELKHOR. 081 000 47
      SHE KEPT HER LOVE-THOUGHTS ON MOST LENTEN DIET, ... 082 00 007
      ABOUT HERSELF SHE IS MOST SENSITIVE, ... 094 00 021
      OF VIRTUES I MOST WARMLY BLESS, ... 096 01 001
      MOST RARELY SEE, UNSELFISHNESS, ... 096 01 002
      A STAR MOST SPIRITUAL, PRINCIPAL, PREEMINENT 098 27 001
      MOST ILL-CONTENT, THIS LEAST LEAST THING I DO. 102 01 054
      MOST LIKE THE TUFT OF PLIGHTED SILVER ROUND V 102 01 068
      MOST DENTED) LAY SYLVESTER, READING KEATS' 107 04 021
      MAN IS MOST LOW, GOD IS MOST HIGH. 133 00 005
      MAN IS MOST LOW, GOD IS MOST HIGH. 133 00 005
      OF VIRTUE AND VICE: BUT MOST (IT SEEMED HIS SENSE)   .   .   . 136 00 027
      DENIS, WHOSE MOTIONABLE, ALERT, MOST VAULTING WIT 143 00 001
      APART WIDE AND NEW-NESTLE AT HEAVEN MOST HIGH.   .   .   .   . 149 A 006
      NO PIECE MATCHED THOSE EYES KEPT MOST PART MUCH CAST DOWN   .   . 152 02 026
      WITH NO NOW, NO GWENVREWI. I MUST MISS HER MOST 152 02 053
      AS SURE AS WHAT IS MOST SURE, SURE AS THAT SPRING PRIMROSES   . 152 C 027
      THE SELFLESS SELF OF SELF, MOST STRANGE, MOST STILL,   .   .   . 157 00 027
      THE SELFLESS SELF OF SELF, MOST STRANGE, MOST STILL,   .   .   . 157 00 027
      YOUR FEAST OF: THAT MOST IN YOU EARNEST EYE 157 00 029
MOTE-LIKE
      MOTE-LIKE IN THY MIGHTY GLOW. 155 00 004
MOTES
      THE MOTES IN CEASELESS EDDY SHINE AND FALL 001 12 004
      THE MILLION SORTS OF UNACCOUNTED MOTES 098 22 002
MOTH
      ALL AS THE MOTH CALL'D UNDERWING ALIGHTED. 108 00 001
MOTHER
      HERE PLAY'D THE VIRGIN MOTHER WITH HER CHILD 001 10 004
      ONE WORD -- AS WHEN A MOTHER SPEAKS 023 00 050
      OH THOU, PROUD MOTHER AND MUCH PROUD MAIDEN -- 026 00 019
      MAID YET MOTHER AS MAY HATH BEEN -- 026 00 020
      SALUTE THEE, MOTHER, THE MAID-MONTH'S QUEEN! 026 00 024
      FIND ME A PLACE BY THEE, MOTHER OF MINE. 027 00 006
      I SHALL LOOK ON THY LOVELINESS, MOTHER OF MINE. 027 00 012
      I SHALL KEEP TIME WITH THEE, MOTHER OF MINE. 027 00 018
      I SHALL COME HOME TO THEE, MOTHER OF MINE. 027 00 024
      SHEW ME THY SON, MOTHER, MOTHER OF MINE. 027 00 030
      SHEW ME THY SON, MOTHER, MOTHER OF MINE. 027 00 030
      I SHALL WORSHIP HIS WOUNDS WITH THEE, MOTHER OF MINE.   .   . 027 00 036
      MAKE ME A LEAF IN THEE, MOTHER OF MINE. 027 00 042
      DRAW ME BY CHARITY, MOTHER OF MINE. 027 00 048
      DO YOU! -- MOTHER OF BEING IN ME, HEART. 028 18 004
      CHRIST HOME, CHRIST AND HIS MOTHER AND ALL HIS HALLOWS.   .   .   . 032 00 014
      O WELL WEPT, MOTHER HAVE LOST SON: 041 00 105
      ASK OF HER, THE MIGHTY MOTHER: 042 00 013
      MOTHER TO AN ENGLISH SIRE (HE 048 00 003
      A MOTHER CAME TO MOULD 060 00 104
      MOTHER, MY ATMOSPHERE: 060 00 115
      MARY, MOTHER OF US, WHERE IS YOUR RELIEF? 065 00 004
      AMONG STRANGERS, FATHER AND MOTHER DEAR, ... 066 00 002
      LEAVES YET THE MIND A MOTHER OF IMMORTAL SONG. 076 00 004
      RIGHT OFFSPRING OF YOUR GRIMY MOTHER EARTH! 077 00 002
      AND MOTHER HAVE NO MILK FOR CHILD, ... 114 00 007
      AND WRECK IN RUINS OF HIS MOTHER 145 00 041
      NEXT MARY MOTHER OF MAID AND NUN, ... 145 00 043
      AH YES! WHY, GET THEE GONE THEN: TELL THY MOTHER I WANT HER.   . 152 01 010
      THIS IS TOO MUCH THE FATHER; NAY THE MOTHER, FANCIFUL!   .   . 152 01 023
      HAPPY THE FATHER, MOTHER OF THESE! TOO FAST: 157 00 005
      FATHER, MOTHER, BROTHERS, SISTERS, FRIENDS 159 00 049
      A COUNTLESS LAUGHTER, EARTH MOTHER OF ALL, ... 160 00 003
MOTHERHOOD
      NATURE'S MOTHERHOOD. 042 00 028
      SHE HOLDS HIGH MOTHERHOOD 060 00 047
MOTHERING
      ALL OVER, AS A BEVY OF EGGS THE MOTHERING WING 034 00 006
      THIS ECSTASY ALL THROUGH MOTHERING EARTH 042 00 045
MOTHER-GROUND
      WITH HEAVEN'S LIGHTS HIGH HUNG ROUND, OR, MOTHER-GROUND   .   . 070 00 011
MOTHER'S
      A MAID WITH MOTHER'S BLISS. '   .   .   .   . APPEN D 30
MOTHERS
      BUT MOTHERS EACH NEW GRACE 060 00 022

                                171

MOTHERS   (CONTINUED)
    MOTHERS ARE DOUBTLESS HAPPIER FOR THEIR BABES   • • • • • • • 123 00 001
MOTH-SOFT
    WITH BELLED FIRE AND THE MOTH-SOFT MILKY WAY,   • • • • • • • 028 26 006
MOTION
    FAST, BUT MINED WITH A MOTION, A DRIFT,   • • • • • • • 028 04 003
    OFF HIM, BUT MEANING MOTION FANS FRESH OUR WITS WITH WONDER.   • • 045 00 014
    RESIGN THEM, SIGN THEM, SEAL THEM, SEND THEM, MOTION THEM WITH BREATH,   059 06 016
    IN MOTION IS NO WEIGHT OR PAIN,   • • • • • • • 130 00 015
    THE MOTION OF THAT MAN'S HEART IS FINE   • • • • • • • 142 00 006
MOTIONABLE
    STANCHING QUENCHING OCEAN OF A MOTIONABLE MIND;   • • • • 028 32 005
    DENIS, WHOSE MOTIONABLE, ALERT, MOST VAULTING WIT   • • • • 143 00 001
MOULD
    COULD MOULD, IF ANY TEARS THERE WERE,   • • • • • • • 018 00 014
    IT WAS MADE OF EARTH'S MOULD BUT IT WENT FROM MEN'S EYES   • • 027 00 003
    IN MOULD OR MIND OR WHAT NOT ELSE MAKES RARE;   • • • • 040 00 006
    HE WAS ALL OF LOVELY MANLY MOULD,   • • • • • • • 041 00 074
    WHO HAVE WATCHED HIS MOULD OF MAN, BIG-BONED AND HARDY-HANDSOME   • 053 00 002
    NAY, WHAT WE HAD LIGHTHANDED LEFT IN SURLY THE MERE MOULD   • • 059 06 022
    A MOTHER CAME TO MOULD   • • • • • • • • • 060 00 104
    HER MOULD OF FEATURES MATED WELL.   • • • • • • • 145 00 016
MOULDED
    MEAL-DRIFT MOULDED EVER AND MELTED ACROSS SKIES?   • • • • 038 00 004
    AS WATER MOULDED TO THE DUCT IT RUNS IN;   • • • • • 101 00 004
MOULDING
    WILL ON THE MOULDING STRIKE AND CLING,   • • • • • • 130 00 010
MOULD'RING
    UPON THE MOULD'RING TERRACES AMAIN;   • • • • • • • 001 13 004
MOUNDED
    KNEADING THE MOUNDED MIRE THAT STOPS   • • • • • • 003 00 010
MOUNDS
    OR ANCIENT MOUNDS THAT COVER BONES,   • • • • • • • 015 00 037
MOUNTAIN
    BUT FROM THE MOUNTAIN GLENS IN AUTUMN LATE   • • • • • 001 13 001
    NEXT MORN A PEASANT FROM THE MOUNTAIN SIDE   • • • • • 001 14 001
    YET GOD (THAT HEWS MOUNTAIN AND CONTINENT,   • • • • • 073 00 009
    BEAT, HEAVE AND THE STRONG MOUNTAIN TIRE   • • • • • 080 05 002
    I CRY ' O ROCKS AND MOUNTAIN MAKE ME ROOM '   • • • • • 080 07 005
    BEFORE THE MOUNTAIN? -- NO, NOT ONE,   • • • • • • 081 00 143
    THE BARROW OF DARK MAENEFA THE MOUNTAIN; C   • • • • • 137 00 004
MOUNTAIN-BOUND
    AMONGST CASTILIAN BARRENS MOUNTAIN-BOUND;   • • • • • 001 01 002
MOUNTAIN-ECHO'D
    THEN PASS'D THE WIND, AND SOBB'D WITH MOUNTAIN-ECHO'D WOE.   • • 001 13 009
MOUNTAIN-SIDE
    LOVE I WAS SHEWN UPON THE MOUNTAIN-SIDE   • • • • • • 020 00 001
MOUNTAINS
    O THE MIND, MIND HAS MOUNTAINS; CLIFFS OF FALL   • • • • 065 00 009
    BETWEENPIE MOUNTAINS -- LIGHTS A LOVELY MILE.   • • • • 069 00 014
MOUNTING
    THEN, LIKE A FLOCK OF SEA-FOWL MOUNTING HIGHER,   • • • • 002 00 082
    MAN'S MOUNTING SPIRIT IN HIS BONE-HOUSE, MEAN HOUSE, DWELLS --   • 039 00 002
    BEAUTY'S BEARING OR MUSE OF MOUNTING VEIN.   • • • • • 047 00 010
MOUNTS
    MOUNTS; THEN TO ALIGHT DISARMING, NO ONE DREAMS,   • • • • 050 00 013
MOURN
    IT IS MARGARET YOU MOURN FOR,   • • • • • • • • 055 00 015
MOURNFUL
    DOWN? NO WAVING OFF OF THESE MOST MOURNFUL MESSENGERS, C   • • 059 0L 004
MOURNING
    I CEASE THE MOURNING AND THE ABJECT FAST,   • • • • • 014 01 008
    HOPE HAD MOURNING ON,   • • • • • • • • • 028 15 002
MOUTH
    HE HATH PUT A NEW SONG IN MY MOUTH,   • • • • • • • 008 00 004
    THE DEWDROP ON THE LARKSPUR'S MOUTH   • • • • • • 010 00 015
    THE DEWBELL IN THE MALLOW'S MOUTH   • • • • • • • 025 00 015
    NOR MOUTH HAD, NO NOR MIND, EXPRESSED   • • • • • • 055 00 012
    HE! HAND TO MOUTH HE LIVES, AND VOIDS WITH SHAME;   • • • • 075 00 009
    ACCEPTANCE ROUND HIS MISTRESS' MOUTH;   • • • • • • 083 00 008
    ANG.   THE BELL-DROPS IN MY MALLOW'S MOUTH   • • • • • APPEN A 15
MOUTHED
    WILL, MOUTHED TO FLESH-BURST,   • • • • • • • • 028 08 004
    THE MOUTHED CENTRE OF A VIOLET,   • • • • • • • 102 01 071
MOVE
    BY OTHER EYES, AND OTHER SUITORS MOVE,   • • • • • • 012 01 012
    I MOVE ALONG LIFE'S TOMB-DECKED WAY   • • • • • • 023 00 039
    I INLY SAID; BUT COULD NOT MOVE   • • • • • • • 081 00 115
MOVED
    OF GOD'S DEAR PLEADINGS HAVE AS YET NOT MOVED THEE, --   • • • 013 00 010
    HIS LIPS MOVED FAST IN SENSE TOO THICK!   • • • • • 081 00 100
    THEIR CHEEKS MOVED AND THE BONES THEREIN.   • • • • • 092 00 003
MOVES
    SOMETIMES A LANTERN MOVES ALONG THE NIGHT,   • • • • • 040 00 001
    THE VIOLET MOVES AND COPSES ROCK.   • • • • • • • 098 03 004
MUCH
    FROM TOO MUCH FRAGRANCE EVERYWHERE: --   • • • • • • 004 00 004

172

MUCH   (CONTINUED)
       OH THOU, PROUD MOTHER AND MUCH PROUD MAIDEN -- 026 00 019
       MUCH, HAD MUCH TO SAY 042 00 035
       MUCH, HAD MUCH TO SAY 042 00 035
       THOUGH MUCH THE MYSTERY HOW, ...   060 00 057
       MUCH DEARER TO MANKIND! 060 00 107
       WHEN WAKING HEARTS CAN PARDON MUCH 077 00 029
       I PLEAD: AND AH! HOW MUCH IN VAIN! 081 00 029
       MISS STORY'S CHARACTER! TOO MUCH YOU ASK, ...   094 00 001
       GOLD GALLANT, FLOWERS MUCH LOOKED AT IN APRIL-WEATHER 098 16 002
       TOO LATE OR ELSE MUCH, MUCH TOO SOON, ...   105 00 016
       TOO LATE OR ELSE MUCH, MUCH TOO SOON, ...   105 00 016
       GAVE THE MUCH MUSIC OF OUR OXFORD BELLS? 107 02 008
       TO DREAM I DARED SO MUCH FOR THEE. 118 00 006
       MUCH CAUSE TO GO BECAUSE CASTARA GOES. 125 00 059
       WORK WHICH TO SEE SCARCE SO MUCH AS BEGUN 150 00 007
       THIS IS TOO MUCH THE FATHER; NAY THE MOTHER, FANCIFUL! 152 01 023
       NO PIECE MATCHED THOSE EYES KEPT MOST PART MUCH CAST DOWN 152 02 026
       THOU CANST NOT HATE SO MUCH AS I DO LOVE THEE. 161 00 004
       JESU SO MUCH IN LOVE WITH ME? 170 00 014
MUCH-DREADED
       YOUR FOOTING NOW TO THE MUCH-DREADED DUST, ...   107 03 002
MUCH-THICK
       THEY RAIN AGAINST OUR MUCH-THICK AND MARSH AIR 040 00 007
MULTIPLY
       THEY MULTIPLY, MULTIPLY, WHO CAN TELL HOW? 027 00 040
       THEY MULTIPLY, MULTIPLY, WHO CAN TELL HOW? 027 00 040
MULTITUDE
       SIR! CHRIST! AGAINST THIS MULTITUDE I STRAIN. -- 080 08 005
       TO WASH BEFORE THE MULTITUDE 080 10 002
       I HEAR THE MULTITUDE TRAMP BY. 080 11 001
       WITH THE MULTITUDE OF THE LILY-BUDS 098 19 003
MURDER
       TO THE MURDER OF MARGARET CLITHEROE. 145 00 047
       MUST ALL DAY LONG TASTE MURDER. WHAT DO NOW THEN? DO? NAY,   .   .   .   152 02 065
MURDEROUS
       IN THE MOST MURDEROUS PASSAGE OF HIS BOOK; 014 02 011
       AND SPEEDS UNCHECK'D HER MURDEROUS GUILE 120 00 030
MUSE
       MUSE AT THAT AND WONDER WHY; 042 00 002
       I MUSE AT HOW ITS BEING PUTS BLISSFUL BACK 046 00 002
       BEAUTY'S BEARING OR MUSE OF MOUNTING VEIN, ...   047 00 010
       SWEET FIRE THE SIRE OF MUSE, MY SOUL NEEDS THIS; 076 00 009
MUSES
       HEARD YET, THE MUSES' MAN, TODAY 166 00 003
MUSIC
       I HAVE FOUND MY MUSIC IN A COMMON WORD, ...   019 00 005
       THE MUSIC MUST BE DEATH. 021 00 039
       THE MUSIC THAT I CARE TO HEAR. 022 00 004
       AND PELT MUSIC, TILL NONE'S TO SPILL NOR SPEND. 035 00 008
       IN FITS OF MUSIC TILL SUNSET 077 00 087
       GAVE THE MUCH MUSIC OF OUR OXFORD BELLS? 107 02 008
       (BECAUSE THE MUSIC FROM HIS BILL FORTH-DRIVEN 113 00 003
       AT ONCE THE SENSES GIVE THE MUSIC BACK, ...   113 00 010
       HAD LET SUCH MUSIC DOWN, WITHOUT IMPEDIMENT 122 00 008
       [THE MUSIC OF HIS MIND, ...   148 00 010
       [THE MUSIC OF HIS MIND, ...   148 00 038
MUSICAL
       THE TOWERS MUSICAL, QUIET-WALLED GROVE, ...   012 01 010
       THIS DRY DEAN, NOW NO LONGER DRY NOR DUMB, BUT MOIST AND MUSICAL   .   .   152 C 012
MYRIAD
       WITH GROWTHS OF MYRIAD FEELERS, CRYSTALLINE 002 00 070
       NIGHT TO A MYRIAD WORLDS GIVES BIRTH, ...   023 00 009
MYRRHY-THREADED
       GIVE MYRRHY-THREADED GOLDEN FOLDS OF EASE. 011 00 012
MYRTLE
       BRING NATURAL MYRTLE, AND HAVE DONE; 165 00 005
       MYRTLE WILL SUIT YOUR PLACE AND MINE; 165 00 006
MYRTLE-BEND
       THEO.   AH MYRTLE-BEND NEVER SIT, ...   APPEN A 37
MYSTERIES
       THE VEIL THAT COVERS MYSTERIES; 077 00 036
       WENT FORTH TO COMPASS MYSTERIES; 077 00 052
       IN THE SHARING OF THY MYSTERIES; 169 00 007
MYSTERIOUS
       BREATHES IN THE MYSTERIOUS AIR; 077 00 128
MYSTERY
       THE ROSE IN A MYSTERY -- WHERE IS IT FOUND? 027 00 001
       SHE IS THE MYSTERY, SHE IS THAT ROSE. 027 00 022
       HIS MYSTERY MUST BE INSTRESSED, STRESSED; 028 05 007
       THOUGH MUCH THE MYSTERY HOW, ...   060 00 057
       AND TO THE MYSTERY OF THOSE THINGS 077 00 047

                                         173

NEAR   (CONTINUED)
    HE HAS A SIN OF MINE, HE ITS NEAR BROTHER! 016 00 009
    TO SHOW THEE THAT THOU ART, AND NEAR, ...   023 00 044
    PROCONSUL! -- IS SAPRICIUS NEAR? -- 025 00 041
    TWO THOUSANDS OF YEARS ARE NEAR UPON PAST 027 00 015
    NOW NEAR BY VENTNOR TOWN 041 00 031
    BROTHERS AND SISTERS ARE IN CHRIST NOT NEAR 066 00 003
    AND THEN MY HEART GOES NEAR TO BREAK. 080 06 007
    YOU SHOULD HAVE BEEN WITH ME AS NEAR 081 00 043
    SAVE ME! AND YOU WERE STANDING NEAR. 081 00 103
    THAT I WAS SO NEAR LAUGHTER? ALAS NOW 102 01 030
    TOO NEAR THEE, AND THOU MUST ABIDE 106 00 003
    NEAR BY IS PAUL'S FREE TARSUS, FABLED WHERE 136 00 007
    A MAN'S VOICE AND A NEW VOICE SPEAKING NEAR.   .   .   .   136 00 022
    FLEDGED THINGS DO RUSTLE NEAR! 160 00 033
    IS TO COME NEAR AND TAKE HIM HOME. 167 00 004
    THEO. PROCONSUL, -- CALL HIM NEAR --   .   .   .   .   .   APPEN A 47
NEAREST
    WHO MADE CONJECTURE NEAREST FAR 077 00 045
    I SPY THE NEAREST DAISIES THROUGH THE DARK, ...   135 00 023
NEARNESS
    THEY ARE NEIGHBOURS! BUT (WHAT NEARNESS COULD NOT DO)   .   .   136 00 011
NECK
    SHE PILLOWING LOW HER LILY NECK 021 00 055
    FOR LOVE HE LEANS FORTH, NEEDS HIS NECK MUST FALL ON, KISS,   .   063 00 012
    ARE STILL! HER NECK IS CREASED IN CLOSE-PLY RINGS!   .   .   099 00 010
    I ALL MY BEING HAVE HACKED IN HALF WITH HER NECK! ONE PART,   .   152 02 060
NECTAR
    HIS SWEETEST NECTAR HIDES BEHIND.] 148 00 042
NEED
    THIS MEANS YOU NEED NOT FEAR THE STORMS, THE CRIES,   .   .   014 03 002
    NOT TODAY WE NEED LAMENT 029 00 013
    DEEPLY SURELY I NEED TO DEPLORE IT, ...   041 00 097
    THAT NE'ER NEED HUNGER, TOM! TOM SELDOM SICK,   .   .   .   070 00 006
    TAKE COURAGE! THIS SHALL NEED NO FURTHER ART.   .   .   .   080 11 005
    I NEED NOT, LOVE, I NEED NOT BREAK 081 00 138
    I NEED NOT, LOVE, I NEED NOT BREAK 081 00 138
    AND KIND COMPASSION, AT HIS LIFE'S LAST NEED   .   .   .   140 00 004
    WHAT NEED I STRAIN MY HEART BEYOND MY KEN? 157 00 034
NEEDFUL
    THIS NEEDFUL, NEVER SPENT, ...   060 00 009
NEEDS
    NOT THAT THE SWEET-FOWL, SONG-FOWL, NEEDS NO REST --   .   .   039 00 009
    TO MAN, THAT NEEDS WOULD WORSHIP BLOCK OR BARREN STONE,   .   062 00 009
    FOR LOVE HE LEANS FORTH, NEEDS HIS NECK MUST FALL ON, KISS,   .   063 00 012
    SWEET FIRE THE SIRE OF MUSE, MY SOUL NEEDS THIS!   .   .   .   076 00 009
    HAVE ALL THINGS READY IN HIS ROOM. THERE NEEDS BUT LITTLE DOING.   .   152 01 006
    LET WHAT THERE NEEDS BE DONE. STAY! WITH HIM ONE COMPANION,   .   152 01 007
NEGLECTFUL
    I KNOW WHAT YOU WILL TELL ME -- NEGLECTFUL THAT YOU WERE NOT.   .   128 00 005
NEIGHBOUR
    IN A NEIGHBOUR DEFT-HANDED? ARE YOU THAT LIAR   .   .   .   046 00 013
    MIGHT COVER THE NEIGHBOUR DOWNS WITH A SPAN OF SINGING,   .   .   098 28 002
NEIGHBOURING
    THAT HE HIES TO A POOL NEIGHBOURING! SEES IT IS THE BEST   .   .   159 00 022
NEIGHBOUR-NATURE
    THAT NEIGHBOUR-NATURE THY GREY BEAUTY IS GROUNDED   .   .   .   044 00 006
NEIGHBOURS
    THEY ARE NEIGHBOURS! BUT (WHAT NEARNESS COULD NOT DO)   .   .   136 00 011
NEREID
    FAR OFF A NEREID COMPANY, AND SHAKE 002 00 075
NERVE
    BREATHE O'ER MY BARE NERVE RATHER. I DESIRE 080 05 005
    WHEN LIFE REVISITS ME, NERVE AND VEIN. 080 08 002
    OF NERVE! THE CLAMMY BALL WAS DRY. 081 00 098
NERVELESS
    AND PRIDE IS NERVELESS AND HEARTS MEEK. 077 00 038
NE'ER
    MAY WHO NE'ER HUNG THERE, NOR DOES LONG OUR SMALL   .   .   .   065 00 011
    THAT NE'ER NEED HUNGER, TOM! TOM SELDOM SICK,   .   .   .   070 00 006
    THE ESSENCE NE'ER FORGOT THE FOLD! 081 00 082
NEST
    WHY, HEAR HIM, HEAR HIM BABBLE AND DROP DOWN TO HIS NEST,   .   .   039 00 010
    BUT HIS OWN NEST, WILD NEST, NO PRISON. 039 00 011
    BUT HIS OWN NEST, WILD NEST, NO PRISON. 039 00 011
    THAT NEST WITHIN CLOSE-BARRED DOORS, ...   077 00 054
    AND IN THE DEWS BESIDE HIS NEST 077 00 091
NESTED
    THROSTLE ABOVE HER NESTED 042 00 020
NESTLIKE
    WITH CENTRES DULY TOUCH'D AND NESTLIKE SPOTS, --   .   .   .   107 04 007
NESTLING
    NESTLING ME EVERYWHERE, ...   060 00 002
NEST'S
    TO THE NEST'S NOOK I BALANCE AND BUOY 138 00 043
NETS
    BROIDERS THE NETS WITH FANS OF AMETHYST 002 00 066

NEVER
    BUT EARTH HAS NEVER FELT THE SNOW. 003 00 002
    I NEVER SAW HER SO DIVINE. 003 00 019
    AND NEVER THIRST OR DEARTH. 005 00 048
    AND NEVER TURNED TO CORN, ... 007 00 008
    WHERE ART THOU FRIEND, WHOM I SHALL NEVER SEE, ... 013 00 001
    I NEVER PROMISED SUCH PERSISTENCY 014 01 002
    OR ONCE OR NEVER TOOK LOVE'S PROPER FOOD; 020 00 010
    THE COPSE WAS NEVER MORE THAN GREY. 021 00 002
    OR NEVER LODGES THERE; 021 00 025
    YOUR PASSING STEPS, I NEVER HEARD 021 00 048
    NEVER ASK IF MEANING IT, WANTING IT, WARNED OF IT -- MEN GO. . 028 08 008
    THE TREASURE NEVER EYESIGHT GOT, C 028 26 008
    AND FOR ALL THIS, NATURE IS NEVER SPENT; 031 00 009
    NEVER FLEETS MORE, FASTENED WITH THE TENDEREST TRUTH . 059 06 012
    THIS NEEDFUL, NEVER SPENT, ... 060 00 009
    NOW KNOWN AND HAND AT WORK NOW NEVER WRONG. . . . 076 00 008
    HOW SHALL I SEARCH, WHO NEVER SOUGHT? 081 00 173
    BUT CANDOUR NEVER HURT THE DEAREST FRIEND. 094 00 008
    PRUDENCE SHE HAS, BUT WISE SHE'LL NEVER BE; . . . 094 00 024
    AND, THINKING THAT SHE THINKS, HAS NEVER THOUGHT; . . 094 00 030
    SHE NEVER HAD THE WIT. 095 00 002
    OR NEVER BEEN AT ALL; 105 00 015
    AND THERE SHE NEVER SAW THE KING, ... 109 24 003
    I NEVER SAW THOSE FIELDS WHEREON THEIR BEST . . . 119 00 011
    IT NEVER YET SO SWEETLY WAS PUT ON 125 00 025
    AND IF YOU WRITE AT LAST, IT NEVER CAN BE THE SAME; . 128 00 003
    HAMPSTEAD WAS NEVER BRIGHT; AND WHATEVER MISS CULLY'S CHARMS 128 00 011
    BUT LATE IS BETTER THAN NEVER; YOU SEE YOU HAVE MANAGED SO, 128 00 017
    ARE NEVER KNOWN FOR FAIR. 133 00 016
    THE ROOKERY NEVER STIRRED A WING, ... 135 00 014
    NEVER, NEVER, NEVER IN THEIR BLUE BANKS AGAIN. . . . 152 02 016
    NEVER, NEVER, NEVER IN THEIR BLUE BANKS AGAIN. . . . 152 02 016
    NEVER, NEVER, NEVER IN THEIR BLUE BANKS AGAIN. . . . 152 02 016
    LIKE THE THING THAT NEVER KNEW THE EARTH, NEVER OFF ROOTS . 159 00 027
    LIKE THE THING THAT NEVER KNEW THE EARTH, NEVER OFF ROOTS . 159 00 027
    THEY TEASE ME. NEVER KNOW THE PART 165 00 003
    GRACE LOVE YOUR LIPS! -- WHAT NEVER EAR 166 00 002
    SONG NEVER WAS SO SWEET IN EAR, ... 167 00 005
    WORD NEVER WAS SUCH NEWS TO HEAR, ... 167 00 006
    THEO. AH MYRTLE-BEND NEVER SIT, ... APPEN A 37
NEVER-ELDERING
    NEVER-ELDERING REVEL AND RIVER OF YOUTH, ... 028 18 007
NEVER-NEEDED
    WHEN I WITH NEVER-NEEDED WILES 135 00 003
NEW
    HE HATH PUT A NEW SONG IN MY MOUTH, ... 008 00 004
    THE WORDS ARE OLD, THE PURPORT NEW, ... 008 00 005
    LEAVES SPENT, NEW SEASONS, ALTER'D SKY; 015 00 002
    AND SOON I SAW IT SHEWING NEW 021 00 005
    NOW BURN, NEW BORN TO THE WORLD, ... 028 34 001
    OF NEW YEAR'S MONTH OR SURLY YULE 030 00 030
    WILL, OR MILD NIGHTS THE NEW MORSELS OF SPRING; . . 034 00 007
    BUT MOTHERS EACH NEW GRACE 060 00 022
    NEW NAZARETHS IN US, ... 060 00 060
    NEW BETHLEMS, AND HE BORN 060 00 063
    NEW SELF AND NOBLER ME 060 00 069
    IT MELTS, NEW LIGHTS ARISE AS FAIR, ... 077 00 118
    ONLY WITH US IS OLD AND NEW. ' 081 00 063
    HER FINGER-LONG NEW HORNS ARE CAPP'D WITH BLACK; . 099 00 007
    NEW LOVE IS FREE LOVE, OR TRUE LOVE 'TIS NOT. . . 102 03 020
    NEW LOVE IS FREE LOVE, OR TRUE LOVE 'TIS NOT. V . 102 03 027
    AND FEEDS NEW LEAVES UPON THE WINDS OF FALL; . . 105 00 010
    MET A NEW SHOWER, AND SAW THE RAINBOW FILL . . . 107 03 010
    THEN OFTEN THE EARS IN A NEW FASHION HARK, . . . 113 00 007
    A MAN'S VOICE AND A NEW VOICE SPEAKING NEAR. . . 136 00 022
    SAYING ' THIS WAS YOURS ' WITH HER, BUT NEW ONE, WORSE, 153 00 010
    HATH DEVIS'D NEW PAINS FOR ME 160 00 012
    THE LADES DISCHARGED AND LADED NEW, ... 166 00 035
NEWBORN
    TO NEWBORN PRINCE, AND ROYAL CORSE INANIMATE. . . 001 04 009
NEW-BASILISK
    MORN DOES NOT NOW NEW-BASILISK HIS STARE, . . . 099 00 017
NEW-DAPPLE
    SHALL NEW-DAPPLE NEXT YEAR, SURE AS TO-MORROW MORNING, . 152 C 028
NEW-DATED
    NEW-DATED FROM THE TERMS THAT REAPPEAR, ... 012 01 001
NEW-NESTLE
    APART WIDE AND NEW-NESTLE AT HEAVEN MOST HIGH. . . 149 A 006
NEW-SKEINED
    HIS RASH-FRESH RE-WINDED NEW-SKEINED SCORE . . . 035 00 006
NEW-WORLD
    AND SHE SHALL CHILD THEM ON THE NEW-WORLD STRAND. ' . 158 00 004
NEWLY
    WHICH IN NEWLY DRAWN GREEN LITTER 025 00 005
NEWLY-DRAWN
    WHERE IN A NEWLY-DRAWN GREEN LITTER 010 00 005

176

NEWLY-DRAWN   (CONTINUED)
    ANG.   WHICH IN NEWLY-DRAWN GREEN LITTER • • • • • • • • • APPEN A 05
NEWS
    NEWS FROM BELLEISLE, EVEN SUCH A SWEETNESS BLOWS • • • • • 119 00 006
    BUT BOTH WILL SHARE ONE CELL. -- THIS WAS GOOD NEWS, GWENVREWI. • • 152 01 009
    WORD NEVER WAS SUCH NEWS TO HEAR. • • • • • • • • 167 00 006
NEXT
    NEXT MORN A PEASANT FROM THE MOUNTAIN SIDE • • • • • 001 14 001
    THEN NEXT I HUNGERED: LOVE WHEN HERE, THEY SAY, • • • • 020 00 009
    HE HAS LOST COUNT WHAT CAME NEXT, POOR BOY. -- • • • • 041 00 072
    BUT EACH A HAND'S BREADTH FURTHER THAN THE NEXT. • • • • 091 00 007
    NEXT TO MEADOWS ABUNDANT, PIERCED WITH FLOWERS. • • • • 098 12 002
    THOUGH THEY TOOK TILL THE SEVENTEENTH OF NEXT OCTOBER TO READ. • 128 00 008
    TIME WAS, NEXT WHITEST AFTER MARY'S OWN. • • • • • 136 00 004
    NEXT MARY MOTHER OF MAID AND NUN, • • • • • • 145 00 043
    NEXT AFTER SWEET SUCCESS. I AM NOT LEFT EVEN THIS: • • • 152 02 059
    SHALL NEW-DAPPLE NEXT YEAR, SURE AS TO-MORROW MORNING, • • 152 C 028
NICHE
    WITH THE GNARLS OF THE NAILS IN THEE, NICHE OF THE LANCE, HIS • • 028 23 003
NIGH
    GAZES ASLANT HIS SHOULDER, VIEWING NIGH • • • • • • 001 11 006
    TILL THE LIFTED CLOUDS WERE NIGH. • • • • • • • 077 00 072
NIGHT
    CAME MIDST THE DRIZZLE TELLING HOW LAST NIGHT • • • • 001 14 002
    THE DARKNESS DID NOT CLOSE THAT NIGHT • • • • • 021 00 003
    NIGHT TO A MYRIAD WORLDS GIVES BIRTH, • • • • • • 023 00 009
    DEEP CALLS TO DEEP, AND BLACKEST NIGHT • • • • • 023 00 027
    THOU KNOWEST THE WALLS, ALTAR AND HOUR AND NIGHT: • • • 028 02 005
    BUT THE COMBS OF A SMOTHER OF SAND: NIGHT DREW HER • • • 028 14 003
    NIGHT ROARED, WITH THE HEART-BREAK HEARING A HEART-BROKE RABBLE, • 028 17 005
    BLUE-BEATING AND HOARY-GLOW HEIGHT: OR NIGHT, STILL HIGHER, • • 028 26 005
    READ THE UNSHAPEABLE SHOCK NIGHT • • • • • • 028 29 003
    WHAT WAS THE FEAST FOLLOWED THE NIGHT • • • • • 028 30 003
    SOMETIMES A LANTERN MOVES ALONG THE NIGHT, • • • • 040 00 001
    DAY AND NIGHT I DEPLORE • • • • • • • • 041 00 086
    NOW THE NIGHT COME: ALL • • • • • • • • 054 00 010
    WOMB-OF-ALL, HOME-OF-ALL, HEARSE-OF-ALL NIGHT, C • • • 061 00 002
    OUR NIGHT WHELMS, WHELMS, AND WILL END US. C • • • 061 00 008
    IS IT EACH ONE? THAT NIGHT, THAT YEAR C • • • • 064 00 013
    THIS NIGHT! WHAT SIGHTS YOU, HEART, SAW: WAYS YOU WENT! • • 067 00 003
    COME WHEN NIGHT CLINGS TO WHAT IS HERS • • • • 077 00 021
    THAT NIGHT THE JUDGMENT DAY BEGAN: • • • • • 081 00 090
    HOW LOOKS THE NIGHT? THERE DOES NOT MISS A STAR. • • • 098 22 001
    THE STARS WERE PACKED SO CLOSE THAT NIGHT • • • • 098 29 001
    NOR NIGHT IS BLOWN WITH FLAME-RINGS EVERYWHERE. • • • 099 00 018
    GILDS WITH SOME SPARKY FANCIES HIS BLACK NIGHT • • • 102 03 030
    GILDS WITH SOME SPARKY FANCIES BLINDING NIGHT, V • • • 102 03 036
    AS SHE LAY WEEPING AT THE NIGHT • • • • • • 109 29 001
    SHOT LIGHTNING TO THE STIFLING LID OF NIGHT • • • • 125 00 050
    I AWOKE IN THE MIDSUMMER NOT-TO-CALL NIGHT, C • • • 137 00 001
    WITH THE UPROLL AND THE DOWNCAROL OF DAY AND NIGHT DELIVERING • 152 C 013
    BEAT FROM OUR BRAINS THE THICKY NIGHT • • • • • 167 00 023
NIGHTFALL
    AND FRIGHTFUL A NIGHTFALL FOLDED RUEFUL A DAY • • • • 028 15 005
    THE TIMES ARE NIGHTFALL, LOOK, THEIR LIGHT GROWS LESS: • • 150 00 001
NIGHTINGALE
    ' YOU KNOW YOU SAID THE NIGHTINGALE • • • • • 021 00 022
    MISS M.'S A NIGHTINGALE. 'TIS WELL • • • • • • 096 03 001
NIGHT'S
    WITH YELLOWY MOISTURE MILD NIGHT'S BLEAR-ALL BLACK, • • • 046 00 003
    NIGHT'S LANTERN • • • • • • • • • • 098 24 001
NIGHTS
    WILL, OR MILD NIGHTS THE NEW MORSELS OF SPRING: • • • 034 00 007
    OF RIVERS, LEAD, THRO' STORMS AND NIGHTS, • • • • 083 00 004
NILE
    NOT GOSHEN. WASTEFUL WIDE HUGE-GIRTHED NILE • • • • 005 00 031
    SURE, THIS IS NILE: I SICKEN, I KNOW NOT WHY, • • • 005 00 059
NIMBLE
    O HIS NIMBLE FINGER, HIS GNARLED GRIP! • • • • • 041 00 081
NINE
    ' FROM NINE O'CLOCK TILL MORNING LIGHT • • • • • 021 00 001
    NINE MONTHS SHE THEN, NAY YEARS, NINE YEARS SHE LONG • • 076 00 005
    NINE MONTHS SHE THEN, NAY YEARS, NINE YEARS SHE LONG • • 076 00 005
NIPS
    WITH DRAUGHT OF THIN AND PURSUANT COLD SO NIPS • • • 011 00 006
NIX
    SHE SOUR WHO SEEMS THE SLIGHTED NIX. • • • • • 120 00 017
    WHEN MADDEST LOOKS THE SLIGHTED NIX.] • • • • • 120 00 019
NO
    NO FINISH'D PROOF WAS THIS OF GOTHIC GRACE • • • • 001 06 001
    THIS WAS NO CLASSIC TEMPLE ORDER'D ROUND • • • • 001 07 001
    THE MONKS LEFT LONG AGO: SINCE WHICH NO MORE • • • 001 15 004
    WHENCE OFT I WATCH BUT SEE THOSE MERMAIDS NOW NO MORE. • • 002 00 143
    AUTUMN-TIME NO EARLIER CAME. • • • • • • • 004 00 026
    AND FEAR NO IRON ROD. • • • • • • • • 005 00 012
    PART FOUND NO ROOT UPON THE FLINTY ROAD, -- • • • • 007 00 009
    TO FIELDS WHERE FLIES NO SHARP AND SIDED HAIL • • • 009 00 003

```
WHERE NO STORMS COME,  .    .    .    .    .    .    .    .    .    .    .    .    .    009 00 006
NO, BUT FOR CHRIST WHO HATH FOREKNOWN AND LOVED THEE.    .    .    .    .    .    013 00 014
IN ITS CONDITION. NO, THE TROPIC TREE    .    .    .    .    .    .    .    .    014 01 003
INTO ALL SEASONS, THOUGH NO WINTER CAST    .    .    .    .    .    .    .    014 01 005
NO INFLUENTIAL HEAVEN EVER WORE;    .    .    .    .    .    .    .    .    .    014 02 007
THAT NO RECORDED DEVILISH THING WAS DONE    .    .    .    .    .    .    .    014 02 008
MY BANKRUPT HEART HAS NO MORE TEARS TO SPEND.    .    .    .    .    .    .    014 03 004
GROWS LESS AND LESS SWEET TO HIM, AND KNOWS NO CAUSE.    .    .    .    .    014 03 014
NO, I SHOULD LOVE THE CITY LESS    .    .    .    .    .    .    .    .    .    015 00 021
THAT HOLDS NO PROMISE OF SUCCESS;    .    .    .    .    .    .    .    .    015 00 034
NO BETTER SERVES ME NOW, SAVE BEST; NO OTHER    .    .    .    .    .    .    016 00 013
NO BETTER SERVES ME NOW, SAVE BEST; NO OTHER    .    .    .    .    .    .    016 00 013
AFFLICTS NO LESS, WHAT YET I HOPE MAY BLOW,    .    .    .    .    .    .    017 00 006
NO ANSWERING VOICE COMES FROM THE SKIES;    .    .    .    .    .    .    .    023 00 002
BUT NO FORGIVING VOICE REPLIES;    .    .    .    .    .    .    .    .    .    023 00 004
WHERE STANDS NO HOST AT DOOR OR HEARTH    .    .    .    .    .    .    .    023 00 011
IS SET IN ANY ORCHARD; NO,    .    .    .    .    .    .    .    .    .    .    025 00 010
O NO IT IS THE SIZING MOON.    .    .    .    .    .    .    .    .    .    .    025 00 020
NO, BUT IT WAS NOT THESE.    .    .    .    .    .    .    .    .    .    .    028 27 001
NO NOT UNCOMFORTED; LOVELY-FELICITOUS PROVIDENCE    .    .    .    .    .    028 31 005
THOUGH NO HIGH-HUNG BELLS OR DIN    .    .    .    .    .    .    .    .    .    029 00 001
TO ME, GOD KNOWS, DESERVING NO SUCH THING;    .    .    .    .    .    .    034 00 002
NO WONDER OF IT: SHEER PLOD MAKES PLOUGH DOWN SILLION    .    .    .    036 00 012
NOT THAT THE SWEET-FOWL, SONG-FOWL, NEEDS NO REST --    .    .    .    039 00 009
BUT HIS OWN NEST, WILD NEST, NO PRISON.    .    .    .    .    .    .    .    039 00 011
NO ATLANTIC SQUALL OVERWROUGHT HER    .    .    .    .    .    .    .    .    041 00 017
AT DOWNRIGHT ' NO OR YES? '    .    .    .    .    .    .    .    .    .    .    041 00 055
BUT HIS EYE NO CLIFF, NO COAST OR    .    .    .    .    .    .    .    .    041 00 067
BUT HIS EYE NO CLIFF, NO COAST OR    .    .    .    .    .    .    .    .    041 00 067
OF RUINOUS SHRINE NO HAND OR, WORSE,    .    .    .    .    .    .    .    041 00 090
THOUGH GRIEF YIELD THEM NO GOOD    .    .    .    .    .    .    .    .    .    041 00 107
BUT A PRICK WILL MAKE NO EYE AT ALL,    .    .    .    .    .    .    .    043 00 015
NOTHING ELSE IS LIKE IT, NO, NOT ALL SO STRAINS    .    .    .    .    .    048 00 029
LET ME THOUGH SEE NO MORE OF HIM, AND NOT DISAPPOINTMENT    .    .    048 00 036
MOUNTS; THEN TO ALIGHT DISARMING, NO ONE DREAMS,    .    .    .    .    050 00 013
HE HAD NO WORK TO HOLD    .    .    .    .    .    .    .    .    .    .    .    054 00 026
NOW NO MATTER, CHILD, THE NAME;    .    .    .    .    .    .    .    .    .    055 00 010
NOR MOUTH HAD, NO NOR MIND, EXPRESSED    .    .    .    .    .    .    .    055 00 012
TO, WITH NO TONGUE TO PLEAD, NO HEART TO FEEL;    .    .    .    .    .    058 00 003
TO, WITH NO TONGUE TO PLEAD, NO HEART TO FEEL;    .    .    .    .    .    058 00 003
O IS THERE NO FROWNING OF THESE WRINKLES, RANKED WRINKLES DEEP,    .    059 0L 003
DOWN? NO WAVING OFF OF THESE MOST MOURNFUL MESSENGERS, C    .    .    059 0L 004
NO THERE 'S NONE, THERE 'S NONE, O NO THERE 'S NONE,    .    .    .    059 0L 005
NO THERE 'S NONE, THERE 'S NONE, O NO THERE 'S NONE,    .    .    .    059 0L 005
BE BEGINNING; SINCE, NO, NOTHING CAN BE DONE    .    .    .    .    .    059 0L 009
O THERE 'S NONE; NO NO NO THERE 'S NONE;    .    .    .    .    .    .    059 0L 014
O THERE 'S NONE; NO NO NO THERE 'S NONE;    .    .    .    .    .    .    059 0L 014
O THERE 'S NONE; NO NO NO THERE 'S NONE;    .    .    .    .    .    .    059 0L 014
GREAT AS NO GODDESS'S    .    .    .    .    .    .    .    .    .    .    .    060 00 027
OFF, AND NO WAY BUT SO.    .    .    .    .    .    .    .    .    .    .    .    060 00 033
YET NO PART BUT WHAT WILL    .    .    .    .    .    .    .    .    .    .    060 00 053
IT DOES NO PREJUDICE.    .    .    .    .    .    .    .    .    .    .    .    060 00 082
TO WEND AND MEET NO SIN;    .    .    .    .    .    .    .    .    .    .    060 00 117
THAT, HOPES THAT, MAKESBELIEVE, THE MEN MUST BE NO LESS;    .    .    063 00 005
IN ME OR, MOST WEARY, CRY I CAN NO MORE. I CAN;    .    .    .    .    064 00 003
NO WORST, THERE IS NONE. PITCHED PAST PITCH OF GRIEF,    .    .    .    065 00 001
THEN LULL, THEN LEAVE OFF. FURY HAD SHRIEKED ' NO LING-    .    .    065 00 007
I CAST FOR COMFORT I CAN NO MORE GET    .    .    .    .    .    .    .    069 00 005
THAT MAMMOCKS, MIGHTY FOOT. BUT NO WAY SPED,    .    .    .    .    .    070 00 012
WITH, PERILOUS, O NO; NOR YET PLOD SAFE SHOD SOUND;    .    .    .    070 00 014
OF EARTH'S GLORY, EARTH'S EASE, ALL; NO ONE, NOWHERE,    .    .    .    070 00 016
EARTH HEARS NO HURTLE THEN FROM FIERCEST FRAY.    .    .    .    .    073 00 008
THEM; BIRDS BUILD -- BUT NOT I BUILD; NO, BUT STRAIN,    .    .    .    074 00 012
FROM GOD AND MAN, IS HELL NO DOUBT.    .    .    .    .    .    .    .    080 01 004
AND FEEL NO BLAST. -- THE FRETFUL FIRE    .    .    .    .    .    .    .    080 05 004
TAKE COURAGE! THIS SHALL NEED NO FURTHER ART. . '  .    .    .    .    080 11 005
BUT YOU, SO SPHERED, SEE NO MORE --    .    .    .    .    .    .    .    081 00 039
NO LOUDER, WHEN I WAS WITH YOU.    .    .    .    .    .    .    .    .    081 00 060
NO HOUSE OF RIMMON MAY I TAKE,    .    .    .    .    .    .    .    .    .    081 00 140
BEFORE THE MOUNTAIN? -- NO, NOT ONE,    .    .    .    .    .    .    .    081 00 143
NO FLOWERS TO FIND, NO PLACE TO HALT,    .    .    .    .    .    .    .    081 00 159
NO FLOWERS TO FIND, NO PLACE TO HALT,    .    .    .    .    .    .    .    081 00 159
NO COLOUR IN THE OVERHEAD,    .    .    .    .    .    .    .    .    .    .    081 00 160
NO RUNNING IN THE RIVER-BED;    .    .    .    .    .    .    .    .    .    081 00 161
ARE WASTE, AND HAD NO WHOLESOME FOODS,    .    .    .    .    .    .    081 00 166
NO; SHEWN TO HER IT CANNOT BUT OFFEND;    .    .    .    .    .    .    094 00 007
HERCLOT'S PREACHINGS I'LL NO LONGER HEAR;    .    .    .    .    .    .    096 05 001
THERE IS NO PARTING OR BARE INTERSTICE    .    .    .    .    .    .    .    098 22 004
NO I'LL NOT HAZARD IT. ONLY HIS HAND,    .    .    .    .    .    .    .    102 01 025
NO TIME TO THINK. I'LL KNOT IT ON THIS RIBBON,    .    .    .    .    .    102 01 027
NO, LET THAT GO; I HAVE SAID GOODNIGHT TO SHAME.    .    .    .    .    102 01 042
YET THIS COULD BE NO OTHER'S HAND THAN HIS,    .    .    .    .    .    102 01 045
BUT SINCE I HAVE NO SCOPE FOR BENEFITS    .    .    .    .    .    .    .    102 01 052
THERE WAS NO CREASE OR GATHER IN THE CLOUDS    .    .    .    .    .    102 02 006
NO, LOVE PRESCRIPTIVE, LOVE WITH PLACE ASSIGN'D,    .    .    .    .    102 03 013
BY HEADY ELEMENTS, FOR NO MAN KNOWS;    .    .    .    .    .    .    .    103 00 005
```

```
NO, THEY ARE COME! THEIR HORN IS LIFTED UP!        .   .   .   .   .   .   104 00 001
SO LATE THERE IS NO FORCE IN SAP OR BLOOD!         .   .   .   .   .   .   105 00 011
THERE WAS NO BLEAT OF EWE, NO CHIME OF WETHER,     .   .   .   .   .   .   107 01 005
THERE WAS NO BLEAT OF EWE, NO CHIME OF WETHER,     .   .   .   .   .   .   107 01 005
' O I HAVE HERE NO FOREIGN LADY     .   .   .   .   .   .   .   .   .   .   109 08 001
' NO TRUTH BETWEEN YOU THREE.       .   .   .   .   .   .   .   .   .   .   109 28 002
SO TAKES THE SISTER SENSE ) CAN FIND NO MARK,      .   .   .   .   .   .   113 00 004
AND MOTHER HAVE NO MILK FOR CHILD,     .   .   .   .   .   .   .   .   .   114 00 007
NO RAINS SHALL FRESH THE FLATS OF SEA,     .   .   .   .   .   .   .   .   114 00 013
I'LL CITE NO FURTHER WHAT THE INITIATE KNOW.       .   .   .   .   .   .   119 00 010
AH NO! AND SHE WHO SITS BESIDE      .   .   .   .   .   .   .   .   .   .   120 00 014
OF WHICH I SAY THERE IS NO JOY IN THEM.    .   .   .   .   .   .   .   .   125 00 047
WILL NO ONE SHOW    .   .   .   .   .   .   .   .   .   .   .   .   .   .   127 00 011
AND WITH THE LAST POST OVER I KNEW NO LETTER WAS SENT.    .   .   .   .   128 00 002
IT'S THE DAY THAT MAKES THE CHARM! NO AFTER-WORDS COULD SUCCEED   .   .   128 00 007
PAST, THE PAST, NO MORE BE SEEN!    .   .   .   .   .   .   .   .   .   .   129 00 002
IN MOTION IS NO WEIGHT OR PAIN,     .   .   .   .   .   .   .   .   .   .   130 00 015
NO TUMBLER WOKE AND SHOOK THE COT,     .   .   .   .   .   .   .   .   .   135 00 013
NO WONDER THEREFORE WAS NOT SLOW    .   .   .   .   .   .   .   .   .   .   145 00 019
GOD LIGHTEN YOUR DARK HEART -- BUT NO,     .   .   .   .   .   .   .   .   145 00 027
SHE NOT CONSIDERED WHETHER OR NO    .   .   .   .   .   .   .   .   .   .   145 00 033
NO! WHAT THE POET DID WRITE RAN,    .   .   .   .   .   .   .   .   .   .   147 00 005
NO MORE THAN RED AND BLUE,          .   .   .   .   .   .   .   .   .   .   148 00 033
NO MORE THAN RE AND MI,             .   .   .   .   .   .   .   .   .   .   148 00 034
NO MAN HAS SUCH A DAUGHTER. THE FATHERS OF THE WORLD     .   .   .   .   152 01 011
CALL NO SUCH MAIDEN ' MINE ' . THE DEEPER GROWS HER DEARNESS     .   .   152 01 012
WHAT WORK? WHAT HARM'S DONE? THERE IS NO HARM DONE, NONE YET;    .   .   152 02 008
PERHAPS WE STRUCK NO BLOW, GWENVREWI LIVES PERHAPS;      .   .   .   .   152 02 009
IN ALL HER BODY, I SAY, NO PLACE WAS LIKE HER EYES,      .   .   .   .   152 02 025
NO PIECE MATCHED THOSE EYES KEPT MOST PART MUCH CAST DOWN    .   .   .   152 02 026
LOYAL TO HIS OWN SOUL, LAYING HIS OWN LAW DOWN, NO LAW NOR   .   .   .   152 02 040
DESPATCHES WITH NO FLINCHING. BUT WILL FLESH, O CAN FLESH    .   .   .   152 02 045
SECOND THIS FIERY STRAIN? NOT ALWAYS! O NO NO!     .   .   .   .   .   .   152 02 046
SECOND THIS FIERY STRAIN? NOT ALWAYS! O NO NO!     .   .   .   .   .   .   152 02 046
WITH NO NOW, NO GWENVREWI. I MUST MISS HER MOST    .   .   .   .   .   .   152 02 053
WITH NO NOW, NO GWENVREWI. I MUST MISS HER MOST    .   .   .   .   .   .   152 02 053
WHOSE BLOODS I RECK NO MORE OF, NO MORE RANK WITH HERS   .   .   .   .   152 02 069
WHOSE BLOODS I RECK NO MORE OF, NO MORE RANK WITH HERS   .   .   .   .   152 02 069
THIS DRY DEAN, NOW NO LONGER DRY NOR DUMB, BUT MOIST AND MUSICAL .   .   152  C 012
FIELD-FLOWN, THE DEPARTED DAY NO MORNING BRINGS    .   .   .   .   .   .   153 00 009
OUT ON THE GIANT AIR! TELL SUMMER NO.      .   .   .   .   .   .   .   .   154 00 003
NO WISDOM CAN FORECAST BY GAUGE OR GUESS,  .   .   .   .   .   .   .   .   157 00 026
FAST FURLED AND ALL FOREDRAWN TO NO OR YES.        .   .   .   .   .   .   157 00 028
NO MORE! OFF WITH -- DOWN HE DINGS C    .   .   .   .   .   .   .   .   .   159 00 028
AH CHILD, NO PERSIAN-PERFECT ART!   .   .   .   .   .   .   .   .   .   .   165 00 001
TO SPEAK OF THAT NO TONGUE WILL DO     .   .   .   .   .   .   .   .   .   167 00 013
ON THE CROSS THY GODHEAD MADE NO SIGN TO MEN;      .   .   .   .   .   .   168 00 009
ANG.  IS SET IN ANY ORCHARD, NO!    .   .   .   .   .   .   .   .   .   .   APPEN A 10
CAT.  O NO, IT IS THE SIZING MOON.     .   .   .   .   .   .   .   .   .   APPEN A 20
THEO.  SIT NO MORE THESE BOOKISH BROWS!    .   .   .   .   .   .   .   .   APPEN A 38
NOBLER
   NEW SELF AND NOBLER ME            .   .   .   .   .   .   .   .   .   .   060 00 069
NOBS
   HOAR MESSMATE, HOBS AND NOBS WITH HIM      .   .   .   .   .   .   .   030 00 011
NOCTURNS
   NOCTURNS I THOUGHT WERE HURRIED THROUGH.   .   .   .   .   .   .   .   081 00 092
NOISE
   I HEAR A NOISE OF WATERS DRAWN AWAY,       .   .   .   .   .   .   .   112 00 001
   A NOISE OF FALLS I AM POSSESSED BY    .   .   .   .   .   .   .   .   121 00 001
   BY THERE COMES A LISTLESS STRANGER: BECKONED BY THE NOISE  .   .   .   159 00 014
NOISES
   ON EAR AND EAR TWO NOISES TOO OLD TO END   .   .   .   .   .   .   .   035 00 001
NO-MAN-FATHOMED
   FRIGHTFUL, SHEER, NO-MAN-FATHOMED. HOLD THEM CHEAP     .   .   .   .   065 00 010
NONE
   LILIES I SHEW YOU, LILIES NONE,    .   .   .   .   .   .   .   .   .   010 00 007
   NONE IN CAESAR'S GARDENS BLOW, --    .   .   .   .   .   .   .   .   010 00 008
   NONE BESIDES ME THIS BYE-WAYS BEAUTY TRY.     .   .   .   .   .   .   012 02 009
   SEE MY LILIES: LILIES NONE,        .   .   .   .   .   .   .   .   .   025 00 007
   NONE IN CAESAR'S GARDEN BLOW.      .   .   .   .   .   .   .   .   .   025 00 008
   WHAT NONE WOULD HAVE KNOWN OF IT, ONLY THE HEART, BEING HARD AT BAY,  028 07 008
   NONE BUT YOU THIS HER TRUE,        .   .   .   .   .   .   .   .   .   029 00 011
   AND NONE RECK OF WORLD AFTER, THIS BIDS WEAR   .   .   .   .   .   .   058 00 013
   HOW TO KEEP -- IS THERE ANY ANY, IS THERE NONE SUCH, C     .   .   .   059 0L 001
   NO THERE 'S NONE, THERE 'S NONE, O NO THERE 'S NONE,       .   .   .   059 0L 005
   NO THERE 'S NONE, THERE 'S NONE, O NO THERE 'S NONE,       .   .   .   059 0L 005
   NO THERE 'S NONE, THERE 'S NONE, O NO THERE 'S NONE,       .   .   .   059 0L 005
   O THERE 'S NONE! NO NO NO THERE 'S NONE:       .   .   .   .   .   .   059 0L 014
   O THERE 'S NONE! NO NO NO THERE 'S NONE:       .   .   .   .   .   .   059 0L 014
   NO WORST, THERE IS NONE. PITCHED PAST PITCH OF GRIEF,      .   .   .   065 00 001
   'TWAS SAID OF NONE BUT ALL MEN KNEW;   .   .   .   .   .   .   .   .   081 00 091
   IT MIGHT BE NONE OF THE THREE.     .   .   .   .   .   .   .   .   .   095 00 026
   AS VOID AS CLOUDS THAT HOUSE AND HARBOUR NONE,     .   .   .   .   .   107 01 001
   IF YOU ARE SILENT, THAT I KNOW OF, NONE.   .   .   .   .   .   .   .   125 00 018
   I NONE CAN SHEW    .   .   .   .   .   .   .   .   .   .   .   .   .   127 00 006
   AND OTHER TRUTH IS NONE,           .   .   .   .   .   .   .   .   .   133 00 002
```

NONE   (CONTINUED)
    FLUNG RIDER AND WINGS AWAY; THOUGH THESE WERE NONE, ... 136 00 009
    HAS SHADES, IS NOWHERE NONE; 148 00 026
    GOES MARCHING THRO' MY MIND. WHAT SENSE IS THIS? IT HAS NONE. . . 152 01 022
    WHAT WORK? WHAT HARM'S DONE? THERE IS NO HARM DONE, NONE YET; . . 152 02 008
    THERE'S NONE BUT TRUTH CAN STEAD YOU. CHRIST IS TRUTH. 157 00 020
    THERE'S NONE BUT GOOD CAN BE GOOD, BOTH FOR YOU 157 00 021
    NONE GOOD BUT GOD -- A WARNING WAVED TO 157 00 023
    ANG. SEE MY LILIES; LILIES NONE, ... APPEN A 07
    ANG. NONE IN CAESAR'S GARDENS BLOW -- . . . . . . APPEN A 08
NONE'S
    AND PELT MUSIC, TILL NONE'S TO SPILL NOR SPEND. 035 00 009
NOOK
    TO THE NEST'S NOOK I BALANCE AND BUOY 138 00 043
NOON
    HIM, MORNING, NOON, AND EVE; 060 00 062
    THERE, EVENING, NOON, AND MORN -- 060 00 064
NOONDAY
    AND NOONDAY HAVE A SHALLOW SHINE. 114 00 004
NOSE
    CRISP LIPS, STRAIGHT NOSE, AND TENDER-SLANTED CHEEK. . . . 136 00 016
NOSTRIL
    HER NOSTRIL GLISTENS; AND HER WET BLACK EYE 099 00 005
NOSTRILS
    YOUR PARCHED NOSTRILS SNUFF EGYPTIAN AIR, ... 005 00 027
    NOSTRILS, YOUR CARELESS BREATH THAT SPEND 022 00 017
NOTE
    FROM BOTH OF WHOM A CHANGELESS NOTE IS HEARD. 019 00 004
    BEING NOT FORGOTTEN, FOR PRIMROSES NOTE 107 03 019
    SO IS IT WITH MY FRIENDS, I NOTE, TO HEAR 119 00 005
    UPON THIS ONLY GAMBOLLING AND ECHOING-OF-EARTH NOTE -- . . . 159 00 005
NOTES
    A SIMPLE PASSAGE OF WEAK NOTES 003 00 013
    OR LOVE OR PITY OR ALL THAT SWEET NOTES NOT HIS MIGHT NURSLES; . 045 00 006
    A TURN OF SEVEN NOTES OR FIVE, ... 081 00 007
    FIVE NOTES OR SEVEN, LATE AND FEW; 081 00 023
    HE SHOOK WITH RACING NOTES THE STANDING AIR. 098 38 001
    HAD BEEN MORE FERTILE AND HAD SOWN WITH NOTES 122 00 005
    [HAD BEEN EFFECTUAL TO HAVE SOWN WITH NOTES] 122 00 012
NOTHING
    WITH LONG-SUPERFLUOUS TIES, FOR NOTHING HERE 012 01 004
    SHAPE NOTHING, LIPS; BE LOVELY-DUMB; 022 00 005
    NOTHING IS SO BEAUTIFUL AS SPRING -- 033 00 001
    NOTHING ELSE IS LIKE IT, NO, NOT ALL SO STRAINS 048 00 029
    BE BEGINNING; SINCE, NO, NOTHING CAN BE DONE 059 0L 009
    WHAT WERE WORTH NOTHING IF ALL COMPLIMENT! 094 00 006
    IS TASTELESS NOTHING; AND IN MY DEGREE 117 00 010
    AND MATCHED WITH THEE THERE 'S NOTHING GLAD 167 00 019
    MASKED BY THESE BARE SHADOWS, SHAPE AND NOTHING MORE, . . 168 00 002
    TRUTH HIMSELF SPEAKS TRULY OR THERE 'S NOTHING TRUE. . . . 168 00 008
    THEO. NOTHING GREEN OR GROWING BUT . . . . . . APPEN A 41
NOT-BY-MORNING-M
    OF US, THE WIMPLED-WATER-DIMPLED, NOT-BY-MORNING-MATCHED FACE, . 059 0G 010
NOT-STALED
    TO THY NOT-STALED UNCHARTED MEMORY. 117 00 014
NOT-TO-CALL
    I AWOKE IN THE MIDSUMMER NOT-TO-CALL NIGHT, [. . . . 137 00 001
NOUGHT
    THE ANGEL SAID; ' O DREAD THEE NOUGHT. . . . . . APPEN D 15
NOURISHES
    SHE INLY NOURISHES A WISH TO SHINE; 094 00 012
NOWHERE
    NOWHERE KNOWN SOME, BOW OR BROOCH OR BRAID OR BRACE, [. . 059 0L 001
    NOWHERE. NATURAL HEART'S IVY, PATIENCE MASKS 068 00 006
    OF EARTH'S GLORY, EARTH'S EASE, ALL; NO ONE, NOWHERE, . . . 070 00 016
    HAS SHADES, IS NOWHERE NONE; 148 00 026
NUMB
    NOW I GROW NUMB. MY TONGUE STRIKES ON THE GUM 080 10 006
NUMBER
    FIVE IS THEIR NUMBER BY NATURE, BUT NOW 027 00 039
    SORROWS PASSING NUMBER. 170 00 009
NUMBERED
    IS, HAIR OF THE HEAD, NUMBERED. 059 0G 021
NUMBS
    AND NUMBS AND STARVES, AS BETWEEN ICY WHARVES 080 03 006
NUN
    EARS, AND THE CALL OF THE TALL NUN 028 19 007
    THOU HADST GLORY OF THIS NUN? -- 028 30 004
    NEXT MARY MOTHER OF MAID AND NUN, ... 145 00 043
NURSING
    AND NURSING ELEMENT; 060 00 010
NURSLES
    OR LOVE OR PITY OR ALL THAT SWEET NOTES NOT HIS MIGHT NURSLES; . 045 00 006

```
OAK
      FELLED AND FURLED THEM, THE HEARTS OF OAK!   .   .   .   .   .   .   .   041 00 006
OAKS
      AND OAKS. -- BUT THESE WERE LEAVED IN SHARPER KNOTS.   .   .   .   .   107 04 008
      THERE WAS A WOOD OF DWARF AND SOURED OAKS .   .   .   .   .   .   .   125 00 002
OAR
      THAT FROCKS AN OAR IN PENMAEN POOL.   .   .   .   .   .   .   .   .   030 00 036
OATH
      PHILIP TOOK OATH, WHILE GLORY OR DEFEAT   .   .   .   .   .   .   .   001 02 003
OBEY
      MAIDEN COULD OBEY SO, BE A BELL TO, RING OF IT, AND   .   .   .   028 31 007
      TO DO WITHOUT, TAKE TOSSES, AND OBEY.   .   .   .   .   .   .   .   068 00 004
      TO SWEEP AND MUST OBEY.   .   .   .   .   .   .   .   .   .   .   148 00 016
OBSCUR'D
      AND SILVER DAMASQU'D PLATES OBSCUR'D IN AGE'S CRUST.   .   .   .   001 12 009
OBSOLETE
      WHAT SPIRIT IS THAT MAKES STILLNESS OBSOLETE   .   .   .   .   .   122 00 016
OBSTRUCTION
      SO LOADING WITH OBSTRUCTION THAT THRESHOLD   .   .   .   .   .   017 00 008
OCCASION
      CAPS OCCASION WITH AN INTELLECTUAL FIT.   .   .   .   .   .   .   143 00 002
OCEAN
      THE ABYSMAL OCEAN HOARDS OF STRANGE AND RARE.   .   .   .   .   002 00 055
      BUT WHEN THE SUN HAD LAPSED TO OCEAN, LO   .   .   .   .   .   .   002 00 136
      STANCHING QUENCHING OCEAN OF A MOTIONABLE MIND!   .   .   .   .   028 32 005
OCTOBER
      THOUGH THEY TOOK TILL THE SEVENTEENTH OF NEXT OCTOBER TO READ.   .   128 00 008
OFF
      FAR OFF A NEREID COMPANY, AND SHAKE   .   .   .   .   .   .   .   002 00 075
      HOVERS OFF, THE JAY-BLUE HEAVENS APPEARING   .   .   .   .   .   028 26 003
      AND THOUGH THE LAST LIGHTS OFF THE BLACK WEST WENT   .   .   .   031 00 011
      FETCHED FRESH, AS I SUPPOSE, OFF SOME SWEET WOOD.   .   .   .   034 00 004
      LEFT HAND, OFF LAND, I HEAR THE LARK ASCEND.   .   .   .   .   035 00 005
      IN CRISPS OF CURL OFF WILD WINCH WHIRL, AND POUR   .   .   .   035 00 007
      IN HIS ECSTASY! THEN OFF, OFF FORTH ON SWING,   .   .   .   .   036 00 005
      IN HIS ECSTASY! THEN OFF, OFF FORTH ON SWING,   .   .   .   .   036 00 005
      AND HURLS FOR HIM, O HALF HURLS EARTH FOR HIM OFF UNDER HIS FEET. .   038 00 014
      AND FLOCKBELLS OFF THE AERIAL   .   .   .   .   .   .   .   .   041 00 007
      IT HURLS, HURLS OFF BONIFACE DOWN.   .   .   .   .   .   .   .   041 00 032
      THE RIVING OFF THAT RACE   .   .   .   .   .   .   .   .   .   041 00 099
      OFF HIM, BUT MEANING MOTION FANS FRESH OUR WITS WITH WONDER.   .   045 00 014
      O FOR NOW CHARMS, ARMS, WHAT BANS OFF BAD   .   .   .   .   .   048 00 034
      HER INJURY'S, LOOKS OFF BY BOTH HORNS OF SHORE,   .   .   .   .   050 00 003
      DOWN? NO WAVING OFF OF THESE MOST MOURNFUL MESSENGERS, C   .   .   059 0L 004
      OFF, AND NO WAY BUT SO.   .   .   .   .   .   .   .   .   .   060 00 033
      OFF HER ONCE SKEINED STAINED VEINED VARIETY C   .   .   .   .   061 00 011
      THESE TWO TELL, EACH OFF THE OTHER! OF A RACK C   .   .   .   061 00 013
      WORLD'S LOVELIEST -- MEN'S SELVES. SELF FLASHES OFF FRAME AND FACE.   .   062 00 011
      THEN LULL, THEN LEAVE OFF, FURY HAD SHRIEKED ' NO LING- .   .   .   065 00 007
      YOU, JADED, LET BE! CALL OFF THOUGHTS AWHILE   .   .   .   .   069 00 010
      SHEER OFF, DISSEVERAL, A STAR, DEATH BLOTS BLACK OUT! NOR MARK   .   072 00 014
      HONOUR IS FLASHED OFF EXPLOIT, SO WE SAY!   .   .   .   .   .   073 00 001
      FOLDS OFF ALOOF, THAT SIGNAL IS AND PROOF   .   .   .   .   .   080 06 003
      THE FALL IS O'ER, TOLD OFF THE LEAVES.   .   .   .   .   .   .   081 00 009
      TOLD OFF THEIR LEAVES ALONG THE PIERCING GALE,   .   .   .   .   098 05 002
      THE HAND DRAWS OFF THE GLOVE; THE ACORN-CUP   .   .   .   .   101 00 009
      BUT THEN HER TETHER CALLS HER! SHE FALLS OFF,   .   .   .   .   103 00 012
      LIES IN HER LAP, WHICH SHE ANON SWEEPS OFF,   .   .   .   .   111 00 009
      DIES OFF IN HYACINTHED GROUND.   .   .   .   .   .   .   .   135 00 033
      AND AFTER THAT OFF THE BOUGH   .   .   .   .   .   .   .   .   138 00 039
      THAT HERE PERSONAL TELLS OFF THESE HEART-SONG POWERFUL PEALS? --   .   141 00 002
      FALLOW, FOAM-FALLOW, HANKS -- FALL'N OFF THEIR RANKS,   .   .   144 00 007
      A DAY OFF SHEARING DAY.   .   .   .   .   .   .   .   .   .   144 00 012
      OFF TRUNDLED TIMBER AND SCOOPS OF THE HILLSIDE GROUND, C   .   .   146 00 004
      AND BREATHES THE BLOTS OFF ALL WITH SIGHS ON SIGHS.   .   .   151 00 006
      STRUCK OFF IT HAS! WRITTEN UPON LOVELY LIMBS,   .   .   .   .   152 02 003
      LIKE THE THING THAT NEVER KNEW THE EARTH, NEVER OFF ROOTS .   .   159 00 027
      NO MORE! OFF WITH -- DOWN HE DINGS C   .   .   .   .   .   .   159 00 028
      FAST HE OPENS, LAST HE OFF WRINGS   .   .   .   .   .   .   .   159 00 034
OFFEND
      ELSE I AM WELL ASSURED I SHOULD OFFEND   .   .   .   .   .   .   014 03 005
      NO! SHEWN TO HER IT CANNOT BUT OFFEND!   .   .   .   .   .   .   094 00 007
OFFENDED
      TENDERED TO HIM. AH WELL, GOD REST HIM ALL ROAD EVER HE OFFENDED! .   053 00 008
OFFER
      RETURNING THANKS, MIGHT OFFER SUCH ARRAY.   .   .   .   .   .   089 00 004
OFFERING
      TO OFFERING MARY MAY.   .   .   .   .   .   .   .   .   .   042 00 036
      YOUR OFFERING, WITH DESPATCH, OF!   .   .   .   .   .   .   .   049 00 021
OFFERINGS
      AND BRING YOUR OFFERINGS TO A GRATEFUL GOD.   .   .   .   .   .   005 00 011
OFFSPRING
      RIGHT OFFSPRING OF YOUR GRIMY MOTHER EARTH!   .   .   .   .   .   077 00 002
OFT
      WHENCE OFT I WATCH BUT SEE THOSE MERMAIDS NOW NO MORE.   .   .   002 00 143
OFTEN
      OFTEN WHEN WINDS IMPENITENT   .   .   .   .   .   .   .   .   080 06 001
```

OFTEN   (CONTINUED)
    THINGS THAT SHE LIKES SEEMS OFTEN TO DESPISE, ... 094 00 017
    TO THE OFTEN TAKINGS OF DESIROUS WINDS, ... 111 00 003
    THEN OFTEN THE EARS IN A NEW FASHION HARK, ... 113 00 007
OH
    OH! EVEN FOR THE WEAKNESS OF THE PLEA 013 00 008
    OH! TILL THOU GIVEST THAT SENSE BEYOND, ... 023 00 043
    OH THOU, PROUD MOTHER AND MUCH PROUD MAIDEN -- 026 00 019
    THEE, OH MAIDEN, MOST WORTHY OF PRAISE! 026 00 036
    IS OUT WITH IT! OH, ... 028 08 001
    OUR KING BACK, OH, UPON ENGLISH SOULS! 028 35 004
    OH, MORNING, AT THE BROWN BRINK EASTWARD, SPRINGS -- . . . 031 00 012
    BRUTE BEAUTY AND VALOUR AND ACT, OH, AIR, PRIDE, PLUME, HERE . 036 00 009
    AND HE BOARDS HER IN OH! SUCH JOY 041 00 071
    LET HIM OH! WITH HIS AIR OF ANGELS THEN LIFT ME, LAY ME! ONLY I'LL 045 00 009
    DEFEAT, THWART ME? OH, THE SOTS AND THRALLS OF LUST . . . 074 00 007
    HER EYES, OH AND HER EYES! 152 02 022
OIL
    AND THEY WHO CRUSH THE OIL 005 00 052
    WITH OIL OF GLADNESS! FOR SACKCLOTH AND FRIEZE 011 00 010
    IT GATHERS TO A GREATNESS, LIKE THE OOZE OF OIL 031 00 003
OILS
    THAN SEWERS WITH SACRED OILS. MANKIND, THAT MOB, COMES, COME! . 152 02 070
    AND OILS OF SHUSHAN COMFORT NOT, ... 166 00 044
OINTMENT
    O NOW WELL WORK THAT SEALING SACRED OINTMENT! 048 00 033
O-SEAL-THAT-SO
    ING BLOOD -- THE O-SEAL-THAT-SO FEATURE, FLUNG PROUDER FORM . . 062 00 002
OLD
    HE HATH ABOLISHED THE OLD DROUTH, ... 008 00 001
    THE WORDS ARE OLD, THE PURPORT NEW, ... 008 00 005
    CHILLING REMEMBRANCE OF MY DAYS OF OLD 017 00 005
    MY NATIONAL OLD EGYPTIAN REED GAVE WAY! 020 00 007
    ON EAR AND EAR TWO NOISES TOO OLD TO END 035 00 001
    SO GOD WAS GOD OF OLD! 060 00 103
    THIS OUTER COLD, MY EXILE FROM OF OLD 080 01 003
    ONLY WITH US IS OLD AND NEW, ... 081 00 063
    THE LAWLESS HONEY EATEN OF OLD 092 00 004
    OF GREENERY: IT IS OLD EARTH'S GROPING TOWARDS THE STEEP . . 149 A 010
    OF GREENERY AND OLD EARTH GROPES FOR, GRASPS AT STEEP V . . 149 B 012
OLDER
    AH! AS THE HEART GROWS OLDER 055 00 005
OLIVE-BRANCH
    AN OLIVE-BRANCH WHENCE RICHLY REEK 077 00 015
ONCE
    OF BATTLE ONCE UPON ST. LAWRENCE' DAY 001 02 002
    THAT SEED WHICH THE GOOD SOWER ONCE DID SOW, ... 017 00 007
    OR ONCE OR NEVER TOOK LOVE'S PROPER FOOD! 020 00 010
    I MUST O'ERTAKE THEE AT ONCE AND UNDER HEAVEN 020 00 015
    ' FOR HE BEGAN AT ONCE AND SHOOK, ... 021 00 029
    THAT WAS BLEST IN IT ONCE, THOUGH NOW IT IS NOT? -- . . . 027 00 008
    WHETHER AT ONCE, AS ONCE AT A CRASH PAUL, ... 028 10 005
    WHETHER AT ONCE, AS ONCE AT A CRASH PAUL, ... 028 10 005
    WANTING! WHICH TWO WHEN THEY ONCE MEET, ... 038 00 012
    ONCE ENCOUNTER IN, HERE COPED AND POISED POWERS! 044 00 004
    LOVE-LACED! -- WHAT ONCE I WELL 054 00 003
    WHAT WOULD THE WORLD BE, ONCE BEREFT 056 00 013
    OFF HER ONCE SKEINED STAINED VEINED VARIETY C 061 00 011
    THOSE LOVELY LADS ONCE, WET-FRESH WINDFALLS OF WAR'S STORM, . . 062 00 006
    I AM ALL AT ONCE WHAT CHRIST IS, SINCE HE WAS WHAT I AM, AND . 072 00 022
    AND THOSE STROKES ONCE THAT GASHED FLESH OR GALLED SHIELD . . 073 00 002
    BREATHES ONCE AND, QUENCHED FASTER THAN IT CAME, ... 076 00 003
    ONCE IT WAS SCARCE PERCEIVED LENT 081 00 011
    ONCE, JOSTLING THICK, THE BLUEBELL SHEAVES 081 00 013
    AT ONCE I STRUGGLE WITH MY BREATH. 081 00 058
    ONCE IN A DRAWER OF INDIAN WOOD 081 00 080
    WHICH ONCE WERE DISOBEDIENT . . . . 093 A 003
    TO SPEAK SO, YET I'LL SPEAK IT FOR THIS ONCE, ... 102 01 038
    LIKE SCALDED BANKS TOPP'D ONCE WITH PRINCIPAL FLOWERS! . . . 102 02 012
    AT ONCE THE SENSES GIVE THE MUSIC BACK, ... 113 00 010
    AT ONCE PERCEIVED, WITH EXCESS 118 00 010
    ALL TIME AT ONCE AND SPAN THE DISTANT GOALS, ... 126 00 004
    UPWARDS AT ONCE AND WIN THEIR AUREOLES. 126 00 008
    AND SHEATHE AT ONCE HIS LEGER WING. 130 00 012
    THE RUINS OF, RIFLED, ONCE A WORLD OF ART? 153 00 004
    ONCE I TURNED FROM THEE AND HID, ... 155 00 009
    ONE ONCE THAT WAS FOUND WANTING WHEN GOOD WEIGHED. . . . 157 00 024
ONEWHERE
    THAT ONEWHERE CURDED, ONEWHERE SUCKED OR SANK -- SOARED OR SANK -- , 071 00 006
    THAT ONEWHERE CURDED, ONEWHERE SUCKED OR SANK -- SOARED OR SANK -- , 071 00 006
ONLY
    ONLY WITH UTTERANCE OF SWEET BREATH THEY SUNG 002 00 130
    AND I HAVE ONLY SET THE SAME TO PEN. 012 02 014
    WHICH ENDS THOSE ONLY STRAINS THAT I APPROVE, ... 019 00 010
    I ONLY FEARED THE WET FOR YOU 021 00 013
    WHICH ONLY MAKES YOU ELOQUENT. 022 00 008
    WHAT NONE WOULD HAVE KNOWN OF IT, ONLY THE HEART, BEING HARD AT BAY, 028 07 008

ONLY   (CONTINUED)
    NOR RESCUE, ONLY ROCKET AND LIGHTSHIP, SHONE, ...   028 15 006
    IPSE, THE ONLY ONE, CHRIST, KING, HEAD! 028 28 005
    ONLY THE INMATE DOES NOT CORRESPOND! 034 00 011
    ONLY THE BREATHING TEMPLE AND FLEET 041 00 093
    IS IT ONLY ITS BEING BRIGHTER 042 00 009
    TEN OR TWELVE, ONLY TEN OR TWELVE. 043 00 020
    LET HIM OH! WITH HIS AIR OF ANGELS THEN LIFT ME, LAY ME! ONLY I'LL   045 00 009
    NOT GRANTED! -- ONLY . . . O ON THAT PATH YOU PACE   .   .   .   047 00 013
    RECORDED ONLY, I HAVE PUT MY LIPS ON PLEAS 048 00 045
    THAT CANST BUT ONLY BE, BUT DOST THAT LONG -- 058 00 004
    ONLY NOT WITHIN SEEING OF THE SUN. 059 06 003
    OF HER WHO NOT ONLY 060 00 017
    ONLY THE BEAKLEAVED BOUGHS DRAGONISH C 061 00 009
    KIND LOVE BOTH GIVE AND GET, ONLY WHAT WORD 066 00 011
    WHO ASKS NOT LIFE BUT ONLY PLACE TO DIE. 079 00 009
    ONLY WITH US IS OLD AND NEW. ' 081 00 063
    THE RAINBOW SHINES, BUT ONLY IN THE THOUGHT 091 00 002
    NO I'LL NOT HAZARD IT, ONLY HIS HAND. 102 01 025
    THE TEMPER'D SOIL WHERE ONLY HER FLOWER IS FOUND.   .   .   102 03 004
    FOR ONLY TRY BY GAZING TO DIVIDE 102 03 009
    ONLY THE BELLED FOXGLOVES LISP'D TOGETHER. 107 01 006
    ONLY THE DAHLIAS BLOW, AND ALL IS AUTUMN HERE.   .   .   .   128 00 010
    CHRIST'S ONLY CHARITY CHARMED AND CHAINED THESE TWO.   .   .   136 00 012
    WHAT IS VIRTUE? VALOUR! ONLY THE HEART VALIANT.   .   .   .   152 02 042
    AND RIGHT? ONLY RESOLUTION! WILL, HIS WILL UNWAVERING   .   .   152 02 043
    AND NOT FROM PURPLE WALES ONLY NOR FROM ELMY ENGLAND,   .   152 C 019
    UPON THIS ONLY GAMBOLLING AND ECHOING-OF-EARTH NOTE --   .   159 00 045
    I LOOK ALL WAYS BUT ONLY SEE 160 00 017
ONYX-CORONALS
    THE DAINTY ONYX-CORONALS DEFLOWERS, ...   002 00 092
OOZE
    IT GATHERS TO A GREATNESS, LIKE THE OOZE OF OIL   .   .   .   031 00 003
    SQUANDERING OOZE TO SQUEEZED DOUGH, CRUST, DUST; STANCHES, STARCHES   .   072 00 007
OPAL
    HITHER BRING PEARL, OPAL, SARD! 024 00 003
OPE
    FLOWERS DO OPE THEIR HEAVENWARD EYES 024 00 015
OPEN
    SPEAR'D OPEN LUSTROUS GASHES, CRIMSON-WHITE! 002 00 008
    OPEN WIDE YOUR HEARTS THAT THEY 024 00 023
    OPEN THE DOOR TO ME. ' 109 29 004
    SAID ! OPEN, OPEN TO ME. ' 109 30 002
    SAID ! OPEN, OPEN TO ME. ' 109 30 002
    LAY OPEN THINE ESTATES. 115 00 007
    CUCKOO, BIRD, AND OPEN EAR WELLS, HEART-SPRINGS, DELIGHTFULLY SWEET,   146 00 002
OPENING
    THINK OF AN OPENING PAGE ILLUMINED   .   .   .   .   .   .   093 B 001
OPEN'D
    BUT OPEN'D TWICE, IN LIFE AND DEATH, TO STATE,   .   .   .   001 04 008
    SHEWN TO EZEKIEL'S OPEN'D SIGHT 077 00 048
OPENS
    SEE HOW SPRING OPENS WITH DISABLING COLD, ...   017 00 001
    FAST HE OPENS, LAST HE OFF WRINGS 159 00 034
OPPORTUNEST
    IS IT OPPORTUNEST 042 00 011
OPPOSITION
    SUCH OPPOSITION TO THE LADY-STAR 014 02 010
OPPRESSED
    AND BEEN IN THEIR RUINOUS REIGNS OPPRESSED, ...   026 00 010
OPPRESSION
    THY IMPALPABLE OPPRESSION, PIN HIM DOWN, ...   102 01 018
ORACLE
    EVER SO BLACK ON IT. OUR TALE, O OUR ORACLE! C   .   .   .   061 00 010
ORB'D
    TO AN ORB'D ROSE, WHICH, BY HOT PANTINGS BLOWN   .   .   .   002 00 020
    PLUNGE ORB'D IN RAINBOW ARCS, AND TRAMPLE AND TREAD   .   .   002 00 078
ORCHARD
    IS SET IN ANY ORCHARD! NO, ...   025 00 010
    LOOK, LOOK! A MAY-MESS, LIKE ON ORCHARD BOUGHS!   .   .   .   032 00 010
    ANG. IS SET IN ANY ORCHARD, NO!   .   .   .   .   .   .   APPEN A 10
ORCHARD-APPLE
    BLOOM LIGHTS THE ORCHARD-APPLE 042 00 038
ORCHARDS
    IN SUMMER ARE OUR ORCHARDS KNOPT 124 00 019
ORDER
    DRESS HIS DAYS TO A DEXTEROUS AND STARLIGHT ORDER.   .   .   048 00 020
ORDER'D
    THIS WAS NO CLASSIC TEMPLE ORDER'D ROUND 001 07 001
ORIENCE
    FOR ORIENCE OF THE DAFFODIL! 081 00 012
    THE HEIGHTENING DAWN WITH MILKY ORIENCE 098 30 002
ORIGINAL
    BREATHE, ARCH AND ORIGINAL BREATH. 028 25 002
    ALL THINGS COUNTER, ORIGINAL, SPARE, STRANGE!   .   .   .   037 00 007
ORINDA
    SELVAGGIA, ORINDA, AND ADELA, AND THE REST. 125 00 038

ORION
    GNASHED: BUT THOU ART ABOVE, THOU ORION OF LIGHT; 028 21 005
O'CLOCK
    ' FROM NINE O'CLOCK TILL MORNING LIGHT 021 00 001
O'ER
    OF FORC'D PERSUASION ISSUE O'ER THE FREE. -- 001 05 007
    MARKING THE SPOT, WHEN THEY HAVE GURGLED O'ER, ... 002 00 003
    DROOP'D O'ER THE BROWS LIKE HECTOR'S CASQUE, AND SWAY'D . . . 002 00 042
    ONE BOUND O'ER DRIPPING GOLD A TURQUOISE-GEMM'D 002 00 060
    WHICH, LIGHTENING O'ER THE BODY ROSY-PALE, ... 002 00 072
    DOWN THAT DANK ROCK O'ER WHICH THEIR LUSH LONG TRESSES WEEP. . . 002 00 115
    WHITE LOOM'D MY ROCK, THE WATER GURGLING O'ER, ... 002 00 142
    SPREAD O'ER THE SWART FACE OF THIS PRODIGAL EARTH. . . . 005 00 045
    TILL DIMPLED JOY STEALS O'ER ITS CHEEKS. 023 00 052
    THY RIVER, AND O'ER GIVES ALL TO RACK OR WRONG. 058 00 008
    WERE I COME O'ER AGAIN ' CRIES CHRIST ' IT SHOULD BE THIS ' . 063 00 014
    MIX O'ER THE NOT UNMOVED EARTH, -- 077 00 130
    BREATHE O'ER MY BARE NERVE RATHER. I DESIRE 080 05 005
    THEY SWATHE AND LACE THE SHROUD-PLAITS O'ER MY FACE, . . . 080 05 006
    I TRY THE CHRISTUS O'ER AGAIN. 080 08 004
    THE FALL IS O'ER, TOLD OFF THE LEAVES. 081 00 009
    SAY, O'ER IT HANGS A WATER-CLOUD 081 00 056
    O'ER PASSES BLEAK, O'ER PERILOUS BARS 083 00 003
    O'ER PASSES BLEAK, O'ER PERILOUS BARS 083 00 003
    GLAZED WATER VAULTED O'ER A DROWSY STONE. 098 39 001
    TO SPILL O'ER FIELDS OF LILIES. SO COULD I 102 01 034
    ALONE UPON THE HILL-TOP, HEAVEN O'ER HIM, ... 107 01 008
O'ER-BRIM
    GOD SHALL O'ER-BRIM THE MEASURES YOU HAVE SPENT . . . 011 00 009
O'ER-HEAD
    AND LONG, THE TREES WERE COLOUR'D, BUT THE O'ER-HEAD, . . . 107 04 012
O'ERTAKE
    I MUST O'ERTAKE THEE AT ONCE AND UNDER HEAVEN . . . 020 00 015
OUTER
    THIS OUTER COLD, MY EXILE FROM OF OLD 080 01 003
OUTGOINGS
    THE OUTGOINGS OF THE VALE DOES BLOCK. 092 00 011
OUT-FLEECED
    OUT-FLEECED BUSHES LIKE A SPANIEL'S EAR V 098 11 001
OUTLINE
    HE SAT AND WROUGHT HIS OUTLINE ON A CLOUD. 107 01 010
OUTRAGE
    I OUTRAGE IT WITH TREASONABLE KISSING. 102 01 049
OUTRIDES
    WITH A MERCY THAT OUTRIDES 028 33 001
OUTRIGHT
    WORD, THAT HEARD AND KEPT THEE AND UTTERED THEE OUTRIGHT. . . 028 30 008
    SHE WAS A WOMAN, UPRIGHT, OUTRIGHT; 145 00 036
OUTWARD
    OF THE OUTWARD SENTENCE LOW LAYS HIM, LISTED TO A HERESY, HERE. . 045 00 004
    NOT SO FAR OUTWARD IN THE SEA: 120 00 021
OUTWARD-STEELED
    UNSEEN, THE HEROIC BREAST NOT OUTWARD-STEELED, ... 073 00 007
OUTWARDS
    ARE MEASURED OUTWARDS FROM MY BREAST. 130 00 002
OVER
    TO BE JUDGE AND RULER OVER US? 005 00 002
    OVER AGAIN I FEEL THY FINGER AND FIND THEE. 028 01 008
    WITH THE SEA-ROMP OVER THE WRECK. 028 17 004
    TO THE MEN IN THE TOPS AND THE TACKLE RODE OVER THE STORM'S BRAWLING. 028 19 008
    BECAUSE THE HOLY GHOST OVER THE BENT 031 00 013
    ALL OVER, AS A BEVY OF EGGS THE MOTHERING WING . . . 034 00 006
    A BUGLER BOY FROM BARRACK (IT IS OVER THE HILL . . . 048 00 001
    OVER GOLDENGROVE UNLEAVING? 055 00 002
    TURNS AND TWINDLES OVER THE BROTH 056 00 006
    AND THE BEADBONNY ASH THAT SITS OVER THE BURN. . . . 056 00 012
    AS TUMBLED OVER RIM IN ROUNDY WELLS 057 00 002
    WITH: OUR EVENING IS OVER US: C 061 00 008
    A DROP OF SHADE ROLLS OVER FIELD AND FLOCK: 098 03 002
    SO WASTE IN TEARS OVER THIS BED OF SWEETNESS, . . . 102 01 035
    ' WHEN HE IS OVER THE SEA? ' 109 04 004
    COME WITH YOU FROM OVER THE SEA? ' 109 07 004
    COME WITH ME FROM OVER THE SEA. ' 109 08 002
    OVER FIELD AND TREE. 109 17 002
    CAME RUNNING OVER THE LEA. 109 17 004
    OR COME FROM OVER THE SEA? ' 109 31 004
    NOR YET FROM OVER THE SEA. 109 32 002
    FROM TEARS SHED OVER CHILDREN'S GRAVES. 123 00 003
    AND WITH THE LAST POST OVER I KNEW NO LETTER WAS SENT. . . 128 00 002
    AND A FEW LEAVES NOT LILY-WHITE BUT CHARACTERED OVER WITH BLACKS. . 128 00 016
    ALL OVER, SOME SUCH WORDS AS THESE, THOUGH DARK, . . . 136 00 029
    THEN OVER HIS TURNED TEMPLES -- HERE -- 144 00 013
    IT IS OVER, MARGARET CLITHEROE. 145 00 061
    HIS DEACON, DIRVAN. WARM TWICE OVER MUST THE WELCOME BE, . . 152 01 008
    OVER FINGER-TEASING TASK, HIS TWINY BOOTS 159 00 033
    AND THE WATER WARBLES OVER INTO, C 159 00 038
    ENTRIES OR BANKS ALL OVER SHADE 166 00 023

OVERBEND
WASTE! HER EARLIEST STARS, EARLSTARS, STARS PRINCIPAL, OVERBEND US, . 061 00 004
OVERFLOW
WHICH THE TIDES COVER IN THEIR OVERFLOW. 002 00 002
AND UNDIVULGED LOVE DOES OVERFLOW. 119 00 012
OVERFLOWING
MY LATE BEING THERE BEGGED OF ME, OVERFLOWING 048 00 006
OVERHEAD
AGAIN, LOOK OVERHEAD 060 00 073
ALL THE WELKIN OVERHEAD, ... 077 00 096
NO COLOUR IN THE OVERHEAD, ... 081 00 160
OVERSPREAD
SOON THE WHOLE WORLD IS OVERSPREAD! 006 00 025
OVERSTOOD
WILD WYCHELM, HORNBEAM FRETTY OVERSTOOD C 159 00 024
OVERTAKE
IF I SHALL OVERTAKE THEE AT LAST ABOVE. 020 00 016
OVERTAKING
HAVE, AT THE AWFUL OVERTAKING, ... 041 00 114
OVERVAULTED
WHICH OVERVAULTED VOICE. 148 00 020
OVERVAULTS
NOW IT OVERVAULTS APPLEDURCOMBE! 041 00 030
OVERWORN
AND FATHER BE OVERWORN. 114 00 008
OVERWROUGHT
NO ATLANTIC SQUALL OVERWROUGHT HER 041 00 017
OWN
EACH IN HIS OWN IMAGINING 023 00 015
WHAT CAN IT BE, THIS GLEE? THE GOOD YOU HAVE THERE OF YOUR OWN? . 028 18 008
BUT HE SCORES IT IN SCARLET HIMSELF ON HIS OWN BESPOKEN, . . 028 22 005
KIND, BUT ROYALLY RECLAIMING HIS OWN! 028 34 007
BUT HIS OWN NEST, WILD NEST, NO PRISON. 039 00 011
MY PEOPLE AND BORN OWN NATION. 041 00 087
FAST FOUNDERING OWN GENERATION. 041 00 088
OF OWN, OF ABRUPT SELF THERE SO THRUSTS ON, SO THRONGS THE EAR. . 045 00 008
YOU THERE ARE MASTER, DO YOUR OWN DESIRE! 046 00 011
TO ITS OWN FINE FUNCTION, WILD AND SELF-INSTRESSED, . . . 047 00 007
AN OUR DAY'S GOD'S OWN GALAHAD, THOUGH THIS CHILD'S DRIFT . . 048 00 040
TO OWN MY HEART! I YIELD YOU DO COME SOMETIMES! BUT . . . 051 00 004
TO HIS OWN SELFBENT SO BOUND, SO TIED TO HIS TURN, . . . 058 00 011
TO ITS OWN BEST BEING AND ITS LOVELINESS OF YOUTH C . . . 059 06 013
WHAT DO THEN? HOW MEET BEAUTY? MERELY MEET IT! OWN, . . . 062 00 012
MY OWN HEART LET ME MORE HAVE PITY ON! LET 069 00 001
YOU WOULD NOT HOUSE BENEATH MY OWN! 081 00 004
I OWN A PREFERENCE FOR PRIDE. 096 01 004
SWEETER THY KISSES, MY OWN LOVE, ... 109 38 003
TIME WAS, NEXT WHITEST AFTER MARY'S OWN. 136 00 004
HOPE HOLDS TO CHRIST THE MIND'S OWN MIRROR OUT 151 00 001
LOYAL TO HIS OWN SOUL, LAYING HIS OWN LAW DOWN, NO LAW NOR . 152 02 040
LOYAL TO HIS OWN SOUL, LAYING HIS OWN LAW DOWN, NO LAW NOR . 152 02 040
HIS LOOKS, THE SOUL'S OWN LETTERS, SEE BEYOND, ... 157 00 015
MILDLY, OF HER OWN MILD MOOD, ... APPEN D 23
REDEEMED US FOR HIS OWN, ... APPEN D 38
OWNS
THE SHEPHERD'S BROW, FRONTING FORKED LIGHTNING, OWNS . . . 075 00 001
OXEYE
SUNSPURGE AND OXEYE 138 00 028
OXFORD
FROM OXFORD COMES THE THRONG AND HUM OF BELLS 098 03 006
GAVE THE MUCH MUSIC OF OUR OXFORD BELLS? 107 02 008

PACE
NOT GRANTED! -- ONLY . . . O ON THAT PATH YOU PACE 047 00 013
AND MILLBROOK-SLIPS WITH PRETTY PACE 130 00 025
PACES
TEACH ME THE PACES THAT YOU WENT 081 00 125
PACING
TURNING AND PACING, SO BY SLIPS DISCLOSES 108 00 002
PACK
UPON, ALL ON TWO SPOOLS; PART, PEN, PACK C 061 00 011
PACKED
THE STARS WERE PACKED SO CLOSE THAT NIGHT 098 29 001
THE STARS ARE PACKED SO THICK TO-NIGHT 135 00 019
FAIRYLAND! SILK-BEECH, SCROLLED ASH, PACKED SYCAMORE, C . . 159 00 024
PACKS
MANWOLF, WORSE! AND THEIR PACKS INFEST THE AGE. 070 00 020
PACTOLUS
A GOLD-WATER PACTOLUS FRETS 003 00 027
PAGE
THINK OF AN OPENING PAGE ILLUMINED . . . . . . 093 B 001
PAGEANT
SOME PAGEANT WHICH TAKES TEARS AND I MUST FOOT WITH FEELING THAT . 152 01 020

PAIN
    AS POETS SING: OR THAT IT IS A PAIN • • • • • • • • • • 002 00 121
    THE DAY THAT BROUGHT MY LASTING PAIN • • • • • • • • • 021 00 010
    FROM ALL THE PAIN OF THE PAST'S UNREST: • • • • • • • • 026 00 012
    WELL, SHE HAS THEE FOR THE PAIN, FOR THE • • • • • • • 028 31 001
    MY EVIL WORDS THORNY WITH PAIN: • • • • • • • • • 081 00 027
    YOU HEAR NOR CARE OF LOVE AND PAIN. • • • • • • • • 081 00 035
    BUT MINE IS DREADFUL LEAPING PAIN, • • • • • • • • 081 00 051
    LED RICHARD WITH A SWEET UNDOING PAIN • • • • • • • 107 04 017
    TAKE THEIR PECULIAR THORNS AND NATURAL PAIN • • • • • 123 00 005
    IN MOTION IS NO WEIGHT OR PAIN, • • • • • • • • • 130 00 015
    AND BOUGHT US OUT OF PAIN, • • • • • • • • • APPEN D 39
PAINED
    AFAR IN CORRIDORS WITH PAINED STRAIN • • • • • • • 001 13 007
PAINFUL
    WHO RISING LATE HAD MISS'D HER PAINFUL WAY • • • • • 079 00 005
PAINS
    BUT HALF THE PAINS HE SPENDS UPON HIS BOY, • • • • • 097 00 004
    HATH DEVIS'D NEW PAINS FOR ME • • • • • • • • • 160 00 012
    THE DREAR DULL BURTHEN OF UNENDING PAINS. • • • • • • 160 00 018
PAINT
    HOW DARE I PAINT MISS STORY TO MISS MAY? • • • • • • 094 00 003
PAINTED
    DEALT SO, PAINTED ON THE AIR, C • • • • • • • • • 159 00 025
PAINTING
    WITH PAINTING GLEAM'D THE RICH PILASTER'D WALLS -- • • • • 001 10 003
PAIR
    SHIVELIGHTS AND SHADOWTACKLE IN LONG LASHES LACE, LANCE, AND PAIR. • 072 00 004
PAIR'D
    SHE PUTS IN LEASH HER PAIR'D LIPS LEST SURPRISE • • • 082 00 003
PALACE
    HARD BY A ROYAL PALACE AND A ROYAL TOMB. • • • • • • 001 01 009
    THE STRETCHING PALACE LAY AS HANDLE FIX'D. • • • • • • 001 04 004
    FELL ON THE PALACE, AND THE LUST OF RABBLE RUDE,) • • • 001 14 009
PALATE
    PALATE, THE HUTCH OF TASTY LUST, • • • • • • • • • 022 00 013
PALE
    THE VEX'D ELM-HEADS ARE PALE WITH THE VIEW • • • • • 078 00 001
    THE LORN MOON, PALE WITH PITEOUS DISMAY, • • • • • • 079 00 004
    BUT IN PALE WATER, FRAIL WATER, WILD RASH AND REELING WATER, • 152 C 015
    BID JOY BACK, HAVE AT THE HARVEST, KEEP HOPE PALE. • • • 154 00 004
    THEO. A PALE AND PERISHED PALMTREE-CUT, • • • • • • APPEN A 42
PALING
    THE SHOCKS. THIS PIECE-BRIGHT PALING SHUTS THE SPOUSE • • • 032 00 013
PALM
    AND TO MY PALM THE POINT APPLY, • • • • • • • • • 080 14 002
    INTO HIS HOLLOW'D PALM SHOULD MOAN THE BLAST: • • • • 090 00 002
    BRING ME PALM WITH PEARLED KNOPS, • • • • • • • • 098 18 002
PALMS
    AND SEVENTY PALMS THERE STAND. • • • • • • • • • 005 00 024
    THY UNCHANCELLING POISING PALMS WERE WEIGHING THE WORTH, • • 028 21 006
    AS STRUCK WITH RINGS OF SOUND THE CLOSE-SHUT PALMS • • • 122 00 010
    [AS MIGHT HAVE STRUCK AND SHOOK THE CLOSE-SHUT PALMS] • • 122 00 013
PALMTREE
    AH DIP IN BLOOD THE PALMTREE PEN • • • • • • • • 025 00 037
PALMTREE-CUT
    THEO. A PALE AND PERISHED PALMTREE-CUT. • • • • • • APPEN A 42
PALMTREE-PEN
    THEO. DIP IN BLOOD THE PALMTREE-PEN • • • • • • • APPEN A 43
PALMY
    IN SOME BROAD PALMY MEAD, AND SAINTLY SMILED, • • • • 001 10 005
    IF A WUTHERING OF HIS PALMY SNOW-PINIONS SCATTER A COLOSSAL SMILE • 045 00 013
PALSY
    STONE, PALSY, CANCER, COUGH, LUNG-WASTING, WOMB-NOT-BEARING, • 152 C 008
PANE
    I STEADY AS A WATER IN A WELL, TO A POISE, TO A PANE, • • 028 04 005
PANG
    THE PANG OF TARTARUS, CHRISTIANS HOLD, • • • • • • 080 01 001
PANGS
    ALL WHILE HER PATIENCE, MORSELLED INTO PANGS, • • • • 050 00 012
    MORE PANGS WILL, SCHOOLED AT FOREPANGS, WILDER WRING. • • 065 00 002
PANSY-DARK
    THEIR PANSY-DARK OR BRONZEN LOCKS WERE STRUNG • • • • 002 00 053
PANTINGS
    TO AN ORB'D ROSE, WHICH, BY HOT PANTINGS BLOWN • • • • 002 00 020
PAPA
    BID YOUR PAPA GOODNIGHT. SWEET EXHIBITION! • • • • • 097 00 007
PAR
    WHO STOPS HIS ASKING MOOD AT PAR • • • • • • • • 166 00 025
PARACLETE
    IN THE HOLY GHOST THE PARACLETE • • • • • • • • 169 00 010
PARADISAICAL
    OR PARING OF PARADISAICAL FRUIT, LOVELY IN WANING BUT LUSTRELESS, • 137 00 003
PARADISE
    IF I WERE COME FROM PARADISE, • • • • • • • • • 109 32 003
    IF IT WERE A FLOWER OF PARADISE, • • • • • • • • 109 34 003
    ' IF IT WERE A CROWN OF PARADISE, • • • • • • • • 109 35 003

PARADISE   (CONTINUED)
    SHE HAS GONE WITH HIM TO PARADISE. 109 39 003
PARADOX
    HEAR YET MY PARADOX: LOVE, WHEN ALL IS GIVEN, ... 020 00 013
PARALLEL
    AND STRAIGHT SHOWERS PARALLEL SHOULD FOLLOW FAST: 090 00 004
    WITH PARALLEL SHAFTS, -- AS UPWARD-PARTED ASHES, --   .   .   . 107 04 005
PARAPET
    ECLIPSING PARAPET: YET ABOVE THE WALL 012 02 007
PARCHED
    YOUR PARCHED NOSTRILS SNUFF EGYPTIAN AIR, ... 005 00 027
PARCHES
    OF YESTERTEMPEST'S CREASES: IN POOL AND RUTPEEL PARCHES   .   . 072 00 006
PARDON
    WHEN WAKING HEARTS CAN PARDON MUCH 077 00 029
    AND I MUST TAKE YOUR AMENDS, CRY PARDON, AND THEN BE DUMB.   .   . 128 00 020
PARE
    DIAMONDS ARE BETTER CUT: WHO PARE, REPAIR: 096 07 005
PARING
    OR PARING OF PARADISAICAL FRUIT, LOVELY IN WANING BUT LUSTRELESS, . 137 00 003
PARIS
    HERE IN SOME DARKEN'D LANDSCAPE PARIS FAIR 001 11 001
PARK
    THIS IS MY PARK, MY PLEASAUNCE: THIS TO ME 012 01 006
    THE AIR SMELLS STRONG OF SWEETBRIAR IN THE PARK. 135 00 024
PARLEY
    YOUR PARLEY WAS NOT DONE AND THERE! 025 00 029
    THEO. YOUR PARLEY WAS NOT DONE AND THERE!   .   .   .   .   . APPEN A 29
PARLOUR-PASTIME
    YOU'VE PARLOUR-PASTIME LEFT AND (WHO'LL 030 00 034
PART
    THE WINGED FOWLS TOOK PART, PART FELL IN THORN 007 00 007
    THE WINGED FOWLS TOOK PART, PART FELL IN THORN 007 00 007
    PART FOUND NO ROOT UPON THE FLINTY ROAD, -- 007 00 009
    PART WAS PICKED FOR JOHN, ... 054 00 007
    AND PLAYS IN GRACE HER PART 060 00 049
    YET NO PART BUT WHAT WILL 060 00 053
    UPON, ALL ON TWO SPOOLS: PART, PEN, PACK C 061 00 011
    OUR REDCOATS, OUR TARS? BOTH THESE BEING, THE GREATER PART,   . 063 00 002
    O HERE IS THE MOST PITEOUS PART, ... 080 11 002
    AND WITH SHARP FLINT WILL PART MY FEET AND DINT   .   .   . 080 13 003
    AND ROSING PART, ON PART DISPENSES GREEN: 100 00 003
    AND ROSING PART, ON PART DISPENSES GREEN: 100 00 003
    ALLOW AT LEAST IT HAS ONE TERM AND PART 102 03 005
    NO PIECE MATCHED THOSE EYES KEPT MOST PART MUCH CAST DOWN   . 152 02 026
    I ALL MY BEING HAVE HACKED IN HALF WITH HER NECK: ONE PART,   . 152 02 060
    THE TELLING TIME OUR TASK IS: TIME'S SOME PART, ... 153 00 005
    THEY TEASE ME, NEVER KNOW THE PART 165 00 003
PARTED
    AN AGE IS NOW SINCE PASSED, SINCE PARTED: WITH THE REVERSAL   .   . 045 00 003
    OF STREAMS: AND CLOUDS LIKE MESH'D AND PARTED MOSS V   .   . 121 00 002
    OF WATER, CLOUDS LIKE PARTED MOSS V 121 00 002
    PARTED ME LEAF AND LEAF, DIVIDED ME, EYELID AND EYELID OF SLUMBER. 137 00 007
    AND PARTED FROM HER SIGHT   .   .   .   . APPEN D 32
PARTING
    AND THRO' THEIR PARTING LIDS THERE CAME AND WENT   .   .   . 002 00 011
    AND HE MY PEACE / MY PARTING, SWORD AND STRIFE.   .   .   . 066 00 004
    THERE IS NO PARTING OR BARE INTERSTICE 098 22 004
PARTLESS
    YOU WENT INTO THE PARTLESS AIR. 025 00 030
    THEO. YOU FELL INTO THE PARTLESS AIR, ... APPEN A 30
PARTS
    FROM PARTS UNLOOK'D FOR, ALTER'D, SPENT, ... 081 00 024
    I KNEW THE BROOK THAT PARTS IN TWO 135 00 025
PASHED
    SELF IN SELF STEEPED AND PASHED -- QUITE C 061 00 006
PASS
    THRO' CRIMSON-GOLDEN FLOODS PASS SWALLOW'D INTO FIRE.   .   . 002 00 083
    THAT MEN MUST WONDER AS I PASS 010 00 003
    MEN ARE AMAZED TO WATCH ME PASS 025 00 003
    LOW-COVERED PASS, AND BRACE THE WOODLAND CLODS   .   .   . 112 00 006
    I HAVE DESIRED, DESIRED TO PASS 130 00 028
    ANG. MEN MUST START TO SEE ME PASS   .   .   .   .   .   . APPEN A 03
PASSAGE
    A SIMPLE PASSAGE OF WEAK NOTES 003 00 013
    IN THE MOST MURDEROUS PASSAGE OF HIS BOOK: 014 02 011
PASSAGES
    AND PASSAGES WHERE WE USED TO MEET, -- 081 00 162
PASSED
    BUT DAY PASSED INTO DAY. 021 00 004
    AN AGE IS NOW SINCE PASSED, SINCE PARTED: WITH THE REVERSAL   .   . 045 00 003
PASSES
    THE WHOLE WORLD PASSES: I STAND BY. 015 00 004
    WHERE WHATEVER'S PRIZED AND PASSES OF US, C 059 06 008
    O'ER PASSES BLEAK, O'ER PERILOUS BARS 083 00 003
    THE WIND, THAT PASSES BY SO FLEET, ... 098 01 001
    WITH WAVED PASSES THERE SHALL GLIDE 106 00 002

PASSING
    YOUR PASSING STEPS, I NEVER HEARD 021 00 048
    AND LISTEN TO THE PASSING BELL 023 00 040
    PRECIOUS PASSING MEASURE, ... 041 00 011
    SORROWS PASSING NUMBER, ... 170 00 009
PASSION
    AND LET HIM PROVE MY PASSION WAS BEGUN 014 02 004
    THE DENSE AND THE DRIVEN PASSION, AND FRIGHTFUL SWEAT; . . . 028 07 005
    THE APPEALING OF THE PASSION IS TENDERER IN PRAYER APART; . . 028 27 006
    MY PASSION LIKE A FOOLISH WIND 081 00 037
    MANTLING PASSION IN A GRANDEUR, CRIMSON GRANDEUR. 152 02 037
PASSIONFLOWER
    GREAT THECLA, THE PLUMED PASSIONFLOWER, ... 145 00 042
PASSION-PASTURED
    HOW, TURN MY PASSION-PASTURED THOUGHT 081 00 174
PASSION-PLUNGED
    OUR PASSION-PLUNGED GIANT RISEN, ... 028 33 007
PASSION-SAKE
    THAT MIGHT HAVE SPARED HER WERE IT BUT FOR PASSION-SAKE. YES, . 152 02 054
PASSION'S
    YOU SEE THAT I HAVE COME TO PASSION'S END; 014 03 001
PASS'D
    THEN PASS'D THE WIND, AND SOBB'D WITH MOUNTAIN-ECHO'D WOE. . . 001 13 009
    BUT THE SPRING-TIDE PASS'D THE SAME; 004 00 024
PAST
    MY LOVE IS LESSENED AND MUST SOON BE PAST. 014 01 001
    TWO THOUSANDS OF YEARS ARE NEAR UPON PAST 027 00 015
    BEYOND SAYING SWEET, PAST TELLING OF TONGUE, ... 028 09 005
    WORDING IT HOW BUT BY HIM THAT PRESENT AND PAST, ... 028 29 005
    GROUND OF BEING, AND GRANITE OF IT; PAST ALL 028 32 006
    WAYLAY HER AT EBB, PAST PENMAEN POOL. 030 00 024
    HAVE LOST THAT CHEER AND CHARM OF EARTH'S PAST PRIME; . . . 035 00 012
    HE FATHERS-FORTH WHOSE BEAUTY IS PAST CHANGE: 037 00 010
    TIME PAST SHE HAS BEEN ATTEMPTED AND PURSUED 050 00 005
    TWO TEDIOUS ACTS WERE PAST! 054 00 029
    NO WORST, THERE IS NONE. PITCHED PAST PITCH OF GRIEF, . . . 065 00 001
    OUR RUINS OF WRECKED PAST PURPOSE, THERE SHE BASKS . . . 068 00 007
    THE BITTERNESS OF DEATH WAS PAST, ... 081 00 120
    BUT THE LILY IS PAST, AS I SAY, AND THE ROSE IS NOT IN ITS PRIME; . 128 00 014
    PAST, THE PAST, NO MORE BE SEEN! 129 00 002
    PAST, THE PAST, NO MORE BE SEEN! 129 00 002
    AND GRAVE PAST GIRLHOOD EARNEST IN HER EYES. 136 00 020
PAST-PRAYER
    A VEIN FOR THE VISITING OF THE PAST-PRAYER, PENT IN PRISON, . . 028 33 005
PASTORAL
    ON A PASTORAL FOREHEAD OF WALES, ... 028 24 002
    EPISTLES, WHILE THE RUNNING PASTORAL BLEATS 107 04 022
PAST'S
    FROM ALL THE PAIN OF THE PAST'S UNREST; 026 00 012
PASTURES
    RAVES THROUGH SICILIAN PASTURES MANY A MILE; 001 11 004
    PIPE ME TO PASTURES STILL AND BE 022 00 003
PATCH
    THIS JACK, JOKE, POOR POTSHERD, PATCH, MATCHWOOD, IMMORTAL DIAMOND, 072 00 023
PATH
    NOT GRANTED! -- ONLY . . . O ON THAT PATH YOU PACE 047 00 013
    I BETTER'D ALL OUR PATH WITH SANGUINE EYES. 125 00 016
PATHLESS
    THEN WAS DISCOVER'D IN THE PATHLESS SKY, ... 079 00 007
PATIENCE
    LET PATIENCE WITH HER CHASTENING WAND 023 00 045
    PATIENCE; BUT PITY OF THE REST OF THEM! 028 31 002
    BUY THEN! BID THEN! -- WHAT? -- PRAYER, PATIENCE, ALMS, VOWS. . . 032 00 009
    ALL WHILE HER PATIENCE, MORSELLED INTO PANGS, ... 050 00 012
    SOME GOOD! AND SO HE DOES LEAVE PATIENCE EXQUISITE, . . . 051 00 008
    OF PATIENCE, PENANCE, PRAYER; 060 00 123
    PATIENCE, HARD THING! THE HARD THING BUT TO PRAY, . . . 068 00 001
    BUT BID FOR, PATIENCE IS! PATIENCE WHO ASKS 068 00 002
    BUT BID FOR, PATIENCE IS! PATIENCE WHO ASKS 068 00 002
    RARE PATIENCE ROOTS IN THESE, AND, THESE AWAY, ... 068 00 005
    NOWHERE. NATURAL HEART'S IVY, PATIENCE MASKS 068 00 006
    DELICIOUS KINDNESS? -& HE IS PATIENT. PATIENCE FILLS . . . 068 00 013
PATIENT
    DELICIOUS KINDNESS? -- HE IS PATIENT. PATIENCE FILLS . . . 068 00 013
PATRONIZE
    AND LOVES -- A FATAL FAULT -- TO PATRONIZE; 094 00 018
PATTERN
    AND VIRTUES THAT THY PATTERN SHOWS, ... 169 00 006
PAUL
    WHETHER AT ONCE, AS ONCE AT A CRASH PAUL, ... 028 10 005
    AND PAUL IS TARSUS' TRUE BELLEROPHON. 136 00 010
    SHE LOOKED, SHE LISTENED; PAUL TAUGHT LONG THAT DAY. . . . 136 00 024
PAUL'S
    NEAR BY IS PAUL'S FREE TARSUS, FABLED WHERE 136 00 007
PAUSE
    TO PAUSE -- THEN FROM HIS GURGLING BILL 077 00 083
PAVES
    PAVES THE CLOUDS ON THE SWEPT AZURE. 078 00 010

PAY
  ' SO I AM VICTOR NOW, I SWEAR TO PAY 001 02 005
  YEA A DEBT TO PAY THEE YET: 155 00 019
  NOT THE PLEASURE, THE PAY, THE PLUNDER, ... 156 00 006
PEACE
  PEACE AND FOOD CHEERED ME WHERE FOUR ROUGH WAYS MEET.   .   .   . 020 00 012
  A SON FOR KING, WHOSE NAME WAS PEACE. 026 00 032
  THEN COME WHO PINE FOR PEACE OR PLEASURE 030 00 037
  HE HAUNTED WHO OF ALL MEN MOST SWAYS MY SPIRITS TO PEACE: .   . 044 00 011
  WHEN WILL YOU EVER, PEACE, WILD WOODDOVE, SHY WINGS SHUT,   .   . 051 00 001
  WHEN, WHEN, PEACE, WILL YOU, PEACE? I'LL NOT PLAY HYPOCRITE   .   . 051 00 003
  WHEN, WHEN, PEACE, WILL YOU, PEACE? I'LL NOT PLAY HYPOCRITE   .   . 051 00 003
  THAT PIECEMEAL PEACE IS POOR PEACE. WHAT PURE PEACE ALLOWS   .   . 051 00 005
  THAT PIECEMEAL PEACE IS POOR PEACE. WHAT PURE PEACE ALLOWS   .   . 051 00 005
  THAT PIECEMEAL PEACE IS POOR PEACE. WHAT PURE PEACE ALLOWS   .   . 051 00 005
  O SURELY, REAVING PEACE, MY LORD SHOULD LEAVE IN LIEU   .   .   . 051 00 007
  THAT PLUMES TO PEACE THEREAFTER. AND WHEN PEACE HERE DOES HOUSE   . 051 00 009
  THAT PLUMES TO PEACE THEREAFTER. AND WHEN PEACE HERE DOES HOUSE   . 051 00 009
  AND HE MY PEACE / MY PARTING, SWORD AND STRIFE. 066 00 004
  GRANT THAT CLOSE-FOLDED PEACE THAT CLAD 077 00 041
PEACH
  YIELDS TENDER AS A PUSHED PEACH, ... 048 00 023
PEACOCK'D
  THE PEACOCK'D COPSE WERE KNOWN TO FILL: 081 00 014
PEACOCK'S
  MARK YOU HOW THE PEACOCK'S EYE 086 00 001
PEAK
  SURROUND THE PEAK FROM WHICH WE GAZE. 023 00 026
PEAK'D
  SKY PEAK'D WITH TINY FLAMES. 098 25 005
PEALED
  SHOULD HAVE PEALED WITH WELCOME, WALES, ... 029 00 018
PEALS
  THAT HERE PERSONAL TELLS OFF THESE HEART-SONG POWERFUL PEALS? --   . 141 00 002
PEARL
  HITHER BRING PEARL, OPAL, SARD: 024 00 003
  THAT SWINISHLY REFUSES SUCH A PEARL! 102 03 033
  THAT SWINISHLY REFUSES SUCH A PEARL! V 102 03 039
PEARLED
  BRING ME PALM WITH PEARLED KNOPS, ... 098 18 002
PEARLY
  AND SILVER FILMS, BENEATH WITH PEARLY MIST, ... 002 00 067
PEARTREE
  THE GLASSY PEARTREE LEAVES AND BLOOMS, THEY BRUSH 033 00 006
PEASANT
  NEXT MORN A PEASANT FROM THE MOUNTAIN SIDE 001 14 001
PEBBLY
  DAWN THAT THE PEBBLY LOW-DOWN EAST 098 31 001
  DAWN THAT THE LOW-DOWN PEBBLY EAST 098 31 004
PECTORAL
  AND WEAR IT THUS, A PECTORAL, BY MY HEART. 102 01 028
PECULIAR
  THE ONE PECULIAR OF THEIR PLEASURED EYE, ... 012 02 013
  TAKE THEIR PECULIAR THORNS AND NATURAL PAIN 123 00 005
PEELED
  OF PIED AND PEELED MAY! 028 26 004
PEER
  ALL MINE, YET COMMON TO MY EVERY PEER. 012 01 008
PEERS
  WHEN THOU AT THE RANDOM GRIM FORGE, POWERFUL AMIDST PEERS,   .   . 053 00 013
  FALLEN FROM MY PEERS. 160 00 010
PEGASUS
  SPENT PEGASUS DOWN THE STARK-PRECIPITOUS AIR 136 00 008
PELICAN
  BRING THE TENDER TALE TRUE OF THE PELICAN: 168 00 021
PELT
  AND PELT MUSIC, TILL NONE'S TO SPILL NOR SPEND. 035 00 008
PELTED
  QUAINT MOONMARKS, TO HIS PELTED PLUMAGE UNDER C 045 00 010
PELTING
  WITH ROSY FOAM AND PELTING BLOSSOM AND MISTS 002 00 090
PEN
  AND I HAVE ONLY SET THE SAME TO PEN. 012 02 014
  AH DIP IN BLOOD THE PALMTREE PEN 025 00 037
  UPON, ALL ON TWO SPOOLS: PART, PEN, PACK C 061 00 011
  THAT WILL NOT WEAR A PRINT, THAT WILL NOT STAIN A PEN,   .   .   . 152 C 016
PENALTIES
  AND THESE ARE FROM THE GODS MY PENALTIES. 160 00 006
PENANCE
  OF PATIENCE, PENANCE, PRAYER: 060 00 123
  PENANCE SHALL CLOTHE ME TO THE BONE. 081 00 135
PENCE
  LIKE THAT POOR POCKET OF PENCE, POOR PENCE OF MINE.   .   .   . 142 00 009
  LIKE THAT POOR POCKET OF PENCE, POOR PENCE OF MINE.   .   .   . 142 00 009
PENCILLED
  AND PENCILLED BLUE SO DAINTILY, ... 003 00 018
PENDANT
  PENDANT IN FORMAL LINE FROM CORNICE TALL 001 12 007

PENETRATIVE
    THE PENETRATIVE ELEMENT • • • • • • • • • • • 081 00 132
PENITENCE
    BUT GRANT MY PENITENCE BEGUN; • • • • • • • 081 00 137
PENITENT
    THE-LAST-BREATH PENITENT SPIRITS -- THE UTTERMOST MARK • • • 028 33 006
PENMAEN
    BUT HERE AT, HERE AT PENMAEN POOL? • • • • • • 030 00 004
    COME, SWING THE SCULLS ON PENMAEN POOL. • • • • • 030 00 008
    TO HALVE THE BOWL OF PENMAEN POOL. • • • • • • 030 00 012
    IN FRANK, IN FAIRY PENMAEN POOL. • • • • • • • 030 00 016
    SHEW BRIGHTER SHAKEN IN PENMAEN POOL. • • • • • 030 00 020
    WAYLAY HER AT EBB, PAST PENMAEN POOL. • • • • • 030 00 024
    THAT LACE THE FACE OF PENMAEN POOL. • • • • • • 030 00 028
    FROM DARKSOME DARKSOME PENMAEN POOL. • • • • • 030 00 032
    THAT FROCKS AN OAR IN PENMAEN POOL. • • • • • • 030 00 036
    AND TASTE THE TREATS OF PENMAEN POOL. • • • • • 030 00 040
PENNON
    A QUIVERING PENNON; THEN, FOR EYE TOO KEEN, • • • • 002 00 017
    HIS LITTLE PENNON IS UNFURLED. • • • • • • • 130 00 014
PENT
    A VEIN FOR THE VISITING OF THE PAST-PRAYER, PENT IN PRISON; • • 028 33 005
    I CAN STAND PENT IN THE MONSTROUS ELEMENT • • • • 080 05 003
    OR THORN-ENGAGED, IMPALED AND PENT • • • • • • 081 00 019
PEOPLE
    THAT CORDIAL AIR MADE THOSE KIND PEOPLE A HOOD • • • • 034 00 005
    MY PEOPLE AND BORN OWN NATION, • • • • • • • 041 00 087
PERCEIVED
    ONCE IT WAS SCARCE PERCEIVED LENT • • • • • • 081 00 011
    AT ONCE PERCEIVED, WITH EXCESS • • • • • • • 118 00 010
PERCH
    THOUGH ALOFT ON TURF OR PERCH OR POOR LOW STAGE, • • • 039 00 005
PERFECT
    TRIUMPH OF AIRY GRACE AND PERFECT HARMONY. • • • • 001 07 009
    PERFECT, NOT ALTER IT. • • • • • • • • • 060 00 089
    AFTER THAT IN PERFECT HUSH • • • • • • • • 145 00 058
    THIS PIECE OF PERFECT SONG. • • • • • • • • 148 00 030
    NOW BE MY PRIDE THEN PERFECT, ALL ONE PIECE. HENCEFORTH • • 152 02 038
PERFUMES
    PERFUMES FOR THE GARB OF WOE. • • • • • • • 024 00 020
PERHAPS
    AND I -- PERHAPS IF MY INTENT • • • • • • • 015 00 009
    PERHAPS IT WAS FOR THIS SHE CHOSE THE PLACE. • • • • 111 00 015
    OUR SEX SHOULD BE BORN IN APRIL PERHAPS OR THE LILY-TIME; • • 128 00 013
    PERHAPS WE STRUCK NO BLOW, GWENVREWI LIVES PERHAPS; • • 152 02 009
    PERHAPS WE STRUCK NO BLOW, GWENVREWI LIVES PERHAPS; • • 152 02 009
PERIL
    ------ THERE IS MORE PERIL FROM MY LAUGHTER. V • • • • 102 01 009
PERILOUS
    IN HOT SANDS PERILOUS • • • • • • • • • 005 00 004
    WITH, PERILOUS, O NO; NOR YET PLOD SAFE SHOD SOUND; • • • 070 00 014
    O'ER PASSES BLEAK, O'ER PERILOUS BARS • • • • • 083 00 003
    METHINKS MY LAUGHTER IS MORE PERILOUS V • • • • • 102 01 008
PERISHABLE
    IN THE LODGES OF THE PERISHABLE SOULS • • • • • 126 00 001
PERISHED
    THEO. A PALE AND PERISHED PALMTREE-CUT. • • • • • APPEN A 42
PERISHING
    WOKE THEE WITH A WE ARE PERISHING IN THE WEATHER OF GENNESARETH. • • 028 25 006
PERISH'D
    TWO MAZED SHEPHERDS PERISH'D IN THE TIDE; • • • • 001 14 003
PERMANENCE
    NOR PERMANENCE IN THE SOLID WORLD. • • • • • • 130 00 016
PERPETUAL
    BLOT THE PERPETUAL FESTIVAL OF DAY? • • • • • • 089 00 002
PERSEUS
    HER PERSEUS LINGER AND LEAVE HER TO HER EXTREMES? -- • • • 050 00 009
PERSIAN-PERFECT
    AH CHILD, NO PERSIAN-PERFECT ART! • • • • • • 165 00 001
PERSISTENCY
    I NEVER PROMISED SUCH PERSISTENCY • • • • • • 014 01 002
    BUT WITH A SWEET PERSISTENCY • • • • • • • 110 00 005
PERSONAL
    THAT HERE PERSONAL TELLS OFF THESE HEART-SONG POWERFUL PEALS? -- • 141 00 002
PERSUASION
    OF FORC'D PERSUASION ISSUE O'ER THE FREE. -- • • • • 001 05 007
PETALL'D
    APART, BETWIXT TEN THOUSAND PETALL'D LIPS • • • • 002 00 021
PETER
    THE SIMON PETER OF A SOUL! TO THE BLAST • • • • 028 29 007
PHANTASIES
    SPLENDID WITH PHANTASIES AERIAL, • • • • • • 001 08 002
PHANTASY
    'TWIXT REAL HUE AND PHANTASY, • • • • • • • 077 00 122
PHAROH'S
    LIKE PHAROH'S EARS OF WINDY HARVEST DRY • • • • • 117 00 006
PHILIP
    PHILIP TOOK OATH, WHILE GLORY OR DEFEAT • • • • • 001 02 003

PHILIP   (CONTINUED)
    PHILIP, SUPPOSING THAT THE GIFT MOST MEET, ...   001 03 006
PHILOMEL
    IT IS THE WAY WITH PHILOMEL 096 03 003
PHOEBUS
    WHERE PHOEBUS WEEPS FOR HIM WHOM ZEPHYR'S GUILE 001 11 007
    PHOEBUS' LOOSEN'D TRESSES, SWIM! 077 00 102
PHOSPHOR
    WHILE PHOSPHOR, RISEN UPON THE SHALLOWING DARK, ...   098 28 003
PHRENZY
    PHRENZY, BUT EDGED AND CLEAR OF BRAIN 081 00 052
PHRYGIAN
    O IF THERE'S THAT WHICH PHRYGIAN STONE 166 00 041
PICK
    TOM! THEN TOM'S FALLOWBOOTFELLOW PILES PICK 070 00 002
PICKED
    PART WAS PICKED FOR JOHN, ...   054 00 007
PIECE
    HER FLOWER, HER PIECE OF BEING, DOOMED DRAGON FOOD. 050 00 004
    AND THE PIECE THAT'S LIKE A BEAN, ...   086 00 004
    THAT PIECE THEMSELVES INTO A RACE OF DROPS 102 01 033
    AND SLENDER ELEMENT TO PIECE AND PLOT. V 102 03 025
    THIS PIECE OF PERFECT SONG. 148 00 030
    NO PIECE MATCHED THOSE EYES KEPT MOST PART MUCH CAST DOWN   .   .   .   152 02 026
    NOW BE MY PRIDE THEN PERFECT, ALL ONE PIECE. HENCEFORTH   .   .   .   152 02 038
PIECED
    THOSE CROOKED ROUGH-SCORED CHEQUERS MAY BE PIECED 011 00 004
    LANDSCAPE PLOTTED AND PIECED -- FOLD, FALLOW, AND PLOUGH;   .   .   037 00 005
    IN LAKES OF BLUEBELLS, PIECED WITH PRIMROSES. 098 09 003
PIECE-BRIGHT
    THE SHOCKS. THIS PIECE-BRIGHT PALING SHUTS THE SPOUSE   .   .   .   032 00 013
PIECEMEAL
    THAT PIECEMEAL PEACE IS POOR PEACE. WHAT PURE PEACE ALLOWS   .   .   051 00 005
PIECING
    PIECING THE ELEMENTS OUT BY PLAN AND PLOT. 102 03 018
PIED
    OF PIED AND PEELED MAY! 028 26 004
PIERCE
    AND PIERCE THE YELLOW WAXEN LIGHT 015 00 043
    PIERCE HER! SHE HANGS UPON THE FLAME-CASED SUN;   .   .   .   -   .   103 00 010
PIERCED
    NEXT TO MEADOWS ABUNDANT, PIERCED WITH FLOWERS, ...   098 12 002
    POINTED WITH PIERCED LIGHTS, AND BREAKS OF RAYS 098 24 002
PIERCING
    TOLD OFF THEIR LEAVES ALONG THE PIERCING GALE, ...   098 05 002
PIETY
    SO, GROWN FANTASTIC IN HIS PIETY, ...   001 03 005
    WHENCE WITH THE SCOURGE OF READY PIETY 001 05 004
    THE PRIDE OF FAITH, AND HOME OF STERNEST PIETY. 001 08 009
PIGEONS
    I SEE THE CITY PIGEONS VEER, ...   015 00 027
PILASTER'D
    WITH PAINTING GLEAM'D THE RICH PILASTER'D WALLS -- 001 10 003
PILATES
    WOULD I COULD HEAR THE OTHER PILATES SHOUT. 080 01 005
PILE
    THERE IS A MASSY PILE ABOVE THE WASTE 001 01 001
PILED
    AND DAMASQU'D ARMS AND FOLIAG'D CARVING PILED. -- 001 10 002
PILES
    TOM! THEN TOM'S FALLOWBOOTFELLOW PILES PICK 070 00 002
PILGRIMAGES
    HERE TO THIS HOLY WELL SHALL PILGRIMAGES BE, ...   152 C 018
PILGRIMS
    PILGRIMS, STILL PILGRIMS, MORE PILGRIMS, STILL MORE POOR PILGRIMS.   .   152 C 021
    PILGRIMS, STILL PILGRIMS, MORE PILGRIMS, STILL MORE POOR PILGRIMS.   .   152 C 021
    PILGRIMS, STILL PILGRIMS, MORE PILGRIMS, STILL MORE POOR PILGRIMS.   .   152 C 021
    PILGRIMS, STILL PILGRIMS, MORE PILGRIMS, STILL MORE POOR PILGRIMS.   .   152 C 021
PILLARS
    WITH MASSY PILLARS OF THE DORIC MOOD 001 07 002
PILLOWING
    SHE PILLOWING LOW HER LILY NECK 021 00 055
PILLOWS
    TOSSED PILLOWS FLAUNT FORTH, THEN CHEVY ON AN AIR- C   .   .   .   072 00 001
PILLOWY
    PILLOWY AIR HE TREADS A TIME AND HANGS 050 00 010
PIN
    THY IMPALPABLE OPPRESSION. PIN HIM DOWN, ...   102 01 018
PINE
    THEN COME WHO PINE FOR PEACE OR PLEASURE 030 00 037
    WHOM WANT COULD NOT MAKE PINE, PINE 142 00 007
    WHOM WANT COULD NOT MAKE PINE, PINE 142 00 007
PINES
    IN THE QUICK FRAGRANCE OF TALL ROLLING PINES, ...   084 00 005
    AND, SWARTER STILL, THE ROLLING PINES SHOULD CAST 090 00 005
PINING
    PINING, PINING, TILL TIME WHEN REASON RAMBLED IN IT AND SOME   .   .   053 00 003

                            191

193

PLOT   (CONTINUED)
    PIECING THE ELEMENTS OUT BY PLAN AND PLOT. 102 03 018
    AND SLENDER ELEMENT TO PIECE AND PLOT. V 102 03 025
    YOU SPOIL THE PLOT I FIND MY TRUE LOVE BY. 135 00 036
PLOTS
    IN BEDS, IN GARDENS, IN THICK PLOTS I STAND, ... 005 00 037
PLOTTED
    LANDSCAPE PLOTTED AND PIECED -- FOLD, FALLOW, AND PLOUGH; . . 037 00 005
    WITH HIS PULL'D AND PLOTTED LEAF. 098 18 004
    TOOK PRIMROSES, THEIR PULL'D AND PLOTTED LEAF 107 03 018
PLOUGH
    NO WONDER OF IT: SHEER PLOD MAKES PLOUGH DOWN SILLION . . . 036 00 012
    LANDSCAPE PLOTTED AND PIECED -- FOLD, FALLOW, AND PLOUGH; . . 037 00 005
    IN HIM, ALL QUAIL TO THE WALLOWING O' THE PLOUGH. C . . . 071 00 010
    THEY PLOUGH OUR VALES: YOU SEE THE UNSTEADY FLARE 104 00 009
PLUCK
    PLUCK THE HARP AND BREATHE THE HORN: 024 00 011
PLUMAGE
    QUAINT MOONMARKS, TO HIS PELTED PLUMAGE UNDER C 045 00 010
    THE SHAKEN PLUMAGE OF MY SPIRIT'S WINGS. 077 00 010
    GATHER THE SOOTY PLUMAGE FROM DEATH'S WINGS 089 00 006
PLUME
    BRUTE BEAUTY AND VALOUR AND ACT, OH, AIR, PRIDE, PLUME, HERE . 036 00 009
PLUMED
    THE THUNDER-PURPLE SEABEACH PLUMED PURPLE-OF-THUNDER. . . . 045 00 012
    GREAT THECLA, THE PLUMED PASSIONFLOWER, ... 145 00 042
PLUMES
    SLIM-POINTED SEA-GULL PLUMES, AND DROOP BEHIND 002 00 080
    THAT PLUMES TO PEACE THEREAFTER. AND WHEN PEACE HERE DOES HOUSE . 051 00 009
PLUM-PURPLE
    PLUM-PURPLE WAS THE WEST: BUT SPIKES OF LIGHT 002 00 007
PLUMY
    TO COOL HIS PLUMY THROBBING BREAST. 077 00 092
PLUNDER
    NOT THE PLEASURE, THE PAY, THE PLUNDER, ... 156 00 006
PLUNGE
    PLUNGE ORB'D IN RAINBOW ARCS, AND TRAMPLE AND TREAD . . . 002 00 078
PLUNGING
    TO KEEP THE LOADED BOLT FROM PLUNGING BACK. 135 00 006
PLUSH-CAPPED
    WORD LAST! HOW A LUSH-KEPT PLUSH-CAPPED SLOE 028 08 003
PLUSHY
    THAT WANT THE YIELD OF PLUSHY SWARD. 022 00 022
PLY
    BY THAT WINDOW WHAT TASK WHAT FINGERS PLY, ... 046 00 005
    PLY FOLD ON FOLD ACROSS HIS DANGEROUS EYES, ... 102 01 019
POCKET
    LIKE THAT POOR POCKET OF PENCE, POOR PENCE OF MINE. . . . 142 00 009
POET
    A BOY FEELS WHEN THE POET HE PORES UPON 014 03 013
    NO: WHAT THE POET DID WRITE RAN. 147 00 005
POETRY
    POETRY TO IT, AS A TREE WHOSE BOUGHS BREAK IN THE SKY. . . 149 A 003
POETS
    AS POETS SING: OR THAT IT IS A PAIN 002 00 121
POINT
    THE POINT FAST IN, AND MY LEFT HAND 080 13 004
    AND TO MY PALM THE POINT APPLY, ... 080 14 002
    TO THE POINT OF SILENCE IN THE AIR 135 00 032
POINTED
    OF POINTED WING AND SILVER STOLE; 077 00 012
    POINTED WITH PIERCED LIGHTS, AND BREAKS OF RAYS 098 24 002
POINTING
    AND FOLIAG'D CROWNALS (POINTING HOW THE WAYS 001 06 004
POINTS
    I GATHER POINTS OF LOTE-FLOWER FROM AN ISLE 005 00 033
POISE
    THE SUMPTUOUS RIDGE-CREST LEAVE TO POISE AND RIDE. 012 02 008
    I STEADY AS A WATER IN A WELL, TO A POISE, TO A PANE, . . 028 04 005
POISED
    ONCE ENCOUNTER IN, HERE COPED AND POISED POWERS: 044 00 004
    HE SWUNG TO HIS FIRST POISED PURPORT OF REPLY. 047 00 004
POISING
    THY UNCHANCELLING POISING PALMS WERE WEIGHING THE WORTH, . . 028 21 006
POLE
    NOT SO FAR FROM THE POLE. 088 00 008
    NOT SO FAR FROM THE POLE. V 088 00 012
POMP
    THAN CHANGEFUL POMP OF COURTS IS AYE MORE WONDERFUL. . . . 001 15 009
POMPEII
    AT RED POMPEII ON MEDALLION'D WALLS. 002 00 051
POND
    THAT STILL MAKES COUNTER-ROUNDELS IN THE POND. 107 03 005
PONDEROUS
    TO KNOW THE DUSK DEPTHS OF THE PONDEROUS SEA, ... 002 00 122
POOL
    BUT HERE AT, HERE AT PENMAEN POOL? 030 00 004

POOL   (CONTINUED)
    COME, SWING THE SCULLS ON PENMAEN POOL. 030 00 008
    TO HALVE THE BOWL OF PENMAEN POOL. 030 00 012
    IN FRANK, IN FAIRY PENMAEN POOL. 030 00 016
    SHEW BRIGHTER SHAKEN IN PENMAEN POOL. 030 00 020
    WAYLAY HER AT EBB, PAST PENMAEN POOL. 030 00 024
    THAT LACE THE FACE OF PENMAEN POOL. 030 00 028
    FROM DARKSOME DARKSOME PENMAEN POOL. 030 00 032
    THAT FROCKS AN OAR IN PENMAEN POOL. 030 00 036
    AND TASTE THE TREATS OF PENMAEN POOL. 030 00 040
    OF A POOL SO PITCHBLACK, FELL-FROWNING, ...   056 00 007
    OF YESTERTEMPEST'S CREASES; IN POOL AND RUTPEEL PARCHES   .   .   072 00 006
    FALLING ALONG THE BREAKLESS POOL OF AIR, ...   122 00 009
    THAT HE HIES TO A POOL NEIGHBOURING; SEES IT IS THE BEST   .   .   159 00 022
POOLS
    THE SAPPHIRE POOLS ARE SMIT WITH WHITE 078 00 007
POOR
    THEN FAIL'D THE TONGUE; THE POOR COLLAPSING FRAME,   .   .   .   001 03 003
    FOR POOR LOVE'S FAILURE THAN HIS HOPELESS RISE. 014 03 007
    FROM FURROWS OF THE POOR AND STINTING WEALD. 017 00 013
    RECK NOT WHAT THE POOR HAVE LOST; 024 00 004
    STARTLE THE POOR SHEEP BACK! IS THE SHIPWRACK THEN A HARVEST, C   028 31 008
    THOUGH ALOFT ON TURF OR PERCH OR POOR LOW STAGE,   .   .   .   039 00 005
    HE HAS LOST COUNT WHAT CAME NEXT, POOR BOY. -- 041 00 072
    THAT PIECEMEAL PEACE IS POOR PEACE. WHAT PURE PEACE ALLOWS   .   051 00 005
    THY TEARS THAT TOUCHED MY HEART, CHILD, FELIX, POOR FELIX RANDAL;   053 00 011
    SOUL, SELF; COME, POOR JACKSELF, I DO ADVISE 069 00 009
    THIS JACK, JOKE, POOR POTSHERD, PATCH, MATCHWOOD, IMMORTAL DIAMOND,   072 00 023
    AND THE POOR CORSE IMPALE WITH IT AND FRAY 089 00 007
    ' SOME ARE PRETTY ENOUGH, AND SOME ARE POOR INDEED. '   .   .   098 15 004
    I HEARD HER SAY, POOR POOR AFFLICTED SOUL, -- 111 00 011
    I HEARD HER SAY, POOR POOR AFFLICTED SOUL, -- 111 00 011
    THE COUNTRY SONG OF WILLOW. ' THE POOR SOUL --   .   .   .   111 00 013
    LIKE THAT POOR POCKET OF PENCE, POOR PENCE OF MINE,   .   .   142 00 009
    LIKE THAT POOR POCKET OF PENCE, POOR PENCE OF MINE,   .   .   142 00 009
    ' WHAT, TERYTH! WHAT, THOU POOR FOND FATHER! C   .   .   .   152 01 016
    PILGRIMS, STILL PILGRIMS, MORE PILGRIMS, STILL MORE POOR PILGRIMS.   152 C 021
POPPIES
    AND CRUSH-SILK POPPIES AFLASH, ...   138 00 021
PORE
    THAT A QUINCE I PORE UPON? 025 00 019
    CAT. THAT A QUINCE WE PORE UPON?   .   .   .   .   APPEN A 19
PORES
    UNBAKES MY PORES, AND STREAMS, AND MAKES ALL FRESH,   .   .   .   005 00 032
    A BOY FEELS WHEN THE POET HE PORES UPON 014 03 013
    WHO LIES ON GRASS AND PORES UPON THE SKY 117 00 003
PORTENDING
    US; FRESH YOUTH FRETTED IN A BLOOMFALL ALL PORTENDING   .   .   048 00 030
PORTENDS
    ARE AFOOT; HEAVEN-VAULT FAST PURPLING PORTENDS, C   .   .   .   152 02 031
PORTHOLES
    DEATH TEEMING IN BY HER PORTHOLES 041 00 039
PORTION
    HE HAS HIS PORTION. GOD, WHO STRETCH'D APART 126 00 002
PORTS
    THY RIBBED PORTS, O DEATH 115 00 005
POSSESSED
    A NOISE OF FALLS I AM POSSESSED BY 121 00 001
POST
    AND WITH THE LAST POST OVER I KNEW NO LETTER WAS SENT.   .   .   128 00 002
POSTS
    ENRICHED POSTS ARE CHAMFER'D; EVERYWHERE 096 07 003
    AND ALL WITHIN THE HOUSE WERE SOUND AS POSTS, ...   135 00 017
POSTUR'D
    THEN LAVER'D FOUNTS AND POSTUR'D STONE HE MIX'D.   .   .   .   001 04 005
POT
    BUT NOW BEFORE THE POT CAN GLOW 015 00 013
POTENT
    WITH POTENT LIPS CALL DOWN CEMENTED TOWERS; 104 00 005
POTENTIAL
    WITH JUST SUCH SWEET POTENTIAL SKILL, ...   081 00 020
POTSHERD
    THIS JACK, JOKE, POOR POTSHERD, PATCH, MATCHWOOD, IMMORTAL DIAMOND,   072 00 023
POUR
    IN CRISPS OF CURL OFF WILD WINCH WHIRL, AND POUR   .   .   .   035 00 007
POURTRAY'D
    POURTRAY'D ALONG THE FRIEZE WITH TITAN'S BROOD 001 07 004
POVERTY
    AND, POVERTY, BE THOU THE BRIDE 022 00 025
POWER
    THAT BEAT AND BREATHE IN POWER -- 049 00 011
    WHOSE PRESENCE, POWER IS 060 00 026
    MISS STORY HAS A MODERATE POWER OF WILL, ...   094 00 009
    THAT LEVEL POWER WHOSE WORD IS MUST 166 00 014
    AND EVERY POWER IN US THAT IS 169 00 008
    AGAINST THY POWER PUT UNDER FEET 169 00 009
POWERFUL
    WHEN THOU AT THE RANDOM GRIM FORGE, POWERFUL AMIDST PEERS,   .   .   053 00 013

```
POWERFUL      (CONTINUED)
    THAT HERE PERSONAL TELLS OFF THESE HEART-SONG POWERFUL PEALS? --  •   •    141 00 002
POWERLESS
    MORE POWERLESS THAN THE BLIND OR LAME.  •   •   •   •   •   •   •   •    015 00 020
POWERS
    ONCE ENCOUNTER IN, HERE COPED AND POISED POWERS;   •   •   •   •    044 00 004
    HIS POWERS SEEMED FREE TO PLAY;   •   •   •   •   •   •   •   •    148 00 014
PRAISE
    THE PRAISE OF THE LIPS AND THE HEARTS OF US BRING TO THEE,   •   •    026 00 035
    THEE, OH MAIDEN, MOST WORTHY OF PRAISE;   •   •   •   •   •    026 00 036
    PRAISE HIM.  •   •   •   •   •   •   •   •   •   •   •   •    037 00 011
    NOW BUT TO BREATHE ITS PRAISE.   •   •   •   •   •   •   •   •    060 00 015
    CATCH SUNLIGHT AND ONE STRAIN OF STUPID PRAISE.   •   •   •   •    098 32 002
    FLATTERY'S ALL OUT OF PLACE WHERE PRAISE IS TRUE.   •   •   •   •    125 00 030
    MISSING PROSPERITY AND PRAISE.   •   •   •   •   •   •   •   •    133 00 015
PRAISED
    AND EVERY PRAISED SEQUENCE OF SWEET STRINGS,   •   •   •   •    019 00 007
    HE PRAISED THE LOVELY LOT OF CONTINENCE;   •   •   •   •   •    136 00 028
PRAISES
    MINGLE PRAISES, PRAYER AND SONG,   •   •   •   •   •   •   •    024 00 027
PRAIS'D
    FOR THAT STAUNCH SAINT STILL PRAIS'D HIS MASTER'S NAME   •   •   •    001 03 001
PRANKED
    ON PRANKED SCALE; OR THREADS OF CARMINE, SHOT   •   •   •   •    002 00 106
PRAY
    MY PRAYERS I SCARCELY CALL TO PRAY.   •   •   •   •   •   •    018 00 004
    PATIENCE, HARD THING! THE HARD THING BUT TO PRAY,   •   •   •   •    068 00 001
    ' I PRAY YOU TELL TO ME.  '   •   •   •   •   •   •   •   •    109 25 004
    NOT HOPE, NOT PRAY; DESPAIR; AY, THAT; BRAZEN DESPAIR OUT,   •   •    152 02 067
    AND I PRAY THE PRAYER OF THE DYING THIEF.   •   •   •   •   •    168 00 012
    PRAY FOR US TO HIM THAT HE   •   •   •   •   •   •   •   •    APPEN D 43
PRAYER
    BATTLING WITH GOD, IS NOW MY PRAYER.   •   •   •   •   •   •    018 00 016
    OUR PRAYER SEEMS LOST IN DESERT WAYS.   •   •   •   •   •   •    023 00 005
    MINGLE PRAISES, PRAYER AND SONG,   •   •   •   •   •   •   •    024 00 027
    THE APPEALING OF THE PASSION IS TENDERER IN PRAYER APART;   •   •    028 27 006
    BUY THEN! BID THEN! -- WHAT? -- PRAYER, PATIENCE, ALMS, VOWS,   •    032 00 009
    AND THE PRAYER THOU HEARST ME MAKING   •   •   •   •   •   •    041 00 113
    PRAYER SHALL FETCH PITY ETERNAL   •   •   •   •   •   •   •    041 00 120
    PRAYER GO DISREGARDED;   •   •   •   •   •   •   •   •   •    048 00 047
    OF PATIENCE, PENANCE, PRAYER;   •   •   •   •   •   •   •   •    060 00 123
    SHE HELD HER HANDS TO, LIKE IN PRAYER;   •   •   •   •   •   •    145 00 048
    AND I PRAY THE PRAYER OF THE DYING THIEF.   •   •   •   •   •    168 00 012
PRAYERS
    MY PRAYERS MUST MEET A BRAZEN HEAVEN   •   •   •   •   •   •    018 00 001
    MY PRAYERS I SCARCELY CALL TO PRAY.   •   •   •   •   •   •    018 00 004
    HER PRAYERS HIS PROVIDENCE;   •   •   •   •   •   •   •   •    060 00 041
PRAYING
    WHICH PRAYING FAILS TO DO AWAY.   •   •   •   •   •   •   •    018 00 012
PRAYS
    TO THEE THE TREMBLING SINNER PRAYS   •   •   •   •   •   •    023 00 003
PREACHINGS
    HERCLOT'S PREACHINGS I'LL NO LONGER HEAR;   •   •   •   •   •    096 05 001
PRECEDENTS
    I RECKON PRECEDENTS OF LOVE,   •   •   •   •   •   •   •   •    018 00 007
PRECIOUS
    FIVE WAYS THE PRECIOUS BRANCHES TORN;   •   •   •   •   •   •    006 00 014
    PRECIOUS PASSING MEASURE,   •   •   •   •   •   •   •   •   •    041 00 011
    AND NOW I GET SOME PRECIOUS SLIPS.   •   •   •   •   •   •   •    081 00 084
    THOUGH ILL-CONTENTED, PRECIOUS PRECIOUS FLORIS,   •   •   •   •    102 01 053
    THOUGH ILL-CONTENTED, PRECIOUS PRECIOUS FLORIS,   •   •   •   •    102 01 053
PRECIPICE
    OR FRAY A GRANITE FROM THE PRECIPICE;   •   •   •   •   •   •    080 12 005
PRECISELY
    NOW MORE PRECISELY TOUCHED IN LIGHT AND GLOOM,   •   •   •   •    098 30 004
PRECISION
    IN MORE PRECISION NOW OF LIGHT AND DARK   •   •   •   •   •    098 30 001
PREDILUVIAN
    COULD COUNT ON PREDILUVIAN AGE,   •   •   •   •   •   •   •    015 00 010
PREEMINENT
    A STAR MOST SPIRITUAL, PRINCIPAL, PREEMINENT   •   •   •   •    098 27 001
PREENED
    ' BOUGHS BEING PRUNED, BIRDS PREENED, SHOW MORE FAIR;   •   •   •    096 07 001
PREFERENCE
    I OWN A PREFERENCE FOR PRIDE.   •   •   •   •   •   •   •   •    096 01 004
PREFERRED
    AND KNOW INFALLIBLY WHICH I PREFERRED.   •   •   •   •   •   •    019 00 008
    BUT THAT SWEET SOUND WHICH I PREFERRED,   •   •   •   •   •   •    021 00 047
PREJUDICE
    IT DOES NO PREJUDICE.   •   •   •   •   •   •   •   •   •   •    060 00 082
PRENATAL
    LOVE BY PRENATAL SERFDOM STILL CONFINED   •   •   •   •   •   •    102 03 015
PREPARE
    THE VERY VICTIM WOULD PREPARE.   •   •   •   •   •   •   •   •    145 00 008
PRESCRIPTIVE
    NO, LOVE PRESCRIPTIVE, LOVE WITH PLACE ASSIGN'D,   •   •   •   •    102 03 013
PRESENCE
    WHOSE PRESENCE, POWER IS   •   •   •   •   •   •   •   •   •    060 00 026
```

PRESENT
    WORDING IT HOW BUT BY HIM THAT PRESENT AND PAST, ... 028 29 005
    APPEAR'D NOT FOR THE PRESENT, TILL 092 00 008
PRESENTED
    UNSOUGHT, PRESENTED SO EASILY, C 137 00 006
PRESS
    A PRESS OF WINGED THINGS COMES DOWN THIS WAY; 005 00 015
    THE WINE WAS RACKED FROM THE PRESS; 006 00 018
    TOO PROUD, TOO PROUD, WHAT A PRESS SHE BORE! 041 00 033
    AND PRESS IT DOWN, ON EITHER SIDE A BONE, ... 080 14 003
    OF THE PRESS OF ROSES. 098 19 008
    OF ALL THE GOLDEN PRESS. 098 27 002
    TO ALL THE STARRY PRESS. -- 098 28 006
    THEY SEEMED TO PRESS AND STARE 098 29 002
    THEY SEEM TO PRESS AND DROOP AND STARE, ... 135 00 020
PRESSED
    WITH THE SWEETEST AIR THAT SAID, STILL PLIED AND PRESSED, . . 047 00 003
    AND PRESSED VIOLETS IN THE FOLDS APPEAR, ... 119 00 004
    PRESSED TO DEATH. HE PLANTS THE YEAR; 145 00 004
PRESSURE
    OF THE GOSPEL PROFFER, A PRESSURE, A PRINCIPLE, CHRIST'S GIFT. . 028 04 008
PRETEND
    AND I'LL PRETEND THE CREDIT GIVEN OF YORE; 014 02 003
PRETTY
    ' SOME ARE PRETTY ENOUGH, AND SOME ARE POOR INDEED. ' . . . 098 15 004
    BACKWARD ARE LAID HER PRETTY BLACK-FLEECED EARS; . . . 099 00 013
    AND MILLBROOK-SLIPS WITH PRETTY PACE 130 00 025
PREY
    INTO MY HAND HE GIVES A HOST FOR PREY, ... 005 00 017
    AND THEY THE PREY OF THE GALES; 028 24 004
PRICE
    HERE ARE SWEET MESSES WITHOUT PRICE OR WORTH, ... 005 00 047
PRICED
    BEFORE-TIME-TAKEN, DEAREST PRIZED AND PRICED -- . . . 028 22 006
PRICK
    BUT A PRICK WILL MAKE NO EYE AT ALL, ... 043 00 015
PRICKPROOF
    SELDOMER HEARTSORE; THAT TREADS THROUGH, PRICKPROOF, THICK . . 070 00 007
PRIDE
    THE PRIDE OF FAITH, AND HOME OF STERNEST PIETY, ... 001 08 009
    UPON THE STIR AND KEEP OF PRIDE, ... 022 00 018
    AND FIVE-LIVED AND LEAVED FAVOUR AND PRIDE, ... 028 23 006
    LET HIM RIDE, HER PRIDE, IN HIS TRIUMPH, C 028 28 008
    PRIDE, ROSE, PRINCE, HERO OF US, HIGH-PRIEST, ... 028 35 007
    BEING PURE! WE, LIFE'S PRIDE AND CARED-FOR CROWN, . . . 035 00 011
    BRUTE BEAUTY AND VALOUR AND ACT, OH, AIR, PRIDE, PLUME, HERE . 036 00 009
    FOR DID SHE PRIDE HER, FREIGHTED FULLY, ON 041 00 009
    THIS PRIDE OF PRIME'S ENJOYMENT 049 00 012
    AND PRIDE IS NERVELESS AND HEARTS MEEK. 077 00 038
    I OWN A PREFERENCE FOR PRIDE. 096 01 004
    NOW BE MY PRIDE THEN PERFECT, ALL ONE PIECE. HENCEFORTH . . 152 02 038
PRIME
    ' I MARK THE FLOWERS ERE THE PRIME 004 00 014
    HAVE LOST THAT CHEER AND CHARM OF EARTH'S PAST PRIME; . . 035 00 012
    BUT THE LILY IS PAST, AS I SAY, AND THE ROSE IS NOT IN ITS PRIME; . 128 00 014
PRIME'S
    THIS PRIDE OF PRIME'S ENJOYMENT 049 00 012
PRIMROSE
    WERE EYES OF CENTRAL PRIMROSE; BLUEBELLS RAN . . . 098 10 002
    AND PRIMROSE BRING, AND MAKE A SHEAF 098 18 003
PRIMROSES
    IN LAKES OF BLUEBELLS, PIECED WITH PRIMROSES. . . . 098 09 003
    TOOK PRIMROSES, THEIR PULL'D AND PLOTTED LEAF . . . 107 03 018
    BEING NOT FORGOTTEN, FOR PRIMROSES NOTE 107 03 019
    AS SURE AS WHAT IS MOST SURE, SURE AS THAT SPRING PRIMROSES . 152 C 027
PRINCE
    TO NEWBORN PRINCE, AND ROYAL CORSE INANIMATE. . . . 001 04 009
    LIKE AN ASSYRIAN PRINCE, WITH BUDS UNSHEATH'D . . . 002 00 062
    PRIDE, ROSE, PRINCE, HERO OF US, HIGH-PRIEST, . . . 028 35 007
PRINCELY
    NOW LET ME SEE YOU, YOU LARGE PRINCELY HAND, . . . 102 01 043
PRINCES
    PRINCES STRONG FOR THE SWORD AND SLAUGHTER, ... 026 00 027
PRINCIPAL
    WASTE: HER EARLIEST STARS, EARLSTARS, STARS PRINCIPAL, OVERBEND US, . 061 00 004
    A STAR MOST SPIRITUAL, PRINCIPAL, PREEMINENT 098 27 001
    LIKE SCALDED BANKS TOPP'D ONCE WITH PRINCIPAL FLOWERS; . . 102 02 012
PRINCIPLE
    OF THE GOSPEL PROFFER, A PRESSURE, A PRINCIPLE, CHRIST'S GIFT. . 028 04 008
PRINT
    THAT WILL NOT WEAR A PRINT, THAT WILL NOT STAIN A PEN, . . 152 C 016
PRISM
    MOST LIKE THOSE HUES THAT IN THE PRISM 077 00 061
PRISON
    A VEIN FOR THE VISITING OF THE PAST-PRAYER, PENT IN PRISON, . . 028 33 005
    BUT HIS OWN NEST, WILD NEST, NO PRISON. 039 00 011
PRIVACY
    AS PUBLIC IS MY GREATER PRIVACY, ... 012 01 007

PRIZE
    AH WELL! IT IS ALL A PURCHASE, ALL IS A PRIZE. 032 00 008
    DULY, DEAR LORD, MY PRIZE IS WON. 081 00 109
    I MUST HUNT DOWN THE PRIZE 088 00 001
    AS BY AND BY OUR PRIZE ART THOU, ... 167 00 026
PRIZED
    BEFORE-TIME-TAKEN, DEAREST PRIZED AND PRICED -- 028 22 006
    WHERE WHATEVER'S PRIZED AND PASSES OF US, C 059 06 008
    THIS WAS THE PRIZED, THE DESIRABLE SIGHT, C 137 00 006
PROCESSION
    WARN'D BY THE BRIGHT PROCESSION OF THE STARS. 102 01 056
PROCONSUL
    PROCONSUL! -- IS SAPRICIUS NEAR? -- 025 00 041
    THEO. PROCONSUL, -- CALL HIM NEAR -- . . . . APPEN A 47
PRODIGAL
  SPREAD O'ER THE SWART FACE OF THIS PRODIGAL EARTH. . . . 005 00 045
PROFESS
  AH! SURELY ALL WHO HAVE WRITTEN WILL PROFESS 117 00 008
PROFFER
  OF THE GOSPEL PROFFER, A PRESSURE, A PRINCIPLE, CHRIST'S GIFT. . 028 04 008
PROFIT
  THUS WE SHALL PROFIT, WHILE GOLD COINAGE STILL 096 07 007
PROFOUND
  THE MILES PROFOUND OF SOLID GREEN, AND BE 002 00 123
PROMISE
  OR FAR-OFF PROMISE OF A TIME TO BE; 013 00 004
  THAT HOLDS NO PROMISE OF SUCCESS; 015 00 034
  WHICH MAKES SO SMALL THE PROMISE OF THAT YIELD 017 00 011
  AND THE PROMISE OF SUMMER WITHIN HER BREAST! 026 00 016
PROMISED
  I NEVER PROMISED SUCH PERSISTENCY 014 01 002
  BUT IS NOT THAT MY GRIEVANCE -- YOU PROMISED AND YOU FORGOT? . 128 00 006
PROMISES
  AND HAPPY PROMISES FULFILL'D. 015 00 008
PROOF
  NO FINISH'D PROOF WAS THIS OF GOTHIC GRACE 001 06 001
  MUST YOU BE GORGED WITH PROOF? DID EVER SAND 005 00 041
  FOLDS OFF ALOOF, THAT SIGNAL IS AND PROOF 080 06 003
PROPER
  OR ONCE OR NEVER TOOK LOVE'S PROPER FOOD; 020 00 010
  THE PROPER SWEET RE-ATTRIBUTING ABOVE. V 113 00 011
  IT IS HARDLY A PROPER TREAT FOR A BIRTHDAY TO REST IN HER ARMS. . 128 00 012
PROPHETESS
  A PROPHETESS TOWERED IN THE TUMULT, A VIRGINAL TONGUE TOLD. . . 028 17 008
PROPORTION
  THAT THOU HADST BORNE PROPORTION IN MY BLISS, ... 013 00 006
PROSPER
  WHY DO SINNERS' WAYS PROSPER? AND WHY MUST 074 00 003
PROSPERITY
  MISSING PROSPERITY AND PRAISE, ... 133 00 015
PROSPEROUSLY-BOD
  RAVENS, FOR PROSPEROUSLY-BODED CURSES 089 00 003
PROUD
  OH THOU, PROUD MOTHER AND MUCH PROUD MAIDEN -- . . . 026 00 019
  OH THOU, PROUD MOTHER AND MUCH PROUD MAIDEN -- . . . 026 00 019
  TOO PROUD, TOO PROUD, WHAT A PRESS SHE BORE! . . . 041 00 033
  TOO PROUD, TOO PROUD, WHAT A PRESS SHE BORE! . . . 041 00 033
  NOT MOOD IN HIM NOR MEANING, PROUD FIRE OR SACRED FEAR, . . 045 00 005
  SINCE, PROUD, IT CALLS THE CALLING MANLY, GIVES A GUESS . . 063 00 004
PROUDER
  ING BLOOD -- THE O-SEAL-THAT-SO FEATURE, FLUNG PROUDER FORM . . 062 00 002
PROUDEST
  A CLOISTER'D CONVENT FIRST, THE PROUDEST HOME 001 01 006
PROVE
  AND LET HIM PROVE MY PASSION WAS BEGUN 014 02 004
  I PROVE IT. WHAT THEN WHEN THESE LINES ARE DEAD . . . 117 00 011
  IF HE WOULD PROVE 127 00 016
PROVERB
  YOU HAVE MADE ME QUOTE ALMOST THE DISMALEST PROVERB I KNOW; . . 128 00 018
PROVIDE
  AND LILY-COLOURED CLOTHES PROVIDE 022 00 027
PROVIDENCE
  NO NOT UNCOMFORTED: LOVELY-FELICITOUS PROVIDENCE . . . 028 31 005
  HER PRAYERS HIS PROVIDENCE; 060 00 041
PRUDENCE
  PRUDENCE SHE HAS, BUT WISE SHE'LL NEVER BE; 094 00 024
PRUNED
  ' BOUGHS BEING PRUNED, BIRDS PREENED, SHOW MORE FAIR; . . 096 07 001
PSALM
  GOD, THOUGH TO THEE OUR PSALM WE RAISE 023 00 001
PUBLIC
  AS PUBLIC IS MY GREATER PRIVACY, ... 012 01 007
PULL
  DID YOU PULL IT IN THE KING'S GARDEN 109 33 003
  ' I DID NOT PULL IT IN KING'S GARDEN 109 34 001
  THE SKY IS BLUE, AND THE WINDS PULL 130 00 022
PULL'D
  WITH HIS PULL'D AND PLOTTED LEAF. 098 18 004

QUARTER   (CONTINUED)
    FOR A QUARTER OF AN HOUR OR SO 145 00 059
QUARTZ-FRET
    QUARTZ-FRET, OR SPARKS OF SALT, ... 060 00 101
QUEEN
    SALUTE THEE, MOTHER, THE MAID-MONTH'S QUEEN! 026 00 024
    SHE PLEASED THE QUEEN AND COUNCIL, SO 145 00 034
QUELL
    THE BREAST'S DESPONDING SOB I QUELL! 023 00 038
    THOSE SWEET HOPES QUELL WHOSE LEAST ME QUICKENINGS LIFT, . . . 048 00 037
QUELLED
    MY ASPENS DEAR, WHOSE AIRY CAGES QUELLED, ... 043 00 001
    QUELLED OR QUENCHED IN LEAVES THE LEAPING SUN, ... 043 00 002
QUENCH
    BUT QUENCH HER BONNIEST, DEAREST TO HER, HER CLEAREST-SELVED SPARK . 072 00 010
    TO QUENCH THE FINE-DRAWN CATARACT! 077 00 090
QUENCHED
    O SHOULD IT THEN BE QUENCHED NOT? 010 00 016
    IS IT QUENCHED OR NOT? 025 00 016
    QUELLED OR QUENCHED IN LEAVES THE LEAPING SUN, ... 043 00 002
    MY TONGUE HAD TAUGHT THEE COMFORT, TOUCH HAD QUENCHED THY TEARS, . . 053 00 010
    BREATHES ONCE AND, QUENCHED FASTER THAN IT CAME, ... 076 00 003
    WHEN ITS LIGHT I QUENCHED! ITS ROSE, TIME'S ONE RICH ROSE, MY HAND, . 152 02 050
    ANG.   HOW ARE THEY QUENCHED NOT? -- . . . . APPEN A 16
QUENCHING
    STANCHING QUENCHING OCEAN OF A MOTIONABLE MIND! 028 32 005
QUENCH'D
    THE FLOATING BLOOMS AND WITH TIDE FLOWING QUENCH'D 002 00 139
QUEST
    BE THIS THY QUEST OR OTHER, SEE 160 00 026
QUESTION
    ERE I HAD FURTHER QUESTION MADE 004 00 016
    QUESTION: WHAT IS SPRING? -- 042 00 015
QUESTIONING
    QUESTIONING WINDS AROUND THE HILLS! 077 00 044
QUESTS
    ALL QUESTS SAVE THE RECITAL OF THEIR GREATNESS! 104 00 003
QUICK
    IN THE QUICK FRAGRANCE OF TALL ROLLING PINES, ... 084 00 005
    WITHIN HER WOMB THE CHILD WAS QUICK. 145 00 039
    LIFE'S QUICK, THIS KIND, THIS KEEN SELF-FEELING, ... 152 02 063
QUICKEN
    NOW QUICKEN, SHEATHED IN THE YELLOW GALAXY. 098 22 003
QUICKENINGS
    THOSE SWEET HOPES QUELL WHOSE LEAST ME QUICKENINGS LIFT, . . . 048 00 037
QUICKGOLD
    THE GREY LAWNS COLD WHERE GOLD, WHERE QUICKGOLD LIES! . . . 032 00 005
QUICKLY
    WAS CALLING ' O CHRIST, CHRIST, COME QUICKLY ' : 028 24 007
    BREATHE IN SUCH ETHER? OR THE QUICKLY ELMS 100 00 007
QUICKSILVERY
    FILLETED WITH GLASSY GRASSY QUICKSILVERY SHIVES AND SHOOTS C . . 159 00 038
QUIET-WALLED
    THE TOWERS MUSICAL, QUIET-WALLED GROVE, ... 012 01 010
QUILL
    OUR SWANS ARE NOW OF SUCH REMORSELESS QUILL, ... 096 02 001
QUILLS
    WITH SPIKED QUILLS ALL OF INTENSEST HUE! 002 00 044
QUILS
    -- AND ON THEIR BRITTLE GREEN QUILS 098 07 001
QUINCE
    AND A QUINCE IN HAND, -- NOT ONE 010 00 009
    HAD SHE A QUINCE IN HAND? YET GAZE! 010 00 019
    THAT A QUINCE I PORE UPON? 025 00 019
    CAT.   THAT A QUINCE WE PORE UPON? . . . . APPEN A 19
QUINCES
    QUINCES, LOOK, WHEN NOT ONE 025 00 009
    ANG.   QUINCES, LOOK, WHEN NOT ONE . . . . APPEN A 09
QUIT
    A FLUKE YET FANGED HIM, ENTANGLED HIM, NOT QUIT UTTERLY. C . . 137 00 005
QUITE
    RICH BEAMS, TILL DEATH OR DISTANCE BUYS THEM QUITE. . . . 040 00 008
    SELF IN SELF STEEPED AND PASHED -- QUITE C 061 00 006
    TO HOLD ME QUITE FIX'D IN THE SELFSAME PLIGHT! 080 13 006
    HIS STEADY WHEEL QUITE TO THE FULL AGAIN. 107 03 012
    GUILTY OF SILENCE? QUITE, AS LADIES GO. 125 00 023
    AND THESE ARE SPENT AND ENDED QUITE! 130 00 021
    THE BURLY SEA MAY QUITE FORGET 166 00 026
QUITS
    CLIMB QUITS! ONE BOARDS THE MASTER THERE 166 00 038
QUIVERING
    A QUIVERING PENNON! THEN, FOR EYE TOO KEEN, ... 002 00 017
QUOTE
    AND TAUGHT MY LIPS TO QUOTE THIS WORD 008 00 006
    YOU MAY QUOTE WORDSWORTH, IF YOU LIKE, TO ME. ' 107 03 008
    YOU HAVE MADE ME QUOTE ALMOST THE DISMALEST PROVERB I KNOW! . . 128 00 018

RABBLE
    FELL ON THE PALACE, AND THE LUST OF RABBLE RUDE,) • • • • • 001 14 009
    NIGHT ROARED, WITH THE HEART-BREAK HEARING A HEART-BROKE RABBLE, • • 028 17 005
    BRAVE ALL, AND TAKE WHAT COMES -- AS HERE THIS RABBLE IS COME, • • 152 02 068
RACE
    THE RIVING OFF THAT RACE • • • • • • • • 041 00 099
    RUN ALL YOUR RACE, O BRACE STERNER THAT STRAIN! • • • • 047 00 014
    THAT DOES NOW REACH OUR RACE -- • • • • • • 060 00 023
    THAT PIECE THEMSELVES INTO A RACE OF DROPS • • • • 102 01 033
    THE RACE OF MAN! AND HENCE I FELL. • • • • • 160 00 031
RACED
    RACED DOWN DECKS, ROUND MESSES OF MORTALS. • • • • 041 00 040
    THEM -- BROAD IN BLUFF HIDE HIS FROWNING FEET LASHED! RACED • • 071 00 013
RACING
    WITH RICHNESS! THE RACING LAMBS TOO HAVE FAIR THEIR FLING. • • 033 00 008
    HE SHOOK WITH RACING NOTES THE STANDING AIR. • • • 098 38 001
RACK
    HACK AND RACK THE GROWING GREEN! • • • • • • 043 00 011
    FOR, WRUNG ALL ON LOVE'S RACK, • • • • • • 054 00 017
    THY RIVER, AND O'ER GIVES ALL TO RACK OR WRONG. • • • 058 00 008
    THESE TWO TELL, EACH OFF THE OTHER; OF A RACK C • • • 061 00 013
    BREATHED ROUND! THE RACK OF RIBS! THE SCOOPED FLANK! LANK • • 071 00 002
RACKED
    THE WINE WAS RACKED FROM THE PRESS; • • • • • 006 00 018
RADIANCE
    WERE LIMN'D ABOUT WITH RADIANCE RARE • • • • • 077 00 060
RAFTS
    BY, RAFTS AND RAFTS OF FLAKE LEAVES LIGHT, C • • • • 159 00 025
    BY, RAFTS AND RAFTS OF FLAKE LEAVES LIGHT, C • • • • 159 00 025
RAGE
    OR WRING THEIR BARRIERS IN BURSTS OF FEAR OR RAGE. • • • 039 00 008
    THIS, BY DESPAIR, BRED HANGDOG DULL; BY RAGE, • • • 070 00 019
RAGING
    HIS INJURY SHE'LL AVENGE WITH RAGING SHAME. • • • • 082 00 006
RAIL
    THE FLANGE AND THE RAIL; FLAME, • • • • • • 028 11 002
RAIN
    ADOWN THE CLATTERING GULLIES SWEPT THE RAIN! • • • 001 13 002
    ' A CRIMSON EAST, THAT BIDS FOR RAIN. • • • • 021 00 008
    THEY RAIN AGAINST OUR MUCH-THICK AND MARSH AIR • • 040 00 007
    MINE, O THOU LORD OF LIFE, SEND MY ROOTS RAIN. • • 074 00 014
    ON THE TUMBLINGS OF THE RAIN, • • • • • 077 00 104
    MY TEARS ARE BUT A CLOUD OF RAIN; • • • • 081 00 036
    AND RAVELL'D INTO STRINGS OF RAIN. • • • • 081 00 057
    -- NOW THE RAIN, • • • • • • 098 06 00!
    WHILE THERE IS NEITHER SUN NOR RAIN! • • • • 105 00 006
    TO THESE CASTARA IS RAIN OR BREEZE OR SPRING, • • 125 00 048
    FOLLOWING FALLS AND FALLS OF RAIN. • • • • 142 00 003
RAINBOW
    PLUNGE ORB'D IN RAINBOW ARCS, AND TRAMPLE AND TREAD • 002 00 078
    FOR A RAINBOW FOOTING IT NOR HE FOR HIS BONES RISEN. • 039 00 014
    TRESSES DIPP'D IN RAINBOW FIRE, • • • • • 077 00 014
    WHEN THE RAINBOW ARCHING HIGH • • • • • 077 00 107
    THE RAINBOW SHINES, BUT ONLY IN THE THOUGHT • • 091 00 002
    A RAINBOW ALSO SHAPES ITSELF BEYOND • • • • 107 03 006
    MET A NEW SHOWER, AND SAW THE RAINBOW FILL • • 107 03 010
    FOAMFALLING IS NOT FRESH TO IT, RAINBOW BY IT NOT BEAMING, • • 152 02 024
RAINBOW'S
    IN THE ASCENDANCY OF RAINBOW'S HORNS, • • • • 084 00 002
RAINBOWS
    FOR WHO MAKES RAINBOWS BY INVENTION? • • • • 091 00 004
RAINDROP-ROUNDEL
    WHY, RAINDROP-ROUNDELS LOOPED TOGETHER • • • 030 00 027
RAIN-BLASTS
    BUT IF THE RAIN-BLASTS BE UNBOUND • • • • 003 00 007
RAIN-BORN
    THEN WHILE THE RAIN-BORN ARC GLOWS HIGHER • • • 077 00 123
RAINS
    WHEATFIELDS TUMBLED WITH THE RAINS, • • • • 077 00 136
    AT MORN THEY COME UPON OUR LANDS LIKE RAINS; • • 104 00 008
    NO RAINS SHALL FRESH THE FLATS OF SEA, • • • 114 00 013
    SAVE IN THE BODY OF THE RAINS. • • • • • 130 00 020
    WHILE RUSHY RAINS SHALL FALL OR BROOKS SHALL FLEET FROM FOUNTAINS, • 152 C 002
RAISE
    GOD, THOUGH TO THEE OUR PSALM WE RAISE • • • • 023 00 001
RAISED
    LINGER'D, THEN RAISED THE WASHING WAVES AND DRENCH'D • • 002 00 138
RAIS'D
    HE RAIS'D THE CONVENT AS A MONSTROUS GRATE! • • • 001 04 001
RAMBLED
    PINING, PINING, TILL TIME WHEN REASON RAMBLED IN IT AND SOME • 053 00 003
RAMPS
    TRENCH -- RIGHT, THE TIDE THAT RAMPS AGAINST THE SHORE! • 035 00 002
RAN
    WHEN THE ROSE RAN IN CRIMSONINGS DOWN THE CROSS-WOOD! • 027 00 034
    ' ALL HANDS FOR THEMSELVES ' THE CRY RAN THEN! • • 041 00 042
    RAN REVEL IN THE ELDER BOY. • • • • • • 054 00 009

RAN   (CONTINUED)
    NAY, ROGUISH RAN THE VEIN, ... 054 00 028
    [AND AND] INTO THE DUOMO RAN: 081 00 088
    WERE EYES OF CENTRAL PRIMROSE: BLUEBELLS RAN 098 10 002
    RAN THROUGH IT, FOLLOWING WHICH WE SHOULD HAVE SIGHT .   .   . 125 00 006
    NO: WHAT THE POET DID WRITE RAN, ... 147 00 005
    IT STOOPED AND FLASHED AND FELL AND RAN LIKE WATER AWAY. .   .   . 152 00 021
    BATHE ME, JESU LORD, IN WHAT THY BOSOM RAN -- 168 00 022
RANDAL
    FELIX RANDAL THE FARRIER, O IS HE DEAD THEN? MY DUTY ALL ENDED, .   . 053 00 001
    THY TEARS THAT TOUCHED MY HEART, CHILD, FELIX, POOR FELIX RANDAL: . 053 00 011
RANDOM
    WHEN THOU AT THE RANDOM GRIM FORGE, POWERFUL AMIDST PEERS, .   .   . 053 00 013
RANGE
    I HAVE FOUND THE DOMINANT OF MY RANGE AND STATE -- 019 00 013
    WHILE ALL THINGS ELSE MAY STIR AND RANGE 130 00 007
RANGED
    THEN THEY, THUS RANGED, 'GAN MAKE FULL PLAINTIVELY 002 00 126
RANG'D
    HE RANG'D LONG CORRIDORS AND CORNIC'D HALLS, ... 001 10 001
    BLADES OF MILAN IN CIRCLES RANG'D, GREW RUST 001 12 008
RANK
    RANTERS SCREAM'D RANK REBELLION, THIS SHOULD BE 001 05 002
    OF A FRESH AND FOLLOWING FOLDED RANK 043 00 004
    THOUGH AS A BEECHBOLE FIRM, FINDS HIS, AS AT A ROLLCALL, RANK . 071 00 007
    YOU RANK AND REEKING THINGS, ... 077 00 005
    WHILE THE BREEZE BY RANK AND MEASURE 078 00 009
    WHOSE BLOODS I RECK NO MORE OF, NO MORE RANK WITH HERS .   .   . 152 02 069
    SAY MAN THAN MAN MAY RANK HIS ROWS 166 00 009
RANKED
    O IS THERE NO FROWNING OF THESE WRINKLES, RANKED WRINKLES DEEP, . 059 0L 003
    RANKED ROUND THE BOWER 159 00 051
RANKING
    SEXING AND RANKING WITH OUR RUDER FILES V 102 01 063
RANK-OLD
    WHAT BEING IN RANK-OLD NATURE SHOULD EARLIER HAVE THAT BREATH BEEN 141 00 001
RANKLE
    DISASTER THERE: BUT MAY HE NOT RANKLE AND ROAM 048 00 042
RANKS
    SQUANDER THE HELL-ROOK RANKS SALLY TO MOLEST HIM: 048 00 018
    FALLOW, FOAM-FALLOW, HANKS -- FALL'N OFF THEIR RANKS, .   .   . 144 00 007
RANSOM
    THEIR RANSOM, THEIR RESCUE, AND FIRST, FAST, LAST FRIEND. .   . 040 00 014
    MONTHS EARLIER, SINCE I HAD OUR SWEET REPRIEVE AND RANSOM .   . 053 00 007
RANSOM'D
    BUT TO BE RANSOM'D FROM THIS PLACE. 080 05 007
RANTERS
    RANTERS SCREAM'D RANK REBELLION, THIS SHOULD BE 001 05 002
RAPTURE
    I WANT THE ONE RAPTURE OF AN INSPIRATION. 076 00 010
RAPTUROUS
    RAPTUROUS LOVE'S GREETING OF REALER, OF ROUNDER REPLIES? .   . 038 00 008
RARE
    THE ABYSMAL OCEAN HOARDS OF STRANGE AND RARE, ... 002 00 055
    CRUSHES AND TEARS THE RARE ENJEWELLING, ... 002 00 085
    IN ALL OUR WESTERN SHIRES WAS RARE, ... 021 00 023
    IN MOULD OR MIND OR WHAT NOT ELSE MAKES RARE: 040 00 006
    RARE PATIENCE ROOTS IN THESE, AND, THESE AWAY, ... 068 00 005
    IN WIDE THE WORLD'S WEAL: RARE GOLD, BOLD STEEL, BARE .   .   . 070 00 017
    WERE LIMN'D ABOUT WITH RADIANCE RARE 077 00 060
    MELTING INTO AETHER RARE 077 00 074
    WHILE A SUBTLE SPIRIT AND RARE 077 00 127
    THEIR ROCKY LODGES. THEN THE WEATHER RARE 080 04 005
RARE-DEAR
    MORE BRIGHTENING HER, RARE-DEAR BRITAIN, AS HIS REIGN ROLLS, . 028 35 006
RARELY
    BUT THROUGH BLACK BRANCHES, RARELY DREST 003 00 020
    EACH HUE SO RARELY WROUGHT THAT WHERE 077 00 117
    MOST RARELY SEE, UNSELFISHNESS. 096 01 002
RAREST
    UPON HIS ALTAR, AND WITH RAREST STORE 001 02 008
RAREST-VEINED
    OF REALTY THE RAREST-VEINED UNRAVELLER: A NOT 044 00 012
RASH
    THE RASH SMART SLOGGERING BRINE 028 19 004
    BUT IN PALE WATER, FRAIL WATER, WILD RASH AND REELING WATER, . 152 _C 015
RASH-FRESH
    HIS RASH-FRESH RE-WINDED NEW-SKEINED SCORE 035 00 006
RATED
    IS STATUARY RATED BY ITS INCHES? 096 07 006
RATHER
    I READ THE STORY RATHER 007 00 003
    RATHER IT IS THE SIZING MOON. 010 00 020
    OR RATHER, RATHER THEN, STEALING AS SPRING 028 10 003
    OR RATHER, RATHER THEN, STEALING AS SPRING 028 10 003
    HAND RATHER, MY HEART LO! LAPPED STRENGTH, C 064 00 011
    'S NOT WRUNG, SEE YOU; UNFORESEEN TIMES RATHER -- AS SKIES .   . 069 00 013

202

RATHER   (CONTINUED)
    BREATHE O'ER MY BARE NERVE RATHER. I DESIRE 080 05 005
    THESE RATHER ARE THE ARC WHERE BEAUTY SHINES, ... 102 03 003
    RATHER TO EAR THAN EYE SHEWS WHERE THEY STRAY, ... 112 00 004
RATION
    JUST SUCH SLIPS OF SOLDIERY CHRIST'S ROYAL RATION. 048 00 028
RAVAGE
    TILL, (FEARING RAVAGE WORSE THAN IN HIS FLIGHT, ... 001 14 007
RAVE
    ALAS! I RAVE, WHERE CALM IS DUE; 081 00 070
RAVEL-ROPE'S-END
    HIS LOCKS LIKE ALL A RAVEL-ROPE'S-END, ... 144 00 005
RAVELL'D
    AND RAVELL'D INTO STRINGS OF RAIN. 081 00 057
RAVENS
    RAVENS, FOR PROSPEROUSLY-BODED CURSES 089 00 003
RAVES
    RAVES THROUGH SICILIAN PASTURES MANY A MILE; 001 11 004
RAVISHMENT
    AND CARRIED ME WITH RAVISHMENT, ... 081 00 016
RAY
    ---- -- LESSEN'D STARS RAY --. V 085 00 006
RAY'D
    IN SILKEN UNDULATION, SPURR'D AND RAY'D 002 00 043
RAYS
    WITH FLOWING TRACERY ENGEMMING RAYS 001 06 002
    THE SHEARING RAYS CONTRACT ME WITH THEIR BLAZE 080 02 006
    STARS WAVING THEIR INDIVISIBLE RAYS. 098 23 001
    POINTED WITH PIERCED LIGHTS, AND BREAKS OF RAYS 098 24 002
    TO FIELDS OF LIGHT! MILLIONS OF TRAVELLING RAYS 103 00 009
RE
    NO MORE THAN RE AND MI, ... 148 00 034
REACH
    REACH ME A . . . FANCY, COME FASTER -- 028 28 002
    THAT DOES NOW REACH OUR RACE -- 060 00 023
    HERE AT THE VERY FURTHEST REACH AWAY 107 04 019
    (THE FURTHEST REACH THIS SIDE, ON THAT THE BAY 107 04 020
    AND BRIGHT ICONIUM EASTWARDS REACH MY RHYMES. 136 00 006
    DIDST REACH THINE ARMS OUT DYING, ... 170 00 006
REACHES
    OF MILE-LONG REACHES OF OUR ROAD BELOW US. 125 00 007
REACH'D
    ROWING, I REACH'D A ROCK -- THE SEA WAS LOW -- 002 00 001
    IN FORTY DAYS REACH'D HEAVEN FROM EARTH; 006 00 024
    SOUNDS REACH'D HIM. RICHARD CAME. SYLVESTER SMILED 107 04 024
READ
    I READ THE STORY RATHER 007 00 003
    READ THE UNSHAPEABLE SHOCK NIGHT 028 29 003
    WHEN YOU WERE LEARNER AND I READ, ... 081 00 165
    I READ THAT THE RECITAL OF THY SIN, ... 102 02 002
    THE SWEETEST SONNET FIVE OR SIX TIMES READ 117 00 009
    THOUGH THEY TOOK TILL THE SEVENTEENTH OF NEXT OCTOBER TO READ. . 128 00 008
READING
    MOST DENTED) LAY SYLVESTER, READING KEATS' 107 04 021
READINGS
    THE UNQUESTION'D READINGS OF A BLOTLESS BOOK. 016 00 006
READS
    THAT READS OR HOLDS THE ASTROLOGIC LORE, ... 014 02 002
READY
    WHENCE WITH THE SCOURGE OF READY PIETY 001 05 004
    WITH THE READY AZURE AND HIGH CARMINE; -- THINK 093 8 002
    I FIND I AM AS READY WITH MY TEARS 102 01 031
    AND BRIDEGROOM WAITS AND READY ARE BOWER AND BED, ... 136 00 018
    HAVE ALL THINGS READY IN HIS ROOM. THERE NEEDS BUT LITTLE DOING. . 152 01 006
REAL
    'TWIXT REAL HUE AND PHANTASY. 077 00 122
REALER
    RAPTUROUS LOVE'S GREETING OF REALER, OF ROUNDER REPLIES?   .   . 038 00 008
REALIZE
    HER CHARACTER SHE DOES NOT REALIZE, ... 094 00 025
REALM
    REALM BOTH CHRIST IS HEIR TO AND THERE REIGNS. 048 00 032
    BARE THE CONDITION OF A REALM AT RIOT. 082 00 004
REALTY
    OF REALTY THE RAREST-VEINED UNRAVELLER; A NOT 044 00 012
REAPPEAR
    NEW-DATED FROM THE TERMS THAT REAPPEAR, ... 012 01 001
REARING
    OR REARING BILLOW OF THE BISCAY WATER; 041 00 018
REARS
    HAS ONE FETCH IN HER; SHE REARS HERSELF TO DIVINE 028 19 006
    THE HEART REARS WINGS BOLD AND BOLDER 038 00 013
REASON
    HER FEASTS FOLLOW REASON, ... 042 00 003
    PINING, PINING, TILL TIME WHEN REASON RAMBLED IN IT AND SOME   . 053 00 003
    REASON, SELFDISPOSAL, CHOICE OF BETTER OR WORSE WAY,   .   .   . 152 02 061
REASON'D
    I REASON'D THE FUTILITY. 081 00 113

REAVE
    TO THRIFTLESS REAVE BOTH OUR RICH ROUND WORLD BARE   • • • • •   058 00 012
REAVING
    O SURELY, REAVING PEACE, MY LORD SHOULD LEAVE IN LIEU   • • •   051 00 007
REBEL
    WRING THY REBEL, DOGGED IN DEN,   • • • • • • • 028 09 003
    WHAT STROKE HAS CARADOC'S RIGHT ARM DEALT? WHAT DONE? HEAD OF A REBEL   152 02 002
REBELLION
    RANTERS SCREAM'D RANK REBELLION, THIS SHOULD BE   • • •   001 05 002
    THIS ROYAL MANHOOD. -- 'TIS IN ME REBELLION   • • • •   102 01 037
REBELLIOUS
    TO BRUISE THEM DEARER, YET THE REBELLIOUS WILLS   • • •   068 00 010
REBOUND
    WITH A BALLAD, WITH A BALLAD, A REBOUND   • • • •   146 00 003
REBUFF
    THE STABBING COLDNESS OF REBUFF. • • • • •   083 00 028
REBUFFED
    REBUFFED THE BIG WIND, MY HEART IN HIDING   • • • •   036 00 007
RECITAL
    I READ THAT THE RECITAL OF THY SIN,   • • • •   102 02 002
    ALL QUESTS SAVE THE RECITAL OF THEIR GREATNESS!   • • •   104 00 003
RECK
    RECK NOT WHAT THE POOR HAVE LOST! • • • •   024 00 004
    CRUSHED. WHY DO MEN THEN NOW NOT RECK HIS ROD?   • • •   031 00 004
    AND NONE RECK OF WORLD AFTER, THIS BIDS WEAR   • • •   058 00 013
    -- BLACK, WHITE; RIGHT, WRONG; RECKON BUT, RECK BUT, MIND C • • 061 00 012
    LITTLE I RECK HO! LACKLEVEL IN, IF ALL HAD BREAD! • • • 070 00 009
    WHOSE BLOODS I RECK NO MORE OF, NO MORE RANK WITH HERS   • • 152 02 069
RECKON
    I RECKON PRECEDENTS OF LOVE,   • • • •   018 00 007
    -- BLACK, WHITE; RIGHT, WRONG; RECKON BUT, RECK BUT, MIND C • • 061 00 012
RECLAIMING
    KIND, BUT ROYALLY RECLAIMING HIS OWN!   • • •   028 34 007
RECONCILED
    FATHER, BE THOU RECONCILED.   • • • • •   155 00 014
RECORD
    THY VENERABLE RECORD, VIRGIN, IS RECORDED) .   • • •   152 C 017
RECORDED
    THAT NO RECORDED DEVILISH THING WAS DONE   • • •   014 02 008
    RECORDED ONLY, I HAVE PUT MY LIPS ON PLEAS   • • •   048 00 045
    THY VENERABLE RECORD, VIRGIN, IS RECORDED) .   • • •   152 C 017
RECORDS
    MONUMENTS OF MY EARNEST, RECORDS OF MY REVENGE,   • •   152 02 005
RECOVER
    HER FAME TO KEEP, HER FAME TO RECOVER.   • • •   156 00 012
RECOVERY
    THE RECURB AND THE RECOVERY OF THE GULF'S SIDES,   • •   028 32 003
    THINGS WITH A REVIVAL, THINGS WITH A RECOVERY, C   • •   152 C 029
RECURB
    THE RECURB AND THE RECOVERY OF THE GULF'S SIDES,   • •   028 32 003
RED
    AT RED POMPEII ON MEDALLION'D WALLS.   • • •   002 00 051
    HERE HE KNELT THEN IN REGIMENTAL RED.   • • •   048 00 009
    AND SEALS OF RED CARNATION WHICH HAD EACH V   • •   098 12 004
    AND EACH A DINTED CIRCLE. THE GRASS WAS RED   • •   107 04 011
    AND JAMES SHALL HATE HIS FADED RED.   • • •   114 00 011
    LINED ALL WITH SILK OF JUICY RED.   • • •   124 00 016
    ALL SLUMBERED WHOM OUR RUD RED TILES   • • •   135 00 001
    NO MORE THAN RED AND BLUE.   • • • •   148 00 033
REDCOATS
    OUR REDCOATS, OUR TARS? BOTH THESE BEING, THE GREATER PART, • • 063 00 002
REDEEMED
    REDEEMED US FOR HIS OWN.   • • • • •   APPEN D 38
REDEEMING
    NOT THAT HELL KNOWS REDEEMING,   • • • •   041 00 117
REED
    MY NATIONAL OLD EGYPTIAN REED GAVE WAY!   • • •   020 00 007
REEDS
    A MOANING VOICE AMONG THE REEDS.   • • • •   023 00 036
REEF
    SHE STRUCK -- NOT A REEF OR A ROCK   • • •   028 14 002
REEFS
    I SEE LONG REEFS OF VIOLETS   • • • •   003 00 025
REEK
    AN OLIVE-BRANCH WHENCE RICHLY REEK   • • •   077 00 015
REEKING
    YOU RANK AND REEKING THINGS,   • • • •   077 00 005
REEL
    THIS RUCK AND REEL WHICH YOU REMARK   • • •   022 00 011
    THY LOVELY DALE DOWN THUS AND THUS BIDS REEL   • • •   058 00 007
REELING
    BUT IN PALE WATER, FRAIL WATER, WILD RASH AND REELING WATER, •   152 C 015
REELS
    WITH A SOUTH-WESTERLY WIND BLUSTERING, WITH A TIDE ROLLS REELS • 141 00 004
REEVE
    OF THY MERCY NOT REEVE EVEN THEM IN? C   • •   028 12 008
    HE OF ALL CAN REEVE A ROPE BEST. THERE HE BIDES IN BLISS • • • 063 00 010

REFUSED
   RHINE REFUSED THEM, THAMES WOULD RUIN THEM; · · · · · · · 028 21 003
REFUSES
   THAT SWINISHLY REFUSES SUCH A PEARL! · · · · · · · 102 03 033
   THAT SWINISHLY REFUSES SUCH A PEARL! V · · · · · · · 102 03 039
REGIMEN
   IT IS A REGIMEN ON THE IMPERFECT WIND, · · · · · · · 102 03 017
   IS TO GIVE REGIMEN TO THE IMPERFECT WIND, V · · · · · · 102 03 024
REGIMENTAL
   HERE HE KNELT THEN IN REGIMENTAL RED. · · · · · · · 048 00 009
REGISTER
   THE UNCHANGING REGISTER OF CHANGE · · · · · · · 130 00 005
REGRET
   THEIR FALL WAS FULLER OF REGRET; · · · · · · · 004 00 030
REGULAR
   AND THE SEA FLINT-FLAKE, BLACK-BACKED IN THE REGULAR BLOW, · · · 028 13 005
REHEARSAL
   IT IS THE FORGED FEATURE FINDS ME; IT IS THE REHEARSAL · · · 045 00 007
REIGN
   MORE BRIGHTENING HER, RARE-DEAR BRITAIN, AS HIS REIGN ROLLS, · · 028 35 006
REIGNS
   AND BEEN IN THEIR RUINOUS REIGNS OPPRESSED, · · · · · 026 00 010
   REALM BOTH CHRIST IS HEIR TO AND THERE REIGNS. · · · · 048 00 032
REIN
   HIGH THERE, HOW HE RUNG UPON THE REIN OF A WIMPLING WING · · · 036 00 004
RE-ATTRIBUTING
   THE PROPER SWEET RE-ATTRIBUTING ABOVE. V · · · · · · 113 00 011
   THAT SWEETNESS RE-ATTRIBUTING ABOVE. -- V · · · · · · 113 00 012
RE-WINDED
   HIS RASH-FRESH RE-WINDED NEW-SKEINED SCORE · · · · · 035 00 006
RELEASE
   YET AH! THIS AIR I GATHER AND I RELEASE · · · · · · 044 00 009
RELEASED
   A RELEASED SHOWER, LET FLASH TO THE SHIRE, C · · · · · 028 34 008
RELICS
   FAIR RELICS TOO THE CHANGEFUL MOOR HAD LEFT · · · · · 001 08 001
RELIEF
   MARY, MOTHER OF US, WHERE IS YOUR RELIEF? · · · · · 065 00 004
   AND EACH DREW BLUEBELLS UP, AND FOR RELIEF · · · · · 107 03 017
RELIGIOUS
   BELIEVES HERSELF RELIGIOUS, AND IS NOT; · · · · · · 094 00 029
RELISH
   WHAT RELISH SHALL THE CENSERS SEND · · · · · · 022 00 019
   AND RELISH NOT HER LOVELESS KISS · · · · · · · 120 00 011
REMAIN
   YET WHAT YOU ARE, THE WORLD WOULD SAY, REMAIN; · · · · 125 00 024
REMAINDER
   REMAINDER OF A MIRACLE. · · · · · · · 025 00 034
   THEO. REMAINDER OF A MIRACLE. · · · · · · · APPEN A 34
REMARK
   THIS RUCK AND REEL WHICH YOU REMARK · · · · · · 022 00 011
REMEMBER
   REMEMBER US IN THE ROADS, THE HEAVEN-HAVEN OF THE REWARD; · · 028 35 003
   I REMEMBER A HOUSE WHERE ALL WERE GOOD · · · · · · 034 00 001
   TO REMEMBER AND EXULTATION · · · · · · · 042 00 047
   I WOULD REMEMBER, LOVE, FORGIVE. · · · · · · · 081 00 071
   AS EVER I REMEMBER IN MY LIFE. · · · · · · · 102 01 013
REMEMBERETH
   ALWAYS THE TIME REMEMBERETH · · · · · · · 081 00 061
REMEMBERING
   THAT BIRD BEYOND THE REMEMBERING HIS FREE FELLS; · · · · 039 00 003
   WEEPING, -- EVEN NOW I CURSE MYSELF REMEMBERING; -- · · · 102 01 041
REMEMBER'D
   REMEMBER'D SWEETNESS. FOR MY THOUGHT · · · · · · 081 00 139
REMEMBRANCE
   CHILLING REMEMBRANCE OF MY DAYS OF OLD · · · · · · 017 00 005
REMINDER
   O THOU OUR REMINDER OF CHRIST CRUCIFIED, · · · · · 168 00 017
REMNANTS
   THE CHOICEST REMNANTS THENCE; -- SUCH HOME FORLORN · · · 001 15 003
REMORSELESS
   OUR SWANS ARE NOW OF SUCH REMORSELESS QUILL, · · · · 096 02 001
REMOTE
   EXILED MOST REMOTE ELKHOR. · · · · · · · 081 00 47
   THE BLUE WITH BRIGHTER PLACES NOT REMOTE. · · · · · 107 03 020
REMOTEST
   THIS TO REMOTEST AGES WAS TO BE · · · · · · · 001 08 008
REMOVE
   REMOVE. NOT BUT IN ALL REMOVES I CAN · · · · · · 066 00 010
REMOVES
   REMOVE. NOT BUT IN ALL REMOVES I CAN · · · · · · 066 00 010
RENDER'D
   MUST SEE THE EAGLE'S BULK, RENDER'D IN MISTS, · · · · 088 00 003
RENT
   STEEL MAY BE MELTED AND ROCK RENT. · · · · · · 081 00 134
REPAIR
   OR ROCKS WHERE ROCKDOVES DO REPAIR · · · · · · 015 00 038

REPAIR   (CONTINUED)
DIAMONDS ARE BETTER CUT: WHO PARE, REPAIR: 096 07 005
REPEAT
REPEAT THAT, REPEAT, ... 146 00 001
REPEAT THAT, REPEAT, ... 146 00 001
REPEATED
RIDES REPEATED TOPSYTURVY 030 00 015
REPENT
I DID REPENT; I AM FORGIVEN. 081 00 110
ARE HEARD, THAT CRY ' SHE DOES REPENT ' . . 081 00 123
TEACH ME THE WAY; I WILL REPENT. 081 00 136
REPENT HE SINNED AND ALL HIS SINS BE FREED. . 140 00 006
ANY INSTANT FALLS MEANS ME, AND I DO NOT REPENT; . 152 02 032
I DO NOT AND I WILL NOT REPENT, NOT REPENT. . 152 02 033
I DO NOT AND I WILL NOT REPENT, NOT REPENT. . 152 02 033
I REPENT OF WHAT I DID. 155 00 012
REPLIES
BUT NO FORGIVING VOICE REPLIES: 023 00 004
RAPTUROUS LOVE'S GREETING OF REALER, OF ROUNDER REPLIES? . 038 00 008
REPLY
AND YOU SHALL MEET ME WITH REPLY. 008 00 013
HER REPLY PUTS THIS OTHER 042 00 014
HE SWUNG TO HIS FIRST POISED PURPORT OF REPLY. . 047 00 004
REPRIEVE
MONTHS EARLIER, SINCE I HAD OUR SWEET REPRIEVE AND RANSOM . 053 00 007
RESCUE
NOR RESCUE, ONLY ROCKET AND LIGHTSHIP, SHONE, . 028 15 006
THEIR RANSOM, THEIR RESCUE, AND FIRST, FAST, LAST FRIEND. . 040 00 014
ALL IS FROM WRECK, HERE, THERE, TO RESCUE ONE -- . 150 00 006
RESENT
WHAT IF MY SUBJECT, SEEING THIS, RESENT . . 094 00 005
RESIDUARY
FALL TO THE RESIDUARY WORM; WORLD'S WILDFIRE, LEAVE BUT ASH: . 072 00 020
RESIGN
RESIGN THEM, SIGN THEM, SEAL THEM, SEND THEM, MOTION THEM WITH BREATH, 059 06 016
RESOLUTION
AND RIGHT? ONLY RESOLUTION; WILL, HIS WILL UNWAVERING . . . 152 02 043
REST
LOOKS LAID FOR FEASTING AND FOR REST. . . . 003 00 024
BUT I MUST YIELD THE CHASE, OR REST AND EAT, -- . 020 00 011
TO THY BREAST, TO THY REST, TO THY GLORY DIVINE . 027 00 047
I WAS UNDER A ROOF HERE, I WAS AT REST, . . 028 24 003
PATIENCE: BUT PITY OF THE REST OF THEM! . . 028 31 002
WHO LONG FOR REST, WHO LOOK FOR PLEASURE . . 030 00 001
NOT THAT THE SWEET-FOWL, SONG-FOWL, NEEDS NO REST -- 039 00 009
DOFF DARKNESS, HOMING NATURE KNOWS THE REST -- . 047 00 006
TENDERED TO HIM. AH WELL, GOD REST HIM ALL ROAD EVER HE OFFENDED! . 053 00 008
BIRTH, MILK, AND ALL THE REST 060 00 021
LIES DIVINELY STILL, AT REST, ... 077 00 098
MY THOUGHT WAS, THERE TO REST AGAINST THE TREES . 125 00 008
SELVAGGIA, ORINDA, AND ADELA, AND THE REST. . 125 00 038
IT IS HARDLY A PROPER TREAT FOR A BIRTHDAY TO REST IN HER ARMS. . 128 00 012
AT ROOST AND REST THEY SHIFTED NOT, ... 135 00 015
RESURRECTION
BUT VASTNESS BLURS AND TIME BEATS LEVEL. ENOUGH! THE RESURRECTION, . 072 00 016
RETIRE
THE VITAL FIRE DOES SUDDENLY RETIRE 080 10 003
RETIREMENT
TO CANVASS THE RETIREMENT OF THE LARK . . . 113 00 002
RETURNING
RETURNING THANKS, MIGHT OFFER SUCH ARRAY. . . 089 00 004
REVEL
NEVER-ELDERING REVEL AND RIVER OF YOUTH, . . 028 18 007
RAN REVEL IN THE ELDER BOY. 054 00 009
REVENGE
IN BLOODY LETTERS, LESSONS OF EARNEST, OF REVENGE: . 152 02 004
MONUMENTS OF MY EARNEST, RECORDS OF MY REVENGE, . 152 02 005
REVERSAL
AN AGE IS NOW SINCE PASSED, SINCE PARTED: WITH THE REVERSAL . . 045 00 003
REVILED
HE, WHERE THE CROWNALS DROOP'D, HIMSELF REVILED . . . 001 10 007
REVISITS
WHEN LIFE REVISITS ME, NERVE AND VEIN. . . . 080 08 002
REVIVAL
THINGS WITH A REVIVAL, THINGS WITH A RECOVERY, C . . . 152 C 029
REWARD
REMEMBER US IN THE ROADS, THE HEAVEN-HAVEN OF THE REWARD: . . 028 35 003
RHINE
RHINE REFUSED THEM, THAMES WOULD RUIN THEM: . 028 21 003
RHYME
LET THE CHIME OF A RHYME 029 00 019
AND TO THEIR FEET THE NARROW BELLS GAVE RHYME. . 107 01 014
RHYMES
AND BRIGHT ICONIUM EASTWARDS REACH MY RHYMES. . . 136 00 006
RIBBED
THY RIBBED PORTS, O DEATH 115 00 005
RIBBON
NO TIME TO THINK. I'LL KNOT IT ON THIS RIBBON, . . . 102 01 027

206

RIBS
HIS CHARNELHOUSE-GRATE RIBS BETWEEN, ... 004 00 010
BREATHED ROUND: THE RACK OF RIBS; THE SCOOPED FLANK; LANK . . . 071 00 002
RICH
WITH GOLDEN FILLETS AND RICH BLAZONRY, ... 001 07 006
WITH PAINTING GLEAM'D THE RICH PILASTER'D WALLS -- 001 10 003
RICH TITIANS FADED: IN THE STRAYING GLEAM 001 12 003
RICH BEAMS, TILL DEATH OR DISTANCE BUYS THEM QUITE. 040 00 008
TO THRIFTLESS REAVE BOTH OUR RICH ROUND WORLD BARE 058 00 012
SKYWARDS: RICH, RICH IT LAPS 060 00 077
SKYWARDS: RICH, RICH IT LAPS 060 00 077
THAT RIDES THE AIR SO RICH ABOUT THEE, C 152 01 017
WHEN 'TS LIGHT I QUENCHED: ITS ROSE, TIME'S ONE RICH ROSE, MY HAND, 152 02 050
OR THEY GO RICH AS ROSELEAVES HENCE THAT LOATHSOME CAME HITHER! . 152 C 024
A JUICE RIDES RICH THROUGH BLUEBELLS, IN VINE LEAVES, . . . 157 00 003
RICHARD
BUT WHAT DREW SHEPHERD RICHARD FROM HIS DOWNS, ... 107 02 001
LED RICHARD WITH A SWEET UNDOING PAIN 107 04 017
SOUNDS REACH'D HIM. RICHARD CAME: SYLVESTER SMILED . . . 107 04 024
RICHEST
THE RICHEST GIFT ST. LAWRENCE EVER BORE, ... 001 02 006
RICH-PIECED
FROM EASY RUNNELS THE RICH-PIECED LAND 005 00 039
RICHLY
AN OLIVE-BRANCH WHENCE RICHLY REEK 077 00 015
RICHNESS
WITH RICHNESS: THE RACING LAMBS TOO HAVE FAIR THEIR FLING. . . 033 00 008
RID
THERE RID THE DRAGONS, ROOT OUT THERE THE SIN. 150 00 010
RIDDLES
WITH, RIDDLES, AND IS RIFE 060 00 007
RIDE
THE SUMPTUOUS RIDGE-CREST LEAVE TO POISE AND RIDE. 012 02 008
SEE, LOVE, I CREEP AND THOU ON WINGS DOST RIDE: 020 00 003
AND SHE BEAT THE BANK DOWN WITH HER BOWS AND THE RIDE OF HER KEEL: 028 14 005
LET HIM RIDE, HER PRIDE, IN HIS TRIUMPH, C 028 28 008
WOULD BRANDLE ADAMANTINE HEAVEN WITH RIDE AND JAR, DID . . . 048 00 046
RIDER
FLUNG RIDER AND WINGS AWAY: THOUGH THESE WERE NONE, . . . 136 00 009
RIDES
BUT IT RIDES TIME LIKE RIDING A RIVER 028 06 007
RIDES REPEATED TOPSYTURVY 030 00 015
THAT RIDES THE AIR SO RICH ABOUT THEE, C 152 01 017
A JUICE RIDES RICH THROUGH BLUEBELLS, IN VINE LEAVES, . . . 157 00 003
RIDGE
AN AZURE RIDGE: OR CLOUDS OF VIOLET GLOW'D 002 00 105
RIDGE-CREST
THE SUMPTUOUS RIDGE-CREST LEAVE TO POISE AND RIDE. 012 02 008
RIDING
BUT IT RIDES TIME LIKE RIDING A RIVER 028 06 007
DOM OF DAYLIGHT'S DAUPHIN, DAPPLE-DAWN-DRAWN FALCON, IN HIS RIDING . 036 00 002
RIDING: THERE DID STORMS NOT MINGLE? AND 041 00 026
RIFE
RIFE IN HER WRONGS, MORE LAWLESS, AND MORE LEWD. 050 00 008
WITH, RIDDLES, AND IS RIFE 060 00 007
Y OF IDLE A BEING BUT BY WHERE WARS ARE RIFE. 066 00 008
RIFLED
THE RUINS OF, RIFLED, ONCE A WORLD OF ART? 153 00 004
RIGGING
ONE STIRRED FROM THE RIGGING TO SAVE 028 16 001
RIGHT
BUT FURTHER DOWN THE VALLEY, LEFT AND RIGHT, ... 001 14 004
FLICKERING WITH SUNNY SPOKES, AND LEFT AND RIGHT 002 00 077
AH! THERE WAS A HEART RIGHT! 028 29 001
WHY, IT SEEMED OF COURSE: SEEMED OF RIGHT IT SHOULD. . . . 034 00 008
TRENCH -- RIGHT, THE TIDE THAT RAMPS AGAINST THE SHORE: . . . 035 00 002
HOW RING RIGHT OUT OUR SORDID TURBID TIME, ... 035 00 010
CHEEKS: RIGHT, RUDE OF FEATURE, ... 041 00 050
DISREMEMBERING, DISMEMBERING ALL NOW. HEART, YOU ROUND ME RIGHT . 061 00 007
-- BLACK, WHITE; RIGHT, WRONG; RECKON BUT, RECK BUT, MIND C . . 061 00 012
THY WRING-WORLD RIGHT FOOT ROCK? LAY A LIONLIMB AGAINST ME? SCAN . 064 00 006
RIGHT OFFSPRING OF YOUR GRIMY MOTHER EARTH! 077 00 002
LOCK WITH MY RIGHT: THEN KNOT A BARKEN BAND 080 13 005
AND THUS I WILL THRUST IN MY RIGHT: -- 080 13 007
WHO KNELT WERE FOR THE LORD'S RIGHT HAND: 081 00 094
SEES THE RIGHT THING TO DO, AND DOES NOT ACT: 094 00 020
EITHER LEFT EITHER RIGHT 138 00 008
RIGHT ROOTING IN THE BARE BUTT'S WINCING NAVEL C 143 00 005
BUT RIGHT MUST SEEK A SIDE 148 00 027
IS NEITHER RIGHT NOR WRONG, ... 148 00 032
WHAT STROKE HAS CARADOC'S RIGHT ARM DEALT? WHAT DONE? HEAD OF A REBEL 152 02 002
AND RIGHT? ONLY RESOLUTION! WILL, HIS WILL UNWAVERING . . . 152 02 043
RIGHTED
AS HALF SHE HAD RIGHTED AND HOPED TO RISE 041 00 038
RIGHTEOUSNESS
DOFFS ALL, DRIVES FULL FOR RIGHTEOUSNESS. 041 00 056
RIGOUR
WITH BARREN RIGOUR AND A FRIGID GLOOM -- 001 01 008

RIVER   (CONTINUED)
  NEVER-ELDERING REVEL AND RIVER OF YOUTH, ... 028 18 007
  SURF, SNOW, RIVER AND EARTH 028 21 004
  ON MEADOW AND RIVER AND WIND-WANDERING WEED-WINDING BANK. . . 043 00 008
  THY RIVER, AND O'ER GIVES ALL TO RACK OR WRONG. 058 00 008
  THE RIVER WOUND ABOUT IT AS A WAIST. 107 04 002
  BEYOND THE RIVER, ALL THE MEADOW'S ROUND, ... 107 04 010
  THE RIVER SPANS IT WITH SO DEEP A HIP. 107 04 026
  MARBLED RIVER, BOISTEROUSLY BEAUTIFUL, BETWEEN . . . 159 00 006
  HE DROPS TOWARDS THE RIVER: UNSEEN 159 00 015
RIVER-BANKS
  IN SPRING OUR RIVER-BANKS ARE TOPT 124 00 017
RIVER-BED
  NO RUNNING IN THE RIVER-BED: 081 00 161
RIVER-HEADS
  YE RIVER-HEADS, THOU BILLOWY DEEP THAT LAUGH'ST . . . 160 00 002
RIVER-ROUNDED
  ROOK-RACKED, RIVER-ROUNDED: C 044 00 002
RIVERS
  AND RIVERS RUN WHERE ALL WAS DRY, ... 008 00 002
  OF RIVERS, LEAD, THRO' STORMS AND NIGHTS, ... 083 00 004
RIVING
  THE RIVING OFF THAT RACE 041 00 099
  I SEE HER RIVING FINGERS TEAR 120 00 005
RIV'N
  THE RIV'N VINE, LEAFLESS, LIFELESS, DRY: 006 00 022
RIVULET
  STARTING THE SILVER RIVULET: 077 00 088
ROAD
  PART FOUND NO ROOT UPON THE FLINTY ROAD, -- 007 00 009
  TENDERED TO HIM. AH WELL, GOD REST HIM ALL ROAD EVER HE OFFENDED! . 053 00 008
  WHAT WAS IT WE SHOULD STRIKE THE ROAD AGAIN? . . . 125 00 001
  OF MILE-LONG REACHES OF OUR ROAD BELOW US. 125 00 007
  THE CART ROAD WITH A SHALLOWY BED 135 00 026
ROADS
  REMEMBER US IN THE ROADS, THE HEAVEN-HAVEN OF THE REWARD: . . 028 35 003
ROAM
  DISASTER THERE: BUT MAY HE NOT RANKLE AND ROAM . . . 048 00 042
ROAMING
  YOUR ROUND ME ROAMING END, AND UNDER BE MY BOUGHS? . . 051 00 002
ROAR
  WITH A FLOOD OR A FALL, LOW LULL-OFF OR ALL ROAR, . . . 035 00 003
  BY MANY BLOWS AND BANES: BUT NOW HEARS ROAR 050 00 006
ROARED
  NIGHT ROARED, WITH THE HEART-BREAK HEARING A HEART-BROKE RABBLE, . 028 17 005
ROARING
  HIS ROLLROCK HIGHROAD ROARING DOWN, ... 056 00 002
ROB
  SLEEP FLORIS WHILE I ROB YOU. TIGHTEN, O SLEEP, . . . 102 01 017
ROBBERY'S
  ROBBERY'S HAND IS BUSY TO 041 00 091
ROBE
  SHE, WILD WEB, WONDROUS ROBE, ... 060 00 038
ROBES
  EARTH THROWS WINTER'S ROBES AWAY, ... 024 00 017
ROCK
  ROWING, I REACH'D A ROCK -- THE SEA WAS LOW -- . . . 002 00 001
  FROM FLESH-FLOWERS OF THE ROCK: BUT MORE WERE WREATH'D . . 002 00 063
  SO THOSE MERMAIDENS CROWDED TO MY ROCK, ... 002 00 098
  DOWN THAT DANK ROCK O'ER WHICH THEIR LUSH LONG TRESSES WEEP. . 002 00 115
  WHITE LOOM'D MY ROCK, THE WATER GURGLING O'ER, . . . 002 00 142
  WHO WOULD DRINK WATER FROM A STONY ROCK? 005 00 020
  FROM WASTES OF ROCK HE BRINGS 007 00 011
  SHE STRUCK -- NOT A REEF OR A ROCK 028 14 002
  NOW TIME'S ANDROMEDA ON THIS ROCK RUDE, ... 050 00 001
  THY WRING-WORLD RIGHT FOOT ROCK? LAY A LIONLIMB AGAINST ME? SCAN . 064 00 001
  BEFORE THAT ROCK, MY SEAT, HE STANDS: 080 09 001
  STEEL MAY BE MELTED AND ROCK RENT. 081 00 134
  THE VIOLET MOVES AND COPSES ROCK. 098 03 004
  WATER, WHICH KEEPS THY NAME, (FOR NOT IN ROCK WRITTEN, . . 152 C 014
ROCKDOVES
  OR ROCKS WHERE ROCKDOVES DO REPAIR 015 00 038
ROCKET
  NOR RESCUE, ONLY ROCKET AND LIGHTSHIP, SHONE, . . . 028 15 006
ROCKFIRE
  BY HIM AND RIPS OUT ROCKFIRE HOMEFORTH -- STURDY DICK: . . 070 00 003
ROCK-A-HEART
  MORTAL MY MATE, BEARING MY ROCK-A-HEART 153 00 001
ROCKS
  DOWN-SPLINTER'D ROCKS CRUSH'D COTTAGES. -- DREAR SIGHT, . . 001 14 005
  OR ROCKS WHERE ROCKDOVES DO REPAIR 015 00 038
  I CRY ' O ROCKS AND MOUNTAIN MAKE ME ROOM ' . . . 080 07 005
  SOME ICE THAT LOCKS THE GLACIER TO THE ROCKS . . . 080 09 006
  I KNOW OF THE BORED AND BITTEN ROCKS 120 00 020
  ROOTS AND ROCKS IS DANCED AND DANDLED, C 159 00 007
  BUILT OF CHANCEQUARRIED, SELFQUAINED, HOAR-HUSKED ROCKS . . 159 00 037
  MERE EYEBROW ROCKS THIS ROUND OF THINGS. 166 00 008

ROCKY
    THEIR ROCKY LODGES. THEN THE WEATHER RARE • • • • • • • • 080 04 005
ROD
    UPON THE STUBBORN FLEMING; AND THE ROD • • • • • • • 001 05 006
    AND FEAR NO IRON ROD. • • • • • • • • • • 005 00 012
    I TOOK OF VINE A CROSS-BARRED ROD OR ROOD. • • • • • 020 00 008
    O AT LIGHTNING AND LASHED ROD; • • • • • • • 028 02 002
    CRUSHED. WHY DO MEN THEN NOW NOT RECK HIS ROD? • • • • 031 00 004
    NAY IN ALL THAT TOIL, THAT COIL, SINCE (SEEMS) I KISSED THE ROD, • 064 00 010
    THEY KISS THE ROD WITH FILIAL SUBMISSION. • • • • • • 097 00 008
RODE
    WHEREIN BENEATH THE CORNICE, HORSEMEN RODE • • • • • 001 07 007
    TO THE MEN IN THE TOPS AND THE TACKLE RODE OVER THE STORM'S BRAWLING. 028 19 008
RODS
    A BASKET BROAD OF WOVEN WHITE RODS • • • • • • • 098 19 001
    THE BLUEBELLS UP WHOSE CRYSTAL-ENDING RODS • • • • • 112 00 008
ROGUISH
    NAY, ROGUISH RAN THE VEIN. • • • • • • • • 054 00 028
ROLL
    THE THICK STARS ROUND HIM ROLL • • • • • • • 060 00 099
    THE ROLL, THE RISE, THE CAROL, THE CREATION, • • • • 076 00 012
    MUST SEE THE WATERS ROLL • • • • • • • • 088 00 005
    MUST SEE THE GREEN SEAS ROLL V • • • • • • • 088 00 009
    AND LAPPED IN SHINING HAIR, ROLL TO THE BANK'S EDGE: THEN • • 152 02 019
ROLLCALL
    THOUGH AS A BEECHBOLE FIRM, FINDS HIS, AS AT A ROLLCALL, RANK • 071 00 007
ROLLED
    THE BREAKERS ROLLED ON HER BEAM WITH RUINOUS SHOCK; • • • 028 14 006
    (CRUSHED THEM) OR WATER (AND DROWNED THEM) OR ROLLED • 028 17 003
    UNCHRIST, ALL ROLLED IN RUIN -- • • • • • • • 041 00 096
ROLLING
    OF THE ROLLING LEVEL UNDERNEATH HIM STEADY AIR, AND STRIDING • 036 00 003
    IN THE QUICK FRAGRANCE OF TALL ROLLING PINES, • • • • 084 00 005
    AND, SWARTER STILL, THE ROLLING PINES SHOULD CAST • • • 090 00 005
ROLLROCK
    HIS ROLLROCK HIGHROAD ROARING DOWN, • • • • • • 056 00 002
ROLL'D
    HAS LOST ITS SAVOUR AND IS ROLL'D • • • • • • 092 00 005
ROLLS
    MORE BRIGHTENING HER, RARE-DEAR BRITAIN, AS HIS REIGN ROLLS, • 028 35 006
    ROLLS ACROSS THE LABOURING WILLOWS; • • • • • 078 00 004
    A DROP OF SHADE ROLLS OVER FIELD AND FLOCK; • • • • 098 03 002
    SEE WHAT HIS PLACE IS: BUT FOR US THE ROLLS • • • • 126 00 005
    WITH A SOUTH-WESTERLY WIND BLUSTERING, WITH A TIDE ROLLS REELS • 141 00 004
ROME
    ED ROME? BUT GOD TO A NATION DEALT THAT DAY'S DEAR CHANCE. • • 062 00 008
ROOD
    I TOOK OF VINE A CROSS-BARRED ROD OR ROOD. • • • • 020 00 008
    LEFT NOT A ROOD WITH CURSES UNIMPREGNATE; • • • • 102 02 005
ROOF
    THE STEEP-UP ROOF AT LAST BEHIND THE SMALL • • • • 012 02 006
    I WAS UNDER A ROOF HERE, I WAS AT REST, • • • • 028 24 003
    UNDER THE CLOUD-FESTOONED ROOF, • • • • • • 077 00 066
    WHATEVER TIME THIS VAPOUROUS ROOF, • • • • • • 080 06 001
ROOF'D
    WHERE THE UPPER MILL-STONE ROOF'D HIS HEAD, • • • • 006 00 007
ROOK
    EYE-GREETING DOVES BRIGHT-COUNTER TO THE ROOK, • • • 016 00 003
ROOKERY
    THE ROOKERY NEVER STIRRED A WING, • • • • • • 135 00 014
ROOK-RACKED
    ROOK-RACKED, RIVER-ROUNDED: C • • • • • • • 044 00 002
ROOM
    AND BLEEDING SAW. -- THUS HUNG FROM ROOM TO ROOM • • • 001 10 008
    AND BLEEDING SAW. -- THUS HUNG FROM ROOM TO ROOM • • • 001 10 008
    BUT HOW SHALL I • • • MAKE ME ROOM THERE; • • • • 028 28 001
    LET INCENSE HANG ACROSS THE ROOM • • • • • • 077 00 019
    I CRY ' O ROCKS AND MOUNTAIN MAKE ME ROOM ' • • • • 080 07 005
    O GROUNDS OF HELL MAKE ROOM. • • • • • • 115 00 002
    HAVE ALL THINGS READY IN HIS ROOM. THERE NEEDS BUT LITTLE DOING. • 152 01 006
ROOST
    AT ROOST AND REST THEY SHIFTED NOT, • • • • • • 135 00 015
ROOT
    PART FOUND NO ROOT UPON THE FLINTY ROAD, -- • • • • 007 00 009
    MY ROOT IS DRY. • • • • • • • • • • 127 00 004
    THERE RID THE DRAGONS, ROOT OUT THERE THE SIN. • • • 150 00 010
ROOTED
    BUT WE DREAM WE ARE ROOTED IN EARTH -- DUST! • • • • 028 11 005
ROOTING
    RIGHT ROOTING IN THE BARE BUTT'S WINCING NAVEL C • • • 143 00 005
ROOT-ROOM
    ELSEWHERE; LEAVE COMFORT ROOT-ROOM; LET JOY SIZE • • • 069 00 011
ROOTS
    FOR US WAS LIFTED FROM THE ROOTS, • • • • • • 006 00 004
    RARE PATIENCE ROOTS IN THESE, AND, THESE AWAY, • • • 068 00 005
    MINE, O THOU LORD OF LIFE, SEND MY ROOTS RAIN. • • • 074 00 014
    HE DROPS HIS BRIGHT ROOTS IN THE WATER'D SWARD, • • • 100 00 002

ROOTS   (CONTINUED)
   ROOTS AND ROCKS IS DANCED AND DANDLED, C 159 00 007
   LIKE THE THING THAT NEVER KNEW THE EARTH, NEVER OFF ROOTS 159 00 027
ROPE
   HE OF ALL CAN REEVE A ROPE BEST, THERE HE BIDES IN BLISS 063 00 010
ROPED
   BUT ROPED WITH, ALWAYS, ALL THE WAY DOWN FROM THE TALL 028 04 006
ROPE-OVER
   ROPE-OVER THIGH; KNEE-NAVE; AND BARRELLED SHANK -- C 071 00 003
ROPE'S
   WITH A ROPE'S END ROUND THE MAN, HANDY AND BRAVE -- 028 16 003
ROPES
   ROPES, WRESTLES, BEATS EARTH BARE C 072 00 005
ROSE
   TO AN ORB'D ROSE, WHICH, BY HOT PANTINGS BLOWN 002 00 020
   THE ZENITH MELTED TO A ROSE OF AIR; 002 00 023
   NOW RINGING CLARION-CLEAR TO WHENCE IT ROSE 002 00 134
   THE ROSE IN A MYSTERY -- WHERE IS IT FOUND? 027 00 001
   SHE IS THE MYSTERY, SHE IS THAT ROSE. 027 00 022
   IS MARY THE ROSE, THEN? MARY THE TREE? 027 00 025
   WHO CAN HER ROSE BE? IT COULD BE BUT ONE: 027 00 027
   WHEN THE ROSE RAN IN CRIMSONINGS DOWN THE CROSS-WOOD! . . . 027 00 034
   PRIDE, ROSE, PRINCE, HERO OF US, HIGH-PRIEST, ... 028 35 007
   LIKE A WIND-PERPLEXED ROSE; 087 00 004
   EVEN SO MY THOUGHT THE ROSE AND GREY DISPOSES 108 00 007
   IF IT BE A WHITE ROSE IN HIS HAND, ... 109 22 001
   IS IT A ROSE I SEE? 109 33 002
   SMELLS THAT ARE SWEETER-MEMORIED THAN THE ROSE, ... 119 00 003
   BUT THE LILY IS PAST, AS I SAY, AND THE ROSE IS NOT IN ITS PRIME; . 128 00 014
   THEY ROSE AT LAST AND FORCED HER FROM THE SPOT. 136 00 034
   WAS A ROSE, OR, FAILING THAT, ... 144 00 014
   WHEN 'TS LIGHT I QUENCHED; ITS ROSE, TIME'S ONE RICH ROSE, MY HAND, . 152 02 050
   WHEN 'TS LIGHT I QUENCHED; ITS ROSE, TIME'S ONE RICH ROSE, MY HAND, . 152 02 050
   ROSE. HERE HE FEASTS; LOVELY ALL IS! C 159 00 028
ROSE-FLAKE
   FOR LETTERING OF THE LAMB'S FLEECE, RUDDYING OF THE ROSE-FLAKE. . 028 22 008
ROSE-MOLES
   FOR ROSE-MOLES ALL IN STIPPLE UPON TROUT THAT SWIM; 037 00 003
ROSE-RED
   WHAT I DID ASK THEN WAS A CIRCLE OF ROSE-RED SEALING-WAX . . . 128 00 015
ROSELEAVES
   OR THEY GO RICH AS ROSELEAVES HENCE THAT LOATHSOME CAME HITHER! . 152 C 024
ROSES
   -- AN ISLE OF ROSES, -- AND ANOTHER NEAR, -- 002 00 029
   HER CHOICE IN ROSES KNOWS BY HEART; 083 00 022
   OF THE PRESS OF ROSES. 098 19 008
   TO COLOUR AS SMOOTH AND FRESH AS CHEEKS OF ROSES, ... 108 00 004
   WHERE ROSES LINGER LAST. 165 00 004
ROSING
   AND ROSING PART, ON PART DISPENSES GREEN; 100 00 003
ROSY
   NOW ALL THINGS ROSY TURN'D; THE WEST HAD GROWN 002 00 019
   WITH LACE OF ROSY WELD WERE CHAPLETED; 002 00 059
   WITH ROSY FOAM AND PELTING BLOSSOM AND MISTS 002 00 090
   OF FILMY GLOBES AND ROSY FLOATING CLOUD; -- 002 00 097
   THE ROSY ISLES; SO THAT I STOLE AWAY 002 00 140
   AND COUNT THE ROSY CROSS WITH BANN'D DISASTROUS THINGS. . . . 089 00 009
ROSY-BUDDED
   WITH GARNET WREATHS AND BLOOMS OF ROSY-BUDDED FIRE. 002 00 026
ROSY-LIPP'D
   THE WAVES WERE ROSY-LIPP'D; THE CRIMSON GLARE 002 00 024
ROSY-PALE,
   WHICH, LIGHTENING O'ER THE BODY ROSY-PALE, ... 002 00 072
ROUGH
   FROST-FURRED OUR IVIES ARE AND ROUGH 003 00 003
   PEACE AND FOOD CHEERED ME WHERE FOUR ROUGH WAYS MEET. . . . 020 00 012
ROUGHCAST
   DOWN ROUGHCAST, DOWN DAZZLING WHITEWASH, WHEREVER AN ELM ARCHES, 072 00 003
ROUGH-ROBIN
   ROUGH-ROBIN OR FIVE-LIPPED CAMPION CLEAR 144 00 015
ROUGH-SCORED
   THOSE CROOKED ROUGH-SCORED CHEQUERS MAY BE PIECED 011 00 004
ROUND
   AT CORNERS FLANK THE STRETCHING COMPASS ROUND; 001 01 004
   THIS WAS NO CLASSIC TEMPLE ORDER'D ROUND 001 07 001
   AN ENDLESS ROUND OF DEAD'NING SOLITUDE; 001 14 006
   SOME CARRIED THE SEA-FAN; SOME ROUND THE HEAD 002 00 058
   A STEALTHY WIND CREPT ROUND SEEKING TO BLOW, ... 002 00 137
   MANY TREES AND FLOWERS ROUND 004 00 019
   TWO HUNDRED SOULS IN THE ROUND -- 028 12 004
   WITH A ROPE'S END ROUND THE MAN, HANDY AND BRAVE -- . . . 028 16 003
   WHAT IS SOUND? NATURE'S ROUND 029 00 003
   TOIL HAS SHED ROUND YOUR HEAD 029 00 015
   RACED DOWN DECKS, ROUND MESSES OF MORTALS, ... 041 00 040
   NOW HE SHOOTS SHORT UP TO THE ROUND AIR; 041 00 065
   YOUR ROUND ME ROAMING END, AND UNDER BE MY BOUGHS? . . . 051 00 002
   TO THRIFTLESS REAVE BOTH OUR RICH ROUND WORLD BARE . . . 058 00 012

ROUND   (CONTINUED)
WITH MERCY ROUND AND ROUND 060 00 035
WITH MERCY ROUND AND ROUND 060 00 035
ROUND THE FOUR FINGERGAPS. 060 00 078
THE THICK STARS ROUND HIM ROLL 060 00 099
ABOVE ME, ROUND ME LIE 060 00 118
DISREMEMBERING, DISMEMBERING ALL NOW. HEART, YOU ROUND ME RIGHT   .   061 00 007
BY GROPING ROUND MY COMFORTLESS, THAN BLIND 069 00 006
WITH HEAVEN'S LIGHTS HIGH HUNG ROUND, OR, MOTHER-GROUND   .   .   .   070 00 011
BREATHED ROUND: THE RACK OF RIBS: THE SCOOPED FLANK: LANK   .   .   071 00 002
LOOKS FROM THE ZENITH ROUND THE SKY, ...   077 00 108
ALLOWS THE SOUND OF BELLS IN HAMLETS ROUND 080 04 006
ACCEPTANCE ROUND HIS MISTRESS' MOUTH: 083 00 008
TOWARDS WASTES WHERE ROUND THE ICE-BLOCKS TILT AND FRET   .   .   088 00 007
AND MANY STANDING ROUND A WATERFALL 091 00 005
ROUND THIS UNSEXING DOUBLET, -- WHILE I SET 102 01 004
MOST LIKE THE TUFT OF PLIGHTED SILVER ROUND V 102 01 068
LIKE KNOCKING THUNDER ALL ROUND BRITAIN'S WELKIN, ...   102 02 003
WHAT TAUGHT THE HUMANITIES AND THE ROUND OF ARTS?   .   .   .   107 02 006
BEYOND THE RIVER, ALL THE MEADOW'S ROUND, ...   107 04 010
AND ALL ROUND NOT TO BE FOUND 138 00 005
ROUND A RING, AROUND A RING 138 00 014
DAYS AND DAYS CAME ROUND ABOUT 145 00 023
AND MORE AND MORE TIMES LACES ROUND AND ROUND MY HEART,   .   .   152 01 013
AND MORE AND MORE TIMES LACES ROUND AND ROUND MY HEART,   .   .   152 01 013
ROUND AND ROUND THEY CAME AND FLASHED TOWARDS HEAVEN: O THERE,   152 02 029
ROUND AND ROUND THEY CAME AND FLASHED TOWARDS HEAVEN: O THERE,   152 02 029
RANKED ROUND THE BOWER 159 00 051
MERE EYEBROW ROCKS THIS ROUND OF THINGS. 166 00 008
BRING SLEEP ROUND THEN? -- SLEEP NOT AFRAID 166 00 021
ROUNDED
ROUNDED IT, THINNING SKYWARDS BY DEGREES, ...   107 04 004
ROUNDER
RAPTUROUS LOVE'S GREETING OF REALER, OF ROUNDER REPLIES?   .   .   038 00 008
ROUNDING
WORK THROUGH A COVER'D COPSE WHOSE HOLLOW ROUNDING   .   .   .   112 00 003
ROUNDS
NOT VAULT THEM, THE MILLION OF ROUNDS C 028 12 008
IT ROUNDS AND ROUNDS DESPAIR TO DROWNING. 056 00 008
IT ROUNDS AND ROUNDS DESPAIR TO DROWNING. 056 00 008
ROUNDS ITS STILL-PURPLING CENTREINGS OF CLOUD. 098 30 003
ROUNDS ITS STILL-PURPLING CENTRE-DARKS OF CLOUD. 098 30 006
ROUNDY
AS TUMBLED OVER RIM IN ROUNDY WELLS 057 00 002
ROUT
AND THE RIOT OF A ROUT 159 00 011
ROW
THAT WAS HER LARKSPUR ROW. -- SO SOON? 010 00 022
A ROW OF RIPPLES IN THE BROOK, ...   021 00 031
ROWELS
STARS LIKE GOLDEN ROWELS. 098 25 004
HIS GILDED ROWELS. 098 26 001
ROWING
ROWING, I REACH'D A ROCK -- THE SEA WAS LOW -- 002 00 001
ROWS
SAY MAN THAN MAN MAY RANK HIS ROWS 166 00 009
ROYAL
HARD BY A ROYAL PALACE AND A ROYAL TOMB. 001 01 009
HARD BY A ROYAL PALACE AND A ROYAL TOMB. 001 01 009
TO NEWBORN PRINCE, AND ROYAL CORSE INANIMATE. 001 04 009
SINCE TRAMPLED SPAIN BY ROYAL DISCORD TORN 001 15 001
ROYAL, AND ALL HER ROYALS WORE. 041 00 034
JUST SUCH SLIPS OF SOLDIERY CHRIST'S ROYAL RATION.   .   .   .   048 00 028
THIS ROYAL MANHOOD. -- 'TIS IN ME REBELLION 102 01 037
HONOURING AN UNCONTROLLED ROYAL WRATHFUL NATURE, ...   152 02 036
ROYALLY
KIND, BUT ROYALLY RECLAIMING HIS OWN: 028 34 007
ROYALS
ROYAL, AND ALL HER ROYALS WORE. 041 00 034
RUBIES
LIKE SHIVER'D RUBIES DANCE OR SHEEN OF SAPPHIRE HAIL.   .   .   .   002 00 073
RUBY
THE RIM WITH RUBY FRINGES DIGHT, ...   077 00 120
RUCK
THIS RUCK AND REEL WHICH YOU REMARK 022 00 011
RUCK AND WRINKLE, DROOPING, DYING, DEATH'S WORST, C   .   .   .   059 0L 012
RUD
ALL SLUMBERED WHOM OUR RUD RED TILES 135 00 001
RUDDIED
IN THE RUDDIED COUNTY OF THE DAY'S UPBRINGING 098 28 004
RUDDYING
FOR LETTERING OF THE LAMB'S FLEECE, RUDDYING OF THE ROSE-FLAKE.   .   028 22 008
RUDE
BY CONQU'RORS RUDE OF HONOR: AND NOT ALL 001 08 004
FELL ON THE PALACE, AND THE LUST OF RABBLE RUDE,)   .   .   .   001 14 009
CHEEKS: RIGHT, RUDE OF FEATURE, ...   041 00 050
NOW TIME'S ANDROMEDA ON THIS ROCK RUDE, ...   050 00 001

212

RUDE   (CONTINUED)
    BUT AH, BUT O THOU TERRIBLE, WHY WOULDST THOU RUDE ON ME 064 00 005
RUDER
    SEXING AND RANKING WITH OUR RUDER FILES V 102 01 063
RUDER-ROUNDED
    C HIS RUDER-ROUNDED RIND. 148 00 040
RUDRED
    FLAME-RASH RUDRED 138 00 023
RUEFUL
    AND FRIGHTFUL A NIGHTFALL FOLDED RUEFUL A DAY 028 15 005
RUIN
    RHINE REFUSED THEM, THAMES WOULD RUIN THEM; 028 21 003
    UNCHRIST, ALL ROLLED IN RUIN -- 041 00 096
RUINOUS
    AND BEEN IN THEIR RUINOUS REIGNS OPPRESSED, ... 026 00 010
    THE BREAKERS ROLLED ON HER BEAM WITH RUINOUS SHOCK; . . . 028 14 006
    OF RUINOUS SHRINE NO HAND OR, WORSE, ... 041 00 090
    RUINOUS HEART-BEAT, WANDERING, DEATH. 081 00 053
RUINS
    OUR RUINS OF WRECKED PAST PURPOSE. THERE SHE BASKS . . . 068 00 007
    AND WRECK IN RUINS OF HIS MOTHER 145 00 041
    THE RUINS OF, RIFLED, ONCE A WORLD OF ART? 153 00 004
RULE
    AT TRANQUIL TURNS, BY NATURE'S RULE, ... 030 00 014
RULER
    TO BE JUDGE AND RULER OVER US? 005 00 002
RUN
    THE WAXEN COLOURS WEEP AND RUN, ... 003 00 029
    AND RIVERS RUN WHERE ALL WAS DRY, ... 008 00 002
    I MARK THE TOWER SWALLOWS RUN 015 00 028
    WHILE AGES AND WHILE AEONS RUN, ... 023 00 020
    AND THE INBOARD SEAS RUN SWIRLING AND HAWLING; 028 19 003
    FIVE AND TWENTY YEARS HAVE RUN 029 00 005
    RUN ALL YOUR RACE, O BRACE STERNER THAT STRAIN! 047 00 014
    THEY BREATHE NOT WHO ARE LATE TO RUN. -- 081 00 148
    TO NOT UNGENTLE DEATH NOW FORTH I RUN. 103 00 019
    THEY WASTE, THEY WITHER WORSE! THEY AS THEY RUN 150 00 003
RUNG
    HIGH THERE, HOW HE RUNG UPON THE REIN OF A WIMPLING WING . . . 036 00 004
    THERE! THE HALL RUNG! 054 00 033
RUNNEL
    A FREEZING RUNNEL SOBS AND DWARFS. 080 03 007
RUNNELS
    FROM EASY RUNNELS THE RICH-PIECED LAND . . .' . . . 005 00 039
RUNNING
    NO RUNNING IN THE RIVER-BED; 081 00 161
    EPISTLES, WHILE THE RUNNING PASTORAL BLEATS 107 04 022
    CAME RUNNING OVER THE LEA. 109 17 004
    RUPTURE, RUNNING SORES, WHAT MORE? IN BRIEF, IN BURDEN, . . . 152 C 009
RUNS
    THE CLOGGED BROOK RUNS WITH CHOKING SOUND 003 00 009
    RUNS HIS FINGERS THROUGH THE WHEAT, ... 098 01 002
    A BRITTLE SHEEN, RUNS UPWARD LIKE A CLIFF, ... 098 06 002
    AS WATER MOULDED TO THE DUCT IT RUNS IN; 101 00 004
    DROPS THE FRUIT OUT; THE DUCT RUNS DRY OR BREAKS; 101 00 010
RUPTURE
    RUPTURE, RUNNING SORES, WHAT MORE? IN BRIEF, IN BURDEN, . . . 152 C 009
RURAL
    RURAL SCENE, A RURAL SCENE, ... 043 00 023
    RURAL SCENE, A RURAL SCENE, ... 043 00 023
    SWEET ESPECIAL RURAL SCENE. 043 00 024
    RURAL RURAL KEEPING -- FOLK, FLOCKS, AND FLOWERS. 044 00 008
    RURAL RURAL KEEPING -- FOLK, FLOCKS, AND FLOWERS. 044 00 008
RUSH
    LEGATES MIGHT RUSH, ZEAL-RAMPANT, FIERY, ... 001 05 005
    THE DESCENDING BLUE; THAT BLUE IS ALL IN A RUSH 033 00 007
    THE HANGING SNOWS RUSH DOWN AND BARE 080 04 004
RUSHY
    WHILE RUSHY RAINS SHALL FALL OR BROOKS SHALL FLEET FROM FOUNTAINS, . 152 C 002
RUST
    BLADES OF MILAN IN CIRCLES RANG'D, GREW RUST 001 12 008
RUSTLE
    WHEN WHOLESOME SPIRITS RUSTLE ABOUT, ... 077 00 027
    FLEDGED THINGS DO RUSTLE NEAR; 160 00 033
RUTPEEL
    OF YESTERTEMPEST'S CREASES; IN POOL AND RUTPEEL PARCHES . . . 072 00 006

'CAUSE
    SPRING NOT, 'CAUSE WORLD IS WINTERING. 010 00 012
    ANG. SPRING NOT, 'CAUSE WORLD IS WINTERING. . . . . . APPEN A 12
'GAN
    THEN THEY, THUS RANGED, 'GAN MAKE FULL PLAINTIVELY 002 00 126

SANDS   (CONTINUED)
    AND MAZY SANDS ALL WATER-WATTLED 030 00 023
SANDY
    THAT HIS FAST-FLOWING HOURS WITH SANDY SILT 136 00 001
SANG
    ' WOULD IT WERE SUMMER-TIME, ' ANON SHE SANG 111 00 012
SANGUINE
    I BETTER'D ALL OUR PATH WITH SANGUINE EYES. 125 00 016
SANK
    SHADOW THAT SWAM OR SANK 043 00 007
    THAT ONEWHERE CURDED, ONEWHERE SUCKED OR SANK -- SOARED OR SANK -- , 071 00 006
    THAT ONEWHERE CURDED, ONEWHERE SUCKED OR SANK -- SOARED OR SANK -- , 071 00 006
SAP
    HAS NOT A CHARTER THAT ITS SAP SHALL LAST 014 01 004
    SO LATE THERE IS NO FORCE IN SAP OR BLOOD; 105 00 011
    MY SAP IS SEALED, ... 127 00 003
SAPPHIRE
    AND WAS AS THO' SOME SAPPHIRE MOLTEN-BLUE 002 00 045
    LIKE SHIVER'D RUBIES DANCE OR SHEEN OF SAPPHIRE HAIL. . 002 00 073
    FROM A HAZE OF SAPPHIRE LIGHT, ... 077 00 018
    SAPPHIRE, JACINTH, CHRYSOLITE, ... 077 00 119
    THE SAPPHIRE POOLS ARE SMIT WITH WHITE 078 00 007
SAPPHIRE-PALE
    WHERE LIQUID HEAVEN SAPPHIRE-PALE 077 00 099
SAPPHIRE-SHOT
    YET SUCH A SAPPHIRE-SHOT, ... 060 00 079
SAPRICIUS
    PROCONSUL! -- IS SAPRICIUS NEAR? -- 025 00 041
SARD
    HITHER BRING PEARL, OPAL, SARD; 024 00 003
SASH
    THE EAR IN MILK, LUSH THE SASH, ... 138 00 020
SAT
    HE SAT AND WROUGHT HIS OUTLINE ON A CLOUD. 107 01 010
    LOWLY ALICE SAT IN HER BOWER 109 16 001
    (LIKE ME) -- SAT SIGHING BY A SYCAMORE-TREE. ' . . . 111 00 001
    THE EARNEST-HEARTED MAIDEN SAT AND HEARD, ... 136 00 032
SATIN-PURFLED
    THE SATIN-PURFLED SMOOTH TO FOAM, AND SPREAD 002 00 079
SATURDAY
    ON SATURDAY SAILED FROM BREMEN, ... 028 12 001
SATURN
    WITH SUCH A SECONDING, NOR SATURN TOOK 014 02 009
    BAD SATURN WITH A SWART ASPECT 083 00 018
    TO SINGLE SATURN, LAST AND SOLITARY! 103 00 015
SAVE
    SAVE BY TWO STARS, MORE CROWDING LIGHTS ARISE, ... 002 00 032
    AND, SAVE BY DARTING ACCIDENTS, FORGET. 014 01 010
    NO BETTER SERVES ME NOW, SAVE BEST! NO OTHER 016 00 013
    SAVE CHRIST: TO CHRIST I LOOK, ON CHRIST I CALL. . . . 016 00 014
    ONE STIRRED FROM THE RIGGING TO SAVE 028 16 001
    SAVE MY HERO, O HERO SAVEST. 041 00 112
    SAVE WHERE THE UNVEXED WEST 077 00 097
    SAVE ME! AND YOU WERE STANDING NEAR. 081 00 103
    ALL QUESTS SAVE THE RECITAL OF THEIR GREATNESS; . . . 104 00 003
    THE TIME SAVE WHEN HER TEARS WHICH STILL [DESCEND] . 111 00 005
    SAVE IN THE BODY OF THE RAINS. 130 00 020
SAVED
    THE WORLD WAS SAVED BY VIRGINS, MADE THE MARK. 136 00 030
SAVES
    A SCHOONER SIGHTS, WITH ANOTHER, AND SAVES, ... 041 00 070
SAVEST
    SAVE MY HERO, O HERO SAVEST. 041 00 112
SAVIOUR
    DOWN ALL THAT GLORY IN THE HEAVENS TO GLEAN OUR SAVIOUR; 038 00 006
    BE CHRIST OUR SAVIOUR STILL. 060 00 054
SAVIOUR'S
    BUT EVEN OUR SAVIOUR'S AND OUR BLOOD, ... 006 00 032
SAVOUR
    HAS LOST ITS SAVOUR AND IS ROLL'D 092 00 005
SAW
    AND BLEEDING SAW. -- THUS HUNG FROM ROOM TO ROOM . . . 001 10 008
    THEN SAW I SUDDEN FROM THE WATERS BREAK 002 00 074
    I NEVER SAW HER SO DIVINE. 003 00 019
    THEN I SAW THAT HE HAD BOUND 004 00 018
    AND SOON I SAW IT SHEWING NEW 021 00 005
    WHEN WAS THE SUMMER THAT SAW THE BUD BLOW? -- 027 00 014
    THEY SAY WHO SAW ONE SEA-CORPSE COLD 041 00 073
    THIS NIGHT! WHAT SIGHTS YOU, HEART, SAW; WAYS YOU WENT! 067 00 003
    AND SAW THE MEN BEFORE THE FLOOD . . . . 093 A 002
    MET A NEW SHOWER, AND SAW THE RAINBOW FILL 107 03 010
    HE SAW HIS BROTHERS THREE. 109 07 002
    AND THERE SHE NEVER SAW THE KING, ... 109 24 003
    BUT SAW HIS BROTHERS THREE. 109 24 004
    I NEVER SAW THOSE FIELDS WHEREON THEIR BEST 119 00 011
    I SAW THE STARS LIKE FLASH OF FIRE. 135 00 008
    SEVERAL TIMES I SAW THEM, THRICE OR FOUR TIMES TURNING; 152 02 028

SAW   (CONTINUED)
    SINNER WHO SAW THE BLADE THAT HUNG   • •   •   •   •   •   • 166 00 017
    AS TOUCHING ME FULFILLED BE THY SAW;   • •   •   •   •   •   • APPEN D 27
SAY
    WHO IS THIS MOSES? WHO MADE HIM, WE SAY, • •   •   •   •   • 005 00 001
    WHO SAY THAT HAD I KNOWN I HAD APPROVED THEE, -- • • •   •   • 013 00 012
    THEN NEXT I HUNGERED: LOVE WHEN HERE, THEY SAY, • •   •   •   • 020 00 009
    I DID SAY YES   •   •   •   •   •   •   •   •   •   •   •   • 028 02 001
    HE THOUGHT HE HEARD SAY   •   •   •   •   •   •   •   •   •   • 041 00 051
    THEY SAY WHO SAW ONE SEA-CORPSE COLD   •   •   •   •   •   •   • 041 00 073
    THAT A STARLIGHT-WENDER OF OURS WOULD SAY •   •   •   •   •   • 041 00 101
    MUCH, HAD MUCH TO SAY   •   •   •   •   •   •   •   •   •   • 042 00 035
    CAME, I SAY, THIS DAY TO IT -- TO A FIRST COMMUNION.   •   •   •   • 048 00 008
    I SAY MORE: THE JUST MAN JUSTICES;   •   •   •   •   •   •   • 057 00 009
    I SAY THAT WE ARE WOUND   •   •   •   •   •   •   •   •   •   • 060 00 034
    WITH WITNESS I SPEAK THIS. BUT WHERE I SAY   •   •   •   •   • 067 00 005
    HONOUR IS FLASHED OFF EXPLOIT, SO WE SAY;   •   •   •   •   •   • 073 00 001
    BUT YET THEY SAY CHRIST COMES AT THE LAST DAY,   •   •   •   •   • 080 01 006
    AND ALL IN ONE SAY ' CRUCIFY! '   •   •   •   •   •   •   •   • 080 08 007
    SAY, O'ER IT HANGS A WATER-CLOUD   •   •   •   •   •   •   •   • 081 00 056
    WHO SAY THAT ANGELS, IN YOUR EAR   •   •   •   •   •   •   •   • 081 00 122
    HE'S WEDDED TO HIS THEORY, THEY SAY.   •   •   •   •   •   •   • 097 00 001
    DID I SAY BUT LATELY   •   •   •   •   •   •   •   •   •   • 102 01 029
    SAY BEAUTY LIES BUT IN THE MEET OF LINES, V   •   •   •   •   • 102 03 021
    I HEARD HER SAY, POOR POOR AFFLICTED SOUL, --   •   •   •   •   • 111 00 011
    YET WHAT YOU ARE, THE WORLD WOULD SAY, REMAIN;   •   •   •   •   • 125 00 024
    WHAT IF I HATED FLATTERY? SAY YOU DO;   •   •   •   •   •   •   • 125 00 028
    OF WHICH I SAY THERE IS NO JOY IN THEM.   •   •   •   •   •   • 125 00 047
    TO SAY I GO BECAUSE CASTARA GOES.   •   •   •   •   •   •   •   • 125 00 054
    YET I'D NOT SAY IT IS HER FACE ALONE   •   •   •   •   •   •   • 125 00 055
    BUT THE LILY IS PAST, AS I SAY, AND THE ROSE IS NOT IN ITS PRIME: • 128 00 014
    FOR A LETTER COMES AT LAST: (SHALL I SAY BEFORE CHRISTMAS IS COME?) 128 00 019
    SHE, HIGH AT THE HOUSETOP SITTING, AS THEY SAY,   •   •   •   •   • 136 00 013
    SAY IT IS ASHBOUGHS: WHETHER ON A DECEMBER DAY AND FURLED   •   •   • 149 A 004
    IN ALL HER BODY, I SAY, NO PLACE WAS LIKE HER EYES,   •   •   •   • 162 02 025
    SAY MAN THAN MAN MAY RANK HIS ROWS   •   •   •   •   •   •   • 166 00 009
SAYING
    BEYOND SAYING SWEET, PAST TELLING OF TONGUE,   •   •   •   •   • 028 09 005
    SAYING ' THIS WAS YOURS ' WITH HER, BUT NEW ONE, WORSE,   •   •   • 153 00 010
SAYS
    HE SAYS HIS SCIENCE HELPS HIM NOT TO LOOK   •   •   •   •   •   • 014 02 013
    OUR LAW SAYS: LOVE WHAT ARE LOVE'S WORTHIEST, WERE ALL KNOWN;   •   • 062 00 010
    SAYS ' GET YOU, GET YOU A LADY TO WED   •   •   •   •   •   •   • 109 09 001
    SAYS ' ARE YOU NOT LORD WILLIAM'S LOVE   •   •   •   •   •   •   • 109 18 003
    WHICH SAYS AT LEAST THEN GO WHILE ALL IS FRESH, --   •   •   •   • 125 00 058
    SAYS GO ON THEN I GO ON   •   •   •   •   •   •   •   •   •   • 138 00 035
    BUT DOWN DROP, IF IT SAYS STOP,   •   •   •   •   •   •   •   • 138 00 037
    HOW SAYS TRUSTY HEARING? THAT SHALL BE BELIEVED;   •   •   •   •   • 168 00 006
SCAFFOLD
    BUT MAN -- WE, SCAFFOLD OF SCORE BRITTLE BONES;   •   •   •   •   • 075 00 005
SCALDED
    LIKE SCALDED BANKS TOPP'D ONCE WITH PRINCIPAL FLOWERS;   •   •   • 102 02 012
SCALE
    ON PRANKED SCALE: OR THREADS OF CARMINE, SHOT   •   •   •   •   • 002 00 106
    NOW MELTING UPWARD THRO' THE SLOPING SCALE   •   •   •   •   •   • 002 00 132
SCALES
    GOD, LOVER OF SOULS, SWAYING CONSIDERATE SCALES,   •   •   •   •   • 034 00 012
SCAN
    THY WRING-WORLD RIGHT FOOT ROCK? LAY A LIONLIMB AGAINST ME? SCAN   •   • 064 00 006
SCANNED
    YOUNG THECLA, SCANNED THE DAZZLING STREETS ONE DAY;   •   •   •   • 136 00 014
SCANTED
    AS A DARE-GALE SKYLARK SCANTED IN A DULL CAGE   •   •   •   •   • 039 00 001
SCARCE
    AIRWARDS, DISTURB'D: AND THE SCARCE TROUBLED SEA   •   •   •   •   • 002 00 110
    AND MINOR SWEETNESS SCARCE MADE MENTION OF;   •   •   •   •   •   • 019 00 012
    TO SING SCARCE HEARD, AND SINGING FILL   •   •   •   •   •   •   • 077 00 077
    ONCE IT WAS SCARCE PERCEIVED LENT   •   •   •   •   •   •   •   • 081 00 011
    SCARCE WORTH DISCOVERY, IN SOME CORNER SEEN   •   •   •   •   •   • 103 00 002
    WORK WHICH TO SEE SCARCE SO MUCH AS BEGUN   •   •   •   •   •   • 150 00 007
SCARCE-CALL-SILV
    A SILVER SCARCE-CALL-SILVER GLOSS   •   •   •   •   •   •   •   • 098 17 001
SCARCE-SHEATHED
    YOUR SCARCE-SHEATHED BONES ARE WEARY OF BEING BENT;   •   •   •   • 011 00 013
SCARCELY
    AND SCARCELY TRACES WHERE ONE BEAUTY STRAYS   •   •   •   •   •   • 001 06 007
    WE SCARCELY CALL THAT BANQUET FOOD,   •   •   •   •   •   •   •   • 006 00 031
    MY PRAYERS I SCARCELY CALL TO PRAY.   •   •   •   •   •   •   •   • 018 00 004
    MY WINTER WORLD, THAT SCARCELY BREATHES THAT BLISS   •   •   •   • 076 00 013
    AND SCARCELY DOES APPEAR   •   •   •   •   •   •   •   •   •   • 105 00 004
SCARE
    FLAKE-DOVES SENT FLOATING FORTH AT A FARMYARD SCARE! --   •   •   • 032 00 007
SCARLESS
    WITH SWEET AND SCARLESS SKY;   •   •   •   •   •   •   •   •   • 060 00 120
SCARLET
    ONE SCARLET FEATHER TRAILING TO THE WIND;   •   •   •   •   •   • 002 00 081
    BUT HE SCORES IT IN SCARLET HIMSELF ON HIS OWN BESPOKEN,   •   •   • 028 22 005

SCARLET   (CONTINUED)
     IN SCARLET OR SOMEWHERE OF SOME DAY SEEING 048 00 038
     AND SCARLET WEAR THE SPIRIT OF WAR THERE EXPRESS. 063 00 008
     STILL THE SCARLET SWINGS AND DANCES ON THE BLADE. 152 02 013
SCARVES
     IN SCARVES OF SILKY SHOT AND SHINE, ... 003 00 021
SCATTER
     AND FAIL OR SCATTER ALL AWAY. 018 00 002
     IF A WUTHERING OF HIS PALMY SNOW-PINIONS SCATTER A COLOSSAL SMILE . . 045 00 013
SCENE
     THE SWEET ESPECIAL SCENE. 043 00 022
     RURAL SCENE, A RURAL SCENE, ... 043 00 023
     RURAL SCENE, A RURAL SCENE, . \ 043 00 023
     SWEET ESPECIAL RURAL SCENE. 043 00 024
SCENT
     THAT SCENT FROM BREEZES BREATHING BY ME, ... 160 00 021
SCENTED
     HIS LUSTY HANDS, IN GUSTS OF SCENTED WIND 002 00 088
SCEPTIC
     THE SCEPTIC DISAPPOINTMENT AND THE LOSS 014 03 012
SCHOOL
     AWAY FROM COUNTER, COURT, OR SCHOOL 030 00 002
     AWAY FROM COUNTER, COURT, OR SCHOOL, ... 030 00 038
SCHOOLED
     MORE PANGS WILL, SCHOOLED AT FOREPANGS, WILDER WRING. . . . 065 00 002
SCHOOLING
     THE VAULT AND SCOPE AND SCHOOLING 049 00 015
SCHOOLS
     SHE SCHOOLS THE FLIGHTY PUPILS OF HER EYES, ... 082 00 001
SCHOONER
     A SCHOONER SIGHTS, WITH ANOTHER, AND SAVES, ... 041 00 070
SCIENCE
     HE SAYS HIS SCIENCE HELPS HIM NOT TO LOOK 014 02 013
     AND OTHER SCIENCE ALL GONE OUT OF DATE 019 00 011
SCIONS
     WITH LISSOME SCIONS, SWEET SCIONS, ... 052 00 003
     WITH LISSOME SCIONS, SWEET SCIONS, ... 052 00 003
SCOOP
     SCOOP YOU FROM TEEMING FILTH SOME SICKLY HOVEL, ... 077 00 006
SCOOPED
     BREATHED ROUND; THE RACK OF RIBS; THE SCOOPED FLANK; LANK . . 071 00 002
SCOOPS
     OFF TRUNDLED TIMBER AND SCOOPS OF THE HILLSIDE GROUND, C . . 146 00 004
SCOPE
     THE VAULT AND SCOPE AND SCHOOLING 049 00 015
     BUT SINCE I HAVE NO SCOPE FOR BENEFITS 102 01 052
     HE SWEPT WHAT SCOPE HE WAS 148 00 015
SCORE
     HIS RASH-FRESH RE-WINDED NEW-SKEINED SCORE 035 00 006
     BUT MAN -- WE, SCAFFOLD OF SCORE BRITTLE BONES; 075 00 005
SCORES
     BUT HE SCORES IT IN SCARLET HIMSELF ON HIS OWN BESPOKEN, . . 028 22 005
SCORNING
     SWEET SOUL! NOT SCORNING HONEST SWEAT 139 00 005
SCOUR
     I CAN SCOUR THEE, FRESH BURNISH THEE, C 152 02 015
SCOURGE
     WHENCE WITH THE SCOURGE OF READY PIETY 001 05 004
     THE LOST ARE LIKE THIS, AND THEIR SCOURGE TO BE 067 00 013
SCOURGED
     SCOURGED UPON THE THRESHING-FLOOR; 006 00 006
SCREAM'D
     RANTERS SCREAM'D RANK REBELLION, THIS SHOULD BE 001 05 002
SCREEN
     THE SCREEN OF MY CAPTIVITY, ... 080 06 002
SCROLLED
     FIRM ACCENTS STRIKE HER FINE AND SCROLLED EAR, ... 136 00 021
     FAIRYLAND; SILK-BEECH, SCROLLED ASH, PACKED SYCAMORE, C . . 159 00 024
SCROLL-LEAVED
     STORM FLAKES WERE SCROLL-LEAVED FLOWERS, C 028 21 008
SCULLS
     COME, SWING THE SCULLS ON PENMAEN POOL. 030 00 008
SCULPTUR'D
     THE SCULPTUR'D IMAGE OF SUCH FAITH WOULD BE, ... 001 03 007
SCYTHE
     THE SOUR SCYTHE CRINGE, AND THE BLEAR SHARE COME. 028 11 008
SCYTHES
     THEIR HARNESS BEAMS LIKE SCYTHES IN MORNING GRASS; 104 00 006
SEA
     ROWING, I REACH'D A ROCK -- THE SEA WAS LOW -- 002 00 001
     SUN-FLUSH'D, UNTIL IT SEEM'D THEIR FATHER SEA 002 00 100
     AIRWARDS, DISTURB'D; AND THE SCARCE TROUBLED SEA 002 00 110
     TO KNOW THE DUSK DEPTHS OF THE PONDEROUS SEA, ... 002 00 122
     A PITEOUS SIREN SWEETNESS ON THE SEA, ... 002 00 127
     AND OUT OF THE SWING OF THE SEA. 009 00 008
     WORLD'S STRAND, SWAY OF THE SEA; 028 01 003
     AND THE SEA FLINT-FLAKE, BLACK-BACKED IN THE REGULAR BLOW, . . 028 13 005

218

SEA   (CONTINUED)
    AND WATCHES CHANGE UPON THE SEA; 077 00 032
    AROUND IT BALANCES THE LEVEL SEA. 098 04 002
    BEFORE HE WENT TO SEA. 109 01 004
    ' WHEN ARE YOU HOME FROM SEA? ' 109 02 002
    ' WHEN HE IS OVER THE SEA? ' 109 04 004
    WHEN I COME HOME FROM SEA. ' 109 05 004
    COME WITH YOU FROM OVER THE SEA? ' 109 07 004
    COME WITH ME FROM OVER THE SEA. ' 109 08 002
    THAT WAS BESIDE THE SEA. 109 15 002
    OR COME FROM OVER THE SEA? ' 109 31 004
    NOR YET FROM OVER THE SEA. 109 32 002
    NO RAINS SHALL FRESH THE FLATS OF SEA, ... 114 00 013
    NOT SO FAR OUTWARD IN THE SEA; 120 00 021
    THE SEA TOOK PITY; IT INTERPOSED WITH DOOM: 158 00 001
    THE BURLY SEA MAY QUITE FORGET 166 00 026
SEAMARK
    WHERE LIES YOUR LANDMARK, SEAMARK, OR SOUL'S STAR? . . . 157 00 019
SEABEACH
    THE THUNDER-PURPLE SEABEACH PLUMED PURPLE-OF-THUNDER, . . 045 00 012
SEA-CORPSE
    THEY SAY WHO SAW ONE SEA-CORPSE COLD 041 00 073
SEA-FAN
    SOME CARRIED THE SEA-FAN; SOME ROUND THE HEAD 002 00 058
SEA-FOWL
    THEN, LIKE A FLOCK OF SEA-FOWL MOUNTING HIGHER, ... 002 00 082
SEA-GULL
    SLIM-POINTED SEA-GULL PLUMES, AND DROOP BEHIND 002 00 080
SEA-GUST
    SHE LISTENED HOW THE SEA-GUST SHOOK 021 00 052
SEA-ROMP
    WITH THE SEA-ROMP OVER THE WRECK. 028 17 004
SEA-SWILL
    LEND HIM A LIFT FROM THE SEA-SWILL. 041 00 064
SEAL
    AND SEAL OF HIS SERAPH-ARRIVAL! AND THESE THY DAUGHTERS . . 028 23 005
    RESIGN THEM, SIGN THEM, SEAL THEM, SEND THEM, MOTION THEM WITH BREATH, 059 06 016
SEALED
    ARE SISTERLY SEALED IN WILD WATERS. 028 23 007
    MY SAP IS SEALED, ... 127 00 003
SEALING
    O NOW WELL WORK THAT SEALING SACRED OINTMENT! 048 00 033
SEALING-WAX
    WHAT I DID ASK THEN WAS A CIRCLE OF ROSE-RED SEALING-WAX . . 128 00 015
SEALS
    AND SEALS OF RED CARNATION WHICH HAD EACH V 098 12 004
SEAMANSHIP
    LEAGUES, LEAGUES OF SEAMANSHIP 041 00 082
SEAMEN
    OF SEAMEN WHELM'D IN CHASMS OF THE MID-MAIN, ... 002 00 120
    TAKE SETTLER AND SEAMEN, TELL MEN WITH WOMEN, ... 028 12 003
    SHE HAD COME FROM A CRUISE, TRAINING SEAMEN -- 041 00 013
SEAR
    THAT STRUGGLING SHOULD NOT SEAR HIM, A GIFT SHOULD CHEER HIM . 142 00 008
SEARCH
    HOW SHALL I SEARCH, WHO NEVER SOUGHT? 081 00 173
    AND SEARCH ME THROUGH 127 00 017
SEARCHING
    THAT DARES TO CAST ITS SEARCHING SIGHT 023 00 029
SEARED
    AND ALL IS SEARED WITH TRADE; BLEARED, SMEARED WITH TOIL; . . 031 00 006
SEAS
    AND THE INBOARD SEAS RUN SWIRLING AND HAWLING; 028 19 003
    BURDEN, IN WIND'S BURLY AND BEAT OF ENDRAGONED SEAS. . . 028 27 008
    TAKES TO THE SEAS AND SNOWS 041 00 059
    PURPLE EYES AND SEAS OF LIQUID LEAVES ALL DAY. 068 00 008
    AND KEEPS THE BREEZE AND CLEARS THE SEAS 083 00 013
    WHERE THE SEAS SET 088 00 006
    MUST SEE THE GREEN SEAS ROLL V 088 00 009
    OF CRUMBLING, FORE-FOUNDERING, THUNDERING ALL-SURFY SEAS IN; SEEN . 141 00 005
    BEUNO. O NOW WHILE SKIES ARE BLUE, NOW WHILE SEAS ARE SALT, . . 152 C 001
    BUT FROM BEYOND SEAS, ERIN, FRANCE AND FLANDERS, EVERYWHERE, . 152 C 020
SEASON
    AT THIS SPRING SEASON OF THE YEAR? ' 004 00 013
    WHAT WAS ITS SEASON THEN? HOW LONG AGO? 027 00 013
    DATED DUE TO SEASON -- 042 00 004
    ON SUCH A SEASON OF THE DAY AND YEAR. 107 01 004
SEASONS
    INTO ALL SEASONS, THOUGH NO WINTER CAST 014 01 005
    LEAVES SPENT, NEW SEASONS, ALTER'D SKY, ... 015 00 002
    HAD CALLED THE SEASONS' CHANGEFUL MOODS 023 00 023
SEAT
    SETS UP A SHADOW IN THY SEAT; 023 00 016
    BEFORE THAT ROCK, MY SEAT, HE STANDS; 080 09 001
SEATS
    SITS TO THE BEAST THAT SEATS HIM -- CARE. 166 00 040
SECOND
    SECOND THIS FIERY STRAIN? NOT ALWAYS; O NO NO! 152 02 046

SEEING   (CONTINUED)
```
ONLY NOT WITHIN SEEING OF THE SUN.  .   .   .   .   .   .   .   .   .   059 0G 003
YES. WHY DO WE ALL, SEEING OF A SOLDIER, BLESS HIM? BLESS  .   .   .   063 00 001
NOW, AND SEEING SOMEWHERE SOME MAN DO ALL THAT MAN CAN DO,  .   .   .   063 00 011
WHAT IF MY SUBJECT, SEEING THIS, RESENT  .   .   .   .   .   .   .   .   094 00 005
OF MY BEING AND AS SEEING  .   .   .   .   .   .   .   .   .   .   .   .   155 00 007
SEEING, TOUCHING, TASTING ARE IN THEE DECEIVED!  .   .   .   .   .   .   168 00 005
```
SEEK
```
WHERE SEEK THEE WITH UNSANDALLED FEET.  .   .   .   .   .   .   .   .   023 00 018
SEEK GOD'S HOUSE IN HAPPY THRONG!  .   .   .   .   .   .   .   .   .   .   024 00 025
THEN I SEEK OUT THE SHADOW OF STONES  .   .   .   .   .   .   .   .   .   080 03 001
BUT RIGHT MUST SEEK A SIDE  .   .   .   .   .   .   .   .   .   .   .   .   148 00 027
```
SEEKING
```
A STEALTHY WIND CREPT ROUND SEEKING TO BLOW,  .   .   .   .   .   .   002 00 137
```
SEEM
```
TO SEEM THE STRANGER LIES MY LOT, MY LIFE .   .   .   .   .   .   .   .   066 00 001
WELL, I KNOW NOT, BUT ALL THINGS SEEM TO-NIGHT  .   .   .   .   .   .   102 01 010
THEY SEEM TO FOLD THE HILLS WITH GOLDEN CAPES!  .   .   .   .   .   .   104 00 011
THEY SEEM TO PRESS AND DROOP AND STARE,  .   .   .   .   .   .   .   .   135 00 020
```
SEEMED
```
WHY, IT SEEMED OF COURSE! SEEMED OF RIGHT IT SHOULD.  .   .   .   .   034 00 008
WHY, IT SEEMED OF COURSE! SEEMED OF RIGHT IT SHOULD.  .   .   .   .   034 00 008
THEY SEEMED TO PRESS AND STARE  .   .   .   .   .   .   .   .   .   .   098 29 002
OF VIRTUE AND VICE! BUT MOST ( IT SEEMED HIS SENSE )  .   .   .   .   136 00 027
HIS POWERS SEEMED FREE TO PLAY!  .   .   .   .   .   .   .   .   .   .   148 00 014
```
SEEMING
```
UNCLEAN AND SEEMING UNFORGIVEN  .   .   .   .   .   .   .   .   .   .   018 00 003
BUT FOR SOULS SUNK IN SEEMING  .   .   .   .   .   .   .   .   .   .   .   041 00 118
C THEN SWEETEST SEEMS THE SEEMING BRIDE  .   .   .   .   .   .   .   120 00 018
```
SEEM'D
```
FAIR BEDS THEY SEEM'D OF WATER-LILY FLAKES  .   .   .   .   .   .   .   002 00 013
SUN-FLUSH'D, UNTIL IT SEEM'D THEIR FATHER SEA  .   .   .   .   .   .   002 00 100
IT SEEM'D AN EVENING IN THE SPRING!  .   .   .   .   .   .   .   .   .   004 00 002
HE SEEM'D A DISMAL MIRKY STAMP  .   .   .   .   .   .   .   .   .   .   004 00 008
IT SEEM'D SO HARD AND DISMAL THING,  .   .   .   .   .   .   .   .   .   004 00 031
SHE STOOD BEFORE A LIGHT NOT HERS, AND SEEM'D  .   .   .   .   .   .   079 00 003
I C DREAM'D J MY COUNTERPART. IT SEEM'D  .   .   .   .   .   .   .   .   081 00 086
SOME KNELT, SOME STOOD! I SEEM'D TO FEEL  .   .   .   .   .   .   .   081 00 093
BUT ALL THE WHILE IT SEEM'D TO ME .   .   .   .   .   .   .   .   .   .   081 00 112
HIS SHEEP SEEM'D TO COME FROM IT AS THEY STEPT,  .   .   .   .   .   107 01 011
```
SEEMS
```
IT SEEMS! FOR GRANDEUR BARREN LEFT AND DULL  .   .   .   .   .   .   001 15 008
THEN SWEETEST SEEMS THE HOUSELESS SHORE,  .   .   .   .   .   .   .   015 00 035
OUR PRAYER SEEMS LOST IN DESERT WAYS,  .   .   .   .   .   .   .   .   023 00 005
SEEMS BY A DIVINE DOOM CHANNELLED, NOR DO I CRY  .   .   .   .   .   048 00 041
HIS THOUGHTS ON HER, FORSAKEN THAT SHE SEEMS,  .   .   .   .   .   .   050 00 011
SEEMS TO US SWEET OF US AND SWIFTLY AWAY WITH, C  .   .   .   .   .   059 0G 008
NAY IN ALL THAT TOIL, THAT COIL, SINCE ( SEEMS ) I KISSED THE ROD,  .   064 00 010
WHILE THE UPGAZING COUNTRY SEEMS  .   .   .   .   .   .   .   .   .   .   077 00 125
THINGS THAT SHE LIKES SEEMS OFTEN TO DESPISE,  .   .   .   .   .   .   094 00 017
THEN SHE SEEMS SWEET WHO SEEMS HIS BRIDE,  .   .   .   .   .   .   .   120 00 016
THEN SHE SEEMS SWEET WHO SEEMS HIS BRIDE,  .   .   .   .   .   .   .   120 00 016
SHE SOUR WHO SEEMS THE SLIGHTED NIX.  .   .   .   .   .   .   .   .   .   120 00 017
C THEN SWEETEST SEEMS THE SEEMING BRIDE  .   .   .   .   .   .   .   120 00 018
AT HIGHEST WHEN HE SEEMS TO BRUSH THE CLOUDS,  .   .   .   .   .   .   122 00 004
WIPED I AM SURE THIS WAS! IT SEEMS, NOT WELL! FOR STILL,  .   .   .   152 02 012
```
SEEN
```
ON THE FLOWERS THAT WERE SEEN  .   .   .   .   .   .   .   .   .   .   004 00 009
JUST SEEN, MAY BE TO MANY UNKNOWN MEN  .   .   .   .   .   .   .   .   012 02 012
THE GLADDEST THING THAT OUR EYES HAVE SEEN  .   .   .   .   .   .   026 00 018
IT IS EVEN SEEN, TIME'S SOMETHING SERVER,  .   .   .   .   .   .   .   103 00 053
SCARCE WORTH DISCOVERY, IN SOME CORNER SEEN  .   .   .   .   .   .   129 00 002
PAST, THE PAST, NO MORE BE SEEN!  .   .   .   .   .   .   .   .   .   .   131 00 006
TOLD OF THE WONDERS HE HAD SEEN.  .   .   .   .   .   .   .   .   .   .   141 00 005
OF CRUMBLING, FORE-FOUNDERING, THUNDERING ALL-SURFY SEAS IN! SEEN  .   .   152 02 001
MY HEART, WHERE HAVE WE BEEN? WHAT HAVE WE SEEN, MY MIND?  .   .   152 02 001
WHAT HAVE WE SEEN? HER HEAD, SHEARED FROM HER SHOULDERS, FALL,  .   152 02 018
```
SEES
```
SOFT, WHEN SHE SEES HER INFANT START,  .   .   .   .   .   .   .   .   023 00 051
BLINDS HER! BUT SHE THAT WEATHER SEES ONE THING, ONE!  .   .   .   028 19 005
MARY SEES, SYMPATHISING  .   .   .   .   .   .   .   .   .   .   .   .   042 00 026
WHEN HIS MELLOW SMILE HE SEES  .   .   .   .   .   .   .   .   .   .   077 00 105
SEES THE RIGHT THING TO DO, AND DOES NOT ACT!  .   .   .   .   .   .   094 00 020
HE SEES HER, O BUT HE MUST MISS  .   .   .   .   .   .   .   .   .   .   120 00 009
SO SHE! ONE SEES THAT HERE AND THERE  .   .   .   .   .   .   .   .   145 00 011
BETWEENWHILES, BUT SHE SEES HERSELF NOT HIM.  .   .   .   .   .   .   151 00 012
SEES THE BEVY OF THEM, HOW THE BOYS  .   .   .   .   .   .   .   .   159 00 016
THAT HE HIES TO A POOL NEIGHBOURING! SEES IT IS THE BEST  .   .   .   159 00 022
```
SELDOM
```
THAT NE'ER NEED HUNGER, TOM! TOM SELDOM SICK,  .   .   .   .   .   .   070 00 006
```
SELDOMER
```
SELDOMER HEARTSORE! THAT TREADS THROUGH, PRICKPROOF, THICK  .   .   070 00 007
```
SELF
```
OF OWN, OF ABRUPT SELF THERE SO THRUSTS ON, SO THRONGS THE EAR.  .   .   045 00 008
BACK TO GOD, BEAUTY'S SELF AND BEAUTY'S GIVER. C  .   .   .   .   .   059 0G 019
THE SWEET ALMS' SELF IS HER  .   .   .   .   .   .   .   .   .   .   .   060 00 043
NEW SELF AND NOBLER ME  .   .   .   .   .   .   .   .   .   .   .   .   060 00 069
```

SELF   (CONTINUED)
SELF IN SELF STEEPED AND PASHED -- QUITE C 061 00 006
SELF IN SELF STEEPED AND PASHED -- QUITE C 061 00 006
WORLD'S LOVELIEST -- MEN'S SELVES, SELF FLASHES OFF FRAME AND FACE. 062 00 011
ME LIVE TO MY SAD SELF HEREAFTER KIND, ... 069 00 002
SOUL, SELF; COME, POOR JACKSELF, I DO ADVISE 069 00 009
THAT THIS IS TRUE OF: 'TIS CASTARA'S SELF: 125 00 056
FROM THE SELF THAT I HAVE BEEN, ... 129 00 005
IS CORPSE NOW, CANNOT CHANGE; MY OTHER SELF, THIS SOUL, . . 152 02 062
THE SELFLESS SELF OF SELF, MOST STRANGE, MOST STILL, . . . 157 00 027
THE SELFLESS SELF OF SELF, MOST STRANGE, MOST STILL, . . . 157 00 027
SELFBENT
TO HIS OWN SELFBENT SO BOUND, SO TIED TO HIS TURN, . . . 058 00 011
SELFDISPOSAL
REASON, SELFDISPOSAL, CHOICE OF BETTER OR WORSE WAY, . . . 152 02 061
SELFISH
IS SLIGHTLY SELFISH IN HER INMOST SOUL) 094 00 028
SELF-EMBRACED
AS A SELF-EMBRACED SWEET THOUGHTS:V 085 00 003
SELF-FEELING
LIFE'S QUICK, THIS KIND, THIS KEEN SELF-FEELING, ... 152 02 063
SELF-INSTRESSED
TO ITS OWN FINE FUNCTION, WILD AND SELF-INSTRESSED, . . . 047 00 007
SELF-MADE
THOUGH SELF-MADE BANDS AT LAST MAY TRUE LOVE BIND, . . . 102 03 019
SELF-OUTWITTED
AND LIKE A SELF-OUTWITTED BLAST 081 00 074
SELF-SACRIFICE
TALKS OF SELF-SACRIFICE, YET CAN'T FORGIVE: 094 00 022
SELF-SENTENCED
SELF-SENTENCED, STILL 127 00 014
SELF-WILL
HIES HEADSTRONG TO ITS WELLBEING OF A SELF-WISE SELF-WILL! . . 048 00 024
SELF-WISE
HIES HEADSTRONG TO ITS WELLBEING OF A SELF-WISE SELF-WILL! . . 048 00 024
SELFLESS
THE SELFLESS SELF OF SELF, MOST STRANGE, MOST STILL, . . . 157 00 027
SELFQUAINED
BUILT OF CHANCEQUARRIED, SELFQUAINED, HOAR-HUSKED ROCKS . . 159 00 037
SELFSAME
TO HOLD ME QUITE FIX'D IN THE SELFSAME PLIGHT: 080 13 006
SELFSTRUNG
WHERE, SELFWRUNG, SELFSTRUNG, SHEATHE- AND SHELTERLESS, C . . . 061 00 014
SELFWRUNG
WHERE, SELFWRUNG, SELFSTRUNG, SHEATHE- AND SHELTERLESS, C . . . 061 00 014
SELFYEAST
SELFYEAST OF SPIRIT A DULL DOUGH SOURS. I SEE 067 00 012
SELVAGGIA
SELVAGGIA, ORINDA, AND ADELA, AND THE REST. 125 00 038
SELVES
SELVES -- GOES ITSELF; MYSELF IT SPEAKS AND SPELLS, . . . 057 00 007
WORLD'S LOVELIEST -- MEN'S SELVES, SELF FLASHES OFF FRAME AND FACE. 062 00 011
AS I AM MINE, THEIR SWEATING SELVES: BUT WORSE. 067 00 014
SEND
BUT NOW I AM SO TIRED I SOON SHALL SEND 014 03 008
WHAT RELISH SHALL THE CENSERS SEND 022 00 019
RESIGN THEM, SIGN THEM, SEAL THEM, SEND THEM, MOTION THEM WITH BREATH, 059 06 016
MINE, O THOU LORD OF LIFE, SEND MY ROOTS RAIN. 074 00 014
FOR HE WHOM I SEND FORTH TO CRUCIFY, ... 080 11 003
I CAN SEND UP AN ESAU'S CRY: 081 00 126
SPEND ME OR END ME WHAT GOD SHALL SEND ME, ... 156 00 013
I BESEECH THEE SEND ME WHAT I THIRST FOR SO, ... 168 00 026
SENDINGS
THERE! AND YOUR SWEETEST SENDINGS, AH DIVINE, ... 048 00 013
SENDS
HEAVEN COMFORT SENDS, BUT HARRY IT AWAY, ... 089 00 005
SENSE
OH! TILL THOU GIVEST THAT SENSE BEYOND, ... 023 00 043
HIS LIPS MOVED FAST IN SENSE TOO THICK! 081 00 100
WITH TWICE AS FINE A SENSE TO APPREHEND THEM, ... 102 01 012
AND BROUGHT THE SENSE OF GENTLE FELLOWSHIP, ... 107 02 004
SO TAKES THE SISTER SENSE) CAN FIND NO MARK, ... 113 00 004
OF VIRTUE AND VICE! BUT MOST (IT SEEMED HIS SENSE) . . 136 00 027
SUCK ANY SENSE FROM THAT WHO CAN: 147 00 003
GOES MARCHING THRO' MY MIND. WHAT SENSE IS THIS? IT HAS NONE. . 152 01 022
SENSES
FIVE LIKE THE SENSES AND MEMBERS OF MEN: 027 00 038
AT ONCE THE SENSES GIVE THE MUSIC BACK, ... 113 00 010
SENSITIVE
ABOUT HERSELF SHE IS MOST SENSITIVE, ... 094 00 021
OF THE WOOD-SORREL AND ALL THINGS SENSITIVE? 122 00 011
AS THE WOOD-SORREL AND ALL THINGS SENSITIVE 122 00 014
SENSUAL
HENCE SENSUAL GROSS DESIRES, ... 077 00 001
SENT
IT IS THE SHUT, THE CURFEW SENT 022 00 006
FLAKE-DOVES SENT FLOATING FORTH AT A FARMYARD SCARE! -- . . 032 00 007

222

SENT   (CONTINUED)
    IS CRIES COUNTLESS, CRIES LIKE DEAD LETTERS SENT • • • • • • 067 00 007
    YET THERE CAME ONE WHO SENT HIS FLOCK BEFORE HIM, • • • • • 107 01 007
    AND WITH THE LAST POST OVER I KNEW NO LETTER WAS SENT. • • • 128 00 002
    SENT TO THE MAIDEN SWEET, • • • • • • • • • • • APPEN D 02
SENTENCE
    OF THE OUTWARD SENTENCE LOW LAYS HIM, LISTED TO A HERESY, HERE. • • 045 00 004
SEPULCHRE
    -- BEFORE THE SEPULCHRE THERE STOOD A GATE, • • • • 001 04 006
SEQUENCE
    AND EVERY PRAISED SEQUENCE OF SWEET STRINGS, • • • • • 019 00 007
SEQUENCES
    OR CAREFUL-SPACED SEQUENCES OF SOUND, • • • • • • 102 03 002
    IN CAREFUL-SPACED SEQUENCES OF SOUND V • • • • • 102 03 022
SEQUINS
    THE SKY MINTED INTO GOLDEN SEQUINS. • • • • • • 098 25 001
SERAPH
    THE SERAPH BROWS OF GALAHAD, • • • • • • • 077 00 042
SERAPH-ARRIVAL
    AND SEAL OF HIS SERAPH-ARRIVAL! AND THESE THY DAUGHTERS • • • 028 23 005
SERFDOM
    LOVE BY PRENATAL SERFDOM STILL CONFINED • • • • • 102 03 015
SERGED
    BREATHE EASTER NOW; YOU SERGED FELLOWSHIPS, • • • • 011 00 007
SERMONS
    THEY'RE OUT OF DATE -- LENT SERMONS ALL THE YEAR. • • • • 096 05 002
SERVANTS
    BE IN THY SERVANTS' HEARTS AS WELL, • • • • • • 169 00 002
SERVE
    THAT HERE WILL SERVE ME FOR COMPARISON? • • • • • 014 03 011
    AND DO SERVE GOD TO SERVE TO • • • • • • • 048 00 027
    AND DO SERVE GOD TO SERVE TO • • • • • • • 048 00 027
    WITH GRACE TO SERVE HIM BY • • • • • • • APPEN D 49
SERVED
    SERVED BY MESSENGER? • • • • • • • • • 025 00 028
    MARK CHRIST OUR KING. HE KNOWS WAR, SERVED THIS SOLDIERING THROUGH; • 063 00 009
    YOU CRIED ' BUT I HAVE SERVED THEE WELL, • • • • • 081 00 107
    THEO. SERVED BY SWEET SECONDER? -- • • • • • APPEN A 28
SERVER
    IT IS EVEN SEEN, TIME'S SOMETHING SERVER, • • • • • 041 00 053
SERVES
    NO BETTER SERVES ME NOW, SAVE BEST; NO OTHER • • • • 016 00 013
    TO WHAT SERVES MORTAL BEAUTY -- DANGEROUS; DOES SET DANC- • • 062 00 001
    WRETCH. UNDER A COMFORT SERVES IN A WHIRLWIND: ALL • • • 065 00 013
    ASK WHOM HE SERVES OR NOT • • • • • • • • 148 00 023
    SERVES AND WHAT SIDE HE TAKES. • • • • • • • 148 00 024
SERVICE
    THEY SHRIVE THEMSELVES AND CRY, ' GOOD SERVICE TO OUR GOD. ' • • 001 05 009
    SEE, LORD, AT THY SERVICE LOW LIES HERE A HEART • • • • 168 00 003
SERVINGMAN
    AND SHE WAS WARE OF A SERVINGMAN • • • • • • 109 17 003
    ' O WHAT WILL YOU NOW, GOOD SERVINGMAN, • • • • • 109 18 001
SET
    IS SET UPON YOUR BOUGHS BELOW; • • • • • • 010 00 010
    NOT SET, BECAUSE THEIR BUDS NOT SPRING; • • • • • 010 00 011
    AND I HAVE ONLY SET THE SAME TO PEN. • • • • • 012 02 014
    IS SET IN ANY ORCHARD; NO, • • • • • • • 025 00 010
    NOT SET BECAUSE THEIR BUDS NOT SPRING! • • • • • 025 00 011
    WIND-BEAT WHITEBEAM! AIRY ABELES SET ON A FLARE! • • • • 032 00 006
    TO WHAT SERVES MORTAL BEAUTY -- DANGEROUS; DOES SET DANC- • • 062 00 001
    IS NOT SOME LITTLE BELA SET • • • • • • • 081 00 142
    WHERE THE SEAS SET • • • • • • • • • 088 00 006
    WHERE WATERS SET V • • • • • • • • • 088 00 010
    ROUND THIS UNSEXING DOUBLET, -- WHILE I SET • • • • 102 01 004
    THEN HE SET SAIL IN A GOLDEN SHIP • • • • • • 109 06 003
    OR EVER HE SET HIS FOOT TO THE LAND • • • • • 109 07 001
    ERE YOU SET SAIL THE KING WAS DEAD. • • • • • 109 09 003
    AND SET THE GLASSES FROM THE SUN • • • • • • 165 00 007
    ANG. IS SET IN ANY ORCHARD, NO; • • • • • • APPEN A 10
    ANG. NOT SET BECAUSE THEIR BUDS NOT SPRING; • • • • APPEN A 11
SETS
    SETS UP A SHADOW IN THY SEAT; • • • • • • • 023 00 016
    WHEN 'TIS THE CONFIDANTE THAT SETS THE TASK. • • • • 094 00 002
SETTING
    AND IT WAS AT THE SETTING OF THE DAY. • • • • • 002 00 006
SETTLE
    WILL CRISP ITSELF OR SETTLE AND SPIN • • • • • • 145 00 010
SETTLER
    TAKE SETTLER AND SEAMEN, TELL MEN WITH WOMEN, • • • • 028 12 003
SEVEN
    I GAZED UNHINDER'D: MERMAIDS SIX OR SEVEN, • • • • 002 00 034
    AND CHARLES'S WAIN, THE WONDROUS SEVEN, • • • • • 030 00 017
    THE SEVEN OR SEVEN TIMES SEVEN • • • • • • 060 00 087
    THE SEVEN OR SEVEN TIMES SEVEN • • • • • • 060 00 087
    THE SEVEN OR SEVEN TIMES SEVEN • • • • • • 060 00 087
    LIT WITH EXQUISITE TINTS SEVEN • • • • • • • 077 00 109
    A TURN OF SEVEN NOTES OR FIVE, • • • • • • • 081 00 007

223

SEVEN   (CONTINUED)
     FIVE NOTES OR SEVEN, LATE AND FEW: 081 00 023
       ' I THINK IT IS SEVEN DAYS,' SHE SAID, ... 109 16 003
     AND SEVEN EARS CROWN THE LODGED CORN, ... 114 00 006
SEVENFOLD-SINGLE
     ALL A SEVENFOLD-SINGLE GEM, ... 077 00 116
SEVENTEENTH
     THOUGH THEY TOOK TILL THE SEVENTEENTH OF NEXT OCTOBER TO READ. .   . 128 00 008
SEVENTY
     AND SEVENTY PALMS THERE STAND. 005 00 024
SEVERAL
     MY SEVERAL MOANS COME DISTANT IN THEIR TONES 080 03 003
     IN THE FIRST SIGNALS OF THE SEVERAL DROPS 084 00 003
     SEVERAL TIMES I SAW THEM, THRICE OR FOUR TIMES TURNING; .   .   . 152 02 028
SEVERANCE
     [THEN SEVERANCE AND SORROW.] 110 00 008
SEW
     THE LAST THING MARGARET'S FINGERS SEW 145 00 013
SEWERS
     THAN SEWERS WITH SACRED OILS, MANKIND, THAT MOB, COMES, COME! .   . 152 02 070
SEX
     OUR SEX SHOULD BE BORN IN APRIL PERHAPS OR THE LILY-TIME; .   .   . 128 00 013
SEXED
     ENROLL'D AND SEXED WITH -- ---- ---- V 102 01 064
SEXING
     SEXING AND RANKING WITH OUR RUDER FILES V 102 01 063
     ENROLL'D AND SEXING WITH -- ---- ---- V 102 01 064
SHADE
     YE WEARY, COME INTO THE SHADE. 006 00 026
     A DROP OF SHADE ROLLS OVER FIELD AND FLOCK; 098 03 002
     ENTRIES OR BANKS ALL OVER SHADE 166 00 023
SHADES
     MORE SWEETLY SHADES HER STOLEN HAIR 120 00 007
     HAS SHADES, IS NOWHERE NONE: 148 00 026
SHADOW
     SETS UP A SHADOW IN THY SEAT; 023 00 016
     SHADOW THAT SWAM OR SANK 043 00 007
     EACH SHAPE AND SHADOW SHOWS. 060 00 085
     STREAKS OF SHADOW, THISTLED LEAS, ... 077 00 137
     THEN I SEEK OUT THE SHADOW OF STONES 080 03 001
     SPANN'D WITH SHADOW EVERY ONE, ... 098 08 003
     IN HOLLOWS OF HER FORM THE SHADOW CLINGS; 099 00 008
     MAKING THE SHADOW SWEETER, A SPIRITUAL GRACE 107 04 015
     [WHERE SHAKE SHADOW IS SUN'S-EYE-RINGED] 138 00 042
SHADOWIEST
     THERE! SWEETEST, FRESHEST, SHADOWIEST; 159 00 023
SHADOWS
     MASKED BY THESE BARE SHADOWS, SHAPE AND NOTHING MORE, .   .   . 168 00 002
SHADOWTACKLE
     SHIVELIGHTS AND SHADOWTACKLE IN LONG LASHES LACE, LANCE, AND PAIR. . 072 00 004
SHAFTS
     BROAD-FLUTED, NOR WITH SHAFTS ACANTHUS-CROWN'D, ... 001 07 003
     WITH PARALLEL SHAFTS, -- AS UPWARD-PARTED ASHES, -- 107 04 005
SHAKE
     FAR OFF A NEREID COMPANY, AND SHAKE 002 00 075
     SHALL SHAKE HER FRUIT AS LIBANUS, ... 006 00 028
     HIS FIRE, THE SUN WOULD SHAKE, ... 060 00 096
     SHAKE THE BALANCED DAFFODILS. 098 07 002
     SHAKE AND UNSET YOUR MORTICED METAPHORS. V 101 00 008
     [WHERE SHAKE SHADOW IS SUN'S-EYE-RINGED] 138 00 042
SHAKEN
     SHEW BRIGHTER SHAKEN IN PENMAEN POOL. 030 00 020
     THE SHAKEN PLUMAGE OF MY SPIRIT'S WINGS. 077 00 010
SHAKES
     WITH FRETTY CHERVIL, LOOK, AND FRESH WIND SHAKES 074 00 011
     SHAKES ITS COCOONING MISTS; AND SO SHE COMES 103 00 008
SHAKESPEARE'S
     HOW SHAKESPEARE'S ENGLAND WEDS WITH DANTE'S ITALY. 098 35 002
SHALLOW
     HOW THESE TWO SHAME THIS SHALLOW AND FRAIL TOWN! 035 00 009
     -- THE SHALLOW FOLDS OF THE WOOD 098 09 001
     COVERS WITH SHALLOW SILVER, THAT UNSETS 098 31 002
     COVERS WITH SHALLOW SILVER, THE LOCK OF CLOUDS 098 31 005
     AND NOONDAY HAVE A SHALLOW SHINE, ... 114 00 004
     AND WONDER AT HER SHALLOW SMILE. 120 00 012
SHALLOWING
     WHILE PHOSPHOR, RISEN UPON THE SHALLOWING DARK, ... 098 28 003
SHALLOWY
     THE CART ROAD WITH A SHALLOWY BED 135 00 026
SHAME
     THE INCAPABLE AND CUMBROUS SHAME 015 00 018
     HOW THESE TWO SHAME THIS SHALLOW AND FRAIL TOWN! 035 00 009
     FOR FOND LOVE AND FOR SHAME. 054 00 037
     HE! HAND TO MOUTH HE LIVES, AND VOIDS WITH SHAME; 075 00 009
     HIS INJURY SHE'LL AVENGE WITH RAGING SHAME. 082 00 006
     DEEP SHAME IT WERE TO BE DISCOVER'D SO, ... 102 01 039
     NO, LET THAT GO; I HAVE SAID GOODNIGHT TO SHAME. 102 01 042

SHAME   (CONTINUED)
    ' IT IS FOR THE SHAME OF THE LOWLY WOMAN 109 14 003
SHANK
    HEAD AND FOOT, SHOULDER AND SHANK -- C 071 00 003
    ROPE-OVER THIGH; KNEE-NAVE; AND BARRELLED SHANK -- C 071 00 003
SHAPE
    OF MAZY SHAPE AND HUE, BUT NOW BEREFT 001 08 003
    SHAPE NOTHING, LIPS; BE LOVELY-DUMB; 022 00 005
    EACH SHAPE AND SHADOW SHOWS. 060 00 085
    AND I SHALL SHAPE ONE TO MY THOUGHT. 080 12 007
    SHAPE ON THE UNDER SIDE AND SIZE AND DROP. 111 00 007
    AT LAST THE BIRD IS FOUND A FLICKERING SHAPE AND SLIM.   .   .   . 113 00 009
    MASKED BY THESE BARE SHADOWS, SHAPE AND NOTHING MORE,   .   .   . 168 00 002
SHAPED
    TO GRACE THEM SPIRES ARE SHAPED WITH CORNER SQUINCHES;   .   .   . 096 07 002
    [WHO SHAPED THESE WALLS HAS SHEWN 148 00 009
SHAPEN
    THE SHAPEN FLAGS AND DRILLED HOLES OF SKY, ... 012 02 011
SHAPES
    THAT SHAPES IN HALF-LIGHT HIS DEPARTING RINGS, ... 019 00 003
    WHEN STRANGELY LOOM ALL SHAPES THAT BE, ... 077 00 031
    NOW LIKE THE BIRD THAT SHAPES ALONE 081 00 006
    -- -- -- ---- -- MAIL'D SHAPES OF BRONZE, V 102 02 010
    A RAINBOW ALSO SHAPES ITSELF BEYOND 107 03 006
    IT SHAPES ITSELF IN TAPER SKEINS; 130 00 018
SHARDED
    NOR CLOSE THE CLAYFIELD'S SHARDED SORES, ... 114 00 014
SHARE
    THE SOUR SCYTHE CRINGE, AND THE BLEAR SHARE COME.   .   .   . 028 11 008
    AND MEN ARE MEANT TO SHARE 060 00 044
    IN BOTH; CARE, BUT SHARE CARE -- 070 00 018
    BUT BOTH WILL SHARE ONE CELL. -- THIS WAS GOOD NEWS, GWENVREWI.   . 152 01 009
SHARES
    AND WEARS MAN'S SMUDGE AND SHARES MAN'S SMELL; THE SOIL   .   . 031 00 007
    SHARES THEIR BEST GIFTS SURELY, FALL HOW THINGS WILL)   .   . 048 00 004
SHARING
    IN THE SHARING OF THY MYSTERIES; 169 00 007
SHARP
    TO FIELDS WHERE FLIES NO SHARP AND SIDED HAIL 009 00 003
    SHARP WITH HER, SHORTEN SAIL; 041 00 035
    AND WITH SHARP FLINT WILL PART MY FEET AND DINT   .   .   . 080 13 003
    YOUR COMFORT IS AS SHARP AS SWORDS; 081 00 032
    DOUBLE AS SHARP, MEANING AND FORCIBLE, ... 102 01 011
SHARPER
    AND OAKS, -- BUT THESE WERE LEAVED IN SHARPER KNOTS.   .   .   . 107 04 008
SHEAF
    WHEN HE HAS SHEAVED US IN HIS SHEAF. 006 00 029
    AND PRIMROSE BRING, AND MAKE A SHEAF 098 18 003
    AND THE CORN IS CORDED AND SHOULDERS ITS SHEAF,   .   .   . 138 00 019
SHEARED
    IS ALL, ALL SHEARED AWAY, THUS! ' THEN I SWEAT FOR FEAR.   .   . 152 01 018
    WHAT HAVE WE SEEN? HER HEAD, SHEARED FROM HER SHOULDERS, FALL,   . 152 02 018
SHEARING
    THE SHEARING RAYS CONTRACT ME WITH THEIR BLAZE   .   .   . 080 02 006
    A DAY OFF SHEARING DAY. 144 00 012
SHEATH
    IN SOD OR SHEATH OR SHELL. 042 00 024
SHEATHE
    WHERE, SELFWRUNG, SELFSTRUNG, SHEATHE- AND SHELTERLESS, C   .   . 061 00 014
    AND SHEATHE AT ONCE HIS LEGER WING. 130 00 012
    SHEATHE THEE IN THY DARK LAIR; THESE DROPS C   .   .   . 152 02 015
SHEATHED
    NOW QUICKEN, SHEATHED IN THE YELLOW GALAXY.   .   .   . 098 22 003
SHEAVED
    SHEAVED IN CRUEL BANDS, BRUISED SORE, ... 006 00 005
    WHEN HE HAS SHEAVED US IN HIS SHEAF, ... 006 00 029
    WE SHALL BE SHEAVED WITH ONE BAND 008 00 014
    OF BLUEBELLS SHEAVED IN MAY 144 00 010
SHEAVES
    ONCE, JOSTLING THICK, THE BLUEBELL SHEAVES   .   .   . 081 00 013
SHED
    TO MANTLE-O'ER THE TAIL, SUCH AS IS SHED   .   .   . 002 00 049
    GRAPES GREW AND DROPS OF WINE WERE SHED.   .   .   . 007 00 005
    FOOD FOR FIVE THOUSAND; ON THE THORNS HE SHED   .   . 007 00 012
    BREAK THE BOX AND SHED THE NARD; 024 00 001
    TOIL HAS SHED ROUND YOUR HEAD 029 00 015
    YET SHED WHAT TEARS SAD TRUELOVE SHOULD.   .   .   . 041 00 108
    FROM TEARS SHED OVER CHILDREN'S GRAVES.   .   .   . 123 00 003
SHEEN
    LIKE SHIVER'D RUBIES DANCE OR SHEEN OF SAPPHIRE HAIL.   .   . 002 00 073
    A BRITTLE SHEEN, RUNS UPWARD LIKE A CLIFF,   .   .   . 098 06 002
SHEENY
    WHILE SHEENY TEARS AND SUNLIT MIRTH 077 00 129
    HER SILKY COAT IS SHEENY, LIKE A HILL.   .   .   . 099 00 003
SHEEP
    STARTLE THE POOR SHEEP BACK! IS THE SHIPWRACK THEN A HARVEST, C   . 028 31 008
    HIS SHEEP SEEM'D TO COME FROM IT AS THEY STEPT.   .   . 107 01 011

SHEEP   (CONTINUED)
     OF SHEEP FROM THE HIGH FIELDS AND OTHER WILD 107 04 023
SHEEP-BELLS
     TO HEAR THE SHEEP-BELLS DIMLY DIE 077 00 071
SHEEP-FLOCK
     AND SHEEP-FLOCK CLOUDS LIKE WORLDS OF WOOL, ... 030 00 018
SHEER
     NO WONDER OF IT; SHEER PLOD MAKES PLOUGH DOWN SILLION . . . 036 00 012
     AS SHEER DOWN THE SHIP GOES. 041 00 060
     WHY? THAT MY CHAFF MIGHT FLY; MY GRAIN LIE, SHEER AND CLEAR. . 064 00 009
     FRIGHTFUL, SHEER, NO-MAN-FATHOMED, HOLD THEM CHEAP 065 00 010
     SHEER OFF, DISSEVERAL, A STAR, DEATH BLOTS BLACK OUT; NOR MARK . 072 00 014
SHEETS
     WINDING SHEETS, TOMBS AND WORMS AND TUMBLING TO DECAY; C . . 059 0L 012
SHELL
     OR STRETCH'D CHORDS TUNEABLE ON TURTLE'S SHELL; 002 00 129
     IN SOD OR SHEATH OR SHELL. 042 00 024
SHELLED
     BE SHELLED, EYES, WITH DOUBLE DARK 022 00 009
SHELLING
     BUD SHELLING OR BROAD-SHED 138 00 024
SHELLS
     WITH CORAL, SHELLS, THICK-PEARLED CORDS, WHATE'ER 002 00 054
SHELLY
     THAT LICK THE SHELLY LEAVES WHICH FLOOR THE COPSE, ... 084 00 004
     TOGETHER, AS THE CRISS-CROSS'D SHELLY CUP 101 00 002
SHELTER
     A SHELTER FOR THIS FLOCK? 005 00 022
     WHO WOULD NOT SHELTER FROM THE HAIL? 081 00 076
     HER LIDS HALF-MESHING SHELTER FROM THE SKY. 099 00 006
     THEN SOUGHT SUCH LEAFY SHELTER AS IT YIELDS, ... 107 03 016
SHELTERLESS
     WHERE, SELFWRUNG, SELFSTRUNG, SHEATHE- AND SHELTERLESS, C . . 061 00 014
SHEPHERD
     LEAD SHEPHERD, NOW WE FOLLOW, SHEPHERD LEAD. 098 15 007
     LEAD SHEPHERD, NOW WE FOLLOW, SHEPHERD LEAD. 098 15 007
     HE WAS A SHEPHERD OF THE ARCADIAN MOOD 107 01 016
     BUT WHAT DREW SHEPHERD RICHARD FROM HIS DOWNS, ... 107 02 001
SHEPHERD'S
     THE SHEPHERD'S BROW, FRONTING FORKED LIGHTNING, OWNS . . . 075 00 001
SHEPHERDS
     TWO MAZED SHEPHERDS PERISH'D IN THE TIDE; 001 14 003
     THE SHEPHERDS, WHOM I VALUE NOT, ... 124 00 023
SHEW
     TO SHEW THE CRIMSON STREAMS THAT INWARD SHINE, ... 002 00 071
     WITH BILLS OF RIME THE BRAMBLES SHEW, ... 003 00 004
     LILIES I SHEW YOU, LILIES NONE, ... 010 00 007
     SHEW ME THY SON, MOTHER, MOTHER OF MINE. 027 00 030
     SHEW BRIGHTER SHAKEN IN PENMAEN POOL. 030 00 020
     TOUCH ME AND PURIFY, AND SHEW 077 00 039
     I NONE CAN SHEW 127 00 006
     ME SHEW MERCY FROM MY HEART 155 00 022
SHEWED
     CHRIST AT ALL HAZARDS FRUIT HATH SHEWED. 007 00 010
SHEWING
     AND SOON I SAW IT SHEWING NEW 021 00 005
SHEWN
     LOVE I WAS SHEWN UPON THE MOUNTAIN-SIDE 020 00 001
     SHEWN TO EZEKIEL'S OPEN'D SIGHT 077 00 048
     NO: SHEWN TO HER IT CANNOT BUT OFFEND; 094 00 007
     SHEWN HIM BOTH GOLD AND FEE: 109 11 002
     C WHO SHAPED THESE WALLS HAS SHEWN 148 00 009
     C YET HERE HE HAS BUT SHEWN 148 00 039
SHEWS
     RATHER TO EAR THAN EYE SHEWS WHERE THEY STRAY, ... 112 00 004
SHIELD
     AND THOSE STROKES ONCE THAT GASHED FLESH OR GALLED SHIELD . . 073 00 002
SHIFT
     BUT THEN I MAKE AN EAGER SHIFT TO SEE 080 06 005
SHIFTED
     AT ROOST AND REST THEY SHIFTED NOT, ... 135 00 015
SHILLING
     THERE IS THE SHILLING THAT FINDS ME WILLING 156 00 008
SHINE
     THE MOTES IN CEASELESS EDDY SHINE AND FALL 001 12 004
     TO SHEW THE CRIMSON STREAMS THAT INWARD SHINE, ... 002 00 071
     IN SCARVES OF SILKY SHOT AND SHINE, ... 003 00 021
     FOR ALL THEY SHINE SO, HIGH IN HEAVEN, ... 030 00 019
     SHINE, AND BLUE-BLEAK EMBERS, AH MY DEAR, ... 036 00 013
     WITH BRINE AND SHINE AND WHIRLING WIND, ... 041 00 080
     SHE INLY NOURISHES A WISH TO SHINE: 094 00 012
     THE MOONLIGHT-MATED GLOWLESS GLOWWORMS SHINE. 098 36 001
     THEY STAND, THEY SHINE IN THE SUN: FAME HAS FOREGONE . . . 104 00 002
     BY SHINE OF CANDLES THREE, ... 109 01 002
     AND NOONDAY HAVE A SHALLOW SHINE, ... 114 00 004

SHINES
    THE RAINBOW SHINES, BUT ONLY IN THE THOUGHT • • • • • • 091 00 002
    THESE RATHER ARE THE ARC WHERE BEAUTY SHINES, • • • • • 102 03 003
SHINING
    IT WILL FLAME OUT, LIKE SHINING FROM SHOOK FOIL; • • • • 031 00 002
    THE SHINING SLATES AND HOUSES. COME AND SEE. • • • • • 107 03 007
    HIS CAP SHALL BE SHINING FUR, • • • • • • • • 124 00 013
    AND LAPPED IN SHINING HAIR, ROLL TO THE BANK'S EDGE; THEN • • 152 02 019
SHINING-HILTED
    WITH SHINING-HILTED CURVES, THAT THEY MAY STAY • • • 112 00 007
SHINING-SHOT
    WITH-A-FOUNTAIN'S SHINING-SHOT FURLS. C • • • • • 071 00 014
SHIP
    AS SHEER DOWN THE SHIP GOES. • • • • • • • 041 00 060
    THEN HE SET SAIL IN A GOLDEN SHIP • • • • • • 109 06 003
SHIPWRACK
    STARTLE THE POOR SHEEP BACK! IS THE SHIPWRACK THEN A HARVEST, C • 028 31 008
SHIRE
    IN STARRY, STARRY SHIRE IT GREW; • • • • • • 025 00 017
    A RELEASED SHOWER, LET FLASH TO THE SHIRE, C • • • • 028 34 008
    ANG. THESE DROPS IN STARRY SHIRE THEY DREW! • • • • APPEN A 17
SHIRES
    IN ALL OUR WESTERN SHIRES WAS RARE, • • • • • • 021 00 023
SHIRT
    AND THE EVER-FRETTING SHIRT OF PUNISHMENT • • • • • 011 00 011
SHIVELIGHTS
    SHIVELIGHTS AND SHADOWTACKLE IN LONG LASHES LACE, LANCE, AND PAIR. • 072 00 004
SHIVER'D
    LIKE SHIVER'D RUBIES DANCE OR SHEEN OF SAPPHIRE HAIL. • • • 002 00 073
SHIVES
    FILLETED WITH GLASSY GRASSY QUICKSILVERY SHIVES AND SHOOTS C • • 159 00 038
SHOAL
    THE GOAL WAS A SHOAL, OF A FOURTH THE DOOM TO BE DROWNED; • • 028 12 006
SHOALS
    IN SHOALS OF BLOOM; AS IN UNPEOPLED SKIES, • • • • 002 00 031
    ON TANGLED SHOALS THAT BAR THE BROOK -- A CROWD • • • 002 00 096
    DROWNED, AND AMONG OUR SHOALS, • • • • • • 028 35 002
SHOALY
    FRESH BROOKS TO SALT SAND-TEASING WATERS SHOALY; -- • • • 016 00 004
SHOCK
    THE BREAKERS ROLLED ON HER BEAM WITH RUINOUS SHOCK; • • • 028 14 006
    READ THE UNSHAPEABLE SHOCK NIGHT • • • • • • 028 29 003
    I STORM AND SHOCK YOU. SO I FAIL, • • • • • 081 00 073
    STAND SHOCK AND SILVER-COATED. • • • • • • 098 13 002
    OR LIKE A JUICY AND JOSTLING SHOCK • • • • • 144 00 009
SHOCKS
    BUT I SHALL WHEN THE SHOCKS ARE STORED • • • • 008 00 008
    THE SHOCKS, THIS PIECE-BRIGHT PALING SHUTS THE SPOUSE • • 032 00 013
    LIKE A CONTENTED WIND, OR GENTLE SHOCKS • • • • • 098 02 002
SHOD
    IS BARE NOW, NOR CAN FOOT FEEL, BEING SHOD. • • • • 031 00 008
    WITH, PERILOUS, O NO! NOR YET PLOD SAFE SHOD SOUND; • • 070 00 014
SHONE
    NOR RESCUE, ONLY ROCKET AND LIGHTSHIP, SHONE, • • • 028 15 006
    DROWNED. O PITY AND INDIGNATION! MANSHAPE, THAT SHONE • • 072 00 013
    ACROSS MY FOUNDERING DECK SHONE • • • • • • 072 00 018
SHOOK
    AN INTENSE LINE OF THROBBING BLOOD-LIGHT SHOOK • • • 002 00 016
    AND SO MY TRUST, CONFUSED, STRUCK, AND SHOOK • • • 016 00 007
    ' FOR HE BEGAN AT ONCE AND SHOOK • • • • • 021 00 029
    SHE LISTENED HOW THE SEA-GUST SHOOK • • • • • 021 00 052
    -- THEY SHOOK IN THE HURLING AND HORRIBLE AIRS. C • • 028 15 008
    IT WILL FLAME OUT, LIKE SHINING FROM SHOOK FOIL; • • • 031 00 002
    HE SHOOK WITH RACING NOTES THE STANDING AIR. • • • 098 38 001
    C AS MIGHT HAVE STRUCK AND SHOOK THE CLOSE-SHUT PALMS] • • 122 00 013
    MY HEART IRREGULARLY SHOOK, • • • • • • 135 00 009
    NO TUMBLER WOKE AND SHOOK THE COT, • • • • • 135 00 013
SHOOT
    WHEN WEEDS, IN WHEELS, SHOOT LONG AND LOVELY AND LUSH; • • 033 00 002
SHOOTS
    NOW HE SHOOTS SHORT UP TO THE ROUND AIR; • • • • 041 00 065
    FILLETED WITH GLASSY GRASSY QUICKSILVERY SHIVES AND SHOOTS C • 159 00 038
SHORE
    OR WEEDED LANDSLIPS OF THE SHORE. • • • • • • 015 00 024
    THEN SWEETEST SEEMS THE HOUSELESS SHORE, • • • • 015 00 035
    TRENCH -- RIGHT, THE TIDE THAT RAMPS AGAINST THE SHORE; • • 035 00 002
    HER INJURY'S, LOOKS OFF BY BOTH HORNS OF SHORE, • • • 050 00 003
SHORES
    A MILE ASTERN LAY THE BLUE SHORES AWAY; • • • • 002 00 005
SHORT
    NOW HE SHOOTS SHORT UP TO THE ROUND AIR; • • • • 041 00 065
    CRISP'D UP AND STARCHY FROM A SHORT HALF-HOUR • • • 107 03 003
    ' HEAVEN MAKE THE TIME BE SHORT, ' SHE SAID, • • • 109 03 001
    ' AND MAKE IT SHORT TO ME. • • • • • • 109 03 004
    ' AND WHY SO SHORT WITH ME? • • • • • • 109 31 002
SHORTEN
    SHARP WITH HER, SHORTEN SAIL! • • • • • • 041 00 035

SHORTER
    AND HOW LONG WAS THE WAY? THIS SHORTER WAY? 125 00 011
SHORTEST
    AND THEN THAT LAST AND SHORTEST 153 00 011
SHOT
    ON PRANKED SCALE: OR THREADS OF CARMINE, SHOT 002 00 106
    IN SCARVES OF SILKY SHOT AND SHINE, ... 003 00 021
    SHOT LIGHTNING TO THE STIFLING LID OF NIGHT 125 00 050
    AND CRIMSON WEAR OF STARRY SHOT 166 00 042
SHOULDER
    GAZES ASLANT HIS SHOULDER, VIEWING NIGH 001 11 006
    A TINTED FIN ON EITHER SHOULDER HUNG: 002 00 052
    AND THE AZUROUS HUNG HILLS ARE HIS WORLD-WIELDING SHOULDER . . 038 00 009
    HEAD, HEART, HAND, HEEL, AND SHOULDER 049 00 010
    HEAD AND FOOT, SHOULDER AND SHANK -- C 071 00 003
SHOULDERING
    SHOULDERING, DOWN VALLEYS SMOKES THE GLOOM. 080 07 002
SHOULDERS
    AND THE CORN IS CORDED AND SHOULDERS ITS SHEAF, ... 138 00 019
    WHAT HAVE WE SEEN? HER HEAD, SHEARED FROM HER SHOULDERS, FALL, . 152 02 018
SHOUT
    WE SHOUT WITH THEM THAT TREAD THE GRAPES: 006 00 012
    WOULD I COULD HEAR THE OTHER PILATES SHOUT. 080 01 005
    WE ARE THERE, WHEN WE HEAR A SHOUT 159 00 008
SHOW
    I MUST FEED FANCY. SHOW ME ANY ONE 014 02 001
    TO SHOW THEE THAT THOU ART, AND NEAR, ... 023 00 044
    ' BOUGHS BEING PRUNED, BIRDS PREENED, SHOW MORE FAIR: . . . 096 07 001
    WILL NO ONE SHOW 127 00 011
    AND BREATH IMMORTAL THRONGED THAT SHOW: 145 00 045
SHOWER
    A RELEASED SHOWER, LET FLASH TO THE SHIRE. C 028 34 008
    OR, IF A SUDDEN SILVER SHOWER 077 00 093
    I FALL, I TEAR AND SHOWER THE WEED, ... 081 00 064
    OF STANDING TO THE BLOSSOM-HITTING SHOWER 107 03 004
    MET A NEW SHOWER, AND SAW THE RAINBOW FILL 107 03 010
SHOWERING
    SHOWERING SILVER JUBILEE. 029 00 008
SHOWER'D
    SHOWER'D THE CLIFFS AND EVERY FRET AND SPIRE 002 00 025
SHOWERS
    A GLORIOUS WANTON; -- ALL THE WRECKS IN SHOWERS 002 00 093
    LILY SHOWERS -- SWEET HEAVEN WAS ASTREW IN THEM. C 028 21 008
    WHEN GREY SHOWERS GATHER AND GUSTS ARE COOL? -- 030 00 026
    AND STRAIGHT SHOWERS PARALLEL SHOULD FOLLOW FAST: 090 00 004
SHOW'D
    THEIR FILMY TAILS ADOWN WHOSE LENGTH THERE SHOW'D 002 00 104
SHOWS
    MY WINDOW SHOWS THE TRAVELLING CLOUDS, ... 015 00 001
    EACH SHAPE AND SHADOW SHOWS. 060 00 085
    FAIRER? THESE ARE THE FLARING SHOWS UNLOVELY 125 00 039
    AND VIRTUES THAT THY PATTERN SHOWS, ... 169 00 006
SHOWY
    HER SHOWY LEAVES STAID WATCHET COUNTERFOILING V 108 00 005
    HER SHOWY LEAVES WITH GENTLE WATCHET FOILING V 108 00 006
SHREDS
    AND AS SHE DWINDLES SHREDS HER SMOCK OF GOLD 103 00 013
SHREWSBURY
    SHREWSBURY MAY SEE OTHERS KEEP: 029 00 010
SHRIEKED
    THEN LULL, THEN LEAVE OFF. FURY HAD SHRIEKED ' NO LING- . . 065 00 007
SHRINE
    BUILD HIS CHURCH AND DECK HIS SHRINE, ... 024 00 007
    OF RUINOUS SHRINE NO HAND OR, WORSE, ... 041 00 090
SHRINES
    DRESS, HOAR-HALLOWED SHRINES UNVISITED: 041 00 092
SHRIVE
    THEY SHRIVE THEMSELVES AND CRY, ' GOOD SERVICE TO OUR GOD. ' . 001 05 009
SHROUD
    I BITE MY HANDS, MY LOOKS I SHROUD: 081 00 065
    IS A SHROUD FOR MARGARET CLITHEROE. 145 00 014
SHROUDED
    JESU WHOM I LOOK AT SHROUDED HERE BELOW, ... 168 00 025
SHROUD-PLAITS
    THEY SWATHE AND LACE THE SHROUD-PLAITS O'ER MY FACE, . . . 080 05 006
SHROUDS
    TO THE SHROUDS THEY TOOK, C 028 15 008
SHROVETIDE
    WHEN SHROVETIDE, TWO YEARS GONE, ... 054 00 005
SHUNS
    THAT MORE HE SHUNS OUR SPECIAL DALE 021 00 024
SHUSHAN
    AND OILS OF SHUSHAN COMFORT NOT, ... 166 00 044
SHUT
    IT IS THE SHUT, THE CURFEW SENT 022 00 006
    AND ITS PLACE IS A SECRET AND SHUT IN THE SKIES. 027 00 004
    SPRANG, THAT BUT NOW WERE SHUT, ... 029 00 007

SHUT   (CONTINUED)
    WHEN WILL YOU EVER, PEACE, WILD WOODDOVE, SHY WINGS SHUT, ... 051 00 001
    IS THIS, FROM CHRIST TO BE SHUT OUT. 080 01 002
    WITH HOPE, WITH SHUT EYES, FIXEDLY; 080 14 004
    HER WHITE WEED-BATHED KNEES ARE SHUT TOGETHER, ... 099 00 002
    ARE SHUT AGAINST THE CANVASSING OF ART. 126 00 006
    UNVALVE OR SHUT HIS VANED TAIL 130 00 011
SHUTS
    THE SHOCKS. THIS PIECE-BRIGHT PALING SHUTS THE SPOUSE 032 00 013
SHUTTLES
    LIKE SHUTTLES FLEET THE CLOUDS, AND AFTER 098 03 001
SHY
    WHEN WILL YOU EVER, PEACE, WILD WOODDOVE, SHY WINGS SHUT, . . . 051 00 001
SICILIAN
    RAVES THROUGH SICILIAN PASTURES MANY A MILE; 001 11 004
SICILY
    VERTICAL HOME, COULD SICILY FARE 166 00 018
SICK
    THIS SEEING THE SICK ENDEARS THEM TO US, US TOO IT ENDEARS. . . 053 00 009
    THAT NE'ER NEED HUNGER, TOM; TOM SELDOM SICK, ... 070 00 006
    WHEN SICK MEN TURN, AND LIGHTS ARE LOW, ... 077 00 025
    THO' FAR OR SICK OR HEAVY OR STILL 081 00 018
    HIS SICK STARS FALTER, MORE HE MAY 083 00 025
    FAMILIAR AND SO HATED BY THE SICK; V 125 00 042
    WHILE SICK MEN SHALL CAST SIGHS, OF SWEET HEALTH ALL DESPAIRING, . 152 C 003
SICKEN
    SURE, THIS IS NILE: I SICKEN, I KNOW NOT WHY, ... 005 00 059
SICKEN'D
    SICKEN'D AND THICKEN'D BY THE GLARE AND SAND 005 00 019
SICKLY
    SCOOP YOU FROM TEEMING FILTH SOME SICKLY HOVEL, ... 077 00 006
SICKNESS
    -- A LITTLE SICKNESS IN THE AIR 004 00 003
    SICKNESS BROKE HIM. IMPATIENT, HE CURSED AT FIRST, BUT MENDED . 053 00 005
SIDE
    NEXT MORN A PEASANT FROM THE MOUNTAIN SIDE 001 14 001
    ALONG THE SANCTUARY SIDE! 022 00 020
    YET DID THE DARK SIDE OF THE BAY OF THY BLESSING 028 12 007
    THIS SIDE, THAT SIDE HURLING A HEAVYHEADED HUNDREDFOLD 069 06 024
    THIS SIDE, THAT SIDE HURLING A HEAVYHEADED HUNDREDFOLD 059 06 024
    AND PRESS IT DOWN, ON EITHER SIDE A BONE, ... 080 14 003
    (THE FURTHEST REACH THIS SIDE, ON THAT THE BAY 107 04 020
    SHAPE ON THE UNDER SIDE AND SIZE AND DROP. 111 00 007
    SERVES AND WHAT SIDE HE TAKES. 148 00 024
    BUT RIGHT MUST SEEK A SIDE 148 00 027
SIDED
    TO FIELDS WHERE FLIES NO SHARP AND SIDED HAIL 009 00 003
SIDES
    THE RECURB AND THE RECOVERY OF THE GULF'S SIDES, ... 028 32 003
SIDLED
    AND THE SUNLIGHT SIDLED, LIKE DEWDROPS, LIKE DANDLED DIAMONDS . 144 00 017
SIEGE
    YIELDS TO THE SULTRY SIEGE OF MELANCHOLY. 016 00 008
SIEVE
    THROUGH THE SIEVE OF THE STRAW OF THE PLAIT. 144 00 018
SIFT
    I AM SOFT SIFT 028 04 001
SIFTED
    SIFTED TO SUIT OUR SIGHT. 060 00 113
SIGH
    BARELY A SIGH TO THOUGHT OF HOPES FORGONE. 014 03 009
    BY AND BY, NOR SPARE A SIGH 055 00 007
    IF HE SUSPECT THAT SHE HAS OUGHT TO SIGH AT 082 00 005
SIGHED
    THUS FRANCES SIGHED AT HOME, WHILE LUKE 021 00 050
SIGHING
    BECAUSE THE SIGHING WIND IS LOW, ... 003 00 006
    (LIKE ME) -- SAT SIGHING BY A SYCAMORE-TREE. ' 111 00 014
SIGHS
    AND WITH SIGHS SOARING, SOARING SIGHS, DELIVER 059 06 017
    AND WITH SIGHS SOARING, SOARING SIGHS, DELIVER 059 06 017
    NOW, YIELDS YOU, WITH SOME SIGHS, OUR EXPLANATION. 076 00 014
    IS ANYTHING A MILK TO THE MIND SO, SO SIGHS DEEP . . . . . 149 A 002
    AND BREATHES THE BLOTS OFF ALL WITH SIGHS ON SIGHS. 151 00 006
    AND BREATHES THE BLOTS OFF ALL WITH SIGHS ON SIGHS. 151 00 006
    WHILE SICK MEN SHALL CAST SIGHS, OF SWEET HEALTH ALL DESPAIRING, . 152 C 003
SIGHT
    DOWN-SPLINTER'D ROCKS CRUSH'D COTTAGES. -- DREAR SIGHT, . . . 001 14 005
    THOSE CYCLADS MADE THAT THICKEN'D ON MY SIGHT. 002 00 037
    OR SUNDER'D FROM MY SIGHT IN THE AGE THAT IS 013 00 003
    COILS, KEEPS, AND TEASES SIMPLE SIGHT. 022 00 012
    THAT DARES TO CAST ITS SEARCHING SIGHT 023 00 029
    FLESH FALLS WITHIN SIGHT OF US, WE, THOUGH OUR FLOWER THE SAME, . 028 11 006
    THOU MARTYR-MASTER: IN THY SIGHT 028 21 007
    STRIKE YOU THE SIGHT OF IT? LOOK AT IT LOOM THERE, ... 028 28 003
    I CANNOT, AND OUT OF SIGHT IS OUT OF MIND. 040 00 011
    SIFTED TO SUIT OUR SIGHT. 060 00 113

SIGHT   (CONTINUED)
```
        BE DISCOVER'D TO MY SIGHT . . . . . . . . . . . . . 077 00 017
        SHEWN TO EZEKIEL'S OPEN'D SIGHT . . . . . . . . . . 077 00 048
        THUS HE TIES SPIDER'S WEB ACROSS HIS SIGHT . . . . . 102 03 028
        SUCH SPIDER'S WEB HE TIES ACROSS HIS SIGHT, V . . . 102 03 034
        RAN THROUGH IT, FOLLOWING WHICH WE SHOULD HAVE SIGHT . 125 00 006
        TO THE SIGHT OF HIM WHO FREED ME . . . . . . . . . 129 00 004
        THIS WAS THE PRIZED, THE DESIRABLE SIGHT, C . . . . 137 00 006
        IN THE SIGHT OF THE SUN. C . . . . . . . . . . . . 143 00 005
        AND BE BLEST FOR EVER WITH THY GLORY'S SIGHT. . . . 168 00 028
        AND PARTED FROM HER SIGHT . . . . . . . . . . . . . APPEN D 32
SIGHTS
        A SCHOONER SIGHTS, WITH ANOTHER, AND SAVES, . . . . 041 00 070
        IT WILL COME TO SUCH SIGHTS COLDER . . . . . . . . 055 00 006
        THIS NIGHT! WHAT SIGHTS YOU, HEART, SAW! WAYS YOU WENT! 067 00 003
        BUT WHEN SHE SIGHTS THE SUN SHE GROWS AND SIZES . . 103 00 006
        WHAT SIGHTS SHALL BE WHEN SOME THAT SWUNG, WRETCHES, ON CRUTCHES . 152 C 022
SIGN
        RESIGN THEM, SIGN THEM, SEAL THEM, SEND THEM, MOTION THEM WITH BREATH, 059 06 016
        SPED OF GODS, OR MORTAL SIGN, . . . . . . . . . . . 160 00 022
        ON THE CROSS THY GODHEAD MADE NO SIGN TO MEN: . . . 168 00 009
SIGNAL
        STIGMA, SIGNAL, CINQUEFOIL TOKEN . . . . . . . . . 028 22 007
        FOLDS OFF ALOOF, THAT SIGNAL IS AND PROOF . . . . . 080 06 003
        YOUR SIGNAL, WHEN APART WE STOOD, . . . . . . . . . 081 00 017
SIGNALLING
        MY SIGNALLING TEARS MIGHT RING UP FLORIS: NOW . . . 102 01 007
SIGNALS
        IN THE FIRST SIGNALS OF THE SEVERAL DROPS . . . . . 084 00 003
SILENCE
        AND SILENCE AND A GULF OF AIR. . . . . . . . . . . 015 00 040
        ELECTED SILENCE, SING TO ME . . . . . . . . . . . . 022 00 001
        OUR HYMN IN THE VAST SILENCE DIES. . . . . . . . . 023 00 006
        AND STILL TH' UNBROKEN SILENCE BROODS . . . . . . . 023 00 019
        SILENCE HOLDS BREATH UPON HER THRONE, . . . . . . . 077 00 033
        WHO COULD KEEP SILENCE, THO' THE SMART . . . . . . 077 00 063
        O WHAT A SILENCE IS THIS WILDERNESS! . . . . . . . 122 00 001
        IN COPYING YOUR SWEET SILENCE, AM I SO . . . . . . 125 00 022
        GUILTY OF SILENCE? QUITE, AS LADIES GO. . . . . . . 125 00 025
        TO THE POINT OF SILENCE IN THE AIR . . . . . . . . 135 00 032
SILENT
        AND THOU ART SILENT, WHILST THY WORLD . . . . . . . 023 00 031
        TO DEATH'S MORE SILENT, DARKER SPELL . . . . . . . 023 00 042
        AND WHEN THE SILENT HEIGHT WERE WON, . . . . . . . 077 00 075
        IF YOU ARE SILENT, THAT I KNOW OF, NONE. . . . . . 125 00 018
SILK
        LINED ALL WITH SILK OF JUICY RED, . . . . . . . . . 124 00 016
        SHE WAS DRESSED IN SILK ATTIRE . . . . . . . . . . 131 00 003
SILKEN
        IN SILKEN UNDULATION, SPURR'D AND RAY'D . . . . . . 002 00 043
        AS SILKEN GARDEN-POPPIES DO. . . . . . . . . . . . 021 00 007
SILK-ASH
        IN SILK-ASH KEPT FROM COOLING, . . . . . . . . . . 049 00 017
SILK-BEECH
        FAIRYLAND: SILK-BEECH, SCROLLED ASH, PACKED SYCAMORE, C . 159 00 024
SILK-SACK
        OF SILK-SACK CLOUDS! HAS WILDER, WILFUL-WAVIER . . . 038 00 003
SILKY
        IN SCARVES OF SILKY SHOT AND SHINE, . . . . . . . . 003 00 021
        AND BARED IS THE ASPEN'S SILKY SKIRTING: . . . . . 078 00 006
        HER SILKY COAT IS SHEENY, LIKE A HILL, . . . . . . 099 00 003
SILLION
        NO WONDER OF IT: SHEER PLOD MAKES PLOUGH DOWN SILLION . 036 00 012
SILT
        THAT HIS FAST-FLOWING HOURS WITH SANDY SILT . . . . 136 00 001
SILVER
        AND SILVER DAMASQU'D PLATES OBSCUR'D IN AGE'S CRUST. . 001 12 009
        FROM THEIR WHITE WAISTS A SILVER SKIRT WAS SPREAD . 002 00 048
        AND SILVER FILMS, BENEATH WITH PEARLY MIST, . . . . 002 00 067
        THRO' SILVER, GLOOM'D TO A BLOOD-VIVID CLOT. . . . 002 00 107
        MAKES THE SILVER JUBILEE. . . . . . . . . . . . . . 029 00 004
        SHOWERING SILVER JUBILEE. . . . . . . . . . . . . . 029 00 008
        THIS HER SILVER JUBILEE. . . . . . . . . . . . . . 029 00 012
        SILVER BUT FOR JUBILEE. . . . . . . . . . . . . . . 029 00 016
        UTTER SILVER JUBILEE. . . . . . . . . . . . . . . . 029 00 020
        OF POINTED WING AND SILVER STOLE, . . . . . . . . . 077 00 012
        STARTING THE SILVER RIVULET: . . . . . . . . . . . 077 00 088
        OR, IF A SUDDEN SILVER SHOWER . . . . . . . . . . . 077 00 093
        AND THO' THE SILVER SEED THAT FLITS . . . . . . . . 083 00 011
        TINGLING BETWEEN DUSK AND SILVER. . . . . . . . . . 098 01 004
        A SILVER SCARCE-CALL-SILVER GLOSS . . . . . . . . . 098 17 001
        COVERS WITH SHALLOW SILVER, THAT UNSETS . . . . . . 098 31 002
        COVERS WITH SHALLOW SILVER, THE LOCK OF CLOUDS . . . 098 31 005
        WHOSE SILVER SKINS LIE LEVEL AND THICK IN FIELD. . . 102 01 022
        MOST LIKE THE TUFT OF PLIGHTED SILVER ROUND V . . . 102 01 068
        ---- ---- -- SILVER PLIGHTED TUFT ABOUT V . . . . . 102 01 070
        BUT MANY A SILVER VISIONARY SPARK . . . . . . . . . 113 00 005
```

SILVER-COATED
    STAND SHOCK AND SILVER-COATED. 098 13 002
SILVER-SHOT
    AND SILVER-SHOT WITH GUSTY LIGHT; 078 00 008
SILVER-SURFED
    WITH SILVER-SURFED CHERRY 042 00 040
SIMILE
    YOUR SIMILE I KEEP. 096 03 002
SIMON
    THE SIMON PETER OF A SOUL! TO THE BLAST 028 29 007
SIMOOM
    MOST WIDE YE ARE WHO CALL THIS GUST SIMOOM. 005 00 026
SIMPLE
    A SIMPLE PASSAGE OF WEAK NOTES 003 00 013
    COILS, KEEPS, AND TEASES SIMPLE SIGHT. 022 00 012
    TO GENTLE MANNA AND SIMPLE BREAD? 081 00 175
    HER SOBER SIMPLE COVERLID UNDERPLIGHTED 108 00 003
    JOVE OF THE GIANTS; SIMPLE JOVE'S 166 00 007
SIN
    HE HAS A SIN OF MINE, HE ITS NEAR BROTHER! 016 00 009
    BUT FEEL THE LONG SUCCESS OF SIN. 018 00 008
    TO WEND AND MEET NO SIN; 060 00 117
    THAT SHALL UNGLUE THE CRUST OF SIN. 081 00 133
    INTO THE BITTERNESS OF SIN. 092 00 006
    I READ THAT THE RECITAL OF THY-SIN. 102 02 002
    SUCH HEATHENISH MISADVENTURE DOGS ONE SIN. V 102 02 013
    SUCH HEATHENISH MISADVENTURE DOGG'D ONE SIN. V 102 02 013
    MAKE WIDE; -- THOU, O LORD OF SIN 115 00 006
    (EXCEPT FOR SIN) 127 00 007
    THERE RID THE DRAGONS, ROOT OUT THERE THE SIN. . . . 150 00 010
    ALL THE WORLD FORGIVENESS OF ITS WORLD OF SIN. . . . 168 00 024
    OF SIN AND DEVIL'S MIGHT.' . . . . APPEN D 10
    AWAY OUR SIN AND GUILT SHOULD TAKE, ... APPEN D 45
SINCE
    SINCE TRAMPLED SPAIN BY ROYAL DISCORD TORN 001 15 001
    THE MONKS LEFT LONG AGO; SINCE WHICH NO MORE 001 15 004
    SINCE ITS BIRTH, AND ITS BLOOM, AND ITS BREATHING ITS LAST. . 027 00 016
    SINCE, THO' HE IS UNDER THE WORLD'S SPLENDOUR AND WONDER, . 028 05 006
    SINCE SACRED FOUNTAINS TO THE SUN 029 00 006
    SINCE COUNTRY IS SO TENDER 043 00 012
    AN AGE IS NOW SINCE PASSED, SINCE PARTED; WITH THE REVERSAL . 045 00 003
    AN AGE IS NOW SINCE PASSED, SINCE PARTED; WITH THE REVERSAL . 045 00 003
    MONTHS EARLIER, SINCE I HAD OUR SWEET REPRIEVE AND RANSOM . 053 00 007
    BE BEGINNING; SINCE, NO, NOTHING CAN BE DONE 059 0L 009
    SINCE GOD HAS LET DISPENSE 060 00 040
    SINCE, PROUD, IT CALLS THE CALLING MANLY, GIVES A GUESS . 063 00 004
    NAY IN ALL THAT TOIL, THAT COIL, SINCE (SEEMS) I KISSED THE ROD, . 064 00 010
    I AM ALL AT ONCE WHAT CHRIST IS, SINCE HE WAS WHAT I AM, AND . 072 00 022
    SINCE ON THE FACE IT IS UNSAFE TO LOOK; 102 01 044
    BUT SINCE I HAVE NO SCOPE FOR BENEFITS 102 01 052
    SINCE ALL THE MAKE OF MAN 148 00 007
    SPARE THOU ME, SINCE I SEE 155 00 015
    ENOUGH NOW; SINCE THE SACRED MATTER THAT I MEAN . . . 159 00 043
    THAT I, SINCE HIS WILL IS, ... APPEN D 28
SINEW
    BONES, THIS SINEW, AND WILL NOT WAKEN. 041 00 084
SINEW-SERVICE
    EACH MUST DO -- HIS SINEW-SERVICE WHERE DO. C 071 00 008
SING
    AS POETS SING! OR THAT IT IS A PAIN 002 00 121
    STRIKE TIMBRELS, SING, EAT, DRINK, BE FULL OF MIRTH. . . 005 00 043
    WITH CORN THAT THEY SHALL LAUGH AND SING. 008 00 017
    ELECTED SILENCE, SING TO ME 022 00 001
    WHEREFORE WE LOVE THEE, WHEREFORE WE SING TO THEE, . . 026 00 033
    THE EAR, IT STRIKES LIKE LIGHTNINGS TO HEAR HIM SING! . . 033 00 005
    BOTH SING SOMETIMES THE SWEETEST, SWEETEST SPELLS; . . 039 00 006
    WOE, WORLD-SORROW! ON AN AGE-OLD ANVIL WINCE AND SING -- . 065 00 006
    TO SING SCARCE HEARD, AND SINGING FILL 077 00 077
    TO SING WHILE OTHERS SLEEP. 096 03 004
    WHEN THE WIND DROPS YOU HEAR THE SKYLARKS SING! . . . 098 03 005
    BUT LET ME SING THAT WHICH IS KNOWN TO ME. 116 00 004
    BUT SING CONTENTED AS THE DOVE 124 00 003
    AND WHILE I SAIL (MUST LISTEN) I SING. 138 00 015
SINGEING
    NOT WITHIN THE SINGEING OF THE STRONG SUN, ... 059 06 004
SINGING
    A SINGING BIRD IN MORNING CLEAR 021 00 041
    SINGING TO THE TRINITY. 024 00 028
    TO SING SCARCE HEARD, AND SINGING FILL 077 00 077
    THEMSELVES LIVE SINGING AND THEIR HEARERS KILL. . . . 096 02 002
    MIGHT COVER THE NEIGHBOUR DOWNS WITH A SPAN OF SINGING, . 098 28 002
SINGLE
    THERE WAS SINGLE EYE! 028 29 002
    BUT SINGLE, LEAD A MISDIRECTED LIFE. 094 00 032
    TO SINGLE SATURN, LAST AND SOLITARY; 103 00 015
SINGS
    TRYING EACH PLEASURABLE THROAT THAT SINGS 019 00 006

SKEINED
    OFF HER ONCE SKEINED STAINED VEINED VARIETY C   • • • • • • 061 00 011
SKEINS
    IN SKEINS ABOUT THE BRAKES. • • • • • • • • • 098 10 003
    IT SHAPES ITSELF IN TAPER SKEINS: • • • • • • • 130 00 018
SKIES
    IN SHOALS OF BLOOM: AS IN UNPEOPLED SKIES, • • • • • 002 00 031
    NO ANSWERING VOICE COMES FROM THE SKIES: • • • • • 023 00 002
    GATHER GLADNESS FROM THE SKIES: • • • • • • • 024 00 013
    AND ITS PLACE IS A SECRET AND SHUT IN THE SKIES. • • • 027 00 004
    LOOK AT THE STARS! LOOK, LOOK UP AT THE SKIES! • • • 032 00 001
    FOR SKIES OF COUPLE-COLOUR AS A BRINDED COW: • • • 037 00 002
    MEAL-DRIFT MOULDED EVER AND MELTED ACROSS SKIES? • • • 038 00 004
    'S NOT WRUNG, SEE YOU: UNFORESEEN TIMES RATHER -- AS SKIES • • 069 00 013
    WHEN THE FIERCE SKIES ARE BLUE TO BLACK, ALBEIT • • • 080 02 005
    NOT OF CLEAR SKIES, BUT STORM TO BE. • • • • • • 080 06 004
    WHEN SKIES ARE HARD AS ANY STONE. • • • • • • 081 00 008
    SPRINGS IN THE FLOATING AIR AND THE SKIES SWIM, -- • • 113 00 006
    BEUNO. O NOW WHILE SKIES ARE BLUE, NOW WHILE SEAS ARE SALT, • 152 C 001
SKIFF
    YOU'LL DARE THE ALP? YOU'LL DART THE SKIFF? • • • • 030 00 005
SKILL
    THE SKILL OF DREAMY CLAUDE, AND TITIAN'S MELLOW GLOOM. • • 001 10 009
    THAT I MAY WIN WITH LATE-LEARNT SKILL UNCOUTH • • • 017 00 012
    OR AS AUSTIN, A LINGERING-OUT SWEET SKILL, • • • • 028 10 006
    WITH JUST SUCH SWEET POTENTIAL SKILL. • • • • • • 081 00 020
    THOU JACINTH: NOR HAVE SKILL OF ALL THY VIRTUES, • • • 102 01 059
SKINS
    WHOSE SILVER SKINS LIE LEVEL AND THICK IN FIELD. • • • 102 01 022
SKIRRING
    WITH LIGHT PULSE OF PINIONS SKIRRING, • • • • • 160 00 035
SKIRT
    FROM THEIR WHITE WAISTS A SILVER SKIRT WAS SPREAD • • • 002 00 048
    THOU HAST A BASE AND BRICKISH SKIRT THERE, SOURS • • • 044 00 005
SKIRTING
    AND BARED IS THE ASPEN'S SILKY SKIRTING: • • • • 078 00 006
SKIRTS
    AND SPINS HER SKIRTS OUT, WHILE HER CENTRAL STAR • • • 103 00 007
SKY
    SO GLASSY WHITE ABOUT THE SKY, • • • • • • • 003 00 016
    THE SHAPEN FLAGS AND DRILLED HOLES OF SKY, • • • • 012 02 011
    LEAVES SPENT, NEW SEASONS, ALTER'D SKY: • • • • 015 00 002
    IN TUFTS OF EVENING SKY. -- SO SOON? • • • • 025 00 022
    THE DEUTSCHLAND, ON SUNDAY: AND SO THE SKY KEEPS, • • 028 13 003
    CHARGED, STEEPED SKY WILL NOT • • • • • • 060 00 080
    WITH SWEET AND SCARLESS SKY: • • • • • • 060 00 120
    LOOKS FROM THE ZENITH ROUND THE SKY, • • • • 077 00 108
    THEN WAS DISCOVER'D IN THE PATHLESS SKY, • • • 079 00 007
    THEY WEBB'D THE SKY WITH GLASSY LIGHT. • • • 087 00 002
    SKY FLEECED WITH THE MILKY WAY. • • • • • 098 23 002
    THE SKY MINTED INTO GOLDEN SEQUINS. • • • • 098 25 001
    SKY PEAK'D WITH TINY FLAMES. • • • • • • 098 25 005
    HER LIDS HALF-MESHING SHELTER FROM THE SKY. • • • 099 00 006
    TO SPREAD THE COMPASS ON THE ALL-STARR'D SKY: • • 102 03 008
    TO TURN THE COMPASS ON THE ALL-STARR'D SKY V • • 102 03 023
    WHO LIES ON GRASS AND PORES UPON THE SKY • • • 117 00 003
    ATTAIN THE WINDY LEVELS OF THE SKY • • • • 121 00 004
    THE SKY IS BLUE, AND THE WINDS PULL • • • • 130 00 022
    TO-DAY THE SKY IS TWO AND TWO • • • • • 138 00 016
    POETRY TO IT, AS A TREE WHOSE BOUGHS BREAK IN THE SKY. • • 149 A 003
    CAT. IN FLOATS OF EVENING SKY. -- SO SOON? • • • • APPEN A 22
SKYLARK
    AS A DARE-GALE SKYLARK SCANTED IN A DULL CAGE • • • 039 00 001
    OR EVER THE EARLY STIRRINGS OF SKYLARK • • • 098 28 001
    OF THE FLOWN SKYLARK, AND HIS TRAVERSE FLIGHT • • 122 00 003
    THE SKYLARK IS MY COUSIN AND HE • • • • • 138 00 012
SKYLARK'S
    WHERE THE STINT COMPASS OF A SKYLARK'S WINGS • • • 098 22 005
SKYLARKS
    WHEN THE WIND DROPS YOU HEAR THE SKYLARKS SING: • • • 098 03 005
SKYWARDS
    SKYWARDS: RICH, RICH IT LAPS • • • • • • 060 00 077
    ROUNDED IT, THINNING SKYWARDS BY DEGREES, • • • 107 04 004
SLABBY
    THE DRENCHED HAIR OF SLABBY WEEDS THAT SWUNG • • • 002 00 113
SLABS
    ARE YOU SANDBLIND? SLABS OF WATER MANY A MILE • • • 005 00 035
SLACK
    NOT UNTWIST -- SLACK THEY MAY BE -- THESE LAST STRANDS OF MAN • 064 00 002
    HER MILK-WHITE THROAT AND FOLDED DEW-LAP SLACK • • • 099 00 009
SLAKE
    THIS BATH OF BLUE AND SLAKE • • • • • • 060 00 095
SLAKED
    DRY UP THE BLUE AND BE NOT SLAKED THEREBY. • • • • 117 00 007
SLAMM'D
    DOORS SLAMM'D TO THE BLASTS CONTINUALLY: MORE LOW, • • 001 13 008
SLATES
    THE SHINING SLATES AND HOUSES. COME AND SEE. • • • 107 03 007

SLATY
    AND TANTALEAN SLATY ASHINESS   •   •   •   •   •   •   •   •   •   117 00 005
SLAUGHTER
    PRINCES STRONG FOR THE SWORD AND SLAUGHTER,   •   •   •   •   •   026 00 027
SLAY
    COME UP, ARISE AND SLAY.   •   •   •   •   •   •   •   •   005 00 018
SLEEK
    THAT, LIKE THIS SLEEK AND SEEING BALL   •   •   •   •   •   043 00 014
    EARTHLESS DEWS ON ANCLES SLEEK;   •   •   •   •   •   •   077 00 016
    NOT SLEEK AWAY; FALERNIAN-GROWN   •   •   •   •   •   •   166 00 043
SLEEP
    ' I DID NOT MEAN TO SLEEP, BUT FOUND   •   •   •   •   021 00 015
    AND THEN LAY BACK TO SLEEP.   •   •   •   •   •   •   021 00 053
    LIFE DEATH DOES END AND EACH DAY DIES WITH SLEEP.   •   •   065 00 014
    BUT SLEEP AGAIN ERE DAY BE BORN;   •   •   •   •   •   077 00 024
    TO SING WHILE OTHERS SLEEP.   •   •   •   •   •   •   096 03 004
    SLEEP FLORIS WHILE I ROB YOU. TIGHTEN, O SLEEP,   •   •   102 01 017
    SLEEP FLORIS WHILE I ROB YOU. TIGHTEN, O SLEEP,   •   •   102 01 017
    BRING SLEEP ROUND THEN? -- SLEEP NOT AFRAID   •   •   •   166 00 021
    BRING SLEEP ROUND THEN? -- SLEEP NOT AFRAID   •   •   •   166 00 021
SLENDER
    TO TOUCH, HER BEING SO SLENDER,   •   •   •   •   •   043 00 013
    WHO CAN BUT BARTER SLENDER SUMS   •   •   •   •   •   081 00 146
    BY SLENDER LOSSES ARE UNDONE;   •   •   •   •   •   081 00 147
    AND SLENDER ELEMENT TO PIECE AND PLOT. V   •   •   •   102 03 025
    BRIDGING THE SLENDER DIFFERENCE OF TWO STARS,   •   •   103 00 003
SLENDERING
    AND SLENDERING TO HIS BURNING RIM   •   •   •   •   •   003 00 030
SLEPT
    I HAD SLEPT A LITTLE AND WAS CHILL.   •   •   •   •   021 00 016
    WITH THE WIND WHAT WHILE WE SLEPT, C   •   •   •   •   059 06 023
SLEW
    HE SLEW THE EGYPTIAN YESTERDAY. TO-DAY   •   •   •   005 00 003
SLIGHT
    WITH SUCH A VIOLET SLIGHT THEIR DISTANCED GREEN? V   •   100 00 008
    SLIGHT WITH SUCH VIOLET THEIR BRIGHT-MASK'D GREEN? V   •   100 00 009
SLIGHTED
    SHE SOUR WHO SEEMS THE SLIGHTED NIX.   •   •   •   •   120 00 017
    WHEN MADDEST LOOKS THE SLIGHTED NIX.]   •   •   •   120 00 019
SLIGHTLY
    IS SLIGHTLY SELFISH IN HER INMOST SOUL)   •   •   •   094 00 028
SLIM
    AT LAST THE BIRD IS FOUND A FLICKERING SHAPE AND SLIM.   •   113 00 009
SLIME
    TO MAN'S LAST DUST, DRAIN FAST TOWARDS MAN'S FIRST SLIME.   •   035 00 014
    'MID FEVER'D FUMES AND SLIME AND CAKED CLOT;   •   •   077 00 008
SLIM-POINTED
    SLIM-POINTED SEA-GULL PLUMES, AND DROOP BEHIND   •   •   002 00 080
SLIP
    -- I AM LIKE A SLIP OF COMET,   •   •   •   •   •   •   103 00 001
SLIPS
    JUST SUCH SLIPS OF SOLDIERY CHRIST'S ROYAL RATION.   •   048 00 028
    AND NOW I GET SOME PRECIOUS SLIPS,   •   •   •   •   081 00 084
    TURNING AND PACING, SO BY SLIPS DISCLOSES   •   •   •   108 00 002
SLIPT
    SOMEWHERE WE SLIPT ASTRAY, YOU CANNOT DOUBT.   •   •   125 00 014
SLOE
    WORD LAST! HOW A LUSH-KEPT PLUSH-CAPPED SLOE   •   •   028 08 003
SLOGGERING
    THE RASH SMART SLOGGERING BRINE   •   •   •   •   •   028 19 004
SLOPE
    GREAT BUTTER-BURR LEAVES FLOOR'D THE SLOPE CORPSE GROUND   •   •   107 04 009
SLOPING
    NOW MELTING UPWARD THRO' THE SLOPING SCALE   •   •   •   002 00 132
SLOP'D
    SLOP'D ON THE GALLERIES; UPON THE WALL   •   •   •   •   001 12 002
SLOW
    LOUDER THE MONKS DRON'D OUT GREGORIANS SLOW;   •   •   001 13 006
    IS IT A WONDER IF THE BUDS ARE SLOW?   •   •   •   •   017 00 003
    DANCES FOR SAD FOOTSTEPS SLOW;   •   •   •   •   •   024 00 022
    WITH SWIFT, SLOW; SWEET, SOUR; ADAZZLE, DIM;   •   •   037 00 009
    NO WONDER THEREFORE WAS NOT SLOW   •   •   •   •   145 00 019
SLOWLY
    INTO THE COOLING GLOOM; TILL SLOWLY ALL   •   •   •   001 12 005
SLUMBER
    SLUMBER IN THESE FORSAKEN   •   •   •   •   •   •   041 00 083
    PARTED ME LEAF AND LEAF, DIVIDED ME, EYELID AND EYELID OF SLUMBER.   137 00 007
SLUMBERED
    WHAT WHILE WE, WHILE WE SLUMBERED.   •   •   •   •   059 06 025
    ALL SLUMBERED WHOM OUR RUD RED TILES   •   •   •   •   135 00 001
SLUMBER'D
    SLUMBER'D AT LAST IN ONE SWEET, DEEP, HEART-BROKEN CLOSE.   •   002 00 135
SMALL
    THE GLAUCUS CLEPED; OTHERS SMALL BRAIDS ENCLUSTER'D   •   002 00 068
    THE STEEP-UP ROOF AT LAST BEHIND THE SMALL   •   •   •   012 02 006
    WHICH MAKES SO SMALL THE PROMISE OF THAT YIELD   •   •   017 00 011
    MAY WHO NE'ER HUNG THERE. NOR DOES LONG OUR SMALL   •   •   065 00 011

SMALL   (CONTINUED)
    THEREWITH TO HANKER FOR THE SMALL! 081 00 153
    OF SMALL AND SUGAR FLINTS, I KNEW 135 00 027
    SMALL MATTER OF THAT THEN! LET HIM SMOTHER 145 00 040
    YOUR WILL IS LAW IN THAT SMALL COMMONWEAL. 150 00 011
SMART
    ARE YOU! TURNED FOR AN EXQUISITE SMART, ...   028 18 002
    THE RASH SMART SLOGGERING BRINE 028 19 004
    AND FAIN WILL FIND AS STERLING ALL AS ALL IS SMART, ...   063 00 007
    WHO COULD KEEP SILENCE, THO' THE SMART 077 00 063
    IS COMFORT'S CAROL OF ALL OR WOE'S WORST SMART. 153 00 008
SMEARED
    AND ALL IS SEARED WITH TRADE; BLEARED, SMEARED WITH TOIL; .   .   .   031 00 006
SMELL
    DOES IT SMELL SWEET TOO IN THAT HOLY PLACE? -- 027 00 043
    AND WEARS MAN'S SMUDGE AND SHARES MAN'S SMELL: THE SOIL .   .   .   031 00 007
    COMFORTING SMELL BREATHED AT VERY ENTERING, ...   034 00 003
SMELLS
    SMELLS THAT ARE SWEETER-MEMORIED THAN THE ROSE, ...   119 00 003
    THE AIR SMELLS STRONG OF SWEETBRIAR IN THE PARK. 135 00 024
SMILE
    STRETCHES THE ENVIED FRUIT WITH FATAL SMILE 001 11 002
    WITH EYES THAT SMILE THRO' THE TEARS OF THE HOURS, ...   026 00 014
    IF A WUTHERING OF HIS PALMY SNOW-PINIONS SCATTER A COLOSSAL SMILE .   045 00 013
    AT GOD KNOWS WHEN TO GOD KNOWS WHAT; WHOSE SMILE 069 00 012
    WHEN HIS MELLOW SMILE HE SEES 077 00 105
    HE MEETS HER, STINTLESS OF HER SMILE; 083 00 021
    CLINGS ON THE STROKE OF DEATH, THAT I CAN SMILE. 102 01 002
    AND WONDER AT HER SHALLOW SMILE. 120 00 012
    BRIGHT-LIFTING WITH A LITTLE-LASTING SMILE 125 00 051
SMILED
    IN SOME BROAD PALMY MEAD, AND SAINTLY SMILED, ...   001 10 005
    SMILED, BLUSHED, AND BIT HIS LIP! 054 00 019
    SOUNDS REACH'D HIM. RICHARD CAME. SYLVESTER SMILED 107 04 024
SMILES
    THEY WOUND THEIR WINCH OF WICKED SMILES 145 00 025
SMIT
    THE SAPPHIRE POOLS ARE SMIT WITH WHITE 078 00 007
SMITTEN
    APOLLO VIEWS THE SMITTEN PYTHON WRITHE AND DIE. 001 11 009
SMOCK
    AND AS SHE DWINDLES SHREDS HER SMOCK OF GOLD 103 00 013
SMOKES
    SHOULDERING, DOWN VALLEYS SMOKES THE GLOOM. 080 07 002
SMOOTH
    THE SATIN-PURFLED SMOOTH TO FOAM, AND SPREAD 002 00 079
    THE LANGUENT SMOOTH WITH DIMPLING DROPS, AND FLASH 002 00 103
    AS A SKATE'S HEEL SWEEPS SMOOTH ON A BOW-BEND; THE HURL AND GLIDING .   036 00 006
    THAT . . IN SMOOTH SPOONS SPY LIFE'S MASQUE MIRRORED; TAME .   .   075 00 013
    TO COLOUR AS SMOOTH AND FRESH AS CHEEKS OF ROSES, ...   108 00 004
SMOOTH-LIPP'D
    TUGG'D THE BOSS'D, SMOOTH-LIPP'D, GIANT STROMBUS-SHELL. .   .   .   002 00 057
SMOTE
    AND LIKE THE STORM-MONTHS SMOTE THE EARTH 026 00 029
SMOTHER
    BUT THE COMBS OF A SMOTHER OF SAND: NIGHT DREW HER 028 14 003
    SMALL MATTER OF THAT THEN! LET HIM SMOTHER 145 00 040
SMOULDERING
    THE SMOULDERING ENORMOUS WINTER WELKIN! MAY .   .   .   .   .   .   149 A 008
    THE SMOULDERING ENORMOUS WINTER WELKIN. G EYE, V .   .   .   .   149 B 009
SMUDGE
    AND WEARS MAN'S SMUDGE AND SHARES MAN'S SMELL: THE SOIL .   .   .   031 00 007
SNATCH
    WHAT HELL HOPES SOON THE SNATCH OF, ...   049 00 020
SNOW
    BUT EARTH HAS NEVER FELT THE SNOW. 003 00 002
    AND HUNTING WINDS AND THE LONG-LYING SNOW. 017 00 002
    WIRY AND WHITE-FIERY AND WHIRLWIND-SWIVELLED SNOW 028 13 007
    SURF, SNOW, RIVER AND EARTH 028 21 004
    AND DEATH FALLS GENTLY AS THE SNOW; 077 00 026
    UNCHILL'D I HANDLE STINGING SNOW! 080 02 001
SNOWFLAKE
    SNOWFLAKE! THAT'S FAIRLY MIXED 060 00 006
SNOW-PINIONS
    IF A WUTHERING OF HIS PALMY SNOW-PINIONS SCATTER A COLOSSAL SMILE .   045 00 013
SNOWS
    INTO THE SNOWS SHE SWEEPS, ...   028 13 001
    FURRED SNOWS, CHARGED TUFT ABOVE TUFT, TOWER 030 00 031
    TAKES TO THE SEAS AND SNOWS 041 00 059
    THE HANGING SNOWS RUSH DOWN AND BARE 080 04 004
    AND SPITING SNOWS TO CHOKE THE GREEN. 166 00 032
SNOWSTORM
    MARK MAKES IN THE RIVELLING SNOWSTORM. .   .   .   -   .   .   .   041 00 068
SNOWWHITE
    MELLS BLUE AND SNOWWHITE THROUGH THEM, A FRINGE AND FRAY .   .   .   149 A 009
    MELLS BLUE WITH SNOWWHITE THROUGH THEIR FRINGE AND FRAY V .   .   149 B 011
SNOWY
    EBB'D BACK BENEATH ITS SNOWY LIDS, UNSEEN. 002 00 018

235

SNUFF
    YOUR PARCHED NOSTRILS SNUFF EGYPTIAN AIR, ... 005 00 027
SOARED
    THAT ONEWHERE CURDED, ONEWHERE SUCKED OR SANK -- SOARED OR SANK -- , 071 00 006
SOARING
    AND WITH SIGHS SOARING, SOARING SIGHS, DELIVER 059 0G 017
    AND WITH SIGHS SOARING, SOARING SIGHS, DELIVER 059 0G 017
SOB
    THE BREAST'S DESPONDING SOB I QUELL; 023 00 038
SOBB'D
    THEN PASS'D THE WIND, AND SOBB'D WITH MOUNTAIN-ECHO'D WOE. . . . 001 13 009
SOBER
    AND SOBER LUSTRES TAKE THE GLOOM; 077 00 020
    HER SOBER SIMPLE COVERLID UNDERPLIGHTED 108 00 003
SOBS
    A FREEZING RUNNEL SOBS AND DWARFS. 080 03 007
SOD
    IN SOD OR SHEATH OR SHELL. 042 00 024
SODDEN-WITH-ITS-
    OF THE SODDEN-WITH-ITS-SORROWING HEART, ... 028 27 004
SODS
    . . . . . IN THEIR NATURAL SODS. 112 00 009
SOFT
    SOFT, WHEN SHE SEES HER INFANT START, ... 023 00 051
    I AM SOFT SIFT 028 04 001
    OR IF THERE DOES SOME SOFT, ... 060 00 090
SOFTENING
    AND HARD MEN FEEL A SOFTENING TOUCH; 077 00 030
SOIL
    TO PLASH WITH COOL FEET THE CLAY JUICY SOIL. 005 00 050
    AND WEARS MAN'S SMUDGE AND SHARES MAN'S SMELL: THE SOIL . . . 031 0U 007
    THE TEMPER'D SOIL WHERE ONLY HER FLOWER IS FOUND. 102 03 004
SOLDIER
    YES, WHY DO WE ALL, SEEING OF A SOLDIER, BLESS HIM? BLESS . . . 063 00 001
SOLDIERING
    MARK CHRIST OUR KING. HE KNOWS WAR, SERVED THIS SOLDIERING THROUGH; . 063 0U 009
SOLDIERS
    HOW SOLDIERS PLATTING THORNS AROUND CHRIST'S HEAD 007 00 004
SOLDIERY
    JUST SUCH SLIPS OF SOLDIERY CHRIST'S ROYAL RATION. . . . 048 00 028
SOLELY
    AND THEY ARE PURER, BUT ALAS! NOT SOLELY 016 0U 005
SOLEMN
    AROSE IN GLOOM, A SOLEMN MOCKERY 001 08 006
SOLID
    THE MILES PROFOUND OF SOLID GREEN, AND BE 002 00 123
    NOR PERMANENCE IN THE SOLID WORLD. 130 00 016
SOLITARY
    TO SINGLE SATURN, LAST AND SOLITARY; 103 0U 015
SOLITUDE
    AN ENDLESS ROUND OF DEAD'NING SOLITUDE; 001 14 006
    AFFINED WELL TO THAT SWEET SOLITUDE, ... 107 01 015
SOMBRE
    A SOMBRE LENGTH OF GREY; FOUR TOWERS PLACED 001 01 003
SOMETIMES
    BOTH SING SOMETIMES THE SWEETEST, SWEETEST SPELLS, . . . 039 0U 006
    YET BOTH DROOP DEADLY SOMETIMES IN THEIR CELLS . . . 039 00 007
    SOMETIMES A LANTERN MOVES ALONG THE NIGHT, . . . 040 00 001
    TO OWN MY HEART: I YIELD YOU DO COME SOMETIMES; BUT . . 051 00 004
    SOMETIMES I SEE THE SUMMIT STAKE 080 04 001
    WE CANNOT LIVE THIS LIFE OUT; SOMETIMES WE MUST WEARY . . 152 02 047
SOMEWHERE
    SOME CANDLE CLEAR BURNS SOMEWHERE I COME BY. . . . 046 0U 001
    IN SCARLET OR SOMEWHERE OF SOME DAY SEEING . . . 048 0U 038
    SOMEWHERE ELSEWHERE THERE IS AH WELL WHERE! ONE, . . 059 0G 006
    NOW, AND SEEING SOMEWHERE SOME MAN DO ALL THAT MAN CAN DO, . 063 00 011
    SOMEWHERE WE SLIPT ASTRAY, YOU CANNOT DOUBT. . . . 125 00 014
    WE ARE LEAFWHELMED SOMEWHERE WITH THE HOOD . . . 159 00 002
SON
    A SON FOR KING, WHOSE NAME WAS PEACE. . . . 026 00 032
    CHRIST JESUS, OUR LORD, HER GOD AND HER SON. . . . 027 00 028
    SHEW ME THY SON, MOTHER, MOTHER OF MINE. . . . 027 00 030
    JESU, MAID'S SON, ... 028 30 002
    O WELL WEPT, MOTHER HAVE LOST SON; 041 00 105
    BOTH GOD'S AND MARY'S SON. . . . 060 00 072
    ' O I AM THE KING'S SON, ' HE SAID, . . . 109 05 001
    HE SPOKE OF GOD THE FATHER AND HIS SON, . . 136 00 025
    GOD'S SON; THESE (THEY DID NOT KNOW) . . 145 0U 053
    AS JESUS GOD THE FATHER'S SON. . . 167 0U 008
    WHAT GOD'S SON HAS TOLD ME, TAKE FOR TRUTH I DO; . 168 00 007
    FOR SO GOD'S SON, THE HEAVEN'S LIGHT, . . APPEN D 06
    AND STRAIGHTWAY SHE CONCEIVED A SON . . APPEN D 33
SONG
    HE HATH PUT A NEW SONG IN MY MOUTH, . . 008 00 004
    MINGLE PRAISES, PRAYER AND SONG, . . . 024 00 027
    LEAVES YET THE MIND A MOTHER OF IMMORTAL SONG. . . 076 00 004
    AND YIELD A SONG TO THE DECAYING YEAR; . . 105 0U 002

237

SOUL   (CONTINUED)
     LOYAL TO HIS OWN SOUL, LAYING HIS OWN LAW DOWN, NO LAW NOR   •   •   •   152 02 040
     IS CORPSE NOW, CANNOT CHANGE! MY OTHER SELF, THIS SOUL,   •   •   •   •   152 02 062
     CAT.   SPHERED SO FAST, SWEET SOUL? -- WE SEE   •   •   •   •   •   APPEN A 23
SOUL'S
     HIS LOOKS, THE SOUL'S OWN LETTERS, SEE BEYOND,   •   •   •   •   •   157 00 015
     WHERE LIES YOUR LANDMARK, SEAMARK, OR SOUL'S STAR?   •   •   •   •   157 00 019
SOULS
     HENCEFORTH LET YOUR SOULS ALWAY   •   •   •   •   •   •   •   024 00 029
     TWO HUNDRED SOULS IN THE ROUND --   •   •   •   •   •   •   •   028 12 004
     OUR KING BACK, OH, UPON ENGLISH SOULS!   •   •   •   •   •   •   028 35 004
     GOD, LOVER OF SOULS, SWAYING CONSIDERATE SCALES,   •   •   •   •   034 00 012
     THREE HUNDRED SOULS, O ALAS! ON BOARD,   •   •   •   •   •   •   041 00 002
     BUT FOR SOULS SUNK IN SEEMING   •   •   •   •   •   •   •   •   041 00 118
     WHICH TO PURE SOULS ALONE MAY BE.   •   •   •   •   •   •   •   077 00 142
     IN THE LODGES OF THE PERISHABLE SOULS   •   •   •   •   •   •   126 00 001
     FOR SOULS THAT MIGHT HAVE BLESSED THE TIME   •   •   •   •   •   133 00 009
SOUND
     THE CLOGGED BROOK RUNS WITH CHOKING SOUND   •   •   •   •   •   003 00 009
     THAT I HAVE TAKEN TO PLEAD WITH, -- IF THE SOUND   •   •   •   •   013 00 009
     AND I COULD HEAR THE TINIEST SOUND,   •   •   •   •   •   •   •   021 00 017
     BUT THAT SWEET SOUND WHICH I PREFERRED,   •   •   •   •   •   •   021 00 047
     WHAT IS SOUND? NATURE'S ROUND   •   •   •   •   •   •   •   •   029 00 003
     WITH, PERILOUS, O NO; NOR YET PLOD SAFE SHOD SOUND;   •   •   •   070 00 014
     ALLOWS THE SOUND OF BELLS IN HAMLETS ROUND   •   •   •   •   •   080 00 006
     OR CAREFUL-SPACED SEQUENCES OF SOUND,   •   •   •   •   •   •   102 03 002
     IN CAREFUL-SPACED SEQUENCES OF SOUND V   •   •   •   •   •   •   102 03 022
     HAVE HERE A TRUE ONE, ECHOING THE SOUND;   •   •   •   •   •   116 00 002
     AS STRUCK WITH RINGS OF SOUND THE CLOSE-SHUT PALMS   •   •   •   122 00 010
     AND ALL WITHIN THE HOUSE WERE SOUND AS POSTS,   •   •   •   •   135 00 017
     AS WHERE THE LITTLE HURLING SOUND   •   •   •   •   •   •   •   135 00 031
     THE WHOLE LANDSCAPE FLUSHES ON A SUDDEN AT A SOUND,   •   •   •   146 00 005
SOUNDING
     AND, HEADED ALWAYS DOWNWARDS, WITH LESS SOUNDING   •   •   •   •   112 00 002
SOUNDS
     SOUNDS REACH'D HIM. RICHARD CAME. SYLVESTER SMILED   •   •   •   107 04 024
SOUR
     GUSH! -- FLUSH THE MAN, THE BEING WITH IT, SOUR OR SWEET,   •   •   028 08 005
     THE SOUR SCYTHE CRINGE, AND THE BLEAR SHARE COME.   •   •   •   028 11 008
     BEFORE IT CLOUD, CHRIST, LORD, AND SOUR WITH SINNING,   •   •   033 00 012
     WITH SWIFT, SLOW; SWEET, SOUR; ADAZZLE, DIM;   •   •   •   •   037 00 009
     SHE SOUR WHO SEEMS THE SLIGHTED NIX.   •   •   •   •   •   •   120 00 017
     WITH DREADFUL DISTILLATION OF THOUGHTS SOUR AS BLOOD,   •   •   152 02 064
SOURED
     THERE WAS A WOOD OF DWARF AND SOURED OAKS   •   •   •   •   •   125 00 002
SOURS
     THOU HAST A BASE AND BRICKISH SKIRT THERE, SOURS   •   •   •   044 00 005
     SELFYEAST OF SPIRIT A DULL DOUGH SOURS. I SEE   •   •   •   •   067 00 012
SOUTH
     BUT THESE WERE FOUND IN THE EAST AND SOUTH   •   •   •   •   •   010 00 013
     BUT THEY CAME FROM THE SOUTH,   •   •   •   •   •   •   •   •   025 00 013
     OR FATHER'D BY THE SUNDER'D SOUTH,   •   •   •   •   •   •   •   083 00 006
     THEO.   BUT THEY CAME FROM THE SOUTH,   •   •   •   •   •   •   APPEN A 13
SOUTHERN
     SOUTHERN DEAN OR LANCASHIRE CLOUGH OR DEVON CLEAVE,   •   •   •   159 00 004
SOUTH-WESTERLY
     WITH A SOUTH-WESTERLY WIND BLUSTERING, WITH A TIDE ROLLS REELS   •   141 00 004
SOVEREIGN
     BATHING: IT IS SUMMER'S SOVEREIGN GOOD.   •   •   •   •   •   •   159 00 013
SOVEREIGNTY
     DEATH WITH A SOVEREIGNTY THAT HEEDS BUT HIDES, BODES BUT ABIDES;   •   028 32 008
SOW
     THAT SEED WHICH THE GOOD SOWER ONCE DID SOW,   •   •   •   •   017 00 007
     SOW THE WIND I WOULD; I SINNED;   •   •   •   •   •   •   •   155 00 011
     LET WINTER WED ONE, SOW THEM IN HER WOMB,   •   •   •   •   •   158 00 003
SOWED
     THOUGH WHEN THE SOWER SOWED,   •   •   •   •   •   •   •   •   007 00 006
SOWER
     THOUGH WHEN THE SOWER SOWED,   •   •   •   •   •   •   •   •   007 00 006
     THAT SEED WHICH THE GOOD SOWER ONCE DID SOW,   •   •   •   •   017 00 007
SOWN
     I FOUND THE WAYS WERE SOWN WITH SALT   •   •   •   •   •   •   081 00 155
     HAD BEEN MORE FERTILE AND HAD SOWN WITH NOTES   •   •   •   •   122 00 005
     [HAD BEEN EFFECTUAL TO HAVE SOWN WITH NOTES]   •   •   •   •   122 00 012
SPACE
     COME OUT OF SPACE, OR SUDDENLY ENGENDER'D   •   •   •   •   •   103 00 004
SPAIN
     SINCE TRAMPLED SPAIN BY ROYAL DISCORD TORN   •   •   •   •   •   001 15 001
SPAKE
     THEN UP AND SPAKE THE THIRD BROTHER,   •   •   •   •   •   •   109 27 001
SPAN
     MIGHT COVER THE NEIGHBOUR DOWNS WITH A SPAN OF SINGING,   •   •   098 28 002
     ALL TIME AT ONCE AND SPAN THE DISTANT GOALS,   •   •   •   •   126 00 004
SPANIEL'S
     OUT-FLEECED BUSHES LIKE A SPANIEL'S EAR V   •   •   •   •   •   098 11 001
SPANN'D
     SPANN'D WITH SHADOW EVERY ONE.   •   •   •   •   •   •   •   •   098 08 003

                                   238

SPANS
  THE RIVER SPANS IT WITH SO DEEP A HIP. 107 04 026
SPARE
  ALL THINGS COUNTER, ORIGINAL, SPARE, STRANGE; 037 00 007
  BY AND BY, NOR SPARE A SIGH 055 00 007
  SPARE! 059 06 001
  DO IN SPARE HOURS MORE THRIVE THAN I THAT SPEND, ... 074 00 008
  SPARE THOU ME, SINCE I SEE 155 00 015
SPARED
  NOT SPARED, NOT ONE 043 00 005
  THAT MIGHT HAVE SPARED HER WERE IT BUT FOR PASSION-SAKE. YES, . . 152 02 054
SPARK
  BUT QUENCH HER BONNIEST, DEAREST TO HER, HER CLEAREST-SELVED SPARK . 072 00 010
  BUT MANY A SILVER VISIONARY SPARK 113 00 005
SPARKLING
  THE THUNDER BRAGS, IN JOINTS AND SPARKLING JAGS 080 07 003
SPARKS
  QUARTZ-FRET, OR SPARKS OF SALT, ... 060 00 101
SPARKY
  THE SPARKY AIR 098 33 001
  GILDS WITH SOME SPARKY FANCIES HIS BLACK NIGHT 102 03 030
  GILDS WITH SOME SPARKY FANCIES BLINDING NIGHT, V 102 03 036
SPATTER'D
  ARE SPATTER'D. WE DESIRE THE YOKE WE BORE, ... 005 00 053
SPEAK
  SPEAK! WHISPER TO MY WATCHING HEART 023 00 049
  STIR IN MY EARS, SPEAK THERE 060 00 121
  WITH WITNESS I SPEAK THIS. BUT WHERE I SAY 067 00 005
  TO SPEAK SO, YET I'LL SPEAK IT FOR THIS ONCE, ... 102 01 038
  TO SPEAK SO, YET I'LL SPEAK IT FOR THIS ONCE, ... 102 01 038
  AH FLORIS, FLORIS, LET ME SPEAK THIS LITTLE 102 01 050
  TO SPEAK OF THAT NO TONGUE WILL DO 167 00 013
SPEAKETH
  MAN FROM THE LIPS OF HIM SPEAKETH AND SAITH, ... 026 00 005
SPEAKING
  A MAN'S VOICE AND A NEW VOICE SPEAKING NEAR. 136 00 022
SPEAKS
  ONE WORD -- AS WHEN A MOTHER SPEAKS 023 00 050
  SELVES -- GOES ITSELF; MYSELF IT SPEAKS AND SPELLS, ... 057 00 007
  TRUTH HIMSELF SPEAKS TRULY OR THERE 'S NOTHING TRUE. 168 00 011
SPEAR'D
  SPEAR'D OPEN LUSTROUS GASHES, CRIMSON-WHITE; 002 00 008
SPECIAL
  THAT MORE HE SHUNS OUR SPECIAL DALE 021 00 024
SPECIAL-GENERAL
  THEIR SPECIAL-GENERAL TITLE TO THY LOVE. 012 01 014
SPED
  THAT MAMMOCKS, MIGHTY FOOT. BUT NO WAY SPED, ... 070 00 012
  FOR ALL THE MILES THAT THEY WERE SPED; 081 00 158
  SPED OF GODS, OR MORTAL SIGN, ... 160 00 022
SPEECH
  WITH EAR-CARESSING SPEECH? WHERE IS THE TONGUE 122 00 017
  BY SPEECH SO SWEETLY BROKEN UP AND GONE. 125 00 027
SPEECHLESS
  SUMMONING MEN FROM SPEECHLESS DAY 023 00 041
SPEEDS
  AND SPEEDS UNCHECK'D HER MURDEROUS GUILE 120 00 030
SPELL
  TO DEATH'S MORE SILENT, DARKER SPELL. 023 00 042
  I WHIRLED OUT WINGS THAT SPELL 028 03 004
  BARS OR HELL'S SPELL THWARTS. THIS TO HOARD UNHEARD, ... 066 00 013
  THE SPELL OF WOE IF ANY COULD. 081 00 079
  ONE SPELL AND WELL THAT ONE. THERE, AH THEREBY 153 00 007
  NOR LETTERS SUIT TO SPELL IT TRUE; 167 00 014
SPELLS
  BOTH SING SOMETIMES THE SWEETEST, SWEETEST SPELLS, ... 039 00 006
  SELVES -- GOES ITSELF; MYSELF IT SPEAKS AND SPELLS, ... 057 00 007
SPEND
  MY BANKRUPT HEART HAS NO MORE TEARS TO SPEND. 014 03 004
  NOSTRILS, YOUR CARELESS BREATH THAT SPEND 022 00 017
  SPEND HERE YOUR MEASURE OF TIME AND TREASURE 030 00 039
  AND PELT MUSIC, TILL NONE'S TO SPILL NOR SPEND. 035 00 008
  DO IN SPARE HOURS MORE THRIVE THAN I THAT SPEND, ... 074 00 008
  SPEND ME OR END ME WHAT GOD SHALL SEND ME, ... 156 00 013
SPENDS
  BUT HALF THE PAINS HE SPENDS UPON HIS BOY, ... 097 00 004
SPENDSAVOUR
  AND, CAST BY CONSCIENCE OUT, SPENDSAVOUR SALT? 046 00 014
SPENT
  GOD SHALL O'ER-BRIM THE MEASURES YOU HAVE SPENT 011 00 009
  LEAVES SPENT, NEW SEASONS, ALTER'D SKY; 015 00 002
  THE LABOURS I SHOULD THEN HAVE SPENT 015 00 011
  YOUR WEALTH OF LIFE IS SOME WAY SPENT; 029 00 014
  AND FOR ALL THIS, NATURE IS NEVER SPENT; 031 00 009
  THIS NEEDFUL, NEVER SPENT, ... 060 00 009
  WHAT HOURS, O WHAT BLACK HOURS WE HAVE SPENT 067 00 002
  DOUBTLESS THE VOICE: NOW FALL'N NOW SPENT, ... 081 00 002

SPENT   (CONTINUED)
     FROM PARTS UNLOOK'D FOR, ALTER'D, SPENT, ... 081 00 024
     MAKE IT TO GOD. I AM NOT SPENT 081 00 130
     AND THESE ARE SPENT AND ENDED QUITE: 130 00 021
     SPENT PEGASUS DOWN THE STARK-PRECIPITOUS AIR 136 00 008
SPHERED
     SPHERED SO FAST, SWEET SOUL? -- WE SEE 010 00 023
     SPHERED SO FAST, SWEET SOUL? -- WE SEE 025 00 023
     BUT YOU, SO SPHERED, SEE NO MORE -- 081 00 039
     CAT. SPHERED SO FAST, SWEET SOUL? -- WE SEE . . . . . . APPEN A 23
SPIDER'S
     THUS HE TIES SPIDER'S WEB ACROSS HIS SIGHT 102 03 028
     SUCH SPIDER'S WEB HE TIES ACROSS HIS SIGHT, V 102 03 034
SPIKED
     WITH SPIKED QUILLS ALL OF INTENSEST HUE: 002 00 044
SPIKES
     PLUM-PURPLE WAS THE WEST; BUT SPIKES OF LIGHT 002 00 007
SPILL
     AND PELT MUSIC, TILL NONE'S TO SPILL NOR SPEND, ... 035 00 008
     TO SPILL O'ER FIELDS OF LILIES. SO COULD I 102 01 034
SPIN
     WILL CRISP ITSELF OR SETTLE AND SPIN 145 00 010
SPINE
     FROM CROWN TO TAIL-FIN FLOATING, FRINGED THE SPINE, . . . 002 00 041
SPINS
     SPINS TO THE WIDOW-MAKING UNCHILDING UNFATHERING DEEPS. . . 028 13 008
     AND SPINS HER SKIRTS OUT, WHILE HER CENTRAL STAR 103 00 007
SPIRE
     SHOWER'D THE CLIFFS AND EVERY FRET AND SPIRE 002 00 025
SPIRES
     TO GRACE THEM SPIRES ARE SHAPED WITH CORNER SQUINCHES: . . 096 07 002
SPIRIT
     MY SOUL DOES LOATHE IT AND MY SPIRIT FAILS. 005 00 014
     THE SPIRIT HOVERED ERE THE SUN 023 00 022
     MAN'S MOUNTING SPIRIT IN HIS BONE-HOUSE, MEAN HOUSE, DWELLS -- 039 00 002
     MAN'S SPIRIT WILL BE FLESH-BOUND WHEN FOUND AT BEST, . . . 039 00 012
     TO ME, SO ARCH-ESPECIAL A SPIRIT AS HEAVES IN HENRY PURCELL, . 045 00 002
     NOT FLESH BUT SPIRIT NOW 060 00 058
     AND SCARLET WEAR THE SPIRIT OF WAR THERE EXPRESS. 063 00 008
     SELFYEAST OF SPIRIT A DULL DOUGH SOURS. I SEE 067 00 012
     MY SPIRIT HATH A BIRTH 077 00 003
     WHO KNEW THE INNER SPIRIT THAT FILLS 077 00 043
     WHILE A SUBTLE SPIRIT AND RARE 077 00 127
     WHAT SPIRIT IS THAT MAKES STILLNESS OBSOLETE 122 00 016
     SHE WAS ADMIRED. THE SPIRIT OF HELL 145 00 017
     IN THE SPIRIT OF THY HOLINESS, ... 169 00 003
SPIRIT'S
     THE SHAKEN PLUMAGE OF MY SPIRIT'S WINGS. 077 00 010
SPIRITS
     THE-LAST-BREATH PENITENT SPIRITS -- THE UTTERMOST MARK . . 028 33 006
     HE HAUNTED WHO OF ALL MEN MOST SWAYS MY SPIRITS TO PEACE; . 044 00 011
     WHEN WHOLESOME SPIRITS RUSTLE ABOUT, ... 077 00 027
     NOT THIS. SOME SPIRITS, IT IS TOLD, ... 118 00 002
     SOMETHING WE GUESS OR KNOW: SOME SPIRITS START 126 00 007
SPIRITUAL
     A STAR MOST SPIRITUAL, PRINCIPAL, PREEMINENT 098 27 001
     MAKING THE SHADOW SWEETER. A SPIRITUAL GRACE 107 04 015
SPITING
     AND SPITING SNOWS TO CHOKE THE GREEN, ... 166 00 032
SPLAY'D
     WHO TREAD THE GRAPES ARE SPLAY'D WITH STRIPES OF GORE, . . 005 00 051
SPLENDID
     SPLENDID WITH PHANTASIES AERIAL, ... 001 08 002
SPLENDOUR
     ANON, ACROSS THEIR SWIMMING SPLENDOUR STROOK, ... 002 00 015
     BY INTERCHANGE GASP'D SPLENDOUR AND ECLIPSE. 002 00 022
     SINCE, THO' HE IS UNDER THE WORLD'S SPLENDOUR AND WONDER, . 028 05 006
SPLENDOURS
     DOES INTO AMBER SPLENDOURS FAIL, ... 077 00 100
SPOIL
     YOU SPOIL THE PLOT I FIND MY TRUE LOVE BY. 135 00 036
SPOKE
     THE MORE SHE ASK'D, THE MORE HE SPOKE, ... 109 36 001
     THE MORE HE TOLD, THE LESS SHE SPOKE, ... 109 36 003
     HE SPOKE OF GOD THE FATHER AND HIS SON, ... 136 00 025
SPOKES
     FLICKERING WITH SUNNY SPOKES, AND LEFT AND RIGHT 002 00 077
SPOOLS
     UPON, ALL ON TWO SPOOLS; PART, PEN, PACK C 061 00 011
SPOONS
     THAT . . . IN SMOOTH SPOONS SPY LIFE'S MASQUE MIRRORED: TAME . 075 00 013
SPORT
     EACH SPORT HAS HERE ITS TACKLE AND TOOL: 030 00 006
SPORTED
     CARELESS OF ME THEY SPORTED; SOME WOULD PLASH 002 00 102
SPOT
     MARKING THE SPOT, WHEN THEY HAVE GURGLED O'ER, ... 002 00 003

240

SPOT   (CONTINUED)
   (WHERE THE EYE FIX'D, FLED THE ENCRIMSONING SPOT, ...   002 00 009
   FROM THE SPOT WHERE HE HAD BEEN. 004 00 023
   ONE SPOT AND HUNGER TO BE THERE. 015 00 032
   BUT WHERE WAS IT FORMERLY? WHICH IS THE SPOT 027 00 007
   WHO FIRED FRANCE FOR MARY WITHOUT SPOT. 044 00 014
   EVEN TO THE TILLAGE OF THE SWEETEST SPOT, -- 102 03 016
   SHE LOVES HIS FACE, SHE KNOWS THE SPOT: 120 00 002
   THEY ROSE AT LAST AND FORCED HER FROM THE SPOT. 136 00 034
   SO LONG TO THIS SWEET SPOT, THIS LEAFY LEAN-OVER, ...   152   C 011
SPOTS
   IN THE GREEN SPOTS OF THAT WOOD 098 10 001
   WITH CENTRES DULY TOUCH'D AND NESTLIKE SPOTS, -- 107 04 007
   WITH FICKLE SPOTS OF SADNESS: ACCESSORIES 125 00 041
SPOUSAL
   WEDLOCK. WHAT THE WATER? SPOUSAL LOVE. 159 00 047
SPOUSE
   YOUR SPOUSE NOT LABOURED-AT NOR SPUN. 022 00 028
   THE SHOCKS. THIS PIECE-BRIGHT PALING SHUTS THE SPOUSE   .   .   .   032 00 013
SPRANG
   SPRANG, THAT BUT NOW WERE SHUT, ...   029 00 007
SPRAY
   WITH HEMPEN STRANDS IN SPRAY -- 144 00 006
SPRAYS
   THEIR HIGHEST SPRAYS WERE DRAWN AS FINE AS LASHES,   .   .   .   107 04 006
SPREAD
   FROM THEIR WHITE WAISTS A SILVER SKIRT WAS SPREAD 002 00 048
   THE SATIN-PURFLED SMOOTH TO FOAM, AND SPREAD 002 00 079
   SPREAD O'ER THE SWART FACE OF THIS PRODIGAL EARTH. 005 00 045
   AND WITH WEEPING CLOUD IS SPREAD 077 00 095
   TO SPREAD THE COMPASS ON THE ALL-STARR'D SKY: 102 03 008
   DO COVER FROM THE STARRY SPREAD, ...   135 00 002
SPREADING
   SPREADING STILL ITS SUNNED GIRTH! 077 00 070
SPRING
   SOON -- AS WHEN SUMMER OF HIS SISTER SPRING 002 00 084
   IT SEEM'D AN EVENING IN THE SPRING! 004 00 002
   AT THIS SPRING SEASON OF THE YEAR? ' 004 00 013
   DEATH, TO MARK THEM IN THE SPRING. 004 00 032
   NOT SET, BECAUSE THEIR BUDS NOT SPRING! 010 00 011
   SPRING NOT, 'CAUSE WORLD IS WINTERING. 010 00 012
   SEE HOW SPRING OPENS WITH DISABLING COLD, ...   017 00 001
   NOT SET BECAUSE THEIR BUDS NOT SPRING! 025 00 011
   SPRING NOT FOR WORLD IS WINTERING. 025 00 012
   FOR THE FALLEN RISE AND THE STRICKEN SPRING TO THEE,   .   .   .   026 00 039
   OR RATHER, RATHER THEN, STEALING AS SPRING 028 10 003
   NOTHING IS SO BEAUTIFUL AS SPRING -- 033 00 001
   WILL, OR MILD NIGHTS THE NEW MORSELS OF SPRING! 034 00 007
   QUESTION: WHAT IS SPRING? -- 042 00 015
   WHENCE SPRING THE JEWELL'D HARMONIES 077 00 138
   BREAKING THE . . . AIR OF SPRING. 098 03 007
   THESE SHOULD HAVE STARV'D WITH THE GREEN BROODS OF SPRING,   .   .   105 00 014
   IN SPRING OUR RIVER-BANKS ARE TOPT 124 00 017
   TO THESE CASTARA IS RAIN OR BREEZE OR SPRING, ...   125 00 048
   BEFORE THE SPRING WAS DONE. 144 00 004
   AS SURE AS WHAT IS MOST SURE, SURE AS THAT SPRING PRIMROSES   .   .   152   C 027
   ANG.   NOT SET BECAUSE THEIR BUDS NOT SPRING!   .   .   .   .   APPEN A 11
   ANG.   SPRING NOT, 'CAUSE WORLD IS WINTERING.   .   .   .   .   APPEN A 12
SPRINGING
   JESU, A SPRINGING WELL THOU ART, ...   167 00 017
SPRING-BROIDERY
   HAD GOTTEN HIM A WREATH OF SWEET SPRING-BROIDERY. 002 00 101
SPRING-TIDE
   BUT THE SPRING-TIDE PASS'D THE SAME: 004 00 024
SPRING-TIME
   AND A SPRING-TIME JOY HAVE FOUND! 024 00 016
SPRING'S
   SPRING'S ONE DAUGHTER, THE SWEET CHILD MAY. 026 00 002
   SPRING'S UNIVERSAL BLISS 042 00 034
SPRINGS
   WHERE SPRINGS NOT FAIL, ...   009 00 002
   SPRINGS THE STRESS FELT 028 06 002
   OH, MORNING, AT THE BROWN BRINK EASTWARD, SPRINGS --   .   .   .   031 00 012
   SORROW'S SPRINGS ARE THE SAME. 055 00 011
   SPRINGS IN THE FLOATING AIR AND THE SKIES SWIM, -- 113 00 006
SPRINGTIME
   AND FAIN IN THE SPRINGTIME SURCEASE WOULD BORROW 026 00 011
SPUN
   YOUR SPOUSE NOT LABOURED-AT NOR SPUN. 022 00 028
SPUR
   SPUR, LIVE AND LANCING LIKE THE BLOWPIPE FLAME, ...   076 00 002
SPURR'D
   IN SILKEN UNDULATION, SPURR'D AND RAY'D 002 00 043
SPY
   THAT . . . IN SMOOTH SPOONS SPY LIFE'S MASQUE MIRRORED: TAME   .   .   075 00 013
   I SPY THE NEAREST DAISIES THROUGH THE DARK, ...   135 00 023
SQUADRONED
   SQUADRONED MASKS AND MANMARKS TREADMIRE TOIL THERE   .   .   .   072 00 008

241

242

STAR   (CONTINUED)
   ONE STAR BY DAYLIGHT FROM THE STRONG BLUE AIR, • • • • • • 102 03 010
   AND SPINS HER SKIRTS OUT, WHILE HER CENTRAL STAR • • • • • 103 00 007
   BUT THE BETHLEHEM STAR MAY LEAD ME • • • • • • • 129 00 003
   WHERE LIES YOUR LANDMARK, SEAMARK, OR SOUL'S STAR? • • • • 157 00 019
STARCHES
   SQUANDERING OOZE TO SQUEEZED DOUGH, CRUST, DUST; STANCHES, STARCHES • 072 00 007
STARCHY
   CRISP'D UP AND STARCHY FROM A SHORT HALF-HOUR • • • • • 107 03 003
STARE
   THEY SEEMED TO PRESS AND STARE • • • • • • • • 098 29 002
   MORN DOES NOT NOW NEW-BASILISK HIS STARE. • • • • • • 099 00 017
   THEY SEEM TO PRESS AND DROOP AND STARE. • • • • • • 135 00 020
STARING
   IN THE STARING DARKNESS • • • • • • • • • • 132 00 001
STAR-EYED
   STAR-EYED STRAWBERRY-BREASTED • • • • • • • • 042 00 019
STARK
   IS ANY OF HIM AT ALL SO STARK • • • • • • • • 072 00 015
STARK-PRECIPITOU
   SPENT PEGASUS DOWN THE STARK-PRECIPITOUS AIR • • • • • 136 00 008
STARLIGHT
   STARLIGHT, WAFTING HIM OUT OF IT; AND • • • • • • 028 05 003
   DRESS HIS DAYS TO A DEXTEROUS AND STARLIGHT ORDER. • • • • 048 00 020
   HEAVEN TURNED ITS STARLIGHT EYES BELOW • • • • • • 145 00 046
STARLIGHT-WENDER
   THAT A STARLIGHT-WENDER OF OURS WOULD SAY • • • • • • 041 00 101
STARRY
   IN STARRY WATER-MEADS THEY DREW • • • • • • • 010 00 017
   IN STARRY, STARRY SHIRE IT GREW; • • • • • • • 025 00 017
   IN STARRY, STARRY SHIRE IT GREW; • • • • • • • 025 00 017
   TO ALL THE STARRY PRESS. -- • • • • • • • • 098 28 006
   DO COVER FROM THE STARRY SPREAD, • • • • • • • 135 00 002
   AND CRIMSON WEAR OF STARRY SHOT • • • • • • • 166 00 042
   ANG. THESE DROPS IN STARRY SHIRE THEY DREW; • • • • • APPEN A 17
STARS
   SAVE BY TWO STARS, MORE CROWDING LIGHTS ARISE, • • • • • 002 00 032
   THESE DROPS: WHICH BE THEY? STARS OR DEW? • • • • • 010 00 018
   TO THE STARS, LOVELY-ASUNDER • • • • • • • • 028 05 002
   STROKE AND A STRESS THAT STARS AND STORMS DELIVER, • • • • 028 06 005
   LOOK AT THE STARS! LOOK, LOOK UP AT THE SKIES! • • • • 032 00 001
   THE THICK STARS ROUND HIM ROLL • • • • • • • 060 00 099
   WASTE! HER EARLIEST STARS, EARLSTARS, STARS PRINCIPAL, OVERBEND US, • 061 00 004
   WASTE! HER EARLIEST STARS, EARLSTARS, STARS PRINCIPAL, OVERBEND US, • 061 00 004
   AND THE WAKED STARS ARE ALL ALONE. • • • • • • 077 00 034
   THE DESTINED LOVER, WHOM HIS STARS • • • • • • 083 00 001
   HIS SICK STARS FALTER, MORE HE MAY • • • • • • 083 00 025
   AND THE THIN STARS TREMBLE NOT. V • • • • • • 085 00 005
   ---- -- LESSEN'D STARS RAY --. V • • • • • • 085 00 006
   STARS FLOAT FROM THE BORDERS OF THE MAIN. • • • • • 098 20 001
   THE VAST OF HEAVEN STUNG WITH BRILLIANT STARS. • • • • 098 21 002
   STARS WAVING THEIR INDIVISIBLE RAYS. • • • • • • 098 23 001
   STARS LIKE GOLD TUFTS. • • • • • • • • 098 25 002
   STARS LIKE GOLDEN BEES. • • • • • • • • 098 25 003
   STARS LIKE GOLDEN ROWELS. • • • • • • • 098 25 004
   NOW STARS OF BLOOD. • • • • • • • • • 098 26 002
   THE STARS WERE PACKED SO CLOSE THAT NIGHT • • • • • 098 29 002
   WARN'D BY THE BRIGHT PROCESSION OF THE STARS, • • • • • 102 01 056
   BRIDGING THE SLENDER DIFFERENCE OF TWO STARS, • • • • • 103 00 003
   WHO CAME FROM FURTHER THAN THE STARS • • • • • • 115 00 003
   OR TAKE IT THUS -- THAT THE CONCORDING STARS • • • • • 122 00 007
   I SAW THE STARS LIKE FLASH OF FIRE. • • • • • • 135 00 008
   THE STARS ARE PACKED SO THICK TO-NIGHT • • • • • • 135 00 019
   AS THE STARS OR AS THE ANGELS THERE. C • • • • • 153 00 026
   ANG. WHICH ARE THEY? STARS OR DEW? • • • • • • APPEN A 18
START
   SOFT, WHEN SHE SEES HER INFANT START. • • • • • • 023 00 051
   WHY, TEARS! IS IT? TEARS; SUCH A MELTING, A MADRIGAL START! • • 028 18 006
   SOMETHING WE GUESS OR KNOW; SOME SPIRITS START • • • • 126 00 007
   ANG. MEN MUST START TO SEE ME PASS • • • • • • APPEN A 03
STARTING
   STARTING THE SILVER RIVULET; • • • • • • • 077 00 088
STARTLE
   STARTLE THE POOR SHEEP BACK! IS THE SHIPWRECK THEN A HARVEST, C • 028 31 008
   AND LEARNT HER NOT TO STARTLE AT HIS NAME. • • • • • 082 00 008
STARVES
   AND NUMBS AND STARVES, AS BETWEEN ICY WHARVES • • • • 080 03 006
STARVEST
   THOU THAT ON SIN'S WAGES STARVEST, • • • • • • 006 00 001
STARV'D
   THESE SHOULD HAVE STARV'D WITH THE GREEN BROODS OF SPRING, • • 105 00 014
STATE
   FORMED BARS OF STONE; BEYOND IN STIFFEN'D STATE • • • • 001 04 003
   BUT OPEN'D TWICE, IN LIFE AND DEATH, TO STATE, • • • • 001 04 008
   I HAVE FOUND THE DOMINANT OF MY RANGE AND STATE -- • • • 019 00 013
STATUARY
   IS STATUARY RATED BY ITS INCHES? • • • • • • 096 07 006

STATUARY   (CONTINUED)
-- GILT AND BLAZON -- BRONZE STATUARY, V 102 02 010
STATUE
BY ANY LAUDED STATUE, NOR AGAIN 125 00 026
STAUNCH
FOR THAT STAUNCH SAINT STILL PRAIS'D HIS MASTER'S NAME . . 001 03 001
STAY
THEN WILL HE KEEP IN THIS STAY? 080 01 007
WITH SHINING-HILTED CURVES, THAT THEY MAY STAY . . . 112 00 007
LET WHAT THERE NEEDS BE DONE. STAY! WITH HIM ONE COMPANION, . . 152 01 007
STAYS
OR IF I GO, SHE STAYS MEANWHILE, ... 120 00 028
STEAD
THERE'S NONE BUT TRUTH CAN STEAD YOU, CHRIST IS TRUTH. . . 157 00 020
STEADY
I STEADY AS A WATER IN A WELL, TO A POISE, TO A PANE, . . 028 04 005
OF THE ROLLING LEVEL UNDERNEATH HIM STEADY AIR, AND STRIDING . 036 00 003
HIS STEADY WHEEL QUITE TO THE FULL AGAIN. 107 03 012
STEAL
DID HELEN STEAL MY LOVE FROM ME? 095 00 001
STEALING
OR RATHER, RATHER THEN, STEALING AS SPRING 028 10 003
STILL MESSENGERS, SAD AND STEALING MESSENGERS OF GREY? -- C . 059 OL 004
STEALS
TILL DIMPLED JOY STEALS O'ER ITS CHEEKS. 023 00 052
HERE THY VERY MANHOOD STEALS FROM HUMAN KEN: . . . 168 00 010
STEALTHY
A STEALTHY WIND CREPT ROUND SEEKING TO BLOW, ... 002 00 137
STEEL
TOM -- GARLANDED WITH SQUAT AND SURLY STEEL 070 00 001
IN WIDE THE WORLD'S WEAL: RARE GOLD, BOLD STEEL, BARE . . 070 00 017
THIS ICE, THIS LEAD, THIS STEEL, THIS STONE, ... 081 00 128
STEEL MAY BE MELTED AND ROCK RENT. 081 00 134
SO BE IT. THOU STEEL, THOU BUTCHER, ... 152 02 014
O WELCOME THERE THEIR STEEL OR CANNON. 156 00 017
STEEP
DURANCE DEAL WITH THAT STEEP OR DEEP. HERE! CREEP, . . 065 00 012
GLIMMER'D ALONG THE SQUARE-CUT STEEP. 092 00 001
BEYOND, THE BANKS WERE STEEP; A BRUSH OF TREES . . . 107 04 003
OF GREENERY: IT IS OLD EARTH'S GROPING TOWARDS THE STEEP . 149 A 010
OF GREENERY AND OLD EARTH GROPES FOR, GRASPS AT STEEP V . 149 B 012
STEEPED
CHARGED, STEEPED SKY WILL NOT 060 00 080
SELF IN SELF STEEPED AND PASHED -- QUITE C 061 00 006
STEEP-UP
THE STEEP-UP ROOF AT LAST BEHIND THE SMALL 012 02 006
STEERED
BY A GREY EYE'S HEED STEERED WELL, ONE CREW, FALL TO: . . 071 00 004
STEM
LOOSE ON THE STEM HAS DONE ITS SUMMERING: 105 00 013
STEPHEN
THE FOOTWAY, STEPHEN SAID, ... 135 00 028
STEPPED
STEPPED FROM THE STOOL, DREW BACK FROM C 137 00 004
STEPS
YOUR PASSING STEPS, I NEVER HEARD 021 00 048
STEPT
HIS SHEEP SEEM'D TO COME FROM IT AS THEY STEPT, . . . 107 01 011
STERLING
AND FAIN WILL FIND AS STERLING ALL AS ALL IS SMART, . . 063 00 007
STERNER
RUN ALL YOUR RACE, O BRACE STERNER THAT STRAIN! . . . 047 00 014
STERNEST
THE PRIDE OF FAITH, AND HOME OF STERNEST PIETY. . . . 001 08 009
STEWARD
ONE HAS GONE TO THE KING'S STEWARD, ... 109 11 001
STICK
WITH BUBBLES BUGLE-EYED, STRUGGLE AND STICK 002 00 095
STIFFEN'D
FORMED BARS OF STONE: BEYOND IN STIFFEN'D STATE . . . 001 04 003
STIFLING
SHOT LIGHTNING TO THE STIFLING LID OF NIGHT 125 00 050
STIGMA
STIGMA, SIGNAL, CINQUEFOIL TOKEN 028 22 007
STILL
FOR THAT STAUNCH SAINT STILL PRAIS'D HIS MASTER'S NAME . . 001 03 001
AND STILL THOU BIND'ST ME TO FRESH FEALTY 012 01 003
THE MORNING WAS SO STILL -- 021 00 018
BETWEENS I HEARD THE WATER STILL 021 00 044
PIPE ME TO PASTURES STILL AND BE 022 00 003
AND STILL TH' UNBROKEN SILENCE BROODS 023 00 019
AND STILL TH' ABYSSES INFINITE 023 00 025
IF STILL IN DARKNESS NOT IN FEAR. 023 00 048
THROUGH HIM, MELT HIM BUT MASTER HIM STILL: 028 10 004
BLUE-BEATING AND HOARY-GLOW HEIGHT! OR NIGHT, STILL HIGHER, . 028 26 005
WITH THE SWEETEST AIR THAT SAID, STILL PLIED AND PRESSED, . 047 00 003
STILL MESSENGERS, SAD AND STEALING MESSENGERS OF GREY? -- C . 059 OL 004

244

STILL   (CONTINUED)
 BE CHRIST OUR SAVIOUR STILL. 060 00 054
 SPREADING STILL ITS SUNNED GIRTH; 077 00 070
 LIES DIVINELY STILL, AT REST, ... 077 00 098
 THO' FAR OR SICK OR HEAVY OR STILL 081 00 018
 HEAVEN AND EVERY FIELD, ARE STILL 085 00 002
 AND IN GREY BANDS THE SUN SHOULD LIE STILL BORN; . . . 090 00 003
 AND, SWARTER STILL, THE ROLLING PINES SHOULD CAST . . . 090 00 005
 BUT, HAVING THAT, BELIEVES IT GREATER STILL; 094 00 010
 THUS WE SHALL PROFIT, WHILE GOLD COINAGE STILL . . . 096 07 007
 ARE STILL; HER NECK IS CREASED IN CLOSE-PLY RINGS; . . 099 00 010
 LOVE BY PRENATAL SERFDOM STILL CONFINED 102 03 015
 THAT STILL MAKES COUNTER-ROUNDELS IN THE POND. . . . 107 03 005
 THE TIME SAVE WHEN HER TEARS WHICH STILL [DESCEND] . . 111 00 005
 SELF-SENTENCED, STILL 127 00 014
 A CUSP STILL CLASPED HIM, C 137 00 005
 WIPED I AM SURE THIS WAS; IT SEEMS, NOT WELL; FOR STILL, . . 152 02 012
 STILL THE SCARLET SWINGS AND DANCES ON THE BLADE. . . 152 02 013
 PILGRIMS, STILL PILGRIMS, MORE PILGRIMS, STILL MORE POOR PILGRIMS. 152 C 021
 PILGRIMS, STILL PILGRIMS, MORE PILGRIMS, STILL MORE POOR PILGRIMS. 152 C 021
 I HAVE LIFE LEFT WITH ME STILL 155 00 017
 THE SELFLESS SELF OF SELF, MOST STRANGE, MOST STILL, . . 157 00 027
 HANG AS STILL AS HAWK OR HAWKMOTH, C 159 00 026
 AND WITH HEAVENFALLEN FRESHNESS DOWN FROM MOORLAND STILL BRIMS, 159 00 039
STILLING
 WITH LEVELL'D LASHES STILLING THEIR DISQUIET; . . . 082 00 002
STILL-PURPLING
 ROUNDS ITS STILL-PURPLING CENTREINGS OF CLOUD. . . . 098 30 003
 ROUNDS ITS STILL-PURPLING CENTRE-DARKS OF CLOUD. . . . 098 30 006
STILLNESS
 WHAT SPIRIT IS THAT MAKES STILLNESS OBSOLETE . . . 122 00 016
STILLY
 AS I WALK'D A STILLY WOOD. 004 00 005
STINGING
 UNCHILL'D I HANDLE STINGING SNOW; 080 02 001
STINT
 WHERE THE STINT COMPASS OF A SKYLARK'S WINGS . . . 098 22 005
STINTING
 FROM FURROWS OF THE POOR AND STINTING WEALD. . . . 017 00 013
STINTLESS
 HE MEETS HER, STINTLESS OF HER SMILE; 083 00 021
STIPPLE
 FOR ROSE-MOLES ALL IN STIPPLE UPON TROUT THAT SWIM; . . 037 00 003
STIR
 UPON THE STIR AND KEEP OF PRIDE, ... 022 00 018
 STIR IN MY EARS, SPEAK THERE 060 00 121
 WHILE ALL THINGS ELSE MAY STIR AND RANGE 130 00 007
STIRLESS
 AND GAIN'D THRO' GROWING DUSK THE STIRLESS BAY; . . . 002 00 141
STIRRED
 ONE STIRRED FROM THE RIGGING TO SAVE 028 16 001
 STIRRED FOR A BIRD, -- THE ACHIEVE OF, THE MASTERY OF THE THING! . 036 00 008
 THE ROOKERY NEVER STIRRED A WING, ... 135 00 014
STIRRING
 WHISPERS OF THE MID-AIR STIRRING 160 00 034
STIRRINGS
 OR EVER THE EARLY STIRRINGS OF SKYLARK 098 28 001
STIRS
 CLOSER BECAUSE FAINT MORNING STIRS; 077 00 022
STOCK-STILL
 FORWARD SHE LEANS, WITH HOLLOWING BACK, STOCK-STILL. . . 099 00 001
STOLE
 THE ROSY ISLES: SO THAT I STOLE AWAY 002 00 140
 STOLE JOY, WOULD LAUGH, CHEER. C 064 00 011
 OF POINTED WING AND SILVER STOLE, ... 077 00 012
STOLED
 BEING A STOLED APPAREL'D STAR. 081 00 042
STOLEN
 MORE SWEETLY SHADES HER STOLEN HAIR 120 00 007
STONE
 FORMED BARS OF STONE; BEYOND IN STIFFEN'D STATE . . . 001 04 003
 THEN LAVER'D FOUNTS AND POSTUR'D STONE HE MIX'D. . . . 001 04 005
 TO MAN, THAT NEEDS WOULD WORSHIP BLOCK OR BARREN STONE, . . 062 00 009
 I'LL TAKE IN HAND THE BLADY STONE 080 14 001
 WHEN SKIES ARE HARD AS ANY STONE. 081 00 008
 THIS ICE, THIS LEAD, THIS STEEL, THIS STONE, ... 081 00 128
 GLAZED WATER VAULTED O'ER A DROWSY STONE. 098 39 001
 THEY HAVE HAPP'D HIM WITH THE SAND AND STONE . . . 109 15 001
 [MADE KNOWN, THOUGH THICK THROUGH STONE, ... 148 00 011
 STONE, PALSY, CANCER, COUGH, LUNG-WASTING, WOMB-NOT-BEARING, . 152 C 008
 O IF THERE'S THAT WHICH PHRYGIAN STONE 166 00 041
STONES
 AND TREES OF TEREBINTH AND STONES 015 00 039
 STONES RING; LIKE EACH TUCKED STRING TELLS, EACH HUNG BELL'S . 057 00 003
 THEN I SEEK OUT THE SHADOW OF STONES 080 03 001
 AND TO THOSE STONES BECOME AKIN 080 03 002
STONY
 WHO WOULD DRINK WATER FROM A STONY ROCK? 005 00 020

STONY   (CONTINUED)
    HIGH UP THE BALANCED STONY AIR -- 080 04 002
    WHICH DRIVES THE STONY AIR TO UTTERANCE? -- 122 00 018
STOOD
    -- BEFORE THE SEPULCHRE THERE STOOD A GATE, ...   001 04 006
    SUDDEN, DEATH BEFORE ME STOOD: 004 00 006
    AND DANCED THE BALLS OF DEW THAT STOOD 021 00 004
    BUT WHAT A WILD FLUSH ON THE FLAKES OF IT STOOD 027 00 033
    AND ALL IN LONE AIR STOOD THE SUN, ...   077 00 076
    SHE STOOD BEFORE A LIGHT NOT HERS, AND SEEM'D 079 00 003
    YOUR SIGNAL, WHEN APART WE STOOD, ...   081 00 017
    SOME KNELT, SOME STOOD: I SEEM'D TO FEEL 081 00 093
    I STOOD: BUT DOES SHE STAND OR KNEEL? 081 00 096
    STOOD CAPITAL, EMINENT, . . . GONFALON BEARER 098 28 005
    SHE STOOD BEFORE THEM IN THE GLEN, ...   109 25 001
STOOKS
    SUMMER ENDS NOW; NOW, BARBAROUS IN BEAUTY, THE STOOKS RISE   .   .   .   038 00 001
STOOL
    THE TRIPLE-HUMMOCKED GIANT'S STOOL, ...   030 00 010
    STEPPED FROM THE STOOL, DREW BACK FROM C 137 00 004
STOOPED
    IT STOOPED AND FLASHED AND FELL AND RAN LIKE WATER AWAY.   .   .   .   152 02 021
STOP
    STOP NOT NOW TO COUNT THE COST: 024 00 002
    BUT DOWN DROP, IF IT SAYS STOP, ...   138 00 037
STOPS
    KNEADING THE MOUNDED MIRE THAT STOPS 003 00 010
    ' YET AS HE CHANGED HIS MIGHTY STOPS 021 00 043
    WHO STOPS HIS ASKING MOOD AT PAR 166 00 025
STORE
    UPON HIS ALTAR, AND WITH RAREST STORE 001 02 008
    EIGHTH WONDER OF THE EARTH, IN SIZE, IN STORE 001 15 005
STORED
    NOW IN OUR ALTAR-VESSELS STORED 006 00 019
    BUT I SHALL WHEN THE SHOCKS ARE STORED 008 00 008
    HOW SHE DID IN HER STORED 042 00 031
    FOR LEARNING STORED AND GARNERED? 081 00 169
STORM
    THE DRIVING STORM AT HOUR OF VESPERS BEAT 001 13 003
    MAN'S MALICE, WITH WRECKING AND STORM, ...   028 09 004
    STORM FLAKES WERE SCROLL-LEAVED FLOWERS, C 028 21 008
    FETCHED IN THE STORM OF HIS STRIDES, C 028 33 008
    THOSE LOVELY LADS ONCE, WET-FRESH WINDFALLS OF WAR'S STORM,   .   .   062 00 006
    NOT OF CLEAR SKIES, BUT STORM TO BE, ...   080 06 004
    I STORM AND SHOCK YOU, SO I FAIL, ...   081 00 073
    JARR'D DOWN THE BALANCED STORM: THE BLEEDING HEAVENS   .   .   .   102 02 004
    TO HUNGER AND NOT HAVE, YET HOPE ON FOR, TO STORM AND STRIVE AND   .   152 02 055
STORMFOWL
    WINGS! SO SOME GREAT STORMFOWL, WHENEVER HE HAS WALKED HIS WHILE   .   045 00 011
STORM-MONTHS
    AND LIKE THE STORM-MONTHS SMOTE THE EARTH 026 00 029
STORM'S
    TO THE MEN IN THE TOPS AND THE TACKLE RODE OVER THE STORM'S BRAWLING.   028 19 008
STORMS
    WHERE NO STORMS COME, ...   009 00 006
    THIS MEANS YOU NEED NOT FEAR THE STORMS, THE CRIES,   .   .   .   014 03 002
    STROKE AND A STRESS THAT STARS AND STORMS DELIVER, ...   028 06 005
    AND STORMS BUGLE HIS FAME. 028 11 004
    RIDING! THERE DID STORMS NOT MINGLE? AND 041 00 026
    OF RIVERS, LEAD, THRO' STORMS AND NIGHTS, ...   083 00 004
STORMY
    BUT WHAT'S TO SEE IN STORMY WEATHER, ...   030 00 025
    THEIR HEADS TOGETHER IN A STORMY BLOT. 090 00 006
STORY
    THEY TELL ITS STORY THUS: AMIDST THE HEAT 001 02 001
    I READ THE STORY RATHER 007 00 003
    OF IT. ANGELS FALL, THEY ARE TOWERS, FROM HEAVEN -- A STORY   .   .   075 00 003
    HOW DARE I PAINT MISS STORY TO MISS MAY? 094 00 003
    MISS STORY HAS A MODERATE POWER OF WILL, ...   094 00 009
STORY'S
    MISS STORY'S CHARACTER! TOO MUCH YOU ASK, ...   094 00 001
STRAIGHT
    AND STRAIGHT SHOWERS PARALLEL SHOULD FOLLOW FAST: 090 00 004
    CRISP LIPS, STRAIGHT NOSE, AND TENDER-SLANTED CHEEK.   .   .   .   136 00 016
STRAIGHTWAY
    AND STRAIGHTWAY SHE CONCEIVED A SON   .   .   .   .   APPEN D 33
STRAIN
    AFAR IN CORRIDORS WITH PAINED STRAIN 001 13 007
    SWELL'D THE SWEET STRAIN TO A MELODIOUS WAIL: 002 00 133
    ' I THOUGHT THE AIR MUST CUT AND STRAIN 021 00 036
    A STRAIN OF THE EARTH'S SWEET BEING IN THE BEGINNING   .   .   .   033 00 010
    RUN ALL YOUR RACE, O BRACE STERNER THAT STRAIN! 047 00 014
    HIS HEART UP AT THE STRAIN: 054 00 027
    THEM: BIRDS BUILD -- BUT NOT I BUILD: NO, BUT STRAIN,   .   .   .   074 00 012
    TO HEAR HIS STRAIN DESCEND LESS LOUD 077 00 079
    SIR! CHRIST! AGAINST THIS MULTITUDE I STRAIN. -- 080 08 005
    CATCH SUNLIGHT AND ONE STRAIN OF STUPID PRAISE. 098 32 002

STRAIN   (CONTINUED)
    SECOND THIS FIERY STRAIN? NOT ALWAYS; O NO NO! 152 02 046
    WHAT NEED I STRAIN MY HEART BEYOND MY KEN? 157 00 034
STRAINED
    IS STRUNG BY DUTY, IS STRAINED TO BEAUTY, ...   041 00 078
STRAINS
    WHICH ENDS THOSE ONLY STRAINS THAT I APPROVE, ...   019 00 010
    NOTHING ELSE IS LIKE IT, NO, NOT ALL SO STRAINS 048 00 029
    EVENING STRAINS TO BE TIME'S VAST, C 061 00 002
    WITH WHITE STROKES AND STRAINS OF THE BLUE, ...   138 00 017
    STRAINS THEM, STRAINS THEM; C 152 01 015
    STRAINS THEM, STRAINS THEM; C 152 01 015
STRAND
    WORLD'S STRAND, SWAY OF THE SEA; 028 01 003
    AND SHE SHALL CHILD THEM ON THE NEW-WORLD STRAND. ' 158 00 004
STRANDED
    THE STRANDED KEEL AND KELSON WARP APART; 101 00 011
STRANDS
    NOT UNTWIST -- SLACK THEY MAY BE -- THESE LAST STRANDS OF MAN   .   064 00 002
    WITH HEMPEN STRANDS IN SPRAY -- 144 00 006
STRANGE
    THE ABYSMAL OCEAN HOARDS OF STRANGE AND RARE, ...   002 00 055
    ALL THINGS COUNTER, ORIGINAL, SPARE, STRANGE; 037 00 007
    FROM HANDS NOW CLAMMY WITH STRANGE BLOOD. 080 10 004
    THO' APT TO THROW IT IN A STRANGE DIRECTION; 094 00 014
    THE SELFLESS SELF OF SELF, MOST STRANGE, MOST STILL, ...   157 00 027
STRANGELY
    WHEN STRANGELY LOOM ALL SHAPES THAT BE, ...   077 00 031
    SO STRANGELY ELEMENTED IS MY MIND'S WEATHER, ...   102 01 015
STRANGER
    TO SEEM THE STRANGER LIES MY LOT, MY LIFE 066 00 001
    BY THERE COMES A LISTLESS STRANGER; BECKONED BY THE NOISE   .   .   .   159 00 014
STRANGERS
    AMONG STRANGERS, FATHER AND MOTHER DEAR, ...   066 00 002
STRAW
    BRING IN THE GLISTERY STRAW. 005 00 046
    THROUGH THE SIEVE OF THE STRAW OF THE PLAIT. 144 00 018
STRAWBERRY-BREAS
    STAR-EYED STRAWBERRY-BREASTED 042 00 019
STRAWY
    THAN FAN OR HOOD OR STRAWY PLAIT. 120 00 008
STRAY
    WHEREIN HE MAKES US STRAY. 005 00 006
    RATHER TO EAR THAN EYE SHEWS WHERE THEY STRAY, ...   112 00 004
STRAYING
    RICH TITIANS FADED; IN THE STRAYING GLEAM 001 12 003
STRAYS
    AND SCARCELY TRACES WHERE ONE BEAUTY STRAYS 001 06 007
STREAK'D
    WERE VEIN'D AND STREAK'D WITH DUSK-DEEP LAZULI, ...   002 00 046
STREAKS
    STREAKS OF SHADOW, THISTLED LEAS, ...   077 00 137
STREAM
    CROWD DOWN UPON A STREAM, AND, JOSTLING THICK 002 00 094
STREAM'D
    WITH ARM AND FIN; THE ARGENT BUBBLES STREAM'D 002 00 109
    DRY WERE HER SAD EYES THAT WOULD FAIN HAVE STREAM'D   .   .   .   079 00 002
STREAMS
    TO SHEW THE CRIMSON STREAMS THAT INWARD SHINE, ...   002 00 071
    UNBAKES MY PORES, AND STREAMS, AND MAKES ALL FRESH,   .   .   .   005 00 032
    WHILE THE SUN STREAMS FORTH AMAIN 077 00 103
    OF STREAMS; AND CLOUDS LIKE MESH'D AND PARTED MOSS V   .   .   .   121 00 002
    BEYOND THE WORLD; THE STREAMS ARE FULL 130 00 024
STREET
    BUT YOU SHALL WALK THE GOLDEN STREET 022 00 023
STREETS
    YOUNG THECLA, SCANNED THE DAZZLING STREETS ONE DAY;   .   .   .   136 00 014
STRENGTH
    RISE! MATCH YOUR STRENGTH WITH MONSTROUS TALMAI 005 00 057
    OR WHERE IS STRENGTH TO MAKE THE LEAF UNFOLD? 017 00 004
    HAND RATHER, MY HEART LO! LAPPED STRENGTH, C 064 00 011
    I THOUGHT; BEFORE I GATHER STRENGTH 118 00 013
STRENGTHEN
    LO, GOD SHALL STRENGTHEN ALL THE FEEBLE KNEES. 011 00 014
STRESS
    AND THE MIDRIFF ASTRAIN WITH LEANING OF, LACED WITH FIRE OF STRESS.   .   028 02 008
    SPRINGS THE STRESS FELT 028 06 002
    STROKE AND A STRESS THAT STARS AND STORMS DELIVER,   .   .   .   028 06 005
    TOLD TALES WITH WHAT HEART'S STRESS 054 00 023
    STAND AT STRESS. EACH LIMB'S BARROWY BRAWN, HIS THEW   .   .   .   071 00 005
    MILKY AND DARK, WITH AN ATTUNING STRESS 107 04 013
    CONFIRMED BEAUTY WILL NOT BEAR A STRESS; -- 117 00 001
    AS ACKNOWLEDGING THY STRESS 155 00 006
    IN THE FULLNESS OF THY FORCE AND STRESS, ...   169 00 004
STRESSED
    HIS MYSTERY MUST BE INSTRESSED, STRESSED; 028 05 007
STRETCHES
    STRETCHES THE ENVIED FRUIT WITH FATAL SMILE 001 11 002

247

STRETCHING
    AT CORNERS FLANK THE STRETCHING COMPASS ROUND;   • • • • • • 001 01 004
    THE STRETCHING PALACE LAY AS HANDLE FIX'D. • • • • • • 001 04 004
STRETCH'D
    OR STRETCH'D CHORDS TUNEABLE ON TURTLE'S SHELL; • • • 002 00 129
    HE HAS HIS PORTION. GOD, WHO STRETCH'D APART • • • 126 00 002
STREWED
    THE MIST UPON THE LEAVES HAVE STREWED, • • • • • 021 00 033
STRICKEN
    FOR THE FALLEN RISE AND THE STRICKEN SPRING TO THEE, • • • 026 00 039
STRIDES
    FETCHED IN THE STORM OF HIS STRIDES. C • • • • 028 33 008
STRIDING
    OF THE ROLLING LEVEL UNDERNEATH HIM STEADY AIR, AND STRIDING • 036 00 003
STRIFE
    AND HE MY PEACE / MY PARTING, SWORD AND STRIFE. • • • 066 00 004
STRIKE
    STRIKE TIMBRELS, SING, EAT, DRINK, BE FULL OF MIRTH. • • 005 00 043
    STRIKE YOU THE SIGHT OF IT? LOOK AT IT LOOM THERE, • • 028 28 003
    WHAT WAS IT WE SHOULD STRIKE THE ROAD AGAIN? • • • 125 00 001
    WILL ON THE MOULDING STRIKE AND CLING, • • • • 130 00 010
    FIRM ACCENTS STRIKE HER FINE AND SCROLLED EAR, • • • 136 00 021
    STRIKE, CHURL; HURL, CHEERLESS WIND, THEN! HELTERING HAIL • 154 00 001
STRIKES
    THE EAR, IT STRIKES LIKE LIGHTNINGS TO HEAR HIM SING; • • 033 00 005
    NOW I GROW NUMB. MY TONGUE STRIKES ON THE GUM • • 080 10 006
STRING
    STONES RING; LIKE EACH TUCKED STRING TELLS, EACH HUNG BELL'S • 057 00 003
STRINGS
    AND EVERY PRAISED SEQUENCE OF SWEET STRINGS, • • • 019 00 007
    AND RAVELL'D INTO STRINGS OF RAIN. • • • • • 081 00 057
STRINGY
    THEY WATCHED THE BRUSH OF THE SWIFT STRINGY DROPS, • • 107 03 013
STRIPED
    YOU STRIPED IN SECRET WITH BREATH-TAKING WHIPS, • • 011 00 003
STRIPES
    WHO TREAD THE GRAPES ARE SPLAY'D WITH STRIPES OF GORE, • • 005 00 051
STRIPS
    AND THE FLOWER STRIPS, • • • • • • • 098 14 002
STRIVE
    TO HUNGER AND NOT HAVE, YET HOPE ON FOR, TO STORM AND STRIVE AND • 152 02 055
STRIVEN
    O LORD! BUT I HAVE WROUGHT AND STRIVEN! • • • 081 00 108
STROKE
    SWINGS THE STROKE DEALT -- • • • • • 028 06 004
    STROKE AND A STRESS THAT STARS AND STORMS DELIVER, • • 028 06 005
    WHERE SHE FOUNDERED! ONE STROKE • • • • • 041 00 005
    CLINGS ON THE STROKE OF DEATH, THAT I CAN SMILE. • • 102 01 002
    WHAT STROKE HAS CARADOC'S RIGHT ARM DEALT? WHAT DONE? HEAD OF A REBEL 152 02 002
STROKES
    STROKES OF HAVOC UNSELVE • • • • • • 043 00 021
    AND THOSE STROKES ONCE THAT GASHED FLESH OR GALLED SHIELD • 073 00 002
    AND MARCHING TO FALSE COLOURS! THOSE FEW STROKES • • 102 01 065
    WITH WHITE STROKES AND STRAINS OF THE BLUE. • • • 138 00 017
STROMBUS-SHELL
    TUGG'D THE BOSS'D, SMOOTH-LIPP'D, GIANT STROMBUS-SHELL. • • 002 00 057
STRONG
    WHEN A SISTER, BORN FOR EACH STRONG MONTH-BROTHER, • • 026 00 001
    PRINCES STRONG FOR THE SWORD AND SLAUGHTER, • • • 026 00 027
    THOU CANST BUT BE, BUT THAT THOU WELL DOST; STRONG • • 058 00 005
    NOT WITHIN THE SINGEING OF THE STRONG SUN, • • • 059 06 004
    THE FINE DELIGHT THAT FATHERS THOUGHT; THE STRONG • • 076 00 001
    BEAT, HEAVE AND THE STRONG MOUNTAIN TIRE • • • • 080 05 002
    THE LOVE OF WOMEN IS NOT SO STRONG, -- • • • • 081 00 048
    KNOWLEDGE IS STRONG BUT LOVE IS SWEET. -- • • • 081 00 154
    IS VERY CAPABLE OF STRONG AFFECTION • • • • • 094 00 013
    ONE STAR BY DAYLIGHT FROM THE STRONG BLUE AIR, • • • 102 03 010
    THE AIR SMELLS STRONG OF SWEETBRIAR IN THE PARK. • • • 135 00 024
STROOK
    ANON, ACROSS THEIR SWIMMING SPLENDOUR STROOK, • • • 002 00 015
STROVE
    OF THOSE WHO STROVE GOD'S GOSPEL TO CONFOUND • • • 001 01 007
    I STROVE TO LOOK; I LOST THE TRICK • • • • • 081 00 097
STRUCK
    AND SO MY TRUST, CONFUSED, STRUCK, AND SHOOK • • • 016 00 007
    SHE STRUCK -- NOT A REEF OR A ROCK • • • • • 028 14 002
    AS STRUCK WITH RINGS OF SOUND THE CLOSE-SHUT PALMS • 122 00 010
    [AS MIGHT HAVE STRUCK AND SHOOK THE CLOSE-SHUT PALMS] • 122 00 013
    STRUCK OFF IT HAS! WRITTEN UPON LOVELY LIMBS, • • • 152 02 003
    PERHAPS WE STRUCK NO BLOW, GWENVREWI LIVES PERHAPS! • • 152 02 009
STRUGGLE
    WITH BUBBLES BUGLE-EYED, STRUGGLE AND STICK • • • 002 00 095
    AND CLEAVES, I STRUGGLE AND AM DUMB, • • • • 080 10 007
    AT ONCE I STRUGGLE WITH MY BREATH. • • • • • 081 00 058
STRUGGLING
    THAT STRUGGLING SHOULD NOT SEAR HIM, A GIFT SHOULD CHEER HIM • 142 00 008
STRUNG
    THEIR PANSY-DARK OR BRONZEN LOCKS WERE STRUNG • • • 002 00 053

STRUNG   (CONTINUED)
    MY HEAD TO HEAR. HE MIGHT HAVE STRUNG 021 00 030
    IS STRUNG BY DUTY, IS STRAINED TO BEAUTY, ...   041 00 078
STUBBORN
    UPON THE STUBBORN FLEMING: AND THE ROD 001 05 006
STUMBLING
    AND STUMBLING SWEARS HE WALKS BY LIGHT OF DAY. 102 03 031
    AND STUMBLING SWEARS HE WALKS BY LIGHT OF DAY. V 102 03 037
STUNG
    BECAUSE SHE FEARS HER FINGERS WILL BE STUNG. 096 04 002
    THE VAST OF HEAVEN STUNG WITH BRILLIANT STARS. 098 21 002
STUPENDOUS
    VAULTY, VOLUMINOUS, . . . STUPENDOUS C 061 00 001
STUPID
    CATCH SUNLIGHT AND ONE STRAIN OF STUPID PRAISE. 098 32 002
STURDY
    BY HIM AND RIPS OUT ROCKFIRE HOMEFORTH -- STURDY DICK: .   .   .   070 00 003
SUBJECT
    WHAT IF MY SUBJECT, SEEING THIS, RESENT 094 00 005
    KINGS HERD IT ON THEIR SUBJECT DROVES 166 00 005
SUBMISSION
    THEY KISS THE ROD WITH FILIAL SUBMISSION. 097 00 008
SUBTLE
    OF TREMULOUS FILM, MORE SUBTLE THAN THE VEST 002 00 039
    WITH A SUBTLE WEB OF BLACK, ...   004 00 020
    AND SOUL IS SUBTLE AND FLESH WEAK 077 00 037
    WHILE A SUBTLE SPIRIT AND RARE 077 00 127
SUCCEED
    IT'S THE DAY THAT MAKES THE CHARM: NO AFTER-WORDS COULD SUCCEED   .   128 00 007
SUCCESS
    THAT HOLDS NO PROMISE OF SUCCESS: 015 00 034
    BUT FEEL THE LONG SUCCESS OF SIN. 018 00 008
    HE HUNG ON THE IMP'S SUCCESS. 054 00 024
    AND I NOT HELP, NOR WORD NOW OF SUCCESS: 150 00 005
    NEXT AFTER SWEET SUCCESS. I AM NOT LEFT EVEN THIS: .   .   .   152 02 069
SUCH
    THE SCULPTUR'D IMAGE OF SUCH FAITH WOULD BE, ...   001 03 007
    THE CHOICEST REMNANTS THENCE: -- SUCH HOME FORLORN   .   .   .   001 15 003
    MORE WONDROUS TO HAVE BORNE SUCH HOPE BEFORE 001 15 007
    TO MANTLE-O'ER THE TAIL, SUCH AS IS SHED 002 00 049
    AND THAT SUCH A SABLE TRACK 004 00 021
    I NEVER PROMISED SUCH PERSISTENCY 014 01 002
    WITH SUCH MALIGN CONJUNCTIONS AS BEFORE 014 02 006
    WITH SUCH A SECONDING, NOR SATURN TOOK 014 02 009
    SUCH OPPOSITION TO THE LADY-STAR 014 02 010
    BEYOND THE HURST WITH SUCH A HUE 021 00 006
    INDEED WHILE SUCH A WONDER'S WARM. 025 00 036
    WHY, TEARS! IS IT? TEARS: SUCH A MELTING, A MADRIGAL START!   .   028 18 006
    TO ME, GOD KNOWS, DESERVING NO SUCH THING: 034 00 002
    AND HE BOARDS HER IN OH! SUCH JOY 041 00 071
    JUST SUCH SLIPS OF SOLDIERY CHRIST'S ROYAL RATION.   .   .   .   048 00 028
    IT WILL COME TO SUCH SIGHTS COLDER 055 00 006
    EARTH BROWS OF SUCH CARE, CARE AND DEAR CONCERN.   .   .   .   058 00 014
    ONE. YES I CAN TELL SUCH A KEY, I DO KNOW SUCH A PLACE,   .   .   059 06 007
    ONE. YES I CAN TELL SUCH A KEY, I DO KNOW SUCH A PLACE,   .   .   059 06 007
    HOW TO KEEP -- IS THERE ANY ANY, IS THERE NONE SUCH, C   .   .   059 0L 001
    YET SUCH A SAPPHIRE-SHOT, ...   060 00 079
    WITH JUST SUCH SWEET POTENTIAL SKILL, ...   081 00 020
    RETURNING THANKS, MIGHT OFFER SUCH ARRAY. 089 00 004
    HER FACE WAS SUCH, AS BEING DIAPERED 093 8 003
    OUR SWANS ARE NOW OF SUCH REMORSELESS QUILL, ...   096 02 001
    AND I COME LADEN FROM SUCH FLOODS 098 19 005
    BREATHE IN SUCH ETHER? OR THE QUICKLY ELMS 100 00 007
    WITH SUCH A VIOLET SLIGHT THEIR DISTANCED GREEN? V   .   .   .   100 00 008
    SLIGHT WITH SUCH VIOLET THEIR BRIGHT-MASK'D GREEN? V   .   .   .   100 00 009
    MASK'D WITH SUCH VIOLET DISALLOW THEIR GREEN? V 100 00 010
    SUCH HEATHENISH MISADVENTURE DOGS ONE SIN. V 102 02 013
    SUCH HEATHENISH MISADVENTURE DOGG'D ONE SIN. V 102 02 013
    THAT SWINISHLY REFUSES SUCH A PEARL! 102 03 033
    SUCH SPIDER'S WEB HE TIES ACROSS HIS SIGHT, V 102 03 034
    THAT SWINISHLY REFUSES SUCH A PEARL! V 102 03 039
    ON SUCH A SEASON OF THE DAY AND YEAR. 107 01 004
    THEN SOUGHT SUCH LEAFY SHELTER AS IT YIELDS, ...   107 03 016
    NEWS FROM BELLEISLE, EVEN SUCH A SWEETNESS BLOWS   .   .   .   119 00 006
    HAD LET SUCH MUSIC DOWN, WITHOUT IMPEDIMENT 122 00 008
    ALL OVER, SOME SUCH WORDS AS THESE, THOUGH DARK,   .   .   .   136 00 029
    I WILL APPEAR, LOOKING SUCH CHARITY 140 00 003
    NO MAN HAS SUCH A DAUGHTER. THE FATHERS OF THE WORLD   .   .   152 01 011
    CALL NO SUCH MAIDEN ' MINE ' . THE DEEPER GROWS HER DEARNESS   152 01 012
    SHE LEANS ON HIM WITH SUCH CONTENTMENT FOND 157 00 013
    INTO SUCH A SUDDEN ZEST 159 00 020
    WORD NEVER WAS SUCH NEWS TO HEAR. 167 00 006
    THEO. WHILE SUCH A WONDER'S WET AND WARM!   .   .   .   .   APPEN A 36
SUCK
    HANDLE THE FIG, SUCK THE FULL-SAPP'D VINE-SHOOT.   .   .   .   005 00 038
    THEY DRAW ALL COVERTS, CUT THE FIELDS, AND SUCK   .   .   .   104 00 012
    SUCK ANY SENSE FROM THAT WHO CAN: 147 00 003

SUN   (CONTINUED)
    AND PUT AWAY MY SUN. 021 00 011
    THE SPIRIT HOVERED ERE THE SUN 023 00 022
    SINCE SACRED FOUNTAINS TO THE SUN 029 00 006
    BRIGHT SUN LANCED FIRE IN THE HEAVENLY BAY; 041 00 022
    QUELLED OR QUENCHED IN LEAVES THE LEAPING SUN, ... 043 00 002
    ONLY NOT WITHIN SEEING OF THE SUN. 059 06 003
    NOT WITHIN THE SINGEING OF THE STRONG SUN. 059 06 004
    HIS FIRE, THE SUN WOULD SHAKE, ... 060 00 096
    AND ALL IN LONE AIR STOOD THE SUN, ... 077 00 076
    WHILE THE SUN STREAMS FORTH AMAIN 077 00 103
    THE SUN WHOSE VAST AFFLICTIVE HEAT 080 02 002
    AND IN GREY BANDS THE SUN SHOULD LIE STILL BORN; 090 00 003
    THE SUN ON FALLING WATERS WRITES THE TEXT 091 00 008
    DEWY FIELDS IN THE MORNING UNDER THE SUN 098 13 001
    THE SUN JUST RISEN 098 34 001
    BUT WHEN SHE SIGHTS THE SUN SHE GROWS AND SIZES 103 00 006
    PIERCE HER; SHE HANGS UPON THE FLAME-CASED SUN, ... 103 00 010
    I HAVE DRAWN HEAT FROM THIS CONTAGIOUS SUN; 103 00 018
    THEY STAND, THEY SHINE IN THE SUN; FAME HAS FOREGONE 104 00 002
    WHILE THERE IS NEITHER SUN NOR RAIN; 105 00 006
    IN THE SIGHT OF THE SUN. C 143 00 005
    HIS CHEEKS THE FORTH-AND-FLAUNTING SUN 144 00 002
    THOU SUN, ALLSEEING EYEBALL OF THE DAY, ... 160 00 004
    AND SET THE GLASSES FROM THE SUN 165 00 007
SUNBEAM
    HUED SUNBEAM WILL TRANSMIT 060 00 088
SUNDAY
    THE DEUTSCHLAND, ON SUNDAY; AND SO THE SKY KEEPS, ... 028 13 003
SUNDER'D
    OR SUNDER'D FROM MY SIGHT IN THE AGE THAT IS 013 00 003
    OR FATHER'D BY THE SUNDER'D SOUTH, ... 083 00 006
SUNG
    ONLY WITH UTTERANCE OF SWEET BREATH THEY SUNG 002 00 130
    SO FORCIBLY HE SUNG, ... 021 00 032
SUN-FLUSH'D
    SUN-FLUSH'D, UNTIL IT SEEM'D THEIR FATHER SEA 002 00 100
SUNK
    GURGLED, WHERE THEY HAD SUNK, MELODIOUSLY. 002 00 111
    BUT FOR SOULS SUNK IN SEEMING 041 00 118
SUNLIGHT
    CATCH SUNLIGHT AND ONE STRAIN OF STUPID PRAISE. 098 32 002
    ANYWHERE IN THE SUNLIGHT. 138 00 009
    AND THE SUNLIGHT SIDLED, LIKE DEWDROPS, LIKE DANDLED DIAMONDS . 144 00 017
    IN ALL HER BEAUTY, AND SUNLIGHT TO IT IS A PIT, DEN, DARKNESS, . 152 02 023
SUNLIT
    WHILE SHEENY TEARS AND SUNLIT MIRTH 077 00 129
SUNNED
    SPREADING STILL ITS SUNNED GIRTH; 077 00 070
SUNNY
    FLICKERING WITH SUNNY SPOKES, AND LEFT AND RIGHT 002 00 077
    AND LOOK ABROAD ON SUNNY CLUSTERS 077 00 134
SUN'S
    TALL SUN'S TINGEING, OR TREACHEROUS THE TAINTING OF THE EARTH'S AIR, 059 06 005
SUN'S-EYE-RINGED
    [WHERE SHAKE SHADOW IS SUN'S-EYE-RINGED] 138 00 042
SUNSET
    AFTER THE SUNSET I WOULD LIE, ... 015 00 042
    IN FITS OF MUSIC TILL SUNSET 077 00 087
    HAS DRENCH'D THE MOLTEN SUNSET HOUR, ... 077 00 094
SUNSPURGE
    SUNSPURGE AND OXEYE 138 00 028
SUPPLIED
    (AND, WELL SUPPLIED WITH VIRTUES ON THE WHOLE, ... 094 00 027
SUPPLY
    THERE MUST BE SOMETHING TO SUPPLY 133 00 007
SUPPOSE
    FETCHED FRESH, AS I SUPPOSE, OFF SOME SWEET WOOD. 034 00 004
SUPPOSING
    PHILIP, SUPPOSING THAT THE GIFT MOST MEET, ... 001 03 006
SURCEASE
    AND FAIN IN THE SPRINGTIME SURCEASE WOULD BORROW 026 00 011
SURE
    SURE, THIS IS NILE; I SICKEN, I KNOW NOT WHY, ... 005 00 059
    SURE, 'S BED NOW. LOW BE IT; LUSTILY HE HIS LOW LOT (FEEL .   . 070 00 005
    AS SURE AS HEAVEN IT IS 133 00 006
    WIPED I AM SURE THIS WAS; IT SEEMS, NOT WELL; FOR STILL, .   .   . 152 02 012
    AS SURE AS WHAT IS MOST SURE, SURE AS THAT SPRING PRIMROSES . 152 C 027
    AS SURE AS WHAT IS MOST SURE, SURE AS THAT SPRING PRIMROSES . 152 C 027
    AS SURE AS WHAT IS MOST SURE, SURE AS THAT SPRING PRIMROSES . 152 C 027
    SHALL NEW-DAPPLE NEXT YEAR, SURE AS TO-MORROW MORNING, .   . 152 C 028
SURELY
    DEEPLY SURELY I NEED TO DEPLORE IT. 041 00 097
    SHARES THEIR BEST GIFTS SURELY, FALL HOW THINGS WILL), .   .   . 048 00 004
    O SURELY, REAVING PEACE, MY LORD SHOULD LEAVE IN LIEU .   .   . 051 00 007
    AH! SURELY ALL WHO HAVE WRITTEN WILL PROFESS 117 00 008
SURF
    SURF, SNOW, RIVER AND EARTH 028 21 004

251

SURLY
    OF NEW YEAR'S MONTH OR SURLY YULE 030 00 030
    NAY, WHAT WE HAD LIGHTHANDED LEFT IN SURLY THE MERE MOULD 059 06 022
    TOM -- GARLANDED WITH SQUAT AND SURLY STEEL 070 00 001
SURPRISE
    SHE PUTS IN LEASH HER PAIR'D LIPS LEST SURPRISE 082 00 003
SURRENDERS
    FROM THERE WHERE ALL SURRENDERS COME 022 00 007
SURROUND
    SURROUND THE PEAK FROM WHICH WE GAZE. 023 00 026
SURVEY
    AND ALL THE LANDSCAPE UNDER SURVEY. 030 00 013
SUSPECT
    IF HE SUSPECT THAT SHE HAS OUGHT TO SIGH AT 082 00 005
SUSPECTS
    FOR FABIAN THAT SUSPECTS HER NOT. 120 00 004
SWALLOW
    THE SWALLOW, FAVOURITE OF THE GALE, ... 130 00 009
SWALLOWING
    I CANNOT MEET THE SWALLOWING MAIN. 120 00 027
SWALLOW'D
    THRO' CRIMSON-GOLDEN FLOODS PASS SWALLOW'D INTO FIRE. . . . 002 00 083
SWALLOWS
    I MARK THE TOWER SWALLOWS RUN 015 00 028
SWAM
    SHADOW THAT SWAM OR SANK 043 00 007
SWAN-FLEDGED
    FROM WINGS SWAN-FLEDGED A WHEEL OF WATERY LIGHT 002 00 076
SWANS
    OUR SWANS ARE NOW OF SUCH REMORSELESS QUILL, ... 096 02 001
SWARD
    THAT WANT THE YIELD OF PLUSHY SWARD, ... 022 00 022
    HE DROPS HIS BRIGHT ROOTS IN THE WATER'D SWARD, ... 100 00 002
SWARM
    O THIS IS BRINGING! TEARS MAY SWARM 025 00 035
    THEO. O THIS IS BRINGING! TEARS MAY SWARM . . . . . . APPEN A 35
SWARMED
    HOW THEN SHOULD GREGORY, A FATHER, HAVE GLEANED ELSE FROM SWARM-
    ED ROME? BUT GOD TO A NATION DEALT THAT DAY'S DEAR CHANCE. . . 062 00 007
                                                                    062 00 008
SWART
    SPREAD O'ER THE SWART FACE OF THIS PRODIGAL EARTH. 005 00 045
    BAD SATURN WITH A SWART ASPECT 083 00 018
SWARTER
    AND, SWARTER STILL, THE ROLLING PINES SHOULD CAST 090 00 005
SWARTHED
    HAD SWARTHED ABOUT WITH LION-BROWN 144 00 003
SWATHE
    THEY SWATHE AND LACE THE SHROUD-PLAITS O'ER MY FACE, . . . 080 05 006
SWAY
    WORLD'S STRAND, SWAY OF THE SEA; 028 01 003
SWAYED
    FROM THY HAND OUT, SWAYED ABOUT 155 00 003
SWAYING
    HUNG IN THE SWAYING OF THE FIERCE MELEE. 001 02 004
    GOD, LOVER OF SOULS, SWAYING CONSIDERATE SCALES, ... 034 00 012
SWAY'D
    DROOP'D O'ER THE BROWS LIKE HECTOR'S CASQUE, AND SWAY'D . . 002 00 042
    HIS BODY SWAY'D UPON TIPTOES, ... 087 00 003
SWAYS
    HE HAUNTED WHO OF ALL MEN MOST SWAYS MY SPIRITS TO PEACE; . . 044 00 011
    AND WHAT SWAYS WITH YOU, MAYBE THIS SWEET MAID; 157 00 022
SWEAR
    ' SO I AM VICTOR NOW, I SWEAR TO PAY 001 02 005
    THE TURMOIL AND THE TORMENT, IT HAS, I SWEAR, A SWEETNESS, . . 152 02 057
SWEARS
    AND STUMBLING SWEARS HE WALKS BY LIGHT OF DAY. 102 03 031
    AND STUMBLING SWEARS HE WALKS BY LIGHT OF DAY. V 102 03 037
SWEAT
    THE DENSE AND THE DRIVEN PASSION, AND FRIGHTFUL SWEAT; . . . 028 07 005
    SWEET SOUL! NOT SCORNING HONEST SWEAT 139 00 005
    IS ALL, ALL SHEARED AWAY, THUS! ' THEN I SWEAT FOR FEAR. . . 152 01 018
    SWEAT AND CARE AND CUMBER, ... 170 00 010
SWEATING
    AS I AM MINE, THEIR SWEATING SELVES; BUT WORSE. 067 00 014
SWEATS
    BUT HERE, HERE IS A WORKMAN FROM HIS DAY'S TASK SWEATS. . . . 152 02 011
SWEEP
    THE SWOON OF A HEART THAT THE SWEEP AND THE HURL OF THEE TROD . 028 02 006
    TO SWEEP AND MUST OBEY. 148 00 016
    THEY TOUCH HEAVEN, TABOUR ON IT; HOW THEIR TALONS SWEEP . . 149 A 007
    WITH TALONS SWEEP V . . . . 149 B 008
SWEEPS
    INTO THE SNOWS SHE SWEEPS, ... 028 13 001
    AS A SKATE'S HEEL SWEEPS SMOOTH ON A BOW-BEND; THE HURL AND GLIDING . 036 00 006
    LIES IN HER LAP, WHICH SHE ANON SWEEPS OFF. 111 00 009
SWEET
    HAD GOTTEN HIM A WREATH OF SWEET SPRING-BROIDERY. 002 00 101

252

SWEET   (CONTINUED)
AND A SWEET SADNESS DWELT ON EVERYONE: 002 00 117
ONLY WITH UTTERANCE OF SWEET BREATH THEY SUNG 002 00 130
SWELL'D THE SWEET STRAIN TO A MELODIOUS WAIL: 002 00 133
SLUMBER'D AT LAST IN ONE SWEET, DEEP, HEART-BROKEN CLOSE.   .   .   .   002 00 135
HERE ARE SWEET MESSES WITHOUT PRICE OR WORTH, ...   005 00 047
IS THE SWEET VINTAGE OF OUR LORD. 006 00 020
SWEET FLOWERS I CARRY, -- SWEETS FOR BITTER. 010 00 006
SPHERED SO FAST, SWEET SOUL? -- WE SEE 010 00 023
GROWS LESS AND LESS SWEET TO HIM, AND KNOWS NO CAUSE.   .   .   .   014 03 014
TO THE SWEET LIVING OF MY FRIENDS I LOOK -- 016 00 002
AND EVERY PRAISED SEQUENCE OF SWEET STRINGS, ...   019 00 007
BUT THAT SWEET SOUND WHICH I PREFERRED, ...   021 00 047
THE CAN MUST BE SO SWEET, THE CRUST 022 00 015
CARRIES TREATS OF SWEET FOR BITTER. 025 00 006
SPHERED SO FAST, SWEET SOUL? -- WE SEE 025 00 023
SPRING'S ONE DAUGHTER, THE SWEET CHILD MAY. 026 00 002
DOES IT SMELL SWEET TOO IN THAT HOLY PLACE? -- 027 00 043
SWEET UNTO GOD, AND THE SWEETNESS IS GRACE: 027 00 044
GUSH! -- FLUSH THE MAN, THE BEING WITH IT, SOUR OR SWEET,   .   .   028 08 005
BEYOND SAYING SWEET, PAST TELLING OF TONGUE, ...   028 09 005
OR AS AUSTIN, A LINGERING-OUT SWEET SKILL. 028 10 006
LILY SHOWERS -- SWEET HEAVEN WAS ASTREW IN THEM. C   .   .   .   028 21 008
A STRAIN OF THE EARTH'S SWEET BEING IN THE BEGINNING   .   .   .   033 00 010
FETCHED FRESH, AS I SUPPOSE, OFF SOME SWEET WOOD. 034 00 004
WITH SWIFT, SLOW; SWEET, SOUR; ADAZZLE, DIM; 037 00 009
LIFE, THIS WILDWORTH BLOWN SO SWEET, ...   041 00 094
THE SWEET ESPECIAL SCENE, ...   043 00 022
SWEET ESPECIAL RURAL SCENE. 043 00 024
OR LOVE OR PITY OR ALL THAT SWEET NOTES NOT HIS MIGHT NURSLES;   .   045 00 006
THOSE SWEET HOPES QUELL WHOSE LEAST ME QUICKENINGS LIFT,   .   .   048 00 037
WITH LISSOME SCIONS, SWEET SCIONS, ...   052 00 003
MONTHS EARLIER, SINCE I HAD OUR SWEET REPRIEVE AND RANSOM   .   .   053 00 007
EARTH, SWEET EARTH, SWEET LANDSCAPE, WITH LEAVES THRONG   .   .   058 00 001
EARTH, SWEET EARTH, SWEET LANDSCAPE, WITH LEAVES THRONG   .   .   058 00 001
SEEMS TO US SWEET OF US AND SWIFTLY AWAY WITH, C   .   .   .   059 06 008
AND YET DEARLY AND DANGEROUSLY SWEET C 059 06 009
SWEET LOOKS, LOOSE LOCKS, LONG LOCKS, LOVELOCKS, C   .   .   .   059 06 015
THE SWEET ALMS' SELF IS HER 060 00 043
WITH SWEET AND SCARLESS SKY: 060 00 120
HOME AT HEART, HEAVEN'S SWEET GIFT; THEN LEAVE, LET THAT ALONE.   .   062 00 013
SWEET FIRE THE SIRE OF MUSE, MY SOUL NEEDS THIS;   .   .   .   076 00 009
ENDING IN SWEET UNCERTAINTY 077 00 121
TOUCH'D FROM HEAVEN IN SWEET DREAMS; 077 00 126
AY, SWEET TO TASTE BESIDE THIS WOE; 080 07 007
WITH JUST SUCH SWEET POTENTIAL SKILL, ...   081 00 020
MY LOVE; AND ALL WAS SWEET AND WELL. 081 00 121
KNOWLEDGE IS STRONG BUT LOVE IS SWEET. -- 081 00 154
AS A SELF-EMBRACED SWEET THOUGHTS:V 085 00 003
MARRIED, WILL MAKE A SWEET AND MATCHLESS WIFE, ...   094 00 031
BID YOUR PAPA GOODNIGHT. SWEET EXHIBITION! 097 00 007
THIS SWEET DESERTER LISTS HERSELF ANEW 102 01 062
SO I GO OUT; MY LITTLE SWEET IS DONE; 103 00 017
AFFINED WELL TO THAT SWEET SOLITUDE, ...   107 01 015
LED RICHARD WITH A SWEET UNDOING PAIN 107 04 017
HEAVEN MAKE IT SWEET TO YOU, ' SHE SAID. 109 03 003
BUT WITH A SWEET PERSISTENCY 110 00 005
THE PROPER SWEET RE-ATTRIBUTING ABOVE. V 113 00 011
THEN SHE SEEMS SWEET WHO SEEMS HIS BRIDE. 120 00 016
MIGHT WE NOT THINK THE SWEET (?) AND DARING RISES   .   .   .   122 00 002
IN COPYING YOUR SWEET SILENCE. AM I SO 125 00 022
WHY, THERE'S AN INTEREST AND SWEET SOUL IN BEAUTY   .   .   .   125 00 035
AND DAYLIGHT AND SWEET AIR, ...   133 00 014
SHOULD CHOKE SWEET VIRTUE'S GLORY IS TIME'S GREAT GUILT.   .   .   136 00 002
WITH A SWEET JOY OF A SWEET JOY, ...   138 00 044
WITH A SWEET JOY OF A SWEET JOY, ...   138 00 044
SWEET, OF A SWEET, OF A SWEET JOY 138 00 045
SWEET, OF A SWEET, OF A SWEET JOY 138 00 045
SWEET, OF A SWEET, OF A SWEET JOY 138 00 045
OF A SWEET -- A SWEET -- SWEET -- JOY. ' 138 00 046
OF A SWEET -- A SWEET -- SWEET -- JOY. ' 138 00 046
OF A SWEET -- A SWEET -- SWEET -- JOY. ' 138 00 046
AS WISHING ALL ABOUT US SWEET, ...   139 00 001
SWEET SOUL! NOT SCORNING HONEST SWEAT 139 00 005
CUCKOO, BIRD, AND OPEN EAR WELLS, HEART-SPRINGS, DELIGHTFULLY SWEET,   146 00 002
OR SWEET THE GOLDEN GLUE 148 00 035
TAMPERING WITH THOSE SWEET BINES, DRAWS THEM OUT, C   .   .   152 01 015
NEXT AFTER SWEET SUCCESS. I AM NOT LEFT EVEN THIS;   .   .   .   152 02 059
WHILE SICK MEN SHALL CAST SIGHS, OF SWEET HEALTH ALL DESPAIRING,   .   152 C 003
SO LONG TO THIS SWEET SPOT, THIS LEAFY LEAN-OVER,   .   .   .   152 C 011
AND WHAT SWAYS WITH YOU, MAYBE THIS SWEET MAID;   .   .   .   157 00 022
LOVE ME AS I LOVE THEE, O DOUBLE SWEET! 161 00 001
SONG NEVER WAS SO SWEET IN EAR, ...   167 00 005
THOUGHT HALF SO SWEET THERE IS NOT ONE 167 00 007
ANG. CARRIES TREATS OF SWEET FOR BITTER.   .   .   .   .   .   APPEN A 06
CAT. SPHERED SO FAST, SWEET SOUL? -- WE SEE   .   .   .   .   .   APPEN A 23
THEO. SERVED BY SWEET SECONDER? --   .   .   .   .   .   .   APPEN A 28

253

SWEET   (CONTINUED)
      SENT TO THE MAIDEN SWEET, ... APPEN D 02
      BY THY SWEET CHILDBEARING, ... APPEN D 19
SWEETBRIAR
      THE AIR SMELLS STRONG OF SWEETBRIAR IN THE PARK. 135 00 024
SWEETER
      THAT SWEET'S SWEETER ENDING; 048 00 031
      MADE SWEETER, NOT MADE DIM. 060 00 111
      MAKING THE SHADOW SWEETER, A SPIRITUAL GRACE 107 04 015
      SWEETER THY KISSES, MY OWN LOVE, ... 109 38 003
SWEETER-MEMORIED
      SMELLS THAT ARE SWEETER-MEMORIED THAN THE ROSE, ... 119 00 003
SWEETEST
      THEN SWEETEST SEEMS THE HOUSELESS SHORE, ... 015 00 035
      BOTH SING SOMETIMES THE SWEETEST, SWEETEST SPELLS, . . . 039 00 006
      BOTH SING SOMETIMES THE SWEETEST, SWEETEST SPELLS, . . . 039 00 006
      WITH THE SWEETEST AIR THAT SAID, STILL PLIED AND PRESSED, . 047 00 003
      THERE! AND YOUR SWEETEST SENDINGS, AH DIVINE, ... 048 00 013
      EVEN TO THE TILLAGE OF THE SWEETEST SPOT, -- 102 03 016
      THE SWEETEST SONNET FIVE OR SIX TIMES READ 117 00 009
      C THEN SWEETEST SEEMS THE SEEMING BRIDE 120 00 018
      HIS SWEETEST NECTAR HIDES BEHIND. J 148 00 042
      THERE! SWEETEST, FRESHEST, SHADOWIEST! 159 00 023
SWEETHEART
      WEPT, WIFE! WEPT, SWEETHEART WOULD BE ONE! 041 00 106
SWEET-AND-SOUR
      WHEN THE AIR WAS SWEET-AND-SOUR OF THE FLOWN FINEFLOUR OF . 142 00 004
SWEET-FAMILIAR
      MORE SWEET-FAMILIAR GROWS MY LOVE TO THEE, ... 012 01 002
SWEET-FOWL
      NOT THAT THE SWEET-FOWL, SONG-FOWL, NEEDS NO REST -- . . 039 00 009
SWEET-PEA-BLOSSO
      AS HALVES OF SWEET-PEA-BLOSSOM ARE! 081 00 044
SWEETLY
      SWEETLY THEN AND OF FREE ACT 077 00 089
      MORE SWEETLY SHADES HER STOLEN HAIR 120 00 007
      IT NEVER YET SO SWEETLY WAS PUT ON 125 00 025
      BY SPEECH SO SWEETLY BROKEN UP AND GONE. 125 00 027
SWEETNESS
      A PITEOUS SIREN SWEETNESS ON THE SEA, ... 002 00 127
      GOD COMES ALL SWEETNESS TO YOUR LENTEN LIPS. 011 00 002
      NOR ELSEWHERE CAN THY SWEETNESS UNENDEAR. 012 01 005
      AND MINOR SWEETNESS SCARCE MADE MENTION OF; 019 00 012
      SWEET UNTO GOD, AND THE SWEETNESS IS GRACE; 027 00 044
      LET THE WARBLED SWEETNESS RILL, ... 077 00 084
      SWEETNESS FROM THE HOUR, AND DIP 077 00 132
      REMEMBER'D SWEETNESS. FOR MY THOUGHT 081 00 139
      SO WASTE IN TEARS OVER THIS BED OF SWEETNESS, ... 102 01 035
      THAT SWEETNESS RE-ATTRIBUTING ABOVE. -- V 113 00 012
      NEWS FROM BELLEISLE, EVEN SUCH A SWEETNESS BLOWS 119 00 006
      THE TURMOIL AND THE TORMENT, IT HAS, I SWEAR, A SWEETNESS, . 152 02 057
      THERE BE THOU THE SWEETNESS MAN WAS MEANT TO FIND. . . . 168 00 020
SWEET'S
      THAT SWEET'S SWEETER ENDING; 048 00 031
SWEETS
      SWEET FLOWERS I CARRY, -- SWEETS FOR BITTER. 010 00 006
      HE SHALL HAVE SUMMER SWEETS AND DRESS 124 00 005
      C AND I SHALL KNOW OF SWEETS FOR HIM 124 00 011
SWELL
      SOME TRAIL'D THE NAUTILUS; OR ON THE SWELL 002 00 056
      WHERE THE GREEN SWELL IS IN THE HAVENS DUMB, ... 009 00 007
      AND BIRD AND BLOSSOM SWELL 042 00 023
SWELLING
      THENCE THE DISCHARGE OF IT, THERE ITS SWELLING TO BE, . . 028 07 006
SWELL'D
      SWELL'D THE SWEET STRAIN TO A MELODIOUS WAIL; 002 00 133
SWELLS
      AND FOR THE TINKLINGS ON THE FALLS AND SWELLS 107 02 007
SWEPT
      ADOWN THE CLATTERING GULLIES SWEPT THE RAIN! 001 13 002
      WHAT TIME THE BAFFLED FRANK SWEPT BACK PURSU'D 001 14 008
      PAVES THE CLOUDS ON THE SWEPT AZURE. 078 00 010
      HE SWEPT WHAT SCOPE HE WAS 148 00 015
SWIFT
      WITH SWIFT, SLOW; SWEET, SOUR; ADAZZLE, DIM; 037 00 009
      THEY WATCHED THE BRUSH OF THE SWIFT STRINGY DROPS, . . . 107 03 013
SWIFTLY
      SEEMS TO US SWEET OF US AND SWIFTLY AWAY WITH, C 059 06 008
SWIM
      FOR ROSE-MOLES ALL IN STIPPLE UPON TROUT THAT SWIM; . . . 037 00 003
      PHOEBUS' LOOSEN'D TRESSES, SWIM; 077 00 102
      SPRINGS IN THE FLOATING AIR AND THE SKIES SWIM, -- . . . 113 00 006
SWIMMING
      ANON, ACROSS THEIR SWIMMING SPLENDOUR STROOK, ... 002 00 015
      SWIMMING, AND LANGUISH'D GREEN UPON THE DEEP 002 00 114
SWIMS
      WHILE HE LOOKS ABOUT HIM, LAUGHS, SWIMS. C 159 00 042

254

SWING
    AND OUT OF THE SWING OF THE SEA, ... 009 00 008
    COME, SWING THE SCULLS ON PENMAEN POOL, ... 030 00 008
    IN HIS ECSTASY! THEN OFF, OFF FORTH ON SWING, ... 036 00 005
SWINGS
    SWINGS THE STROKE DEALT -- 028 06 004
    THOUSANDS OF THORNS, THOUGHTS) SWINGS THOUGH, COMMONWEAL . . 070 00 008
    STILL THE SCARLET SWINGS AND DANCES ON THE BLADE. 152 02 013
SWINISHLY
    THAT SWINISHLY REFUSES SUCH A PEARL! 102 03 033
    THAT SWINISHLY REFUSES SUCH A PEARL! V 102 03 039
SWIRLING
    SWIRLING OUT BLOOM TILL ALL THE AIR IS BLIND 002 00 089
    AND THE INBOARD SEAS RUN SWIRLING AND HAWLING; 028 19 003
SWOLL'N
    SWOLL'N IS THE WIND THAT IN ARGENT BILLOWS 078 00 003
SWOON
    THE SWOON OF A HEART THAT THE SWEEP AND THE HURL OF THEE TROD . . 028 02 006
SWOONED
    SOMETHING I SAID! I SWOONED AND FELL. 081 00 118
SWORD
    TAKE CANAAN WITH YOUR SWORD AND WITH YOUR BOW. 005 00 056
    PRINCES STRONG FOR THE SWORD AND SLAUGHTER, ... 026 00 027
    ' SOME FIND ME A SWORD; SOME 028 11 001
    AND HE MY PEACE / MY PARTING, SWORD AND STRIFE. 066 00 004
SWORDS
    YOUR COMFORT IS AS SHARP AS SWORDS; 081 00 032
SWUNG
    THE DRENCHED HAIR OF SLABBY WEEDS THAT SWUNG 002 00 113
    HE SWUNG TO HIS FIRST POISED PURPORT OF REPLY. 047 00 004
    BOW SWUNG FINDS TONGUE TO FLING OUT BROAD ITS NAME; 057 00 004
    SWUNG DOWN AT A DISARRAY, ... 144 00 008
    WHAT SIGHTS SHALL BE WHEN SOME THAT SWUNG, WRETCHES, ON CRUTCHES . 152 C 022
SYCAMORE
    -- SHE BY A SYCAMORE, ... 111 00 001
    FAIRYLAND; SILK-BEECH, SCROLLED ASH, PACKED SYCAMORE, C . . . 159 00 024
SYCAMORE-TREE
    (LIKE ME) -- SAT SIGHING BY A SYCAMORE-TREE. ' 111 00 014
SYDNEY
    SYDNEY FLETCHER, BRISTOL-BRED, ... 041 00 057
SYLVESTER
    ' SYLVESTER, COME, SYLVESTER; YOU MAY TRUST 107 03 001
    ' SYLVESTER, COME, SYLVESTER; YOU MAY TRUST 107 03 001
    SYLVESTER CAME: THEY WENT BY CUMNOR HILL, ... 107 03 009
    MOST DENTED) LAY SYLVESTER, READING KEATS' 107 04 021
    SOUNDS REACH'D HIM. RICHARD CAME. SYLVESTER SMILED 107 04 024
SYMPATHISING
    MARY SEES, SYMPATHISING 042 00 026

TABLE
    CROWDED LET HIS TABLE BE; 024 00 026
TABOUR
    THEY TOUCH HEAVEN, TABOUR ON IT; HOW THEIR TALONS SWEEP . . 149 A 007
    THEY TOUCH, THEY TABOUR ON IT, HOVER ON IT [; HERE, THERE HURLED] ,V 149 B 007
TACKLE
    TO THE MEN IN THE TOPS AND THE TACKLE RODE OVER THE STORM'S BRAWLING. 028 19 008
    EACH SPORT HAS HERE ITS TACKLE AND TOOL; 030 00 006
    AND ALL TRADES, THEIR GEAR AND TACKLE AND TRIM. 037 00 006
TACKLED
    BENEATH THE TACKLED VINE. 165 00 008
TACT
    HAS WIT ENOUGH, BUT LESS THAN FEMALE TACT, ... 094 00 019
TAIL
    TO MANTLE-O'ER THE TAIL, SUCH AS IS SHED 002 00 049
    UNVALVE OR SHUT HIS VANED TAIL 130 00 011
TAIL-FIN
    FROM CROWN TO TAIL-FIN FLOATING, FRINGED THE SPINE, . . . 002 00 041
TAILS
    THEIR FILMY TAILS ADOWN WHOSE LENGTH THERE SHOW'D 002 00 104
TAINTING
    TALL SUN'S TINGEING, OR TREACHEROUS THE TAINTING OF THE EARTH'S AIR, 059 06 005
TAKE
    TAKE CANAAN WITH YOUR SWORD AND WITH YOUR BOW. 005 00 056
    TAKE A LESSON FROM THE GROUND; 024 00 014
    TAKE SETTLER AND SEAMEN, TELL MEN WITH WOMEN, ... 028 12 003
    TO HIS YOUNGSTER TAKE HIS TREAT! 048 00 011
    TAKE AS FOR TOOL, NOT TOY MEANT 049 00 013
    HE DOES TAKE FRESH AND FRESH, ... 060 00 056
    TO DO WITHOUT, TAKE TOSSES, AND OBEY. 068 00 004
    AND SOBER LUSTRES TAKE THE GLOOM; 077 00 020

TAKE   (CONTINUED)
    TAKE COURAGE; THIS SHALL NEED NO FURTHER ART. 080 11 005
    I'LL TAKE IN HAND THE BLADY STONE 080 14 001
    NO HOUSE OF RIMMON MAY I TAKE, ... 081 00 14D
    BUT HAS NOT LEARNT TO TAKE IT GRACEFULLY; 094 00 016
    NOW I AM MINDED TO TAKE PIPE IN HAND 105 00 001
    AND WILL NOT TAKE DENIAL. 110 00 007
    OR TAKE IT THUS -- THAT THE CONCORDING STARS 122 00 007
    TAKE THEIR PECULIAR THORNS AND NATURAL PAIN 123 00 005
    AND I MUST TAKE YOUR AMENDS, CRY PARDON, AND THEN BE DUMB. .   .   . 128 00 020
    TO TAKE HER; WHILE THEIR TONGUES WOULD GO 145 00 026
    TO TAKE HIS LOVELY LIKENESS MORE AND MORE. 151 00 002
    BRAVE ALL, AND TAKE WHAT COMES -- AS HERE THIS RABBLE IS COME, .   . 152 02 068
    IS TO COME NEAR AND TAKE HIM HOME. 167 00 004
    WHAT GOD'S SON HAS TOLD ME, TAKE FOR TRUTH I DO; 168 00 007
    LOVES MAN, THAT HE A MAN WILL BE AND TAKE   .   .   .   . APPEN D 07
    AWAY OUR SIN AND GUILT SHOULD TAKE, ... APPEN D 45
    TILL HE US TO HIM TAKE,   AMEN.   .   .   .   . APPEN D 50
TAKEN
    THAT I HAVE TAKEN TO PLEAD WITH, -- IF THE SOUND 013 00 009
    THEY HAVE TAKEN OUT THEIR LONG BRANDS, ... 109 14 001
TAKES
    TAKES TO THE SEAS AND SNOWS 041 00 059
    SO TAKES THE SISTER SENSE) CAN FIND NO MARK, ... 113 00 004
    SERVES AND WHAT SIDE HE TAKES. 148 00 024
    SOME PAGEANT WHICH TAKES TEARS AND I MUST FOOT WITH FEELING THAT .   . 152 01 020
    HER URN TAKES ALL, HER DEAL IS JUST. 166 00 016
TAKINGS
    TO THE OFTEN TAKINGS OF DESIROUS WINDS, ... 111 00 003
TALE
    GIVE US THE TALE OF BRICKS AS HERETOFORE; 005 00 049
    EVER SO BLACK ON IT, OUR TALE, O OUR ORACLE! C 061 00 010
    HIS TALE AND TELLING HAS BEEN GIVEN TO ME. 107 01 018
    BRING THE TENDER TALE TRUE OF THE PELICAN; 168 00 021
TALES
    TOLD TALES WITH WHAT HEART'S STRESS 054 00 023
TALKS
    TALKS OF SELF-SACRIFICE, YET CAN'T FORGIVE; 094 00 022
TALL
    PENDANT IN FORMAL LINE FROM CORNICE TALL 001 12 007
    BUT ROPED WITH, ALWAYS, ALL THE WAY DOWN FROM THE TALL   .   .   . 028 04 006
    EARS, AND THE CALL OF THE TALL NUN 028 19 007
    TALL SUN'S TINGEING, OR TREACHEROUS THE TAINTING OF THE EARTH'S AIR, 059 06 005
    VEINS VIOLETS AND TALL TREES MAKES MORE AND MORE) 073 00 011
    IN THE QUICK FRAGRANCE OF TALL ROLLING PINES, ... 084 00 005
    HIS THREE BROTHERS ARE EACH AS TALL 109 21 003
    ' I HAVE TALL DAUGHTERS DEAR THAT HEED MY HAND; 158 00 002
TALMAI
    RISE; MATCH YOUR STRENGTH WITH MONSTROUS TALMAI 005 00 057
TALONS
    THEY TOUCH HEAVEN, TABOUR ON IT; HOW THEIR TALONS SWEEP   .   .   . 149 A 007
    WITH TALONS SWEEP V   .   .   .   . 149 B 008
TAME
    THAT . . . IN SMOOTH SPOONS SPY LIFE'S MASQUE MIRRORED; TAME   .   . 075 00 013
TAMPERING
    TAMPERING WITH THOSE SWEET BINES, DRAWS THEM OUT, C 152 01 015
TANGLED
    ON TANGLED SHOALS THAT BAR THE BROOK -- A CROWD 002 00 096
TANGLES
    AND TANGLES ON A DOWN OF FRANCE, ... 083 00 014
TANTALEAN
    AND TANTALEAN SLATY ASHINESS 117 00 005
TAPER
    IT SHAPES ITSELF IN TAPER SKEINS; 130 00 018
TAR
    EVERY INCH A TAR, ... 041 00 075
TARPEIAN-FAST
    TARPEIAN-FAST, BUT A BLOWN BEACON OF LIGHT. 028 29 008
TARS
    OUR REDCOATS, OUR TARS? BOTH THESE BEING, THE GREATER PART,   .   . 063 00 002
    AND HATE THE ILL-VISAGED CURSING TARS, ... 114 00 010
TARSUS
    NEAR BY IS PAUL'S FREE TARSUS, FABLED WHERE 136 00 007
    AND PAUL IS TARSUS' TRUE BELLEROPHON. 136 00 010
TARTARUS
    THE PANG OF TARTARUS, CHRISTIANS HOLD, ... 080 01 001
TASK
    BY THAT WINDOW WHAT TASK WHAT FINGERS PLY, ... 046 00 005
    WHEN 'TIS THE CONFIDANTE THAT SETS THE TASK. 094 00 002
    BUT HERE, HERE IS A WORKMAN FROM HIS DAY'S TASK SWEATS. .   .   . 152 02 011
    THE TELLING TIME OUR TASK IS; TIME'S SOME PART, ... 153 00 005
    OVER FINGER-TEASING TASK, HIS TWINY BOOTS 159 00 033
TASKING
    TIME'S TASKING, IT IS FATHERS THAT ASKING FOR EASE 028 27 003
TASKS
    WANTS WAR, WANTS WOUNDS; WEARY HIS TIMES, HIS TASKS;   .   .   . 068 00 003
TASTE
    AND TASTE THE TREATS OF PENMAEN POOL. 030 00 040

```
TASTE          (CONTINUED)
    BITTER WOULD HAVE ME TASTE: MY TASTE WAS ME;      •   •   •   •   •   • 067 00 010
    BITTER WOULD HAVE ME TASTE: MY TASTE WAS ME;      •   •   •   •   •   • 067 00 010
    AY, SWEET TO TASTE BESIDE THIS WOE.               •   •   •   •   •   • 080 07 007
    I DARE NOT TASTE THE THICKENING SALT,             •   •   •   •   •   • 120 00 026
    MUST ALL DAY LONG TASTE MURDER. WHAT DO NOW THEN? DO? NAY,  •   •   • 152 02 065
TASTED
    BUT THEY CAN GUESS WHO HAVE TASTED OF             •   •   •   •   •   • 167 00 015
TASTELESS
    IS TASTELESS NOTHING: AND IN MY DEGREE            •   •   •   •   •   • 117 00 010
TASTING
    SEEING, TOUCHING, TASTING ARE IN THEE DECEIVED:   •   •   •   •   •   • 168 00 005
TASTY
    PALATE, THE HUTCH OF TASTY LUST,                  •   •   •   •   •   • 022 00 013
    BE MANAGED TASTY TO THAT TONGUE?                  •   •   •   •   •   • 166 00 019
TATTER-TANGLED
    TATTER-TANGLED AND DINGLE-A-DANGLED               •   •   •   •   •   • 138 00 025
TAUGHT
    AND TAUGHT MY LIPS TO QUOTE THIS WORD             •   •   •   •   •   • 008 00 006
    FALLS LIGHT AS TEN YEARS LONG TAUGHT HOW TO AND WHY.  •   •   •   •   • 047 00 008
    MY TONGUE HAD TAUGHT THEE COMFORT, TOUCH HAD QUENCHED THY TEARS,  •   • 053 00 010
    WHAT PUT TAUGHT GRACES ON HIS COUNTRY LIP,        •   •   •   •   •   • 107 02 003
    WHAT TAUGHT THE HUMANITIES AND THE ROUND OF ARTS?  •   •   •   •   •   • 107 02 006
    SHE LOOKED, SHE LISTENED: PAUL TAUGHT LONG THAT DAY.  •   •   •   •   • 136 00 024
    HE TAUGHT ANOTHER TIME THERE AND A THIRD:         •   •   •   •   •   • 136 00 031
TAUNTLESS
    TONGUE TRUE, VAUNT- AND TAUNTLESS:               •   •   •   •   •   • 048 00 015
TEACH
    WHEN LIMBER LIQUID YOUTH, THAT TO ALL I TEACH    •   •   •   •   •   • 048 00 022
    TEACH ME THE PACES THAT YOU WENT                  •   •   •   •   •   • 081 00 125
    TEACH ME THE WAY: I WILL REPENT.                  •   •   •   •   •   • 081 00 136
    AND I CAN TEACH HIM HAPPINESS                     •   •   •   •   •   • 124 00 007
TEAR
    DISPEL THE DOUBT AND DRY THE TEAR:                •   •   •   •   •   • 023 00 046
    I FALL, I TEAR AND SHOWER THE WEED,               •   •   •   •   •   • 081 00 064
    I SEE HER RIVING FINGERS TEAR                     •   •   •   •   •   • 120 00 005
TEAR-TRICKED
    HIS TEAR-TRICKED CHEEKS OF FLAME                  •   •   •   •   •   • 054 00 036
TEARS
    CRUSHES AND TEARS THE RARE ENJEWELLING,           •   •   •   •   •   • 002 00 085
    MY BANKRUPT HEART HAS NO MORE TEARS TO SPEND.     •   •   •   •   •   • 014 03 004
    NOR TEARS, NOR TEARS THIS CLAY UNCOUTH            •   •   •   •   •   • 018 00 013
    NOR TEARS, NOR TEARS THIS CLAY UNCOUTH            •   •   •   •   •   • 018 00 013
    COULD MOULD, IF ANY TEARS THERE WERE.             •   •   •   •   •   • 018 00 014
    AND TRUTH IS HEARD, WITH TEARS IMPEARLED,         •   •   •   •   •   • 023 00 036
    O THIS IS BRINGING! TEARS MAY SWARM               •   •   •   •   •   • 025 00 035
    WITH EYES THAT SMILE THRO' THE TEARS OF THE HOURS, •   •   •   •   •   • 026 00 014
    TRENCHED WITH TEARS, CARVED WITH CARES.           •   •   •   •   •   • 028 15 003
    WHY, TEARS! IS IT? TEARS! SUCH A MELTING, A MADRIGAL START!  •   •   • 028 18 006
    WHY, TEARS! IS IT? TEARS! SUCH A MELTING, A MADRIGAL START!  •   •   • 028 18 006
    YET SHED WHAT TEARS SAD TRUELOVE SHOULD.          •   •   •   •   •   • 041 00 108
    I TO HIM TURN WITH TEARS                          •   •   •   •   •   • 052 00 010
    MY TONGUE HAD TAUGHT THEE COMFORT, TOUCH HAD QUENCHED THY TEARS,  •   • 053 00 010
    THY TEARS THAT TOUCHED MY HEART, CHILD, FELIX, POOR FELIX RANDAL!  •   • 053 00 011
    WHILE SHEENY TEARS AND SUNLIT MIRTH               •   •   •   •   •   • 077 00 129
    I PLEAD: AND YOU WILL GIVE YOUR TEARS!            •   •   •   •   •   • 081 00 028
    MY TEARS ARE BUT A CLOUD OF RAIN!                 •   •   •   •   •   • 081 00 036
    INTOLERABLE TEARS I BLEED.                        •   •   •   •   •   • 081 00 067
    MY SIGNALLING TEARS MIGHT RING UP FLORIS: NOW     •   •   •   •   •   • 102 01 007
    LAUGHING OR TEARS. I THINK I COULD DO EITHER --   •   •   •   •   •   • 102 01 014
    THAT TEARS AND LAUGHTER ARE HUNG CLOSE TOGETHER.  •   •   •   •   •   • 102 01 016
    I FIND I AM AS READY WITH MY TEARS                •   •   •   •   •   • 102 01 031
    SO WASTE IN TEARS OVER THIS BED OF SWEETNESS,     •   •   •   •   •   • 102 01 035
    THE TIME SAVE WHEN HER TEARS WHICH STILL [ DESCEND ]  •   •   •   •   • 111 00 005
    FROM TEARS SHED OVER CHILDREN'S GRAVES.           •   •   •   •   •   • 123 00 003
    WITH TEARS TO PUT HER CANDLE OUT:                 •   •   •   •   •   • 145 00 024
    SOME PAGEANT WHICH TAKES TEARS AND I MUST FOOT WITH FEELING THAT  •   • 152 01 020
    AND BEAUTY'S DEAREST VERIEST VEIN IS TEARS.       •   •   •   •   •   • 157 00 004
    THEO.  O THIS IS BRINGING!  TEARS MAY SWARM       •   •   •   •   •   • APPEN A 35
TEASE
    THEY TEASE ME. NEVER KNOW THE PART                •   •   •   •   •   • 165 00 003
TEASES
    COILS, KEEPS, AND TEASES SIMPLE SIGHT.            •   •   •   •   •   • 022 00 012
TEDIOUS
    TWO TEDIOUS ACTS WERE PAST:                       •   •   •   •   •   • 054 00 029
TEEMING
    IF FLOODTIDE TEEMING THRILLS HER FULL,            •   •   •   •   •   • 030 00 022
    DEATH TEEMING IN BY HER PORTHOLES                 •   •   •   •   •   • 041 00 039
    SCOOP YOU FROM TEEMING FILTH SOME SICKLY HOVEL,   •   •   •   •   •   • 077 00 006
TEEVO
    TEEVO CHEEVO CHEEVIO CHEE:                        •   •   •   •   •   • 138 00 001
TELL
    THEY TELL ITS STORY THUS: AMIDST THE HEAT         •   •   •   •   •   • 001 02 001
    WHICH I MAY TELL AT AUTUMN-TIME. '               •   •   •   •   •   • 004 00 015
    TELL ME THE NAME NOW, TELL ME ITS NAME.           •   •   •   •   •   • 027 00 019
    TELL ME THE NAME NOW, TELL ME ITS NAME.           •   •   •   •   •   • 027 00 019
    THEY MULTIPLY, MULTIPLY, WHO CAN TELL HOW?        •   •   •   •   •   • 027 00 040
```

TELL   (CONTINUED)
     MY HEART, BUT YOU WERE DOVEWINGED, I CAN TELL, ... 028 03 006
     TAKE SETTLER AND SEAMEN, TELL MEN WITH WOMEN, ... 028 12 003
     THEY COULD TELL HIM FOR HOURS, DANDLED THE TO AND FRO . . . 028 16 006
     ' BUT TELL ME, CHILD, YOUR CHOICE: WHAT SHALL I BUY . . . 047 00 001
     ONE. YES I CAN TELL SUCH A KEY, I DO KNOW SUCH A PLACE, . . 059 06 007
     A CARE KEPT. -- WHERE KEPT? DO BUT TELL US WHERE KEPT, WHERE. -- . 059 06 030
     THESE TWO TELL, EACH OFF THE OTHER: OF A RACK C 061 00 013
     AND THEN -- I CHOKE TO TELL THIS OUT -- 080 09 002
     GIVE HIM THE GIFT. ' I CANNOT TELL 081 00 111
     AND TRULY TELL TO ME. 109 11 004
     ' I PRAY YOU TELL TO ME. ' 109 25 004
     I KNOW WHAT YOU WILL TELL ME -- NEGLECTFUL THAT YOU WERE NOT. . 128 00 005
     AH YES! WHY, GET THEE GONE THEN: TELL THY MOTHER I WANT HER. . 152 01 010
     OUT ON THE GIANT AIR: TELL SUMMER NO, ... 154 00 003
TELLING
     CAME MIDST THE DRIZZLE TELLING HOW LAST NIGHT 001 14 002
     BEYOND SAYING SWEET, PAST TELLING OF TONGUE, ... 028 09 005
     HIS TALE AND TELLING HAS BEEN GIVEN TO ME. 107 01 018
     A JAUNTING VAUNTING ASSAULTING TRUMPET TELLING. V . . . 141 00 007
     THE TELLING TIME OUR TASK IS: TIME'S SOME PART, ... 153 00 005
TELLS
     TELLS MARY HER MIRTH TILL CHRIST'S BIRTH 042 00 046
     THERE) -- BOY BUGLER, BORN, HE TELLS ME, OF IRISH . . . 048 00 002
     STONES RING: LIKE EACH TUCKED STRING TELLS, EACH HUNG BELL'S . 057 00 003
     THAT HERE PERSONAL TELLS OFF THESE HEART-SONG POWERFUL PEALS? -- . 141 00 002
TEMPE
     OR TEMPE WITH THE WEST TO BLOW. 166 00 024
TEMPERATENESS
     CONTROLL'D THEM TO A GREY-GREEN TEMPERATENESS, ... 107 04 014
TEMPER'D
     THE TEMPER'D SOIL WHERE ONLY HER FLOWER IS FOUND. . . . 102 03 004
TEMPEST
     DOES TEMPEST CARRY THE GRAIN FOR THEE? C 028 31 008
     O IN TURNS OF TEMPEST, ME HEAPED THERE: C 064 00 008
TEMPESTS
     MY TEMPESTS THERE, MY FIRE AND FEVER FUSSY. 075 00 014
TEMPLE
     THIS WAS NO CLASSIC TEMPLE ORDER'D ROUND 001 07 001
     ONLY THE BREATHING TEMPLE AND FLEET 041 00 093
TEMPLES
     THEN OVER HIS TURNED TEMPLES -- HERE -- 144 00 013
TEMPT
     BUT IF I CANNOT TEMPT HIS THOUGHT 124 00 021
TEN
     APART, BETWIXT TEN THOUSAND PETALL'D LIPS 002 00 021
     TEN OR TWELVE, ONLY TEN OR TWELVE 043 00 020
     TEN OR TWELVE, ONLY TEN OR TWELVE 043 00 020
     FALLS LIGHT AS TEN YEARS LONG TAUGHT HOW TO AND WHY. . . 047 00 008
     CHRIST. FOR CHRIST PLAYS IN TEN THOUSAND PLACES, . . . 057 00 012
TENDER
     OR TENDER PINKS WITH BLOODY TYRIAN DYE. 002 00 047
     OR BAT WITH TENDER AND AIR-CRISPING WINGS 019 00 002
     TO THEE WE TENDER THE BEAUTIES ALL 026 00 021
     FINGER OF A TENDER OF, O OF A FEATHERY DELICACY, THE BREAST OF THE . 028 31 006
     SINCE COUNTRY IS SO TENDER 043 00 012
     OR TO-FRO TENDER TRAMBEAMS TRUCKLE AT THE EYE. . . . 046 00 004
     YIELDS TENDER AS A PUSHED PEACH, ... 048 00 023
     TURN MOST ON TENDER BYPLAY. 054 00 016
     BRING THE TENDER TALE TRUE OF THE PELICAN: 168 00 021
TENDERED
     TENDERED TO HIM. AH WELL, GOD REST HIM ALL ROAD EVER HE OFFENDED! . 053 00 008
TENDERER
     THE APPEALING OF THE PASSION IS TENDERER IN PRAYER APART: . . 028 27 006
TENDEREST
     NEVER FLEETS MORE, FASTENED WITH THE TENDEREST TRUTH . . 059 06 012
TENDER-SLANTED
     CRISP LIPS, STRAIGHT NOSE, AND TENDER-SLANTED CHEEK. . . 136 00 016
TENDERNESS
     BUT IS THERE A PLACE FOR TENDERNESS, ... 081 00 077
TENT-POLES
     YOUR HANDS HAVE BORNE THE TENT-POLES: ON YOU PLOD: . . . 005 03 007
TEREBINTH
     AND TREES OF TEREBINTH AND STONES 015 00 039
TERM
     ALLOW AT LEAST IT HAS ONE TERM AND PART 102 03 005
TERMS
     NEW-DATED FROM THE TERMS THAT REAPPEAR, ... 012 01 001
TERRACES
     UPON THE MOULD'RING TERRACES AMAIN: 001 13 004
TERRIBLE
     TERRIBLE FRUIT WAS ON THE TREE 006 00 015
     TO ME WAS TERRIBLE TO HEAR. 021 00 042
     BUT AH, BUT O THOU TERRIBLE, WHY WOULDST THOU RUDE ON ME . . 064 00 005
TERROR
     THY TERROR, O CHRIST, O GOD: 028 02 004
TERYTH
     ' WHAT, TERYTH! WHAT, THOU POOR FOND FATHER! C . . . 152 01 016

258

TETHER
    BUT THEN HER TETHER CALLS HER; SHE FALLS OFF, ... 103 00 012
TEXT
    THE SUN ON FALLING WATERS WRITES THE TEXT 091 00 008
    THESE ARE MY VERY TEXT OF DISCONTENT; 125 00 044
TH'
    AND STILL TH' UNBROKEN SILENCE BROODS 023 00 019
    AND STILL TH' ABYSSES INFINITE 023 00 025
    THROUGH TH' HOLY GHOST HIS MIGHT. . . . . . . APPEN D 34
THAMES
    RHINE REFUSED THEM, THAMES WOULD RUIN THEM; 028 21 003
THAN
    TILL, (FEARING RAVAGE WORSE THAN IN HIS FLIGHT, ... 001 14 007
    THAN CHANGEFUL POMP OF COURTS IS AYE MORE WONDERFUL. . . . 001 15 009
    OF TREMULOUS FILM, MORE SUBTLE THAN THE VEST 002 00 039
    AND BOASTING ' I HAVE FAIRER THINGS THAN THESE ' 002 00 086
    SOONER THAN THEIR MATES; AND YET 004 00 029
    THAN TREBLE-FERVENT MORE OF OTHER MEN, ... 014 01 013
    FOR POOR LOVE'S FAILURE THAN HIS HOPELESS RISE. 014 03 007
    MORE POWERLESS THAN THE BLIND OR LAME. 015 00 020
    EVEN THAN THIS MY THANKLESS LORE! 015 00 022
    THE COPSE WAS NEVER MORE THAN GREY. 021 00 002
    FAIRER THAN THIS ONE TO BRIGHTEN OUR DAY? 026 00 008
    THOU HEARDST ME TRUER THAN TONGUE CONFESS 028 02 003
    LOWER THAN DEATH AND THE DARK; 028 33 004
    MORE, MORE THAN WAS WILL YET BE. -- 041 00 104
    THAN THE MOST ARE MUST DELIGHT HER? 042 00 010
    WELL BUT THERE WAS MORE THAN THIS; 042 00 033
    MANNERLY-HEARTED! MORE THAN HANDSOME FACE -- 047 00 009
    A WILDER BEAST FROM WEST THAN ALL WERE, MORE 050 00 007
    DEEP, DEEPER THAN DIVINED, ... 052 00 006
    FONDER A CARE KEPT THAN WE COULD HAVE KEPT IT, KEPT . . . 059 06 028
    MY MORE THAN MEAT AND DRINK, ... 060 00 011
    NAY, MORE THAN ALMONER, ... 060 00 042
    THAN PURCELL TUNE LETS TREAD TO? SEE; IT DOES THIS; KEEPS WARM . 062 00 003
    MASTER MORE MAY THAN GAZE, GAZE OUT OF COUNTENANCE. . . . 062 00 005
    BY GROPING ROUND MY COMFORTLESS, THAN BLIND 069 00 006
    HOW WOULDST THOU WORSE, I WONDER, THAN THOU DOST . . . 074 00 006
    DO IN SPARE HOURS MORE THRIVE THAN I THAT SPEND, . . . 074 00 008
    BREATHES ONCE AND, QUENCHED FASTER THAN IT CAME, . . . 076 00 003
    DOUBLE, AND HIGHER THAN HIS WONT, ... 077 00 111
    WHAT HAVE I MORE THAN OTHER MEN, ... 081 00 168
    MORE GOLDEN THAN THE WORLD OF LIGHTS, ... 083 00 002
    BUT EACH A HAND'S BREADTH FURTHER THAN THE NEXT. . . . 091 00 007
    HAS WIT ENOUGH, BUT LESS THAN FEMALE TACT. 094 00 019
    WORSE THAN WHEN FLORIS FOUND ME IN THE GARDEN . . . 102 01 040
    YET THIS COULD BE NO OTHER'S HAND THAN HIS, . . . 102 01 045
    THAN ALL THE CROWNS TO ME. 109 38 004
    RATHER TO EAR THAN EYE SHEWS WHERE THEY STRAY, . . . 112 00 004
    WHO CAME FROM FURTHER THAN THE STARS 115 00 003
    THAN WE IN THE EAST DARE LOOK FOR BUDS, DISCLOSE . . . 119 00 002
    SMELLS THAT ARE SWEETER-MEMORIED THAN THE ROSE, . . . 119 00 003
    THAN FAN OR HOOD OR STRAWY PLAIT, ... 120 00 008
    THAT HAS IT; AND SHE IS FAIRER THAN COLOMB; . . . 125 00 037
    BUT LATE IS BETTER THAN NEVER; YOU SEE YOU HAVE MANAGED SO, . 128 00 017
    IS KNOWN TO MEN MORE THAN ME. 138 00 013
    NO MORE THAN RED AND BLUE, ... 148 00 033
    NO MORE THAN RE AND MI, ... 148 00 034
    A GROWING BURNISH BRIGHTER THAN BEFORE . . . 151 00 004
    THAN SEWERS WITH SACRED OILS. MANKIND, THAT MOB, COMES. COME! . 152 02 070
    SAY MAN THAN MAN MAY RANK HIS ROWS . . . 166 00 009
    BUT MORE THAN HONEY AND HONEYCOMB 167 00 003
THANKLESS
    EVEN THAN THIS MY THANKLESS LORE; 015 00 022
THANKS
    RETURNING THANKS, MIGHT OFFER SUCH ARRAY. 089 00 004
THECLA
    WHO THINKS OF THECLA? YET HER NAME WAS KNOWN, . . . 136 00 003
    YOUNG THECLA, SCANNED THE DAZZLING STREETS ONE DAY; . . . 136 00 014
    GREAT THECLA, THE PLUMED PASSIONFLOWER, . . . 145 00 042
THE-LAST-BREATH
    THE-LAST-BREATH PENITENT SPIRITS -- THE UTTERMOST MARK . . . 028 33 006
THENCE
    THE CHOICEST REMNANTS THENCE; -- SUCH HOME FORLORN . . . 001 15 003
    THENCE THE DISCHARGE OF IT, THERE ITS SWELLING TO BE, . . 028 07 006
THEORY
    HE'S WEDDED TO HIS THEORY, THEY SAY. 097 00 001
THEREAFTER
    THAT PLUMES TO PEACE THEREAFTER. AND WHEN PEACE HERE DOES HOUSE . 051 00 009
THEREBY
    DRY UP THE BLUE AND BE NOT SLAKED THEREBY. . . . 117 00 007
    ONE SPELL AND WELL THAT ONE. THERE, AH THEREBY . . . 153 00 007
THEREFORE
    THEREFORE HOW BITTER, AND LEARNT HOW LATE, THE TRUTH! . . 017 00 014
    AND FIND IT WILL NOT THEREFORE BE DESCRIED . . . 102 03 011
    NO WONDER THEREFORE WAS NOT SLOW 145 00 019
    THEREFORE THIS MASTERHOOD, ... 148 00 029

THEREFORE   (CONTINUED)
      LORD BEUNO COMES TONIGHT. TONIGHT, SIR! SOON, NOW; THEREFORE   •   •   152 01 005
      THERE THEY DID APPEAL. THEREFORE AIRY VENGEANCES   •   •   •   •   •   152 02 030
THEREIN
      THEIR CHEEKS MOVED AND THE BONES THEREIN.   •   •   •   •   •   •   092 00 003
THEREON
      THE ANGEL WENT AWAY THEREON   •   •   •   •   •   •   •   •   APPEN D 31
THEREWITH
      THEREWITH TO HANKER FOR THE SMALL!   •   •   •   •   •   •   •   081 00 153
THEW
      FOR ALL HIS DREADNOUGHT BREAST AND BRAIDS OF THEW;   •   •   •   028 16 005
      BOTH THOUGHT AND THEW NOW BOLDER   •   •   •   •   •   •   049 00 008
      STAND AT STRESS. EACH LIMB'S BARROWY BRAWN, HIS THEW   •   •   071 00 005
THICK
      CROWD DOWN UPON A STREAM, AND, JOSTLING THICK   •   •   •   002 00 094
      IN BEDS, IN GARDENS, IN THICK PLOTS I STAND,   •   •   •   •   005 00 037
      WHEN HEAVENLY VALES SO THICK SHALL STAND   •   •   •   •   008 00 016
      THE THICK STARS ROUND HIM ROLL   •   •   •   •   •   •   060 00 099
      SELDOMER HEARTSORE; THAT TREADS THROUGH, PRICKPROOF, THICK   •   070 00 007
      NOW, LEAVED HOW THICK! LACED THEY ARE AGAIN   •   •   •   •   074 00 010
      ONCE, JOSTLING THICK, THE BLUEBELL SHEAVES   •   •   •   •   081 00 013
      HIS LIPS MOVED FAST IN SENSE TOO THICK!   •   •   •   •   •   081 00 100
      WHOSE SILVER SKINS LIE LEVEL AND THICK IN FIELD.   •   •   •   102 01 022
      THE STARS ARE PACKED SO THICK TO-NIGHT   •   •   •   •   •   135 00 019
      C MADE KNOWN, THOUGH THICK THROUGH STONE,   •   •   •   •   148 00 011
THICKEN
      AND MORE, ON EACH HAND, THICKEN, AND APPEAR   •   •   •   •   002 00 030
THICKENING
      I DARE NOT TASTE THE THICKENING SALT,   •   •   •   •   •   120 00 026
THICKEN'D
      THOSE CYCLADS MADE THAT THICKEN'D ON MY SIGHT.   •   •   •   002 00 037
      AND THICKEN'D, LIKE THAT DRIFTED BLOOM, THE FLOCK   •   •   002 00 099
      SICKEN'D AND THICKEN'D BY THE GLARE AND SAND   •   •   •   005 00 019
THICKEST
      FOR, WHERE THE MARTYR'S BONES WERE THICKEST TROD,   •   •   •   001 05 008
THICKET
      AND THICKET AND THORP ARE MERRY   •   •   •   •   •   •   042 00 039
THICK-FLEECED
      THICK-FLEECED BUSHES LIKE A HEIFER'S EAR V   •   •   •   •   098 11 001
THICK-PEARLED
      WITH CORAL, SHELLS, THICK-PEARLED CORDS, WHATE'ER   •   •   002 00 054
THICKLY
      SHE TO THE BLACK-ABOUT AIR, TO THE BREAKER, THE THICKLY   •   •   028 24 005
THICKY
      BEAT FROM OUR BRAINS THE THICKY NIGHT   •   •   •   •   •   167 00 023
THIEF
      AND I PRAY THE PRAYER OF THE DYING THIEF.   •   •   •   •   168 00 012
THIGH
      ROPE-OVER THIGH; KNEE-NAVE; AND BARRELLED SHANK -- C   •   •   071 00 003
THIN
      WITH A THIN FLOATING VEIL OF WATER HOAR.   •   •   •   •   002 00 004
      WITH DRAUGHT OF THIN AND PURSUANT COLD SO NIPS   •   •   •   011 00 006
      CLUSTER OF BUGLE BLUE EGGS THIN   •   •   •   •   •   •   042 00 021
      AND FOR THAT FEARFUL HOUR LIFE IS MORE THIN   •   •   •   •   080 03 005
      AND THE THIN STARS TREMBLE NOT. V   •   •   •   •   •   •   085 00 005
      BRIGHT HUES LONG LOOK'D AT THIN, DISSOLVE AND FLY;   •   •   117 00 002
THINE
      LAY OPEN THINE ESTATES.   •   •   •   •   •   •   •   •   115 00 007
      DIDST REACH THINE ARMS OUT DYING,   •   •   •   •   •   •   170 00 006
THING
      OF THAT JACINTHINE THING, THAT, WHERE IT LINGERS,   •   •   •   002 00 065
      I HAD A DREAM, A WONDROUS THING,   •   •   •   •   •   •   004 00 001
      IT SEEM'D SO HARD AND DISMAL THING,   •   •   •   •   •   004 00 031
      THAT NO RECORDED DEVILISH THING WAS DONE   •   •   •   •   014 02 008
      WITH NOT A THING TO MAKE ME FEAR,   •   •   •   •   •   •   021 00 040
      THE GLADDEST THING THAT OUR EYES HAVE SEEN,   •   •   •   026 00 018
      BLINDS HER! BUT SHE THAT WEATHER SEES ONE THING, ONE!   •   •   028 19 005
      THING THAT SHE...THERE THEN! THE MASTER,   •   •   •   •   028 28 004
      TO ME, GOD KNOWS, DESERVING NO SUCH THING!   •   •   •   •   034 00 002
      STIRRED FOR A BIRD, -- THE ACHIEVE OF, THE MASTERY OF THE THING!   •   036 00 008
      EACH MORTAL THING DOES ONE THING AND THE SAME;   •   •   057 00 005
      EACH MORTAL THING DOES ONE THING AND THE SAME;   •   •   057 00 005
      WHEN THE THING WE FREELY FORFEIT IS KEPT WITH FONDER A CARE,   •   059 06 027
      PATIENCE, HARD THING! THE HARD THING BUT TO PRAY,   •   •   068 00 001
      PATIENCE, HARD THING! THE HARD THING BUT TO PRAY,   •   •   068 00 001
      A THING THAT WEEPS, ENDURING LONG: •   •   •   •   •   081 00 050
      IT WAS A HARD THING TO UNDO THIS KNOT.   •   •   •   •   091 00 001
      IT WAS A HARD THING TO UNDO THIS KNOT.   •   •   •   •   091 00 010
      SEES THE RIGHT THING TO DO, AND DOES NOT ACT;   •   •   •   094 00 020
      WHAT I DO NOW IS BUT THE LEAST LEAST THING.   •   •   •   102 01 051
      MOST ILL-CONTENT, THIS LEAST LEAST THING I DO,   •   •   •   102 01 054
      THE KING'S FRIEND TOLD THE THING THAT WAS HID   •   •   •   109 12 001
      THE LAST THING MARGARET'S FINGERS SEW   •   •   •   •   145 00 013
      HOW ALL'S TO ONE THING WROUGHT!   •   •   •   •   •   148 00 001
      LIKE THE THING THAT NEVER KNEW THE EARTH, NEVER OFF ROOTS   •   •   159 00 027
      SHALL BE THIS THING WHEREOF TIDING I BRING;   •   •   •   APPEN D 17
THING'S
      IN EVERY LEAST THING'S LIFE;   •   •   •   •   •   •   •   060 00 008

THINGS
    NOW ALL THINGS ROSY TURN'D: THE WEST HAD GROWN   •   •   •   •   •   • 002 00 019
    AND BOASTING ' I HAVE FAIRER THINGS THAN THESE '   •   •   •   •   • 002 00 086
    A PRESS OF WINGED THINGS COMES DOWN THIS WAY: •   •   •   •   • 005 00 015
    AND WOULD NOT HAVE THAT LEGION OF WINGED THINGS   •   •   •   •   • 007 00 014
    THERE LIVES THE DEAREST FRESHNESS DEEP DOWN THINGS;   •   •   •   • 031 00 010
    ALL THE AIR THINGS WEAR THAT BUILD THIS WORLD OF WALES;   •   •   • 034 00 010
    GLORY BE TO GOD FOR DAPPLED THINGS --   •   •   •   •   •   •   • 037 00 001
    ALL THINGS COUNTER, ORIGINAL, SPARE, STRANGE;   •   •   •   •   • 037 00 007
    THESE THINGS, THESE THINGS WERE HERE AND BUT THE BEHOLDER   •   • 038 00 011
    THESE THINGS, THESE THINGS WERE HERE AND BUT THE BEHOLDER   •   • 038 00 011
    LOOK, FOOT TO FORELOCK, HOW ALL THINGS SUIT! HE   •   •   •   • 041 00 077
    ALL THINGS RISING, ALL THINGS SIZING   •   •   •   •   •   •   • 042 00 025
    ALL THINGS RISING, ALL THINGS SIZING   •   •   •   •   •   •   • 042 00 025
    SHARES THEIR BEST GIFTS SURELY, FALL HOW THINGS WILL) •   •   • 048 00 004
    LEAVES, LIKE THE THINGS OF MAN, YOU   •   •   •   •   •   •   • 055 00 003
    ON THINGS ALOOF, ALOFT,   •   •   •   •   •   •   •   •   • 060 00 091
    MEN'S WITS TO THE THINGS THAT ARE: WHAT GOOD MEANS -- WHERE A GLANCE 062 00 004
    YOU RANK AND REEKING THINGS,   •   •   •   •   •   •   •   •   • 077 00 005
    AND TO THE MYSTERY OF THOSE THINGS   •   •   •   •   •   •   • 077 00 047
    AND COUNT THE ROSY CROSS WITH BANN'D DISASTROUS THINGS.   •   • 089 00 009
    THINGS THAT SHE LIKES SEEMS OFTEN TO DESPISE,   •   •   •   •   • 094 00 017
    WELL, I KNOW NOT. BUT ALL THINGS SEEM TO-NIGHT   •   •   •   • 102 01 010
    OF THE WOOD-SORREL AND ALL THINGS SENSITIVE?   •   •   •   •   • 122 00 011
    AS THE WOOD-SORREL AND ALL THINGS SENSITIVE   •   •   •   •   • 122 00 014
    THAT MAKE MY EYES SORE AND CROSS-COLOUR THINGS   •   •   •   • 125 00 040
    WHILE ALL THINGS ELSE MAY STIR AND RANGE   •   •   •   •   •   • 130 00 007
    HEAVEN WITH IT WHOM SHE CHILDS THINGS BY. V   •   •   •   •   • 149 8 013
    HAVE ALL THINGS READY IN HIS ROOM. THERE NEEDS BUT LITTLE DOING. • 152 01 006
    AMONGST COME-BACK-AGAIN THINGS, C   •   •   •   •   •   •   • 152 C 029
    THINGS WITH A REVIVAL, THINGS WITH A RECOVERY, C   •   •   •   • 152 C 029
    THINGS WITH A REVIVAL, THINGS WITH A RECOVERY, C   •   •   •   • 152 C 029
    FLEDGED THINGS DO RUSTLE NEAR: •   •   •   •   •   •   •   • 160 00 033
    MERE EYEBROW ROCKS THIS ROUND OF THINGS.   •   •   •   •   •   • 166 00 008
THINK
    I THINK: WHERE FROM AND BOUND, I WONDER, WHERE;   •   •   •   • 040 00 003
    WHEN CHILL WOODS WAKE AND THINK OF MORN,   •   •   •   •   •   • 077 00 023
    THINK OF AN OPENING PAGE ILLUMINED   •   •   •   •   •   •   • 093 8 001
    WITH THE READY AZURE AND HIGH CARMINE: -- THINK   •   •   •   • 093 8 002
    LAUGHING OR TEARS. I THINK I COULD DO EITHER --   •   •   •   • 102 01 014
    NO TIME TO THINK. I'LL KNOT IT ON THIS RIBBON,   •   •   •   • 102 01 027
    ' I THINK IT IS SEVEN DAYS, ' SHE SAID,   •   •   •   •   •   • 109 16 003
    AND EVERY HEART THINK LOATHINGLY   •   •   •   •   •   •   •   • 114 00 015
    MIGHT WE NOT THINK THE SWEET (?) AND DARING RISES   •   •   • 122 00 002
    I THINK HE WILL NOT TIRE OF ME,   •   •   •   •   •   •   •   • 124 00 002
    WE HAVE COME FOUR, DO YOU THINK?   •   •   •   •   •   •   • 125 00 013
    THINK THIS, MY BIRTHDAY FALLS IN SADDENING TIME OF YEAR: •   • 128 00 009
    THINK YOU WANT DAFFODILS AND FOLLOW AS FAR   •   •   •   •   • 135 00 030
    THAT I DO THINK THERE IS NOT TO BE HAD   •   •   •   •   •   • 138 00 032
    TO MAKE BELIEVE MY MOOD WAS -- MOCK. O I MIGHT THINK SO   •   • 152 02 010
THINKING
    AND, THINKING THAT SHE THINKS, HAS NEVER THOUGHT;   •   •   •   • 094 00 030
THINKS
    AND, THINKING THAT SHE THINKS, HAS NEVER THOUGHT;   •   •   •   • 094 00 030
    WHO THINKS OF THECLA? YET HER NAME WAS KNOWN,   •   •   •   • 136 00 003
THINLY
    COME BECAUSE THEN MOST THINLY LIES   •   •   •   •   •   •   • 077 00 035
THINNED
    THE MOON, DWINDLED AND THINNED TO THE FRINGE C   •   •   •   • 137 00 002
THINNING
    ROUNDED IT, THINNING SKYWARDS BY DEGREES.   •   •   •   •   •   • 107 04 004
THIRD
    I AM IN IRELAND NOW: NOW I AM AT A THIRD   •   •   •   •   •   • 066 00 009
    THEN UP AND SPAKE THE THIRD BROTHER,   •   •   •   •   •   • 109 27 001
    HE TAUGHT ANOTHER TIME THERE AND A THIRD: •   •   •   •   • 136 00 031
THIRST
    AND NEVER THIRST OR DEARTH.   •   •   •   •   •   •   •   •   • 005 00 048
    EYES IN THEIR DARK CAN DAY OR THIRST CAN FIND   •   •   •   • 069 00 007
    WHILE BLIND MEN'S EYES SHALL THIRST C   •   •   •   •   •   • 152 C 004
    I BESEECH THEE SEND ME WHAT I THIRST FOR SO,   •   •   •   • 168 00 026
THIRST'S
    THIRST'S ALL-IN-ALL IN ALL A WORLD OF WET.   •   •   •   •   • 069 00 008
THISTLED
    STREAKS OF SHADOW, THISTLED LEAS.   •   •   •   •   •   •   • 077 00 137
THISTLES
    ON THISTLES THAT MEN LOOK NOT GRAPES TO GATHER,   •   •   •   • 007 00 002
THITHER
    BUT SHE WHO HAD HOUSED THEM THITHER   •   •   •   •   •   • 041 00 043
THOMAS
    I AM NOT LIKE THOMAS, WOUNDS I CANNOT SEE,   •   •   •   •   • 168 00 013
THONGS
    WITH GORGON'S GEAR AND BAREBILL / THONGS AND FANGS.   •   •   • 050 00 014
THORN
    FOR US THE VINE WAS FENCED WITH THORN,   •   •   •   •   •   • 006 00 013
    THE WINGED FOWLS TOOK PART, PART FELL IN THORN   •   •   •   • 007 00 007
THORN-ENGAGED
    OR THORN-ENGAGED, IMPALED AND PENT   •   •   •   •   •   •   • 081 00 019

261

THORNS
    HOW SOLDIERS PLATTING THORNS AROUND CHRIST'S HEAD 007 00 004
    FOOD FOR FIVE THOUSAND: ON THE THORNS HE SHED 007 00 012
    THOUSANDS OF THORNS, THOUGHTS) SWINGS THOUGH. COMMONWEAL . . . 070 00 008
    TAKE THEIR PECULIAR THORNS AND NATURAL PAIN 123 00 005
THORNY
    MY EVIL WORDS THORNY WITH PAIN: 081 00 027
THOROUGHFARE
    BUILT THOROUGHFARE: HEAVEN ROYSTERERS, IN GAY GANGS C . . . 072 00 002
THORP
    AND THICKET AND THORP ARE MERRY 042 00 039
THOUGHT
    THOSE CHARMS ACCEPTED OF MY INMOST THOUGHT, ... 012 01 009
    BARELY A SIGH TO THOUGHT OF HOPES FORGONE. 014 03 009
    AND I HAD THOUGHT SO HITHERTO -- 021 00 026
    ' I THOUGHT THE AIR MUST CUT AND STRAIN 021 00 036
    HE THOUGHT HE HEARD SAY 041 00 051
    BOTH THOUGHT AND THEW NOW BOLDER 049 00 008
    TO MY CREATING THOUGHT, WOULD NEITHER HEAR 066 00 006
    THE FINE DELIGHT THAT FATHERS THOUGHT: THE STRONG . . . 076 00 001
    AND I SHALL SHAPE ONE TO MY THOUGHT. 080 12 007
    NOCTURNS I THOUGHT WERE HURRIED THROUGH. 081 00 092
    REMEMBER'D SWEETNESS. FOR MY THOUGHT 081 00 139
    I CALL'D THEM AND I THOUGHT THEM THEN -- 081 00 164
    HOW TURN MY PASSION-PASTURED THOUGHT 081 00 174
    THE RAINBOW SHINES, BUT ONLY IN THE THOUGHT 091 00 002
    WHICH YET IS IN THE EYE OR IN THE THOUGHT. 091 00 009
    AND, THINKING THAT SHE THINKS, HAS NEVER THOUGHT; . . 094 00 030
    TO TRACE SOME TRACELESS LOSS OF THOUGHT AGAIN. . . 107 04 018
    EVEN SO MY THOUGHT THE ROSE AND GREY DISPOSES . . . 108 00 007
    AND COLDLY DO BELIE THE THOUGHT OF THEE? 117 00 012
    WAKING I THOUGHT; AND IT SUFFICED: 118 00 008
    I THOUGHT: BEFORE I GATHER STRENGTH 118 00 013
    BUT IF I CANNOT TEMPT HIS THOUGHT 124 00 021
    MY THOUGHT WAS, THERE TO REST AGAINST THE TREES . . 125 00 008
    DOOMSDAY AND DEATH -- WHOSE DATELESS THOUGHT MUST CHART . . 126 00 003
    I THOUGHT THAT YOU WOULD HAVE WRITTEN: MY BIRTHDAY CAME AND WENT, . 128 00 001
    OR LISTENING THOUGHT OF LINEN-WINDED GHOSTS. 135 00 018
    TO HIM WHO EVER THOUGHT WITH LOVE OF ME 140 00 001
    O WHAT A TUNE THE THOUGHT 148 00 003
    HARK, HEARER, HEAR WHAT I DO: LEND A THOUGHT NOW, MAKE BELIEVE . 159 00 001
    JESUS TO CAST ONE THOUGHT UPON 167 00 001
    THOUGHT HALF SO SWEET THERE IS NOT ONE 167 00 007
THOUGHTS
    OUR THOUGHTS' CHIVALRY'S THRONG'S LORD. C 028 35 008
    HIS THOUGHTS ON HER, FORSAKEN THAT SHE SEEMS, . . . 050 00 011
    WITH YOUR FRESH THOUGHTS CARE FOR, CAN YOU? 055 00 004
    THOUGHTS AGAINST THOUGHTS IN GROANS GRIND. C . . . 061 00 014
    THOUGHTS AGAINST THOUGHTS IN GROANS GRIND. C . . . 061 00 014
    YOU, JADED, LET BE: CALL OFF THOUGHTS AWHILE . . . 069 00 010
    THOUSANDS OF THORNS, THOUGHTS) SWINGS THOUGH. COMMONWEAL . 070 00 008
    AS A SELF-EMBRACED SWEET THOUGHTS:V 085 00 003
    I HERE FORBID MY THOUGHTS TO FOOL THEMSELVES WITH FEARS. . 152 01 024
    WITH DREADFUL DISTILLATION OF THOUGHTS SOUR AS BLOOD, . . 152 02 064
THOUSAND
    APART, BETWIXT TEN THOUSAND PETALL'D LIPS 002 00 021
    AND, ON A THOUSAND ALTARS LAID, ... 006 00 009
    FOOD FOR FIVE THOUSAND: ON THE THORNS HE SHED . . . 007 00 012
    CHRIST. FOR CHRIST PLAYS IN TEN THOUSAND PLACES, . . 057 00 012
    EIGHT THOUSAND FURLONGS IN ADVANCE. 083 00 016
    I A THOUSAND THOUSAND YEARS 160 00 008
    I A THOUSAND THOUSAND YEARS 160 00 008
THOUSANDS
    TWO THOUSANDS OF YEARS ARE NEAR UPON PAST 027 00 015
    HE WAS BUT ONE LIKE THOUSANDS MORE. 041 00 085
    THOUSANDS OF THORNS, THOUGHTS) SWINGS THOUGH. COMMONWEAL . 070 00 008
THRALLS
    DEFEAT, THWART ME? OH, THE SOTS AND THRALLS OF LUST . . 074 00 007
THREAD
    A THREAD OF LIGHT BETRAY'D THE HILL 092 00 009
    AND STAINED, AND KNOTS OF GOLDEN THREAD. 124 00 014
THREADS
    ON PRANKED SCALE: OR THREADS OF CARMINE, SHOT . . . 002 00 106
THREE
    MID-NUMBERED HE IN THREE OF THE THUNDER-THRONE! . . . 028 34 005
    THREE HUNDRED SOULS, O ALAS! ON BOARD, ... 041 00 002
    THREE RIVALS THRONG HER GARDEN CHAIR, ... 083 00 010
    IT MIGHT BE NONE OF THE THREE: 095 00 006
    BUT WITH HIS OTHER FOOT THREE MILES BEYOND 100 00 004
    BY SHINE OF CANDLES THREE, ... 109 01 002
    ' IN TWO YEARS OR IN THREE. ' 109 02 004
    ' ALTHOUGH IT WERE YEARS THREE. 109 03 002
    FOR TWO YEARS AND FOR THREE. 109 06 002
    HE SAW HIS BROTHERS THREE. 109 07 002
    IT WAS BUT ONE TO THREE. 109 13 004
    BESIDE HIS BROTHERS THREE? ' 109 20 002
    BESIDE HIS BROTHERS THREE? 109 21 002
    HIS THREE BROTHERS ARE EACH AS TALL 109 21 003

THREE   (CONTINUED)
      BESIDE HIS BROTHERS THREE: 109 22 004
      AMONG HIS BROTHERS THREE, ...   109 23 002
      BUT SAW HIS BROTHERS THREE, ...   109 24 004
      ' NO TRUTH BETWEEN YOU THREE, ...   109 26 002
      SHE HEARD BUT KNOCKINGS THREE. 109 29 002
      IF I GIVE THEE KISSES THREE? 109 37 002
      GIVE ME THY KISSES THREE. 109 38 002
      THREE MILES INDEED. 125 00 012
      THE HOLY THREE IN ONE. 133 00 004
      SHE CAUGHT THE CRYING OF THOSE THREE. 145 00 029
      SHE TOLD HIS NAME TIMES-OVER THREE: 145 00 056
THREEFOLD
      A PIOUS WORK WITH THREEFOLD PURPOSE CROWN'D -- 001 01 005
THREE-HEELED
      YET ARTHUR IS A BOWMAN: HIS THREE-HEELED TIMBER'LL HIT 143 00 003
THREE-NUMBERED
      GOD, THREE-NUMBERED FORM: 028 09 002
THRESHING-FLOOR
      SCOURGED UPON THE THRESHING-FLOOR: 006 00 006
THRESHOLD
      SO LOADING WITH OBSTRUCTION THAT THRESHOLD 017 00 008
THREW
      IN JOSEPH'S GARDEN THEY THREW BY 006 00 021
THRICE
      AND THRICE AND FOUR TIMES AND AGAIN. 098 37 002
      SEVERAL TIMES I SAW THEM, THRICE OR FOUR TIMES TURNING: 152 02 028
THRIFTLESS
      TO THRIFTLESS REAVE BOTH OUR RICH ROUND WORLD BARE 058 00 012
THRILL
      THROUGH OTHER BARS IT USED TO THRILL, ...   081 00 015
THRILLS
      IF FLOODTIDE TEEMING THRILLS HER FULL, ...   030 00 022
THRIVE
      DO IN SPARE HOURS MORE THRIVE THAN I THAT SPEND, ...   074 00 008
      THAT THRIVE IN THE LOAMY GREENNESS OF THIS PLACE? 122 00 015
THRO
      AND THRO' THEIR PARTING LIDS THERE CAME AND WENT 002 00 011
      OF SOMETHING DRIFTING THRO' DELIGHTED AIR, ...   002 00 028
      THRO' CRIMSON-GOLDEN FLOODS PASS SWALLOW'D INTO FIRE. 002 00 083
      THRO' SILVER, GLOOM'D TO A BLOOD-VIVID CLOT. 002 00 107
      NOW MELTING UPWARD THRO' THE SLOPING SCALE 002 00 132
      AND GAIN'D THRO' GROWING DUSK THE STIRLESS BAY: 002 00 141
      WITH EYES THAT SMILE THRO' THE TEARS OF THE HOURS, ...   026 00 014
      WE, ALL WE, THRO' THE LENGTH OF OUR DAYS, ...   026 00 034
      OF RIVERS, LEAD, THRO' STORMS AND NIGHTS, ...   083 00 004
      FLUSH THRO' THEIR HEAVING COLUMNS; WHEN THEY HALT 104 00 010
      GOES MARCHING THRO' MY MIND. WHAT SENSE IS THIS? IT HAS NONE.   .   .   .   152 01 022
THROAT
      TRYING EACH PLEASURABLE THROAT THAT SINGS 019 00 006
      HER MILK-WHITE THROAT AND FOLDED DEW-LAP SLACK 099 00 009
THROBBING
      AN INTENSE LINE OF THROBBING BLOOD-LIGHT SHOOK 002 00 016
      TO COOL HIS PLUMY THROBBING BREAST. 077 00 092
THRONE
      SILENCE HOLDS BREATH UPON HER THRONE, ...   077 00 033
THRONED
      GRASP GOD, THRONED BEHIND 028 32 007
THRONG
      SEEK GOD'S HOUSE IN HAPPY THRONG: 024 00 025
      FALLING FLAKES, TO THE THRONG THAT CATCHES AND QUAILS 028 24 006
      EARTH, SWEET EARTH, SWEET LANDSCAPE, WITH LEAVES THRONG 058 00 001
      IN GAY-GANGS THEY THRONG: THEY GLITTER IN MARCHES. C 072 00 002
      THREE RIVALS THRONG HER GARDEN CHAIR, ...   083 00 010
      FROM OXFORD COMES THE THRONG AND HUM OF BELLS 098 03 006
      THAT WONT TO THRONG ZEUS' BANQUET-HALL, ...   160 00 029
THRONGED
      OUR COMPANY THRONGED THE HALL, ...   054 00 011
      AND BREATH IMMORTAL THRONGED THAT SHOW: 145 00 045
THRONG'S
      OUR THOUGHTS' CHIVALRY'S THRONG'S LORD. C 028 35 008
THRONGS
      OF OWN, OF ABRUPT SELF THERE SO THRUSTS ON, SO THRONGS THE EAR.   .   .   045 00 008
      TRAY OR ASWARM, ALL THROUGHTHER, IN THRONGS: C 061 00 006
THROSTLE
      THROSTLE ABOVE HER NESTED 042 00 020
THROTTLED
      THE MAWDDACH, HOW SHE TRIPS! THOUGH THROTTLED 030 00 021
THROUGHTHER
      TRAY OR ASWARM, ALL THROUGHTHER, IN THRONGS: C 061 00 006
THROW
      UPON CHRIST THROW ALL AWAY: 024 00 005
      THO' APT TO THROW IT IN A STRANGE DIRECTION: 094 00 014
      TO THE BARGAIN OF ITS HATE TO THROW 145 00 020
THROWS
      EARTH THROWS WINTER'S ROBES AWAY, ...   024 00 017
THRUSH
      THRUSH'S EGGS LOOK LITTLE LOW HEAVENS, AND THRUSH 033 00 003

TIME   (CONTINUED)
    I SHALL KEEP TIME WITH THEE, MOTHER OF MINE.   •   •   •   •   •   •   •   027 00 018
    BUT IT RIDES TIME LIKE RIDING A RIVER   •   •   •   •   •   •   •   028 06 007
    SPEND HERE YOUR MEASURE OF TIME AND TREASURE   •   •   •   •   •   •   030 00 039
    HOW RING RIGHT OUT OUR SORDID TURBID TIME,   •   •   •   •   •   •   035 00 010
    SO AT HOME, TIME WAS, TO HIS TRUTH AND GRACE   •   •   •   •   •   •   041 00 100
    TIME PAST SHE HAS BEEN ATTEMPTED AND PURSUED   •   •   •   •   •   •   050 00 005
    PILLOWY AIR HE TREADS A TIME AND HANGS   •   •   •   •   •   •   •   050 00 010
    PINING, PINING, TILL TIME WHEN REASON RAMBLED IN IT AND SOME   •   •   053 00 003
    BUT VASTNESS BLURS AND TIME BEATS LEVEL. ENOUGH! THE RESURRECTION,   072 00 016
    SHOULD TONGUE THAT TIME NOW, TRUMPET NOW THAT FIELD,   •   •   •   •   073 00 003
    WHATEVER TIME THIS VAPOUROUS ROOF.   •   •   •   •   •   •   •   •   080 06 001
    ALWAYS THE TIME REMEMBERETH   •   •   •   •   •   •   •   •   •   •   081 00 061
    THE TIME WAS LATE AND THE WET YELLOW WOODS   •   •   •   •   •   098 05 001
    -- YES FOR A TIME THEY HELD AS WELL   •   •   •   •   •   •   •   101 00 001
    NO TIME TO THINK, I'LL KNOT IT ON THIS RIBBON,   •   •   •   •   •   102 01 027
    THEIR CHANGING FEET IN FLICKER ALL THE TIME   •   •   •   •   •   •   107 01 013
    ' HEAVEN MAKE THE TIME BE SHORT, ' SHE SAID,   •   •   •   •   •   109 03 001
    THE TIME SAVE WHEN HER TEARS WHICH STILL [DESCEND]   •   •   •   •   111 00 005
    ALL TIME AT ONCE AND SPAN THE DISTANT GOALS,   •   •   •   •   •   126 00 004
    THINK THIS, MY BIRTHDAY FALLS IN SADDENING TIME OF YEAR;   •   •   •   128 00 009
    FOR SOULS THAT MIGHT HAVE BLESSED THE TIME   •   •   •   •   •   •   133 00 009
    TIME WAS, NEXT WHITEST AFTER MARY'S OWN.   •   •   •   •   •   •   •   136 00 004
    HE TAUGHT ANOTHER TIME THERE AND A THIRD: •   •   •   •   •   •   136 00 031
    THE TELLING TIME OUR TASK IS: TIME'S SOME PART,   •   •   •   •   •   153 00 005
    BORN OF HER TOO WHEN TIME WAS DUE: WHO THEN   •   •   •   •   •   •   APPEN D 37
    AND HEAVEN'S BLISS, WHEN OUR TIME IS TO DIE,   •   •   •   •   •   •   APPEN D 47
TIMED
    TIMED HER SAD VISIONS WITH HIS WRECK.   •   •   •   •   •   •   •   021 00 056
TIME'S
    TIME'S TASKING, IT IS FATHERS THAT ASKING FOR EASE   •   •   •   •   028 27 003
    IT IS EVEN SEEN, TIME'S SOMETHING SERVER,   •   •   •   •   •   •   041 00 053
    NOW TIME'S ANDROMEDA ON THIS ROCK RUDE,   •   •   •   •   •   •   •   050 00 001
    EVENING STRAINS TO BE TIME'S VAST, C   •   •   •   •   •   •   •   061 00 002
    TIME'S EUNUCH, AND NOT BREED ONE WORK THAT WAKES.   •   •   •   •   074 00 013
    SHOULD CHOKE SWEET VIRTUE'S GLORY IS TIME'S GREAT GUILT.   •   •   •   136 00 002
    WHEN 'TS LIGHT I QUENCHED: ITS ROSE, TIME'S ONE RICH ROSE, MY HAND,   152 02 060
    THE TELLING TIME OUR TASK IS: TIME'S SOME PART,   •   •   •   •   •   153 00 005
    IN ONE FAIR FALL: BUT, FOR TIME'S AFTERCAST,   •   •   •   •   •   •   157 00 007
TIMES
    TIMES TOLD LOVELIER, MORE DANGEROUS, O MY CHEVALIER!   •   •   •   •   036 00 011
    THE SEVEN OR SEVEN TIMES SEVEN   •   •   •   •   •   •   •   •   •   060 00 087
    WANTS WAR, WANTS WOUNDS: WEARY HIS TIMES, HIS TASKS: •   •   •   •   068 00 003
    'S NOT WRUNG, SEE YOU: UNFORESEEN TIMES RATHER -- AS SKIES   •   •   069 00 013
    AND THRICE AND FOUR TIMES AND AGAIN.   •   •   •   •   •   •   •   •   098 37 002
    THE SWEETEST SONNET FIVE OR SIX TIMES READ   •   •   •   •   •   •   117 00 009
    TO THAT FIRST GOLDEN AGE OF GOSPEL TIMES   •   •   •   •   •   •   •   136 00 005
    THE TIMES ARE NIGHTFALL, LOOK, THEIR LIGHT GROWS LESS: •   •   •   150 00 001
    THE TIMES ARE WINTER, WATCH, A WORLD UNDONE: •   •   •   •   •   150 00 002
    AND MORE AND MORE TIMES LACES ROUND AND ROUND MY HEART,   •   •   •   152 01 013
    SEVERAL TIMES I SAW THEM, THRICE OR FOUR TIMES TURNING: •   •   •   152 02 028
    SEVERAL TIMES I SAW THEM, THRICE OR FOUR TIMES TURNING: •   •   •   152 02 028
TIMES-OVER
    SHE TOLD HIS NAME TIMES-OVER THREE: •   •   •   •   •   •   •   •   145 00 056
TINGEING
    TALL SUN'S TINGEING, OR TREACHEROUS THE TAINTING OF THE EARTH'S AIR,   059 06 005
TINGLING
    TINGLING BETWEEN DUSK AND SILVER.   •   •   •   •   •   •   •   •   098 01 004
TINIEST
    AND I COULD HEAR THE TINIEST SOUND,   •   •   •   •   •   •   •   •   021 00 017
TINKLINGS
    AND FOR THE TINKLINGS ON THE FALLS AND SWELLS   •   •   •   •   •   107 02 007
TINTED
    A TINTED FIN ON EITHER SHOULDER HUNG: •   •   •   •   •   •   •   002 00 052
    TWICE LOVELY, TINTED EASTERN, TURNED GREEK --   •   •   •   •   •   136 00 015
TINTS
    LIT WITH EXQUISITE TINTS SEVEN   •   •   •   •   •   •   •   •   •   077 00 109
TINY
    WOULD NOT PUT OUT SOME TINY GOLDEN CENTRE.   •   •   •   •   •   •   098 22 006
    SKY PEAK'D WITH TINY FLAMES.   •   •   •   •   •   •   •   •   •   098 25 005
    SO TINY A TRICKLE OF SONG-STRAIN: •   •   •   •   •   •   •   •   138 00 004
TIPTOES
    HIS BODY SWAY'D UPON TIPTOES,   •   •   •   •   •   •   •   •   •   087 00 003
TIRE
    BEAT, HEAVE AND THE STRONG MOUNTAIN TIRE   •   •   •   •   •   •   •   080 05 002
    I THINK HE WILL NOT TIRE OF ME.   •   •   •   •   •   •   •   •   124 00 002
TIRED
    THE TRUMPET WAXES LOUD: TIRED ARE YOUR FEET.   •   •   •   •   •   005 00 008
    BUT NOW I AM SO TIRED I SOON SHALL SEND   •   •   •   •   •   •   •   014 03 008
TIRES
    THE CITY TIRES TO DEATH,   •   •   •   •   •   •   •   •   •   •   133 00 012
TITAN'S
    POURTRAY'D ALONG THE FRIEZE WITH TITAN'S BROOD   •   •   •   •   •   001 07 004
TITIAN'S
    THE SKILL OF DREAMY CLAUDE, AND TITIAN'S MELLOW GLOOM.   •   •   •   001 10 009
TITIANS
    RICH TITIANS FADED: IN THE STRAYING GLEAM   •   •   •   •   •   •   001 12 003

265

TITLE
    AND ART AND BEAUTY: TITLE NOW TOO FULL -- 001 15 006
    THEIR SPECIAL-GENERAL TITLE TO THY LOVE. 012 01 014
    THAT FORGE HER TITLE OF INHERITANCE 102 01 066
TODAY
    NOT TODAY WE NEED LAMENT 029 00 013
    HEARD YET, THE MUSES' MAN, TODAY 166 00 003
TOGETHER
    WE MEET TOGETHER, YOU AND I, ...   008 00 010
    WHY, RAINDROP-ROUNDELS LOOPED TOGETHER 030 00 027
    BLAST BOLE AND BLOOM TOGETHER? 041 00 016
    GRASS AND GREENWORLD ALL TOGETHER! 042 00 018
    THEIR HEADS TOGETHER IN A STORMY BLOT. 090 00 006
    HER WHITE WEED-BATHED KNEES ARE SHUT TOGETHER. .   .   .   099 00 002
    TOGETHER, AS THE CRISS-CROSS'D SHELLY CUP 101 00 002
    THAT TEARS AND LAUGHTER ARE HUNG CLOSE TOGETHER. .   .   102 01 016
    ONLY THE BELLED FOXGLOVES LISP'D TOGETHER. 107 01 006
TOIL
    TOIL HAS SHED ROUND YOUR HEAD 029 00 015
    AND ALL IS SEARED WITH TRADE; BLEARED, SMEARED WITH TOIL; .   031 00 006
    NAY IN ALL THAT TOIL, THAT COIL, SINCE (SEEMS) I KISSED THE ROD, 064 00 010
    SQUADRONED MASKS AND MANMARKS TREADMIRE TOIL THERE .   .   072 00 008
TO-DAY
    HE SLEW THE EGYPTIAN YESTERDAY. TO-DAY 005 00 003
    WITH JOY FOR TO-DAY AND HOPE FOR TO-MORROW 026 00 015
    TO-DAY THE SKY IS TWO AND TWO 138 00 016
TO-FRO
    OR TO-FRO TENDER TRAMBEAMS TRUCKLE AT THE EYE. .   .   .   046 00 004
TO-MORROW
    WITH JOY FOR TO-DAY AND HOPE FOR TO-MORROW 026 00 015
    SHALL NEW-DAPPLE NEXT YEAR, SURE AS TO-MORROW MORNING, .   152 C 028
TO-NIGHT
    WELL, I KNOW NOT. BUT ALL THINGS SEEM TO-NIGHT .   .   .   102 01 010
    THE STARS ARE PACKED SO THICK TO-NIGHT 135 00 019
TOKEN
    STIGMA, SIGNAL, CINQUEFOIL TOKEN 028 22 007
TOLD
    A PROPHETESS TOWERED IN THE TUMULT, A VIRGINAL TONGUE TOLD. .   028 17 008
    TIMES TOLD LOVELIER, MORE DANGEROUS, O MY CHEVALIER! .   .   036 00 011
    AND TOLD BY NATURE: TOWER! 049 00 009
    TOLD TALES WITH WHAT HEART'S STRESS 054 00 023
    THE FALL IS O'ER, TOLD OFF THE LEAVES, ...   081 00 009
    TOLD OFF THEIR LEAVES ALONG THE PIERCING GALE, .   .   .   098 05 002
    THE KING'S FRIEND TOLD THE THING THAT WAS HID .   .   .   109 12 001
    THE MORE HE TOLD, THE LESS SHE SPOKE, ...   109 36 003
    NOT THIS. SOME SPIRITS, IT IS TOLD, ...   118 00 002
    HAVE TOLD ME I AM FAIR TO SEE. 124 00 024
    TOLD OF THE WONDERS HE HAD SEEN. 131 00 006
    SHE TOLD HIS NAME TIMES-OVER THREE; 145 00 056
    I TOLD YOU THAT SHE TURNED HER MIRROR DIM 151 00 011
    WHAT GOD'S SON HAS TOLD ME, TAKE FOR TRUTH I DO; .   .   168 00 007
TOM
    TOM -- GARLANDED WITH SQUAT AND SURLY STEEL 070 00 001
    TOM; THEN TOM'S FALLOWBOOTFELLOW PILES PICK 070 00 002
    TOM HEART-AT-EASE, TOM NAVVY; HE IS ALL FOR HIS MEAL .   .   070 00 004
    TOM HEART-AT-EASE, TOM NAVVY; HE IS ALL FOR HIS MEAL .   .   070 00 004
    THAT NE'ER NEED HUNGER, TOM; TOM SELDOM SICK, .   .   .   070 00 006
    THAT NE'ER NEED HUNGER, TOM; TOM SELDOM SICK, .   .   .   070 00 006
TOMB
    HARD BY A ROYAL PALACE AND A ROYAL TOMB. 001 01 009
TOMB-DECKED
    I MOVE ALONG LIFE'S TOMB-DECKED WAY 023 00 039
TOMBS
    WINDING SHEETS, TOMBS AND WORMS AND TUMBLING TO DECAY; C .   059 OL 012
TOMORROW
    ' LORD WILLIAM COMES HUNTING TOMORROW MORNING, .   .   .   109 19 003
    TOMORROW MEET YOU? O NOT TOMORROW. 110 00 001
    TOMORROW MEET YOU? O NOT TOMORROW. 110 00 001
TOM'S
    TOM; THEN TOM'S FALLOWBOOTFELLOW PILES PICK 070 00 002
TONES
    WHAT BASS IS OUR VIOL FOR TRAGIC TONES? 075 00 008
    MY SEVERAL MOANS COME DISTANT IN THEIR TONES 080 03 003
TONGUE
    THEN FAIL'D THE TONGUE; THE POOR COLLAPSING FRAME, .   .   001 03 003
    AN ANTIQUE CHAUNT AND IN AN UNKNOWN TONGUE. 002 01 131
    THOU HEARDST ME TRUER THAN TONGUE CONFESS 028 02 003
    BEYOND SAYING SWEET, PAST TELLING OF TONGUE, ...   028 09 005
    A PROPHETESS TOWERED IN THE TUMULT, A VIRGINAL TONGUE TOLD. .   028 17 008
    TONGUE TRUE, VAUNT- AND TAUNTLESS; 048 00 015
    MY TONGUE HAD TAUGHT THEE COMFORT, TOUCH HAD QUENCHED THY TEARS, 053 00 010
    DOG, HE DID GIVE TONGUE! 054 00 034
    BOW SWUNG FINDS TONGUE TO FLING OUT BROAD ITS NAME; .   .   057 00 004
    TO, WITH NO TONGUE TO PLEAD, NO HEART TO FEEL; .   .   .   058 00 003
    AND WHAT IS EARTH'S EYE, TONGUE, OR HEART ELSE, WHERE .   058 00 009
    SHOULD TONGUE THAT TIME NOW, TRUMPET NOW THAT FIELD, .   .   073 00 003
    NOW I GROW NUMB. MY TONGUE STRIKES ON THE GUM .   .   .   080 10 006

TONGUE   (CONTINUED)
    MY FAST-LODGED TONGUE. ' [TO HER THE GIFT] 081 00 116
    YOU ASK WHY CAN'T CLARISSA HOLD HER TONGUE. 096 04 001
    WITH EAR-CARESSING SPEECH? WHERE IS THE TONGUE 122 00 017
    IN COPYING? HOW? MUST I GIVE TONGUE AGAIN? 125 00 021
    MEANTIME SOME TONGUE CRIES C 152 01 016
    BE MANAGED TASTY TO THAT TONGUE? 166 00 019
    TO SPEAK OF THAT NO TONGUE WILL DO 167 00 013
TONGUES
    TWO TONGUES LIKE BUTTERFLIES. 098 12 007
    TO TAKE HER; WHILE THEIR TONGUES WOULD GO 145 00 026
TONIGHT
    LORD BEUNO COMES TONIGHT. TONIGHT, SIR! SOON, NOW; THEREFORE   .   .   152 01 005
    LORD BEUNO COMES TONIGHT. TONIGHT, SIR! SOON, NOW; THEREFORE   .   .   152 01 005
TOOK
    PHILIP TOOK OATH, WHILE GLORY OR DEFEAT 001 02 003
    THE WINGED FOWLS TOOK PART, PART FELL IN THORN 007 00 007
    WITH SUCH A SECONDING, NOR SATURN TOOK 014 02 009
    I TOOK OF VINE A CROSS-BARRED ROD OR ROOD. 020 00 008
    OR ONCE OR NEVER TOOK LOVE'S PROPER FOOD; 020 00 010
    TO THE SHROUDS THEY TOOK, C 060 00 055
    OF HER FLESH HE TOOK FLESH; 060 00 055
    TOOK PRIMROSES, THEIR PULL'D AND PLOTTED LEAF 107 03 018
    THOUGH THEY TOOK TILL THE SEVENTEENTH OF NEXT OCTOBER TO READ.   .   .   128 00 008
    THE SEA TOOK PITY; IT INTERPOSED WITH DOOM; 158 00 001
TOOL
    EACH SPORT HAS HERE ITS TACKLE AND TOOL; 030 00 006
    TAKE AS FOR TOOL, NOT TOY MEANT 049 00 013
TOOLSMOOTH
    DAMASK THE TOOLSMOOTH BLEAK LIGHT; BLACK, C 061 00 009
TOPP'D
    LIKE SCALDED BANKS TOPP'D ONCE WITH PRINCIPAL FLOWERS;   .   .   .   102 02 012
TOPS
    TO THE MEN IN THE TOPS AND THE TACKLE RODE OVER THE STORM'S BRAWLING.   028 19 008
TOPSYTURVY
    RIDES REPEATED TOPSYTURVY 030 00 015
TOPT
    IN SPRING OUR RIVER-BANKS ARE TOPT 124 00 017
TORMENT
    THE TURMOIL AND THE TORMENT, IT HAS, I SWEAR, A SWEETNESS,   .   .   152 02 057
TORMENTED
    CHARITABLE; NOT LIVE THIS TORMENTED MIND 069 00 003
    WITH THIS TORMENTED MIND TORMENTING YET. 069 00 004
TORMENTING
    WITH THIS TORMENTED MIND TORMENTING YET. 069 00 004
TORN
    SINCE TRAMPLED SPAIN BY ROYAL DISCORD TORN 001 15 001
    FIVE WAYS THE PRECIOUS BRANCHES TORN; 006 00 014
    CLOUD-PUFFBALL, TORN TUFTS, C 072 00 001
TOSSED
    TOSSED PILLOWS FLAUNT FORTH, THEN CHEVY ON AN AIR- C   .   .   .   072 00 001
TOSSES
    TO DO WITHOUT, TAKE TOSSES, AND OBEY. 068 00 004
TOUCH
    AT THE TOUCH OF HER WANDERING WONDERING BREATH 026 00 006
    THY DOING; AND DOST THOU TOUCH ME AFRESH? 028 01 007
    TO TOUCH, HER BEING SO SLENDER, ...   043 00 013
    MY TONGUE HAD TAUGHT THEE COMFORT, TOUCH HAD QUENCHED THY TEARS,   .   053 00 010
    AND HARD MEN FEEL A SOFTENING TOUCH; 077 00 030
    TOUCH ME AND PURIFY, AND SHEW 077 00 039
    THEY TOUCH HEAVEN, TABOUR ON IT; HOW THEIR TALONS SWEEP   .   .   149   A 007
    THEY TOUCH, THEY TABOUR ON IT, HOVER ON IT [; HERE, THERE HURLED] ,V   149   B 007
TOUCHED
    AH, TOUCHED IN YOUR BOWER OF BONE, ...   028 18 001
    THY TEARS THAT TOUCHED MY HEART, CHILD, FELIX, POOR FELIX RANDAL;   .   053 00 011
    NOW MORE PRECISELY TOUCHED IN LIGHT AND GLOOM, ...   098 30 004
TOUCHING
    SEEING, TOUCHING, TASTING ARE IN THEE DECEIVED; 168 00 005
    AS TOUCHING ME FULFILLED BE THY SAW;   .   .   .   .   .   .   APPEN D 27
TOUCH'D
    TOUCH'D FROM HEAVEN IN SWEET DREAMS; 077 00 126
    WITH CENTRES DULY TOUCH'D AND NESTLIKE SPOTS, -- 107 04 007
TOWARDS
    TO MAN'S LAST DUST, DRAIN FAST TOWARDS MAN'S FIRST SLIME.   .   .   035 00 014
    TOWARDS ALL OUR GHOSTLY GOOD 060 00 048
    I WALK TOWARDS EVE OUR WALKS AGAIN; 081 00 054
    TOWARDS WASTES WHERE ROUND THE ICE-BLOCKS TILT AND FRET   .   .   088 00 007
    TOWARDS THOSE WASTES WHERE THE ICE-BLOCKS TILT AND FRET, V   .   .   088 00 011
    OF GREENERY: IT IS OLD EARTH'S GROPING TOWARDS THE STEEP   .   .   149   A 010
    ROUND AND ROUND THEY CAME AND FLASHED TOWARDS HEAVEN; O THERE,   .   152 02 029
    TOWARDS MY BROTHER, EVERY OTHER 155 00 023
    HE DROPS TOWARDS THE RIVER; UNSEEN 159 00 015
TOWER
    I MARK THE TOWER SWALLOWS RUN 015 00 028
    TOWER FROM THE GRACE TO THE GRACE. C 028 03 008
    FURRED SNOWS, CHARGED TUFT ABOVE TUFT, TOWER 030 00 031
    AND TOLD BY NATURE: TOWER; 049 00 009

267

TOWERED
 A PROPHETESS TOWERED IN THE TUMULT. A VIRGINAL TONGUE TOLD. • • • 028 17 008
TOWER-TOP
 BETWEEN THE TOWER-TOP AND THE GROUND • • • • • • 015 00 029
TOWERS
 A SOMBRE LENGTH OF GREY; FOUR TOWERS PLACED • • • • 001 01 003
 THE TOWERS MUSICAL, QUIET-WALLED GROVE; • • • • 012 01 010
 I SEE THE CROWNING OF THEIR TOWERS, • • • • • 015 00 007
 TOWERY CITY AND BRANCHY BETWEEN TOWERS; • • • • 044 00 001
 OF IT. ANGELS FALL, THEY ARE TOWERS, FROM HEAVEN -- A STORY • • 075 00 003
 WITH POTENT LIPS CALL DOWN CEMENTED TOWERS; • • • • 104 00 005
TOWERY
 TOWERY CITY AND BRANCHY BETWEEN TOWERS; • • • • 044 00 001
TOWN
 BUT GERTRUDE, LILY, AND LUTHER, ARE TWO OF A TOWN, • • • 028 20 005
 HOW THESE TWO SHAME THIS SHALLOW AND FRAIL TOWN! • • • 035 00 009
 NOW NEAR BY VENTNOR TOWN • • • • • • • 041 00 031
 THE DAPPLE-EARED LILY BELOW THEE; THAT COUNTRY AND TOWN DID • • 044 00 003
 [A BELL] AT MIDNIGHT WOKE THE TOWN • • • • 081 00 087
 OF, IT MUST BE, BOYS FROM THE TOWN • • • • • 159 00 012
TOWNS
 AND BRED ACQUAINTANCE OF UNUSED TOWNS? • • • • 107 02 002
TOY
 TAKE AS FOR TOOL, NOT TOY MEANT • • • • • 049 00 013
TRACE
 TO TRACE SOME TRACELESS LOSS OF THOUGHT AGAIN. • • • 107 04 018
TRACED
 THERE WAS A MEADOW LEVEL ALMOST; YOU TRACED • • • 107 04 001
TRACELESS
 TO TRACE SOME TRACELESS LOSS OF THOUGHT AGAIN. • • • 107 04 018
TRACERY
 WITH FLOWING TRACERY ENGEMMING RAYS • • • • • 001 06 002
TRACES
 AND SCARCELY TRACES WHERE ONE BEAUTY STRAYS • • • 001 06 007
TRACK
 AND THAT SUCH A SABLE TRACK • • • • • • 004 00 021
TRADE
 AND ALL IS SEARED WITH TRADE; BLEARED, SMEARED WITH TOIL; • • 031 00 006
TRADES
 AND ALL TRADES, THEIR GEAR AND TACKLE AND TRIM. • • • 037 00 006
TRAGIC
 WHAT BASS IS OUR VIOL FOR TRAGIC TONES? • • • • 075 00 008
TRAILING
 ONE SCARLET FEATHER TRAILING TO THE WIND; • • • • 002 00 081
TRAIL'D
 SOME TRAIL'D THE NAUTILUS; OR ON THE SWELL • • • • 002 00 056
TRAINING
 SHE HAD COME FROM A CRUISE, TRAINING SEAMEN -- • • • 041 00 013
TRAMBEAMS
 OR TO-FRO TENDER TRAMBEAMS TRUCKLE AT THE EYE. • • • 046 00 004
TRAMP
 I HEAR THE MULTITUDE TRAMP BY. • • • • • 080 11 001
TRAMPLE
 PLUNGE ORB'D IN RAINBOW ARCS, AND TRAMPLE AND TREAD • • 002 00 078
TRAMPLED
 SINCE TRAMPLED SPAIN BY ROYAL DISCORD TORN • • • 001 15 001
TRAMPLERS
 DISCOVERING YOU, DARK TRAMPLERS, TYRANT YEARS. • • • 157 00 002
TRANQUIL
 AT TRANQUIL TURNS, BY NATURE'S RULE, • • • • 030 00 014
TRANSLUCENT
 THIS WAS THEIR MANNER; ONE TRANSLUCENT CREST • • • 002 00 038
TRANSMIT
 HUED SUNBEAM WILL TRANSMIT • • • • • • 060 00 088
TRASH
 A BEACON, AN ETERNAL BEAM. FLESH FADE, AND MORTAL TRASH • • 072 00 019
TRAVELLING
 MY WINDOW SHOWS THE TRAVELLING CLOUDS, • • • • 015 00 001
 TO FIELDS OF LIGHT; MILLIONS OF TRAVELLING RAYS • • • 103 00 009
TRAVELL'D
 NOT FURTHER'D FAR MY TRAVELL'D FEET • • • • • 081 00 157
TRAVERSE
 OF THE FLOWN SKYLARK, AND HIS TRAVERSE FLIGHT • • • 122 00 003
TREACHEROUS
 TALL SUN'S TINGEING, OR TREACHEROUS THE TAINTING OF THE EARTH'S AIR, 059 06 005
TREAD
 PLUNGE ORB'D IN RAINBOW ARCS, AND TRAMPLE AND TREAD • • 002 00 078
 WHO TREAD THE GRAPES ARE SPLAY'D WITH STRIPES OF GORE, • • 005 00 051
 WE SHOUT WITH THEM THAT TREAD THE GRAPES; • • • • 006 00 012
 THEN THOUGH I SHOULD TREAD TUFTS OF CONSOLATION • • • 048 00 025
 THEN LET THE MARCH TREAD OUR EARS: • • • • • 052 00 009
 O THEN, WEARY THEN WHY SHOULD WE TREAD? [• • • • 059 06 026
 THAN PURCELL TUNE LETS TREAD TO? SEE: IT DOES THIS: KEEPS WARM 062 00 003
 WHERE YOU AND I WERE WONT TO TREAD; • • • • • 081 00 156
 TREAD BACK -- AND BACK, THE LEWD AND LAY! -- • • • 166 00 001
TREADMIRE
 SQUADRONED MASKS AND MANMARKS TREADMIRE TOIL THERE • • 072 00 008

TREADS
PILLOWY AIR HE TREADS A TIME AND HANGS 050 00 010
ARE THE GROINS OF THE BRAES THAT THE BROOK TREADS THROUGH, . . . 056 00 010
SELDOMER HEARTSORE; THAT TREADS THROUGH, PRICKPROOF, THICK 070 00 007
DEED-BOUND I AM! ONE DEED TREADS ALL DOWN HERE C 152 02 066

TREASONABLE
I OUTRAGE IT WITH TREASONABLE KISSING. 102 01 049

TREASURE
THE TREASURE NEVER EYESIGHT GOT, C 028 26 008
SPEND HERE YOUR MEASURE OF TIME AND TREASURE 030 00 039
LADS AND MEN HER LADE AND TREASURE. 041 00 012
THE TREASURE FROM ALL CITIES. 104 00 013

TREAT
TO HIS YOUNGSTER TAKE HIS TREAT! 048 00 011
IT IS HARDLY A PROPER TREAT FOR A BIRTHDAY TO REST IN HER ARMS. . 128 00 012
DAYLIGHT TO HEAD AND TREAT TO HEART, ... 167 00 018

TREATS
CARRIES TREATS OF SWEET FOR BITTER. 025 00 006
AND TASTE THE TREATS OF PENMAEN POOL. 030 00 040
ANG. CARRIES TREATS OF SWEET FOR BITTER. . . . . APPEN A 06

TREBLE
HANG OF A TREBLE SIZE. 088 00 004

TREBLE-FERVENT
THAN TREBLE-FERVENT MORE OF OTHER MEN, ... 014 01 013

TREE
TERRIBLE FRUIT WAS ON THE TREE 006 00 015
ON EASTER MORN THE TREE WAS FORTH, ... 006 00 023
IN ITS CONDITION. NO, THE TROPIC TREE 014 01 003
WHO TO US ARE AS DEW UNTO GRASS AND TREE, ... 026 00 038
IS MARY THE ROSE, THEN? MARY THE TREE? 027 00 025
OVER FIELD AND TREE, ... 109 17 002
THAT COMES AGAIN TO THE WOODLAND TREE. 124 00 004
POETRY TO IT, AS A TREE WHOSE BOUGHS BREAK IN THE SKY. . . . . 149 A 003

TREE-TOPS
OF WRINGING TREE-TOPS, CHALKY LANES, ... 077 00 135

TREES
MANY TREES AND FLOWERS ROUND 004 00 019
AND TREES OF TEREBINTH AND STONES 015 00 039
VEINS VIOLETS AND TALL TREES MAKES MORE AND MORE) 073 00 011
CAUGHT ON THE DANK-YTRESSED TREES. 077 00 106
WHEN THIS IS SOUGHT TREES WILL BE WANTING NOT, ... 080 12 006
OR ELSE THEIR COOINGS CAME FROM BAYS OF TREES, ... 098 02 001
DAPPLED WITH DIMINISH*D TREES 098 08 002
AND BLUER GREY THE FLOCKS OF TREES LOOK IN THE PLAIN. 105 00 008
BEYOND, THE BANKS WERE STEEP; A BRUSH OF TREES 107 04 003
AND LONG, THE TREES WERE COLOUR*D, BUT THE O'ER-HEAD, ... 107 04 012
MY THOUGHT WAS, THERE TO REST AGAINST THE TREES 125 00 008
TREES BY THEIR YIELD 127 00 001
INTO FAIRY TREES, WILDFLOWERS, WOODFERNS 159 00 050

TREETOP
TO THE ALL-A-LEAF OF THE TREETOP. 138 00 038

TREMBLE
AND THE THIN STARS TREMBLE NOT. V 085 00 005

TREMBLING
TO THEE THE TREMBLING SINNER PRAYS 023 00 003
CREPT TREMBLING OUT OF BED. 135 00 004

TREMULOUS
OF TREMULOUS FILM, MORE SUBTLE THAN THE VEST 002 00 039

TRENCH
TRENCH -- RIGHT, THE TIDE THAT RAMPS AGAINST THE SHORE; . . . 035 00 002

TRENCHED
TRENCHED WITH TEARS, CARVED WITH CARES, ... 028 15 003

TRESSES
DOWN THAT DANK ROCK O'ER WHICH THEIR LUSH LONG TRESSES WEEP. . 002 00 115
TRESSES DIPP*D IN RAINBOW FIRE; 077 00 014
PHOEBUS' LOOSEN*D TRESSES, SWIM; 077 00 102
YET WHEN MY UNSET TRESSES HUNG LOOSE-TRACED 102 01 003

TRIAL
I WOULD NOT MAKE THE TRIAL. 110 00 002

TRICK
I STROVE TO LOOK; I LOST THE TRICK 081 00 097

TRICKLE
SO TRICKLE FROM YOUR HAND? 005 00 042
AND FAINTER, FINER, TRICKLE FAR 077 00 081
SO TINY A TRICKLE OF SONG-STRAIN; 138 00 004

TRICKLING
EARTH, ALL, OUT; WHO, WITH TRICKLING INCREMENT, ... 073 00 010

TRIM
AND ALL TRADES, THEIR GEAR AND TACKLE AND TRIM. 037 00 006
C HE SHALL HAVE SUMMER GOODS AND TRIM 124 00 009

TRINITY
SINGING TO THE TRINITY. 024 00 028

TRIP
I HOPE THAT ALL THE PLACES ON OUR TRIP 107 04 027

TRIPLE-HUMMOCKED
THE TRIPLE-HUMMOCKED GIANT'S STOOL, ... 030 00 010

TRIPS
THE MAWDDACH, HOW SHE TRIPS! THOUGH THROTTLED 030 00 021

TRIUMPH
    TRIUMPH OF AIRY GRACE AND PERFECT HARMONY, ... 001 07 009
    LET HIM RIDE, HER PRIDE, IN HIS TRIUMPH, C 028 28 008
    DEALS TRIUMPH AND IMMORTAL YEARS. 052 00 012
    SHE'S FRAMED TO TRIUMPH IN ADVERSITY; 094 00 023
TROD
    FOR, WHERE THE MARTYR'S BONES WERE THICKEST TROD, ... 001 05 008
    THE SWOON OF A HEART THAT THE SWEEP AND THE HURL OF THEE TROD . . 028 02 006
    GENERATIONS HAVE TROD, HAVE TROD, HAVE TROD; 031 00 005
    GENERATIONS HAVE TROD, HAVE TROD, HAVE TROD; 031 00 005
    GENERATIONS HAVE TROD, HAVE TROD, HAVE TROD; 031 00 005
    CHEER WHOM THOUGH? THE HERO WHOSE HEAVEN-HANDLING FLUNG ME, FOOT TROD 064 00 012
TROOPS
    CLUSTER'D IN TROOPS AND HALO'D BY THE LIGHT, ... 002 00 036
TROPES
    AND GIVES FOR TROPES HIS JUDGMENT ALL AWAY, ... 102 03 029
    AND GIVES FOR TROPES HIS JUDGMENT ALL AWAY, V 102 03 035
TROPIC
    IN ITS CONDITION. NO, THE TROPIC TREE 014 01 003
TROUBLED
    AIRWARDS, DISTURB'D; AND THE SCARCE TROUBLED SEA 002 00 110
TROUT
    FOR ROSE-MOLES ALL IN STIPPLE UPON TROUT THAT SWIM; . . . 037 00 003
TRUCKLE
    OR TO-FRO TENDER TRAMBEAMS TRUCKLE AT THE EYE. 046 00 004
TRUE
    A FORTRESS OF TRUE FAITH, AND CENTRAL STAND 001 05 003
    AND NOW I WISH THAT IT WERE TRUE. 021 00 028
    IS IT ANYTHING TRUE? DOES IT GROW UPON GROUND? 027 00 002
    NONE BUT YOU THIS HER TRUE, ... 029 00 011
    TONGUE TRUE, VAUNT- AND TAUNTLESS; 048 00 015
    THAT SHOULD HAVE BEEN TRUE TO ME. 095 00 008
    IF THAT WERE TRUE, IT COULD NOT LIVE A DAY,] 097 00 002
    ['TIS SO CONCEIVED IN HIS TRUE LINEAMENT.] 102 01 047
    THOUGH SELF-MADE BANDS AT LAST MAY TRUE LOVE BIND, . . . 102 03 019
    NEW LOVE IS FREE LOVE, OR TRUE LOVE 'TIS NOT. 102 03 020
    NEW LOVE IS FREE LOVE, OR TRUE LOVE 'TIS NOT. V 102 03 027
    AND WHAT IS YOUR TRUE NAME? ' SHE SAID, ... 109 04 001
    HER TRUE LOVE SHE MIGHT SEE. 109 30 004
    ' WILT THOU FOLLOW ME, MY TRUE LOVE, ... 109 37 001
    WILT THOU FOLLOW ME, MY TRUE LOVE? 109 37 003
    ' O I WILL FOLLOW THEE, MY TRUE LOVE. 109 38 001
    HAVE HERE A TRUE ONE, ECHOING THE SOUND; 116 00 002
    TRUE, MADAM. I AM SORRY NOW TO SEE 125 00 015
    ILL MEANT, YET TRUE, I BEST SHOULD FLATTER THEN, ... 125 00 019
    FLATTERY'S ALL OUT OF PLACE WHERE PRAISE IS TRUE. . . . 125 00 030
    THAT THIS IS TRUE OF; 'TIS CASTARA'S SELF; 125 00 056
    THE BEST IDEAL IS THE TRUE 133 00 001
    YOU SPOIL THE PLOT I FIND MY TRUE LOVE BY. 135 00 036
    AND PAUL IS TARSUS' TRUE BELLEROPHON, ... 136 00 010
    NOR LETTERS SUIT TO SPELL IT TRUE; 167 00 014
    TRUTH HIMSELF SPEAKS TRULY OR THERE 'S NOTHING TRUE. . . . 168 00 008
    BRING THE TENDER TALE TRUE OF THE PELICAN; 168 00 021
    TRUE GOD, TRUE MAN, IN FLESH AND BONE; . . . . . . APPEN D 36
    TRUE GOD, TRUE MAN, IN FLESH AND BONE; . . . . . . APPEN D 36
TRUELOVE
    YET SHED WHAT TEARS SAD TRUELOVE SHOULD. 041 00 108
TRUER
    THOU HEARDST ME TRUER THAN TONGUE CONFESS 028 02 003
TRULY
    AND TRULY TELL TO ME. ' 109 11 004
    TRUTH HIMSELF SPEAKS TRULY OR THERE 'S NOTHING TRUE. . . . 168 00 008
TRUMPET
    THE TRUMPET WAXES LOUD; TIRED ARE YOUR FEET. 005 00 008
    FORGET THE WAKING TRUMPET, THE LONG LAW. 005 00 044
    IN A FLASH, AT A TRUMPET CRASH, ... 072 00 021
    SHOULD TONGUE THAT TIME NOW, TRUMPET NOW THAT FIELD, . . . 073 00 003
    A JAUNTING VAUNTING VAULTING ASSAULTING TRUMPET TELLING. V . . 141 00 007
TRUNDLED
    OFF TRUNDLED TIMBER AND SCOOPS OF THE HILLSIDE GROUND, C . . 146 00 004
TRUST
    AND SO MY TRUST, CONFUSED, STRUCK, AND SHOOK 016 00 007
    ' SYLVESTER, COME, SYLVESTER; YOU MAY TRUST 107 03 001
    I KEEP MY TRUST. 127 00 015
TRUSTY
    HOW SAYS TRUSTY HEARING? THAT SHALL BE BELIEVED; 168 00 006
TRUTH
    THEREFORE HOW BITTER, AND LEARNT HOW LATE, THE TRUTH! . . . 017 00 014
    A WARFARE OF MY LIPS IN TRUTH, ... 018 00 015
    AND TRUTH IS HEARD, WITH TEARS IMPEARLED, ... 023 00 035
    O UNTEACHABLY AFTER EVIL, BUT UTTERING TRUTH, ... 028 18 005
    SO AT HOME, TIME WAS, TO HIS TRUTH AND GRACE 041 00 100
    NEVER FLEETS MORE, FASTENED WITH THE TENDEREST TRUTH . . . 059 06 012
    ' NO TRUTH BETWEEN YOU THREE. 109 28 002
    AND OTHER TRUTH IS NONE. 133 00 002
    THERE'S NONE BUT TRUTH CAN STEAD YOU. CHRIST IS TRUTH. . . . 157 00 020
    THERE'S NONE BUT TRUTH CAN STEAD YOU. CHRIST IS TRUTH. . . . 157 00 020

TRUTH   (CONTINUED)

    WHAT GOD'S SON HAS TOLD ME, TAKE FOR TRUTH I DO; 168 00 007
    TRUTH HIMSELF SPEAKS TRULY OR THERE 'S NOTHING TRUE. 168 00 008

TRY

    IS ALL THE WINTER BIRD DARE TRY. 003 00 014
    NONE BESIDES ME THIS BYE-WAYS BEAUTY TRY. 012 02 009
    OR IF THEY TRY IT, I AM HAPPIER THEN; 012 02 010
    I TRY THE CHRISTUS O'ER AGAIN. 080 08 004
    FOR ONLY TRY BY GAZING TO DIVIDE 102 03 009

TRYING

    TRYING EACH PLEASURABLE THROAT THAT SINGS 019 00 006

TUCKED

    STONES RING; LIKE EACH TUCKED STRING TELLS, EACH HUNG BELL'S . . 057 00 003

TUFT

    FURRED SNOWS, CHARGED TUFT ABOVE TUFT, TOWER 030 00 031
    FURRED SNOWS, CHARGED TUFT ABOVE TUFT, TOWER 030 00 031
    MOST LIKE THE TUFT OF PLIGHTED SILVER ROUND V 102 01 068
    ---- ---- -- PLIGHTED TUFT OF ---- ---- V 102 01 069
    ---- ---- -- SILVER PLIGHTED TUFT ABOUT V 102 01 070

TUFTS

    IN TUFTS OF EVENING SKY. -- SO SOON? 025 00 022
    THEN THOUGH I SHOULD TREAD TUFTS OF CONSOLATION 048 00 025
    CLOUD-PUFFBALL, TORN TUFTS, C 072 00 001
    STARS LIKE GOLD TUFTS. 098 25 002

TUGG'D

    TUGG'D THE BOSS'D, SMOOTH-LIPP'D, GIANT STROMBUS-SHELL. . . . 002 00 057

TUMBLED

    AS TUMBLED OVER RIM IN ROUNDY WELLS 057 00 002
    WHEATFIELDS TUMBLED WITH THE RAINS, ... 077 00 136

TUMBLED-TO

    ALL LIE TUMBLED-TO; THEN WITH LOOP-LOCKS 159 00 031

TUMBLER

    NO TUMBLER WOKE AND SHOOK THE COT, ... 135 00 013

TUMBLING

    WINDING SHEETS, TOMBS AND WORMS AND TUMBLING TO DECAY; C . . 059 OL 012

TUMBLINGS

    ON THE TUMBLINGS OF THE RAIN, ... 077 00 104

TUMULT

    A PROPHETESS TOWERED IN THE TUMULT, A VIRGINAL TONGUE TOLD. . . 028 17 008

TUNE

    THAN PURCELL TUNE LETS TREAD TO? SEE: IT DOES THIS; KEEPS WARM . 062 00 003
    TUNE IT TO WORDS OF GOOD INTENT. 081 00 127
    O WHAT A TUNE THE THOUGHT 148 00 003

TUNEABLE

    OR STRETCH'D CHORDS TUNEABLE ON TURTLE'S SHELL; 002 00 129

TUNED

    WE TUNED TO ONE KEY AND MADE THEIR HARMONIES. 098 02 004

TURBID

    HOW RING RIGHT OUT OUR SORDID TURBID TIME, ... 035 00 010

TURF

    THOUGH ALOFT ON TURF OR PERCH OR POOR LOW STAGE, ... 039 00 005

TURMOIL

    THE TURMOIL AND THE TORMENT, IT HAS, I SWEAR, A SWEETNESS, . . 152 02 057

TURN

    AND PLANETS BUD WHERE'ER WE TURN OUR MAZED EYES. 002 00 033
    AND I WILL TURN MY LOOKS TO YOU, ... 008 00 012
    I TO HIM TURN WITH TEARS 052 00 010
    TURN MOST ON TENDER BYPLAY. 054 00 016
    TO HIS OWN SELFBENT SO BOUND, SO TIED TO HIS TURN, ... 058 00 011
    WHEN SICK MEN TURN, AND LIGHTS ARE LOW, ... 077 00 025
    A TURN OF SEVEN NOTES OR FIVE, ... 081 00 007
    HOW TURN MY PASSION-PASTURED THOUGHT 081 00 174
    I MUST NOT TURN THE LANTERN ON HIS FACE. -- 102 01 024
    TO TURN THE COMPASS ON THE ALL-STARR'D SKY V 102 03 023
    AND BARLEY TURN TO WEED AND WILD, ... 114 00 005
    SHALL SEE THE AZURE TURN EXPRESSIONLESS 117 00 004
    I'LL LAY THEM BY, AND FRESHLY TURN INSTEAD 117 00 013
    HER HAND FROM HEAVEN TO TURN A MILL -- 139 00 004
    ALL BY TURN AND TURN ABOUT. C 159 00 018
    ALL BY TURN AND TURN ABOUT. C 159 00 018

TURNED

    AND NEVER TURNED TO CORN, ... 007 00 008
    AND WHEN HE TURNED IT BACK AGAIN 021 00 038
    ARE YOU! TURNED FOR AN EXQUISITE SMART, ... 028 18 002
    TWICE LOVELY, TINTED EASTERN, TURNED GREEK -- 136 00 015
    THEN OVER HIS TURNED TEMPLES -- HERE -- 144 00 013
    HEAVEN TURNED ITS STARLIGHT EYES BELOW 145 00 046
    I TOLD YOU THAT SHE TURNED HER MIRROR DIM 151 00 011
    ONCE I TURNED FROM THEE AND HID, ... 155 00 009

TURNING

    THAT WITH A TURNING OF THE WINGS 077 00 067
    TURNING AND PACING, SO BY SLIPS DISCLOSES 108 00 002
    SEVERAL TIMES I SAW THEM, THRICE OR FOUR TIMES TURNING; . . 152 02 028

TURN'D

    NOW ALL THINGS ROSY TURN'D: THE WEST HAD GROWN 002 00 019
    ABANDONED BY HER SAINTS, TURN'D BLACK AND BLASTED, ... 102 02 011

TURNS

    AT TRANQUIL TURNS, BY NATURE'S RULE, ... 030 00 014

TURNS   (CONTINUED)
     TURNS AND TWINDLES OVER THE BROTH 056 00 006
     O IN TURNS OF TEMPEST, ME HEAPED THERE; C 064 00 008
     AND TURNS TO WASH IT FROM HER WELLING EYES 151 00 005
     TURNS 159 00 048
TURQUOISE-GEMM'D
     ONE BOUND O'ER DRIPPING GOLD A TURQUOISE-GEMM'D 002 00 060
TURTLE'S
     OR STRETCH'D CHORDS TUNEABLE ON TURTLE'S SHELL; 002 00 129
TWELVE
     HOPE WAS TWELVE HOURS GONE; 028 15 004
     TEN OR TWELVE, ONLY TEN OR TWELVE 043 00 020
     TEN OR TWELVE, ONLY TEN OR TWELVE 043 00 020
TWENTY
     FIVE AND TWENTY YEARS HAVE RUN 029 00 005
TWICE
     BUT OPEN'D TWICE, IN LIFE AND DEATH, TO STATE, ... 001 04 008
     WITH TWICE AS FINE A SENSE TO APPREHEND THEM, ... 102 01 012
     TWICE LOVELY, TINTED EASTERN, TURNED GREEK -- 136 00 015
     HIS DEACON, DIRVAN, WARM TWICE OVER MUST THE WELCOME BE, . 152 01 008
TWINDLES
     TURNS AND TWINDLES OVER THE BROTH 056 00 006
TWINY
     OVER FINGER-TEASING TASK, HIS TWINY BOOTS 159 00 033
TWO
     TWO MAZED SHEPHERDS PERISH'D IN THE TIDE; 001 14 003
     SAVE BY TWO STARS, MORE CROWDING LIGHTS ARISE, ... 002 00 032
     TWO THOUSANDS OF YEARS ARE NEAR UPON PAST 027 00 015
     TWO HUNDRED SOULS IN THE ROUND -- 028 12 004
     BUT GERTRUDE, LILY, AND LUTHER, ARE TWO OF A TOWN, . . 028 20 005
     ON EAR AND EAR TWO NOISES TOO OLD TO END 035 00 001
     HOW THESE TWO SHAME THIS SHALLOW AND FRAIL TOWN! . . . 035 00 009
     WANTING; WHICH TWO WHEN THEY ONCE MEET, ... 038 00 012
     WHEN SHROVETIDE, TWO YEARS GONE, ... 054 00 005
     TWO TEDIOUS ACTS WERE PAST; 054 00 029
     UPON, ALL ON TWO SPOOLS; PART, PEN, PACK C 061 00 011
     NOW HER ALL IN TWO FLOCKS, TWO FOLDS C 061 00 012
     NOW HER ALL IN TWO FLOCKS, TWO FOLDS C 061 00 012
     BUT THESE TWO; WARE OF A WORLD WHERE BUT C 061 00 013
     THESE TWO TELL, EACH OFF THE OTHER; OF A RACK C 061 00 013
     TWO TONGUES LIKE BUTTERFLIES. 098 12 007
     AND YOUR TWO ETC. 101 00 012
     BRIDGING THE SLENDER DIFFERENCE OF TWO STARS, ... 103 00 003
     ' IN TWO YEARS OR IN THREE. ' 109 02 004
     FOR TWO YEARS AND FOR THREE. 109 06 002
     WITH A TWO YEARS CHILD AT HER KNEE. 109 16 002
     TWO MADE ANSWER IN ONE BREATH 109 26 001
     I KNEW THE BROOK THAT PARTS IN TWO 135 00 025
     CHRIST'S ONLY CHARITY CHARMED AND CHAINED THESE TWO. . 136 00 012
     TO-DAY THE SKY IS TWO AND TWO 138 00 016
     TO-DAY THE SKY IS TWO AND TWO 138 00 016
TYRANT
     DISCOVERING YOU, DARK TRAMPLERS, TYRANT YEARS. 157 00 002
TYRIAN
     OR TENDER PINKS WITH BLOODY TYRIAN DYE. 002 00 047

UNACCOUNTED
     THE MILLION SORTS OF UNACCOUNTED MOTES 098 22 002
UNALTER'D
     NOW WHILE THE FULL-LEAVED HURSTS UNALTER'D STAND, . . 105 00 003
UNAWAKENED
     SOME ASLEEP UNAWAKENED, ALL UN- 041 00 003
UNAWARE
     ALL OF HER GLORIOUS GAININGS UNAWARE. 151 00 010
UNBAKES
     UNBAKES MY PORES, AND STREAMS, AND MAKES ALL FRESH. . 005 00 032
UNBLOWN
     C HIS BRIGHTEST BLOOMS LIE THERE UNBLOWN, ... 148 00 041
UNBOUND
     BUT IF THE RAIN-BLASTS BE UNBOUND 003 00 007
UNBROKEN
     AND STILL TH' UNBROKEN SILENCE BROODS 023 00 019
UNCERTAINTY
     ENDING IN SWEET UNCERTAINTY 077 00 121
UNCHALLENGED
     ALTHO' UNCHALLENGED, WHERE SHE SITS, ... 083 00 009
UNCHANCELLING
     THY UNCHANCELLING POISING PALMS WERE WEIGHING THE WORTH, . 028 21 006
UNCHANGING
     THE UNCHANGING REGISTER OF CHANGE 130 00 005
UNCHARTED
     TO THY NOT-STALED UNCHARTED MEMORY. 117 00 014

273

UNDONE   (CONTINUED)
    BY SLENDER LOSSES ARE UNDONE; 081 00 147
    THE TIMES ARE WINTER, WATCH, A WORLD UNDONE; 150 00 002
UNDULATION
    IN SILKEN UNDULATION, SPURR'D AND RAY'D 002 00 043
UNENDEAR
    NOR ELSEWHERE CAN THY SWEETNESS UNENDEAR. 012 01 005
UNENDING
    THE DREAR DULL BURTHEN OF UNENDING PAINS. 160 00 018
UNENDURING
    THE UNENDURING FALLOWS OF THE HEAVEN? 122 00 006
UNESPIED
    THE COLD WHIP-ADDER UNESPIED 106 00 001
UNFATHERING
    SPINS TO THE WIDOW-MAKING UNCHILDING UNFATHERING DEEPS. 028 13 008
UNFATHOMABLE
    BOTH ARE IN AN UNFATHOMABLE, ALL IS IN AN ENORMOUS DARK 072 00 012
UNFOLD
    OR WHERE IS STRENGTH TO MAKE THE LEAF UNFOLD? 017 00 004
UNFORESEEN
    'S NOT WRUNG, SEE YOU; UNFORESEEN TIMES RATHER -- AS SKIES .   .   . 069 00 013
UNFORGIVEN
    UNCLEAN AND SEEMING UNFORGIVEN 018 00 003
UNFURLED
    AND HOSTS CONFRONT WITH FLAGS UNFURLED 023 00 033
    HIS LITTLE PENNON IS UNFURLED. 130 00 014
UNGENTLE
    TO NOT UNGENTLE DEATH NOW FORTH I RUN. 103 00 019
UNGIRDLED
    YET LEAVES HIM IN UNGIRDLED EASE 083 00 015
UNGLUE
    THAT SHALL UNGLUE THE CRUST OF SIN. 081 00 133
UNHEARD
    BARS OR HELL'S SPELL THWARTS. THIS TO HOARD UNHEARD, ... 066 00 013
UNHEEDED
    HEARD UNHEEDED, LEAVES ME A LONELY BEGAN. 066 00 014
UNHINDER'D
    I GAZED UNHINDER'D: MERMAIDS SIX OR SEVEN, ... 002 00 034
UNHOLY
    MYSELF UNHOLY, FROM MYSELF UNHOLY 016 00 001
    MYSELF UNHOLY, FROM MYSELF UNHOLY 016 00 001
UNHOUSE
    AND YOU UNHOUSE AND HOUSE THE LORD. 022 00 024
UNIMPERILL'D
    IN UNIMPERILL'D HAVEN IS WRECK'D. 083 00 020
UNIMPREGNATE
    LEFT NOT A ROOD WITH CURSES UNIMPREGNATE; 102 02 005
UNIVERSAL
    SPRING'S UNIVERSAL BLISS 042 00 034
UNKIND
    FOR THE INFINITE AIR IS UNKIND, ... 028 13 004
UNKNOWN
    AN ANTIQUE CHAUNT AND IN AN UNKNOWN TONGUE. 002 00 131
    JUST SEEN, MAY BE TO MANY UNKNOWN MEN 012 02 012
UNLEAVING
    OVER GOLDENGROVE UNLEAVING? 055 00 002
UNLOOK'D
    FROM PARTS UNLOOK'D FOR, ALTER'D, SPENT, ... 081 00 024
UNLOVELY
    FAIRER? THESE ARE THE FLARING SHOWS UNLOVELY 125 00 039
UNMADE
    AND AFTER IT ALMOST UNMADE, WHAT WITH DREAD, ... 028 01 006
UNMINDFUL
    UNMINDFUL OF THEIR GRACE, THE ESCORIAL 001 08 005
UNMOVED
    MIX O'ER THE NOT UNMOVED EARTH, -- 077 00 130
UNPALATEABLE
    UNPALATEABLE FRUITS TO EAT. 081 00 167
UNPASSION'D
    EVEN YOUR UNPASSION'D EYELIDS MIGHT BE WET. 014 01 014
UNPEOPLED
    IN SHOALS OF BLOOM: AS IN UNPEOPLED SKIES, ... 002 00 031
UNPINNED
    I PUT THE DOOR TO WITH THE BOLTS UNPINNED, ... 135 00 011
UNQUESTION'D
    THE UNQUESTION'D READINGS OF A BLOTLESS BOOK. 016 00 006
UNRAVELLER
    OF REALTY THE RAREST-VEINED UNRAVELLER: A NOT 044 00 012
UNREST
    FROM ALL THE PAIN OF THE PAST'S UNREST; 026 00 012
UNRETICENT
    IT IS THE WASTE DONE IN UNRETICENT YOUTH 017 00 010
UNSAFE
    SINCE ON THE FACE IT IS UNSAFE TO LOOK: 102 01 044
UNSANDALLED
    WHERE SEEK THEE WITH UNSANDALLED FEET. 023 00 018
UNSEEMLINESS
    LOOK WITH WHAT UNSEEMLINESS 160 00 007

274

UNSEEN
    EBB'D BACK BENEATH ITS SNOWY LIDS, UNSEEN. 002 00 018
    WE GUESS: WE CLOTHE THEE, UNSEEN KING. 023 00 013
    UNSEEN, THE HEROIC BREAST NOT OUTWARD-STEELED, ... 073 00 007
    HE DROPS TOWARDS THE RIVER: UNSEEN 159 00 015
UNSELFISHNESS
    MOST RARELY SEE, UNSELFISHNESS. 096 01 002
UNSELVE
    STROKES OF HAVOC UNSELVE 043 00 021
UNSET
    SHAKE AND UNSET YOUR MORTICED METAPHORS. V 101 00 008
    YET WHEN MY UNSET TRESSES HUNG LOOSE-TRACED 102 01 003
UNSETS
    COVERS WITH SHALLOW SILVER, THAT UNSETS 098 31 002
UNSEXING
    ROUND THIS UNSEXING DOUBLET, -- WHILE I SET 102 01 004
UNSHAPEABLE
    READ THE UNSHAPEABLE SHOCK NIGHT 028 29 003
UNSHEATH'D
    LIKE AN ASSYRIAN PRINCE, WITH BUDS UNSHEATH'D 002 00 062
UNSHOD
    COME BY THE FLESH-POTS: YOU SHALL SIT UNSHOD 005 00 009
UNSOUGHT
    UNSOUGHT, PRESENTED SO EASILY, C 137 00 006
UNSTEADY
    THEY PLOUGH OUR VALES: YOU SEE THE UNSTEADY FLARE . . . 104 00 009
UNSTINTED
    YET FOUND UNSTINTED PLACE FOR MIRTH: 077 00 056
UNSWERVING
    UNSWERVING THROUGH THE FIRMAMENT: 077 00 050
UNTAUGHT
    I WHO WAS WISE WOULD BE UNTAUGHT, ... 081 00 171
UNTAINTED
    DURING THE EASTERING OF UNTAINTED MORNS, ... 084 00 001
UNTEACHABLY
    O UNTEACHABLY AFTER EVIL, BUT UTTERING TRUTH, ... 028 18 005
UNTIL
    SUN-FLUSH'D, UNTIL IT SEEM'D THEIR FATHER SEA 002 00 100
    IN WANDERING UNTIL BROAD LIGHT OF DAY: 079 00 006
    AND WATCH UNTIL OUR HORSES AND THE MEN 125 00 009
UNTO
    PURE FASTED FACES DRAW UNTO THIS FEAST: 011 00 001
    THAT WAS UNTO JUDAH AS MAY, AND BROUGHT HER 026 00 031
    WHO TO US ARE AS DEW UNTO GRASS AND TREE, ... 026 00 038
    SWEET UNTO GOD, AND THE SWEETNESS IS GRACE: 027 00 044
    THE CROWN SHOULD BE UNTO HER HEAD 109 10 003
    ' FIE, ' SHE SAID UNTO THEM ALL, ... 109 28 001
UNTWIST
    NOT UNTWIST -- SLACK THEY MAY BE -- THESE LAST STRANDS OF MAN . . 064 00 002
UNUSED
    AND BRED ACQUAINTANCE OF UNUSED TOWNS? 107 02 002
UNVALVE
    UNVALVE OR SHUT HIS VANED TAIL 130 00 011
UNVEINED
    AFTER THE SANDFIELD AND THE UNVEINED GLARE! 005 00 029
UNVEXED
    SAVE WHERE THE UNVEXED WEST 077 00 097
UNVISITED
    DRESS, HOAR-HALLOWED SHRINES UNVISITED: 041 00 092
UNWARNED
    SOME ASLEEP UNAWAKENED, ALL UN- 041 00 003
    WARNED, ELEVEN FATHOMS FALLEN 041 00 004
UNWAVERING
    AND RIGHT? ONLY RESOLUTION: WILL, HIS WILL UNWAVERING . . 152 02 043
UNWET
    AND THERE SHE WAITS WITH LOCKS UNWET 120 00 003
UNWORTHINESS
    MY HOPES AND MY UNWORTHINESS, ... 118 00 009
UP
    COME UP, ARISE AND SLAY. 005 00 018
    UP TILL THAT MORNING'S FALL OF DEW, ... 021 00 027
    SETS UP A SHADOW IN THY SEAT: 023 00 016
    LOOK AT THE STARS! LOOK, LOOK UP AT THE SKIES! 032 00 001
    AROUND: UP ABOVE, WHAT WIND-WALKS! WHAT LOVELY BEHAVIOUR . 038 00 002
    I WALK, I LIFT UP, I LIFT UP HEART, EYES, ... 038 00 005
    I WALK, I LIFT UP, I LIFT UP HEART, EYES, ... 038 00 005
    NOW HE SHOOTS SHORT UP TO THE ROUND AIR: 041 00 065
    HIS HEART UP AT THE STRAIN: 054 00 027
    THEN WOULD I FLING ME UP TO SIP 077 00 131
    HIGH UP THE BALANCED STONY AIR -- 080 04 002
    CUCKOO CALLS CUCKOO UP THE WOOD, ... 081 00 022
    I CAN SEND UP AN ESAU'S CRY: 081 00 126
    AT LAST UP THE BLUE ELEMENT. 087 00 006
    LEAPS UP BEFORE MY VISION, -- THOU ART GONE. 098 33 002
    MY SIGNALLING TEARS MIGHT RING UP FLORIS: NOW 102 01 007
    NO, THEY ARE COME: THEIR HORN IS LIFTED UP: 104 00 001
    CRISP'D UP AND STARCHY FROM A SHORT HALF-HOUR 107 03 003

UP   (CONTINUED)
    AND EACH DREW BLUEBELLS UP, AND FOR RELIEF 107 03 017
    THEN UP AND SPAKE THE THIRD BROTHER. 109 27 001
    WHOSE ALL-BELATED LEAVES YIELD UP THEMSELVES 111 00 002
    THE BLUEBELLS UP WHOSE CRYSTAL-ENDING RODS 112 00 008
    LIFT UP YOUR HEADS, O GATES! 115 00 008
    BE YE LIFT UP, YE EVERLASTING DOORS 115 00 009
    DRY UP THE BLUE AND BE NOT SLAKED THEREBY. 117 00 007
    BY SPEECH SO SWEETLY BROKEN UP AND GONE. 125 00 027
    AND FILL THE WORLD UP WITH DELIGHT. 167 00 024
UPBRINGING
    IN THE RUDDIED COUNTY OF THE DAY'S UPBRINGING 098 28 004
UPGAZING
    WHILE THE UPGAZING COUNTRY SEEMS 077 00 125
UPLANDS
    TO WHERE THE LISTENING UPLANDS ARE! 077 00 082
UPPER
    WHERE THE UPPER MILL-STONE ROOF'D HIS HEAD, ...   006 00 007
    IN BREEZY BELTS OF UPPER AIR 077 00 073
    TO MANHOOD, ON THE UPPER LIP, -- THEY LOOK'D 102 01 067
UPRAIS'D
    UPRAIS'D AN EMBLEM OF THAT FIERY CONSTANCY. 001 03 008
UPRIGHT
    SHE WAS A WOMAN, UPRIGHT, OUTRIGHT! 145 00 036
UPROLL
    WITH THE UPROLL AND THE DOWNCAROL OF DAY AND NIGHT DELIVERING   .   .   152 C 013
UPWARD
    NOW MELTING UPWARD THRO' THE SLOPING SCALE 002 00 132
    A BRITTLE SHEEN, RUNS UPWARD LIKE A CLIFF, ...   098 06 002
UPWARD-PARTED
    WITH PARALLEL SHAFTS, -- AS UPWARD-PARTED ASHES, -- 107 04 005
UPWARDS
    THEN MAY I UPWARDS GAZE AND SEE 077 00 113
    UPWARDS AT ONCE AND WIN THEIR AUREOLES. 126 00 008
URN
    HER URN TAKES ALL, HER DEAL IS JUST. 166 00 016
USED
    THROUGH OTHER BARS IT USED TO THRILL, ...   081 00 015
    AND PASSAGES WHERE WE USED TO MEET, -- 081 00 162
UTTER
    UTTER SILVER JUBILEE. 029 00 020
UTTERANCE
    ONLY WITH UTTERANCE OF SWEET BREATH THEY SUNG 002 00 130
    WHICH DRIVES THE STONY AIR TO UTTERANCE? -- 122 00 018
UTTERED
    WORD, THAT HEARD AND KEPT THEE AND UTTERED THEE OUTRIGHT.   .   .   .   028 30 008
    THE UTTERER, UTTERED, UTTERING, ...   145 00 031
UTTERER
    THE UTTERER, UTTERED, UTTERING, ...   145 00 031
UTTERING
    O UNTEACHABLY AFTER EVIL, BUT UTTERING TRUTH, ...   028 18 005
    THE UTTERER, UTTERED, UTTERING, ...   145 00 031
UTTERLY
    OF A MASTERING HEAVEN UTTERLY BLUE! 078 00 002
    A FLUKE YET FANGED HIM, ENTANGLED HIM, NOT QUIT UTTERLY. C   .   .   137 00 005
UTTERMOST
    THE-LAST-BREATH PENITENT SPIRITS -- THE UTTERMOST MARK   .   .   .   028 33 006

VACANT
    VACANT CREATION'S LAMPS APPAL. 023 00 012
    ON BEING'S DREAD AND VACANT MAZE. 023 00 030
VAIN
    THE ALTAR-TAPERS FLAR'D IN GUSTS! IN VAIN 001 13 005
    I PLEAD! AND AH! HOW MUCH IN VAIN! 081 00 029
VALE
    THE OUTGOINGS OF THE VALE DOES BLOCK. 092 00 011
VALERIAN
    COME, DAPHNIS, GOOD VALERIAN, I WILL COME. 125 00 031
    I DO NOT, BUT TO PLEASE VALERIAN. 125 00 033
VALES
    WHEN HEAVENLY VALES SO THICK SHALL STAND 008 00 016
    THEN FOR HER WHOSE VELVET VALES 029 00 017
    LOVELY THE WOODS, WATERS, MEADOWS, COMBES, VALES, ...   034 00 009
    THEY PLOUGH OUR VALES! YOU SEE THE UNSTEADY FLARE 104 00 009
VALIANT
    WHAT IS VIRTUE? VALOUR! ONLY THE HEART VALIANT. 152 02 042
VALLEY
    BUT FURTHER DOWN THE VALLEY, LEFT AND RIGHT, ...   001 14 004
    EGYPT, THE VALLEY OF OUR PLEASANCE, THERE! 005 00 025
VALLEYS
    SHOULDERING. DOWN VALLEYS SMOKES THE GLOOM. 080 07 002
VALOUR
    BRUTE BEAUTY AND VALOUR AND ACT, OH, AIR, PRIDE, PLUME, HERE   .   .   036 00 009

VALOUR   (CONTINUED)
    WHAT IS VIRTUE? VALOUR: ONLY THE HEART VALIANT. • • • • • • • 152 02 042
VALUE
    THE SHEPHERDS, WHOM I VALUE NOT, • • • • • • • • • 124 00 023
VANED
    UNVALVE OR SHUT HIS VANED TAIL • • • • • • • • • 130 00 011
VANISHING
    • • • FROM VANISHING AWAY? C • • • • • • • • 059 0L 002
VANISH'D
    DEATH WAS VANISH'D FROM THE GLADE. • • • • • • • • 004 00 017
VANTAGE
    THAT GAVE YOU VANTAGE WHEN YOU WOULD DESPISE: • • • • • 014 03 003
VAPOUR
    THERE IS A VAPOUR STANDS IN THE WIND: • • • • • • 130 00 017
VAPOUROUS
    WHATEVER TIME THIS VAPOUROUS ROOF, • • • • • • • • 080 06 001
VARIETY
    OFF HER ONCE SKEINED STAINED VEINED VARIETY C • • • • • 061 00 011
VARIOUS
    HER HUE'S A VARIOUS BROWN WITH CREAMY LAKES, • • • • • 099 00 011
VAST
    OUR HYMN IN THE VAST SILENCE DIES. • • • • • • • 023 00 006
    EVENING STRAINS TO BE TIME'S VAST, C • • • • • • • 061 00 002
    THE SUN WHOSE VAST AFFLICTIVE HEAT • • • • • • • 080 02 002
    THE VAST OF HEAVEN STUNG WITH BRILLIANT STARS. • • • • • 098 21 002
VASTNESS
    BUT VASTNESS BLURS AND TIME BEATS LEVEL. ENOUGH! THE RESURRECTION, • 072 00 016
VASTY
    IN GRIMY VASTY VAULT. • • • • • • • • • • 060 00 102
VAULT
    NOT VAULT THEM, THE MILLION OF ROUNDS C • • • • • • 028 12 008
    MEND FIRST AND VITAL CANDLE IN CLOSE HEART'S VAULT: • • • • 046 00 010
    THE VAULT AND SCOPE AND SCHOOLING • • • • • • • • 049 00 015
    IN GRIMY VASTY VAULT. • • • • • • • • • • 060 00 102
VAULTED
    GLAZED WATER VAULTED O'ER A DROWSY STONE. • • • • • • 098 39 001
VAULTING
    A JAUNTING VAUNTING VAULTING ASSAULTING TRUMPET TELLING. V • • 141 00 007
    DENIS. WHOSE MOTIONABLE, ALERT, MOST VAULTING WIT • • • • 143 00 001
VAULTY
    VAULTY, VOLUMINOUS, • • • STUPENDOUS C • • • • • • 061 00 001
VAUNT
    TONGUE TRUE, VAUNT- AND TAUNTLESS: • • • • • • • 048 00 015
VAUNTING
    A JAUNTING VAUNTING VAULTING ASSAULTING TRUMPET TELLING. V • • 141 00 007
VEER
    I SEE THE CITY PIGEONS VEER, • • • • • • • • 015 00 027
    AND LEAVES THE BLADES, WHERE'ER HE WILL VEER, • • • • • 098 01 003
VEIL
    WITH A THIN FLOATING VEIL OF WATER HOAR. • • • • • • 002 00 004
    THE VEIL THAT COVERS MYSTERIES: • • • • • • • • 077 00 036
VEIN
    FELLS OR FLANKS OF THE VOEL, A VEIN • • • • • • • 028 04 007
    HEART, GO AND BLEED AT A BITTERER VEIN FOR THE • • • • 028 31 003
    A VEIN FOR THE VISITING OF THE PAST-PRAYER, PENT IN PRISON, • • 028 33 005
    BEAUTY'S BEARING OR MUSE OF MOUNTING VEIN, • • • • • 047 00 010
    NAY, ROGUISH RAN THE VEIN. • • • • • • • • 054 00 028
    WHEN LIFE REVISITS ME, NERVE AND VEIN. • • • • • • 080 08 002
    AND BEAUTY'S DEAREST VERIEST VEIN IS TEARS. • • • • • 157 00 004
VEINED
    OFF HER ONCE SKEINED STAINED VEINED VARIETY C • • • • • 061 00 011
VEIN'D
    WERE VEIN'D AND STREAK'D WITH DUSK-DEEP LAZULI, • • • • • 002 00 046
VEINS
    THOU HAST BOUND BONES AND VEINS IN ME, FASTENED ME FLESH, • • 028 01 005
    VEINS VIOLETS AND TALL TREES MAKES MORE AND MORE) • • • 073 00 011
    WITH LOOPS OF VEINS: NOT OF AN EVEN PINK, • • • • • 093 8 004
VELVET
    THEN FOR HER WHOSE VELVET VALES • • • • • • • 029 00 017
VELVETY
    THROUGH THE VELVETY WIND V-WINGED • • • • • • • 138 00 041
VENERABLE
    THY VENERABLE RECORD, VIRGIN, IS RECORDED) • • • • • 152 C 017
VENGEANCES
    THERE THEY DID APPEAL. THEREFORE AIRY VENGEANCES • • • • 152 02 030
VENTNOR
    NOW NEAR BY VENTNOR TOWN • • • • • • • • • 041 00 031
VENUS
    FRONTS VENUS. -- HIS ILL-LAUNCHED HOPE • • • • • • 083 00 019
VERIEST
    AND BEAUTY'S DEAREST VERIEST VEIN IS TEARS. • • • • • 157 00 004
VERMEIL-RAIN
    OF DRIVING VERMEIL-RAIN; AND, AS HE LISTS, • • • • • 002 00 091
VERTICAL
    VERTICAL HOME, COULD SICILY FARE • • • • • • • 166 00 018
VERY
    COMFORTING SMELL BREATHED AT VERY ENTERING, • • • • • 034 00 003

VERY   (CONTINUED)
    THIS VERY VERY DAY CAME DOWN TO US AFTER A BOON HE ON 048 00 005
    THIS VERY VERY DAY CAME DOWN TO US AFTER A BOON HE ON 048 00 005
    HIS VERY LOOKS IN OTHER YEARS, ...   081 00 062
    IS VERY CAPABLE OF STRONG AFFECTION 094 00 013
    HERE AT THE VERY FURTHEST REACH AWAY 107 04 019
    THESE ARE MY VERY TEXT OF DISCONTENT; 125 00 044
    THERE WAS A LADY VERY GAY, ...   131 00 002
    AND I'M VERY GLAD 132 00 005
    I AM SO VERY, O SO VERY GLAD 138 00 031
    I AM SO VERY, O SO VERY GLAD 138 00 031
    THE VERY VICTIM WOULD PREPARE. 145 00 008
    HERE THY VERY MANHOOD STEALS FROM HUMAN KEN: 168 00 010
    IN THE VERY WAYS THAT THY LIFE GOES 169 00 005
VERY-VIOLET-SWEE
    MAJESTIC -- AS A STALLION STALWART, VERY-VIOLET-SWEET! --   .   .   .   038 00 010
VESPERS
    THE DRIVING STORM AT HOUR OF VESPERS BEAT 001 13 003
VESPILLO
    VESPILLO MY CENTURION HACKS OUT 080 09 005
VEST
    OF TREMULOUS FILM, MORE SUBTLE THAN THE VEST 002 00 039
VEX'D
    THE VEX'D ELM-HEADS ARE PALE WITH THE VIEW 078 00 001
VICE
    O HIDEOUS VICE TO HAGGLE YET 081 00 149
    OF VIRTUE AND VICE; BUT MOST (IT SEEMED HIS SENSE) 136 00 027
VICTIM
    THE VERY VICTIM WOULD PREPARE. 145 00 008
VICTOR
    ' SO I AM VICTOR NOW, I SWEAR TO PAY 001 02 005
VIEW
    THE VEX'D ELM-HEADS ARE PALE WITH THE VIEW 078 00 001
VIEWING
    GAZES ASLANT HIS SHOULDER, VIEWING NIGH 001 11 006
VIEWS
    APOLLO VIEWS THE SMITTEN PYTHON WRITHE AND DIE. 001 11 009
VIGIL-KEEPERS
    YOU VIGIL-KEEPERS WITH LOW FLAMES DECREASED, ...   011 00 008
VIGIL-ORGAN
    HER JAILOR WITH HIS VIGIL-ORGAN DEAD? 099 00 016
VIGOROUS
    THE VIGOROUS HORIZONTALS, EACH WAY FALL 012 02 003
VILLAGES
    HE RISES FROM THE FLOCKS OF VILLAGES 100 00 005
VINE
    FOR US THE VINE WAS FENCED WITH THORN, ...   006 00 013
    THE RIV'N VINE, LEAFLESS, LIFELESS, DRY: 006 00 022
    I TOOK OF VINE A CROSS-BARRED ROD OR ROOD. 020 00 008
    A JUICE RIDES RICH THROUGH BLUEBELLS, IN VINE LEAVES,   .   .   .   157 00 003
    BENEATH THE TACKLED VINE. 165 00 008
    FOR HAIL UPON THE VINE NOR BREAK 166 00 029
VINE-SHOOT
    HANDLE THE FIG, SUCK THE FULL-SAPP'D VINE-SHOOT. 005 00 038
VINES
    UNDER THE CLOISTER-LIGHT OF GREENHOUSE VINES, ...   084 00 006
VINTAGE
    IS THE SWEET VINTAGE OF OUR LORD. 006 00 020
VIOL
    WHAT BASS IS OUR VIOL FOR TRAGIC TONES? 075 00 008
    OR BIRD WITH PIPE, WITH VIOL WITH AIR 166 00 020
VIOLENT
    THE BLAME BEAR WHO AROUSED ME. WHAT I HAVE DONE VIOLENT   .   .   152 02 034
    NOR FEAR THE VIOLENT CALENDAR 166 00 027
VIOLET
    AN AZURE RIDGE; OR CLOUDS OF VIOLET GLOW'D 002 00 105
    TO WIN A LOOK OF VIOLET. 086 00 006
    THE VIOLET MOVES AND COPSES ROCK. 098 03 004
    WITH SUCH A VIOLET SLIGHT THEIR DISTANCED GREEN? V 100 00 008
    SLIGHT WITH SUCH VIOLET THEIR BRIGHT-MASK'D GREEN? V   .   .   .   100 00 009
    MASK'D WITH SUCH VIOLET DISALLOW THEIR GREEN? V 100 00 010
    THE MOUTHED CENTRE OF A VIOLET. 102 01 071
VIOLETS
    I SEE LONG REEFS OF VIOLETS 003 00 025
    VEINS VIOLETS AND TALL TREES MAKES MORE AND MORE) 073 00 011
    AND PRESSED VIOLETS IN THE FOLDS APPEAR, ...   119 00 004
VIRGIN
    HERE PLAY'D THE VIRGIN MOTHER WITH HER CHILD 001 10 004
    MARY THE VIRGIN, WELL THE HEART KNOWS, ...   027 00 021
    AND FAVOURING VIRGIN FRESHNESS YET. 139 00 006
    THY VENERABLE RECORD, VIRGIN, IS RECORDED)   .   .   .   .   .   152 C 017
VIRGINAL
    OF THE MONTH BY MEN CALLED VIRGINAL. 026 00 022
    A PROPHETESS TOWERED IN THE TUMULT, A VIRGINAL TONGUE TOLD.   .   028 17 008
VIRGINS
    THE WORLD WAS SAVED BY VIRGINS, MADE THE MARK. 136 00 030
VIRTUE
    OF VIRTUE AND VICE; BUT MOST (IT SEEMED HIS SENSE) 136 00 027

VIRTUE   (CONTINUED)
      BEING TO HER VIRTUE CLINCHING-BLIND 145 00 018
      WHAT IS VIRTUE? VALOUR; ONLY THE HEART VALIANT. 152 02 042
VIRTUE'S
      SHOULD CHOKE SWEET VIRTUE'S GLORY IS TIME'S GREAT GUILT. 136 00 002
VIRTUES
      AND FOR THOSE VIRTUES I IN THEE HAVE FOUND, ... 013 00 011
      FOR THESE, MAKE ALL THE VIRTUES TO ABOUND, -- 013 00 013
      (AND, WELL SUPPLIED WITH VIRTUES ON THE WHOLE, ... 094 00 027
      OF VIRTUES I MOST WARMLY BLESS, ... 096 01 001
      THOU JACINTH; NOR HAVE SKILL OF ALL THY VIRTUES, ... 102 01 059
      WHERE ALL THE VIRTUES WERE ILLUSTRATED 102 02 009
      AND VIRTUES THAT THY PATTERN SHOWS, ... 169 00 006
VISION
      FAIR, BUT OF FAIRNESS AS A VISION DREAM'D; 079 00 001
      LEAPS UP BEFORE MY VISION, -- THOU ART GONE. 098 33 002
VISIONARY
      BUT MANY A SILVER VISIONARY SPARK 113 00 005
VISIONS
      TIMED HER SAD VISIONS WITH HIS WRECK. 021 00 056
VISITING
      A VEIN FOR THE VISITING OF THE PAST-PRAYER, PENT IN PRISON, . . 028 33 005
      HOW IT DOES MY HEART GOOD, VISITING AT THAT BLEAK HILL, . . . 048 00 021
VISUAL
      BY VISUAL COMPULSION, TILL I HIDE 012 02 005
VITAL
      MEND FIRST AND VITAL CANDLE IN CLOSE HEART'S VAULT; 046 00 010
      THE VITAL FIRE DOES SUDDENLY RETIRE 080 10 003
VIVE
      -- ---- -- VIVE ------ ---- -- ---- V 098 12 006
V-WINGED
      THROUGH THE VELVETY WIND V-WINGED 138 00 041
VOEL
      FELLS OR FLANKS OF THE VOEL, A VEIN 028 04 007
VOICE
      NO ANSWERING VOICE COMES FROM THE SKIES; 023 00 002
      BUT NO FORGIVING VOICE REPLIES; 023 00 004
      A MOANING VOICE AMONG THE REEDS. 023 00 036
      IN WHOSE DEAD LAKE EVEN A VOICE MAY MAKE 080 04 003
      AT LAST I HEAR THE VOICE WELL KNOWN; 081 00 001
      DOUBTLESS THE VOICE; NOW FALL'N NOW SPENT, ... 081 00 002
      AT LAST I HEAR THE VOICE I KNEW, ... 081 00 025
      A MAN'S VOICE AND A NEW VOICE SPEAKING NEAR. 136 00 022
      A MAN'S VOICE AND A NEW VOICE SPEAKING NEAR. 136 00 022
      WHICH OVERVAULTED VOICE. 148 00 020
VOID
      AS VOID AS CLOUDS THAT HOUSE AND HARBOUR NONE, ... 107 01 001
      AS VOID AS THOSE THE GENTLE DOWNS APPEAR 107 01 003
VOIDS
      HE! HAND TO MOUTH HE LIVES, AND VOIDS WITH SHAME; . . . 075 00 00?
VOLUMINOUS
      VAULTY, VOLUMINOUS, ... STUPENDOUS C 061 00 00
VOWS
      BUY THEN! BID THEN! -- WHAT? -- PRAYER, PATIENCE, ALMS, VOWS, . . 032 00 009

WADING
      WITH, ALL DOWN DARKNESS WIDE, HIS WADING LIGHT? 040 00 004
WAFT
      IDLE FOR EVER TO WAFT HER OR WIND HER WITH, THESE SHE ENDURED. . . 028 14 008
WAFTING
      STARLIGHT, WAFTING HIM OUT OF IT; AND 028 05 003
WAG
      WAG OR CROSSBRIDLE, IN A WIND LIFTED, WINDLACED -- C . . . 071 00 011
WAGES
      THOU THAT ON SIN'S WAGES STARVEST, ... 006 00 001
WAIL
      SWELL'D THE SWEET STRAIN TO A MELODIOUS WAIL; 002 00 133
WAILING
      THE WOMAN'S WAILING, THE CRYING OF CHILD WITHOUT CHECK -- . . 028 17 006
WAIN
      AND CHARLES'S WAIN, THE WONDROUS SEVEN, ... 030 00 017
WAIST
      HE LEANS TO IT, HARRY BENDS, LOOK. BACK, ELBOW, AND LIQUID WAIST . . 071 00 009
      THE RIVER WOUND ABOUT IT AS A WAIST. 107 04 002
WAISTS
      FROM THEIR WHITE WAISTS A SILVER SKIRT WAS SPREAD 002 00 048
WAIT
      I'LL WAIT TILL MORN ETERNAL BREAKS. 023 00 054
WAITS
      AND THERE SHE WAITS WITH LOCKS UNWET 120 00 003
      AND BRIDEGROOM WAITS AND READY ARE BOWER AND BED. . . . 136 00 018
WAKE
      I WAKE AND FEEL THE FELL OF DARK, NOT DAY. 067 00 001

WAKE   (CONTINUED)
    WHEN CHILL WOODS WAKE AND THINK OF MORN, ... 077 00 023
    WISH US GOOD MORNING WHEN WE WAKE 167 00 021
WAKED
    WILL HAVE WAKED AND HAVE WAXED AND HAVE WALKED C 059 06 023
    AND THE WAKED STARS ARE ALL ALONE. 077 00 034
WAKEN
    BONES, THIS SINEW, AND WILL NOT WAKEN. 041 00 084
WAKES
    TIME'S EUNUCH, AND NOT BREED ONE WORK THAT WAKES. 074 00 013
WAKING
    FORGET THE WAKING TRUMPET, THE LONG LAW. 005 00 044
    WHEN WAKING HEARTS CAN PARDON MUCH 077 00 029
    WAKING I THOUGHT; AND IT SUFFICED; 118 00 008
WALES
    ON A PASTORAL FOREHEAD OF WALES. 028 24 002
    SHOULD HAVE PEALED WITH WELCOME, WALES, ... 029 00 018
    ALL THE AIR THINGS WEAR THAT BUILD THIS WORLD OF WALES; . . . 034 00 010
    AND NOT FROM PURPLE WALES ONLY NOR FROM ELMY ENGLAND, . . . 152 C 019
WALK
    I WALK MY BREEZY BELVEDERE 015 00 025
    BUT YOU SHALL WALK THE GOLDEN STREET 022 00 023
    I WALK, I LIFT UP, I LIFT UP HEART, EYES, ... 038 00 005
    I WALK TOWARDS EVE OUR WALKS AGAIN; 081 00 054
    IN THE WHITE AND THE WALK OF THE MORNING; C 137 00 001
    TILL WALK THE WORLD HE CAN WITH BARE HIS FEET 159 00 035
WALKED
    WINGS; SO SOME GREAT STORMFOWL, WHENEVER HE HAS WALKED HIS WHILE . 045 00 011
    WILL HAVE WAKED AND HAVE WAXED AND HAVE WALKED C 059 06 023
WALK'D
    AS I WALK'D A STILLY WOOD, ... 004 00 005
WALKS
    I WALK TOWARDS EVE OUR WALKS AGAIN; 081 00 054
    AND STUMBLING SWEARS HE WALKS BY LIGHT OF DAY. 102 03 031
    AND STUMBLING SWEARS HE WALKS BY LIGHT OF DAY. V 102 03 037
    ONE AND THEN ONE, ALONG THEIR WALKS, AND KEPT 107 01 012
WALL
    SLOP'D ON THE GALLERIES; UPON THE WALL 001 12 002
    ECLIPSING PARAPET; YET ABOVE THE WALL 012 02 007
    IN AN HOURGLASS -- AT THE WALL 028 04 002
    THE GIRTH OF IT AND THE WHARF OF IT AND THE WALL; 028 32 004
    HENRY, BY THE WALL, ... 054 00 012
    THE FRUIT AGAINST THE WALL 105 00 012
WALLOWING
    IN HIM, ALL QUAIL TO THE WALLOWING O' THE PLOUGH. C 071 00 010
WALLS
    WITH PAINTING GLEAM'D THE RICH PILASTER'D WALLS -- 001 10 003
    AT RED POMPEII ON MEDALLION'D WALLS. 002 00 051
    YOU HAVE YOUR WISH; ENTER THESE WALLS, ONE SAID; 020 00 017
    THOU KNOWEST THE WALLS, ALTAR AND HOUR AND NIGHT; 028 02 005
    HE LIVED ON; THESE WEEDS AND WATERS, THESE WALLS ARE WHAT . . 044 00 010
    C WHO SHAPED THESE WALLS HAS SHEWN 148 00 009
    C WHO BUILT THESE WALLS MADE KNOWN 148 00 037
WALNUT
    A BRANCH OF WALNUT LEAVES, AND THAT 120 00 006
WALSINGHAM
    THE MARVELLOUS MILK WAS WALSINGHAM WAY 041 00 102
WAN
    ' O WHY ART THOU SO WAN, ' SHE SAID, ... 109 31 001
WAND
    LET PATIENCE WITH HER CHASTENING WAND 023 00 045
    MORE WILL WEAR THIS WAND AND THEN 025 00 039
    THEO. AND MORE SHALL WEAR THIS WAND AND THEN . . . . . APPEN A 45
WANDERING
    AT THE TOUCH OF HER WANDERING WONDERING BREATH 026 00 006
    IN WANDERING UNTIL BROAD LIGHT OF DAY; 079 00 006
    RUINOUS HEART-BEAT, WANDERING, DEATH. 081 00 053
    NOT OF ALL MY EYES SEE, WANDERING ON THE WORLD, ... 149 A 001
WANED
    IT WANED INTO THE WORLD OF LIGHT, ... 025 00 031
    LET LIFE, WANED, AH LET LIFE WIND C 061 00 010
    THE WANNER WANED SHE. 109 36 004
    THEO. YOU WANED INTO THE WORLD OF LIGHT, ... APPEN A 31
WANING
    OR PARING OF PARADISAICAL FRUIT, LOVELY IN WANING BUT LUSTRELESS, . 137 00 003
WANNER
    THE WANNER WANED SHE. 109 36 004
WANT
    THAT WANT THE YIELD OF PLUSHY SWARD, ... 022 00 022
    I WANT THE ONE RAPTURE OF AN INSPIRATION. 076 00 010
    THINK YOU WANT DAFFODILS AND FOLLOW AS FAR 135 00 030
    WHOM WANT COULD NOT MAKE PINE, PINE 142 00 007
    AH YES! WHY, GET THEE GONE THEN; TELL THY MOTHER I WANT HER. . 152 01 010
    THEO. I WANT, I WANT, IF I WERE FIT; . . . . APPEN A 39
    THEO. I WANT, I WANT, IF I WERE FIT, ... APPEN A 39
WANTED
    GRACE THAT DAY GRACE WAS WANTED, ' 041 00 116

WANTING
    NEVER ASK IF MEANING IT, WANTING IT, WARNED OF IT -- MEN GO,   028 08 008
    WANTING; WHICH TWO WHEN THEY ONCE MEET,   038 00 012
    WHEN THIS IS SOUGHT TREES WILL BE WANTING NOT,   080 12 006
    ONE ONCE THAT WAS FOUND WANTING WHEN GOOD WEIGHED.   157 00 024
WANTON
    A GLORIOUS WANTON; -- ALL THE WRECKS IN SHOWERS   002 00 093
    AGAINST THE WILD AND WANTON WORK OF MEN.   157 00 036
WANTS
    THERE, EYES THEM, HEART WANTS, CARE HAUNTS, FOOT FOLLOWS KIND,   040 00 013
    WANTS WAR, WANTS WOUNDS; WEARY HIS TIMES, HIS TASKS;   068 00 003
    WANTS WAR, WANTS WOUNDS; WEARY HIS TIMES, HIS TASKS;   068 00 003
WANWOOD
    THOUGH WORLDS OF WANWOOD LEAFMEAL LIE;   055 00 008
WAR
    AND SCARLET WEAR THE SPIRIT OF WAR THERE EXPRESS.   063 00 008
    MARK CHRIST OUR KING. HE KNOWS WAR, SERVED THIS SOLDIERING THROUGH;   063 00 009
    WANTS WAR, WANTS WOUNDS; WEARY HIS TIMES, HIS TASKS;   068 00 003
    BUT BE THE WAR WITHIN, THE BRAND WE WIELD   073 00 006
WARBLED
    LET THE WARBLED SWEETNESS RILL,   077 00 084
WARBLES
    AND THE WATER WARBLES OVER INTO, C   159 00 038
WARBLING
    FOR WARBLING OF THE WARBLING BIRD. '   021 00 049
    FOR WARBLING OF THE WARBLING BIRD. '   021 00 049
WARE
    THEN, LOOKING ON THE WATERS, I WAS WARE   002 00 027
    BUT THESE TWO; WARE OF A WORLD WHERE BUT C   061 00 013
    AND SHE WAS WARE OF A SERVINGMAN   109 17 003
WARFARE
    A WARFARE OF MY LIPS IN TRUTH,   018 00 015
WARM
    INDEED WHILE SUCH A WONDER'S WARM.   025 00 036
    WARM ON HIS BROW; LO! WHERE IS ANOTHER   026 00 007
    THOU ART LIGHTNING AND LOVE, I FOUND IT, A WINTER AND WARM;   028 09 006
    WORLD BROODS WITH WARM BREAST AND WITH AH! BRIGHT WINGS.   031 00 014
    THAN PURCELL TUNE LETS TREAD TO? SEE: IT DOES THIS; KEEPS WARM   062 00 003
    THIS HEART IS WARM TO YOU ALONE;   081 00 129
    HE SHALL BE WARM WITH MINIVER   124 00 015
    HIS DEACON, DIRVAN, WARM TWICE OVER MUST THE WELCOME BE,   152 01 008
    WARM BEAT WITH COLD BEAT COMPANY, SHALL I   153 00 002
    THEO. WHILE SUCH A WONDER'S WET AND WARM!   APPEN A 36
WARM-LAID
    WARM-LAID GRAVE OF A WOMB-LIFE GREY;   028 07 003
WARMLY
    OF VIRTUES I MOST WARMLY BLESS,   096 01 001
    I AM WARMLY CLAD.   132 00 004
WARM'D
    WITH THE WARM'D AND THE WATER'D BUDS   098 19 007
WARMS
    FORMS AND WARMS THE LIFE WITHIN;   042 00 022
WARMTH
    WHISPERS ' IF THOU HAVE WARMTH AT HEART   080 11 004
WARNED
    NEVER ASK IF MEANING IT, WANTING IT, WARNED OF IT -- MEN GO.   028 08 008
    ON ONE THAT WENT AGAINST ME WHEREAS I HAD WARNED HER --   152 02 006
    WARNED HER! WELL SHE KNEW I WARNED HER OF THIS WORK.   152 02 007
    WARNED HER! WELL SHE KNEW I WARNED HER OF THIS WORK.   152 02 007
WARNING
    NONE GOOD BUT GOD -- A WARNING WAVED TO   157 00 023
WARN'D
    WARN'D BY THE BRIGHT PROCESSION OF THE STARS.   102 01 056
WARP
    THE STRANDED KEEL AND KELSON WARP APART;   101 00 011
WARPED
    THE WARPED WORLD WE SHALL UNDO.   025 00 040
    THEO. THE WARPED WORLD IT WILL UNDO. --   APPEN A 46
WARRANTS
    AND WORDY WARRANTS ARE FLAWED THROUGH.   025 00 038
    THEO. AND WORDY WARRANTS ARE FLAWED THROUGH;   APPEN A 44
WARRING
    THAT, WARRING, WASTED THE LAND'S INCREASE,   026 00 028
WAR'S
    THOSE LOVELY LADS ONCE, WET-FRESH WINDFALLS OF WAR'S STORM,   062 00 006
WARS
    ALARMS OF WARS, THE DAUNTING WARS, THE DEATH OF IT?   051 00 006
    ALARMS OF WARS, THE DAUNTING WARS, THE DEATH OF IT?   051 00 006
    Y OF IDLE A BEING BUT BY WHERE WARS ARE RIFE.   066 00 008
    GROWN WICKED IN THE WICKED WARS.   114 00 012
WASH
    WOOD BANKS AND BRAKES WASH WET LIKE LAKES   042 00 042
    TO WASH BEFORE THE MULTITUDE   080 10 002
    AND TURNS TO WASH IT FROM HER WELLING EYES   151 00 005
WASHING
    LINGER'D, THEN RAISED THE WASHING WAVES AND DRENCH'D   002 00 138
    WHILE HE WAS WASHING FROM ON DECK   021 00 054

WASHING   (CONTINUED)
     AND LIVES AT LAST WERE WASHING AWAY: 028 15 007
WASTE
     THERE IS A MASSY PILE ABOVE THE WASTE 001 01 001
     THEY DO NOT WASTE THEIR METED HOURS, ...   015 00 005
     IT IS THE WASTE DONE IN UNRETICENT YOUTH 017 00 010
     CHRIST'S LILY AND BEAST OF THE WASTE WOOD: 028 20 006
     WASTE: HER EARLIEST STARS, EARLSTARS, STARS PRINCIPAL, OVERBEND US, . 061 00 004
     ARE WASTE, AND HAD NO WHOLESOME FOODS, ...   081 00 166
     SO WASTE IN TEARS OVER THIS BED OF SWEETNESS, ...   102 01 035
     THEY WASTE, THEY WITHER WORSE; THEY AS THEY RUN 150 00 003
WASTED
     THAT, WARRING, WASTED THE LAND'S INCREASE, ...   026 00 028
WASTEFUL
     NOT GOSHEN, WASTEFUL WIDE HUGE-GIRTHED NILE 005 00 031
WASTES
     FROM WASTES OF ROCK HE BRINGS 007 00 011
     TOWARDS WASTES WHERE ROUND THE ICE-BLOCKS TILT AND FRET   .   .   .   088 00 007
     TOWARDS THOSE WASTES WHERE THE ICE-BLOCKS TILT AND FRET, V   .   .   088 00 011
WATCH
     WHENCE OFT I WATCH BUT SEE THOSE MERMAIDS NOW NO MORE.   .   .   .   002 00 143
     TO WATCH THE LOW OR LEVANT SUN, ...   015 00 026
     MEN ARE AMAZED TO WATCH ME PASS 025 00 003
     AND WATCH UNTIL OUR HORSES AND THE MEN 125 00 009
     THE TIMES ARE WINTER, WATCH, A WORLD UNDONE: 150 00 002
     MUST WATCH DOWN WITH WEARINESS 160 00 009
WATCHED
     WHO HAVE WATCHED HIS MOULD OF MAN, BIG-BONED AND HARDY-HANDSOME   .   053 00 002
     THAT IN MAJORCA ALFONSO WATCHED THE DOOR. 073 00 014
     THEY WATCHED THE BRUSH OF THE SWIFT STRINGY DROPS,   .   .   .   107 03 013
WATCHES
     AND WATCHES CHANGE UPON THE SEA: 077 00 032
WATCHET
     HER SHOWY LEAVES STAID WATCHET COUNTERFOILING V 108 00 005
     HER SHOWY LEAVES WITH GENTLE WATCHET FOILING V 108 00 006
WATCHING
     BUT WATCHING WHILE THE COLOUR GREW 021 00 012
     SPEAK! WHISPER TO MY WATCHING HEART 023 00 049
WATCH'D
     BUT MOST IN A HALF-CIRCLE WATCH'D THE SUN: 002 00 116
WATER
     WITH A THIN FLOATING VEIL OF WATER HOAR. 002 00 004
     WHITE LOOM'D MY ROCK, THE WATER GURGLING O'ER,   ,   .   .   .   002 00 142
     WHO WOULD DRINK WATER FROM A STONY ROCK? 005 00 020
     ARE YOU SANDBLIND? SLABS OF WATER MANY A MILE 005 00 035
     I WATER WITH MY FOOT. 005 00 040
     AND WATER DRAINING THROUGH AND THROUGH 021 00 020
     BETWEENS I HEARD THE WATER STILL 021 00 044
     I STEADY AS A WATER IN A WELL, TO A POISE, TO A PANE,   .   .   .   028 04 005
     (CRUSHED THEM) OR WATER (AND DROWNED THEM) OR ROLLED   .   .   028 17 003
     THE ALL OF WATER, AN ARK 028 33 002
     OR REARING BILLOW OF THE BISCAY WATER: 041 00 018
     I GIVE COMMANDS FOR WATER FOR MY HANDS: 080 09 003
     OF FALLING WATER. THIS AND ALL OF THESE 098 02 003
     GLAZED WATER VAULTED O'ER A DROWSY STONE. 098 39 001
     AS WATER MOULDED TO THE DUCT IT RUNS IN: 101 00 004
     OF WATER, CLOUDS LIKE PARTED MOSS V 121 00 003
     LIKE WATER SOON TO BE SUCKED IN 145 00 009
     DOWN THE BEETLING BANKS, LIKE WATER IN WATERFALLS,   .   .   .   152 02 020
     IT STOOPED AND FLASHED AND FELL AND RAN LIKE WATER AWAY.   .   .   152 02 021
     WATER, WHICH KEEPS THY NAME, (FOR NOT IN ROCK WRITTEN,   .   .   152 C 014
     BUT IN PALE WATER, FRAIL WATER, WILD RASH AND REELING WATER,   .   152 C 015
     BUT IN PALE WATER, FRAIL WATER, WILD RASH AND REELING WATER,   .   152 C 015
     BUT IN PALE WATER, FRAIL WATER, WILD RASH AND REELING WATER,   .   152 C 015
     AND THE WATER WARBLES OVER INTO, C 159 00 038
     WEDLOCK. WHAT THE WATER? SPOUSAL LOVE. 159 00 047
WATERBLOWBALLS
     ALL IN FROTH AND WATERBLOWBALLS, DOWN. C 159 00 007
WATERFALL
     AND MANY STANDING ROUND A WATERFALL 091 00 005
WATERFALLS
     DOWN THE BEETLING BANKS, LIKE WATER IN WATERFALLS,   .   .   .   152 02 020
WATERFEARERS
     FALLERS IN DREADFUL FROTHPITS, WATERFEARERS WILD,   .   .   .   152 C 007
WATER-CLOUD
     SAY, O'ER IT HANGS A WATER-CLOUD 081 00 056
WATER-IN-A-WALLO
     HIS CHARGE THROUGH THE CHAMP-WHITE WATER-IN-A-WALLOW,   .   .   .   041 00 048
WATER-LILY
     FAIR BEDS THEY SEEM'D OF WATER-LILY FLAKES 002 00 013
WATER-MEADS
     IN STARRY WATER-MEADS THEY DREW 010 00 017
WATER-NYMPHS
     AROUND THE WATER-NYMPHS IN FRETTED FALLS, ...   002 00 050
WATER-PIERCED
     FIT FOR FLOWERS, WATER-PIERCED AND RILLY. 098 15 006
WATER-WATTLED
     AND MAZY SANDS ALL WATER-WATTLED 030 00 023

WATER'D
    WITH THE WARM'D AND THE WATER'D BUDS   •   •   •   •   •   •   •   098 19 007
    HE DROPS HIS BRIGHT ROOTS IN THE WATER'D SWARD,   •   •   •   •   100 00 002
WATERS
    THEN, LOOKING ON THE WATERS, I WAS WARE   •   •   •   •   002 00 027
    THEN SAW I SUDDEN FROM THE WATERS BREAK   •   •   •   •   002 00 074
    FRESH BROOKS TO SALT SAND-TEASING WATERS SHOALY; --   •   016 00 004
    ARE SISTERLY SEALED IN WILD WATERS,   •   •   •   •   •   028 23 007
    LOVELY THE WOODS, WATERS, MEADOWS, COMBES, VALES,   •   •   034 00 009
    HE LIVED ON: THESE WEEDS AND WATERS, THESE WALLS ARE WHAT   •   •   044 00 010
    MUST SEE THE WATERS ROLL   •   •   •   •   •   •   •   088 00 005
    WHERE WATERS SET V   •   •   •   •   •   •   •   088 00 010
    THE SUN ON FALLING WATERS WRITES THE TEXT   •   •   •   091 00 008
    I HEAR A NOISE OF WATERS DRAWN AWAY,   •   •   •   •   112 00 001
    FISH FEEL THEIR WATERS DRAWING TO   •   •   •   •   •   166 00 033
WATERWORLD
    ARE EARTHWORLD, AIRWORLD, WATERWORLD THOROUGH HURLED, C   •   •   159 00 018
WATERY
    FROM WINGS SWAN-FLEDGED A WHEEL OF WATERY LIGHT   •   •   •   002 00 076
    THE WEBBED AND THE WATERY WEST   •   •   •   •   •   003 00 022
    (LOW LIE HIS MATES NOW ON WATERY BED)   •   •   •   •   041 00 058
WATERY-PLATED
    LIGHTED THE WATERY-PLATED LEAVES. V   •   •   •   •   098 17 002
    THE WATERY-PLATED PLANE-LEAVES LIT. V   •   •   •   098 17 003
WAVE
    WAVE WITH THE MEADOW, FORGET THAT THERE MUST   •   •   •   028 11 007
    WITH THE BURL OF THE FOUNTAINS OF AIR, BUCK AND THE FLOOD OF THE WAVE?   028 16 008
WAVED
    WITH WAVED PASSES THERE SHALL GLIDE   •   •   •   •   106 00 002
    NONE GOOD BUT GOD -- A WARNING WAVED TO   •   •   •   •   157 00 023
WAVER
    (AND HERE THE FAITHFUL WAVER, THE FAITHLESS FABLE AND MISS)   •   •   028 06 008
WAVES
    THE WAVES WERE ROSY-LIPP'D; THE CRIMSON GLARE   •   •   •   002 00 024
    LINGER'D, THEN RAISED THE WASHING WAVES AND DRENCH'D   •   •   002 00 138
    WITH LIGHT ON HER FACE LIKE THE WAVES AT PLAY,   •   •   •   026 00 004
    HIM, AFTER AN HOUR OF WINTRY WAVES,   •   •   •   •   041 00 069
WAVING
    DOWN? NO WAVING OFF OF THESE MOST MOURNFUL MESSENGERS, C   •   •   059 0L 004
    STARS WAVING THEIR INDIVISIBLE RAYS.   •   •   •   •   098 23 001
WAXED
    WILL HAVE WAKED AND HAVE WAXED AND HAVE WALKED C   •   •   059 0G 023
    THE FAIRER WAXED HE.   •   •   •   •   •   •   •   109 36 002
WAXEN
    THE WAXEN COLOURS WEEP AND RUN,   •   •   •   •   •   003 00 029
    AND PIERCE THE YELLOW WAXEN LIGHT   •   •   •   •   015 00 043
WAXES
    THE TRUMPET WAXES LOUD; TIRED ARE YOUR FEET.   •   •   •   005 00 008
WAY
    HE HIDES OUR CORPSES DROPPING BY THE WAY   •   •   •   005 00 005
    A PRESS OF WINGED THINGS COMES DOWN THIS WAY;   •   •   •   005 00 015
    THE VIGOROUS HORIZONTALS, EACH WAY FALL   •   •   •   012 02 003
    MY NATIONAL OLD EGYPTIAN REED GAVE WAY: •   •   •   020 00 007
    I MOVE ALONG LIFE'S TOMB-DECKED WAY   •   •   •   •   023 00 039
    BUT ROPED WITH, ALWAYS, ALL THE WAY DOWN FROM THE TALL   •   028 04 006
    WITH BELLED FIRE AND THE MOTH-SOFT MILKY WAY,   •   •   •   028 26 006
    YOUR WEALTH OF LIFE IS SOME WAY SPENT: •   •   •   029 00 014
    ' HER COMMANDER! AND THOU TOO, AND THOU THIS WAY. '   •   041 00 052
    THE MARVELLOUS MILK WAS WALSINGHAM WAY   •   •   •   041 00 102
    OFF, AND NO WAY BUT SO.   •   •   •   •   •   •   060 00 033
    THAT MAMMOCKS, MIGHTY FOOT. BUT NO WAY SPED,   •   •   070 00 012
    WHO RISING LATE HAD MISS'D HER PAINFUL WAY   •   •   •   079 00 005
    LIFTS THEM A LITTLE WAY ABOVE.   •   •   •   •   •   081 00 038
    TEACH ME THE WAY: I WILL REPENT.   •   •   •   •   081 00 136
    IT IS THE WAY WITH PHILOMEL   •   •   •   •   •   096 03 003
    SKY FLEECED WITH THE MILKY WAY.   •   •   •   •   098 23 002
    BIDS HIM THIS WAY HIS GAZES FIX.   •   •   •   •   120 00 015
    AND HOW LONG WAS THE WAY? THIS SHORTER WAY?   •   •   125 00 011
    AND HOW LONG WAS THE WAY? THIS SHORTER WAY?   •   •   125 00 011
    THE WORDS CAME FROM A COURT ACROSS THE WAY.   •   •   136 00 023
    SHE MENDS THE WAY SHE MEANS TO GO.   •   •   •   •   145 00 012
    REASON, SELFDISPOSAL, CHOICE OF BETTER OR WORSE WAY.   •   152 02 061
    SO KIND TO THOSE WHO ASK THE WAY,   •   •   •   •   167 00 010
    BUT JUST THE WAY THAT THOU DIDST ME   •   •   •   •   170 00 018
WAYLAY
    WAYLAY HER AT EBB, PAST PENMAEN POOL.   •   •   •   030 00 024
WAYS
    AND FOLIAG'D CROWNALS (POINTING HOW THE WAYS   •   •   001 06 004
    FIVE WAYS THE PRECIOUS BRANCHES TORN;   •   •   •   006 00 014
    LO, LINKED HEAVENS WITH MILKY WAYS!   •   •   •   •   010 00 021
    PEACE AND FOOD CHEERED ME WHERE FOUR ROUGH WAYS MEET.   •   020 00 012
    OUR PRAYER SEEMS LOST IN DESERT WAYS,   •   •   •   023 00 005
    THEE, MAY-HOPE OF OUR DARKENED WAYS!   •   •   •   •   026 00 040
    COME THEN, YOUR WAYS AND AIRS AND LOOKS, LOCKS, C   •   •   059 0G 014
    WINNING WAYS, AIRS INNOCENT, MAIDEN MANNERS, C   •   •   059 0G 015
    MINDS ME IN MANY WAYS   •   •   •   •   •   •   060 00 016
    THIS NIGHT! WHAT SIGHTS YOU, HEART, SAW; WAYS YOU WENT!   •   067 00 003

WAYS   (CONTINUED)
    HIS CRISP COMBS, AND THAT COMES THOSE WAYS WE KNOW. 068 00 014
    WHY DO SINNERS' WAYS PROSPER? AND WHY MUST 074 00 003
    I FOUND THE WAYS WERE SOWN WITH SALT 081 00 155
    WITHAL HER MIEN IS MODEST, WAYS ARE WISE. 136 00 019
    I LOOK ALL WAYS BUT ONLY SEE 160 00 017
    IN THE VERY WAYS THAT THY LIFE GOES 169 00 005
WEAK
    A SIMPLE PASSAGE OF WEAK NOTES 003 00 013
    AND SOUL IS SUBTLE AND FLESH WEAK 077 00 037
WEAKNESS
    OH! EVEN FOR THE WEAKNESS OF THE PLEA 013 00 008
WEAL
    IN WIDE THE WORLD'S WEAL; RARE GOLD, BOLD STEEL, BARE   .   .   .   070 00 017
WEALD
    FROM FURROWS OF THE POOR AND STINTING WEALD. 017 00 013
WEALTH
    YOUR WEALTH OF LIFE IS SOME WAY SPENT: 029 00 014
    WITH WEALTH THAT MOCKS HIS HIGH DEGREE, ...   124 00 022
    FOR WEALTH AS WIDE AS WEARINESS? 166 00 048
WEAR
    BEAUTY NOW FOR ASHES WEAR, ...   024 00 019
    MORE WILL WEAR THIS WAND AND THEN 025 00 039
    ALL THE AIR THINGS WEAR THAT BUILD THIS WORLD OF WALES;   .   .   .   034 00 010
    FREQUENTING THERE WHILE MOON SHALL WEAR AND WEND. 035 00 004
    AND NONE RECK OF WORLD AFTER, THIS BIDS WEAR 058 00 013
    AND SCARLET WEAR THE SPIRIT OF WAR THERE EXPRESS. 063 00 008
    AND WEAR IT THUS, A PECTORAL, BY MY HEART. 102 01 028
    IF HE WEAR THE CROWN UPON HIS HEAD 109 23 001
    IF HE WEAR A CROWN UPON HIS HEAD 109 23 003
    THAT WILL NOT WEAR A PRINT, THAT WILL NOT STAIN A PEN,   .   .   .   152 C 016
    HIS BLEACHED BOTH AND WOOLWOVEN WEAR: 159 00 029
    AND CRIMSON WEAR OF STARRY SHOT 166 00 042
    THEO. AND MORE SHALL WEAR THIS WAND AND THEN   .   .   .   .   .   APPEN A 45
WEARIEST
    THEN EVEN IN WEARIEST WINTRY HOUR 030 00 029
WEARINESS
    MUST WATCH DOWN WITH WEARINESS 160 00 009
    FOR WEALTH AS WIDE AS WEARINESS? 166 00 048
WEARS
    AND WEARS MAN'S SMUDGE AND SHARES MAN'S SMELL: THE SOIL   .   .   .   031 00 007
    WITHIN HER WEARS, BEARS, CARES AND COMBS THE SAME: 076 00 006
WEARY
    YE WEARY, COME INTO THE SHADE. 006 00 026
    YOUR SCARCE-SHEATHED BONES ARE WEARY OF BEING BENT: .   .   .   011 00 013
    O THEN, WEARY THEN WHY SHOULD WE TREAD? C 059 06 026
    IN ME OR, MOST WEARY, CRY I CAN NO MORE. I CAN; 064 00 003
    ME, WERE I PLEADING, PLEAD NOR DO I: I WEAR- 066 00 007
    Y OF IDLE A BEING BUT BY WHERE WARS ARE RIFE. 066 00 008
    WANTS WAR, WANTS WOUNDS; WEARY HIS TIMES, HIS TASKS;   .   .   .   068 00 003
    ' THIS WEARY MARTINMAS, WOULD IT WERE SUMMER ' 111 00 010
    WE CANNOT LIVE THIS LIFE OUT; SOMETIMES WE MUST WEARY   .   .   .   152 02 047
WEATHER
    BLINDS HER; BUT SHE THAT WEATHER SEES ONE THING, ONE;   .   .   .   028 19 005
    WOKE THEE WITH A WE ARE PERISHING IN THE WEATHER OF GENNESARETH.   .   028 25 006
    BUT WHAT'S TO SEE IN STORMY WEATHER, ...   030 00 025
    MUST IT, WORST WEATHER, ...   041 00 015
    THEIR ROCKY LODGES, THEN THE WEATHER RARE 080 04 005
    GEM-FLEECED AT MORN, SO BRILLIANT IS THE WEATHER. 099 00 004
    SO STRANGELY ELEMENTED IS MY MIND'S WEATHER, ...   102 01 015
WEB
    WITH A SUBTLE WEB OF BLACK. 004 00 020
    SHE, WILD WEB, WONDROUS ROBE, ...   060 00 038
    THUS HE TIES SPIDER'S WEB ACROSS HIS SIGHT 102 03 028
    SUCH SPIDER'S WEB HE TIES ACROSS HIS SIGHT, V 102 03 034
WEBBED
    THE WEBBED AND THE WATERY WEST 003 00 022
WEBB'D
    THEY WEBB'D THE SKY WITH GLASSY LIGHT. 087 00 002
WEBS
    OF THOSE GILT WEBS THAT LANGUISH'D IN A FALL. 001 08 007
WED
    ' THEN WILL YOU WED WITH AN ENGLISH LADY, ...   109 08 003
    SAYS ' GET YOU, GET YOU A LADY TO WED 109 09 001
    ' AND IF I CHOSE A LOVE TO WED 109 10 001
    SAID, IT WAS NOT MEET THE KING SHOULD WED 109 12 003
    WHO MEANS TO WED OR MEANS TO KILL, ...   120 00 029
    HER WEEDS ALL MARK HER MAIDEN, THOUGH TO WED, ...   136 00 017
    LET WINTER WED ONE, SOW THEM IN HER WOMB, ...   158 00 003
WEDDED
    HE'S WEDDED TO HIS THEORY, THEY SAY. 097 00 001
    THEY WERE WEDDED AT MIDNIGHT 109 01 001
    AS WEDDED YOU MUST BE? ' 109 08 004
WEDLOCK
    WHO TO WEDLOCK, HIS WONDER WEDLOCK, ...   052 00 011
    WHO TO WEDLOCK, HIS WONDER WEDLOCK, ...   052 00 011
    WEDLOCK. WHAT THE WATER? SPOUSAL LOVE. 159 00 047

284

WEDS
    HOW SHAKESPEARE'S ENGLAND WEDS WITH DANTE'S ITALY. • • • • • 098 35 002
WEED
    WITH LACE OF ROSY WEED WERE CHAPLETED; • • • • • • • 002 00 059
    I FALL, I TEAR AND SHOWER THE WEED, • • • • • • • 081 00 064
    AND BARLEY TURN TO WEED AND WILD, • • • • • • • 114 00 005
WEEDED
    OR WEEDED LANDSLIPS OF THE SHORE. • • • • • • • 015 00 024
WEEDIO-WEEDIO
    WEEDIO-WEEDIO: THERE AGAIN! • • • • • • • • 138 00 003
WEED-BATHED
    HER WHITE WEED-BATHED KNEES ARE SHUT TOGETHER, • • • • 099 00 002
WEED-WINDING
    ON MEADOW AND RIVER AND WIND-WANDERING WEED-WINDING BANK. • • • 043 00 008
WEEDS
    THE DRENCHED HAIR OF SLABBY WEEDS THAT SWUNG • • • • 002 00 113
    WHEN WEEDS, IN WHEELS, SHOOT LONG AND LOVELY AND LUSH; • • • 033 00 002
    HE LIVED ON: THESE WEEDS AND WATERS, THESE WALLS ARE WHAT • • 044 00 010
    LONG LIVE THE WEEDS AND THE WILDERNESS YET. • • • • 056 00 016
    HER WEEDS ALL MARK HER MAIDEN, THOUGH TO WED, • • • • 136 00 017
WEEK
    YOU MAY DEPEND THAT ERE A WEEK WAS FLED. • • • • • 097 00 005
WEEKS
    LATE IN THE GREEN WEEKS OF APRIL • • • • • • • 081 00 021
    THE WEIGHTY WEEKS WITHOUT HANDS GROW, • • • • • • 145 00 005
WEEP
    DOWN THAT DANK ROCK O'ER WHICH THEIR LUSH LONG TRESSES WEEP. • • 002 00 115
    THE WAXEN COLOURS WEEP AND RUN, • • • • • • • 003 00 029
    AND YET YOU WILL WEEP AND KNOW WHY. • • • • • • 055 00 009
    MAIDENS SHALL WEEP AT MERRY MORN, • • • • • • • 114 00 001
WEEPING
    AND WITH WEEPING CLOUD IS SPREAD • • • • • • • 077 00 095
    WEEPING, -- EVEN NOW I CURSE MYSELF REMEMBERING: -- • • • 102 01 041
    AS SHE LAY WEEPING AT THE NIGHT • • • • • • • 109 29 001
WEEPINGS
    WITH FIERCER WEEPINGS OF THESE DESPERATE EYES • • • • 014 03 006
WEEPS
    WHERE PHOEBUS WEEPS FOR HIM WHOM ZEPHYR'S GUILE • • • 001 11 007
    A THING THAT WEEPS, ENDURING LONG; • • • • • • 081 00 050
WEIGH
    BUT WHY THEN SHOULD CASTARA WEIGH WITH ME? • • • • 125 00 034
WEIGHED
    ONE ONCE THAT WAS FOUND WANTING WHEN GOOD WEIGHED. • • • 157 00 024
WEIGHING
    THY UNCHANCELLING POISING PALMS WERE WEIGHING THE WORTH, • • • 028 21 006
WEIGHT
    IN MOTION IS NO WEIGHT OR PAIN, • • • • • • • 130 00 015
WEIGHTY
    THE WEIGHTY WEEKS WITHOUT HANDS GROW, • • • • • • 145 00 005
WELCOME
    SHOULD HAVE PEALED WITH WELCOME, WALES, • • • • • 029 00 018
    WELCOME IN WOMB AND BREAST, • • • • • • • • 060 00 020
    MAKES WELCOME DEATH, DOES DEAR FORGETFULNESS. • • • • 150 00 008
    HIS DEACON, DIRVAN, WARM TWICE OVER MUST THE WELCOME BE, • • 152 01 008
    O WELCOME THERE THEIR STEEL OR CANNON. • • • • • 156 00 017
WELKIN
    AND DOWN THE WELKIN, GUSHING FREE, • • • • • • 077 00 085
    ALL THE WELKIN OVERHEAD, • • • • • • • • 077 00 096
    LIKE KNOCKING THUNDER ALL ROUND BRITAIN'S WELKIN, • • • 102 02 003
    THE SMOULDERING ENORMOUS WINTER WELKIN! MAY • • • • 149 A 008
    THE SMOULDERING ENORMOUS WINTER WELKIN. [EYE, V • • • 149 B 009
WELL
    ELSE I AM WELL ASSURED I SHOULD OFFEND • • • • • 014 03 005
    KNOWING THEM WELL I CAN BUT SEE THE FALL. • • • • 016 00 010
    YET MADE ITS MARKET HERE AS WELL; • • • • • • 025 00 032
    MARY THE VIRGIN, WELL THE HEART KNOWS, • • • • • 027 00 021
    I STEADY AS A WATER IN A WELL, TO A POISE, TO A PANE, • • 028 04 005
    WELL, SHE HAS THEE FOR THE PAIN, FOR THE • • • • 028 31 001
    O WHERE LIVE WELL YOUR LEASE OF LEISURE • • • • • 030 00 003
    AH WELL! IT IS ALL A PURCHASE, ALL IS A PRIZE. • • • 032 00 008
    O WELL WEPT, MOTHER HAVE LOST SON: • • • • • • 041 00 105
    WELL BUT THERE WAS MORE THAN THIS: • • • • • • 042 00 033
    O NOW WELL WORK THAT SEALING SACRED OINTMENT! • • • • 048 00 033
    TENDERED TO HIM. AH WELL, GOD REST HIM ALL ROAD EVER HE OFFENDED! • 053 00 008
    LOVE-LACED! -- WHAT ONCE I WELL • • • • • • • 054 00 003
    THOU CANST BUT BE, BUT THAT THOU WELL DOST; STRONG • • • 058 00 005
    SOMEWHERE ELSEWHERE THERE IS AH WELL WHERE! ONE, • • • 059 06 006
    BY A GREY EYE'S HEED STEERED WELL, ONE CREW, FALL TO; • • 071 00 004
    AT LAST I HEAR THE VOICE WELL KNOWN: • • • • • 081 00 001
    YOU CRIED ' BUT I HAVE SERVED THEE WELL, • • • • • 081 00 107
    MY LOVE: AND ALL WAS SWEET AND WELL. • • • • • 081 00 121
    (AND, WELL SUPPLIED WITH VIRTUES ON THE WHOLE, • • • 094 00 027
    MISS M.'S A NIGHTINGALE. 'TIS WELL • • • • • • 096 03 001
    -- YES FOR A TIME THEY HELD AS WELL • • • • • 101 00 001
    WELL, I KNOW NOT, BUT ALL THINGS SEEM TO-NIGHT • • • 102 01 010
    AFFINED WELL TO THAT SWEET SOLITUDE, • • • • • 107 01 015
    IN COPYING WELL WHAT YOU HAVE BEST BEGUN. • • • • 125 00 020

WELL   (CONTINUED)

WELL, AFTER ALL! AH BUT HARK -- 138 00 010
HER MOULD OF FEATURES MATED WELL. 145 00 016
IT WILL NOT WELL, SO SHE WOULD BRING ABOUT 151 00 003
WARNED HER! WELL SHE KNEW I WARNED HER OF THIS WORK.   .   .   .   152 02 007
WIPED I AM SURE THIS WAS: IT SEEMS, NOT WELL; FOR STILL,   .   .   .   152 02 012
HERE TO THIS HOLY WELL SHALL PILGRIMAGES BE, ...   152 C 018
ONE SPELL AND WELL THAT ONE. THERE, AH THEREBY 153 00 007
AS WELL THE SISTER SITS, WOULD WELL THE WIFE; 157 00 014
AS WELL THE SISTER SITS, WOULD WELL THE WIFE; 157 00 014
AH WELL A DAY! -- 160 00 019
SITH I LOV'D AND LOV'D TOO WELL 160 00 030
JESU, A SPRINGING WELL THOU ART, ...   167 00 017
BE IN THY SERVANTS' HEARTS AS WELL, ...   169 00 002
THEO. YET MADE YOUR MARKET HERE AS WELL;   .   .   .   .   .   APPEN A 32

WELLBEING
HIES HEADSTRONG TO ITS WELLBEING OF A SELF-WISE SELF-WILL!   .   .   048 00 024

WELLING
AND TURNS TO WASH IT FROM HER WELLING EYES 151 00 005

WELL-BRED
BLINDNESS! A LEARNED FOOL AND WELL-BRED CHURL 102 03 032
A LEARNED FOOL INDEED AND WELL-BRED CHURL V 102 03 038

WELLS
BEHOLD AT ELIM WELLS ON EVERY HAND 005 00 023
AS TUMBLED OVER RIM IN ROUNDY WELLS 057 00 002
CUCKOO, BIRD, AND OPEN EAR WELLS, HEART-SPRINGS, DELIGHTFULLY SWEET,   146 00 002

WEND
FREQUENTING THERE WHILE MOON SHALL WEAR AND WEND. 035 00 004
TO WEND AND MEET NO SIN; 060 00 117

WENT
AND THRO' THEIR PARTING LIDS THERE CAME AND WENT 002 00 011
YOU WENT INTO THE PARTLESS AIR. 025 00 030
IT WAS MADE OF EARTH'S MOULD BUT IT WENT FROM MEN'S EYES   .   .   027 00 003
AND THOUGH THE LAST LIGHTS OFF THE BLACK WEST WENT   .   .   .   031 00 011
THIS NIGHT! WHAT SIGHTS YOU, HEART, SAW; WAYS YOU WENT!   .   .   067 00 003
COULD CROWD CAREER WITH CONQUEST WHILE THERE WENT   .   .   .   073 00 012
ON CHEBAR'S BANKS, AND WHY THEY WENT 077 00 049
WENT FORTH TO COMPASS MYSTERIES; 077 00 052
TO ALIEN EAVES YOU FLED AND WENT, -- 081 00 005
TEACH ME THE PACES THAT YOU WENT 081 00 125
IN EDDIES OF THE WIND HE WENT 087 00 005
SYLVESTER CAME; THEY WENT BY CUMNOR HILL, ...   107 03 009
BEFORE HE WENT TO SEA. 109 01 004
I THOUGHT THAT YOU WOULD HAVE WRITTEN: MY BIRTHDAY CAME AND WENT,   .   128 00 001
WORD WENT SHE SHOULD BE CRUSHED OUT FLAT 145 00 038
ON ONE THAT WENT AGAINST ME WHEREAS I HAD WARNED HER --   .   .   152 02 006
THE ANGEL WENT AWAY THEREON   .   .   .   .   APPEN D 31

WEPT
O WELL WEPT, MOTHER HAVE LOST SON; 041 00 105
WEPT, WIFE; WEPT, SWEETHEART WOULD BE ONE; 041 00 106
WEPT, WIFE; WEPT, SWEETHEART WOULD BE ONE; 041 00 106

WEST
PLUM-PURPLE WAS THE WEST; BUT SPIKES OF LIGHT 002 00 007
NOW ALL THINGS ROSY TURN'D; THE WEST HAD GROWN 002 00 019
THE WEBBED AND THE WATERY WEST 003 00 022
KISS MY HAND TO THE DAPPLED-WITH-DAMSON WEST; 028 05 005
AWAY IN THE LOVEABLE WEST, ...   028 24 001
AND THOUGH THE LAST LIGHTS OFF THE BLACK WEST WENT   .   .   .   031 00 011
A WILDER BEAST FROM WEST THAN ALL WERE, MORE 050 00 007
HER FOND YELLOW HORNLIGHT WOUND TO THE WEST, C 061 00 003
SAVE WHERE THE UNVEXED WEST 077 00 097
WHEN LILY-YELLOW IS THE WEST. 081 00 055
OR IF HE LEAVE THE WEST BEHIND, ...   083 00 005
AND JUSTIFY THE EAST AND WEST; 130 00 004
OR TEMPE WITH THE WEST TO BLOW. 166 00 024

WESTERN
IN ALL OUR WESTERN SHIRES WAS RARE, ...   021 00 023

WESTER'D
THERE IS AN ISLAND, WESTER'D IN THE MAIN, ...   098 04 001

WESTWARD
WESTWARD ON HIS SINKING SIRE; 077 00 124

WET
EVEN YOUR UNPASSION'D EYELIDS MIGHT BE WET. 014 01 014
I ONLY FEARED THE WET FOR YOU 021 00 013
WOOD BANKS AND BRAKES WASH WET LIKE LAKES 042 00 042
OF WET AND OF WILDNESS? LET THEM BE LEFT, ...   056 00 014
O LET THEM BE LEFT, WILDNESS AND WET; 056 00 015
THIRST'S ALL-IN-ALL IN ALL A WORLD OF WET. 069 00 008
THE TIME WAS LATE AND THE WET YELLOW WOODS 098 05 001
FLARES HIS WET BRILLIANCE IN THE DINTLESS HEAVEN.   .   .   .   098 34 002
HER NOSTRIL GLISTENS; AND HER WET BLACK EYE 099 00 005
THEO. WHILE SUCH A WONDER'S WET AND WARM!   .   .   .   .   APPEN A 36

WETHER
THERE WAS NO BLEAT OF EWE, NO CHIME OF WETHER,   .   .   .   107 01 005

WET-FRESH
THOSE LOVELY LADS ONCE, WET-FRESH WINDFALLS OF WAR'S STORM,   .   062 00 006

WHARF
THE GIRTH OF IT AND THE WHARF OF IT AND THE WALL;   .   .   .   028 32 004

WHARVES
    ITS BRINDLED WHARVES AND YELLOW BRIM.   •   •   •   •   •   •   003 00 028
    AND NUMBS AND STARVES, AS BETWEEN ICY WHARVES   •   •   •   •   080 03 006
WHATEVER
    WHATEVER IS FICKLE, FRECKLED (WHO KNOWS HOW?)   •   •   •   •   037 00 008
    WHATEVER TIME THIS VAPOUROUS ROOF,   •   •   •   •   •   •   080 06 001
    HAMPSTEAD WAS NEVER BRIGHT; AND WHATEVER MISS CULLY'S CHARMS   •   128 00 011
WHATEVER'S
    WHERE WHATEVER'S PRIZED AND PASSES OF US, C   •   •   •   •   059 06 008
WHEAT
    RUNS HIS FINGERS THROUGH THE WHEAT,   •   •   •   •   •   •   098 01 002
WHEATFIELDS
    WHEATFIELDS TUMBLED WITH THE RAINS,   •   •   •   •   •   077 00 136
WHEAT-ACRE
    THE BLUE WHEAT-ACRE IS UNDERNEATH   •   •   •   •   •   •   138 00 018
WHEEL
    FROM WINGS SWAN-FLEDGED A WHEEL OF WATERY LIGHT   •   •   •   002 00 076
    AND CANVAS AND COMPASS, THE WHORL AND THE WHEEL   •   •   028 14 007
    HIS STEADY WHEEL QUITE TO THE FULL AGAIN.   •   •   •   •   107 03 012
WHEELS
    WHEN WEEDS, IN WHEELS, SHOOT LONG AND LOVELY AND LUSH;   •   •   033 00 002
WHELM'D
    OF SEAMEN WHELM'D IN CHASMS OF THE MID-MAIN,   •   •   •   002 00 120
WHELMS
    OUR NIGHT WHELMS, WHELMS, AND WILL END US. C   •   •   •   061 00 008
    OUR NIGHT WHELMS, WHELMS, AND WILL END US. C   •   •   •   061 00 008
WHENCE
    WHENCE WITH THE SCOURGE OF READY PIETY   •   •   •   •   •   001 05 004
    NOW RINGING CLARION-CLEAR TO WHENCE IT ROSE   •   •   •   002 00 134
    WHENCE OFT I WATCH BUT SEE THOSE MERMAIDS NOW NO MORE.   •   •   002 00 143
    AN OLIVE-BRANCH WHENCE RICHLY REEK   •   •   •   •   •   077 00 015
    WHENCE SPRING THE JEWELL'D HARMONIES   •   •   •   •   077 00 138
WHENEVER
    WINGS: SO SOME GREAT STORMFOWL, WHENEVER HE HAS WALKED HIS WHILE   •   045 00 011
WHEREAS
    WHEREAS DID AIR NOT MAKE   •   •   •   •   •   •   •   060 00 094
    ON ONE THAT WENT AGAINST ME WHEREAS I HAD WARNED HER --   •   •   152 02 006
WHEREFORE
    WHEREFORE WE LOVE THEE, WHEREFORE WE SING TO THEE,   •   •   026 00 033
    WHEREFORE WE LOVE THEE, WHEREFORE WE SING TO THEE,   •   •   026 00 033
WHEREIN
    WHEREIN BENEATH THE CORNICE, HORSEMEN RODE   •   •   •   •   001 07 007
    WHEREIN HE MAKES US STRAY.   •   •   •   •   •   •   005 00 006
    MY HAPPIER WORLD, WHEREIN.   •   •   •   •   •   •   060 00 116
WHEREOF
    SHALL BE THIS THING WHEREOF TIDING I BRING;   •   •   •   •   APPEN D 17
WHEREON
    I NEVER SAW THOSE FIELDS WHEREON THEIR BEST   •   •   •   •   119 00 011
WHEREVER
    DOWN ROUGHCAST, DOWN DAZZLING WHITEWASH, WHEREVER AN ELM ARCHES,   072 00 003
WHETHER
    ON MERMAIDS -- WHETHER THAT THEY RING THE KNELLS   •   •   •   002 00 119
    WHETHER AT ONCE, AS ONCE AT A CRASH PAUL,   •   •   •   •   028 10 005
    SHE NOT CONSIDERED WHETHER OR NO   •   •   •   •   •   145 00 033
    SAY IT IS ASHBOUGHS: WHETHER ON A DECEMBER DAY AND FURLED   •   •   149 A 004
WHILE
    PHILIP TOOK OATH, WHILE GLORY OR DEFEAT   •   •   •   •   001 02 003
    WHILE HIS CRACK'D FLESH LAY HISSING ON THE GRATE;   •   •   001 03 002
    WHILE FROM THE PULPIT IN A HERETIC LAND   •   •   •   •   001 05 001
    BUT, HAPLESS YOUTH, ANTINOUS THE WHILE   •   •   •   •   001 11 005
    BLAZE FOR HIM ALL THIS WHILE.   •   •   •   •   •   •   005 00 036
    AND SO, THOUGH EACH HAVE ONE WHILE I HAVE ALL,   •   •   •   016 00 012
    BUT WATCHING WHILE THE COLOUR GREW   •   •   •   •   •   021 00 012
    THUS FRANCES SIGHED AT HOME, WHILE LUKE   •   •   •   •   021 00 050
    WHILE HE WAS WASHING FROM ON DECK   •   •   •   •   •   021 00 054
    WHILE AGES AND WHILE AEONS RUN,   •   •   •   •   •   023 00 020
    WHILE AGES AND WHILE AEONS RUN,   •   •   •   •   •   023 00 020
    INDEED WHILE SUCH A WONDER'S WARM.   •   •   •   •   •   025 00 036
    FREQUENTING THERE WHILE MOON SHALL WEAR AND WEND.   •   •   035 00 004
    WINGS: SO SOME GREAT STORMFOWL, WHENEVER HE HAS WALKED HIS WHILE   •   045 00 011
    GIVE GOD WHILE WORTH CONSUMING.   •   •   •   •   •   049 00 007
    ALL WHILE HER PATIENCE, MORSELLED INTO PANGS,   •   •   •   050 00 012
    WITH THE WIND WHAT WHILE WE SLEPT, C   •   •   •   •   059 06 023
    WHAT WHILE WE, WHILE WE SLUMBERED.   •   •   •   •   •   059 06 025
    WHAT WHILE WE, WHILE WE SLUMBERED.   •   •   •   •   •   059 06 025
    COULD CROWD CAREER WITH CONQUEST WHILE THERE WENT   •   •   073 00 012
    WHILE THE SUN STREAMS FORTH AMAIN   •   •   •   •   •   077 00 103
    THEN WHILE THE RAIN-BORN ARC GLOWS HIGHER   •   •   •   077 00 123
    WHILE THE UPGAZING COUNTRY SEEMS   •   •   •   •   •   077 00 125
    WHILE A SUBTLE SPIRIT AND RARE   •   •   •   •   •   077 00 127
    WHILE SHEENY TEARS AND SUNLIT MIRTH   •   •   •   •   077 00 129
    WHILE THE BREEZE BY RANK AND MEASURE   •   •   •   •   078 00 009
    BUT ALL THE WHILE IT SEEM'D TO ME   •   •   •   •   •   081 00 112
    HAS DANCED WITH HER; AND ALL THE WHILE   •   •   •   •   083 00 023
    TO SING WHILE OTHERS SLEEP.   •   •   •   •   •   •   096 03 004
    THUS WE SHALL PROFIT, WHILE GOLD COINAGE STILL   •   •   •   096 07 007
    WHILE PHOSPHOR, RISEN UPON THE SHALLOWING DARK,   •   •   098 28 003

WHILE   (CONTINUED)
    ROUND THIS UNSEXING DOUBLET, -- WHILE I SET 102 01 004
    SLEEP FLORIS WHILE I ROB YOU. TIGHTEN, O SLEEP, ... 102 01 017
    AND SPINS HER SKIRTS OUT, WHILE HER CENTRAL STAR 103 00 007
    NOW WHILE THE FULL-LEAVED HURSTS UNALTER'D STAND, ... 105 00 003
    WHILE THERE IS NEITHER SUN NOR RAIN: 105 00 006
    EPISTLES, WHILE THE RUNNING PASTORAL BLEATS 107 04 022
    WHICH SAYS AT LEAST THEN GO WHILE ALL IS FRESH, -- 125 00 058
    WHILE ALL THINGS ELSE MAY STIR AND RANGE 130 00 007
    AND WHILE I SAIL (MUST LISTEN) I SING. 138 00 015
    TO TAKE HER; WHILE THEIR TONGUES WOULD GO 145 00 026
    BEUNO. O NOW WHILE SKIES ARE BLUE, NOW WHILE SEAS ARE SALT, ... 152 C 001
    BEUNO. O NOW WHILE SKIES ARE BLUE, NOW WHILE SEAS ARE SALT, ... 152 C 001
    WHILE RUSHY RAINS SHALL FALL OR BROOKS SHALL FLEET FROM FOUNTAINS, .   . 152 C 002
    WHILE SICK MEN SHALL CAST SIGHS, OF SWEET HEALTH ALL DESPAIRING, .   .   . 152 C 003
    WHILE BLIND MEN'S EYES SHALL THIRST C .   .   .   . 152 C 004
    WHILE CRIPPLES ARE, WHILE LEPERS, DANCERS IN DISMAL LIMBDANCE, .   .   . 152 C 006
    WHILE CRIPPLES ARE, WHILE LEPERS, DANCERS IN DISMAL LIMBDANCE, .   .   . 152 C 006
    WHILE HE LOOKS ABOUT HIM, LAUGHS, SWIMS. C 159 00 042
    THEO. WHILE SUCH A WONDER'S WET AND WARM! .   .   .   . APPEN A 36
WHILST
    AND THOU ART SILENT, WHILST THY WORLD 023 00 031
WHIP-ADDER
    THE COLD WHIP-ADDER UNESPIED 106 00 001
WHIPS
    YOU STRIPED IN SECRET WITH BREATH-TAKING WHIPS, ... 011 00 003
WHIRL
    IN CRISPS OF CURL OFF WILD WINCH WHIRL, AND POUR 035 00 007
    ALL ELSE MAY WHIRL OR DIVE OR FLY. 130 00 008
WHIRLED
    I WHIRLED OUT WINGS THAT SPELL 028 03 004
WHIRLING
    WITH BRINE AND SHINE AND WHIRLING WIND. 041 00 080
WHIRLWIND
    WRETCH, UNDER A COMFORT SERVES IN A WHIRLWIND: ALL 065 00 013
WHIRLWIND-SWIVEL
    WIRY AND WHITE-FIERY AND WHIRLWIND-SWIVELLED SNOW 028 13 007
WHISPER
    SPEAK! WHISPER TO MY WATCHING HEART 023 00 049
WHISPERS
    WHISPERS ' IF THOU HAVE WARMTH AT HEART 080 11 004
    WHISPERS OF THE MID-AIR STIRRING 160 00 034
WHITE
    FROM THEIR WHITE WAISTS A SILVER SKIRT WAS SPREAD 002 00 048
    OTHERS WITH FINGERS WHITE WOULD COMB AMONG 002 00 112
    WHITE LOOM'D MY ROCK, THE WATER GURGLING O'ER, ... 002 00 142
    SO GLASSY WHITE ABOUT THE SKY, ... 003 00 016
    WHITE TO BEGIN WITH, IMMACULATE WHITE. 027 00 032
    WHITE TO BEGIN WITH, IMMACULATE WHITE. 027 00 032
    -- BLACK, WHITE; RIGHT, WRONG; RECKON BUT, RECK BUT, MIND C 061 00 012
    THE SAPPHIRE POOLS ARE SMIT WITH WHITE 078 00 007
    A BASKET BROAD OF WOVEN WHITE RODS 098 19 001
    HER WHITE WEED-BATHED KNEES ARE SHUT TOGETHER, ... 099 00 002
    IF IT BE A WHITE ROSE IN HIS HAND, ... 109 22 001
    THEIR CLOUDS WITH BREATHING EDGES WHITE 130 00 023
    IN THE WHITE AND THE WALK OF THE MORNING: C 137 00 001
    WITH WHITE STROKES AND STRAINS OF THE BLUE. 138 00 017
WHITEBEAM
    WIND-BEAT WHITEBEAM! AIRY ABELES SET ON A FLARE! 032 00 006
WHITE-FACED
    WHITE-FACED, AS ONE IN SAD ASSAY TO FLY 079 00 008
WHITE-FIERY
    WIRY AND WHITE-FIERY AND WHIRLWIND-SWIVELLED SNOW 028 13 007
WHITEST
    TIME WAS, NEXT WHITEST AFTER MARY'S OWN. 136 00 004
WHITEWASH
    DOWN ROUGHCAST, DOWN DAZZLING WHITEWASH, WHEREVER AN ELM ARCHES, 072 00 003
WHOLE
    SOON THE WHOLE WORLD IS OVERSPREAD: 006 00 025
    THE WHOLE WORLD PASSES; I STAND BY. 015 00 004
    (AND, WELL SUPPLIED WITH VIRTUES ON THE WHOLE, ... 094 00 027
    THERE WOULD NOT BE A WHOLE PLACE IN HIS HEAD. 097 00 006
    THE WHOLE LANDSCAPE FLUSHES ON A SUDDEN AT A SOUND. 146 00 005
WHOLESALE
    WIDER, MORE WHOLESALE: ONE WITH CLAIM 166 00 010
WHOLESOME
    WHEN WHOLESOME SPIRITS RUSTLE ABOUT, ... 077 00 027
    ARE WASTE, AND HAD NO WHOLESOME FOODS, ... 081 00 166
WHOLLY
    OR WHOLLY WINDS HIM TO HER WILL. 120 00 031
WHORL
    AND CANVAS AND COMPASS, THE WHORL AND THE WHEEL 028 14 007
WHORLED
    AND BEAT UPON MY WHORLED EAR, ... 022 00 002
WICKED
    GROWN WICKED IN THE WICKED WARS. 114 00 012
    GROWN WICKED IN THE WICKED WARS. 114 00 012

288

WICKED   (CONTINUED)
    THEY WOUND THEIR WINCH OF WICKED SMILES 145 00 025
WICKET
    FLING TO THE CONVENT WICKET FAST. 081 00 075
WIDE
    MOST WIDE YE ARE WHO CALL THIS GUST SIMOOM. 005 00 026
    NOT GOSHEN. WASTEFUL WIDE HUGE-GIRTHED NILE 005 00 031
    OPEN WIDE YOUR HEARTS THAT THEY 024 00 023
    O WORLD WIDE OF ITS GOOD! 028 20 004
    WITH, ALL DOWN DARKNESS WIDE, HIS WADING LIGHT? 040 00 004
    IN WIDE THE WORLD'S WEAL: RARE GOLD, BOLD STEEL, BARE .   .   . 070 00 017
    WHEN SHE HAD MADE THE DOOR WIDE 109 30 003
    MAKE WIDE: -- THOU, O LORD OF SIN, ... 115 00 006
    THEY HAD THEM OUT AND LAID THEM WIDE 145 00 049
    FOR GOOD GROWS WILD AND WIDE, ... 148 00 025
    APART WIDE AND NEW-NESTLE AT HEAVEN MOST HIGH. .   .   .   . 149 A 006
    IN A WIDE WORLD OF DEFIANCE CARADOC LIVES ALONE, ... 152 02 039
    FOR WEALTH AS WIDE AS WEARINESS? 166 00 048
WIDER
    WIDER, MORE WHOLESALE: ONE WITH CLAIM 166 00 010
WIDOW
    THE WIDOW OF AN INSIGHT LOST SHE LIVES, WITH AIM 076 00 007
WIDOW-MAKING
    SPINS TO THE WIDOW-MAKING UNCHILDING UNFATHERING DEEPS. .   .   . 028 13 008
WIELD
    BUT BE THE WAR WITHIN, THE BRAND WE WIELD 073 00 006
WIFE
    WEPT, WIFE: WEPT, SWEETHEART WOULD BE ONE: 041 00 106
    ENGLAND, WHOSE HONOUR O ALL MY HEART WOOS, WIFE 066 00 005
    MARRIED, WILL MAKE A SWEET AND MATCHLESS WIFE, ... 094 00 031
    AS WELL THE SISTER SITS, WOULD WELL THE WIFE: 157 00 014
WILD
    BUT WHAT A WILD FLUSH ON THE FLAKES OF IT STOOD 027 00 033
    THE WILD WOMAN-KIND BELOW, ... 028 16 002
    ARE SISTERLY SEALED IN WILD WATERS, ... 028 23 007
    IN CRISPS OF CURL OFF WILD WINCH WHIRL, AND POUR .   .   . 035 00 007
    BUT HIS OWN NEST, WILD NEST, NO PRISON. 039 00 011
    TO ITS OWN FINE FUNCTION, WILD AND SELF-INSTRESSED, .   .   . 047 00 007
    WHEN WILL YOU EVER, PEACE, WILD WOODDOVE, SHY WINGS SHUT, .   . 051 00 001
    WILD AIR, WORLD-MOTHERING AIR, ... 060 00 001
    SHE, WILD WEB, WONDROUS ROBE, ... 060 00 038
    WORLD-MOTHERING AIR, AIR WILD, ... 060 00 124
    HER WILD HOLLOW HOARLIGHT HUNG TO THE HEIGHT C 061 00 003
    OF SHEEP FROM THE HIGH FIELDS AND OTHER WILD 107 04 023
    AND BARLEY TURN TO WEED AND WILD, ... 114 00 005
    HOW CAN HE BE? THE WORDS ARE WILD. 147 00 002
    HOW CAN HE BE? THE WORDS ARE WILD. 147 00 008
    FOR GOOD GROWS WILD AND WIDE, ... 148 00 025
    FALLERS IN DREADFUL FROTHPITS, WATERFEARERS WILD, .   .   . 152 C 007
    BUT IN PALE WATER, FRAIL WATER, WILD RASH AND REELING WATER, . 152 C 015
    MAY'S BEAUTY MASSACRE AND WISPED WILD CLOUDS GROW .   .   . 154 00 002
    AGAINST THE WILD AND WANTON WORK OF MEN. 157 00 036
    WILD WYCHELM, HORNBEAM FRETTY OVERSTOOD C 159 00 024
WILDER
    OF SILK-SACK CLOUDS! HAS WILDER, WILFUL-WAVIER 038 00 003
    A WILDER BEAST FROM WEST THAN ALL WERE, MORE 050 00 007
    MORE PANGS WILL, SCHOOLED AT FOREPANGS, WILDER WRING. .   . 065 00 002
WILDERNESS
    BUT I DESIRE THE WILDERNESS 015 00 023
    THEN FREE AND KIND THE WILDERNESS. 015 00 036
    LONG LIVE THE WEEDS AND THE WILDERNESS YET. 056 00 016
    O WHAT A SILENCE IS THIS WILDERNESS! 122 00 001
WILDFIRE
    FALL TO THE RESIDUARY WORM: WORLD'S WILDFIRE, LEAVE BUT ASH: . 072 00 020
WILDFLOWERS
    INTO FAIRY TREES, WILDFLOWERS, WOODFERNS 159 00 050
WILD-WORST
    CHRISTENS HER WILD-WORST BEST. C 028 24 008
WILDNESS
    OF WET AND OF WILDNESS? LET THEM BE LEFT, ... 056 00 014
    O LET THEM BE LEFT, WILDNESS AND WET: 056 00 015
WILDWORTH
    LIFE, THIS WILDWORTH BLOWN SO SWEET, ... 041 00 094
WILES
    WHEN I WITH NEVER-NEEDED WILES 135 00 003
WILFUL-WAVIER
    OF SILK-SACK CLOUDS! HAS WILDER, WILFUL-WAVIER 038 00 003
WILL
    IT IS GALILEE'S GROWTH: IT GREW AT GOD'S WILL 027 00 009
    AND WITH FIRE IN HIM FORGE THY WILL 028 13 002
    TILL A LIFEBELT AND GOD'S WILL 041 00 063
    THE AIRY EMPIRE AT HIS WILL: 077 00 078
    MISS STORY HAS A MODERATE POWER OF WILL, ... 094 00 009
    OR WHOLLY WINDS HIM TO HER WILL. 120 00 031
    SHE LENDS, IN AID OF WORK AND WILL, ... 139 00 003
    HER WILL WAS BENT AT GOD. FOR THAT 145 00 037
    YOUR WILL IS LAW IN THAT SMALL COMMONWEAL. 150 00 011

                            289

WILL   (CONTINUED)
            I DO NOT AND I WILL NOT REPENT, NOT REPENT. 152 02 033
            MAN LIVES THAT LIST, THAT LEANING IN THE WILL 157 00 025
            WORST WILL THE BEST. WHAT WORM WAS HERE WE CRY, ... 157 00 031
WILLIAM
            ' LORD WILLIAM THEY CALL ME. 109 05 002
            ' LORD WILLIAM COMES HUNTING TOMORROW MORNING, ... 109 19 003
            BUT HOW WILL YOU LORD WILLIAM KNOW 109 20 001
            ' YET HOW WILL YOU LORD WILLIAM KNOW 109 21 001
            ' O WHERE IS LORD WILLIAM, MY LORDS, ' SHE SAID, ... 109 25 003
            ' FIE, YOU ARE NOT LORD WILLIAM, ' SHE SAID; 109 26 003
            LORD WILLIAM IS KING OF ALL THIS LAND 109 27 003
WILLIAM'S
            SAYS ' ARE YOU NOT LORD WILLIAM'S LOVE 109 18 003
            ' I AM LORD WILLIAM'S LOVE, ' SHE SAID, ... 109 19 001
WILLING
            THERE IS THE SHILLING THAT FINDS ME WILLING 156 00 008
WILLOW
            THE COUNTRY SONG OF WILLOW. ' THE POOR SOUL -- 111 00 013
WILLOWS
            ROLLS ACROSS THE LABOURING WILLOWS; 078 00 004
WILL'D
            HAVE WILL'D TO BE DISPARADISED 118 00 003
WILLS
            TO BRUISE THEM DEARER. YET THE REBELLIOUS WILLS 068 00 010
WIMPLED
            CHEEK AND THE WIMPLED LIP, ... 049 00 002
WIMPLED-WATER-DI
            OF US, THE WIMPLED-WATER-DIMPLED, NOT-BY-MORNING-MATCHED FACE,   .   . 059 06 010
WIMPLING
            HIGH THERE, HOW HE RUNG UPON THE REIN OF A WIMPLING WING 036 00 004
WIN
            THAT I MAY WIN WITH LATE-LEARNT SKILL UNCOUTH 017 00 012
            ABOVE IT CANNOT ENTRANCE WIN. 018 00 006
            OR LESS WOULD WIN MAN'S MIND. 060 00 109
            NOT WIN, IF THIS BE NOT ENOUGH. 083 00 026
            TO WIN A LOOK OF VIOLET. 086 00 006
            THERE LIVES THE WITCH SHALL WIN MY LOCKS 120 00 022
            NOR LOCKS NOR EYES SHALL WIN AGAIN. 120 00 025
            UPWARDS AT ONCE AND WIN THEIR AUREOLES. 126 00 008
            BLOOD THAT BUT ONE DROP OF HAS THE WORTH TO WIN 168 00 023
WINCE
            WOE, WORLD-SORROW; ON AN AGE-OLD ANVIL WINCE AND SING --   .   .   . 065 00 006
WINCH
            IN CRISPS OF CURL OFF WILD WINCH WHIRL, AND POUR 035 00 007
            THEY WOUND THEIR WINCH OF WICKED SMILES 145 00 025
WINCING
            RIGHT ROOTING IN THE BARE BUTT'S WINCING NAVEL C 143 00 005
WIND
            THEN PASS'D THE WIND, AND SOBB'D WITH MOUNTAIN-ECHO'D WOE.   .   .   . 001 13 009
            ONE SCARLET FEATHER TRAILING TO THE WIND; 002 00 081
            HIS LUSTY HANDS, IN GUSTS OF SCENTED WIND 002 00 088
            A STEALTHY WIND CREPT ROUND SEEKING TO BLOW, ... 002 00 137
            BECAUSE THE SIGHING WIND IS LOW. 003 00 006
            SITTING EASTNORTHEAST, IN CURSED QUARTER, THE WIND; 028 13 006
            IDLE FOR EVER TO WAFT HER OR WIND HER WITH, THESE SHE ENDURED.   .   . 028 14 008
            REBUFFED THE BIG WIND, MY HEART IN HIDING 036 00 007
            DEATH OR DISTANCE SOON CONSUMES THEM: WIND 040 00 009
            HEAVENGRAVEL? WOLFSNOW, WORLDS OF IT, WIND THERE? 041 00 028
            WITH BRINE AND SHINE AND WHIRLING WIND. 041 00 080
            WITH THE WIND WHAT WHILE WE SLEPT, C 059 06 023
            LET LIFE, WANED, AH LET LIFE WIND C 061 00 010
            WAG OR CROSSBRIDLE, IN A WIND LIFTED, WINDLACED -- C 071 00 011
            DELIGHTFULLY THE BRIGHT WIND BOISTEROUS C 072 00 005
            WITH FRETTY CHERVIL, LOOK, AND FRESH WIND SHAKES 074 00 011
            SWOLL'N IS THE WIND THAT IN ARGENT BILLOWS 078 00 003
            MY PASSION LIKE A FOOLISH WIND 081 00 037
            ' THE LIGHT WAS SO, THE WIND SO LOUD 081 00 059
            IN EDDIES OF THE WIND HE WENT 087 00 005
            THE WIND, THAT PASSES BY SO FLEET, ... 098 01 001
            LIKE A CONTENTED WIND, OR GENTLE SHOCKS 098 02 002
            THE WIND COMES BREAKING HERE AND THERE WITH LAUGHTER; 098 03 003
            WHEN THE WIND DROPS YOU HEAR THE SKYLARKS SING; 098 03 005
            IT IS A REGIMEN ON THE IMPERFECT WIND. 102 03 017
            IS TO GIVE REGIMEN TO THE IMPERFECT WIND, V 102 03 024
            HE DROPS UPON THE WIND AGAIN; 130 00 013
            THERE IS A VAPOUR STANDS IN THE WIND; 130 00 017
            OF THE COLD WIND BLOWING. 132 00 003
            UPON MY FOREHEAD HIT THE BURLY WIND. 135 00 012
            THROUGH THE VELVETY WIND V-WINGED 138 00 041
            WITH A SOUTH-WESTERLY WIND BLUSTERING, WITH A TIDE ROLLS REELS   .   . 141 00 004
            STRIKE, CHURL; HURL, CHEERLESS WIND, THEN; HELTERING HAIL 154 00 001
            SOW THE WIND I WOULD; I SINNED; 155 00 011
WINDFALLS
            THOSE LOVELY LADS ONCE, WET-FRESH WINDFALLS OF WAR'S STORM,   .   .   . 062 00 006
WINDING
            WINDING SHEETS, TOMBS AND WORMS AND TUMBLING TO DECAY; C 059 0L 012

WIND-BEAT
    WIND-BEAT WHITEBEAM! AIRY ABELES SET ON A FLARE!   • • • • • •   032 00 006
WIND-LONG
    OR WIND-LONG FLEECES ON THE FLOCK • • • • • • •   144 00 011
WIND-PERPLEXED
    LIKE A WIND-PERPLEXED ROSE; • • • • • • • •   087 00 004
WIND-WALKS
    AROUND; UP ABOVE, WHAT WIND-WALKS! WHAT LOVELY BEHAVIOUR • •   038 00 002
WIND-WANDERING
    ON MEADOW AND RIVER AND WIND-WANDERING WEED-WINDING BANK. • •   043 00 008
WINDLACED
    SEE HIS WIND- LILYLOCKS -LACED; C • • • • • • •   071 00 011
    WAG OR CROSSBRIDLE, IN A WIND LIFTED, WINDLACED -- C • • •   071 00 011
WINDOW
    MY WINDOW SHOWS THE TRAVELLING CLOUDS, • • • • •   015 00 001
    BY THAT WINDOW WHAT TASK WHAT FINGERS PLY, • • • • •   046 00 005
WINDOW-CIRCLES
    THE WINDOW-CIRCLES, THESE MAY ALL BE SOUGHT • • • •   012 01 011
WINDPIPE
    THE WINDPIPE WHEN HE SUCKED HIS BREATH • • • • •   021 00 037
WINDPUFF-BONNET
    A WINDPUFF-BONNET OF FAWN-FROTH • • • • • • •   056 00 005
WIND'S
    BURDEN, IN WIND'S BURLY AND BEAT OF ENDRAGONED SEAS. • •   028 27 008
WINDS
    AND HUNTING WINDS AND THE LONG-LYING SNOW. • • • • •   017 00 002
    QUESTIONING WINDS AROUND THE HILLS; • • • • • •   077 00 044
    OFTEN WHEN WINDS IMPENITENT • • • • • • •   080 06 001
    AND FEEDS NEW LEAVES UPON THE WINDS OF FALL; • • •   105 00 010
    TO THE OFTEN TAKINGS OF DESIROUS WINDS, • • • •   111 00 003
    AND JOHN SHALL LIE, WHERE WINDS ARE DEAD, • • •   114 00 009
    OR WHOLLY WINDS HIM TO HER WILL. • • • • •   120 00 031
    THE SKY IS BLUE, AND THE WINDS PULL • • • •   130 00 022
WINDY
    LIKE PHAROH'S EARS OF WINDY HARVEST DRY • • •   117 00 006
    ATTAIN THE WINDY LEVELS OF THE SKY • • • • •   121 00 004
WINE
    THE WINE WAS RACKED FROM THE PRESS; • • • • •   006 00 018
    GRAPES GREW AND DROPS OF WINE WERE SHED. • • • •   007 00 006
    DESIRE NOT TO BE RINSED WITH WINE; • • • • •   022 00 014
    YE HAVE KEPT YOUR CHOICEST WINE -- • • • • •   024 00 009
WING
    ALL OVER, AS A BEVY OF EGGS THE MOTHERING WING •   034 00 006
    HIGH THERE, HOW HE RUNG UPON THE REIN OF A WIMPLING WING • •   036 00 004
    OF POINTED WING AND SILVER STOLE, • • • • • •   077 00 012
    AND SHEATHE AT ONCE HIS LEGER WING. • • • • •   130 00 012
    THE ROOKERY NEVER STIRRED A WING, • • • • •   135 00 014
WINGED
    A PRESS OF WINGED THINGS COMES DOWN THIS WAY; • •   005 00 015
    THE WINGED FOWLS TOOK PART, PART FELL IN THORN • •   007 00 007
    AND WOULD NOT HAVE THAT LEGION OF WINGED THINGS •   007 00 014
WINGS
    FROM WINGS SWAN-FLEDGED A WHEEL OF WATERY LIGHT • •   002 00 076
    BEAR HIM TO HEAVEN ON EASEFUL WINGS. • • • •   007 00 015
    OR BAT WITH TENDER AND AIR-CRISPING WINGS • •   019 00 002
    SEE, LOVE, I CREEP AND THOU ON WINGS DOST RIDE; •   020 00 003
    THE BATS' WINGS LISPING AS THEY FLEW • • • •   021 00 019
    I WHIRLED OUT WINGS THAT SPELL • • • • •   028 03 004
    WORLD BROODS WITH WARM BREAST AND WITH AH! BRIGHT WINGS. •   031 00 014
    FRESH-FIRECOAL CHESTNUT-FALLS; FINCHES' WINGS! •   037 00 004
    THE HEART REARS WINGS BOLD AND BOLDER • • •   038 00 013
    WINGS: SO SOME GREAT STORMFOWL, WHENEVER HE HAS WALKED HIS WHILE •   045 00 011
    WHEN WILL YOU EVER, PEACE, WILD WOODDOVE, SHY WINGS SHUT, •   051 00 001
    THE SHAKEN PLUMAGE OF MY SPIRIT'S WINGS. • • •   077 00 010
    THAT WITH A TURNING OF THE WINGS • • • •   077 00 067
    CAUGHT FROM ANGELS' WINGS IN HEAVEN, • • •   077 00 110
    HE PLAY'D HIS WINGS AS THOUGH FOR FLIGHT; • •   087 00 001
    GATHER THE SOOTY PLUMAGE FROM DEATH'S WINGS • •   089 00 006
    WHERE THE STINT COMPASS OF A SKYLARK'S WINGS • •   098 22 005
    FLUNG RIDER AND WINGS AWAY; THOUGH THESE WERE NONE, •   136 00 009
WINKS
    WINKS AWAY ITS RING OF GREEN. • • • • • •   086 00 002
WINNING
    MOST, O MAID'S CHILD, THY CHOICE AND WORTHY THE WINNING. •   033 00 014
    WINNING WAYS, AIRS INNOCENT, MAIDEN MANNERS, C • •   059 06 015
WINTER
    IS ALL THE WINTER BIRD DARE TRY. • • • • •   003 00 014
    WHERE WINTER IS THE CLIME FORGOT. -- • • • •   010 00 014
    INTO ALL SEASONS, THOUGH NO WINTER CAST • •   014 01 005
    WE HAVE SUFFERED THE SONS OF WINTER IN SORROW • •   026 00 009
    THOU ART LIGHTNING AND LOVE, I FOUND IT, A WINTER AND WARM; •   028 09 006
    MY WINTER WORLD, THAT SCARCELY BREATHES THAT BLISS •   076 00 013
    THE SMOULDERING ENORMOUS WINTER WELKIN! MAY • •   149 A 008
    THE SMOULDERING ENORMOUS WINTER WELKIN. L EYE, V •   149 B 009
    THE TIMES ARE WINTER, WATCH, A WORLD UNDONE; • •   150 00 002
    HIDEOUS DASHED DOWN, LEAVING EARTH A WINTER WITHERING •   152 02 052

292

WITHOUT   (CONTINUED)
    THE WOMAN'S WAILING, THE CRYING OF CHILD WITHOUT CHECK -- 028 17 006
    FEAST OF THE ONE WOMAN WITHOUT STAIN. 028 30 005
    WHO FIRED FRANCE FOR MARY WITHOUT SPOT. 044 00 014
    TO DO WITHOUT, TAKE TOSSES, AND OBEY. 068 00 004
    THOSE YEARS AND YEARS BY OF WORLD WITHOUT EVENT 073 00 013
    WHO COULD FORGIVE WITHOUT GRUDGE AFTER 077 00 057
    ' IT IS AS COLD AS DEATH WITHOUT: 109 29 003
    SAID ' WHO IS THIS THAT STANDS WITHOUT? ' 109 30 001
    SITS WITHOUT CONSOLATION, MARKING NOT 111 00 004
    HAD LET SUCH MUSIC DOWN, WITHOUT IMPEDIMENT 122 00 008
    THE WEIGHTY WEEKS WITHOUT HANDS GROW, ...   145 00 005
    WORLD WITHOUT END ALONE IN THEE. 167 00 028
WITHOUTEN
    WITHOUTEN INSTRUMENT, OR CONCH, OR BELL, ...   002 00 128
WITNESS
    WITH WITNESS I SPEAK THIS, BUT WHERE I SAY 067 00 005
    AND WITNESS IN HER PLACE WOULD SHE. 145 00 032
    O BUT I BEAR MY BURNING WITNESS THOUGH 157 00 035
    WITNESS TO ME! LOOK YOU, I AM A GOD, ...   160 00 005
WITNESSED
    WITNESSED: SO FORTUNE FELL. 054 00 004
WITS
    OFF HIM, BUT MEANING MOTION FANS FRESH OUR WITS WITH WONDER.   .   .   045 00 014
    MEN'S WITS TO THE THINGS THAT ARE: WHAT GOOD MEANS -- WHERE A GLANCE   062 00 004
WOE
    THEN PASS'D THE WIND, AND SOBB'D WITH MOUNTAIN-ECHO'D WOE.   .   .   001 13 009
    PERFUMES FOR THE GARB OF WOE. 024 00 020
    AY, SWEET TO TASTE BESIDE THIS WOE. 080 07 007
    THE SPELL OF WOE IF ANY COULD. 081 00 079
    SHE WAS WITH THE CHOKE OF WOE. -- 145 00 060
    ENOUGH: CORRUPTION WAS THE WORLD'S FIRST WOE. 157 00 033
    WOE IS ME, WHAT DO I HEAR? 160 00 032
WOEFUL
    THE WOEFUL, CRADOCK, O THE WOEFUL WORD! THEN WHAT,   .   .   .   152 02 017
    THE WOEFUL, CRADOCK, O THE WOEFUL WORD! THEN WHAT,   .   .   .   152 02 017
WOE'S
    IS COMFORT'S CAROL OF ALL OR WOE'S WORST SMART. 153 00 008
WOES
    BUT DROPP'D ITS COIL OF WOES: ARTHUR'S BRITAIN, ...   102 02 007
WOKE
    WOKE THEE WITH A WE ARE PERISHING IN THE WEATHER OF GENNESARETH.   .   028 25 006
    [A BELL] AT MIDNIGHT WOKE THE TOWN 081 00 087
    NO TUMBLER WOKE AND SHOOK THE COT, ...   135 00 013
WOLFSNOW
    HEAVENGRAVEL? WOLFSNOW, WORLDS OF IT, WIND THERE? 041 00 028
WOMAN
    FEAST OF THE ONE WOMAN WITHOUT STAIN. 028 30 005
    MERELY A WOMAN, YET 060 00 025
    SAID ' WHO THEN IS THIS LOWLY WOMAN, ...   109 11 003
    ' IT IS FOR THE SHAME OF THE LOWLY WOMAN 109 14 003
    SHE WAS A WOMAN, UPRIGHT, OUTRIGHT: 145 00 036
WOMAN-KIND
    THE WILD WOMAN-KIND BELOW, ...   028 16 002
WOMAN'S
    THE WOMAN'S WAILING, THE CRYING OF CHILD WITHOUT CHECK --   .   .   028 17 006
WOMB
    WELCOME IN WOMB AND BREAST, ...   060 00 020
    WITHIN HER WOMB THE CHILD WAS QUICK. 145 00 039
    LET WINTER WED ONE, SOW THEM IN HER WOMB, ...   158 00 003
WOMB-LIFE
    WARM-LAID GRAVE OF A WOMB-LIFE GREY: 028 07 003
WOMB-NOT-BEARING
    STONE, PALSY, CANCER, COUGH, LUNG-WASTING, WOMB-NOT-BEARING,   .   152 C 008
WOMB-OF-ALL
    WOMB-OF-ALL, HOME-OF-ALL, HEARSE-OF-ALL NIGHT. C 061 00 002
WOMEN
    TAKE SETTLER AND SEAMEN, TELL MEN WITH WOMEN, ...   028 12 003
    THE LOVE OF WOMEN IS NOT SO STRONG, -- 081 00 048
WON
    AND LIFE'S FIRST GERMS FROM DEATH HAD WON. 023 00 024
    AND WHEN THE SILENT HEIGHT WERE WON, ...   077 00 075
    DULY, DEAR LORD, MY PRIZE IS WON. 081 00 109
    OF WORLD MADE, MARRED, AND MENDED, LOST AND WON: 136 00 026
WONDER
    EIGHTH WONDER OF THE EARTH, IN SIZE, IN STORE 001 15 005
    THAT MEN MUST WONDER AS I PASS 010 00 003
    IS IT A WONDER IF THE BUDS ARE SLOW? 017 00 003
    SINCE, THO' HE IS UNDER THE WORLD'S SPLENDOUR AND WONDER,   .   .   028 05 006
    NO WONDER OF IT: SHEER PLOD MAKES PLOUGH DOWN SILLION   .   .   .   036 00 012
    I THINK: WHERE FROM AND BOUND, I WONDER, WHERE, ...   040 00 003
    MUSE AT THAT AND WONDER WHY: 042 00 002
    OFF HIM, BUT MEANING MOTION FANS FRESH OUR WITS WITH WONDER.   .   045 00 014
    WHO TO WEDLOCK, HIS WONDER WEDLOCK, ...   052 00 011
    HOW WOULDST THOU WORSE, I WONDER, THAN THOU DOST   .   .   .   074 00 006
    AND WONDER AT HER SHALLOW SMILE. 120 00 012
    A WONDER IN THE COUNTRY, AND A LANDMARK 125 00 004

                                        293

WONDER   (CONTINUED)
    NO WONDER THEREFORE WAS NOT SLOW 145 00 019
    LOST, ALL LOST IN WONDER AT THE GOD THOU ART. 168 00 004
WONDERFUL
    THAN CHANGEFUL POMP OF COURTS IS AYE MORE WONDERFUL. 001 15 009
WONDERING
    AT THE TOUCH OF HER WANDERING WONDERING BREATH 026 00 006
    WONDERING WHY MY MASTER BORE IT, ... 041 00 098
    I PLOD WONDERING, A-WANTING, JUST FOR LACK 046 00 006
WONDER'S
    INDEED WHILE SUCH A WONDER'S WARM. 025 00 036
    THEO. WHILE SUCH A WONDER'S WET AND WARM! . . . . . . APPEN A 36
WONDERS
    TOLD OF THE WONDERS HE HAD SEEN. 131 00 006
    HOLDS TILL HAND ACHES AND WONDERS WHAT IS THERE; 151 00 008
WONDROUS
    MORE WONDROUS TO HAVE BORNE SUCH HOPE BEFORE 001 15 007
    I HAD A DREAM, A WONDROUS THING; 004 00 001
    AND CHARLES'S WAIN, THE WONDROUS SEVEN, ... 030 00 017
    SHE, WILD WEB, WONDROUS ROBE, ... 060 00 038
WONT
    DOUBLE, AND HIGHER THAN HIS WONT, ... 077 00 111
    WHERE YOU AND I WERE WONT TO TREAD; 081 00 156
    THAT WONT TO THRONG ZEUS' BANQUET-HALL; 160 00 029
WOOD
    AS I WALK'D A STILLY WOOD, ... 004 00 005
    WE ARE SO GRAFTED ON HIS WOOD. 006 00 033
    THE WOOD; BUT NOT A DOVE WOULD COO. 021 00 021
    IN ACRES ALL ABOVE THE WOOD. 021 00 035
    CHRIST'S LILY AND BEAST OF THE WASTE WOOD: 028 20 006
    FETCHED FRESH, AS I SUPPOSE, OFF SOME SWEET WOOD. 034 00 004
    WOOD BANKS AND BRAKES WASH WET LIKE LAKES 042 00 042
    CUCKOO CALLS CUCKOO UP THE WOOD, ... 081 00 022
    ONCE IN A DRAWER OF INDIAN WOOD 081 00 080
    -- THE SHALLOW FOLDS OF THE WOOD 098 09 001
    IN THE GREEN SPOTS OF THAT WOOD 098 10 001
    THERE WAS A WOOD OF DWARF AND SOURED OAKS 125 00 002
    OF SOME BRANCHY BUNCHY BUSHYBOWERED WOOD, ... 159 00 003
WOODDOVE
    WHEN WILL YOU EVER, PEACE, WILD WOODDOVE, SHY WINGS SHUT, . . 051 00 001
WOODFERNS
    INTO FAIRY TREES, WILDFLOWERS, WOODFERNS 159 00 050
WOOD-SORREL
    OF THE WOOD-SORREL AND ALL THINGS SENSITIVE? 122 00 011
    AS THE WOOD-SORREL AND ALL THINGS SENSITIVE 122 00 014
WOODLAND
    LOW-COVERED PASS, AND BRACE THE WOODLAND CLODS 112 00 006
    THAT COMES AGAIN TO THE WOODLAND TREE. 124 00 004
WOODLARK
    ' I AM THE LITTLE WOODLARK. 138 00 011
WOODS
    DOWN IN DIM WOODS THE DIAMOND DELVES! THE ELVES'-EYES! . . . 032 00 004
    LOVELY THE WOODS, WATERS, MEADOWS, COMBES, VALES, ... 034 00 009
    WHEN CHILL WOODS WAKE AND THINK OF MORN, ... 077 00 023
    FRUIT-CLOISTERING HYACINTH-WARDING WOODS, ... 081 00 163
    THE TIME WAS LATE AND THE WET YELLOW WOODS 098 05 001
WOOL
    AND SHEEP-FLOCK CLOUDS LIKE WORLDS OF WOOL, ... 030 00 018
WOOLWOVEN
    HIS BLEACHED BOTH AND WOOLWOVEN WEAR! 159 00 029
WOOS
    ENGLAND, WHOSE HONOUR O ALL MY HEART WOOS, WIFE 066 00 005
WORD
    AND TAUGHT MY LIPS TO QUOTE THIS WORD 008 00 006
    I HAVE FOUND MY MUSIC IN A COMMON WORD, ... 019 00 005
    ONE WORD -- AS WHEN A MOTHER SPEAKS 023 00 050
    WORD LAST! HOW A LUSH-KEPT PLUSH-CAPPED SLOE 028 08 003
    AND THE WORD OF IT SACRIFICED. 028 22 004
    HEAVEN AND EARTH ARE WORD OF, WORDED BY? -- 028 29 006
    WORD, THAT HEARD AND KEPT THEE AND UTTERED THEE OUTRIGHT. . . 028 30 008
    KIND LOVE BOTH GIVE AND GET. ONLY WHAT WORD 066 00 011
    NOW ONE WORD MORE AND THEN I AM GONE INDEED, ... 102 01 055
    WORD WENT SHE SHOULD BE CRUSHED OUT FLAT 145 00 038
    AND I NOT HELP, NOR WORD NOW OF SUCCESS: 150 00 005
    THE WOEFUL, CRADOCK, O THE WOEFUL WORD! THEN WHAT, ... 152 02 017
    THAT LEVEL POWER WHOSE WORD IS MUST 166 00 014
    WORD NEVER WAS SUCH NEWS TO HEAR, ... 167 00 006
WORDED
    HEAVEN AND EARTH ARE WORD OF, WORDED BY? -- 028 29 006
WORDING
    WORDING IT HOW BUT BY HIM THAT PRESENT AND PAST, ... 028 29 005
WORDS
    THE WORDS ARE OLD, THE PURPORT NEW, ... 008 00 005
    HAVE YOU! MAKE WORDS BREAK FROM ME HERE ALL ALONE, ... 028 18 003
    MY EVIL WORDS THORNY WITH PAIN: 081 00 027
    I KNOW I MAR MY CAUSE WITH WORDS: 081 00 030
    TUNE IT TO WORDS OF GOOD INTENT. 081 00 127

WORLD'S
WORLD'S STRAND, SWAY OF THE SEA; 028 01 003
SINCE, THO' HE IS UNDER THE WORLD'S SPLENDOUR AND WONDER, ... 028 05 006
WORLD'S LOVELIEST -- MEN'S SELVES. SELF FLASHES OFF FRAME AND FACE. 062 00 011
IN WIDE THE WORLD'S WEAL; RARE GOLD, BOLD STEEL, BARE 070 00 017
FALL TO THE RESIDUARY WORM; WORLD'S WILDFIRE, LEAVE BUT ASH; . . 072 00 020
ENOUGH; CORRUPTION WAS THE WORLD'S FIRST WOE. 157 00 033
TO THE WORLD'S END, TO THE LAST HILL 160 00 024
WORLDS
NIGHT TO A MYRIAD WORLDS GIVES BIRTH, ... 023 00 009
AND SHEEP-FLOCK CLOUDS LIKE WORLDS OF WOOL, ... 030 00 018
HEAVENGRAVEL? WOLFSNOW, WORLDS OF IT, WIND THERE? 041 00 028
THOUGH WORLDS OF WANWOOD LEAFMEAL LIE; 055 00 008
WORM
FALL TO THE RESIDUARY WORM; WORLD'S WILDFIRE, LEAVE BUT ASH; . . 072 00 020
WORST WILL THE BEST. WHAT WORM WAS HERE, WE CRY, ... 157 00 031
WORMS
WINDING SHEETS, TOMBS AND WORMS AND TUMBLING TO DECAY; C . . . 059 OL 012
WORSE
TILL, (FEARING RAVAGE WORSE THAN IN HIS FLIGHT, ... 001 14 007
OF RUINOUS SHRINE NO HAND OR, WORSE, ... 041 00 090
AS I AM MINE, THEIR SWEATING SELVES; BUT WORSE. 067 00 014
MANWOLF, WORSE! AND THEIR PACKS INFEST THE AGE. 070 00 020
HOW WOULDST THOU WORSE, I WONDER, THAN THOU DOST 074 00 006
WORSE THAN WHEN FLORIS FOUND ME IN THE GARDEN 102 01 040
THEY WASTE, THEY WITHER WORSE; THEY AS THEY RUN 150 00 003
BE AT EVERY ASSAULT FRESH FOILED, WORSE FLUNG, DEEPER DISAPPOINTED, 152 02 056
REASON, SELFDISPOSAL, CHOICE OF BETTER OR WORSE WAY, . . . 152 02 061
SAYING ' THIS WAS YOURS ' WITH HER, BUT NEW ONE, WORSE, . . 153 00 010
WORSHIP
I SHALL WORSHIP HIS WOUNDS WITH THEE, MOTHER OF MINE. . . 027 00 036
TO MAN, THAT NEEDS WOULD WORSHIP BLOCK OR BARREN STONE, . . 062 00 009
TO BOW BUT LITTLE, AND WORSHIP NOT? 081 00 141
WORST
IN THE WORST HOUR THAT'S MEASURED BY THE SUN, ... 014 02 005
WE LASH WITH THE BEST OR WORST 028 08 002
MUST IT, WORST WEATHER, ... 041 00 015
RUCK AND WRINKLE, DROOPING, DYING, DEATH'S WORST, C . . . 059 OL 012
NO WORST, THERE IS NONE. PITCHED PAST PITCH OF GRIEF, . . 065 00 001
IS COMFORT'S CAROL OF ALL OR WOE'S WORST SMART. . . . 153 00 008
WORST WILL THE BEST. WHAT WORM WAS HERE, WE CRY, . . 157 00 031
WORTH
HERE ARE SWEET MESSES WITHOUT PRICE OR WORTH, . . . 005 00 047
THY UNCHANCELLING POISING PALMS WERE WEIGHING THE WORTH, . 028 21 006
GIVE GOD WHILE WORTH CONSUMING. 049 00 007
WHAT WERE WORTH NOTHING IF ALL COMPLIMENT! 094 00 006
HE HEIGHTENS WORTH WHO GUARDEDLY DIMINISHES; . . . 096 07 004
IS WORTH AND CURRENT WITH A LESSEN'D MILL. ' . . . 096 07 008
FLORIS; SHE WILL NOT HIT THY SUM OF WORTH. . . . 102 01 058
SCARCE WORTH DISCOVERY, IN SOME CORNER SEEN . . . 103 00 002
BLOOD THAT BUT ONE DROP OF HAS THE WORTH TO WIN . . 168 00 023
WORTHIEST
OUR LAW SAYS: LOVE WHAT ARE LOVE'S WORTHIEST, WERE ALL KNOWN; . 062 00 010
WORTHY
THEE, OH MAIDEN, MOST WORTHY OF PRAISE! 026 00 036
MOST, O MAID'S CHILD, THY CHOICE AND WORTHY THE WINNING. . . 033 00 014
WOUND
WAS AROUND THEM, BOUND THEM OR WOUND THEM WITH HER. . . 041 00 044
I SAY THAT WE ARE WOUND 060 00 034
WOUND WITH THEE, IN THEE ISLED, ... 060 00 125
HER FOND YELLOW HORNLIGHT WOUND TO THE WEST, C . . . 061 00 003
THE RIVER WOUND ABOUT IT AS A WAIST. 107 04 002
THEY WOUND THEIR WINCH OF WICKED SMILES 145 00 025
WOUNDED
AND I CRY OUT FOR WOUNDED LOVE. 081 00 033
WOUNDS
I SHALL WORSHIP HIS WOUNDS WITH THEE, MOTHER OF MINE. . 027 00 036
WANTS WAR, WANTS WOUNDS; WEARY HIS TIMES, HIS TASKS; . 068 00 003
I AM NOT LIKE THOMAS, WOUNDS I CANNOT SEE. . . . 168 00 013
WOVEN
A BASKET BROAD OF WOVEN WHITE RODS 098 19 001
WRAPPED
KEPT TO HER -- CARE-DROWNED AND WRAPPED IN . . . 041 00 046
WRATHFUL
HONOURING AN UNCONTROLLED ROYAL WRATHFUL NATURE, . . 152 02 036
WREATH
HAD GOTTEN HIM A WREATH OF SWEET SPRING-BROIDERY. . 002 00 101
WREATH'D
FROM FLESH-FLOWERS OF THE ROCK; BUT MORE WERE WREATH'D . 002 00 063
WREATHS
WITH GARNET WREATHS AND BLOOMS OF ROSY-BUDDED FIRE. . 002 00 026
WRECK
HUNG LIKE A WRECK THAT FLAMES NOT BILLOWS BEAT -- . 001 03 004
TIMED HER SAD VISIONS WITH HIS WRECK. 021 00 056
WITH THE SEA-ROMP OVER THE WRECK. 028 17 004
AND WRECK IN RUINS OF HIS MOTHER 145 00 041
ALL IS FROM WRECK, HERE, THERE, TO RESCUE ONE -- . 150 00 006

WRECKED
      BUT WHAT BLACK BOREAS WRECKED HER? HE • • • • • • • 041 00 023
      OUR RUINS OF WRECKED PAST PURPOSE, THERE SHE BASKS • • • • 068 00 007
WRECKING
      MAN'S MALICE, WITH WRECKING AND STORM. • • • • • • 028 09 004
WRECK'D
      IN UNIMPERILL'D HAVEN IS WRECK'D. • • • • • • • 083 00 020
WRECKS
      A GLORIOUS WANTON: -- ALL THE WRECKS IN SHOWERS • • • • 002 00 093
      AS WRECKS OF MINED EMBERS WILL. • • • • • • • 092 00 013
WRESTLES
      ROPES, WRESTLES, BEATS EARTH BARE C • • • • • • 072 00 005
WRESTLING
      OF NOW DONE DARKNESS I WRETCH LAY WRESTLING WITH (MY GOD!) MY GOD. 064 00 014
WRETCH
      OF NOW DONE DARKNESS I WRETCH LAY WRESTLING WITH (MY GOD!) MY GOD. 064 00 014
      WRETCH, UNDER A COMFORT SERVES IN A WHIRLWIND: ALL • • 065 00 013
WRETCHES
      WHAT SIGHTS SHALL BE WHEN SOME THAT SWUNG, WRETCHES, ON CRUTCHES • 152 C 022
WRING
      AND FROM DANK FEATHERS WRING THE DROPS • • • • • 003 00 008
      WRING THY REBEL, DOGGED IN DEN, • • • • • • • 028 09 003
      THROUGH THE ECHOING TIMBER DOES SO RINSE AND WRING • • • 033 00 004
      OR WRING THEIR BARRIERS IN BURSTS OF FEAR OR RAGE. • • • 039 00 008
      MORE PANGS WILL, SCHOOLED AT FOREPANGS, WILDER WRING. • • • 065 00 002
WRINGING
      OF WRINGING TREE-TOPS, CHALKY LANES, • • • • • 077 00 135
WRING-WORLD
      THY WRING-WORLD RIGHT FOOT ROCK? LAY A LIONLIMB AGAINST ME? SCAN • 064 00 006
WRINGS
      NOW HE WRINGS FOR BREATH WITH THE DEATHGUSH BROWN: • • • 041 00 062
      FAST HE OPENS, LAST HE OFF WRINGS • • • • • • 159 00 034
WRINKLE
      RUCK AND WRINKLE, DROOPING, DYING, DEATH'S WORST, C • • • 059 OL 012
WRINKLES
      O IS THERE NO FROWNING OF THESE WRINKLES, RANKED WRINKLES DEEP, • 059 OL 003
      O IS THERE NO FROWNING OF THESE WRINKLES, RANKED WRINKLES DEEP, • 059 OL 003
WRIT
      DOROTHEA -- OR WAS YOUR WRIT • • • • • • • 025 00 027
      THEO. DOROTHEA -- OR WAS YOUR WRIT • • • • • • APPEN A 27
WRITE
      AND IF YOU WRITE AT LAST, IT NEVER CAN BE THE SAME: • • • 128 00 003
      NO: WHAT THE POET DID WRITE RAN, • • • • • • 147 00 005
WRITES
      THE SUN ON FALLING WATERS WRITES THE TEXT • • • • • 091 00 008
WRITHE
      APOLLO VIEWS THE SMITTEN PYTHON WRITHE AND DIE. • • • 001 11 009
WRITTEN
      AH! SURELY ALL WHO HAVE WRITTEN WILL PROFESS • • • • 117 00 008
      I THOUGHT THAT YOU WOULD HAVE WRITTEN: MY BIRTHDAY CAME AND WENT, • 128 00 001
      STRUCK OFF IT HAS: WRITTEN UPON LOVELY LIMBS, • • • • 152 02 003
      WATER, WHICH KEEPS THY NAME, (FOR NOT IN ROCK WRITTEN, • • 152 C 014
WRONG
      THY RIVER, AND O'ER GIVES ALL TO RACK OR WRONG. • • • 058 00 008
      -- BLACK, WHITE: RIGHT, WRONG: RECKON BUT, RECK BUT, MIND C • 061 00 012
      NOW KNOWN AND HAND AT WORK NOW NEVER WRONG. • • • • 076 00 008
      IS NEITHER RIGHT NOR WRONG, • • • • • • • 148 00 032
WRONGING
      I SHOULD BE WRONGING LONGER LEAVING IT TO FLOAT • • • 159 00 044
WRONG'D
      I HAVE WRONG'D IT OF ITS CORONET, AND NOW • • • • • 102 01 048
WRONGS
      RIFE IN HER WRONGS, MORE LAWLESS, AND MORE LEWD. • • • 050 00 008
WROUGHT
      BUT NOT THE HAND THAT WROUGHT THEM ALL: • • • • 023 00 008
      THE WROUGHT RIM OF HEAVEN'S FONT, -- • • • • • 077 00 112
      EACH HUE SO RARELY WROUGHT THAT WHERE • • • • • 077 00 117
      O LORD! BUT I HAVE WROUGHT AND STRIVEN: • • • • • 081 00 108
      HE SAT AND WROUGHT HIS OUTLINE ON A CLOUD. • • • • 107 01 010
      HOW ALL'S TO ONE THING WROUGHT! • • • • • • 148 00 001
      'TIS THROUGH THE HOLY GHOST THAT WROUGHT • • • • APPEN D 16
WRUNG
      FATHER AND FONDLER OF HEART THOU HAST WRUNG: • • • 028 09 007
      FOR, WRUNG ALL ON LOVE'S RACK, • • • • • • • 054 00 017
      'S NOT WRUNG, SEE YOU: UNFORESEEN TIMES RATHER -- AS SKIES • • 069 00 013
WUTHERING
      IF A WUTHERING OF HIS PALMY SNOW-PINIONS SCATTER A COLOSSAL SMILE • 045 00 013
WYCHELM
      WILD WYCHELM, HORNBEAM FRETTY OVERSTOOD C • • • • • 159 00 024

YAWN'D
      YAWN'D LIKE LONG FURROW IN THE HEART: • • • • • • 077 00 064

YEA
```
    YEA IRON IS MINGLED WITH MY CLAY, . . . . . . . . . 018 00 010
    STAIN LIGHT. YEA, MARK YOU THIS: . . . . . . . . . 060 00 081
    YEA, WISH THAT THOUGH, WISH ALL, GOD'S BETTER BEAUTY, GRACE. . . 062 00 014
    AS THE LAST PLEIAD, YEA BEHIND . . . . . . . . . 081 00 046
    YEA, TO MYSELF I ANSWER MAKE: . . . . . . . . . 081 00 145
    YEA, CRUSH'D MY HEART, AND MADE ME DUMB, . . . . . . . 118 00 012
    YEA A DEBT TO PAY THEE YET: . . . . . . . . . . 155 00 019
    YEA AND DEATH, AND THIS FOR ME, . . . . . . . . . 170 00 011
```
YEAR
```
    AT THIS SPRING SEASON OF THE YEAR? ' . . . . . . . 004 00 013
    IS IT EACH ONE? THAT NIGHT, THAT YEAR C . . . . . . 064 00 013
    THERE IS A DAY OF ALL THE YEAR . . . . . . . . . 080 08 001
    THEY'RE OUT OF DATE -- LENT SERMONS ALL THE YEAR. . . . . 096 05 002
    AND YIELD A SONG TO THE DECAYING YEAR: . . . . . . . 105 00 002
    ON SUCH A SEASON OF THE DAY AND YEAR, . . . . . . . 107 01 004
    AS DEVONSHIRE LETTERS, EARLIER IN THE YEAR . . . . . . 119 00 001
    THINK THIS, MY BIRTHDAY FALLS IN SADDENING TIME OF YEAR: . . 128 00 009
    PRESSED TO DEATH, HE PLANTS THE YEAR: . . . . . . . 145 00 004
    SHALL NEW-DAPPLE NEXT YEAR, SURE AS TO-MORROW MORNING, . . 152  C 028
```
YEAR-MOTHER
```
    LIES IN THE BREAST OF THE YOUNG YEAR-MOTHER . . . . . 026 00 003
```
YEARN'D
```
    HE YEARN'D, HE YEARN'D TO HAVE HIS LOVE, . . . . . . 109 06 001
    HE YEARN'D, HE YEARN'D TO HAVE HIS LOVE, . . . . . . 109 06 001
```
YEAR'S
```
    OF THE YORE-FLOOD, OF THE YEAR'S FALL: . . . . . . 028 32 002
    OF NEW YEAR'S MONTH OR SURLY YULE . . . . . . . . 030 00 030
```
YEARS
```
    TWO THOUSANDS OF YEARS ARE NEAR UPON PAST . . . . . 027 00 015
    FIVE AND TWENTY YEARS HAVE RUN . . . . . . . . . 029 00 005
    FALLS LIGHT AS TEN YEARS LONG TAUGHT HOW TO AND WHY. . . 047 00 008
    DEALS TRIUMPH AND IMMORTAL YEARS. . . . . . . . . 052 00 012
    HOW FAR FROM THEN FORETHOUGHT OF, ALL THY MORE BOISTEROUS YEARS, 053 00 012
    WHEN SHROVETIDE, TWO YEARS GONE, . . . . . . . . 054 00 005
    HOURS I MEAN YEARS, MEAN LIFE. AND MY LAMENT . . . . 067 00 006
    THOSE YEARS AND YEARS BY OF WORLD WITHOUT EVENT . . . . 073 00 013
    THOSE YEARS AND YEARS BY OF WORLD WITHOUT EVENT . . . . 073 00 013
    NINE MONTHS SHE THEN, NAY YEARS, NINE YEARS SHE LONG . . 076 00 005
    NINE MONTHS SHE THEN, NAY YEARS, NINE YEARS SHE LONG . . 076 00 005
    HIS VERY LOOKS IN OTHER YEARS, . . . . . . . . . 081 00 062
    ' IN TWO YEARS OR IN THREE. . . . . . . . . . 109 02 004
    ' ALTHOUGH IT WERE YEARS THREE. . . . . . . . . 109 03 002
    FOR TWO YEARS AND FOR THREE. . . . . . . . . . 109 06 002
    WITH A TWO YEARS CHILD AT HER KNEE. . . . . . . . 109 16 002
    DISCOVERING YOU, DARK TRAMPLERS, TYRANT YEARS. . . . . 157 00 002
    I A THOUSAND THOUSAND YEARS . . . . . . . . . . 160 00 008
```
YELLOW
```
    ITS BRINDLED WHARVES AND YELLOW BRIM, . . . . . . . 003 00 028
    AND PIERCE THE YELLOW WAXEN LIGHT . . . . . . . . 015 00 043
    HER FOND YELLOW HORNLIGHT WOUND TO THE WEST, C . . . . 061 00 003
    THE TIME WAS LATE AND THE WET YELLOW WOODS . . . . . 098 05 001
    NOW QUICKEN, SHEATHED IN THE YELLOW GALAXY. . . . . . 098 22 003
    THE AUTUMN YELLOW FEATHER IN THE BOUGHS . . . . . . 105 00 005
    WITH YELLOW FLAGS WILL SUIT HIS BROW, . . . . . . . 124 00 018
```
YELLOWY
```
    WITH YELLOWY MOISTURE MILD NIGHT'S BLEAR-ALL BLACK, . . . 046 00 003
```
YES
```
    I DID SAY YES . . . . . . . . . . . . . . 028 02 001
    AT DOWNRIGHT ' NO OR YES? ' . . . . . . . . . . 041 00 055
    THERE IS ONE, YES I HAVE ONE ( HUSH THERE! ) , . . . 059 06 002
    ONE. YES I CAN TELL SUCH A KEY, I DO KNOW SUCH A PLACE, . 059 06 007
    NOW WE FOLLOW. -- YONDER, YES YONDER, YONDER, C . . . 059 06 011
    YES. WHY DO WE ALL, SEEING OF A SOLDIER, BLESS HIM? BLESS . 063 00 001
    -- YES FOR A TIME THEY HELD AS WELL . . . . . . . 101 00 001
    AH YES! WHY, GET THEE GONE THEN; TELL THY MOTHER I WANT HER. 152 01 010
    THAT MIGHT HAVE SPARED HER WERE IT BUT FOR PASSION-SAKE, YES, 152 02 054
    FAST FURLED AND ALL FOREDRAWN TO NO OR YES. . . . . . 157 00 028
```
YESTERDAY
```
    HE SLEW THE EGYPTIAN YESTERDAY. TO-DAY . . . . . . 005 00 003
```
YESTERTEMPEST'S
```
    OF YESTERTEMPEST'S CREASES: IN POOL AND RUTPEEL PARCHES . . 072 00 006
```
YET
```
    SOONER THAN THEIR MATES; AND YET . . . . . . . . 004 00 029
    HAD SHE A QUINCE IN HAND? YET GAZE: . . . . . . . 010 00 019
    ALL MINE, YET COMMON TO MY EVERY PEER. . . . . . . 012 01 008
    ECLIPSING PARAPET: YET ABOVE THE WALL . . . . . . . 012 02 007
    OF GOD'S DEAR PLEADINGS HAVE AS YET NOT MOVED THEE, -- . . 013 00 010
    THAT LESS IS HEAVENS HIGHER EVEN YET . . . . . . . 014 01 012
    YET IT IS NOW TOO LATE TO HEAL . . . . . . . . . 015 00 017
    AFFLICTS NO LESS, WHAT YET I HOPE MAY BLOW, . . . . . 017 00 006
    HEAR YET MY PARADOX: LOVE, WHEN ALL IS GIVEN, . . . . 020 00 013
    ' YET AS HE CHANGED HIS MIGHTY STOPS . . . . . . . 021 00 043
    YET LIKE A LIGHTED EMPTY HALL . . . . . . . . . 023 00 010
    YET KNOW NOT HOW OUR GIFTS TO BRING, . . . . . . . 023 00 017
    YET MADE ITS MARKET HERE AS WELL: . . . . . . . . 025 00 032
    MY EYES HOLD YET THE RINDS AND BRIGHT . . . . . . . 025 00 033
```

299

YONDER   (CONTINUED)
     YONDER. 059 06 032
YORE
     THE EASY BURDEN OF YORE. 005 00 054
     AND I'LL PRETEND THE CREDIT GIVEN OF YORE: 014 02 003
YORE-FLOOD
     OF THE YORE-FLOOD, OF THE YEAR'S FALL: 028 32 002
YOUNG
     LIES IN THE BREAST OF THE YOUNG YEAR-MOTHER 026 00 003
     YOUNG JOHN: THEN FEAR, THEN JOY 054 00 008
     YOUNG THECLA, SCANNED THE DAZZLING STREETS ONE DAY: 136 00 014
     THEIR YOUNG DELIGHTFUL HOUR DO FEATURE DOWN 157 00 010
     THE YOUNG CHIEF OF THE BLESS'D OF HEAVEN 160 00 011
YOUNGSTER
     TO HIS YOUNGSTER TAKE HIS TREAT! 048 00 011
YOUTH
     BUT, HAPLESS YOUTH, ANTINOUS THE WHILE 001 11 005
     IT IS THE WASTE DONE IN UNRETICENT YOUTH 017 00 010
     NEVER-ELDERING REVEL AND RIVER OF YOUTH, ...   028 18 007
     WHEN LIMBER LIQUID YOUTH, THAT TO ALL I TEACH 048 00 022
     US: FRESH YOUTH FRETTED IN A BLOOMFALL ALL PORTENDING .   .   .   048 00 030
     IT IS AN EVERLASTINGNESS OF, O IT IS AN ALL YOUTH! C   .   .   .   059 06 013
     TO ITS OWN BEST BEING AND ITS LOVELINESS OF YOUTH C   .   .   .   059 06 013
     OF FAVOURED MAKE AND MIND AND HEALTH AND YOUTH, ...   157 00 018
YULE
     OF NEW YEAR'S MONTH OR SURLY YULE 030 00 030

ZEAL
     AND ZEAL IS FLUSHED AND PITY BLEEDS 023 00 034
ZEAL-RAMPANT
     LEGATES MIGHT RUSH, ZEAL-RAMPANT, FIERY, ...   001 05 005
ZENITH
     THE ZENITH MELTED TO A ROSE OF AIR: 002 00 023
     LOOKS FROM THE ZENITH ROUND THE SKY, ...   077 00 108
ZENITH'D
     SHALL, WHEN HIS STAR IS ZENITH'D, FIND 083 00 007
ZEPHYR'S
     WHERE PHOEBUS WEEPS FOR HIM WHOM ZEPHYR'S GUILE '. 001 11 007
ZEST
     KEEPS A KIND OF JOY IN IT, A ZEST, AN EDGE, AN ECSTASY, .   .   .   152 02 058
     INTO SUCH A SUDDEN ZEST 159 00 020
ZEUS
     FOE OF ZEUS AND HATE OF ALL 160 00 028
     THAT WONT TO THRONG ZEUS' BANQUET-HALL, ...   160 00 029
ZONE
     I AM THE MIDST OF EVERY ZONE 130 00 003

Word FREQUENCY
Table

Word		Word		Word		Word	
ALL	241	FIND	24	BEING	15	MISS	12
AS	174	HOME	24	BLACK	15	OH	12
NO	144	MAKES	24	BLOW	15	PATIENCE	12
LIKE	95	PLACE	24	CARE	15	PRIDE	12
MORE	95	ABOVE	23	CRY	15	SPENT	12
LOVE	94	FATHER	23	DAYLIGHT	15	STRAIN	12
SWEET	89	NEW	23	DROPS	15	SUMMER	12
YET	75	SEA	23	GOLDEN	15	TIMES	12
SEE	70	SPRING	23	HONOUR	15	TRUTH	12
COME	69	ABOUT	22	KEEP	15	WILL	12
HEART	68	AFTER	22	LAND	15	AGAINST	11
AIR	63	EVER	22	MORNING	15	BESIDE	11
GOD	62	FAIR	22	PEACE	15	BIRD	11
DAY	60	HIGH	22	REST	15	BONES	11
THAN	50	NAME	22	SEEMS	15	BREAK	11
WHILE	50	O'ER	22	SOON	15	BREAST	11
HEAVEN	48	SKY	22	THINK	15	CAST	11
SUCH	47	FOUND	21	ALONG	14	DARKNESS	11
EYES	43	FRESH	21	BEAT	14	FEAR	11
LET	43	GOD'S	21	BOUND	14	FIELDS	11
LIGHT	43	JOY	21	BRING	14	FINE	11
ROUND	43	RIGHT	21	CROWN	14	FIVE	11
WORLD	43	SILVER	21	EAR	14	FOOT	11
MAKE	42	WILD	21	ELSE	14	FRUIT	11
HAND	41	CHILD	20	FOLLOW	14	GAZE	11
MEN	41	HEARD	20	FREE	14	HEARTS	11
OFF	41	HOPE	20	GOES	14	LEAVE	11
CHRIST	40	MUCH	20	JUST	14	LIES	11
MAN	40	POOR	20	KEPT	14	LILIES	11
MOST	40	ROSE	20	KING	14	MAIDEN	11
NEVER	40	SIGHT	20	KNEW	14	MUSIC	11
LORD	39	SINCE	20	LITTLE	14	NOTHING	11
WELL	39	TONGUE	20	LOOKS	14	OLD	11
CAME	38	BACK	19	MORN	14	PAIN	11
DEATH	38	BOTH	19	POOL	14	PRAYER	11
LOOK	37	BREATH	19	ROCK	14	RAIN	11
LAST	36	EVEN	19	SELF	14	RICH	11
SAID	36	FACE	19	SIN	14	SAME	11
BEAUTY	35	FIRE	19	SING	14	SAVE	11
STILL	35	FLOWERS	19	SOUND	14	SHINE	11
LONG	34	LOST	19	SPIRIT	14	STONE	11
ONLY	34	LOVELY	19	TOLD	14	STOOD	11
WIND	34	MEET	19	VERY	14	STRONG	11
EARTH	33	TELL	19	WHITE	14	THICK	11
KNOW	33	ANY	18	WONDER	14	THRO	11
MOTHER	33	BEST	18	WORD	14	WATERS	11
THINGS	33	BRIGHT	18	WORK	14	WINTER	11
HEAR	32	CALL	18	BARE	13	BETWEEN	10
ONCE	32	CLOUDS	18	BEAR	13	BOUGHS	10
SAY	32	EVERY	18	BEHIND	13	CLOUD	10
GOOD	31	FAR	18	BLOOM	13	DEW	10

Word		Word		Word		Word	
OVER	31	GIVE	18	COMFORT	13	ENOUGH	10
THOUGHT	31	GONE	18	DAYS	13	FEEL	10
AWAY	30	LAY	18	DESPAIR	13	FIELD	10
LEAVES	30	LEFT	18	DRY	13	FLAME	10
NONE	30	LIPS	18	END	13	GARDENS	10
SUN	30	LIVE	18	FORTH	13	GRASS	10
TEARS	30	NEAR	18	FULL	13	LILY	10
NIGHT	29	SAW	18	HANDS	13	MARGARET	10
STARS	29	SOUL	18	HUNG	13	MASTER	10
TRUE	29	WINGS	18	LIE	13	NATURE	10
AH	28	YEARS	18	MAN'S	13	NAY	10
GRACE	28	COLD	17	MANY	13	NEXT	10
GREEN	28	DEAR	17	SKIES	13	PENMAEN	10
LIFE	28	DIVINE	17	SON	13	PUT	10
TIME	28	FEET	17	SWEETNESS	13	RAN	10
UNDER	28	FIRST	17	TREES	13	RARE	10
FALL	27	FLESH	17	WEAR	13	RIVER	10
LOW	27	HARD	17	WEST	13	RUN	10
MIND	27	PART	17	WIDE	13	'S	10
TILL	27	PAST	17	WITHOUT	13	SEAS	10
UP	27	SET	17	WOOD	13	SEEM'D	10
EYE	26	WENT	17	ACROSS	12	SEEN	10
MADE	26	WITHIN	17	ALONE	12	SEES	10
OWN	26	BEYOND	16	BLOOD	12	SEVEN	10
THING	26	DEEP	16	BORN	12	SHOOK	10
TWO	26	FELL	16	BREATHE	12	SIDE	10
BEFORE	25	GLORY	16	DEAD	12	SILENCE	10
BLUE	25	GOLD	16	DIE	12	SPOT	10
COMES	25	GREY	16	FALLS	12	STAR	10
GO	25	KNOWN	16	GATHER	12	SWEETEST	10
HEAD	25	LATE	16	GROUND	12	THOUGHTS	10
TAKE	25	LESS	16	HOUR	12	TOOK	10
THREE	25	MARK	16	HOUSE	12	VOICE	10
WATER	25	STAND	16	KNOWS	12	WARM	10
WAY	25	TURN	16	LOCKS	12	WET	10
DARK	24	WAYS	16	MARY	12	WORDS	10
FAST	24			MAY	12	WORSE	10

YEAR	10	SURE	8	WORLD'S	7	SNOW	6
YES	10	TALL	8	WORST	7	SOMETIMES	6
YIELD	10	TOUCH	8	WROUGHT	7	SOMEWHERE	6
BANNER	9	TREE	8	YELLOW	7	SOUR	6
BROTHERS	9	TURNED	8	YONDER	7	SPELL	6
CHRIST'S	9	WASTE	8	ALAS	6	SPEND	6
COUNTRY	9	WEARY	8	ALWAYS	6	SPREAD	6
DESIRE	9	WINDS	8	ANGEL	6	STEEL	6
EAST	9	YEA	8	ANGELS	6	STORMS	6
ERE	9	YOUTH	8	BAY	6	STRAINS	6
FINGERS	9	AMONG	7	BEGINNING	6	STRIKE	6
FLORIS	9	APART	7	BEGUN	6	STRUCK	6
FLOWER	9	AROUND	7	BENEATH	6	TASTE	6
GLOOM	9	ART	7	BLUEBELLS	6	THEREFORE	6
HAIR	9	ASK	7	BODY	6	THIN	6
HILL	9	BASKET	7	BORE	6	TOM	6
HOLD	9	BED	7	BREAD	6	TOWERS	6
HOLY	9	BELOW	7	BREAKS	6	TOWN	6
HOURS	9	BLIND	7	BROOK	6	TROD	6
INDEED	9	BOLD	7	BROW	6	UNTO	6
JESU	9	BOW	7	CALLED	6	VINE	6
KEEPS	9	BROUGHT	7	CAUSE	6	WALK	6
LEAST	9	CHANGE	7	CHEEKS	6	WALL	6
LIFE'S	9	CLEAR	7	COLOUR	6	WATCH	6
LIGHTS	9	COMPASS	7	CRIES	6	WOUND	6
LIVES	9	CRIMSON	7	DARE	6	AIRY	5
NEED	9	DEAREST	7	DARKSOME	6	AMIDST	5
PRESS	9	DEGREE	7	DAWN	6	ANSWER	5
RATHER	9	DOOR	7	DEAL	6	APPEAR	5
RING	9	DRAW	7	DIM	6	ARMS	5
SEEING	9	EVERYWHERE	7	DRAWN	6	AZURE	5
SHADOW	9	FAIL	7	DREW	6	BANDS	5
SHUT	9	FEAST	7	DROP	6	BEAUTY'S	5
SLEEP	9	FOLD	7	ELEMENT	6	BELLS	5
SMILE	9	FOND	7	FAIRER	6	BIRTHDAY	5
SOULS	9	FOUR	7	FALLEN	6	BITTER	5
STORM	9	FURTHER	7	FEW	6	BLAST	5
STRESS	9	GARDEN	7	FILL	6	BLESS	5
TENDER	9	GET	7	FINDS	6	BLEST	5
TIME'S	9	GIFT	7	FLASH	6	BLOSSOM	5
TOGETHER	9	GIVES	7	FLED	6	BREAKING	5
TOWARDS	9	HALF	7	FLEET	6	BREATHING	5
TREAD	9	HATE	7	FLOATING	6	BROAD	5
WIN	9	HEAVENLY	7	FLOOD	6	BROWN	5
WORTH	9	HEAVENS	7	GENTLE	6	BUILD	5
AGE	8	JESUS	7	GUESS	6	CASTARA	5
BANKS	8	LADY	7	HAIL	6	CAUGHT	5
BETTER	8	LAUGHTER	7	HANGS	6	CHEER	5
BID	8	LAW	7	HEART'S	6	CHOICE	5
BIRTH	8	LEAD	7	HOLDS	6	CLAY	5
BLISS	8	LEAF	7	HOLLOW	6	COMBS	5
BOY	8	MOUNTAIN	7	HOPES	6	COMPANY	5
BUDS	8	MOUTH	7	KING'S	6	COVER	5
CALLS	8	NOTES	7	KISS	6	CRISP	5
CHARITY	8	OPEN	7	LEVEL	6	CROSS	5
CLITHEROE	8	PIECE	7	LIFTED	6	DEALT	5
CLOSE	8	PITY	7	LIGHTNING	6	DEARLY	5
COPSE	8	PLEAD	7	LOVE'S	6	DECK	5
DOWN	8	PRAISE	7	MAKING	6	DELIGHT	5
EARS	8	PURE	7	MEANS	6	DISCOVER'D	5
EARTH'S	8	QUENCHED	7	MERCY	6	DOOM	5
EASTER	8	QUITE	7	MET	6	DOUBLE	5
EITHER	8	RANK	7	MILKY	6	DULL	5
EVENING	8	ROD	7	MONTH	6	DUMB	5
FLOCK	8	ROOM	7	MOOD	6	DUST	5
GAVE	8	SALT	7	MORTAL	6	EARLIER	5
GREAT	8	SHAPE	7	MYSTERY	6	EARNEST	5
GROWS	8	SHED	7	NATURE'S	6	EASE	5
HEAVEN'S	8	SICK	7	NEEDS	6	ENGLISH	5
HELL	8	SIGHS	7	PASS	6	FAIN	5
IMMORTAL	8	SITS	7	PLAIN	6	FALLING	5
LIFT	8	SONG	7	POWER	6	FAME	5
MEAN	8	SPEAK	7	PRAY	6	FAULT	5
MOON	8	STARRY	7	PROUD	6	FLEECE	5
MOULD	8	SUDDEN	7	QUOTE	6	FLING	5
RAINBOW	8	TAUGHT	7	REACH	6	FLOCKS	5
RED	8	THOUSAND	7	READ	6	FLUNG	5
REPENT	8	THRONG	7	RECK	6	FLY	5
RISE	8	VEIN	7	ROOTS	6	FOLDED	5
ROCKS	8	VIOLET	7	ROSY	6	FOLDS	5
ROYAL	8	VIRTUES	7	SCARCE	6	FOOD	5
SAD	8	WALLS	7	SENT	6	FORGE	5
SAYS	8	WANT	7	SHAKE	6	FORGOT	5
SEND	8	WEATHER	7	SHALLOW	6	FRAY	5
SENSE	8	WED	7	SHAPES	6	FRIEND	5
SHAME	8	WILLIAM	7	SHEWN	6	GHOST	5
SHEW	8	WISH	7	SIR	6	GIVEN	5
SMALL	8	WOE	7	SISTER	6	GLASSY	5

GREW	5	SPRINGS	5	DISMAL	4	PERILOUS	4
HANG	5	STANDING	5	DOWNS	4	PILGRIMS	4
HARVEST	5	STANDS	5	DRESS	4	PLOD	4
HEIGHT	5	STEEP	5	DRINK	4	PLOT	4
HELD	5	STORY	5	DROWNED	4	PLOUGH	4
HERO	5	STRANGE	5	EARLY	4	PRIMROSES	4
HIGHER	5	STREAMS	5	ENGLAND	4	PRIZE	4
HILLS	5	STROKE	5	ETERNAL	4	PROMISE	4
HUE	5	SUCCESS	5	FACES	4	QUINCE	4
HURLS	5	SUIT	5	FAITH	4	RIDES	4
ILL	5	SWUNG	5	FEARS	4	ROOF	4
JUBILEE	5	SYLVESTER	5	FEATURE	4	RUINOUS	4
KNEE	5	TAKES	5	FEED	4	RUNNING	4
KNOT	5	TASK	5	FELLED	4	SADNESS	4
LACE	5	TELLING	5	FELT	4	SAIL	4
LAID	5	TEN	5	FIERY	4	SAND	4
LANDSCAPE	5	TIDE	5	FIT	4	SAT	4
LEANS	5	TRUMPET	5	FIX'D	4	SCENE	4
LETTERS	5	TRY	5	FLAKES	4	SEASON	4
LINED	5	TUFT	5	FOAM	4	SEEK	4
LIP	5	TURNS	5	FONDER	4	SEEM	4
LIQUID	5	WEEDS	5	FORCE	4	SERVE	4
LO	5	WELCOME	5	FORGET	4	SERVED	4
LOWLY	5	WELKIN	5	FORM	4	SHARE	4
MAID	5	WHENCE	5	FRAIL	4	SHEAVED	4
MEANT	5	WHOLE	5	FRESHNESS	4	SHELTER	4
MEASURE	5	WING	5	FRETTED	4	SHEPHERD	4
MEN'S	5	WISE	5	FRINGE	4	SHINING	4
MIGHTY	5	WOMAN	5	FROWNING	4	SHORE	4
MILK	5	WOODS	5	GIANT	4	SHOT	4
MIRTH	5	WRECK	5	GRANDEUR	4	SHOWERS	4
MONSTROUS	5	WRING	5	GRAPES	4	SHOWS	4
MOTION	5	YOUNG	5	GREATER	4	SILENT	4
NEST	5	ALMOST	4	GRIEF	4	SIZE	4
PALE	5	ANON	4	GROW	4	SIZING	4
PARTED	5	BAD	4	GROWING	4	SKYLARK	4
PASSES	5	BARS	4	GROWN	4	SOUGHT	4
PASSION	5	BEGAN	4	GROWTH	4	SOUTH	4
PERFECT	5	BELL	4	HAPPY	4	SPHERED	4
PERHAPS	5	BENT	4	HARK	4	STAIN	4
PLAY	5	BIDS	4	HEAT	4	START	4
PLAYS	5	BLESSED	4	HENCE	4	STONES	4
PLEASURE	5	BLOOMS	4	HOAR	4	STORED	4
PRECIOUS	5	BLOWN	4	HURLING	4	STRENGTH	4
RACE	5	BONE	4	ICE	4	STROKES	4
RACK	5	BOWER	4	INSIGHT	4	SUBTLE	4
RAINS	5	BOYS	4	ITALY	4	SUCKED	4
RAYS	5	BRAKES	4	JACK	4	SUNLIGHT	4
READY	5	BREATHES	4	JUDGMENT	4	SURELY	4
REMEMBER	5	BRED	4	KEEN	4	SWEAT	4
RIDE	5	BREEZE	4	KISSES	4	SWEEP	4
RIM	5	BRIDE	4	KNOWING	4	SWEETER	4
RISEN	5	BRIGHTER	4	LAKES	4	SWEETLY	4
ROAD	5	BRITTLE	4	LARK	4	SWEPT	4
ROLL	5	BROTHER	4	LENGTH	4	SWORD	4
ROLLS	5	BROWS	4	LETTER	4	TALE	4
ROSES	5	BRUSH	4	LIMBS	4	TEACH	4
ROUNDS	5	BUD	4	LINES	4	TELLS	4
RUDE	5	BUILT	4	LITTER	4	THIRST	4
RUNS	5	BURDEN	4	LIVING	4	THORNS	4
RURAL	5	BURLY	4	LONGER	4	THUNDER	4
SACRED	5	BURN	4	LOT	4	TOIL	4
SAKE	5	BUY	4	LOUD	4	TOWER	4
SAPPHIRE	5	CANDLE	4	LOVER	4	TREADS	4
SCARCELY	5	CATCH	4	LOVES	4	TREASURE	4
SCARLET	5	CHOKE	4	LUSH	4	TRESSES	4
SEEMED	5	CHOOSE	4	MAIN	4	TRIUMPH	4
SERVES	5	CITY	4	MANKIND	4	TUFTS	4
SHARP	5	CLAMMY	4	MARCH	4	TWICE	4
SHEER	5	CONCEIVED	4	MEADOW	4	UNDERNEATH	4
SHOCK	5	CORN	4	MEANING	4	UNDO	4
SHORT	5	COUNT	4	MELTED	4	UNDONE	4
SHOULDER	5	COURT	4	MELTING	4	UNSEEN	4
SHOW	5	CRIED	4	MIGHT	4	VALES	4
SHOWER	5	CRUCIFIED	4	MILD	4	VAST	4
SIGHTS	5	CRUST	4	MILE	4	VAULT	4
SIMPLE	5	CUCKOO	4	MILES	4	VIRGIN	4
SINGING	5	CURSE	4	MULTITUDE	4	WALES	4
SIT	5	DANDLED	4	MUSE	4	WALKS	4
SKILL	5	DAPPLED	4	NATURAL	4	WANDERING	4
SLENDER	5	DAUGHTER	4	NECK	4	WANED	4
SLOW	5	DAY'S	4	NOTE	4	WANTING	4
SMART	5	DEARER	4	NOWHERE	4	WAR	4
SMOOTH	5	DEATH'S	4	OFTEN	4	WARNED	4
SNOWS	5	DEED	4	PALMS	4	WARS	4
SORROW	5	DEEPER	4	PARADISE	4	WAVES	4
SPARE	5	DIED	4	PASSING	4	WEB	4
SPIRITS	5	DIP	4	PEN	4	WEEP	4

Word		Word		Word		Word	
WHETHER	4	CROWD	3	GIRL	3	MIST	3
WIFE	4	CRUCIFY	3	GLAD	3	MISTS	3
WILDERNESS	4	CRUSHED	3	GLADNESS	3	MOUNTING	3
WINE	4	CRYING	3	GLARE	3	MOVE	3
WITNESS	4	CUT	3	GLORIOUS	3	MOVED	3
WON	4	DAFFODILS	3	GLOVE	3	MYSTERIES	3
WONDROUS	4	DALE	3	GLOW	3	NERVE	3
WORLDS	4	DANCED	3	GODHEAD	3	NE'ER	3
WRITTEN	4	DANCES	3	GODS	3	NEWS	3
WRONG	4	DANGEROUS	3	GOSPEL	3	NINE	3
YIELDS	4	DEAN	3	GRANT	3	NOISE	3
ACT	3	DELIGHTFUL	3	GRATE	3	NUN	3
ADMIRE	3	DELIVER	3	GROSS	3	OBEY	3
ADORED	3	DESCENDING	3	GUILE	3	OCEAN	3
AGO	3	DESIRED	3	GUILT	3	OIL	3
AIRS	3	DIAMOND	3	GUSTS	3	ORCHARD	3
ALICE	3	DIES	3	GWENVREWI	3	OVERHEAD	3
ALIEN	3	DISAPPOINTMENT	3	HALL	3	PACKED	3
ALLOWS	3	DISTANCE	3	HANDLE	3	PAINS	3
ALOOF	3	DOING	3	HAPPIER	3	PALACE	3
ALTER'D	3	DOORS	3	HARRY	3	PALM	3
AMEN	3	DOROTHY	3	HATED	3	PARTING	3
APRIL	3	DOUBT	3	HAVEN	3	PAUL	3
ARISE	3	DREAD	3	HEADS	3	PAY	3
ASH	3	DREADFUL	3	HEARING	3	PEARL	3
ASK'D	3	DREAM	3	HEED	3	PENT	3
ASTRAY	3	DREAMS	3	HENRY	3	PIECED	3
AUTUMN	3	DRIFT	3	HID	3	PIETY	3
AY	3	DROOP	3	HIDE	3	PINE	3
BALANCED	3	DROVE	3	HIDES	3	PIPE	3
BALL	3	DRUM	3	HIT	3	PITEOUS	3
BARREN	3	DUE	3	HITHER	3	PLACES	3
BEAM	3	DUSK	3	HOLLOWS	3	PLIGHTED	3
BEAMS	3	DUTY	3	HOOD	3	PLOTTED	3
BEARING	3	DWELLS	3	HORN	3	PLUMAGE	3
BEAST	3	DYING	3	HORNS	3	POINT	3
BEGIN	3	EASY	3	HORROR	3	PORES	3
BEHOLD	3	EAT	3	HOST	3	PRAYERS	3
BETWIXT	3	ECSTASY	3	HOVER	3	PRESSED	3
BLAZON	3	EGGS	3	HUES	3	PRETTY	3
BLEAK	3	EGYPTIAN	3	HUNGER	3	PRIME	3
BLEEDING	3	ELEMENTS	3	HURL	3	PRINCE	3
BLINDING	3	ELSEWHERE	3	INNER	3	PRINCIPAL	3
BLOCK	3	ENDEARS	3	INTEREST	3	PRIZED	3
BLOODY	3	ENDS	3	IRON	3	PROOF	3
BOAST	3	ENORMOUS	3	JOHN	3	PROPER	3
BOON	3	EQUAL	3	JOSTLING	3	PROVE	3
BORNE	3	EVERYTHING	3	JUICY	3	PULL	3
BOUGH	3	EXQUISITE	3	KEEL	3	PURPLE	3
BRACE	3	FAILS	3	KEN	3	PURPOSE	3
BRAIN	3	FAIRY	3	KEY	3	PUTS	3
BREATHED	3	FANCIES	3	KINGS	3	QUICK	3
BRINGING	3	FATAL	3	KNEES	3	RARELY	3
BRINGS	3	FATHERS	3	KNELT	3	REACH'D	3
BRONZE	3	FEASTS	3	LACED	3	REASON	3
BROODS	3	FEATHER	3	LAKE	3	RECORDED	3
BUGLE	3	FEATURES	3	LANCE	3	REPLY	3
BURNING	3	FEE	3	LANTERN	3	RESCUE	3
BURNS	3	FELIX	3	LASHES	3	RICHARD	3
CAESAR'S	3	FETCHED	3	LEARNT	3	RIDING	3
CALLING	3	FIE	3	LEAVED	3	RIFE	3
CARELESS	3	FILLS	3	LED	3	RINGS	3
CARRIED	3	FINGER	3	LEND	3	RISING	3
CENTRAL	3	FLAGS	3	LIDS	3	ROLLED	3
CENTRE	3	FLAMES	3	LINE	3	ROLLING	3
CHANGED	3	FLANK	3	LISTEN	3	ROOT	3
CHANGEFUL	3	FLASHED	3	LISTS	3	RUINS	3
CHANGING	3	FLIGHT	3	LOCK	3	RUSH	3
CHARGED	3	FLOODS	3	LODGES	3	SANK	3
CHARM	3	FLOW	3	LOOKING	3	SAP	3
CHARMS	3	FLUSH	3	LOOK'D	3	SATURN	3
CHEEK	3	FOLLOWING	3	LORE	3	SCOPE	3
CHURL	3	FOOL	3	LOSS	3	SEAMEN	3
CLIFF	3	FOREHEAD	3	LUST	3	SEASONS	3
CLIFFS	3	FORGIVE	3	MAJESTY	3	SEEMING	3
CLIME	3	FORWARD	3	MANHOOD	3	SELVES	3
CLINGS	3	FOUNTAINS	3	MARY'S	3	SENSITIVE	3
COMMON	3	FRAMED	3	MASTERY	3	SEVERAL	3
CONCEIVE	3	FRANCE	3	MATE	3	SHADE	3
CONTENTED	3	FRET	3	MATTER	3	SHEAF	3
CONVENT	3	FRIENDS	3	MEADOWS	3	SHEATHE	3
COOL	3	FRIGHTFUL	3	MELT	3	SHEEP	3
COPYING	3	FURLED	3	MERCIFUL	3	SHIRE	3
COUNTER	3	FURROW	3	MERMAIDS	3	SHOALS	3
COVERS	3	GALE	3	MESSENGER	3	SHOCKS	3
CREEP	3	GAZES	3	MESSENGERS	3	SHONE	3
CREPT	3	GIFTS	3	MILL	3	SHOUT	3
CREW	3	GILT	3	MIND'S	3	SIGH	3

Word	N	Word	N	Word	N	Word	N
SIGN	3	WEEPING	3	BLAZE	2	CONSOLATION	2
SIGNAL	3	WELLS	3	BLAZONED	2	COO	2
SILKY	3	WEPT	3	BLEAR	2	COOLING	2
SINGLE	3	WHATEVER	3	BLEAT	2	CORNER	2
SINS	3	WHEEL	3	BLEED	2	CORNERS	2
SIRE	3	WHEREIN	3	BLISSFUL	2	CORNICE	2
SITTING	3	WICKED	3	BLOCKS	2	CORPSE	2
SLEEK	3	WILDER	3	BLOT	2	CORRIDORS	2
SLIPS	3	WINGED	3	BLOTS	2	CORSE	2
SMELL	3	WINTERING	3	BLOWS	2	COUNTENANCE	2
SMILED	3	WIT	3	BOARDS	2	COUNTERPART	2
SOFT	3	WOKE	3	BODIES	2	COUNTLESS	2
SOIL	3	WOMB	3	BOISTEROUS	2	COURTS	2
SORES	3	WONDERING	3	BOLDER	2	COUSIN	2
SOW	3	WONT	3	BOOK	2	CRASH	2
SOWN	3	WORSHIP	3	BOUGHT	2	CREASED	2
SPARKY	3	WOUNDS	3	BOW'D	2	CREST	2
SPEAKS	3	WRUNG	3	BOWS	2	CROWDED	2
SPED	3	ABROAD	2	BRAGGART	2	CROWDING	2
SPLENDOUR	3	ACRE	2	BRAIDS	2	CROWDS	2
SPOKE	3	ACTS	2	BRAINS	2	CROWNALS	2
SPOTS	3	ADOWN	2	BRANCHES	2	CROWNING	2
STARE	3	AERIAL	2	BRANCHY	2	CROWNS	2
STARLIGHT	3	AGE'S	2	BRAVE	2	CRUSH	2
STATE	3	AGES	2	BRAZEN	2	CRUSH'D	2
STAY	3	A-WANTING	2	BREEZY	2	CRUTCHES	2
STEADY	3	ALBEIT	2	BRIEF	2	CUMBER	2
						CURRENT	2
STIR	3	ALIVE	2	BRILLIANT	2	CURSED	2
STIRRED	3	ALL-STARR'D	2	BRIM	2	CURSES	2
STOLE	3	ALL'S	2	BRIMS	2	DAINTY	2
STONY	3	ALMS	2	BRINE	2	DAMASQU'D	2
STOPS	3	ALOFT	2	BRITAIN	2	DANCING	2
STRUGGLE	3	ALSO	2	BROKE	2	DANK	2
STRUNG	3	ALTAR	2	BROOD	2	DARED	2
SUCK	3	ALWAY	2	BROOKS	2	DARING	2
SUNSET	3	AMAIN	2	BROTH	2	DARKER	2
SURLY	3	AMBER	2	BRUISED	2	DATE	2
SWEEPS	3	AMONGST	2	BUBBLES	2	DAUGHTERS	2
SWEETS	3	ANGEL'S	2	BUGLER	2	DAZZLING	2
SWELL	3	ANYTHING	2	BUOY	2	DEALS	2
SWIM	3	ANYWHERE	2	BURNISH	2	DEARTH	2
SWING	3	APPEAL	2	BUSHES	2	DEBT	2
SWINGS	3	APPROVED	2	CAERWYS	2	DECKS	2
TACKLE	3	APT	2	CALL'D	2	DEEPLY	2
TEAR	3	ARC	2	CALM	2	DEEPS	2
TEEMING	3	ARGENT	2	CAPS	2	DEFEAT	2
TERRIBLE	3	ARM	2	CAREFUL-SPACED	2	DELIGHTFULLY	2
TH	3	AROSE	2	CARES	2	DELVE	2
THECLA	3	ASHES	2	CARMINE	2	DEN	2
THEW	3	ASKING	2	CAROL	2	DEPARTING	2
THICKEN'D	3	ASKS	2	CARRIES	2	DEPLORE	2
THIRD	3	ASLEEP	2	CARRY	2	DESCEND	2
THOUSANDS	3	ATTAIN	2	CART	2	DESPATCH	2
THROW	3	AUTUMN-TIME	2	CEASE	2	DESPERATE	2
TIES	3	BABBLE	2	CENTRES	2	DESPISE	2
TINY	3	BALLAD	2	CHANNEL	2	DEUTSCHLAND	2
TITLE	3	BALLS	2	CHARACTER	2	DEWS	2
TO-DAY	3	BAND	2	CHARGE	2	DEWY	2
TOMORROW	3	BANES	2	CHEEVIO	2	DIAMONDS	2
TORN	3	BANK	2	CHESTNUT	2	DISTANT	2
TOUCHED	3	BARELY	2	CHIEF	2	DISTRESS	2
TREAT	3	BARROW	2	CHILDS	2	DOGGED	2
TREATS	3	BASE	2	CHILL	2	DOOMED	2
TRICKLE	3	BATH	2	CHIME	2	DOROTHEA	2
TRUST	3	BATHE	2	CHOICEST	2	DOUBTLESS	2
TUNE	3	BEACON	2	CHORDS	2	DOUGH	2
TURNING	3	BEAD	2	CHOSE	2	DOVE	2
TWELVE	3	BEATS	2	CHRISTIAN	2	DRAUGHT	2
UNDERSTOOD	3	BEAUTIFUL	2	CHRISTMAS	2	DRAWS	2
UNTIL	3	BECKONED	2	CIRCLE	2	DREAMED	2
UPPER	3	BEDS	2	CIRCLED	2	DREAM'D	2
VEINS	3	BEETLING	2	CLAD	2	DREAR	2
VIOLETS	3	BEING'S	2	CLASPED	2	DRENCH'D	2
VIRTUE	3	BELIEVE	2	CLEARS	2	DRIVES	2
WAKE	3	BELIEVES	2	CLEAVES	2	DRIVING	2
WAKING	3	BELLED	2	CLOSE-SHUT	2	DROOPING	2
WAND	3	BEREFT	2	CLOT	2	DROOP'D	2
WANTS	3	BEUNO	2	CLOTHE	2	DUCT	2
WARE	3	BEVY	2	CLUSTER	2	DULY	2
WASH	3	BILL	2	COIL	2	DWELT	2
WASHING	3	BILLOW	2	COLOURS	2	DWINDLED	2
WASTES	3	BILLOWS	2	COMB	2	DYE	2
WATCHED	3	BILLOWY	2	COMFORTING	2	EARLIEST	2
WATERY	3	BIND	2	COMFORTLESS	2	EARTHLESS	2
WEALTH	3	BIRDS	2	COMING	2	EASILY	2
WEDDED	3	BITTERNESS	2	COMMONWEAL	2	EAVES	2
WEDLOCK	3	BLADE	2	CONDITION	2	ECHOING	2
WEED	3	BLADES	2	CONSCIENCE	2	ECSTACY	2

EDGE	2	FURLS	2	INNOCENT	2	MAZED	2
ELDER	2	FURTHEST	2	INSTEAD	2	MAZY	2
EMBERS	2	GALAHAD	2	INSTRUMENT	2	MEAD	2
EMPTY	2	GALES	2	INTENT	2	MEANWHILE	2
ENDED	2	GALL	2	ISLE	2	MEASURED	2
ENDING	2	GALLANT	2	ISLED	2	MEAT	2
ENROLL'D	2	GARLANDED	2	JACINTH	2	MEEK	2
ESPECIAL	2	GEAR	2	JANE	2	MEETS	2
EVE	2	GENTLY	2	JAR	2	MELLOW	2
EVERLASTING	2	GILDS	2	JEWS	2	MELLS	2
EVERYONE	2	GIRTH	2	JOVE'S	2	MELTS	2
EVIL	2	GIVER	2	JUICE	2	MEMBERS	2
EYELASH	2	GLASS	2	KELSON	2	MEND	2
EYELID	2	GLEAM'D	2	KILL	2	MENDED	2
FABIAN	2	GLIDE	2	KNEEL	2	MERE	2
FADED	2	GLOWS	2	KNOTS	2	MERELY	2
FAINT	2	GOING	2	LACK	2	MERRY	2
FAITHFUL	2	GOODNIGHT	2	LAD	2	MESSES	2
FALLOW	2	GOSHEN	2	LADS	2	MID-AIR	2
FALL'N	2	GOT	2	LAMENT	2	MIDNIGHT	2
FAMILIAR	2	GRACES	2	LANDMARK	2	MIDST	2
FAN	2	GRAIN	2	LANGUISH'D	2	MIDSUMMER	2
FANCY	2	GRANITE	2	LAPPED	2	MILLION	2
FANG	2	GRANTED	2	LARGE	2	MINDS	2
FANS	2	GRAVE	2	LASH	2	MINED	2
FASTENED	2	GREATNESS	2	LASHED	2	MINGLE	2
FASTER	2	GREENERY	2	LATCH	2	MIRACLE	2
FAWNING	2	GREET	2	LATELY	2	MIRROR	2
FEARING	2	GRIMY	2	LAUGH	2	MISADVENTURE	2
FEASTING	2	GRIND	2	LAWLESS	2	MOISTURE	2
FEATHERS	2	GROANS	2	LAWRENCE	2	MOLTEN	2
FEATHERY	2	GROINS	2	LAYING	2	MONKS	2
FEEDS	2	GROPES	2	LEAFY	2	MONTHS	2
FEELING	2	GROPING	2	LEAGUES	2	MORNING'S	2
FELLOWSHIP	2	GROVE	2	LEANING	2	MORSELS	2
FELLS	2	GUESSED	2	LEAPING	2	MOSS	2
FETCH	2	GUILTY	2	LEARNED	2	MOTES	2
FICKLE	2	GULLIES	2	LEAVING	2	MOTHERHOOD	2
FIERCE	2	GURGLED	2	LEISURE	2	MOTHERING	2
FIGHT	2	GURGLING	2	LENT	2	MOTHERS	2
FILLED	2	HALT	2	LENTEN	2	MOTIONABLE	2
FILMY	2	HANGING	2	LESSEN'D	2	MOULDED	2
FIN	2	HARBOUR	2	LEVELS	2	MOUNTAINS	2
FINER	2	HARM	2	LEWD	2	MOURNING	2
FINISH'D	2	HARMONIES	2	LIAR	2	MOUTHED	2
FIRM	2	HAVING	2	LIBERTIES	2	MOVES	2
FIRMAMENT	2	HAVOC	2	LIFTS	2	MULTIPLY	2
FLAG	2	HAZARD	2	LIGHTED	2	MURDER	2
FLANKS	2	HEALTH	2	LIGHTNINGS	2	MURDEROUS	2
FLARE	2	HEARS	2	LINEAMENT	2	MUSICAL	2
FLASHES	2	HEATHENISH	2	LINGER	2	MYRIAD	2
FLAT	2	HEAVE	2	LISTENED	2	MYRTLE	2
FLATTERY	2	HEDGES	2	LISTENING	2	NAILS	2
FLAWED	2	HEEL	2	LIT	2	NATION	2
FLEECED	2	HEIR	2	LIVED	2	NAZARETH	2
FLICKERING	2	HELEN	2	LOOKED	2	NEAREST	2
FLIES	2	HELP	2	LOOM	2	NEIGHBOUR	2
FLINT	2	HENCEFORTH	2	LOOSE	2	NEWLY-DRAWN	2
FLINTY	2	HERD	2	LORDLY	2	NIGH	2
FLOAT	2	HERITAGE	2	LOUDER	2	NIGHTFALL	2
FLOATS	2	HEW	2	LOVELESS	2	NIGHTINGALE	2
FLOWING	2	HIDEOUS	2	LOVELIEST	2	NIGHT'S	2
FLOWN	2	HIDING	2	LOVELINESS	2	NIGHTS	2
FLUSHED	2	HIES	2	LOV'D	2	NILE	2
FLYING	2	HIGHEST	2	LOW-DOWN	2	NIX	2
FOLIAG'D	2	HISSING	2	LUSTRES	2	NOON	2
FOOLISH	2	HOARD	2	MAIDENS	2	NOSTRILS	2
FOOTING	2	HOLINESS	2	MAID'S	2	NUMBER	2
FORBID	2	HONEY	2	MALLOW-ROW	2	NURSLES	2
FORECAST	2	HOPELESS	2	MALLOW'S	2	OAKS	2
FOREIGN	2	HOT	2	MANAGED	2	OFFEND	2
FORELOCK	2	HOUSES	2	MANLY	2	OFFERING	2
FORGOTTEN	2	HOWEVER	2	MANNA	2	OILS	2
FORLORN	2	HUNDRED	2	MAR	2	ONEWHERE	2
FORSAKEN	2	HUNT	2	MARCHING	2	OOZE	2
FOUGHT	2	HUNTING	2	MARKET	2	OPEN'D	2
FOUL	2	HURDLES	2	MARKING	2	OPENS	2
FOUNDERING	2	HURLED	2	MARK'D	2	ORB'D	2
FRAGRANCE	2	HURTLE	2	MARRED	2	ORIENCE	2
FRAME	2	HUSH	2	MARVELLOUS	2	ORIGINAL	2
FRANK	2	ICE-BLOCKS	2	MASKS	2	OUTRIGHT	2
FREED	2	IDLE	2	MASSY	2	OUTWARD	2
FREELY	2	IMMACULATE	2	MASTERING	2	OVERFLOW	2
FRETTY	2	IMPERFECT	2	MASTERS	2	OXFORD	2
FRIEZE	2	INDOORS	2	MATCHED	2	PACE	2
FRONTING	2	INFINITE	2	MATCHLESS	2	PALMY	2
FUNERAL	2	INLY	2	MATES	2	PANGS	2
FUR	2	INMOST	2	MAZE	2	PARALLEL	2

PARDON	2	REGIMEN	2	SINNER	2	TABOUR	2
PARK	2	REIGNS	2	SINNING	2	TAIL	2
PARLEY	2	RE-ATTRIBUTING	2	SISTERS	2	TAKEN	2
PARTLESS	2	RELIEF	2	SIX	2	TALONS	2
PARTS	2	RELISH	2	SKEINS	2	TARS	2
PASSAGE	2	REMAINDER	2	SKIRT	2	TARSUS	2
PASSED	2	REMEMBERING	2	SKYWARDS	2	TASTY	2
PASS'D	2	REMOTE	2	SLACK	2	TEMPEST	2
PASTORAL	2	REPAIR	2	SLEPT	2	TEMPLE	2
PASTURES	2	REPEAT	2	SLIGHT	2	TEXT	2
PATH	2	REPLIES	2	SLIGHTED	2	THENCE	2
PEBBLY	2	REVEL	2	SLIME	2	THEREBY	2
PECULIAR	2	REVENGE	2	SLUMBER	2	THINE	2
PEERS	2	RHYME	2	SLUMBERED	2	THINKS	2
PENANCE	2	RIBS	2	SMELLS	2	THORN	2
PENCE	2	RIND	2	SMOTHER	2	THREAD	2
PENNON	2	RINDS	2	SMOULDERING	2	THRICE	2
PEOPLE	2	RIOT	2	SNOWWHITE	2	THRIVE	2
PERCEIVED	2	RISES	2	SOARING	2	THROAT	2
PERSISTENCY	2	RIVERS	2	SOBER	2	THROBBING	2
PHILIP	2	RIVING	2	SOLID	2	THRONGED	2
PHOEBUS	2	ROAR	2	SOLITUDE	2	THRONGS	2
PIERCE	2	RODE	2	SONS	2	TIDES	2
PIERCED	2	RODS	2	SORE	2	TIDING	2
PINES	2	ROOD	2	SOUL'S	2	TIED	2
PINING	2	ROUGH	2	SOURS	2	TILT	2
PITCHED	2	ROW	2	SOWER	2	TIMBER	2
PLAIT	2	ROWELS	2	SPAN	2	TINTED	2
PLAN	2	RUCK	2	SPARED	2	TIRE	2
PLANETS	2	RUIN	2	SPARK	2	TIRED	2
PLASH	2	RUNG	2	SPEECH	2	TODAY	2
PLAY'D	2	RUSTLE	2	SPELLS	2	TO-MORROW	2
PLEA	2	'CAUSE	2	SPIDER'S	2	TO-NIGHT	2
PLEASE	2	'GAN	2	SPILL	2	TONES	2
PLUMED	2	SAFE	2	SPINS	2	TONGUES	2
PLUMES	2	SAINT	2	SPIRITUAL	2	TONIGHT	2
PLY	2	SALVATION	2	SPOUSE	2	TOOL	2
POET	2	SANDAL	2	SPRING'S	2	TORMENTED	2
POINTED	2	SANDS	2	SPY	2	TOUCHING	2
POISE	2	SAVIOUR	2	ST	2	TOUCH'D	2
POISED	2	SAYING	2	STAINED	2	TRAVELLING	2
POLE	2	SCALE	2	STARTLE	2	TREMBLING	2
PORE	2	SCATTER	2	STATUARY	2	TRIM	2
POSTS	2	SCHOOL	2	STEALING	2	TROPES	2
POWERFUL	2	SCIENCE	2	STEALS	2	TRULY	2
POWERS	2	SCIONS	2	STEEPED	2	TUMBLED	2
PRAISED	2	SCORE	2	STILL-PURPLING	2	TURN'D	2
PREFERRED	2	SCOURGE	2	STOOL	2	UNCLE	2
PRESENT	2	SCROLLED	2	STOP	2	UNCOUTH	2
PREY	2	SEAL	2	STORE	2	UNDERSTAND	2
PRIMROSE	2	SEALED	2	STORMY	2	UNFURLED	2
PRISON	2	SEARCH	2	STRAIGHT	2	UNHOLY	2
PROCONSUL	2	SEAT	2	STRAND	2	UNKNOWN	2
PROMISED	2	SECRET	2	STRANDS	2	UNSET	2
PROVIDENCE	2	SEED	2	STRANGELY	2	UPWARD	2
PULL'D	2	SENSES	2	STRANGER	2	UPWARDS	2
PURCELL	2	SEQUENCES	2	STRAW	2	USED	2
PURPORT	2	SERVICE	2	STRAY	2	UTTERANCE	2
QUAILS	2	SERVINGMAN	2	STREAM'D	2	UTTERED	2
QUARTER	2	SETS	2	STRETCHING	2	UTTERING	2
QUEEN	2	SEXING	2	STRETCH'D	2	UTTERLY	2
QUELL	2	SHADES	2	STRIKES	2	VACANT	2
QUELLED	2	SHAFTS	2	STRINGS	2	VAIN	2
QUENCH	2	SHAKEN	2	STROVE	2	VALERIAN	2
QUESTION	2	SHAKES	2	STUMBLING	2	VALLEY	2
QUICKLY	2	SHANK	2	STUNG	2	VALOUR	2
QUINCES	2	SHAPED	2	SUBJECT	2	VAULTING	2
RACED	2	SHARES	2	SUCKS	2	VEER	2
RACING	2	SHEARED	2	SUDDENLY	2	VEIL	2
RAFTS	2	SHEARING	2	SUITING	2	VICE	2
RAGE	2	SHEEN	2	SUMMERTIME	2	VIOL	2
RANDAL	2	SHEENY	2	SUNDER'D	2	VIOLENT	2
RANGE	2	SHELL	2	SUNG	2	VIRGINAL	2
RANG'D	2	SHELLY	2	SUNK	2	VISION	2
RANKED	2	SHEPHERDS	2	SUNNY	2	VISITING	2
RANKS	2	SHINES	2	SWARD	2	VITAL	2
RANSOM	2	SHIP	2	SWARM	2	VOID	2
RASH	2	SHOD	2	SWART	2	WAIST	2
REALM	2	SHOOTS	2	SWAYING	2	WAITS	2
REARS	2	SHOULDERS	2	SWAY'D	2	WAKED	2
REBEL	2	SHOWY	2	SWAYS	2	WALKED	2
REBELLION	2	SHRINE	2	SWEAR	2	WANTON	2
RECITAL	2	SHROUD	2	SWEARS	2	WARBLING	2
RECKON	2	SICKNESS	2	SWIFT	2	WARMLY	2
RECOVERY	2	SIGHING	2	SWIMMING	2	WARPED	2
REEL	2	SILK	2	SWINISHLY	2	WARRANTS	2
REEVE	2	SILKEN	2	SWIRLING	2	WATCHET	2
REFUSES	2	SINNED	2	SYCAMORE	2	WATCHING	2

WATER'D	2	ACORN-CUP	1	ANVIL-DING	1	BALDBRIGHT	1
WATERY-PLATED	2	ACQUAINTANCE	1	APOLLO	1	BALES	1
WAVE	2	ACRES	1	APPAL	1	BALM	1
WAVED	2	ADAMANTINE	1	APPAREL'D	1	BAN	1
WAVING	2	ADAZZLE	1	APPEALING	1	BANKRUPT	1
WAXED	2	ADD	1	APPEARING	1	BANK'S	1
WAXEN	2	ADELA	1	APPEAR'D	1	BANNED	1
WEAK	2	ADMIRED	1	APPLEDURCOMBE	1	BANN'D	1
WEARINESS	2	ADORE	1	APPLE-TREES	1	BANQUET	1
WEARS	2	ADVANCE	1	APPLES	1	BANQUET-HALL	1
WEEKS	2	ADVERSITY	1	APPLY	1	BANS	1
WEEPS	2	ADVISE	1	APPREHEND	1	BAR	1
WELL-BRED	2	AEOLIS	1	APPROVE	1	BARBAROUS	1
WEND	2	AEONS	1	APRIL-WEATHER	1	BAREBILL	1
WHARVES	2	AETHER	1	ARCADIA	1	BARED	1
WHELMS	2	AFAR	1	ARCADIAN	1	BARGAIN	1
WHEREAS	2	AFFECTION	1	ARCH	1	BARGE	1
WHEREFORE	2	AFFINED	1	ARCHED	1	BARKEN	1
WHIRL	2	AFFLICTED	1	ARCHES	1	BARLEY	1
WHISPERS	2	AFFLICTIVE	1	ARCHING	1	BARN	1
WHOLESOME	2	AFFLICTS	1	ARCH-ESPECIAL	1	BARRACK	1
WILDNESS	2	AFLASH	1	ARCS	1	BARRED	1
WILLIAM'S	2	AFOOT	1	ARCTURUS-SET	1	BARREL	1
WINCH	2	AFRAID	1	ARGUED	1	BARRELLED	1
WINDLACED	2	AFRESH	1	ARIGHT	1	BARRENS	1
WINDOW	2	AFTERCAST	1	ARK	1	BARRIERS	1
WINDY	2	AFTERDRAUGHT	1	AROUSED	1	BARROWY	1
WINNING	2	AFTER-COMERS	1	ARRAY	1	BARR'D	1
WINTER-TIME	2	AFTER-WORDS	1	ARTHUR	1	BARTER	1
WINTER'S	2	AFTERNOON	1	ARTHUR'S	1	BARTER'D	1
WINTRY	2	AGE-OLD	1	ARTIST	1	BASKS	1
WIRY	2	AGGRANDISE	1	ARTS	1	BASON	1
WISDOM	2	AID	1	ASCEND	1	BASS	1
WITS	2	AIDENN	1	ASCENDANCY	1	BAST	1
WOEFUL	2	AIM	1	ASCRIBED	1	BAT	1
WOMEN	2	AIRBUILT	1	ASHBOUGHS	1	BATHED	1
WONDER'S	2	AIR-BLENDED	1	ASHINESS	1	BATHES	1
WONDERS	2	AIR-CRISPING	1	ASH-TOPS	1	BATHING	1
WOOD-SORREL	2	AIR'S	1	ASIDE	1	BATS	1
WOODLAND	2	AIRWARDS	1	ASKED	1	BATTERING	1
WORDSWORTH	2	AIRWORLD	1	ASLANT	1	BATTLE	1
WORDY	2	AIRY-GREY	1	ASPECT	1	BATTLED	1
WORE	2	AKIN	1	ASPEN'S	1	BATTLING	1
WORLD-MOTHERING	2	ALARMS	1	ASPENS	1	BAYS	1
WORM	2	ALE	1	ASSAULT	1	BEACH	1
WORTHY	2	ALERT	1	ASSAULTING	1	BEADBONNY	1
WRECKED	2	ALFONSO	1	ASSAY	1	BEAKLEAVED	1
WRECKS	2	ALIGHT	1	ASSIGN'D	1	BEAMING	1
WRETCH	2	ALIGHTED	1	ASSURED	1	BEAM-BLIND	1
WRINGS	2	ALIKE	1	ASSYRIAN	1	BEAN	1
WRINKLES	2	ALL-ACCEPTING	1	ASTERN	1	BEARER	1
WRIT	2	ALL-A-LEAF	1	ASTRAIN	1	BEARS	1
WRITE	2	ALL-BELATED	1	ASTRAL	1	BEATING	1
YEARN'D	2	ALL-FIRE	1	ASTREW	1	BEAUTIES	1
YEAR'S	2	ALL-HEAL	1	ASTROLOGIC	1	BEAUTY-BOW	1
YORE	2	ALL-IN-ALL	1	ASWARM	1	BEAUTY-IN-THE-GH	1
ZENITH	2	ALL-SURFY	1	ATLANTIC	1	BECOME	1
ZEST	2	ALLOW	1	ATMOSPHERE	1	BEDDED	1
ZEUS	2	ALLSEEING	1	ATONE	1	BEE	1
ABAKE	1	ALMONER	1	ATTEMPTED	1	BEECHBOLE	1
ABANDONED	1	ALP	1	ATTIRE	1	BEES	1
ABEL	1	ALTAR-TAPERS	1	ATTRIBUTES	1	BEETLE-BROWED	1
ABELES	1	ALTAR-VESSELS	1	ATTUNEABLE	1	BEFAL	1
ABIDE	1	ALTARS	1	ATTUNING	1	BEFALL	1
ABIDES	1	ALTER	1	AUREOLES	1	BEFORE-TIME-TAKE	1
ABJECT	1	ALTHO	1	AUSTIN	1	BEGGED	1
ABODE	1	ALTOGETHER	1	AUTHENTIC	1	BEHAVIOUR	1
ABOLISHED	1	AMANSSTRENGTH	1	AVENGE	1	BEHOLDER	1
ABOUND	1	AMAZE	1	AVOID	1	BELA	1
ABREAST	1	AMAZED	1	AVOW	1	BELIE	1
ABRUPT	1	AMEND	1	AWFUL	1	BELIEF	1
ABUNDANT	1	AMENDS	1	AWHILE	1	BELIEVED	1
ABUTMENTS	1	AMERICAN-OUTWARD	1	AWOKE	1	BELLBRIGHT	1
ABYSMAL	1	AMETHYST	1	AYE	1	BELLEISLE	1
ABYSSES	1	AMISS	1	AZURED	1	BELLEROPHON	1
ACANTHUS-CROWN'D	1	ANCIENT	1	AZURING-OVER	1	BELLISLE	1
ACCENTS	1	ANCLES	1	AZUROUS	1	BELL-DROPS	1
ACCEPT	1	ANDROMEDA	1	BABES	1	BELL-SWARMED	1
ACCEPTANCE	1	ANEW	1	BABYHOOD	1	BELLOWS	1
ACCEPTED	1	ANGEL-WARDER	1	BACKED	1	BELL'S	1
ACCESSORIES	1	ANIGH	1	BACKWARD	1	BELONG	1
ACCIDENTS	1	ANOINTED	1	BACKWHEELS	1	BELTS	1
ACCUMULATED	1	ANSWERED	1	BAFFLE	1	BELVEDERE	1
ACHES	1	ANSWERING	1	BAFFLED	1	BEND	1
ACHIEVE	1	ANTINOUS	1	BAFFLING	1	BENDS	1
ACHING	1	ANTIPODES	1	BALANCE	1	BENEDICTION	1
ACKNOWLEDGING	1	ANTIQUE	1	BALANCES	1	BENEFITS	1
ACORN	1	ANVIL	1	BALD	1	BERG	1

BERYL	1	BOOKISH	1	BURSTS	1	CHAOTIC	1
BERYL-COVERED	1	BOONS	1	BURTHEN	1	CHAPEL-SIDE	1
BESEECH	1	BOOTS	1	BURY	1	CHAPLETED	1
BESIDES	1	BORDERS	1	BUSH-BROWED	1	CHAPLETS	1
BESPOKEN	1	BOREAS	1	BUSHYBOWERED	1	CHAPTERED	1
BESTOWING	1	BORED	1	BUSINESS	1	CHARACTERED	1
BETHLEHEM	1	BORES	1	BUSY	1	CHARITABLE	1
BETHLEM	1	BOROUGHS	1	BUTCHER	1	CHARITY'S	1
BETHLEMS	1	BORROW	1	BUTTERFLIES	1	CHARLES'S	1
BETIMES	1	BOSOM	1	BUTTER-BURR	1	CHARMED	1
BETRAY	1	BOSS'D	1	BUTT'S	1	CHARNELHOUSE-GRA	1
BETRAY'D	1	ROUNDEN	1	BUYS	1	CHART	1
BETTER'D	1	BOW-BEND	1	BYE-WAYS	1	CHARTED	1
BETWEENPIE	1	BOWL	1	BYGONES	1	CHARTER	1
BETWEENS	1	BOWMAN	1	BYPLAY	1	CHASE	1
BETWEENWHILES	1	BOX	1	CADAIR	1	CHASMS	1
BIDDER'S	1	BRAES	1	CADENCE	1	CHASTENING	1
BIDES	1	BRAGS	1	CAGE	1	CHASTITY	1
BIDST	1	BRAID	1	CAGES	1	CHAUNT	1
BIG	1	BRAIDED	1	CAIN'S	1	CHEAP	1
BIG-BONED	1	BRAMBLES	1	CAKED	1	CHEBAR'S	1
BILLION	1	BRANCH	1	CALENDAR	1	CHECK	1
BILLS	1	BRAND	1	CALVARY	1	CHEE	1
BIND'ST	1	BRANDLE	1	CALVARY'S	1	CHEERED	1
BINES	1	BRANDS	1	CAMPION	1	CHEERING	1
BISCAY	1	BRASS	1	CANAAN	1	CHEERLESS	1
BIT	1	BRASS-BOLD	1	CANCER	1	CHEER'S	1
BITE	1	BRAVEST	1	CANDLEMAS	1	CHEEVO	1
BITTEN	1	BRAWLING	1	CANDLES	1	CHEQUERS	1
BITTERER	1	BRAWN	1	CANDOUR	1	CHERRY	1
BLACKEST	1	BRAZED	1	CANDYCOLOURED	1	CHERVIL	1
BLACK-ABOUT	1	BREADTH	1	CANNON	1	CHESTNUT-FALLS	1
BLACK-BACKED	1	BREAKER	1	CANVAS	1	CHESTNUT-FANS	1
BLACK-FLEECED	1	BREAKERS	1	CANVASS	1	CHEVALIER	1
BLACKNESS	1	BREAKLESS	1	CANVASSING	1	CHEVY	1
BLACKS	1	BREASTING	1	CAP	1	CHEW'D	1
BLADE-GASH	1	BREAST'S	1	CAPABLE	1	CHIEFS	1
BLADE'S	1	BREASTS	1	CAPES	1	CHIEFTAIN	1
BLADY	1	BREATH-TAKING	1	CAPITAL	1	CHIEFWOE	1
BLAME	1	BREED	1	CAPP'D	1	CHILDBEARING	1
BLASTED	1	BREEDS	1	CAPSIZE	1	CHILD-LIKE	1
BLASTS	1	BREEZES	1	CAPTAIN	1	CHILDLESS	1
BLAZONRY	1	BREMEN	1	CAPTIVITY	1	CHILDREN	1
BLEACHED	1	BRICKISH	1	CARADOC	1	CHILDREN'S	1
BLEARED	1	BRICKS	1	CARADOC'S	1	CHILD'S	1
BLEAR-ALL	1	BRIDEGROOM	1	CARED-FOR	1	CHILLING	1
BLEATS	1	BRIDGE	1	CAREER	1	CHIPS	1
BLEEDS	1	BRIDGING	1	CARE-COILED	1	CHIVALRY	1
BLESSING	1	BRIER	1	CARE-DROWNED	1	CHIVALRY'S	1
BLESS'D	1	BRIGHTEN	1	CARE-KILLED	1	CHOIR	1
BLIGHT	1	BRIGHTENING	1	CARISBROOK	1	CHOKING	1
BLINDFOLD	1	BRIGHTEST	1	CARNATION	1	CHRISM	1
BLINDNESS	1	BRIGHT-COUNTER	1	CAROUSE	1	CHRISTENS	1
BLINDS	1	BRIGHT-LIFTING	1	CARRIER-WITTED	1	CHRISTIANS	1
BLINDWORM	1	BRIGHT-MASK'D	1	CARRIERS	1	CHRIST-DONE	1
BLINKING	1	BRIGHTNESS	1	CARRION	1	CHRIST-ED	1
BLOOD-GUSH	1	BRILLIANCE	1	CARVED	1	CHRISTUS	1
BLOOD-LIGHT	1	BRILLIANT-HUED	1	CARVING	1	CHRIST.'S	1
BLOOD-VIVID	1	BRIMMED	1	CASE	1	CHRYSOLITE	1
BLOODS	1	BRINDED	1	CASEMENTS	1	CHURCH	1
BLOOMFALL	1	BRINDLED	1	CASQUE	1	CHURCH-TOWER	1
BLOOMING	1	BRINK	1	CASTARA'S	1	CHURLSGRACE	1
BLOSSOM-HITTING	1	BRISTOL-BRED	1	CASTILIAN	1	CHURNING	1
BLOTLESS	1	BRITAIN'S	1	CATARACT	1	CIEL'D	1
BLOWING	1	BROAD-FLUTED	1	CATCHES	1	CINQUEFOIL	1
BLOWPIPE	1	BROAD-SHED	1	CAVERNOUS	1	CIPHER	1
BLUEBELL	1	BROIDERS	1	CEASELESS	1	CIRCLE-CITADELS	1
BLUE-BEATING	1	BROKEN	1	CELL	1	CIRCLES	1
BLUE-BLEAK	1	BRONZEN	1	CELLS	1	CIRCLET	1
BLUER	1	BROOCH	1	CEMENTED	1	CIRCLING	1
BLUFF	1	BROTHER'S	1	CENSERS	1	CITE	1
BLURR'D	1	BROWN-AS-DAWNING	1	CENTREINGS	1	CITHERN	1
BLURS	1	BROWZED	1	CENTRE-DARKS	1	CITIES	1
BLUSHED	1	BRUISE	1	CENTURION	1	CLAIM	1
BLUSTERING	1	BRUTE	1	CERES	1	CLAMMYISH	1
BOARD	1	BUCK	1	CERTAINTY	1	CLANK	1
BOASTING	1	BUCKLE	1	CHAFF	1	CLARION-CLEAR	1
BOATMAN	1	BUGLE-EYED	1	CHAINED	1	CLARIONS	1
BODES	1	BUGLES	1	CHAINS	1	CLARISSA	1
BOISTEROUSLY	1	BULK	1	CHAIR	1	CLASP'D	1
BOLDBOYS	1	BULKY	1	CHALKY	1	CLASSIC	1
BOLE	1	BULLION	1	CHAMFER'D	1	CLATTERING	1
BOLT	1	BUNCHY	1	CHAMP-WHITE	1	CLAUDE	1
BOLTS	1	BURIAL	1	CHANCE	1	CLAYFIELD'S	1
BONE-HOUSE	1	BURL	1	CHANCEQUARRIED	1	CLEAN	1
BONFIRE	1	BURLING	1	CHANGELESS	1	CLEANER	1
BONIFACE	1	BURNISH'D	1	CHANG'D	1	CLEAREST-SELVED	1
BONNIEST	1	BURST	1	CHANNELLED	1	CLEAVE	1

CLEPED 1	CONQU'RORS 1	CROUCH 1	DEADLY-ELECTRIC 1
CLICKING 1	CONSIDERATE 1	CROWNED 1	DEAD'NING 1
CLIMB 1	CONSIDERED 1	CROWN'D 1	DEAF 1
CLINCHES 1	CONSTANCY 1	CRUEL 1	DEARNESS 1
CLINCHING-BLIND 1	CONSUMES 1	CRUISE 1	DEARS 1
CLING 1	CONSUMING 1	CRUMBLED 1	DEATHDANCE 1
CLODS 1	CONTAGIOUS 1	CRUMBLING 1	DEATHGUSH 1
CLOGGED 1	CONTAINED 1	CRUSHES 1	DEATHS 1
CLOISTER-LIGHT 1	CONTEND 1	CRUSH-SILK 1	DECAY 1
CLOISTER'D 1	CONTENDED 1	CRYSTAL-ENDING 1	DECAYING 1
CLOISTERS 1	CONTENDS 1	CRYSTALLINE 1	DECEIVED 1
CLOSE-BARRED 1	CONTENTMENT 1	CUCKOOCALL 1	DECEMBER 1
CLOSE-FOLDED 1		CUCKOO-ECHOING 1	DECREASED 1
CLOSE-PLY 1	CONTINENCE 1	CUD 1	DECREE 1
CLOSE-ROOTED 1	CONTINENT 1	CUE 1	DEED-BOUND 1
CLOSER 1	CONTINUALLY 1	CULLY'S 1	DEEM 1
CLOSES 1	CONTRACT 1	CUMBERED 1	DEEMED 1
CLOTHES 1	CONTROLL'D 1	CUMBROUS 1	DEEMS 1
CLOUD-FESTOONED 1	COOINGS 1	CUMNOR 1	DEEPENING 1
CLOUD-PUFFBALL 1	COOP 1	CUP 1	DEEP-GROVED 1
CLOUGH 1	COPED 1	CUPBOARD 1	DEFIANCE 1
CLOY 1	COPSES 1	CUPP'D 1	DEFLOWERS 1
CLUSTERING 1	CORAL 1	CURB 1	DEFT-HANDED 1
CLUSTER'D 1	CORDED 1	CURDED 1	DEGGED 1
CLUSTERS 1	CORDIAL 1	CURE 1	DEGREES 1
CLUTCHED 1	CORDS 1	CURFEW 1	DEJECTION 1
COAL 1	CORNIC'D 1	CURL 1	DELAY 1
COAST 1	CORONET 1	CURL'D 1	DELICACY 1
COAT 1	CORPSES 1	CURLS 1	DELICIOUS 1
COATS 1	CORRESPOND 1	CURSING 1	DELIGHTED 1
COBBLED 1	CORRUPTION 1	CURVES 1	DELIVERING 1
COCOONING 1	COST 1	CUSP 1	DELL 1
COFFER 1	COT 1	CUSTOMARY 1	DELVES 1
COFFIN-BLACK 1	COTTAGES 1	CYCLADS 1	DENIAL 1
COGGED 1	COUGH 1	CYPRIS 1	DENIS 1
COIFED 1	COULDST 1	DABBLED 1	DENSE 1
COILS 1	COUNCIL 1	DAFFODIL 1	DENTED 1
COINAGE 1	COUNSEL 1	DAFFODILLIES 1	DEPARTED 1
COLDER 1	COUNTERFEIT 1	DAHLIAS 1	DEPEND 1
COLDLY 1	COUNTERFOILING 1	DAILY 1	DEPTHS 1
COLDNESS 1	COUNTER-ROUNDELS 1	DAINTILY 1	DESCRIED 1
COLLAPSING 1		DAINTY-DELICATE 1	DESERT 1
COLOMB 1	COUNTERVAIL 1	DAISIES 1	DESERTER 1
COLOSSAL 1	COUNTING 1	DALLIES 1	DESERVE 1
COLOURED 1	COUNTY 1	DAMASK 1	DESERVING 1
COLOURING 1	COUPLE-COLOUR 1	DAMASK'D 1	DESIRABLE 1
COLOUR'D 1	COURAGE 1	DAME 1	DESIRES 1
COLUMNAR-SEVERE 1	COURSE 1	DAMP 1	DESIROUS 1
COLUMNS 1	COURSES 1	DANCE 1	DESPAIRING 1
COMBATING 1	COURTESIES 1	DANCERS 1	DESPATCHES 1
COMBES 1	COVERLID 1	DANDY-HUNG 1	DESPONDING 1
COME-BACK-AGAIN 1	COVER'D 1	DANGER 1	DESTINED 1
COMET 1	COVERTS 1	DANGEROUSLY 1	DESTINY 1
COMFORTABLE 1	COW 1	DANK-YTRESSED 1	DEVICE 1
COMFORTER 1	CRACK'D 1	DANTE'S 1	DEVILISH 1
COMFORT'S 1	CRADOCK 1	DAPHNIS 1	DEVIL'S 1
COMMANDER 1	CRAGIRON 1	DAPPLE 1	DEVIS'D 1
COMMANDS 1	CRAGS 1	DAPPLED-WITH-DAM 1	DEVON 1
COMMUNION 1	CRAMPS 1	DAPPLE-DAWN-DRAW 1	DEVONSHIRE 1
COMPANION 1	CRAWL 1	DAPPLE-EARED 1	DEVOURING 1
COMPARISON 1	CREAMY 1	DAREDEATHS 1	DEWBELL 1
COMPASSION 1	CREASE 1	DARE-GALE 1	DEWDROP 1
COMPASSIONATE 1	CREASES 1	DARES 1	DEWDROPS 1
COMPLAISANT 1	CREATING 1	DARKENED 1	DEW-LAP 1
COMPLETE 1	CREATION 1	DARKEN'D 1	DEXTEROUS 1
COMPLIMENT 1	CREATION'S 1	DARKLES 1	DIADEM 1
COMPOSITE 1	CREATURE 1	DARLING 1	DIADEM'D 1
COMPULSION 1	CREATURES 1	DART 1	DIAPERED 1
COMRADE 1	CREDIT 1	DARTING 1	DIAPERS 1
CONCAVITY 1	CREEDS 1	DASHED 1	DICK 1
CONCEIVING 1	CRIME 1	DATED 1	DIE-AWAY 1
CONCERN 1	CRIMSONINGS 1	DATELESS 1	DIET 1
CONCERNED 1	CRIMSON-CRESSETE 1	DATES 1	DIFFERENCE 1
CONCH 1	CRIMSON-GOLDEN 1	DAUNTING 1	DIGHT 1
CONCORDING 1	CRIMSON-WHITE 1	DAUNTLESS 1	DIMINISHES 1
CONFESS 1	CRINGE 1	DAUPHIN 1	DIMINISH'D 1
CONFESSION 1	CRIPPLES 1	DAVID'S 1	DIMLY 1
CONFIDANTE 1	CRISP'D 1	DAY-BREAK 1	DIMM'D 1
CONFIDENCE 1	CRISPS 1	DAY-DISSOLVED 1	DIMNESS 1
CONFINED 1	CRISS-CROSS'D 1	DAY-LABOURING-OU 1	DIMPLED 1
CONFIRMED 1	CROCODILES 1	DAYLIGHT'S 1	DIMPLING 1
CONFOUND 1	CROOKED 1	DAYSPRING 1	DIN 1
CONFOUNDED 1	CROSSBRIDLE 1	DAYSTAR 1	DINGLE-A-DANGLED 1
CONFRONT 1	CROSSES 1	DAZE 1	DINGS 1
CONFUSED 1	CROSS-BARRED 1	DAZZLE 1	DINT 1
CONJECTURE 1	CROSS-COLOUR 1	DEACON 1	DINTED 1
CONJUNCTIONS 1	CROSS-WOOD 1	DEAD-ALIVE 1	DINTLESS 1
CONQUEST 1	CROSS'D 1	DEADLY 1	DIPP'D 1

312

DIRECTION	1	DRAWER	1	ENDEAVOUR	1	FALSIFIED	1
DIRECTLY	1	DRAWING	1	ENDLESS	1	FALTER	1
DIRVAN	1	DRAYHORSE	1	ENDLESSLY	1	FAME'S	1
DISMAY	1	DREADNOUGHT	1	ENDRAGONED	1	FAMILIARNESS	1
DISABLING	1	DREAMY	1	ENDURED	1	FANCIED	1
DISALLOW	1	DRENCHED	1	ENDURING	1	FANCIFUL	1
DISAPPOINTED	1	DRESSED	1	ENEMY	1	FANGED	1
DISARMING	1	DREST	1	ENGEMMING	1	FANGS	1
DISARRAY	1	DRIFTED	1	ENGENDER'D	1	FANTASTIC	1
DISASTER	1	DRIFTING	1	ENGLAND'S	1	FARE	1
DISASTROUS	1	DRILLED	1	ENJEWELLING	1	FAR-OFF	1
DISCHARGE	1	DRINKS	1	ENJOY	1	FARMING	1
DISCHARGED	1	DRIPPING	1	ENJOYMENT	1	FARMYARD	1
DISCHARGING	1	DRIVEN	1	ENRICHED	1	FARRIER	1
DISCLOSE	1	DRIZZLE	1	ENTANGLED	1	FASHED	1
DISCLOSES	1	DRON'D	1	ENTER	1	FASHION	1
DISCONTENT	1	DROP-OF-BLOOD-AN	1	ENTERING	1	FASTED	1
DISCORD	1	DROPPED	1	ENTRANCE	1	FASTEN	1
DISCOVERED	1	DROPPING	1	ENTRANCINGLY	1	FAST-FLOWING	1
DISCOVERING	1	DROPP'D	1	ENTRIES	1	FAST-LODGED	1
DISCOVERY	1	DROUTH	1	ENVIED	1	FASTS	1
DISHEVELLED	1	DROVES	1	EPISTLES	1	FATHER'D	1
DISMALEST	1	DROWNING	1	EQUIPPED	1	FATHER'S	1
DISMEMBERING	1	DROWSY	1	ERIN	1	FATHERS-FORTH	1
DISOBEDIENT	1	DRUDGERY	1	ERST	1	FATHOMS	1
DISORDERS	1	DUOMO	1	ESAU'S	1	FAULT-NOT-FOUND-	1
DISPARADISED	1	DURANCE	1	ESCAPE	1	FAVOUR	1
DISPEL	1	DURING·	1	ESCORIAL	1	FAVOURABLE	1
DISPENSE	1	DUSK-DEEP	1	ESPIAL	1	FAVOURED	1
DISPENSES	1	DUTY-SWERVER	1	ESSENCE	1	FAVOURING	1
DISPOSES	1	DWARF	1	ESTATES	1	FAVOURITE	1
DISQUIET	1	DWARFS	1	ESTEEM'D	1	FAWN-FROTH	1
DISREGARDED	1	DWELL	1	ETC	1	FEALTY	1
DISREMEMBERING	1	DWELLEST	1	ETHER	1	FEARED	1
DISSEVERAL	1	DWINDLES	1	EUCHARIST	1	FEARFUL	1
DISSOLVE	1	DWINDLING	1	EUNUCH	1	FEAR'D	1
DISTANCED	1	DYPHWYS	1	EURYDICE	1	FED	1
DISTEMPER'D	1	EAGER	1	EVENT	1	FEEBLE	1
DISTILLATION	1	EAGERER	1	EVER-FRETTING	1	FEELERS	1
DISTILLS	1	EAGLE'S	1	EVERLASTINGNESS	1	FEEL-OF-PRIMROSE	1
DISTINCTION	1	EAR-CARESSING	1	EVERMORE	1	FEELS	1
DISTRESSED	1	EARLSTARS	1	EVIL-HEAVEN'D	1	FEIGNS	1
DISTURB'D	1	EARNEST-HEARTED	1	EVILS	1	FELL-FROWNING	1
DITHER	1	EARTHWORLD	1	EWE	1	FELLOWSHIPS	1
DIVE	1	EASEFUL	1	EXCEPT	1	FEMALE	1
DIVER'S	1	EASTERING	1	EXCESS	1	FENCED	1
DIVIDE	1	EASTERN	1	EXHIBITION	1	FENS	1
DIVIDED	1	EASTNORTHEAST	1	EXILE	1	FERN	1
DIVINED	1	EASTWARD	1	EXILED	1	FERTILE	1
DIVINELY	1	EASTWARDS	1	EXPLANATION	1	FESTIVAL	1
DIVING	1	EATEN	1	EXPLOIT	1	FETTLE	1
DIVINITY	1	EBB	1	EXPRESS	1	FEVER	1
DIZZY	1	EBB'D	1	EXPRESSED	1	FEVER'D	1
DOFF	1	ECHO	1	EXPRESSIONLESS	1	FIELD-FLOWERS	1
DOFFS	1	ECHOING-OF-EARTH	1	EXTREMES	1	FIELD-FLOWN	1
DOG	1	ECLIPSE	1	EXTREMITY	1	FIERCER	1
DOGEARED	1	ECLIPSING	1	EXULTATION	1	FIERCEST	1
DOGG'D	1	EDDIES	1	EYEBALL	1	FIG	1
DOG-STAR	1	EDDY	1	EYEBROW	1	FIGHTER	1
DOGROSE	1	EDEN	1	EYED	1	FILES	1
DOGS	1	EDGED	1	EYE-ATTENTIVE	1	FILIAL	1
DOMAIN	1	EDGES	1	EYE-GREETING	1	FILLETED	1
DOMINANT	1	EFFECTUAL	1	EYELIDS	1	FILLETS	1
DOOMFIRE	1	EGYPT	1	EYE'S	1	FILL'D	1
DOOMSDAY	1	EIGHT	1	EYESIGHT	1	FILM	1
DOOMS-DAY	1	EIGHTH	1	EZEKIEL'S	1	FILMS	1
DORIC	1	ELBOW	1	FABLE	1	FILTH	1
DOUBLE-MUSICAL	1	ELECTED	1	FABLED	1	FINCHES	1
DOUBLE-NATURED	1	ELECTRICAL	1	FABLING	1	FINDING	1
DOUBLET	1	ELEMENTED	1	FADE	1	FINEFLOUR	1
DOVES	1	ELEVEN	1	FADING	1	FINE-DRAWN	1
DOVEWINGED	1	ELIM	1	FAGGED	1	FINGERGAPS	1
DOWNCAROL	1	ELKHOR	1	FAILING	1	FINGERING	1
DOWNDOLPHINRY	1	ELM	1	FAIL'D	1	FINGER-LONG	1
DOWN-DUGGED	1	ELM-HEADS	1	FAILURE	1	FINGER-TEASING	1
DOWN-SPLINTER'D	1	ELMS	1	FAINTER	1	FINGERNAIL	1
DOWNRIGHT	1	ELMY	1	FAIRLY	1	FIREBALL	1
DOWNWARD	1	ELOQUENT	1	FAIRNESS	1	FIRED	1
DOWNWARD-HOLLOWI	1	ELSE-MINDED	1	FAIRYLAND	1	FIREDINT	1
DOWNWARDS	1	ELVES'-EYES	1	FAITHLESS	1	FIRE-FOLK	1
DOWNY	1	EMBLEM	1	FALCON	1	FIRST-FRUITS	1
DRAGON	1	EMINENT	1	FALERNIAN-GROWN	1	FISH	1
DRAGONFLIES	1	EMPIRE	1	FALLERS	1	FISHES	1
DRAGONISH	1	EMPLOYMENT	1	FALL-GOLD	1	FITS	1
DRAGONS	1	ENCHAIN'D	1	FALLOWBOOTFELLOW	1	FIVE-LIPPED	1
DRAIN	1	ENCLUSTER'D	1	FALLOWS	1	FIVE-LIVED	1
DRAINING	1	ENCOUNTER	1	FALSE	1	FIX	1
DRAUGHTS	1	ENCRIMSONING	1	FALSELY	1	FIXED	1

FIXEDLY 1
FLAKE 1
FLAKE-DOVES 1
FLAME-CASED 1
FLAME-RASH 1
FLAME-RINGS 1
FLANDERS 1
FLANGE 1
FLARES 1
FLARING 1
FLAR'D 1
FLASHING 1
FLATS 1
FLATTER 1
FLATTERY'S 1
FLAUNT 1
FLECKS 1
FLEDGED 1
FLEECES 1
FLEECIEST 1
FLEES 1
FLEETED 1
FLEET-FEATHER'D 1
FLEETS 1
FLEMING 1
FLESHED 1
FLESH-BOUND 1
FLESH-BURST 1
FLESH-FLOWERS 1
FLESH-POTS 1
FLETCHER 1
FLEW 1
FLICKER 1
FLIGHTY 1
FLINCHING 1
FLINGS 1
FLINT-FLAKE 1
FLINTS 1
FLIRTING 1
FLITCHES 1
FLITS 1
FLOATED 1
FLOCKBELLS 1
FLOODTIDE 1
FLOOR 1
FLOOR'D 1
FLOWERETS 1
FLUE 1
FLUKE 1
FLUSHES 1

FLUTES 1
FOAMFALLING 1
FOAM-FALLOW 1
FOAM-FLEECE 1
FOAM-TUFT 1
FOE 1
FOIL 1
FOILED 1
FOILING 1
FOLIAGE 1
FOLK 1
FOLLOWED 1
FOLLOWS 1
FONDLER 1
FONT 1
FOODS 1
FOOTFRETTED 1
FOOTREST 1
FOOTSTEPS 1
FOOTWAY 1
FORCED 1
FORCIBLE 1
FORCIBLY 1
FORC'D 1
FOREDRAWN 1
FOREFALLS 1
FOREFENDING 1
FOREGONE 1
FORE-FOUNDERING 1
FORE-MOTIONS 1
FOREKNOWN 1
FOREPANGS 1
FORETHOUGHT 1
FORFEIT 1
FORGED 1
FORGETFULNESS 1
FORGIVEN 1
FORGIVENESS 1

FORGIVES 1
FORGIVING 1
FORGONE 1
FORKED 1
FORMAL 1
FORMED 1
FORMERLY 1
FORMS 1
FORTH-AND-FLAUNT 1
FORTH-DRIVEN 1
FORTRESS 1
FORTUNE 1
FORTY 1
FORWARD-LIKE 1
FOULED 1
FOUNDERED 1
FOUNTAIN 1
FOUNTS 1
FOURTH 1
FOWLS 1
FOXGLOVES 1
FRAILEST-FLIXED 1
FRAILTY 1
FRANCES 1
FRANCIS 1
FRANTIC 1
FRAUGHT 1
FRECKLED 1
FREEZE 1
FREEZING 1
FREIGHTED 1
FRENZIED 1
FREQUENTING 1
FRESHEST 1
FRESH-FIRECOAL 1
FRESH-LEAVED 1
FRESHLY 1
FRETFUL 1
FRETS 1
FRIGATE 1
FRIGID 1
FRINGED 1
FRINGES 1
FRO 1
FROCKS 1
FROLICLAVISH 1
FRONTS 1
FROST-FURRED 1
FROTH 1
FROTHPITS 1

FROTHY 1
FROWARD 1
FROWN 1
FRUIT-CLOISTERIN 1
FRUITS 1
FULFIL 1
FULFILLED 1
FULFILL'D 1
FULLER 1
FULL-LEAVED 1
FULL-SAPP'D 1
FULLNESS 1
FULLY 1
FUMES 1
FUMING 1
FUMITORY 1
FUNCTION 1
FURL 1
FURLONGS 1
FURNACE 1
FURRED 1
FURROWS 1
FURTHER'D 1
FURY 1
FUSSY 1
FUTILITY 1
GABRIEL 1
GAIETY 1
GAIN 1
GAININGS 1
GAIN'D 1
GAINS 1
GALAXY 1
GALILEE 1
GALILEE'S 1
GALLANTRY 1
GALLED 1
GALLERIES 1

GALLOP 1
GAMBOL 1
GAMBOLLING 1
GAPES 1
GAPS 1
GARB 1
GARDEN-POPPIES 1
GARLAND 1
GARNERED 1
GARNERING 1
GARNET 1
GASH 1
GASHED 1
GASHES 1
GASP 1
GASPING 1
GASP'D 1
GASPS 1
GATE 1
GATES 1
GATHERING 1
GATHER'D 1
GATHERS 1
GAUGE 1
GAY 1
GAYGEAR 1
GAY-GANGS 1
GAYLINKS 1
GAZED 1
GAZING 1
GEM 1
GEM-FLEECED 1
GENERATION 1
GENERATIONS 1
GENNESARETH 1
GERMS 1
GERTRUDE 1
GETHSEMANE 1
GHOSTLY 1
GHOSTS 1
GIANT'S 1
GIANTS 1
GIDDIES 1
GIDEON'S 1
GILDED 1
GIRDER 1
GIRDLES 1
GIRLGRACE 1
GIRLHOOD 1
GIVEST 1

GLACIER 1
GLADDEST 1
GLADE 1
GLANCE 1
GLANCES 1
GLASSES 1
GLASS-BLUE 1
GLASSY-CLEAR 1
GLAUCUS 1
GLAZED 1
GLEAM 1
GLEAN 1
GLEANED 1
GLEE 1
GLEN 1
GLENS 1
GLIDES 1
GLIDING 1
GLIMMER'D 1
GLIMPSES 1
GLISTENS 1
GLISTERY 1
GLITTER 1
GLOBES 1
GLOOM'D 1
GLORIES 1
GLORIFY 1
GLORYING 1
GLORY'S 1
GLOSS 1
GLOWLESS 1
GLOW'D 1
GLOWWORMS 1
GLUE 1
GLUEGOLD-BROWN 1
GNARLED 1
GNARLS 1
GNASHED 1

GOAL 1
GOALS 1
GOATS 1
GODDESS'S 1
GOD-MADE-FLESH 1
GODLESS 1
GOINGS 1
GOLDENGROVE 1
GOLDEN-GIRDLED 1
GOLDISH 1
GOLD-VERMILION 1
GOLD-WATER 1
GOLD-WISP 1
GOLDNAILS 1
GOLDY 1
GONFALON 1
GOODS 1
GORE 1
GORGED 1
GORGON'S 1
GORSE 1
GOSSAMER 1
GOSSAMERS 1
GOTHIC 1
GOTTEN 1
GRACEFULLY 1
GRACELESS 1
GRAFTED 1
GRAINS 1
GRASP 1
GRASPS 1
GRASSES 1
GRASSY 1
GRATEFUL 1
GRAVER 1
GRAVES 1
GREECE 1
GREEK 1
GREENEST 1
GREENHOUSE 1
GREEN-WHITE 1
GREENNESS 1
GREENWORLD 1
GREETING 1
GREGORIANS 1
GREGORY 1
GREYBELL 1
GREY-GREEN 1
GRIEF'S 1
GRIEVANCE 1

GRIEVES 1
GRIEVING 1
GRIM 1
GRIP 1
GRIZZLED 1
GROOM 1
GROUNDED 1
GROUND-HUGGED 1
GROUNDLONG 1
GROUNDS 1
GROVEL 1
GROWTHS 1
GRUDGE 1
GUARD 1
GUARDEDLY 1
GUESSES 1
GUESSING 1
GUINEVERE 1
GULF 1
GULF'S 1
GUM 1
GUSH 1
GUSHING 1
GUST 1
GUSTY 1
GWEN 1
HACK 1
HACKED 1
HACKS 1
HAEDUS-RISE 1
HAEMONY 1
HAGGARD 1
HAGGLE 1
HAILROPES 1
HAIR-BOUND 1
HAIRS 1
HALF-CIRCLE 1
HALF-DIVINE 1

HALF-HOUR	1	HEAVEN-ROYSTERER	1	HUDDLING	1	INTERCHANGE	1
HALF-HUMAN	1	HEAVEN-VAULT	1	HUED	1	INTERESTS	1
HALF-LIGHT	1	HEAVENLIER	1	HUE'S	1	INTERPOSED	1
HALF-LIT	1	HEAVENWARD	1	HUGE	1	INTERSTICE	1
HALF-MESHING	1	HEAVES	1	HUGE-GIRTHED	1	INTOLERABLE	1
HALLOWED	1	HEAVING	1	HUM	1	INVENTION	1
HALLOWING	1	HEAVY	1	HUMAN	1	INWARD	1
HALLOWS	1	HEAVYHEADED	1	HUMANITIES	1	IPSE	1
HALLS	1	HECTOR'S	1	HUNDREDFOLD	1	IRELAND	1
HALO'D	1	HEDGE	1	HUNDREDWEIGHTS	1	IRISH	1
HALVE	1	HEDGEROW	1	HUNGERED	1	IRREGULARLY	1
HALVES	1	HEEDS	1	HUNG-HEAVENWARD	1	ISLAND	1
HAMLETS	1	HEELS	1	HUNTERS	1	ISLES	1
HAMPSTEAD	1	HEFT	1	HURDLE	1	ISSUE	1
HANDMAIDEN	1	HEIFER'S	1	HURRIED	1	IVIES	1
HAND'S	1	HEIGHTENING	1	HURST	1	IVY	1
HANDSOME	1	HEIGHTENS	1	HURSTS	1	-CARESS'D	1
HANDY	1	HEIGHTS	1	HURT	1	JACINTHINE	1
HANGDOG	1	HELL-ROOK	1	HUSHED	1	JACK'S	1
HANKER	1	HELL'S	1	HUSH'D	1	JACKSELF	1
HANKS	1	HELP'D	1	HUSSY	1	JADED	1
HAPLESS	1	HELPS	1	HUSTINGS	1	JADING	1
HAPPINESS	1	HELTERING	1	HUSTLE	1	JAGGED	1
HAPP'D	1	HEMPEN	1	HUTCH	1	JAGS	1
HARDEN'D	1	HERCLOT'S	1	HYACINTHED	1	JAILOR	1
HARDER	1	HERDS-LONG	1	HYACINTH-WARDING	1	JAMES	1
HARDEST	1	HEREAFTER	1	HYACINTHS	1	JARR'D	1
HARD-HURLED	1	HERESY	1	HYALINE	1	JAUNTING	1
HARDLY	1	HERETIC	1	HYMN	1	JAY-BLUE	1
HARDY-HANDSOME	1	HERETOFORE	1	HYPOCRITE	1	JESSY	1
HARE	1	HEROIC	1	ICONIUM	1	JESU'S	1
HARMONY	1	HEWS	1	ICY	1	JET	1
HARM'S	1	HIGH-HUNG	1	IDEAL	1	JEWELL'D	1
HARNESS	1	HIGH-PRIEST	1	IGNORANTLY	1	JOINTS	1
HARP	1	HIGHROAD	1	ILL-BALANCED	1	JOKE	1
HARSHNESS	1	HILL-TOP	1	ILL-CONTENT	1	JOLT	1
HASTEN'D	1	HILLSIDE	1	ILL-CONTENTED	1	JOSEPH'S	1
HAT	1	HINDERS	1	ILL-LAUNCHED	1	JOVE	1
HATRED	1	HINDRANCE	1	ILL-VISAGED	1	JOY-LADEN	1
HAUNT	1	HIP	1	ILLUMINED	1	JOYLESS	1
HAUNTED	1	HITHERTO	1	ILLUSTRATED	1	JOYS	1
HAUNTS	1	HO	1	IMAGE	1	JUDAH	1
HAVENS	1	HOARDS	1	IMAGES	1	JUDGE	1
HAVERING	1	HOAR-HALLOWED	1	IMAGINING	1	JUSTICES	1
HAVOC-POCKED	1	HOAR-HUSKED	1	IMMORTALS	1	JUSTIFY	1
HAWK	1	HOARLIGHT	1	IMPALE	1	KATE	1
HAWKMOTH	1	HOARSE	1	IMPALED	1	KEATS	1
HAWLING	1	HOARY	1	IMPALPABLE	1	KEENER	1
HAZARDS	1	HOARY-GLOW	1	IMPATIENT	1	KEEPING	1
HAZE	1	HOBS	1	IMPEACHED	1	KENTISH	1
HAZELS	1	HOLDING	1	IMPEARLED	1	KILLED	1
HEADED	1	HOLES	1	IMPEDIMENT	1	KILL-WEIGHTS	1
HEADSTRONG	1	HOLIER	1	IMPENITENT	1	KILLS	1
HEADWAY	1	HOLIEST	1	IMP'S	1	KINDCOLD	1
HEADY	1	HOLLOWING	1	INANIMATE	1	KINDNESS	1
HEAL	1	HOLLOW'D	1	INBOARD	1	KINDRED	1
HEAPED	1	HOMEFORTH	1	INCAPABLE	1	KINE	1
HEARDST	1	HOME-OF-ALL	1	INCENSE	1	KINGDOM	1
HEARER	1	HOMES	1	INCH	1	KINGFISHERS	1
HEARERS	1	HOMING	1	INCHES	1	KIRJATH-ARBA	1
HEARINGS	1	HONEST	1	INCREASE	1	KISSED	1
HEARSE-OF-ALL	1	HONEYCOMB	1	INCREMENT	1	KISSING	1
HEARSES	1	HONEYSUCK	1	INDIAN	1	KNEADING	1
HEARST	1	HONEYSUCKLE	1	INDIFFERENCE	1	KNEE-NAVE	1
HEARTBURN	1	HONOR	1	INDIGNATION	1	KNEELED	1
HEARTH	1	HONOURING	1	INDIGNITY	1	KNELLS	1
HEARTH'S	1	HOPED	1	INDIVISIBLE	1	KNOCK	1
HEARTILY	1	HORIZON-ROUND	1	INEXPLICABLY	1	KNOCKING	1
HEART-AT-EASE	1	HORIZONTALS	1	INFALLIBLY	1	KNOCKINGS	1
HEART-BEAT	1	HORNBEAM	1	INFANCY	1	KNOPS	1
HEART-BREAK	1	HORNLIGHT	1	INFANT	1	KNOPT	1
HEART-BROKE	1	HOROSCOPE	1	INFEST	1	KNOWEST	1
HEART-BROKEN	1	HORRIBLE	1	INFINITELY	1	KNOWLEDGE	1
HEART-FLESHED	1	HORSEBACK	1	INFINITY	1	LABOURED-AT	1
HEART-FORSOOK	1	HORSEMEN	1	INFLUENTIAL	1	LABOURING	1
HEART-SONG	1	HORSES	1	INHERITANCE	1	LABOURS	1
HEART-SPRINGS	1	HOSTS	1	INITIATE	1	LACE-LEAVED	1
HEART-THROE	1	HOURGLASS	1	INJURY	1	LACES	1
HEART'S-CLARION	1	HOUSED	1	INJURY'S	1	LACKLEVEL	1
HEARTSORE	1	HOUSEL	1	INMATE	1	LADE	1
HEATHPACKS	1	HOUSELESS	1	INSPIRATION	1	LADED	1
HEAVED	1	HOUSETOP	1	INSTANT	1	LADEN	1
HEAVENFALLEN	1	HOVEL	1	INSTRESSED	1	LADES	1
HEAVENGRAVEL	1	HOVERED	1	INSUFFICIENCIES	1	LADIES	1
HEAVEN-ENFORCED	1	HOVERINGS	1	INTELLECTUAL	1	LADY-STAR	1
HEAVEN-FLUNG	1	HOVER-FLOAT	1	INTENSE	1	LAG	1
HEAVEN-HANDLING	1	HOVERS	1	INTENSEST	1	LAGGING	1
HEAVEN-HAVEN	1	HUDDLE	1	INTENSITY	1	LAIR	1

Word		Word		Word		Word	
LAMB'S	1	LIMN'D	1	MAGNIFY	1	METHINKS	1
LAMBS	1	LINEN-WINDED	1	MAGNIFYING	1	MI	1
LAME	1	LINGERER	1	MAIDENGEAR	1	MICHAELMAS	1
LAMENTABLE	1	LINGERING	1	MAIDEN-FURLED	1	MID-MAIN	1
LAMENTS	1	LINGERING-OUT	1	MAIDEN-MOTHER	1	MID-NUMBERED	1
LAMPS	1	LINGER'D	1	MAIDEN'S	1	MIDRIFF	1
LANCASHIRE	1	LINGERS	1	MAID-MONTH'S	1	MIEN	1
LANCED	1	LINKED	1	MAIL'D	1	MILAN	1
LANCING	1	LION	1	MAIM	1	MILDLY	1
LAND'S	1	LIONESS	1	MAINSTRENGTH	1	MILE-LONG	1
LANDS	1	LION-BROWN	1	MAJESTIC	1	MILK-WHITE	1
LANDSLIPS	1	LIONLIKE	1	MAJESTICAL	1	MILLBROOK-SLIPS	1
LANES	1	LIONLIMB	1	MAJORCA	1	MILLION-FUELED	1
LANGUENT	1	LIPMUSIC	1	MAKESBELIEVE	1	MILLIONS	1
LANK	1	LISPING	1	MALICE	1	MILL-STONE	1
LAP	1	LISP'D	1	MALIGN	1	MINDED	1
LAPS	1	LISSOME	1	MAMMOCKS	1	MINGLED	1
LAPSED	1	LIST	1	MANMARKS	1	MINION	1
LARK-CHARMED	1	LISTED	1	MANGER	1	MINIVER	1
LARKSPUR	1	LISTENER	1	MANKIND'S	1	MINOR	1
LARKSPUR'S	1	LISTLESS	1	MANNA-BUSHES	1	MINT	1
LASHTENDER	1	LITTLE-LASTING	1	MANNER	1	MINTED	1
LASTING	1	LOADED	1	MANNERLY-HEARTED	1	MIRACLE-IN-MARY-	1
LATE-FOUND	1	LOADING	1	MANNERS	1	MIRE	1
LATE-LEARNT	1	LOAMY	1	MANSEX	1	MIRKY	1
LAUDED	1	LOATHE	1	MANSHAPE	1	MIRRORED	1
LAUGHING	1	LOATHED	1	MANTLE-O'ER	1	MISDIRECTED	1
LAUGH'ST	1	LOATHINGLY	1	MANTLES	1	MISERY	1
LAUGHS	1	LOATH'D	1	MANTLING	1	MISLIKE	1
LAVER'D	1	LOATHSOME	1	MANWOLF	1	MISSING	1
LAWNS	1	LODGE	1	MARBLED	1	MISS'D	1
LAW'S	1	LODGED	1	MARCHES	1	MISTRESS	1
LAYS	1	LOINS	1	MARCH-BLOOM	1	MIX	1
LAZULI	1	LONE	1	MARCUS	1	MIXED	1
LEA	1	LONELY	1	MARGARET'S	1	MIX'D	1
LEAFING	1	LONGING	1	MARRIAGE	1	M.'S	1
LEAF-LIGHT	1	LONG-LYING	1	MARRIED	1	MOAN	1
LEAFLESS	1	LONG-SUPERFLUOUS	1	MARSH	1	MOANING	1
LEAFMEAL	1	LOOKER'S	1	MARTINMAS	1	MOANS	1
LEAFWHELMED	1	LOOM'D	1	MARTYR	1	MOB	1
LEAN-OVER	1	LOOPED	1	MARTYR-MASTER	1	MOCK	1
LEAP	1	LOOP-LOCKS	1	MARTYR'S	1	MOCKED	1
LEAPS	1	LOOPS	1	MARVEL	1	MOCKERY	1
LEARN	1	LOOSE-TRACED	1	MASKED	1	MOCKS	1
LEARNER	1	LOOSELY	1	MASK'D	1	MODERATE	1
LEARNING	1	LOOSEN'D	1	MASON'S	1	MODEST	1
LEAS	1	LORD'S	1	MASQUE	1	MOIST	1
LEASE	1	LORDS	1	MASSACRE	1	MOLEST	1
LEASH	1	LORN	1	MASTERHOOD	1	MOLTEN-BLUE	1
LEDGES	1	LOSE	1	MASTER'S	1	MONARCHS	1
LEEWARD	1	LOSSES	1	MATCH	1	MONITION	1
LEGATES	1	LOTE-FLOWER	1	MATCHWOOD	1	MONTH-BROTHER	1
LEGER	1	LOTS	1	MATED	1	MONUMENTS	1
LEGION	1	LOUCHED	1	MAWDDACH	1	MOODS	1
LENDS	1	LOVEABLE	1	MAYBE	1	MOONLESS	1
LEPERS	1	LOVED	1	MAYDAY	1	MOONLIGHT	1
LESSENED	1	LOVE-LACED	1	MAY-HOPE	1	MOONLIGHT-MATED	1
LESSON	1	LOVE-THOUGHTS	1	MAY-MESS	1	MOONMARKS	1
LESSONS	1	LOVELIER	1	MAY'S	1	MOOR	1
LEST	1	LOVELOCKS	1	MEADOW-DOWN	1	MOORLAND	1
LETS	1	LOVELY-ASUNDER	1	MEADOW'S	1	MORI	1
LETTERING	1	LOVELY-DUMB	1	MEAL	1	MORNS	1
LEVANT	1	LOVELY-FELICITOU	1	MEALED-WITH-YELL	1	MORROW	1
LEVELL'D	1	LOVESCAPE	1	MEAL-DRIFT	1	MORSELLED	1
LIBANUS	1	LOVING	1	MEALTIME	1	MORTALS	1
LICK	1	LOWER	1	MEANTIME	1	MORTICED	1
LID	1	LOW-COVERED	1	MEANWHILES	1	MOSES	1
LIEU	1	LOW-LATCHED	1	MEASURES	1	MOTE-LIKE	1
LIFEBELT	1	LOYAL	1	MEDALLION'D	1	MOTH	1
LIFELESS	1	LUKE	1	MEDLEY	1	MOTHER-GROUND	1
LIGHTEN	1	LULL	1	MELANCHOLY	1	MOTHER'S	1
LIGHTENING	1	LULL-OFF	1	MELEE	1	MOTH-SOFT	1
LIGHTHANDED	1	LUNG	1	MELODIOUS	1	MOULDING	1
LIGHT'S	1	LUNG-WASTING	1	MELODIOUSLY	1	MOULD'RING	1
LIGHTSHIP	1	LURCH	1	MELODY	1	MOUNDED	1
LIKENESS	1	LUSH-KEPT	1	MEMENTO	1	MOUNDS	1
LIKES	1	LUSTILY	1	MEMORY	1	MOUNTAIN-BOUND	1
LIKEST	1	LUSTRELESS	1	MENDS	1	MOUNTAIN-ECHO'D	1
LILY-BUDS	1	LUSTROUS	1	MENTION	1	MOUNTAIN-SIDE	1
LILY-COLOURED	1	LUSTY	1	MERCIES	1	MOUNTS	1
LILY-TIME	1	LUTHER	1	MERMAIDENS	1	MOURN	1
LILY-WHITE	1	MADAM	1	MERRILY	1	MOURNFUL	1
LILY-YELLOW	1	MADDEST	1	MESH'D	1	MUCH-DREADED	1
LILYLOCKS	1	MADRID	1	MESSAGE	1	MUCH-THICK	1
LIMBDANCE	1	MADRIGAL	1	MESSMATE	1	MUSES	1
LIMBER	1	MAENEFA	1	METAL-LUSTRED	1	MYRRHY-THREADED	1
LIMB'S	1	MAGDALEN	1	METAPHORS	1	MYRTLE-BEND	1
LIME	1	MAGIC	1	METED	1	MYSTERIOUS	1

Word		Word		Word		Word	
NAMES	1	O'ERTAKE	1	PEGASUS	1	PLUNGE	1
NARD	1	OUTER	1	PELICAN	1	PLUNGING	1
NARROW	1	OUTGOINGS	1	PELT	1	PLUSH-CAPPED	1
NATIONAL	1	OUT-FLEECED	1	PELTED	1	PLUSHY	1
NAUTILUS	1	OUTLINE	1	PELTING	1	POCKET	1
NAVEL	1	OUTRAGE	1	PENALTIES	1	POETRY	1
NAVVY	1	OUTRIDES	1	PENCILLED	1	POETS	1
NAZARETHS	1	OUTWARD-STEELED	1	PENDANT	1	POINTING	1
NEARNESS	1	OUTWARDS	1	PENETRATIVE	1	POINTS	1
NECTAR	1	OVERBEND	1	PENITENCE	1	POISING	1
NEEDFUL	1	OVERFLOWING	1	PENITENT	1	POMP	1
NEGLECTFUL	1	OVERSPREAD	1	PERCH	1	POMPEII	1
NEIGHBOURING	1	OVERSTOOD	1	PERFUMES	1	POND	1
NEIGHBOUR-NATURE	1	OVERTAKE	1	PERIL	1	PONDEROUS	1
NEIGHBOURS	1	OVERTAKING	1	PERISHABLE	1	POOLS	1
NEREID	1	OVERVAULTED	1	PERISHED	1	POPPIES	1
NERVELESS	1	OVERVAULTS	1	PERISHING	1	PORTENDING	1
NESTED	1	OVERWORN	1	PERISH'D	1	PORTENDS	1
NESTLIKE	1	OVERWROUGHT	1	PERMANENCE	1	PORTHOLES	1
NESTLING	1	OWNS	1	PERPETUAL	1	PORTION	1
NEST'S	1	OXEYE	1	PERSEUS	1	PORTS	1
NETS	1	PACES	1	PERSIAN-PERFECT	1	POSSESSED	1
NEVER-ELDERING	1	PACING	1	PERSONAL	1	POST	1
NEVER-NEEDED	1	PACK	1	PERSUASION	1	POSTUR'D	1
NEWBORN	1	PACKS	1	PETALL'D	1	POT	1
NEW-BASILISK	1	PACTOLUS	1	PETER	1	POTENT	1
NEW-DAPPLE	1	PAGE	1	PHANTASIES	1	POTENTIAL	1
NEW-DATED	1	PAGEANT	1	PHANTASY	1	POTSHERD	1
NEW-NESTLE	1	PAINED	1	PHAROH'S	1	POUR	1
NEW-SKEINED	1	PAINFUL	1	PHILOMEL	1	POURTRAY'D	1
NEW-WORLD	1	PAINT	1	PHOSPHOR	1	POVERTY	1
NEWLY	1	PAINTED	1	PHRENZY	1	POWERLESS	1
NICHE	1	PAINTING	1	PHRYGIAN	1	PRAISES	1
NIMBLE	1	PAIR	1	PICK	1	PRAIS'D	1
NIPS	1	PAIR'D	1	PICKED	1	PRANKED	1
NOBLER	1	PALATE	1	PIECE-BRIGHT	1	PRAYING	1
NOBS	1	PALING	1	PIECEMEAL	1	PRAYS	1
NOCTURNS	1	PALMTREE	1	PIECING	1	PREACHINGS	1
NOISES	1	PALMTREE-CUT	1	PIED	1	PRECEDENTS	1
NO-MAN-FATHOMED	1	PALMTREE-PEN	1	PIERCING	1	PRECIPICE	1
NONE'S	1	PALSY	1	PIGEONS	1	PRECISELY	1
NOOK	1	PANE	1	PILASTER'D	1	PRECISION	1
NOONDAY	1	PANG	1	PILATES	1	PREDILUVIAN	1
NOSE	1	PANSY-DARK	1	PILE	1	PREEMINENT	1
NOSTRIL	1	PANTINGS	1	PILED	1	PREENED	1
NOT-BY-MORNING-M	1	PAPA	1	PILES	1	PREFERENCE	1
NOT-STALED	1	PAR	1	PILGRIMAGES	1	PREJUDICE	1
NOT-TO-CALL	1	PARACLETE	1	PILLARS	1	PRENATAL	1
NOUGHT	1	PARADISAICAL	1	PILLOWING	1	PREPARE	1
NOURISHES	1	PARADOX	1	PILLOWS	1	PRESCRIPTIVE	1
NUMB	1	PARAPET	1	PILLOWY	1	PRESENCE	1
NUMBERED	1	PARCHED	1	PIN	1	PRESENTED	1
NUMBS	1	PARCHES	1	PINIONS	1	PRESSURE	1
NURSING	1	PAPE	1	PINK	1	PRETEND	1
OAR	1	PARING	1	PINKS	1	PRICE	1
OATH	1	PARIS	1	PIOUS	1	PRICED	1
OBSCUR'D	1	PARLOUR-PASTIME	1	PIT	1	PRICK	1
OBSOLETE	1	PASHED	1	PITCH	1	PRICKPROOF	1
OBSTRUCTION	1	PASSAGES	1	PITCHBLACK	1	PRIME'S	1
OCCASION	1	PASSIONFLOWER	1	PLACED	1	PRINCELY	1
OCTOBER	1	PASSION-PASTURED	1	PLACID	1	PRINCES	1
OFFENDED	1	PASSION-PLUNGED	1	PLAINLY	1	PRINCIPLE	1
OFFER	1	PASSION-SAKE	1	PLAINTIVELY	1	PRINT	1
OFFERINGS	1	PASSION'S	1	PLANE-LEAVES	1	PRISM	1
OFFSPRING	1	PAST-PRAYER	1	PLANT	1	PRIVACY	1
OFT	1	PAST'S	1	PLANTED	1	PROCESSION	1
OINTMENT	1	PATCH	1	PLANTS	1	PRODIGAL	1
O-SEAL-THAT-SO	1	PATHLESS	1	PLASHES	1	PROFESS	1
OLDER	1	PATIENT	1	PLATES	1	PROFFER	1
OLIVE-BRANCH	1	PATRONIZE	1	PLATTING	1	PROFIT	1
ONYX-CORONALS	1	PATTERN	1	PLEADING	1	PROFOUND	1
OPAL	1	PAUL'S	1	PLEADINGS	1	PROMISES	1
OPE	1	PAUSE	1	PLEAS	1	PROPHETESS	1
OPENING	1	PAVES	1	PLEASANCE	1	PROPORTION	1
OPPORTUNEST	1	PEACH	1	PLEASAUNCE	1	PROSPER	1
OPPOSITION	1	PEACOCK'D	1	PLEASED	1	PROSPERITY	1
OPPRESSED	1	PEACOCK'S	1	PLEASURABLE	1	PROSPEROUSLY-BOD	1
OPPRESSION	1	PEAK	1	PLEASURED	1	PROUDER	1
ORACLE	1	PEAK'D	1	PLEDGED	1	PROUDEST	1
ORCHARD-APPLE	1	PEALED	1	PLEIAD	1	PROVERB	1
ORCHARDS	1	PEALS	1	PLIED	1	PROVIDE	1
ORDER	1	PEARLED	1	PLIGHT	1	PRUDENCE	1
ORDER'D	1	PEARLY	1	PLOTS	1	PRUNED	1
ORINDA	1	PEARTREE	1	PLUCK	1	PSALM	1
ORION	1	PEASANT	1	PLUME	1	PUBLIC	1
O'CLOCK	1	PECTORAL	1	PLUM-PURPLE	1	PULPIT	1
O'ER-BRIM	1	PEELED	1	PLUMY	1	PULSE	1
O'ER-HEAD	1	PEER	1	PLUNDER	1	PUNISHMENT	1

PUPIL	1	REBUFFED	1	RIPS	1	SACRIFICE	1
PUPILS	1	RECLAIMING	1	RIS*N	1	SACRIFICED	1
PURCHASE	1	RECONCILED	1	RIVAL	1	SADDENING	1
PURER	1	RECORD	1	RIVALLED	1	SAILED	1
PURIFY	1	RECORDS	1	RIVALS	1	SAILORS	1
PURPLE-OF-THUNDE	1	RECOVER	1	RIVELLING	1	SAINTLY	1
PURPLING	1	RECURB	1	RIVER-BANKS	1	SAINTS	1
PURPLY	1	REDCOATS	1	RIVER-BED	1	SAITH	1
PURSUANT	1	REDEEMED	1	RIVER-HEADS	1	SAKES	1
PURSUED	1	REDEEMING	1	RIVER-ROUNDED	1	SALLOWS	1
PURSU*D	1	REED	1	RIV*N	1	SALLY	1
PUSHED	1	REEDS	1	RIVULET	1	SALUTE	1
PUSHING	1	REEF	1	ROADS	1	SANCTUARY	1
PYTHON	1	REEFS	1	ROAM	1	SANDALLED	1
QUAIL	1	REEK	1	ROAMING	1	SANDBLIND	1
QUAINT	1	REEKING	1	ROARED	1	SANDFIELD	1
QUARTZ-FRET	1	REELING	1	ROARING	1	SAND-TEASING	1
QUENCHING	1	REELS	1	ROB	1	SANDY	1
QUENCH*D	1	REFUSED	1	ROBBERY*S	1	SANG	1
QUEST	1	REGIMENTAL	1	ROBE	1	SANGUINE	1
QUESTIONING	1	REGISTER	1	ROBES	1	SAPPHIRE-PALE	1
QUESTS	1	REGRET	1	ROCKDOVES	1	SAPPHIRE-SHOT	1
QUICKEN	1	REGULAR	1	ROCKET	1	SAPRICIUS	1
QUICKENINGS	1	REHEARSAL	1	ROCKFIRE	1	SARD	1
QUICKGOLD	1	REIGN	1	ROCK-A-HEART	1	SASH	1
QUICKSILVERY	1	REIN	1	ROCKY	1	SATIN-PURFLED	1
QUIET-WALLED	1	RE-WINDED	1	ROGUISH	1	SATURDAY	1
QUILL	1	RELEASE	1	ROLLCALL	1	SAVED	1
QUILLS	1	RELEASED	1	ROLLROCK	1	SAVES	1
QUILS	1	RELICS	1	ROLL*D	1	SAVEST	1
QUIT	1	RELIGIOUS	1	ROME	1	SAVIOUR*S	1
QUITS	1	REMAIN	1	ROOF*D	1	SAVOUR	1
QUIVERING	1	REMARK	1	ROOK	1	SCAFFOLD	1
RACKED	1	REMEMBERETH	1	ROOKERY	1	SCALDED	1
RADIANCE	1	REMEMBER*D	1	ROOK-RACKED	1	SCALES	1
RAGING	1	REMEMBRANCE	1	ROOST	1	SCAN	1
RAIL	1	REMINDER	1	ROOTED	1	SCANNED	1
RAINBOW*S	1	REMNANTS	1	ROOTING	1	SCANTED	1
RAINBOWS	1	REMORSELESS	1	ROOT-ROOM	1	SCARCE-CALL-SILV	1
RAINDROP-ROUNDEL	1	REMOTEST	1	ROPE	1	SCARCE-SHEATHED	1
RAIN-BLASTS	1	REMOVE	1	ROPED	1	SCARE	1
RAIN-BORN	1	REMOVES	1	ROPE-OVER	1	SCARLESS	1
RAISE	1	RENDER*D	1	ROPE*S	1	SCARVES	1
RAISED	1	RENT	1	ROPES	1	SCENT	1
RAIS*D	1	REPEATED	1	ROSE-FLAKE	1	SCENTED	1
RAMBLED	1	REPRIEVE	1	ROSE-MOLES	1	SCEPTIC	1
RAMPS	1	RESENT	1	ROSE-RED	1	SCHOOLED	1
RANDOM	1	RESIDUARY	1	ROSELEAVES	1	SCHOOLING	1
RANGED	1	RESIGN	1	ROSING	1	SCHOOLS	1
RANKING	1	RESOLUTION	1	ROSY-BUDDED	1	SCHOONER	1
RANK-OLD	1	RESURRECTION	1	ROSY-LIPP*D	1	SCOOP	1
RANKLE	1	RETIRE	1	ROSY-PALE	1	SCOOPED	1
RANSOM*D	1	RETIREMENT	1	ROUGHCAST	1	SCOOPS	1
RANTERS	1	RETURNING	1	ROUGH-ROBIN	1	SCORES	1
RAPTURE	1	REVERSAL	1	ROUGH-SCORED	1	SCORNING	1
RAPTUROUS	1	REVILED	1	ROUNDED	1	SCOUR	1
RARE-DEAR	1	REVISITS	1	ROUNDER	1	SCOURGED	1
RAREST	1	REVIVAL	1	ROUNDING	1	SCREAM*D	1
RAREST-VEINED	1	REVIVAL	1	ROUNDY	1	SCREEN	1
RASH-FRESH	1	RHINE	1	ROUT	1	SCROLL-LEAVED	1
RATED	1	RHYMES	1	ROWING	1	SCULLS	1
RATION	1	RIBBED	1	ROWS	1	SCULPTUR*D	1
RAVAGE	1	RIBBON	1	ROYALLY	1	SCYTHE	1
RAVE	1	RICHEST	1	ROYALS	1	SCYTHES	1
RAVEL-ROPE*S-END	1	RICH-PIECED	1	RUBIES	1	SEAMARK	1
RAVELL*D	1	RICHLY	1	RUBY	1	SEABEACH	1
RAVENS	1	RICHNESS	1	RUD	1	SEA-CORPSE	1
RAVES	1	RID	1	RUDDIED	1	SEA-FAN	1
RAVISHMENT	1	RIDDLES	1	RUDDYING	1	SEA-FOWL	1
RAY	1	RIDER	1	RUDER	1	SEA-GULL	1
RAY*D	1	RIDGE	1	RUDER-ROUNDED	1	SEA-GUST	1
RE	1	RIDGE-CREST	1	RUDRED	1	SEA-ROMP	1
REACHES	1	RIFLED	1	RUEFUL	1	SEA-SWILL	1
READING	1	RIGGING	1	RULE	1	SEALING	1
READINGS	1	RIGHTED	1	RULER	1	SEALING-WAX	1
READS	1	RIGHTEOUSNESS	1	RUNNEL	1	SEALS	1
REAL	1	RIGOUR	1	RUNNELS	1	SEAMANSHIP	1
REALER	1	RILL	1	RUPTURE	1	SEAR	1
REALIZE	1	RILLY	1	RUSHY	1	SEARCHING	1
REALTY	1	RIME	1	RUST	1	SEARED	1
REAPPEAR	1	RIMMON	1	RUTPEEL	1	SEATS	1
REARING	1	RINGED	1	*MID	1	SECOND	1
REASON*D	1	RINGING	1	*SCUTCHEON	1	SECONDER	1
REAVE	1	RINGLET-RACE	1	*SPERSES	1	SECONDING	1
REAVING	1	RINSE	1	*TWIXT	1	SECRETS	1
REBELLIOUS	1	RINSED	1	SABINE	1	SEEKING	1
REBOUND	1	RIPEST	1	SABLE	1	SELDOM	1
REBUFF	1	RIPPLES	1	SACKCLOTH	1	SELDOMER	1

SELFBENT 1
SELFDISPOSAL 1
SELFISH 1
SELF-EMBRACED 1
SELF-FEELING 1
SELF-INSTRESSED 1
SELF-MADE 1
SELF-OUTWITTED 1
SELF-SACRIFICE 1
SELF-SENTENCED 1
SELF-WILL 1
SELF-WISE 1
SELFLESS 1
SELFQUAINED 1
SELFSAME 1
SELFSTRUNG 1
SELFWRUNG 1
SELFYEAST 1
SELVAGGIA 1
SENDINGS 1

SENDS 1
SENSUAL 1
SENTENCE 1
SEPULCHRE 1
SEQUENCE 1
SEQUINS 1
SERAPH 1
SERAPH-ARRIVAL 1
SERFDOM 1
SERGED 1
SERMONS 1
SERVANTS 1
SERVER 1
SETTING 1
SETTLE 1
SETTLER 1
SEVENFOLD-SINGLE 1
SEVENTEENTH 1
SEVENTY 1
SEVERANCE 1
SEW 1
SEWERS 1
SEX 1
SEXED 1
SHADOWIEST 1
SHADOWS 1
SHADOWTACKLE 1
SHAKESPEARE'S 1
SHALLOWING 1
SHALLOWY 1
SHAPEN 1
SHARDED 1
SHARING 1
SHARPER 1
SHEATH 1
SHEATHED 1
SHEAVES 1
SHEEP-BELLS 1
SHEEP-FLOCK 1
SHEETS 1
SHELLED 1
SHELLING 1
SHELLS 1
SHELTERLESS 1
SHEPHERD'S 1
SHEWED 1
SHEWING 1
SHEWS 1
SHIELD 1
SHIFT 1
SHIFTED 1
SHILLING 1
SHINING-HILTED 1
SHINING-SHOT 1
SHIPWRACK 1
SHIRES 1
SHIRT 1
SHIVELIGHTS 1
SHIVER'D 1
SHIVES 1
SHOAL 1
SHOALY 1
SHOOT 1
SHORES 1
SHORTEN 1

SHORTER 1
SHORTEST 1
SHOULDERING 1

SHOWERING 1
SHOWER'D 1
SHOW'D 1
SHREDS 1
SHREWSBURY 1
SHRIEKED 1
SHRINES 1
SHRIVE 1
SHROUDED 1
SHROUD-PLAITS 1
SHROUDS 1
SHROVETIDE 1
SHUNS 1
SHUSHAN 1
SHUTS 1
SHUTTLES 1
SHY 1
SICILIAN 1
SICILY 1
SICKEN 1

SICKEN'D 1
SICKLY 1
SIDED 1
SIDES 1
SIDLED 1
SIEGE 1
SIEVE 1
SIFT 1
SIFTED 1
SIGHED 1
SIGNALLING 1
SIGNALS 1
SILK-ASH 1
SILK-BEECH 1
SILK-SACK 1
SILLION 1
SILT 1
SILVER-COATED 1
SILVER-SHOT 1
SILVER-SURFED 1
SIMILE 1
SIMON 1
SIMOOM 1
SINEW 1
SINEW-SERVICE 1
SINGEING 1
SINGS 1
SINKING 1
SINNERS 1
SIN'S 1
SIP 1
SIREN 1
SISTERHOOD 1
SISTERING 1
SISTERLY 1
SITH 1
SIZES 1
SKATE'S 1
SKEINED 1
SKIFF 1
SKINS 1
SKIRRING 1
SKIRTING 1
SKIRTS 1
SKYLARK'S 1
SKYLARKS 1
SLABBY 1
SLABS 1
SLAKE 1
SLAKED 1
SLAMM'D 1
SLATES 1
SLATY 1
SLAUGHTER 1
SLAY 1
SLENDERING 1
SLEW 1
SLIGHTLY 1
SLIM 1
SLIM-POINTED 1
SLIP 1
SLIPT 1
SLOE 1
SLOGGERING 1
SLOPE 1

SLOPING 1
SLOP'D 1
SLOWLY 1

SLUMBER'D 1
SMEARED 1
SMILES 1
SMIT 1
SMITTEN 1
SMOCK 1
SMOKES 1
SMOOTH-LIPP'D 1
SMOTE 1
SMUDGE 1
SNATCH 1
SNOWFLAKE 1
SNOW-PINIONS 1
SNOWSTORM 1
SNOWY 1
SNUFF 1
SOARED 1
SOB 1
SOBB'D 1
SOBS 1

SOD 1
SOODEN-WITH-ITS- 1
SODS 1
SOFTENING 1
SOLDIER 1
SOLDIERING 1
SOLDIERS 1
SOLDIERY 1
SOLELY 1
SOLEMN 1
SOLITARY 1
SOMBRE 1
SONG-FOWL 1
SONG-STRAIN 1
SONNET 1
SOONER 1
SOONEST 1
SOOTY 1
SOPP'D 1
SORDID 1
SORDIDNESS 1
SORROW'S 1
SORROWS 1
SORRY 1
SORT 1
SORTS 1
SOTS 1
SOUNDING 1
SOUNDS 1
SOURED 1
SOUTHERN 1
SOUTH-WESTERLY 1
SOVEREIGN 1
SOVEREIGNTY 1
SOWED 1
SPACE 1
SPAIN 1
SPAKE 1
SPANIEL'S 1
SPANN'D 1
SPANS 1
SPARKLING 1
SPARKS 1
SPATTER'D 1
SPEAKETH 1
SPEAKING 1
SPEAR'D 1
SPECIAL 1
SPECIAL-GENERAL 1
SPEECHLESS 1
SPEEDS 1
SPENDS 1
SPENDSAVOUR 1
SPIKED 1
SPIKES 1
SPIN 1
SPINE 1
SPIRE 1
SPIRES 1
SPIRIT'S 1
SPITING 1
SPLAY'D 1
SPLENDID 1
SPLENDOURS 1
SPOIL 1

SPOKES 1
SPOOLS 1
SPOONS 1

SPORT 1
SPORTED 1
SPOUSAL 1
SPRANG 1
SPRAY 1
SPRAYS 1
SPREADING 1
SPRINGING 1
SPRING-BROIDERY 1
SPRING-TIDE 1
SPRING-TIME 1
SPRINGTIME 1
SPUN 1
SPUR 1
SPURR'D 1
SQUADRONED 1
SQUALL 1
SQUANDER 1
SQUANDERING 1
SQUARED 1

SQUARE-CUT 1
SQUAT 1
SQUEEZED 1
SQUINCHES 1
STABBING 1
STAFF 1
STAGE 1
STAID 1
STAIR-WAY 1
STAKE 1
STALK 1
STALLION 1
STALWART 1
STAMP 1
STANCHES 1
STANCHING 1
STARCHES 1
STARCHY 1
STARING 1
STAR-EYED 1
STARK 1
STARK-PRECIPITOU 1
STARLIGHT-WENDER 1
STARTING 1
STARVES 1
STARVEST 1
STARV'D 1
STATUE 1
STAUNCH 1
STAYS 1
STEAD 1
STEAL 1
STEALTHY 1
STEEP-UP 1
STEERED 1
STEM 1
STEPHEN 1
STEPPED 1
STEPS 1
STEPT 1
STERLING 1
STERNER 1
STERNEST 1
STEWARD 1
STICK 1
STIFFEN'D 1
STIFLING 1
STIGMA 1
STILLING 1
STILLNESS 1
STILLY 1
STINGING 1
STINT 1
STINTING 1
STINTLESS 1
STIPPLE 1
STIRLESS 1
STIRRING 1
STIRRINGS 1
STIRS 1
STOCK-STILL 1
STOLED 1
STOLEN 1
STOOKS 1
STOOPED 1

STORMFOWL 1
STORM-MONTHS 1
STORM'S 1

Word		Word		Word		Word	
STORY*S	1	SWAYED	1	THICKLY	1	TRACK	1
STRAIGHTWAY	1	SWEATING	1	THICKY	1	TRADE	1
STRAINED	1	SWEATS	1	THIEF	1	TRADES	1
STRANDED	1	SWEETBRIAR	1	THIGH	1	TRAGIC	1
STRANGERS	1	SWEETER-MEMORIED	1	THING*S	1	TRAILING	1
STRAWBERRY-BREAS	1	SWEETHEART	1	THINKING	1	TRAIL*D	1
STRAWY	1	SWEET-AND-SOUR	1	THINLY	1	TRAINING	1
STRAYING	1	SWEET-FAMILIAR	1	THINNED	1	TRAMBEAMS	1
STRAYS	1	SWEET-FOWL	1	THINNING	1	TRAMP	1
STREAK*D	1	SWEET-PEA-BLOSSO	1	THIRST*S	1	TRAMPLE	1
STREAKS	1	SWEET*S	1	THISTLED	1	TRAMPLED	1
STREAM	1	SWELLING	1	THISTLES	1	TRAMPLERS	1
STREET	1	SWELL*D	1	THITHER	1	TRANQUIL	1
STREETS	1	SWELLS	1	THOMAS	1	TRANSLUCENT	1
STRENGTHEN	1	SWIFTLY	1	THONGS	1	TRANSMIT	1
STRESSED	1	SWIMS	1	THORN-ENGAGED	1	TRASH	1
STRETCHES	1	SWOLL*N	1	THORNY	1	TRAVELL*D	1
STREWED	1	SWOON	1	THOROUGHFARE	1	TRAVERSE	1
STRICKEN	1	SWOONED	1	THORP	1	TREACHEROUS	1
STRIDES	1	SWORDS	1	THRALLS	1	TREADMIRE	1
STRIDING	1	SYCAMORE-TREE	1	THREADS	1	TREASONABLE	1
STRIFE	1	SYDNEY	1	THREEFOLD	1	TREBLE	1
STRING	1	SYMPATHISING	1	THREE-HEELED	1	TREBLE-FERVENT	1
STRINGY	1	TABLE	1	THREE-NUMBERED	1	TREE-TOPS	1
STRIPED	1	TACKLED	1	THRESHING-FLOOR	1	TREETOP	1
STRIPES	1	TACT	1	THRESHOLD	1	TREMBLE	1
STRIPS	1	TAIL-FIN	1	THREW	1	TREMULOUS	1
STRIVE	1	TAILS	1	THRIFTLESS	1	TRENCH	1
STRIVEN	1	TAINTING	1	THRILL	1	TRENCHED	1
STROMBUS-SHELL	1	TAKINGS	1	THRILLS	1	TRIAL	1
STROOK	1	TALES	1	THRONE	1	TRICK	1
STRUGGLING	1	TALKS	1	THRONED	1	TRICKLING	1
STUBBORN	1	TALMAI	1	THRONG*S	1	TRINITY	1
STUPENDOUS	1	TAME	1	THROSTLE	1	TRIP	1
STUPID	1	TAMPERING	1	THROTTLED	1	TRIPLE-HUMMOCKED	1
STURDY	1	TANGLED	1	THROUGHTHER	1	TRIPS	1
SUBMISSION	1	TANGLES	1	THROWS	1	TROOPS	1
SUCCEED	1	TANTALEAN	1	THRUSH	1	TROPIC	1
SUFFER	1	TAPER	1	THRUSH*S	1	TROUBLED	1
SUFFERED	1	TAR	1	THRUST	1	TROUT	1
SUFFEREDST	1	TARPEIAN-FAST	1	THRUSTS	1	TRUCKLE	1
SUFFERING	1	TARTARUS	1	THUNDERING	1	TRUELOVE	1
SUFFERS	1	TASKING	1	THUNDER-PURPLE	1	TRUER	1
SUFFICED	1	TASKS	1	THUNDER-THRONE	1	TRUNDLED	1
SUGAR	1	TASTED	1	THWART	1	TRUSTY	1
SUITORS	1	TASTELESS	1	THWARTS	1	TRYING	1
SULPHUR-COLOUR*D	1	TASTING	1	TIGHTEN	1	TUCKED	1
SULTRY	1	TATTER-TANGLED	1	TILES	1	TUGG*D	1
SUM	1	TAUNTLESS	1	TILLAGE	1	TUMBLED-TO	1
SUMMERING	1	TEAR-TRICKED	1	TIMBER*LL	1	TUMBLER	1
SUMMER-TIME	1	TEASE	1	TIMBRELS	1	TUMBLING	1
SUMMER*S	1	TEASES	1	TIMED	1	TUMBLINGS	1
SUMMIT	1	TEDIOUS	1	TIMES-OVER	1	TUMULT	1
SUMMONING	1	TEEVO	1	TINGEING	1	TUNEABLE	1
SUMPTUOUS	1	TEMPE	1	TINGLING	1	TUNED	1
SUMS	1	TEMPERATENESS	1	TINIEST	1	TURBID	1
SUNBEAM	1	TEMPER*D	1	TINKLINGS	1	TURF	1
SUNDAY	1	TEMPESTS	1	TINTS	1	TURMOIL	1
SUN-FLUSH*D	1	TEMPLES	1	TIPTOES	1	TURQUOISE-GEMM*D	1
SUNLIT	1	TEMPT	1	TIRES	1	TURTLE*S	1
SUNNED	1	TENDERED	1	TITAN*S	1	TWENTY	1
SUN*S	1	TENDERER	1	TITIAN*S	1	TWINDLES	1
SUN*S-EYE-RINGED	1	TENDEREST	1	TITIANS	1	TWINY	1
SUNSPURGE	1	TENDER-SLANTED	1	TO-FRO	1	TYRANT	1
SUPPLIED	1	TENDERNESS	1	TOKEN	1	TYRIAN	1
SUPPLY	1	TENT-POLES	1	TOMB	1	UNACCOUNTED	1
SUPPOSE	1	TEREBINTH	1	TOMB-DECKED	1	UNALTER*D	1
SUPPOSING	1	TERM	1	TOMBS	1	UNAWAKENED	1
SURCEASE	1	TERMS	1	TOM*S	1	UNAWARE	1
SURF	1	TERRACES	1	TOOLSMOOTH	1	UNBAKES	1
SURPRISE	1	TERROR	1	TOPP*D	1	UNBLOWN	1
SURRENDERS	1	TERYTH	1	TOPS	1	UNBOUND	1
SURROUND	1	TETHER	1	TOPSYTURVY	1	UNBROKEN	1
SURVEY	1	THAMES	1	TOPT	1	UNCERTAINTY	1
SUSPECT	1	THANKLESS	1	TORMENT	1	UNCHALLENGED	1
SUSPECTS	1	THANKS	1	TORMENTING	1	UNCHANCELLING	1
SWALLOW	1	THE-LAST-BREATH	1	TOSSED	1	UNCHANGING	1
SWALLOWING	1	THEORY	1	TOSSES	1	UNCHARTED	1
SWALLOW*D	1	THEREAFTER	1	TOWERED	1	UNCHECK*D	1
SWALLOWS	1	THEREIN	1	TOWER-TOP	1	UNCHILDING	1
SWAM	1	THEREON	1	TOWERY	1	UNCHILL*D	1
SWAN-FLEDGED	1	THEREWITH	1	TOWNS	1	UNCHRIST	1
SWANS	1	THICKEN	1	TOY	1	UNCLEAN	1
SWARMED	1	THICKENING	1	TRACE	1	UNCOMFORTED	1
SWARTER	1	THICKEST	1	TRACED	1	UNCONFESSED	1
SWARTHED	1	THICKET	1	TRACELESS	1	UNCONTROLLED	1
SWATHE	1	THICK-FLEECED	1	TRACERY	1	UNCREATED	1
SWAY	1	THICK-PEARLED	1	TRACES	1	UNCUMBERED	1